ROBERTS' DICTIONARY of INDUSTRIAL RELATIONS

Third Edition

ROBERTS' DICTIONARY of INDUSTRIAL RELATIONS

Third Edition

Harold S. Roberts
Senior Professor of Business Economics
and Industrial Relations
Director, Industrial Relations Center
1949-1970

Third Edition
Prepared by
Industrial Relations Center
University of Hawaii at Manoa

The Bureau of National Affairs, Inc. Washington, D.C. 20037

The Bureau of National Affairs, Inc.
Washington, D.C.

Library of Congress Cataloging-in-Publication Data

Roberts, Harold Selig, 1911–1970.
Roberts' Dictionary of industrial relations.

Bibliography: p.
1. Industrial relations—Dictionaries. I. University of Hawaii at Manoa. Industrial Relations Center. II. Title. III. Title: Dictionary of industrial relations.
HD4839.R612 1986 331'.03'21 85-29100
ISBN 0-87179-488-8

Printed in the United States of America
International Standard Book Number: 0-87179-488-8

A word is not a crystal, transparent and unchanged; it is the skin of a living thought and may vary greatly in color and content according to the circumstances and the time in which it is used.

Mr. Justice Holmes
[*Towne* v. *Eisner*,
245 U.S. 418, 425 (1918)]

The family of Harold S. Roberts
lovingly dedicate this book to his memory

Foreword to the Third Edition

The first edition of *Roberts' Dictionary* was prepared two decades ago, and its last revision was published nearly 15 years ago. Since then, the changes accompanying the developments in the American workplace, the growth and recognition of women and minorities in the labor force, and the rise of public sector collective bargaining have generated a host of new terms in the industrial relations vocabulary. Terms such as *dislocated worker, concession bargaining,* and *employee giveback* only hint at the effects, for example, of the shift from manufacturing to service industries in the economic base. Equal employment opportunity and affirmative action, seen as emerging employment issues during the early 1970s, have indeed developed into major areas, replete with unique terminology—from *adverse impact* to *utilization analysis.* Public sector bargaining gained momentum with the passage of numerous enabling statutes during the past 15 years, including the first law governing federal employees—Title VII of the Civil Service Reform Act of 1978. Terms such as *blue flu, tri-offer arbitration,* and *compelling need* originate out of the public sector. In addition to all of these developments, the language of labor-management relations has become more technical: we hear such phrases as *costing labor contracts, productivity bargaining,* or *wage spillovers.*

The third edition enables us to continue the work of Professor Harold S. Roberts and, like the previous edition, it is a memorial to Dr. Roberts. It attempts to maintain Dr. Roberts' endeavor, which he explained in his Introduction was

> . . . to provide a simple yet reasonably accurate explanation of terms and phrases currently used in the field of labor-management relations, brief summaries of important cases, short notes on international unions, and other items which might be of interest and help to a person seeking concise information in a single reference volume. . . . Since most entries are brief, we have frequently provided source references so that individuals interested in obtaining more detailed information or desirous of consulting primary sources may do so with a minimum of research.

To keep *Roberts' Dictionary* as current as possible, we have made certain alterations to selected terms found in earlier editions, attempting throughout, however, to retain the nature and flavor of Dr. Roberts' work at all times. A few terms have been deleted; most of these are *See* terms, primarily labor union and university industrial relations center entries. Others have been changed to reflect current usage; terms such as *Public Contracts (Walsh-Healey) Act, required collective bargaining,* and *workmen's compensation* have been retitled to utilize the more current or popular term, i.e., *Walsh-Healey Act, mandatory subjects of bargaining,* and *workers compensation,* respectively.

In addition, in the interest of citing current works, an extensive literature search was conducted for the source reference titles accompanying the various items. Where possible, the source references for existing terms were revised and current titles included.

Standard references, including a number of new sources, were consulted in developing definitions of new terms and in revising definitions of existing terms. New sources include, among others, a number of journals—*Employee Relations Law Journal, Industrial Relations Law Journal, Journal of Collective Negotiations in the Public Sector,* and *Journal of Labor Research.*

Standard reference tools were utilized for information on labor union, agency, and other organization entries. Citations to these various volumes are not entered under the individual entries, and instead are noted here for convenient reference. They include:

Lloyd G. Reynolds and Charles C. Killingsworth, *Trade Union Publications* (3 vol., Baltimore: Johns Hopkins Press, 1944–1945).

U.S. Dept. of Labor, Bureau of Labor Statistics, *Directory of National Unions and Employee Associations, 1947–1979* (Washington: 1947–1980).

Bureau of National Affairs, *Directory of U.S. Labor Organizations, 1982–83 Edition, 1984–85 Edition* (Washington: 1982, 1984).

U.S. Office of the Federal Register, *United States Government Manual, 1965–1966 — 1983–84* (Washington: 1966–1984).

Gale Research, *Encyclopedia of Associations, Volume 1 — National Organizations of the U.S.* (18th ed., Detroit: 1983).

New titles also have been added to the General Source References found at the end of the volume reflecting the latest additions to the group of "classics" in industrial relations literature.

Over 600 new entries appear in the third edition. In all, *Roberts' Dictionary* contains over 4,400 entries, some 3,800 cross references, and nearly 9,300 references to sources.

As in previous editions, this volume represents the work of many individuals, including those who contributed their comments and suggestions in the early preparation of the third edition. We wish to acknowledge the help received from the members of the Committee of Industrial Relations Librarians who devoted time during their May 1983 meeting to discuss the revision of *Roberts' Dictionary.* We appreciate the helpful ideas and suggestions made at the meeting. We want to specially thank Georgianna Herman, Industrial Relations Center, University of Minnesota, who served as hostess of the meeting; and to Margaret Chaplan, Institute of Labor and Industrial Relations, University of Illinois; James Danky, State Historical Society of Wisconsin; Dawn Dobson, Canadian Labour Congress; Bernard Downey, Institute of Management and Labor Relations, Rutgers University; Shirley Harper, New York State School of Industrial and Labor Relations, Cornell University; Dora Kelenson, AFL-CIO; and Nancy J. Sedmak, BNA Labor Indexing Unit; who kindly provided advice and informational and reference materials.

We also wish to acknowledge the work of Craig A. Olson, State University of New York, Buffalo, and Helen Remick, University of Washington, in the review of the new terms added to *Roberts' Dictionary*; and for his editorial assistance, we are grateful to Dennis T. Ogawa, University of Hawaii at Manoa. We also benefitted from the advice of our good friends Alice H. Cook, New York State School of Industrial and Labor Relations, Cornell University; Derek Robinson, Oxford University; and James L. Stern, University of Wisconsin-Madison; who kindly provided us good sense and comfort while visiting with us. We are indebted to Mary Green Miner, BNA Books & Conferences, for her support.

The unstinting devotion and effort of the members of the staff of the Industrial Relations Center—Eva L. Goo, Stephanie E. Hokushin, Gail F. Inaba, Joyce Y. Nakahara, Mark E. Nakamura, and, in particular, Helene S. Tanimoto for her mighty work in seeing to it that the job was finished according to schedule—are gratefully acknowledged. Finally, we are most indebted to the University of Hawaii at Manoa for the support that was needed and given us to continue this important work of Harold S. Roberts, our teacher, friend, and founder of the Industrial Relations Center.

Joyce M. Najita, Director
Industrial Relations Center
University of Hawaii at Manoa
October 1984

Foreword to the Second Edition

Since the publication of the first edition of the *Dictionary* a number of developments have emerged or assumed greater importance. Among these are the growing interest in public employee bargaining and the host of areas related to manpower development and training: the disadvantaged worker, equal employment opportunities, the poor, the black worker, minority youth, and unemployment in general. New reference titles have become available to report these new developments, among them BNA's *Government Employee Relations Report*, the *Journal of Human Resources, Poverty and Human Resources Abstracts*, the University of Michigan-Wayne State University Institute of Labor and Industrial Relations' *Policy Papers in Human Resources and Industrial Relations*, and the Public Personnel Administration's *Public Employee Relations Library* series. These and other titles will be found in the source references under the individual entries. We have attempted to include new developments in this second edition, but at the same time to retain the nature and flavor of the *Dictionary* as Dr. Roberts would have prepared it. In this revision the page references to the loose-leaf reporting services of The Bureau of National Affairs, Inc., have been omitted because they are subject to change. Current page numbers can be obtained from the indexes of the specific services cited.

Additionally, we have altered in two ways the General Source References at the back of the volume. We eliminated titles to avoid duplicating works cited under individual entries, with the exception of those works which we felt were "classics" or which we felt belonged in a basic library of books and periodicals. We incorporated more recent titles to reflect the current interest in areas which have presented themselves since the publication of the first edition.

This *Dictionary* is a form of memorial to Harold S. Roberts, who died in February 1970. For their work in readying the material for publication, grateful acknowledgement is made to Eva L. Goo, Helene Shimaoka, Joyce Najita, and Vickie Triplett.

John B. Ferguson, Acting Director
Industrial Relations Center
University of Hawaii
October 1971

Introduction to the First Edition

Labor-management relations, like other subjects which seek to enshroud themselves in the mantle of science, has over the years developed a language peculiar to its needs and problems. Unlike many other disciplines, however, it has not yet developed a protective jargon which has the effect of confusing the general public. Among the disciplines its vocabulary might be labeled "lowbrow," having acquired expressions reflective of the practices of industry and trade. Terms like fink, roping, hooking, rough shadowing, quickie, scab, shape-up, stool pigeon, etc., are part and parcel of the history of labor-management relations.

The tremendous growth in unionization during the last three decades; specialized labor legislation including the Norris-LaGuardia Act, the Wage and Hour Law, the Wagner Act, the Taft-Hartley Act, and the Labor-Management Reporting and Disclosure Act; greater emphasis on personnel practices resulting from management integration; increased automation; and the use of more specialized tools in hiring and placement have led to the use of more technical phraseology. The growth of job evaluation, time and motion study, the rapid expansion and development of the collective bargaining process, decisions by federal and state courts, and by arbitrators have been responsible for the widespread use of technical expressions which are unfamiliar to the layman and occasionally even to the general practitioner who is not a specialist in any particular field. Terms like affirmative order, appropriate unit, decertification, Balleisen contracts, Bedeaux system, unfair labor practices, consent decrees, constructive discharges, leveling, and fatigue factor are referred to more frequently in the general press but are not generally understood by the public.

If the general practitioner encounters difficulty at times, the problem of the layman who tries to keep abreast of developments in industrial relations is pathetic. The various media of communication including television, radio, newspapers, and magazines seek to simplify the subject, but the issues in labor-management relations are becoming more and more complex. We are confronted with health and welfare plans, pensions, guaranteed wage plans, job classifications and evaluations, supplementary unemployment benefits, compliance with the Taft-Hartley Act and other labor laws, secondary boycotts, featherbedding, jurisdictional disputes, sympathetic strikes, non-Communist affidavits, trust-fund regulation, and a host of other concepts which are not part of the working vocabulary of the intelligent layman.

An attempt is made in this volume to provide a simple yet reasonably accurate explanation of terms and phrases currently used in the field of labor-management relations, brief summaries of important cases, short notes on international unions, and other items which might be of interest and help to a person seeking concise information in a single reference volume.

Some users of the Dictionary may find it helpful to read the brief "Guide to Users" following this Introduction. Since most entries are brief, we have frequently provided source references so that individuals interested in obtaining more detailed information or desirous of consulting primary sources may do so with a minimum of further research. We have tried to provide references which are generally available in public or university libraries, or libraries of personnel or research departments of trade unions, employers associations, or large companies. We have sought also to use citations to journals which are widely distributed and which are generally accessible. Among these are the U.S. Department of Labor *Monthly Labor Review*, the *Personnel Journal*, the *Labor Law Journal*, the *Industrial and Labor Relations Review*, and the industrial relations services. Frequent references also have been made to the specialized publications of university "industrial relations centers" throughout the country. Now and again we have made reference to historical studies or "classics" which may be out of print or found only in the larger or more specialized collections. We believe that these references may be especially helpful to individuals who have convenient access to large metropolitan libraries or universities whose libraries contain fairly large collections of volumes in the field of industrial relations. We have tried to make the Dictionary as comprehensive as possible. It contains more than 3,000 entries, 2,000 cross references, and 5,000 source references, plus cross indexing by The Bureau of National Affairs, Inc.

In addition to references to books, periodicals, and historical studies, entries in the Dictionary are cross indexed to volume and page of the loose-leaf and reporting services published by The Bureau of National Affairs, Inc., Washington, D.C., publisher of the Dictionary. These services include such established publications as *Labor Relations Reporter, Wage and Hour Manual, Labor Policy and Practice, Collective Bargaining Negotiations and Contracts,* and *Daily Labor Report.*

The response from users of the advance installments of the Dictionary, issued in pamphlet form and covering one or more letters which began in June 1957, suggests that it meets a definite need among laymen, supervisors, shop stewards, as well as practitioners, students, and teachers in the field of industrial relations. For individuals or groups which have need for a basic library of books and periodicals, we have appended at the back of the volume a list of *General Source References* from which such a collection might be assembled. This bibliography may be helpful to those who have limited financial resources, but at the same time feel the need of a working collection in this field.

A dictionary is not the product of one man's work. It may be written by one man, but the spade work and the wide variety of sources he has to draw upon play a crucial role in the preparation of such a volume. This, of course, is true of this Dictionary, and by the very nature of the project, the author has had to rely on the able and extensive research of many students in the field of labor-management relations. Some notion of the importance and pervasiveness of this reliance may be gathered from the more than 5,000 references to these sources appended to many entries. Since it is impossible to quote extensively or to use more than a few references, the author has included only those which seem likely to be useful. Where possible, he has endeavored to cite sources which present varying points of view. The number of publications, services, books, and manuals of one sort or another in the labor-management field has grown so rapidly in recent years that it has become almost impossible to keep abreast of its literature. Persons planning to do specialized research will avail themselves of the bibliographies, digests, and subject indexes available at most university industrial relations centers and in the larger university libraries.

The author is keenly aware of the limitations of this undertaking. He hopes that the Dictionary will prove to be a source of useful information of the literature in this field and at the same time serve as a medium for a better understanding of the language of labor-management relations.

The first installment of the Dictionary (covering the letter "A") was published in June of 1957; other sections were published from time to time. These "separates" were distributed and comments were solicited and received from users. These comments have been reviewed and, where useful, incorporated into this one-volume edition. In the present edition the author has updated these earlier sections and where possible has made the material current to 1965. In addition a number of students have reviewed and commented on the volume in draft form. The author extends his warm thanks to Benjamin Sigal, Murray Weisz and Phil Arnow, who have reviewed one or more sections of the volume. Paul F. Brissenden and Al Weiss have read the manuscript in its entirety and commented extensively on it. They have added immeasurably to the content of the final product.

The Bureau of National Affairs has assisted in the final review of copy and has keyed in references to the BNA Indexes so that the volume will be more helpful to those subscribing to its services. Editorial suggestions were made by Paul Brissenden, Al Weiss, Joy Roberts, John D. Stewart and Edward H. Donnel, Jr.

It is, of course, impossible to acknowledge the debt owed by the author to the numerous individuals working in the field of industrial relations from whom he has borrowed or whose ideas he may have absorbed. He is particularly indebted to E. Wight Bakke, Paul F. Brissenden, David Cole, Nathan Feinsinger, Frank Graham, Clark Kerr, William Leiserson, Harry Millis, Wayne Morse, Selig Perlman, William G. Rice, Jr., David J. Saposs, Harry Shulman, Philip Taft, George Taylor, Edwin E. Witte, W. Willard Wirtz, and Dale Yoder. Wherever possible specific acknowledgments have been made at appropriate points in the source references. It goes without saying, of course, that they are in no way responsible for any of the limitations or shortcomings of the volume.

Special thanks are due to the members of the staff of the Industrial Relations Center of the University of Hawaii. More specifically, the author would like to extend his thanks to Norma Nekota and Eva Lee Goo for their assistance in the typing of manuscript, and to Helene Shimaoka and Joyce Matsumoto Najita for their unstinting help on many aspects of the undertaking.

The author, of necessity, must accept the responsibility for all errors of omission or commission.

Harold S. Roberts
December 1965

Guide to Users

1. *Selection of terms*

In selecting terms for inclusion in *Roberts' Dictionary*, the general goal was to provide within practical limits a fairly extensive list of terms. Where a choice of descriptive titles had to be made, the currently popular terminology was used as the main title with *See* references to it noted under the other titles. Some titles, although not in common use at the present time, have been included for historical significance.

All terms, except for proper terms, have been entered in the lower case to follow a dictionary format. Proper terms include titles of laws; case citations; names of administrative agencies, labor unions, and other organizations; titles of journals and publications; and names of programs and projects.

In the definitions, the use of "he/she" was avoided, and it is intended that all references to "he," where they are found, are to be read without regard to gender.

2. *Arrangement of terms and source references*

Popular abbreviations of names of labor unions, as well as other abbreviations/acronyms, precede nonabbreviated terms in each section. All other terms, including case names and statutes are listed alphabetically, letter-by-letter, regardless of whether the entry contains more than one word. Thus, for example, terms are arranged according to the following order:

Adair v. United States	industrial hygiene
Adamson Act	industrialization
Adams v. Tanner	industrial journalism

For inverted terms, however, the alphabetization is carried up to the comma or semicolon used to invert the heading, as for example:

labor	Education, Department of
labor, common	educational leave
labor, indirect	Education Association; National (Ind)
labor agreement	Education Association, Inc.; Overseas

Punctuation is ignored in all other cases, e.g.:

old age insurance
old age, survivors, and disability insurance
older worker
on-call time pay
one big union
on-site labor

Source references are placed in alphabetical order according to the name of the author. However, citations to laws, cases, and rules and regulations have been arranged to precede the titles arranged according to the author's name.

References to the loose-leaf reporting services of the Bureau of National Affairs, Inc., have been omitted from the individual entries of the *Dictionary* because page references are subject to change. A complete list of the BNA labor services follows the General Source References.

3. *Labor union entries*

Labor unions are entered under the craft or trade designations contained in their names. Thus, the International Longshoremen's Association, is entered as—Longshoremen's Association; International (AFL-CIO). A complete list of unions included in *Roberts' Dictionary* may be found under the term *national and international unions*. The list is arranged according to the formal name of the union, and the trade or craft designation is set out in italics to assist the reader in locating the individual union entry.

The respective state federations of labor with their addresses are entered under the term *state federations of labor*.

4. *Cross references*

In the cross-referencing of entries, or the referral and designation of related terms to be found in *Roberts' Dictionary*, references were made from the general or broad term to the specific or narrow term(s). In some cases, however, *See also* references from the specific to the general are given, especially where it was thought helpful to inform the reader about other terms related to specific entries. *See* references were made wherever possible to current preferred terminology.

5. *List of abbreviations/acronyms*

A number of abbreviations/acronyms are used in *Roberts' Dictionary*, primarily in the bibliographic material included in the source references at the end of entries. Full titles of these abbreviations/acronyms follow:

AAA	American Arbitration Association
AEI	American Enterprise Institute for Public Policy Research
AER	American Economic Review
AFL	American Federation of Labor
AFL-CIO	American Federation of Labor-Congress of Industrial Organizations
AJ	Arbitration Journal
A/M	Annual Meeting
AMA	American Management Association
Annals	Annals of the American Academy of Political and Social Science
BES	Bureau of Employment Security
BILA	Bureau of International Labor Affairs

BJIR	British Journal of Industrial Relations
BLS	Bureau of Labor Statistics
BNA	Bureau of National Affairs, Inc.
Bull.	Bulletin
CCH	Commerce Clearing House, Inc.
CED	Committee for Economic Development
CIO	Congress of Industrial Organizations
CSC	Civil Service Commission
EEOC	Equal Employment Opportunity Commission
ETA	Employment and Training Administration
FEP	Fair Employment Practice (Bureau of National Affairs)
FLRA	Federal Labor Relations Authority
FLRC	Federal Labor Relations Council
FMCS	Federal Mediation and Conciliation Service
FSA	Federal Security Agency
GAO	General Accounting Office
Harvard BR	Harvard Business Review
HEW	Health, Education, and Welfare
HHS	Health and Human Services
ILO	International Labor Organization and/or Office
ILR	International Labour Review
ILRR	Industrial and Labor Relations Review
IPMA	International Personnel Management Association
IR	Industrial Relations, a journal of economy and society Industrial Relations
IRC	Industrial Relations Center
IRRA	Industrial Relations Research Association
IRRI	Industrial Relations Research Institute
IUD	Industrial Union Department (AFL-CIO)
LA	Labor Arbitration Reports (Bureau of National Affairs)
LJ	Law Journal (generally preceded by name of university, e.g., Duke LJ)
LLJ	Labor Law Journal
LMSA	Labor-Management Services Administration
LQ	Law Quarterly (generally preceded by name of university, e.g., Temple LQ)
LR	Law Review (generally preceded by name of university, e.g., Iowa LR)
LRPP	Labor Relations and Public Policy series, Wharton School
LRRM	Labor Relations Reference Manual (Bureau of National Affairs)
MLR	Monthly Labor Review
NAA	National Academy of Arbitrators
NAM	National Association of Manufacturers

NBER	National Bureau of Economic Research
NFI	National Foremen's Institute, Inc.
NICB	National Industrial Conference Board
NLRB	National Labor Relations Board
NMB	National Mediation Board
NPA	National Planning Association
NYSSILR	New York State School of Industrial and Labor Relations
NYU	New York University
OECD	Organization for Economic Co-Operation and Development
OFCCP	Office of Federal Contract Compliance Programs
OMAT	Office of Manpower, Automation and Training
OPM	Office of Personnel Management
PERL	Public Employee Relations Library (International Personnel Management Association)
PH	Prentice-Hall, Inc.
PJ	Personnel Journal
PPA	Public Personnel Association
PPF	Personnel Policies Forum (Bureau of National Affairs)
SLF	Southwestern Legal Foundation
SPIDR	Society of Professionals in Dispute Resolution
SSA	Social Security Administration
Univ.	University; e.g., Univ. of Michigan
UC	University of California
UP	University Press (preceded by name of university, e.g., Cornell UP)
WH	Wage and Hour (Bureau of National Affairs)
WLR	War Labor Reports (Bureau of National Affairs)
WP	Working Paper

Contents

Foreword to the Third Edition	vii
Foreword to the Second Edition	xi
Introduction to the First Edition	xiii
Guide to Users	xvii
Dictionary of Industrial Relations	1
General Source References	803

A

AA *See* AFFIRMATIVE ACTION.

AAA *See* AMERICAN ARBITRATION ASSOCIATION.

AAAA *See* ACTORS AND ARTISTES OF AMERICA; ASSOCIATED (AFL-CIO).

AACSE *See* CLASSIFIED SCHOOL EMPLOYEES; AMERICAN ASSOCIATION OF (IND).

AAE *See* AERONAUTICAL EXAMINERS; NATIONAL ASSOCIATION OF (IND).

AAUP *See* AMERICAN ASSOCIATION OF UNIVERSITY PROFESSORS (AAUP) (IND).

ABGW *See* ALUMINUM, BRICK AND GLASS WORKERS INTERNATIONAL UNION (AFL-CIO).

ACTWU *See* CLOTHING AND TEXTILE WORKERS UNION; AMALGAMATED (AFL-CIO).

ADEA *See* AGE DISCRIMINATION IN EMPLOYMENT ACT OF 1967.

AEA *See* ACTORS' EQUITY ASSOCIATION.

AFA *See* FLIGHT ATTENDANTS; ASSOCIATION OF.

AFGE *See* GOVERNMENT EMPLOYEES; AMERICAN FEDERATION OF (AFL-CIO).

AFGM *See* GRAIN MILLERS; AMERICAN FEDERATION OF (AFL-CIO).

AFGW *See* GLASS WORKERS' UNION OF NORTH AMERICA; AMERICAN FLINT (AFL-CIO).

AFL *See* AMERICAN FEDERATION OF LABOR.

AFL-CIO *See* AMERICAN FEDERATION OF LABOR-CONGRESS OF INDUSTRIAL ORGANIZATIONS.

AFM *See* MUSICIANS; AMERICAN FEDERATION OF (AFL-CIO).

AFSA *See* SCHOOL ADMINISTRATORS; AMERICAN FEDERATION OF (AFL-CIO).

AFSCME *See* STATE, COUNTY AND MUNICIPAL EMPLOYEES; AMERICAN FEDERATION OF (AFL-CIO).

AFT *See* TEACHERS; AMERICAN FEDERATION OF (AFL-CIO).

AFTRA *See* TELEVISION AND RADIO ARTISTS; AMERICAN FEDERATION OF.

AGE *See* ASSEMBLY OF GOVERNMENTAL EMPLOYEES.

AGLIW *See* ATLANTIC, GULF, LAKES AND INLAND WATERS DISTRICT.

AGMA *See* MUSICAL ARTISTS, INC.; AMERICAN GUILD OF.

AGVA *See* VARIETY ARTISTS; AMERICAN GUILD OF.

AIU *See* ATLANTIC INDEPENDENT UNION (IND).

AIW *See* INDUSTRIAL WORKERS OF AMERICA; INTERNATIONAL UNION, ALLIED (AFL-CIO).

ALA *See* ALLIANCE FOR LABOR ACTION (ALA).

ALEA *See* AIR LINE EMPLOYEES ASSOCIATION; INTERNATIONAL.

ALJ *See* ADMINISTRATIVE LAW JUDGE (ALJ).

ALO *See* LACE OPERATIVES OF AMERICA; AMALGAMATED (IND).

ALPA *See* AIR LINE PILOTS ASSOCIATION; INTERNATIONAL (AFL-CIO).

ANA *See* AMERICAN NURSES' ASSOCIATION (IND).

APCA *See* AERONAUTICAL PRODUCTION CONTROLLERS; NATIONAL ASSOCIATION OF (IND).

APWU *See* POSTAL WORKERS UNION; AMERICAN (AFL-CIO).

ASCSE *See* ASCS COUNTY OFFICE EMPLOYEES; NATIONAL ASSOCIATION OF (IND).

ATU *See* TRANSIT UNION; AMALGAMATED (AFL-CIO).

AWIU *See* ALLIED WORKERS INTERNATIONAL UNION; UNITED (IND).

AWWU *See* WATCH WORKERS UNION; AMERICAN (IND).

ability Training, skill, aptitude, and other factors essential in the performance of a job. It is the factor considered most important by employers in promotion and generally ranks with length of service in layoffs, rehires, and transfers. The relative importance of ability (in connection with such factors as length of service, training, etc.) will vary from contract to contract. Where job performance is based on acquired skills with a minimum of discretion as on some mass production jobs, length of service plays a greater role. Where substantial discretion and careful judgment are important, the factor of ability looms greater.

A contract clause which combines ability and length of service may read as follows: "Promotions to all vacancies and positions created during the term of this agreement will be made from the group of present employees on the basis of ability and seniority. Among employees whose ability is relatively equal, seniority will determine the choice for promotion."

Ability has been measured by performance on the job, by work records, and other ratings designed to measure an employee's day-to-day handling of his job.

Source references: Frank Elkouri and Edna A. Elkouri, *How Arbitration Works* (4th ed., Washington: BNA, 1985); J. Healy, "The Ability Factor in Labor Relations," *AJ*, Vol. 10, no. 1, 1955; Wayne E. Howard, "The Arbitration of the Ability Qualification to Exercise of Contractual Seniority Rights" (Unpublished Ph.D. dissertation, Univ. of Pennsylvania, 1957); Thomas J. McDermott, "Types of Seniority Provisions and the Measurement of Ability," *AJ*, Vol. 25, no. 2, 1970; Philip E. Vernon, *The Measurement of Abilities* (2d ed., New York: Philosophical Library, 1961).

See also SKILL.

ability tests Tests to measure capacity to perform work or to determine aptitudes to pursue certain vocations are in widespread use. General intelligence tests used in vocational education have been adapted and modified to meet industrial needs. Current batteries of tests are being utilized for perceptiveness, manipulative ability, verbal facility, and a wide variety of factors which may be of particular interest to a company in the performance of a particular service or productive operation.

Source references: "Ability Tests," *Across the Board*, July/Aug. 1982; Robert M. Guion and Andrew S. Imada, "Eyeball Measurement of Dexterity: Tests as Alternatives to Interviews," *Personnel Psychology*, Spring 1981; John B. Hunter and Frank L. Schmidt, "Ability Tests: Economic Benefits Versus the Issue of Fairness," *IR*, Fall 1982; John H. Metzler and E. V. Kohrs, "Tests and 'The Requirements of the Job,' " *AJ*, Vol. 20, no. 2, 1965; Lois C. Northrup, *The Definition and Measurement of Judgment* (Washington: U.S. CSC, Technical Memorandum 76–17, 1976); Benjamin Schneider, "Increasing the Validity of Ability Measures," *Personnel*, May/June 1978.

See also APTITUDE TESTS, INTELLIGENCE TESTS, TEST, UNIFORM GUIDELINES ON EMPLOYEE SELECTION PROCEDURES.

ability to pay A factor generally considered in labor-management negotiations. It is almost always an "implied" item to be kept in mind. Occasionally it becomes a major "overt" criterion in wage determination. It has received widespread public consideration where the employer has claimed that he is unable to bear the brunt of the wage increase requested by the union. The detailed consideration of a company's financial ability or inability leads to a maze of complexities. For example, would a company's cash or profit picture permit an increase if it had not "expanded" or developed or purchased new equipment the previous year? Has it invested for the purpose of showing a limited ability to absorb a large wage increase? Does the company's ability to pay depend on future developments which it is difficult to assess at the time negotiations are taking place?

What constitutes a company's ability to pay may be a highly controversial issue. For example, does a company's other expansion, which results in a poor liquid showing and high interest payment, show that it is unable to pay? An examination of union briefs on this point indicates that many issues have been raised which touch on the methods of company accounting and go much beyond the mere existence of a cash surplus out of which a wage increase may be met.

The ability-to-pay argument has been used by both labor and management to support a specific position in specific negotiations. Invariably the financial position of a company cannot help but be in the background of any wage negotiation.

During World War II the National War Labor Board in a series of cases following passage of the Wage Stabilization Act indicated that because of the necessity to stabilize wages it could not consider the company's ability to pay as a factor in determining what would constitute a proper wage adjustment. The Board also took the position that a company's financial inability to pay, during the stabilization period, should not deny the employees wage adjustments otherwise appropriate.

In contract negotiations where the company claims inability to pay as a basis for denying a wage increase or seeking to reduce it, the NLRB has held that the union bargaining committee may insist that the employer offer documentation or proof to that effect.

Source references: NLRB v. Truitt Mfg. Co., 351 US 149, 38 LRRM 2042 (1956); Jules Bachman, *Economics of Fourth Round Wage Increase*, Testimony on behalf of the Steel companies before the Presidential Steel Board (n.p., 1949); Ernest Dale, *Sources of Economic Information for Collective Bargaining* (New York: AMA, Research Report no. 17, 1951); Fred R. Fairchild, *Profits and the Ability to Pay Wages* (Irvington-on-Hudson: Foundation for Economic Education, 1946); Philip A. Miscimarra, "Inability to Pay: The Problem of Contract Enforcement in Public Sector Collective Bargaining," *Univ. of Pittsburgh LR*, Vol. 43, no. 3, Spring 1982; Charles C. Mulcahy, "Ability to Pay: The Public Employee Dilemma," *AJ*, June 1976; Charles C. Mulcahy and Marion Cartwright Smith, *Problems & Solutions Resulting from Inability to Pay in the Public Sector* (Washington: IPMA, PERL 57, 1978); Philip Murray, *The CIO Case for Substantial Pay Increases* (Washington: CIO, 1945); Sumner H. Slichter, *Basic Criteria Used in Wage Negotiations* (Chicago: Chicago Assn. of Commerce & Industry, 1947).

See also ACCESS TO COMPANY BOOKS AND RECORDS, REFUSAL TO BARGAIN.

able and willing to work Criterion generally applied in state laws providing unemployment benefits to those out of work in covered occupations who report to the employment offices as "able and willing" to take employment.

See also UNEMPLOYMENT BENEFITS.

able-bodied labor A term generally applied to workers who possess the physical strength to perform a variety of manual tasks. The term excludes the very young and very old in the population as well as those incapacitated through physical or mental disability.

"Ability to work" under unemployment compensation statutes has been defined variously to determine the claim by the individual for benefit payments.

Source references: Ralph Altman, *Availability for Work* (Cambridge: Harvard UP, 1950); John H. Person, *Full Employment* (New Haven: Yale UP, 1941).

Abood v. Detroit Board of Education A Supreme Court decision which held that a state law authorizing an agency shop agreement in the public sector requiring nonunion employees to render service fees equal to union dues is constitutionally valid. The Court, however, ruled that service fees may not be used to finance union activities which are not related to collective bargaining, contract administration, and grievance adjustment.

Source references: Abood v. Detroit Board of Education, 431 US 209, 95 LRRM 2411 (1977); Michael S. Mitchell, "Public Sector Union Security: The Impact of *Abood*," *LLJ*, Nov. 1978; Mark S. Pulliam, "Union Security

Clauses in Public Sector Labor Contracts and *Abood v. Detroit Board of Education*: A Dissent," *LLJ*, Sept. 1980; Charles M. Rehmus and Benjamin A. Kerner, "The Agency Shop After *Abood*: No Free Ride, But What's the Fare?" *ILRR*, Oct. 1980; Robert H. Wilde, "Abood v. Detroit Board of Education," *Journal of Collective Negotiations in the Public Sector*, Vol. 7, no. 3, 1978.

See also AGENCY SHOP, REBATE PLAN, SERVICE FEE.

abrogation of agreement The cancellation or setting aside of a collective bargaining agreement or any portion of it. This may be implied in the signing of new contract terms which differ from the preceding agreement or may be spelled out by including a specific clause which sets aside all previous agreements or understandings.

Some contracts set forth conditions under which the agreement may be voided. For example: "Should either party to this agreement violate any of its provisions, same shall be deemed sufficient cause for cancellation of this agreement by the other party."

Title III, Section 301 of the Taft-Hartley amendments to the National Labor Relations Act provides specific remedies in the federal courts for contract violations.

Source references: Herbert Burstein, "Enforcement of Collective Agreements by the Courts," *NYU 6th Annual Conference on Labor*, ed. by Emanuel Stein (Albany: Bender, 1953); Sherman L. Cohn, "Suing the Unincorporated Union," *LLJ*, Jan. 1960; Dagmar F. Harris, "Practice and Procedure Under Section 301 and 303 of the Taft-Hartley Act," *NYU 10th Annual Conference on Labor*, ed. by Emanuel Stein (Albany: Bender, 1957); S. P. Kaye and E. G. Allen, "The Suability of Unions," *LLJ*, June 1950; Philip G. Marshall, "Enforcing the Labor Contract," *LLJ*, April 1963; Peter Seitz, "The Enforcement of Collective Bargaining Contracts by Arbitration," *NYU 6th Annual Conference on Labor*, ed. by Emanuel Stein (Albany: Bender, 1953); U.S. Dept. of Labor, BLS, *Collective Bargaining Provisions: Strikes and Lockouts; Contract Enforcement* (Washington: Bull. 908–13, 1949).

See also AGREEMENT ENFORCEMENT, ENFORCEMENT OF AGREEMENT, ENFORCEMENT OF ARBITRATION AGREEMENT, ENFORCEMENT STRIKE, SAVINGS CLAUSE, SECTION 301, SEPARABILITY CLAUSE, SUITS FOR CONTRACT VIOLATION.

absence A temporary unavailability for work lasting for one or more days or shifts. It is to be distinguished from lateness which is of a lesser duration than one day or shift, even though the employee may be unavailable when needed for work assignment.

Source references: Hilde Behrend, "Voluntary Absence from Work," *ILR*, Feb. 1959; Maurice D. Kilbridge, "Turnover, Absence, and Transfer Rates as Indicators of Employee Dissatisfaction with Repetitive Work," *ILRR*, Oct. 1961; Carol Boyd Leon, "Employed But Not at Work: A Review of Unpaid Absences," *MLR*, Nov. 1981; Metropolitan Life Insurance Co., Policyholders Service Bureau, *Control of Absence* (New York: 1951); Daniel E. Taylor, "Absences from Work Among Full-Time Employees," *MLR*, March 1981; U.S. Dept. of HEW, Public Health Service, *Time Lost From Work Among the Currently Employed Population, United States—1968* (Washington: 1972).

absence rate A measure, usually in the form of a statistical estimate, to determine the time lost (in terms of hours or man-days) by being away from the job as against the time worked, or the time employees could have worked had they all been present.

BLS maintains data on absence rates. The formula used by BLS is as follows:

$$\text{A.R.} = \frac{\text{man-days lost (per month)}}{\text{man-days worked plus man-days lost}}$$

BLS records a "man-day lost" when the employee is absent on a day he was scheduled to work.

Comparability of company or industry data privately maintained will depend upon the definition of such factors as: man-days, time worked, normal work period, work schedule, workday available.

Source references: J. K. Chadwick-Jones et al., "Absence Measures: Their Reliability and Stability in an Industrial Setting," *Personnel Psychology*, Autumn 1971; John B. Fox and Jerome F. Scott, *Absenteeism: Management's Problem* (Cambridge: Harvard School of Business Administration, Business Research Studies no. 29, 1943); Janice Neipert Hedges,

Absence from Work—Measuring the Hours Lost, May 1973–76 (Washington: U.S. Dept. of Labor, BLS, Special Labor Force Report 207, 1977); Herbert G. Heneman, Jr. et al., "Standardized Absence Rates: A First Step Toward Comparability," *PJ*, July/Aug. 1961; U.S. Dept. of Labor, BLS, *The ABC of Absenteeism* (Washington: Special Bull. no. 17, 1944).

absentee A worker who is unavailable for work for one or more days or shifts, when he has been assigned to or scheduled for or expected to report for work.

absentee interview A meeting or conference with a worker who has been absent from his shift for one or more days. The purpose for such meeting is to determine the reason or reasons for such absence and to work out procedures to avoid their future occurrence and to reduce unnecessary absenteeism.

absenteeism The practice of a worker of failing to report for work for a period of one or more days or shifts, when he has been assigned to or scheduled for work.

During war periods government agencies have sought to reduce absenteeism in order to increase the productive potential of industry.

Collective bargaining agreements sometimes provide disciplinary action and discharge for excessive absenteeism. Where no standard has been established, the interpretation of "excessive" may give rise to difficulty and require occasional submission to arbitration.

Source references: Steven G. Allen, "Compensation, Safety, and Absenteeism: Evidence From the Paper Industry," *ILRR*, Jan. 1981; Howard Block and Richard Mittenthal, "Paper on Discipline for Absenteeism . . . Before National Academy of Arbitrators," *Daily Labor Report*, No. 104, May 31, 1984; Paul F. Brissenden and Emil Frankel, *Labor Turnover in Industry* (New York: Macmillan, 1922); BNA, *Job Absence and Turnover Control* (Washington: PPF Survey no. 132, 1981); Raymond Dreyfack, *How to Control Absenteeism* (Chicago: Dartnell, 1972); John B. Fox and Jerome F. Scott, *Absenteeism: Management's Problem* (Cambridge: Harvard School of Business Administration, Business Research Studies no. 29, 1943); W. M. Gafafer, *Sickness Absenteeism Among Male and Female Industrial Workers 1937–1946* (Washington: U.S. Public Health Service, Public Health Report no. 2817, 1947); Frederick J. Gaudet, *Solving the Problems of Employee Absence* (New York: AMA, Research Study 57, 1963); Frank E. Kuzmits, "No Fault: A New Strategy for Absenteeism Control," *PJ*, May 1981; J. Paul Leigh, "The Effects of Union Membership on Absence from Work Due to Illness," *Journal of Labor Research*, Fall 1981; Mary Green Miner, "Job Absence and Turnover: A New Source of Data," *MLR*, Oct. 1977; Rhoda Rosenthal, "Arbitral Standards for Absentee Discharges," *LLJ*, Dec. 1979; Miriam Rothman, "Can Alternatives to Sick Pay Plans Reduce Absenteeism?" *PJ*, Oct. 1981; John Scherba and Lyle Smith, "Computerization of Absentee Control Programs," *PJ*, May 1973; Doris M. Thompson, *Controls for Absenteeism* (New York: NICB, Studies in Personnel Policy no. 126, 1952); U.S. Dept. of Labor, BLS, *Improving Productivity: Labor and Management Approaches* (Washington: Bull. no. 1715, 1971).

absolute majority A vote in which 51 percent of those eligible to cast their vote do so in favor of or in opposition to a specific proposition.

See also MAJORITY RULE, REPRESENTATION ELECTIONS.

absolute minimum standard of living *See* BARE (MINIMUM) SUBSISTENCE LEVEL.

academic tenure The 1940 Statement of Principles on Academic Freedom and Tenure of the American Association of University Professors and the Association of American Colleges states that "After the expiration of a probationary period, teachers or investigators should have permanent or continuous tenure, and their service should be terminated only for adequate cause, except in the case of retirement for age, or under extraordinary circumstances because of financial exigencies."

Among other practices, the principles require that the probationary period prior to granting of tenure not exceed seven years, termination for cause be considered by both a faculty committee and the governing board of the institution, "the accused teacher should be informed before the hearing in writing of the charges against him and should have the opportunity to be heard in his own defense by all bodies that pass judgment upon his case," and termination due to financial exigency should be "demonstrably bona fide."

Source references: American Association of University Professors, *Policy Documents and Reports* (Washington: 1971); Frank J. Atelsek and Irene L. Gomberg, *Tenure Practices at Four-Year Colleges and Universities* (Washington: American Council on Education, Higher Education Panel Report no. 48, 1980); Richard P. Chait and Andrew T. Ford, *Beyond Traditional Tenure, A Guide to Sound Policies and Practices* (San Francisco: Jossey-Bass, 1982); Commission on Academic Tenure in Higher Education, *Faculty Tenure; A Report and Recommendations* (San Francisco: Jossey-Bass, 1973); Louis Joughin (ed.), *Academic Freedom and Tenure; A Handbook of the American Association of University Professors* (Madison: Univ. of Wisconsin, 1967); Lionel S. Lewis, "Academic Tenure: Its Recipients and Its Effects," *Annals*, March 1980; James O'Toole, William W. Van Alstyne, and Richard Chait, *Three Views, Tenure* (New Rochelle: Change Magazine Press, 1979); "A Recent Survey on Tenure Practices at Four-Year Institutions," *Change*, March 1981; Bardwell L. Smith and Associates, *The Tenure Debate* (San Francisco: Jossey-Bass, 1973); "Tenure and Retrenchment Practices in Higher Education—A Technical Report," *Journal of the College and University Personnel Association*, Fall/Winter 1980.

See also JOB TENURE, ROTH CASE, SINDERMANN CASE, TENURE.

"AC" cases A designation used by the NLRB for petitions filed by a certified representative of a bargaining unit or by an employer of such bargaining unit employees to amend an outstanding certification of a bargaining representative.

Source reference: U.S. NLRB, *A Guide to Basic Law and Procedures Under the National Labor Relations Act* (Washington: 1978).

See also "R" CASES, "U" CASES.

accelerating premium pay A wage incentive system under which the bonus or premium progressively rises as the production standard is exceeded. An employee who exceeds his standard production by 5 percent may receive a 5 percent bonus, while one who exceeds his standard by 10 percent may receive a 15 percent bonus, and one who exceeds his standard by 20 percent may receive a 30 percent bonus.

Source references: Dale S. Beach, "Wage Incentives on the Wane?" *Personnel*, Nov./Dec. 1962; Aaron Levenstein, "The Incentive to Produce," *Management Review*, July 1962; J. K. Louden, "Management's Search for Precision in Measuring a Fair Day's Work," *Advanced Management*, Jan. 1942; Charles W. Lyttle, *Wage Incentive Methods* (New York: Ronald Press, 1929); National Conference Board, *Systems of Wage Payment* (New York: 1930).

See also INCENTIVE WAGE, PREMIUM PAY.

accession Addition to the work force of a new employee or the rehiring of a former employee. Information on accession is maintained by employers in order to measure turnover in the plant. BLS computes the turnover rates by dividing the number of separations and accessions by the total number working during a specified period.

Source references: Paul F. Brissenden and Emil Frankel, *Labor Turnover in Industry* (New York: Macmillan, 1922); "Labor Turnover—Meaning and Measurement," *ILR*, June 1960; Sumner H. Slichter, *The Turnover of Factory Labor* (New York: Appleton, 1921); Dale Yoder, *Labor Market Research* (Minneapolis: Univ. of Minnesota Press, 1948).

See also ACCESSION RATE, LABOR TURNOVER, SEPARATION.

accession rate The number of new or rehired employees added to the work force per hundred employees. It is generally computed on a monthly basis.

$$\text{A.R.} = \frac{\text{Total Accessions} \times 100}{\text{Number Working During Period}}$$

access to company books and records This issue may come up in contract negotiations when there is a question of the company's ability to pay, or when the union claims that the company's profits are greater than those actually reported. When employers claim an inability to pay, they incur a legal obligation to provide access to financial books and records. Historically, employers have claimed unwillingness to pay and have been reluctant to show their books and records. However, current economic condition and concession bargaining developments have prompted employers to provide such information to unions.

In the public utility field, state public utility commissions in most cases have access to the records and books of companies within their jurisdiction. Such provisions flow from the rate-fixing powers of the commissions.

The problem comes up in collective bargaining and may come before the NLRB when negotations break down and the unions file an unfair labor practice charge alleging "refusal to bargain" or failure to bargain in "good faith," because the company withheld basic financial data.

Access to company records may also be involved in seniority problems. Although company books and records generally are not accessible to union representatives, companies generally will permit union representatives to examine the service and other employment records in connection with promotion, transfer, or discharge of employees. The collective bargaining agreement may specify the type of records available to the union.

Source references: Florian Bartosic and Roger C. Hartley, "The Employer's Duty to Supply Information to the Union—A Study of the Interplay of Administrative and Judicial Rationalization," *IR Law Digest*, July 1973; Ernest Dale, *Sources of Economic Information for Collective Bargaining* (New York: AMA Research Report no. 17, 1951); Max J. Miller, "Employer's Duty to Furnish Economic Data to Unions—Revisited," *LLJ*, May 1966; Winifred D. Morio, *"Detroit Edison Co. v. NLRB*: Confidentiality and the Duty to Furnish Information," *NYU 32d Annual National Conference on Labor*, ed. by Richard Adelman (New York: Bender, 1980); Samuel Morris, "Standards for Supplying Information Under the National Labor Relations Act," *Industrial and Labor Relations Forum*, Vol. 13, no. 3, 1979; James T. O'Reilly and Gale P. Simon, *Unions' Rights to Company Information* (Philadelphia: Univ. of Pennsylvania, Wharton School, Industrial Research Unit, LRPP Series no. 21, 1980).

See also ABILITY TO PAY.

access to company property by employees and company representatives Rights, variously applied, protecting employees not on strike to enter company premises for the purpose of working. These rights may be safeguarded by limiting the number of pickets at the plant entrance or providing police protection for those desiring to work during a labor dispute.

See also PICKETING, STRIKE.

access to plant by union representatives Provision often is made to permit union officers or agents other than those working on the premises access to the place of work of employees. The purpose of such permission may be to allow them to collect dues or to handle or investigate grievances.

The details as to time, place of entrance, method of escort, etc., will vary from plant to plant and the conditions which are present in the particular industry. Frequently the agreement may require a specific pass for the union representatives, and assurances from them that there will be no interference with production.

accident *See* INDUSTRIAL ACCIDENT.

accident and sick benefits Payments made to workers because of time lost from work because of disabilities caused by sickness or accident. Many collective bargaining contracts provide for such benefits. Financing may be joint or fully supported by, the employer.

Source references: Dorothy Kittner Greene and Harry E. Davis, "Accident and Sickness Benefits Under Collective Bargaining, 1958," *MLR*, June 1959; David McCahan, *Accident and Sickness Insurance* (Philadelphia: Univ. of Pennsylvania Press, 1954).

See also DISABILITY INSURANCE, HEALTH BENEFIT PROGRAMS, HEALTH INSURANCE, PERMANENT DISABILITY, SICK LEAVE, TEMPORARY DISABILITY INSURANCE, WORKERS COMPENSATION.

accident frequency rate A statistical measure showing the rate of accidents. This is usually in the form of a ratio of the number of man-hours (employee hours) worked to the number of disabling accidents or injuries per one million man-hours worked. The number of hours actually worked sometimes is referred to as the number of hours the employees are "exposed" to accidents. The formula used by BLS is the total number of disabling injuries per one million man-hours actually worked.

Source references: Roland P. Blake (ed.), *Industrial Safety* (2d ed., New York: PH, 1953); "Industrial Industry Trends Over Three Decades," *ILR*, March 1961; Norman Root, "Injuries at Work are Fewer Among Older Employees," *MLR*, March 1981; R. H. Simonds, *Safety Management: Accident Cost and Control* (Homewood: Irwin, 1956); Robert S. Smith, "Intertemporal Changes in Work Injury Rates," *Proceedings of the 25th A/M, IRRA*, ed. by Gerald Somers (Madison: 1973); U.S. Dept. of Labor, BLS, *Injury Rates by Industry, 1970* (Washington: Report 406, 1972).

See also ACCIDENT SEVERITY RATE, ILLNESS FREQUENCY RATE.

accident insurance Laws in effect in most states providing for payments to employees injured on the job.

Accidents are regarded as one of the normal costs considered in the production of goods. The charges are made against the employer and ultimately are borne by the consumer.

Workers compensation laws may provide for medical and surgical treatment as well as hospital care; compensation for loss of wages for temporary, partial, or permanent disability; funeral allowances and pensions to dependents in case of death.

Source references: Earl F. Cheit, "Work Injuries and Recovery. I. Survivors' Benefits—A Plan to Make Them Equitable," *MLR*, Oct. 1961; Harry A. Millis and Royal E. Montgomery, *Labor's Risk and Social Insurance* (New York: McGraw-Hill, 1938).

See also WORKERS COMPENSATION.

accident prevention Efforts on the part of government, employers, and labor-management committees to eliminate and reduce the causes of industrial injuries and accidents. The work to prevent accidents has gone along not only on humane grounds but also on economic ones. It has been found that accident prevention is cheaper than accident compensation.

Accident prevention efforts have been responsible for economic savings in the form of increased production; decreased overhead costs; reduced labor turnover; and maintenance of skill and experience.

Source references: Roland P. Blake (ed.), *Industrial Safety* (2d ed., New York: PH, 1953); Russell De Reamer, *Modern Safety Practices* (New York: Wiley, 1958); H. W. Heinrich, *Industrial Accident Prevention* (4th ed., New York: McGraw-Hill, 1959); ILO, *Accident Prevention, A Workers' Education Manual* (Geneva: 1961); Frederick G. Lippert, *Accident Prevention Administration* (New York: McGraw-Hill, 1947); Alan McLean, "Accidents and the 'Human Factor,'" *PJ*, Feb. 1956; W. D. Okrongley, "Attitude Development and Accident Prevention," *PJ*, March 1966.

See also JOB SAFETY TRAINING, OCCUPATIONAL SAFETY AND HEALTH ACT (OSHA) OF 1970, SAFETY, SAFETY EDUCATION, SAFETY PROGRAMS.

accident prone Term applied to workers who are involved in an unusually large number of accidents. These workers, although small in number, are responsible for a substantial number of industrial accidents.

Workers who show this tendency toward "accident proneness" may be transferred to less hazardous occupations or to plant areas which are potentially less dangerous. Studies constantly are in progress to determine the factors which may be involved, such as poor coordination, short concentration spans, lack of adequate vision, and personal problems.

Source references: A. G. Arbous and J. E. Kerrich, "The Phenomenon of Accident Proneness," *Industrial Medicine and Surgery*, April 1953; Charles A. Drake, "Detecting Accident Prone Workers," *Personnel*, March 1942; Thomas N. Jenkins, "Identifying the Accident-Prone Employee," *Personnel*, July/Aug. 1961; K. T. Johnstone, "The Identification of Accident Proneness," *Industrial Medicine and Surgery*, July 1955; Wayne K.

Kirchner, "A Fresh Look at the Safety Program: II. The Fallacy of Accident-Proneness," *Personnel*, Nov./Dec. 1961; Joseph T. Kunce, "Vocational Interest and Accident Proneness," *Journal of Applied Psychology*, June 1967.

accident reporting laws Provisions in many state statutes which require employers to report all disabling accidents marking absence from the job for more than one day or shift.

See also WORKERS COMPENSATION.

accident severity rate A statistical measure of the total number of days lost because of industrial accident per 1,000 man-hours of exposure.

See also ACCIDENT FREQUENCY RATE.

accommodation Under federal laws prohibiting discrimination on the basis of religion or handicap, employers are required to accommodate the religious needs, beliefs, and practices, or physical and mental handicaps of employees or prospective employees. With respect to religious accommodation, Sections 701(j) and 703(a) of Title VII of the Civil Rights Act of 1964 require employers, labor organizations, employment agencies, or joint labor-management committees controlling apprenticeship or other training or retraining "to reasonably accommodate" the religious practices of an employee or prospective employee unless it can be demonstrated that such accommodation would result in "undue hardship" on the employer. The reasonable accommodation duty has been held by the Supreme Court to mean that only a minimum of additional costs need be incurred by the employer, otherwise discrimination against other employees would result from the accommodation efforts. Examples of alternative measures the employer must offer to satisfy this duty include voluntary substitutions and swaps, flexible scheduling, lateral transfer, and change of job assignments.

With respect to the physically and mentally disabled, OFCCP regulations issued in compliance with Section 503 of the Rehabilitation Act of 1973 require employers with government contracts in excess of $2,500 to make "reasonable accommodation to the physical and mental limitations of an employee or applicant" unless to do so would impose an "undue hardship" on the conduct of business. The extent of a contractor's accommodation obligations will be determined by, among other considerations, "business necessity and financial cost and expenses." Some alternative means of accommodation include changing job requirements, modifying equipment, and moving supplies to a more convenient and accessible location. Similarly, under the Vietnam Era Veterans Readjustment Assistance Act of 1974, if accommodations to the physical and mental limitations of disabled veterans can be made without imposing an undue hardship on the business in terms of safety and efficiency or financial costs and expenses, the contractor is required to make such arrangements.

Source references: Rehabilitation Act of 1973, as amended, 29 U.S.C. 701 et seq. (1982); Civil Rights Act of 1964, as amended, 42 U.S.C. 2000e et seq. (1982); U.S. EEOC, "Guidelines on Discrimination Because of Religion," 29 C.F.R. 1605; U.S. OFCCP, "Affirmative Action Obligations of Contractors and Subcontractors for Handicapped Workers," 41 C.F.R. 60–741; ———, "Affirmative Action Program for Disabled Veterans and Veterans of Vietnam Era," 41 C.F.R. 60–250.6; Roger B. Jacobs, "Reasonable Accommodation in Public Employment," *LLJ*, Nov. 1978; John M. Livingood, "The Status of Religious Accommodation After the *Hardison* Case," *LLJ*, April 1978; James C. Oldham, "Reflections on Title VII from the Standpoint of Customer Preference and Management Prerogative," *Industrial Relations LJ*, Fall 1976; Stephen Sahlein, *The Affirmative Action Handbook* (New York: Executive Enterprises, 1978).

See also HANDICAPPED INDIVIDUAL, RELIGIOUS DISCRIMINATION, UNDUE HARDSHIP.

accretion The addition of new employees to an existing bargaining unit. Unions may negotiate provisions which automatically extend a contract to cover plants or operations acquired by an employer after an agreement is signed. Disputes over questions of accretion are brought before the NLRB.

Source reference: Illinois Malleable Iron Co., 120 NLRB 451, 41 LRRM 1510 (1958).

achievement test Examination which seeks to measure, through established norms or standards, the progress of an employee after specialized education or training programs.

Source reference: Dorothy C. Adkins, *Construction and Analysis of Achievement Tests* (Washington: 1947).

See also TEST.

across-the-board increase A wage adjustment given at one time to all or a significant group of the workers in a plant, company, or industry. The increase may be applied as a percentage or expressed as a fixed cents-per-hour.

Where a uniform percentage is given, higher rated employees will receive a greater absolute adjustment, thus a 10 percent across-the-board increase will give the employee with a $1 rate, 10 cents per hour, while the employee who receives $2 an hour will receive a 20-cent adjustment.

Generally speaking a fixed cents-per-hour adjustment favors the lower-skilled employee whereas the percentage adjustment favors the more highly skilled workers.

During World War II "tapered" adjustments were made so the "internal wage structure" would not be seriously disturbed. Though the adjustments were general, the cents-per-hour figure differed from group to group, thus one group might receive 15 cents, another 12, a third 9, etc.

See also GENERAL WAGE INCREASE, TAPERED WAGE INCREASES.

act Frequently used interchangeably with the word "law." It is a statute enacted by a federal or state legislative body. Some distinguish the two terms by holding that the statute or act becomes law when it has been upheld by the courts. Such a distinction, however, is not widely accepted.

active employees A phrase sometimes used to distinguish employees who have been on layoff status from those who have been retired. Individuals who are retired technically may not be employees of the company although they may have certain retirement benefits. Employees on layoff status, however, are generally considered employees, eligible for rehire under the terms of the collective bargaining contract.

See also LAYOFF, RETIREMENT, RETIREMENT AGE.

Actors and Artistes of America, Associated (AFL-CIO) A national union chartered by the American Federation of Labor in July 1919. The Actors' Equity request for a charter in 1916 was turned down because the AFL had granted jurisdiction covering the theatrical field to the White Rats Actors' Union of America. The White Rats Actors' Union of America was an amalgamation of the Actors' International Union and the White Rats Union in 1910.

The union has membership in the following nine branches:

(1) Actors' Equity Association,
(2) American Federation of Television and Radio Artists,
(3) American Guild of Musical Artists, Inc.,
(4) American Guild of Variety Artists,
(5) Asociacion Puertorriquena de Artistas y Technicos del Espectaculo,
(6) Hebrew Actors Union, Inc.,
(7) Italian Actors Union,
(8) Screen Actors Guild,
(9) Screen Extras Guild.

Address: 165 West 46th Street, New York, N.Y. 10036. Tel. (212) 869–0358

Source references: Alfred Harding, *The Revolt of the Actors* (New York: Wm. Morrow & Co., 1929); Murray Ross, *Stars and Strikes* (New York: Columbia UP, 1941).

See also ACTORS' EQUITY ASSOCIATION; HEBREW ACTORS UNION, INC.; ITALIAN ACTORS UNION; MUSICAL ARTISTS, INC., AMERICAN GUILD OF; SCREEN ACTORS GUILD; SCREEN EXTRAS GUILD; TELEVISION AND RADIO ARTISTS, AMERICAN FEDERATION OF; VARIETY ARTISTS, AMERICAN GUILD OF.

Actors' Equity Association A branch of the Associated Actors and Artistes of America (AFL-CIO). Originally launched in 1913. Affiliated with the American Federation of Labor in 1919. It applied to the Federation for a charter in 1919, and when the White Rats Actors' Union surrendered its charter, the Federation chartered Actors' Equity and the White Rats as the "Associated Actors and Artistes of America"—which then became a federation of autonomous groups, which included Actors' Equity Association. The monthly publication is the *Equity News*. The union has a membership of approximately 30,000.

Address: 165 West 46th St., New York, N.Y. 10036. Tel. (212) 869–0358

actual hours worked The number of hours spent by an employee on the job during a fixed reporting period, weekly or monthly. Actual hours worked include regularly scheduled as well as overtime hours worked.

In determining company or industry data, total man-hours worked are divided by the number of workers employed.

actual wages The term has been used synonymously with "real" wages, or the actual purchasing power of the dollar—generally measured by changes in the Consumer Price Index (cost-of-living index).

The term has also been used to define the wages in the pay envelope at the end of a pay period (take-home pay).

The term offers little in usefulness and might well be set aside in favor of the more clearly understood phrases "real wages," or "nominal wages," or "take-home pay."

Source references: Paul H. Douglas, *Real Wages in the United States* (Boston: Houghton Mifflin, 1930); I. M. Rubinow, "The Recent Trend of Real Wages," *AER*, Dec. 1914; U.S. Dept. of Commerce, Bureau of the Census, *Historical Statistics of the United States, Colonial Times to 1970, Bicentennial Edition, Parts 1 & 2* (Washington: 1975).

See also CONSUMER PRICE INDEX, REAL WAGES, TAKE-HOME PAY.

actuarial equivalent Equivalent pension rates established after equating such factors as interest, form of pension, and mortality. A pension of equivalent value from an actuarial standpoint—i.e., giving adequate consideration to actuarial factors such as, interest, form of pension, incidence of mortality, etc.

actuarial reserve Funds set aside to meet pension payments upon the death or survival of those covered under a plan. Reserves are established on the basis of set mortality rates and specified interest earnings.

actuary An individual trained or engaged in the practice of applying probability in the field of mortality to determine the financial risk involved.

Actuarial (longevity) tables are revised on the basis of experience. Sufficient latitude (safety factors) is provided so those who agree to provide the insurance are protected adequately.

Adair v. United States A major labor case in which the Supreme Court, in 1908, held that section 10 of the Erdman Act of 1898 (30 Stat. 424, c. 370) was unconstitutional. Section 10 of the Act forbade an agent of an interstate carrier to discharge a worker because of membership in a union.

Section 10 read as follows: ". . . That any employer subject to the provisions of this Act and any officer, agent, or receiver of such employer who shall require any employee, or any person seeking employment, as a condition of such employment, to enter into an agreement, either written or verbal, not to become or remain a member of any labor corporation, association, or organization; or shall threaten any employee with loss of employment, or shall unjustly discriminate against any employee because of his membership in such a labor corporation, association, or organization, or who shall require any employee or any person seeking employment, as a condition of such employment, to enter into a contract whereby such employee or applicant for employment shall agree to contribute to any fund for charitable, social, or beneficial purposes; to release such employer from legal liability for any personal injury by reason of any benefit received from such fund beyond the proportion of the benefit arising from the employer's contribution to such fund; or who shall, after having discharged an employee, attempt or conspire to prevent such employee from obtaining employment, is hereby declared to be guilty of a misdemeanor, and, upon conviction thereof in any court of the United States of competent jurisdiction in the district in which such offense was committed, shall be punished for each offense by a fine of not less than one hundred dollars and not more than one thousand dollars."

O. B. Coppage, a fireman on the Louisville and Nashville Railroad, was discharged by William Adair. Adair was convicted and fined under the Erdman Act. On appeal, the Supreme Court held the Erdman Act unconstitutional.

The Supreme Court based its decision on two points: (1) union membership had no relation to interstate commerce ("But what possible legal or logical connection," said Justice Harlan, "is there between an employee's membership in a labor organization and the carrying on of interstate commerce?"), and (2) the Erdman Act deprived the employer of his freedom to contract. ("In our opinion," said Justice Harlan, "That section, [section 10] in the particular mentioned, is an invasion of the personal liberty, as well as the right of property, guaranteed by that [fifth] Amendment. Such liberty and right embraces the right to make contracts for the purchase of the labor of others and equally the right to make contracts for the sale of one's own labor; . . ."

Source references: Adair v. United States, 208 US 161 (1908); Edward Berman, "The Supreme Court Interprets the Railway Labor Act," *AER*, Dec. 1930; Charles R. Darling, "The Adair Case," 42 *American LR* 884 (1908); Richard Olney, "Discrimination Against Union Labor—Legal?" 42 *American LR* 161 (1908).

Adamson Act Act of Congress passed in 1916 at the request of President Woodrow Wilson. It provided the eight-hour day for interstate railroad employees. Congressional action followed a demand by the Railway Brotherhoods for a basic eight-hour day. Following a strike vote, the union threatened to stop work on Labor Day, September 1916.

On August 29, President Wilson appeared before a joint session of Congress and urged that train employees be granted the eight-hour day. Congress passed the Adamson Act on September 2 and the President signed it.

The Supreme Court upheld the constitutionality of the Act in *Wilson v. New* (243 US 332 (1917)).

Source references: Hours of Service Acts (Railroads), as amended, 45 U.S.C. 65, 66 (1982); *Bunting v. Oregon*, 243 US 426 (1917), Economic Briefs by Felix Frankfurter and Josephine Goldmark before U.S. Supreme Court; *Muller v. Oregon*, 208 US 412 (1908), Economic Briefs by Louis D. Brandeis and Josephine Goldmark before U.S. Supreme Court; Marian C. Cahill, *Shorter Hours* (New York: Columbia UP, 1932); Felix Frankfurter, *The Case for the Shorter Workday* (New York: National Consumers League, 1916); John P. Frey, "The Economics of Wages and Hours," *American Federationist*, March 1931; Samuel Gompers, "The Eight-Hour Workday," *American Federationist*, April 1897; Wayne McNaughton and Joseph Lazar, *Industrial Relations and the Government* (New York: McGraw-Hill, 1954); Sumner H. Slichter, "Implications of the Shorter Hour Movement," *Proceedings of the Academy of Political Science*, Vol. 15, 1934; Harry D. Wolf, *The Railroad Labor Board* (Chicago: Univ. of Chicago Press, 1927).

Adams v. Tanner Decision by the Supreme Court in 1917 holding unconstitutional a statute passed by the State of Washington which prohibited employment agencies in the state from collecting fees from employees.

The Court held that private employment agencies could be regulated but could not be prohibited. The Court held that the state law was arbitrary and oppressive and deprived the individuals of property and freedom of contract in violation of the 14th Amendment.

Source reference: Adams v. Tanner, 244 US 590 (1917).

adequate remedy at law A solution or remedy which is as practical, efficient, plain, and complete to achieve the ends of justice and its prompt administration as a remedy in equity. The phrase frequently is found in discussions of use of the injunction and provisions of the Norris-LaGuardia (Anti-Injunction) Act. One of the conditions which has to be met for the granting of an injunction in a labor dispute is that there is "no adequate remedy at law."

Source references: Norris-LaGuardia Anti-Injunction Act, as amended, Section 7(d), 29 U.S.C. 107(d) (1982); Benjamin Aaron, "Strikes in Breach of Collective Agreements: Some Unanswered Questions," 63 *Columbia LR* 1027 (1963); Henry C. Black, *Black's Law Dictionary* (abridged 5th ed., St. Paul: West Publishing, 1983); Walter A. Shumaker and George F. Longsdorf, *Cyclopedia Law Dictionary* (Chicago: Callaghan, 1940); Edwin E. Witte, "The Federal Anti-Injunction Act," 16 *Minnesota LR* 63 (1962).

See also EQUITY, INJUNCTION.

ad hoc arbitration *See* ARBITRATION, AD HOC.

adjustment board An agency to deal with a specific set of labor-management problems. In the handling of plant grievances a board consisting of union and management representatives may screen problems before submission to an arbitrator. These boards may be given authority to adjust or resolve the grievance by majority or unanimous agreement.

It may be a government tribunal, sometimes tripartite in representation, to resolve specific problems in an industry—such as the Wage Adjustment Board set up by the National War Labor Board to handle wage problems in the building and construction industry.

See also NATIONAL RAILROAD ADJUSTMENT BOARD.

Adkins v. Children's Hospital The Supreme Court decision in 1923 which held unconstitutional a law passed by Congress in 1918 providing for the fixing of minimum wages for women and children in the District of Columbia. The Supreme Court in 1937 overruled its previous position.

In the *Parrish* case the Court held that ". . . the decision in the *Adkins* case was a departure from the true application of the principles governing the regulation by the state of the relationship of employer and employee. . . . Our conclusion is that the case of *Adkins v. Children's Hospital* should be, and it is, overruled."

Source references: Adkins v. Children's Hospital, 261 US 525 (1923); *West Coast Hotel v. Parrish*, 300 US 391, 1 WH Cases 38 (1937).

See also MINIMUM WAGE.

administration In collective bargaining, the machinery established to effectuate or administer the provisions of the labor-management contract. The term is also applied to the process of carrying out or enforcing a statute, or management procedures to effectuate a policy set out by the executive.

Source references: Marshall E. Dimock, *A Philosophy of Administration* (New York: Harper, 1958); Ordway Tead, *Administration: Its Purpose and Performance* (New York: Harper, 1959); ______, *The Art of Administration* (New York: McGraw-Hill, 1951).

administration of the agreement *See* AGREEMENT, ADMINISTRATION OF.

administrative employees A class of management employees exempt from the provisions of the Fair Labor Standards Act (Wage-Hour Law). Regulations established by the wage-hour administrator set out the tests to be met by these white-collar employees under the law.

Source references: Fair Labor Standards Act of 1938, Section 13(a)(1), 29 U.S.C. 213 (a)(1) (1982); U.S. Dept. of Labor, BLS, *National Survey of Professional, Administrative, Technical, and Clerical Pay, March 1982* (Washington: Bull. no. 2145, 1982).

administrative law A body of law established by rules, regulations, and court interpretations of actions by an administrative agency established by the federal government or state legislature.

The administrative agencies serve as specialized subjudicial tribunals to administer statutes. The administrative agency, because of its specialized knowledge and continuing concern with the problems of a particular law, gives body and substance to the law, and seeks to effectuate the purpose and intent of the statute.

The growth of administrative agencies, such as the Interstate Commerce Commission, Federal Communications Commission, Federal Trade Commission, Securities and Exchange Commission, the National Labor Relations Board, etc., led Congress to enact the Administrative Procedure Act in June 1946. Purpose of the law is to provide a uniform set of procedures for administrative tribunals.

administrative law judge (ALJ) The rules and regulations of the NLRB define administrative law judge as "the agent of the Board conducting the hearing in an unfair labor practice or Telegraph Merger Act proceeding." Administrative law judges were formerly known as trial examiners. The change in title was made on August 19, 1972.

Hearings officers of other agencies, such as the Occupational Safety and Health Review Commission, are also called administrative law judges.

Source references: U.S. NLRB, *Rules and Regulations and Statements of Procedure, Series 8, as Amended* (Washington: 1982); ———, *Thirty-Eighth Annual Report . . . for the Fiscal Year Ended June 30, 1973* (Washington: 1973).

See also TRIAL EXAMINER, TRIAL EXAMINER'S DECISION.

administrative order (rulings or interpretation) A regulation or order issued by an administrative agency or administrator setting forth detailed procedures and interpretations of the law. These may be issued as a result of misunderstanding of a particular section of the law or as a clarification to indicate how the law will be interpreted and applied by the agency. These orders have the effect of law, but are subject to review by the courts.

Under Sections 9 and 10 of the Portal-to-Portal Act of 1947 an employer may plead as a defense to an alleged violation of the Fair Labor Standards Act that he relied on and conformed in good faith to the ruling, interpretation, or order of the administrator. This also applies to the Equal Pay Act of 1963, an amendment to FLSA.

Administrative Procedure Act A law passed by Congress in June 1946 (5 U.S.C. 1001), to establish uniform procedures for administrative and quasi-judicial agencies. The statute requires the agency to promulgate and publish rules of procedure, including provisions for fair hearings and review of decisions.

The Act was amended in 1967 and 1974 to provide the public with greater access to federal agency information.

Source references: U.S. Congress, Senate, *Administrative Procedure in Government Agencies* (Washington: Senate Doc. no. 8, 1941); U.S. Congress, Senate, Committee on the Judiciary, *Amending the Administrative Procedure Act and Eliminating Certain Exemptions Therefrom, Report* (Washington: 1951).

See also FREEDOM OF INFORMATION ACT (FOIA) OF 1966.

administrator A person who has the responsibility of carrying out the purposes or provisions of a law. The Wage and Hour Law is enforced by an administrator. The National Labor Relations Act, as amended by Taft-Hartley, is administered by a general counsel and five NLRB members. In most administrative or quasi-judicial agencies the powers are not divided.

admission to union *See* UNION MEMBERSHIP ELIGIBILITY.

adoption leave Type of leave which allows an employee to be absent on annual leave or on leave without pay to process an adoption.

Source references: Mitchell Meyer, *Women and Employee Benefits* (New York: The Conference Board, Report no. 752, 1978); U.S. CSC, *A Survey of Leave Provisions in Federal Labor Agreements* (Washington: 1977).

advance on wages Payment of earnings prior to the regular payday. Employees who work on a commission basis may receive an advance on their wages prior to having earned them. Some firms may provide a fixed allowance or advance for a period of weeks or months, to be repaid when earnings or commissions are received.

adverse action In the federal service it includes removals, suspensions for more than 30 days, furloughs without pay, and reductions in rank or pay, as promulgated by the rules and regulations of the former Civil Service Commission.

Currently, under Title II of the Civil Service Reform Act of 1978, adverse action procedures may be initiated by federal agencies against employees in accordance with the regulations of the Office of Personnel Management but "only for such cause as will promote the efficiency of the service." Employees may appeal adverse actions through the negotiated grievance procedure or to the Merit Systems Protection Board.

Although frequently used in reference to disciplinary measures, the term may also refer to actions taken because of a lack of work or funds, or for other nondisciplinary reasons.

Source references: Civil Service Reform Act of 1978, 5 U.S.C. 7501 et seq. (1982); U.S. CSC, *Federal Personnel Manual*, Chapter 752, Subpart B, January 3, 1972.

adverse impact Defined by the EEOC as "a substantially different rate of selection in hiring, promotion, or other employment decision which works to the disadvantage of members of a race, sex, or ethnic group." EEOC sometimes uses as a gross measure of adverse impact whether the selection rate for any race, sex, or ethnic group is less than four-fifths (or 80 percent) of the selection rate for the group with the highest selection rate. According to the EEOC, this measure is a rule of thumb, not a legal definition.

Sometimes referred to as "disparate impact," it is considered a more complicated type of discrimination than disparate treatment. It involves employment practices that are facially neutral in their treatment of different groups but that in fact fall more harshly on one group than another and cannot be justified by business necessity.

Employee selection procedures which may have adverse impact on a protected class include such measures as: scored tests; height, weight, and physical requirements; nonscored objective criteria such as specific education, license, performance, or experience; and such subjective criteria as "leadership," "aggressiveness," interest, or personality.

Source references: U.S. EEOC, "Adoption of Questions and Answers to Clarify and Provide a Common Interpretation of the Uniform Guidelines on Employee Selection Procedures," 44 F.R. 11996; ———, "Uniform Guidelines on Employee Selection Procedures," 29 C.F.R. 1607; John Klinefelter and James Thompkins, "Adverse Impact in Employment Selection," *Public Personnel Management*, May/June 1976; John D. Kraft, "Adverse Impact Determination in Federal Examination," *Public Personnel Management*, Nov./Dec. 1978.

See also EIGHTY PERCENT (80%) RULE, PROTECTED CLASS, UNIFORM GUIDELINES ON EMPLOYEE SELECTION PROCEDURES.

advisory arbitration *See* ARBITRATION, ADVISORY.

advisory council An agency, generally tripartite in structure, to assist in a consultative or advisory capacity on major policy matters.

advisory councils on employment security State employment service agencies operating under the Wagner-Peyser Act are required to establish tripartite advisory councils. These councils act in a consultative or advisory capacity to the agency administering the state law.

A federal council similar in structure advises the United States Employment Service.

Source references: Joseph M. Becker, "Advisory Councils in Employment Security," *ILRR*, April 1959; ———, *Shared Government in Employment Security: A Study of Advisory Councils* (New York: Columbia UP, 1959).

Aeronautical Examiners; National Association of (Ind) 1938 Miner Ave., San Pablo, Calif. 94806. Tel. (415) 869–3476

Aeronautical Production Controllers; National Association of (Ind) Formerly known as the Aeronautical Production Controlmen Association (Ind).

Address: 743 Red Mill Rd., Norfolk, Va. 23502. Tel. (804) 461–3451

affected class According to the OFCCP, class consisting of "one or more employees, former employees, or applicants who have been denied employment opportunities or benefits because of discriminatory practices and/or policies by the contractor, its employees, or agents. Evidence of the existence of an affected class requires: (1) identification of the discriminatory practices; (2) identification of the effects of discrimination; and (3) identification of those suffering from the effects of discrimination."

Revised Order No. 4 refers to affected class members as those "who by virtue of past discrimination continue to suffer the present effects of that discrimination."

Source references: U.S. OFCCP, "Revised Order No. 4," 41 C.F.R. 60–2; ———, *Federal Contract Compliance Manual* (Washington: 1979).

See also EXECUTIVE ORDER 11246, MINORITY GROUPS, PROTECTED CLASS, REVISED ORDER NO. 4.

affecting commerce Much of federal legislation regulating labor-management relations is based on the authority of Congress to regulate commerce among the states. The term is incorporated in many of the statutes. The National Labor Relations Act, as amended by Taft-Hartley, states: "The term 'affecting commerce' means in commerce, or burdening or obstructing commerce or the free flow of commerce, or having led or tending to lead to a dispute burdening or obstructing commerce or the free flow of commerce." (Section 2(7)).

See also COMMERCE CLAUSE.

affidavit A written statement given under oath and accepted as evidence when no better proof is available. Hearings before an NLRB trial examiner may be in the form of affidavits when the individuals have left the employ of the company, are ill, etc., and are not available as witnesses.

Strict rules of evidence are not required in hearings before NLRB. The character and source of the evidence are considered by the trial examiner and the Board. The Board makes its decision on the preponderance of evidence in the whole record.

See also EVIDENCE.

Affiliated Schools for Workers A group of summer schools first organized during the 1920s, such as Bryn Mawr and Oberlin, to provide women wage earners with college guidance and training in economics, labor history, etc. The work of these groups were enlarged and both men and women received training at worker schools in Bryn Mawr, Pennsylvania; Berkeley, California; Madison, Wisconsin; Asheville, North Carolina; and Chicago, Illinois.

AFL-CIO and several affiliated unions assisted in financing and organizing the summer schools. Classroom and faculty facilities were provided by some of the universities.

The organization was later known as the American Labor Education Service.

See also LABOR EDUCATION, NATIONAL INSTITUTE OF LABOR EDUCATION (NILE).

affiliation The joining or association of a group with a parent or national organization. For example, a local union may be affiliated with the national union, and the national union in turn may be affiliated with the AFL-CIO.

affirmative action A remedial concept involving positive actions taken by an employer in areas such as recruitment, hiring, transfer, upgrading, rates of pay, and selection for training to improve work opportunities of groups considered to have been deprived of these opportunities because of discrimination. Affirmative action-type remedies may be directed by the courts or negotiated by the EEOC in the form of conciliation agreements settling employment discrimination charges brought under Title VII of the Civil Rights Act of 1964.

The term is defined by OFCCP as "results-oriented actions which a contractor by virtue of its contracts must take to ensure equal employment opportunity. Where appropriate, it includes goals to correct underutilization, correction of problem areas, etc. It may also include relief such as back pay, retroactive seniority, make-up goals and timetables, etc." Written affirmative action plans are required of certain categories of federal contractors as specified under Executive Order 11246. Federal contractors are required under Section 503 of the Rehabilitation Act of 1973 to take affirmative action to employ and advance in employment handicapped persons; veterans are to be given similar attention by the terms of the Vietnam Era Veterans Readjustment Assistance Act of 1974.

State and local governmental units may be subject to special affirmative action requirements through receipt of federal funds under the Revenue Sharing Act of 1972 and the Intergovernmental Personnel Act.

Source references: E.O. 11246, 3 C.F.R. (1964–65 comp.) 339; U.S. OFCCP, "Revised Order No. 4," 41 C.F.R. 60–2; Clement J. Berwitz, *The Job Analysis Approach to Affirmative Action* (New York: Wiley, 1975); Robert Freiberg (ed.), *The Manager's Guide to Equal Employment Opportunity* (New York: Executive Enterprises, 1977); Gregory D. Squires, *Affirmative Action: A Guide for the Perplexed* (East Lansing: Institute for Community Development, Michigan State Univ., 1977); John Clayton Thomas, "Budget-Cutting and Minority Employment in City Governments: Lessons from Cincinnati," *Public Personnel Management*, May/June 1978.

See also EXECUTIVE ORDER 11246, PRESIDENT'S COMMITTEE ON EQUAL EMPLOYMENT OPPORTUNITY, REVISED ORDER NO. 4, UNDERREPRESENTATION, UNDERUTILIZATION, WEBER CASE.

affirmative order An order issued by the NLRB or state labor boards requiring an employer or union to take specific action to undo a wrong committed in violation of law.

An example of an affirmative order of NLRB is one which requires the employer to reinstate an improperly discharged employee and make him whole for any loss of pay he may have suffered, reestablish his seniority and other rights, and so far as possible undo the harm which resulted from the unfair labor practice. Board orders also have a negative or cease-and-desist section which requires the employer to stop unfair labor practices.

A typical decision of NLRB will illustrate the negative and affirmative aspects of the Board order:

> Upon the entire record in the case, and pursuant to section . . . of the National Labor Relations Act as amended, the National Labor Relations Board hereby orders the Respondent (name of company) and its officers, agents, successors, and assigns, (to):
>
> (1) *Cease and desist* from:
>
> (a) Discouraging membership in (union) or in any other labor organization of its employees, by discharging or refusing to reinstate any of its employees, or in any other manner discriminating in regard to their hire or tenure of employment, or any term or condition of their employment; . . .
>
> (2) Take the following *affirmative action*, which the Board finds will effectuate the policies of the Act:
>
> (a) Offer (name) full reinstatement to his former or substantially equivalent position, without prejudice to his seniority or other rights or privileges . . . .
>
> (b) Make whole (name) for any loss of pay he may have suffered because of the Respondent's discrimination against him, by payment of a sum equal to the amount which he normally would have earned as wages during the period . . . (of discrimination) . . . less his net earnings, if any, during the same period.

Among unusual remedial orders, NLRB in the *H. W. Elson Bottling Co.* and *Teamsters, Local 328* (155 NLRB 714, 60 LRRM 1381 (1965)), case held that the employer had prevented the union from obtaining a majority through coercive practices. To remedy the situation the Board in its affirmative order required the company to provide the employees a one-hour meeting on company premises; the use of a company bulletin board to post notices for a three-month period; and the sending of notices by the company to each of its employees to inform them of their statutory right to be "free from interference, coercion and restraint." NLRB noted the *Local 60 Carpenters* case in which the U.S. Supreme Court held that the Board must "take measures designed to recreate the conditions and relationships that would have been had there been no unfair labor practice."

Source references: Local 60, Carpenters Union v. NLRB, 365 US 651, 47 LRRM 2900 (1961); *NLRB v. Seven-Up Bottling Co.*, 344 US 344, 31 LRRM 2237 (1953); *NLRB v. Erie Resistor Corp.*, 373 US 221, 53 LRRM 2121 (1963).

See also CEASE AND DESIST ORDER, MAKE WHOLE.

AFL-CIO COPE The Committee on Political Education was formed with the merger of the AFL-CIO in 1955. It was an outgrowth of the AFL Labor's League for Political Education (LLPE) and the CIO Political Action Committee (PAC). Its major purpose is to persuade members of unions, their families and friends that they should take an active part in the political life of the community in order to protect their rights as union members and citizens.

COPE organizations also participate actively in nomination, support, and election of candidates COPE has endorsed as those who favor organized labor's legislative objectives.

In one of its publications COPE stated its position in these words: "There is not a single labor-management contract anywhere in America that is worth the paper it is written on if there is a Congress or state legislature that wants to weaken or destroy it. That, in substance, is the principal reason organized labor entered the political field—and will remain active in it." In another publication it quoted with favor the statement of Professor Lloyd Reynolds of Yale as follows: "It is often debated whether unions should 'go into politics'; really, they have no choice in the matter. They are automatically in politics because they exist under a legal and political system which has been generally critical of union activities. . . . A minimum of political activity is essential in order that unions may be able to engage in collective bargaining on even terms."

Its official publication, the biweekly *Memo from COPE*, was discontinued after the June 28, 1982 issue and incorporated into the *AFL-CIO News*.

Source references: AFL-CIO, *First Constitutional Convention Proceedings, 1955* (Washington: 1956); ———, *Union Political Activity Spans 230 Years of U.S. History* (Washington: Pub. no. 106, 1960); AFL-CIO, Committee on Political Education, *Labor and Politics* (Washington: COPE Pub. no. 59, n.d.); J. David Greenstone, *Labor in American Politics* (New York: Knopf, 1969); James L. McDevitt, *The Role of AFL in Politics* (Washington: AFL, Labor's League for Political Education, n.d.); Edwin E. Witte, "The New Federation and Political Action," *ILRR*, April 1956.

See also POLITICAL ACTION, UNION; POLITICAL EDUCATION, UNION.

AFL-CIO departments The merged AFL-CIO trade and industrial departments include the following: Building and Construction Trades, Food and Allied Service Trades, Industrial Union, Maritime Trades, Metal Trades, Professional Employees, Public Employee, and Union Label and Service Trades. All departments are located in the AFL-CIO Building.

Address: 815 16th St., N.W., Washington, D.C. 20006. Tel. (202) 637-5000

Source reference: Albert T. Helbing, *The Departments of the American Federation of Labor* (Baltimore: Johns Hopkins Press, 1931).

AFL-CIO Executive Committee An advisory body consisting of eight vice-presidents selected by the Executive Council of the AFL-CIO which meets with the president and secretary-treasurer every two months on matters of policy.

The Committee was disbanded by the AFL-CIO 1967 convention.

AFL-CIO Executive Council The governing body of the AFL-CIO consists of the president, secretary-treasurer and 33 vice-presidents. It meets at least three times a year. The council is concerned with all of the problems which affect the labor movement. It deals with legislation, bargaining goals, relations among unions, and numerous other problems which are of concern to affiliates and their members. The council may assist unions in organization, charter new national and international unions, and take such other action as necessary, subject to approval by the biennial AFL-CIO convention.

AFL-CIO General Board Meets upon the call of the president and is composed of all 35 members of the Executive Council and a principal officer of each affiliated international and national union and department. It acts on problems presented to it by the Executive Council or the president and secretary-treasurer. Voting strength is based on per-capita payments to the AFL-CIO.

AFL-CIO merger The unification of the American Federation of Labor and the Congress of Industrial Organizations as one federation. The Committee for Industrial Organization was formed in 1935 by seven unions affiliated with the AFL. Following expulsion from the AFL in 1938, these unions reorganized as the Congress of Industrial Organizations.

Goldberg notes that from 1935 to 1952, "unity remained a desirable symbol; but unity was not achieved because the practical factors pulling labor away from unity were stronger than the general pro-unity sentiment." The selection of George Meany as president of the AFL and Walter Reuther as president of the CIO in 1952, and the ratification of the no-raiding agreement by the AFL and CIO on June 9, 1954, brought the federations closer to achieving labor unity.

On January 4, 1955, the AFL and CIO leadership agreed to appoint a subcommittee to prepare a merger agreement. The agreement was ratified by the AFL executive council on February 9, 1955, and by the CIO executive board on February 24, 1955. The AFL-CIO merger became a reality on December 5, 1955, when the first constitutional convention of the AFL-CIO was called to order. George Meany, nominated by Walter Reuther to be the first AFL-CIO president, was unanimously elected together with William Schnitzler as secretary-treasurer.

Source references: "AFL-CIO Convention Approval of Merger Plan," 37 *LRRM* 59; "The AFL-CIO Merger," *ILRR*, April 1956; "Constitution of Merged AFL-CIO Federation," 36 *LRRM* 164; Arthur J. Goldberg, *AFL-CIO, Labor United* (New York: McGraw-Hill, 1956); Donald George Klisares, "An Analysis of the Recent AFL-CIO Merger" (M.A. thesis, Univ. of Iowa, 1956); Sidney Lens, "Will Merged Labor Set New Goals?" *Harvard BR*, March/April 1956.

See also AMERICAN FEDERATION OF LABOR-CONGRESS OF INDUSTRIAL ORGANIZATIONS.

AFL-CIO News The merged publication of the former AFL clip-sheet and *The CIO News*. The newspaper is published weekly by the AFL-CIO at Washington, D.C. *The American Federationist* and *Memo from COPE* were discontinued as separate publications and incorporated in the *News* beginning in July 1982.

AFL-CIO no-raiding agreement *See* NO-RAIDING AGREEMENT.

AFL-CIO unity Steps taken to reestablish unity in the labor movement, following the secession of the CIO. In December 1955 the AFL and CIO reunited as the AFL-CIO.

Source references: Arthur J. Goldberg, *AFL-CIO: Labor United* (New York: McGraw-Hill, 1956); "Merger Documents," *ILRR*, April 1956; "Merger Implementation Pact," 37 *LRRM* 61.

See also AFL-CIO MERGER, AMERICAN FEDERATION OF LABOR-CONGRESS OF INDUSTRIAL ORGANIZATIONS.

AFSCME v. State of Washington Case in which the state of Washington was found guilty under Title VII of "pervasive and intentional" discrimination by paying employees in predominantly female classifications approximately 20 percent less than that for predominantly male classifications requiring equal or less overall levels of effort, skill, and responsibility. United States District Court Judge Jack E. Tanner ruled that the state showed discriminatory intent by, among other factors, perpetuating the wage disparity despite several state studies which established that the predominantly female jobs were not compensated at their full evaluated worth.

Source references: AFSCME v. State of Washington, 33 FEP Cases 808 (1983) (Overruled, 38 FEP Cases 1353 (CA 9, 1985).

afternoon shift A schedule where work starts at 3 or 4 o'clock in the afternoon and continues until 11 or 12 midnight. It is sometimes referred to as the second, swing, or relief shift.

See also GRAVEYARD SHIFT, MULTIPLE SHIFT, ROTATING SHIFT, SHIFT, SWING SHIFT.

age certificate *See* CERTIFICATE OF AGE.

aged *See* OLDER WORKER.

Age Discrimination Act of 1975 Federal statute prohibiting discrimination based on age and protecting individuals from being excluded from participation in, being denied the benefits of, or being subjected to discrimination on the basis of age in programs or activities receiving federal financial assistance. State and local programs or activities are covered by the law.

Noncompliance with the law may result in termination of federal funds. The Department of Health and Human Services has issued regulations to implement provisions of the law.

This law, unlike the Age Discrimination in Employment Act of 1967 which protects individuals who are 40 but less than 70 years of age, does not specify any age limit.

Source reference: Age Discrimination Act of 1975, as amended, 42 U.S.C. 6101–6107 (1982).

Age Discrimination in Employment Act of 1967 Federal law prohibiting employers, unions, employment agencies, and apprenticeship and training programs from discriminating against employees and job applicants on the basis of age. The law, which was amended in 1974 and 1978, protects individuals who are at least 40 but less than 70 years of age.

Employers with 20 or more workers employed for at least 20 weeks a year are subject to the Act, as are labor unions with 25 members, employment agencies, and apprenticeship and training programs which operate to provide referral services to employers in interstate commerce. States and political subdivisions and federal employees, except military personnel, are also covered by the Act.

Employee selection, discharge, classification, and compensation on the basis of age, among other practices, are prohibited by the law. Age-based employment practices are permitted if age is a bona fide occupational qualification.

Mandatory retirement of employees under 65 and before 70 years of age is illegal and employees in this age grouping are due the same health benefits as other employees, regardless of Medicare entitlement.

The ADEA has its origin in a study conducted by the Secretary of Labor pursuant to the mandate contained in Section 715 of the Civil Rights Act of 1964, which directed the Secretary of Labor to conduct a study "of the factors which might tend to result in discrimination in employment because of age and of the consequences of such discrimination on the economy and individuals affected. . . . [which] shall include . . . such recommendations for legislation to prevent arbitrary discrimination in employment because of age as he determines advisable." The study, titled *The Older American Worker, Age Discrimination in Employment*, concluded that age discrimination was based not on "evidence of prejudice based on dislike or intolerance for the older worker," but rather on erroneous assumptions about the effects of age on ability adopted by businesses out of concerns for economic efficiency.

The enforcement responsibilities of the law were transferred by Reorganization Plan No. 1 of 1978 from the Secretary of Labor and the Civil Service Commission (for federal employees) to the Equal Employment Opportunity Commission on July 1, 1979.

Source references: Age Discrimination in Employment Act of 1967, as amended, 29 U.S.C. 621–634 (1982); "The Age Discrimination in Employment Act of 1967," *IR Law Digest*, Spring 1977; Robert W. Cuddy, "Age Discrimination Amendments and Their Impact on Personnel," *Employee Relations LJ*, Winter 1978/79; William J. Isaacson, "Age Discrimination: The New Amendments and Recent Developments," *Labor Law Developments 1979*, Proceedings of the 25th Annual Institute on Labor Law, SLF (New York: Bender, 1979); Robert M. Macdonald, *Mandatory Retirement and the Law* (Washington: AEI, Studies 204, 1978); Marc Rosenblum and George Biles, "The Aging of Age Discrimination—Evolving ADEA Interpretations and Employee Relations Policies," *Employee Relations LJ*, Summer 1982; Lawrence T. Smedley, "The Impact of Raising the Mandatory Retirement Age: A Brief Assessment," *LLJ*, Aug. 1979; Julia E. Stone, "Age Discrimination in Employment Act: A Review of Recent Changes," *MLR*, March 1980; U.S. Dept. of Labor, *The Older American Worker, Age Discrimination in Employment* (Washington: 1965); Dennis H. Vaughn, "The ADEA—A Statute Coming of Age," *Labor Law Developments 1978*, Proceedings of 24th Annual Institute on Labor Law, SLF (New York: Bender, 1978); Herbert D. Werner, "The Age Discrimination in Employment Act Amendments of 1978 and their Effect on Collective Bargaining," *LLJ*, Aug. 1979.

See also BONA FIDE OCCUPATIONAL QUALIFICATION (BFOQ); EXECUTIVE ORDER 11141; RETIREMENT, COMPULSORY.

agency shop A union security provision to eliminate "free riders." All employees in the bargaining unit are required to pay dues or service charges to the collective bargaining agent. Nonunion employees, however, are not required to join the union as a condition of employment. Payment of dues is to defray the expenses of the bargaining agent in negotiations, contract administration, etc.

The Supreme Court in the *Schermerhorn* case, decided June 3, 1963, held that the agency shop is legal under Section 8(a)(3) of the Taft-Hartley amendments to the National Labor Relations Act dealing with the union shop, but is within the authority of the states to outlaw under the priority given them in Section 14(b).

"The prevailing administrative and judicial view under the Wagner Act," the Court said, was that the proviso to Section 8(3) "covered both the closed and union shop, as well as less onerous union security arrangements, if they were otherwise legal . . . We find nothing in the legislative history of the Act indicating that Congress intended the amended proviso to Section 8(a)(3) to validate only the union shop and simultaneously to abolish, in addition to the closed shop, all other union-security arrangements permissible under state law. There is much to be said for the Board's view that, if Congress desired in the Wagner Act to permit a closed or union shop and in the Taft-Hartley Act the union shop, then it also intended to preserve the status of less vigorous, less compulsory contracts which demanded less adherence to the union."

The Court noted a difference between the union shop and agency shop, in that the union may insist on an employee being placed "on its rolls" (joining) under the former, while the choice is up to the employee under the latter, while still requiring the same monetary support as does the union shop. "Such a difference between the union and agency shop may be of great importance in some contexts, but for present purposes it is more formal than real. To the extent that it has any significance at all it serves, rather than violates, the desire of Congress to reduce the evils of compulsory unionism while allowing financial support for the bargaining agent."

The *General Motors* case "rules" the Florida case, the Court said in its second opinion. "At the very least," the Court pointed out, "the agreements requiring 'membership' in a labor union which are expressly permitted by Section 8(a)(3) are the same 'membership' agreements expressly placed within the reach of state law by Section 14(b) . . . the 'agency shop' arrangement involved here . . . is the 'practical equivalent' of an 'agreement requiring membership in a labor organization as a condition of employment.'"

Source references: NLRB v. General Motors, 373 US 734, 53 LRRM 2313 (1963); *Retail Clerks, Local 1625 v. Schermerhorn*, 373 US 746, 53 LRRM 2318 (1963); James T. Bennett and Manuel H. Johnson, "Free Riders in U.S. Labour Unions: Artifice of Affliction?" *BJIR*, July 1979; George W. Cassidy, "Equity Considerations in Public Sector Union Security Arrangements: Should 'Free-Riders' Pay?" *Journal of Collective Negotiations in the Public Sector*, Vol. 5, no. 1, 1976; Kurt L. Hanslowe, David Dunn, and Jay Erstling, *Union Security in Public Employment or Free Riding and Free Association* (Ithaca: NYSSILR, Cornell Univ., Institute of Public Employment, IPE Monograph no. 8, 1978); Norman E. Jones, "The Agency Shop," *LLJ*, Nov. 1959; Dale D. McConkey, "Was the Agency Shop Prematurely Scrapped?" *LLJ*, Feb. 1958; Joyce M. Najita, "The Mandatory Agency Shop in Hawaii's Public Sector," *ILRR*, April 1974; Robert T. Noonan, "The Agency Shop Under State and Federal Law," *Univ. of Cincinnati LR*, Sept. 1963; Daniel Orr, "The Free Rider and Labor Law: Introduction and Overview," *Journal of Labor Research*, Fall 1980; Morgan O. Reynolds, "The Free Rider Argument for Compulsory Union Dues," *Journal of Labor Research*, Fall 1980; U.S. Dept. of Labor, BLS, *Union Security and Checkoff Provisions in Major Union Contracts, 1958–59* (Washington: Bull. no. 1272, 1960); Jay W. Waks, "Impact of the Agency Shop on Labor Relations in the Public Sector," *IR Law Digest*, Jan. 1971.

See also ABOOD V. DETROIT BOARD OF EDUCATION, FAIR SHARE AGREEMENT, FREE RIDERS, RAND FORMULA, REBATE PLAN, RELIGIOUS DISCRIMINATION, SERVICE FEE, UNION SECURITY CLAUSES.

agent A person who acts, or is held responsible for the acts of another. Under the Taft-Hartley amendments to the National Labor Relations Act, the NLRB's findings of unfair labor practices against employers because of the action of supervisory employees, were modified so that agents had to be authorized to act on behalf of the employers.

The status of agent under the Norris-LaGuardia Act also has a direct bearing on the issuance of injunctions in a labor dispute.

agent provocateur An individual who incites, or is hired to induce or start, open resistance or trouble in a plant, usually for the purpose of discrediting or weakening a union.

aggregate wages *See* WAGES, AGGREGATE.

agitator A troublemaker, one who stirs up the group to rebel against existing conditions. During early organizational efforts, labor organizers generally were labeled "outside agitators."

See also OUTSIDE AGITATORS.

agreement, administration of The day-to-day activity used to carry out the intent and substance of the terms and conditions of employment in the collective bargaining agreement.

The effectiveness and maturity of the parties to the agreement are demonstrated in the way in which they implement the contract language.

Source references: Mollie H. Bowers, *Contract Administration in the Public Sector* (Chicago: IPMA, PERL no. 53, 1976); James A. Craft, "Notes on the Administration of Collective Bargaining Agreements," *Personnel Administration/Public Personnel Review*, July/Aug. 1972; Harold W. Davey, *Contemporary Collective Bargaining* (3d ed., Englewood Cliffs: PH, 1972); Francis D. Ferris, "Contract Interpretation—A Bread-And-Butter Talent," *Public Personnel Management*, July/Aug. 1975; Charles O. Gregory, "The Law of Collective Agreement," *Michigan LR*, March 1959; Indiana Univ., Midwest Center for Public Sector Labor Relations, *Questions and Answers on Contract Administration, A Practitioner's Guide* (Bloomington: 1978); Harry Kershen, "After You've Signed the Contract, What's Next?" *Journal of Collective Negotiations in the Public Sector*, Winter 1974; Richard Mittenthal, "Past Practice and the Administration of Collective Bargaining Agreements," *Arbitration and Public Policy*, Proceedings of the 14th A/M, NAA, ed. by Spencer Pollard (Washington: BNA, 1961); William B. Werther, "Reducing Grievances Through Effective Contract Administration," *LLJ*, April 1974; Fred Whitney, *The Collective Bargaining Agreement: Its Negotiation and Administration* (Bloomington: Indiana Univ., School of Business, Bureau of Business Research, Indiana Business Report no. 25, 1957).

agreement, area *See* AREA AGREEMENT.

agreement, association *See* ASSOCIATION AGREEMENT.

agreement, blanket *See* BLANKET AGREEMENT.

agreement, closed shop *See* CLOSED SHOP AGREEMENT.

agreement, collective A contract or mutual understanding between a union and company or their representatives setting forth the terms and conditions of employment, usually for a specific period of time. The scope and coverage of the agreement will depend on the parties. Most agreements include sections dealing with the bargaining unit, union security, seniority, wages and hours, and other working conditions, such as vacation pay, grievance procedures, and holidays.

The Supreme Court in 1941 in the *Heinz* case held that where agreement has been reached on the terms, the employer is required to enter into a signed agreement if requested by the union.

The Supreme Court in 1960 in one of the "trilogy" arbitration decisions stated that "a collective bargaining agreement is an effort to erect a system of industrial self government. . . ."

Source references: H. J. Heinz v. NLRB, 311 US 514, 7 LRRM 291 (1941); *Steelworkers v. Warrior & Gulf Navigation Co.*, 363 US 574, 46 LRRM 2416 (1960); AFL-CIO, *Comparative Survey of Major Collective Bargaining Agreements, Manufacturing and Nonmanufacturing, May, 1971* (Washington: 1971); BNA, *Basic Patterns in Union Contracts* (10th ed., Washington: 1983); ———, *Construction Craft Jurisdiction Agreements, 1979 Edition* (Washington: 1979); Frederick D. Braid, "*Wiley* and Its Aftermath: Survival of Contract Rights Beyond the Expiration of Collective Bargaining Agreements," *LLJ*, Nov. 1976; Abraham Desser, *Trends in Collective Bargaining and Union Contracts* (New York: NICB, Studies in Personnel Policy no. 71, 1946); David E. Feller, "A General Theory of the Collective Bargaining Agreement," *Industrial Relations LJ*, Spring 1974; Ralph Fuchs, "Labor Contract," *Encyclopedia of the Social Sciences*, ed. by Edwin R. A. Seligman (Vol. 8, New York: Macmillan, 1932); Paul S. Kuelthau, "Rights on Contract Termination," *NYU 22d Annual Conference on Labor*, ed. by Thomas Christensen and Andrea Christensen (New York: Bender, 1970); Addison Mueller, "The Law of Contracts—A Changing Legal Environment," *Truth, Lie Detectors, and Other Problems in Labor Arbitration*, Proceedings of the 31st A/M, NAA, ed. by James Stern and Barbara Dennis (Washington: BNA, 1979); Warren C. Ogden, John R. Arthur, and J. Martin Smith, "The Survival of Contract Terms

Beyond the Expiration of a Collective Bargaining Agreement," *LLJ*, Feb. 1981; Rudolph Oswald, "Contracts: Some Recent Trends," *American Federationist*, March 1970; Selig Perlman, "Trade Agreements," *Encyclopedia of the Social Sciences*, ed. by Edwin R. A. Seligman (Vol. 14, New York: Macmillan, 1934); U.S. Dept. of Labor, BLS, *Bargaining Calendar 1983* (Washington: BLS Bull. 2165, 1983); ———, *Characteristics of Major Collective Bargaining Agreements, January 1, 1980* (Washington: BLS Bull. 2095, 1981); U.S. NLRB, Division of Economic Research, *The Written Trade Agreement* (Washington: Bull. no. 4, 1939); Samuel C. Walker, "The Dynamics of Clear Contract Language," *PJ*, Jan. 1981; Arnold M. Zack and Richard I. Bloch, *The Labor Agreement in Negotiation and Arbitration* (Washington: BNA, 1983); David Ziskind, *The Law Behind Union Agreements* (Washington: U.S. Dept. of Labor, 1941).

See also AGREEMENT, INDUSTRYWIDE; AGREEMENT, MASTER; AGREEMENT, NATIONAL; ASSOCIATION AGREEMENT; HEINZ CASE; INTERIM AGREEMENT; LABOR CONTRACT; LABOR MANAGEMENT RELATIONS ACT OF 1947; MEMORANDUM OF UNDERSTANDING.

agreement, individual *See* INDIVIDUAL AGREEMENT.

agreement, industrywide Collective bargaining contracts or agreements which involve a majority of the employers as well as the employees working in a particular industry. Such agreements are not very common. In recent years, however, collective bargaining negotiations have involved large segments of an industry which are called multiemployer, or as in the steel industry, industrywide bargaining. Such negotiations seek to set up reasonably uniform standards and conditions of employment which may be the pattern for other companies in the industry.

There was much debate, during the discussions on the Taft-Hartley Act, urging the elimination or invalidation of agreements negotiated on an industrywide basis.

agreement, interim *See* INTERIM AGREEMENT.

agreement, ironclad *See* IRONCLAD AGREEMENT (CONTRACT).

agreement, joint *See* JOINT AGREEMENT.

agreement, jurisdictional *See* JURISDICTIONAL AGREEMENT.

agreement, labor *See* AGREEMENT, COLLECTIVE; LABOR AGREEMENT; LABOR CONTRACT.

agreement, master A collective bargaining agreement which serves as the pattern for major terms and conditions for an entire industry or segment thereof. Local terms may be negotiated in addition to the terms set forth in the master contract.

The master agreement helps to establish uniform conditions of employment throughout an industry or company. Some international unions suggest the master agreement as a guide but will permit variations to meet special circumstances of a union or company.

See also COLLECTIVE BARGAINING, INDUSTRYWIDE; COLLECTIVE BARGAINING, MULTIEMPLOYER; PATTERN BARGAINING.

agreement, model *See* MODEL AGREEMENT.

agreement, "more favorable terms" *See* "FAVORED NATIONS" CLAUSE, "MORE FAVORABLE TERMS" AGREEMENTS.

agreement, national A collective bargaining agreement which is national in scope or covers a major industry, trade, or occupational group.

The coal and steel agreements are sometimes referred to as national agreements although no single agreement in coal or steel covers the entire industry. However, the term generally is applied to an agreement which sets a national pattern even though it may not cover all of the plants within a particular industry or all of the occupations or trades.

agreement, open-end *See* OPEN-END AGREEMENT.

agreement, regional *See* REGIONAL LABOR AGREEMENTS.

agreement, submission A statement agreed to by union and employer setting out the specific items which they wish the arbitrator to act on in a particular dispute.

See also ARBITRATION.

agreement, sweetheart In not-so-polite union terminology, the accusation by one union (the one without the agreement) that the collective bargaining agreement between an employer and another union is not in the best interest of the employees, does not represent majority wishes of the employees, or that the organization is in actuality a "kept" or "company union," is presumably entered into collusively between an employer and a union in order to bar another union, which provides less-than-standard wages and benefits; or one which is not enforced intentionally; or one which is negotiated by a "racketeer" union; or one whose existence is unknown to the employees it presumably covers; or one which may embody several of these characteristics.

The term also is used occasionally to describe a collective bargaining agreement where both sides express, in writing, a mutual desire to live harmoniously and cooperate fully.

See also COMPANY UNION, TOP-DOWN CONTRACT.

agreement coverage The provisions generally found in most collective bargaining agreements include: recognition; bargaining unit; union security; wages, hours, and working conditions, including seniority, layoffs, transfers, promotions, vacations, overtime; the grievance machinery and provisions for duration.

The coverage will vary with industry and occupation, but generally attempts to meet the specific needs of the parties to the agreement.

Source references: BNA, *Basic Patterns in Union Contracts* (10th ed., Washington: 1983); Elias Lieberman, *Collective Labor Agreement* (New York: Harper, 1939); C. W. Randle and Max S. Wortman, Jr., *Collective Bargaining: Principles and Practices* (2d ed., Boston: Houghton-Mifflin, 1966); S. H. Torff, *Collective Bargaining: Negotiations and Agreements* (New York: McGraw-Hill, 1953).

See also BARGAINING UNIT, MANAGEMENT RIGHTS, SCOPE OF BARGAINING.

agreement duration The period during which a collective bargaining agreement is in effect. Agreements in effect today generally have long duration periods (two years or longer).

See also LONG-TERM CONTRACT.

agreement enforcement Most collective bargaining agreements are observed by labor and management within the spirit, as well as the letter, of the contract. Where differences of opinion arise which cannot be resolved by mutual consent, they may be processed through the grievance machinery.

Occasionally, however, labor and management may seek to enforce the agreement through appeal to the courts or through the use of economic sanctions, such as the strike or lockout. Some agreements for example permit a union to call a strike to enforce an arbitration award.

Although the courts have accorded legal status to the collective bargaining agreement, early agreements were regarded as unenforceable contracts at law following English precedent.

The Taft-Hartley Act provides for enforcement in the federal courts without the usual criteria of diversity of citizenship and the amount of money involved (Section 301).

The best agreement enforcement, however, is still the good will of the parties to the agreement.

Source references: Archibald Cox, "Individual Enforcement of Collective Bargaining Agreements," *LLJ*, Dec. 1957; Frank Cummings, "Individual Enforcement of Rights Under Collective Bargaining Agreements," *LLJ*, Aug. 1962; Richard L. Epstein, "Disengagement from the Labor Contract: The Problem and a Proposal," *California LR*, Oct. 1962; David E. Feller, "A General Theory of the Collective Bargaining Agreement," *IR Law Digest*, Summer 1974; William J. Isaacson, "Enforcement of Labor Agreements by Economic Action," *NYU 6th Annual Conference on Labor*, ed. by Emanuel Stein (Albany: Bender, 1953); Warren C. Ogden, John R. Arthur, and J. Marvin Smith, "The Survival of Contract Terms Beyond the Expiration of a Collective Bargaining Agreement," *LLJ*, Feb. 1981.

See also ARBITRATION AWARD, ENFORCEMENT OF AGREEMENT, NO-STRIKE CLAUSE, SECTION 301.

agreement nullification *See* NULLIFICATION OF AGREEMENT.

agreement ratification Formal approval of a newly negotiated agreement by vote of the general membership or union members affected as required in union constitutions, bylaws, or by tradition.

Source references: Donald R. Burke and Lester Rubin, "Is Contract Rejection a Major Collective Bargaining Problem?" *ILRR*, Jan. 1973; M. Sami Kassem, "Contract Rejection by the Rank and File Member," *Management of Personnel Quarterly*, Winter 1970; Matthew A. Kelly, "The Contract Rejection Problem: A Positive Labor-Management Approach," *LLJ*, July 1969; Francis J. Loevi, "The Problem of Unnecessary Legislative Contract Rejections in Public Employment: An Alternative System for Ratification," *Public Personnel Review*, April 1970; Joyce M. Najita and Sonia Faust, "When a University Faculty Rejects a Contract," *IR*, Feb. 1976; Charles A. Odewahn and Joseph Krislov, "Contract Rejections: Testing the Explanatory Hypotheses," *IR*, Oct. 1972; Joel Seidman (ed.), *Trade Union Government and Collective Bargaining: Some Critical Issues* (New York: Praeger, 1970); Gilbert J. Seldin, "The Law and Practice of Contract Ratification," *NYU 22d Annual Conference on Labor*, ed. by Thomas Christensen and Andrea Christensen (New York: Bender, 1970); David I. Shair, "The Mythology of Labor Contract Rejections," *LLJ*, Feb. 1970.

agreement revision Provision made in the collective bargaining agreement to modify or change its terms. Generally, major revisions are made at the expiration period when the parties negotiate the terms of the new agreement. With the advent of more long-term contracts—those in excess of one year—provision may be made allowing either party to reopen the contract on a limited number of issues, such as basic wage adjustment.

Changes, of course, may be made at any time by mutual consent of the parties, through exchange of letters, memoranda of understanding, amendments, or supplementary agreements.

It has been contended that arbitration awards may have the effect of "revising" the agreement. Most contracts, however, provide that the arbitrator shall have no authority to revise, amend, or change the terms of the contract. Where an arbitrator "interprets" a disputed term, the party unhappy with the result may feel that the arbitrator has changed the terms of the contract.

See also REOPENING CLAUSE.

Agricultural Workers Union; National (AFL-CIO) Formerly known as the National Farm Labor Union (AFL). The union surrendered its charter and in August 1960 joined the Amalgamated Meat Cutters and Butcher Workmen of North America (AFL-CIO).

Source references: National Advisory Committee on Farm Labor, *Farm Labor Organizing, 1905–1967: A Brief History* (New York: 1967); U.S. Dept. of Labor, BLS, *Labor Unionism in American Agriculture* (Washington: Bull. no. 836, 1945).

See also MEAT CUTTERS AND BUTCHER WORKMEN OF NORTH AMERICA; AMALGAMATED (AFL-CIO).

Agriculture Employees; National Association of (Ind) Formerly known as the Federal Plant Quarantine Inspectors National Association (Ind). The current name was adopted in the early 1980s. It publishes *The News Letter* (quarterly) and *Hotline* (periodically).

Address: P.O. Box 73–A, Metairie, La. 70033. Tel. (504) 887–1549

Airline Communications Employees Association (Ind) A former independent labor organization with headquarters in Denver, Colorado. It merged with the Communications Workers of America (AFL-CIO) in February 1960.

See also COMMUNICATIONS WORKERS OF AMERICA (AFL-CIO).

Air Line Dispatchers Association (AFL-CIO) A labor organization chartered by the AFL in 1939. On March 15, 1977, the union merged with the Transport Workers Union of America (AFL-CIO).

Source reference: Karl M. Ruppenthal, *The Air Line Dispatcher in North America* (Stanford: Stanford Univ., Graduate School of Business, 1962).

See also TRANSPORT WORKERS UNION OF AMERICA (AFL-CIO).

Air Line Employees Association; International Founded in 1951, it is a division of the Air Line Pilots Association (AFL-CIO). It issues *The Air Line Employee* (bimonthly).

Address: 5600 South Central Ave., Chicago, Ill. 60638. Tel. (312) 767–3333

Air Line Pilots Association; International (AFL-CIO) A labor organization chartered by the AFL in 1931.

The union has three divisions: Pilots and Flight Attendants divisions are located in Washington, D.C., and the Air Line Employees Association is located in Chicago. A fourth division, the Union of Professional Airmen, disbanded on December 11, 1981, and joined the Pilots division.

The Pilots division issues *The Air Line Pilot* (monthly), the Flight Attendants division issues the *Flightlog* (quarterly), and the Air Line Employees division issues *The Air Line Employee* (bimonthly).

Address: 1625 Massachusetts Ave., N.W., Washington, D.C. 20036. Tel. (202) 797–4000

See also AIR LINE EMPLOYEES ASSOCIATION, INTERNATIONAL; FLIGHT ATTENDANTS, ASSOCIATION OF.

Air Line Stewards and Stewardesses Association; International Formerly a division of the Air Line Pilots Association, the union merged with the Transport Workers Union of America (AFL-CIO) in 1961.

See also TRANSPORT WORKERS UNION OF AMERICA (AFL-CIO).

Air Traffic Specialists; National Association of (Ind) An organization founded in 1960. Its bimonthly publication is the *NAATS Bulletin*.

Address: Wheaton Plaza North, Suite 415, Wheaton, Md. 20902. Tel. (301) 946–0882

Alabama State Employees Association (Ind) An organization affiliated with the Assembly of Governmental Employees, it publishes the monthly *ASEA News*.

Address: 110 North Jackson St., Montgomery, Ala. 36104. Tel. (205) 834–6965

Alabama v. Arizona A decision by the Supreme Court in February 1934 which denied a petition by the state of Alabama requesting an injunction to restrain the enforcement of state laws which prevented prison-made goods from Alabama from being sold in other states.

Source reference: Alabama v. Arizona, 291 US 286 (1934).

See also PRISON LABOR.

Alaska Public Employees Association (Ind) Formerly known as the Alaska State Employees Association (Ind), it is affiliated with the Assembly of Governmental Employees. Its official monthly publication is the *Reporter*.

Address: 340 North Franklin St., Juneau, Alaska 99801. Tel. (907) 586–2334

Albemarle Paper Co. v. Moody A Supreme Court decision that set standards for back pay awards under Title VII of the 1964 Civil Rights Act, and supported the application of EEOC guidelines to determine the validity or job-relatedness of employment tests.

The case originated out of a class action challenge to a racially segregated seniority system and an employment testing program established by a North Carolina paper mill. A lower court had ordered implementation of a "plantwide" system of seniority, but denied back pay and refused to enjoin the testing program.

The Supreme Court held that the standards set by the NLRA are to be followed in awarding back pay in Title VII cases. The Court ruled that "back pay should be denied only for reasons which, if applied generally, would not frustrate the central statutory purposes of eradicating discrimination throughout the economy and making persons whole for injuries suffered through past discrimination." The Court further ruled that the absence of bad faith on the part of the employer was not sufficient reason for denying back pay under Title VII.

The Court also gave deference to the EEOC Uniform Guidelines on Employee Selection Procedures in determining the validity of employment tests. Applying the provisions of the guidelines, the Court found the validation study conducted by the employer to be deficient.

Source reference: Albemarle Paper Co. v. Moody, 422 US 405, 10 FEP Cases 1181 (1975).

alcoholism Problem drinking that can result in unacceptable job performance, including excessive tardiness, absenteeism, and workplace accidents.

Alcoholism has been estimated to cost $20 billion annually in lost productivity involving 6 to 10 percent of the employed population. Some companies have alcohol treatment programs, with or without union participation.

Alcoholism was certified as a disease by the American Medical Association during the 1950s. Although the Rehabilitation Act of 1973 once included alcoholism within the broad definition of "handicap," the 1978 amendments expressly exclude alcoholics from the protection of the Act.

Source references: Tia Schneider Denenberg and R. V. Denenberg, *Alcohol and Drugs: Issues in the Workplace* (Washington: BNA, 1983); Michael Marmo, "Arbitrators View Alcoholic Employees: Discipline or Rehabilitation?" *AJ*, March 1982; Glendel J. Provost et al., "Alcohol in the Workplace: A Review of Recent Arbitration Cases," *Employee Relations LJ*, Winter 1978/79; Gerald G. Somers, "Alcohol and the Just Cause for Discharge," *Arbitration—1975*, Proceedings of the 28th A/M, NAA, ed. by Barbara Dennis and Gerald Somers (Washington: BNA, 1976); Harrison M. Trice, *Applied Research Studies: Job Based Alcoholism and Employee Assistance Programs* (Ithaca: Cornell Univ., NYSSILR, Reprint no. 514, 1980); Harrison Trice and Paul M. Roman, *Spirits and Demons at Work: Alcohol and Other Drugs on the Job* (Ithaca: Cornell Univ., NYSSILR, 1972); Richard M. Weiss, *Dealing with Alcoholism in the Workplace* (New York: The Conference Board, Report no. 784, 1980).

See also REHABILITATION ACT OF 1973.

Alexander v. Gardner-Denver A Supreme Court decision holding that arbitration of a discrimination claim does not bar a Title VII (Civil Rights Act) suit of the same claim.

The Court held that Title VII was "designed to supplement, rather than supplant, existing laws and institutions relating to employment discrimination," and that an employee covered by a collective bargaining agreement had both a contractual right under that agreement and an independent statutory right accorded by Congress. The doctrine of election of remedies thus does not apply. The Court noted that an employee instituting a Title VII action after the grievance is denied in arbitration is not seeking review of the arbitrator's decision, but is "asserting a statutory right independent of the arbitration process."

Source references: Alexander v. Gardner-Denver, 415 US 36, 7 FEP Cases 81 (1974); Julia P. Cooper, "The Gardner-Denver Decision: The View from EEOC," *NYU 27th Annual Conference on Labor*, ed. by David Raff (New York: Bender, 1975); Robert Coulson, "Another Seat at the Table: Gardner-Denver 1974," *NYU 27th Annual Conference on Labor*, ed. by David Raff (New York: Bender, 1975); Frank J. Madden, *Gardner-Denver, Arbitration and Title VII, A Critical Analysis* (Bloomington, Minn.: IR Service Bureau, 1975); Bernard D. Meltzer, "The Impact of Alexander v. Gardner-Denver on Labor Arbitration," *NYU 27th Annual Conference on Labor*, ed. by David Raff (New York: Bender, 1975); Peter G. Nash, "Board Referral to Arbitration and *Alexander v. Gardner-Denver*: Some Preliminary Observations," *LLJ*, May 1974; Bonnie L. Siber, "The Gardner-Denver Decision: Does It Put Arbitration in a Bind?" *LLJ*, Nov. 1974; Gary R. Siniscalco, "Title VII Disputes: Impact of the Gardner-Denver Case," *Proceedings of the 27th A/M, IRRA*, ed. by James Stern and Barbara Dennis (Madison: 1975).

alien A foreigner. A person not resident in the community. Technically a person who is not a naturalized citizen or national. Labor organizers occasionally were referred to as "alien or foreign agitators."

See also AGITATOR.

Alien Contract Law A federal statute of 1885 which was designed to stop alien labor from entering the United States. The law prohibited recruiting through the advancement of money, including payment of transportation.

alien labor Foreign-born individuals in the labor force who are not citizens of the country.

Reubens separates aliens into three main categories: "First are the 'resident aliens,' or legal immigrants, admitted for permanent settlement under statutory quotas and preferences. . . . Second are the 'temporary workers,' such as doctors, scientists, entertainers, and other particularly qualified persons, admitted for specific periods. . . . Third and largest in number are the rising streams of illegals. . . ."

Concern about alien labor largely centers on economic issues, i.e., that aliens compete for jobs, depress wages and working conditions, and use social services without contributing taxes for their support.

Alien labor, including illegal immigrants, enjoy many of the protections accorded to U.S. citizens; legislation requires employers to extend protection to all workers. Aliens, therefore, are covered by the National Labor Relations Act, the Occupational Safety and Health Act, and the Fair Labor Standards Act. In addition, employers are required to contribute social security taxes for these workers.

The noncitizen status of aliens is not protected by Title VII of the Civil Rights Act of 1964, as the Supreme Court ruled in *Espinoza v. Farah Manufacturing Co.*, that "nothing in the Act makes it illegal to discriminate on the basis of citizenship or alienage." The Court, however, found that employment practices discriminating among aliens based on race, color, religion, sex, or national origin, i.e., hiring Anglo-Saxon aliens over aliens of Mexian ancestry, is prohibited by Title VII. The EEOC guidelines state: "In those circumstances, where citizenship requirements have the purpose or effect of discriminating against an individual on the basis of national origin, they are prohibited by Title VII."

In federal employment, the Supreme Court in *Hampton v. Wong*, ruled that although the President and Congress could restrict employment of aliens in the national interest, a ban on employment of resident aliens must be based on adequate showing of legitimate reasons. Executive Order 11935 (Sept. 2, 1976), requiring citizenship status for federal employment, has been upheld by the courts on the basis that the President has the authority to issue executive orders to bar aliens from civil service employment.

Source references: E. O. 11935, 41 F.R. 37301; *Espinoza v. Farah Manufacturing Co.*, 414 US 86, 6 FEP Cases 933 (1973); *Hampton v. Wong*, 426 US 88, 12 FEP Cases 1377 (1976); U.S. EEOC, "Guidelines on Discrimination Because of National Origin," 29 C.F.R. 1606; Robert L. Bach and Jennifer B. Bach, "Employment Patterns of Southeast Asian Refugees," *MLR*, Oct. 1980; George J. Borjas, "The Earnings of Male Hispanic Immigrants in the United States," *ILRR*, April 1982; Barry R. Chiswick, "Immigrant Earnings Patterns by Sex, Race, and Ethnic Grouping," *MLR*, Oct. 1980; Walter Fogel, "Illegal Alien Workers in the United States," *IR*, Oct. 1977; ———, *Mexican Illegal Alien Workers in the United States* (Los Angeles: UC, Institute of IR, Monograph series 20, 1978); Philip L. Martin and Mark Miller, "Regulating Alien Labor in Industrial Societies," *Proceedings of the 32d A/M, IRRA*, ed. by Barbara Dennis (Madison: 1980); David S. North, "The Access of the Foreign-Born to Jobs and Labor Market Protection in the U.S.," *Proceedings of the 34th A/M, IRRA*, ed. by Barbara Dennis (Madison: 1982); Edwin P. Reubens, "Aliens, Jobs, and Immigration Policy," *The Public Interest*, Spring 1978; ———, *Temporary Admission of Foreign Workers: Dimensions and Policies* (Washington: U.S. National Commission for Manpower Policy, Special Report no. 34, 1979); Jose A. Rivera, "Aliens Under the Law—A Legal Perspective," *Employee Relations LJ*, Summer 1977; Refugio I. Rochin, "Illegal Aliens in Agriculture: Some Theoretical Considerations," *LLJ*, March 1978; U.S. GAO, *Administrative Changes Needed to Reduce Employment of Illegal Aliens* (Washington: 1981).

See also GUESTWORKER PROGRAM, NATIONAL ORIGIN DISCRIMINATION, UNDOCUMENTED WORKERS.

allegiance Loyalty to or support of a union member to his labor organization. Although efforts are made to have the individual support "either" the employer "or" union, most workers have divided allegiance. There is general recognition that such division of allegiance is not tantamount to disloyalty, either to the company or the union.

See also LOYAL WORKERS; PATERNALISM, EMPLOYER.

Allen-Bradley case Case in which the Supreme Court carved out an exception to the Hutcheson doctrine exempting union activities from the Sherman Anti-Trust Act regardless of the "rightness or wrongness" of the object of the union activities. The exemption does not apply, the Court said, where union action to affect prices or suppress competition is taken in combination with a nonlabor group, such as an employer association. Thus, union participation with a group of employers in a scheme to monopolize a local market by boycotting out-of-city and nonunion goods was held to violate the Sherman Act.

Source reference: Allen-Bradley Co. v. Electrical Workers, IBEW, 325 US 797, 16 LRRM 798 (1945).

See also ANTITRUST LAWS, PENNINGTON CASE.

Alliance for Labor Action (ALA) A "labor action group" formed by the United Auto Workers and Teamsters through which unions work together to carry out specific joint action programs. The following goals were outlined in its Program for Action adopted by the International Executive Boards of the Teamsters and the UAW in joint meeting in Chicago, Ill., on July 23, 1968: assist in organizing the unorganized; strengthen collective bargaining to make it a more effective instrument; explore the establishment of an emergency defense fund to support workers involved with management refusals to bargain; organize farm workers; organize community unions; and social and community action, including expanded educational opportunities, rebuilding of cities, encouragement of voluntary health plans, advancement of consumer interests, guaranteed income, and improvement in the quality of American life.

The first AFL-CIO affiliate, the International Chemical Workers Union, to join the ALA in August 1969 was expelled by the AFL-CIO Convention on October 3, 1969, on the ground that the union's affiliation with ALA did "violence to the objectives and principles of the federation." The National Council of Distributive Workers of America joined the ALA in May 1970.

According to Treckel, the "view most frequently advanced in explaining the demise of the ALA is that the organization collapsed because of the death of Walter Reuther" in 1970. The ALA existed until the Spring of 1972.

The Chemical Workers Union withdrew from the ALA on May 5, 1971, and was readmitted to the AFL-CIO on May 12, 1971.

Source references: "AFL-CIO Expels Chemical Union for Affiliation with Rival ALA," *AFL-CIO News*, October 11, 1969; "Reuther-Fitzsimmons Propose No-Raiding Agreement to AFL-CIO," *Daily Labor Report*, No. 229, Nov. 22, 1968; Karl F. Treckel, *The Rise and Fall of the Alliance for Labor Action (1968–1972)* (Kent: Kent State Univ., Center for Business and Economic Research, Labor and IR Series no. 3, 1975); "UAW and Teamsters Form Alliance for Labor Action With Reform Objectives," *Daily Labor Report*, No. 143, July 23, 1968.

allied labor (craft) councils National, state, or local organizations of craft groups federated for the purpose of meeting mutual craft or industry problems. Building and printing trades councils exist in many cities throughout the United States.

Allied Workers International Union; United (Ind) It publishes the *News and Views* (semiannually).

Address: 5506 Calumet Ave., Hammond, Ind. 46320. Tel. (219) 932–9400

allowed time The number of minutes set or allowed to complete a task under an incentive wage plan. The term also has been used to note the number of minutes of nonwork time permitted for such factors as fatigue, cleaning of tools, rest periods, and other personal needs. The allowed time added to actual work or operating time constitutes the full time used in setting piece rates or production bonuses or standards.

Source references: Ralph M. Barnes, *Motion and Time Study* (6th ed., New York: Wiley, 1968); W. G. Holmes, *Applied Time and Motion Study* (New York: Ronald Press, 1938).

See also CLEAN-UP PERIOD, DEAD TIME, DELAY ALLOWANCES, DRESSING TIME, LEVELING, MAKE-READY ACTIVITIES, MOTION STUDY, PIECE RATE, REST PERIOD, SET-UP TIME.

all-union shop Union security agreements in which all employees of a company are union members. The term is not widely used since other terms such as closed shop, union shop, maintenance of membership, more definitely distinguish the nature of the union security relationship in the plant.

See also AGENCY SHOP, CLOSED SHOP, MAINTENANCE OF MEMBERSHIP, MODIFIED UNION SHOP, UNION SECURITY CLAUSES, UNION SHOP.

alternative work schedules *See* FLEXTIME/FLEXITIME.

Alton Railroad Co. v. Railroad Retirement Board *See* RAILROAD RETIREMENT ACT, RAILROAD RETIREMENT BOARD V. ALTON RAILROAD CO.

Aluminum, Brick and Clay Workers International Union (AFL-CIO) Union formed in 1981 by the merger of the Aluminum Workers International Union (AFL-CIO) and The United Brick and Clay Workers of America (AFL-CIO). In September 1982, the union merged with the United Glass and Ceramic Workers of North America (AFL-CIO) to form the Aluminum, Brick and Glass Workers International Union (AFL-CIO).

See also ALUMINUM, BRICK AND GLASS WORKERS INTERNATIONAL UNION (AFL-CIO).

Aluminum, Brick and Glass Workers International Union (AFL-CIO) Union created by the merger of the Aluminum, Brick and Clay Workers International Union (AFL-CIO) and the United Glass and Ceramic Workers of North America (AFL-CIO) in September 1982. Its bimonthly publication is *Aluminum Light.*

Address: 3362 Hollenberg Dr., Bridgeton, Mo. 63044. Tel. (314) 739–6142

Aluminum Workers International Union (AFL-CIO) The union merged with The United Brick and Clay Workers of America (AFL-CIO) to form the Aluminum, Brick and Clay Workers International Union (AFL-CIO) on September 1, 1981.

See also ALUMINUM, BRICK AND CLAY WORKERS INTERNATIONAL UNION (AFL-CIO).

amalgamated craft unions Consolidated or merged trade unions performing similar work absorbed in a new homogeneous organization. It is a form of unionism between the industrial and craft union. Employees in an amalgamated craft group work with a common material such as glass, wood, or pottery, but the trade skills are not identical.

American Anti-Boycott Association An organization formed in 1902–1903 to bring unions within the ambit of the antitrust laws. It was successful when the Supreme Court in the famous *Danbury Hatters* case held that labor organizations came within the scope of the Sherman Anti-Trust Act of 1890.

D. E. Loewe, one of the employers boycotted by the United Hatters of America, was instrumental in forming the Association. He obtained the assistance of a Bridgeport, Conn., lawyer named Daniel Davenport, who became an active figure in the organization.

The Association changed its name to the League for Industrial Rights in 1919. Its official publication was *Law and Order.*

Source reference: Edward Berman, *Labor and the Sherman Act* (New York: Harper, 1930).

See also LAWLOR V. LOEWE, SHERMAN ACT OF 1890.

American Arbitration Association A private nonprofit organization formed in 1926 to encourage the use of arbitration in the settlement of disputes. Devoted largely to commercial arbitration at its inception, it developed and sponsored facilities for resolving disputes in the international area—and with the development of large scale unionization and collective bargaining agreements, the encouragement of labor-management arbitration.

Its functions are education, research, and service. The Association sponsors conferences; publishes a quarterly journal, *The Arbitration Journal*; puts out digests of arbitration cases; and has developed panels of arbitrators in most large American cities. It developed a Code of Ethics for Arbitrators and recommends special arbitration clauses for inclusion in contracts. It also publishes a manual of procedures.

In 1968, the National Center for Dispute Settlement of the AAA was established to apply the "techniques of arbitration, mediation, and fact-finding to the solution of conflicts in urban areas." The Center seeks "to develop impartial machinery and to train mediators within local communities to deal with such matters as landlord-tenant disputes, urban renewal conflicts, complaints against welfare agency procedures, dissension between merchants and consumers and 'confrontations by civil rights units.'"

Source references: Noble Braden, "Policy and Practice of American Arbitration Association," *Management Rights and the Arbitration Process*, Proceedings of 9th A/M, NAA, ed. by Jean McKelvey (Washington: BNA, 1956); "Center for Dispute Settlement Established . . . ," *Arbitration News*, Sept. 1968; "Code of Ethics and Procedural Standards of Labor-Management Arbitration," *The Profession of Labor Arbitration*, Selected papers from the First Seven A/M, NAA, ed. by Jean McKelvey (Washington: BNA, 1957); Michael F. Hoellering, "Recent Developments at the American Arbitration Association," *LLJ*, Aug. 1978; Samuel C. Jackson, "Community Conflict and Fair Employment Relations," *Arbitration and Social Change*, Proceedings of 22d A/M, NAA, ed. by Gerald Somers (Washington: BNA, 1970); Frances Kellor, *American Arbitration: Its History, Functions and Achievements* (New York: Harper, 1948).

See also ARBITRATION, NATIONAL ACADEMY OF ARBITRATORS.

American Association for Labor Legislation A section of the International Association for Labor Legislation formed in 1900 to investigate labor conditions in all countries. The organization formed in the United States in 1906 did much to cumulate information and draft model bills to aid legislatures in enacting better social and labor legislation. It has sponsored conferences and published research materials to encourage governmental protection of health, employment, and other labor standards.

The official journal of the Association was the *American Labor Legislation Review*, a quarterly started in 1909. John B. Andrews was one of its leaders.

The New York State School of Industrial and Labor Relations Library, Cornell University, received in 1962 a gift from the Princeton University Library collection of approximately 5,000 pamphlets dealing with the early development of protective labor legislation and social security in the United States. These pamphlets were part of the collection of the American Association for Labor Legislation which had gone to Princeton in 1944. Cornell University in 1945 acquired the records and office files of the Association which are now part of the Cornell Labor-Management Documentation Center. With the additional 5,000 pamphlets from Princeton University, the Cornell University collection has the complete existing archives of the American Association for Labor Legislation and of John B. Andrews.

Source reference: John R. Commons and John B. Andrews, *Principles of Labor Legislation* (4th rev. ed., New York: Harper, 1936).

American Association of University Professors (AAUP) (Ind) According to Metzger, "In the spring of 1913, a letter signed by eighteen full professors on the faculty of the Johns Hopkins University was sent to persons of equal rank at nine other leading universities, urging them to join in the formation of a national association of professors. The letter stated that the specialized interests of academics were served by the disciplinary societies, but that their institutional and societal interests, which were equally important and pressing, were not being adequately cared for; and that for this purpose an ecumenical society was required. Many of the recipients agreed. Committees of eminent professors were formed to advance the project; 650 persons, chosen for their prominence in their disciplines, accepted the invitation to become charter members; in January, 1915, at a convention of academic luminaries, the American Association of University Professors was born."

Initially, the AAUP atttempted to evolve into a professional society with functions akin to that of the American Medical Association. However, in 1965, it began to engage in collective bargaining, and in 1968, the AAUP affirmed the appropriateness of a faculty strike in certain situations. By 1972, the AAUP voted to "pursue collective bargaining as a major additional way of realizing the Association's goals in higher education. . . ."

In the 1983 revision of its Statement on Collective Bargaining adopted in 1973, the Association states: "As a national organization which has historically played a major role in formulating and implementing the principles that govern relationships in academic life, the Association promotes collective bargaining to reinforce the best features of higher education. The principles of academic freedom and tenure, fair procedures, faculty participation in governance, and the primary responsibility of the faculty for determining academic policy will thereby be secured. For these reasons, the Association supports efforts of local chapters to pursue collective bargaining." Included in the Statement is the Association's "Policy for Collective Bargaining Chapters."

In 1982, the AAUP had 1,372 chapters and 66,000 members. It publishes *Academe: The Bulletin of the AAUP*, six times annually.

Address: 1 Dupont Circle, N.W., Suite 500, Washington, D.C. 20036. Tel. (202) 737-5900

Source references: AAUP, *Policy Documents and Reports* (Washington: 1971); Tracy H. Ferguson, "Collective Bargaining in Universities and Colleges," *LLJ*, Dec. 1968; Eileen B. Hoffman, *Unionization of Professional Societies* (New York: The Conference Board, Report 690, 1976); Walter P. Metzger, "Origins of the Association," *AAUP Bulletin*, June 1965; "Statement on Collective Bargaining," *AAUP Bulletin*, Summer 1973; "Statement on Collective Bargaining," *Academe*, Vol. 69, no. 5 (1983); George Strauss, "The AAUP as a Professional Occupational Association," *IR*, Oct. 1965.

American Civil Liberties Union An organization formed around 1920 for the purpose, among others, of protecting individuals and organizations by providing legal counsel and taking action to protect and promote civil rights. It is not a labor organization or union but is composed of private citizens opposed to infringement of civil rights because of racial or other prejudice. It publishes *First Principles* (monthly) and *Civil Liberties* (bimonthly).

Address: 132 W. 43rd St., New York, N.Y. 10036.

American Federationist, The The official monthly magazine of the AFL-CIO. It is devoted mainly to economic and social problems affecting labor. It was discontinued in its magazine format after the April/June 1982 issue and is now issued as a periodic supplement to the weekly *AFL-CIO News*.

American Federation of Labor Organized in 1881 as the Federation of Organized Trades and Labor Unions of the United States of America and Canada. It changed its name in 1886.

On July 1, 1954, just before the merger with CIO, the AFL claimed 10,200,000 dues-paying members. It comprised 110 national and international unions with 45,000 local unions, and 900 local trade and federal labor unions of 165,000 directly affiliated with the AFL.

Many of the national unions also were affiliated with one or more of the five trades departments—Building Trades, Metal Trades, Railway Employees, Maritime Employees, and the Union Label Trades Department.

There also were 50 state federations of labor and 825 city central bodies.

With the exception of one year, Samuel Gompers was president of the AFL from 1886 until his death in 1924. William Green succeeded Gompers and remained president of the Federation until his death on November 21, 1952. George Meany was elected president by the executive council on November 25, 1952.

Source references: Jack Barbash, *American Unions: Structure, Government and Politics* (New York: Random House, 1967); Mary Erb (comp.), *American Federation of Labor: History, Encyclopedia and Reference Book* (Washington: AFL-CIO, 1960); Herbert Harris, *American Labor* (New Haven: Yale UP, 1938); Lewis L. Lorwin, *The American Federation of Labor* (Washington: Brookings Institution, 1933); Harry A. Millis and Royal E. Montgomery, *Organized Labor* (New York: McGraw-Hill, 1945); James O. Morris, *Conflict Within the A.F. of L.: A Study of Craft Versus Industrial Unionism, 1891–1938* (Ithaca: NYSSILR, Cornell Univ., Cornell Studies in Industrial and Labor Relations, Vol. X, 1958); Florence Peterson, *American*

Labor Unions (New York: Harper, 1963); Louis Schultz Reed, *The Labor Philosophy of Samuel Gompers* (Port Washington, N.Y.: Kennikat Press, 1966); Philip Taft, *The A.F. of L. From the Death of Gompers to the Merger* (New York: Harper, 1959); ———, *The A.F. of L. in the Time of Gompers* (New York: Harper, 1957); Lloyd Ulman, *The Rise of the National Trade Union* (Cambridge: Harvard UP, 1966).

See also AMERICAN FEDERATION OF LABOR-CONGRESS OF INDUSTRIAL ORGANIZATIONS.

American Federation of Labor-Congress of Industrial Organizations The merger of the AFL and the CIO in 1955 brought together approximately 130 international unions. The CIO organization which had been formed by a split within the AFL, largely on the issue of organization along industrial lines, was brought back into the fold. Since agreement on a new name could not be reached, the new name merely combined the two. For convenience the organization is referred to as the AFL-CIO.

The AFL-CIO is made up of 99 national unions and more than 49,000 local unions. It has a membership of approximately 15 million.

Lane Kirkland was elected president of the AFL-CIO on November 19, 1979, following the retirement of its first president George Meany. It publishes the *AFL-CIO News* and *Free Trade Union News*.

Address: 815 16th St., N.W., Washington, D.C. 20006. Tel. (202) 637–5000

Source references: AFL-CIO, *Convention Proceedings* (Washington: 1955); "The AFL-CIO Merger," *ILRR*, April 1956; Jack Barbash, *American Unions: Structure, Government and Politics* (New York: Random House, 1967); Joseph W. Bloch, "Founding Convention of the AFL-CIO," *MLR*, Feb. 1956; Carroll R. Daugherty, "Import of the AFL-CIO Merger for Management," *MLR*, Dec. 1956; Arthur J. Goldberg, *AFL-CIO: Labor United* (New York: McGraw-Hill, 1956); John Hutchinson, "The Constitution and Government of the AFL-CIO," *California LR*, Dec. 1958; Florence Peterson, *American Labor Unions* (2d rev. ed., New York: Harper, 1963); Archie Robinson, *George Meany and His Times, a Biography* (New York: Simon and Schuster, 1981).

See also AFL-CIO MERGER.

American Federation of Labor v. National Labor Relations Board A case in which the Supreme Court was asked to review and set aside a determination by the NLRB as to the "unit appropriate for purposes of collective bargaining." The petitioners before the court, two AFL longshore unions on the west coast, claimed that the NLRB had deprived them of their bargaining rights in areas where they "had been selected as bargaining representatives by a majority of the employees of their respective employers. . . ." The certification by the National Labor Relations Board in the case (*Shipowners' Association of the Pacific Coast*, 7 NLRB 1002) had the bargaining unit include, in a single unit, all of the longshore employees of the members of the employer associations doing business at the west coast ports of the United States.

The Board claimed that it had discretion under the statute to determine the appropriate bargaining unit and that such certifications were not subject to review by the federal appellate courts.

In an opinion delivered by Justice Stone, the court upheld the NLRB's contention, saying in part:

> The conclusion is unavoidable that Congress, as the result of a deliberate choice of conflicting policies, has excluded representation certifications of the Board from review by federal appellate courts authorized by the Wagner Act except in the circumstances specified in section 9(d).

Source reference: American Federation of Labor v. National Labor Relations Board, 308 US 401, 5 LRRM 670 (1940).

See also BARGAINING UNIT.

American Federation of Labor v. Swing A Supreme Court decision in which the Court affirmatively answered the question: "Is the constitutional guarantee of freedom of discussion infringed by the common law policy of a state forbidding resort to peaceful persuasion through picketing merely because there is no immediate employer-employee dispute?"

The issue arose when an AFL union sought to organize Swing's beauty parlor. Placards and picketing were used by the union. Swing sought and obtained a preliminary injunction, and later a final decree. The final decree of the Illinois state appellate court held that ". . . this Court and the Supreme Court of this State have held in this case, that, under the law of this State, peaceful picketing or peaceful persuasion are unlawful when conducted by strangers to the employer (i.e., where there is not a proximate relation of employees and employer), and that appellants are entitled in this case to relief by injunction against the threat of such peaceful picketing or persuasion by appellees."

The Supreme Court decision delivered by Justice Frankfurter held that "Such a ban of free communication is inconsistent with the guarantee of freedom of speech. . . . A State cannot exclude workingmen from peacefully exercising the right of free communication by drawing the circle of economic competition between employers and workers so small as to contain only an employer and those directly employed by him. The interdependence of economic interest of all engaged in the same industry has become a commonplace."

Source references: AFL v. Swing, 312 US 321, 7 LRRM 307 (1941). Law review notes on the *Swing* case are to be found in 28 *California LR* 733 (1940); 25 *Minnesota LR* 238 (1941).

See also FREEDOM OF SPEECH, STRANGER PICKETING.

American Indian or Alaskan Native According to OFCCP, "A person with origins in any of the original peoples of North America and who maintains cultural identification through tribal affiliation or community recognition." Under Title VII, this is a protected class and one of the racial/ethnic categories for which data are reported to the federal government.

Source reference: U.S. OFCCP, *Federal Contract Compliance Manual* (Washington: 1979).

See also AFFECTED CLASS, PROTECTED CLASS.

American Institute for Free Labor Development An education program started in 1959 by the Communications Workers of America (AFL-CIO) to train Latin American labor leaders. It subsequently received support from the AFL-CIO, private business concerns, and some foreign aid funds. Classes began in Washington in 1962 with 40 students under the directorship of William C. Doherty, Jr., who currently serves as its executive director. The Institute issues the *AIFLD Report*.

Address: 1015 20th St., N.W., Washington, D.C. 20036. Tel. (202) 659–6300

Source reference: Eugene H. Methvin, "Labor's New Weapon for Democracy," *Reader's Digest*, Oct. 1966.

Americanization The process which a foreign or immigrant worker goes through in accepting the language, customs, and traditions of American life and culture.

Many unions which have a large immigrant membership provide courses to make it easier for the worker to adjust to American life. Many unions help workers with courses in language, American history and government, as well as assistance in obtaining their citizenship papers.

See also LABOR EDUCATION.

American Labor Education Service *See* AFFILIATED SCHOOLS FOR WORKERS.

American Management Association An organization of companies, trade associations, and professional people concerned with the problems of personnel and management. The organization prior to 1923 was known as the National Association of Employment Managers.

The Association pursues an active publication program which includes the monthly, *Management Review*, and bimonthly, *Personnel*. Among other publications, it issues the *Management Briefing, Research Study*, and *Survey Report* series. The scope of the publications are much broader than the field of industrial relations.

Address: 135 West 50th Street, New York, N.Y. 10020. Tel. (212) 568–8100

American National Insurance case Case in which the Supreme Court rejected an NLRB holding that the company violated its good-faith bargaining duty under the Taft-Hartley Act by conditioning the execution of a contract on the union's acceptance of a so-called management functions clause. The Board had ruled that the company's action was a *per se* violation of the Act, since the management functions clause covered conditions of employment that were subjects of collective bargaining. But the Court said that the "Board may not, either directly or indirectly, compel concessions or otherwise sit in judgment upon the substantive terms of collective bargaining agreements."

Source reference: NLRB v. American National Insurance Co., 343 US 395, 30 LRRM 2147 (1952).

See also BORG-WARNER CASE, MANAGEMENT RIGHTS.

American Nurses' Association (Ind) A professional organization of registered nurses organized in 1896, consisting of 53 constituent associations in states and territories and 860 local associations. It carries on a variety of programs devoted to nursing education, nursing services, and nursing practice, in addition to economic and general welfare. The latter is carried out under the leadership of its Commission on Economic and General Welfare. In the ANA's view, collective bargaining is necessary if nurses are to achieve professional status. According to Stieber, the ANA was the first professional association to support collective bargaining. In 1946, the ANA urged its state associations to seek recognition as exclusive representatives of nurses in negotiations. It issues *The American Nurse* (monthly).

Address: 2420 Pershing Road, Kansas City, Mo. 64108. Tel. (816) 474–5720

Source references: Joel Seidman, "Nurses and Collective Bargaining," *ILRR*, April 1970; Jack Stieber, *Public Employee Unionism: Structure, Growth, Policy* (Washington: Brookings Institution, 1973).

American Plan The term applied to efforts by American industry to maintain the open-shop movement in the 1920s.

The term "American Plan" was adopted at a conference in 1921, by 22 state employer associations convened for the purpose of preventing the closed shop in American industry.

See also OPEN SHOP.

American Ship Building case Case in which the Supreme Court held that a company did not violate the Taft-Hartley Act when, after an impasse had been reached in contract negotiations, the company temporarily shut down its plant and laid off its employees for the sole purpose of bringing economic pressure to bear in support of its legitimate bargaining position. The Court said that the company's action was not demonstrably destructive of employee rights, and there was no evidence that the company was motivated by anti-union purposes. The NLRB had held that the company's action was an unfair labor practice under the Act.

Source reference: American Ship Building Co. v. NLRB, 380 US 300, 58 LRRM 2672 (1965).

See also LOCKOUT.

American shop A company which operated under the so-called American or open-shop plan.

Source reference: Paul K. Crosser, *Ideologies and American Labor* (Oxford: Oxford UP, 1941).

See also OPEN SHOP.

American Steel Foundries v. Tri-City Central Trades Council A decision of the Supreme Court which held that the right of peaceful persuasion, or peaceful picketing, protected in Section 20 of the Clayton Act must be examined on the merits of each case and the circumstances surrounding it. The Court in an opinion by Chief Justice Taft held that strikebreakers and new employees were to be permitted "clear passage" to the plant. The Court limited the number of pickets and restricted the right of the pickets to ". . . observation, communication and persuasion." The pickets were, moreover, admonished not to be "abusive, libelous, or threatening, and they not approach individuals together but singly. . . ."

The Court reviewed the applicability of Section 20 of the Clayton Act (c. 323, 38 Stat. 738, 29 USCA) which was passed October 15, 1914, while the case was pending in the Circuit Court of Appeals. Section 20 provided, among other things, that

> . . . no restraining order or injunction . . . shall prohibit any person or persons, whether single or in concert, from terminating any relation of employment . . . or from recommending, advising, or persuading others by peaceful means so to do or from attending any place where any such person or persons may lawfully be, for the purpose of peacefully persuading any person to work or to abstain from working; . . . or from peaceably assembling in a lawful manner, and for lawful purposes; . . .

Chief Justice Taft said in part: "How far may men go in persuasion and communication and still not violate the right of those whom they would influence? In going to and from work men have a right to as free a passage without obstruction as the streets afford consistent with the right of others to enjoy the same privilege. . . ." Influencing the action of others the Court held proper if done in an "inoffensive way," but ". . . persistence, importunity, following and dogging become unjustifiable annoyance and obstruction which is likely soon to savor of intimidation."

The Court said further:

> Each case must turn on its own circumstances. It is a case for the flexible remedial power of a court of equity which may try one mode of restraint, and if it fails or proves to be too drastic, may change it. We think that the strikers and their sympathizers engaged in the economic struggle should be limited to one representative for each point of ingress and egress in the plant or place of business and that all others be enjoined from congregating or loitering at the plant or in the neighboring streets by which access is had to the plant, that such representatives should have the right of observation, communication and persuasion but with special admonition that their communication, arguments and appeals shall not be abusive, libelous or threatening, and that they shall not approach individuals together but singly, and shall not in their single efforts at communication or persuasion obstruct an unwilling listener by importunate following or dogging his steps.

The *American Steel Foundries* decision contains a much-quoted passage by the Chief Justice in praise of unionism and the need for its existence.

Said the Chief Justice:

> Labor unions are recognized by the Clayton Act as legal when instituted for mutual help and lawfully carrying out their legitimate objects. They have long been thus recognized by the courts. They were organized out of the necessities of the situation. A single employee was helpless in dealing with an employer. He was dependent ordinarily on his daily wage for the maintenance of himself and family. If the employer refused to pay him the wages that he thought fair, he was nevertheless unable to leave the employ and to resist arbitrary and unfair treatment. Union was essential to give laborers opportunity to deal on equality with their employer. They united to exert influence upon him and to leave him in a body in order by this inconvenience to induce him to make better terms with them. . . . The strike became a lawful instrument in a lawful economic struggle or competition between employer and employees as to the share or division between them of the joint product of labor and capital. . . .

Source references: American Steel Foundries v. Tri-City Trade Council, 257 US 184 (1921). For law review notes on the *American Steel Foundries* case see: 70 *Univ. of Pennsylvania LR* 101 (1922) and 8 *Virginia LR* 401 (1922).

See also FREEDOM OF SPEECH, PEACEFUL PERSUASION, PEACEFUL PICKETING.

American Vocational Association An organization formed in 1926 to promote vocational education throughout the United States. Its official publication is the *A.V.A. Journal.*

amnesty clause An agreement between management and union that no reprisal or discrimination would be taken against strikers or nonstrikers after a dispute is settled.

In the public sector, management may grant general amnesty in order to restore essential public services.

Source reference: Carmen D. Saso, *Coping with Public Employee Strikes* (Chicago: PPA, 1970).

anarchism Although there are many sects among the anarchists—collectivist, individualist, communistic, or philosophical—they are all based primarily on the rejection of all external authority. All relationships are to be based on the consent of the person concerned.

Anarchism as a philosophy was never accepted by American labor, although there were efforts in the 1880s and 1890s to use terroristic methods in achieving gains for the "downtrodden" workingman.

Source references: Paul K. Crosser, *Ideologies and American Labor* (Oxford: Oxford UP, 1941); Bertrand Russell, *Roads to Freedom: Socialism, Anarchism and Syndicalism* (London: Allen & Unwin, 1966); David J. Saposs, "Impact of Labor Ideology on Industrial Relations," *MLR*, Oct. 1962.

See also HAYMARKET RIOT.

angelfood Industrial Workers of the World description of mission preaching.

Source reference: Joyce L. Kornbluh (ed.), *Rebel Voices* (Ann Arbor: Univ. of Michigan Press, 1964).

See also INDUSTRIAL WORKERS OF THE WORLD.

annual earnings Total compensation received by an employee from whatever source during a calendar year. It may include such earnings as wages, overtime, vacation pay, etc., at one or more companies.

annual improvement factor A term which came into prominence following a collective bargaining agreement between General Motors and the UAW (CIO) which provided a yearly wage adjustment based on the premise that employees should be permitted to improve their standard of living. The improvement factor was to be the cents-per-hour equivalent of the yearly increase in productivity to be shared with the employees. It was 3 cents in 1948 when first negotiated.

Source references: Frederick H. Harbison, "The General Motors-United Auto Workers Agreement of 1950," *Journal of Political Economy*, Oct. 1950; Dale D. McConkey, "Why the Annual Improvement Factor?" *LLJ*, Aug. 1959; "New Wage Formula in Auto Contract," 22 *LRRM* 18 (1948), 26 *LRRM* 3, 6 (1950).

See also PRODUCTIVITY, WAGE ADJUSTMENT PLANS.

annual wage plan *See* GUARANTEED ANNUAL WAGE, SUPPLEMENTAL UNEMPLOYMENT BENEFITS.

annuity A fixed payment to a specific person at stated intervals, either for a definite number of years or for life. The term is also applied to the contract under which the annuity is paid.

Immediate annuities are those which are purchased with a single premium. Annuity payments begin within six months or a year.

Deferred annuities are those purchased with a single premium or annual premiums over a number of years. Annuity payments do not begin for a period of years.

Annuity certain is one where the annuitant receives the annuity for a fixed period regardless of the length of his life.

A *life annuity* is one where the annuitant receives fixed payments for the duration of his life.

There is a large variety of annuity contracts offered by insurance companies.

Source references: R. G. Olmsted, "The Variable Annuity," *NYU 10th Annual Conference on Labor*, ed. by Emanuel Stein (Albany: Bender, 1957); Michael Puchek, *Pension Plan Policies and Practices* (Ithaca: NYSSILR, Cornell Univ., Bull. no. 21, 1952).

See also MODIFIED CASH REFUND ANNUITY.

Anthracite Coal Commission A board appointed by President Theodore Roosevelt in 1902 to settle the severe strike in the anthracite coal mines of Pennsylvania. The miners returned to work after the employers agreed to accept the award of the Commission.

Source references: Robert J. Cornell, *The Anthracite Coal Strikes of 1902* (Washington: The Catholic Univ. of America Press, 1957); Chris Evans, *History of the United Mine Workers of America* (2 vols., Indianapolis: United Mine Workers of America, 1918); Elsie Gluck, *John Mitchell, Miner* (New York: John Day, 1929); A. E. Suffern, *Conciliation and Arbitration in the Coal Industry of America* (Boston: Houghton Mifflin, 1915).

anti-certification strike Work stoppage conducted by a union seeking recognition to force an employer to no longer recognize another union which has been certified as bargaining agent. This is an unfair labor practice under the Taft-Hartley Act.

anti-communist affidavit *See* NONCOMMUNIST AFFIDAVIT.

Anti-Injunction Act (Norris LaGuardia Act) *See* NORRIS-LAGUARDIA ACT.

Anti-Kickback Law (Copeland Act) Legislation passed by the Congress in 1934 to eliminate the widespread practice of employers to require workers on federally financed projects to return part of their wages as a condition of employment. The law prohibits, on penalty of fine, employers or their agents from using force, threats, or other means against workers to return any part of their wages in order to retain their job.

Source references: "Anti-Kickback Legislation," *MLR*, May 1939; Donald R. Herzog, "Labor Laws Applicable to Federal Government Contracts," *LLJ*, Jan. 1968.

See also KICKBACK.

anti-labor legislation Enactments by Congress, state, or local legislative bodies which are considered by organized labor to be directed against legitimate trade union activities and interests. Laws which in the eyes of labor are designed to restrict organization or trade union efforts to achieve better wages, hours, or working conditions. Legislation limiting or circumscribing the right to strike or picket, or the passage of "right to work laws" are examples.

anti-leaflet ordinance A municipal ordinance or statute which attempts to prohibit or regulate the distribution of handbills, circulars, and other union organization or campaign literature.

Source reference: Schneider v. State, 308 US 147, 5 LRRM 659 (1939).

See also FREEDOM OF SPEECH.

Anti-Petrillo Act *See* LEA ACT (ANTI-PETRILLO ACT).

Anti-Racketeering Act (Hobbs Act) A federal statute passed in 1934 (49 Stat. 979), but subsequently amended to cover labor organizations, forbidding the use of extortion, force, or violence in interstate commerce.

The Act made it illegal for unscrupulous labor unions to blackmail employers or accept bribes for not calling strikes.

Source references: U.S. v. Teamsters, Local 807, 315 US 521, 10 LRRM 368 (1942); Charles O. Gregory, *Labor and the Law* (2d rev. ed., New York: Norton, 1961); William Eric Minamyer, "The Labor Activity Exemption to the Hobbs Act: An Analysis of the Appropriate Scope," *LLJ*, Jan. 1983; A. Howard Myers, *Labor Law and Legislation* (4th ed., Cincinnati: South-Western, 1968).

See also FEATHERBEDDING.

Anti-Strikebreaking Act (Byrnes Act) A federal statute passed in 1936 (49 Stat. 1899), to prevent employers from transporting strikebreakers across state lines. The law was amended in 1938 and forbids interstate transportation of any person for the purpose of interfering with peaceful picketing during a labor dispute.

Source references: "Industrial Strikebreaking—The Byrnes Act," 4 *Univ. of Chicago LR* 657 (1937).

See also MOHAWK VALLEY FORMULA, STRIKEBREAKER.

Anti-Trust Act, 1890 (Sherman Act) *See* SHERMAN ACT OF 1890.

Anti-Trust Act, 1914 (Clayton Act) *See* CLAYTON ACT OF 1914.

antitrust laws Statutes intended to limit interference with free trade and competition. Frequently applied to labor organizations, as agencies acting in restraint of trade.

Source references: "The Antitrust Laws and the Single-Firm Conduct," *Law and Contemporary Problems*, Summer 1965; Dale G. Brickner, "Labor and Antitrust Action," *ILRR*, Jan. 1960; Emanuel Celler, "Should Unions Be Made Subject to the Anti-Trust Laws?" *American Federationist*, Nov. 1959; Laurence J. Cohen, "Labor Law and Antitrust Law: The Impact of *Connell Construction*," *NYU 32d Annual National Conference on Labor*, ed. by Richard Adelman (New York: Bender, 1980); Malcolm Cohen, "Unions and the Antitrust Strawman," *LLJ*, Feb. 1963; Archibald Cox, "Labor and Antitrust Laws—A Preliminary Analysis," *Univ. of Pennsylvania LR*, Nov. 1955; Walter L. Daykin, "The Status of Unions Under Our Antitrust Laws," *LLJ*, March 1960; Mary L. Dooley, "Antitrust Legislation and Labor Unions," *LLJ*, Oct. 1960; Victor R. Hansen, "Applying Antitrust Laws to Labor Unions' Activities," 41 *LRRM* 91; George H. Hildebrand, "Collective Bargaining and the Antitrust Laws," *Public Policy and Collective Bargaining*, ed. by Joseph Shister, Benjamin Aaron, and Clyde W. Summers (New York: Harper, IRRA Pub. no. 27, 1962); Julia E. Johnsen (comp.), *Trade Unions and the Antitrust Laws* (New York: Wilson, 1940); Luis Kutner, "Due Process of Economy: Anti-trust Control of Labor," *Univ. of Pittsburgh LR*, Oct. 1962; "Labor and the Anti-Trust Laws," *American Federationist*, Oct. 1961; Andrew Laidlaw, "Labor Antitrust Problems: Trap for the Unwary," *Employee Relations LJ*, Spring 1978; Sar A. Levitan, "An Appraisal of the Antitrust Approach,"

Annals, Jan. 1961; Jesse W. Markham, "Antitrust Trends and New Constraints," *Harvard BR*, May/June 1963; A. Neale, *The Antitrust Laws of the United States of America: A Study of Competition Enforced by Law* (Cambridge: Cambridge UP, 1960); Edward G. Posniak, "Looking Around: Effectiveness of Antitrust," *Harvard BR*, March/April 1959; Harold S. Roberts (ed.), *Labor and Antitrust Legislation* (Honolulu: Univ. of Hawaii, IRC, 1961); Theodore St. Antoine, "Collective Bargaining and the Antitrust Laws," *Proceedings of the 19th A/M, IRRA*, ed. by Gerald Somers (Madison: 1967); George W. Stocking and Myron W. Watkins, *Monopoly and Free Enterprise* (New York: Twentieth Century Fund, 1951); Jerrold G. Van Cise, "How to Live with Antitrust," *Harvard BR*, Nov./Dec. 1962; Jerre S. Williams, "Labor and the Antitrust Laws," *Labor Law Developments*, Proceedings of the 12th Annual Institute on Labor Law, SLF (Washington: BNA, 1966).

See also CLAYTON ACT OF 1914, SHERMAN ACT OF 1890.

anti-union agreement *See* YELLOW DOG CONTRACT.

anti-union practices Activities and practices of employers or employer associations interfering with the rights of self-organization and collective bargaining. Prior to the National Labor Relations Act of 1935 these practices were not prohibited by law. Section 8 of the NLRA held some of these to be contrary to federal labor policy.

Source references: Jules Bernstein, "Union Busting: From Benign Neglect to Malignant Growth," *NYU 33d Annual National Conference on Labor*, ed. by Richard Adelman (New York: Bender, 1981); William E. Fulmer, "Step by Step Through a Union Campaign," *Harvard BR*, July/Aug. 1981; G. T. 99 (pseud.), *Labor Spy* (Indianapolis: Bobbs-Merrill, 1937); Tommy W. Jarrett, "'Outsiders' as Agents of the Employer," *IR Law Digest*, April 1968; John G. Kilgour, *Preventive Labor Relations* (New York: AMACOM, 1981); William A. Krupman, "Election Campaign Strategy: NLRB Expands Employer Rights," *Employee Relations LJ*, Spring 1976; Steve Lagerfeld, *The Ideology of Union Busting* (New York: League for Industrial Democracy, Labor Issues Papers, 1981[?]); Edward Levinson, *I Break Strikes* (New York: Robert McBride & Co., 1935); Charles McDonald and Dick Wilson, "Peddling the 'Union-Free' Guarantee," *American Federationist*, April 1979; Phillis Payne, "The Consultants Who Coach the Violators," *American Federationist*, Sept. 1977; D. J. Saposs and E. T. Bliss, *Current Anti-Labor Activities* (Pittsburgh: NLRB, Release Z–207, Jan. 11, 1938); J. M. Servais, "Anti-Union Discrimination in the Field of Employment," *ILR*, May/June 1977; Anna Stewart, "The Business Offensive in the United States—Will it Spread?" *Journal of IR*, Dec. 1980; Frederick L. Sullivan, "Limiting Union Organizing Activity Through Supervisors," *Personnel*, July/Aug. 1978; U.S. Congress, Senate, Committee on Education and Labor, *Violations of Free Speech and Rights of Labor* (Washington: 1939–42); W. Willard Wirtz, "Board Policy and Labor-Management Relations: 'Employer Persuasion,'" *NYU 7th Annual Conference on Labor*, ed. by Emanuel Stein (Albany: Bender, 1954).

Apex Hosiery Co. v. Leader A decision of the Supreme Court which substantially limited the application of the Sherman Anti-Trust Act to labor unions.

The case arose out of a three-month strike. Failure of a union demand for a closed shop resulted in a sit-down strike, forceable seizure of the plant by employees, and destruction of machinery. The strikers were ejected under an injunction.

The company brought suit to obtain treble damages, alleging that the union was engaged in a conspiracy in violation of the Sherman Anti-Trust Act. Following a jury trial a verdict of $237,310 was returned for the company. The trial judge trebled the verdict to $711,932.55 in conformity with the provisions of the Sherman Act. The Court of Appeals of the Third Circuit reversed the decision, and the Supreme Court granted certiorari February 26, 1940, since the questions presented were "of importance in the administration of the Sherman Act (309 US 644)."

The Supreme Court held, in part, that the mere decline in the volume of goods moving in interstate commerce because of the strike did not constitute a "restraint" of interstate commerce. Restraint, the Court stated, required a showing of actual or intended effect on competition in the marketplace for the employer's product.

Source references: Apex Hosiery v. Leader, 310 US 469, 6 LRRM 647 (1940); Dale G. Brickner, "The Apex Decision: A New Look at Unions Under Antitrust Action," *LLJ*, Feb. 1960; Arthur L. Brown, "The Apex Case and Its Effect Upon Labor Activities and the Anti-Trust Laws," 21 *Boston Univ. LR* 48 (1941); Charles O. Gregory, "Labor's Coercive Activities Under the Sherman Act—The Apex Case," 7 *Univ. of Chicago LR* 347 (1940).

See also ANTITRUST LAWS.

appeal The procedures, normally set out in a law, which provide for the review of a decision of a lower court by a higher body. Under the Labor Management Relations Act (LMRA), also known as the Taft-Hartley Act, appeals may be taken from the district court to the circuit court, to the Supreme Court, in certain cases. Unfair labor practice cases normally go to circuit courts of appeals from the NLRB. The appellate decisions may be reviewed by the Supreme Court.

Appeals may of course be provided on administrative, as well as on legal levels. Thus under the LMRA appeals may be taken from action by the NLRB regional office, by the General Counsel, or by the administrative law judge (formerly known as the trial examiner). The NLRB is the final administrative authority. Reviews of its decisions are before the federal courts.

See also ADMINISTRATIVE PROCEDURE ACT.

appeal procedure Machinery set up to permit review of a case by a higher tribunal. Under NLRB procedure, Board decisions may be appealed to the U.S. courts of appeals and finally to the Supreme Court.

apple polishing The process of shining up to a supervisor or minor official to get into his good graces. The expression probably stems from the practice of bringing an apple for the teacher.

applicant flow data According to OFCCP, "A statistical compilation of employment applicants showing the specific numbers of each racial, ethnic, and sex group who applied for each job title (or group of job titles requiring similar qualifications) during a specified time period." These data are to be gathered to ascertain whether recruitment policies and practices need improvement.

Source references: U.S. OFCCP, "EEO Duties of Contractors," 41 C.F.R. 60–1.40(b); Howard R. Bloch and Robert L. Pennington, "The Use of Applicant Flow Data in a Discrimination Suit," *Public Personnel Management*, Jan./Feb. 1980; U.S. OFCCP, *Federal Contract Compliance Manual* (Washington: 1979).

application, employment *See* EMPLOYMENT APPLICATION.

apprenticeship A method of perpetuating the skills of a trade and regulating the entrance of craftsmen into the trade. It is designed to maintain standards of workmanship and skill as well as to protect the employment opportunities of the journeymen.

The apprentice generally signs an agreement for a fixed period of time during which he will learn the skills of the trade and ultimately become a journeyman. The scope, duration, and content of the training program under the apprenticeship is carefully worked out in each craft.

Manpower legislation such as the Comprehensive Employment and Training Act has provided funds for apprenticeship programs. The Job Training Partnership Act also provides that funds may be used for pre-apprenticeship programs.

Source references: Thomas A. Barocci, "The Determinants of Completion in Apprenticeship," *Proceedings of the 26th A/M, IRRA*, ed. by Gerald Somers (Madison: 1974); Paul Bergevin, *Industrial Apprenticeship* (New York: McGraw-Hill, 1947); Vernon M. Briggs, Jr. and Felician F. Foltman (ed.), *Apprenticeship Research: Emerging Findings and Future Trends*, Proceedings of a Conference on Apprenticeship Training Held April 30 and May 1, 1980, in Washington, D.C. (Ithaca: NYSSILR, Cornell Univ., 1981); William S. Franklin, "Are Construction Apprenticeships Too Long?" *LLJ*, Feb. 1976; Robert W. Glover, "Apprenticeship in America: An Assessment," *Proceedings of the 27th A/M, IRRA*, ed. by James Stern and

Barbara Dennis (Madison: 1975); Reese Hammond, "Effective Preparation for Apprenticeship," *Proceedings of the 22d A/M, IRRA*, ed. by Gerald Somers (Madison: 1970); William Patterson and Marion Hedges, *Educating for Industry Through Apprenticeship* (New York: PH, 1946); Gerald G. Somers, *Innovations in Apprenticeship, The Feasibility of Establishing Demonstration Centers for Apprenticeship and other Industrial Training* (Madison: Univ. of Wisconsin, Manpower and Training Research Unit, IRRI, 1972); U.S. Dept. of Labor, Bureau of Apprenticeship and Training, *Apprenticeship—Past and Present* (rev. ed., Washington: 1962); ———, *The National Apprenticeship Program* (Washington: 1966); U.S. Dept. of Labor, BLS, *Jobs for Which Apprenticeships are Available* (Washington: 1976); ———, *Jobs for Which You Can Train Through Apprenticeship* (Washington: 1979); U.S. Dept. of Labor, ETA, *Apprenticeship: Past and Present* (rev. ed., Washington: 1977); ———, *The National Apprenticeship Program* (Washington: 1980); U.S. Dept. of Labor, Manpower Administration, *Apprenticeship Training in the 1970's: Report of a Conference* (Washington: Research Monograph no. 37, 1974); U.S. Dept. of Labor, Women's Bureau, *A Woman's Guide to Apprenticeship* (Washington: Pamphlet 17, 1980).

See also FEDERAL COMMITTEE ON APPRENTICESHIP TRAINING, INDENTURED APPRENTICESHIP, JOURNEYMAN, LEARNER.

apprenticeship committee A group of employers and union representatives who are responsible for administering an apprenticeship program.

See also JOINT APPRENTICESHIP COMMITTEE OR COUNCIL.

appropriate unit The designation by the National Labor Relations Board and state and local government boards of the group or type of employees who are to constitute the "appropriate unit" for collective bargaining purposes. Although the Taft-Hartley amendments to the National Labor Relations Act place certain limitations on the Board with regard to supervisors, foremen, plant guards, and watchmen, NLRB still has the prime responsibility for determining the unit appropriate for collective bargaining.

The Board's delineation of the bargaining unit, craft, plant, multiplant, or other, frequently determines the union to be selected as the "exclusive bargaining agent" for the employees. Over the years, NLRB has established criteria for determining the appropriate unit for collective bargaining.

Source references: John E. Abodeely, Randi C. Hammer, and Andrew L. Sander, *The NLRB and the Appropriate Bargaining Unit* (rev. ed., Philadelphia: Univ. of Pennsylvania, Wharton School, Industrial Research Unit, LRPP Series no. 3, 1981); Michael I. Berstein, "Appropriate Bargaining Unit Determinations: Affirmative Action Now!" *Employee Relations LJ*, Autumn 1979; Neil W. Chamberlain, "The Structure of Bargaining Units in the United States," *ILRR*, Oct. 1956; William Feldesman, "Current Principles Governing Unit Determination," *NYU 6th Annual Conference on Labor*, ed. by Emanuel Stein (Albany: Bender, 1953); Howard Jenkins, Jr., "A Jurisprudential View of Unit Determination," *Labor Law Developments*, Proceedings of 11th Annual Institute on Labor Law, SLF (Washington: BNA, 1965); Joyce M. Najita and Helene S. Tanimoto, *Guide to Statutory Provisions in Public Sector Collective Bargaining—Unit Determination* (4th issue, Honolulu: Univ. of Hawaii, IRC, 1981); Benjamin B. Naumoff, "Current Practices and Procedures in the Handling of Unit Problems in Representation Cases Under the National Labor Relations Act," *NYU 6th Annual Conference on Labor*, ed. by Emanuel Stein (Albany: Bender, 1953); Norman W. Weiner, "The Appropriate Bargaining Unit," *NYU 6th Annual Conference on Labor*, ed. by Emanuel Stein (Albany: Bender, 1953); James E. Youngdahl, "Crafty Industriousness—Determining the Appropriate Bargaining Unit," *Labor Law Developments*, Proceedings of 14th Annual Institute on Labor Law, SLF (New York: Bender, 1968).

See also BARGAINING UNIT.

aptitude tests Examinations to determine the abilities of individuals to perform certain activities or to measure their capacity to learn or be trained for specific jobs. Some measure general ability while others deal with specific manual dexterity.

See also TEST.

arbitrability Refers to the question of whether a disputed issue is subject to grievance arbitration. Challenges of arbitrability are usually determined by an arbitrator or a court.

Source references: Maurice C. Benewitz, "On Timely Grievances and Arbitrability," *AJ*, June 1979; Kurt H. Decker, "Arbitrability of Public Sector Grievances After Expiration of a Contract," *Journal of Collective Negotiations in the Public Sector*, Vol. 7, no. 4, 1978; Frank Elkouri and Edna A. Elkouri, *How Arbitration Works* (4th ed., Washington: BNA, 1985); Harry H. Rains, "*Boys Market* Injunctions: Strict Scrutiny of the Presumption of Arbitrability," *LLJ*, Jan. 1977; Ralph R. Smith, "Resolving Grievability and Arbitrability Questions in the Federal Sector: Current Policy and Procedure and Recommendations for Change," *Journal of Collective Negotiations in the Public Sector*, Vol. 7, no. 4, 1978.

arbitration A procedure whereby parties unable to agree on a solution to a problem indicate their willingness to be bound by the decision of a third party. The parties usually agree, in advance, on the issues which the third party (the arbitrator) is to decide. This agreement is usually known as the "submission" and the arbitrator is limited and confined by the scope of the submission.

Collective bargaining agreements generally provide for arbitration as the final step in the machinery set up to handle plant grievances. The arbitrator, under an agreement, is generally limited to the interpretation and application of the agreement, and he is required not to add to or amend the contract in his award. Where the arbitrator is appointed for a single case, it is generally referred to as *ad hoc*, or temporary, arbitration. Where the same arbitrator handles all arbitrations under the contract, the procedure may be referred to as permanent arbitration. The term "permanent" is used in a relative sense, since arbitrators are generally appointed only for the duration of the agreement, and occasionally for shorter periods. In some cases they remain only so long as both parties are satisfied with them. Considering the life expectancy of arbitrators under agreements, it is somewhat confusing to apply the term "permanent" to such "impermanent" machinery. There are, however, many instances where arbitrators have served for substantial periods. In some cases the parties have used other terms to describe this third party. George Taylor, for example, was *impartial chairman* under the Full Fashioned Hosiery Industry Agreement for a number of years. Harry Shulman was *umpire* under the Ford Agreement.

Source references: Benjamin Aaron, "Arbitration in the Federal Courts: Aftermath of the Trilogy," *Collective Bargaining and the Arbitrator's Role*, Proceedings of the 15th A/M, NAA, ed. by Mark Kahn (Washington: BNA, 1962); ———, "Current Trends and Developments in Arbitration," *Labor Law Developments 1978*, Proceedings of the 24th Annual Institute on Labor Law, SLF (New York: Bender, 1978); Benjamin Aaron et al., *The Future of Labor Arbitration in America* (New York: AAA, 1976); Walter E. Baer, *The Labor Arbitration Guide* (Homewood, Ill.: Dow Jones-Irwin, 1974); Gerald A. Brown, "The National Labor Policy, the NLRB and Arbitration," *IR Law Digest*, April 1968; Robert Coulson, *Labor Arbitration; What You Need to Know* (New York: AAA, 1973); Harry T. Edwards, "Labor Arbitration at the Crossroads: The 'Common Law of the Shop' v. External Law," *AJ*, June 1977; Frank Elkouri, "Informal Observations on Labor Arbitration Today," *AJ*, Sept. 1980; Frank Elkouri and Edna Asper Elkouri, *How Arbitration Works* (4th ed., Washington: BNA, 1985); Owen Fairweather, *Practice and Procedure in Labor Arbitration* (2d ed., Washington: BNA, 1983); David E. Feller, "The Coming End of Arbitration's Golden Age," *Arbitration—1976*, Proceedings of the 29th A/M, NAA, ed. by Barbara Dennis and Gerald Somers (Washington: BNA, 1976); R. W. Fleming, *The Labor Arbitration Process* (Urbana: Univ. of Illinois Press, 1965; Arthur J. Goldberg, "A Supreme Court Justice Looks at Arbitration," *AJ*, Vol. 20, No. 1, 1965; Paul R. Hays, *Labor Arbitration: A Dissenting View* (New Haven: Yale UP, 1966); Marvin Hill, Jr. and Anthony V. Sinicropi, *Evidence in Arbitration* (Washington: BNA,

1980); ———, *Remedies in Arbitration* (Washington: BNA, 1981); ILO, *Conciliation and Arbitration Procedures in Labour Disputes, A Comprehensive Study* (Geneva: 1980); Edgar A. Jones, Jr., "The Decisional Thinking of Judges and Arbitrators as Triers of Fact," *Decisional Thinking of Arbitrators and Judges*, Proceedings of the 33d A/M, NAA, ed. by James Stern and Barbara Dennis (Washington: BNA, 1981); ———, "The Role of Arbitration in State and National Labor Policy," *Arbitration and the Public Interest*, Proceedings of the 24th A/M, NAA, ed. by Gerald Somers and Barbara Dennis (Washington: BNA, 1971); Frances Kellor, *American Arbitration* (New York: Harper, 1948); Michael J. Klapper, "The Scholarship of Paul Hays: A Critical Study," *Industrial and Labor Relations Forum*, Oct. 1974; John A. Lapp, *Labor Arbitration: Principles and Procedures* (Deep River: National Foremen's Institute, Inc., 1946); Herbert L. Marx, Jr., "Arbitration as an Ethical Institution in Our Society," *AJ*, Sept. 1982; Charles J. Morris, "Twenty Years of Trilogy: A Celebration," *Decisional Thinking of Arbitrators and Judges*, Proceedings of the 33d A/M, NAA, ed. by James Stern and Barbara Dennis (Washington: BNA, 1981); Joyce M. Najita (ed.), *Labor Arbitration for Union and Management Representatives*, Proceedings of Seminar, AAA, May 27–28, 1976 (Honolulu: Univ. of Hawaii, IRC, 1976); Paul Prasow and Edward Peters, *Arbitration and Collective Bargaining: Conflict Resolution in Labor Relations* (New York: McGraw-Hill, 1970); Harold S. Roberts, *Essentials of Labor Arbitration* (Honolulu: Univ. of Hawaii, IRC, 1956); Donald P. Rothschild, Leroy S. Merrifield, and Harry T. Edwards, *Collective Bargaining and Labor Arbitration, Materials on Collective Bargaining and Labor Arbitration and Discrimination in Employment* (2d ed., Indianapolis: Bobbs-Merrill, 1979); William E. Simkin and Van Dusen Kennedy, *Arbitration of Grievances* (Washington: U.S. Dept. of Labor, Division of Labor Standards, Bull. no. 82, 1946); Donald B. Straus, "Labor Arbitration and Its Critics," *AJ*, Vol. 20, No. 4, 1965; Wesley Sturges, *Cases in Arbitration Law* (Albany: Bender, 1953); U.S. Dept. of Labor, BLS, *Major Collective Bargaining Agreements: Arbitration Procedures* (Washington: Bull. no. 1425–6, 1966); Cla ence M. Updegraff, *Arbitration and Lab Relations* (3d ed., Washington: BNA, 197 Clarence Updegraff and Whitley McCo *Arbitration of Labor Disputes* (Chicag CCH, 1946).

See also AGREEMENT, SUBMISSION; AME CAN ARBITRATION ASSOCIATION; NATION ACADEMY OF ARBITRATORS.

arbitration, ad hoc Temporary, single c arbitration, as distinguished from "per nent" arbitration systems or where so-cal permanent arbitrators are named in the c tract to resolve unsettled disputes under terms of the collective bargaining areeme

arbitration, advisory A relatively new c cept to the area of dispute settlement. It developed primarily to meet the needs of public service. It was incorporated into federal Executive Order issued by Presid Kennedy on January 17, 1962. The order d with many aspects of employee-managem cooperation in the federal service. Sec 8(b) provided for the use of grievance arbi tion on the following three conditions:

(1) Shall be advisory in nature with decisions or recommendations sub to the approval of the agency head;
(2) Shall extend only to the interpreta or application of agreements or age policy and not to changes in or propo changes in agreements or agency icy; and
(3) Shall be invoked only with the appr of the individual employee or emp ees concerned.

In actuality advisory arbitration is arbitration in the normally accepted us which entails a "final and binding decisi In this sense an advisory arbitration is n "decision" but is more in the nature of a ommendation—one, however, that would difficult for the agency head to turn dow

Advisory arbitration was also used in gaining unit determination under Execu Order 10988. Executive Order 11491, iss October 1969, replaced advisory arbitra with final and binding arbitration.

Advisory arbitration as an impasse res tion procedure is utilized in some state local government jurisdictions.

Source references: Ezra K. Bryan, "Advisory Arbitration of New Contracts: A Case Study. I. Avoiding Confrontation by Advisory Arbitration," *Arbitration and the Expanding Role of Neutrals*, Proceedings of the 23d A/M, NAA, ed. by Gerald Somers and Barbara Dennis (Washington: BNA, 1970); Isaac N. Groner, "Advisory Arbitration of New Contracts: A Case Study. II. Why Advisory Arbitration of New Contracts?" *Arbitration and the Expanding Role of Neutrals*, Proceedings of the 23d A/M, NAA, ed. by Gerald Somers and Barbara Dennis (Washington: BNA, 1970); Robert G. Howlett, "Arbitration in the Public Sector," *Labor Law Developments 1969*, Proceedings of the 15th Annual Institute on Labor Law, SLF (New York: Bender, 1969); Joseph Krislov, "Prospects for the Use of Advisory Grievance Arbitration in Federal Service," *ILRR*, April 1965; Stanley Mosk, "Arbitration in Government," *Arbitration and Public Policy*, Proceedings of the 14th A/M, NAA, ed. by Spencer Pollard (Washington: BNA, 1961); James M. Ringer, "Legality and Propriety of Agreements to Arbitrate Major and Minor Disputes in Public Employment," *IR Law Digest*, July 1969; Harold S. Roberts, *Labor-Management Relations in the Public Service* (Honolulu: Univ. of Hawaii Press, 1970); David B. Ross, "The Arbitration of Public Employee Wage Disputes," *ILRR*, Oct. 1969.

arbitration, binding *See* ARBITRATION AWARD.

arbitration, compulsory Third party dispute settlement required by law—state or federal. Governmental compulsion of labor dispute settlement has been accepted in Australia and New Zealand for many years. It was indirectly accepted in the United States during World War II. The National War Labor Board acted as the tribunal whose decisions were final and binding. It should be noted, however, that the Board was established after a labor-management conference agreed that there should be no strikes or lockouts during the war, and that disputes affecting the war effort be submitted to a national tribunal for settlement.

Some states following the end of World War II provided for compulsory arbitration or seizure in public utility labor disputes. Subsequent Supreme Court decisions held that the federal government had preempted the field of labor-management relations insofar as these disputes affected interstate commerce.

A number of state and local government employee collective bargaining laws mandate arbitration, most notably of disputes involving police, firefighters, and guard employees.

Source references: Paul A. Abodeely, *Compulsory Arbitration and the NLRB, A Study of Congressional Intent and Administration Policy* (Philadelphia: Univ. of Pennsylvania, Wharton School of Finance and Commerce, Industrial Research Unit, LRPP Series Report no. 1, 1968); Arvid Anderson, "Compulsory Arbitration Under State Statutes," *NYU 22d Annual Conference on Labor*, ed. by Thomas Christensen and Andrea Christensen (New York: Bender, 1970); Edward Berman, "The Supreme Court and Compulsory Arbitration," *AER*, March 1928; D. S. Chauhan, "The Political and Legal Issues of Binding Arbitration in Government," *MLR*, Sept. 1979; R. Theodore Clark, Jr., *Compulsory Arbitration in Public Employment* (Chicago: PPA, PERL no. 37, 1972); Peter Feuille, "Selected Benefits and Costs of Compulsory Arbitration," *ILRR*, Oct. 1979; M. L. Friedman, "Compulsory Arbitration of Labor Disputes in Public Utilities," *George Washington LR*, April 1949; Walter J. Gershenfeld, "Compulsory Arbitration Is Ready When You Are," *LLJ*, March 1972; Kingsley Laffer, "Compulsory Arbitration and Collective Bargaining," *Journal of IR*, Oct. 1962; J. Joseph Loewenberg, "The Effect of Compulsory Arbitration on Collective Negotiations," *Journal of Collective Negotiations in the Public Sector*, May 1972; J. Joseph Loewenberg et al., *Compulsory Arbitration, An International Comparison* (Lexington, Mass.: Lexington Books, 1976); NAM, *A Study of Compulsory Arbitration in Six Foreign Countries With Applications for the United States* (New York: 1960); Herbert R. Northrup, *Compulsory Arbitration and Government Intervention in Labor Disputes; An Analysis of Experience* (Washington: Labor Policy Assn., 1966); Orme W. Phelps, "Compulsory Arbitration: Some Perspectives," *ILRR*, Oct. 1964; Harold S. Roberts, "Compulsory Arbitration of Labor Disputes

in Public Utilities," *LLJ*, June 1950; ———, *Compulsory Arbitration: Panacea or Millstone?* (Honolulu: Univ. of Hawaii, IRC, 1967); Benjamin Rubenstein, "The Bugaboo of Compulsory Arbitration," *LLJ*, March 1972; Paul D. Staudohar, "Compulsory Arbitration of Interest Disputes in the Protective Services," *LLJ*, Nov. 1970; Carl M. Stevens, "Is Compulsory Arbitration Compatible With Bargaining?" *IR*, Feb. 1966; George W. Taylor, "Is Compulsory Arbitration Inevitable?" *Proceedings of the 1st A/M, IRRA*, ed. by Milton Derber (Champaign: 1949); Hoyt N. Wheeler, "Compulsory Arbitration: A 'Narcotic Effect'?" *IR*, Feb. 1975.

See also ARBITRATION, FINAL OFFER; ARBITRATION, INTEREST; MEDIATION WITH FINALITY.

arbitration, expedited A simplified arbitration procedure to get decisions quickly and at reduced cost which was first incorporated as a contract provision in the 1971 Steel Industry/Steelworkers collective bargaining agreement. In the same year, the American Arbitration Association recommended the establishment of expedited procedures under which arbitration cases could be scheduled promptly and awards rendered within five days of the hearing.

Expedited arbitration procedures generally provide for informal hearings without transcripts, briefs, and extensive opinions. The hearing is normally completed within one to two days. A panel of arbitrators is established and arbitrators are assigned on a rotation basis. Under the steel industry arrangement, each plant selects its own panel of arbitrators.

Effective January 1, 1984, the AAA offered new "Streamlined Labor Arbitration Rules," that specify cost and time limits of the expedited arbitration procedure.

Source references: AAA, *Expedited Labor Arbitration Rules* (New York: n.d.); ———, *Streamlined Labor Arbitration Rules* (New York: 1984); Michael F. Hoellering, "Expedited Arbitration," *NYU 28th Annual Conference on Labor*, ed. by Richard Adelman (New York: Bender, 1976); ———, "Expedited Labor Arbitration Tribunal: A New AAA Forum for Companies and Unions," *LLJ*, Nov. 1972; Matthew E. Murray and Charles J. Griffin, Jr., "Expedited Arbitration of Discharge Cases," *AJ*, Dec. 1976; Marcus H. Sandver, Harry R. Blaine, and Mark N. Woyar, "Time and Cost Savings Through Expedited Arbitration Procedures," *AJ*, Dec. 1981; W. L. Schlager, Jr., "Expedited Arbitration on the LIRR," *AJ*, Dec. 1975; Lawrence Stessin, "Expedited Arbitration: Less Grief Over Grievances," *Harvard BR*, Jan./Feb. 1977.

arbitration, final offer An interest arbitration procedure requiring the arbitrator, or panel, to select either the union or management proposal; the arbitrator is not free to fashion a compromise position. Generally found as an impasse resolution procedure in public sector bargaining laws covering police and firefighters.

There are two types of final offer arbitration: whole package and issue-by-issue. Under the package concept, the arbitrator must choose the final offer package of either the employer or the union. Under the issue-by-issue procedure, the arbitrator must select the offer of either party on each issue.

Source references: Henry S. Farber, "Does Final-Offer Arbitration Encourage Bargaining?" *Proceedings of the 33d A/M, IRRA*, ed. by Barbara Dennis (Madison: 1981); Peter Feuille, *Final Offer Arbitration; Concepts, Developments, Techniques* (Chicago: PERL no. 50, 1975); Joseph R. Grodin, "Either-or Arbitration for Public Employee Disputes," *IR*, May 1972; Nels E. Nelson, "Final-Offer Arbitration: Some Problems," *AJ*, March 1975; Rena C. Seplowitz, "Final Offer Arbitration: The Last Word in Public Sector Labor Disputes," 10 *Columbia Journal of Law and Social Problems* 525 (1974); James L. Stern et al., *Final-Offer Arbitration, the Effects on Public Safety Employee Bargaining* (Lexington, Mass.: Lexington Books, 1975); Carl M. Stevens, "Is Compulsory Arbitration Compatible with Bargaining?" *IR*, Feb. 1966; Arnold M. Zack, "Final Offer Selection—Panacea or Pandora's Box?" *IR Law Digest*, Fall 1974.

See also ARBITRATION, TRI-OFFER.

arbitration, forced choice A variety of experimental proposals for resolving impasses in collective bargaining by which the arbitrator must make a decision from among the final offers made by the parties in a dispute. In 1969 the Tennessee Valley Authority Engineers Association suggested a system whereby the arbitrator's decision would be limited to either the last offer of the union or of management. In 1970 the TVA, which had rejected the Association's plan, proposed its own version of the forced-choice idea. Before either side could call upon an arbitrator, the parties would be required to submit the dispute to mediation. If mediation failed, each side would be required to submit a brief to the other side and responses to each would be prepared. The arbitrator would have to limit his decision to these briefs and responses.

Source references: BNA, *What's New in Collective Bargaining Negotiations and Contracts*, No. 646, March 5, 1970; No. 652, May 28, 1970.

See also ARBITRATION, FINAL OFFER.

arbitration, grievance A voluntary means of settling grievances which arise from the interpretation or application of an existing contract. The arbitrator clarifies the meaning of contract provisions and renders a decision when disagreements cannot be settled at the lower levels of grievance procedure.

Source references: Robert Coulson, "Grievance Arbitration: Too Much Trivia on the Table," *Labor Law Developments 1981*, Proceedings of the 27th Annual Institute on Labor Law, SLF (New York: Bender, 1981); Harold W. Davey, *Improving Grievance Arbitration: The Practitioners Speak* (Ames: Iowa State Univ., IRC, WP 1973–07, 1973); ———, "What's Right and What's Wrong With Grievance Arbitration: The Practitioners Air Their Views," *AJ*, Dec. 1973; Harry T. Edwards, *Contributions of Grievance Arbitration in Industrial Relations and Industrial Peace* (Amherst: Univ. of Massachusetts, Labor Relations and Research Center, 1977); Harry E. Graham, Brian P. Heshizer, and David B. Johnson, "Grievance Arbitration: Labor Officials' Attitudes," *AJ*, June 1978; Raymond L. Hilgert, "An Arbitrator Looks at Grievance Arbitration," *PJ*, Oct. 1978; ILO, *Grievance Arbitration, A Practical Guide* (Geneva: 1977); William B. Leahy, "Arbitration of Disputes Over Grievance Processing By Union Representatives," *AJ*, Vol. 26, no. 2, 1971; Peter Seitz, "The Gotterdammerung of Grievance Arbitration," *Employee Relations LJ*, Spring 1977; Russell A. Smith and Dallas L. Jones, "The Impact of the Emerging Federal Law of Grievance Arbitration on Judges, Arbitrators, and Parties," 52 *Virginia LR* 831 (1966); U.S. Dept. of Labor, BLS, *Major Collective Bargaining Agreements: Grievance Procedures* (Washington: Bull. no. 1425–1, 1965); U.S. GAO, *Grievance Arbitration Awards Made Under the Federal Labor Relations Program* (Washington: 1975); ———, *Improved Grievance-Arbitration Systems: A Key to Better Labor Relations in the Postal Service* (Washington: 1979); Arnold M. Zack, "Avoiding the Arbitrator: Some New Alternatives to the Conventional Grievance Procedure. III. Suggested New Approaches to Grievance Arbitration," *Arbitration—1977*, Proceedings of the 30th A/M, NAA, ed. by Barbara Dennis and Gerald Somers (Washington: BNA, 1978); Frank P. Zeidler, *Grievance Arbitration in the Public Sector* (Chicago: PPA, PERL no. 38, 1972).

See also ARBITRATION, RIGHTS.

arbitration, industrial In general usage, it is the same as labor arbitration, that is, arbitration involving the relationship between labor and management, particularly in the application and interpretation of the collective bargaining agreement. It also applies to arbitration involving new contract terms. It is distinguished from other types of arbitration such as commercial arbitration, international arbitration, civil arbitration.

Source references: Ruth G. Gilbert, *Analysis of the Scope of Private Industrial Arbitration* (Cambridge: MIT, 1946); Joseph Lowell, *Industrial Arbitration and Conciliation* (New York: Putnam, 1894); Carl Mote, *Industrial Arbitration* (Indianapolis: Bobbs-Merrill, 1916); Wesley A. Sturges, *Cases on Arbitration Law* (Albany: Bender, 1953); "The Use of Tri-partite Boards in Labor, Commercial and International Arbitration," 68 *Harvard LR* 293 (1954).

arbitration, interest An impasse resolution procedure in which one or more neutrals renders a binding decision to resolve a dispute over new contract terms. Interest arbitration procedures may differ in terms of the number of arbitrators (single or panel), the rules governing the nature of the decision, and the nature of the proceedings (voluntary or compulsory, by law or contract).

Source references: Thomas A. Kochan, "The Politics of Interest Arbitration," *AJ*, March 1978; Charles J. Morris, "The Role of Interest Arbitration in a Collective Bargaining System," *Industrial Relations LJ*, Fall 1976; Charles A. Myers, "Voluntary Arbitration of Disputes Over New Labor Contracts," *Sloan Management Review*, Fall 1976; Rutgers Univ., Institute of Management and Labor Relations, *Interest Arbitration*, Proceedings of an IMLR Conference (New Brunswick: 1980); Clifford Scharman, "Interest Arbitration in the Private Sector," *AJ*, Sept. 1981; Joseph P. Tonelli, "What is Happening in Interest Arbitration?" *NYU 28th Annual Conference on Labor*, ed. by Richard Adelman (New York: Bender, 1976).

See also ARBITRATION, FINAL OFFER; ARBITRATION, TRI-OFFER; EXPERIMENTAL NEGOTIATING AGREEMENT (ENA); MED-ARB.

arbitration, justiciable *See* ARBITRATION, RIGHTS.

arbitration, labor Third party dispute settlement affecting labor-management relations. The grievance procedure of the collective bargaining agreement almost invariably provides for arbitration of disputes arising out of the terms of the contract.

arbitration, nonjusticiable The phrase used occasionally to describe new contract arbitration; that is, the arbitration of the terms of the new collective bargaining agreement as distinguished from arbitration involving the interpretation and the application of the current agreement or grievance arbitration.

See also ARBITRATION, INTEREST; MAJOR DISPUTES.

arbitration, obligatory Arbitration which results from the voluntary agreement of parties under a collective bargaining contract to submit future disputes under the terms of the contract to a third party for settlement. The parties have obligated themselves to arbitrate. Some collective contracts may also contain provisions obligating the parties to settle new contract terms by arbitration. In current usage the phrase "obligatory arbitration" is encompassed in the phrase "voluntary arbitration."

arbitration, rights Arbitration which involves the interpretation or application of the agreement and sometimes referred to as justiciable arbitration. The arbitrator in this type of dispute interprets and applies the contract and acts in a quasi-judicial capacity concerning the meaning and intent of the contract on the basis of the presentation or record made by the parties before him.

Arbitration involving the handling of grievances under the terms of the contract is referred to as arbitration over the *rights* of the parties under the negotiated contract. Arbitration of such disputes is distinguished from that involving the determination of new contract provisions or nonjusticiable disputes. These are referred to as disputes involving *interests* rather than rights under the terms of the contract.

Under the Railway Labor Act they are known as "minor" disputes.

See also ARBITRATION, INTEREST; MINOR DISPUTES.

arbitration, secondary A phrase sometimes used to describe grievance arbitration; that is, arbitration involving the interpretation or application of the provisions of the collective bargaining agreement. Primary arbitration would be arbitration designed to establish the terms and conditions of employment for the new collective bargaining contract (new contract arbitration).

See also ARBITRATION, NONJUSTICIABLE; ARBITRATION, RIGHTS.

arbitration, terminal The provisions in a collective bargaining agreement, providing for arbitration as the final (terminal) step in the grievance procedure.

arbitration, tri-offer A variation of final offer arbitration which requires the arbitrator to choose from among the final positions of management, the union, or the recommendations of a factfinder.

Tri-offer arbitration has been adopted in Iowa to resolve public employee collective bargaining disputes. The procedure is also used in New Jersey for impasses involving police and firefighters.

Source references: Frederic C. Champlin and Daniel G. Gallagher, *Bargaining Under Tri-Offer Arbitration, A Theory and Proposed Test* (Minneapolis: Univ. of Minnesota, IRC, WP 81–05, 1981); Daniel G. Gallagher and M. D. Chaubey, "Impasse Behavior and Tri-Offer Arbitration in Iowa," *IR*, Spring 1982; Daniel G. Gallagher and Richard Pegnetter, "Impasse Resolution Under the Iowa Multistep Procedure," *ILRR*, April 1979.

arbitration, twilight Grievance arbitration which involves the application and interpretation of the contract, but where the dispute does not set out clearly the particular language which has been violated.

arbitration, voluntary Third party settlement where labor and management mutually request that an issue be submitted to arbitration. This may be done by a voluntary submission agreement or by language in the agreement to permit all future disputes, as qualified by the definition of what constitutes an arbitrable grievance, to go to arbitration.

Source references: Bernard Cushman, "Voluntary Arbitration of New Contract Terms—A Forum in Search of a Dispute," *LLJ*, Dec. 1965; Paul M. Herzog and Morris Stone, "Voluntary Labour Arbitration in the United States," *ILR*, Oct. 1960; Carl M. Stevens, "The Analytics of Voluntary Arbitration: Contract Disputes," *IR*, Oct. 1967; George W. Taylor, "The Voluntary Arbitration of Labor Disputes," *Michigan LR*, April 1951.

arbitration, wage The referral and determination by a neutral person or body of any dispute involving wages which has been unresolved by employer and union. The submission generally is voluntary and may include either a wage dispute involving the interpretation and application of the agreement or, less often, the determination of basic wages for a new contract.

Source reference: Irving Bernstein, *Arbitration of Wages* (Los Angeles: UC Press, 1954).

arbitration agreement An arrangement or contract provision entered into by the parties to submit their dispute to a third party for final and binding decision.

arbitration award The final and binding decision of an arbitrator or arbitration tribunal. In labor-management arbitration the award is in writing and is usually at the end of the opinion setting out the reasons for the award.

Although the award is final and binding on the parties, most state arbitration statutes provide for appeal on specific grounds. These grounds generally include:

(1) An award procured by corruption, fraud, or undue means;
(2) An award based on partiality or corruption of the arbitrator;
(3) An award based on failure to provide either party with a fair and impartial hearing;
(4) An award where the arbitrator exceeded his power, or so imperfectly executed it that a mutual, final, and definitive award was not made.

Source references: Howard Abrahams, "Vacating an Arbitrator's Award: A Procedural Solution," *IR Law Digest*, April 1970; Thomas G. S. Christensen, "The Disguised Review of the Merits of Arbitration Awards," *Labor Arbitration at the Quarter-Century Mark*, Proceedings of the 25th A/M, NAA, ed. by Barbara Dennis and Gerald Somers (Washington: BNA, 1973); Barbara D. Dennis, "The Publication of Arbitration Awards," *Arbitration—1975*, Proceedings of the 28th A/M, NAA, ed. by Barbara Dennis and Gerald Somers (Washington: BNA, 1976); Bernard Dunau, "Scope of Judicial Review of Labor Arbitration Awards," *NYU 24th Annual Conference on Labor* (New York: Bender, 1972); Frank Elkouri and Edna Asper Elkouri, *How Arbitration Works* (4th ed., Washington: BNA, 1985); "Employee Challenges to Arbitral Awards: A Model for Protecting Individual Rights Under the Collective Bargaining Agreement," *IR Law Digest*, Winter 1978; George H. Friedman, "Correcting Arbitrator Error: The Limited Scope of Judicial Review," *AJ*, Dec. 1978; Philip Harris, "The Use of Precedent in Labor Arbitration," *AJ*, March 1977; Raymond L. Hogler, "Industrial Due Process and Judicial Review of Arbitration Awards," *LLJ*, Sept. 1980; Frances Kellor, *American Arbitration* (New York: Harper, 1948); Margaret Oppenheimer and

Helen LaVan, "Arbitration Awards in Discrimination Disputes: An Empirical Analysis," *AJ*, March 1979; Theodore J. St. Antoine, "Judicial Review of Labor Arbitration Awards: A Second Look at *Enterprise Wheel* and its Progeny," *Arbitration—1977*, Proceedings of the 30th A/M, NAA, ed. by Barbara Dennis and Gerald Somers (Washington: BNA, 1978); Anthony V. Sinicropi and Peter A. Veglahn, "Dicta in Arbitration Awards: An Aid or Hinderance?" *LLJ*, Sept. 1972; Morris Stone, *Labor Grievances and Decisions; New Series* (New York: AAA, 1970); Judith H. Toole, "Judicial Activism in Public Sector Grievance Arbitration: A Study of Recent Developments," *AJ*, Sept. 1978.

arbitration board A group of three, five, or seven members serving as the arbitration tribunal. The group may consist of all neutral members, or representatives of labor and management, with one neutral member acting as chairman.

Source reference: Elinore Jackson, *Industrial Arbitration* (New York: McGraw-Hill, 1952).

arbitration clause A provision in the collective bargaining agreement stipulating that disputes arising out of the application of the contract be subject to arbitration. The arbitration clause may be broad enough to include "any dispute" or be confined by the parties to specific areas or issues.

Source reference: U.S. Dept. of Labor, BLS, *Major Collective Bargaining Agreements—Arbitration Procedures* (Washington: Bull. no. 1425–6, 1966).

arbitration committee *See* ARBITRATION BOARD.

arbitration tribunal The agency established to handle a dispute submitted to arbitration. Generally any body or group which is established to make a final and binding decision. Thus the three judges constituting the Court of Industrial Relations, established by the Kansas Industrial Relations Act of 1920, acted as an arbitration tribunal.

Source reference: J. H. Wooten, "The Role of the Tribunals," *Journal of IR*, July 1970.

arbitration under duress An agreement entered into by labor and management to submit a dispute to a third party for final and binding decision, but one of the parties may have done so involuntarily. The pressure may have come from the press, public opinion, or governmental agency. This is not duress in its legal sense, otherwise the agreement to arbitrate would be void.

arbitrator The individual who has been designated by the parties (judge, referee, arbiter, umpire) to make a final and binding decision on the basis of evidence presented to him. In compulsory arbitration the arbitrator may be designated by the court or by procedure set out in the law.

Source references: Benjamin Aaron, "Should Arbitrators be Licensed or 'Professionalized'?" *Arbitration—1976*, Proceedings of the 29th A/M, NAA, ed. by Barbara Dennis and Gerald Somers (Washington: BNA, 1976); Gerald Aksen, "Some Legal and Practical Problems of Labor Arbitrators," *NYU 22d Annual Conference on Labor*, ed. by Thomas Christensen and Andrea Christensen (New York: Bender, 1970); Gabriel N. Alexander, "Discretion in Arbitration," *Arbitration and the Public Interest*, Proceedings of the 24th A/M, NAA, ed. by Gerald Somers and Barbara Dennis (Washington: BNA, 1971); Richard I. Bloch, "Future Directions for Labor Arbitration and for the Academy. II. Some Far-Sighted Views of Myopia," *Arbitration—1977*, Proceedings of the 30th A/M, NAA, ed. by Barbara Dennis and Gerald Somers (Washington: BNA, 1978); Steven Stambaugh Briggs and John C. Anderson, "An Empirical Investigation of Arbitrator Acceptability," *IR*, Spring 1980; Robert Coulson, "Certification and Training of Labor Arbitrators: Should Arbitrators be Certified? Dead Horse Rides Again," *Arbitration—1977*, Proceedings of the 30th A/M, NAA, ed. by Barbara Dennis and Gerald Somers (Washington: BNA, 1978); Louis A. Crane, "The Use and Abuse of Arbitral Power," *Labor Arbitration at the Quarter-Century Mark*, Proceedings of the 25th A/M, NAA, ed. by Barbara Dennis and Gerald Somers (Washington: BNA, 1973); John Van N. Dorr, III, "Labor Arbitrator Training: The Internship," *AJ*, June 1981; Joel

M. Douglas, "The Scope of Arbitrator Immunity," *AJ*, June 1981; "Education and Training of Arbitrators," *The Profession of Labor Arbitration*, Selected papers from the First Seven A/M, NAA, ed. by Jean McKelvey (Washington: BNA, 1957); Robben W. Fleming, "Arbitrators and Arbitrability," *Washington Univ. LQ*, Vol. 1963, No. 2; ———, "Some Problems of Evidence Before the Labor Arbitrator," *Michigan LR*, Dec. 1961; Charlotte Gold and Ruth E. Lyons (ed.), *Dispute Resolution Training, the State of the Art*, Selected Proceedings of the Second Wingspread Conference, June 9–10, 1977 (New York: AAA, 1978); James A. Gross, "Value Judgments in the Decisions of Labor Arbitrators," *ILRR*, Oct. 1967; Peter Seitz, "How Arbitrators Decide Cases: A Study in Black Magic," *Collective Bargaining and the Arbitrator's Role*, Proceedings of the 15th A/M, NAA, ed. by Mark Kahn (Washington: BNA, 1962); ———, "Some Observations on the Role of an Arbitrator," *AJ*, Sept. 1979; Saul Wallen, "Arbitrators and Judges—Dispelling the Hays' Haze," *Labor Law Developments*, Proceedings of the 12th Annual Institute on Labor Law, SLF (Washington: BNA, 1966); Barbara M. Wertheimer and Anne H. Nelson (ed.), *Women as Third-Party Neutrals: Gaining Acceptability, Proceedings from a Conference* (Ithaca: NYSSILR, Cornell Univ., 1978); Arnold M. Zack, "Who is Responsible for the Development of Arbitrators—The Parties or the Arbitrators?" *AJ*, June 1981.

See also CONCILIATOR, FACTFINDER, IMPARTIAL CHAIRPERSON, INDUSTRY ARBITRATOR, MASTER, MEDIATOR, PANEL OF ARBITRATORS, PERMANENT ARBITRATOR, REFEREE, TEMPORARY ARBITRATOR, UMPIRE.

Architects' and Draftsmen's Unions; International Federation of Technical Engineers (AFL) An international union, affiliated with the AFL, founded in 1918. It has since changed its name to the American Federation of Technical Engineers (AFL-CIO).

See also TECHNICAL ENGINEERS; AMERICAN FEDERATION OF (AFL-CIO).

area agreement A collective bargaining agreement whose terms and conditions cover many employers and workers in a large geographical area. It generally covers most of the employees in a given industry in a locality. The bargaining unit is usually more extensive than a city or metropolitan center.

area of production The administrator of the Wage and Hour Law has the authority to define "area of production" under the Law (Fair Labor Standards Act). The definition is used to provide partial or complete exemption of employees working on specified agricultural commodities.

See also FAIR LABOR STANDARDS ACT OF 1938.

Area Redevelopment Act of 1961 Bill signed by President John F. Kennedy on May 1, 1961, aimed at expanding economic growth in chronic labor surplus areas. The provisions of the Act dealt with four related programs: "(1) long-term loans at low rates of interest providing venture capital to attract new business to locate in depressed areas or to help expand established businesses; (2) financial aid to help communities develop the public facilities needed to attract business; (3) training programs to help the unemployed and underemployed secure jobs; and (4) technical assistance to help communities plan constructive development programs which will stimulate their economic growth." Replaced by the Public Works and Economic Development Act in August 1965.

Source references: Area Redevelopment Act, as amended, Pub. L. 87–27, May 1, 1961, 75 Stat. 47 (codified as amended in scattered sections of 15, 40, and 42 U.S.C.); Sanford Cohen, "Achieving Full Employment: The Outlook As of 1962," *LLJ*, Jan. 1962; "Eight Months' Training Experience Under the Area Redevelopment Act," *MLR*, Dec. 1962; Lowell E. Gallaway, "Proposals for Federal Aid to Depressed Industrial Areas: A Critique," *ILRR*, April 1961; Phyllis Groom, "Retraining the Unemployed: II. Federal and State Legislation on Retraining," *MLR*, Sept. 1961; Sar Levitan, "Area Redevelopment: An Analysis of the Program," *IR*, May 1964; ———, *Federal Aid to Depressed Areas* (Baltimore: Johns Hopkins Press, 1964); Moses Lukaczer, "Reflections on the Problem of Depressed Areas—1962," *LLJ*, Jan. 1962; U.S. Dept. of Labor, BLS, *Proceedings of the 19th Interstate Conference on Labor Statistics, July 11–14, 1961, Bloomington, Indiana*

(Washington: 1962); U.S. Dept. of Labor, OMAT, *Training for Jobs in Redevelopment Areas* (Washington: 1962).

See also DEPRESSED AREA, PUBLIC WORKS AND ECONOMIC DEVELOPMENT ACT OF 1965.

areawide bargaining *See* COLLECTIVE BARGAINING, AREAWIDE.

aristocracy of labor A loose term seeking to describe workers whose earnings or salary are above the average. At one stage in labor history the aristocrats were craftsmen and highly skilled workers who felt they did not have anything in common with the large masses of unskilled laborers.

Arizona Public Employees Association An organization once affiliated with the Assembly of Governmental Employees, it merged with the American Federation of State, County and Municipal Employees (AFL-CIO) in October 1982. Its monthly publication is the *Arizona Public Employee.*

Address: 420 North 15th Ave., Phoenix, Ariz. 85007. Tel. (602) 252–6501

arsenal of weapons approach (choice of procedures) A suggestion elaborated by the then Senator Kennedy during his debates with Vice President Nixon in October 1960, on labor proposals and the handling of national emergency disputes. Kennedy indicated a preference for giving the President a wider variety of alternatives (choice of procedures) and methods of dispute settlement in the national emergency field. Among the arsenals of weapons suggested were:

(1) Greater use of factfinding boards and impartial commissions with the power to make recommendations;
(2) More extensive use of the Federal Mediation and Conciliation Service but not competitive with the Emergency Boards of Inquiry;
(3) Flexible rather than fixed use of injunctions for cooling-off periods;
(4) Extended use of arbitration and explanation for failure to use the procedure when one side offers it as an alternative;
(5) Use of seizure by the government in case a plant is struck and the product is needed for the safety of the public.

The arsenal of weapons proposal is based on the assumption that flexible remedies are more effective in bringing pressure on the parties. They may, however, raise the question of "fairness and equity" in the type of remedy used by the President or the agencies of government. Where the law is clear (even though it may favor one or the other side), the Executive cannot be held responsible for the application of the remedy. Some flexibility is, of course, available even within the national emergency provisions of the Taft-Hartley Act.

Source references: W. Willard Wirtz, "The 'Choice of Procedure' Approach to National Emergency Disputes," *Emergency Disputes and National Policy*, ed. by Irving Bernstein et al. (New York: Harper, IRRA Pub. 15, 1955).

See also BOARD OF INQUIRY, NATIONAL EMERGENCY DISPUTES.

articulate industrial unrest Open dissatisfaction, criticism, and attacks against the existing social and economic order, and against long hours, poor wages, and working conditions. When the discontent manifests itself in oral or written form it has been termed "articulate." The resort to strikes and other forms of industrial warfare are overt forms of industrial unrest.

Source references: R. S. Baker, *The New Industrial Unrest* (New York: Doubleday, 1920); John A. Fitch, *The Causes of Industrial Unrest* (New York: Harper, 1924); Dale Yoder, "Economic Changes and Industrial Unrest in the United States," *Journal of Political Economy*, April 1940.

artisan A worker employed in the industrial arts, a skilled craftsman. During the artisan-apprenticeship period he worked for himself. If he had accumulated sufficient capital he became a master and hired other journeymen.

Source references: Carl Bridenbaugh, *The Colonial Craftsman* (New York: NYU Press, 1950); W. Hasbach, *A History of the English Agricultural Laborer* (London: P. S. King & Son, 1908).

See also JOURNEYMAN.

asbestosis A disabling lung disease characterized by extensive scarring of the lung tissue and progressive shortness of breath. No specific treatment presently exists for asbestosis.

From the 1940s through the 1960s, asbestos was used heavily in shipyards and in the construction industry. The National Institute for Occupational Safety and Health estimates that between 8 and 11 million workers were exposed to asbestos during that period.

Exposure to asbestos may also result in various types of cancer. These include lung cancer and mesothelioma, a cancer of the lung lining and abdominal cavity.

Source reference: U.S. Dept. of Labor, *An Interim Report to Congress on Occupational Diseases* (Washington: 1980).

Asbestos Workers; International Association of Heat and Frost Insulators and (AFL-CIO) The union had its origin in 1904. Its official quarterly publication is *The Asbestos Worker.*

Address: 1300 Connecticut Avenue, N.W., Washington, D.C. 20036. Tel. (202) 785–2388

ASCS County Office Employees; National Association of (Ind) The *NASCOE Newsletter* issued semimonthly is its official publication.

Address: Clay County ASCS Office, 218 W. Mill, Liberty, Mo. 64068. Tel. (816) 781–5566

Ashurst-Sumners Act A federal law enacted in 1935 forbidding the shipping in interstate commerce of prison-made goods into states which prohibit convict labor. If the state has no law prohibiting the sale of goods made by convict labor, the federal law requires that such goods be labeled, showing the name and address of the shipper, the consignee, the nature of the goods, and the name of the prison where the goods were produced.

See also PRISON LABOR.

Asian or Pacific Islander According to OFCCP, "A person with origins in any of the original peoples of the Far East, Southeast Asia, the Indian Subcontinent, or the Pacific Islands." These areas include, among others, China, Japan, Korea, the Philippine Islands, Vietnam, Laos, Cambodia, and Samoa. The Indian Subcontinent includes India, Pakistan, Bangladesh, Sri Lanka, Nepal, Sikkim, and Bhutan. Under Title VII, this is a protected class and one of the racial/ethnic categories for which data is reported to the federal government.

Source references: Daniel E. Jaco and George L. Wilber, "Asian Americans in the Labor Market," *MLR*, July 1975; U.S. OFCCP, *Federal Contract Compliance Manual* (Washington: 1979).

See also AFFECTED CLASS, PROTECTED CLASS.

assembly line production A procedure widely used in mass production industries where the worker performs a single specialized task. The materials and parts are conveyed on mechanical belts and the worker performs his task as the material or equipment moves past his workplace.

Assembly of Governmental Employees The federation was founded in 1952 as the National Conference of Independent Public Employee Organizations and is made up of 30 state, county, and local affiliated organizations. It is primarily concerned with establishing and maintaining the merit principle. Its affiliates, however, have considerable autonomy on specific policy issues, including work stoppages. Its publication is *Hotline AGE.*

Address: 1522 K St., N.W., Washington, D.C. 20005. Tel. (202) 371–1123

assessment center An employee selection and promotion program utilizing a series of simulations, or exercises, that require the performance of skills necessary for the job. The exercises are observed by specially trained individuals, who then pool their observations and arrive at a consensus evaluation of each candidate.

The objective of an assessment center is to match the right person with available positions. Assessment centers may be used to help management in the early identification of employee potential and in career planning programs.

Boehm notes that an assessment center has six key elements: "(1) a measuring process (2) using multiple measurement techniques (3) focusing on the measurement of behavior relevant to 'real world' situations (4) conducted by multiple assessors (5) who are specifically trained to observe and evaluate behavior, and (6) where the processes of observing and evaluating behavior are separated."

Industrial application of assessment centers was first utilized by AT&T in 1956.

Source references: Virginia R. Boehm, "Assessment Centers and Their Use in Management Development," *Personnel Management*, ed. by Kendrith M. Rowland and Gerald R. Ferris (Boston: Allyn and Bacon, 1982); Stephen L. Cohen, "Pre-Packaged vs. Tailor-Made: The Assessment Center Debate," *PJ*, Dec. 1980; ———, "Validity and Assessment Center Technology: One and the Same?" *Human Resource Management*, Winter 1980; George F. Dreher and Paul R. Sackett, *Some Problems With Applying Content Validity Evidence to Assessment Center Procedures [with rejoinder to Norton]* (Lawrence: Univ. of Kansas, School of Business, Reprint no. 211, 1981); Richard J. Klimoski and William J. Strickland, "Assessment Centers—Valid or Merely Prescient," *Personnal Psychology*, Autumn 1977; Allen I. Kraut, "New Frontiers for Assessment Centers," *Personnel*, July/Aug. 1976; Leland C. Nichols and Joseph Hudson, "Dual-Role Assessment Center: Selection and Development," *PJ*, May 1981; Joyce D. Ross, "A Current Review of Public Sector Assessment Centers: Cause for Concern," *Public Personnel Management*, Jan./Feb. 1979; Ed Yager, "When New Hires Don't Make the Grade (The Case for Assessment Centers)," *PJ*, May 1980.

assessments Usually special charges made against union members for the purpose of raising funds to meet an urgent need, such as assessments to help maintain a strike, start an organizing campaign, etc. The power to levy assessments usually is limited by the union constitution and bylaws.

Assessments are not to be confused with the regular, periodic union dues.

In a 1967 decision, the NLRB drew a distinction between "regular" dues which a "member must pay toward the support of the society (union) in order to retain his membership therein," and assessments (in this case so-called "working dues") which the union had set up for establishing a credit union and a building fund. The NLRB said in part:

> The "working dues" herein are clearly not for the support and maintenance of the Respondent as an organization but are special purpose funds established . . . to accomplish ends not encompassed in its duties as a collective bargaining agent of the employees. This is not to say that the purposes of the funds are not beneficial to the membership or that the Respondent cannot organize and administer such funds on a voluntary basis. We find only that the support of such funds cannot come from "periodic dues" as that term is used in the Act, which are made payable under the terms of a union-security provision, and thus may be collected from the employees upon pain of discharge.

Source references: Local 959, Teamsters and P. Stephen Treadwell, 167 NLRB 1042, 66 LRRM 1203 (1967); Joel Seidman, *Union Rights and Union Duties* (New York: Harcourt, Brace, 1943).

See also CHECK-OFF, FEES, SERVICE FEE.

assignment of contract Provision in some collective bargaining agreements that in case of sale or merger the terms of the contract be assigned to the new owner. The terms and conditions of employment are thereby maintained for the duration of the contract.

See also RUNAWAY SHOP, SUCCESSOR EMPLOYER.

assignment of wages Provisions by a worker to set aside a certain portion of his wages for payment of debts. The employer turns these monies over to the creditor. Where a court orders the employer to pay a certain percent of the employee's wages to a creditor, it is known as garnishment.

Source reference: J. C. Wood, "Attachment of Wages," *Modern LR*, Jan. 1963.

See also GARNISHMENT.

Associated Unions of America (Ind) An independent labor union organized in 1938. It merged with the Office and Professional Employees International Union (AFL-CIO) on April 27, 1972.

See also OFFICE AND PROFESSIONAL EMPLOYEES INTERNATIONAL UNION (AFL-CIO).

association agreement A collective bargaining agreement which covers the terms and conditions of employment for all members of the employer's organization representing the companies in a particular industry and locality. The members of the association may operate in a particular locality or in a number of localities—statewide, areawide, or nationally. The association may cover employers in a particular industry, or in a variety of industries.

assumption of risk One of the defenses by employers against claims of employees who had been injured on the job. The employers claimed that the worker who accepted a contract of employment was aware of the hazards of the jobs and thereby assumed the risks incident to the job. Existing workers compensation laws largely have discarded the doctrine.

See also FELLOW SERVANT DOCTRINE, WORKERS COMPENSATION.

Atchison Topeka & Santa Fe R.R. v. Gee A decision of federal Judge McPherson dealing with peaceful picketing. "There is," he said, "and can be no such thing as peaceful picketing any more than there can be chaste vulgarity, or peaceful mobbing or lawful lynching; when men want to converse and persuade, they do not form a picket line."

Source reference: Atchison Topeka & Santa Fe R.R. v. Gee, 139 Fed. 582 (SD Iowa, 1905).

See also FREEDOM OF SPEECH, PEACEFUL PICKETING, PICKETING.

Athletes; Federation of Professional (AFL-CIO) 1300 Connecticut Ave., N.W., Washington, D.C. 20036. Tel. (202) 463–2200

Atkins v. Kansas Supreme Court decision which upheld the right of government to fix the hours of private contractors working for the government.

Source reference: Atkins v. Kansas, 191 US 207 (1903).

Atlantic, Gulf, Lakes and Inland Waters District A division of the Seafarers' International Union of North America (AFL-CIO). In June 1978, the Marine Cooks and Stewards' Union, also a division of the SIU, merged with the Atlantic, Gulf, Lakes and Inland Waters District. Its monthly publication is the *Seafarers' Log*.

Address: 675 4th Ave., Brooklyn, N.Y. 11232. Tel. (212) 499–6600

Source reference: Seafarers International Union, Atlantic, Gulf, Lakes and Inland Waters District, *The Deep Sea Sailor's Handbook: Constitution, Welfare, Vacations, Contracts, How to Conduct a Meeting, Delegate's Guide, General Information* (San Francisco: 1961).

Atlantic Independent Union (Ind) Its official publication is *AIU News*, published quarterly.

Address: 3207 U Centre Sq. E., 1500 Market St., Philadelphia, Pa. 19101. Tel. (215) 204–3790

Atomic Energy Labor-Management Relations Panel A special mediation disputes settlement panel which developed out of the unusual circumstances of the Atomic Energy Commission and the need for tight security relations as well as a minimum of strike activity. It developed out of the Commission's action setting up a Labor Relations Panel in 1949. Cyrus Ching was chairman of the Panel for many years.

Source references: David L. Cole, "Government in the Bargaining Process: The Role of Mediation," *Annals*, Jan. 1961; H. T. Herrick, "A Brief Comparison of Two Special Panels in the Atomic Energy Industry," *Proceedings of the 1964 Annual Spring Meeting, IRRA*, ed. by Gerald Somers (Madison: 1964); T. E. Lane, "Special Government Dispute Panel," *Proceedings of the 1964 Annual Spring Meeting, IRRA*, ed. by Gerald Somers (Madison: 1964); P. L. Siemiller, "Special Government Dispute Settlement Panels," *Proceedings of the 1964 Annual Spring Meeting, IRRA*, ed. by Gerald Somers (Madison: 1964); U.S. Atomic Energy Commission, Division of Labor Relations, *Maximizing the Effectiveness of Collective Bargaining Within the Atomic Energy Program* (Washington: 1965).

See also MISSILE SITES LABOR COMMISSION.

attendance bonus Extra compensation in the form of a bonus to employees who establish an exceptional record of attendance. Fines for absences and bonuses for attendance are not widespread.

Source reference: Z. Clark Dickinson, *Compensating Industrial Effort* (New York: Ronald Press, 1937).

See also BONUS, OVERTIME.

attitude measurement Procedures to determine an employee's opinion or feeling toward his employer, supervisor, company policy, or other items about which the employer desires to know the general attitude of his workers.

Measurement is generally made through use of personal interviews, questionnaires, or both.

See also MORALE SURVEY, OPINION SURVEY.

attorney general Chief law officer and legal adviser of the federal or state government. The attorney general of the United States has specific duties under the Taft-Hartley Act to petition the federal courts for injunctions in national emergency disputes. He is a member of the Cabinet and head of the Department of Justice.

attrition A term which has received much attention largely because of the real concern of employers and unions in protecting the job rights of individuals whose jobs have been eliminated through automation or whose jobs are threatened by developing mechanization.

Attrition seeks in large part to protect the individual who is presently on the job so that the elimination of the job does not apply to the individual.

It is somewhat similar to the red-circle-rate concept in which the individual following a job evaluation or review of wage rates finds that he is receiving a rate higher than the job calls for. The individual on the job will receive that red circle rate but the new employee coming to that job when the present employee either retires, quits, or is transferred will receive the existing rate of pay.

The attrition approach providing for gradual reduction in employment through resignation, retirement, and death has been widely discussed and was particularly prominent during the 1959–1963 dispute involving the railroad employees and the railroad carriers, two issues which ultimately went to arbitration as a result of congressional action in 1963.

Source references: U.S. v. Lowden, 308 US 255 (1939); Jack Frye, "Attrition in Job Elimination," *LLJ*, Sept. 1963; John Grimes, "Compensatory Benefits, Federal Pressure Nudge Grudging Unions Toward Reality," *Wall Street Journal*, Dec. 21, 1962; U.S. Dept. of Labor, BLS, *Major Collective Bargaining Agreements: Severance Pay and Layoff Benefit Plans* (Washington: Bull. 1425–2, 1965); U.S. National Center for Productivity and Quality of Working Life, *Productivity and Job Security: Attrition—Benefits and Problems* (Washington: 1977).

See also DISMISSAL COMPENSATION, RAILWAY LABOR ACT, RED CIRCLE RATE, TECHNOLOGICAL UNEMPLOYMENT.

authorization card During an organizing campaign a union may obtain a statement from employees indicating that they authorize the union to act as their representative. Authorization cards are not as difficult to obtain as signatures to a membership card. Membership usually involves payment of initiation fees and dues. Signing an authorization card does not obligate the employee to vote for the union in a representation election. Authorization cards may be used to establish union bargaining rights even though the union loses an election.

Source references: Joseph Barbash, "Authorization Card Problems and Their Cure," *NYU 22d Annual Conference on Labor*, ed. by Thomas Christensen and Andrea Christensen (New York: Bender, 1970); Charles B. Burch, "Employer Recognition of Unions on the Basis of Authorization Cards: The 'Independent Knowledge' Standard," *IR Law Digest*, Jan. 1973; Daniel F. Gruender and Philip M. Prince, "Union Authorization Cards: Why Not Laboratory Conditions?" *LLJ*, Jan. 1981; Alan Roberts McFarland and Wayne S. Bishop, *Union Authorization Cards and the NLRB* (Philadelphia: Univ. of Pennsylvania, Wharton School of Finance and Commerce, Industrial Research Unit, LRPP series, Report no. 2, 1969); Marcus Hart Sandver, "The Validity of Union Authorization Cards as a Predictor of Success in NLRB Certification Elections," *LLJ*, Nov. 1977; Victor Schachter and Andrew Peterson, "Lawful Employer Participation in the Revocation of Union Authorization Cards," *LLJ*, Sept. 1980; LeRoy H. Schramm, "Authorization Cards as Valid Indicators of Union Majority," 20 *Syracuse LR* 577 (1969).

See also CARD CHECK, CERTIFICATION, GISSEL PACKING CO. CASE.

automatic check-off A procedure whereby the employer deducts from the pay of all employees, members of the union in the bargaining unit, membership dues and assessments and turns these monies over to the union. Under the automatic, or so-called compulsory check-off, the deductions are made without prior authorization or written individual assignment by the employee. It is presumed that since the union represents the employees for bargaining purposes, the employees have given the union prior authorization to negotiate the terms of employment, including the check-off.

Under the Taft-Hartley Act, the automatic check-off is invalid. Section 302 provides for the voluntary check-off: ". . . provided, that the employer has received a written assignment . . ." from each employee on whose account such deductions are made.

Source references: Labor Management Relations Act of 1947, as amended, Section 302, 29 U.S.C. 186 (1982).

See also CHECK-OFF.

automatic progression A method of wage adjustment in companies which use job classification rate ranges. The employee moves from the minimum of the rate range to the maximum on the basis of fixed periods of service. Thus an employee may receive an automatic adjustment of 5 cents every six months in his range until he reaches the maximum. In some companies the adjustments may be automatic up to the mid-point, but with the discretion of the employer beyond the middle of the range. In some cases a formal merit rating scheme will determine adjustments beyond the mid-point. In some plans the progression is automatic from minimum to maximum rate, provided the work performance is satisfactory.

See also LONGEVITY PAY, MERIT RATING, RATE RANGE.

automatic wage adjustment A procedure for raising or lowering wage rates conditioned on the occurrence of certain events, such as the increase or decrease in the Consumer Price Index, the price of the product, profits, or other predetermined factors.

The increase in the number of long-term contracts is accompanied by automatic annual increments or wage adjustments. These are negotiated by the union and company and are designed to avoid annual contract reopening. Sometimes these adjustments are based on increased productivity—the General Motors annual improvement factor was an automatic adjustment of this type.

Source references: Z. Clark Dickinson, *Collective Wage Determination* (New York: Ronald Press, 1941); J. W. Garbarino, "The Economic Significance of Automatic Wage Adjustments," *New Dimension in Collective Bargaining* (New York: Harper, IRRA Pub. no. 21, 1959); Benson Soffer, "Cost of Living Wage Policy," *ILRR*, Jan. 1954; U.S. Dept. of Labor, BLS, *Collective Bargaining Provisions: Wage Adjustment Plans* (Washington: Bull. 908–9, 1948).

See also ANNUAL IMPROVEMENT FACTOR, CONSUMER PRICE INDEX, COST-OF-LIVING ADJUSTMENT, LONGEVITY PAY.

automation Generally, a process which substitutes a mechanical function for a human function, with automatic or mechanical controls of the operation—machines operating machines. The term frequently is applied loosely to most types of technological advance, although distinguished from simple mechanization. Proponents claim that automation increases employment in the long run; opponents usually have taken the view that automation decreases employment, at least in the short run.

Source references: "Automation Commission's Report on Technological Development," *MLR*, March 1966; Howard R. Bowen and Garth L. Mangum (ed.), *Automation and Economic Progress* (Englewood Cliffs: PH, 1966); Arch R. Dooley and Thomas M. Stout, "Rise of the Blue-Collar Computer," *Harvard BR*, July/ Aug. 1971; George Friedmann, *The Anatomy of Work: Labor, Leisure and the Implications of Automation* (New York: Free Press of Glencoe, 1961); Robert L. Heilbroner, *Automation in the Perspective of Long-Term Technological Change* (Washington: U.S. Dept. of Labor, Manpower Administration, Seminar on Manpower Policy and Program, 1966); Charles C. Killingsworth, "Industrial Relations and Automation," *Annals*, March 1962; Margaret Mangus, "Office Automation, Personnel and the New Technology," *PJ*, Oct. 1980; Kristen Nygaard, "Unemployment and Computer Technology," *Free Labour World*, March/ April 1979; Martin M. Perline and Kurtis L. Tull, "Automation: Its Impact on Organized Labor," *PJ*, May 1969; Julius Rezler, *Automation: Its Impacts on the Organization & Functions of Personnel Management* (Chicago:

Loyola Univ., Institute of IR, Reprint, 1972); Herbert E. Striner, "An Evaluation of the Report of the National Commission on Technology, Automation and Economic Progress," *Proceedings of the 19th A/M, IRRA*, ed. by Gerald Somers (Madison: 1967); Gerald I. Susman, "Process Design, Automation, and Worker Alienation," *IR*, Feb. 1972; U.S. Dept. of Labor, BES, *Background Information on Impact of Automation and Technological Change on Employment and Unemployment* (Washington: Pub. no. R–206, 1961); U.S. National Commission on Technology, Automation, and Economic Progress, *Technology and the American Economy* (7 vols., Washington: 1966); U.S. President's Advisory Committee on Labor-Management Policy, *Automation* (Washington: 1962); Michael D. Zisman, "Office Automation: Revolution or Evolution?" *Sloan Management Review*, Spring 1978.

See also MECHANIZATION, ROBOTICS, TECHNOLOGICAL CHANGE.

Automobile, Aerospace and Agricultural Implement Workers of America; International Union, United (AFL-CIO) One of the largest unions in the United States, it originally was organized in Detroit, Michigan, in August 1935 by the AFL organization in the automobile industry following passage of the National Industrial Recovery Act. The protection of Section 7(a) of the law led to the formation of more than 100 federal labor unions which became the National Council of Automobile Workers.

Following formation of the CIO it joined and remained a member of the CIO until the merger of the AFL-CIO on December 5, 1955.

On July 1, 1968, the Auto Workers disaffiliated itself from the AFL-CIO because of disagreement on internal policy. The union reaffiliated on July 1, 1978. In June 1979, the Distributive Workers of America (Ind) merged with the union. Its publication, *Solidarity*, is issued every three weeks.

Address: 8000 East Jefferson Ave., Detroit, Mich. 48214. Tel. (313) 926–5000

Source references: AFL-CIO, *To Clear the Record*, AFL-CIO Executive Council Report on the Disaffiliation of the UAW (Washington: 1969); Ely Chinoy, *Automobile Workers and the American Dream* (Boston: Beacon, 1965); Frank Cormier and William J. Eaton, *Reuther* (Englewood Cliffs: PH, 1970); Sidney Fine, "The Origins of the United Automobile Workers, 1933–1935," *Journal of Economic History*, Sept. 1958; ———, *Sit-Down, The General Motors Strike of 1936–37* (Ann Arbor: Univ. of Michigan Press, 1969); Nancy Gabin, "Women Workers and the UAW in the Post–World War II Period: 1945–1954," *Labor History*, Winter 1979–80; Jean Gould and Lorena Hickok, *Walter Reuther; Labor's Rugged Individualist* (New York: Dodd, Mead, 1972); Alfred O. Hero, Jr. and Emil Starr, *The Reuther-Meany Foreign Policy Dispute: Union Leaders and Members View World Affairs* (Dobbs Ferry, N.Y.: Oceana, 1970); Irving Howe and B. J. Widick, *The UAW and Walter Reuther* (New York: Random House, 1949); Roger R. Keeran, "Communist Influence in the Automobile Industry, 1920–1933: Paving the Way for an Industrial Union," *Labor History*, Spring 1979; Frank Marquart, *An Automobile Worker's Journal, the UAW Crusade to One-Party Union* (University Park: Pennsylvania State UP, 1975); "Meany Charges UAW Officers Unwilling to 'Live in Harmony' Within AFL-CIO," *Daily Labor Report*, No. 136, July 12, 1968; Wyndham Mortimer, *Organize! My Life as a Union Man* (Boston: Beacon, 1971); Al Nash, *The Local Union: Center of Life in the UAW* (Ithaca: NYSSILR, Cornell Univ., Reprint 450, 1978); ———, *The Walter and May Reuther UAW Family Center* (Ithaca: NYSSILR, Cornell Univ., Reprint 337, 1973); Victor G. Reuther, *The Brothers Reuther and the Story of the UAW, A Memoir* (Boston: Houghton Mifflin, 1976); William Serrin, *The Company and the Union; the "Civilized Relationship" of the General Motors Corporation and the United Automobile Workers* (New York: Knopf, 1973); Jack Skeels, "The Background of the UAW Factionalism," *Labor History*, Spring 1961; Carl Dean Snyder, *White-Collar Workers and the UAW* (Urbana: Univ. of Illinois Press, 1973); Jack Stieber, *Governing the United Auto Workers* (New York: Wiley, 1962).

See also ALLIANCE FOR LABOR ACTION (ALA).

Automobile Workers of America; International Union, United (AFL-CIO) The AFL counterpart of the CIO auto workers which did not merge with the CIO group in the new AFL-CIO organization but affiliated with the AFL-CIO as a separate entity. Following the AFL-CIO merger in 1955, it changed its name to the International Union, Allied Industrial Workers of America (AFL-CIO).

See also INDUSTRIAL WORKERS OF AMERICA; INTERNATIONAL UNION, ALLIED (AFL-CIO).

autonomy Self government. The national and international unions affiliated with the AFL-CIO are generally regarded as autonomous bodies, although closely associated with the parent organization. The jurisdiction of the unions is set forth in their charters and is subject to some degree of control by the parent organization, through the executive council and the convention of the AFL-CIO.

Source references: Jack Barbash, *American Unions: Structure, Government and Politics* (New York: Random House, 1967); Sidney E. Cohn, "The International and the Local Union," *NYU 11th Annual Conference on Labor*, ed. by Emanuel Stein (Albany: Bender, 1958); Alice H. Cook, "Dual Governments in Unions—A Tool for Analysis," *ILRR*, April 1962; Patricia Eames, "The Relationship Between International and Local Unions," *NYU 15th Annual Conference on Labor*, ed. by Emanuel Stein (Albany: Bender, 1962); William J. Isaacson, "The Local and the International," *NYU 5th Annual Conference on Labor*, ed. by Emanuel Stein (Albany: Bender, 1952); Herbert J. Lahne et al., "The Local Union: A Regulating Problem," *LLJ*, Dec. 1961; Reed C. Richardson, *American Labor Unions, An Outline of Growth and Structure* (2d ed., Ithaca: NYSSILR, Cornell Univ., Bull. 30, 1970); Joel Seidman, *Union Rights and Union Duties* (New York: Harcourt, Brace, 1943); Leo Troy, *Management and the Local Independent Union* (New York: Industrial Relations Counselors, Inc., Memo no. 145, 1966).

See also AMERICAN FEDERATION OF LABOR-CONGRESS OF INDUSTRIAL ORGANIZATIONS; JURISDICTION, UNION.

availability A technical term in EEO/AA usage referring to the percentage of minorities and women in an employer's relevant labor market who are qualified under valid, job-related criteria for employment in particular job groups.

The term is generally used in reference to Revised Order No. 4 and its requirements for determining underutilization of minorities and women. Revised Order No. 4 specifies eight basic factors to be considered in a utilization analysis. For minorities, these factors include:

(1) The minority population,
(2) The number of minority unemployed in the labor area surrounding the facility,
(3) The percentage of the minority workforce compared to the total workforce,
(4) The general availability of minorities with requisite skills in the immediate labor area,
(5) The availability of minorities with requisite skills in an area in which the contractor can reasonably recruit,
(6) The availability of promotable and transferable minorities within the contractor's organization,
(7) The existence of institutions capable of training persons in the requisite skills, and
(8) The extent of training the contractor is reasonably able to undertake as a means of qualifying minorities for all job classes.

The same factors are used for women but consideration of the availability of women seeking employment in the labor or recruitment area is substituted for the population criterion.

Source references: U.S. OFCCP, "Revised Order No. 4," 41 C.F.R. 60–2; George T. Milkovich, *An Analysis of Issues Relating to Availability* (Minneapolis: Univ. of Minnesota, IRC, WP 77–12, 1977); U.S. OFCCP, *Federal Contract Compliance Manual* (Washington: 1979).

See also RELEVANT LABOR MARKET AREA, REVISED ORDER NO. 4, UNDERUTILIZATION, UTILIZATION ANALYSIS.

average hourly earnings The amount of money actually received by an employee per hour of work during a pay period. It is computed by dividing total pay (gross compensation) by the total number of hours actually worked and paid for. Hourly earnings include compensation for overtime and other monetary payments. Hourly wage rates do not include overtime and other payments.

BLS publishes gross average hourly earnings in manufacturing. These data are also adjusted to eliminate the effect of overtime payments at premium rates after 40 hours per week.

Source references: Overnight Motor Transportation Co. v. Missel, 316 US 572, 2 WH Cases 47 (1942); *Bay Ridge Operating Co. v. Aaron*, 334 US 446, 8 WH Cases 20 (1948).

See also OVERTIME, PREMIUM PAY.

average straight-time hourly earnings The amount of money received by an employee per hour exclusive of premium overtime payments and shift differentials. It includes such payments as cost-of-living and production bonus, and commissions. It does not include nonproduction bonus, such as Christmas and attendance bonuses, tips, or payments in kind.

average working force An estimated average of the number of workers on a payroll during a stated period, such as monthly or annually. The average may be obtained by a daily tally or more conveniently (though less accurately) by adding the number of employees at the beginning and end of the period and dividing the total by two.

B

BAC *See* BRICKLAYERS AND ALLIED CRAFTSMEN; INTERNATIONAL UNION OF (AFL-CIO).

BAT *See* BUREAU OF APPRENTICESHIP AND TRAINING (BAT).

BBF *See* BOILERMAKERS, IRON SHIP BUILDERS, BLACKSMITHS, FORGERS AND HELPERS; INTERNATIONAL BROTHERHOOD OF (AFL-CIO).

BCTWU *See* BAKERY, CONFECTIONERY AND TOBACCO WORKERS INTERNATIONAL UNION (AFL-CIO).

BEU *See* BAKERY EMPLOYEES UNION; INDEPENDENT (IND).

BFOQ *See* BONA FIDE OCCUPATIONAL QUALIFICATION (BFOQ).

BLE *See* LOCOMOTIVE ENGINEERS; BROTHERHOOD OF (IND).

BLFE *See* LOCOMOTIVE FIREMEN AND ENGINEMEN; BROTHERHOOD OF (AFL-CIO).

BLS *See* BUREAU OF LABOR STATISTICS.

BMO *See* MARINE OFFICERS; BROTHERHOOD OF.

BMWE *See* MAINTENANCE OF WAY EMPLOYES; BROTHERHOOD OF (AFL-CIO).

BNA *See* BUREAU OF NATIONAL AFFAIRS, INC.; THE

BRASC *See* RAILWAY, AIRLINE AND STEAMSHIP CLERKS, FREIGHT HANDLERS, EXPRESS AND STATION EMPLOYES; BROTHERHOOD OF (AFL-CIO).

BRC *See* RAILWAY CARMEN OF THE UNITED STATES AND CANADA; BROTHERHOOD OF (AFL-CIO).

BRS *See* RAILROAD SIGNALMEN; BROTHERHOOD OF (AFL-CIO).

BSAC *See* SHOE AND ALLIED CRAFTSMEN; BROTHERHOOD OF (IND).

BSOIW *See* IRON WORKERS; INTERNATIONAL ASSOCIATION OF BRIDGE, STRUCTURAL AND ORNAMENTAL (AFL-CIO).

B Standard output per minute in the Bedeaux wage incentive system. "B" is defined as one minute consisting of "relative proportions of work and rest" as set by the requirements of the entire task. Sixty "B's" constitute the task per hour. Premium payments are made for production in excess of 60 "B's."

Source reference: NICB, *Some Problems in Wage Incentive Administration* (New York: Studies in Personnel Policy 19, 1940).

See also BEDEAUX WAGE PLAN, INCENTIVE WAGE.

baby Wagner acts State and local labor laws based on the National Labor Relations Act, also known as the Wagner Act, these statutes deal primarily with representation procedures and unfair labor and management practices.

Source references: Sanford Cohen, *State Labor Legislation, 1937–1947* (Columbus: Bureau of Business Research, Ohio State Univ., 1948); Charles Killingsworth, *State Labor Relations Acts* (Chicago: Univ. of Chicago Press, 1948); Russell A. Smith and William J. DeLancy, "The State Legislatures and Unionism," 38 *Michigan LR* 987 (1940).

See also NATIONAL LABOR RELATIONS ACT, STATE LABOR RELATIONS ACT.

back pay Wages or earnings due to an employee because of (a) improper layoff or discharge under the collective bargaining agreement, (b) piece rate adjustments following a grievance under the contract, (c) violation of the legal minimum wage under federal, state, or local law, (d) violation of federal, state, or local laws prohibiting unfair labor practices.

Back pay under (a) and (b) generally is pursuant to an arbitration award. Back pay under (c) and (d) results from action under the minimum wage or labor-relations laws and is enforced by the courts.

Some authors distinguish between back pay and retroactive pay, holding the latter to apply to a delayed wage payment resulting from collective bargaining negotiations where increases are applied retroactively.

Source references: George A. Davidson, " 'Back Pay' Awards Under Title VII of the Civil Rights Act of 1964," *IR Law Digest*, Spring 1974; David J. Farber, "Reversion to Individualism: The Back Pay Doctrines of the NLRB," *ILRR*, Jan. 1954; Patrick J. Fisher, "Ramifications of Back Pay in Suspension and Discharge Cases," *Arbitration and Social Change*, Proceedings of the 22d A/M, NAA, ed. by Gerald Somers (Washington: BNA, 1970); James L. Hughes et al., "Back Pay in Employment Discrimination Cases," 35 *Vanderbilt LR* 893 (1982); Dallas L. Jones, "Ramifications of Back-Pay Awards in Discharge Cases," *Arbitration and Social Change*, Proceedings of the 22d A/M, NAA, ed. by Gerald Somers (Washington: BNA, 1970); Herbert J. Lahne, "The NLRB and 'Willful Idleness,' " *LLJ*, Oct. 1957; C. Richard Miserendino, "Back Pay Arbitration Awards in the Federal Service," *Journal of Collective Negotiations in the Public Sector*, Vol. 7, no. 2, 1978; Sylvester Petro, "Union Liability for Back Pay Under the NLRA," *LLJ*, Feb. 1951; Robert J. Pleasure, "Allocation of Back-Pay Liability in Equal Employment Opportunity," *Labor Law Developments 1977*, Proceedings of the 23d Annual Institute on Labor Law, SLF (New York: Bender, 1977); Robert H. Sand, "Back Pay Liability Under Title VII," *Proceedings of the 27th A/M, IRRA*, ed. by James Stern and Barbara Dennis (Madison: 1975); ———, "Back Pay Problems Under Title VII," *NYU 27th Annual Conference on Labor*, ed. by David Raff (New York: Bender, 1975); U.S. Dept. of Labor, BLS, *Glossary of Current Industrial Relations and Wage Terms* (Washington: Bull. no. 1438, 1965); James E. Youngdahl, "Deducting Unemployment Compensation from Back Pay: Erosion of a Rational Policy," *LLJ*, Sept. 1977.

See also FAIR LABOR STANDARDS ACT OF 1938, MAKE WHOLE, NET EARNINGS, RETROACTIVE PAY.

back room boys Employees who are hired by detective agencies and assigned to shadowing, sleuthing, or general investigative work which does not require the use of a "cover." The LaFollette Committee investigation of detective agency activities in labor relations reported on these activities.

Source references: U.S. Congress, Senate, Committee on Education and Labor, *Violations of Free Speech and Rights of Labor, Hearings* (Washington: 1936–1940); ———, *Violations of Free Speech and Rights of Labor, Report no. 6—Strikebearing Services* (Washington: 1939); ———, *Violations of Free Speech and Rights of Labor, Report no. 46, Part 3—Industrial Espionage* (Washington: 1938).

See also ANTI-UNION PRACTICES, ESPIONAGE.

back-to-work movement Any organized effort to get employees out on strike to return to work. Frequently the action is instituted by employers to persuade the workers to abandon the strike. Unions generally regard such efforts as strike breaking.

Source references: In the Matter of Remington Rand, Inc., 2 NLRB 626, 1 LRRM 88 (1937); Robert R. R. Brooks, *When Labor Organizes* (New Haven: Yale UP, 1937); "Industrial Strikebreaking—The Byrnes Act," 4 *Univ. of Chicago LR* 657 (1937); James E. Youngdahl, "Baccalaureates in Strike-Breaking," *The Nation*, Oct. 15, 1955.

See also MOHAWK VALLEY FORMULA, STRIKEBREAKER.

backtracking *See* BUMPING.

Bailey v. Drexel Furniture Company A decision of the Supreme Court which held invalid a federal statute which sought to tax the net profits of a company as a device to regulate child labor. The Supreme Court held invalid the right of Congress to use its taxing power to regulate matters which were within the jurisdiction of the police powers of the state.

Source reference: Bailey v. Drexel Furniture Co., 259 US 20 (1922).

Bakery and Confectionery Workers' International Union; American (AFL-CIO) A former national union of the AFL-CIO. The union merged with the Bakery and Confectionery Workers' International Union of America (AFL-CIO) on December 4, 1969.

See also BAKERY AND CONFECTIONERY WORKERS' INTERNATIONAL UNION OF AMERICA (AFL-CIO).

Bakery and Confectionery Workers' International Union of America (AFL-CIO) Following expulsion from the AFL-CIO in December 1957, the union affiliated with the Teamsters Union. In October 1969, the union became an AFL-CIO affiliate. Merger with the American Bakery and Confectionery Workers' International Union (AFL-CIO) was effected on December 4, 1969.

It merged with the Tobacco Workers International Union on August 16, 1978, to form the Bakery, Confectionery and Tobacco Workers International Union (AFL-CIO).

See also BAKERY, CONFECTIONERY AND TOBACCO WORKERS INTERNATIONAL UNION (AFL-CIO).

Bakery, Confectionery and Tobacco Workers International Union (AFL-CIO) Union formed with the merger of the Tobacco Workers International Union and the Bakery and Confectionery Workers' International Union of America on August 16, 1978.

It publishes the *BC and T News* (10 issues a year) and the monthly *BC and T Report*.

Address: 10401 Connecticut Ave., Kensington, Md. 20895. Tel. (301) 933–8600

Bakery Employees Union; Independent (Ind) Founded in 1954.

Address: P.O. Box 188, Alexandria, La. 71301. Tel. (318) 448–1600

Bakke case The first Supreme Court decision to address the legality of a program voluntarily undertaken by a school to remedy enrollment imbalances by giving preferential treatment to minority groups. The so-called "reverse discrimination" case was initiated by a white male who was denied admission to a medical school that had reserved openings for minority students as part of a special admissions program to increase minority enrollment.

The Court held that the admissions plan violated Title VI of the 1964 Civil Rights Act since it used race as the sole basis to exclude a nonminority applicant from a federally funded program. However, the Court also ruled that race or ethnic origin could be considered as "one element—to be weighed fairly against other elements—in the selection process." The Court noted that a substantial interest may be served by a properly devised admissions program involving the competitive consideration of race and ethnic origin.

Source references: Regents of the University of California v. Bakke, 438 US 265 (1978); Charles G. Bakaly and Gordon E. Krischer, "*Bakke:* Its Impact on Public Employment Discrimination," *Employee Relations LJ*, Spring 1979; George Emery Biles and Michael A. Mass, "*Bakke:* Death Knell of 'Equal Opportunity'?" *Employee Relations LJ*, Autumn 1977; Thomas R. Knight, "Title VII and Private Voluntary Remedial Preferences: The Impact of *Weber* and *Bakke*," *Industrial and Labor Relations Forum*, June 1980; U.S. Commission on Civil Rights, *Toward an Understanding of Bakke* (Washington: Clearinghouse Publication 58, 1979).

See also WEBER CASE.

Ball-Burton-Hatch bill A bill to replace the National Labor Relations Act through the use of factfinding, mediation, and voluntary arbitration. It was opposed by labor because it was designed to remove many of the rights enjoyed by unions under the protection of the NLRA.

Source references: Congressional Record, 79th Cong., 1st Sess., Jan. 3, 1945–Dec. 21, 1945; "The Gentlemen Try It Again," *American Federationist*, Feb. 1946.

Balleisen contracts A form of individual contract, attempts to eliminate the role of unions in collective bargaining. In its origin a variation of the yellow dog contract. The employee agrees as a condition of employment not to demand any form of union security, or a written collective bargaining agreement, but to handle his own grievances and to avoid the use of any labor organization while employed with the company.

Baltimore and Ohio Railroad Company v. Interstate Commerce Commission A decision of the Supreme Court which upheld the right of Congress to regulate the hours of work as a safety measure within the scope of the commerce clause.

Source reference: Baltimore and Ohio Railroad Co. v. Interstate Commerce Commission, 221 US 612 (1911).

B. and O. plan A well-known plan of labor-management cooperation developed in the shops of the Baltimore and Ohio Railroad. Otto S. Beyer has been given credit for developing the plan following the 1922 shopman's strike.

Under the B. & O. plan, committees of union representatives and supervisors handled employee grievances and discussed all questions relating to greater efficiency of railroad service. The joint committees operated on local, regional, and system bases. The Machinists Union was the first to agree to this program, the other shop crafts following.

See also LABOR-MANAGEMENT COOPERATION.

Barbers and Beauty Culturists Union of America (AFL-CIO) A union active in barber shops and beauty parlors. It merged with the Journeymen Barbers, Hairdressers, Cosmetologists and Proprietors' International Union of America (AFL-CIO) during July 1956.

See also BARBERS, HAIRDRESSERS, COSMETOLOGISTS AND PROPRIETORS' INTERNATIONAL UNION OF AMERICA; JOURNEYMEN (AFL-CIO).

Barbers, Beauticians, and Allied Industries International Association (AFL-CIO) Formerly known as the Journeymen Barbers, Hairdressers, Cosmetologists and Proprietors' International Union of America (AFL-CIO).

On September 1, 1980, the union merged with the United Food and Commercial Workers International Union (AFL-CIO).

See also FOOD AND COMMERCIAL WORKERS INTERNATIONAL UNION; UNITED (AFL-CIO).

Barbers, Hairdressers, Cosmetologists and Proprietors' International Union of America; Journeymen (AFL-CIO) The Barbers and Beauty Culturists Union of America (AFL-CIO) merged with this union in July 1956. It later changed its name to the Barbers, Beauticians, and Allied Industries International Association (AFL-CIO).

Source reference: William S. Hall, *The Journeymen Barbers International Union of North America* (Baltimore: Johns Hopkins UP, 1936).

See also BARBERS, BEAUTICIANS, AND ALLIED INDUSTRIES INTERNATIONAL ASSOCIATION (AFL-CIO).

bare (minimum) subsistence level A standard of living just sufficient to provide food, clothing, and shelter with no provision for insurance, medicine, recreation, and other incidental expenditures. It is sometimes referred to as the absolute minimum level sufficient to permit physical survival of the family.

See also FAMILY BUDGET, STANDARD OF LIVING.

bargaining, areawide *See* COLLECTIVE BARGAINING, AREAWIDE.

bargaining, concession *See* CONCESSION BARGAINING.

bargaining, decision/effects *See* DECISION/EFFECTS BARGAINING.

bargaining, individual *See* INDIVIDUAL BARGAINING.

bargaining, industrywide *See* COLLECTIVE BARGAINING, INDUSTRYWIDE.

bargaining, multilateral *See* MULTILATERAL BARGAINING.

bargaining, multiplant *See* MULTIPLANT BARGAINING.

bargaining, multi-union *See* MULTI-UNION BARGAINING.

bargaining, pattern *See* PATTERN BARGAINING.

bargaining, productivity *See* PRODUCTIVITY BARGAINING.

bargaining, single-employer *See* SINGLE-EMPLOYER BARGAINING.

bargaining, single-plant *See* SINGLE-PLANT BARGAINING.

bargaining, single-union *See* SINGLE-UNION BARGAINING.

bargaining agent The union certified by a national, state, or local government labor agency to represent a majority of the employees in an appropriate bargaining unit and to be the exclusive bargaining agent for those employees. Employers may recognize an organization as the bargaining agent without an election or official certification. Such a procedure may not protect the employer if there is a competing labor organization which claims to represent a majority of the employees.

The employer is obligated to meet and negotiate the wages, hours, and other terms and conditions of employment with the bargaining agent.

Source reference: Joseph Rosenfarb, *The National Labor Policy and How it Works* (New York: Harper, 1940).

See also AUTHORIZATION CARD, EXCLUSIVE BARGAINING AGENT.

bargaining agent, for members only A form of union security in which the employer recognizes the union for its members only. Such bargaining arrangements are not widespread, since certification by national, state, or local government labor relations boards carries with it "exclusive" bargaining rights for all employees in the appropriate bargaining unit. Such a members-only clause might read:

> The employer recognizes the union as the collective bargaining agency for all of its employees who are members of the union on all matters affecting those employees who are members.

Source references: U.S. Dept. of Labor, BLS, *Union Agreement Provisions* (Washington: Bull. 686, 1942); ______, *Union-Security Provisions in Collective Bargaining* (Washington: Bull. 908, 1947).

bargaining history One of the criteria relied on by the NLRB in determining the unit appropriate for collective bargaining purposes. It also may have a bearing on charges of unfair labor practices where there is a claim of refusal to bargain. In the interpretation or application of a collective bargaining agreement, an arbitrator may go behind the language of the contract to find out if there was any specific intent or understanding during the negotiation of the agreement.

bargaining rights The legal authority of the union certified as the duly authorized bargaining agent to collectively negotiate, for all employees including nonmembers in the bargaining unit, the terms and conditions of employment and to act as the agent of the employees to protect those rights in the administration, enforcement, and renegotiation of the collective bargaining contract.

See also SOLE BARGAINING RIGHTS.

bargaining strength The relative power positions of management and labor during the negotiating process. The nature of the settlement frequently, though not always, is a factor of the relative bargaining power of the two parties. There are many factors which enter into the determination of the relative strength. These may include: union membership and support of the leadership and its policy; employer economic strength to withstand strike pressure for a period of time; relative flexibility of the market to absorb or to shift to alternative supplies; solidarity of employer group, particularly in multiplant, geographic, or industrywide bargaining; extent of the insecurity of the two parties; attitude of the public and its response to economic pressure from both sides.

bargaining structure Defined by Kochan "as the scope of the employees and employers covered or affected by the bargaining agreement. The formal structure of bargaining is defined as the negotiations unit. . . . The informal structure is defined as the employees or employers that are affected by the results of a negotiated settlement through pattern bargaining or some other nonbinding process."

Weber views the "informal work group" as the basic element of any bargaining structure. This informal work group becomes an appropriate bargaining unit for union representation purposes, which in turn may become "the *negotiation unit*, or the unit within which formal collective bargaining takes place." Bargaining structure may be centralized (consolidation of bargaining units) or decentralized (autonomous work units).

Source references: Thomas A. Kochan, *Collective Bargaining and Industrial Relations*

(Homewood: Irwin, 1980); Arnold R. Weber, "Stability and Change in the Structure of Collective Bargaining," *Challenges to Collective Bargaining* (Englewood Cliffs: PH, 1967).

See also BARGAINING UNIT; COLLECTIVE BARGAINING, COALITION.

bargaining theory of wages An attempt to explain wage payments on the basis of the supply and demand for labor. Labor is considered as a commodity whose price fluctuates in the marketplace on the basis of the bargaining power of employers and workers.

Source references: George De Menil, *Bargaining: Monopoly Power Versus Union Power* (Cambridge, Mass.: MIT Press, 1971); Paul H. Douglas, *The Theory of Wages* (New York: Macmillan, 1934); Henry S. Farber, "The Determinants of Union Wage Demands: Some Preliminary Empirical Evidence," *Proceedings of the 30th A/M, IRRA*, ed. by Barbara Dennis (Madison: 1978); J. R. Hicks, *The Theory of Wages* (New York: Macmillan, 1932); Lawrence M. Kahn, *Bargaining Power, Search Theory and the Phillips Curve* (Urbana: Univ. of Illinois, Institute of Labor and IR, Reprint series no. 287, 1980); Clark Kerr, "Trade Unionism and Distributive Shares," *AER*, May 1954; Richard A. Lester, *Economics of Labor* (2d ed., New York: Macmillan, 1964); Harold M. Levinson, *Determining Forces in Collective Wage Bargaining* (New York: Wiley, 1966); ______, "Unionism, Concentration and Wage Changes: Toward a Unified Theory," *ILRR*, Jan. 1967; William J. Moore and Douglas K. Pearce, "A Comparative Analysis of Strike Models During Periods of Rapid Inflation: 1967–1977," *Journal of Labor Research*, Winter 1982; Melvin Reder, *The Theory of Employment and Wages in Non-Profit Industry* (Princeton: Princeton Univ., IR Section, WP no. 42A, 1973); ______, "Wage Determination in Theory and Practice," *A Decade of Industrial Relations Research 1946–1956*, ed. by Neil W. Chamberlain, Frank C. Pierson, and Theresa Wolfson (New York: Harper, IRRA Pub. 19, 1958); Arthur Ross, *Trade Union Wage Policy* (Berkeley: UC Press, 1948); Sumner H. Slichter, *Basic Criteria Used in Wage Negotiations* (Chicago: Chicago Assn. of Commerce & Industry, 1947); Edwin E. Witte, "Criteria in Wage Rate Determinations," 1 *Washington Univ. LQ* 24 (1949).

See also WAGE BARGAINING.

bargaining unit The group of employees held by national, state, or local government labor boards to constitute the unit appropriate for bargaining purposes. Where no official designation or certification is made, it is the unit accepted by the employer for bargaining purposes.

Since the size and skill grouping of workers affects the numbers eligible to bargain in a unit, it also may determine which union competing for the right to represent the employees will get the advantage in an election. There is substantial conflict therefore in the problem of designating the unit appropriate for collective bargaining.

The NLRB and the state and local government boards have attempted to establish criteria to assist in making reasonable and uniform decisions. The standards frequently used by these agencies include the following:

(1) The desire of the employees,
(2) Functional coherence,
(3) Mutuality of interest based on occupation or skill,
(4) The history of collective bargaining.

The effort by the Board to balance the equities in any particular case where rival unions are competing poses serious difficulties. In the long run the Board must make reasonable and equitable decisions which at the same time will promote effective collective bargaining.

Source references: Matthew W. Finkin, "An Intervenor's Standing to Propose a Bargaining Unit: A Comment on the Vagaries of Decisional Rule-Making," *LLJ*, July 1974; Thomas P. Gilroy and Anthony C. Russo, *Bargaining Unit Issues: Problems, Criteria, Tactics* (Chicago: IPMA, PERL no. 43, 1973); Hiram S. Hall, "Impact of the Bargaining Unit on Labor-Management Relations," *NYU 2d Annual Conference on Labor*, ed. by Emanuel Stein (Albany: Bender, 1949); Dallas L. Jones, "Self-Determination vs. Stability of Labor Relations," *Michigan LR*, Jan. 1960; Michael F. Mayer, "Determination of the Appropriate Bargaining Unit in Multi-Plant Enterprises," *Yale LJ*, May 1950; Benjamin

B. Naumoff, "Judicial Review of NLRB Representation Proceedings," *NYU 11th Annual Conference on Labor*, ed. by Emanuel Stein (Albany: Bender, 1958); James L. Perry and Harold L. Angle, "Bargaining Unit Structure and Organizational Outcomes," *IR*, Winter 1981; Berton B. Subrin, "Conserving Energy at the Labor Board: The Case for Making Rules on Collective Bargaining Units," *LLJ*, Feb. 1981; Andrew W. J. Thomson, *Unit Determination in Public Employment* (Ithaca: NYSSILR, Cornell Univ., Public Employee Relations Reports no. 1, 1967); U.S. Dept. of Labor, LMSA, *Public Sector Unit Determination, Administrative Procedures and Case Law* (Washington: 1979); Fred Witney, "The Appropriate Bargaining Unit Controversy," *Southern Economic Journal*, Oct. 1949.

See also APPROPRIATE UNIT, CRAFT UNION, EMPLOYEE UNIT, GLOBE DOCTRINE, INDUSTRIAL UNION, MULTI-EMPLOYER UNITS, MULTIPLANT UNIT.

Barth premium plan A method of wage payment which averages both piece rate and time rate in order to arrive at the wages paid. It seeks to compensate both for the amount of production and the time spent on the job. The formula for the plan is:

$$E = R_H \sqrt{H_S H_A}$$

Where,

E = Earnings for a period of time
R_H = Hourly rate of pay
H_S = Standard hours produced
H_A = Actual hours worked.

Source reference: Gordon Watkins et al., *The Management of Personnel and Labor Relations* (New York: McGraw-Hill, 1950).

Baseball Players Association; Major League (Ind) The first of the major professional sports to enter into collective bargaining, the Major League Baseball Players Association and the club owners negotiated a two-year agreement in February 1968.

Address: 805 Third Ave., New York, N.Y. 10022. Tel. (212) 826–0808

Source references: James R. Chelius and James B. Dworkin, "Arbitration and Salary Determination in Baseball," *Proceedings of the 33d A/M, IRRA*, ed. by Barbara Dennis (Madison: 1981); ———, "Free Agency and Salary Determination in Baseball," *LLJ*, August 1982; James B. Dworkin, *The Shortest Season—The Baseball Strike of 1981* (Minneapolis: Univ. of Minnesota, IRC, WP 81–10, 1981); Robert B. Hoffman, "Is the NLRB Going to Play the Ball Game?" *LLJ*, April 1969; Peter Seitz, "Footnotes to Baseball Salary Arbitration," *AJ*, June 1974; ———, "The Transplanting of Industrial Relations Tissues and Organs or, Is the Baseball Salary Arbitration System Compatible with Interest Arbitration in the Private Sector Generally," *NYU 28th Annual Conference on Labor*, ed. by Richard Adelman (New York: Bender, 1976); Arthur A. Sloane, "Collective Bargaining in Major League Baseball: A New Ball Game and Its Genesis," *LLJ*, April 1977; Paul M. Sommers and Noel Quinton, "Pay and Performance in Major League Baseball: The Case of the First Family of Free Agents," *Journal of Human Resources*, Summer 1982; Paul D. Staudohar, "Player Salary Issues in Major League Baseball," *AJ*, Dec. 1978.

base pay *See* BASE RATE.

base period The period during which an employee fulfills the employment requirement in order to receive the benefits of the state unemployment insurance system. This is designed to limit the benefits to those in the labor force.

Also the period used in statistical measurement, i.e., by index numbers (the base period may be a month, year, or years, measured as 100) where changes in the series are measured from the base period.

base rate The pay of an employee for a fixed unit of time, i.e., hour, day, etc., apart from the payment of overtime or other premiums.

Under piece rate it is the amount of pay guaranteed per hour or day. Under other wage incentive systems it is the amount of pay received for production at the "standard" set for the established task. Extra pay or earnings are received for production beyond the standard.

See also GUARANTEED BASE RATE.

basic rate of pay Same as basic hourly rate. The "regular rate" of pay on which overtime (time and one half) is computed under the Fair Labor Standards Act and the Walsh-Healey Public Contracts Act.

basic workday The number of hours set out in collective bargaining agreements or statutory overtime provisions, in excess of which premium payments are made. The eight-hour day is widely accepted as the standard or basic workday.

Source references: Fair Labor Standards Act of 1938, 29 U.S.C. 201 et seq. (1982); BNA, *The New Wage and Hour Law* (Washington: 1961); CCH, *New 1966 Minimum Wage Law, With Explanation* (Chicago: 1966).

See also HOURS OF WORK, WORKDAY.

basic workweek Most collective bargaining agreements specify eight hours as the basic workday and 40 hours as the basic workweek. Overtime or premium pay is provided for hours worked in excess of those specified. Federal and state minimum wage and maximum overtime provisions set the standard workweek. Premium overtime is paid for hours worked in excess of the basic workday or workweek.

The Fair Labor Standards Act setting the 40-hour workweek provided for gradual attainment of that goal. In 1938–39 it was 44 hours, in 1939–40, 42 hours, and after October 1940, 40 hours. FLSA does not apply to intrastate companies and exempts groups such as seasonal workers and those covered by certain annual wage plans.

Source reference: Fair Labor Standards Act of 1938, 29 U.S.C. 201 et seq. (1982).

See also HOURS OF WORK.

Basketball Players Association; National (Ind) An association of professional athletes with a reported membership of 270. Its monthly publication is *Time Out.*

Address: c/o Lawrence Fleisher, 15 Columbus Circle, New York, N.Y. 10023. Tel. (212) 541–7118

battery tests A series or combination of examinations to measure a person's ability in a particular area or his potential to perform certain work. The development of psychological testing in personnel work has led to the development of measures to assist in more effective hiring, training, and promotion of employees.

See also HIRING, TEST, TRAINING.

Bay Ridge case Supreme Court case involving overtime payments under the Fair Labor Standards Act. The Court held that premium payments under collective bargaining agreements were to be considered in computing the basic rate of pay ("regular rate") for overtime computation.

Source reference: Bay Ridge Company v. Aaron, 334 US 446, 8 WH Cases 20 (1948).

See also OVERTIME-ON-OVERTIME.

Bedeaux wage plan A wage incentive plan popular in the 1920s, named after its sponsor, Charles Bedeaux, French engineer and industrialist. The plan gave emphasis to the movement to increase production through use of standards and techniques of measurement.

Bedeaux engineers used the letter "B" to designate the unit of measurement. "B" was the equivalent of one minute, and 60 B's constituted the standard task to be performed per hour. Premiums were paid for performance above 60 B's. Savings were divided in the ratio of 3 to 1 between direct and indirect labor. This division later gave way so that direct labor received 100 percent of the bonus.

The system was viewed by its proponents as a method for comparing unit costs among varying operations since all work presumably was reduced to a common denominator, the B standard.

Source references: Z. Clark Dickinson, *Compensating Industrial Effort* (New York: Ronald Press, 1937); William Gomberg, "Union Attitudes on the Application of Industrial Engineering Techniques to Collective Bargaining," *Personnel,* May 1948; Van Dusen Kennedy, *Union Policy and Incentive Wage Methods* (New York: Columbia UP, 1945); J. K. Louden, *Wage Incentives* (New York: Wiley, 1944).

Bedford Cut Stone Co. v. Journeymen Stone Cutters' Association A decision of the Supreme Court in 1927 holding the Journeymen Stone Cutters union in violation of the Sherman Anti-Trust Act. In issue was a union rule which provided that no member should work on stone cut by nonunion labor. Although there were no threats, picketing, or violence, the Court held that the union's action was calculated to destroy the company's interstate markets.

Source reference: Bedford Cut Stone v. Journeymen Stone Cutters' Association, 174 US 37 (1927).

See also SHERMAN ACT OF 1890.

beginner's rate The scheduled pay for an inexperienced employee. More generally set up as a trainee rate. The regular rate for the job is received as soon as the minimum training period is completed.

See also ENTRANCE RATE, JOB RATE, LEARNER RATE, STARTING RATE.

bell-horses *See* PACERS.

Belo wage plan A wage plan held by the Supreme Court to meet the overtime provisions of the Fair Labor Standards Act. The individual or collective bargaining contract provides a constant guaranteed weekly wage for fluctuating workweeks. A Belo-type wage plan to come within the protection of the Court decision must meet the conditions of (a) irregularity of hours inherent in the nature of the job, (b) a regular rate of pay, with compensation of time and one half after 40 hours, and (c) a weekly wage guarantee for work of no more than 60 hours.

Source references: Walling v. Belo, 316 US 624 (1942); "Wages, Hours—Rulings, Decisions, Problems," *LLJ*, Sept. 1956.

benchmarks *See* FACTOR COMPARISON METHOD, PEG POINT.

benefit plans Programs developed by many unions to protect their members from special hardships, due to unemployment, sickness, accidents, disability, and other risks of workers in modern society. Some of these plans were financed out of regular dues payments. However, most of the insurance plans had to be financed out of special assessments, or through voluntary membership in a particular plan.

See also EMPLOYEE BENEFITS, FRINGE BENEFITS.

benefit year The period of time set in unemployment compensation laws to permit a person covered by the law to meet one of the qualifications for benefit payments. Section 2(c) of the Social Security Act (1937) defined the "benefit year" as ". . . the fifty-two consecutive week period beginning with the first day of the week with respect to which benefits are next payable to him after the termination of his last preceding benefit year."

Source reference: Gilman G. Udell (comp.), *Laws Relating to Social Security and Unemployment Compensation* (Washington: U.S. Congress, House, 1967).

Bennett Amendment Section 703(h) of Title VII of the Civil Rights Act of 1964, proposed by Senator Wallace F. Bennett of Utah, reads:

> It shall not be unlawful employment practice under this title for any employer to differentiate upon the basis of sex in determining the amount of the wages or compensation paid or to be paid to employees of such employer if such differentiation is authorized by the provisions of Section 6(d) of the Fair Labor Standards Act of 1938, as amended (29 U.S.C. 206(d)) [Equal Pay Act of 1963].

The Bennett Amendment became a source of controversy because it was not clear whether the amendment restricted the Title VII prohibition of sex-based wage discrimination to an equal pay for equal work standard, or whether the amendment was intended only to incorporate the four affirmative defenses of the Equal Pay Act, thus permitting to be heard wage discrimination claims based on sex. In *County of Washington v. Gunther*, the Supreme Court held that female former guards, even though they did not perform work equal to that of male officers, have stated a claim that is not barred under Title VII when it claimed that the county evaluated the worth of their jobs; that the county determined that they should be paid approximately 95 percent as much as male jail guards; that it paid them only about 70 percent as much, while paying the male officers the full evaluated worth of their jobs; and that the failure of the county to pay them the full evaluated worth of their jobs can be proven to be attributable to intentional sex discrimination.

Source references: Ruth G. Blumrosen, "Wage Discrimination, Job Segregation, and Title VII of the Civil Rights Act of 1964," 12 *Univ. of Michigan Journal of Law Reform* 399 (1979); Laura N. Gasaway, "Comparable Worth: A Post-Gunther View," 69 *Georgetown LJ* 1123 (1981); Michael Evan Gold, "A Tale of Two Amendments: The Reasons Congress Added Sex to Title VII and Their Implication for the Issue of Comparable Worth," 19 *Duquesne LR* 453 (1981); Winn Newman and Jeanne M. Vonhoff, " 'Separate But Equal'—Job Segregation and Pay Equity in the Wake of Gunther," *Univ. of Illinois LR,* Vol. 1981, no. 2 (1981).

See also COMPARABLE WORTH, EQUAL PAY ACT OF 1963, GUNTHER CASE, PAY EQUITY.

Bergoff technique Technique ascribed or credited to Pearl L. Bergoff, one of the most notorious strikebreakers in American history. He provided professional services to assist employers in preventing unionism and where it had obtained a foothold, to dispose of it. His services were particularly effective during industrial strife. The Bergoff technique, in addition to creating strife, involved the setting up of "loyal" back-to-work movements, engineered by Bergoff men and assisted by the press. Its effect was to demoralize the workers by casting suspicion on fellow workers and to break the strike by fear and sometimes by force.

See also BACK ROOM BOYS, BACK-TO-WORK MOVEMENT.

bidding A procedure for permitting employees of a company to make known their interest in a vacant position. Following posting of the vacancy on bulletin boards or through other channels, individuals may bid for the position by applying for the opening. The filling of the position will depend on seniority and such other factors as the company and union have agreed on, or upon the policy of the company where there is no union.

See also JOB OPEN FOR BID, POSTING.

big four The major railroad brotherhoods which dominated the railroad industry. The big four included: the Brotherhood of Locomotive Engineers, the Brotherhood of Locomotive Firemen and Enginemen, the Brotherhood of Railroad Trainmen, and the Order of Railway Conductors and Brakemen.

In January 1969, the United Transportation Union (AFL-CIO) was formed with the merger of the Brotherhood of Railroad Trainmen, the Switchmen's Union of North America, the Order of Railway Conductors and Brakemen, and the Brotherhood of Locomotive Firemen and Enginemen.

See also TRANSPORTATION UNION; UNITED (AFL-CIO).

big steel U.S. Steel Corporation—the major steel producer in the United States.

See also LITTLE STEEL.

bilateral action Distinguished from "unilateral" action, where the employer (usually) takes action without discussion or agreement with the bargaining agent. Bilateral action involves the joint action of the parties to collective bargaining before final action is taken.

Bill Posters, Billers and Distributors of the United States and Canada; International Alliance of (AFL-CIO) A former AFL union, it relinquished its charter and dissolved in the early 1970s.

bindle stiffs *See* BUNDLE STIFFS.

bipartite board Sometimes referred to as a joint board where it is used as a step in the grievance machinery, at the step prior to arbitration. The board consists of equal numbers from labor and management, with a majority needed to dispose of a grievance. Where the board is deadlocked, a neutral member steps in as the third member (if there are four on the board as the fifth member) in order to break the deadlock.

A bipartisan board also may be set up as an arbitration tribunal. The difficulty of tie votes creates the same problems as in the joint mediation (bipartite) boards.

See also NATIONAL WAR LABOR BOARD, TRIPARTITE BOARDS.

Bituminous Coal Act of 1937 A federal law to regulate the sales and distribution of bituminous coal in interstate commerce, to protect the coal resources of the country, to regulate prices, and to eliminate unfair methods of competition. The act also protected the right to organize and bargain collectively, similar to provisions of the National Labor Relations Act.

black According to OFCCP, "A person with origins in any of the black racial groups of Africa who is also not of Hispanic origin." Under Title VII, this is a protected class and one of the racial/ethnic categories for which data is reported to the federal government.

Source reference: U.S. OFCCP, *Federal Contract Compliance Manual* (Washington: 1979).

See also AFFECTED CLASS, PROTECTED CLASS.

Black-Connery bill *See* FAIR LABOR STANDARDS ACT OF 1938.

black death A pestilence which reached Europe in the middle of the 14th century (1348) and killed more than one third of the population. Wage and price regulations which began with the emergency carried through during the next two centuries and did much to change the manorial system and also limit the rights of individuals to determine their wages, hours, and conditions of employment. The conspiracy doctrine which was applied against individuals and combinations which sought to organize remained an effective weapon until the middle of the 19th century.

black employment Following the Civil War, blacks were restricted to unskilled, low-status, and low-paying jobs. Until World War II, they were rarely hired in factories except as janitors or as laborers. Since 1960, black employment has been increasing with the gains concentrated in white-collar, artisan, and operative occupations. Many blacks are in business for themselves, most operating small service-oriented businesses.

In 1983, some 10.4 percent of the U.S. labor force was black; yet some 19.5 percent of blacks were unemployed compared to 8.4 percent for whites. Among teenagers, the unemployment rate was 48.5 percent for blacks and 19.3 percent for whites. The labor force participation rate of women 25 years and older is greater for black women than white women. In 1981, the median income for black families was 56 percent of that for white families.

Federal legislation has created programs focusing on the improvement of employment conditions and work opportunities for disadvantaged workers, the majority of whom are nonwhite. Such programs have included the Neighborhood Youth Corps, Job Corps, Upward Bound, the National Alliance of Business-JOBS project, and various on-the-job training programs. Employers themselves, who previously had covertly discriminated against black workers, have joined with the federal government in programs geared to upgrading and training disadvantaged workers and have also devised training programs on their own.

The Civil Rights Act of 1964 banned discrimination in apprenticeship programs and in employment because of race, color, religion, national origin, or sex, and created an Equal Employment Opportunity Commission, which reviews and attempts to settle complaints of racial discrimination. Although 26 labor unions had formal race bars to membership in 1930, when the Civil Rights Act was passed only two unions had such restrictive clauses. Some unions have continued to deny blacks and other minority group workers full participation, and the problem of labor union discrimination has been attacked by such groups as the AFL-CIO Civil Rights Department, the Workers Defense League, the NAACP, and black workers in union locals.

Source references: "Annual Averages—Household Data," *Employment and Earnings*, Jan. 1984; Alfred W. Blumrosen, *Black Employment and the Law* (New Brunswick: Rutgers UP, 1971); Louis A. Ferman, *The Negro and Equal Employment Opportunities* (New York: Praeger, 1968); Philip S. Foner, *Organized Labor and the Black Worker, 1619–1973* (New York: Praeger, 1974); Richard Freeman, "Black Economic Progress Since 1964," *The Public Interest*, Summer 1978; Jack G. Gourlay, *The Negro Salaried Worker* (New York: AMA, Research Study no. 70, 1964); Stephen Habbe, *Company Experience with Negro Employment* (2 vol., New York: NICB, Studies in Personnel Policy no. 201, 1966); Julius Jacobson (ed.), *The Negro and the American Labor Movement* (Garden City: Doubleday, 1968); F. Ray Marshall, *The Negro Worker* (New York: Random House, 1967); Harold L. Sheppard and Herbert E. Striner, *Civil Rights, Employment and the Social Status of American Negroes* (Kalamazoo: Upjohn Institute, 1966); Twentieth Century Fund, *Task Force on Employment Problems of Black Youth, The Job Crisis for Black Youth, Report* (New York: Praeger, 1971); U.S. Dept. of Commerce, Bureau of the Census, *Population Profile of the United States: 1982* (Washington: Current Population Reports, P–23, no. 130, 1983); ———, *The Social and Economic Status of the Black Population in the United States: An Historical View, 1790–1978* (Washington: Current Population Reports, P–23, no. 80, 1979); Benjamin W. Wolkinson, *Blacks, Unions, and the*

EEOC: A Study of Administrative Futility (Lexington, Mass.: Lexington Books, 1973).

blackleg The British equivalent for the term scab.

blacklist A procedure whereby employers or employers' associations circulated the name or names of "undesirable" employees, mostly those who were active union men, "disrupters," or "outside agitators." Such employees had a difficult time finding employment at their usual occupation in their locality. With the growth and wider acceptance of unionism this practice is becoming outmoded. In practice, of course, it is difficult to prevent the exchange of information from personnel office to personnel office which may affect the employment of a person. Discrimination because of union membership or activity is now subject to unfair labor practice charges under federal, state, and local government laws.

Many state laws specifically prohibit the blacklist. As a matter of enforcement it has been difficult to prosecute violations.

The term has also been applied to contractors who have been denied the opportunity to receive federal contracts because of violations of the Walsh-Healey Act.

Source reference: U.S. Congress, House, Committee on Un-American Activities, *Investigation of So-Called "Blacklisting" in Entertainment Industry* (Washington: 1956).

See also WALSH-HEALEY ACT OF 1936.

blacklisting The practice and procedure of using the blacklist.

Black Lung Benefits Reform Act of 1977 Statute which liberalized the eligibility requirements in the black lung benefits program established by Title IV of the Federal Coal Mine and Safety Act of 1969 and the Black Lung Benefits Act of 1972.

The Black Lung Benefits Reform Act of 1977 facilitated access to benefits, including monthly payments and medical treatment for coal miners totally disabled by pneumoconiosis, or black lung disease. Benefits were also provided to dependents and survivors of coal miners with the disease. Other major changes contained in the law included (1) reconsideration of claims previously rejected under more restrictive criteria, (2) a redefinition of total disability, and (3) alteration of the standards of evidence proving disability.

The Act was amended by the Black Lung Benefits Amendments of 1981, which tightened the eligibility requirements for claims filed after December 29, 1981.

Source references: Black Lung Benefits Reform Act of 1977, 30 U.S.C. 901 et seq. (1982); Carvin Cook, "The 1977 Amendments to the Black Lung Benefits Law," *MLR*, May 1978; Arnold R. Miller, "UMWA Recommendations for Black Lung Amendments," *LLJ*, April 1975; Jennings Randolph and Robert R. Humphreys, "Black Lung Benefits Reform: Mirage or Reality?" *LLJ*, Sept. 1977.

Blacksmiths, Drop Forgers and Helpers; International Brotherhood of (AFL) *See* BOILERMAKERS, IRON SHIP BUILDERS, BLACKSMITHS, FORGERS AND HELPERS; INTERNATIONAL BROTHERHOOD OF (AFL-CIO).

blanket agreement A collective bargaining agreement whose terms cover an entire industry or large geographic area within an industry.

"blanket" injunction A court order issued during a strike or to prevent a strike which is so broad in its sweep of restraints that it encompasses activities which have little relation to the dispute within its blanket. The Norris-LaGuardia Act sets forth safeguards in the issuance of injunctions in labor disputes.

Source references: Paul F. Brissenden, "Campaign Against the Labor Injunction," *AER*, March 1933; Edwin E. Witte, "Value of Injunctions in Labor Disputes," *Journal of Political Economy*, June 1924.

See also NORRIS-LAGUARDIA ACT.

blind alley jobs Jobs accepted by workers which offer little if any opportunity for advancement. Such jobs lead nowhere in terms of wages, prestige, or satisfaction.

See also DEAD-END JOB.

blue-collar worker Term used to describe production and maintenance workers employed in a plant as distinguished from white-collar employees employed in an office. Blue-collar workers are usually paid by the hour or on an incentive basis. The U.S. Department of Labor projects a continuing decline of blue-collar employment and an increase in white-collar employment.

Source references: Peter M. Blau and Otis Dudley Duncan, *The American Occupational Structure* (New York: Wiley, 1967); Charles Brecher, *Upgrading Blue Collar and Service Workers* (Baltimore: Johns Hopkins UP, 1972); Mitchell Fein, "The Real Needs and Goals of Blue Collar Workers," *Conference Board Record*, Feb. 1973; Christopher G. Gellner, "Occupational Characteristics of Urban Workers," *MLR*, Oct. 1971; Irving Howe (ed.), *The World of the Blue Collar Worker* (New York: Quadrangle Books, 1972); David B. Johnson and James L. Stern, "Blue Collar Workers: A Recruitment Source for White Collar Openings," *PJ*, June 1970; ———, "Why and How Workers Shift From Blue-Collar to White-Collar Jobs," *MLR*, Oct. 1969; Andrew Levison, *The Working Class Majority* (New York: Coward, McCann & Geoghegan, 1974); Sar A. Levitan (ed.), *Blue Collar Workers: A Symposium on Middle America* (New York: McGraw-Hill, 1971); Stanley E. Seashore and J. Thad Barnowe, "Behind the Averages: A Closer Look at America's Lower-Middle-Income Workers," *Proceedings of the 24th A/M, IRRA*, ed. by Gerald Somers (Madison: 1972); Patricia Cayo Sexton and Brendan Sexton, *Blue Collars and Hard Hats; The Working Class and the Future of American Politics* (New York: Random House, 1971); Harold L. Sheppard and Neal Q. Herrick, *Where Have All the Robots Gone?* (New York: Free Press, 1972); Curt Tausky, "Meanings of Work Among Blue Collar Men," *Pacific Sociological Review*, Spring 1969; David A. Weeks, "Salaries for Blue Collar Workers," *Conference Board Record*, Nov. 1965.

See also WHITE-COLLAR EMPLOYEE.

blue eagle The insignia of the National Industrial Recovery Act.

See also NATIONAL INDUSTRIAL RECOVERY ACT, SECTION 7(A).

blue flu Usually refers to mass sick calls made by police officers to express dissatisfaction with wages or working conditions. A mass sick call by firefighters is sometimes referred to as "red flu" or "red rash."

Since public sector strikes are prohibited in most jurisdictions, this tactic has been used to exert pressure on public employers.

Source references: Casey Ichniowski, "Arbitration and Police Bargaining: Prescriptions for the Blue Flu," *IR*, Spring 1982; Carmen D. Saso, *Coping with Public Employee Strikes* (Chicago: PPA, 1970).

See also JOB ACTION, SICKOUT.

blue sky bargaining Unrealistic and unreasonable demands in negotiations by either or both labor and management, where neither concedes anything and demands the impossible, is sometimes referred to as blue sky bargaining. In actuality it is not collective bargaining at all.

See also COLLECTIVE BARGAINING.

board of inquiry A board generally set up to investigate the facts involved in a labor dispute. Under the Taft-Hartley Act, the board of inquiry is appointed by the President to report to him on the issues involved in disputes under the national emergency provisions of the law. Section 206 reads in part:

> Whenever in the opinion of the President of the United States, a threatened or actual strike or lockout affecting an entire industry or a substantial part thereof engaged in trade, commerce, transportation, transmission, or communication among the several States or with foreign nations, or engaged in the production of goods for commerce, will, if permitted to occur or to continue, imperil the national health or safety, he may appoint a board of inquiry to inquire into the issues involved in the dispute and to make a written report to him within such time as he shall prescribe.

Source references: Labor Management Relations Act of 1947, Sections 206–210, 29 U.S.C. 176–180 (1982); Arthur A. Sloane, "Presidential Boards of Inquiry in National Emergency Disputes—An Assessment After 20 Years of Performance," *LLJ*, Nov. 1967.

bogey Efforts by employees to restrict output by setting up an informal standard (bogey) beyond which the employees do not go. Since such limitations are presumed to result in production below normal or par, some authors believe the term is derived from the golf course. Bogey on a hole is a stroke in excess of par for that hole. Excess production (strokes) on the golf course becomes lower production in the plant to achieve a bogey.

See also RESTRICTION OF OUTPUT.

bogus (type) work Refers to the "make work" practice in composing rooms by typesetters, who reset type which is not necessary in order to print the article or advertising. (The advertiser may have supplied mats for making the ad.)

Setting of bogus type was held not to be in violation of the featherbedding provisions of the Taft-Hartley Act.

Source references: Labor Management Relations Act of 1947, Section 8(b)(6), 29 U.S.C. 158(b)(6) (1982); *American Newspaper Publishers v. NLRB*, 345 US 100, 31 LRRM 2422 (1953); *U.S. v. International Hod Carriers*, 313 US 539 (1941); William L. Brach, "Legislative Shackles on Featherbedding Practices," 34 *Cornell LQ* 255 (1948).

See also FEATHERBEDDING.

bohunk Any foreigner who is disliked. A dull or stupid individual.

Boilermakers, Iron Ship Builders, Blacksmiths, Forgers and Helpers; International Brotherhood of (AFL-CIO) Organized in Chicago on October 1, 1880. In September 1893, the International Brotherhood of Boiler Makers merged with the National Brotherhood of Boiler Makers to form the Brotherhood of Boiler Makers and Iron Ship Builders of America.

The International Brotherhood of Blacksmiths, Drop Forgers and Helpers (AFL) merged with the union in July 1953 and adopted its current name. In April 1984 the union merged with the United Cement, Lime, Gypsum, and Allied International Union (AFL-CIO). Its official publication is the *Boilermaker-Blacksmiths Reporter* (monthly).

Address: 570 New Brotherhood Bldg., Kansas City, Kan. 66101. Tel. (913) 371–2640

Bolshevism The extreme form of socialism or communism. Extremists in the labor movement have sometimes been referred to as Bolshevists or Bolsheviks.

bona fide occupational qualification (BFOQ) An employment standard or job qualification which allows employment on the basis of an individual's sex, religion, national origin, or age, if it is shown to be "reasonably necessary to the normal operation of that particular business or enterprise." Title VII of the Civil Rights Act of 1964 and the Age Discrimination in Employment Act both provide for BFOQ; however, an employer must establish that sex, religion, national origin, or age is required for performing the job.

The EEOC and the courts have narrowly construed the BFOQ application. Gender or race may be used as a proper job qualification in the case of actors or actresses, and sex for work in restrooms or fitting rooms. In *Dothard v. Rawlinson*, the Supreme Court decided that under certain conditions, the use of women as prison guards would pose security problems in an all-male penitentiary. In most other situations, however, BFOQs are not granted.

Source references: Age Discrimination in Employment Act of 1967, as amended, 29 U.S.C. 621 et seq. (1982); Civil Rights Act of 1964, as amended, 42 U.S.C. 2000e et seq. (1982); *Dothard v. Rawlinson*, 433 US 321, 15 FEP Cases 10 (1977); Thomas Stephen Neuberger, "Sex as a Bona Fide Occupational Qualification Under Title VII," *LLJ*, July 1978; Butler D. Shaffer, "Some Economic Considerations in Sex Discrimination Cases," *LLJ*, May 1975; Jeffrey M. Shaman, "Toward Defining and Abolishing the Bona Fide Occupational Qualification Based on Class Status," *LLJ*, June 1971; Michael L. Sirota, "Sex Discrimination: Title VII and the Bona Fide Occupational Qualification," *IR Law Digest*, Spring 1978; U.S. Commission on Civil Rights, *A Guide to Federal Laws Prohibiting Sex Discrimination* (Washington: 1974).

bona fide seniority system A seniority system which is free of discrimination or intent to discriminate against specific groups of employees. The district court in *Quarles v. Philip Morris* held that the employer's seniority system was not bona fide because its "departmental seniority system . . . has its genesis in racial discrimination. . . ." In *Teamsters v. U.S.*, the Supreme Court found the employer's seniority system bona fide because it was not based on racial discrimination and "it was negotiated and has been maintained free from any illegal purposes."

Source references: Quarles v. Philip Morris, 1 FEP Cases 260 (DC Va 1968); *Teamsters v. U.S.*, 431 US 324, 14 FEP Cases 1514 (1977).

See also MEMPHIS FIRE DEPARTMENT V. STOTTS, TEAMSTERS V. U.S.

bonus Any payments in excess of the regular rate or in excess of base or guaranteed rate in an incentive plan. Bonuses also are paid for attendance, overtime, hazardous or unpleasant work, or night work. Christmas bonuses and other annual allotments fall in the same category.

Source references: John T. Bourke, "Performance Bonus Plans: Boon for Managers and Stockholders," *Management Review*, Nov. 1975; Timothy W. Costello and Sheldon S. Zalkind, "Merit Raise or Merit Bonus: A Psychological Approach," *Personnel Administration*, Nov./Dec. 1962; John Dearden, "How to Make Incentive Plans Work," *Harvard BR*, July/Aug. 1972; John Dearden and William S. Edgerly, "Bonus Formula for Division Heads," *Harvard BR*, Sept./Oct. 1965; Herbert F. Floyd, "Profit Center Incentives: Stimulants or Depressants?" *Management Review*, April 1979; Harland Fox, "Top Executive Bonus Arithmetic," *Conference Board Record*, April 1967; ———, *Top Executive Bonus Plans* (New York: The Conference Board, Report no. 760, 1979); Robert A. Pitts, "Incentive Compensation and Organization Design," *PJ*, May 1974; Ray Stata and Modesto A. Maidique, "Bonus System for Balanced Strategy," *Harvard BR*, Nov./Dec. 1980; Robert M. Tomasko, "Focusing Company Reward Systems to Help Achieve Business Objectives," *Management Review*, Oct. 1982; George W. Torrence, *The Motivation and Measurement of Performance* (Washington: BNA, 1967); ———, *Prevalence of Bonus Plans in Manufacturing* (New York: NICB, Studies in Personnel Policy no. 185, 1962); N. B. Winstanley, "Management 'Incentive' Bonus Plan Realities," *Conference Board Record*, Jan. 1970.

See also ATTENDANCE BONUS, CHRISTMAS BONUS, DANGER ZONE BONUS, GROUP BONUS, NIGHT PREMIUM, NONPRODUCTION BONUS, PRODUCTION BONUS, QUALITY BONUS, QUOTA-BONUS PLAN, SUGGESTION BONUS.

Bonwit Teller rule *See* CAPTIVE AUDIENCE, FREEDOM OF SPEECH.

Bookbinders; International Brotherhood of (AFL-CIO) Bookbinders were organized as early as 1850. Some of the members joined the International Typographical Union when it was formed in 1852. The bookbinders, however, formed their own organization in 1892 as the International Brotherhood of Bookbinders. They joined the AFL in 1898. In September 1972, the union merged with the Lithographers and Photoengravers International Union (AFL-CIO) to form the Graphic Arts International Union (AFL-CIO).

See also GRAPHIC ARTS INTERNATIONAL UNION (AFL-CIO).

boomer *See* FLOATER.

boondoggling Work of an unnecessary or useless character designed primarily to keep the employee busy. The term was applied to some of the projects during the depression which involved the expenditure of public funds with little public benefit.

Joseph Shipley in his *Dictionary of Word Origins* suggests that "boondoggle means to be as busy as a puppy—doing nothing; and that the relief was a great boon."

bootleg wages Wages received by employees above or below the contract rate or in violation of rates established by law or wage regulations as during the period of wage stabilization in World War II.

Basically improper or illegal wage payments. The concept is similar to that of bootleggers during the Prohibition period who peddled liquor illegally.

Borderland Coal Corporation v. United Mine Workers A case which arose from a petition by the Borderland Coal Corporation of West Virginia and some 60 other companies to restrain, by injunction, certain activities by the United Mine Workers, allegedly in violation of the Sherman Act. Judge Anderson of the District Court of Indiana granted a temporary injunction on October 21, 1921, which restrained officers of the union from "advising, assisting, encouraging, aiding, abetting, or in any way or manner, and by any and all means whatsoever by the use of any funds or money however collected by the International Union

United Mine Workers of America, its officers, members, agents, or representatives the unionization or the attempted unionization of the nonunion mines in Mingo County, West Virginia, and Pike County, Kentucky. . . ." In addition the district court restrained the operators from collecting union dues under the check-off.

The case was appealed to the 7th Circuit Court of Appeals which reversed the district court insofar as the dues check-off was concerned.

Source reference: Edward Berman, *Labor and the Sherman Act* (New York: Harper, 1930).

Borg-Warner case Case in which the Supreme Court recognized three categories of bargaining proposals under the Taft-Hartley Act and established three sets of rules for them. They are:

(1) *Illegal subjects.* These are proposals that would be illegal and forbidden under the Act, such as a proposal for a closed shop. Bargaining on such proposals is not required, and they may not be included in the contract even if the other party agrees.

(2) *Mandatory subjects.* Under Section 8(d) of the Act, both employers and unions are required to bargain in good faith with respect to "wages, hours, and other terms and conditions of employment." Either party must bargain about proposals falling in this category, and the party advancing them may insist on their inclusion in any contract executed.

(3) *Voluntary subjects.* These are proposals that fall outside the mandatory category of "wages, hours, and other terms and conditions of employment." They may be placed on the table for voluntary bargaining and agreement. But the other party may not be required either to bargain on them or to agree to their inclusion in the contract. Insistence on them as a condition to the execution of a contract is a violation of the bargaining duty under the Act.

Source references: NLRB v. Wooster Division of Borg-Warner Corp., 356 US 342, 42 LRRM 2034 (1958); Robben W. Fleming, "The Changing Duty to Bargain," *LLJ*, April 1963; Joseph P. McManemin, "Subject Matter of Collective Bargaining," *LLJ*, Dec. 1962; Donald H. Wollett, "The Borg-Warner Case and the Role of the NLRB in the Bargaining Process," *NYU 12th Annual Conference on Labor*, ed. by Emanuel Stein (Albany: Bender, 1959).

See also MANDATORY SUBJECTS FOR BARGAINING, PERMISSIVE SUBJECTS FOR BARGAINING, PROHIBITED SUBJECTS FOR BARGAINING.

boring from within A procedure used by the Socialists, but more effectively by the Communists, to gain their objectives within the trade union movement. During the period in which the policy called for "boring from within," no separate, militant, or identified Communist union was set up. Instead, the objectives were to be achieved by infiltrating the existing conservative organizations, building opposition groups and an effective minority to disrupt or to establish a policy sympathetic to the Communist Party program.

See also COMMUNISM IN AMERICAN LABOR UNIONS.

boss The person who gives orders and is to be obeyed. A foreman may function as the boss to the employees in his gang. A plant superintendent may be the boss to the supervisors under him, while the board of directors may be the boss to the president of the company.

"bottom line" The standard set forth in the EEOC Uniform Guidelines on Employee Selection Procedures that, where it is found that the total employee selection process does not have an adverse impact, the federal enforcement agencies in the exercise of their prosecutorial discretion, in usual circumstances, will not expect users of the procedures to evaluate the individual components or to validate such individual components. The measure is a result of a decision by the various enforcement agencies that, as a matter of prosecutorial discretion, they will devote their limited enforcement resources to the most serious offenders of EEO laws. It is not a rule of law and does not apply to the processing of individual charges, but to the initiation of enforcement action.

Blumrosen supports the "bottom line" because, among other reasons, it permits employers to "avoid expensive, time-consuming, and uncertain test validation efforts." However, the "bottom line" may not excuse the adverse impact of any unvalidated procedure. The Guidelines specify that under certain circumstances, including instances in which the selection procedure was a significant factor in continuing employment patterns caused by prior discriminatory practices, the employer is expected to evaluate the individual components for adverse impact and take appropriate action.

In *Connecticut v. Teal*, the Supreme Court rejected an employer's nondiscriminatory "bottom line" as a defense under Title VII. The Court ruled that if a "non-job-related" test had adverse impact, then Title VII was violated, even if the overall number of minorities or women hired or promoted showed no discriminatory effect.

Source references: Connecticut v. Teal, 457 US 440, 29 FEP Cases 1 (1982); U.S. EEOC, "Adoption of Questions and Answers to Clarify and Provide a Common Interpretation of the Uniform Guidelines on Employee Selection Procedures," 44 F.R. 11996; ———, "Uniform Guidelines on Employee Selection Procedures," 29 C.F.R. 1607; Alfred W. Blumrosen, "The 'Bottom Line' After *Connecticut v. Teal*," *Employee Relations LJ*, Spring 1983; ———, "Equal Employment Opportunity in the Eighties: The Bottom Line," *Employee Relations LJ*, Spring 1981; Duane E. Thompson and Patricia S. Christiansen, "Court Acceptance of Uniform Guidelines Provisions: The Bottom Line and the Search for Alternatives," *Employee Relations LJ*, Spring 1983; U.S. OPM, *Applicant Data Systems in State and Local Governments* (Washington: 1981).

Boulwarism A collective bargaining approach followed by General Electric Company and named after its vice president for employee and public relations, Lemuel Boulware. It was described by Professor Herbert Northrup as follows: "After careful research, and a full exchange of views with the union bargaining agents for many days, or even weeks before an offer is made, the company puts what it believes proper on the table and changes it only on the basis of what is considered 'new information'."

It was described in more detail by NLRB trial examiner Arthur Leff as embracing the following:

(1) The same basic offer is made to substantially all of the unions with which the company negotiates.
(2) The company, however, does not initially present its offer on a "take-it-or-leave-it" basis. It states "a willingness to make prompt adjustments whenever (but only when) new information from any source or a significant change in facts indicates that its initial offer fell short of being right." But the company also emphasizes that "it will not make any change it believes to be incorrect because of a strike or a threat of a strike. . . ."
(3) As a basic part of the approach, the company "markets" its positions directly to the employees through "an elaborate employee communications system, making use of plant newspapers, daily news digests, employee bulletins, letters to employees' homes, television and radio broadcasts, and other media of mass communication, as well as personal contacts." It is the company's belief that the employees, in turn, may influence union acceptance of the offer.
(4) Finally, it is the company's policy to make certain that no union receives favored treatment. Moreover, it applies the terms of the basic offer made to the unions to the employees who are not represented by a union.

Source references: General Electric Co., 150 NLRB 192, 57 LRRM 1491 (1964); Lemuel R. Boulware, *The Truth About Boulwarism* (Washington: BNA, 1969); Morris D. Forkosch, "Take It or Leave It as a Bargaining Technique," *LLJ*, Nov. 1967; Kenneth A. Housman, "Final Offer Selection: An Arbitration Technique," *Personnel Administration*, Jan./Feb. 1972; James W. Kuhn, "A New Glance of Boulwarism: The Significance of the GE Strike," *LLJ*, Sept. 1970; Herbert R. Northrup, *Boulwarism* (Ann Arbor: Univ. of

Michigan, Bureau of IR, 1964); ———, "Boulwarism vs. Coalitionism—The 1966 GE Negotiations," *Management of Personnel Quarterly*, Summer 1966; ———, "The Case for Boulwarism," *Harvard BR*, Sept./Oct. 1963.

See also GENERAL ELECTRIC CASE.

bourbon Generally a person opposed to liberal or progressive labor legislation. The term is used more frequently in its political connotation as the equivalent of Tory, Rightist, Conservative, or Standpatter—a person opposed to change.

boycott Concerted action on the part of employees and a union to refuse to patronize or do business with an employer. The action is generally part of economic or strike strategy against an employer because of unfair labor practices or action which the union thinks inimical to its welfare. Where the refusal to patronize is directed against the employer directly involved in the dispute it is a *primary boycott*. Where the economic pressure is exerted through parties not directly involved in the dispute, or where failure to patronize or handle the products or supply the services affect third parties, they are generally held to be *secondary boycotts*. The courts have not always agreed where the line between primary and secondary boycotts is to be drawn.

The Taft-Hartley Act proscribes the secondary boycott and makes it an enjoinable act unprotected by the general provisions of the Norris-LaGuardia Act.

The origin of the term is attributed to the agrarian land agitation in Ireland around 1880–1881. The procedure adopted by irate tenants against Captain Boycott, an agent for an Irish landlord, who was harsh in his treatment of his tenants, was effective and widely used. A person given the Boycott treatment was cut off from all social intercourse with his neighbors; no one was permitted to take his land, work for him, supply him with goods or services, or to aid him in any other way.

Source references: Paul A. Brinker, "The Ally Doctrine," *LLJ*, Sept. 1972; William L. Dennis, "The Supreme Court and the Taft-Hartley Boycott Provisions," *NYU 5th Annual Conference on Labor*, ed. by Emanuel Stein (Albany: Bender, 1952); William Feldesman, "Restrictions on Picketing and Boycotts: 'Proviso, and Proviso, and Proviso,—'," *LLJ*, April 1963; Michael A. Gordon, "The Labor Boycott in New York City, 1880–1886," *Labor History*, Spring 1975; Harry W. Laidler, *Boycotts and the Labor Struggle* (New York: John Lane Co., 1914); Michael Henry Levin, " 'Wholly Unconcerned': The Scope and Meaning of the Ally Doctrine Under Section 8(b)(4) of the NLRA," *IR Law Digest*, Oct. 1971; David S. Lindau, "Picketing and Boycott: A Functional Analysis—Management Viewpoint," *NYU 15th Annual Conference on Labor*, ed. by Emanuel Stein (Albany: Bender, 1962); Robert H. I. Palgrave, *Palgrave's Dictionary of Political Economy*, ed. by Henry Higgs (3 vols., London: Macmillan, 1926); Arthur B. Smith, Jr., "Work Preservation Boycotts: 'The Drawing of Lines More Nice than Obvious,' " *Industrial Relations LJ*, Fall 1976; Donald H. Wollett, "The Weapons of Conflict: Picketing and Boycotts," *Public Policy and Collective Bargaining*, ed. by Joseph Shister, Benjamin Aaron, and Clyde W. Summers (New York: Harper, IRRA Pub. 27, 1962); Leo Wolman, *The Boycott in American Trade Unions* (Baltimore: Johns Hopkins Press, 1916).

See also PRIMARY BOYCOTT, SECONDARY BOYCOTT.

Boys Markets case A Supreme Court decision holding that an employer is to be ordered to arbitrate as a condition of obtaining an injunction against union violation of a contractual no-strike clause. The Court emphasized that the *Boys Markets* decision was a narrow ruling, but that an injunction may issue if the agreement contains a mandatory grievance arbitration procedure, the strike concerns a grievance that is subject to the contractual grievance arbitration procedure, and the court determines that the employer would incur irreparable injury more from the denial of the injunction than the union would from its issuance.

The Court thus overturned its ruling in *Sinclair Refining v. Atkinson* and adopted the principles stated in the *Sinclair* dissent.

Source references: Boys Markets, Inc. v. Retail Clerks, Local 770, 389 US 235, 74 LRRM 2257 (1970); John D. Canoni, "Unauthorized Strikes and Illegal Actions: A Management View," *NYU 36th Annual National*

Conference on Labor, ed. by Richard Adelman (New York: Bender, 1983); Martin H. Dodd, "Of *Mastro* and *Marathon*: Waiver of the Right to Strike Over Unfair Labor Practices in a *Boys Markets* World," *Industrial Relations LJ*, Vol. 5, No. 2, 1983; Alan I. Horowitz, "The Applicability of *Boys Markets* Injunctions to Refusals to Cross a Picket Line," *IR Law Digest*, Fall 1976; Harry H. Rains, "*Boys Market* Injunctions: Strict Scrutiny of the Presumption of Arbitrability," *LLJ*, Jan. 1977; William C. Zifchak, "Coping with Sympathy Strikes After *Buffalo Forge*: Never Send a *Boys* to do a Man's Job," *Employee Relations LJ*, Spring 1977.

See also SINCLAIR REFINING CO. V. ATKINSON.

bracero system A program initiated during World War II to relieve manpower shortages in American agriculture, involving the importation of Mexican field hands or braceros ("the Mexican who works with his hand") as seasonal farm laborers, chiefly in California and Texas. Long opposed by organized labor and the American farm worker, Public Law 78, which legalized the bracero system in July 1951, was terminated by Congress in December 1964.

Source references: Lamar B. Jones, "Public Law 78 and Farm Manpower Problems," *LLJ*, Feb. 1966; Michael Kelly Schutz, "The Bracero and California Agriculture," *Industrial and Labor Relations Forum*, Nov. 1965.

See also CALIFORNIA FARM LABOR PANEL.

brass chills A metal fume fever first commonly associated with brass foundries which used zinc. It has been reported that similar fever is produced by other metals, including cadmium, lead, manganese, mercury, and magnesium. The inhaling of heavy concentrations of the metal fumes has led to this industrial disease. Workers frequently know the disease under such other names as brass founders ague, oxide chills, galvo and zinc oxide fever, metal ague, spelter shakes (chills).

Source references: William B. Gafafer (ed.), *Manual of Industrial Hygiene and Medical Services in War Industries* (Philadelphia: Saunder, 1943); R. T. Johnstone and Seward E. Miller, *Occupational Diseases and Industrial Medicine* (Philadelphia: Saunders, 1960).

breach of contract *See* ABROGATION OF AGREEMENT, ENFORCEMENT OF AGREEMENT, NULLIFICATION OF AGREEMENT.

bread and butter unionism *See* BUSINESS UNIONISM.

break-in time The period of time allowed under a group incentive plan to permit the necessary adjustment for new employees added to the group. Also the time allowed an employee to adjust to a new job.

Brewery, Flour, Cereal, Soft Drink and Distillery Workers of America; International Union of United (AFL-CIO) The earliest labor union of brewery workers was organized in Cincinnati on December 26, 1879. In 1886 delegates from a number of cities formed the National Union of Brewers of the United States. It affiliated with the AFL in March 1887. It changed its name to the National Union of the United Brewers Workmen of the United States in the same year and extended its jurisdiction.

The brewery workers early adopted the principle of industrial unionism and this led to constant jurisdictional battles within the AFL. In June 1907 the AFL revoked the union's charter. The AFL Convention restored it in November 1907, recognizing the union's jurisdiction over all workers employed in the brewing industry. Prohibition led to many difficulties and the necessity to organize the soft-drink industry.

Because of its industrial union attitude and organization it joined the CIO. Its official publication was *The Brewery Worker*.

On November 6, 1973, the union merged with the International Brotherhood of Teamsters, Chauffeurs, Warehousemen and Helpers of America (Ind).

See also TEAMSTERS, CHAUFFEURS, WAREHOUSEMEN AND HELPERS OF AMERICA; INTERNATIONAL BROTHERHOOD OF (IND).

Brick and Clay Workers of America; The United (AFL-CIO) The union was organized in Chicago on May 18, 1894. It was known as the National Brick Makers' Alliance and held that name until 1909. In that year it extended its jurisdiction over the terra-cotta industry and changed its name to the International Alliance of Brick, Tile, and Terra-Cotta Workers. Dissension in the organization led to the formation of a second organization known as the United Brick and Clay Workers. It operated as a dual union, but agreement finally was reached with the officers of the International Alliance. It merged with the Aluminum Workers International Union (AFL-CIO) on September 1, 1981, to form the Aluminum, Brick and Clay Workers International Union (AFL-CIO).

See also ALUMINUM, BRICK AND CLAY WORKERS INTERNATIONAL UNION (AFL-CIO).

Bricklayers and Allied Craftsmen; International Union of (AFL-CIO) Formerly known as the Bricklayers, Masons and Plasterers' International Union of America (AFL-CIO), the union adopted its present name in the early 1970s.

The official monthly publications are *The Journal of the International Union of Bricklayers and Allied Craftsmen* and *Chalkline.*

Address: 815 15th St., N.W., Washington, D.C. 20005. Tel (202) 783–3788

Bricklayers, Masons and Plasterers' International Union of America (AFL-CIO) Organized on October 17, 1865, as the International Bricklayers' Union of North America. It changed its name to the National Bricklayers' Union in 1868. It reorganized in 1881 and permitted masons to enter the union. In 1883 it changed its name to Bricklayers and Masons' International Union. It later absorbed the Stone Masons' International Union. In 1910, the union extended its jurisdiction to plasterers and changed its name to Bricklayers, Masons, and Plasterers' International Union of America. It remained independent until 1916, when it joined the AFL and absorbed marble setters, who belonged to the International Association of Marble Workers. The union changed its name to the International Union of Bricklayers and Allied Craftsmen (AFL-CIO) in the early 1970s.

See also BRICKLAYERS AND ALLIED CRAFTSMEN; INTERNATIONAL UNION OF (AFL-CIO).

bridging Early retirement payments designed to supplement the retirement income of an eligible employee until social security or other regular benefit becomes payable. Under plans found in private sector agreements, the employer pays early retirees a supplement equal to social security until the retiree qualifies for the normal benefit.

Under the Washington University "bridge benefit" plan, eligible employees retiring at age 65 may elect to defer receipt of annuity benefits until age 70. During the interim, the employer pays a "bridge benefit" equal to 80 percent of the employee's average final five years of salary less the primary social security benefit.

Source references: Mitchell Meyer and Harland Fox, *Early Retirement Programs* (New York: The Conference Board, 1971); Gloria W. White, "Bridge Over Troubled Waters: An Approach to Early Retirement," *Journal of the College and University Personnel Association,* Summer 1981.

British Trades Union Congress (TUC) The central coordinating body of the British trade union movement founded in 1868. Its functions are similar to those of the American Federation of Labor, prior to its merger with the CIO.

The TUC operates primarily through its General Council and six major departments—Economic, Education, International, Organization, Production, and Social Insurance. It is an active member of the International Labour Organization and was one of the founding members of the International Confederation of Free Trade Unions in 1949. Its 12.1 million membership represents 93 percent of union members in the United Kingdom. Some 100 organizations are affiliated with the TUC.

Source references: J. Rojot, "Background Notes on Major Industrial Countries," *Comparative Labour Law and Industrial Relations,* ed. by R. Blanpain (Washington: BNA, 1982); George Smith, "British Trades Union Congress," *Free Labour World,* July/Aug. 1972; TUC, *Trade Unionism: The Evidence of the Trades Union Congress to the Royal Commission on Trade Unions and Employers' Associations* (London: 1966).

Broadcast Employees and Technicians; National Association of (AFL-CIO) A union formerly known as the National Association of Broadcast Engineers and Technicians (CIO). Its bimonthly publication is *NABET News.*

Address: 7101 Wisconsin Ave., Suite 1303, Bethesda, Md. 20814. Tel. (301) 657–8420

broken time Any work schedule or shift where the employee works for a certain period, then is off duty and returns for another period of work. It was not uncommon in industries or services which had peak loads, such as restaurants and local transportation companies which required large work forces during rush hours. More frequently called a split shift.

Brook Farm A cooperative communal effort in the 1840s in West Roxbury, Massachusetts. Established as the Brook Farm Institute for Agriculture and Education, it attracted New England intellectuals and radicals dissatisfied with the existing social and economic order. Among its leaders were George Ripley, Nathaniel Hawthorne, and Charles A. Dana. It went out of existence around 1847.

Source references: Harold U. Faulkner, *American Political and Social History* (4th ed., New York: Crofts, 1945); Vernon L. Parrington, "Brook Farm," *Encyclopedia of the Social Sciences*, ed. by Edwin R. A. Seligman (Vol. 3, New York: Macmillan, 1930).

Brookings Institution A privately financed research agency, located in Washington, D.C. Concerned primarily with problems of public concern in the field of economics and business. Occasional studies deal with industrial relations.

Source references: E. R. Livernash, "Brookings Research Project on the Influence of Unions Upon Management: A Reappraisal of Union Policies and Industrial Management," *Proceedings of the 12th A/M, IRRA*, ed. by David Johnson (Madison: 1960); Lewis L. Lorwin, *The American Federation of Labor* (Washington: Brookings Institution, 1933); Harold Metz, *Labor Policy of the Federal Government* (Washington: Brookings Institution, 1943).

Brookwood Labor College One of the best known resident schools for the training of leadership of trade unions. It was established in 1921 near Katonah, New York. It provided a two-year course including economics, English, public speaking, American history, statistics, labor law, labor journalism, and problems of trade unionism. It expected students to return to the labor movement after graduation.

It received support from the garment unions and other progressive labor groups. In 1927, at the insistence of Matthew Woll, the Executive Council of the AFL urged its affiliates to withdraw their support of the College. The attack came not only from the right, but also from the left. The Communists attacked the College in 1929. In 1932 A. J. Muste, Director of the College, and a group of teachers withdrew. The College closed in 1937. During its 16 years it had graduated some 400 workers.

Broom and Whisk Makers' Union of America; International (AFL-CIO) The union organized in 1893 and affiliated with the AFL. It disbanded in August 1962.

brother Organized workers frequently refer to their co-workers as "brothers." With expansion of the labor movement and the influx of women, union correspondence to members, formerly addressed "Dear Sir and Brother," will frequently start out "Dear Brothers and Sisters."

brotherhood Many of the older labor organizations used the term "Brotherhood" in their official name to indicate solidarity and common interest. They regarded themselves as members or brothers of the same organization or union.

Source reference: Samuel Gompers, *Seventy Years of Life and Labor* (New York: Dutton, 1925).

Brown-Olds doctrine The NLRB in the *Brown-Olds Plumbing and Heating Corp.* case held that any collective bargaining agreement which contained a union security provision which was unlawful would be remedied by reimbursing or returning all of the dues collected under the unlawful union security provision. The employer or the union or both could be held responsible for making the reimbursement to the employees.

Source references: Brown-Olds Plumbing & Heating Corp., 115 NLRB 594, 37 LRRM 1360 (1956); Jerome D. Fenton, "NLRB's 'Brown-Olds' Remedy for Illegal Hiring Arrangements," *MLR*, Feb. 1959.

Bryn Mawr summer school One of the interesting efforts in the field of worker education started in 1921 with the establishment of a summer school for wage-earning women which provided a regular program of courses to assist workers in meeting their trade union problems. It was forced to close in 1937 when the Depression impaired scholarship support. In 1939, the school was moved to West Park, New York, where it operated as the Hudson Shore Labor School. The school closed because of the lack of financial support.

Source reference: Barbara Mayer Wertheimer (ed.), *Labor Education for Women Workers* (Philadelphia: Temple UP, 1981).

Bucks' Stove and Range case A leading court case involving the use of the unfair list. After a strike at the Bucks' Stove and Range Company's plant in St. Louis, its products were put on the unfair list by a local union and later by the St. Louis Trades and Labor Assembly. *The American Federationist* included its name on the unfair list in May 1907. In December the company obtained an injunction against the AFL and its affiliated bodies restraining them from boycotting the company's products. When the officers of the AFL refused to comply with the injunction they were held in contempt and sentenced to serve jail terms. Contempt action was against Gompers (President), Morrison (Secretary), and Mitchell (Vice-President). The Supreme Court set aside the contempt order on technical grounds.

Source references: Gompers v. Bucks' Stove & Range Co., 221 US 418 (1911); Selig Perlman and Philip Taft, *History of Labor in the United States, 1896–1932* (Vol. 4, New York: Macmillan, 1935); E. E. Witte, *The Government in Labor Disputes* (New York: McGraw-Hill, 1932).

budget submission date Negotiations in the public sector may lead to agreement by the agency and union to an adjustment of wages as well as other cost items. Since the agency or department may have no authority to levy or obtain funds except through some other state or municipal agency, agreements which involve funds must be submitted to the budget agency for presentation to the authority which can properly appropriate the funds to implement the agreement. Negotiations provided under certain statutes require that sufficient time be allowed to permit the parties to reach agreement in advance of the budget submission date.

The Pennsylvania Public Employee Relations Act (Act 195, L. 1970) defines it as:

> . . . the date by which under the law or practice a public employer's proposed budget, or budget containing proposed expenditures applicable to such public employer is submitted to the Legislature or other similar body for final action. For the purposes of this act, the budget submission date for the Commonwealth shall be February 1 of each year and for a nonprofit organization or institution, the last day of its fiscal year.

Source reference: Harold S. Roberts, *Labor-Management Relations in the Public Service* (Honolulu: Univ. of Hawaii Press, 1970).

bug *See* UNION LABEL (BUG).

Building and Construction Trades Department The Building and Construction Trades Department of the AFL-CIO was established by the AFL in 1908. It encourages the formation of local organizations in the building and construction trades, the adjustment of existing trade disputes, the advancement of the interests of the industry, and the development of greater harmony between employers and employees in the industry. Its publication is *The Builders*.

Organizations affiliated with the Department are: Asbestos Workers; Boilermakers; Bricklayers; Carpenters; Electrical Workers; Elevator Constructors; Operating Engineers; Iron Workers; Laborers; Painters; Plasterers; Plumbers; Roofers; Sheet Metal Workers; and Tile, Marble and Terrazzo Finishers.

Address: AFL-CIO Bldg., 815 16th St., N.W., Washington, D.C. 20006. Tel. (202) 347–1461

Source references: A. T. Helbing, *The Departments of the American Federation of Labor* (Baltimore: Johns Hopkins Press, 1931); Lewis L. Lorwin, *The American Federation of Labor* (Washington: Brookings Institution, 1933).

See also AFL-CIO DEPARTMENTS.

Building Service Employees' International Union (AFL-CIO) Organized in 1917 and affiliated with the AFL in 1921. It changed its name to the Service Employees' International Union (AFL-CIO) in 1968.

See also SERVICE EMPLOYEES' INTERNATIONAL UNION (AFL-CIO).

building trades The skilled trades in the building industry. These include: carpenters, painters, electricians, plumbers, hod carriers, bricklayers, stone masons, etc. These crafts are generally highly organized with a well-developed apprenticeship system.

bulletin boards One of the frequently used procedures in plants of any major size is the use of bulletin boards. These may be provided by the employer, or the union may be permitted to set up bulletin boards at various places in the plant. The bulletin boards serve as a convenient place for posting union notices of meetings and other union activities. They also are used for posting job vacancies, seniority lists, shop rules, layoff notices, etc. Some contracts may require employer authorization before posting.

bumping The procedure used during layoffs where an employee with greater seniority has the right to displace an employee of lesser seniority. This process is more widely used in companies with plantwide seniority in which jobs are somewhat interchangeable or the work not too highly skilled. It is designed to protect the job rights of the employees with greater length of service. In some plants the right to bump a lower seniority employee is limited to employees in the same department.

The bumping process is utilized during periods of layoff, reorganization, or mechanization causing job elimination.

See also SENIORITY.

bundle stiffs Migratory workers who go from job to job carrying their possessions in a bundle. The term is outdated.

See also MIGRATORY WORKER.

Bunting v. Oregon A decision of the Supreme Court which upheld legislation by the state of Oregon which prohibited as a "health measure" the employment of workers in mills, factories, and manufacturing establishments in excess of 10 hours a day, except under specified conditions.

The case came to the Supreme Court on appeal from the Supreme Court of Oregon, which had upheld the state law. The Supreme Court dismissed the argument that the hours limitation was essentially a wage regulation (provision was made for overtime up to three hours) and that the law deprived persons of property without due process of law.

Source reference: Bunting v. Oregon, 243 US 426 (1916).

burdening or obstructing commerce *See* AFFECTING COMMERCE, COMMERCE CLAUSE.

burden of proof According to Fairweather, the general rule in nondisciplinary proceedings is that the grieving party, typically the union, bears the initial burden of presenting sufficient evidence to prove its contention. In a discharge case, the burden of proceeding first, to establish proof of cause for discharge, is on the employer.

The initial burden of proof in employment discrimination cases rests with the complainant. If a prima facie case of discrimination is shown, the burden of producing nondiscriminatory reasons for the challenged action is borne by the defendant. If this burden is met, it shifts back to the complainant to show either that the defendant's argument is pretextual or that there are other procedures which could be used and which have less impact on protected classes.

Source references: Texas Dept. of Community Affairs v. Burdine, 450 US 248, 25 FEP Cases 113 (1981); Maurice C. Benewitz, "Discharge, Arbitration and the Quantum of Proof," *AJ*, June 1973; Alan A. Blakeboro, "Allocation of Proof in ADEA Cases: A Critique of the Prima Facie Case Approach," *Industrial Relations LJ*, Vol. 4, no. 1, 1980; Owen Fairweather, *Practice and Procedure in Labor Arbitration* (2d ed., Washington: BNA, 1983); Ronald F. Miller, "Evidence and Proof in Arbitration," *Journal of Collective Negotiations in the Public Sector*, Vol. 5, no. 4, 1976; Martin F. Scheinman, *Evidence and Proof in Arbitration* (Ithaca: Cornell Univ., NYSSILR, 1977).

Bureau of Apprenticeship and Training (BAT) Established in 1937 as the Apprenticeship and Training Service, BAT is a division of the Employment and Training Administration, U.S. Department of Labor. The Bureau carries out the objectives of the National Apprenticeship Act to promote the establishment and improvement of apprenticeship and other forms of allied industrial training.

Source reference: U.S. Dept. of Labor, Manpower Administration, *The National Apprenticeship Program* (Washington: 1966).

See also APPRENTICESHIP, FEDERAL COMMITTEE ON APPRENTICESHIP TRAINING.

Bureau of Employees' Compensation Provided workers compensation protection, safety, and accident-prevention programs. The Bureau was transferred from the Federal Security Agency to the Department of Labor by Reorganization Plan No. 19 of 1950.

It was abolished on March 13, 1972, and its functions are currently carried out by the Employment Standards Administration.

Source reference: U.S. Dept. of Labor, *The Anvil and the Plow: A History of the United States Department of Labor* (Washington: 1963).

Bureau of Employment Security Under Reorganization Plan No. 2 of 1949, the Bureau was transferred from the Federal Security Agency to the U.S. Department of Labor. The Bureau, abolished by Secretary of Labor's Order 14–69, effective March 17, 1969, was responsible for two major programs—the U.S. Employment Service and the Unemployment Insurance Service. Both programs are presently administered by the Employment and Training Administration.

The major publications of the Bureau included:

Area Trends in Employment and Unemployment (monthly) (currently issued by the Employment and Training Administration),
Benefit Series Service (monthly),
Dictionary of Occupational Titles (currently issued by the Employment and Training Administration),
Employment and Wages of Workers Covered by State Unemployment Insurance Laws (quarterly),
Employment Service Statistics,
Farm Labor Developments,
Unemployment Insurance Claims (weekly),
Unemployment Insurance Statistics (monthly).

Source reference: Federal Register, April 15, 1969.

See also EMPLOYMENT AND TRAINING ADMINISTRATION (ETA), U.S. EMPLOYMENT SERVICE.

Bureau of International Labor Affairs Established within the Department of Labor on December 31, 1959, replacing the Office of International Labor Affairs originally established in 1947. Its functions and responsibilities include advising on the implications of international labor developments in relation to U.S. foreign and domestic policy, analyzing the impact of domestic policy and developments on labor aspects of foreign affairs, and recommending operations designed to promote the U.S. national interest in the foreign labor field. The Deputy Under Secretary responsible for the Bureau serves as the U.S. Government member of the Governing Body of the ILO and as head of the U.S. delegation to the Annual Conference of the ILO. The Bureau assists in carrying out the Department's responsibilities with respect to the labor attaché and Foreign Service labor-reporting programs; representation on delegation to UNESCO, the Organization for Economic Cooperation and Development (OECD), and the General Agreement on Tariffs and Trade (GATT); overseeing the adjustment assistance program under the Trade Act of 1974; and other activities affecting labor which are designed to implement foreign policy.

Bureau of Labor-Management Reports *See* OFFICE OF LABOR-MANAGEMENT STANDARDS ENFORCEMENT.

Bureau of Labor Standards Founded as the Division of Labor Standards, this Labor Department agency was concerned with developing and establishing labor standards, primarily in the field of labor legislation. It worked with state labor agencies and maintained eight regional coordinating offices. It also worked in the areas of grievances, supervision, and safety.

The Bureau celebrated its 30th anniversary on November 17, 1964. The functions of the Bureau were absorbed by the Occupational Safety and Health Administration in May 1971.

Source reference: U.S. Dept. of Labor, Bureau of Labor Standards, *A Report of the Bureau of Labor Standards 30th Anniversary* (Washington: Bull. no. 272, 1965).

See also OCCUPATIONAL SAFETY AND HEALTH ACT (OSHA) OF 1970.

Bureau of Labor Statistics One of the major divisions in the U.S. Department of Labor which is concerned primarily with collection, analysis, and dissemination of statistics in the field of labor. The continuing series on wages, prices, cost of living, strike statistics, employment, etc., are published in the *Monthly Labor Review*. The Bureau conducts special studies of working conditions and publishes the results of these studies in monographs. Summaries of the studies generally are published in the *Monthly Labor Review*. In 1968 it issued a catalog listing its major publications entitled *Publications of the Bureau of Labor Statistics, 1886–1967* (Bull. 1567).

The Bureau, which is headed by the Commissioner of Labor Statistics, has no enforcement or administrative functions. Its basic data is collected from workers, businesses, and from other government agencies on a voluntary basis; the research projects which it conducts grow out of the needs of Congress, the federal government, and the state governments.

The Bureau's regular publications include:

CPI Detailed Report (monthly),
Current Wage Developments (monthly),
Employment and Earnings (monthly),
Monthly Labor Review (monthly),
Occupational Outlook Handbook (biennial),
Occupational Outlook Quarterly (quarterly),
Producer Prices and Price Indexes (monthly).

A number of major publications were discontinued beginning in 1981–82.

Source references: Ewan Clague, *The Bureau of Labor Statistics* (New York: Praeger, 1968); Joseph P. Goldberg and William T. Moye, "The AFL and a National BLS: Labor's Role is Crystallized," *MLR*, March 1982; Geoffrey H. Moore, "Long-Range Program Objectives for BLS," *MLR*, Oct. 1969; "Reagan Budget Slashes Could Mean Elimination of Several BLS Series," *Daily Labor Report*, no. 216, Nov. 9, 1981; Gustavus A. Weber, *The Bureau of Labor Statistics: United States Department of Labor: Its History, Activities and Organization* (Washington: Bull. no. 319, 1922).

See also CONSUMER PRICE INDEX, MONTHLY LABOR REVIEW, WORK STOPPAGE STATISTICS.

Bureau of National Affairs, Inc.; The A private information service established in 1929. It publishes books, special reports, and over 60 daily, weekly, biweekly, and monthly information services on a variety of topics in the labor, legal, economic, environmental, safety, and tax management fields. BNA provides a complete labor service covering federal, state, and local developments. A list of BNA services appears in Appendix A.

Address: 1231 25th St., N.W., Washington, D.C. 20037. Tel. (202) 452–4200

Source reference: Dean Dinwoodey, "BNA Builds Business on Factual Reports," *Christian Science Monitor*, March 6–9, 1957.

Bureau of Old Age and Survivors Insurance Originally a part of the SSA under the Federal Security Administrator in 1946, the Bureau and the SSA were transferred to the Department of Health, Education, and Welfare when HEW was established in 1953. The Bureau was responsible for the administration of benefit payments to those retired workers and their survivors covered by the Social Security Act. In 1963 the SSA was reorganized and the Bureau of Old Age and Survivors Insurance was abolished. Its duties have been assumed by the Bureau of Retirement and Survivors Insurance. The 1979 reorganization of the SSA eliminated the Bureau of Retirement and Survivors Insurance.

Source references: U.S. Dept. of HEW, SSA, *Social Security Sources in Federal Records, 1934–1950*, by Abe Bortz (Washington: Research Report no. 30, 1969); U.S. National Commission on Social Security, *Social Security in America's Future* (Washington: 1981).

See also SOCIAL SECURITY ADMINISTRATION.

Bureau of Retirement and Survivors Insurance *See* BUREAU OF OLD AGE AND SURVIVORS INSURANCE.

Burlesque Artists Association Formerly a branch of the Associated Actors and Artistes of America (AFL-CIO). The Associated Actors and Artistes of America voted on June 19, 1957, to withdraw the Burlesque Artists Association's charter and asked the American Guild of Variety Artists to assume jurisdiction in the burlesque field.

See also VARIETY ARTISTS; AMERICAN GUILD OF.

burnout *See* STRESS.

Burns Detective Agency A private detective agency headed by William Burns which in the past was active in helping employers break strikes.

See also BACK-TO-WORK MOVEMENT, BERGOFF TECHNIQUE.

business agent A full-time local union officer, elected or appointed, who handles the union's financial, administrative, or labor relations problems.

Source reference: Van Dusen Kennedy and Wilma R. Krauss, *The Business Agent and His Union* (2d ed., Berkeley: UC, Institute of IR, 1964).

See also UNION LEADERSHIP.

business cycle Fluctuations in business activity which show major booms and recessions. The growth and decline of the American labor movement historically shows the effect of the business cycle.

Source references: Carl A. Dauten, *Business Cycles and Forecasting* (Cincinnati: Southwestern Publishing, 1961); James A. Estey, *Business Cycles* (New York: PH, 1941); Robert A. Gordon, "Is the Business Cycle Obsolete?" *The Economic Outlook for 1968*, Papers Presented at the 15th Annual Conference on the Economic Outlook (Ann Arbor: Univ. of Michigan, Nov. 16–17, 1967); Wesley C. Mitchell, *Business Cycles: The Problem and Its Setting* (New York: NBER, 1927); Albert T. Sommers, *The Widening Cycle, An Examination of U.S. Experience with Stabilization Policy in the Last Decade* (New York: The Conference Board, Report no. 670, 1975).

business necessity A standard used to justify a facially neutral employment practice that has discriminatory impact. In *Griggs*, the Supreme Court held that a policy that had a discriminatory impact might be justified on grounds of business necessity; the test for business necessity requires a showing that an employment practice is related to job performance. Other courts have added interpretations of business necessity as justification on the basis that (1) the challenged practice is essential for the safe and efficient operation of the business and (2) no acceptable alternative with lesser impact is available. Business necessity is understood to exclude inconvenience, annoyance, or expense to the employer.

The OFCCP defines it as "justification for an otherwise prohibited employment practice based on a contractor's proof that: (1) the otherwise prohibited employment practice is essential for the safety and efficiency of the business, and (2) no reasonable alternative with a lesser impact exists."

Source references: Griggs v. Duke Power Co., 401 US 424, 3 FEP Cases 175 (1971); *Robinson v. Lorillard Corp.*, 444 F2d 791, 3 FEP Cases 653 (1971); "Business Necessity Under Title VII of the Civil Rights Act of 1964: A No-Alternative Approach," *IR Law Digest*, Summer 1975; U.S. OFCCP, *Federal Contract Compliance Manual* (Washington: 1979).

business unionism American trade unions of the conservative variety have been characterized as bread-and-butter or "business" unions. Such unions are considered non-idealistic, businesslike, and conservative in political and economic objectives. Their primary program consists of demands for better wages, hours, and working conditions.

Source references: Philip Taft, "A Labor Historian Views Changes in the Trade Union Movement," *MLR*, Sept. 1969; ———, "On the Origins of Business Unionism," *ILRR*, Oct. 1963.

button The insignia, badge, or button worn by members of a union to indicate membership in the union. Although generally designed to show solidarity of the members in a particular company or department, it is sometimes used as an organizing technique to get those who are not members to join.

Byrnes Act *See* ANTI-STRIKEBREAKING ACT (BYRNES ACT).

C

CCC *See* CIVILIAN CONSERVATION CORPS.

CCH *See* COMMERCE CLEARING HOUSE, INC.

CEP *See* CONCENTRATED EMPLOYMENT PROGRAM (CEP).

CETA *See* COMPREHENSIVE EMPLOYMENT AND TRAINING ACT (CETA) OF 1973.

CIO *See* COMMITTEE FOR INDUSTRIAL ORGANIZATION, CONGRESS OF INDUSTRIAL ORGANIZATIONS.

CISC *See* WORLD CONFEDERATION OF LABOUR (WCL).

CIU *See* COOPERS' INTERNATIONAL UNION OF NORTH AMERICA (AFL-CIO).

CJA *See* CARPENTERS AND JOINERS OF AMERICA; UNITED BROTHERHOOD OF (AFL-CIO).

CLA *See* CHRISTIAN LABOR ASSOCIATION OF THE UNITED STATES OF AMERICA (IND).

CLGA *See* COMPOSERS AND LYRICISTS GUILD OF AMERICA (IND).

CLGW *See* CEMENT, LIME, GYPSUM, AND ALLIED WORKERS INTERNATIONAL UNION; UNITED (AFL-CIO).

CLUW *See* COALITION OF LABOR UNION WOMEN (CLUW).

COIU *See* INDEPENDENT UNIONS; CONGRESS OF (IND).

COLA *See* COST-OF-LIVING ADJUSTMENT.

COPE *See* AFL-CIO COPE.

CPI *See* CONSUMER PRICE INDEX.

CPS *See* CURRENT POPULATION SURVEY (CPS).

CRA *See* CIVIL RIGHTS ACT OF 1964.

CSC *See* U.S. CIVIL SERVICE COMMISSION (CSC).

CSRA *See* CIVIL SERVICE REFORM ACT OF 1978.

CTA *See* CIVILIAN TECHNICIANS; ASSOCIATION OF (IND).

CWA *See* COMMUNICATIONS WORKERS OF AMERICA (AFL-CIO).

ca' canny A procedure used by the British trades unions many years ago to indicate opposition to employer policy or alleged inadequate wages. It has been variously practiced in the United States in the form of slowdown, limitation of output, or other restrictive work practices designed to reduce output. Related to "sabotage."

cafeteria plans Programs that allow employees to tailor a compensation package according to their needs. Sometimes referred to as flexible benefit plans, these plans provide employees with the opportunity to satisfy their own compensation preferences within a given dollar allowance. Cafeteria plans are so termed because, like cafeterias, they provide a limited or extensive range of choices. Some plans may allow employees to choose to increase their retirement income or leave or to better their health or dental insurance or their long-term disability benefit coverage.

Source references: Albert Cole, Jr., "Flexible Benefits Are a Key to Better Employee Relations," *PJ*, Jan. 1983; Richard J. Farrell, "Compensation and Benefits," *PJ*, Nov. 1976; George T. Milkovich and Michael J. Delaney, "A Note on Cafeteria Pay Plans," *IR*, Feb. 1975; James H. Shea, "Cautions About Cafeteria-Style Benefit Plans," *PJ*, Jan. 1981; Gerard Tavernier, "How American Can Manages Its Flexible Benefits Program," *Management Review*, Aug. 1980; David J. Thomsen, "Introducing Cafeteria Compensation in Your

Company," *PJ*, March 1977; John O. Todd, "'Cafeteria Compensation': Making Management Motivators Meaningful," *PJ*, May 1975.

caisson disease Sometimes known as "the bends." The disease results from a sudden change in pressure or from the use of compressed air, as in construction of tunnels, working under water, etc. It is an industrial hazard for certain construction workers required to work in deep water.

California Farm Labor Panel The Secretary of Labor on April 15, 1965, issued an order (Secretary's Order No. 1165) to establish a panel of three members for the purpose of advising him "with respect to certifications at the request of the Attorney General pursuant to the Immigration and Nationality Act, Public Law 414, 82nd Congress (66 Stat. 163) relating to the admission of non-immigrant aliens to perform temporary labor or services in the United States."

The original panel consisted of Benjamin Aaron, a member of the Law School faculty at UCLA and director of the Institute of Industrial Relations, chairman; Daniel G. Aldrich, Jr., Chancellor of the University of California; and Arthur Ross, former director of the Institute of Industrial Relations at Berkeley.

The functions of the panel are set out in sections a, b, and c of Secretary's Order No. 1165:

a. The Panel shall make findings of fact and recommendations to the Secretary of Labor regarding applications for the certification of foreign workers to California growers under Public Law 414. This will be done after such hearings of interested parties as the Panel determines to be appropriate. The provisions of the Immigration and Nationality Act and the Department of Labor Regulations of December 19, 1964 (20 CFR Sec. 602.10), will be the basis for the Panel's findings and recommendations.

b. The Panel shall make recommendations for any further procedures which will effectuate the purpose of serving fully all agricultural labor needs, of relying on domestic workers for this so far as they are available, and of maintaining adequate agricultural wages and working and living conditions.

c. The Panel shall make recommendations for any appropriate arrangements in connection with the hiring of any supplemental laborers certified under Public Law 414.

Source reference: USDL News, No. 6586, April 15, 1965.

California School Employees Association (Ind) An organization affiliated with the American Association of Classified School Employees (Ind). Its monthly publication is the *School Employee*.

Address: P.O. Box 640, 2350 Paragon Dr., San Jose, Calif. 95131. Tel. (408) 263–8000

California State Employees Association (AFL-CIO) A statewide public employee organization of over 105,000 members working in nearly all job classifications in state government and state-run schools. Once affiliated with the Assembly of Governmental Employees, it merged with the Service Employees' International Union in February 1984. It publishes *California State Employee* (bimonthly), *CSUS Campus Voice* (monthly), and *University Voice* (monthly).

Address: 1108 O St., Sacramento, Calif. 95814. Tel. (916) 444–8134

Source reference: California, Dept. of IR and U.S. Dept. of Labor, BLS, *Independent State and Local Public Employee Associations in California, 1968* (n.p., 1969).

call-back pay Extra compensation, frequently at special or premium rates, for employees called back to the job after completion of a regular assignment or work period. Provision is made in some collective agreements that workers called back for such work be guaranteed a minimum number of hours pay. The work performed when called back is usually of a special or emergency nature.

call-in pay The number of hours of pay guaranteed, usually by contract, to a worker who reports to work when there is insufficient work for him to do. In general usage call-in pay applies to situations where workers report at their regularly scheduled time and the employer has not given adequate notice to the employees not to report.

Some writers distinguish call-in pay from reporting pay. They hold that call-in pay applies to a guarantee of a minimum number of hours when the worker is called in on a day on which he otherwise would not be scheduled to work, and reporting pay, a guarantee on days on which normally he is scheduled to work. No such distinction is made in general usage.

Source reference: C. Wilson Randle and Max S. Wortman, Jr., *Collective Bargaining, Principles and Practices* (2d ed., Boston: Houghton Mifflin, 1966).

call pay *See* CALL-IN PAY.

Canada Industrial Relations and Disputes Investigation Act The law, effective September 1, 1948, formed the basis for the governance of labor-management relations, including recognition and collective bargaining. It defined and prohibited unfair labor practices, provided for the certification of trade unions, and established procedures for the negotiation of collective agreements. It prohibited work stoppages and changes in terms of employment while an agreement was in effect and also until collective bargaining and conciliation processes were exhausted. It established the Canada Labour Relations Board and authorized the appointment of Industrial Inquiry Commissions to investigate disputes or complaints concerning violations of the Act. The law was replaced by the Canada Labour Code of 1970.

Source references: A. C. Crysler, *Handbook on Canadian Labour Law* (Toronto: Carswell, 1957); Thomas M. Eberlee, "Labor Law and Its Effects on Collective Bargaining, The Federal Perspective," *Industrial Relations in Canada: Towards a Better Understanding* (Ottawa: The Conference Board in Canada, Canadian Studies no. 49, 1977); H. D. Woods and Sylvia Ostry, *Labour Policy and Labour Economics in Canada* (Toronto: Macmillan of Canada, 1962).

See also CANADIAN INDUSTRIAL DISPUTES INVESTIGATION ACT (1907).

Canada Labour Code Federal law enacted in 1970, governing employment and collective bargaining in industries within the authority of the Parliament of Canada such as navigation, railways, shipping, ships, air transport, telegraph and cable systems, broadcasting, banking, and Crown Corporations such as Post Canada. Some 600,000 employees come under the jurisdiction of the Code.

The Code provides for certification of unions as bargaining agents, unfair practices, conciliation of labor disputes, and prohibits strikes during the term of a collective bargaining agreement. The law is administered by the Minister of Labour and information may be obtained from the Department of Labour, Ottawa.

The Code supersedes the Industrial Relations and Disputes Investigations Act, Canada Fair Employment Practices Act, Female Employees Equal Pay Act, and the Canadian Labour (Standards) Code. In addition to the section titled "Industrial Relations," the Code covers "Fair Employment Practices," "Standard Hours, Wages, Vacations and Holidays," and "Safety of Employees."

Source references: The Conference Board, *Industrial Relations in Canada: Towards a Better Understanding* (Ottawa: Canadian Studies no. 49, 1977); W. P. Kelly, "The Structure and Operation of Conciliation Services in Canada," *Conciliation Services: Structures, Functions and Techniques* (Geneva: ILO, Labor Management Relations series no. 62, 1983); *Martindale-Hubbell Law Directory* (Summit, N.J.: 1983).

Canadian and Catholic Confederation of Labour A labor organization, composed primarily of Catholic workers, bringing together local unions in a number of industries. It was established in 1921.

Earlier organization efforts of Catholic workers occurred around the turn of the century. In 1901 the Quebec union of shoeworkers accepted the labor doctrine of the Catholic church. It was incorporated in 1912 under the name of "La Federation Ouvrière Mutuelle du Nord."

The strength of the CCCL largely has been in Quebec Province. The CCCL, which in 1960 changed its name to the Confederation of National Trade Unions, has always maintained that Canadian unions should remain independent and should avoid affiliation with American unions. This position contrasts to that held by the Canadian Congress of Labour (as of 1956, the Canadian Labour Congress), which parallels the AFL-CIO.

Source references: Samuel H. Baines, "The Evolution of Christian Trade Unionism in Quebec," *ILRR*, July 1959; Harold A. Logan, *The History of Trade Union Organization in Canada* (Toronto: Macmillan, 1948); Bryce

M. Stewart, *Canadian Labor Laws and the Treaty* (New York: Columbia UP, 1926).

See also CONFEDERATION OF NATIONAL TRADE UNIONS.

Canadian Congress of Labour An organization consisting primarily of international unions originally affiliated with the CIO. It was organized in 1927 and known as the All-Canadian Congress of Labour until 1940, when the name was changed. The Congress of Labour merged with the Trades and Labor Congress in 1956 to form the Canadian Labour Congress, which parallels the AFL-CIO in the United States.

See also CANADIAN LABOUR CONGRESS.

Canadian Federation of Labour Members of the Knights of Labor who were in the Trades and Labor Congress, seceded in 1902–3. They organized as the National Trades and Labor Congress, but changed their name to the Canadian Federation of Labour in 1908.

In 1927 the Canadian Federation of Labour joined with other Canadian labor groups to form the All-Canadian Congress of Labour. In 1940 the ACCL joined with the unions which had been expelled from the CIO in the 1930s to form the Canadian Congress of Labour.

Source references: John Crispo, *International Unionism: A Study in Canadian-American Relations* (Toronto: McGraw-Hill, 1967); Alfred C. Crysler, *Labour Relations and Precedents in Canada* (Toronto: Carswell Co., 1949); Harold A. Logan, *The History of Trade Union Organization in Canada* (Chicago: Univ. of Chicago Press, 1928).

Canadian Industrial Disputes Investigation Act (1907) Statute which provided compulsory investigation of disputes affecting public utilities, railroads, and mines. A study of the operation of the Act from 1907 to 1935 indicated that it had been fairly effective except for wildcat disputes in the coal mining industry. It was repealed with the passage of the Industrial Relations and Disputes Investigation Act of 1948.

Source references: Alfred W. R. Carrothers, *Collective Bargaining Law in Canada* (Toronto: Butterworths, 1965); Alfred C. Crysler, *Handbook on Canadian Labour Law* (Toronto: Carswell, 1957); ———, *Labour Relations and Precedents in Canada* (Toronto: Carswell, 1949); Benjamin M. Selekman, *Law and Labor Relations: A Study of the Industrial Disputes Investigation Act of Canada* (Cambridge: Harvard Univ., Business Research Studies no. 14, 1936); H. D. Woods and Sylvia Ostry, *Labour Policy and Labour Economics in Canada* (Toronto: Macmillan, 1962).

Canadian Labour Congress An organization formed in 1956 by the merger of the Trades and Labor Congress of Canada and the Canadian Congress of Labour, paralleling the AFL-CIO merger in the United States. The Congress is composed of approximately 90 national and international unions, with a membership of two million which represents approximately 56 percent of Canada's unionized work force. CLC conventions are held in the spring of every second year. It publishes the bilingual monthly, *Canadian Labour (Travailleur Canadien).*

Address: 2841 Riverside Drive, Ottawa, Ontario, Canada K1V 8X7. Tel. (613) 521–3400

Canadian Trades and Labor Congress An outgrowth of the Toronto Trades Assembly of 1881. The Trades and Labor Congress started in Toronto in 1883. A permanent constitution was obtained in 1886. Its organization paralleled the development of the American Federation of Labor. Most of the membership was affiliated with the AFL. The Trades and Labor Congress merged with the Canadian Congress of Labour in 1956 to form the Canadian Labour Congress, which parallels the AFL-CIO in the United States.

Source references: John Crispo, *International Unionism: A Study in Canadian-American Relations* (Toronto: McGraw-Hill, 1967); Stuart Jamieson, *Industrial Relations in Canada* (Ithaca: Cornell UP, 1957); H. B. Lees-Smith (ed.), *The Encyclopaedia of the Labour Movement* (London: Caxton, 1928); H. A. Marquand, *Organized Labor in Four Continents* (London: Longmans, Green, 1939).

canned music The term of disdain applied by the American Federation of Musicians to music produced by recording machines. Many of the practices of the Musicians Union stem from its efforts to provide more employment opportunities for "live musicians."

captive audience A group of workers assembled by an employer during working hours to listen to the employer discuss unionization, or the employer's point of view during an organization drive, or a statement on how much the employer has done for his workers.

Under the National Labor Relations Act such acts of the employer were held to be unfair labor practices designed to interfere with the rights of employees to organize into unions of their own choosing. Under the Taft-Hartley Act employers have wider latitude in presenting their points of view to employees.

Source references: David I. Shair, "Is the Captive-Audience Doctrine Back?" *LLJ*, July 1952; Thomas E. Silfen, "NLRB Regulation of Employer's Pre-Election Captive Audience Speeches," *IR Law Digest*, Oct. 1967.

captive mines A term applied to the coal mines owned by the steel companies. Generally the term applies to any mine whose output is consumed by the company which owns it. The captive mines became an issue in the organization of the steel industry.

Source reference: Mary Van Kleeck, *Miners and Management* (New York: Russell Sage Foundation, 1934).

captive union *See* COMPANY-DOMINATED UNION.

card carrying members Union members in good standing who have evidence of their membership.

card check Procedure whereby signed union authorization cards are checked against a list of workers in a prospective bargaining unit to determine if the union has majority status. The employer may recognize the union on the basis of this check without the necessity of a formal election. The card check is often conducted by an outside party, e.g., a respected member of the community.

Source references: H. Stephan Gordon, "Union Authorization Cards and the Duty to Bargain," *LLJ*, April 1968; Albert Gore, "Authorization Cards and Required Bargaining," *NYU 21st Annual Conference on Labor*, ed. by Thomas Christensen (New York: Bender, 1969); Eugene A. Kelly, "NLRB Upheld on Cardcheck Rulings," *AFL-CIO News*, June 21, 1969; Robert Lewis, "The Use and Abuse of Authorization Cards in Determining Union Majority," *LLJ*, July 1965; Kenneth C. McGuiness, "Are Union Authorization Cards Consistent With Employee Freedom of Choice?" *NYU 21st Annual Conference on Labor*, ed. by Thomas Christensen (New York: Bender, 1969); Harry H. Rains, "Authorization Cards as an Indefensible Basis for Board Directed Union Representation Status: Fact and Fancy," *LLJ*, April 1967.

See also AUTHORIZATION CARD.

career education Defined, in part, by Hoyt as "a community effort aimed at helping persons—youth and adults—better prepare themselves for work through acquiring adaptability skills that will enable them to change with change in society in such ways that work—paid and unpaid—will become a more meaningful and more rewarding part of their total lifestyle." Career education, is rooted in work and "education/work relationships," is applicable "to *all* persons at *all* age levels—including *all* kinds of educational settings," and requires "the joint participation of the education system *and* the broader community."

Sidney P. Marland, Jr., former Commissioner of Education credited as the prime mover of career education, stated in 1971 that career education "seeks to remove the assumed distinctions between academic and occupational learning programs, blending them to serve all learners at all levels of instruction in their quest for productive careers and rewarding lives."

In contrast to vocational education which is concerned with providing specific occupational skills, career education attempts to develop attributes, such as oral/written communication skills, good work habits, and positive attitudes on work value and motivation.

Source references: Education Commission of the States, *Career Education: The Policies and Priorities of Businesses, Organizations and Agencies* (Denver: Report no. 120, 1979); ———, *Collaboration in State Career Education Policy Development: The Role of Business, Industry and Labor* (Denver: Report no. 117, 1979); ———, *An Overview of State Career Education Laws* (Denver:

Report no. 119, 1979); Lorraine S. Hansen, *An Examination of the Definitions and Concepts of Career Education* (Washington: U.S. National Advisory Council for Career Education, 1977); Edwin L. Herr, *The Emerging History of Career Education, A Summary View* (Washington: U.S. National Advisory Council for Career Education, 1976); Kenneth B. Hoyt, *Career Education and Organized Labor* (Washington: U.S. Dept. of HEW, Office of Education, Monographs on Career Education, 1979); ———, *Career Education and the Business-Labor-Industry Community* (Washington: U.S. Dept. of HEW, Office of Education, 1976); ———, *Career Education: Retrospect and Prospect* (Washington: U.S. Dept. of Education, Monographs on Career Education, 1981); ———, *A Primer for Career Education* (Washington: U.S. Dept. of HEW, Office of Education, Monographs on Career Education, 1977); ———, *Refining the Concept of Collaboration in Career Education* (Washington: U.S. Dept. of HEW, Office of Education, Monographs on Career Education, 1978); Roberta H. Jackson, *Career Education and Minorities* (Washington: U.S. Dept. of HEW, Office of Education, Monographs on Career Education, 1978); Larry McClure and Carolyn Buan (ed.), *Essays on Career Education* (Washington: U.S. Dept. of HEW, Office of Education, 1973); Eleanor Farrar McGowan and David K. Cohen, "'Career Education'—Reforming School Through Work," *The Public Interest*, Winter 1977; John A. Sessions, "Misdirecting Career Education," *American Federationist*, March 1974.

career ladder Jobs which make up a line of progression from an entry-level to a targeted position.

Considered essential to career planning, the construction of a career ladder includes identification of promotion paths and the establishment of criteria for job progress and promotion. Career ladders are considered useful in establishing the organization's policy in equal opportunity matters, the specifications of organizational responsibilities, clarification of individual responsibilities, and the bases for administration of the promotion program.

Source reference: Elmer H. Burack and Nicholas Mathys, "Career Ladders, Pathing and Planning: Some Neglected Basics," *Human Resource Management*, Summer 1979.

Carey v. Westinghouse Electric Corp. A decision of the Supreme Court in January 1961 which held that a dispute involving work assignment was arbitrable. The Court held that arbitration was permitted as an alternative remedy in view of the blurred line between representation and work assignment disputes, the weight which the NLRB had accorded to arbitration awards, and the curative effect which arbitration might have. The Supreme Court reversed the decision of the Court of Appeals in New York. The majority opinion was written by Mr. Justice William O. Douglas and the minority opinion by Mr. Justice Hugo Black.

Source reference: Carey v. Westinghouse Electric Corp., 375 US 261, 55 LRRM 2042 (1964).

"carom" lobbying Tactic employed by public sector unions, after a tentative agreement has been reached with the employer, to improve a package by pressing the chief executive or legislative body for further benefits.

Source reference: Michael H. Moskow, J. Joseph Loewenberg, and Edward Clifford Koziara, *Collective Bargaining in Public Employment* (New York: Random House, 1970).

See also END RUN BARGAINING.

Carpenters and Joiners of America; United Brotherhood of (AFL-CIO) A national union organized in Chicago in August 1881, as the Brotherhood of Carpenters and Joiners of America. In 1888 amalgamation was effected with the New York group of the United Order of American Carpenters and Joiners, and the name was changed to the United Brotherhood of Carpenters and Joiners of America. In 1912 it absorbed the Amalgamated Woodworkers Union, which was a merger of the International Furniture Workers' Union, founded in 1873, and the Machine Wood Workers' International Union, founded in 1890. The Wood, Wire and Metal Lathers International Union (AFL-CIO) merged with the union in August 1979.

The union's official monthly publication is *The Carpenter.*

Address: 101 Constitution Avenue, N.W., Washington, D.C. 20001. Tel. (202) 546–6206

Source references: Thomas R. Brooks, *The Road to Dignity: A Century of Conflict; A History of the United Brotherhood of Carpenters and Joiners of America, AFL-CIO, 1881–1981* (New York: Atheneum, 1981); Paul Bullock, *Building California: The Story of the Carpenters' Union* (Los Angeles: UC, Institute of IR, 1982); Morris A. Horowitz, *The Structure and Government of the Carpenters' Union* (New York: Wiley, 1962).

carryover seniority *See* RETROACTIVE SENIORITY.

cash refund annuity A policy which provides an annual income at retirement for life. Provision is made that upon death prior to full payment of the annuity, the remainder will go to the beneficiary's estate.

casual labor Work occupations in which the demand for employment is highly variable, such as port work, migratory farm work, and other jobs of an unskilled, intermittent nature.

casual worker Workers who work occasionally and intermittently and are not attached to a particular company. They are usually unskilled and move with seasonal fluctuating demands of the labor market. Sometimes applied to temporary employees.

Source references: Paul H. Furfey et al., *Marginal Employability* (Washington: Catholic Univ. of America Press, 1962); Kenneth Lehmann and C. Edward Weber, *Workers on the Move* (Urbana: Univ. of Illinois, Institute of Labor & IR, 1952); Don D. Lescohier, *The Labor Market* (New York: Macmillan, 1919); Carleton Parker, *The Casual Laborer and Other Essays* (New York: Harcourt Brace, 1920).

See also DECASUALIZATION, MIGRATORY WORKER.

caucus A meeting of a small group of influential members of an organization to plan strategy or policy prior to a general meeting. It may also consist of a faction of the organization to plan its own program, support specific candidates, or follow a certain policy on the floor. Such meetings may take place before annual meetings or elections of local unions, or city or state organizations. They also take place prior to the annual or biennial conventions of national or international unions. The term may also apply to collective bargaining negotiations, when one of the groups (union or employer) requests a recess to discuss, by itself, a proposal or offer made by the other party, or by a mediator, if one is in attendance.

"C" cases A designation assigned by the NLRB to cases on its docket involving unfair labor practice complaints. It is distinguished from "R" cases which involve questions of representation (designation of bargaining agent).

Under the Taft-Hartley Act, complaints also may be filed against unions. The "C" designation thus is divided into two broad categories—"CA" cases are complaints against the employer and "CB" cases are complaints against unions.

Other "C" designations include: "CC" cases involving Section 8(b)(4)(i)(A), (B), or (C) filed by an employer, an individual, or a labor organization against a labor organization; "CD" cases involving a jurisdictional dispute charge filed by an employer, an individual, or a labor organization; "CE" cases involving Section 8(e) and hot-cargo contracts; "CG" cases involving failure to notify a health care institution and the FMCS of a strike or picketing action against a health care institution; and "CP" cases involving Section 8(b)(7) and recognition picketing.

Source references: Kenneth C. McGuiness and Jeffrey A. Norris, *How to Take a Case Before the NLRB* (5th ed., Washington: BNA, 1986); U.S. NLRB, *A Guide to Basic Law and Procedures Under the National Labor Relations Act* (Washington: 1978).

cease and desist order An order issued by the NLRB (or state agency) to a labor organization or employer to stop an unfair labor practice held in violation of the law. A cease and desist order states the action which the employer or union is to stop, and the affirmative action to be taken to remedy the situation. Such commands or orders are subject to court appeal.

Source references: Harry A. Millis and Emily C. Brown, *From the Wagner Act to*

Taft-Hartley (Chicago: Univ. of Chicago Press, 1950); Joseph Rosenfarb, *The National Labor Policy and How It Works* (New York: Harper, 1940); Jerre S. Williams (ed.), *Labor Relations and the Law* (3d ed., Boston: Little, Brown, 1965).

See also AFFIRMATIVE ORDER, MAKE WHOLE.

Cement, Lime and Gypsum Workers International Union; United (AFL-CIO) Organized as the National Council of United Cement Workers in 1936. The name was changed to the United Cement, Lime and Gypsum Workers International Union in 1939, and then to the United Cement, Lime, Gypsum, and Allied Workers International Union (AFL-CIO) in February 1981.

See also CEMENT, LIME, GYPSUM, AND ALLIED WORKERS INTERNATIONAL UNION; UNITED (AFL-CIO).

Cement, Lime, Gypsum, and Allied Workers International Union; United (AFL-CIO) Formerly known as the United Cement, Lime and Gypsum Workers International Union. The current name was adopted in February 1981. Its official monthly publication is the *Voice of the Cement, Lime, Gypsum, and Allied Workers.* In April 1984 the union merged with the International Brotherhood of Boilermakers, Iron Ship Builders, Blacksmiths, Forgers and Helpers (AFL-CIO).

Address: 2500 Brickvale Dr., Elk Grove Village, Ill. 60007. Tel. (312) 595–5171

central labor (trades) council An organization of local AFL unions in a locality or city to provide coordination of effort in political, economic, or other areas. It could exercise some power in calling strikes in the area. It might act as a clearinghouse for joint action by unions in the community, or to iron out interunion problems. Occasionally it might agree to support candidates for office in local elections.

The Central Labor Council also has been known as: City Central, Central Trades Council, Federal Trades and Labor Council, Joint Council, City Trade Assembly. The CIO counterpart was known as the Industrial Union Council.

See also STATE FEDERATIONS OF LABOR.

centrist The group in an organization which represents the middle position—between the extremes of the left and right. The reference is rarely applied to American trade union groups. The American counterpart would be the "middle-of-the-roaders."

certificated employees Commonly refers to teachers who are usually required to have teaching certificates in order to qualify for their positions. In some states, school administrators may also be included in this designation.

Source reference: Joyce M. Najita and Helene S. Tanimoto, *Guide to Statutory Provisions in Public Sector Collective Bargaining: Unit Determination* (4th Issue, Honolulu: Univ. of Hawaii, IRC, 1981).

certificate of age A document issued under the Fair Labor Standards Act which limits child labor. The document certifies that the child is of age to perform certain work without violation of the child labor laws.

See also CHILD LABOR.

certificate of intent A statement formerly filed by unions under the registration section of the Taft-Hartley Act (9(f), (g), and (h)) to indicate compliance with the requirements of the law. These sections were repealed, effective September 14, 1959.

certification Official recognition by the NLRB, or a state labor agency, that the labor organization is the duly designated agency for purposes of collective bargaining. A union so certified remains the exclusive bargaining agent for all of the employees in the appropriate bargaining unit.

Source references: National Labor Relations Act, as amended, Section 8(b)(4), Section 9(c)(1), 29 U.S.C. 158(b)(4), 29 U.S.C. 159(c)(1) (1982); Arvid Anderson, "Selection and Certification of Representatives in Public Employment," *NYU 20th Annual Conference on Labor*, ed. by Thomas Christensen (New York: Bender, 1968); Robert R. R. Brooks, *Unions of Their Own Choosing* (New Haven: Yale UP, 1940); Bernard Cushman, "Duration of Certification by the NLRB and the Doctrine of Administrative Stability," *Michigan LR*, Nov. 1946; Eugene G. Goslee, "Clarification of Bargaining Units and Amendments to Certifications," *IR Law Digest*, Oct. 1969;

Aaron Levenstein, *Labor, Today and Tomorrow* (New York: Knopf, 1945); Lewis Lorwin and Arthur Wubnig, *Labor Relations Boards* (Washington: Brookings Institution, 1935); George W. Salem, "Nonmajority Bargaining Orders: A Prospective View in Light of *United Dairy Farmers*," *LLJ*, March 1981.

See also AUTHORIZATION CARD, CARD CHECK, DECERTIFICATION.

certified employee organization Term currently found in state and local government laws governing public employment relations referring to the organization which has been certified by the appropriate government agencies as the official representative of the employees in the bargaining unit for purposes of collective bargaining or negotiations. The New York City Collective Bargaining Law defines the term as follows:

> The term "certified employee organization" shall mean any public employee organization: (1) certified by the board of certification as the exclusive bargaining representative of a bargaining unit determined to be appropriate for such purpose; (2) recognized as such exclusive bargaining representative by a public employer other than a municipal agency; or (3) recognized by a municipal agency, or certified by the department of labor, as such exclusive bargaining representative prior to the effective date of this chapter unless such recognition has been or is revoked or such certificate has been or is terminated.

Source reference: Harold S. Roberts, *Labor-Management Relations in the Public Service* (Honolulu: Univ. of Hawaii Press, 1970).

chain picketing A procedure of marching around a struck company or the entrances to the premises so that the line of pickets forms an impenetrable column to prevent anyone from going through the picket line. The strikers form a continuous moving chain around the establishment being picketed.

Source references: Robert R. R. Brooks, *When Labor Organizes* (New Haven: Yale UP, 1937); E. T. Hiller, *The Strike* (Chicago: Univ. of Chicago Press, 1928); Sylvester Petro, "State Jurisdiction to Regulate Violent Picketing," *LLJ*, Jan. 1952; Samuel Yellen, *American Labor Struggles* (New York: Arno & The New York Times, c.1936, 1969).

See also MASS PICKETING, PICKETING, STRIKE.

challenged ballot A vote that has been questioned by one of the observers at an NLRB election. Challenged ballots are kept sealed and counted separately by the regional office if the number of challenged ballots is sufficient to affect the vote.

chapel Shop clubs found in some old trades, long known among the compositors in the printing trades. These chapels are subordinate to the local union, but they perform a function within the shop or establishment, providing the workers with an opportunity to discuss working conditions and problems in the plant.

Source references: Robert F. Hoxie, *Trade Unionism in the United States* (New York: Appleton, 1931); Sidney and Beatrice Webb, *The History of Trade Unionism* (London: Longmans, Green, 1926).

charge A written claim filed by an employer or union that there has been an unfair labor practice in violation of the Taft-Hartley Act. After investigation of the charge, and if there is merit in the case and it is not settled informally, the NLRB will issue a formal complaint.

Source reference: Louis G. Silverberg, *A Guide to the National Labor Relations Act* (Washington: U.S. Dept. of Labor, Div. of Labor Standards, Bull. no. 81, 1946).

See also COMPLAINT, NATIONAL LABOR RELATIONS BOARD.

charter The grant of jurisdiction by the parent organization to a national or international union or by the international to a local union. American unions, unlike European unions, are given a special grant of jurisdiction which gives them authority to organize employees within the special job, craft, or occupational category, or in a specific geographic territory. In actual practice most national unions constantly broaden their organizational field. Many of the jurisdictional difficulties stem from changes in industrial production and the use of new materials in the handling of work. As a matter of general policy the parent organization will not charter more than one international in a single field.

check-in board Used in some mining operations to hang the identification badge of individual workers, to show they have checked in. It is similar to a card rack used in many companies where the employee checks in by having his time card punched and then placed in the rack.

check-off A procedure whereby the employer deducts from the pay of all employees who are members of the union in the bargaining unit, membership dues and assessments and turns these monies over to the union. Under the Taft-Hartley Act the employee must give a written assignment which is limited to one year, or to the termination date of the collective bargaining agreement, whichever date occurs first. The check-off also may be used under the agency shop to deduct assessments from nonmembers.

Source references: Labor Management Relations Act of 1947, as amended, Section 302, 29 U.S.C. 186 (1982); James J. Bambrick, Jr., *Union Security and Check-Off Provisions* (New York: NICB, Studies in Personnel Policy no. 127, 1952); Efren Cordova, "The Check-Off System: A Comparative Study," *ILR*, May 1969; E. B. McNatt, "Check-Off," *LLJ*, Feb. 1953; U.S. CSC, *Voluntary Dues Allotments in the Federal Government, 1968* (Washington: 1968); U.S. Dept. of Labor, BLS, *Major Collective Bargaining Agreements: Union Security and Dues Checkoff Provisions* (Washington: Bull. 1425–21, 1982).

See also AUTOMATIC CHECK-OFF, INVOLUNTARY CHECK-OFF, RAND FORMULA, VOLUNTARY CHECK-OFF.

Chemical Workers Union, International (AFL-CIO) The Chemical Workers Union voted to join the Alliance for Labor Action at its convention on September 17, 1968. The union was subsequently expelled by the AFL-CIO Convention on October 3, 1969. It reaffiliated with the AFL-CIO in May 1971.

Its official monthly publication is the *International Chemical Worker.*

Address: 1655 West Market St., Akron, Ohio 44313. Tel. (216) 867–2444

See also ALLIANCE FOR LABOR ACTION (ALA).

Chicago, Rock Island and Pacific Railroad Co. v. Arkansas A decision of the Supreme Court upholding the right of a state to set out the minimum number of workers to be employed in operating a train.

Source reference: Chicago, Rock Island & Pacific Railroad Co. v. Arkansas, 219 US 453 (1911).

See also INTERSTATE COMMERCE.

child care Nursery, day care, and after school care needs of children created by the increase in the number of working mothers, one of the fastest growing segments of the labor force. BLS reports that by 1982, 59 percent of women with minor children and 50 percent of women with preschool age children were in the labor force.

Government support for child care services has included federal programs for day care for low-income families, food subsidies for child care centers, and tax credits for child care expenses.

Child care services have been rarely included in employee benefit packages. However, it is expected that the pressure to expand employee benefits, the increase in the number of working mothers, and tax relief for employer-paid day care benefits will motivate companies to provide for such services.

Source references: BNA, *Employers and Child Care: Development of a New Employee Benefit* (Washington: 1984); Sandra L. Burud, Pamela R. Aschbacher, and Jacquelyn McCroskey, *Employer-Supported Child Care* (Boston: Auburn House, 1984); Sheila B. Kamerman, "Child-Care Services: a National Picture," *MLR*, Dec. 1983; Renee Y. Magid, "Parents and Employers: New Partners in Child Care," *Management Review*, March 1982; Oscar Ornati and Carol Buckham, "Day Care: Still Waiting its Turn as a Standard Benefit," *Management Review*, May 1983; M. C. Seguret, "Child-Care Services for Working Parents," *ILR*, Nov./Dec. 1981; U.S. Dept. of Labor, Women's Bureau, *Employers and Child Care: Establishing Services Through the Workplace* (rev. ed., Washington: Pamphlet 23, 1982).

child labor The practice of employing children in gainful occupations. The age of 16 is generally accepted as marking the transition from childhood to youth for purposes of regulation. "Oppressive child labor" is defined by Section 3(l) of the Fair Labor Standards Act of 1938 to include all labor of children under the ages of 16 and 18 in any occupation determined by the Secretary of Labor to be particularly hazardous or detrimental to a child's health or well-being.

When the United States was developing as an industrial nation, child labor was considered necessary to maintain production and, indeed, a valuable institution to keep children from mischief and the immorality of idleness and to prevent orphaned children or the children of poor families from becoming public charges. Children as young as six or seven were employed in factories (often hired along with their parents) and mines. All of the operatives in the first cotton-spinning mill in the United States established in Pawtucket, Rhode Island, about 1790, for example, were children between the ages of seven and 12. Because all workers put in long hours, it was not thought excessive to work children 12 or 13 or more hours per day for six days a week.

Source references: Mark Aldrich, "State Reports on Women and Child Wage Earners, 1870–1906," *Labor History*, Winter 1979/80; Claudia Goldin, *Household and Market Production of Families in a Late Nineteenth Century American City* (Princeton: Princeton Univ., IR Section, WP no. 115, 1978); William James Knight, *The World's Exploited Children: Growing Up Sadly* (Washington: U.S. Dept. of Labor, BILA, Monograph no. 4, 1980); Judson MacLaury, "A Senator's Reaction to Report on Working Women and Children," *MLR*, Oct. 1975; Elias Mendelievich, "Child Labour," *ILR*, Sept./Oct. 1979; Daniel J. B. Mitchell, "A Furor Over Working Children and the Bureau of Labor," *MLR*, Oct. 1975; Gerry Rodgers and Guy Standing, "Economic Roles of Children in Low-Income Countries," *ILR*, Jan./Feb. 1981; Sidney and Beatrice Webb, *Industrial Democracy* (London: Longmans, Green, 1920).

See also CHILD LABOR LAWS, NATIONAL CHILD LABOR COMMITTEE, OPPRESSIVE CHILD LABOR.

child labor laws The first state laws regulating child labor were prompted by concern for the education of factory children. These laws required manufacturing proprietors to provide a basic education for the children they employed; set a maximum working day for children; or established a minimum age, usually between 10 and 13, for factory employment.

As child labor began to be considered exploitative and debilitative rather than an economic necessity and a morally and physically beneficial institution, and as the economic life and educational goals of the United States changed in the 20th century, more and more states, and eventually the federal government, enacted laws regulating child labor and conditions and practices. Most current state child labor laws contain the following standards: a 16-year minimum age for factory work and for all work during school hours, a 14-year minimum age for nonfactory work (other than on farms) outside school hours, an 18-year minimum age for hazardous work, and a 40-hour workweek for minors under 16. They generally prohibit night work and require employment certificates for minors under 18.

Certain types of work which employ children and adolescents are either excluded from most state child labor laws or are covered by separate provisions. These types of work include street trades, such as selling and delivering newspapers, peddling, and shining shoes; agriculture; acting and radio and television entertaining. Also exempted are children under 16 working for their parents in nonhazardous occupations or in work other than mining or manufacturing.

The Fair Labor Standards Act of 1938, as amended, places standards for hiring children insofar as their work is involved in interstate commerce. This Act provides for minimum wage coverage and for overtime for work in excess of 40 hours per week. It prohibits employment in nonhazardous work under age 16 and employment under age 18 in occupations declared hazardous by the Secretary of Labor. As part of the hazardous-occupations designation, minors under 18 cannot legally be employed in mines, sawmills, slaughterhouses; near explosives or radioactive substances; with roofers or excavators, wreckers or demolition crews; or as drivers of motor vehicles, loggers, or operators of power-driven machines used in certain jobs. The Fair Labor Standards Act amendment of 1950 prohibits the employment of children under 16 in agriculture during school hours; a 1966 provision forbids the employment of children under 16 in hazardous farm work, as outlined by the Secretary of Labor.

Source references: Jeremy P. Felt, "The Child Labor Provisions of the Fair Labor Standards Act," *Labor History,* Fall 1970; Arden J. Lee, "Cotton Textiles and the Federal Child Labor Act of 1916," *Labor History,* Fall 1975; Daniel J. B. Mitchell and John Clapp, *Legal Constraints on Teenage Employment, A New Look at Child Labor and School Leaving Laws* (Los Angeles: UC, Institute of IR, Monograph Series 22, 1979); U.S. Dept. of Labor, Bureau of Labor Standards, *Child Labor Laws* (Washington: Bull. no. 312, 1968); U.S. Dept. of Labor, Wage and Hour and Public Contracts Divisions, *Agriculture and Child Labor Requirements Under Fair Labor Standards Act, as Amended in 1966* (rev. ed., Washington: Child-Labor Bull. no. 102, 1969); ———, *Guide to Child Labor Provisions of Fair Labor Standards Act* (Washington: Pub. no. 1258, 1969); Roger W. Walker, "The A.F.L. and Child-Labor Legislation: An Exercise in Frustration," *Labor History,* Summer 1970.

See also FAIR LABOR STANDARDS ACT OF 1938, HAMMER V. DAGENHART, WALSH-HEALEY ACT OF 1936.

Children's Bureau The Children's Bureau was established by Act of Congress on April 9, 1912, and was placed within the Department of Labor in 1913. Except for the division relating to functions under the Fair Labor Standards Act of 1938, which remained in the Department of Labor, it was transferred in 1946 to the Federal Security Agency, where it functioned under SSA. In 1953 the Bureau became a part of the Department of Health, Education, and Welfare, which was established in that year. In 1963 it was transferred to the new Welfare Administration of HEW, and by an HEW reorganization order of 1967 it was reassigned to the newly created Social and Rehabilitation Service. The Children's Bureau was reassigned to the Office of Child Development in 1969. The Bureau currently is in the Office of Human Development Services, Department of Health and Human Services.

The Bureau's major function is to plan, develop, and coordinate those programs which provide for the health and welfare of the nation's children. These programs include welfare services for children and for the families of dependent children; maternal, child health, and infant care; programs for improvement of health and welfare services for mothers and children; and services for adolescent youth and delinquent youth.

See also CHILD LABOR LAWS.

chilling effect The term is used to denote the deterrent effect interest arbitration may have on the parties' incentive to bargain in good faith.

In EEO/AA usage, it refers to any practice or action by an employer which denies, discourages, or inhibits individuals of their employment rights. An employer's alleged reputation for discrimination is sometimes said to have a "chilling effect."

Source references: Senter v. General Motors Corp., 383 FSupp 222, 11 FEP Cases 1068 (1974); Peter Feuille, "Final Offer Arbitration and the Chilling Effect," *IR,* Oct. 1975; Roger B. Jacobs, "The 'Chilling Effect' of Discovery in Labor Proceedings—Employee Interrogation and the Right to Representation," *Employee Relations LJ,* Summer 1980.

See also NARCOTIC EFFECT.

Chinese overtime *See* COOLIE OVERTIME.

Christian Labor Association of the United States of America (Ind) Founded in 1931.

Address: 9820 Gordon St., Box 65, Zeeland, Mich. 49464. Tel. (616) 772–9153

Christmas bonus A special payment or yearly allotment given by some companies to regular employees during the Christmas season. It was designed to give the employees some indication of the employer's interest in the worker and to help in defraying expenses of the Christmas season. It was used by some companies as a profit sharing method, long before profit sharing schemes became popular.

Source references: BNA, *Christmas and Year-End Personnel Practices* (Washington: PPF Survey no. 85, 1968); Richard Hand,

"Keep Cash in Christmas: A Study of Arbitration Cases Involving Christmas Bonuses," *Industrial and Labor Relations Forum,* June 1968; Richard P. Helwig, "The Christmas Bonus: A Gift or a Give-Away?" *PJ,* Nov. 1973; Mitchell Meyer, "The Christmas Bonus for Employees," *Conference Board Record,* Oct. 1965.

Cigar Makers' International Union of America (AFL-CIO) The Cigar Makers were organized in New York in June 1864, as the National Cigar Makers' Union. It changed its name to the Cigar Makers' International Union in 1887. The union was active in the eight-hour day movement and was one of the active members in founding the AFL. On June 1, 1974, the union merged with the Retail, Wholesale and Department Store Union (AFL-CIO).

See also RETAIL, WHOLESALE AND DEPARTMENT STORE UNION (AFL-CIO).

circuit courts of appeals Federal courts which hear appeals from decisions of district courts. There are 14 circuits which serve the United States. Appeals from the circuit courts go to the Supreme Court. Appeals from decisions of the NLRB go to the appropriate circuit court and then to the Supreme Court.

circular picketing A form of picketing where the workers march around the establishment in a circular, unbroken line.

See also CHAIN PICKETING.

citizens' committee *See* BACK-TO-WORK MOVEMENT.

city central *See* CENTRAL LABOR (TRADES) COUNCIL.

city federation *See* CENTRAL LABOR (TRADES) COUNCIL.

Civilian Conservation Corps An agency created by Congress in 1933 to provide employment for young men out of work, and at the same time to conserve natural resources. It was a "make-work" program. The men worked out of camps, carved trails, built roads, planted trees, learned useful crafts, and helped beautify many communities. The program lasted during most of the depression years, and went out of existence in 1943.

civilian labor force All employed or unemployed persons in the civilian noninstitutional population, 16 years of age and older.

Source reference: U.S. Dept. of Labor, BLS, *BLS Handbook of Methods* (Washington: Bull. 2134–1, 1982).

Civilian Technicians; Association of (Ind) Founded in 1960. Its bimonthly publication is *The Technician.*

Address: 932 Hungerford Dr., Suite 34A, Rockville, Md. 20850. Tel. (301) 762–5656

civil liberties Those rights and freedoms which people feel they must have in order to think and act according to their best judgment. This includes many freedoms—some protected by our Constitution, and others protected only by the vigil of free men in a society of free people. Many organizations and groups have banded together to protect what they feel are inalienable rights which must not be abridged either by private groups or public agencies.

Source references: Benjamin Aaron, *Protecting Civil Liberties of Members Within Trade Unions* (Los Angeles: UC, Institute of IR, 1950); American Civil Liberties Union, *Legal Tactics for Labor's Rights* (New York: 1930); William O. Douglas, "The Battle for the Minds of Men," Speech to the Amalgamated Clothing Workers, May 14, 1952; Milton R. Konvitz, "Civil Liberties," *Annals,* May 1967; Joseph L. Rauh, Jr., "Civil Rights and Liberties and Labor Unions," *LLJ,* Dec. 1957; Charles E. Wyzanski, "The Open Window and the Open Door—An Inquiry into Freedom of Association," 35 *California LR* 336 (1947).

See also AMERICAN CIVIL LIBERTIES UNION.

Civil Rights Act of 1866 Also known as Section 1981. Enacted to enforce the 13th Amendment, which was ratified in 1865.

The 13th Amendment reads: "Neither slavery nor involuntary servitude, except as a punishment for crime whereof the party shall have been duly convicted, shall exist within the United States, or any place subject to their jurisdiction."

The Civil Rights Act of 1866 states: "All persons within the jurisdiction of the United States shall have the same right in every State and Territory to make and enforce contracts, to sue, be parties, give evidence, and to the full and equal benefit of all laws and proceedings for the security of persons and property as is enjoyed by white citizens, and shall be subject to like punishment, pains, penalties, taxes, licenses, and exactions of every kind, and to no other."

According to Schlei and Grossman the coverage of this law is "broad with respect to defendants, reaching private as well as public conduct, but narrow with respect to bases of discrimination, reaching only discrimination based on race, color, and alienage."

Source references: Civil Rights Act of 1866, 42 U.S.C. 1981 (1982); "Damages for Federal Employment Discrimination: Section 1981 and Qualified Executive Immunity," *IR Law Digest,* Fall 1976; Daniel J. Hoffheimer, "Employment Discrimination Against Resident Aliens by Private Employers," *LLJ,* March 1984; Barbara Lindemann Schlei and Paul Grossman, *Employment Discrimination Law* (2d ed., Washington: BNA, 1983).

Civil Rights Act of 1871 Also known as Section 1983 or the Ku Klux Klan Act. The law was enacted to enforce the provisions of the 14th Amendment.

The 14th Amendment provides, in part: "No state shall make or enforce any law which shall abridge the privileges or immunities of citizens of the United States; nor shall any State deprive any person of life, liberty, or property, without due process of law; nor deny to any person within its jurisdiction the equal protection of the laws."

The law states: "Every person who, under color of any statute, ordinance, regulation, custom or usage, of any State or Territory, subjects, or causes to be subjected, any citizen of the United States or other person within the jurisdiction thereof to the deprivation of any rights, privileges, or immunities secured by the Constitution and laws, shall be liable to the party injured in an action at law, suit in equity, or other proper proceeding for redress."

According to Schlei and Grossman this law, "only applies where the defendants act under color of state law. However, where it does apply, it covers discrimination based on . . . race, color, sex, religion, or national origin."

Source references: Civil Rights Acts, as amended, 42 U.S.C. 1983 (1982); Barbara Lindemann Schlei and Paul Grossman, *Employment Discrimination Law* (2d ed., Washington: BNA, 1983).

Civil Rights Act of 1964 Statute which includes 11 Titles, one of which, Title VII, undertakes to eliminate all employment discrimination based on race, color, religion, sex, or national origin. The law became effective July 2, 1965, one year after its enactment. During its first year, Title VII applied to employers of 100 or more employees. Currently, employers with 15 or more employees are covered. The law also applies to labor unions, employment agencies, and joint labor-management committees. The administering agency is the five-member Equal Employment Opportunity Commission.

Title VII emphasizes conciliation as the method of settling complaints of discrimination and makes provision for a system of federal-state cooperation in enforcing its mandates by reliance on state laws (or local enactments in some cases) whose terms are compatible with the federal statute. If negotiation or conciliation fails to redress complaints, enforcement is through actions in U.S. district courts. The EEOC is authorized to seek injunctive and other relief in federal court; the Attorney General retains such authority in cases against a government, government agency, or a political subdivision.

Major amendments to Title VII were enacted by the Equal Employment Opportunity Act of 1972, which extended coverage to state and local governments, and the Pregnancy Discrimination Act of 1978.

Source references: Civil Rights Act of 1964, as amended, 42 U.S.C. 2000d et seq. (1982); Arvil V. Adams, *Toward Fair Employment and the EEOC: A Study of Compliance Procedures Under Title VII of the Civil Rights Act of 1964, Final Report* (Washington: U.S. EEOC, 1973); G. William Baab, "Significant Developments in Equal Employment Opportunity from the Union Viewpoint," *Labor Law Developments 1975,* Proceedings of 21st Annual Institute on Labor Law, SLF (New York: Bender, 1975); Maurice C. Benewitz, "Coverage Under Title VII of the Civil Rights Act," *LLJ,* May 1966; BNA, *The Civil Rights*

Act of 1964 (Washington: 1964); _______, *A Current Look at (1) The Negro and Title VII, (2) Sex and Title VII* (Washington: PPF Survey no. 82, 1967); Stanley P. Hebert and Charles L. Reischel, "Title VII and the Multiple Approaches to Eliminating Employment Discrimination," *IR Law Digest,* April 1972; Herbert Hill, "The Equal Employment Opportunity Acts of 1964 and 1972: A Critical Analysis of the Legislative History and Administration of the Law," *Industrial Relations LJ,* Spring 1977; Charles A. Kothe, "Implications of Title VII of the 1964 Civil Rights Act, as Amended from the Employer's Point of View," *Labor Law Developments 1973,* Proceedings of 19th Annual Institute on Labor Law, SLF (New York: Bender, 1973); Gabrielle K. McDonald, "Plaintiff's Remedies for Racial Violations of Title VII of the Civil Rights Act of 1964 and the Civil Rights Act of 1866—Preparation, Trial, and Settlement," *Labor Law Developments 1974,* Proceedings of 20th Annual Institute on Labor Law, SLF (New York: Bender, 1974); Richard B. Miller, *Civil Rights and Your Employment Practices* (Swarthmore: PJ, 1965); John H. Powell, Jr., "Title VII of the Civil Rights Act," *Labor Law Developments 1975,* Proceedings of 21st Annual Institute on Labor Law, SLF (New York: Bender, 1975); Julius Reich, "Implications of Title VII of the Civil Rights Act for Unions," *Labor Law Developments 1973,* Proceedings of 19th Annual Institute on Labor Law, SLF (New York: Bender, 1973); Julius Rezler, *Social and Legal Background of the Equal Employment Opportunity Legislation* (Chicago: Loyola Univ., Institute of IR, Research Series no. 3, 1967); Ruth G. Shaeffer, *Nondiscrimination in Employment: Changing Perspectives, 1963–1972* (New York: The Conference Board, Report no. 589, 1973); Cynthia Shenker, "Protective Labor Legislation: Title VII and the Equal Rights Amendment," *Industrial and Labor Relations Forum,* Vol. 12, no. 2, 1976; Michael Sovern, *Legal Restraints on Racial Discrimination in Employment* (New York: Twentieth Century Fund, 1966); Russell Specter, "The Concept and Theory of Relief for Acts of Employment Discrimination Under Title VII of the Civil Rights Act of 1964 as Amended by the Equal Employment Opportunity Act of 1972," *Labor Law Developments 1973,* Proceedings of 19th Annual Institute on Labor Law, SLF (New York: Bender, 1973); Dennis H. Vaughn, "Choice of Laws and Forums in Employment Discrimination Cases," *Labor Law Developments 1972,* Proceedings of 18th Annual Institute on Labor Law, SLF (New York: Bender, 1972).

See also BENNETT AMENDMENT, EQUAL EMPLOYMENT OPPORTUNITY ACT OF 1972, EQUAL EMPLOYMENT OPPORTUNITY COMMISSION, PREGNANCY DISCRIMINATION ACT.

civil service Used synonymously with merit system, it refers to a governmental employment system that regulates the selection by examination or the assessment of fitness, ability and experience, advancement, and retention based on merit and competence.

Stahl explains, "Erroneously the phrase *civil service* still lingers with a connotation of appointment by examination simply because the subject of reform came to be confused with its nature. But the more accurate designation is merit system. Civil service, after all, merely distinguishes civilian pursuits in government from military. A civil service can literally be manned under either a patronage or a merit system."

Source references: Felix A. Nigro and Lloyd G. Nigro, *The New Public Personnel Administration* (Itasca, Ill.: Peacock Pub., 1976); O. Glenn Stahl, *Public Personnel Administration* (7th ed., New York: Harper & Row, 1976); Herbert J. Storing, "Political Parties and the Bureaucracy," *Political Parties, U.S.A.,* ed. by Robert A. Goldwin (Chicago: Rand McNally, 1964).

See also MERIT PRINCIPLE, MERIT SYSTEM.

Civil Service Act of 1883 Also known as the Pendleton Act, it created the federal merit system. Senator George H. Pendleton of Ohio introduced a bill on December 15, 1880, to reform the civil service. In 1881, Pendleton agreed to introduce a bill drawn up by the New York Civil Service Reform Association to supersede his original bill. Congress passed the measure in 1882 and the Act became law on January 16, 1883 (22 Stat. 403).

The Act was the result of the civil service reform movement of the 1870s and 1880s, led by George William Curtis, who headed the

Civil Service Commission created by President Grant in 1871, and was one of the founders of the National Civil Service Reform League (currently the National Civil Service League). The assassination of President Garfield by a disappointed office seeker was also a factor prompting Congress to enact the law.

Stahl considers as the "outstanding characteristics" of the law, among others, (1) the creation of the U.S. Civil Service Commission, an independent bipartisan commission, appointed by and responsible to the chief executive, charged with the responsibilities for administration of the law; (2) the introduction of the merit principle and selection by open competitive examinations; and (3) the freeing of employees from any obligations to make political contributions, and the strict prohibition on officers from receiving or soliciting such funds for such purposes.

Source references: O. Glenn Stahl, *Public Personnel Administration* (5th ed., New York: Harper & Row, 1962); Paul P. Van Riper, *History of the United States Civil Service* (Evanston: Row, Peterson, 1958).

See also U.S. CIVIL SERVICE COMMISSION (CSC).

Civil Service Commission *See* U.S. CIVIL SERVICE COMMISSION (CSC).

Civil Service Employees Association, Inc. (New York) Founded in 1910, the New York organization was known at one time as the largest independent union of public employees. The CSEA represents some 260,000 blue- and white-collar, professional and nonprofessional state, county, municipal, and school employees. On April 21, 1978, the CSEA affiliated with the American Federation of State, County and Municipal Employees (AFL-CIO). The affiliation agreement granted CSEA a union charter and created a new AFSCME legislative district. It issues the weekly *Civil Service Leader.*

Address: 33 Elk St., Albany, N.Y. 12207. Tel. (518) 434–0191

Source reference: "AFSCME and CSEA Unite; AFSCME Now Largest in AFL-CIO," *Public Employee,* May 1978.

See also STATE, COUNTY AND MUNICIPAL EMPLOYEES; AMERICAN FEDERATION OF (AFL-CIO).

Civil Service Reform Act of 1978 On October 13, 1978, President Carter signed into law the Civil Service Reform Act to revamp the 95-year-old federal civil service structure. The law, consisting of nine titles, became effective on January 1, 1979. It splits the CSC into two bodies—the Office of Personnel Management and the Merit Systems Protection Board. The law also creates a Senior Executive Service for senior level personnel, ties pay for middle level managers to performance rather than longevity, protects whistleblowers, places in law a labor relations program with its own enforcement authority, and streamlines procedures for hiring, firing, and disciplining employees.

Source references: Civil Service Reform Act of 1978, 5 U.S.C. 7101 et seq. (1982); U.S. GAO, *Civil Service Reform After Two Years: Some Initial Problems Resolved But Serious Concerns Remain* (Washington: 1981); ______, *Civil Service Reform—Where It Stands Today* (Washington: 1980).

See also COMPELLING NEED; FEDERAL LABOR RELATIONS AUTHORITY (FLRA); MERIT SYSTEMS PROTECTION BOARD (MSPB); OFFICE OF PERSONNEL MANAGEMENT (OPM); OFFICIAL TIME; REORGANIZATION PLAN NO. 1 OF 1978; REORGANIZATION PLAN NO. 2 OF 1978; SENIOR EXECUTIVE SERVICE (SES); TITLE VII, CIVIL SERVICE REFORM ACT OF 1978; WHISTLEBLOWER.

class action A civil suit brought, or defended, by one or more persons on behalf of other similarly situated persons. Class actions in federal court are subject to Rule 23 of the Federal Rules of Civil Procedure, which provides, in part:

> One or more members of the class may sue or be sued as representative parties on behalf of all only if (1) the class is so numerous that joinder of all members is impracticable, (2) there are questions of law or fact common to the class, (3) the claims or defenses of the representative parties are typical of the claims or defenses of the class, and (4) the representative parties will fairly and adequately protect the interests of the class.

Class actions are frequently brought under Title VII of the Civil Rights Act of 1964.

Source references: Federal Rules of Civil Procedure, 28 U.S.C. App.; Leonard S. Janofsky, "Class Actions Under Title VII," *LLJ,* June 1976; "Recommending Union Class

Representation in Title VII Suits," 95 *Harvard LR* 1627 (1982); Robert H. Rotstein, "Federal Employment Discrimination: Scope of Inquiry and the Class Action Under Title VII," *IR Law Digest*, Jan. 1976; J. Clay Smith, Jr., "Class Actions and the EEOC," *Labor Law Developments 1980*, Proceedings of the 26th Annual Institute on Labor Law, SLF (New York: Bender, 1980); "The Tentative Settlement: Class and Class Action Suits Under Title VII of the Civil Rights Act," *IR Law Digest*, Spring 1975.

class grievance *See* GROUP GRIEVANCE.

Classification Act employees Federal government employees, typically professional, administrative, technical, and clerical employees, excluding employees of the U.S. Postal Service and others exempted by law, whose salary rates and certain other conditions of employment are determined by the Congress. Sometimes referred to as government white-collar or General Schedule employees. The salary schedules of these employees are set out in the Classification Acts; hence, the term "Classification Act" employees.

Source references: William M. Smith, "Federal Pay Procedures and the Comparability Survey," *MLR*, Aug. 1976; U.S. Dept. of Labor, BLS, *Salary Trends: Federal Classified Employees, 1939–60* (Washington: Report no. 200, 1961).

See also FEDERAL PAY COMPARABILITY ACT OF 1970, WAGE BOARD EMPLOYEES.

Classification Act of 1923 Described by Stahl as "one of the great milestones in public personnel legislation," the law established the principles of grouping white-collar positions into classes on the basis of their duties and responsibilities and of equal compensation for equal work, irrespective of sex. It created a central Personnel Classification Board (whose functions were later transferred to the CSC) to administer the provisions of the law.

Source references: Classification Act of 1923, as amended, 5 U.S.C. 661–674, 38 U.S.C. 74 (1982); O. Glenn Stahl, *Public Personnel Administration* (4th ed., New York: Harper, 1956).

See also CLASSIFICATION ACT OF 1949.

Classification Act of 1949 The statute governing administrative management of federal government employees. It replaced the Classification Act of 1923.

According to Stahl, the Act enabled "for the first time . . . a clear distinction between establishment of job evaluation standards (a task assigned to the Civil Service Commission) and classification of individual positions (a function left to the departments and agencies, subject to the commission's postaudit and power to correct misclassifications). . . . It crystallized the trend toward department responsibility for personnel transactions, with the central personnel agency becoming a standard-setting and reviewing agency." The law also provided for a study of compensating hazardous employment, a management improvement program, special awards for superior performance, longevity pay, and efficiency ratings. The pay and classifications provisions of the Act do not apply to postal employees and to blue-collar wage board employees.

Source references: Classification Act of 1949, as amended, Pub. L. 81–429, Oct. 28, 1949, 63 Stat. 954 (codified as amended in scattered sections of 2, 5, 12, 15, 16, 19, 20, 22, 25, 29, 33, 40, 41, 42, 43, 45, 49 app., 50, 50 app. U.S.C.); O. Glenn Stahl, *Public Personnel Administration* (4th ed., New York: Harper and Bros., 1956).

See also CLASSIFICATION ACT OF 1923, FEDERAL PAY COMPARABILITY ACT OF 1970, FEDERAL WAGE SYSTEM.

classification plan A method of describing and evaluating a job so that a fair rate of compensation may be assigned which has some relation to the status of the job and the proficiency required. It attempts to evaluate jobs and assign reasonable wage differentials based on the relative scale of values set up in the classification.

Source references: C. Balderston, *Wage Setting Based on Job Analysis and Evaluation* (New York: Industrial Relations Counselors, Inc., 1943); Tom Basuray and Steven A. Scherling, *Job Classification System and Pay Plan Design for Minot, North Dakota* (Grand Forks: Univ. of North Dakota, Bureau of Business and Economic Research, North Dakota Economic Studies no. 18, 1977); Robert C. Garnier, *The Maintenance of a Classification*

Plan (Chicago: PPA, Personnel Brief no. 7, 1953); Esther C. Lawton and Harold Suskin, *Elements of Position Classification in Local Government* (2d ed., Chicago: IPMA, Personnel Report no. 761, 1976); James M. Meith, Jean S. Austin, and Sharon E. Johnson, "Flex Class—A Different Way to Look at Organizational Structure," *PJ*, Nov. 1977.

See also JOB EVALUATION PLANS.

classified employee *See* CLASSIFIED SERVICE.

Classified School Employees; American Association of (Ind) Founded in 1958. It issues *The California School Employee* (10 issues annually), *The OAPSE Journal* (10 issues annually), *The Journal* (monthly), and *USEA Review* (9 issues annually).

Address: 1925 K St., N.W., Washington, D.C. 20006. Tel. (202) 466–4623

classified service A system of jobs categorized into a structured hierarchy and usually made part of a civil service system.

An act of Congress approved March 27, 1922 (42 Stat. 470; 5 U.S.C. 679) states: "The classified service shall include all persons who have heretofore or may hereafter be given a competitive status in the classified civil service, with or without competitive examination, by legislative enactment, or under the civil-service rules . . . covering groups of employees with their positions into the competitive classified service, or authorizing the appointment of individuals to positions within such service. . . ."

According to Stahl, "under the typical civil service law, the central personnel agency is given jurisdiction over specified groups of positions; according to some civil service parlance, these positions are in the 'classified service.' The term *classified* in this sense has nothing to do with the grouping of positions into classes upon the basis of duties. In the federal service and others the term *classified* has been dropped. Positions subject to the merit system are in the 'competitive service' or the 'career service.'"

Source reference: O. Glenn Stahl, *Public Personnel Administration* (7th ed., New York: Harper & Row, 1976).

See also UNCLASSIFIED SERVICE.

classless society One of the tenets of Marxist doctrine which holds that communism in its pure form would create a classless society—the proletariat. This doctrine has had little support among American trade unions. These unions have decried "class" lines, and have realized that there is no rigid demarcation among economic groups. The aspiration of American workers has been to move up in the economic, social, and political hierarchy.

class struggle A cornerstone of the Marxist philosophy. It holds that the inevitable struggle between the capitalists (owners of the means of production) and the proletariat (the nonpropertied wage earner) will lead to the downfall of the capitalist and establishment of a classless society. Some trade unions premise their policies on the existence of the class struggle and the ultimate control by the workers through the dictatorship of the proletariat.

class war A philosophy adopted by some left-wing unions from the Marxist doctrine that there is a constant class war between the capitalists (the owners of the means of production) and the workers, who are exploited by the capitalists. Trade union policy based on such a proposition will differ radically from one which it based on a "mutuality" of interest between workers and the owners of industry. Mutuality of interest does not imply acceptance or agreement on economic issues in a particular dispute.

The factors in collective bargaining which lead to settlement or strike are too complex to be explained by a philosophic concept. It is true, of course, that acceptance of our economic system by unions and recognition of the problems of management will provide a better climate for resolution of problems as they arise—in collective bargaining and in day-to-day operation of the plant.

Clayton Act of 1914 A law passed by Congress designed to disallow application of the Sherman Anti-Trust Act to combinations of labor and also to limit the jurisdiction of the courts to issue injunctions in labor disputes. Sections 6 and 20 are quoted in part below.

> Section 6. That the labor of a human is not a commodity or article of commerce. Nothing in the antitrust laws shall be construed to forbid the existence and operation of labor, . . . organizations, instituted for the purposes of mutual

help, . . . or to forbid or restrain individual members of such organizations from lawfully carrying out the legitimate objects thereof, nor shall such organizations, or the members thereof be held or construed to be illegal combinations or conspiracies in restraint of trade under the antitrust laws.

Section 20. That no restraining order or injunction shall be granted by any court of the United States, . . . in any case between an employer and employees, . . . involving, or growing out of a dispute concerning terms or conditions of employment, unless necessary to prevent irreparable injury to property, or to a property right, . . . for which injury there is no adequate remedy at law. . . .

The law was hailed as labor's "Magna Carta," but judicial construction changed that opinion and new efforts were made in this direction. The Norris-LaGuardia Act (1932) and the National Labor Relations Act (1935) subsequently were deemed to have served this purpose.

Source references: Clayton Act, as amended, Pub. L. 212 (ch. 323), Oct. 15, 1914, 38 Stat. 730 (codified as amended in scattered sections of 15, 18, and 29 U.S.C.); Felix Frankfurter and Nathan Green, *The Labor Injunction* (New York: Macmillan, 1930); Dallas L. Jones, "The Enigma of the Clayton Act," *ILRR*, Jan. 1957; Stanley I. Kutler, "Labor, the Clayton Act and the Supreme Court," *Labor History*, Winter 1962; Edwin E. Witte, "The Federal Anti-Injunction Act," 16 *Minnesota LR* 638 (1932).

See also ADEQUATE REMEDY AT LAW, NATIONAL LABOR RELATIONS ACT, NORRIS-LAGUARDIA ACT.

Cleaning and Dye House Workers; International Association of (AFL-CIO) An international union which was suspended from the AFL. In May 1956, the union merged with the Laundry Workers' International Union (AFL-CIO).

See also LAUNDRY, DRY CLEANING AND DYE HOUSE WORKERS INTERNATIONAL UNION (IND).

cleansing period The period required under Section 504(a) of the Labor-Management Reporting and Disclosure Act of 1959 during which a union officer has to cleanse himself of previous criminal acts.

In a case involving Harry Serio, a Teamster business agent, the question was put to the court by the Secretary of Labor, who has the responsibility for enforcing the provisions, as to whether the five-year ban on ex-criminals holding union office begins at the end of parole or incarceration. The Third Circuit Court of Appeals held it to be at the end of parole. The court in this particular case did not decide whether the federal or the state law should control since the New Jersey law and the federal law were consistent in that under both statutes a parolee remains in legal custody and, therefore, technically is a prisoner at large.

The court in this case held that both state and federal law should be taken into account in determining the five-year cleansing period so long as the state law is not materially different as to make Section 504(a) ineffective.

Source references: Labor-Management Reporting and Disclosure Act, as amended, Section 504(a), 29 U.S.C. 504(a) (1982); *Harry Serio v. Milton J. Liss*, 300 F2d 386, 47 LRRM 2225 (CA3, 1961).

clean-up period That part of the workday, before meals or at the end of the work shift, allowed the employee to clean his person or clothing, or to clean up the workplace so the person on the next shift will find it in good working condition.

It may also refer to the allowance in the time standard for the job, a recognition that one of the time factors in the particular work involves time to clean up.

See also ALLOWED TIME.

clearance A procedure in public employment offices which provides clearing house procedures so that unfilled job orders and applicants from one office may be transferred to other offices which have job opportunities. Such clearance permits more effective handling of placements and meeting labor market needs of communities. The term also is used to denote that the employee has been checked for loyalty, etc., and has "clearance" to classified materials, secret work, or work performed under "security" regulations.

clear and present danger doctrine The doctrine that the right of freedom of speech is constitutionally protected unless there is a "clear-and-present danger" sufficient to deny that freedom for the protection of the public interest.

Source references: Bakery & Pastry Drivers Union v. Wohl, 315 US 769, 10 LRRM 507 (1942); *Carpenters and Joiners Union v. Ritter's Cafe,* 315 US 722, 10 LRRM 511 (1942); *Hague v. C.I.O.,* 307 US 496, 4 LRRM 501 (1939); *Schenck v. U.S.,* 249 US 47 (1919); *Senn v. Tile Layers Union,* 301 US 468 (1937); *Thornhill v. Alabama,* 310 US 88, 6 LRRM 697 (1940); E. Merrick Dodd, "Picketing and Free Speech," 56 *Harvard LR* 513 (1943); Sylvester Petro, "Picketing and Freedom of Speech," *LLJ,* June 1950; Bernard L. Samoff, "Picketing and the First Amendment: 'Full Circle' and 'Formal Surrender,'" *LLJ,* Dec. 1958; Ludwig Teller, "Picketing and Free Speech," 56 *Harvard LR* 180 (1943).

See also FREEDOM OF SPEECH, PICKETING.

cleavage The NLRB under Section 8(a)(2) of the National Labor Relations Act has authority to "disestablish" organizations supported or assisted or dominated by the employer. Where an organization succeeded the disestablished company-dominated union, the Board insisted that there be a distinct and clear cleavage between the two organizations—that the change was one of substance, not of form only.

See also COMPANY-DOMINATED UNION, DISESTABLISHMENT.

clerical work Occupations which serve to promote certain transactions or assist in reporting or recording such activity. Work ranges from routine, repetitive, and simple tasks to those of a highly complex nature. The range of occupations includes such titles as accountants, bookkeepers, cashiers, office and shipping clerks, stenographers, typists, etc.

Source references: H. D. Anderson and P. E. Davidson, *Occupational Trends* (Stanford: Stanford UP, 1947); Eaton H. Conant, "Worker Efficiency and Wage Differentials in a Clerical Labor Market," *ILRR,* April 1963; W. C. Krautheim, "Setting Standards for Clerical Employees," *PJ,* July 1968; Carroll L. Shartle, *Occupational Information* (New York: PH, 1946); William F. Stansbury, "What Causes Clerical Turnover?" *PJ,* Dec. 1969.

See also OFFICE WORKER.

climb on the bandwagon Getting in with the winning team in the hope that the spoils will be shared. Election of union officers and convention proceedings have some of the characteristics of political elections. Machine politics and the political bandwagon have been adapted from the political arena to the field of union politics.

closed anti-union shop A shop or plant closed to union members or to those who may seek union affiliation or membership. Such a plant or shop is illegal under the Taft-Hartley Act in any company engaged in interstate commerce.

Source references: Adair v. United States, 208 US 161 (1908); Frank T. Carlton, *History and Problems of Organized Labor* (Boston: Heath, 1920).

See also ADAIR V. UNITED STATES, ERDMAN ACT, OPEN SHOP, YELLOW DOG CONTRACT.

closed shop A union-security arrangement where the employer is required to hire only employees who are members of the union. Membership in the union is also a condition of continued employment. The closed shop is illegal under federal labor statutes.

Source references: John Chamberlain, "Democracy and the Closed Shop," *Fortune,* Jan. 1942; George F. Jensen, "The Closed Shop Is Not a Closed Issue," *ILRR,* July 1949; Julia E. Johnsen (comp.), *The Closed Shop* (New York: Wilson, 1942); Frank T. Stockton, *The Closed Shop in American Trade Unions* (Baltimore: Johns Hopkins Press, 1911); Jerome Toner, *The Closed Shop* (Washington: American Council on Public Affairs, 1942); U.S. Dept. of Labor, BLS, *Extent of Collective Bargaining and Union Recognition, 1946* (Washington: Bull. no. 909, 1947); Stephen C. Vladeck, "Open and Closed Shop Unions," *NYU 5th Annual Conference on Labor,* ed. by Emanuel Stein (Albany: Bender, 1952).

See also MODIFIED CLOSED SHOP.

closed shop agreement A collective bargaining agreement which provides that only members in good standing are permitted to work. Membership in good standing is a condition of continued employment. The closed shop agreement is outlawed under the Taft-Hartley Act.

closed shop with closed union A situation in which the union has a closed shop arrangement with the employer, but controls the number of workers in the trade by limiting membership in the union. A closed union can be maintained by unreasonably high entrance fees, membership dues, apprenticeship regulations, or by not accepting applicants for membership by "closing the books," or other factors which would prohibit individuals desirous of joining the union from becoming members. Although some of these restrictions developed from legitimate concern over the limited number of job opportunities, many abuses crept in and such limitations are objected to and opposed by most trade unionists.

Source reference: Marinship Corp. v. James, 155 P2d 329, 15 LRRM 798 (Cal 1945).

See also CLOSED SHOP, MAINTENANCE OF MEMBERSHIP, UNION SHOP.

closed union A union which through various methods seeks to protect the job opportunities of its members by limiting those who may enter the trade and become members. Membership is restricted through unusually high initiation fees and dues, through restrictive membership conditions, and other devices designed to make difficult entrance into the union.

See also CLOSED SHOP.

clothing allowance A special payment in addition to regular wages for the purchase of clothing, uniforms, safety shoes or goggles, or other safety garments required in the regular performance of work.

Clothing and Textile Workers Union; Amalgamated (AFL-CIO) Union formed with the merger of the Amalgamated Clothing Workers of America (AFL-CIO) and the Textile Workers Union of America (AFL-CIO) on June 3, 1976. The United Shoe Workers of America (AFL-CIO), in March 1979, and the United Hatters, Cap and Millinery Workers International Union (AFL-CIO), in December 1982, joined the ACTWU. Its official monthly publication is *ACTWU Labor Unity.*

Address: 15 Union Square, New York, N.Y. 10003. Tel. (212) 242–0700

Clothing Workers of America; Amalgamated (AFL-CIO) Organized in Nashville, Tennessee, as a result of a split in the United Garment Workers of America. It adopted the name Amalgamated Clothing Workers of America in December 1914 and remained outside the AFL until October 1933, when it received its charter from the AFL. When the CIO was formed it joined the group of industrial unions in their effort to organize the mass production industries.

The International Glove Workers' Union of America (AFL-CIO) merged with the union in December 1961.

Its official publication was *The Advance.* The union is now known as the Amalgamated Clothing and Textile Workers Union (AFL-CIO).

Source reference: George Soule, *Sidney Hillman, Labor Statesman* (New York: Macmillan, 1939).

See also CLOTHING AND TEXTILE WORKERS UNION; AMALGAMATED (AFL-CIO).

coalition bargaining *See* COLLECTIVE BARGAINING, COALITION.

Coalition of Labor Union Women (CLUW) A national organization of trade unionists founded in 1974. The Statement of Purpose adopted at its founding conference declared that the primary purpose of CLUW "is to unify all union women in a viable organization to determine . . . our common problems and concerns and to develop action programs within the framework of our unions to deal effectively with our objectives." Among its objectives are unionization of women workers, affirmative action, political action within unions and outside unions, and participation of women in union affairs. It issues the bimonthly *Newsletter.*

Address: 386 Park Avenue S., New York, New York 10016. Tel. (212) 679–0765

Source references: Anne H. Nelson, *Working Women in Organized Labor* (Ithaca: Cornell Univ., NYSSILR, Reprint no. 385, 1975); Barbara M. Wertheimer, *Search for a Partnership Role, Women in Labor Unions Today* (Ithaca: Cornell Univ., NYSSILR, Reprint no. 387, 1976).

codes of ethics Systematically organized standards of behavior established to guide groups in their actions. Thus a code of ethics for arbitrators and those using the arbitration process has been adopted. The CIO, and later the AFL-CIO, set up an ethical practices committee which established a number of codes for behavior of trade unionists and trade union officials in the handling of health and welfare funds, etc.

Source references: "Code of Professional Responsibility for Arbitrators of Labor-Management Disputes," as approved April 28, 1975, NAA, AAA, FMCS; Emanuel Stein, "Ethical Aspects of Union Policy and Conduct," *Annals*, Jan. 1966; "Text of AFL-CIO Code of Ethical Practices," 39 *LRRM* 28, 40 *LRRM* 27.

codetermination A procedure for providing workers a greater degree of responsibility and authority in the production process.

Participative management and industrial democracy are other terms used to describe procedures which attempt to give workers a greater role in decision making.

Source references: Edwin F. Beal, "Codetermination in German Industry, Origins of Codetermination," *ILRR*, July 1955; Dorothea de Schweinitz, *Labor-Management Consultation in the Factory: The Experience of Sweden, England, and the Federal Republic of Germany* (Honolulu: IRC, Univ. of Hawaii, 1966); Milton Derber, *Collective Bargaining, Mutuality, and Workers Participation in Management, an International Analysis* (Urbana: Univ. of Illinois, Institute of Labor and IR, Reprint Series no. 281, 1980); James N. Ellenberger, "The Realities of Co-Determination," *American Federationist*, Oct. 1977; G. David Garson, "The Codetermination Model of Workers' Participation: Where Is It Leading?" *Sloan Management Review*, Spring 1977; Gerry Hunnius, G. David Garson, and John Case (ed.), *Workers' Control, A Reader on Labor and Social Change* (New York: Vintage Books, 1973); Clark Kerr, "Economic Effects of Codetermination," *Proceedings of the 8th A/M, IRRA*, ed. by L. Reed Tripp (Madison: 1956); William H. McPherson, "Co-Determination in Practice," *ILRR*, July 1955; Henry Rutz and Edwin Beal, "The Origins of Codetermination," *ILRR*, July 1958; Douglas Soutar, "Co-Determination, Industrial Democracy and the Role of Management," *Proceedings of the 26th A/M, IRRA*, ed. by Gerald Somers (Madison: 1974); Adolph Sturmthal, "Industrial Democracy in the Affluent Society," *Proceedings of the 17th A/M, IRRA*, ed. by Gerald Somers (Madison: 1965); William W. Winpisinger, "An American Unionist Looks at Co-Determination," *Employee Relations LJ*, Autumn 1976.

See also MULTIPLE MANAGEMENT, PARTICIPATIVE MANAGEMENT, QUALITY CIRCLES, WORKERS' COUNCILS.

coercion Pressures exerted by employers against employees to prevent their joining a union or engaging in concerted activities protected by law. It also includes activities by unions or representatives of unions to force individuals to join a union in violation of the law.

cold storage training A procedure for training employees for advancement or for supervisory positions in advance of any specific opening for promotion. The trainee is kept in "cold storage" until such time as he is needed by the company. It is a training program based on long-range needs of the organization rather than on the specific immediate need for a qualified person in a definite position.

Source references: Helen Baker, *Company Plans for Employee Promotions* (Princeton: Princeton Univ., IR Section, Reprint Series 58, 1939); Palmer Kalsem, *Practical Supervision* (New York: McGraw-Hill, 1945); G. I. MacLaren, "Promotion from the Ranks," *Personnel*, May 1937; William Spriegel and Joseph Towls, *Retail Personnel Management* (New York: McGraw-Hill, 1951).

See also PROMOTION.

collar-to-collar pay *See* PORTAL-TO-PORTAL PAY.

collective actions Suits instituted by an employee or a group of employees under the Fair Labor Standards Act for unpaid wages and damages because of an employer's violation of the statute. The law forbids representative actions by nonemployees with the exception of the Secretary of Labor, who specifically is empowered to bring suit on behalf of an employee or group of employees.

collective bargaining A term used to denote the process whereby representatives of labor and management work out the wages, hours, and other terms and conditions of employment to be embodied in an agreement that is to govern the relations of the parties for a specified period of time. More recently the term has been augmented to include the day-to-day activities involved in effectuating and carrying out the terms of the agreement.

The term has a somewhat narrower meaning as applied to the public sector, due largely to the fact that management is the government. There is a great deal of debate as to what features of the collective bargaining process in the private sector are applicable to the public sector. Some feel that the term collective bargaining is inapplicable to public employment since collective bargaining implies the right to strike when there is no agreement after negotiation. Some have made the effort to use a softer terminology, such as "professional negotiation," "collective dealing," and "collective negotiation."

A number of public sector laws define collective bargaining. The Hawaii law, for example, provides:

> "Collective Bargaining" means the performance of the mutual obligations of the public employer and the exclusive representative to meet at reasonable times, to confer and negotiate in good faith, and to execute a written agreement with respect to wages, hours, and other terms and conditions of employment, except that by any such obligation neither party shall be compelled to agree to a proposal, or be required to make a concession.

Source references: Howard J. Anderson (ed.), *The Labor Board and the Collective Bargaining Process,* A Report on the Labor-Law Seminar of the Kansas City Bar Assn., March 25, 1970, with Editorial Analysis, Additional Text, and Selected NLRB and Court Decisions (Washington: BNA, 1971); Wallace N. Atherton, *Theory of Union Bargaining Goals* (Princeton: Princeton UP, 1973); Samuel B. Bacharach and Edward J. Lawler, *Bargaining; Tactics and Outcomes* (San Francisco: Jossey-Bass, 1981); E. Wight Bakke, Clark Kerr, and Charles W. Anrod (ed.), *Unions, Management and the Public* (3d ed., New York: Harcourt Brace, 1967); Lee Balliet, *Survey of Labor Relations* (Washington: BNA, 1981); Jack Barbash, "Collective Bargaining as an Institution—A Long View," *Proceedings of the 29th A/M, IRRA*, ed. by James Stern and Barbara Dennis (Madison: 1977); Edwin F. Beal and James P. Begin, *The Practice of Collective Bargaining* (6th ed., Homewood, Ill.: Irwin, 1982); BNA, *Labor-Management Relations, 1979–2029* (Washington: 1979); John J. Collins, *Bargaining at the Local Level* (New York: Fordham UP, 1974); Archibald Cox and John T. Dunlop, "Regulation of Collective Bargaining by the National Labor Relations Board," *Harvard LR*, Jan. 1950; Harold W. Davey, *Contemporary Collective Bargaining* (3d ed., Englewood Cliffs, N.J.: PH, 1972); George De Menil, *Bargaining: Monopoly Power Versus Union Power* (Cambridge: MIT Press, 1971); Julius N. Draznin, "Letting the Sunshine into Collective Bargaining," *PJ*, Oct. 1976; Peter Feuille, Wallace E. Hendricks, and Lawrence M. Kahn, *Bargaining Structure and Bargaining Outcomes: Determinants and Tradeoffs* (Washington: U.S. National Technical Information Service, 1981); Audrey Freedman, *Managing Labor Relations* (New York: The Conference Board, Report no. 765, 1979); Wayne L. Horvitz, "Overcoming Rigidity in Collective Bargaining," *NYU 31st Annual National Conference on Labor*, ed. by Richard Adelman (New York: Bender, 1978); Howard D. Marshall and Natalie J. Marshall, *Collective Bargaining* (New York: Random House, 1971); Daniel Quinn Mills, *Labor-Management Relations* (New York: McGraw-Hill, 1978); Richard B. Peterson and Lane Tracy, *Models of the Bargaining Process: With Special Reference to Collective Bargaining* (Seattle: Univ. of Washington, Graduate School of Business Administration, 1977); Reed C. Richardson, *Collective Bargaining by Objectives* (Englewood Cliffs: PH, 1977); George Ruben, "Focus on Bargaining: 25 Years of Progress," *American Federationist*, May 1974; ———, "Organized Labor in 1981: A Shifting of Priorities," *MLR*, Jan. 1982; Benjamin M. Sheiber, "Honesty in Bargaining," *American Federationist*, April 1975; Gerald G. Somers (ed.), *Collective Bargaining: Contemporary American Experience* (Madison: IRRA, 1980); Jack Stieber, Robert B. McKersie, and D. Quinn Mills (ed.), *U.S. Industrial Relations 1950–1980: A Critical Assessment* (Madison: IRRA, 1981); W. J.

Usery, Jr., "The Challenge Facing Free Collective Bargaining," *Labor Law Developments 1980,* Proceedings of the 26th Annual Institute on Labor Law, SLF (New York: Bender, 1980); Arnold R. Weber, "Labor-Management Relations in a Controlled and Rationed Economy," *Arbitration—1974,* Proceedings of the 27th A/M, NAA, ed. by Barbara Dennis and Gerald Somers (Washington: BNA, 1975).

See also COLLECTIVE NEGOTIATION, MANDATORY SUBJECTS FOR BARGAINING, MEET AND CONFER, NEGOTIATING RANGES, PERMISSIVE SUBJECTS FOR BARGAINING, PROHIBITED SUBJECTS FOR BARGAINING, SCOPE OF BARGAINING.

collective bargaining, areawide The process of negotiation between employers and unions which usually covers a wide geographic area. The West Coast longshore and paper industries are illustrative. It differs from industrywide bargaining, which seeks to cover all employers in an industry regardless of its location in the United States.

collective bargaining, blue sky *See* BLUE SKY BARGAINING.

collective bargaining, coalition A procedure developed in the 1966 negotiations between General Electric and Westinghouse and 11 AFL-CIO unions, which involve efforts on the part of a number of unions (of frequently unrelated groups of workers in different parts of a company or industry) which have contracts with a single employer to effect union coordination to meet employer coordination. The objective is to prevent individual agreements and to secure a uniform, centrally directed agreement. It is distinguished from the voluntary joint bargaining which has taken place in reasonably homogeneous parts of a company or industry.

Source references: William N. Chernish, *Coalition Bargaining, A Study of Union Tactics and Public Policy* (Philadelphia: Univ. of Pennsylvania Press, 1969); Abraham Cohen, "Coordinated Bargaining and Structures of Collective Bargaining," *LLJ,* June 1975; ———, "Union Rationale and Objectives of Coordinated Bargaining," *LLJ,* Feb. 1976; "Coordinated-Coalition Bargaining: Theory, Legality, Practice and Economic Effects," *IR Law Digest,* July 1971; Guy Farmer, *Coalition Bargaining and Union Power* (New York: Industrial Relations Counselors, Inc., Research Monograph no. 27, 1967); Stephen B. Goldberg, "Coordinated Bargaining Tactics of Unions," *IR Law Digest,* Jan. 1971; Wallace Hendricks, "Conglomerate Mergers and Collective Bargaining," *IR,* Feb. 1976; George H. Hildebrand, "Cloudy Future for Coalition Bargaining," *Harvard BR,* Nov./Dec. 1968; Herbert J. Lahne, "Coalition Bargaining and the Future of Union Structure," *LLJ,* June 1967; Hank McKinnell, *Coordinated Bargaining, An Antidote for Boulwarism* (n.p.: Steering Committee of the Coordinated Bargaining Committee of GE-Westinghouse Unions, 1974); Robert A. McLean, "Coalition Bargaining & Strike Activity in the Electrical Equipment Industry, 1950–1974," *ILRR,* April 1977; Michael W. Schiefen, "Industrial Union Alliances for Collective Bargaining," *Industrial and Labor Relations Forum,* March 1972; Philip J. Schwarz, *Coalition Bargaining* (Ithaca: NYSSILR, Cornell Univ., Key Issues Series no. 5, 1970); Joel Seidman (ed.), *Trade Union Government and Collective Bargaining: Some Critical Issues* (New York: Praeger, 1970).

See also COLLECTIVE BARGAINING, INDUSTRYWIDE; COLLECTIVE BARGAINING, MULTI-EMPLOYER.

collective bargaining, companywide Collective bargaining agreements which cover all of a company's employees. Collective bargaining which takes place between a company with many plants and a single union representing employees of a particular craft or all employees of an industrial unit. Terms and conditions of employment are generally uniform, except for provisions to handle purely local conditions.

Source reference: Frank C. Pierson, *Collective Bargaining Systems* (Washington: American Council on Public Affairs, 1942).

collective bargaining, industrywide Collective bargaining which takes place on an industrywide basis. In industrywide bargaining, the terms and conditions of employment mutually agreed upon by labor and management cover all or a major portion of the organized employees in the industry. Contracts, of course, may provide for geographic and other variations to meet local conditions. Complete industrywide bargaining doesn't exist in any industry since there are always some companies not organized and under the terms of the agreement. The coal mining industry and steel are typical examples of industries in which industrywide bargaining is approximated.

Source references: Milton Derber, *Labor-Management Relations at the Plant Level Under Industry-Wide Bargaining* (Champaign: Institute of Labor & IR, Univ. of Illinois, 1955); Arlyn J. Melcher, "Central Negotiations and Master Contract: An Analysis of Their Implications for Collective Bargaining," *LLJ*, June 1965; Frank C. Pierson, "Prospects for Industry-Wide Bargaining," *ILRR*, April 1950; John V. Van Sickle, *Industry-Wide Collective Bargaining and the Public Interest* (New York: American Enterprise Association, National Economic Problems Serial 425, 1947); Colston E. Warne, *Industry-Wide Collective Bargaining: Promise or Menace?* (Boston: Heath, 1950); Leo Wolman, *Industry-Wide Bargaining* (Irvington-on-Hudson: Foundation for Economic Education, 1948).

See also ASSOCIATION AGREEMENT.

collective bargaining, multi-employer Collective bargaining which takes place between a union and a group or groups of employers. Bargaining between a union and an employer association sometimes is referred to as "association bargaining."

Quite frequently so-called industrywide bargaining is actually multi-employer bargaining, since there are relatively few industries in which collective bargaining is covered in an industrywide sense. Frequently there are bargaining arrangements which cover large segments of an industry in a particular geographic region.

Source references: Jules Bachman, "How Important is Multi-Employer Bargaining?" *PJ*, March 1952; ———, *Multi-Employer Bargaining* (New York: NYU, Institute of Labor Relations & Social Security, 1951); Peter Feuille et al., "Determinants of Multi-Employer Bargaining in Metropolitan Hospitals," *Employee Relations LJ*, Summer 1978; ———, "Multi-Employer Bargaining Among Local Governments," *Proceedings of the 29th A/M, IRRA*, ed. by James Stern and Barbara Dennis (Madison: 1977); Sylvester Garrett, "Is Multi-Employer Bargaining Right for Your Company?" *The New Climate of Union-Management Relations* (New York: AMA, Personnel Series no. 150, 1953); Clark Kerr and Lloyd H. Fisher, "Multiple-Employer Bargaining: The San Francisco Experience," *Insights Into Labor Issues*, ed. by R. A. Lester and J. Shister (New York: Macmillan, 1948); Richard Pegnetter, *Multi-employer Bargaining in the Public Sector: Purposes and Experiences* (Chicago: IPMA, PERL no. 52, 1975); Harry H. Rains, "Multi-employer Bargaining in the Public Sector: Pros and Cons and the Realities of the Possible," *Employee Relations LJ*, Autumn 1976; Charles M. Rehmus, "Multi-Employer Bargaining," *Current History*, Aug. 1965; Julius Rezler, *Multi-Employer Association Bargaining and Its Impact on the Collective Bargaining Process* (Washington: U.S. Congress, House, Committee on Education and Labor, 1965); Cyrus F. Smythe, Jr., "Public-Private Sector Multi-Employer Collective Bargaining—The Role of the Employer Representative," *LLJ*, Aug. 1971; Lynn E. Wagner, "Multi-Union Bargaining: A Legal Analysis," *LLJ*, Dec. 1968.

See also ASSOCIATION AGREEMENT.

collective bargaining, plantwide Bargaining which encompasses the employees in a single plant. The terms and conditions of employment cover the employees in the bargaining unit in a particular plant, even though the company may have many plants throughout the state or country.

collective bargaining contract *See* AGREEMENT, COLLECTIVE.

collective labor agreement *See* AGREEMENT, COLLECTIVE.

collective negotiation A phrase which has received currency in the discussion of procedures in the public sector and which might serve as the counterpart to the term "collective bargaining" in the private sector. Those who contend that the term collective bargaining is not meaningful in the public sector hold that collective bargaining implies the right to strike when there is an impasse in negotiations. They believe that no such right can be tolerated in the public sector, and hence there is need for a term which distinguishes the two processes.

Those who favor the term "collective bargaining" believe that much of the process in the private sector is applicable to the public sector, and although the limited right to strike is extended in only a few public sector jurisdictions, strikes do occur when there is no adequate procedure for the resolution of impasses.

The issue as to which phrase to use is not likely to be resolved on the semantic front. Because of the wide acceptance of "collective bargaining" following the passage of the National Labor Relations Act, and the psychological attachment of unions to the term, it is likely that it will win out over the phrase "collective negotiation." This, however, does not require the conclusion that collective bargaining in the private and public sectors will have the same ingredients. The bargaining or negotiations which will take place in the public sector will of necessity be basically different because of the existence of state laws, ordinances, civil service regulations, etc., which will have to accommodate the enlarged scope of bargaining in the years ahead.

Source references: Arvid Anderson and Hugh D. Jascourt (ed.), *Trends in Public Sector Labor Relations. Volume 1, 1972–73* (Chicago: IPMA and Public Employment Relations Research Institute, 1975); Tim Bornstein, "Legacies of Local Government Collective Bargaining in the 1970s," *LLJ*, March 1980; Robert H. Chanin, "The United States Constitution and Collective Negotiation in the Public Sector," *Labor Law Developments 1972*, Proceedings of the 18th Annual Institute on Labor Law, SLF (New York: Bender, 1972); Richard M. Cunningham, "Labor-Management Relations in the Federal Sector: Democracy or Paternalism?" *LLJ*, Oct. 1980; Roger E. Dahl, "Public Sector Bargaining Issues in the 1980's: A Management View," *NYU 33d Annual National Conference on Labor*, ed. by Richard Adelman (New York: Bender, 1981); Milton Derber, Peter Pashler, and Mary Beth Ryan, *Collective Bargaining by State Governments in the Twelve Midwestern States* (Urbana: Univ. of Illinois, Institute of Labor & IR, 1974); Harry T. Edwards, "The Emerging Duty to Bargain in the Public Sector," *IR Law Digest*, Jan. 1974; R. W. Fleming, "Public-Employee Bargaining: Problems and Prospects," *Proceedings of the 31st A/M, IRRA*, ed. by Barbara Dennis (Madison: 1979); Michael Grace, "The Chaos in Public Sector Bargaining," *American Federationist*, July 1981; Thomas Y. Hobart, Jr., "Public Sector Bargaining Issues in the 1980's: A Union View," *NYU 33d Annual National Conference on Labor*, ed. by Richard Adelman (New York: Bender, 1981); IRRA, *Public-Sector Bargaining*, ed. by Benjamin Aaron, Joseph R. Grodin, and James L. Stern (Washington: BNA, 1979); Hugh D. Jascourt (ed.), *Government Labor Relations: Trends and Information for the Future, Volume 1, 1975 to 1978* (Oak Park, Ill.: Moore Pub. and Public Employment Relations Research Institute, 1979); Myron Lieberman, *Public-Sector Bargaining, A Policy Reappraisal* (Lexington, Mass.: Lexington Books, 1980); J. Joseph Loewenberg and Michael H. Moskow, *Collective Bargaining in Government: Readings and Cases* (Englewood Cliffs: PH, 1972); Thomas M. Love and George T. Sulzner, "Political Implications of Public Employee Bargaining," *IR*, Feb. 1972; Joyce M. Najita, "State Government Employee Bargaining: Selected Characteristics," *LLJ*, Aug. 1982; Murray B. Nesbitt, *Labor Relations in the Federal Government Service* (Washington: BNA, 1976); Public Employment Relations Service, *Portrait of a Process—Collective Negotiations in Public Employment*, ed. by Muriel K. Gibbons et al. (Fort Washington, Pa.: Labor Relations Press, 1979); Bob F. Repas, *Collective Bargaining in Federal Employment* (2d ed., Honolulu: Univ. of Hawaii, IRC, 1973); Joel Seidman, *Public Sector Collective Bargaining and the Administrative Process* (Honolulu: Univ. of Hawaii, IRC, 1972); Clyde W. Summers, "Public Employee Bargaining: A Political Perspective," 83 *Yale LJ* 1156 (1974); ———, "Public Sector Bargaining: Problems of Governmental Decision-Making," 44 *Cincinnati LR* 669 (1975); Robert S. Summers, *Collective Bargaining and Public Benefit Conferral: A Jurisprudential Critique* (Ithaca: Cornell Univ., NYSSILR, Institute of Public Employment, Monograph 7, 1976); George W. Taylor, "Public Employment: Strikes or Procedures?" *ILRR*, July 1967; U.S. Dept. of

Commerce, Bureau of the Census, *1977 Census of Governments, Vol. 3, Public Employment, no. 3: Management-Labor Relations in State and Local Governments* (Washington: 1979); Kenneth O. Warner and Mary L. Hennessy, *Public Management at the Bargaining Table* (Chicago: PPA, 1967); Joan Weitzman, *City Workers and Fiscal Crisis: Cutbacks, Givebacks and Survival; A Study of the New York City Experience* (New Brunswick: Rutgers Univ., Institute of Management and Labor Relations, 1979); Harry H. Wellington and Ralph K. Winter, Jr., *The Unions and the Cities* (Washington: Brookings Institution, 1972); Donald H. Wollett, "Collective Bargaining in the Public Sector, State Government—Strategies for Negotiations in an Austere Environment: A Management Perspective," *LLJ*, Aug. 1976; Sam Zagoria (ed.), *Public Workers and Public Unions* (Englewood Cliffs: PH, 1972).

See also PROFESSIONAL NEGOTIATION, PUBLIC EMPLOYEE RELATIONS.

Collyer Insulated Wire case An NLRB decision holding that deferral of an unfair labor practice dispute to a collectively bargained grievance/arbitration procedure is a proper exercise of its authority under the National Labor Relations Act. The charge that the company unilaterally effected changes in wages and working conditions was viewed by the Board as a dispute over terms and conditions of work covered by the collective bargaining agreement and hence subject to the grievance/arbitration procedure of the agreement. However, the Board retained jurisdiction for the limited purpose of entertaining a motion for further consideration upon a showing that either (1) the dispute was not, with reasonable promptness after issuance of the Board's decision, resolved by an amicable settlement in the grievance procedure or submitted promptly to arbitration, or (2) the grievance or arbitration procedures were not fair and regular or reached a result repugnant to the Act.

Source references: Collyer Insulated Wire and Local Union 1098, International Brotherhood of Electrical Workers, 192 NLRB 837, 77 LRRM 1931 (1971); Milden J. Fox, Jr. and Huntly E. Shelton, Jr., "The Collyer Case: A Landmark NLRB Decision," *Journal of Collective Negotiations in the Public Sector*, Summer 1973; Dell B. Johannesen and W. Britton Smith, Jr., "*Collyer:* Open Sesame to Deferral," *LLJ*, Dec. 1972; Peter G. Nash, "The NLRB and Arbitration: Some Impressions of the Practical Effect of the Board's Collyer Policy Upon Arbitrators and Arbitration," *Arbitration—1974*, Proceedings of the 27th A/M, NAA, ed. by Barbara Dennis and Gerald Somers (Washington: BNA, 1975); Catherine G. Novack, "Cutting Back on *Collyer*: The First Step in the Right Direction," *LLJ*, Dec. 1977; Rosemary Pye, "Collyer's Effect on the Individual Charging Party," *LLJ*, Sept. 1974; George Schatzki, "Earliest Returns from the NLRB's New Deferral Policy in *Collyer Insulated Wire*," *NYU 25th Annual Conference on Labor* (New York: Bender, 1973); Kenneth J. Simon-Rose, "Deferral Under *Collyer* by the NLRB of Section 8(a)(3) Cases," *LLJ*, April 1976; Michael J. Zimmer, "Wired for Collyer: Rationalizing NLRB and Arbitration Jurisdiction," *IR Law Digest*, Oct. 1973.

Colorado Association of Public Employees (Ind) An organization affiliated with the Assembly of Governmental Employees. Its publication, *The Citizen*, is issued every month.

Address: 1390 Logan St., Room 402, Denver, Colo. 80203. Tel. (303) 832–1001

Colorado Classified School Employees Association (Ind) An organization affiliated with the American Association of Classified School Employees (Ind). Its monthly publication is the *Classified Chronicle*.

Address: 1321 Bannock Street, Denver, Colo. 80204. Tel. (303) 629–7272

Colorado plan Also known as the Rockefeller plan since it involved the Rockefeller-controlled mines and steel plants of the Colorado Fuel and Iron Company, where the plan was put into effect in 1915 after a series of labor disputes.

Sponsored by John D. Rockefeller, Jr., it was designed to provide labor and management committees to consider problems of mutual concern, such as housing, safety, sanitation, and recreation. Wages were not subject to joint review. Issues subject to joint discussion could be taken to a board of arbitration.

The plan was a forerunner of the employee representation plans which flourished following the enactment of section 7(a) of the National Industrial Recovery Act.

Source references: Edward Kirkland, *A History of American Economic Life* (3d ed., New York: Appleton, 1951); Samuel Yellen, *American Labor Struggles* (New York: Arno & The New York Times, c.1936, 1969).

See also EMPLOYEE REPRESENTATION PLANS.

color discrimination Unfair employment practices against persons based on skin pigmentation. Blacks have been the group most discriminated against in employment opportunities, layoffs, and promotions. Some unions also have discriminated against blacks by denying them opportunities to join or by establishing discriminatory "B" locals designed to limit membership only to blacks. Most unions have eliminated such discriminatory practices.

Source references: Paul Bullock, "Employment Problems of the Mexican-American," *IR,* May 1964; Hugh Hafer and John E. Rinehart, Jr., "Blinded by Color—Some Observations on Title VII of the Civil Rights Act of 1964," *Labor Law Developments 1972,* Proceedings of the 18th Annual Institute on Labor Law, SLF (New York: Bender, 1972); Howard Ketcham, "The Influence of Color on the Work Environment," *Personnel Administration,* July/Aug. 1958; Robert B. McKersie, "The Civil Rights Movement and Employment," *IR,* May 1964; Herbert R. Northrup and Richard L. Rowan, *The Negro and Employment Opportunity* (Ann Arbor: Univ. of Michigan, Bureau of IR, 1965); Dawn Wachtel, *The Negro and Discrimination in Employment* (Ann Arbor: Univ. of Michigan-Wayne State Univ., Institute of Labor and IR, 1965).

See also BLACK EMPLOYMENT, CIVIL RIGHTS ACT OF 1964.

Columbia Typographical Union Claimed to be the oldest local union existing in the country, it is affiliated with the International Typographical Union (AFL-CIO). It has been continuously in existence since 1815.

Address: 4626 Wisconsin Ave. N.W., Washington, D.C. 20016. Tel. (202) 362–9413

combinations, labor *See* LABOR COMBINATIONS.

comintern The Communist International organized in 1919 to spread and promote communism throughout the world and to promote proletarian revolutions wherever possible. Meetings of Communists from various countries in Moscow in 1920 led to the formation of a policy of infiltrating the labor movements of the Western countries.

The organization established in the United States in 1921 was the Trade Union Education League, under the leadership of William Z. Foster.

International communism made a strong bid in the 1920s by "boring from within" the AFL through the development of militant and aggressive programs and policies and working to establish class-conscious unions.

The Communist International was officially dissolved in 1943 but reincarnated in the Cominform (Communist Information Bureau) in 1947.

Source references: Edward E. Palmer, *The Communist Problem in America* (New York: Crowell, 1951); John Price, *The International Labor Movement* (Oxford: Oxford UP, 1947); Earl R. Sikes, *Contemporary Economic Systems* (New York: Henry Holt, 1940).

See also THIRD INTERNATIONAL.

commerce clause Article I, section 8 of the Constitution, which provides that Congress shall have the power ". . . to regulate commerce with foreign nations and among the several states. . . ." Much of federal labor legislation, including the National Labor Relations Act and the Labor Management Relations Act, was constitutionally supported by the commerce clause of the Constitution.

See also AFFECTING COMMERCE.

Commerce Clearing House, Inc. A private information service which publishes materials in the field of labor-management relations.

Address: 4025 W. Peterson Ave., Chicago, Ill. 60646. Tel. (312) 267–9010

commerce power The authority granted to Congress by the federal Constitution to regulate commerce between and among the states.

See also AFFECTING COMMERCE.

commission earnings Earnings or compensation by sales personnel based on a percentage of total dollar sales volume. Sales personnel may receive in addition a minimum salary guarantee, in the event sales are inadequate.

See also SALARY AND COMMISSION.

Committee for Industrial Organization A group of unions within the AFL formed in November 1935 to organize unorganized workers in the mass production industries.

These unions were accused of sponsoring "dual unionism" and were suspended from the AFL in 1936. Following their suspension, they met and organized an independent federation, known as the Congress of Industrial Organizations. In 1955, it merged with the AFL to form the AFL-CIO.

See also AFL-CIO MERGER.

committeeman A worker in a plant or department, generally elected by other members of the union, to represent the membership in the handling of grievances, solicitation of new members, and, occasionally, the collection of dues.

See also SHOP STEWARD.

Committee on Fair Employment Practices *See* FAIR EMPLOYMENT PRACTICE COMMITTEE.

Committee on Political Education (AFL-CIO) *See* AFL-CIO COPE.

commodity concept of labor The theory that labor was a commodity similar to other commodities which had a price on the open market, and behaved similarly to other commodities. The Clayton Anti-Trust Act declared that ". . . the labor of a human being is not a commodity or article of commerce."

common labor rate The rate of pay for physical or manual work of a simple nature, which requires no special training, skill, or previous experience, usually the lowest rate in the plant.

common law A system of law based on decided cases, as against one based on statutes. Much of the common law in English history has been enacted and become part of the statutory law.

common-situs picketing *See* PICKETING AT COMMON SITE (SITUS).

Commonwealth v. Hunt One of the landmark cases in labor history which limited the use of the conspiracy doctrine in labor disputes and supported the right of labor organizations to carry out their legitimate functions. Chief Justice Shaw of the Supreme Judicial Court of Massachusetts, said in part:

> . . . a conspiracy must be a combination of two or more persons, by some concerted action, to accomplish some criminal or unlawful purpose, or to accomplish some purpose, not in itself criminal or unlawful, by criminal or unlawful means.
>
> We think, therefore, that associations may be entered into, the object of which is to adopt measures that may have a tendency to impoverish another, that is, to diminish his gains and profits, and yet so far from being criminal or unlawful, the object may be highly meritorious and public spirited. . . .

Source references: Commonwealth v. Hunt, 4 Met. 111 (Mass 1842); J. Holmes dissent in *Vegelahn v. Guntner,* 167 Mass 92, 44 NE 1077 (1896); Walter Nelles, "Commonwealth v. Hunt," 52 *Columbia LR* 1128 (1932); Marjorie S. Turner, *The Early American Labor Conspiracy Cases, Their Place in Labor Law, A Reinterpretation* (San Diego: San Diego State College Press, Social Science Monograph series vol. 1, no. 3, 1967).

communications The policy and procedures used by a company or union to provide a flow of information from top to bottom and an equally effective procedure for permitting the flow of information from bottom to top.

No company personnel policy can be effective without providing an effective method of communications, easily understood and readily transmitted.

Communications, in broad, must also be directed by the company toward its customers, stockholders, and the public. These lines of communication have a direct effect on its public relations policy. In normal usage communications generally apply to workers, supervisors, and lower executives. Any communication system, whether formal or informal, must be a two-way system.

Source references: Glenn A. Bassett, "The Three L's—Still Personnel Basics, Still Neglected," *Personnel,* Sept./Oct. 1972; Adri

G. Boudewyn, "The Open Meeting—A Confidential Forum for Employees," *PJ*, April 1977; BNA, *Employee Communications* (Washington: PPF Survey no. 110, 1975); William G. Dyer, "Encouraging Feedback," *Management Review*, Sept. 1974; Richard V. Farace and Donald MacDonald, "New Direction in the Study of Organizational Communication," *Personnel Psychology*, Spring 1974; Dan H. Fenn, Jr. and Daniel Yankelovich, "Responding to the Employee Voice," *Harvard BR*, May/June 1972; Bruce Harriman, "Up and Down the Communications Ladder," *Harvard BR*, Sept./Oct. 1974; Woodruff Imberman, "Letting the Employee Speak His Mind," *Personnel*, Nov./Dec. 1976; M. Blaine Lee and William L. Zwerman, "Developing a Facilitation System for Horizontal and Diagonal Communication in Organizations," *PJ*, July 1975; Ruth G. Newman, "Case of the Questionable Communiques," *Harvard BR*, Nov./Dec. 1975; Fred A. Olsen, "Corporations Who Succeed Through Communication—Three Case Studies," *PJ*, Dec. 1979; Thomas M. Rohan, "Getting Through to the Troops," *Management Review*, May 1972; Geneva Seybold, *Employee Communication: Policy and Tools* (New York: NICB, Personnel Policy Study no. 200, 1966); J. N. Smith, "Operation Speakeasy: An Experiment in Communication," *Management Review*, March 1973; James B. Strenski, "Two Way Communication—A Management Necessity," *PJ*, Jan. 1970; Gerard Tavernier, "Using Employee Communications to Support Corporate Objectives," *Management Review*, Nov. 1980.

Communications Association; American (Ind) An independent labor organization, once affiliated with the CIO. It merged with the International Brotherhood of Teamsters in December 1966.

See also TEAMSTERS, CHAUFFEURS, WAREHOUSEMEN AND HELPERS OF AMERICA; INTERNATIONAL BROTHERHOOD OF (IND).

Communications Workers of America (AFL-CIO) Formerly known as the National Federation of Telephone Workers (Ind), the union adopted its present name in June 1947 and affiliated with the CIO. In February 1960, the Airline Communications Employees Association (Ind) merged with the union.

During the 1960s, the CWA began organizing public employees in various parts of the country. State and local government employees comprise approximately 10 percent of its membership.

In 1982, the CWA had 883 locals and 550,500 members. It publishes the monthly *CWA News*.

Address: 1925 K St. N.W., Washington, D.C. 20006. Tel. (202) 728–2300

Source references: Jack Barbash, *Unions and Telephones* (New York: Harper, 1952); "CWA Meeting Looks to the Future; Sets Commitment for Public Worker Organizing," *Government Employee Relations Report*, No. 1008, April 11, 1983.

communism in American labor unions Efforts by various organizations to infiltrate the American labor movement. Among the earliest results of such efforts by Communists was the Trade Union Educational League, and later the Trade Union Unity League. At the time of the formation of the CIO there were small Communist groups in many unions within the AFL. Following formation of the CIO the leadership of a number of key unions was in the hands of those whose political sympathies were with the Communists. They were tried before a special committee of the CIO and expelled.

Source references: William D. Andrew, "Factionalism and Anti-Communism: Ford Local 600," *Labor History*, Spring 1979; "Box Score on Communist Influence in U.S. Labor," *Fortune*, June 1951; Donald T. Critchlow, "Communist Unions and Racism," *Labor History*, Spring 1976; Walter Galenson, "Communists and Trade Union Democracy," *IR*, Oct. 1974; Harvey Levenstein, "Leninist Undone by Leninism: Communism and Unionism in the United States and Mexico, 1935–1939," *Labor History*, Spring 1981; August Meier and Elliot Rudwick, "Communist Unions and the Black Community: The Case of the Transport Workers Union, 1934–1944," *Labor History*, Spring 1982; F. S. O'Brien, "The 'Communist-Dominated' Unions in the United States Since 1950," *Labor History*, Spring 1968; James R. Prickett, "Anti-Communism and Labor History," *IR*, Oct. 1974; David J. Saposs, *Communism in American Unions* (New York: McGraw-

Hill, 1959); U.S. Congress, House, Committee on Un-American Activities, *100 Things You Should Know About Communism and Labor* (Washington: 1948); U.S. Congress, Senate, Committee on Labor and Public Welfare, *Communist Domination of Unions and National Security* (Washington: 1952).

See also BORING FROM WITHIN.

communist affidavits *See* NONCOMMUNIST AFFIDAVIT.

Communist Control Act of 1954 A law passed by Congress, designed among other things to lessen the power of unions found to be Communist infiltrated, Communist front, or Communist action groups. Unions found to be so controlled are deprived of all protection under the Labor Management Relations Act.

Communist Information Bureau *See* COMINTERN.

Communist International *See* COMINTERN.

Communist Manifesto A declaration issued in pamphlet form by Karl Marx and Friedrich Engels which sets forth the doctrine of the class struggle and the inevitable triumph of the proletariat. It was addressed to the workers of the world and concluded with the statement: "The proletarians have nothing to lose but their chains. They have a world to win. Workingmen of all countries, unite!"

community of interest A criterion utilized by administrative agencies to determine whether a group of employees constitute an appropriate bargaining unit. Among factors considered are similarities in job duties, wages, hours, fringe benefits, skills, training, working conditions, and common supervision.

community wage survey A statistical study designed to establish the level and structure of wages in a given geographical area. Such surveys are conducted on a scheduled basis by BLS.

See also WAGE SURVEY.

company-dominated union An organization sponsored, supported, or dominated by an employer in violation of the National Labor Relations Act (Section 8(a)(2)), which holds that employees were entitled to form "unions of their own choosing," free from the domination or interference of employers.

Source reference: H. O. Eby, *The Labor Relations Act in the Courts* (New York: Harper, 1943).

See also COMPANY UNION, GREYHOUND CASES.

company loans The practice by some companies to make personal loans to employees to meet emergency needs. The loans usually are made without interest payment.

Source references: George D. Halsey, *Handbook of Personnel Management* (New York: Harper, 1947); J. Roger O'Meara, "Loans to Employees—When and How," *Conference Board Record,* June 1965.

company scout *See* RECRUITING AGENT.

company spy An individual hired by an employer whose sole function is to find out what is going on in a union, keep informed about organizing activity, and report back to the employer. The general purpose of such informants is to prevent or destroy labor organization in the plant. Such activity, prevalent prior to the National Labor Relations Act, has been substantially eliminated, and is contrary to the labor policy of the United States.

Source references: Clinch Calkins, *Spy Overhead* (New York: Harcourt Brace, 1937); Leo Huberman, *The Labor Spy Racket* (New York: Modern Age Books, 1937); Edward Levinson, *I Break Strikes! The Technique of Pearl L. Bergoff* (New York: Robert M. McBride, 1935).

company store A store, usually in a company-controlled town, where the employees have to buy their groceries and food at prices set by the company.

See also SCRIP, STORE ORDER, TRUCK SYSTEM.

company town Towns which grew up in isolated communities and attracted workers who settled in them and became the work force attached to the particular operation or project. The company owned the land, the buildings, the utilities, the stores, and amusement areas. The employee received his wages from the employer, but returned it to him at the company store and through other payments for services performed by the employer.

Since the company exercised control over most of the conditions in the community, no free government existed—the employer even assumed the policing functions in the area. Even where conditions of employment were enlightened, these local conditions led to many abuses and frequently deprived workers of rights which they were able to obtain in free communities. Efforts at organization and unionization were extremely difficult under such conditions.

Source references: James B. Allen, *The Company Town in the American West* (Norman: Univ. of Oklahoma Press, 1966); Joel I. Seidman, *Union Rights and Union Duties* (New York: Harcourt Brace, 1943).

company union An organization of employees of a single plant or company not affiliated with any national organization. In general usage, however, the term has come to be used as synonymous with "company-dominated union." Since most of the company unions were formed, assisted, or dominated by employers, they did not meet the requirements of the National Labor Relations Act, which prohibited interference by employers and protected the right of employees to form "unions of their own choosing." Section 8(2) of the NLRA prohibited employer support or domination of labor organizations.

Some of the early organizations such as the employee representation plans, works councils, and industrial assemblies sought to provide a forum for a limited type of grievance procedure and exchange of information. In more recent years company unions have been organized primarily to avoid "outside" unionization.

Source references: Paul H. Douglas, "Shop Committees: Substitute for, or Supplement to, Trade Unions?" *Journal of Political Economy,* Feb. 1921; Robert W. Dunn, *Company Unions: Employers' Industrial Democracy* (New York: Vanguard Press, 1927); Lincoln Fairley, *The Company Union in Plan and Practice* (New York: Affiliated Schools for Workers, 1936); Carroll E. French, *The Shop Committee in the United States* (Baltimore: Johns Hopkins Univ., Studies in Historical & Political Science, Series 41, 1923); William Green, *The Superiority of Trade Unions Over Company Unions* (Washington: AFL, 1926); NICB, *Collective Bargaining Through Employee Representation* (New York: 1933); ———, *Works Councils in the United States* (New York: 1919); William G. Rice, Jr., "The Determination of Employee Representatives," 5 *Law and Contemporary Problems* 188 (Spring 1938); Henry R. Seager, "Company Unions vs. Trade Unions," *AER,* March 1923; Robert H. Spahr, *Employee Representation or Work Councils* (Washington: Chamber of Commerce of the U.S., 1927); U.S. Dept. of Labor, BLS, *Characteristics of Company Unions, 1935* (Washington: Bull. 634, 1938); Paul Wander, "The Challenge of Company-Made Unionism," *American Labor Dynamics,* ed. by J. B. S. Hardman (New York: Harcourt Brace, 1938).

companywide collective bargaining *See* COLLECTIVE BARGAINING, COMPANYWIDE.

comparable rate Rates used in wage negotiations where it is necessary to compare identical or similar occupations or occupations with similar job characteristics. These may be within the same plant or in other plants in the community or the industry. The comparison of such rates where agreement is reached on the jobs to be compared may provide a basis for settlement where individual job classifications are being considered in wage negotiations.

comparable worth Variously defined, the concept which is generally taken to mean that compensation should be based on the worth of a job to the employer as measured by such factors as skill, effort, responsibility, and working conditions under a bias-free system of job evaluation. Comparable worth theory contemplates "equal pay for work of comparable worth," rather than "equal pay for equal work." The idea dates back to the days of the War Labor Board, which in 1942 issued a general order calling for adjustments to equalize "the wages or salary rates paid to females with the rates paid to males for comparable quality and quantity of work on the same or similar operations. . . ."

Comparable worth is frequently raised as an issue in discussions concerning the earnings gap between male-dominated and female-dominated jobs, e.g., tree trimmers v. nurses, plumbers v. teachers.

Although not ruling on the issue of comparable worth, the Supreme Court in *County of Washington v. Gunther* held that "claims of discriminatory undercompensation are not barred by Sec. 703(h) of Title VII merely because [the claimants] do not perform work equal to that of male jail guards." The Court held that Title VII plaintiffs need not prove that they were working at substantially equal jobs in order to sustain a wage discrimination claim under Title VII; plaintiffs can prevail by proving that their wages were depressed because of intentional sex discrimination even though their jobs were not equal to jobs held by higher-paid men.

Source references: John H. Bunzel, "To Each According to Her Worth?" *The Public Interest,* Spring 1982; BNA, *The Comparable Worth Issue: A BNA Special Report* (Washington: 1981); Alice H. Cook, *Comparable Worth: The Problem and States' Approaches to Wage Equity* (Honolulu: Univ. of Hawaii, IRC, 1983); Equal Employment Advisory Council, *Comparable Worth, A Symposium on the Issues and Alternatives* (Washington: 1981); "Equal Pay, Comparable Work, and Job Evaluation," 90 *Yale LR* 657 (1981); Laura N. Gasaway, "Comparable Worth: A Post-Gunther Overview," 69 *Georgetown LJ* 1123 (1981); "General Order No. 16," *Wartime Wage Control and Dispute Settlement* (Washington: BNA, 1945); Michael Evan Gold, *A Dialogue on Comparable Worth* (Ithaca: ILR Press, NYSSILR, Cornell Univ., 1983); John B. Golper, "The Current Legal Status of 'Comparable Worth' in the Federal Courts," *LLJ,* Sept. 1983; E. Robert Livernash (ed.), *Comparable Worth: Issues and Alternatives* (Washington: Equal Employment Advisory Council, 1980); George T. Milkovich, "Pay Inequities and Comparable Worth," *Proceedings of the 33d A/M, IRRA,* ed. by Barbara Dennis (Madison: 1981); Bruce A. Nelson, Edward M. Opton, Jr., and Thomas E. Wilson, "Wage Discrimination and the 'Comparable Worth' Theory in Perspective," 13 *Univ. of Michigan Journal of Law Reform* 231 (1980); Rosselle Pekelis, "Equal Pay: Comparability vs. Identical Work," *NYU 33d Annual National Conference on Labor,* ed. by Richard Adelman (New York: Bender, 1981); David A. Pierson, Karen S. Koziara, and Russell E. Johannesson, *Equal Pay for Jobs of Comparable Worth: A Quantified Job Content Approach* (Philadelphia: Temple Univ., Dept. of IR and Organizational Behavior, 1981); Helen Remick, "The Comparable Worth Controversy," *Public Personnel Management,* Winter 1981; Richard J. Schonberger and Harry W. Hennessey, Jr., "Is Equal Pay for Comparable Work Fair?" *PJ,* Dec. 1981; "Special Issue: Comparable Worth," *Public Personnel Management,* Winter 1983; Evan J. Spelfogel, "Equal Pay for Work of Comparable Value: A New Concept," *LLJ,* Jan. 1981; Clarence Thomas, "Pay Equity and Comparable Worth," *LLJ,* Jan. 1983; Donald J. Treiman and Heidi I. Hartmann (ed.), *Women, Work, and Wages: Equal Pay for Jobs of Equal Value* (Washington: National Academy Press, 1981); Stanley C. Wisniewski, "Achieving Equal Pay for Comparable Worth Through Arbitration," *Employee Relations LJ,* Autumn 1982.

See also BENNETT AMENDMENT, EQUAL PAY ACT OF 1963, GUNTHER CASE, IUE V. WESTINGHOUSE ELECTRIC CORP., PAY EQUITY.

compelling need Requirement under section 7117(a)(2) of the Civil Service Reform Act of 1978 which renders nonnegotiable proposals conflicting with an agency rule or regulation for which a compelling need exists and which has been issued at the agency headquarters or one of its primary national subdivisions. The concept, which was extracted from Executive Order 11491, was designed to promote meaningful negotiations at the local level on personnel policies and practices and matters affecting working conditions. Section 7117(a)(2) provides:

> The duty to bargain in good faith shall, to the extent not inconsistent with Federal law or any Government-wide rule or regulation, extend to matters which are subject of any agency rule or regulation . . . only if the Authority has determined under subsection (b) of this section that no compelling need (as determined under regulations prescribed by the Authority) exists for the rule or regulation.

The Federal Labor Relations Authority (FLRA) has promulgated final compelling need standards under section 7105(a)(2)(D). With the exception that the goal of uniformity is no longer defined as constituting a compelling need, the FLRA standards resemble the ones promulgated by the Federal Labor Relations Council under Executive Order 11491. According to the standards, a compelling need exists for an agency rule or regulation concerning any condition of employment when the agency demonstrates that the rule or regulation meets one or more of the following "illustrative criteria":

(a) The rule or regulation is essential, as distinguished from helpful or desirable, to the accomplishment of the mission or the execution of functions of the agency or primary national subdivision in a manner which is consistent with the requirements of an effective and efficient government.

(b) The rule or regulation is necessary to insure the maintenance of basic merit principles.

(c) The rule or regulation implements a mandate to the agency or primary national subdivision under law or other outside authority, which implementation is essentially nondiscretionary in nature.

Source references: Civil Service Reform Act of 1978, 5 U.S.C. 7101 et seq. (1982); U.S. FLRA, "Operating Regulations of the Federal Labor Relations Authority," 5 C.F.R. 2400.1; Henry H. Robinson, *Negotiability in the Federal Sector* (Ithaca: NYSSILR, Cornell Univ. and AAA, 1981).

compensable injury A work injury for which compensation indemnity benefits are payable to the injured or his beneficiary under workers compensation laws.

See also WORKERS COMPENSATION.

compensatory time off Special time allowed to employees in lieu of overtime pay, or for extra time put in by the employee for which no overtime can be paid, as in certain government jobs.

competence Proven ability, knowledge or skill for the handling of a specific job.

competitive wage In general usage, the wages which a company must pay its employees in order to be able to hold its employees or recruit employees when needed in carrying out its production schedules. The company's wages are said to be competitive when its wage rates are sufficient to hold its labor supply. Labor mobility, of course, depends on factors other than wages. Where the wage rate is the primary factor in the movement of labor it is easy to compare the competitive positions of respective employers.

complaint Formal statement by the NLRB, after the investigation of a charge, that it has a prima facie case involving a violation of the law. The complaint sets forth the basis for the Board's jurisdiction and the alleged unfair practices committed by the employer or the union.

Section 10(b) of the Labor Management Relations Act provides in part: "Whenever it is charged that any person has engaged in or is engaging in any such unfair labor practice, the Board, or any agent or agency designated by the Board for such purposes, shall have power to issue and cause to be served upon such person a complaint stating the charges in that respect. . . ."

Source references: Joseph Rosenfarb, *The National Labor Policy and How It Works* (New York: Harper, 1940); U.S. NLRB, *A Guide to Basic Law and Procedures Under the National Labor Relations Act* (Washington: 1978).

compliance agencies Under EEO/AA law, agencies with primary responsibility to enforce EEO/AA laws, rules, and regulations. Under Executive Order 11246, compliance responsibility was assigned to 11 federal agencies, until 1978 when Executive Order 12086 consolidated the compliance authority in the OFCCP. EEOC oversees compliance under Title VII of the Civil Rights Act of 1964. Compliance agencies may also be state or local, if so established, to administer and supervise equal opportunity laws and affirmative action plans.

Source references: E.O. 11246, 3 C.F.R. (1964–65 Comp.) 339; Stephen Sahlein, *The Affirmative Action Handbook* (New York: Executive Enterprises, 1978); U.S. OFCCP, "Heads of Agencies Memorandum," *FEP* 401:625; ———, "History of Federal Contract Compliance Programs in Employment, Order 401a1" (Washington: 1979).

compliance notice A statement required by the NLRB from an employer or union found in violation of the law. The compliance notice indicates the actions taken by the employer or the union either as to the cease-and-desist or affirmative-action sections of the Board's order in the particular case. Where a settlement is reached without a formal hearing the settlement agreement indicates the steps to be taken by the employers or union to conform its actions to the provisions of the statute.

See also AFFIRMATIVE ORDER, CEASE AND DESIST ORDER.

compliance review Procedure of compliance agencies to investigate employer practices to ensure that fair employment and affirmative action obligations required under laws, rules, and regulations are met.

The OFCCP compliance procedures are contained in Revised Order No. 4 and Revised Order No. 14 (nonconstruction contractors) and in "Construction Contractors—Affirmative Action Requirements." In addition, the OFCCP *Federal Contract Compliance Manual* details the procedures of a proper compliance review. The basic steps of a compliance review are a desk audit, an on-site review, and, if necessary, an off-site analysis.

The EEOC conducts compliance reviews of conciliation or negotiated settlement agreements, court orders, and consent decrees to implement the remedial and affirmative action provisions of such determinations. The review process includes: "(a) an on-going in-office analysis of written reports submitted by the Respondent (Defendant) on a schedule dictated by the agreement; and (b) the on-site review requiring a facility visit by the reviewing official."

Source references: U.S. OFCCP, "Construction Contractors—Affirmative Action Requirements," 41 C.F.R. 60–4; ———, "Revised Order No. 4," 41 C.F.R. 60–2; ———, "Revised Order No. 14," 41 C.F.R. 60–60; *EEOC Compliance Manual* (Chicago: CCH, 1982); U.S. OFCCP, *Federal Contract Compliance Manual* (Washington: 1979).

Composers and Lyricists Guild of America (Ind) 10999 Riverside Dr., #100, North Hollywood, Calif. 91602. Tel. (213) 985–4102

Comprehensive Employment and Training Act (CETA) of 1973 Law repealing the 1962 Manpower Development and Training Act (MDTA) and restructuring the series of manpower programs that had developed out of the MDTA and the Economic Opportunity Act of 1964.

The central purpose of CETA was "to provide job training and employment opportunities for economically disadvantaged, unemployed or underemployed persons . . . and to assure that training and other services lead to maximum employment opportunities and enhance self-sufficiency by establishing a flexible, coordinated, and decentralized system of Federal, State, and local programs." The responsibility for managing CETA programs was directed to state and local governments, known as "prime sponsors." The federal government provided prime sponsors with block grants, permitting local officials to tailor employment and training programs to fit the needs of their areas.

A major program of CETA dealt with public service employment which by 1978 had accounted for 60 percent of all CETA expenditures. The Act was amended eight times, with the 1978 amendments reauthorizing it through September 1982. CETA was replaced by the Job Training Partnership Act of 1982.

Source references: Comprehensive Employment and Training Act, as amended, Pub. L. 93–203, Dec. 28, 1973, 87 Stat. 839 (codified as amended in scattered sections of 18, 29, and 42 U.S.C.); Paul Bullock, *CETA at the Crossroads: Employment Policy and Politics* (Los Angeles: UC, Institute of IR, Monograph and Research series 29, 1981); Ernest Green, "CETA After Four Years: Achievement and Controversy; Current Program Developments and New Initiatives," *LLJ*, Aug. 1978; Sar A. Levitan and Garth L. Mangum (ed.), *CETA Training, A National Review and Eleven Case Studies* (Kalamazoo: Upjohn Institute for Employment Research, 1981); ———, (ed.), *The T in CETA, Local and National Perspectives* (Kalamazoo: Upjohn Institute for Employment Research, 1981); Garth L. Mangum (ed.), *CETA: Results and Redesign* (Salt Lake City: Olympus Pub., 1981); William Mirengoff et al., *CETA: Accomplishments, Problems, Solutions* (Kalamazoo: Upjohn Institute for Employment Research, 1982); ———, *CETA: Assessment of Public Service Employment Programs* (Washington: National Academy of Sciences, 1980); ———, *The New CETA:*

Effect on Public Service Employment Programs: Final Report (Washington: National Academy of Sciences, 1980); Pawan K. Sawhney, Robert H. Jantzen, and Irwin L. Herrnstadt, "The Differential Impact of CETA Training," *ILRR*, Jan. 1982; U.S. Dept. of Labor, ETA, *Public Service Employment: CETA Program Models* (Washington: 1978); U.S. National Commission for Manpower Policy, *CETA: An Analysis of the Issues* (Washington: Special Report no. 23, 1978).

See also ECONOMIC OPPORTUNITY ACT, JOB TRAINING PARTNERSHIP ACT (JTPA) OF 1982, MANPOWER DEVELOPMENT AND TRAINING ACT OF 1962, PRIVATE INDUSTRY COUNCIL (PIC), PRIVATE SECTOR INITIATIVE PROGRAM (PSIP), PUBLIC SERVICE EMPLOYMENT (PSE).

compressed air illness *See* CAISSON DISEASE.

compulsory arbitration *See* ARBITRATION, COMPULSORY.

compulsory audience *See* CAPTIVE AUDIENCE.

compulsory check-off *See* AUTOMATIC CHECK-OFF.

compulsory investigation A procedure for "cooling off" by postponement of strike or lockout for a definite period of time and the appointment of an investigatory board.

See also COOLING-OFF PERIOD, NATIONAL EMERGENCY DISPUTES, RAILWAY LABOR ACT.

compulsory retirement *See* RETIREMENT, COMPULSORY.

compulsory union membership The term is generally used by those opposed to union security which takes the form of the union shop, or prior to the Taft-Hartley Act, the closed shop. The closed shop required membership in the union, prior to employment by the company. The union shop permits the employer to hire the employee, but the employee is required, under the terms of the agreement, to join the union within a specified period of time.

See also CLOSED SHOP, MAINTENANCE OF MEMBERSHIP, UNION SHOP.

Concentrated Employment Program (CEP) Established in the summer of 1967 by the federal government to provide a coordinated, total system for delivering manpower services to urban and rural poverty areas with the greatest concentration of disadvantaged persons. The first CEPs were started in 20 cities and two rural areas and were oriented to service particular needs of each poverty area by enlisting the support of local organizations and local labor and business interests; providing a wide range of counseling, education, and training services; aiding each enrollee in finding a job or training program suited to his interests and needs; and providing the follow-up necessary to guarantee that the newly obtained job would not be lost. The CEPs were usually sponsored by a local community action agency and worked with that agency in coordinating services.

Source references: Norman Driscoll, "Lessons from Charcoal Valley, The Watt's CEP—What's Happening and Why," *Manpower*, Feb./March 1969; Steven Markowitz, "Training and Job Creation—A Case Study," *LLJ*, Aug. 1968; U.S. Dept. of Labor, Manpower Adm., *Concentrated Employment Program, Total Service for Unemployed and Underemployed* (Washington: 1969); U.S. President, *Manpower Report of the President* (Washington: 1968).

concentration OFCCP defines it as "having substantially more minorities or women in a job area than might reasonably be expected by their overall representation in the contractor's work force, or relevant section of that work force." The identification of a job area exhibiting concentration is part of the required work force analysis in an affirmative action program.

Source reference: U.S. OFCCP, *Federal Contract Compliance Manual* (Washington: 1979).

See also UNDERREPRESENTATION.

concerted activities Action by workers designed to better their wages, hours, and working conditions. By and large such activities are protected by the National Labor Relations Act as well as state labor relations acts.

concession bargaining Collective bargaining in which unions agree to modify or forego improvements in pay, benefits, or working conditions in return for job security or other employment protection. Concession bargaining may also involve employee "givebacks" in which employees agree to cuts in wages and/or other benefits. According to Mills, "Sometimes managerial prerogatives have been surrendered, unions have obtained a future financial claim against the company earnings, and executives have had to face the charge that they traded away the store to the unions to save a few dollars." This is in marked contrast to traditional bargaining in which companies agree to increase wages and benefits to preserve management rights.

Source references: Paul Bosanac, "Concession Bargaining, Work Transfers, and Midcontract Modification: *Los Angeles Marine Hardware Company*," *LLJ*, Feb. 1983; BNA, *Labor Relations in an Economic Recession: Job Losses and Concession Bargaining* (Washington: 1982); D. Quinn Mills, "When Employees Make Concessions," *Harvard BR*, May/June 1983.

See also EMPLOYEE GIVEBACK.

conciliation The process, sometimes called an extension of collective bargaining, whereby the parties seek to reconcile their differences. In the conciliation process a third party acts as the intermediary in bringing the disputing parties together, but acts as a catalytic agent, by being available, but not actually taking an active part in the settlement process. Conciliation is sometimes distinguished from mediation, where the third party actively seeks to assist the parties in reaching a settlement, by making suggestions, providing background information, and noting avenues open to the parties for settlement. He does not actually decide or determine the settlement. He helps the parties find a solution to the problem. In current usage the terms conciliation and mediation are used interchangeably.

As an illustration of the close tie-in of the terms, one may cite the fact that within the U.S. Conciliation Service of the Department of Labor, the individuals were referred to as Commissioners of Conciliation. Under the Taft-Hartley Act, the new agency is known as the Federal Mediation and Conciliation Service (FMCS). Both terms, mediation and conciliation, are used. FMCS representatives perform their duties as conciliators and mediators interchangeably.

Source references: W. Ellison Chalmers, "The Conciliation Process," *ILRR*, April 1948; Royce A. Coffin, *The Negotiator; A Manual for Winners* (New York: AMACOM, 1973); Philip Garmon et al., *Conciliation and Cooperation in Collective Bargaining* (New York: AMA, Personnel Series no. 44, 1940); ILO, *Conciliation and Arbitration Procedures in Labour Disputes, A Comparative Study* (Geneva: 1980); M. M. Kampelman, "The U.S. Conciliation Service," *Minnesota LR*, June 1947; Harold S. Roberts (ed.), *Manual for Mediation and Emergency Boards* (Honolulu: Univ. of Hawaii, IRC, 1948); SPIDR, *Dispute Resolution: Public Policy and the Practitioner*, 1977 Proceedings, 5th A/M (Washington: 1978); B. M. Squires, "Conciliation," *Encyclopedia of the Social Sciences*, ed. by Edwin R. A. Seligman (New York: Macmillan, 1931); U.S. Congress, House, *Compilation of Laws Relating to Mediation, Conciliation, and Arbitration Between Employers and Employees, Vol. II* (Washington: 1978); Edgar L. Warren, "The Conciliation Service: V-J Day to Taft-Hartley," *ILRR*, April 1948.

See also FEDERAL MEDIATION AND CONCILIATION SERVICE (FMCS), MEDIATION.

conciliator The person assigned or who has assumed the responsibility of keeping disputing parties in negotiation so they may reach an amicable settlement of the problem.

See also FEDERAL MEDIATION AND CONCILIATION SERVICE (FMCS), MEDIATOR.

Condon-Wadlin Law *See* TAYLOR LAW.

Confederated Unions of America *See* NATIONAL FEDERATION OF INDEPENDENT UNIONS.

Confédération des Syndicats Nationaux (Confederation of National Trade Unions) A Quebec-based central labor body founded in 1921 as the Confederation of Canadian Catholic Workers. Comprised of a number of denominational unions, its early objective was to launch a trade union movement founded on the social teachings of the Roman Catholic Church, particularly on the principles of the papal encyclical Rerum Novarum. It gradually relinquished its denominational status and in 1960 the constitution was amended and the current name was adopted. The purpose of the Confederation is "to fight for the creation of social, economic, political and cultural structures which will ensure the full development of man and of all mankind."

The Confederation is affiliated with the World Confederation of Labour and claims approximately 25 percent of the trade union membership in Quebec, which represents 6 percent of total Canadian trade union membership.

Address: 1601, av. de Lorimier, Montreal, Quebec, Canada H2K 4M5.

Source references: Samuel R. Barnes, "The Evolution of Christian Trade Unionism in Quebec," *ILRR*, July 1959; John Crispo, *International Unionism: A Study in Canadian-American Relations* (Toronto: McGraw-Hill, 1967).

Conference Board, The A private organization established in 1916 as the National Industrial Conference Board by a number of anti-union associations. It has since then developed into a factfinding organization which acts both as a clearinghouse and agency for dissemination of information, the publication of statistical bulletins, and other services which include information on employer-employee relations. According to a statement in the *Conference Board Record* (February 1967 issue), "The National Industrial Conference Board is one of the great nonprofit factfinding laboratories in the world. Now in its 50th year, it has continuously served as an institution for scientific research in the fields of business economics and business management. Its sole purpose is to promote prosperity and security by assisting in the effective operation and sound development of voluntary productive enterprise."

In 1970, the organization's name was changed to The Conference Board.

The Conference Board publications include the monthly *Across the Board*, and the Information Bulletin, Miscellaneous Publication, Report, and Research Bulletin series. Periodicals, among others, *Consumer Attitudes and Buying Plans, Economic Road Maps,* and *Statistical Bulletin* and the annual *Cumulative Index* are issued by the organization.

Address: 845 Third Avenue, New York, N.Y. 10022.

confidential employee An employee assisting and acting in a confidential capacity to those who formulate, determine, and effectuate labor management relations policies. The NLRB established this definition in *The B.F. Goodrich Company.* The Supreme Court, in *NLRB v. Hendricks County,* ruled that there was "a reasonable basis in law" for excluding confidential employees from bargaining units. Under many public sector bargaining laws, confidential employees are excluded from coverage.

Source references: The B.F. Goodrich Co., 115 NLRB 722, 37 LRRM 1383 (1956); *NLRB v. Hendricks County*, 454 US 170, 108 LRRM 3105 (1981); Melvin K. Bers, *The Status of Managerial, Supervisory and Confidential Employees in Government Employment Relations* (Albany: New York State Public Employment Relations Board, 1970); William L. Keller and Richard Leland Brooks, "NLRB Treatment of Confidential Employees: Renewed Confrontation with Congress and the Courts," *LLJ*, Dec. 1980; "The 'Labor-Nexus' Limitation on the Exclusion of Confidential Employees—NLRB v. Hendricks County Rural Electric Membership Corporation," 16 *Georgia LR* 745 (1982).

Congressional Record The official record of the U.S. Senate and House of Representatives. In addition to all official statements and bills introduced, it contains statements submitted for printing at the back of the *Record* in "Extension of Remarks." In recent years it has also added a section in the back summarizing the activities of the previous day's bills signed and bills introduced, as well as the calendar of the various committees of Congress. It contains discussion and debate on labor and management matters as well as on labor and other legislation.

Congress of Independent Unions (Ind) *See* INDEPENDENT UNIONS; CONGRESS OF (IND).

Congress of Industrial Organizations Originally formed as the Committee for Industrial Organization in November 1935 to help organize the mass production industries along industrial lines, it organized as a permanent organization, following its expulsion from the AFL, as the Congress of Industrial Organizations. After reorganization in November 1938 it consisted of some 32 international unions, a number of organizing committees, as well as city and state organizations that paralleled the AFL structure. John L. Lewis became its first president, and remained head of the organization until 1942 when Philip Murray succeeded him. In 1955 the CIO merged with the AFL to form the AFL-CIO.

Source references: Fay Calkins, *The CIO and the Democratic Party* (Chicago: Univ. of Chicago Press, 1952); Walter Galenson, *The CIO Challenge to the AFL* (Cambridge: Harvard UP, 1960); Max M. Kampelman, *The Communist Party vs. the CIO; A Study in Power Politics* (New York: Praeger, 1957); Art Preis, *Labor's Giant Step, Twenty Years of the CIO* (New York: Pioneer Publishers, 1964); Benjamin Stolberg, *The Story of the C.I.O.* (New York: Viking Press, 1938); J. Raymond Walsh, *Industrial Unionism in Action* (New York: Norton, 1937).

See also AFL-CIO MERGER, COMMITTEE FOR INDUSTRIAL ORGANIZATION.

Congress of Railway Unions *See* RAILWAY UNIONS; CONGRESS OF.

Connecticut State Employees Association (Ind) It issues the quarterly *State Employee* and triweekly *Government News.*

Address: 760 Capital Ave., Hartford, Conn. 06106. Tel. (203) 525–6614

consent decree A procedure used by the NLRB and other administrative agencies to settle a disputed case by having the company or union enter an agreement or understanding on the basis of which litigation will be ended. The litigants consent to the entry of a decree and once a circuit court has reviewed and entered the decree there is no further appeal open to the parties.

In EEO/AA terminology, consent decrees are broad pledges from employers, usually obtained by the Equal Employment Opportunity Commission to implement affirmative employment practices. Two of the more prominent cases involved the voluntary plan of nine major steel companies and the United Steelworkers in 1974 to remedy race and sex discrimination and the consent decree involving the American Telephone and Telegraph Company, the EEOC, and the Department of Labor consummated on January 18, 1973.

Source references: Ben Fischer, *Evaluating the Steel Industry Consent Decree* (Newark: Rutgers Univ., 1975); Casey Ichniowski, "Have Angels Done More? The Steel Industry Consent Decree," *ILRR,* Jan. 1983; Bernard Kleiman and Carl B. Frankel, "Seniority Remedies Under Title VII: The Steel Consent Decree—A Union Perspective," *NYU 28th Annual Conference on Labor,* ed. by Richard Adelman (New York: Bender, 1976); Vincent L. Matera, "Steel Industry Equal Employment Consent Decrees," *Proceedings of the 27th A/M, IRRA,* ed. by James Stern and Barbara Dennis (Madison: 1975); George A. Moore, Jr., "How to Settle a Discrimination Case: The Employer View Point—Steel Industry Consent Decree," *NYU 28th Annual Conference on Labor,* ed. by Richard Adelman (New York: Bender, 1976); ———, "Steel Industry Consent Decrees—A Model for the Future," *Employee Relations LJ,* Autumn 1977; Phyllis A. Wallace (ed.), *Equal Employment Opportunity and the AT&T Case* (Cambridge: MIT Press, 1976).

consent election A procedure for holding elections and determining the wishes of the employees in the bargaining unit without the necessity of a formal hearing. Where the employer and union consent to waive a formal hearing the regional director is given authority to proceed with the election, make his determination, and certify the results.

The Agreement for Consent Election form signed by the parties covers the following items: election procedures, eligible voters, notice of election, observers, tally of ballots, objections, challenges, reports thereon, runoff procedures, and wording of the ballot.

Source references: Kenneth C. McGuiness and Jeffrey A. Norris, *McGuiness' How to Take a Case Before the NLRB* (5th ed., Washington: BNA, 1986); Joseph Rosenfarb, *The National Labor Policy and How It Works* (New York: Harper, 1940); B. F. Tucker, *Guide to National Labor Relations Act* (Chicago: CCH, 1947).

conspiracy doctrine The doctrine developed and nurtured by English common law that some acts, perfectly lawful when performed by an individual, may become unlawful when performed in concert. The doctrine was applied in England and in the United States to prevent the combination of workers to enhance their wages, hours, and conditions of employment. The early conspiracy cases in the United States finally gave rise to a decision by the Massachusetts Supreme Court in *Commonwealth v. Hunt,* which made difficult its further use against labor unions.

Source references: Commonwealth v. Hunt, 4 Met. 111 (Mass 1842); John R. Commons & Associates (ed.), "Labor Conspiracy Cases, 1806–1842," *A Documentary History of American Industrial Society* (Vols. III & IV, New York: Russell & Russell, 1958); Charles O. Gregory, *Labor and the Law* (2nd rev. ed., New York: Norton, 1961).

See also COMMONWEALTH V. HUNT.

constant wage plan A wage plan to give employees a regular weekly income even though there are wide fluctuations in the workweek.

Source references: Arne H. Anderson, "Wage and Employment Guarantees in Major Agreements," *MLR,* Nov. 1964; Jack Chernick and George Hellickson, *Guaranteed Annual Wages* (Minneapolis: Univ. of Minnesota Press, 1945); Leon H. Keyserling, "Employment and the 'New Economics,'" *Annals,* Sept. 1967; Charles A. Myers, "Stable Employment and Flexible Wages," *Personnel,* Aug. 1940; U.S. Dept. of Labor, BLS, *Major Collective Bargaining Agreements; Supplemental Unemployment Benefit Plans and Wage-Employment Guarantees* (Washington: Bull. 1425–3, 1965).

constitution and bylaws Unions, like other private organizations, operate under the specific constitution and bylaws adopted by the membership. The constitution acts as a general guide and policy and frequently insures adequate democratic safeguards to individual members.

Union constitutions will frequently set out the objectives of the organization, its trade jurisdiction, the structure of its government, qualifications for membership, the holding of conventions, apprenticeship regulations, methods of negotiating agreements, benefit payments, procedures for the holding of elections and trials of members, referendum and recall, and other provisions needed by the union to permit it to operate effectively.

Source references: Leo Bromwich, *Union Constitutions* (New York: Fund for the Republic, 1959); John Hutchinson, "The Constitution and Government of the AFL-CIO," *California LR,* Dec. 1958; "National Union Constitutions Before and After LMRA," *MLR,* Dec. 1965; U.S. Dept. of Labor, LMSA, *Local Convention Representation and Constitutional Amendments in National Unions* (Washington: 1965).

Construction Industry Collective Bargaining Commission By Executive Order 11482 a tripartite commission was created in September 1969 to seek solutions to the labor-management and manpower problems which affect the growth of the industry and to develop voluntary tripartite procedures in settling disputes. The general objectives of the Commission were to upgrade skills of those employed in the construction industry and to improve manpower training procedures, to reduce the instability of demand for labor in the construction industry, to provide a greater number of weeks per year of construction work, to strengthen the role of labor organizations and contractors' associations in the dispute settlement process, to establish more effective machinery for the resolution of disputes over the terms of collective bargaining agreements, and to identify means to improve and adapt the structure of collective bargaining in the industry to meet the challenges of technological innovation and changing demands. The Commission had the authority to intercede in any construction industry labor dispute when the dispute over the terms or application of the collective bargaining agreement was likely to have a significant impact on construction activity in a particular locality or localities.

The Commission consisted of four representatives each of the public, management, and labor unions. The public representatives appointed were George P. Shultz, Secretary of Labor and chairman of the Commission; George W. Romney, Secretary of the Department of Housing and Urban Development; J.

Curtis Counts, director of the Federal Mediation and Conciliation Service; and John T. Dunlop of Harvard University.

Source reference: "Construction Industry Bargaining Commission Created by President Nixon; Tripartite Form," *Daily Labor Report*, No. 183, Sept. 22, 1969.

constructive discharge Action by an employer to get rid of an employee, not by actual discharge, but by making conditions so unbearable that the employee is forced to "quit."

Source references: Eric A. Bare, "Handling Claims of Constructive Discharge," *Journal of the College and University Personnel Association*, Summer 1980; Ralph H. Baxter, Jr. and John M. Farrell, "Constructive Discharges—When Quitting Means Getting Fired," *Employee Relations LJ*, Winter 1981/82; Marco L. Colosi, "Who's Pulling the Strings on Employment at Will?" *PJ*, May 1984.

constructive seniority *See* RETROACTIVE SENIORITY.

construct validity One of three validity strategies recognized by the American Psychological Association and the EEOC Uniform Guidelines on Employee Selection Procedures. Constuct validity is a demonstration that a selection procedure, e.g., an employment test, measures a construct (an individual trait or characteristic such as honesty or leadership) and that the construct is important for successful job performance.

Source reference: U.S. EEOC, "Adoption of Questions and Answers to Clarify and Provide a Common Interpretation of the Uniform Guidelines on Employee Selection Procedures," 44 F.R. 11996.

See also CONTENT VALIDITY, CRITERION VALIDITY.

consultation A procedure instituted to provide greater participation by employees and employee organizations in the formulation and implementation of policies which are likely to affect their working conditions. Consultation is aimed at getting individuals or groups to suggest or respond to proposals for policy formulation or implementation without at the same time giving up "management's rights" to make the final decision in these matters. It provides an opportunity to present a point of view or state an objection, but it is not in the nature of a "negotiating" session of two equal parties to arrive at a mutually acceptable decision.

Consultation has taken many forms, from merely informing an organization that a new policy would be instituted and permitting written statements to be presented before the policy is officially announced, to detailed sessions with "draft proposals" for consideration and study and substantial give and take between management and employee organizations before the policy statement is given final form.

Source references: Dorothea de Schweinitz, "Consultation and Negotiation in Swedish Factories," *MLR*, Oct. 1960; ILO, *Consultation and Co-Operation Between Employers and Workers at the Level of the Enterprise* (Geneva: Labour-Management Relations Series no. 13, 1962); Harold S. Roberts, *Labor-Management Relations in the Public Service* (Honolulu: Univ. of Hawaii Press, 1970).

See also MEET AND CONFER, NATIONAL CONSULTATION RIGHTS.

consumer price index Formerly known as the Cost of Living Index. The name was changed following a prolonged dispute during World War II between BLS and the AFL and CIO on the construction of the index and what it measured.

The index, which is issued monthly by BLS, measures the average change in prices of goods and services purchased by moderate-income families, describing shifts in the purchasing power of the consumer's dollar. The "new series" beginning in January 1964 covers all urban wage-earner and clerical-worker consumers, including single workers living alone as well as families of two or more persons. Beginning in January 1978, BLS began publishing a new Consumer Price Index (CPI) for all urban consumers (CPI-U) and a revised CPI for urban wage earners and clerical workers (CPI-W). The CPI-U includes groups previously excluded from CPI coverage such as professional, managerial, and technical workers, the self employed, short-term workers, the unemployed, and retirees. In January 1983, the homeownership component was replaced with a rental equivalent to provide a more accurate reflection of price changes in the CPI-U series; this change will be incorporated in the CPI-W in 1985. The CPI series are widely used in collective bargaining agreements in the form of "escalator" clauses which specify adjustments in wages based on fluctuations of the Consumer Price Index.

Source references: Dorothy Brady and Solomon Fabricant, "Appraisal of the U.S. Bureau of Labor Statistics Cost of Living Index," *Journal of the American Statistical Association,* March 1944; Phillip Cagan and Geoffrey H. Moore, *The Consumer Price Index: Issues and Alternatives* (Washington: AEI, 1981); Ewan Clague, "The Use and Limitations of Cost of Living Data," *NYU 3d Annual Conference on Labor,* ed. by Emanuel Stein (Albany: Bender, 1950); Robert J. Gordon, "The Consumer Price Index: Measuring Inflation and Causing It," *The Public Interest,* Spring 1981; Gloria P. Green, "Relative Importance of CPI Items," *MLR,* Nov. 1965; W. John Layng, "An Examination of the Revised and Unrevised Consumer Price Indexes After Six Months," *Proceedings of the 31st A/M, IRRA,* ed. by Barbara Dennis (Madison: 1979); George Meany and R. J. Thomas, *Recommended Report for the Presidential Committee on the Cost of Living* (Washington: CIO, Pub. no. 101, 1944); NICB, *A Critical Analysis of the Meany-Thomas Report of the Cost of Living* (New York: 1944); "New Features of the Revised CPI," *MLR,* April 1964; Janet L. Norwood, "The CPI Controversy," *LLJ,* March 1980; Rudy Oswald, "The CPI: An Honest Measure," *American Federationist,* June 1980; Lazare Teper, "Observations on the Cost of Living Index of the Bureau of Labor Statistics," *Journal of the American Statistical Association,* Sept. 1943; Jack E. Triplett, "Determining the Effects of Quality Change on the CPI," *MLR,* May 1971; ———, "Reconciling the CPI and PCE Deflator," *MLR,* Sept. 1981; U.S. Congressional Budget Office, *Indexing With the Consumer Price Index: Problems and Alternatives* (Washington: 1981); U.S. Dept. of Labor, BLS, *CPI Issues* (Washington: Report 593, 1980); ———, *The Consumer Price Index: Concepts and Content Over the Years* (Washington: Report 517, 1977); ———, *The Consumer Price Index: History and Techniques* (Washington: Bull. no. 1517, 1966); ———, *The Consumer Price Index Revision—1978. Facts About the Revised Consumer Price Index* (Washington: 1978); ———, *The Consumer Price Index: Technical Notes 1959–63* (Washington: Bull. no. 1554, 1967); U.S. National War Labor Board, *Wage Report on the Wartime Relationship of Wages to the Cost of Living* (Washington: 1945); U.S. Office of Economic Stabilization, *Report of the President's Committee on the Cost of Living* (Washington: 1945).

See also FAMILY BUDGET, STANDARD OF LIVING, WHOLESALE PRICE INDEX.

consumers' cooperative Efforts on the part of consumers or consumer groups to eliminate the middlemen—wholesale and retail merchants and their profits—and to obtain the benefits of cooperative purchases.

The movement began in England and received much impetus from the Rochdale plan.

See also COOPERATIVES (CO-OPS), WORKINGMEN'S PROTECTIVE UNION.

contempt of court An act that obstructs or tends to obstruct administration of justice by a court; also an act that embarrasses, or detracts from the dignity of, a court. In labor disputes, failure to obey an injunction may lead to contempt action that can result in fine or imprisonment, or both.

See also INJUNCTION.

content validity A validity strategy recognized by the American Psychological Association and the EEOC. It is a demonstration that the content of a selection procedure is representative of important aspects of performance on the job. A work sample test, e.g., a typing test for prospective typists, is usually deemed to be content-valid.

Source references: U.S. EEOC, "Adoption of Questions and Answers to Clarify and Provide a Common Interpretation of the Uniform Guidelines on Employee Selection Procedures," 44 F.R. 11996; Richard S. Barrett, "Is the Test Content-Valid: Or, Who Killed Cock Robin?" *Employee Relations LJ,* Spring 1981; Frank J. Dyer, "An Alternative to Validating Selection Tests," *PJ,* April 1978;

Robert D. Gatewood and Lyle F. Schoenfeldt, "Content Validity and EEOC: A Useful Alternative for Selection," *PJ*, Oct. 1977; Stephen J. Mussio and Mary K. Smith, *Content Validity: A Procedural Manual* (Chicago: IPMA, Special Report, 1973); David C. Roth and Philip C. Stahl, "Application of the EEOC Guidelines to Employment Tests Validation: A Uniform Standard for Both Public and Private Employers," *IR Law Digest*, Oct. 1973.

See also CONSTRUCT VALIDITY, CRITERION VALIDITY.

continuous bargaining A term which became popular following the settlement of the steel strike in 1959. The Kaiser Steel Company, which made an early settlement, provided for the sharing of the "fruits of progress" and the setting up of a committee which included labor and management representatives and three public members. It was hoped that problems which needed settlement should not develop in the fury of the countdown in actual contract negotiations, with the possibility of a strike deadline, but that problems which might come up in collective bargaining might be studied and thought through long before the contract reopening period. It was felt that the crisis atmosphere of bargaining was not conducive to settlement and did not enable sufficient thoughtful consideration to basic issues which need to be seen in perspective.

The Kaiser Sharing Plan was put into effect following the special committee's study. The basic steel industry after long meetings of the Human Relations Committee, which is part of the continuous bargaining process, came up with solutions which resulted in an agreement well in advance of the scheduled June 30, 1964, expiration date. Although there was no direct wage increase in the steel settlement, many items were modified and a special sabbatical vacation plan was introduced.

A distinction may be made between the concept of continuous bargaining, which suggests that both sides are ready and willing at all times to meet to review problems of major concern to each other and to the public, and that which provides for a long period of study in anticipation of bargaining or when an issue comes up which obviously needs thoughtful attention for a longer period of time.

continuous bargaining committees Committees established by management and union in a collective bargaining relationship to keep the agreement under constant review, and to discuss possible contract changes, long in advance of the contract expiration date. These committees may include third-party representation.

continuous process Plant operations or production processes which require "round-the-clock" scheduling, because of the nature of the product or the work process. Work schedules are arranged so that production can be kept on a continuous basis, 24 hours a day, 7 days a week. In times of difficulty, or during strikes arrangements usually are made so the machinery is serviced in order to avoid damage to the equipment.

See also NONCONTINUOUS PROCESS.

contract, labor *See* LABOR CONTRACT.

contract, long-term *See* LONG-TERM CONTRACT.

contract, master *See* AGREEMENT, MASTER.

contract, top-down *See* TOP-DOWN CONTRACT.

contract, wage payment A method of wage compensation where the worker agrees to do a fixed job for a specified amount of money.

contract-bar rule A general rule followed by the NLRB that it will not disturb a valid, existing contract during its term. Requests for certification or decertification are tested against this rule. Exceptions to the rule are made when the circumstances warrant—loss of majority, unusually long contract term, effort to avoid a valid test of membership support, etc.

Source references: Walter L. Daykin, "Contract as a Bar to a Representation Election," *LLJ*, April 1959; John J. Fitz-Simons, "Development and Application of the Contract Bar Doctrine by the National Labor Relations Board," *NYU 6th Annual Conference on Labor*, ed. by Emanuel Stein (Albany: Bender, 1953); Joseph Krislov, "Contract-Bar Extension and the Narrowing of the Schism Doctrine," *LLJ*, Nov. 1954;

Benjamin B. Naumoff, "Evolution of the NLRB Contract Bar Doctrine," *LLJ*, Oct. 1959; ———, "The New NLRB Contract Bar Rules (A Summary and Evaluation)," *NYU 12th Annual Conference on Labor*, ed. by Emanuel Stein (Albany: Bender, 1959); Michael A. Roberts, "Duration of the Contract Bar," *NYU 8th Annual Conference on Labor*, ed. by Emanuel Stein (Albany: Bender, 1955).

See also ONE-YEAR RULE, TWO-YEAR RULE.

contracting out *See* SUBCONTRACTING.

contract labor A form of involuntary servitude for a period of time. Existed in the United States to the end of 19th century. Workers contracted to work for a period of time in payment of transportation or other considerations. Contracts were in writing and enforceable and violators were subject to fine and imprisonment.

Source references: Carter Goodrich, "Contract Labor," *Encyclopedia of the Social Sciences*, ed. by Edwin R. A. Seligman (Vol. 4, New York: Macmillan, 1931); Richard B. Morris, *Government and Labor in Early America* (New York: Columbia UP, 1946).

contract ratification *See* AGREEMENT RATIFICATION.

contracts, major union *See* MAJOR UNION CONTRACTS.

Contract Work Hours and Safety Standards Act A federal statute adopted on August 13, 1962, to replace the Eight-Hour Laws applicable to laborers and mechanics on public works and federally financed construction projects. The Eight-Hour Laws required that such workers be paid time and one-half for work in excess of eight hours a day. The Contract Work Hours and Safety Standards Act requires that they be paid time and one-half for work both in excess of eight hours a day and 40 hours a week. There is a penalty of $10 a day for each worker employed in violation of these requirements.

A 1969 amendment to the Act provides that no laborer or mechanic shall be employed in working conditions that are "unsanitary, hazardous, or dangerous to his health and safety," as determined by the Secretary of Labor. The blacklist penalty may be imposed for repeated willful or grossly negligent violations.

Source references: Contract Work Hours and Safety Standards Act of 1962, as amended, 40 U.S.C. 327–333 (1982); BNA, "Contract Work Hours and Safety Standards Act," *WHM* 99:1601.

contributory negligence A common law defense which was used to prevent workers from collecting damages resulting from accidents. A worker had to sue in order to collect and also establish that the accident did not in any way result from his negligence. Negligence was held to exist where the employee continued to work at an obviously hazardous occupation where accidents were not uncommon, or where he did not exercise sufficient care to prevent the occurrence of the accident. These conditions were difficult to meet. The development of workers compensation laws has alleviated the difficulties of the common law defense in industrial accidents.

Source reference: John R. Commons and John B. Andrews, *Principles of Labor Legislation* (4th rev. ed., New York: Harper, 1936).

See also FELLOW SERVANT DOCTRINE, WORKERS COMPENSATION.

contributory pension plan A pension plan jointly financed by employer and employees. Although the pension trust is for the benefit of the employees, the contributions are frequently made entirely by the employer. In the case of contributory plans, the employees share in the cost.

Source references: Fleming Bomar et al., *Handbook for Pension Planning* (Washington: BNA, 1949); BNA, *Pensions and Profit Sharing* (3d ed., Washington: 1964); Joseph J. Melone and Everett T. Allen, Jr., *Pension Planning, Pensions, Profit Sharing, and Other Deferred Compensation Plans* (Homewood: Irwin, 1966); Hugh O'Neill, *Modern Pension Plans* (New York: PH, 1947).

See also EMPLOYEE RETIREMENT INCOME SECURITY ACT (ERISA) OF 1974, NONCONTRIBUTORY PENSION PLAN.

controlled referrals A procedure used primarily during World War II which provided that work referrals be made under war-manpower regulations and only through the official channels of the employment offices. With limited manpower it was necessary to give priority to industries engaged in the war effort. Among industries so engaged, priorities existed which gave preference to those industries and occupations whose products were most urgently needed to prosecute the war effort.

control of job The term refers to efforts on the part of workers to limit the absolute control of employers over the jobs of employees. The extension of collective bargaining has placed many of the previously held employer prerogatives in the area of joint discussion. Grievance procedures provide an opportunity for employees, through collective bargaining, to exercise some restriction over the control of the job.

The term occasionally has been used to describe the job control practiced by certain unions, which limit the right of employers to hire workers, except through union referral. The provisions of the Taft-Hartley Act, insofar as they apply to companies engaged in interstate commerce, have limited the unions' control over job opportunities previously exercised.

See also JOB CONTROL.

convention The national conference held periodically in order to review the activities of the previous year or years, to elect officers, to hear reports on problems facing the union, to pass resolutions on matters affecting the union, to pass on questions of policy affecting the locals (changes in dues, initiation fees, salaries of officers, etc.), to hear appeals on expulsions of members or locals, and to act as the final law-making body of the union until the next convention.

Delegates to the convention are generally elected by the membership of the local unions and voting power is based on the number of dues-paying members. The election of officers, in many conventions, constitutes the highlight of the meeting. The convention has the final word on most matters. Occasionally, some matters also require a referendum vote of the majority before becoming policy.

In ILO usage, a convention is a policy (in the nature of a treaty) adopted first by the delegates at an ILO conference, which has obtained the support of the necessary number of governments to adopt the terms of the convention and put it into effect. Most conventions, however, become effective only for those countries which implement the terms agreed upon in conference.

See also INTERNATIONAL LABOR ORGANIZATION (ILO), LABOR CONVENTION.

convict labor *See* PRISON LABOR.

coolie overtime A method of computing an employee's regular rate of pay under the Fair Labor Standards Act. The procedure applied to salaried employees calculates the overtime by dividing the salary by the number of hours worked. As the number of hours of work increases the rate of pay per hour decreases, resulting in a lower overtime rate as the number of hours worked increases.

See also FAIR LABOR STANDARDS ACT OF 1938, OVERTIME PAY.

coolie system A procedure used in getting unskilled workers from Asian countries, India, and other tropical areas under a contract system to work for low wages and under poor working conditions.

Source references: Mary Roberts Coolidge, *Chinese Immigration* (New York: H. Holt, 1909); E. George Payne, *An Experiment in Alien Labor* (Chicago: Univ. of Chicago Press, 1912).

cooling-off period Provisions of law, federal or state, which postpone strike or lockout action, to give mediation agencies an opportunity to postpone or settle the dispute. It is also designed to give the parties a chance to think things over, and in some cases an opportunity to vote on the company's "last offer," to see whether or not the employees will accept the company proposal as a settlement.

Many feel that procedures which prevent the use of the strike or lockout do not result in "cooling-off," but in "heating-up" periods—the parties becoming more disturbed about the problems which would normally be settled by collective bargaining. Federal procedures for cooling-off and for holding strike votes under the War Labor Disputes Act of 1943 (Smith-Connally Act) did not result in the elimination of strikes. The national emergency provisions of the Taft-Hartley Act, which require a cooling-off period, have not resulted in any strong feeling that the procedure has been conducive to peaceful settlements or avoiding strikes. The public, however, seeks any method which holds out some hope for preventing strikes in industries which seriously affect the public interest.

Source references: War-Labor Disputes Act, Pub. L. 78–89, June 25, 1943, 57 Stat. 163 (War Labor Disputes Act, formerly codified under 50 app. U.S.C. 1501–1511, omitted as terminating six months after Dec. 31, 1946, pursuant to the proclamation of the cessation of hostilities of World War II by Proc. No. 2714, eff. Dec. 31, 1946; see note 50 app. U.S.C. 1501); Labor Management Relations Act, as amended, Sections 8(d) and 206–210, 29 U.S.C. 158(d), 29 U.S.C. 176–180 (1982); Howard S. Kaltenborn, *Government Adjustment of Labor Disputes* (Chicago: Foundations Press, 1943); Princeton Univ., IR Section, *Current Proposals for Dealing with Strikes Affecting the National Interest* (Princeton: 1967).

See also NATIONAL EMERGENCY DISPUTES, RAILWAY LABOR ACT, WAITING PERIOD (TIME), WAR LABOR DISPUTES ACT.

cooperation *See* LABOR-MANAGEMENT COOPERATION.

Cooperative League of the U.S.A. An organization formed in 1915 to aid the consumers' cooperative movement in the United States. Its most active exponent was James Warbasse, for many years president of the league.

Source reference: Leland J. Gordon, *Economics for Consumers* (2d ed., Cincinnati: American Book Co., 1944).

cooperatives (co-ops) Organizations established by groups of consumers or producers for the purpose of reducing costs to themselves by eliminating the profits of middlemen (consumers' cooperatives), or to cut the cost of getting products to the market (producers' cooperatives) in order to get a greater share for the primary producers.

Source references: Paul H. Casselman, *The Cooperative Movement and Some of its Problems* (New York: Philosophical Library, 1952); Ellis Cowling, *Cooperatives in America* (New York: Coward-McCann, 1938); Anna-Stina Ericson, "Consumer Cooperatives in an Expanding Economy," *MLR*, May 1957; W. W. Gaston, "The Big Business of Farm Cooperatives," *Harvard BR*, Sept./Oct. 1978; Ray A. Goldberg, "Profitable Partnerships: Industry and Farmer Co-Ops," *Harvard BR*, March/April 1972; Derek Jones, "U.S. Producer Cooperatives: The Record to Date," *IR*, Fall 1979; F. Ray Marshall and Lamond Godwin, *Cooperatives and Rural Poverty in the South* (Baltimore: Johns Hopkins Press, 1971); Jean Orizet, "The Co-operative Movement Since the First World War," *ILR*, July 1969; Arie Shirom, "The Industrial Relations Systems of Industrial Cooperatives in the United States, 1880–1935," *Labor History*, Fall 1972; Robert N. Stern and Tove Helland Hammer, *Buying Your Job: Factors Affecting the Success or Failure of Employee Acquisition Attempts* (Ithaca: NYSSILR, Cornell Univ., Reprint 451, 1978); U.S. Dept. of Labor, BLS, *Directory of Consumers' Cooperatives in the U.S.* (Washington: Bull. no. 750, 1947).

See also PRODUCERS' COOPERATION.

Coopers' International Union of North America (AFL-CIO) Organized in Titusville, Pennsylvania, in November 1890 and affiliated with the AFL in 1891. Its official semiannual publication is *The Coopers Journal.*

Address: 200 Executive Park, Suite 224, Louisville, Ky. 40207. Tel. (502) 897–3274

coordinated bargaining *See* COLLECTIVE BARGAINING, COALITION.

Copeland Act (Anti-Kickback Law) *See* ANTI-KICKBACK LAW (COPELAND ACT).

Coppage v. Kansas A decision of the Supreme Court, handed down in 1915, holding invalid a Kansas statute which sought to outlaw the yellow-dog contract in private employment. The Court held the statute repugnant to the due process clause of the 14th Amendment, saying:

> . . . conceding the full right of the individual to join the union, he has no inherent right to do this and still remain in the employ of one who is unwilling to employ a union man, any more than the same individual has a right to join the union without the consent of that organization.

Source reference: Coppage v. Kansas, 236 US 1 (1915).

See also ADAIR V. UNITED STATES, ERDMAN ACT.

Coronado Coal v. United Mine Workers Two cases which came before the Supreme Court on the application of the Sherman Act to labor unions. The first time the case came to the Court it found no unlawful conspiracy to restrain commerce (1922). In a second decision it held that there had been illegal interference with the flow of commerce, punishable under the Sherman Act. Following the Court decision new trials were held, but an out-of-court settlement was reached by the parties.

Of importance to labor unions was the general principle enunciated by the Court that unincorporated organizations such as labor unions could be sued as entities and held subject to triple damages under the Sherman Act.

Source references: Coronado Coal v. United Mine Workers, 268 US 295 (1925); *United Mine Workers v. Coronado Coal,* 250 US 344 (1922).

See also SHERMAN ACT OF 1890.

corporate authority The proper official within any city, town or municipality whose duty it is to establish wages, salaries, rates of pay, hours, working conditions, and other terms and conditions of employment of firefighters and police officers. The corporate authority may be the mayor, city manager, city council, director of personnel, or personnel board.

Source references: Fire Fighter's Mediation Act, *Code of Georgia Annotated,* Title 54, Ch. 54–13; Firefighters' and Policemen's Arbitration Law, *Oklahoma Statutes Annotated,* Title 11, Secs. 548.1–548.14; Fire Fighters' Arbitration Act, *General Laws of Rhode Island 1956,* Secs. 28–9.1–1—28–9.1–16; Policemen's Arbitration Act, *General Laws of Rhode Island 1956,* Secs. 28–9.2–1—28–9.2–16.

corporate campaign A concerted union effort to influence negotiations or other labor relations activities of management through corporate strategies such as persuading potential investors to avoid the company or pressing for the removal of key executives by shareholders. A union may use such tactics during organization drives, bargaining sessions, or in strike situations in order to place economic pressure on the employer.

The term is claimed to be a trademark of Corporate Campaign, Inc., a New York-based labor relations consulting firm, which developed strategies, procedures, and materials to help unions and community organizations resolve their disputes.

Source references: "MGM Grand Hotel Targeted by FAST for National Corporate Campaign," *Daily Labor Report,* No. 95, May 16, 1984; "NABET Will Begin Corporate Campaign Against NBC and Parent Company, RCA," *Daily Labor Report,* No. 120, June 21, 1984; "'What's in a Name?'—A Trademark, Asserts Corporate Campaign, Inc.," *White Collar Report,* May 30, 1984.

costing labor contracts Calculating the financial impact of a contract. The process usually involves estimating the cost of wages and fringe benefits over the life of the contract. Among the factors considered important in costing a contract is an assessment of the relationship between labor costs and productivity. Both union and management cost labor contracts in order to develop better contract demands and/or to counter the cost claims of the other party.

Source references: Michael H. Granof, *How to Cost Your Labor Contract* (Washington: BNA, 1973); W. D. Heisel and Gordon S. Skinner, *Costing Union Demands* (Washington: IPMA, PERL 55, 1976); John G. Kilgour, "'Wrapping the Package' of Labor Agreement Costs," *PJ,* June 1977; Noah M. Meltz, *The Use of Information and Data in Collective Bargaining* (Toronto: Univ. of Toronto, Centre for IR, 1980); Gordon S. Skinner and E. Edward Herman, "The Importance of Costing Labor Contracts," *LLJ,* Aug. 1981.

cost items Popularized in public sector collective bargaining, this term includes wages, hours, and other benefits, the implementation of which generally requires appropriation by a legislative body.

Source reference: Richard J. Murphy and Morris Sackman (ed.), *The Crisis in Public Employee Relations in the Decade of the Seventies* (Washington: BNA, 1970).

cost-of-living adjustment An increase or decrease in wages based on the fluctuation of the Consumer Price Index of BLS, or any local measure of changes in prices.

See also CONSUMER PRICE INDEX, ESCALATOR CLAUSE.

cost-of-living allowance (float) Regular cents-per-hour or percentage payments to workers through the operation of escalator clauses or other types of cost-of-living adjustments. A float is a cost-of-living allowance not incorporated into base rates.

cost-of-living index *See* CONSUMER PRICE INDEX.

cost-plus contract An agreement, generally with the government, to produce an article at a price which is not determined. The agreement provides that the government will pay all of the costs, plus a fixed fee to the contractor. Cost-plus contracts were widely used during World War II and in many situations led to "loose" wage incentive systems—since Uncle Sam was paying the bill. Difficulties arose following the end of the war when standards had to be tightened and brought in line with more normal competitive conditions.

Council of Economic Advisers A federal advisory board of three persons set up under the 1946 Employment Act. The Council, among other things, advises the President and maintains and studies economic data on general economic conditions. The data and analysis are brought together in the annual Economic Report of the President.

See also JOINT CONGRESSIONAL COMMITTEE ON THE ECONOMIC REPORT.

counseling A method instituted to help workers find reasonable solutions to problems, largely emotional, which beset them. Trained counselors may merely suggest the avenues for solution. Counseling work has been helpful in assisting workers, and at the same time provides useful information to permit better and more effective handling of personnel problems. Frequently, careful exit interviewing by trained counselors is a helpful device to assist the upset or disturbed employee and gives the Industrial Relations Department a better understanding of plant problems.

In recent years unions have provided some services to their members which approximate counseling.

Source references: Charles E. Barry, "Clinical Counseling—Its Value in Industry," *PJ,* Jan. 1963; Ann K. Baxter, "University Employees as People: A Counseling Service for Faculty and Staff," *Journal of the College and University Personnel Association,* Oct./Nov. 1976; Irwin A. Berg, "Employee Counseling in a Well-Rounded Personnel Program," *Public Personnel Review,* July 1970; BNA, *Employee Counseling* (Washington: PPF, Survey 63, 1961); Edwin J. Busch, Jr., "Developing an Employee Assistance Program," *PJ,* Sept. 1981; Perry A. Constas, "Alienation-Counseling Implications and Management Therapy," *PJ,* May 1973; William J. Dickson and F. J. Roethlisberger, *Counseling in an Organization* (Boston: Harvard Univ., Graduate School of Business Administration, 1966); James A. Finkelstein and James T. Ziegenfuss, Jr., "Diagnosing Employees' Personal Problems," *PJ,* Nov. 1978; M. I. Gould, "Counseling for Self-Development," *PJ,* March 1970; John F. McGowan and Lyle D. Schmidt, *Counseling: Readings in Theory and Practice* (New York: Holt, Rinehart & Winston, 1962); Allen J. Schuh and Milton D. Hakel, "The Counselor in Organizations: A Look to the Future," *PJ,* May 1972; Joseph P. Zima, "Counseling Concepts for Supervisors," *PJ,* June 1971.

See also PERSONAL PROBLEMS CONSULTANT, VOCATIONAL COUNSELOR.

counterproposal Offer made by employers or unions in collective bargaining negotiations designed to assist them in finding mutually satisfactory answers to problems. Under the National Labor Relations Act the NLRB gave weight to the employer's counterproposals or offers when determining whether the employer was bargaining in good faith. Concessions made by the employer were one of the indicia of good faith. Under the Taft-Hartley Act (Section 8(d)) collective bargaining is defined so that there is no obligation on the part of the employer or union ". . . to agree to a proposal or require the making of a concession."

See also GOOD-FAITH BARGAINING.

cover The device employed by a hooker or roper or an ordinary operative to conceal his detective agency connection.

See also HOOKING, ROPING.

covered job A job or class of work which comes within the scope and protection of specific legislation. Since the coverage of a law depends on the desire of Congress, it is frequently spelled out in the statute. As experience is developed, the protection and coverage of the law may be extended to larger groups and classes of workers. This is true of the Social Security Act, the Wage and Hour Law, etc.

covert discrimination *See* SYSTEMIC DISCRIMINATION.

craft A trade or employment or occupation which requires skill, manual ability, an understanding of the principle of the trade, and a fixed training period. Early efforts at unionization began among the skilled craftsmen such as the tailors, printers, boot and shoemakers.

craft-conscious unionism Early organizational attitude of many AFL unions which sought to protect the highly skilled workers and their trade interest. They were not concerned with the unskilled and semiskilled workers in the newly developing mass production industries. The partisan interest in the skilled technician and the rather closed circle created by common interests, social status, and training created a barrier against the broader organization of workers in occupations outside the sphere of interest of the craftsmen.

craft severance In determining units appropriate for collective bargaining, the NLRB has had to deal with the problem of providing a separate unit for identifiable craft unions. The Board has broad authority in bargaining unit determinations under Section 9(b) of the National Labor Relations Act.

In the *National Tube Company* case the Board established the policy that certain basic industries were to be exempt from organization on a craft basis. As a parallel policy the Board had adopted the principle in the *American Potash* case that in other industries a severance election would be required where the employees constituting a true craft or departmental unit desired representation by a union that had historically represented such a craft.

In a 1967 decision, the Board reversed its former policy in a decision involving *Mallinckrodt Chemical Works, Uranium Division.* A majority of the Board decided to abandon the *National Tube* and *American Potash* doctrines and decided that in the future it would consider all relevant factors or "areas of inquiry" in determining a craft severance issue.

Source references: National Tube Co., 76 NLRB 1199, 21 LRRM 1292 (1948); *American Potash & Chemical Corp.*, 107 NLRB 1418, 33 LRRM 1380 (1954); *Mallinckrodt Chemical Works, Uranium Div.*, 162 NLRB 387, 64 LRRM 1011 (1966); *E. I. DuPont de Nemours and Co.*, 162 NLRB 413, 64 LRRM 1021 (1966); *Holmberg, Inc.*, 162 NLRB 407, 64 LRRM 1025 (1966); John H. Fanning, "Representation Law," *Daily Labor Report*, No. 75, April 18, 1969.

See also BARGAINING UNIT.

craftsman *See* ARTISAN.

craft union An organization of workers bound by a common occupation, skill, or trade, or a group of closely related skilled tasks. Organizations may be purely local or national in scope. Many craft unions have enlarged their jurisdiction to include as members other than the highly skilled craftsmen who comprised the membership of the early union. An examination of the jurisdiction and membership of many of the former AFL craft unions indicates that as the production technology of the industry changed, the union had to make similar changes in order to maintain its organization or bargaining position in the industry.

See also HORIZONTAL UNIONS, INDUSTRIAL UNION.

craft unit A primary responsibility of the NLRB and state boards is that of holding elections to determine which union represents the majority of the employees, to decide the unit appropriate for collective bargaining purposes. Under the National Labor Relations Act the Board sought to establish criteria for the appropriate unit, to encourage the process of collective bargaining and to meet the desires of the employees. When the AFL and CIO rift occurred the Board was faced with many problems arising out of the controversy between craft and industrial units for bargaining purposes. The Board's annual reports to Congress note the difficulties which beset it and its efforts to resolve the problem.

Under the Taft-Hartley Act, restrictions were placed on the Board and greater emphasis was given to craft interests. Section 9(b) provides in part ". . . the Board shall not . . . decide that any craft unit is inappropriate for such purposes on the ground that a different unit has been established by a prior Board determination, unless a majority of the employees in the proposed craft unit vote against separate representation, . . ."

Source references: Lawrence J. Cohen, "Two Years Under Mallinckrodt: A Review of the Board's Latest Craft Unit Policy," *LLJ*, April 1969; Jesse Freidin, "Craft and Splinter Units," *NYU 7th Annual Conference on Labor*, ed. by Emanuel Stein (Albany: Bender, 1954); Joseph Krislov, "The NLRB on Craft Severance: One Year of American Potash," *LLJ*, May 1955; Dale D. McConkey, "The NLRB's Craft Severance Rule and Intraplant Truck Drivers," *LLJ*, Feb. 1960; Benjamin Rathbun, Jr., "The Taft-Hartley Act and Craft Unit Bargaining," *Yale LJ*, May 1950; Thomas Page Sharp, "Craft Certification: New Expansion of an Old Concept," *IR Law Digest*, Jan. 1973; Paul R. White, *Craft Severance Under the Wagner and Taft-Hartley Acts, 1935–1962* (Ithaca: NYSSILR, Cornell Univ., 1963); J. A. Willes, *The Craft Bargaining Unit, Ontario and U.S. Labour Board Experience* (Kingston, Ontario: IRC, Queen's Univ., Research Series no. 19, 1970); Albert J. Woll et al., "Craft Unionism and the National Labor Relations Act," *LLJ*, Oct. 1949; James E. Youngdahl, "Crafty Industriousness—Determining the Appropriate Bargaining Unit," *Labor Law Developments 1968*, Proceedings of the 14th Annual Institute on Labor Law, SLF (New York: Bender, 1968).

See also APPROPRIATE UNIT.

credentials committee An important committee at union conventions which examines the authenticity of the credentials submitted by the official delegates and recommends which delegates are to be seated, where more than one group claims to be the duly authorized delegate to the convention. Control of the credentials committee may result in the control of the convention and its election machinery.

credited service The years of employment counted for retirement, severance pay, seniority, etc. The definition of a credited year of service varies among companies and plans.

credit union A form of cooperative organization designed to assist trade union members and others to obtain credit at low rates and without substantial security. Loans are for small amounts and based on the credit of the individual. Loans are restricted to members, but membership is open and shares may be bought in small amounts. Earnings from loans are distributed to the members in the form of dividends.

crew assignment Procedures for designating the size of the crew to operate a machine or perform specified tasks. The time arrangement for work on the machine is generally within the scope of management. Occasionally, however, the collective bargaining agreement may designate the crew assignment.

See also MANNING SCALE.

criminal conspiracy *See* CONSPIRACY DOCTRINE.

crisis bargaining Term used to characterize collective bargaining taking place under the shadow of an imminent strike deadline, as distinguished from extended negotiations in which both parties enjoy ample time to present and discuss their positions.

See also CONTINUOUS BARGAINING COMMITTEES.

criterion validity A validation method recognized by the American Psychological Association and the EEOC in its Uniform Guidelines on Employee Selection Procedures. It is a statistical demonstration of the relationship between the scores received by job candidates in a selection procedure and the job performance of a sample of workers.

Source reference: U.S. EEOC, "Adoption of Questions and Answers to Clarify and Provide a Common Interpretation of the Uniform Guidelines on Employee Selection Procedures," 44 F.R. 11996.

See also CONSTRUCT VALIDITY, CONTENT VALIDITY.

critical occupation Jobs which require two years or more training time and which are in short supply. During World War II these occupations were carefully guarded and training encouraged so that the supply would be sufficient to take care of the most urgent needs of the war effort.

A "List of Critical Occupations" prepared by the Department of Labor listed over 20 occupational titles, including die setters, machinists, osteopaths, and pattern makers. The list was made available to local draft boards of the Selective Service System in making determinations on requests for occupational deferment. It was also used by the Selective Service System in selecting men for enlistment in the Ready Reserve.

See also ESSENTIAL OCCUPATIONS.

cross-check A procedure formerly used by the NLRB and some state boards to determine whether a union's claim of a majority was valid. Where the employer consented, the union's membership cards or other authorizations to act as representative were checked against the company payroll and if a majority had designated the union, according to the cross-check, the union was certified as the bargaining agent without a formal hearing and election.

See also AUTHORIZATION CARD, CARD CHECK.

Crosser-Dill Act *See* RAILWAY LABOR ACT.

cross picketing Picketing engaged in by more than one union claiming to represent the employees.

Cullman Committee A committee appointed in 1931 by the governor of New York to study the operation of workers compensation in the state. The committee issued two reports in 1932 holding that claimants did not receive adequate care in commercial clinics or at clinics maintained by the insurance companies.

Source reference: Walter Dodd, *Administration of Workmen's Compensation* (New York: Commonwealth Fund, 1936).

Current Population Survey (CPS) A program of personal interviews conducted by the Bureau of the Census for BLS. The sample currently consists of approximately 60,000 households selected to represent the noninstitutional population aged 16 years and older. The households are surveyed on a rotating basis so that three-fourths of the sample remains the same for any two consecutive months.

The National Commission on Employment and Unemployment Statistics, established by the Congress to study the labor force data system, states that the CPS

> is the cornerstone of our labor market information system. It is the only monthly survey of a representative sample of the total working-age civilian noninstitutional population; it provides highly reliable current estimates of the employed, the unemployed, and those not in the labor force. Data for these groups are available by age, sex, color, education, occupation, industry, and other characteristics. Monthly, quarterly, and annual average data are readily available (seasonally adjusted where appropriate) and additional socioeconomic and income data are provided in extensive supplements each year. In addition, the CPS is a prime source of information not directly related to labor force activities. Annual supplements collect information on marital and family characteristics, educational attainment, fertility, and health statistics. Nonrecurring supplements have been sponsored by various agencies on pension plan coverage, food stamps, and job search activities of the unemployed.

The program was initiated in March 1940 by the Works Progress Administration to "measure the level and change in the size of the labor force, employment, and unemployment." In August 1942, the Bureau of the Census was selected by the Bureau of the Budget (now the Office of Management and Budget) to continue the program as the Works Progress Administration began to be phased out. Bregger states that by "October 1943, the Bureau of Census had thoroughly revised the sample, coverted it to a full probability basis, and expanded the number of primary sampling units. Within 2 years, the sample size was increased from about 8,000 to 23,000 housing units. The name was changed as well, to the 'Monthly Report on the Labor Force,' and still later (1948) it became known as the Current Population Survey (CPS)." The CPS has also been referred to as the Household Survey.

Labor force data from the CPS are available in the following BLS publications: *Employment and Earnings* (monthly), *Monthly Labor Review, Labor Force Statistics Derived from the Current Population Survey* (BLS Bull. 2096), *Employment and Earnings, United States*, and *Employment and Earnings, States and Areas.*

Source references: John E. Bregger, "The Current Population Survey: A Historical Perspective and BLS' Role," *MLR,* June 1984; ———, "Labor Force Data from the CPS to Undergo Revision in January 1983," *MLR,* Nov. 1982; U.S. National Commission on Employment and Unemployment Statistics, *Counting the Labor Force* (Washington: 1979); U.S. President's Committee to Appraise Employment and Unemployment Statistics, *Measuring Employment and Unemployment* (Washington, 1962).

Customs Service Association; National (Ind) *See* TREASURY EMPLOYEES UNION; NATIONAL (IND).

cutback An unexpected reduction in work which results in laying off employees.

Source references: James J. Bambrick, "Layoff Policies Reconsidered," *Management Record,* July 1949; BNA, *Layoff Problems and Procedures in Collective Bargaining Negotiations and Contracts* (Washington: 1949).

See also LAYOFF.

cyclical unemployment Loss of work resulting from periodic fluctuations of the economy. The fluctuations of business prosperity and depressions have resulted in wide variations of employment. The impact on employment of cyclical economic fluctuations in the past was far greater than that due to seasonal, technological, or other factors in the economy.

Source references: William A. Berridge, *Cycles of Unemployment in the United States, 1903–1922* (Boston: Houghton Mifflin, Pollack Foundation for Economic Research, Pub. 4, 1933); Malcolm S. Cohen and William Gruber, "Variability by Skill in Cyclical Unemployment," *MLR,* August 1967; W. Lee Hansen, *The Cyclical Sensitivity of the Labor Supply* (Los Angeles: UC, Institute of IR, 1961); John A. Hobson, *Economics of Unemployment* (New York: Macmillan, 1931); Wesley C. Mitchell, *Business Cycles and Unemployment* (New York: McGraw-Hill, 1923); A. C. Pigou, *Industrial Fluctuations* (New York: Macmillan, 1927); ———, *The Theory of Unemployment* (New York: Macmillan, 1933).

See also SEASONAL UNEMPLOYMENT, TECHNOLOGICAL UNEMPLOYMENT.

D

DGA *See* DIRECTORS GUILD OF AMERICA, INC. (IND).

DOL *See* LABOR DEPARTMENT, U.S.

DOT *See* DICTIONARY OF OCCUPATIONAL TITLES.

DSC *See* DIE SINKERS' CONFERENCE; INTERNATIONAL (IND).

DWW *See* DISTILLERY, WINE AND ALLIED WORKERS' INTERNATIONAL UNION (AFL-CIO).

dago American slang used to denote contempt for common laborers of Italian, Spanish, or Portuguese extraction.

Dailey Commission A commission set up in 1921 to investigate the building trades in Chicago and the collusion going on in the handling of labor in the building industry which created higher prices for consumers and greater profits for the contractors. A similar investigation was made by the Lockwood Committee in New York.

Source references: Illinois, General Assembly, Joint Building Investigating Commission, *Report on the Illinois Building Investigation Commission Authorized by the 52nd General Assembly 1921* (Springfield: Illinois State Register Printers, 1923); Royal E. Montgomery, *Industrial Relations in the Chicago Building Trades* (Chicago: Univ. of Chicago Press, 1927).

Daily Labor Report One of the special labor services of The Bureau of National Affairs, Inc. It presents daily information on developments shaping the American labor scene which includes, among others, Congressional actions, court decisions, management and union activities, arbitration, NLRB decisions, and contract settlements.

See also BUREAU OF NATIONAL AFFAIRS, INC.; THE

daily rate The amount of pay received for a standard or fixed number of hours per day, exclusive of overtime or premium pay.

damaged work Provisions found in some agreements which seek to protect the employee when damage results to the product or equipment because of a mistake. If the damage is not caused by willful or spiteful action the employee is not docked. Frequently these matters may be taken through the grievance machinery.

damage suits Civil claims for alleged injury resulting from actions in violation of law. Under Section 7 of the Sherman Anti-Trust Act, a company could sue for treble damages if its business was injured by actions in violation of the law. In *Loewe v. Lawlor*, the Supreme Court in 1908 held that individual members were liable for damages suffered by an employer resulting from a violation of the Sherman Act.

Under the Taft-Hartley Act unions and employers may file damage suits for violations of contract. Damages, however, are against the assets of the union, not those of the employee or union member. Section 301(b) of the Taft-Hartley Act provides in part:

> Any money judgment against a labor organization in a district court of the United States shall be enforceable only against the organization as an entity and against its assets, and shall not be enforceable against any individual member or his assets.

Damage suits against unions have also been filed by union as well as nonunion members, who feel that they have been deprived of certain rights protected by the union constitution, or state or federal laws.

Source references: Taft-Hartley Act, as amended, Sections 301 and 303, 29 U.S.C. 185, 187 (1982); C. Paul Barker, "Significant Developments in Damage Suits for Secondary Activity Under Section 303 of Taft-

Hartley," *Labor Law Developments 1975*, Proceedings of the 21st Annual Institute on Labor Law, SLF (New York: Bender, 1975); Edward Berman, *Labor and the Sherman Act* (New York: Harper, 1930).

See also LAWLOR V. LOEWE, SHERMAN ACT OF 1890.

Danbury Hatters' case *See* LAWLOR V. LOEWE.

dangerous occupation *See* HAZARDOUS OCCUPATIONS.

danger zone bonus A premium or bonus paid to workers for working in an area which is unusually hazardous. The handling of high explosives or working in the area where such materials are handled frequently calls for special payments to employees. Such bonuses also were paid in the shipping industry during World War II where cargoes had to be carried over routes that were frequented by submarines or foreign war vessels or that were subject to attack by enemy planes.

Darlington case Landmark case in which the Supreme Court held that an employer has the absolute right to terminate his entire business for any reason he chooses, including antiunion bias. The Court added, however, that an employer does not have a similar right to close part of his business, to transfer work to another plant, or to open a new plant to replace a closed plant. The termination of multiplant business will violate the Taft-Hartley Act, the Court said, if the employer is motivated by a purpose to "chill" unionism in the remaining parts of the business and if he reasonably can foresee that the partial closing will have that effect. The NLRB had held that an employer did not have a right to terminate his business if his purpose was to avoid dealing with a union or to retaliate against his employees for their union activities.

Source references: Textile Workers v. Darlington Manufacturing Co., 380 US 263, 58 LRRM 2657 (1965); Robert A. Bedolis, "The Supreme Court's Darlington Mills Opinion," *Conference Board Record*, June 1965; John W. Edelman, "Turning Point at Darlington?" *American Federationist*, March 1965; Dell Bush Johannesen, "Case of the Runaway Mill: Darlington Manufacturing Company," *LLJ*, Dec. 1961; Arthur Mermin, "The Impact of Darlington-Fibreboard," *NYU 18th Annual Conference on Labor*, ed. by Thomas Christensen (Washington: BNA, 1966); John R. Schoemer, Jr., "Case of the Runaway Author: Professor Johannesen's Article on the Darlington Case," *LLJ*, May 1962.

See also FIBREBOARD CASE, PLANT MIGRATION, RUNAWAY SHOP.

Daughters of Saint Crispin The women's auxiliary of the Knights of Saint Crispin. They were first organized among the women shoemakers in 1869.

See also KNIGHTS OF SAINT CRISPIN.

Davis-Bacon Act A federal statute (46 Stat. 1494, 40 U.S.C. 276a–276a–7) passed in 1931 and amended in 1935, 1940, and 1964 which requires the payment of wage rates and fringe benefits prevailing in the area or locality where public works, repair, or alteration is being done under federal or federally financed contract. Prevailing rates and fringe benefits are determined by the Secretary of Labor and apply to all contracts and subcontracts of more than $2,000 in the United States and the District of Columbia. Violations of the law may result in the withholding of payment to the contractor by the Comptroller General, cancellation of the contract by the government agency and denial of awards of government contracts for a period of three years.

The Wage Appeals Board, established in February 1964 under new regulations changing the Davis-Bacon Act procedures, reviews decisions of the Solicitor of Labor on prevailing wage determinations and enforcement cases.

Source references: Louis A. Cox, "The Davis-Bacon Act and Defense Construction: Problems of Statutory Coverage," *NYU 15th Annual Conference on Labor*, ed. by Emanuel Stein (Albany: Bender, 1962); Donald Elisburg, "Wage Protection Under the Davis-Bacon Act," *LLJ*, June 1977; Robert S. Goldfarb and John F. Morrall III, "The Davis-Bacon Act: An Appraisal of Recent Studies," *ILRR*, Jan. 1981; John P. Gould, *Davis-Bacon Act, The Economics of Prevailing Wage Laws* (Washington: AEI, Special Analysis no. 15, 1971); William A. Keyes, "The Minimum Wage and the Davis-Bacon Act: Employment

Effects on Minorities and Youth," *Journal of Labor Research*, Fall 1982; David Levinson, "The Hard-Hats, the Davis-Bacon Act and Nixon's Income Policy," *LLJ*, June 1971; Phillis Payne, "The Plot to Subvert Labor Standards," *American Federationist*, July 1979; Jerry E. Pohlman, "Hard-Core Unemployment, Public Housing Construction and the Davis-Bacon Act," *LLJ*, April 1971; Armand J. Thieblot, Jr., *The Davis-Bacon Act* (Philadelphia: Univ. of Pennsylvania, Wharton School, Industrial Research Unit, LRPP Series Report no. 10, 1975); U.S. GAO, *The Davis-Bacon Act Should Be Repealed* (Washington: 1979); Stuart Rodney Wolk, "Davis-Bacon: Labor's Anachronism 1974," *LLJ*, July 1974.

day shift Where the plant or company operates on more than one shift, the day shift is the first shift working during daylight hours. It generally starts early in the morning and ends during the afternoon.

day wage The wage paid for a definite number of hours per day.

day work The time put in during a regular day shift and compensated on the basis of a fixed number of hours, rather than on an incentive or piecework basis.

day worker A person hired by the day, usually in casual labor or at an unskilled job.

dead-end job A job which has no future.

deadhead A person passed over in a promotion by a junior employee who may be better qualified. Also an employee of a transportation company (airline, railroad) who is traveling without charge on his employer's vehicle.

deadheading The term has a variety of meanings. In the transportation industry it means a free rider, a person who is being transported back to his place of work. It is also used when applied to empty trucks, buses, or empty cars which are being transported to a terminal or some other station. In the personnel field, it has been applied to the practice of passing over an employee with long seniority who is not qualified for or not able to handle the promotion. It has also been used to apply to the extra time required to get to and from the workplace.

deadheading time *See* TRAVEL TIME.

dead-horse rule A procedure used by printers to increase the amount of make-work in setting up type. Type which has been set up for advertising is required to be melted down and reset by the printers of another newspaper.

Source reference: Paul Jacobs, "Dead Horse and the Featherbird: The Specter of Useless Work," *Harper's*, Sept. 1962.

See also BOGUS (TYPE) WORK, FEATHERBEDDING, LEA ACT (ANTI-PETRILLO ACT), MAKE-WORK PRACTICES.

dead time Periods when an employee on an incentive pay basis is prevented from continuing his work because of factors beyond his control such as material shortages, mechanical breakdowns, power shortage, or other unavoidable delays. He generally receives his base or guaranteed rate during this period.

Some wage incentive systems may allow a number of minutes as a factor to take care of the usual delays in the handling of a particular operation. These factors, however, are not designed to meet unusual or long delays.

See also IDLE TIME.

dead work In mining or quarrying, the nonproductive work (stripping the surface, removal of rocks) necessary to prepare the mine for productive work.

death benefit Payment, usually a lump sum, provided to a worker's beneficiary, in the event of his death. The payment may be provided by a pension plan or another type of employer-sponsored welfare plan, or by a union to its members. When insured, the more common term is life insurance.

deauthorization election A procedure under Section 9(e) of the Taft-Hartley Act which permits employees, on a petition of more than 30 percent in the bargaining unit, to vote on the question of withdrawing from the union the authority to require membership in the union as a condition of continued employment.

This procedure was probably the counterpart of the original Taft-Hartley provision which required the holding of elections to "authorize" the union to bargain for a union shop. Because it was found burdensome and useless, the union shop authorization election was repealed in 1951. However, Section 9(e)(1) was not removed and the law requires the Board to "take a secret ballot of the employees in such a unit and certify the results thereof to such labor organization and to the employer."

Source references: Labor Management Relations Act, as amended, Section 9(e)(1), 29 U.S.C. 159(e)(1) (1982); *NLRB v. Penn Cork & Closures,* 156 NLRB 411, 61 LRRM 1037 (1965), *enf'd,* 376 F2d 52, 64 LRRM 2855 (CA 2, 1967), *cert. denied,* 389 US 843, 66 LRRM 2308 (1967); *W. P Ihrie & Sons, Div. of Sunshine Biscuits and Local 68, American Bakery & Confectionery Workers Int. Union,* 165 NLRB 167, 65 LRRM 1205 (1967); James B. Dworkin and Marian M. Extejt, "Recent Trends in Union Decertification/Deauthorization Elections," *Proceedings of the 32d A/M, IRRA,* ed. by Barbara Dennis (Madison: 1980); Chester A. Morgan, "The Union Shop Deauthorization Poll," *ILRR,* Oct. 1958.

See also DECERTIFICATION, UNION SHOP.

decasualization The process of regularizing employment of the casual worker. In the longshore industry where the "shape-up" led to substantial waste of manpower, much improvement has been made through the use of hiring halls and procedures for providing more regular periods of employment.

Source references: ILO, *Decasualisation of Dock Labour,* Second item on the agenda (Geneva: Report 2, Inland Transport Committee, 3d Session, Brussels, 1949); ———, *Expanded Programme of Technical Assistance, Report to the Government of Malaysia on Decasualisation of Dock Labour in the Port of Penang* (Geneva: 1966); Vernon H. Jensen, "Decasualisation of Employment on the New York Waterfront," *ILRR,* July 1958; Edward E. Swanstrom, *The Waterfront Labor Problem: A Study in Decasualization and Unemployment Insurance* (New York: Fordham UP, 1938).

See also CASUAL WORKER.

decertification The procedure for removing a union as certified bargaining representative of employees in an appropriate bargaining unit. This is done after petition alleging that the union no longer represents the majority of the employees. When the election is lost by the certified agent, or the NLRB determines that the certified agent is no longer a "representative," the union loses its status and is "decertified."

Source references: Taft-Hartley Act, as amended, Section 9(e)(2), 29 U.S.C. 159(e)(2) (1982); John C. Anderson, Charles A. O'Reilly III, and Gloria Busman, "Union Decertification in the U.S.: 1947–1977," *IR,* Winter 1980; John C. Anderson, Gloria Busman, and Charles A. O'Reilly III, "What Factors Influence the Outcome of Decertification Elections?" *MLR,* Nov. 1979; Ralph D. Elliot and Benjamin M. Hawkins, "Do Union Organizing Activities Affect Decertification?" *Journal of Labor Research,* Spring 1982; ———, "Union Decertification—Some Recent Trends," *Employee Relations LJ,* Spring 1980; William E. Fulmer and Tamara A. Gilman, "Why Do Workers Vote for Union Decertification?" *Personnel,* March/April 1981; Joseph Krislov, "Decertification Elections Increase But Remain No Major Burden to Unions," *MLR,* Nov. 1979; ———, "Union Decertification," *ILRR,* July 1956; William A. Krupman and Gregory I. Rasin, "Decertification: Removing the Shroud," *LLJ,* April 1979; William J. Rosenthal, "Issues in Decertification Proceedings," *NYU 34th Annual National Conference on Labor,* ed. by Richard Adelman (New York: Bender, 1982).

See also DEAUTHORIZATION ELECTION.

decision A conclusion, usually by a court, which involves the interpretation or application of law to the facts of a particular case. In arbitration, decisions usually are known as awards, and generally are binding on the parties, subject only to review under limited conditions permitted by law.

See also ARBITRATION AWARD.

decision/effects bargaining Decision bargaining refers to negotiations over employer determinations about business operations; effects or impact bargaining refers to negotiations over the impact of management decisions on the employees.

The courts have held that management is not obligated to bargain over the decision to close a plant or go out of business. Bargaining, however, may be required over other decisions such as the decision to subcontract work.

Employers are generally required to bargain over the "effects" of management decisions on wages, hours, and working conditions. The NLRB in *Shamrock Dairy* held that this requirement "includes the duty to notify the collective bargaining representative and to afford such representative an opportunity to bargain with respect to a contemplated change concerning the tenure of the employees and their conditions of employment." The requirement does not include an obligation to reach an agreement.

Source references: Brockway Motor Trucks v. NLRB, 582 F2d 720, 99 LRRM 2013 (1978); *Shamrock Dairy, Inc.*, 119 NLRB 998, 41 LRRM 1216 (1957); John S. Irving, Jr., "Closing and Sales of Businesses: A Settled Area?" *LLJ*, April 1982; Thomas C. Kohler, "Distinctions Without Differences: Effects Bargaining in Light of *First National Maintenance*," *Industrial Relations LJ*, Vol. 5, no. 3, 1983; Philip A. Miscimarra, *The NLRB and Managerial Discretion: Plant Closing, Relocations, Subcontracting, and Automation* (Philadelphia: Univ. of Pennsylvania, Wharton School, Industrial Research Unit, LRPP no. 24, 1983); Gerard Morales, "The Obligation of a Multiplant Employer to Bargain on the Decision to Close One of its Plants," *LLJ*, Nov. 1979; Marianna M. Perkins, "Economically Motivated Partial Closings: The Duty of Management to Decision-Bargain," *LLJ*, Nov. 1980.

See also FIBREBOARD CASE.

deductions Generally refers to the check-off of union dues, fines, and other assessments. Deductions from the employee's pay check may also include U.S. goverment bonds, stock ownership plans, health and welfare programs, or the "reasonable cost" of board, lodging, and other facilities under the Fair Labor Standards Act.

See also CHECK-OFF.

defendant The individual or organization having the responsibility of defending its position before a tribunal or court.

Defense Mediation Board *See* NATIONAL DEFENSE MEDIATION BOARD.

defense strike *See* NEGATIVE STRIKE.

deferral In grievance arbitration, deferral means the judicial and administrative policy and practice of yielding to the jurisdiction and decisions of arbitrators in cases involving interpretation and application of collective bargaining agreements. Although courts and administering agencies normally defer to arbitration, exceptions occur in the event a dispute involves both contractual rights and rights granted by the National Labor Relations Act.

Deferral also means a procedure under Section 706(c) and (d) of Title VII of the Civil Rights Act of 1964 that requires discrimination complaints to be handled initially by a state agency. EEOC thus defers action on the complaint to the 706 agency, and a charge is processed by the Commission only after the deferral procedure is completed.

Source references: Civil Rights Act of 1964, as amended, 42 U.S.C. 2000e–5(c) and (d) (1982); U.S. EEOC, "Procedural Regulations," 29 C.F.R. 1601; Benjamin Aaron, "Judicial and Administrative Deference to Arbitration," *Labor Law Developments 1972*, Proceedings of the 18th Annual Institute on Labor Law, SLF (New York: Bender, 1972); Reginald Alleyne, "Courts, Arbitrators, and the NLRB: The Nature of the Deferral Beast," *Decisional Thinking of Arbitrators and Judges*, Proceedings of the 33d A/M, NAA, ed. by James Stern and Barbara Dennis (Washington: BNA, 1981); Michael C. Harper, "Union Waiver of Employee Rights Under the NLRA: Part II—A Fresh Approach to Board Deferral to Arbitration," *Industrial Relations LJ*, Vol. 4, no. 4, 1981; Stephen L. Hayford and Lynelle M. Wood, "Deferral to Grievance Arbitration in Unfair Labor Practice Matters: The Public Sector Treatment," *LLJ*, Oct. 1981; Edwin R. Teple, "Deferral to Arbitration: Implications of NLRB Policy," *AJ*, June 1974; Jonathan Yarowsky, "Judicial Deference to Arbitral Determinations: Continuing Problems of Power and Finality," *IR Law Digest*, Winter 1977.

See also ARBITRABILITY, COLLYER INSULATED WIRE CASE, EQUAL EMPLOYMENT OPPORTUNITY COMMISSION, 706 AGENCY, SPIELBERG DOCTRINE, STEELWORKERS TRILOGY.

deferred retirement date The date to which the fixed or normal date set for retirement is postponed.

deferred wage increase General term used for negotiated wage changes which are not to become effective until some specified date in the future, e.g., a year later.

See also ANNUAL IMPROVEMENT FACTOR.

deindustrialization Defined by Bluestone and Harrison as "a widespread, systematic disinvestment in the nation's basic productive capacity," it is evidenced by plant closings, corporate diversification, and plant relocation to another community or to a foreign country.

Source reference: Barry Bluestone and Bennett Harrison, *The Deindustrialization of America* (New York: Basic Books, 1982).

DeJonge case A decision of the Supreme Court which held that "peaceable assembly for lawful discussion" was not a crime. The case resulted from action by Dirk DeJonge in 1934 when he spoke at a meeting arranged by the Communist Party to protest police activity during strikes. DeJonge was convicted under the Oregon Criminal Syndicalism Statute.

The decision of the Supreme Court in 1937, stated in part:

> The right of peaceable assembly is a cognate to those of free speech and free press and is equally fundamental. As this court said in *U.S. v. Cruikshank* (92 U.S. 542 at 552, 23 L. Ed. 588), "The very idea of government, republican in form, implies a right on the part of its citizens to meet peaceably for consultation in respect to public affairs and to petition for a redress of grievances."

Source reference: DeJonge v. Oregon, 299 US 33 (1937).

delay allowances The time factor allowed for unintentional or undue delay caused on the job because of machine or material delay in setting the time standard for an incentive operation.

See also ALLOWED TIME.

delinquent members Those members of the union who have not paid their dues to the union as of a definite date during the month. In some plants where the union did not have the check-off, prior to the Taft-Hartley Act, the employer would deduct the union dues from the next month's pay of those delinquent and turn the funds over to the union.

demarcation dispute The name for a jurisdictional dispute among British unions. It involves a dispute or disputes between two unions over the apportionment or overlapping of work.

Source reference: Sidney and Beatrice Webb, *The History of Trade Unionism* (London: Longmans, Green, 1926).

de minimis doctrine The legal doctrine that the law does not concern itself with minor or trifling matters. (De Minimis non curat lex.) The doctrine has been applied in cases under the Wage-Hour Law and in questions involving predominantly local matters, not subject to federal regulation because the issue or the interstate business involved is of small moment.

Source reference: Anderson v. Mt. Clemens Pottery, 328 US 680, 6 WH Cases 83 (1946).

democracy Term generally applied to political government where control and power rests in the majority of the people. It also implies that the rights of the minority will be respected. Democracy in trade unions has a similar connotation in that the majority of the members should have sufficient power to control and determine policy decisions by the votes of the majority. Protection also must be afforded to minority groups in the union.

Source references: Benjamin Aaron, "Individual Employee Rights and Union Democracy," *Proceedings of the 21st A/M, IRRA,* ed. by Gerald Somers (Madison: 1969); American Civil Liberties Union, *Democracy in Trade Unions* (New York: 1943); John C. Anderson, "A Comparative Analysis of Local Union Democracy, *IR,* Oct. 1978; ———, "Union Participation and Convention Democracy," *Proceedings of the 32d A/M, IRRA,* ed. by Barbara Dennis (Madison: 1980); Herman W. Benson, *Democratic Rights for Union Members; A Guide to Internal Union Democracy* (New York: Association for Union Democracy, 1979); Alice H. Cook, *Union Democracy: Practice and Ideal* (Ithaca: NYSSILR, Cornell Univ., 1963); J. David Edelstein and Malcolm Warner, "Research Areas in National Union Democracy," *IR,* May 1977; Sara Gamm, "The Election Base of National Union Executive Boards," *ILRR,* April 1979; Will Herberg, "Bureaucracy and Democracy in Labor Unions," *Antioch Review,* Fall 1943; Arthur Hochner, Karen Koziara, and Stuart Schmidt, "Thinking About Democracy and

Participation in Unions," *Proceedings of the 32d A/M, IRRA*, ed. by Barbara Dennis (Madison: 1980); John L. Holcombe, "Union Democracy and the LMRDA," *LLJ*, July 1961; Michele Hoyman, "Leadership Responsiveness in Local Unions and Title VII Compliance: Does More Democracy Mean More Representation for Blacks and Women?" *Proceedings of the 32d A/M, IRRA*, ed. by Barbara Dennis (Madison: 1980); Henry A. Landsberger and Charles L. Hulin, "A Problem of Union Democracy: Officers' Attitudes Toward Union Members," *ILRR*, April 1961; William Leiserson, *American Trade Union Democracy* (New York: Columbia UP, 1959); Joel Seidman, *Democracy in the Labor Movement* (2d ed., Ithaca: NYSSILR, Cornell Univ., Bull. 39, 1969); Herbert A. Shepard, "Democratic Control in a Labor Union," *American Journal of Sociology*, Jan. 1949.

See also INDUSTRIAL DEMOCRACY.

demonstration project A term frequently associated with social science research, "demonstration" is defined by the National Research Council Study Project on Social Research and Development as "a small-scale program undertaken in an operational setting for a finite period of time to test the desirability of a proposed course of action."

Under the Job Training Partnership Act, the Secretary of Labor is authorized to establish a research program which includes demonstration projects, "for the purpose of improving techniques and demonstrating the effectiveness of specialized methods in meeting employment and training problems."

The Civil Service Reform Act of 1978 defines "demonstration project" as "a project conducted by the Office of Personnel Management, or under its supervision, to determine whether a specified change in personnel management policies or procedures would result in improved Federal personnel management."

Source references: Civil Service Reform Act of 1978, Section 4701(a)(4), 5 U.S.C. 4701(a)(4) (1982); Job Training Partnership Act of 1982, Section 452(b), 29 U.S.C. 1732(b) (1982); Mark A. Abramson, *The Funding of Social Knowledge Production and Application: A Survey of Federal Agencies* (Washington: National Academy of Sciences, Study Project on Social Research & Development Volume 2, 1978); National Research Council, *The Federal Investment in Knowledge of Social Problems* (Washington: National Academy of Sciences, Study Project on Social Research & Development Volume 1: Study Project Report, 1978).

demotion The process of moving an employee to a position lower in the wage scale or in rank. It may be involuntary, resulting from inefficient or careless work in the form of a penalty, or voluntary resulting from a curtailment of production, and without prejudice to the employee. It is similar to downgrading.

dental care, prepaid One of the efforts in very recent years to extend the comprehensiveness of health care plans negotiated by labor and management. Although unions had pioneered dental plans in the early 1950s, the extensive development of this fringe benefit in the medical care area achieved greater acceptance in the 1960s.

The State of California alone, according to information from the Division of Labor Statistics and Research of the State of California, indicated that approximately 400,000 union members and their families were covered by prepaid dental care during mid-1966.

Source references: Donald R. Bell, "Dental and Vision Care Benefits in Health Insurance Plans," *MLR*, June 1980; J. J. Follmann, Jr., "Current Picture of Insurance Programs for Dental Care," *Journal of the American Dental Association*, May 1962; Mitchell Meyer, *Dental Insurance Plans* (New York: The Conference Board, Report no. 680, 1976); John H. Simons, *Prepaid Dentistry: A Case Study* (Berkeley: Center for Labor Research and Education, Institute of IR, UC, 1967); U.S. Dept. of HEW, Public Health Service, *Survey of Dental Benefit Plans, 1973* (Washington: 1979).

See also FRINGE BENEFITS, HEALTH BENEFIT PROGRAMS.

departmental seniority A seniority procedure in a plant which gives employees with greater length of service in the department preference in matters of promotion, layoff, or transfer. The seniority clause (which may include factors other than length of service) is applied in the first instance to the departmental unit. A departmental seniority clause might read as follows:

> Each employee will have a separate seniority standing in each department in which he has worked. His seniority standing in each department will equal the length of service in that department, dating from the first day of employment in the department.

departmental steward *See* SHOP STEWARD.

departmental unit A group within the plant composed of workers in a particular department. In seniority based on departmental arrangements, promotions, transfers, and layoffs are first adjusted within the department, in line with the policy of the company or the collective bargaining agreement. The departmental unit also may be the basis for collective bargaining, where the NLRB has designated it as the unit appropriate for bargaining purposes.

See also APPROPRIATE UNIT.

Department Store Workers of America; United (CIO) Merged with the Retail, Wholesale and Department Store Union (CIO) during March 1955.

See also RETAIL, WHOLESALE AND DEPARTMENT STORE UNION (AFL-CIO).

dependent One who relies on someone else for his support. Under income tax laws a person who receives more than half his support from a person related to him by blood, marriage, or legal adoption. A state of dependency may be variously defined under state laws which provide relief for wholly or partially dependent persons.

dependent unionism A form of union organization described by Professor Hoxie as "dependent" on the good will of the employer and sponsored or dominated by him.

Source reference: Robert F. Hoxie, *Trade Unionism in the United States* (New York: Appleton, 1917).

See also COMPANY UNION.

deposits, monetary Provisions under some agreements which require the employer or union or both to make a deposit of funds to insure the carrying out of the terms of the agreement. If violation occurs, the money is forfeited. Questions of contract violation may be arbitrated under the terms of the agreement.

See also AGREEMENT ENFORCEMENT, ARBITRATION AWARD, NO-STRIKE CLAUSE.

depressed area Depressed areas in legislation have been defined as certain geographic communities in which the number of unemployed has gone beyond a certain percentage, generally substantially above the average for the country. Special treatment is accorded these depressed areas by way of receiving certain government contracts and other benefits designed to provide additional employment opportunities and to enlarge work opportunities in that particular area.

Under Sections 5(a) and 5(b) of the Area Redevelopment Act of 1961 (ARA), areas were designated by the Area Redevelopment Administrator as eligible for assistance according to the following criteria:

Industrial areas: (1) unemployment in the area averaged at least 6 percent during the qualifying period; and (2) (a) 50 percent above the national average for three of the preceding four calendar years, or (b) 75 percent above the national average for two of the three preceding calendar years, or (c) 100 percent above the national average for one of the preceding two calendar years.

Rural and Smaller Urban Areas: " . . . the number of low income farm families in the various rural areas . . . the relationship of the income levels of the families in each such area to the general levels of income in the United States, . . . the availability of manpower in each such area for supplemental unemployment, . . . the extent of migration out of the area, . . . and the extent to which 'rural development' projects have previously been located in any such area under programs administered by the Department of Agriculture. . . ."

By January 1962, 129 labor market areas, most of which had a minimum labor force of 15,000 in 1960 that included at least 8,000 nonagricultural workers, were designated as eligible to receive ARA assistance under Section 5(a) of the Act. These are sometimes referred to as "5(a) areas" because they were designated as eligible for assistance under Section 5(a) of the Act. Another 657 counties, most of which had a labor force of less than

15,000 in 1960 and containing either small urban centers or were predominantly rural, were designated "5(b) areas" eligible for assistance under the Act.

Sar A. Levitan has suggested that a depressed area is one marked by general economic stagnation and that "a high rate of chronic unemployment is only one of many socioeconomic characteristics signaling distress in an area. A stagnating population [out-migration, particularly of the young and the better educated], deterioration in the quality of available labor resources [low educational attainment among the population and a high rate of unskilled labor], declining labor-force participation rates, low wages and income, inadequate investment in capital outlays, and substandard housing are associated with chronic labor-surplus areas."

The Public Works and Economic Development Act of 1965 set forth criteria similar to Section 5(a) of the ARA in establishing "redevelopment areas" eligible for federal assistance.

Source references: Kenneth O. Alexander, "Employment Shifts in Areas of Persistent Unemployment," *ILRR*, Oct. 1968; Lowell E. Gallaway, "An Economic Analysis of Public Policy for the Depressed Areas," *ILRR*, July 1962; Sar A. Levitan, "Characteristics of Urban Depressed Areas," *MLR*, Jan. 1964; ———, *Federal Aid to Depressed Areas* (Baltimore: Johns Hopkins Press, 1964); John H. Lindauer, "The Accuracy of Area Unemployment Estimates Used to Identify Depressed Areas," *ILRR*, April 1966; ———, "Effects of Selected Methods to Improve Unemployment Rates Used to Identify Depressed Areas," *ILRR*, April 1967; Moses Lukaczer, "Reflections on the Problem of Depressed Areas—1962," *LLJ*, Jan. 1962.

See also AREA REDEVELOPMENT ACT OF 1961, PUBLIC WORKS AND ECONOMIC DEVELOPMENT ACT OF 1965.

depression The period during the business cycle when unemployment is extremely high and the economy is at a low productive level. American labor unions historically have had a difficult time maintaining their organizational strength during periods of depression.

dermatitis, industrial Inflammation of the skin (hands, fingers, forearm, face, and neck) caused by fumes, vapors, irritant dusts, etc., in occupations where acids, dyes, dusts, oils, and waxes are used, which come in contact with the skin or penetrate the clothing through saturation.

Source references: William H. Gafafer (ed.), *Manual of Industrial Hygiene and Medical Services in War Industries* (Philadelphia: Saunders, 1943); Rutherford T. Johnstone and Seward E. Miller, *Occupational Diseases and Industrial Medicine* (Philadelphia: Saunders, 1960); Frederick J. Wampler (ed.), *The Principles and Practice of Industrial Medicine* (Baltimore: William Wood & Co., 1943).

de-skill, to *See* JOB DILUTION, RATIONALIZATION.

Diamond Workers' Protective Union of America (AFL) Merged with the Jewelry Workers to become Diamond Workers Division of Local 1, International Jewelry Workers' Union (AFL) on November 1, 1954.

See also JEWELRY WORKERS' UNION; INTERNATIONAL (AFL-CIO).

dictatorship of the proletariat The term which implies control of the means of production by the workers. It is the ultimate goal of Marxism, the classless society, when power rests in the hands of the toilers, or proletariat.

Dictionary of Occupational Titles A publication of the United States Employment Service (USES) in the Department of Labor that codifies and describes some 20,000 separate jobs or occupations. It is widely used by personnel people and by employment offices throughout the country. The major groups are codified as follows:

- 0/1 Professional, technical, and managerial occupations
- 2 Clerical and sales occupations
- 3 Service occupations
- 4 Agricultural, fishery, forestry, and related occupations
- 5 Processing occupations
- 6 Machine trades occupations
- 7 Bench work occupations
- 8 Structural work occupations
- 9 Miscellaneous occupations

The fourth edition was issued in 1977, followed by a supplement in 1983.

Source references: U.S. Dept. of Labor, ETA, *Conversion Table of Code and Title Changes, Third to Fourth Edition, Dictionary of Occupational Titles* (Washington: 1979); ———, *Dictionary of Occupational Titles* (4th ed., Washington: 1977); ———, *Selected Characteristics of Occupations Defined in the Dictionary of Occupational Titles* (Washington: 1981); Emanuel Weinstein, "A Well-Brewed DOT," *Occupational Outlook Quarterly,* Summer 1978.

Die Sinkers' Conference; International (Ind) The monthly publication is the *News Flash.*

Address: 4807 Rockside Rd., Cleveland, Ohio 44131. Tel. (216) 447–9797

differential piece rate Compensation of labor in which the money rate per piece is based on the total pieces produced during the period (usually one day).

diffential piece-rate plan A method of wage payment designed to speed up production by providing a higher rate for work performed above the standard and a lower rate for work performed below the standard. It has sometimes been referred to as the Taylor differential-piece-rate plan, since Taylor was its most popular proponent.

Thus, if the standard were set for 50 pieces per day at 25 cents per piece, or $12.50 per day for the normal worker, those producing in excess of 50 pieces would receive a rate above 25 cents and those producing below 50 pieces would receive a piece rate below 25 cents.

See also MERRICK MULTIPLE-PIECE RATE PLAN.

differentials *See* WAGE DIFFERENTIALS.

dilution *See* JOB DILUTION.

direct action A procedure used by some unions to achieve their aims, rather than by negotiation or use of the machinery of the collective bargaining agreement. The union uses threats or resorts to slowdowns or other means to get the employer to act in the handling of certain grievances. In some cases, various forms of strike action may be used to force the employer to accede to the union's demands.

See also JOB ACTION.

direct contact method of training A procedure used in training supervisory employees. Instruction is provided largely by direct observation of job performance by the trainee.

direct labor An internal control or accounting device to determine or establish cost factors for labor directly involved in the production operation. "Indirect labor" generally is deemed to refer to work which is not specifically assigned to any operation, but is designed to serve the plant functions generally. In the handling of incentive programs, many problems arise in trying to devise incentive procedures for indirect labor.

See also INDIRECT LABOR, PRODUCTION WORKERS.

Directors Guild of America, Inc. (Ind) An organization formed by the merger of the Radio and Television Directors Guild (AFL-CIO) and the Screen Directors' Guild of America, Inc. (Ind) on January 1, 1960.

It issues the monthly *Directors Guild of America News.*

Address: 7950 Sunset Blvd., Hollywood, Calif. 90046. Tel. (213) 656–1220

Directory of Labor Organizations: Europe The 1965 revised edition is a two-volume publication which gives addresses, membership data, principal offices, publications, and international affiliation of more than 2,500 European labor organizations. The Directory includes a section on European regional organizations of worldwide trade internationals: the International Confederation of Free Trade Unions (ICFTU) and the International Federation of Christian Trade Unions (IFCTU). The revised directory is one in a series of four directories which covers, besides Europe, labor organizations in Africa, Asia-Australasia, and the Western Hemisphere. The various directories are now combined and issued as *Directory of Foreign Labor Organizations,* by the Office of Foreign Relations, Bureau of International Labor Affairs, U.S. Department of Labor.

Source reference: U.S. Dept. of Labor, BILA and BLS, *Directory of Labor Organizations: Europe* (rev. ed., 2 vols., Washington: 1965).

disability The inability of an individual to perform his ordinary or customary work or routine because of injury.

Source references: Richard V. Burkhauser and Robert H. Haveman, *Disability and Work, the Economics of American Policy* (Baltimore: Johns Hopkins UP, 1982); Alfonso Duarte, Jr., *Long-Term Disability: A Report to Management* (New York: AMA, Management Bull. 91, 1966); Lawrence D. Haber, "The Chronology of Disability," *Proceedings of the 24th A/M, IRRA*, ed. by Gerald Somers (Madison: 1972); Research Council for Economic Security, *Disability* (Chicago: 1947); Shell Oil Company, Personnel Dept., *Shell Disability Benefit Plan* (New York: 1949); U.S. Dept. of HEW, Public Health Service, *Disability Among Persons in the Labor Force by Employment Status* (Washington: 1964); U.S. Dept. of HEW, SSA, *Rehabilitated Disability Applicants, 1967* (Washington: Research and Statistics Note no. 26, 1974); ———, *Work Disability in the United States, A Chartbook* (Washington: 1981).

See also INCAPACITY FOR WORK, PERMANENT DISABILITY, PERMANENT PARTIAL DISABILITY, PERMANENT TOTAL DISABILITY, TEMPORARY DISABILITY.

disability insurance A method insuring workers against loss of wages incurred because of inability to perform their ordinary or customary work.

Source references: Monroe Berkowitz and William G. Johnson, "Towards an Economics of Disability: The Magnitude and Structure of Transfer and Medical Costs," *Journal of Human Resources*, Summer 1970; Lawrence D. Haber, *The Disabled Worker Under OASDI* (Washington: U.S. Dept. of HEW, SSA, Research Report no. 6, 1964); William G. Johnson, William P. Curington, and Paul R. Cullinan, "Income Security for the Disabled," *IR*, Spring 1979; Ronald S. Koot and Thomas E. White, *Temporary Disability Insurance: Significant Data, 1960–1961* (Washington: U.S. Dept. of Labor, BES, Pub. no. U–212, 1962); James O'Brien, "Protecting the Worker On and Off the Job," *American Federationist*, Sept. 1972; Robert Tilove, "State Disability Insurance Laws," *Labor and the Nation*, Spring 1950; U.S. Dept. of HHS, SSA, *Experience of Disabled-Worker Benefits Under OASDI, 1974–78* (Washington: Actuarial Study no. 81, 1980); U.S. Dept. of HEW, SSA, *An Analysis of Disability Insurance Benefit Loss Due to Delays in Filing, 1968–76* (Washington: Research and Statistical Note no. 11, 1979); David A. Weeks, "Long Term Disability—Your Next Employee Benefit?" *Conference Board Record*, Jan. 1965.

See also SECOND INJURY PROVISIONS, TEMPORARY DISABILITY INSURANCE.

disability retirement Retirement because of physical inability to perform the job.

See also PERMANENT DISABILITY.

disabled veteran Defined by the Vietnam Era Veterans Readjustment Assistance Act as "(A) a veteran who is entitled to compensation or who, but for the receipt of military retired pay, would be entitled to compensation under laws administered by the Veterans' Administration, or (B) a person who was discharged or released from active duty because of a service-connected disability."

Source reference: Vietnam Era Veterans Readjustment Assistance Act of 1974, Pub. L. 93–508, Dec. 3, 1974, 88 Stat. 1578 (codified throughout scattered sections of 38 U.S.C.).

disabling injury An injury which results in the loss of working time beyond the day or shift during which the injury occurred.

disadvantaged workers The terms disadvantaged workers, hard-core unemployed, and unemployables are frequently used interchangeably in referring to the employment, education, and income problems of those who have the greatest difficulty finding and retaining a job.

The U.S. Department of Labor has defined a disadvantaged worker as one who is poor, unemployed or underemployed, under 22 or over 45 years of age, a minority group member, less than a high school graduate, or handicapped. The five basic combinations of the definitions are: poor school dropout without suitable employment; poor minority member without suitable employment; poor youth without suitable employment; poor older worker without suitable employment; poor handicapped worker without suitable employment.

The disadvantaged worker is usually employed in a job which involves a low wage, no possibility for advancement, undesirable working conditions, and inequitable supervision. Even when a disadvantaged worker is able to find a job, he frequently develops work habits and job expectations that are incompatible with the performance and production standards of a higher wage, higher status job. Consequently, employers have regarded the disadvantaged worker as being irresponsible and prone to a high absentee rate.

During the early 1960s, the federal government, in programs under the Area Redevelopment Act of 1961 and the Manpower Development and Training Act of 1962, instituted programs to provide vocational skills to experienced but unemployed males. In the middle and latter 1960s, federal programs were joined with manpower activities in the private business sector to establish programs geared to providing basic education job skills, instruction in how to get and hold a job, and eventual job placement for disadvantaged workers of both sexes. Such programs included the Job Corps, the NAB-JOBS project, the Model Cities Program, and the Neighborhood Youth Corps. Private companies have also taken the initiative in establishing their own recruiting and training programs for the disadvantaged.

Source references: Grace Aboud, *Hiring and Training the Disadvantaged for Public Employment* (Ithaca: NYSSILR, Cornell Univ., Key Issues Series no. 11, 1973); Elchanan Cohn and Morgan V. Lewis, "Employer's Experience in Retaining Hard-Core Hires," *IR*, Feb. 1975; Jules Cohn, *The Conscience of the Corporations: Business and Urban Affairs, 1967–1970* (Baltimore: Johns Hopkins Press, 1971); Peter B. Doeringer (ed.), *Programs to Employ the Disadvantaged* (Englewood Cliffs: PH, 1969); Richard A. Drabant, "Employing the Unemployable: The Lessons of Experience," *Conference Board Record*, Nov. 1972; Sidney A. Fine, *Guidelines for the Employment of the Culturally Disadvantaged* (Kalamazoo: Upjohn Institute, 1969); Jackie P. Hearns, "New Approaches to Meet Post-Hiring Difficulties of Disadvantaged Workers," *Proceedings of the 21st A/M, IRRA*, ed. by Gerald Somers (Madison: 1969); Deborah A. Heskes, *Supportive Services for Disadvantaged Workers and Trainees* (Ithaca: NYSSILR, Cornell Univ., Key Issues Series no. 12, 1973); William H. Holley, Jr., "Successful Employment of the Disadvantaged," *PJ*, March 1973; Allen R. Janger, *Employing the Disadvantaged: A Company Perspective* (New York: The Conference Board, Report no. 551, 1972); David B. Lipsky, "Employer Role in Hard-Core Trainee Success," *IR*, May 1973; Robert M. Middlekauff, "Industrial Relations Implications in Hiring the Disadvantaged," *Arbitration and Social Change*, Proceedings of the 22d A/M, NAA, ed. by Gerald Somers (Washington: BNA, 1970); Charles R. Milton and James M. Black, "The Disadvantaged—Changing Definitions and Personnel Practice," *Personnel*, March/April 1974; Leonard Nadler, "Helping the Hard-Core Adjust to the World of Work," *Harvard BR*, March/April 1970; NICB, *Education, Training and Employment of the Disadvantaged* (New York: Public Affairs Study no. 4, 1969); Harland Padfield and Roy Williams, *Stay Where You Were, A Study of Unemployables in Industry* (Philadelphia: Lippincott, 1973); V. Lane Rawlins, "Manpower Programs for Disadvantaged Youths," *IR*, May 1972; Joseph B. Shedd, *White Workers and Black Trainees, An Outline of the Issues Raised by Special Training Programs for the Disadvantaged* (Ithaca: NYSSILR, Cornell Univ., Key Issues Series no. 13, 1973); U.S. Dept. of Labor, Manpower Aministration, *Breakthrough for Disadvantaged Youth* (Washington: 1969); Saul Wallen, "Industrial Relations Problems of Employing the Disadvantaged," *Arbitration and Social Change*, Proceedings of the 22d A/M, NAA, ed. by Gerald Somers (Washington: BNA, 1970).

See also COMPREHENSIVE EMPLOYMENT AND TRAINING ACT (CETA) OF 1973, HARD CORE OF UNEMPLOYMENT, NATIONAL ALLIANCE OF BUSINESS (NAB), POOR, UNEMPLOYABLE.

disaffiliation The procedure whereby a local union separates from the national or international union of which it is a member. It is also the procedure which may be followed by a national or international union when it seeks to withdraw from its parent organization. Disaffiliation also may result from action by the parent organization or national union, in which case it usually takes the form of suspension or expulsion.

Source reference: Francis B. Conrad, "The Contract-Bar-Rule and Disaffiliation Cases," *NYU 4th Annual Conference on Labor,* ed. by Emanuel Stein (Albany: Bender, 1951).

discharge Dismissal of an employee, usually for some infraction of the rules or policies of the company, incompetence, or other good reason. Collective bargaining agreements frequently spell out the grounds for discharge. Discharge results in involuntary separation and with prejudice to the employee. A discharge will result in the loss of seniority and other rights.

Source references: Roger I. Abrams, "A Theory for the Discharge Case," *AJ,* Sept. 1981; Walter E. Baer, "Arbitrating the Discharge and Discipline of Union Officials," *MLR,* Sept. 1969; ———, *Discipline and Discharge Under the Labor Agreement* (New York: AMA, 1972); Eric A. Bare, "Handling Claims of Constructive Discharge," *Journal of the College and University Personnel Association,* Summer 1980; Maurice C. Benewitz, "Discharge Arbitration and the Quantum of Proof," *AJ,* June 1973; BNA, *Separation Procedures and Severance Benefits* (Washington: PPF Survey no. 121, 1978); Robert W. Fisher, "Arbitration of Discharges for Marginal Reasons," *MLR,* Oct. 1968; ———, "When Workers are Discharged—An Overview," *MLR,* June 1973; Ken Jennings and Roger Wolters, "Discharge Cases Reconsidered," *AJ,* Sept. 1976; Stephen S. Kaagen, "Terminating People From Key Positions," *PJ,* Feb. 1978; Irving Kovarsky, "Discharges for Events Occurring Away from Work," *LLJ,* May 1962; Edward Mandt, "Employee Termination: Proceed With Care," *Management Review,* Dec. 1980; Harold J. Rood, "Legal Issues in Faculty Termination, An Analysis Based on Recent Court Cases," *Journal of Higher Education,* March/April 1977; George Rose, "Employees' Rights to Damages Upon Wrongful Discharge," *LLJ,* Oct. 1960; Henry S. Sahm, "The Discharge for Union Activities," *LLJ,* April 1961; Richard C. Stapleton, "Terminations: Lower-Level Dismissals," *Personnel,* May/June 1971; Clyde W. Summers, "Protecting *All* Employees Against Unjust Dismissal," *Harvard BR,* Jan./Feb. 1980.

See also CONSTRUCTIVE DISCHARGE, DISCRIMINATORY DISCHARGE, DISMISSAL, RELEASE, RIGHT TO FIRE, SEPARATION, WRONGFUL DISCHARGE.

dischargee A worker who has been discharged.

discharge warning A notice given to a worker that his services will be terminated if he commits infractions or violations of rules or does unsatisfactory work in the future.

disciplinary layoff A temporary removal of a worker from the payroll because of infraction or violation of company rules or policies. It is a warning and notice of possible permanent separation from the payroll if warranted by the employee's future behavior.

See also SUSPENSION.

discipline Action by an employer, short of discharge, against an employee for infraction of company or contract rules. Discipline may take the form of loss of rights under the agreement, being sent home for a period of time, loss of pay, or other penalties set out in the contract or agreed to as a method of avoiding or reducing the incidence of infractions. Discipline of a union member by the union itself for violation of its rules or regulations may take many forms, including loss of membership in good standing, and possibly loss of employment.

Discipline is designed to encourage workers to follow procedures so that the work of the group can go on without undue difficulty. It is designed to set up standards of performance, behavior, fair play, and good morale. Discipline as a form of punishment to obtain conformance may be subject to question—but it is widely used in labor-management relations.

Source references: AMA, *Constructive Discipline in Industry* (New York: Social Research Report 3, 1946); Leon D. Boncarosky, "Guidelines to Corrective Discipline," *PJ,* Oct. 1979; BNA, *Employee Conduct and Discipline* (Washington: PPF Survey no. 102, 1973); Roger E. Dahl, *Discipline: A Supervisor's Guide* (Washington: Labor-Management Relations Service, Strengthening Local Government Through

Better Labor Relations Series, 1978); Joseph C. Graham III, "Arbitration of Insubordination Disputes in the Public Sector," *AJ*, Sept. 1976; P. M. Hammett, "The Power of Trade Unions to Discipline Their Members," *Univ. of Pennsylvania LR*, March 1948; Morrison Handsaker, "Arbitration of Discipline Cases," *PJ*, March 1967; John Huberman, "Discipline Without Punishment," *Harvard BR*, July/Aug. 1964; ———, " 'Discipline Without Punishment' Lives," *Harvard BR*, July/Aug. 1975; William H. Leahy, "Arbitration and Insubordination of Union Stewards," *AJ*, March 1972; John W. Leonard, "Discipline for Off-the-Job Activities," *MLR*, Oct. 1968; Mack A. Moore, "The Conflict Between Union Discipline and Union Security," *LLJ*, Feb. 1967; Rodney L. Oberle, "Administering Disciplinary Actions," *PJ*, Jan. 1978; George S. Odiorne, "Discipline by Objectives," *Management of Personnel Quarterly*, Summer 1971; James R. Redeker, *Discipline: Policies and Procedures* (Washington: BNA, 1983); Carmen D. Saso and Earl Tanis, *Disciplinary Policies and Practices* (Chicago: IPMA, PERL no. 40, 1972); Rosalind Schwartz and Erin-Aine Miller, *Employee Discipline* (Los Angeles: UC, Institute of IR, 1977); Joel Seidman, *A Guide to Discipline in the Public Sector* (Honolulu: Univ. of Hawaii, IRC, 1977); ———, "Discipline of Union Officers by Public Management," *AJ*, Dec. 1977; Clyde Summers, "Disciplinary Powers of Unions," *ILRR*, July 1950; ———, "Disciplinary Procedures of Unions," *ILRR*, Oct. 1950; Irene Unterberger and S. Herbert Unterberger, "Disciplining Professional Employees," *IR*, Oct. 1978; Carl A. Warns, Jr., "Right of Management to Discipline for Refusal to Cross a Picket Line," *Arbitration of Interest Disputes*, Proceedings of the 26th A/M, NAA, ed. by Barbara Dennis and Gerald Somers (Washington: BNA, 1974); June Weisberger, *Recent Developments in Job Security: Layoffs and Discipline in the Public Sector* (Ithaca: NYSSILR, Cornell Univ., Institute of Public Employment Monograph no. 6, 1976); Hoyt N. Wheeler, "Punishment Theory and Industrial Discipline," *IR*, May 1976; Wallace Wohlking, "Effective Discipline in Employee Relations," *PJ*, Sept. 1975; Roger S. Wolters, "Moral Turpitude in the Industrial Environment: A Real Dilemma," *LLJ*, April 1976; Louis Yagoda, "The Discipline Issue in Arbitration: Employer Rules," *LLJ*, Sept. 1964; Arnold M. Zack and Richard I. Bloch, *The Arbitration of Discipline Cases: Concepts and Questions* (New York: AAA, 1979).

See also EXPULSION FROM UNION, GRIEVANCE MACHINERY, INSUBORDINATION, REPRIMAND, SUSPENSION, UNION DISCIPLINE.

disclosure of information *See* ACCESS TO COMPANY BOOKS AND RECORDS.

discount privileges for employees A form of employee fringe benefits through which companies offer their own products and services or sell noncompany products to their employees at a discount rate. Company products sold at discount rates include home furnishings, building supplies, automobile accessories, household appliances, and food and beverages. Noncompany products offered at discount include such job-related items as safety clothing and equipment, salvage material, and tickets for recreational events and travel. Companies offer discount rates to employees in order to save money for employees, improve employee morale, increase employee knowledge of the quality of company products and services, discourage pilfering, aid in recruiting, meet a benefit offered by competitors, increase sales volume, and make shopping more convenient.

Source reference: NICB, *Discount Privileges for Employees* (New York: Studies in Personnel Policy no. 207, 1967).

discouraged worker Defined by BLS as "persons who *want* a job but are *not* searching for employment because they feel that no jobs are available." Discouraged workers are not counted among the unemployed because they are not actively seeking employment.

The discouraged worker is part of a larger group termed the "hidden unemployed." Among the hidden unemployed are persons who want a job, but are not seeking work because of school attendance, and those who do not want employment until suitable job opportunities arise.

Source references: T. Aldrich Finegan, "Discouraged Workers and Economic Fluctuations," *ILRR*, Oct. 1981; Paul O. Flaim, "Discouraged Workers and Changes in

Unemployment," *MLR,* March 1973; Jacob Mincer, "Determining Who Are the 'Hidden Unemployed,' " *MLR,* March 1973; Stuart O. Schweitzer and Ralph E. Smith, "The Persistence of the Discouraged Worker Effect," *ILRR,* Jan. 1974; U.S. Dept. of Labor, BLS, *Questions and Answers on Popular Labor Force Topics* (Washington: Report 522, 1978).

See also SUBEMPLOYMENT.

discretion The nature and the amount of freedom possessed by the employer in the handling of his plant problems. Discretion exists in various forms in many areas of operation—subject to the specific limitations of the contract or past practice. The amount of discretion, for example, in hiring, layoffs, promotions, discharge, etc., will vary from contract to contract.

See also MANAGEMENT RIGHTS.

discrimination The unequal or unfair application of policy to an individual or group. Thus, the Taft-Hartley Act forbids discrimination in hire and tenure of employment because of membership or nonmembership in a union. The federal and most state laws dealing with rights of employers and employees in collective bargaining proscribe certain acts as being discriminatory and in violation of public policy.

It applies also to unfair treatment in employment practices, hiring, promotion, discharge, etc., based on race, creed, color, sex, or national origin, rather than on actual job performance.

Source references: Gary Stanley Becker, *The Economics of Discrimination* (2d ed., Chicago: Univ. of Chicago Press, 1971); Walter L. Daykin, "Legality of Hiring," *LLJ,* Nov. 1959; "Drive to End Job Bias Pledged by 120 Unions," *AFL-CIO News,* Nov. 17, 1962; Zachary D. Fasman and R. Theodore Clark, Jr., "Non-Discriminatory Discrimination: An Overview of the Discrimination Problem," *NYU 26th Annual Conference on Labor,* ed. by Emanuel Stein and S. Theodore Reiner (New York: Bender, 1974); "The Job Ahead in Fair Employment Practices," *Social Action,* Dec. 1962; James E. Long, "Employment Discrimination in the Federal Sector," *Journal of Human Resources,* Winter 1976; Walter H. Maloney, Jr., "Racial and Religious Discrimination in Employment and the Role of the NLRB," *Maryland LR,* Summer 1961; Ray Marshall, "Some Factors Influencing Union Racial Practices," *Proceedings of the 14th A/M, IRRA,* ed. by Gerald Somers (Madison: 1962); Marian Leif Palley and Michael B. Preston, *Race, Sex, and Policy Problems* (Lexington, Mass.: Lexington Books, 1979); U.S. EEOC, *Job Discrimination? Laws and Rules You Should Know* (Washington: 1975).

See also AGE DISCRIMINATION IN EMPLOYMENT ACT OF 1967, CIVIL RIGHTS ACT OF 1964, EXECUTIVE ORDER 11246, REHABILITATION ACT OF 1973, VIETNAM ERA VETERANS READJUSTMENT ASSISTANCE ACT OF 1974.

discrimination, age *See* AGE DISCRIMINATION IN EMPLOYMENT ACT OF 1967.

discrimination, color *See* COLOR DISCRIMINATION.

discrimination, covert *See* SYSTEMIC DISCRIMINATION.

discrimination, handicapped *See* HANDICAPPED INDIVIDUAL, REHABILITATION ACT OF 1973, VIETNAM ERA VETERANS READJUSTMENT ASSISTANCE ACT OF 1974.

discrimination, national origin *See* NATIONAL ORIGIN DISCRIMINATION.

discrimination, race *See* RACIAL DISCRIMINATION.

discrimination, religious *See* RELIGIOUS DISCRIMINATION.

discrimination, reverse *See* REVERSE DISCRIMINATION.

discrimination, sex *See* SEX DISCRIMINATION.

discrimination, "sex-plus" *See* "SEX PLUS" DISCRIMINATION.

discrimination, systemic *See* SYSTEMIC DISCRIMINATION.

discriminatory discharge A discharge not based on job performance or failure to meet the standards set for the job, but on discriminatory reasons. It is generally applied to discharges for union membership or activity or other activities in connection with the protection and betterment of workers' wages, hours, and working conditions. Federal and state laws protect employees from discharges which are discriminatory.

Source references: Herbert A. Moss, "The Requirement of Knowledge in Discriminatory Discharge Cases," *LLJ*, Sept. 1966; Bryan F. Murphy, "Discriminatory Dismissal of Union Adherents During Organizing Campaigns: Suggested Remedial Amendments," *Industrial Relations LJ*, Vol. 4, no. 1, 1980; Bernard Samoff, "NLRB Priority and Injunctions for Discriminatory Discharges," *LLJ*, Jan. 1980.

See also CONSTRUCTIVE DISCHARGE, WRONGFUL DISCHARGE.

disestablishment The procedure used by the NLRB to divest an organization of its claim to represent the employees and its status as a labor organization. This generally follows a finding by the Board that the union was set up in violation of Section 8(a)(2) and was company dominated, supported, or inspired. The remedy of disestablishment is reserved by the Board for cases in which the company actually has dominated the organization by having a hand in its policies and election of officers. In cases of illegal support falling short of such domination, the Board merely cuts off the organization's bargaining rights until the effects of the support have been dissipated.

See also COMPANY-DOMINATED UNION, GREYHOUND CASES.

disguised unemployment The unemployed who would have been looking for work except they believed none was available in their line of work or in their community. Sometimes used to refer to discouraged workers in depressed areas or occupations.

Source reference: Robert L. Stein, "New Definitions for Employment and Unemployment," *Employment and Earnings*, Feb. 1967.

dislocated worker Also known as a displaced worker; a person who has lost a job because of technological change or skill obsolescence, plant closing or relocation, company merger or reorganization, or the impact of imports. Kolberg in his volume on workers in the smokestack industries describes the typical dislocated worker as "male, 40 years old or older, a union member, and the head of a household; although he has no more than a high school education, he has been able to maintain a middle-class salary status for most of his working life." According to Kolberg, such persons comprised approximately one-half to two million of the employed in 1983.

Unions seek to safeguard workers against job loss through job preservation clauses, transfer rights, early retirement plans, and advance notice of plant shutdowns. The federal government has elected to offer aid to workers displaced as a direct result of federal policies; the Trade Act of 1974 provides for such aid.

Source references: William H. Kolberg (ed.), *The Dislocated Worker* (Cabin John, Md.: Seven Locks Press, 1983); Bruce H. Millen, "Providing Assistance to Displaced Workers," *MLR*, May 1979; George P. Shultz and Arnold R. Weber, *Strategies for the Displaced Worker* (New York: Harper & Row, 1966); U.S. Congressional Budget Office, *Dislocated Workers: Issues and Federal Options* (Washington: Background Paper, 1982); U.S. Dept. of Labor, BLS, *Case Studies of Displaced Workers: Experiences of Workers After Layoff* (Washington: Bull. no. 1408, 1964).

See also TRADE ACT OF 1974, TRADE EXPANSION ACT OF 1962.

dismissal Occasionally used as a synonym for discharge. Actually a distinction sometimes is made between a discharge, where the employee leaves with prejudice for actions over which he has some control and responsibility, and a dismissal, where the employee has no control and the separation does not result from infractions or violations of company rules or policy. Dismissals frequently occur because of technological changes or where uneconomic operations are closed down. Employees are separated permanently, occasionally with dismissal compensation, based on length of service with the company.

Source references: Robert L. Aronson, *Layoff Policies and Practices* (Princeton: IR Section, Princeton Univ., 1950); Donald J. Johnston, "Dismissal Notice in Employment

Contracts," *McGill LJ*, Vol. 9, No. 2, 1963; Stanley J. Schwartz, "How to Dehire: A Guide for the Manager," *Human Resource Management*, Winter 1980.

See also DISCHARGE, RELEASE, SEPARATION.

dismissal compensation A payment to a worker upon permanent separation from the company, due to no fault of his own, either in a lump sum or in smaller amounts over a period of time. Separation may be due to technological changes or reductions in force because of cessation of operation of marginal plants. Frequently used as synonym for "dismissal pay" or "severance pay."

Source references: Lawrence M. Baytos, "Easing the Pain of Terminations," *Personnel*, July/Aug. 1979; BNA, *Layoff and Unemployment Compensation Policies* (Washington: PFF Survey no. 128, 1980); ———, *Separation Procedures and Severance Benefits* (Washington: PFF Survey no. 121, 1978); Audrey Freedman, *Security Bargains Reconsidered; SUB, Severance Pay, Guaranteed Work* (New York: The Conference Board, Report no. 736, 1978); E. D. Hawkins, *Dismissal Compensation* (Princeton: Princeton UP, 1940); Stacey J. Hendrickson, "The Priority of Severance Pay Claims Under the Bankruptcy Reform Act," *Industrial Relations LJ*, Fall 1979; NICB, *Dismissal Compensation* (New York: Studies in Personnel Policy no. 50, 1943); U.S. Dept. of Labor, BLS, *Major Collective Bargaining Agreements: Severance Pay and Layoff Benefit Plans* (Washington: Bull. 1425–2, 1965); ———, *The Operation of Severance Pay Plans and Their Implications for Labor Mobility* (Washington: Bull. 1462, 1966); U.S. GAO, *The Federal Government's Severance Pay Programs Need Reform* (Washington: 1978); Dena G. Weiss, "Dismissal Pay Provisions in Major Bargaining Agreements," *MLR*, June 1957.

See also LAYOFF PAY.

disparate impact *See* ADVERSE IMPACT.

disparate treatment The most easily understood type of discrimination, it involves the treatment of some people less favorably than others because of their race, color, religion, sex, or national origin. The classic example of disparate treatment is segregated facilities.

OFCCP defines it as "differential treatment of employees or applicants on the basis of their race, color, religion, sex, national origin, handicap, or veteran's status (including, for example, the situation where applicants or employees of a particular race or sex are required to pass tests or meet educational requirement, etc., which similarly situated contemporary applicants or employees of another race or sex were not required to take or meet)."

Source references: Robert Freiberg (ed.), *The Manager's Guide to Equal Employment Opportunity* (New York: Executive Enterprises, 1977); Jeffrey L. Liddle, "Disparate Treatment Claims Under ADEA: The Negative Impact of *McDonnell Douglas v. Green*," *Employee Relations LJ*, Spring 1980; Stephen Sahlein, *The Affirmative Action Handbook* (New York: Executive Enterprises, 1978); U.S. OFCCP, *Federal Contract Compliance Manual* (Washington: 1979).

See also ADVERSE IMPACT, TEAMSTERS V. U.S.

dispatchers Agents of the union in the hiring halls in the maritime industry, who have the responsibility of assigning individual workers to their jobs in line with agreed-upon rules.

Source references: U.S. Maritime Labor Board, *Report to the President and to the Congress* (Washington: 1940); ———, *Supplemental Report to the President and to the Congress* (Washington: 1942).

See also HIRING HALL.

displaced worker *See* DISLOCATED WORKER.

displacement *See* BUMPING.

displacement of skill The phrase is generally applied to the reduction in employment and decline in the number of skills, resulting from the introduction of machines. The extent and speed with which displacement of skill occurs, according to Professor George E. Barnett, depends on the following factors:

(1) The speed with which machines are introduced,
(2) The mobility of skilled labor,

(3) The effect of the machine on reducing the cost of the product,
(4) The amount of labor saved by the machine,
(5) The extent to which the skilled handcraftsman can be employed in the machine process.

Source reference: George E. Barnett, *Chapters on Machinery and Labor* (Cambridge: Harvard UP, 1926).

disposable income *See* SPENDABLE EARNINGS, TAKE-HOME PAY.

disputants The parties to a labor-management dispute.

dispute A controversy between an employer and a union, or between unions, or a union and its members, which usually leads to conflict in the labor-management field. Sometimes used instead of the term strike. Many disputes, however, are settled before they culminate in a strike.

See also INDUSTRIAL DISPUTES, JURISDICTIONAL DISPUTE, LABOR DISPUTE.

dispute adjustment A labor dispute, generally speaking, includes any controversy concerning the terms and conditions of employment, or concerning the association or representation of persons in negotiating, fixing, maintaining, changing, or seeking to arrange the terms or conditions of employment.

There are many methods used for the settlement of these differences: mediation, conciliation, factfinding, emergency boards, arbitration, or litigation.

The question of whether a "labor dispute" exists within the meaning of the terms of the Norris-LaGuardia Act or the Taft-Hartley Act frequently becomes lost in fine shades of legal argument. The granting of an injunction by the court will frequently rest on the court's determination that a "labor dispute" does not exist within the meaning of the Norris-LaGuardia Act.

Source references: Labor Management Relations Act, as amended, Section 2(9), 29 U.S.C. 152(9) (1982); Norris-LaGuardia Act, as amended, Section 13(c), 29 U.S.C. 113(c) (1982); Howard J. Anderson (ed.), *New Techniques in Labor Dispute Resolution,* A Report of the 23d Conference of the Association of Labor Mediation Agencies (July 28–Aug. 2, 1974) and the 2d Conference of the Society of Professionals in Dispute Resolution (Nov. 11–13, 1974) (Washington: BNA, 1976); Jerome T. Barrett, "Legislative Encouragement of Labor Peace," *LLJ*, Sept. 1967; Kurt Braun, *Labor Disputes and Their Settlement* (Baltimore: Johns Hopkins Press, 1955); Paul F. Brissenden, *Settlement of Disputes Over Grievances in the United States* (Honolulu: Univ. of Hawaii, IRC, 1965); ———, "The Settlement of Labor Disputes Over Interest in the United States," *Journal of IR,* March 1964; R. Theodore Clark, *Coping With Mediation, Fact Finding, and Forms of Arbitration* (Chicago: IPMA, PERL no. 42, 1974); David J. Cole, "Collective Bargaining and Industrial Peace," *American Federationist,* Aug. 1973; ———, "Focus on Bargaining: The Evolving Techniques," *American Federationist,* May 1974; Laurence P. Corbett, "Mediation-Arbitration from the Employer's Standpoint," *MLR,* Dec. 1973; Bernard Cushman, "Current Experiments in Collective Bargaining," *Proceedings of the 26th A/M, IRRA,* ed. by Gerald Somers (Madison: 1974); Michael Dudra (ed.), *Current Developments in Labor Disputes Settlements,* A Symposium, Oct. 8, 1976 (Loretto: Saint Francis College, Graduate School of IR, 1976); Thomas A. Kochan et al., *Dispute Resolution Under Fact-Finding and Arbitration: An Empirical Evaluation* (New York: AAA, 1979); Scott A. Kruse, "Boards of Inquiry in Health Care Disputes: New Options for the Parties," *LLJ*, Oct. 1979; Abbe David Lowell, "Dow Chemical: Restricting the Availability of Self-Help Measures in Labor Disputes," *IR Law Digest,* Summer 1977; James L. Stern, "Declining Utility of the Strike," *ILRR,* Oct. 1964; Donald B. Straus, "Alternatives to Strikes," *NYU 25th Annual Conference on Labor* (New York: Bender, 1973); ———, "How to Stop Strikes By Really Trying," *PJ*, Oct. 1970; John R. Van de Water, "Growth of Third-Party Power in the Settlement of Industrial Disputes," *LLJ*, Dec. 1961; Allan Weisenfeld, "Labor Dispute Settlement—Local or Federal Function?" *LLJ*, Oct. 1959; Donald J. White, "The Council on Industrial Relations for the Electrical Contracting Industry," *Proceedings of the 24th A/M, IRRA,* ed. by Gerald Somers (Madison: 1972).

See also ARBITRATION, CONCILIATION, FACTFINDING, GOVERNMENT SEIZURE, GRIEVANCE ADJUSTMENT, MED-ARB, MEDIATION, NATIONAL EMERGENCY BOARDS, NATIONAL EMERGENCY PROVISIONS, PRESIDENTIAL SEIZURE.

dispute notice Provision in the Taft-Hartley Act which requires employers and employees as a condition of good-faith bargaining to notify the FMCS of the existence of a dispute which has not been resolved by the parties through negotiation. Section 8(d) provides that:

> . . . the duty to bargain collectively shall also mean that no party to such contract shall terminate or modify such contract, unless the party desiring such termination or modification— . . . . (3) notifies the Federal Mediation and Conciliation Service within thirty days after such notice of the existence of a dispute, and simultaneously therewith notifies any State or Territorial agency established to mediate and conciliate disputes within the State or Territory where the dispute occurred, provided no agreement has been reached by that time. . . .

A strike called by a union without giving the required notices is not protected under the Taft-Hartley Act. In addition, Section 8(g) requires a labor union to notify a health care institution and the FMCS of its intention to engage "in any picketing, striking, or other concerted refusal to work . . . not less than ten days prior to such action. . . ."

Source reference: Labor Management Relations Act, as amended, 29 U.S.C. 158(d)(3) and 158(g) (1982).

Distillery, Rectifying, Wine and Allied Workers' International Union of America (AFL-CIO) Founded in 1940, the union changed its name to the Distillery, Wine and Allied Workers' International Union (AFL-CIO) in 1979.

See also DISTILLERY, WINE AND ALLIED WORKERS' INTERNATIONAL UNION (AFL-CIO).

Distillery, Wine and Allied Workers' International Union (AFL-CIO) Formerly known as the Distillery, Rectifying, Wine and Allied Workers' International Union of America (AFL-CIO); the union adopted the present name in 1979. Its quarterly publication is the *DWU Newsletter*.

Address: 66 Grand Ave., Englewood, N.J. 07631. Tel. (201) 569–9212

distressed employee *See* TROUBLED EMPLOYEE.

Distributive, Processing and Office Workers of America (Ind) Merged with and became part of the Retail, Wholesale and Department Store Union (CIO) during May 1954.

See also RETAIL, WHOLESALE AND DEPARTMENT STORE UNION (AFL-CIO).

Distributive Workers of America; National Council of (Ind) Union formed on March 28, 1969, following disaffiliation of District 65 from the Retail, Wholesale and Department Store Union (AFL-CIO). It was affiliated with the Alliance for Labor Action. The union changed its name to Distributive Workers of America (Ind) in the early 1970s.

See also DISTRIBUTIVE WORKERS OF AMERICA (IND).

Distributive Workers of America (Ind) Formerly known as the National Council of Distributive Workers (Ind), the name was changed to Distributive Workers of America (Ind) in the early 1970s. The union merged with the International Union, United Automobile, Aerospace and Agricultural Implement Workers of America in June 1979.

See also AUTOMOBILE, AEROSPACE AND AGRICULTURAL IMPLEMENT WORKERS OF AMERICA; INTERNATIONAL UNION, UNITED (AFL-CIO).

district council An intermediate form of labor organization between the international and local union. It consists of locals in a particular trade or industry within a state or other geographic area and serves to consolidate and coordinate activity designed to help that trade—i.e., carpenters, teamsters, clothing workers, etc. Where an international union has many locals in a particular area these councils may meet to consider establishment of uniformity in wages and other working conditions and may even work out procedures for bargaining purposes.

District 50, Allied and Technical Workers of the United States and Canada; International Union of (Ind) An international union once affiliated with the United Mine Workers of America, District 50 had substantial contracts in heavy and highway construction, as well as contracts in manufacturing, service, and other industries.

On August 9, 1972, the union merged with the United Steelworkers of America (AFL-CIO).

See also STEELWORKERS OF AMERICA; UNITED (AFL-CIO).

District 50, United Mine Workers of America (Ind) Founded in 1936 as a national department of the United Mine Workers of America under the name Gas and By-Products Coke Workers, District 50 of the United Mine Workers of America. The union changed its name to District 50, United Mine Workers of America in 1941.

Generally referred to as the "catch-all" arm of the United Mine Workers of America, District 50 initially covered workers in coal processing and coke ovens but the UMW constitution was changed in 1942 to include "such other industries as may be designated and approved by the Executive Board." A subgroup of District 50, the United Construction Workers of America (UCWA), drew the wrath of the Building and Construction Trades Department of the AFL, with whose craft unions UCWA sought to compete as an industrial union.

In the early 1960s, the union changed its name to the International Union of District 50, United Mine Workers of America and in 1969, disaffiliated from the United Mine Workers. At its April 1970 convention, the union adopted the name, International Union of District 50, Allied and Technical Workers of the United States and Canada.

Source references: Melvyn Dubofsky and Warren Van Tine, *John L. Lewis, A Biography* (New York: Quadrangle/The New York Times Book Co., 1977); James Nelson, *The Mine Workers' District 50: The Story of the Gas, Coke, and Chemical Unions of Massachusetts and Their Growth Into a National Union* (New York: Exposition Press, 1955); Florence Peterson, *American Labor Unions* (rev. ed., New York: Harper, 1952).

See also DISTRICT 50, ALLIED AND TECHNICAL WORKERS OF THE UNITED STATES AND CANADA; INTERNATIONAL UNION OF (IND).

District 925, Service Employees' International Union An autonomous local of the Service Employees' International Union jointly established in 1981 by the SEIU and 9 to 5, National Association of Working Women. District 925 seeks to organize women clerical and secretarial workers.

Jacquelynn Ruff serves as executive director of District 925, and Karen Nussbaum, one of the founders and executive director of 9 to 5, is president.

District 925 offices are located in the SEIU headquarters in Washington, D.C.

division of labor The process whereby a production problem is broken down to its component operations. Each process is then assigned to a separate worker or group of workers. It involves the organization of production, simplification, and increasing mechanization for greater productive output. Modern mass production industries best illustrate the development and extent of division of labor in industrial operations.

Division of Labor Standards *See* BUREAU OF LABOR STANDARDS.

Doak plan A plan designed by Secretary of Labor W. N. Doak in 1931 to improve the public employment offices throughout the United States. The plan was not effective, and was discarded by Secretary of Labor Frances Perkins. The Wagner-Peyser Act was set up in 1933 to provide a nationwide system of free public employment offices under a federal-state cooperation procedure.

See also U.S. EMPLOYMENT SERVICE, WAGNER-PEYSER ACT.

docking Deducting from the pay of a worker an amount equal to the penalty imposed. Employees may be docked for violation of rules on absenteeism, tardiness, breakage, etc. If those deductions reduce the wage below the minimum required by law, they may be illegal.

dole The term used in England for public unemployment relief. The term has been designated in the United States as any relief provided by public authority instead of employment.

Source reference: E. Wight Bakke, *Insurance or Dole?* (New Haven: Yale UP, 1935).

Doll and Toy Workers of the United States and Canada; International Union of (AFL-

CIO) *See* TOYS, PLAYTHINGS, NOVELTIES AND ALLIED PRODUCTS OF THE UNITED STATES AND CANADA; INTERNATIONAL UNION OF DOLLS (AFL-CIO).

domestic system Generally referred to as the putting-out system which featured work at home. The worker would be dependent on the entrepreneur for his material and sometimes for tools and equipment. Control of the product, prices, etc., was in the hands of the owner of the raw materials. The system, with its increasing control over the worker, was replaced by the modern factory. Many of the abuses of the putting-out system could be more effectively controlled by the state in a plant which could be subject to frequent visits and inspection of safety rules, cleanliness, hours of work, and similar factors.

Source references: Carl Bridenbaugh, *The Colonial Craftsman* (Chicago: Univ. of Chicago Press, 1961); Majur S. Chandrashekhar, *Small-Scale and Household Industries in a Developing Economy: A Study of Their Rationale, Structure and Operative Conditions* (New York: Asia Pub. House, 1963); Edwin F. Gay, "Putting Out System," *Encyclopedia of the Social Sciences*, ed. by Edwin R. A. Seligman (Vol. 13, New York: Macmillan, 1934); Richard B. Morris, *Government and Labor in Early America* (New York: Columbia UP, 1946); Rolla M. Tryon, *Household Manufactures in the United States, 1640–1860* (New York: Johnson Reprint, 1966).

domination *See* COMPANY UNION.

Dominion Hotel v. Arizona A decision of the Supreme Court upholding a statute of the state of Arizona that regulated the hours of women, to require their work be confined to a definite period of time.

Source reference: Dominion Hotel v. Arizona, 249 US 265 (1919).

Donham v. West-Nelson Co. A decision of the Supreme Court holding invalid a minimum wage statute of the state of Arkansas.

Source reference: Donham v. West-Nelson Co., 273 US 657 (1927).

Dorchy v. Kansas A decision of the Supreme Court holding that there is no constitutional right to strike.

Source reference: Dorchy v. Kansas, 272 US 306 (1926).

double-breasted operation A company that operates both unionized and nonunionized subsidiaries. A unionized firm may set up a nonunionized unit to compete with open shop employers. Double-breasted employers are most commonly found in the construction industry.

Unions frequently challenge double-breasted operations by bringing Section 8(a)(5) claims before the NLRB. Double-breasting also has been alleged in federal courts as violations of Section 301 of the Labor Management Relations Act and provisions of the Employee Retirement Income Security Act and antitrust laws.

Source reference: John M. Husband and T. Jay Thompson, "Establishing and Operating Both Union and Nonunion Subsidiaries: A Trap for the Unwary," *LLJ*, June 1983.

double employment The practice of holding down two jobs at the same time. During periods of rising prices such practices become more frequent. Companies have sought to control such employment since it tends to reduce productivity and increase accidents. Many employers have cooperated with their unions to control or regulate abuses in double employment. The practice now is called "moonlighting."

Source references: Patrick J. Davey and James K. Brown, "The Corporate Reaction to 'Moonlighting'," *Conference Board Record*, June 1970; Stephen Habbe, "Moonlighting and the Controls," *Management Record*, July 1957; Estelle Hepton, *Moonlighting in Waikiki* (Honolulu: Univ. of Hawaii, IRC, 1961); Kopp Michelotti, "Multiple Jobholders in May 1975," *MLR*, Nov. 1975; Glenn W. Miller, Ronald W. Presley, and Mark S. Sniderman, "Multijobholding by Firemen and Policemen Compared," *Public Personnel Management*, July/Aug. 1973; Glenn W. Miller and Mark S. Sniderman, "Multijobholding of Wichita Public School Teachers," *Public Personnel Management*, Sept./Oct. 1974; "Moonlighting—Its Cause and Effect," *American Federationist*, Sept. 1962; Vera C. Perrella, "Moonlighters: Their Motivations and Characteristics," *MLR*, Aug. 1970; Edward S. Sekscenski, "Womens' Share of Moonlighting

Nearly Doubles During 1969–79," *MLR*, May 1980; Lawrence Stessin, "Moonlighting: The Employer's Dilemma," *Personnel*, Jan./Feb. 1981.

See also SECONDARY EMPLOYMENT.

doubleheading pay Extra pay to railroad engineers who are required to use more than one engine in running over steep grades for any length of time.

doubletime Premium pay for work performed at double the standard or regular rate for the job. Sunday or holiday overtime is usually at doubletime. Variations, of course, depend on the contracts and vary from company to company and industry to industry.

See also OVERTIME.

downgrading *See* DEMOTION.

down periods Shutdowns of plant operation to permit cleaning, repair, and maintenance of equipment. Occasionally to install new equipment or facilities.

down time Pay to an employee on piecework during the period that a machine or equipment is idle due to no fault of the employee. A machine may be idle for repair, set up, breakdown or shortage of materials.

See also DEAD TIME.

drawing account A regular allowance made available to salesmen employed on a straight commission basis. The account will vary with the potential earning power of the salesman. The commission earned by the salesman is balanced against the drawing account at various intervals.

dressing time The allowed period for workers to change from their street clothes to their working clothes or special dress required on the job. Clothes-changing time must be counted as time worked under the Fair Labor Standards Act if it is required by the nature of the employee's work or by a statute or ordinance unless it is excluded from working time by the express terms of or a custom or practice under a collective bargaining contract.

See also ALLOWED TIME.

drifter A worker who moves or floats from job to job.

dropouts Individuals with less than a high school education. As a consequence of dropping out of high school, individuals experience greater unemployment, get lower-paying jobs, are employed in a relatively limited number of occupations, and are less likely to receive post-school training than high school graduates. School dropout rates are found to be higher among low-income and minority groups.

Source references: George Iden, "The Labor Force Experience of Black Youth: A Review," *MLR*, Aug. 1980; Randall Howard King, *The Labor Market Consequences of Dropping Out of High School* (Columbus: Ohio State Univ., Center for Human Resource Research, 1978); Daniel J. B. Mitchell and John Clapp, "The Impact of Child Labor Laws on the Kinds of Jobs Held by Young School-Leavers," *Journal of Human Resources*, Summer 1980; Craig Polhemus and Gregory J. Mounts, "A Renewed Deal for Youth Employment," *Occupational Outlook Quarterly*, Fall 1978; U.S. Congressional Budget Office, *Improving Youth Employment Prospects: Issues and Options* (Washington: 1982); ———, *Youth Employment and Education: Possible Federal Approaches* (Washington: 1980); U.S. Dept. of HEW, Education Div., *Indicators of Youth Unemployment and Education in Industrialized Nations* (Washington: 1978); Work in America Institute, *Job Strategies for Urban Youth, Sixteen Pilot Programs for Action* (Scarsdale: 1979); Anne McDougall Young, "Labor Force Patterns of Students, Graduates, and Dropouts, 1981," *MLR*, Sept. 1982.

drug abuse Inappropriate use of lawfully obtained prescription drugs or over-the-counter drugs (by being taken in too large or too frequent doses or by being combined with alcohol); substances which are not technically drugs or medicine (glue sniffing); so-called "street drugs" such as heroin, the possession, sale, and use of which are prohibited by federal and state laws; or other federally controlled substances, such as prescription drugs which have bona fide medical applications but were obtained illegally and administered without medical authorization (drugs such as amphetamines, tranquilizers, and barbiturates). The increase in workplace drug abuse has become a major concern of both union and management. Although some of the problems raised by employee drug abuse are similar to alcoholism—for example, impaired job performance and adverse effects on the employee's mental and physical health—drug abuse is considered to be different because the drug may be illegal.

Company rules frequently specify actions to be taken in cases of employee drug use, and discharge is commonly specified in cases involving illegal drug use. Some companies provide for programs designed to encourage recognition, treatment, and rehabilitation of drug dependent employees.

Source references: Peter B. Bensinger, "Drugs in the Workplace," *Harvard BR*, Nov./Dec. 1982; Tia Schneider Denenberg, "The Arbitration of Alcohol and Drug Abuse Cases," *AJ*, Dec. 1980; Tia Schneider Denenberg and R. V. Denenberg, *Alcohol and Drugs, Issues in the Workplace* (Washington: BNA, 1983); Robert D. Dugan, "Affirmative Action for Alcoholics and Addicts?" *Employee Relations LJ*, Autumn 1979; Kenneth Jennings, "Arbitrators and Drugs," *PJ*, Oct. 1976; ———, "The Problem of Employee Drug Abuse and Remedial Alternatives," *PJ*, Nov. 1977; Edward Levin and Tia S. Denenberg, "How Arbitrators View Drug Abuse," *AJ*, June 1976; Stephen J. Levy, "Drug Abuse in Business: Telling It Like It Is," *Personnel*, Sept./Oct. 1972; George W. Noblit, Paul H. Radtke, and James G. Ross, *Drug Use and Public Employment: A Personnel Manual* (Chicago: IPMA, Public Employment Practices Bull. no. 9, 1975); Rolf E. Rogers and John T. C. Colbert, "Drug Abuse and Organizational Response: A Review and Evaluation," *PJ*, May 1975; Harold M. F. Rush, "Combating Employee Drug Abuse," *Conference Board Record*, Nov. 1971; Jan P. Wijting, "Employing the Recovered Drug Abuser—Viable?" *Personnel*, May/June 1979; Pat Wynns, "Arbitration Standards in Drug Discharge Cases," *AJ*, June 1979.

See also ALCOHOLISM, REHABILITATION ACT OF 1973.

dry-run picketing Picketing which is used at times other than during a strike to indicate that the plant has been shut down. This type of picketing may be used during negotiations, in organizing, and other ways to bring pressure on the employer to come to terms. It is designed to show strength.

dual allegiance Worker loyalty to both the company and union. Purcell in his study of meatpacking workers defines it as worker acceptance of the company and the union as institutions and the workers' positive allegiance to each institution.

Drucker terms it "twin allegiance," which he views as necessary to the survival of labor and management—"it is to the interest of neither union nor management to press the demand for absolute allegiance, as this can only turn the worker against both."

Source references: Lois R. Dean, "Union Activity and Dual Loyalty," *ILRR*, July 1954; Peter F. Drucker, *The New Society* (New York: Harper, 1950); George W. England, "Dual Allegiance to Company and Union," *Personnel Administration*, March/April 1960; Theodore V. Purcell, *The Worker Speaks His Mind on Company and Union* (Cambridge: Harvard UP, 1953).

dual motive *See* MIXED MOTIVE CASES.

dual-pay system A method of wage payment, largely in the transportation field, whereby compensation is paid on the basis of hours of work and miles traveled. The employee has the choice of the method providing the greatest remuneration. Occasionally the speed of the train or vehicle is a factor in determining the compensation.

dual unionism A term generally applied to any union or organization which is seeking to represent workers in the same trade or industry in which a union already exists. Thus the AFL attacked the Committee for Industrial Organization as sponsoring dual unionism when it was seeking to organize the mass production industries. It is a form of rival unionism, except that dual unionism seems to imply more than rivalry. It is used by the union which is "in" and claims antecedent jurisdiction, holding that the competitor is engaging in dual unionism—an unsavory and undesirable form of trade union activity. Rival unionism, on the other hand, seems to suggest a more competitive activity of two organizations seeking to bring unorganized employees under their respective banners.

Dual unionism may also be used as a charge (usually a punishable offense) leveled at a union member or officer who seeks or accepts membership or position in a rival union, or otherwise attempts to undermine a union by helping its rival.

Source references: George E. Barnett, "Causes of Jurisdictional Disputes in American Trade Unions," *Harvard BR*, July 1931; Walter Galenson, *Rival Unionism in the United States* (Washington: American Council on Public Affairs, 1940); J. Malcolm Walker and John J. Lawler, "Dual Unions and Political Processes in Organizations," *IR*, Winter 1979.

See also JURISDICTION, UNION.

Dubinsky v. Blue Dale Dress A decision by the New York courts upholding the terms of a collective bargaining agreement which was designed to prevent "runaway" shops. The agreement with the union provided that ". . . No member of the association shall . . . move his shop or factory from its present location to any place beyond which the public carrier fare is more than 5 cents."

Source reference: Dubinsky v. Blue Dale Dress, 292 NYS 898 (1936).

due process of law Provisions in the United States Constitution—the 5th and 14th Amendments which read in part:

> No person shall be . . . deprived of life, liberty, or property without due process of law. . . . (5th Amendment)
>
> . . . nor shall any State deprive any person of life, liberty, or property, without due process of law, nor deny to any person within its jurisdiction the equal protection of the laws. (14th Amendment)

What "due process" means ultimately rests with the interpretation placed upon it by the Supreme Court. The meaning has changed to meet changing social and economic conditions. In its narrow sense it is designed to prevent unreasonable and arbitrary legislation or arbitrary application of the laws by public officials. In its broad meaning it has encompassed protection over the health and morals of the American people, which in previous decades were held to be an infringement of the due process provisions of the Constitution. The constitutionality of the National Labor Relations Act, for example, would not have been upheld under the meaning given to "due process" in the Supreme Court decision in the *Adair* case, setting aside the "yellow dog" contract provisions of the Erdman Act of 1898.

Source references: Adair v. United States, 208 US 161 (1908); William M. Evan, "Due Process of Law in Military and Industrial Organizations," *Administrative Science Quarterly*, Sept. 1962.

See also ADAIR V. UNITED STATES.

dues Periodic payments, usually on a monthly basis, paid by members to the union, in order to defray the costs of the organization. The amount of the dues payment is set by either the constitution or bylaws, and is subject to revision by the membership. In the public sector, the amount of dues may be subject to approval by an administrative agency. The dues cover the costs of maintaining the operation of the offices of the union, the publication of the union paper, benefits financed by the union, and such other services as are required by the members.

These regular payments are apart from periodic assessments and initiation fees.

Source references: Leon Applebaum, "Dues and Fees: Structure of Local Unions," *MLR*, Nov. 1966; Edward R. Curtin, *Union Initiation Fees, Dues, and Per Capita Tax, National Union Strike Benefits* (New York: NICB, 1968); Charles W. Hickman, "Labor Organizations' Fees and Dues," *MLR*, May 1977; Irving Kovarsky, "Dues, Initiation Fees and Union Security," *LLJ*, Dec. 1959; Nels E. Nelson, "Union Dues and Political Spending," *LLJ*, Feb. 1977; Edwin R. Render, "Constitutional Questions Involved in the Expenditure of Compulsorily Paid Union Dues Under the Railway Labor Act," *Vanderbilt LR*, Oct. 1962; Charles Sovel, "Service Fees for Union Benefits," *NYU 21st Annual Conference on Labor*, ed. by Thomas Christensen (New York: Bender, 1969).

See also AGENCY SHOP, ASSESSMENTS, FAIR SHARE AGREEMENT, INITIATION FEE, SERVICE FEE.

Duplex Printing Press Co. v. Deering A decision of the Supreme Court that activity by a union to maintain closed-shop conditions through the use of the boycott was not protected by the Clayton Act. The court held that

Section 6 of the Clayton Act did not exempt the union or its members ". . . from accountability where it or they depart from its normal and legitimate objects and engage in an actual combination or conspiracy in restraint of trade."

The union sought to prevent the Duplex Company from changing over to the "open shop," and from continuing on a 10-hour day, when its organized competitors were on an eight-hour day.

Source reference: Duplex Printing Press Co. v. Deering, 254 US 443 (1921).

duration of agreement *See* AGREEMENT DURATION.

duress Physical force, or threat of force or intimidation to make a person do something against his will or better judgment. A contract obtained by duress may be set aside by the court where the court is convinced that force or the threat of force was used to obtain the agreement.

duty of fair representation The obligation of the union imposed by federal labor laws to fairly represent all bargaining unit members in collective bargaining and in the enforcement of the agreement.

The duty of unions to represent employees without discrimination was first spelled out by the Supreme Court in rulings under the Railway Labor Act (*Steele v. Louisville & Nashville R.R. Co.*, 323 US 192, 15 LRRM 708 (1944); *Tunstall v. Locomotive Firemen*, 323 US 210, 15 LRRM 715 (1944)). This principle was later extended to apply also under the Labor Management Relations Act in a case dealing with a union's power to negotiate a contract (*Ford Motor Co. v. Huffman*, 345 US 330, 31 LRRM 2548 (1953)).

In the grievance processing context, the Supreme Court has decided that this duty does not require that every grievance be carried to arbitration (*Vaca v. Sipes*, 386 US 171, 64 LRRM 2369 (1967)). The Court also set out the principle that liability for damages resulting from a breach of duty is to be apportioned between the union and employer according to the damage caused by the fault of each.

Source references: Bowen v. U.S. Postal Service, 459 US 212, 112 LRRM 2281 (1983); *Hines v. Anchor Motor Freight, Inc.*, 424 US 554, 91 LRRM 2481 (1976); *Vaca v. Sipes*, 386 US 171, 64 LRRM 2369 (1967); C. Paul Barker, "The Employer's Stake in the Union's Duty of Fair Representation: A Form of Liability Without Fault—The Employer's Duty to Police the Handling of Employee Grievances," *Labor Law Developments 1978*, Proceedings of 24th Annual Institute on Labor Law, SLF (New York: Bender, 1978); Stuart Bernstein, "Breach of the Duty of Fair Representation: The Appropriate Remedy," *Decisional Thinking of Arbitrators and Judges*, Proceedings of the 33d A/M, NAA, ed. by James Stern and Barbara Dennis (Washington: BNA, 1981); Timothy J. Boyce, *Fair Representation, the NLRB, and the Courts* (Philadelphia: Univ. of Pennsylvania, Wharton School, Industrial Research Unit, LRPP series no. 18, 1978); Charles A. Edwards, "Employers' Liability for Union Unfair Representation: Fiduciary Duty or Bargaining Reality?" *LLJ*, Nov. 1976; Tracy H. Ferguson and Elia M. Desruisseaux, "The Duty of Fair Representation: Exhaustion of Internal Union Remedies," *Employee Relations LJ*, Spring 1982; Irving Friedman, "Breach of the Duty of Fair Representation: One Union Attorney's View," *Decisional Thinking of Arbitrators and Judges*, Proceedings of the 33rd A/M, NAA, ed. by James Stern and Barbara Dennis (Washington: BNA, 1981); Eric Heyden, "Landrum-Griffin Section 101(a)(4)—Its Impact on Employee Rights," *Employee Relations LJ*, Spring 1982; Mark S. Jacobs, "Fair Representation and Binding Arbitration," *LLJ*, June 1977; Roger B. Jacobs, "Time Limitations and Section 301: A New Direction from the Supreme Court," *LLJ*, Jan. 1983; Andrew H. Levi, "The Collective Bargaining Agreement as a Limitation on Union Control of Employee Grievances," *IR Law Digest*, April 1971; William Levin, "Duty of Fair Representation: The Role of the Arbitrator," *Decisional Thinking of Arbitrators and Judges*, Proceedings of the 33d A/M, NAA, ed. by James Stern and Barbara Dennis (Washington: BNA, 1981); Marvin J. Levine and Michael P. Hollander, "The Union's Duty of Fair Representation in Contract Administration," *Employee Relations LJ*, Autumn 1981; J. P. McGuire, "The Individual Employee in Breach of Contract and Duty of Fair Representation Cases: Exhaustion of Remedies,"

AJ, Dec. 1979; Paul H. Tobias, "The Plaintiff's View of '301-DFR' Litigation," *Employee Relations LJ*, Spring 1980.

See also HINES V. ANCHOR MOTOR FREIGHT, VACA V. SIPES.

duty to bargain The obligation under the Taft-Hartley Act and state laws requiring employers and unions to bargain in good faith with respect to the terms and conditions of employment and to embody the agreements reached in collective bargaining contracts. What constitutes a "refusal to bargain" depends on the facts of the case as found by the national or state boards and the courts.

Source references: Thomas P. Brown IV, "Hard Bargaining: The Board Says No, the Courts Say Yes," *Employee Relations LJ*, Summer 1982; Archibald Cox, "The Duty to Bargain Collectively During the Term of an Existing Agreement," *Harvard LR*, May 1950; Milton C. Denbo, "New Problems in Duty to Bargain," *Labor Law Developments*, Proceedings of the 16th Annual Institute on Labor Law, SLF (New York: Bender, 1970); Mary L. Dooley, "Union's Duty to Bargain Collectively with the Employers," *LLJ*, April 1957; Robben W. Fleming, "The Changing Duty to Bargain," *LLJ*, April 1963; Stanley A. Gacek, "The Employer's Duty to Bargain on Termination of Unit Work," *LLJ*, Oct. 1981, Nov. 1981; Gerard Morales, "The Obligation of a Multiplant Employer to Bargain on the Decision to Close One of Its Plants," *LLJ*, Nov. 1979; W. B. Nelson and R. T. Howard, "The Duty to Bargain During the Term of an Existing Agreement," *LLJ*, Sept. 1976; Elihu Platt, "The Duty to Bargain as Applied to Management Decisions," *LLJ*, March 1968; Howard Schulman, "Analysis and Portent of Developing Law of Meaningful Remedies for Employers' Failure to Bargain," *Labor Law Developments 1971*, Proceedings of the 17th Annual Institute on Labor Law, SLF (New York: Bender, 1971); J. Mack Swigert, "The Duty to Bargain in the Absence of Certification," *NYU 19th Annual Conference on Labor*, ed. by Thomas Christensen (Washington: BNA, 1967).

E

ECI *See* EMPLOYMENT COST INDEX (ECI).

EEO *See* EQUAL EMPLOYMENT OPPORTUNITY (EEO).

EEOC *See* EQUAL EMPLOYMENT OPPORTUNITY COMMISSION.

ENA *See* EXPERIMENTAL NEGOTIATING AGREEMENT (ENA).

EPA *See* EQUAL PAY ACT OF 1963.

ERISA *See* EMPLOYEE RETIREMENT INCOME SECURITY ACT (ERISA) OF 1974.

ESA *See* EMPLOYMENT STANDARDS ADMINISTRATION (ESA).

ESC *See* ENGINEERS AND SCIENTISTS OF CALIFORNIA.

ESOP *See* EMPLOYEE STOCK OWNERSHIP PLAN.

ESPO *See* EDUCATION SUPPORT PERSONNEL OF OKLAHOMA (IND).

ETA *See* EMPLOYMENT AND TRAINING ADMINISTRATION (ETA).

ETUC *See* EUROPEAN TRADE UNION CONFEDERATION (ETUC).

early retirement Arrangement by which the worker may cease employment at an age earlier than the normal retirement age.

Source references: Richard Barfield and James Morgan, *Early Retirement: The Decision and the Experience* (Ann Arbor: Univ. of Michigan, Institute for Social Research, 1969); Merton C. Bernstein, "The Arguments Against Early Retirement," *IR,* May 1965; Jeremy I. Bulow, *Early Retirement Pension Benefits* (Cambridge: NBER, WP no. 654, 1981); Jeanne Prial Gordus, *Leaving Early, Perspectives and Problems in Current Retirement Practice and Policy* (Kalamazoo: Upjohn Institute for Employment Research, 1980); Frank M. Kleiler, *Can We Afford Early Retirement?* (Baltimore: Johns Hopkins UP, 1978); Max D. Kossoris, "Early Retirement: An Overview," *IR,* May 1965; Mitchell Meyer and Harland Fox, *Early Retirement Programs* (New York: The Conference Board, Report no. 532, 1971); Charles E. Odell, "The Case for Early Retirement," *IR,* May 1965; Herbert S. Parnes, "Inflation and Early Retirement: Recent Longitudinal Findings," *MLR,* July 1981; Joseph F. Quinn, *The Early Retirement Decision: Evidence from the 1969 Retirement History Study* (Washington: U.S. Dept. of HEW, SSA, Staff Paper no. 29, 1978); Neal Schmitt et al., "Comparison of Early Retirees and Non-Retirees," *Personnel Psychology,* Summer 1979; Richard Shoemaker, "The Quickening Trend Towards Early Retirement," *American Federationist,* March 1965; Lawrence T. Smedley, "The Patterns of Early Retirement," *American Federationist,* Jan. 1974; James N. Walker, "Will Early Retirement Retire Early?" *Personnel,* Jan./Feb. 1976; Gloria W. White, "Bridge Over Troubled Waters: An Approach to Early Retirement," *Journal of the College and University Personnel Association,* Summer 1981; John Zalusky, "Shorter Work Years—Early Retirement," *American Federationist,* Aug. 1977.

See also BRIDGING, NORMAL RETIREMENT AGE, RETIREMENT, RETIREMENT AGE.

earned rate *See* WAGE RATE.

earning power A worker's potential capacity on his job to earn wages over a period of time—generally the normal span of years during which he is productive. In estimating the loss to society of a person killed as a result of an industrial accident, the dollar value of potential earning power of the individual during his lifetime is used. The estimates, of course, are based on average figures of earnings and life expectancy, rather than on those of the individuals involved in the accidents.

Source references: James E. Annable, Jr. and Frederick H. Friutman, "An Earnings Function for High-Level Manpower," *ILRR*, July 1973; Joseph M. Davis, "Health and the Education-Earnings Relationship," *MLR*, April 1973; George Iden, "Factors Affecting Earnings of Southern Migrants," *IR*, May 1974; Mark R. Killingsworth, *'Ability' and 'Training' Over the Life Cycle: Equilibrium Dynamics and Comparative Dynamics in Alternative Models of Human Capital* (Princeton: Princeton Univ., IR Section, WP no. 86, 1976); Allan G. King and Charles B. Knapp, "Race and the Determinants of Lifetime Earnings," *ILRR*, April 1978; Herman P. Miller, "Annual and Lifetime Income in Relation to Education: 1939–1959," *AER*, Dec. 1960; Sherwin Rosen, "Human Capital and the Internal Rate of Return," *Proceedings of the 26th A/M, IRRA*, ed. by Gerald Somers (Madison: 1974); James E. Rosenbaum, "Hierarchical and Individual Effects on Earnings," *IR*, Winter 1980; Theodore W. Schultz, *The Economic Value of Education* (New York: Columbia UP, 1963); U.S. Dept. of HEW, SSA, *1972 Lifetime Earnings by Age, Sex, Race, and Education Level* (Washington: Research and Statistical Note no. 12, 1976); Yoram Weiss and Reuben Gronau, *Expected Interruptions in Labor Force Participation and Sex Related Differences in Earnings Growth* (Cambridge: NBER, WP no. 667, 1981).

earnings The total amount of remuneration received by a worker for a given period as compensation for work performed or services rendered, including bonuses, commissions, overtime pay, shift differentials, etc.

Because a statistical concept is usually involved, earnings figures should be carefully defined, e.g., straight-time average hourly earnings. Gross earnings usually mean total earnings, while the term compensation includes the entire range of earnings and benefits, both current and deferred.

Source references: Robert H. Ferguson, *Wages, Earnings, and Incomes: Definitions of Terms and Sources Data* (Ithaca: NYSSILR, Cornell Univ., Bull. no. 63, 1971); Walter Fogel, "Occupational Earnings: Market and Institutional Influence," *ILRR*, Oct. 1979; James D. Gwartney and James E. Long, "Relative Earnings of Blacks and Other Minorities," *ILRR*, April 1978; Francis W. Horvath, "Tracking Individual Earnings Mobility With the Current Population Survey," *MLR*, May 1980; Lawrence M. Kahn, "Wage Growth and Endogenous Experience," *IR*, Winter 1980; Harold Lydall, *The Structure of Earnings* (Oxford: Oxford UP, 1968); Arthur Sackley, "Trends in Average Annual Earnings and Income," *MLR*, Nov. 1965; Bradley R. Schiller, "Equality, Opportunity, and the 'Good Job,' " *The Public Interest*, Spring 1976; Dixie Sommers, "What Are Earnings?" *Occupational Outlook Quarterly*, Fall 1973; Robert L. Stein and Paul M. Ryscavage, "Measuring Annual Earnings of Household Heads in Production Jobs," *MLR*, April 1974; U.S. Dept. of Commerce, Bureau of the Census, *Lifetime Earnings Estimates for Men and Women in the United States: 1979* (Washington: Current Population Reports, Series P–60, no. 139, 1983); U.S. Dept. of HEW, SSA, *Earnings Distributions in the United States 1974* (Washington: 1982); U.S. Dept. of Labor, BLS, *Weekly and Hourly Earnings Data From the Current Population Survey* (Washington: Special Labor Force Report no. 195, 1977).

See also AVERAGE HOURLY EARNINGS, AVERAGE STRAIGHT-TIME HOURLY EARNINGS, COMMISSION EARNINGS, EXPECTED EARNING LEVEL, GROSS AVERAGE HOURLY EARNINGS, GROSS AVERAGE WEEKLY EARNINGS.

economic action Steps taken by labor organizations to achieve their goals, generally in the form of strikes, picketing, boycotts, or other means at their disposal. Term also is applied to retaliatory steps taken by employers.

See also DIRECT ACTION.

Economic Development Administration *See* PUBLIC WORKS AND ECONOMIC DEVELOPMENT ACT OF 1965.

Economic Opportunity Act First enacted in 1964 and amended in subsequent years, the purpose of the Act was to open "to everyone the opportunity for education and training, the opportunity to work, and the opportunity to live in decency and dignity." In eight divisions, or titles, the Act provided for the establishment of: Title I—Work Training and Work-Study Programs; Title II—Urban and Rural Community Action Programs; Title III—Special Programs to Combat Poverty in Rural Areas; Title IV—Employment and Investment Incentives; Title V—Work Experience, Training, and Day Care Programs; Title VI—Administration and Coordination; Title VII—Treatment of Income for Certain Public Assistance Purposes; and Title VIII—Domestic Volunteer Service Programs.

Controversy surrounded the Act; it was criticized because it went too far and because it did not go far enough. Much criticism also was directed at the administration of the Act. The Act was repealed with the enactment of the Comprehensive Employment and Training Act in 1973.

Source references: Roger H. Davidson and Sar A. Levitan, *Antipoverty Housekeeping: The Administration of the Economic Opportunity Act* (Ann Arbor: Univ. of Michigan-Wayne State Univ., Institute of Labor & IR, Policy Papers in Human Resources & IR, no. 9, 1968); Sar A. Levitan, *Antipoverty Work and Training Efforts: Goals and Reality* (Ann Arbor: Univ. of Michigan-Wayne State Univ., Institute of Labor & IR, Policy Papers in Human Resources & IR, no. 3, 1967); ———, *The Great Society's Poor Law: A New Approach to Poverty* (Baltimore: Johns Hopkins Press, 1969); U.S. Congress, House, Committee on Education and Labor, *Economic Opportunity Amendments of 1965* (Washington: 1965); ———, *1966 Amendments to the Economic Opportunity Act of 1964, Parts 1 and 2* (Washington: 1966); U.S. Office of Economic Opportunity, *The Quiet Revolution* (Washington: 1967).

economic report The annual report to the Congress required of the President by the Employment Act of 1946.

See also COUNCIL OF ECONOMIC ADVISERS, EMPLOYMENT ACT OF 1946, JOINT CONGRESSIONAL COMMITTEE ON THE ECONOMIC REPORT.

economic sanction Generally refers to concerted action undertaken to interrupt the flow of an employer's business. Unions may impose economic sanctions to press employers for the resolution of labor disputes. In addition to the strike, such actions may include persuading customers not to purchase an employer's products. The term may also refer to action undertaken by an employer to penalize the union for certain activities.

In international relations, economic sanction may involve measures calling for the cessation or interruption of economic relations with a nation, through the use of an arms embargo, trade restrictions, or financial embargo.

Source references: Labor Management Relations Act, as amended, Section 301, 29 U.S.C. 185 (1982); Ralph M. Dereshinsky, Alan D. Berkowitz, and Philip A. Miscimarra, *The NLRB and Secondary Boycotts* (rev. ed., Philadelphia: Univ. of Pennsylvania, Wharton School, Industrial Research Unit, LRPP series no. 4, 1981); League of Nations, *The Covenant of the League of Nations, Article XVI* (Washington: GPO, 1920); United Nations, *Charter of the United Nations and Statute of the International Court of Justice* (Berkeley: UC Press, 1945).

See also LEGAL SANCTION, PROFESSIONAL SANCTION, STRIKE.

economic strike A work stoppage which results from inability of an employer and a union to agree on wages, hours, or other conditions of employment. The NLRB distinguishes between economic strikes and unfair labor practice strikes. Strikes or work stoppages which result from or are prolonged by unfair labor practices of the employer are protected, and the Board will order reinstatement of workers after the strike is concluded.

If a strike is for economic purposes alone, the employer is free to hire permanent replacements for the strikers. Economic strikers retain their status as employees and are entitled to reinstatement by the employer until they have obtained other and substantially equivalent employment or until their jobs have been permanently abolished. In an unfair labor practice strike, the government requires the reinstatement of strikers on the ground that the employer's action was in violation of law and against the public interest.

Source references: NLRB v. Fleetwood Trailer Co., 389 US 375, 66 LRRM 2737

(1967); Walter Daykin, "The Distinction Between Economic and Unfair Labor Practice Strikes," *LLJ*, March 1961.

See also UNFAIR LABOR PRACTICE STRIKE.

Education, Department of An executive department created in 1979 when the Department of Health, Education, and Welfare was abolished. It establishes policies for, administers, and coordinates most federal assistance to education. It maintains 10 regional offices.

Address: 400 Maryland Ave., S.W., Washington, D.C. 20202. Tel. (202) 655–4000

educational leave Time granted to employees for educational and professional improvement purposes, with or without pay. Paid educational leave enables workers to pursue education and training without sacrificing job and income. The ILO Convention No. 140 of 1974 established the concept of paid educational leave as covering "any leave granted to a worker for educational purposes whether it be on the employer's initiative or at the worker's request and regardless of whether the education or training in question is acquired inside or outside the undertaking." A number of ILO member nations have adopted paid educational leave as national policy.

Source references: Janet Longmore, *Paid Educational Leave* (Kingston: Queen's Univ., IRC, 1980); Jean-Marie Luttringer and Bernard Pasquier, "Paid Educational Leave in Five European Countries," *ILR*, July/Aug. 1980; Stanley D. Nollen, "Paid Educational Leave: New Element in Firm-Level Manpower Policy?" *Proceedings of the 30th A/M, IRRA*, ed. by Barbara Dennis (Madison: 1978); OECD, *Alternation Between Work and Education, A Study of Educational Leave of Absence at Enterprise Level* (Paris: 1978); Jule M. Sugarman, "Alternative Work Schedules: The Decennial-Sabbatical Plan," *Journal of the College and University Personnel Association*, Summer 1977; U.S. Dept. of HEW, National Institute of Education, *Paid Educational Leave*, by Herbert A. Levine (Washington: NIE Papers in Education and Work no. 6, 1977).

See also SABBATICALS, TUITION AID.

Education Association; National (Ind) *See* NATIONAL EDUCATION ASSOCIATION (IND).

Education Association, Inc.; Overseas (Ind) *See* OVERSEAS EDUCATION ASSOCIATION, INC. (IND).

education of workers *See* INDUSTRIAL EDUCATION, LABOR EDUCATION.

Education Support Personnel of Oklahoma (Ind) An organization affiliated with the American Association of Classified School Employees (Ind). Its monthly publication is *Shoptalk*.

Address: P.O. Box 758, Stillwater, Okla. 74074. Tel (405) 624–9960

EEO reports Annual or biennial reports required by the EEOC from every employer, apprenticeship committee, labor organization, state and local government, school district, and institution of higher education subject to Title VII of the Civil Rights Act of 1964, to allow the EEOC and other agencies to review employment practices. Under Section 709(c) of Title VII and EEOC regulations, the filing of these reports is mandatory and, if necessary, the EEOC may obtain a court order to compel filing.

EEO–1, the employer information report, sometimes referred to as Standard Form 100, must be filed by employers covered by Title VII who have 100 or more employees and by government contractors covered by Executive Order 11246 who have 50 or more employees and government contracts of $50,000 or more. It contains information on the number of employees in nine job categories by ethnicity or race and sex.

EEO–2, the apprenticeship information report, must be filed by joint labor-management apprenticeship committees. For each craft or trade, the number of apprentices by ethnicity or race and sex and the standards and selection procedures for the program must be reported. A similar record on applicants must be maintained.

EEO–2E, the employer apprenticeship report, must be filed for every establishment with 25 or more employees by each employer who (a) has a companywide employment of 100 or more employees, and (b) conducts and controls apprenticeship program, and (c) has five or more apprentices in the establishment. For each craft or trade, the number of apprentices by ethnicity or race and sex must be reported. A record of applicants must also be maintained.

EEO–3, the local union report, must be filed by local unions with 100 or more members. The sex and racial or ethnic composition of the union membership must be reported. Referral unions are required to provide additional data on job referrals and applicants.

EEO–4, the state and local government information report, must be filed by all states and all other political jurisdictions which have 100 or more employees, and on an annually rotating sample by political jurisdictions which have 15 to 99 employees. Data on occupation, salary range, ethnicity or race, and sex must be reported. This information is required according to governmental function, e.g., financial administration, public welfare, police protection, natural resources, health, and housing.

EEO–5, the elementary and secondary schools staff information report, must be maintained by public elementary and secondary school systems or districts, including individually or separately administered districts within a system and separately administered schools with 15 or more employees, and by individual schools regardless of size within such systems or districts. The School Reporting Committee, comprised of representatives of the EEOC, the Office for Civil Rights (OCR) of the U.S. Department of Education, and the National Center for Education Statistics (NCES), annually determines which of the systems, districts, and schools is required to file the EEO–5 report. The report requires staff data by ethnicity or race and sex.

The OCR involvement stems from Title VI of the Civil Rights Act of 1964 and Title IX of the Education Amendments of 1972; the NCES is authorized by Title V, Amendments Relating to Education Administration, Education Amendments of 1974.

EEO–6, the higher education staff information report, must be filed biennially by public and private institutions with 15 or more employees. Statistics by occupation and salary level, race or ethnicity, and by sex must be reported.

Source references: U.S. EEOC, "EEOC Form 164, State and Local Government Information (EEO–4)," *FEP* 441:419; ____, "EEOC Forms 168A and B, Elementary-Secondary Staff Information (EEO–5)," *FEP* 441:433; ____, "EEOC Form 221, Higher Education Staff Information (EEO–6)," *FEP* 441:451; ____, "EEOC Form 272, Apprenticeship Information Report (EEO–2)," *FEP* 441:357; ____, "EEOC Form 273, Apprenticeship Information Report (EEO–2E)," *FEP* 441:379; ____, "EEOC Form 274, Local Union Report (EEO–3)," *FEP* 441:403; ____, "Equal Employment Opportunity, Standard Form 100, Employer Information Report EEO–1," *FEP*, 441:275.

See also EXECUTIVE ORDER 11246, OFFICE OF FEDERAL CONTRACT COMPLIANCE PROGRAMS (OFCCP), TITLE IX OF THE EDUCATION AMENDMENTS OF 1972.

effects bargaining *See* DECISION/EFFECTS BARGAINING.

efficiency expert An individual assigned to review the operations of a plant, department, or other production unit to determine the most effective way to perform job duties. The work may involve review of the equipment used, the layout of facilities, or the methods used in performing the task; investigation of other factors which would permit work simplification; or integration of functions with a view to reducing the cost of operation through the saving of time, equipment, or material.

In general plant parlance, any person assigned by management who goes about with a stopwatch to get more work out of the workers or the machines. Sometimes referred to as the "speed-up boy."

efficiency of labor The productivity of a worker as measured by his output during a definite time span. The productivity of the individual is generally related to his own skill and capacity, as well as to the quality of the tools and equipment he has available to assist him in his task and the caliber of supervision.

efficiency rating The periodic appraisal of an employee's work performance, usually on the basis of a number of factors which seek to measure the most important qualities required on his job. The rating may be used to determine whether the employee is to be promoted, demoted, or dropped. Where it is used in connection with the seniority clause for promotion or other purposes, it is the equivalent of the "ability factor." Sometimes referred to as rating service, merit rating, performance rating, employee rating, or employee appraisal.

Source references: Douglas L. Bartley, "Inefficiency: The Reasons Why," *PJ*, Aug. 1975; Raymond C. Claydon, "Background for Efficiency Rating Reform. II. Let's Improve Efficiency Ratings," *Personnel Administration*, May 1950; Charles W. Eisemann, "Production Performance Measurement and Analysis," *PJ*, Feb. 1972; Buddy L. Jackson, "Determining Efficiency Through Work Sampling," *Management Review*, Jan. 1972; Catherine S. Lott and John Boddie, "Background for Efficiency Rating Reform. I. What Employees and Supervisors Think of Efficiency Ratings," *Personnel Administration*, May 1950; Wesley H. Moulton, "Background for Efficiency Rating Reform. III. A Guide for Performance Evaluation," *Personnel Administration*, May 1950; Jay M. Stein, "Using Group Process Techniques to Develop Productivity Measures," *Public Personnel Management*, March/April 1979.

See also MERIT RATING, PERFORMANCE APPRAISAL, RATING.

effort rating *See* LEVELING.

eight-hour day *See* ADAMSON ACT.

eight-hour leagues Organizations formed in 1865 in Massachusetts (The Grand Eight-Hour Leagues) to get support for the eight-hour day.

eight-hour movement The efforts during various periods, particularly in the 1800s, to obtain public support for the eight-hour day. Strikes by the Knights of Labor focused attention on the efforts by workers to achieve a shorter workday.

It was not until the strike threat of the Railway Brotherhoods in 1916 that Congress went on record for the basic eight-hour day by adopting the Adamson Act.

See also ADAMSON ACT.

eighty percent (80%) rule A rule of thumb used by federal enforcement agencies to determine adverse impact of the selection process. If the selection rate for any race, sex, or ethnic group is less than four-fifths, or 80 percent, of the group with the highest selection rate, adverse impact is indicated. The four-fifths rule may be applied if the affected or protected class constitutes 2 percent or more of the total labor force in the relevant labor area or 2 percent or more of the applicable work force. It is not a legal definition and is used only to establish the initial inference of adverse action; a final determination requires additional information and evidence.

The rule is cited in the Uniform Guidelines on Employee Selection Procedures. The following example illustrates the calculation of the 80 percent standard: If the selection rate for whites is 60 percent (48 of 80 white applicants were hired), American Indians 45 percent, Hispanics 48 percent, and blacks 51 percent, and each of these groups constitutes more than 2 percent of the labor force in the relevant labor area, the impact ratios are 45/60 (or 75 percent) for American Indians, 48/60 (or 80 percent) for Hispanics, and 51/60 (or 85 percent) for blacks. Under this example, adverse impact would be indicated for American Indians whose selection rate is less than four-fifths the rate of whites, the group with the highest selection rate.

Source references: U.S. EEOC, "Adoption of Questions and Answers to Clarify and Provide a Common Interpretation of the Uniform Guidelines on Employee Selection Procedures," 44 F.R. 11996; ———, "Uniform Guidelines on Employee Selection Procedures," 29 C.F.R. 1607.

electioneering Activity designed to influence voting. The NLRB limits electioneering activity near the polling places when elections are held to determine bargaining representatives.

elections *See* CONTRACT-BAR RULE, "R" CASES, REPRESENTATION ELECTIONS, UNION ELECTIONS.

elections, deauthorization *See* DEAUTHORIZATION ELECTION.

elections, decertification *See* DEAUTHORIZATION ELECTION, DECERTIFICATION.

elections, representation *See* "R" CASES, REPRESENTATION ELECTIONS.

Electrical, Radio and Machine Workers; International Union of (AFL-CIO) Organization of electrical workers formed after the expulsion of the United Electrical, Radio and Machine Workers of America (Ind) from the CIO. The union is now known as the International Union of Electronic, Electrical, Technical, Salaried and Machine Workers (AFL-CIO).

See also ELECTRONIC, ELECTRICAL, TECHNICAL, SALARIED AND MACHINE WORKERS; INTERNATIONAL UNION OF (AFL-CIO).

Electrical, Radio and Machine Workers of America; United (Ind) One of the militant left-wing unions which was once part of the CIO but was expelled before the AFL-CIO merger. The organization was formed following the passage of the National Labor Relations Act and built a membership in excess of 400,000.

When the CIO expelled the UE and the International Union of Electrical, Radio and Machine Workers was set up, the UE lost membership rapidly.

Its official semimonthly publication is the *UE News*.

Address: 11 East 51st St., New York, N.Y. 10022. Tel. (212) 753–1960

Electrical Workers; International Brotherhood of (AFL-CIO) Union of electrical workers organized in St. Louis, Mo., in November 1891 as the National Brotherhood of Electrical Workers of America. When its jurisdiction was extended to Canada in 1899, it changed its name to the International Brotherhood of Electrical Workers.

Its official monthly publication is the *IBEW Journal*.

Address: 1125 15th St., N.W., Washington, D.C. 20005. Tel. (202) 833–7000

Electronic, Electrical, Technical, Salaried and Machine Workers; International Union of (AFL-CIO) Formerly known as the International Union of Electrical, Radio and Machine Workers, it adopted its current name in 1983. *IUE News* is the official monthly publication of the union.

Address: 1126 16th St., N.W., Washington, D.C. 20036. Tel. (202) 296–1201

Elevator Constructors; International Union of (AFL-CIO) Organized in July 1901 as the International Union of Elevator Constructors of the United States. It extended its organization to Canada, and in 1903 changed its name to the International Union of Elevator Constructors.

Its official publication is *The Elevator Constructor*, published monthly.

Address: Suite 530, Clarke Building, 5565 Sterrett Place, Columbia, Md. 21044. Tel. (301) 997–9000

Elgin, Joliet & Eastern Ry. v. Burley A decision of the Supreme Court in 1945 upholding the right of 10 employees to object to a compromise settlement made by the grievance committee of the union of Railway Trainmen and the company. The 10 workers contended they had not authorized the grievance committee to act for them.

The employees took the case to the National Railroad Adjustment Board under the Railway Labor Act (Section 3) but were turned down. They then filed suit in federal court claiming that the employer had violated the contract. The district court held for the company. On appeal to the court of appeals, the district court was reversed, largely on the ground that it had not examined the factual question of whether the employees actually had authorized the union (grievance committee) to compromise their claim.

The Supreme Court by a divided vote (5 to 4) upheld the court of appeals. On a petition for rehearing, the Supreme Court upheld its previous ruling.

Justice Rutledge, writing the majority opinion, held that there should have been some showing that the bargaining agent was authorized to act for the employees. Although this was implicit in the negotiation of new contract terms, he said it was not at all clear in grievance disputes, which involved claims of "rights accrued." Said Justice Rutledge in part: "It would be difficult to believe that Congress intended . . . to submerge wholly the individual and minority interest, with all power to act concerning them, in the collective interest and agency. . . . Acceptance of such a view would require the clearest expression of purpose."

Justice Frankfurter wrote the minority opinion. (Chief Justice Stone and Justices

Roberts and Jackson concurred in the opinion.) He held that this decision would undermine the basic purposes of the Railway Labor Act and the "customary" procedures for settling disputes. "It undermines the confidence so indispensable to adjustment by negotiation, which is the vital object of the Act," he said.

Source reference: Elgin, Joliet & Eastern Ry. v. Burley, 325 US 711, 16 LRRM 749 (1945), *reaff'd,* 327 US 661, 17 LRRM 899 (1946).

eligibility date The date (actually a period) used by the NLRB to determine the eligilibity of employees to vote in a representation election. It is usually the payroll period immediately preceding the date of the election.

eligibility for union membership Most unions permit membership to those employees in the trade, occupation, or plant who pay their initiation fees and dues and live up to the union constitution and bylaws. Closed or restrictive unions may impose standards which are difficult to meet or are discriminatory.

See also RESTRICTION OF MEMBERSHIP, UNION MEMBERSHIP ELIGIBILITY.

eligibility list A list generally used by civil service agencies to determine, after written or oral examination, those eligible to be hired in certain categories. Companies may have similar lists of those eligible for promotion. Another form of eligibility list, used in representation elections conducted under federal and state labor relations laws, is a list of employees eligible to vote.

eligibility of strikers to vote The National Labor Relations Act was silent on this matter. The Taft-Hartley Act, however, provided that employees on strike who are not entitled to reinstatement—that is, economic strikers who had been replaced—"shall not be eligible to vote," but the law as amended contained no hint of when an economic striker should be regarded as permanently replaced. Subsequently, the Landrum-Griffin Act further amended Section 9(c)(3) of the statute to provide that economic strikers who are not entitled to reinstatement shall be eligible to vote in representation elections conducted within 12 months after the commencement of the strike "under such regulations as the [National Labor Relations] Board shall find are consistent with the purposes and provisions of this Act. . . ."

Source references: Samuel H. Cohen, "The Strike Ballot and Other Compulsory Union Balloting," *NYU 7th Annual Conference on Labor,* ed. by Emanuel Stein (Albany: Bender, 1954); James V. Constantine, "Economic Strikers' Voting Rights," *LLJ,* Feb. 1960; B. H. Levy, "Eligibility of Strikers to Vote Under the Taft-Hartley Act," *Personnel,* July 1948.

emergency boards *See* NATIONAL EMERGENCY BOARDS.

emergency disputes *See* NATIONAL EMERGENCY DISPUTES.

emergency work Occasionally has reference to work provided during serious periods of unemployment in order to meet the needs of the community. Emergency work of this nature is generally confined to public works projects. During the Great Depression of the 1930s a wide variety of projects was initiated to ameliorate the consequences of widespread unemployment.

The phrase also is used to apply to situations which require work of an employee during mealtime, Sundays, or other periods when he normally is not at work. Unforeseen circumstances in the operation of the plant may require the immediate attention of specific employees. Such work generally is compensated at premium rates.

Emerson efficiency plan A wage incentive system developed by Harrington Emerson which pays the day rate to the worker until he reaches the standard. After he reaches the standard he receives a piece rate which is increased as his production increases. The method is designed to provide higher premiums in an increasing ratio as production is increased. The graduated bonus is paid in addition to the day rate after the standard has been attained.

Source reference: Gordon S. Watkins et al., *The Management of Personnel and Labor Relations* (New York: McGraw-Hill, 1950).

See also INCENTIVE WAGE.

employ To hire or make use of someone's service. It implies an offer of employment for compensation in return for services.

employable Those persons in the population who are able to work (i.e., have no physical, mental, or other disability that prevents them from working) and are within certain age limits. There is no clearly defined area which permits easy determination of when a person is "employable" or "unemployable" within the labor market. A person who may be unemployable during a period when there is great competition for jobs (periods of high unemployment) may be employed when the standards are reduced. Persons with certain physical disabilities which impair their employment may through vocational rehabilitation qualify for certain jobs and become employable.

See also UNEMPLOYABLE.

employed An individual 16 years of age and older who, during the week of the Current Population Survey, worked for pay; worked 15 hours or more in a family-operated enterprise without pay; or was temporarily absent from the job because of illness, vacation, labor dispute, or other similar reasons.

Beginning in January 1983, BLS included members of the armed forces stationed in the United States in the employed category because enlistment is voluntary and "represents a viable job market alternative."

Source references: John E. Bregger, "Labor Force Data from the CPS to Undergo Revision in January 1983," *MLR*, Nov. 1982; John D. Duran, *The Labor Force in the United States, 1890–1960* (New York: Gordon & Breach, 1968); Marvin Friedman, "The Changing Profile of the Labor Force," *American Federationist,* July 1967; Robert L. Stein, "Reasons for Nonparticipation in the Labor Force," *MLR*, July 1967.

See also CURRENT POPULATION SURVEY (CPS), LABOR FORCE, UNEMPLOYED.

employed rate The number of individuals employed as a percent of the (1) civilian labor force or the (2) total labor force. The total labor force includes the civilian labor force and members of the armed forces stationed in the United States.

See also CIVILIAN LABOR FORCE, EMPLOYMENT.

employee In general usage the term "employee" covers all those who work for a wage or salary and perform services for an employer.

In labor-management relations the term has been variously defined to establish rights and obligations under federal laws. Thus under the Taft-Hartley Act, the National Labor Relations Act is amended in Section 2(3) so that the definition of "employee" excludes certain categories of workers, such as supervisors.

Occasionally the same definition is used for more than one statute. For example, the War Labor Disputes Act of 1943 (Smith-Connally Act) stated in Section 2(d): "The terms 'employer,' 'employee,' 'representative,' 'labor organization,' and 'labor dispute' shall have the same meaning as in section 2 of the National Labor Relations Act [Wagner Act]."

For other definitions, one has to turn to the specific statute and the interpretations by the administrative agencies. See, for example, how the term is applied in the Fair Labor Standards Act and in the Social Security Act.

Collective bargaining agreements will define classifications of employees under the agreement. The Montgomery Ward contract ordered by the War Labor Board provided as follows:

> For the purposes of this agreement, the classifications of employees herein set forth are hereby defined as follows:
>
> (a) Regular full-time employees are employees who have been employed in the business on a full-time basis for at least a period of six months.
>
> (b) Regular short-hour employees are employees who have been employed for at least a period of six months working on a part-time basis.
>
> (c) Apprentice full-time employees are employees who have been employed for a period of less than six months, working a full-time basis in the business.
>
> (d) Apprentice short-hour employees are employees who have been employed for a period of less than six months and have been employed less hours per week than a full working week.

(e) Experienced extra help is one employed for temporary work who has had at least six months' experience in the business.

employee assistance programs Employer-provided services to assist workers in handling personal problems such as alcohol or drug abuse. Such programs are initiated because it is recognized that an employee's personal problem may adversely affect job performance and attendance.

An employee assistance program may function as a problem assessment and referral service and not as a treatment program. Unions may take an active role in helping to develop employee assistance programs.

Source references: Sheila H. Akabas and Seth A. Akabas, "Social Services at the Workplace: New Resources for Management," *Management Review,* May 1982; James T. Wrich, *Guidelines for Developing an Employee Assistance Program,* An AMA Management Briefing (New York: AMA, 1982).

employee associations Groups of workers organized in a single plant or establishment for the purpose of meeting common objectives. Although they may be independent and free of employer domination, they sometimes have been set up for the purpose of preventing organization by established unions with membership and affiliation beyond the plant, locality, or even the industry.

In the public sector, employee associations were formed, among other purposes, to establish insurance and retirement plans, to better salaries, or to further professional interests. Many state employee associations affiliated with the Assembly of Governmental Employees (AGE). However, in recent years, a number of employee associations have left AGE to affiliate with unions such as the American Federation of State, County and Municipal Employees (AFL-CIO), Communications Workers of America (AFL-CIO), and Service Employees' International Union (AFL-CIO) to pursue collective bargaining. In 1982, four employee associations—the National Education Association, American Nurses' Association, American Association of Classified School Employees, and Fraternal Order of Police—each reported membership of over 100,000.

Source references: Courtney D. Gifford (ed.), *Directory of U.S. Labor Organizations, 1984–85 Edition* (Washington: BNA, 1984); Jack Stieber, *Public Employee Unionism* (Washington: Brookings Institution, 1973).

See also COMPANY UNION.

employee benefits Nonwage aids instituted to meet some of the problems of insecurity of workers and at the same time to build better morale in the plant. These benefits, such as vacations, holidays, medical care, sick leave, pensions, hospitalization, and other health and welfare programs, have been instrumental in improving the health of employees and frequently have resulted in increased production.

Although originally these measures were adopted by employers unilaterally as part of an enlightened personnel program, or as a means of discouraging the entrance of outside unions, they have been widely adopted and have become one of the important areas in collective bargaining. Decisions by the NLRB, supported by court decisions, have been partly responsible for the extension of the scope of collective bargaining in this area.

Many national unions have programs for sickness and disability payments as well as death benefits. These benefits are generally supplementary to those negotiated with employers.

Source references: Inland Steel Co. v. NLRB, 170 F2d 247, 22 LRRM 2506 (1948), 336 US 960, 24 LRRM 2019 (1949); BNA, *Employee Expense Allowances and Perquisites* (Washington: PPF Survey no. 124, 1979); Arthur J. Deric (ed.), *The Total Approach to Employee Benefits* (New York: AMA, 1967); Walter W. Kolodrubetz, "Growth in Employee-Benefit Plans, 1950–1965," *Social Security Bulletin,* April 1967; Jeffrey D. Mamorsky, "Impact of the 1978 ADEA Amendments on Employee Benefit Plans," *Employee Relations LJ,* Autumn 1978; Mitchell Meyer and Harland Fox, *Profile of Employee Benefits* (New York: The Conference Board, Report no. 645, 1974); Lee M. Modjeska, "Eligibility Clauses in Benefit Plans Under the LMRA—Some Hidden Pitfalls," *LLJ,* Feb. 1973; Martin E. Segal Co., *Employee Benefits Factbook 1970* (New York: Fleet Academic Editions, 1970); Richard R.

Stackpole, "Benefit Plans for Foreign Subsidiaries," *PJ*, April 1978; Robert Tilove, "Employee Benefit Plans," *A Decade of Industrial Relations Research, 1946–1956*, ed. by Neil W. Chamberlain, Frank C. Pierson, and Theresa Wolfson (New York: Harper, IRRA Pub. 19, 1958); Samuel C. Walker, "Improving Cost and Motivational Effectiveness of Employee Benefit Plans," *PJ*, Nov. 1977; David A. Weeks (ed.), *Rethinking Employee Benefits Assumption* (New York: The Conference Board, Report no. 739, 1978).

See also BENEFIT PLANS, FRINGE BENEFITS, HEALTH BENEFIT PROGRAMS, HEALTH INSURANCE.

employee benefit society *See* MUTUAL BENEFIT ASSOCIATIONS.

employee buyout *See* EMPLOYEE OWNERSHIP.

employee committee *See* COMPANY UNION.

employee elections *See* REPRESENTATION ELECTIONS.

employee evaluation The procedure used to determine an individual's fitness and qualifications for a particular job. Among the factors frequently considered are productivity, honesty, reliability, cooperativeness, growth potential, and attitude toward the job.

See also PERFORMANCE APPRAISAL, RATING.

employee giveback The reduction of previously obtained wage levels, fringe benefits, or working conditions. Unions may agree to employee givebacks to avoid layoffs or plant closings.

Source references: Scott A. Kruse, "Giveback Bargaining: One Answer to Current Problems?" *PJ*, April 1983; Joan Weitzman, *City Workers and Fiscal Crisis: Cutbacks, Givebacks and Survival; A Study of the New York City Experience* (New Brunswick: Rutgers Univ., Institute of Management and Labor Relations, 1979); Dale Yoder and Paul D. Staudohar, "Auditing the Labor Relations Function," *Personnel*, May/June 1983.

See also CONCESSION BARGAINING.

employee handbook A booklet provided by employers to new employees as part of the orientation program. It generally contains a brief statement about the company and its organization and growth. It discusses the company's policies on such things as hospital and dispensary facilities, vacations, hours of work, recreation, housing, lunchroom facilities, and general shop rules. Where the plant is organized, reference is made to that fact, but it is generally up to the union to supply information to the employees concerning their rights, duties, and obligations toward the union.

Source references: William B. Cobaugh, "When It's Time to Rewrite Your Personnel Manual," *PJ*, Dec. 1978; Paula Cowan, "Establishing a Communication Chain: The Development and Distribution of An Employee Handbook," *PJ*, June 1975; Robert E. Harmon, *Improving Administrative Manuals, An AMA Research Study* (New York: AMA, 1982); Don E. Jones, "The Employee Handbook," *PJ*, Feb. 1973; William N. McNairn, "Procedures Manuals *Can* Be Useful," *Management Review*, Aug. 1973; NICB, *Personnel Procedure Manuals* (New York: Studies in Personnel Policy no. 180, 1961).

employee magazine A general medium for communication with employees in the plant. It is designed to keep employees informed about the company's activities, about activities of other employees on the job, recreational activities, and other things which might be of interest to workers in the plant. A further purpose is to increase the degree of employee attachment or allegiance to the company.

employee-management cooperation in the federal service *See* EXECUTIVE ORDER 10988, EXECUTIVE ORDER 11491.

employee organization A phrase which has the same connotation as "labor organization," except that it does not have the flavor of "unionism." In the public sector there are many organizations which do not consider themselves "labor" organizations, although they may perform many of the functions of a labor organization, such as representing employees, seeking improvement in wages and working conditions, etc. Some may be professional or technical organizations which want to maintain a clear distinction between the services which they perform for their membership and the general role and function of a labor union. The term is frequently used interchangeably with "public employee organization."

Under Executive Order 10988, the term was defined as:

> any lawful association, labor organization, federation, council, or brotherhood having as a primary purpose the improvement of working conditions among Federal employees, or any craft, trade or industrial union whose memberships include both Federal employees and employees of private organizations; but such terms shall not include any organization (1) which asserts the right to strike against the Government of the U.S. or any agency thereof, or to assist or participate in any such strike, or which imposes a duty or obligation to conduct, assist or participate in any such strike, or (2) which advocates the overthrow of the constitutional form of Government in the United States, or (3) which discriminates with regard to the terms or conditions of membership because of race, color, creed or national origin.

Under Executive Order 11491, the term "labor organization" was substituted for "employee organization" and redefined to exclude organizations of supervisors and managers and to extend the nondiscrimination requirement to include sex and age. A separate system for communication and consultation with associations of supervisors was provided under Section 7(e).

The Civil Service Reform Act of 1978 which replaced Executive Order 11491 utilizes the term "labor organization."

Source reference: Harold S. Roberts, *Labor-Management Relations in the Public Service* (Honolulu: Univ. of Hawaii Press, 1970).

See also EMPLOYEE ASSOCIATIONS, LABOR ORGANIZATION.

employee ownership Financial holdings of employees in the company. Hammer and Stern note: "Employee owned companies in the form of producers' cooperatives in which employees commonly own and manage the business, occurred as early as 1791 in the United States and increased dramatically in the 19th century. Firms organized along traditional lines also have made small amounts of company stock available to selected employees through fringe benefit stock options and bonus plans since the 1920s." The employee stock ownership plan is another form of employee ownership. In recent years some plants have been purchased by employees from the employer to avoid the closing of the plant.

Source references: Michael Conte and Arnold S. Tannenbaum, "Employee-Owned Companies: Is the Difference Measurable?" *MLR,* July 1978; Michael A. Gurdon, "Is Employee Ownership the Answer to Our Economic Woes?" *Management Review,* May 1982; Tove Helland Hammer and Robert N. Stern, *Employee Ownership: Implications for the Organizational Distribution of Power* (Ithaca: Cornell Univ., NYSSILR, Reprint no. 475, 1980); Richard J. Long, "Worker Ownership and Job Attitudes: A Field Study," *IR,* Spring 1982; James O'Toole, "The Uneven Record of Employee Ownership," *Harvard BR,* Nov./Dec. 1979; Robert N. Stern, K. Haydn Wood, and Tove Helland Hammer, *Employee Ownership in Plant Shutdowns, Prospects for Employment Stability* (Kalamazoo: Upjohn Institute for Employment Research, 1979); William Foote Whyte, *In Support of Voluntary Employee Ownership* (Ithaca: Cornell Univ., NYSSILR, Reprint no. 445, 1978); William Foote Whyte and Joseph R. Blasi, *From Research to Legislation on Employee Ownership* (Ithaca: Cornell Univ., NYSSILR, Reprint no. 491, 1980); Linda Wintner, *Employee Buyouts: An Alternative to Plant Closings* (New York: The Conference Board, Research Bull. 140, 1983).

See also EMPLOYEE STOCK OWNERSHIP PLAN.

employee rating *See* EFFICIENCY RATING.

employee representation plans Programs designed to provide some sense of participation by employees in a particular company. They entailed the formation of committees or other bodies elected by the employees to meet with members of management to consider problems of mutual concern, primarily the application or enforcement of company policy, grievances, and working conditions. The plans were not designed to develop machinery for collective bargaining, but rather to provide an opportunity for the exchange of ideas or experience before final decision by management.

These plans were developed during World War I and were designed in part to achieve increased production through cooperation. Some were developed or enlarged during the 1920s. Following the organization drive which came with Section 7(a) of the National Industrial Recovery Act in 1933, employee representation plans multiplied quite rapidly as a means of forestalling unionization by "outside" organizers. These plans fell by the wayside when the National Labor Relations Act was passed and the NLRB held these organizations to be "company dominated" or "company sponsored" and not proper agencies for purposes of collective bargaining.

Source references: Benjamin B. Naumoff, "Developments in the National Labor Relations Board Policy on Employee Representation," *NYU 8th Annual Conference on Labor,* ed. by Emanuel Stein (Albany: Bender, 1955); Benjamin M. Selekman and Mary Van Kleek, *Collective Bargaining Through Employee Representation* (New York: NICB, 1933); ———, *Employee Representation in Steel Works* (New York: Russell Sage Foundation, 1924); ———, *Representation in Coal Mines* (New York: Russell Sage Foundation, 1924).

See also COLORADO PLAN, COMPANY UNION.

employee requisition A procedure used in some companies whereby departments request the personnel office or division to supply the personnel needs of the operating divisions.

Employee Retirement Income Security Act (ERISA) of 1974 The first comprehensive pension reform law passed by Congress, it ensures that employees covered by private pension and welfare plans receive benefits in accordance with their credited years of service. In addition to the establishment of minimum vesting requirements, the law also establishes registration and reporting requirements, rules for the administration of the plans with penalties for violations, fiduciary responsibilities, funding requirements, improvements in provisions covering the self-employed, and provisions for individual retirement accounts. ERISA supersedes the Welfare and Pension Plans Disclosure Act of 1958.

Exemptions to ERISA include government retirement plans, Railroad Retirement Act plans, church plans, unfunded excess benefit plans, and others.

ERISA is administered by the Department of Labor, Internal Revenue Service, and the Pension Benefit Guaranty Corporation.

Source references: Stuart N. Alperin et al., "The Employee Retirement Income Security Act of 1974: Policies and Problems," *IR Law Digest,* Fall 1975; Elliot Bredhoff, "Collective Bargaining for Socially Responsible Investment of Pension and Welfare Fund Assets: Another Look at ERISA," *Proceedings of the 34th A/M, IRRA,* ed. by Barbara Dennis (Madison: 1982); Jeremy I. Bulow, Myron S. Scholes, and Peter Menell, *Economic Implications of ERISA* (Cambridge: NBER, WP 927, 1982); BNA, *Highlights of the New Pension Reform Law* (Washington: 1974); ———, *ERISA: The Law and the Code, 1985 Edition,* ed. by Kathleen D. Gill (Washington: 1985); Francis X. Burkhardt, "ERISA Problems and Programs," *LLJ,* Dec. 1977; Raymond J. Donovan, "Effective Administration of ERISA," *LLJ,* March 1982; Paul J. Fasser, Jr., "New Pension Reform Legislation," *Arbitration—1975,* Proceedings of the 28th A/M, NAA, ed. by Barbara Dennis and Gerald Somers (Washington: BNA, 1976); Robert Frumkin and Donald Schmitt, "Pension Improvements Since 1974 Reflect Inflation, New U.S. Law," *MLR,* April 1979; Bernard Greenberg, "ERISA and Collective Bargaining," *NYU 28th Annual Conference on Labor,* ed. by Richard Adelman (New York: Bender, 1976); Peter Henle and Raymond Schmitt, "Pension Reform: The Long, Hard Road to Enactment," *MLR,* Nov. 1974; Ian D. Lanoff, "The Social Investment of Private Pension Plan Assets: May It be Done Lawfully Under ERISA?" *LLJ,* July 1980; Noel Arnold Levin, "ERISA's Effect on Bargaining Over Pensions," *NYU 28th Annual Conference on Labor,* ed. by Richard Adelman (New York: Bender, 1976); Mary K. Nicholson, "Collections and Settlement Under ERISA," *LLJ,* June 1978; Robert D. Paul, "The Impact of Pension Reform on American Business," *Sloan Management*

Review, Fall 1976; Robin Berman Schwartzman, "Multiemployer Employee-Benefit Plans Under ERISA," *Employee Relations LJ,* Summer 1977; Denis R. Sheil, "Determining the Rights of Pension Claimants: Before and After ERISA," *LLJ,* Feb. 1979; Robert Tilove, "ERISA—Its Effect on Collective Bargaining," *NYU 29th Annual Conference on Labor,* ed. by Richard Adelman (New York: Bender, 1976); U.S. Dept. of Labor, LMSA, *Employee Retirement Income Security Act, 1981 Report to Congress* (Washington: 1982); ———, *Often-Asked Questions About the Employee Retirement Income Security Act of 1974* (Washington: 1975); ———, *What You Should Know About the Pension and Welfare Law, A Guide to the Employee Retirement Income Security Act of 1974* (Washington: 1978); Mark A. Vogel, "Excess Benefits Plans and Other Nonqualified Deferred Compensation Plans Under ERISA," *Employee Relations LJ,* Winter 1977.

See also MULTIEMPLOYER PENSION PLAN AMENDMENTS ACT (MPPAA) OF 1980, PENSION BENEFIT GUARANTY CORP. (PBGC), RETIREMENT EQUITY ACT OF 1984.

employee rule book A booklet setting forth company rules or detailed information on company procedures. Many employee handbooks also contain company rules and policies in addition to other information about the company.

See also EMPLOYEE HANDBOOK.

employees' annual report A report directed primarily to the worker in the plant, in language which he can comprehend and which avoids the technical language of finance or accounting, intended to give him some understanding of the operations of the company. It helps the worker to see how the company operates; how its product is marketed; what the costs of production are; how much is expended on wages, materials, plant maintenance, etc.; and how much is paid out in dividends.

employees' club A group or association set up within a company or plant whose functions are primarily social and recreational and generally open to all employees.

employee skills inventory *See* INVENTORY OF EMPLOYEE SKILLS.

employee stock ownership plan Plan designed to give workers a sense of participation in the management of a company. By encouraging employees to purchase stock, or by issuing stock bonuses, management hopes to instill a sense of ownership and create ties that will result in increased production, low turnover, and possibly opposition to outside unionization.

Employee stock ownership and profit sharing plans have been two major prongs in employers' efforts to have the employee identify his interest with that of the company. In most instances, employee stock purchases are too small to permit the worker any effective say in the management of the company.

The extension of stock dividends, or ownership to executives, however, has provided an incentive to some top executives to stay with a company whose profit prospects are good but whose salaries are below those offered by competing firms.

In the absence of any generally accepted definition, the National Industrial Conference Board adopted three tests: (1) All rank-and-file employees, or all of a substantial group of rank-and-file employees (e.g., all white-collar workers) must be covered. (2) The employee must obtain possession of the stock while he is still employed; ownership must not be deferred until, say, after retirement. (3) The employee must buy the stock from his own funds, not by gift from the company.

ESOPs have been used during periods of recession to stop plant closings.

Source references: Timothy C. Jochin, "Labor-Management Relations and Employee Stock-Ownership Programs," *Personnel,* Nov./Dec. 1978; Mitchell Meyer and Harland Fox, *Employee Stock Ownership Plan* (New York: NICB, Studies in Personnel Policy no. 206, 1967); Profit Sharing Council of America, *ESOPs: An Analytical Report* (Chicago: 1975); W. Robert Reum and Sherry Milliken Reum, "Employee Stock Ownership Plans: Pluses and Minuses," *Harvard BR,* July/Aug. 1976; Robert N. Stern and Philip Comstock, *Employee Stock Ownership Plans (ESOPs): Benefits for Whom?* (Ithaca:

NYSSILR, Cornell Univ., Key Issues series no. 23, 1978); U.S. Congress, Senate, Committee on Finance, *Employee Stock Ownership Plans, An Employer Handbook* (Washington: 1980); U.S. GAO, *Employee Stock Ownership Plans: Who Benefits Most in Closely Held Companies?* (Washington: 1980).

See also EMPLOYEE OWNERSHIP, PAYROLL-BASED EMPLOYEE STOCK OWNERSHIP PLAN (PAYSOP), PROFIT SHARING, TAX REDUCTION ACT STOCK OWNERSHIP PLAN (TRASOP).

employee unit The group of employees determined by the NLRB or a state board, or the parties by agreement, to be the unit appropriate for collective bargaining purposes. Where the unit is on a craft or skill basis, all the employees in the craft in the employ of the employer in a single plant or in all of the plants constitute the unit for bargaining purposes. Where the unit is on an industrial basis, all of the employees, with the exception of exempt employees such as supervisory or confidential employees, are in the bargaining unit.

employee wage suit Action by a worker against an employer for the recovery of unpaid wages, usually under the Fair Labor Standards Act. Section 16(b) of the Act, as amended by the Portal-to-Portal Act of 1947, provides as follows:

> Any employer who violates the provisions of section 6 or section 7 of this Act shall be liable to the employee or employees affected in the amount of their unpaid minimum wages, or their unpaid overtime compensation, as the case may be, and in an additional equal amount as liquidated damages. . . . An action to recover the liability prescribed . . . may be maintained against any employer (including a public agency) in any Federal or state court of competent jurisdiction by any one or more employees for and in behalf of himself or themselves and other employees similarly situated. No employee shall be a party plaintiff to any such action unless he gives his consent in writing to become such a party and such consent is filed in the court in which such action is brought. The court in such action shall, in addition to any judgment awarded to the plaintiff or plaintiffs, allow a reasonable attorney's fee to be paid by the defendant, and costs of the action.

Source references: Fair Labor Standards Act of 1938, as amended, 29 U.S.C. 216 (1982); Portal-to-Portal Act, as amended, 29 U.S.C. 251–262 (1982).

employer Generally a person, association, or corporation having workers in its employ. In a small company the employer is frequently the owner and manager. In a large organization the functions of the employer are divided among foreman, manager, president, and stockholders.

In the labor-management field the term "employer" has a more technical meaning, generally confined to the application of a particular statute. Those drafting legislation set their own definitions in order to meet their objectives, particularly as to the coverage of the statute. For example, the National Labor Relations Act defined employer as:

> any person acting in the interest of an employer, directly or indirectly, but shall not include the United States or any State or political subdivision thereof, or any person subject to the Railway Labor Act, as amended from time to time, or any labor organization (other than when acting as an employer), or anyone acting in the capacity of officer or agent of such labor organization.

When the Taft-Hartley Act was passed in 1947, Congress redefined the term "employer" as:

> any person acting as an agent of an employer, directly or indirectly, but shall not include the United States or any wholly owned Government corporation, or any Federal Reserve Bank, or any State or political subdivision thereof, or any corporation or association operating a hospital, if no part of the net earnings inures to the benefit of any private shareholder or individual, or any person subject to the Railway Labor Act, as amended from time to time, or any labor organization (other than when acting as an employer), or anyone acting in the capacity of officer or agent of such labor organization.

Changes in the definition of the term are important in the administration of the law. Thus discriminatory actions by foremen and supervisors under Section 8 of the National Labor Relations Act constituted actions "in the interest" of the employer. Under the Taft-Hartley Act the foremen or supervisors or other employees must act as "agents" of the employer before the NLRB can make a finding holding the employer responsible for an alleged unfair labor practice.

See also MANAGEMENT, PUBLIC EMPLOYER.

employer association A group or organization sponsored or supported by employers primarily for the purpose of presenting a united front in dealing with organized employees. Normally composed of employers in the same industry and locality, these organizations are intended to permit the employers to meet the union on an equal footing. Some employer organizations may be motivated by a desire to frustrate or avoid unionization, while others may be concerned in resolving problems created by unionism and the growth of collective bargaining.

Source references: Jesse T. Carpenter, *Employers' Associations and Collective Bargaining in New York City* (Ithaca: Cornell UP, 1950); ILO, *Role of Employers' Organisations in the Arab Countries* (Geneva: Labour-Management Relations Series 54, 1979); Peter Jackson and Keith Sisson, "Employers' Confederation in Sweden and the U.K. and the Significance of Industrial Infrastructure," *BJIR*, Nov. 1976; Kenneth M. McCaffree, "A Theory of the Origin and Development of Employer Associations," *Proceedings of the 15th A/M, IRRA*, ed. by Gerald Somers (Madison: 1963); Almon E. Roth et al., *Employer Associations in Collective Bargaining* (New York: AMA, 1939); Max S. Wortman, Jr., "Labor Relations Decision-Making in the Membership of Employers' Associations," *LLJ*, July 1963.

See also AMERICAN MANAGEMENT ASSOCIATION, NATIONAL ASSOCIATION OF MANUFACTURERS (NAM), NATIONAL ERECTORS' ASSOCIATION, NATIONAL FOUNDERS' ASSOCIATION.

employer-employee relations Refers to the entire gamut of relationships that exist in, or arise out of, employment of workers by an employer. The term has been used synonymously with labor-management relations, industrial relations, or labor relations. Some restrict use of "industrial relations" to a formal, organized relationship resulting from collective bargaining and the existence of a labor union acting for the employees, while applying "employer-employee relations" to all plant relationships whether with organized or unorganized employees.

The employer-employee relationship occasionally is defined as the contractual agreement of the employer with the individual employee as to wages and performance of assigned work, as distinguished from the relationship with the union through the collective bargaining agreement which sets out the conditions and standards of employment for all the employees in the bargaining unit.

See also INDUSTRIAL RELATIONS.

employer petition A formal request by an employer to the NLRB or a state board requesting the holding of an election to determine the representative, if any, to be recognized for collective bargaining purposes in the plant, or for a smaller unit within the plant.

The NLRB requires that the employer demonstrate by objective considerations that he has some reasonable grounds for believing the union has lost its majority.

Source references: U.S. Gypsum Co. and United Steelworkers of America, AFL-CIO, 157 NLRB 652, 61 LRRM 1384 (1966); "NLRB Drops Old Rule on Employer Petitions; Company Must Show Reasonable Basis for Vote," *White Collar Report*, No. 471, March 17, 1966.

See also REPRESENTATION ELECTIONS.

employer reserve plan Unemployment tax payments based on the merit rating of the employer. Companies with a high unemployment rate pay the maximum tax, while those with no unemployment in the period pay the minimum tax. Each employer's reserve fund depends on the extent of the use of the fund by those of his employees eligible for unemployment benefits.

See also MERIT RATING, UNEMPLOYMENT COMPENSATION.

employer rights Those prerogatives and activities relating to the operation and management of a business which the employer feels are not subject to collective bargaining. There is much disagreement between management and labor as to where the line should be drawn.

Source references: Neil W. Chamberlain, *The Union Challenge to Management Control* (New York: Harper, 1948); Sumner H. Slichter, *Union Policies and Industrial Management* (Washington: Brookings Institution, 1941).

See also MANAGEMENT RIGHTS.

employer's agent *See* AGENT.

employer's final offer A procedure set forth in the Taft-Hartley Act as part of the handling of national emergency disputes which assumes that if employees are familiar with the employer's last offer, and have an opportunity to vote by secret ballot in an election conducted by an impartial government agency, they are likely to accept the offer. Experience to date has not supported this assumption. Section 209(b) provides that after the Board of Inquiry reports to the President, he ". . . shall make such report available to the public. The National Labor Relations Board, within the succeeding fifteen days, shall take a secret ballot of the employees of such employer involved in the dispute on the question of whether they wish to accept the final offer of settlement made by their employer as stated by him and shall certify the results thereof to the Attorney General within five days thereafter."

Section 203(c) provides similar procedures for the use of the FMCS, stating that the Director shall seek to induce ". . . submission to the employees in the bargaining unit of the employer's last offer of settlement for approval or rejection in a secret ballot."

Similar voting procedures were set up under the War Labor Disputes Act of 1943 (Smith-Connally Act), Section 8(3) of which provided for a secret ballot to determine whether employees would ". . . permit any such interruption of war production." Such voting, contrary to the expectations of the legislators, supported the strike threats of the union.

Source reference: War Labor Disputes Act, Pub. L. 78–89, June 25, 1943, 57 Stat. 163 (War Labor Disputes Act, formerly codified under 50 app. U.S.C. 1501–1511, omitted as terminating six months after Dec. 31, 1946, pursuant to the proclamation of the cessation of hostilities of World War II by Proc. No. 2714, eff. Dec. 31, 1946; see note 50 app. U.S.C. 1501); Labor Management Relations Act, as amended, Sections 8(d) and 206–210, 29 U.S.C. 158(d), 29 U.S.C. 176–180 (1982).

See also ARBITRATION, FINAL OFFER.

employers' liability Statutes which determine the circumstances under which employers are subject or liable for damages for injuries received by their employees.

Source references: Edward Berman, "Employers' Liability," *Encyclopedia of the Social Sciences*, ed. by Edwin R. A. Seligman (Vol. 5, New York: Macmillan, 1931); John H. Munkman, *Employer's Liability at Common Law* (London: Butterworths, 1966).

See also CONTRIBUTORY NEGLIGENCE, WORKERS COMPENSATION.

employer's liability insurance Policies taken out by employers to cover industrial accidents which might occur to employees or to outsiders during employment. Such protection is in addition to that provided by workers compensation laws.

employment For purposes of collecting data on employment and unemployment, a number of fine distinctions must be made. BLS defines an employed person as an individual 16 years of age and older who, during the week in which the survey was made, did any work for pay or profit, did at least 15 hours of unpaid work in a family-operated enterprise, or was temporarily absent from his regular job. An unemployed person is one who had no job during the survey week and who made an effort to find a job during the past four weeks, one who was not working but was waiting to be called back to a job from which he had been laid off, or one who was not working but was waiting to report to a new job within 30 days.

Source references: Robert W. Bednarzik, Marillyn A. Hewson, and Michael A. Urquhart, "The Employment Situation in 1981: New Recession Takes Its Toll," *MLR*, March 1982; Norman Bowers, "Have Employment Patterns in Recessions Changed?" *MLR*, Feb. 1981; N. N. Franklin, "Employment and Unemployment: Views and Policies, 1919–1969," *ILR*, March 1969; Walter Galenson, *A Primer on Employment and Wages* (New York: Random House, 1966); Robert A. Gordon, "Employment and Unemployment," *International Encyclopedia of the Social Sciences*, ed. by David L. Sills (vol. 5, New York: Macmillan & Free Press, 1968); Gloria P. Green, "Comparing Employment Estimates from Household and Payroll Surveys," *MLR*, Dec. 1969; Carol Boyd Leon, "The Employment-Population Ratio: Its Value in Labor Force Analysis," *MLR*, Feb.

1981; Morris J. Newman, "Seasonal Variations in Employment and Unemployment During 1951–75," *MLR*, Jan. 1980; Valerie A. Personick, "Industry Output and Employment: BLS Projections to 1990," *MLR*, April 1979; Richard Ruggles, *Employment and Unemployment Statistics and Indexes of Economic Activity and Capacity Utilization* (Washington: U.S. National Commission on Employment and Unemployment Statistics, Background Paper no. 28, 1979); Robert L. Stein, "New Definitions for Employment and Unemployment," *Employment and Earnings*, Feb. 1967; U.S. Dept. of Labor, BLS, *BLS Handbook of Methods* (Washington: Bull. 2134–1, 1982); ———, *Employment Projections for the 1980's* (Washington: Bull. 2030, 1979); ———, *Geographic Profile of Employment and Unemployment, 1980* (Washington: 1982); ———, *Methodology for Projections of Industry Employment to 1990* (Washington: Bull. 2036, 1980); ———, *State Profile of Employment and Unemployment, 1977* (Washington: 1978); Diane N. Westcott and Robert W. Bednarzik, "Employment and Unemployment: A Report on 1980," *MLR*, Feb. 1981.

See also CURRENT POPULATION SURVEY (CPS), EMPLOYED, LABOR FORCE, UNEMPLOYMENT.

Employment Act of 1946 A federal statute declaring that the government has a responsibility to promote employment opportunities. Provision also is made for continuing study of economic trends and the submission of the President's Economic Report, which is based on studies made by a Council of Economic Advisers.

The Employment Act holds it to be the policy of the government to ". . . use all practicable means consistent with its needs and obligations and other essential considerations of national policy, . . . to coordinate and utilize all its plans, functions and resources for the purpose of creating and maintaining in the manner calculated to foster and promote free competitive enterprise and the general welfare, conditions under which these will be afforded useful employment opportunities, including self-employment, for those able, willing and seeking to work, and to promote maximum employment, production and purchasing power."

Source references: Employment Act of 1946, as amended, 15 U.S.C. 1021–1024 (1982); Leon H. Keyserling, *How Well is the Employment Act of 1946 Achieving Its Goal?* (Washington: U.S. Dept. of Labor, Manpower Administration, Seminar on Manpower Policy and Program, 1966); Sar A. Levitan, "On Reforming the Employment Act," *Conference Board Record*, Sept. 1976; U.S. Congress, Joint Economic Committee, *Achieving the Goals of the Employment Act of 1946—Thirtieth Anniversary Review. Volume 1—Employment, Paper no. 1, On Giving a Job: The Implementation and Allocation of Public Service Employment* (Washington: 1975); ———, *Achieving the Goals of the Employment Act of 1946—Thirtieth Anniversary Review. Volume 2—Energy, Paper no. 2, Energy and Economic Growth* (Washington: 1977); ———, *Employment Act of 1946, as Amended, With Related Laws (Annotated) and Rules* (Washington: 1975); ———, *Twentieth Anniversary of the Employment Act of 1946, An Economic Symposium* (Washington: 1966).

employment agencies Organizations established for the purpose of bringing together employers having employment opportunities and workers in need of employment. State and federal employment offices provide the largest placement service for those seeking employment. The U.S. Employment Service was established under the Wagner-Peyser Act of June 1933. Its purpose was to provide free public employment offices throughout the country under a cooperative arrangement between federal and state governments.

Many commercial agencies provide placement service for a fee paid either by the applicant or by the employer. Some private agencies also provide placement services and counseling. Union hiring halls are also instrumental in placing union workers on jobs in many industries. Under the Taft-Hartley Act unions are prohibited from discriminating against nonunion employees. The practices of many union hiring halls have had to be modified to conform to the requirements of the law.

Source references: Leonard P. Adams, "Employment Agencies: Public vs. Private," *Challenge,* Jan./Feb. 1967; Howard Aldrich, *Resource Dependence and Interorganizational Relations, Local Employment Service Offices and Social Services Sector Organizations* (Ithaca: NYSSILR, Cornell Univ., Reprint Series no. 389, 1976); Robert L. Caleo, "Dealing with Employment Agencies," *Management Review,* April 1963; George J. Carcagno, Robert Cecil, and James C. Ohls, "Using Private Employment Agencies to Place Public Assistance Clients in Jobs," *Journal of Human Resources,* Winter 1982; Terry L. Dennis and David P. Gustafson, "College Campuses vs. Employment Agencies as Sources of Manpower," *PJ,* Aug. 1973; Maxwell Harper and Arthur R. Pell, *Starting and Managing an Employment Agency* (Washington: U.S. Small Business Administration, Starting and Managing Series, vol. 22, 1971); Stephen Rubenfeld and Michael Crino, "Are Employment Agencies Jeopardizing Your Selection Process?" *Personnel,* Sept./Oct. 1981; Jack W. Skeels, "Perspectives on Private Employment Agencies," *IR,* Feb. 1969; U.S. National Commission for Manpower Policy, *Labor Market Intermediaries* (Washington: Special Report no. 22, 1978).

See also HIRING HALL, PUBLIC EMPLOYMENT OFFICE, U.S. EMPLOYMENT SERVICE.

Employment and Training Administration (ETA) An agency of the U.S. Department of Labor. The five major components of the ETA consist of the Office of Employment Security (which includes the Unemployment Insurance Service, U.S. Employment Service, and Office of Trade Adjustment Assistance), Office of Employment and Training Programs (which includes the Bureau of Apprenticeship and Training), Office of Strategic Planning and Policy Development, Office of Financial Control and Management Systems, and the Office of Regional Management.

The ETA administers the Job Training Partnership Act of 1982. It publishes the monthly *Area Trends in Employment and Unemployment* and the annual report entitled *Employment and Training Report of the President* (formerly *Manpower Report of the President*).

Formerly known as the Manpower Administration, the name was changed to the ETA by Secretary of Labor's Order 14–75, dated November 12, 1975. The Order stated that as the statutes administered by the agency "impact upon the employment or training of workers, the Administration within the Department which administers these statutes should reflect these generic concerns."

Address: 200 Constitution Ave., N.W., Washington, D.C. 20210. Tel. (202) 376–6750

Source references: Secretary of Labor Order 14–75, 40 F.R. 54,485; U.S. Dept. of Labor, ETA, *ETA: Helping to Improve American Worklife* (Washington: 1978); U.S. President, *Employment and Training Report of the President* (Washington: 1976 +).

See also BUREAU OF APPRENTICESHIP AND TRAINING (BAT), UNEMPLOYMENT INSURANCE SERVICE (UIS), U.S. EMPLOYMENT SERVICE.

employment application A formal request by an applicant for employment. The application form usually contains sufficient background information to permit the employment officer to make a preliminary evaluation of the candidate and to decide if further interviews should be arranged.

In developing the application form, care should be taken that it does not inadvertently violate federal, state, or local statutes which prohibit various types of discrimination. Information requested on the application blank relating to membership in a union (Taft-Hartley Act) or reference to a specific race, color, nationality, or religion may be a basis for alleged discrimination.

Source references: Lipman G. Feld, "Fifteen Questions You Dare Not Ask Job Applicants," *Management Review,* Nov. 1974; Robert Hershey, "Employees Going and Coming: The Application Form," *Personnel,* Jan./Feb. 1971; Clemm C. Kessler III and George J. Gibbs, "Getting the Most From Application Blanks and References," *Personnel,* Jan./Feb. 1975; Harry Kitson and Juna Newton, *Helping People Find Jobs* (New York: Harper, 1950); Clifford M. Koen, Jr., "The Pre-Employment Inquiry Guide," *PJ,* Oct. 1980; Edward L. Levine and Abram Flory III, "Evaluation of Job Applications—A Conceptual Framework," *Public Personnel*

Management, Nov./Dec. 1975; Laurence Lipsett, "Selecting Personnel Without Tests," *PJ,* Sept. 1972; Frank A. Malinowski, "Job Selection Using Task Analysis," *PJ,* April 1981; Elizabeth Marting (ed.), *AMA Book of Employment Forms* (New York: 1967); Richard H. McKillip and Cynthia L. Clark, *Biographical Data and Job Performance* (Washington: U.S. CSC, Technical Memorandum 74–1, 1974); Robert L. Minter, "Human Rights Laws and Pre-Employment Inquiries," *PJ,* June 1972; Larry A. Pace and Lyle F. Schoenfeldt, "Legal Concerns in the Use of Weighted Applications," *Personnel Psychology,* Summer 1977; Wayne R. Porter and Edward L. Levine, "Improving Applicants' Performance in the Completion of Applications," *Public Personnel Management,* July/Aug. 1974; Edward J. Rogers, "Making the Most of the Employment Application Form," *PJ,* Sept. 1960; J. L. Stone, "Using a Questionnaire With an Employment Application," *Public Personnel Management,* March/April 1973; Harrison M. Trice and William J. Wasmuth, *Effective Hiring in Small Business Organizations* (Ithaca: NYSSILR, Cornell Univ., Bull. 46, 1962).

See also FAIR EMPLOYMENT PRACTICES, FORMS AND RECORDS, POST-EMPLOYMENT QUESTIONNAIRE.

employment at will Common law principle that employees may be discharged at the prerogative of the employer.

A Tennessee court in 1884 explained the principle as: "All may dismiss their employee(s) at-will, be they many or few, for good cause, for no cause, or even for cause morally wrong without being thereby guilty of legal wrong." (*Payne v. Western & A.R.R. Co.,* 81 Tenn 507 (1884)).

Collective bargaining contract provisions and statutory restrictions, including prohibitions against discharge because of race, sex, national origin, or union activity, can restrict the right of employers to discharge employees at will and safeguard the rights of unprotected employees. In some states, courts have ruled that there are public policy exceptions to the common law doctrine. Examples of these exceptions include attendance at jury duty or military service. Courts have also taken the position that company manuals or handbooks or even employment interviews constitute "implied contracts" to which an employer is legally bound to adhere.

Source references: Frederick Brown, "Limiting Your Risks in the New Russian Roulette—Discharging Employees," *Employee Relations LJ,* Winter 1982/83; BNA, *The Employment-at-Will Issue* (Washington: 1982); Michael J. Klinger, "The Future of Employment Security," *LLJ,* Oct. 1976; Gordon E. Krischer, "The Growing Arsenal of Rights of Unrepresented Employees: Recent Trends in the Common-Law Employment At-Will Doctrine and Employee Privacy," *Labor Law Developments 1982,* Proceedings of the 28th Annual Institute on Labor Law, SLF (New York: Bender, 1982); Theodore A. Olsen, "Wrongful Discharge Claims Raised by At Will Employees: A New Legal Concern for Employers," *LLJ,* May 1981; Clyde W. Summers, "Protecting *All* Employees Against Unjust Dismissal," *Harvard BR,* Jan./Feb. 1980; Richard G. Vernon and Peter S. Gray, "Termination At Will—The Employer's Right to Fire," *Employee Relations LJ,* Summer 1980; Stuart A. Youngblood and Gary L. Tidwell, "Termination At Will: Some Changes in the Wind," *Personnel,* May/June 1981.

See also WRONGFUL DISCHARGE.

employment contract The relationship created when an employer hires an employee to perform work.

See also COLLECTIVE BARGAINING.

employment controls Generally applies to those regulations issued during periods of war emergency when the government is seeking to mobilize its manpower into channels producing goods and services for the war effort. The War Manpower Commission had responsibility during World War II to exercise those controls considered necessary to effective prosecution of the war.

employment cost index (ECI) According to BLS, the ECI is

> [a] quarterly measure of the change in the price of labor, free from the influence of employment shifts among occupations and industries. The ECI wage and salary series is limited to changes in wage and salary rates, defined as straight-time average hourly earnings. Straight-time earnings are total earnings before payroll deductions, excluding premium pay for overtime, work on

weekends and holidays, and shift differentials. Production bonuses, incentive earnings, commission payments, and cost-of-living adjustments are included in straight-time earnings, whereas nonproduction bonuses (such as Christmas or year-end bonuses) are excluded. Also excluded are such items as payments-in-kind, free room and board, and tips.

The ECI has been issued since December 1975, and was once referred to as the general wage index. The ECI enables users to compare rates of change by occupation, industry, geographic area, and union coverage; it is reported in *Current Wage Developments*, a BLS monthly publication.

Source references: Daniel M. Kohler, "The Employment Cost Index: A Review of the Statistics," *MLR*, Jan. 1978; Beth Levin, "The Employment Cost Index: Recent Trends and Expansion," *MLR*, May 1982; Victor J. Sheifer, "Employment Cost Index: A Measure of Change in the 'Price of Labor'," *MLR*, July 1975; ———, "How Benefits Will Be Incorporated into the Employment Cost Index," *MLR*, Jan. 1978; Patricia B. Smith, "The Employment Cost Index in 1980: A First Look at Total Compensation," *MLR*, June 1981; U.S. Dept. of Labor, BLS, *BLS Handbook of Methods* (Washington: Bull. 2134–1, 1982); *U.S. Dept. of Labor News*, Feb. 3, 1983; G. Donald Wood, Jr., "Estimation Procedures for the Employment Cost Index," *MLR*, May 1982.

employment division That section of the personnel department of a large company which handles recruitment and placement.

See also PERSONNEL DEPARTMENT.

employment exchanges *See* EMPLOYMENT AGENCIES.

employment forecasting Projecting for either short or long periods estimates of total employment in a particular industry, region, state, or country. Individual companies may desire to determine employment needs over a period of time to adequately take care of their future needs.

employment guarantee A system or plan designed to provide steady employment during the year by assuring a certain fixed number of weeks of work, or an equivalent in wages.

See also GUARANTEED ANNUAL WAGE, SUPPLEMENTAL UNEMPLOYMENT BENEFITS.

employment history The individual personnel record of each employee which contains the most important information about the worker. It should provide all the information necessary to make a decision about the employee in case of transfer, promotion, layoff, or other personnel action. Typical documents may include the original application blank, records of pay changes, promotions, training or education completed, congratulatory or disciplinary notices, and the like.

Source references: Philip G. Benson, "Personal Privacy and the Personnel Record," *PJ*, July 1978; D. Jan Duffy, "Privacy vs. Disclosure: Balancing Employee and Employer Rights," *Employee Relations LJ*, Spring 1982; Felician F. Foltman, *Manpower Information for Effective Management. Part I: Collecting and Managing Employee Information* (Ithaca: Cornell Univ., NYSSILR, Key Issues Series no. 10, 1973); John C. Fox and Paul J. Ostling, "Employee and Government Access to Personnel Files: Rights and Requirements," *Employee Relations LJ*, Summer 1979; Denise Hauselt, "Employee Privacy, Information Needs, and the Law," *Industrial and Labor Relations Forum*, Jan. 1980; Marion G. Hughes and Beverly Nicholson, "As You Were Saying—Handling Personnel History Records," *PJ*, July/Aug. 1961; Ronald A. Leahy, "Four Keys to Information Disclosure," *LLJ*, July 1978; David F. Linowes, "Employee Rights to Privacy and Access to Personnel Records: A New Look," *Employee Relations LJ*, Summer 1978; Mordechai Mironi, "The Confidentiality of Personnel Records: A Legal and Ethical View," *LLJ*, May 1974; Erwin S. Stanton, "The Discharged Employee and the EEO Laws," *PJ*, March 1976.

See also FORMS AND RECORDS, INVENTORY OF EMPLOYEE SKILLS.

employment interview One of the most widely used techniques in the selection of employees. It is generally used after preliminary application forms, tests, background checks, and other measures of fitness have been obtained and a final decision has to be made—usually among a small number of applicants who have survived preliminary screening. The interview may involve individuals at various levels of the administrative hierarchy before the final choice is made.

The employment interview should serve as a final check and summation of pertinent factors needed by the applicant for the job and to make sure that the successful applicant is fully aware of what is needed by him to perform successfully when he reports for work.

Source references: Richard D. Arvey and James E. Campion, "The Employment Interview: A Summary and Review of Recent Research," *Personnel Psychology,* Summer 1982; Glenn A. Bassett, *Practical Interviewing: A Handbook for Managers* (New York: AMA, 1965); Jack Bucalo, "The Balanced Approach to Successful Screening Interviews," *PJ,* Aug. 1978; John W. Cogger, "Are You a Skilled Interviewer," *PJ,* Nov. 1982; Calvin W. Downs, "A Content Analysis of Twenty Selection Interviews," *Personnel Administration/Public Personnel Review,* Sept./Oct. 1972; Barbara Felton and Sue Ries Lamb, "A Model for Systematic Selection Interviewing," *Personnel,* Jan./Feb. 1982; Susan Greco, *The Oral Interview as a Selection Technique: Some Suggested Formats and Guidelines for Structuring the Interview Process* (Chicago: U.S. CSC, 1978); Dennis L. Huett, *Improving the Selection Interview in a Civil Service Setting* (Chicago: IPMA, 1976); Newell C. Kephart, *The Employment Interview in Industry* (New York: McGraw-Hill, 1952); Felix M. Lopez, *Personnel Interviewing, Theory and Practice* (2d ed., New York: McGraw-Hill, 1975); Milton M. Mandell, *The Employment Interview* (New York: AMA, Research Study 47, 1961); Gail M. Martin, "Getting Chosen: The Job Interview and Before," *Occupational Outlook Quarterly,* Spring 1979; Louis A. Ordini, Jr., "Why Interview?" *PJ,* June 1968; Elliott D. Pursell, Michael A. Campion, and Sarah R. Gaylord, "Structured Interviewing: Avoiding Selection Problems," *PJ,* Nov. 1980; Allen J. Schuh, "Effects of Interview Rating Form Content and Rater Experience on the Evaluation of a Job Applicant," *Personnel Psychology,* Summer 1973; Nancy J. Schweitzer and John Deely, "Interviewing the Disabled Job Applicant," *PJ,* March 1982; Claudio R. Serafini, "Interviewer Listening," *PJ,* July 1975; Lawrence L. Steinmetz, *Interviewing Skills for Supervisory Personnel* (Reading, Mass.: Addison-Wesley, 1971).

See also ABSENTEE INTERVIEW, EXIT INTERVIEW, SELECTION INTERVIEW, SELECTION OF EMPLOYEES.

employment manager Sometimes used interchangeably with personnel director or personnel manager. The employment manager's prime function is to coordinate and supervise the operation of the personnel department, including the hiring, training, and discharge of employees. Where substantial responsibility is provided "down the line," general policy coordination is still effected through the central personnel office and the employment manager or director.

The term also has been used to describe the official in charge of the employment division of a large personnel department. The responsibility of such a person relates to the various aspects of employment, such as information dealing with the labor supply in the community, selection, initial introduction of the worker to the job, a follow up, and possibly the handling of exit interviews. In such an organization the employment manager would be under the direction of, and report to, the director of personnel, who will be in charge of all divisions, including employment, promotions, transfers, training, job and wage analysis, health, welfare and safety, research, and contract negotiations and administration.

Source references: AMA, *How to Establish and Maintain a Personnel Department* (New York: Research Report no. 4, 1944); Walter D. Scott, Robert C. Clothier, and William R. Spriegel, *Personnel Management* (6th ed., New York: McGraw-Hill, 1961); Gordon S. Watkins et al., *The Management of Personnel and Labor Relations* (New York: McGraw-Hill, 1950).

See also PERSONNEL DIRECTOR.

employment relations The phrase refers to the broad range of relationships that exist in, or arise out of, employment of workers by an employer. Occasionally the phrase "employer-employee relations" is used instead of employment relations.

The phrase has also been used synonymously with labor-management relations, industrial relations, or labor relations. Some restrict use of "industrial relations" to a formal organized relationship resulting from collective bargaining and the existence of a labor union acting for the employees, while applying "employer-employee relations" to all plant relationships whether with organized or unorganized employees.

Source reference: Harold S. Roberts, *Labor-Management Relations in the Public Service* (Honolulu: Univ. of Hawaii Press, 1970).

See also EMPLOYER-EMPLOYEE RELATIONS, INDUSTRIAL RELATIONS.

Employment Service *See* U.S. EMPLOYMENT SERVICE.

employment stabilization Refers to efforts on the part of employers, employees, and government to achieve greater regularity or stability in employment. Efforts of individual companies are directed toward greater product diversification, producing "off season" items to pick up slack in sales, and similar activities to stabilize production and sales staffs. Efforts of employees have been directed toward some form of guaranteed employment or wage payments to tide them over a period of unemployment. Efforts of government take the form of financial incentives, tax benefits, government contracts, unemployment benefits, and other means to prevent serious fluctuations in employment—particularly when they are downward and may lead to a serious depression.

Basically, employment stabilization programs embody the efforts made by a competitive society to minimize the effect of recurring business fluctuations.

Source references: AEI, *Reducing Unemployment, The Humphrey-Hawkins and Kemp-McClure Bills* (Washington: 1976); Fred Best and Barry Stern, "Education, Work, and Leisure: Must They Come in That Order?" *MLR*, July 1977; Paul H. Douglas and Aaron Director, *The Problem of Unemployment* (New York: Macmillan, 1931); Gary C. Fethke, Andrew J. Policano, and Samuel H. Williamson, *An Investigation of the Conceptual and Qualitative Impact of Employment Tax Credits* (Kalamazoo: Upjohn Institute for Employment Research, 1978); Charles G. Gibbons, *Stabilization of Employment is Good Management* (Kalamazoo: Upjohn Institute for Community Research, 1953); G. William Miller, "The Not Impossible Goal: Full Employment and Price Stability," *Across the Board*, March 1978; National Manpower Policy Task Force, *The Best Way to Reduce Unemployment is to Create More Jobs* (Washington: 1975); Bertil G. Ohlin, *The Problem of Employment Stabilization* (New York: Columbia UP, 1949); Laurence S. Seidman, *The Design of Federal Employment Programs* (Lexington, Mass.: Lexington Books, 1975); U.S. Congress, Senate, Committee on Labor and Public Policy, *Emergency Jobs Programs Extension Act of 1976, Report* (Washington: 1976); U.S. Dept. of Labor, ETA, *Perspectives on Public Job Creation* (Washington: R & D Monograph 52, 1977).

See also FULL EMPLOYMENT, GUARANTEED ANNUAL WAGE, SUPPLEMENTAL UNEMPLOYMENT BENEFITS, UNEMPLOYMENT BENEFITS.

Employment Standards Administration (ESA) An agency within the Department of Labor that oversees minimum wage and overtime programs, registration of farm labor contractors, prevailing wage rates and affirmative action programs of government contractors, and workers compensation programs for federal and certain private employers and employees. These programs are carried out by the Wage and Hour Division, the Office of Federal Contract Compliance Programs, and the Office of Workers' Compensation Programs. The Employment Standards Administration together with the Wage and Hour Division and the OFCCP maintain 10 regional offices; the Workers' Compensation program has 21 district offices.

Address: 200 Constitution Ave., N.W., Washington, D.C. 20210. Tel. (202) 523–8743

employment statistics Data published by governmental and private agencies embodying attempts to estimate the total labor force, employment, and unemployment. BLS and the Bureau of the Census make and publish regular estimates of employment. Data are published in *Employment and Earnings*, *Monthly Labor Review*, and *Survey of Current Business*. Special reports also are issued from time to time.

Source references: Daniel H. Brill, "Unemployment Measures for Government and Business Policy Formulations," *Proceedings of the 27th A/M, IRRA*, ed. by James Stern and Barbara Dennis (Madison: 1975); Ernest J. Eberling and Charles S. Bullock, Jr., "Employment Statistics and Manpower," *ILRR*, Jan. 1952; James Hanna, "The Federal-State Approach to Labor Statistics," *MLR*, Oct. 1977; Wendell D. MacDonald, "The Early History of Labor Statistics in the United States," *Labor History*, Spring 1972; Geoffrey H. Moore, *Improving the Presentation of Employment and Unemployment Statistics* (Washington: U.S. National Commission on Employment and Unemployment Statistics, Background Paper no. 22, 1978); Herbert Morton, A. H. Raskin, and Julius Duscha, *Views on Employment Statistics From the Press, Business, Labor and Congress* (Washington: U.S. National Commission on Employment and Unemployment Statistics, Background Paper no. 23, 1979); National Science Foundation, *Methodology of Statistics on Research and Development* (Washington: 1959); Janet L. Norwood, "Reshaping a Statistical Program to Meet Legislative Priorities," *MLR*, Nov. 1977; Robert L. Stein, "National Commission Recommends Changes in Labor Force Statistics," *MLR*, April 1980; U.S. Dept. of Commerce, *An Error Profile: Employment as Measured by the Current Population Survey* (Washington: Statistical Policy WP 3, 1978); U.S. Dept. of Labor, BLS, *Employment and Earning Statistics for the United States, 1909–1978* (Washington: Bull 1312–11, 1979); ———, *Supplement to Employment and Earning Statistics for States and Areas, 1977–81* (Washington: Bull 1370–16, 1982); James R. Wetzel, "Bureau of Labor Statistics Actions to Improve Current Labor Force Statistics," *Proceedings of the 27th A/M, IRRA*, ed. by James Stern and Barbara Dennis (Madison: 1975); Seymour Wolfbein, *Establishment Reporting in the United States* (Washington: U.S. National Commission on Employment and Unemployment Statistics, Background Paper no. 2, 1978).

See also LABOR FORCE, UNEMPLOYMENT.

enabling legislation A statute passed by a state legislature which makes it possible to receive certain benefits under a federal law, or generally, any act which removes a restriction or disability. Because of the federal-state character of our government, it is frequently necessary to implement legislation through such enabling procedures. In certain other areas, the federal government may grant authority to the states to legislate in fields which the federal government has preempted. For example, under the Taft-Hartley Act Congress has permitted states to pass legislation in the field of union security more stringent than the federal statute.

See also PREEMPTION, DOCTRINE OF; RIGHT TO WORK LAW; UNION SECURITY CLAUSES.

end run bargaining A practice of the union bargaining representative to bypass the chief management negotiator and to negotiate with higher level management officials in order to secure more favorable terms. This occurs most frequently in the public sector where union negotiators may make their appeals directly to the elected government representatives and bypass the appointed management spokesperson.

Source references: Thomas A. Kochan, "A Theory of Multilateral Collective Bargaining in City Governments," *ILRR*, July 1974; Jay S. Siegel and Burton Kainen, "Political Forces in Public Sector Collective Bargaining," 21 *Catholic University LR* 581 (1972).

See also "CAROM" LOBBYING, END RUN LOBBYING, MULTILATERAL BARGAINING.

end run lobbying A strategy used by public sector unions to bring political pressure on elected officials while negotiations are in progress in order to obtain management concessions.

Source references: Michael H. Moskow, J. Joseph Lowenberg, and Edward Clifford Koziara, *Collective Bargaining in Public Employment* (New York: Random House, 1970); Jay S. Siegel and Burton Kainen, "Political Forces in Public Sector Collective Bargaining," 21 *Catholic University LR* 581 (1972).

See also "CAROM" LOBBYING.

end spurt Increased output and effort toward the completion of a task, or the end of a work period. This increased production may occur even though the worker may be tired toward the end of the day or the assignment.

enforced delay *See* COOLING-OFF PERIOD.

enforced membership A procedure, usually under the provisions of the collective bargaining agreement (prior to Taft-Hartley) whereby all new employees were required to be or become members of the union and remain in good standing as a condition of employment. In trades which have not used the written contract, such an arrangement was accomplished as a matter of practice. Under this type of union security (closed shop) it was frequently the practice to have the employer ask the union to provide the employees needed for the various jobs in the plant.

See also CLOSED SHOP, HIRING HALL, UNION SECURITY CLAUSES.

enforcement of agreement Collective bargaining agreements are generally self-enforceable. The provisions of the agreement set forth the conditions of employment during the contract period. Both parties agree to abide by the terms. Differences as to the interpretation or application of the contract generally are subject to the grievance machinery and arbitration. A wide variety of measures exists to protect the contract and to prevent strikes or lockouts during its term.

Some contracts place the responsibility on the union to discipline members for contract violation. One such contract reads:

> The union is charged with the responsibility of enforcing the terms of this agreement on the part of the members of the union, and in the event that any provisions of this agreement are violated by one or more of the employees, members of the union, such employee or employees shall be deemed thereby to have terminated their employment; and the union will undertake to discipline such employee or employees and to take such other action as may be sufficient to prevent recurrence of violation.

Other contracts may permit the parties to use the courts to enforce agreements. For example: "It is agreed that either party hereto shall have the right to have the agreement specifically enforced and to prevent the violation thereof by injunction or other proper decree of any court of competent jurisdiction."

Such a clause is not needed where the parties are in interstate commerce and covered by Title III of the Taft-Hartley Act, which sets up procedures for actions in the district courts of the United States for violation of contracts between employers and labor organizations.

Source references: Richard W. Duesenberg, "Enforcement of Collective Bargaining Agreements in Missouri," *Univ. of Kansas City LR*, Winter 1955/56; Seymour P. Kaye and E. G. Allen, "Union Responsibility and Enforcement of Collective Bargaining Agreements—Study of Background and Application of Section 301 of Labor-Management Relations Act of 1947," *Boston Univ. LR*, Jan. 1950; John H. Kirkwood, "The Enforcement of Collective Bargaining Contracts—A Summary," *LLJ*, Feb. 1964; Paul S. Kuelthau, "Contract Enforcement and the Courts," *LLJ*, Sept. 1964; Fred D. Smith, "Section 301 and State Court Injunctions to Enforce Collective Bargaining Agreements," *Washington LR*, Summer 1962; Benjamin Wyle, "Unions in Search of a Forum to Enforce Contracts," *LLJ*, July 1956.

See also AGREEMENT ENFORCEMENT.

enforcement of arbitration agreement The procedure available to the parties to carry out their agreement for final and binding determination of various types of labor disputes. In general practice the collective bargaining agreement provides machinery for the handling of grievances arising out of the application or interpretation of the agreement with arbitration as the terminal point in the machinery. Labor and management usually abide by the contract provisions.

Occasionally the language in the contract defining a "grievance" limits the scope of arbitration or, according to one of the parties to the agreement, is not intended to permit certain issues to be decided by the arbitration machinery. Where either party contends that an issue is "not arbitrable," the dispute may remain unresolved. The issue may be resolved by enforcing the arbitration agreement—by submission of the question of "arbitrability" to an arbitrator, by taking the issue to the courts to require arbitration, or occasionally by economic action.

Source references: Charles O. Gregory and R. M. Orlikoff, "Enforcement of Labor Arbitration Agreements," *Univ. of Chicago LR*, Winter 1950; Isadore and David Jaffe, "Enforcing Labor Arbitration Clauses by Section 301, Taft-Hartley Act," *AJ*, Vol. 8, no. 2, 1953.

See also ARBITRABILITY, ARBITRATION.

enforcement strike A concerted stoppage of work for the purpose of maintaining existing conditions of employment. Where the union or employees feel that the employer is seeking to change existing practices or acts contrary to the provisions of the agreement they may seek to enforce the contract by refusing to work until such practices are reinstated. Such strikes are generally held by employers to be in violation of the terms of the agreement. They contend that if the employer's actions are in violation of the agreement the union has an adequate remedy by filing a grievance under the terms of the contract.

Occasionally contracts may permit the union to strike where the employer has refused to honor an arbitration award.

engagement *See* HIRING, RECRUITING.

Engel's law A generalization arrived at by Ernst Engel (1821–1896), German economist and statistician, based on studies of Prussian family budgets, that the percentage spent on food is smaller for those in the higher-income brackets than for those in the low-income group. Engel also noted that the percentage spent for sundries increased as the income increased.

Source references: James H. Dodd and Carl W. Hasek, *Economics, Principles and Applications* (3d ed., Cincinnati: South-Western Publishing, 1957); "Engel, Ernst," *International Encyclopedia of the Social Sciences*, ed. by David L. Sills (Vol. 5, New York: Macmillan & Free Press, 1968).

Engineers and Scientists; Association of (Ind) The union merged with the American Federation of Government Employees (AFL-CIO) on April 1, 1971.

See also GOVERNMENT EMPLOYEES; AMERICAN FEDERATION OF (AFL-CIO).

Engineers and Scientists of California A branch of the National Marine Engineers' Beneficial Association (AFL-CIO). Its bimonthly publication is the *ESC Newsletter*.

Address: 340 Fremont St., San Francisco, Calif. 94105. Tel. (415) 433–7280

English workweek The term applied to the working practice in England in the 1920s which set the workweek at eight hours for Monday through Friday and four hours on Saturday morning. This gave the worker additional time off on Saturday afternoon as well as Sunday, the traditional day of rest. It is also referred to at times as the 44-hour week.

Source reference: "Forty-Four Hour Week in New South Wales," *MLR*, May 1931.

Engravers and Sketchmakers, Inc.; Friendly Society of (Ind) An independent group of skilled journeymen organized in January 1874. It remained independent except for the period 1933–1935, when it was affiliated with the AFL. It merged with the Machine Printers' Beneficial Association on October 1, 1960. The union later changed its name to the Machine Printers and Engravers Association of the United States (Ind).

See also MACHINE PRINTERS AND ENGRAVERS ASSOCIATION OF THE UNITED STATES (IND).

enjoin A court action designed to prevent a union from engaging in economic or strike action, or requiring it to take certain action calculated to remedy an inequity. An employer or corporation also may be enjoined during a labor dispute.

Source references: In re Debs, 158 US 564 (1895); Felix Frankfurter and Nathan Greene, *The Labor Injunction* (New York: Macmillan, 1930); Melvin J. Segal, *The Norris-LaGuardia Act and the Courts* (Washington: American Council on Public Affairs, 1942); Edwin E. Witte, *The Government in Labor Disputes* (New York: McGraw-Hill, 1932).

See also INJUNCTION, NORRIS-LAGUARDIA ACT.

enterprise unionism A type of union organization where employees of the same firm, irrespective of whether they are blue-collar, white-collar, or lower-management workers, are organized together in a single union. It differs from the so-called "company union" in that it is organized on the workers' own initiative and by their own free choice; it is favored by employers in that all union members are company employees who can be expected to share similar interests with the management and therefore be less prone to strike. It is characterized by strong independent unions and a lack of control by the federations over the individual unions.

In Japan, enterprise unionism is the principal form of organization, covering more than 90 percent of unionized workers and involving more than 65,000 enterprise unions. Affiliation with national confederations such as *Sohyo* and *Domei* is established primarily to serve informational and political purposes only.

Source references: Tadashi Hanami, *Labor Relations in Japan Today* (Tokyo: Kodansha International, 1979); ILO, *Labour Relations and Development: Country Studies on Japan, the Philippines, Singapore and Sri Lanka* (Geneva: Labour-Management Relations Series 59, 1982); Kazuo Okochi, Bernard Karsh, and Solomon B. Levine (ed.), *Workers and Employers in Japan: The Japanese Employment Relations System* (Princeton: Princeton UP, 1974); OECD, *The Development of Industrial Relations Systems, Some Implications of Japanese Experience* (Paris: 1977); Taishiro Shirai (ed.), *Contemporary Industrial Relations in Japan* (Madison: Univ. of Wisconsin Press, 1983).

See also LIFETIME EMPLOYMENT SYSTEM, SENIORITY WAGE SYSTEM.

entrance rate The hourly rate of pay an employee receives when first hired by the company. The rate of pay may be the entrance rate for the particular job or occupation, or it may be the lowest entrance rate for unskilled labor. The latter is sometimes referred to as the minimum plant rate for common or unskilled work. In skilled jobs which have a definite rate range or fixed minimum with periodic adjustments based on performance or length of service, the entrance rate for the job may be in the nature of a probationary hourly rate. Afted a fixed period during which the employee's performance is watched and is found satisfactory, he will then move to the job rate.

See also BEGINNER'S RATE.

entrepreneur Technically an undertaker or enterpriser, the person, group, or organization which brings together the other factors in production in order to provide goods or services. The entrepreneur may also have a substantial investment in the enterprise, but he contributes more than capital. He may be responsible for initiating, planning, and providing managerial know-how to the functioning of the enterprise.

ephemeral union A labor organization which has only a brief period of existence. It may also have reference to the early precursors of modern unionism, such as the trade clubs. The Webbs have contended that these ephemeral organizations were not actually kin to the modern trade unions which arose out of the problems created by the industrial revolution.

Source reference: Sidney and Beatrice Webb, *The History of Trade Unionism* (rev. ed., London: Longmans, Green, 1920).

equal distribution of work Procedures designed to provide an opportunity for all employees to share equally in the work that is available. During periods of unemployment these procedures may be carried out with the support of the union. Generally the distribution of available work is not so arranged as to make it impossible for those remaining on the payroll to earn a decent weekly income.

Equal-distribution-of-work arrangements also may be designed to provide an opportunity for equitable sharing of available overtime in the plant.

equal employment opportunity (EEO) Policy and practice designed to guarantee individuals fair access to all available jobs and training programs under equal terms and conditions with equal benefits and services and without consideration of the applicants' race, sex, national origin, age, or religion. The term includes equality in recruitment, hiring, layoff, discharge, recall, promotion, training, responsibility, wages, sick leave, vacation, overtime, insurance, retirement and pension benefits, and rest periods.

The EEO concept originated out of legislation passed during the Civil War and Reconstruction era to help former slaves achieve economic freedom. The enactment of the Civil Rights Act of 1964 set in motion the administrative apparatus for achieving equality of employment opportunity.

Source references: BNA, *Equal Employment Opportunity: Programs and Results* (Washington: PPF no. 112, 1976); Robert Freiberg (ed.), *The Manager's Guide to Equal*

Employment Opportunity (New York: Executive Enterprise, 1977); Eli Ginzberg, "EEO's Next Frontier: Assignment, Training, and Promotion," *Employee Relations LJ*, Summer 1978; William H. Holley and Hubert S. Feild, "Equal Employment Opportunity and its Implications for Personnel Practices," *LLJ*, May 1976; William T. Hudson and Walter D. Broadnax, "Equal Employment Opportunity as Public Policy," *Public Personnel Management*, Fall 1982; William J. Kilberg, "Progress and Problems in Equal Employment Opportunity," *LLJ*, Oct. 1973; David H. Rosenbloom, *Federal Equal Employment Opportunity: Politics and Public Personnel Administration* (New York: Praeger, 1977); U.S. Commission on Civil Rights, *A Guide to Federal Laws Prohibiting Sex Discrimination* (Washington: 1974).

See also AFFIRMATIVE ACTION, CIVIL RIGHTS ACT OF 1964.

Equal Employment Opportunity Act of 1972 A law signed on March 24, 1972, amending Title VII of the Civil Rights Act of 1964. The amendment extended coverage of Title VII to include, among others, state and local governments and educational institutions, employers with 15 and more employees, and labor unions with 15 and more members.

The amendment empowers the EEOC to seek injunctive and other relief in federal district court against an employer, union, employment agency, or joint labor-management committee when it is not able to obtain a conciliation agreement. In cases involving state or local governments, the attorney general is authorized to bring the suit. It also requires the EEOC to notify an aggrieved party if a complaint is dimissed by the Commission, a complaint is not issued, or if the Commission does not enter into a conciliation agreement.

The EEOC and the Justice Department retain concurrent jurisdiction for two years to settle unlawful employment practice cases. The Commission has exclusive jurisdiction after the two-year period.

Source reference: BNA, *The Equal Employment Opportunity Act of 1972* (Washington: 1973).

Equal Employment Opportunity Commission A five-member commission appointed by the President of the United States under the provisions of Title VII of the Civil Rights Act of 1964. The function of the Commission is to administer provisions of Title VII which make it unlawful for employers to refuse to hire, or discharge, or otherwise discriminate against, any individual by reason of race, color, religion, sex, or national origin. Employment agencies and unions are also forbidden to engage in such discrimination. In July 1979, the administration of the Equal Pay Act was transferred to the EEOC by Reorganization Plan No. 1 of 1978.

Source references: "A Conversation with Eleanor Holmes Norton," *Employee Relations LJ*, Winter 1978; Alfred W. Blumrosen, "Labor Arbitration, EEOC Conciliation, and Discrimination in Employment," *AJ*, Vol. 24, no. 2, 1969; Luther Holcomb, "The Equal Employment Opportunity Commission and Labor," *NYU 20th Annual Conference on Labor*, ed. by Thomas Christensen (New York: Bender, 1968); Issie L. Jenkins, "Developments at the Equal Employment Opportunity Commission," *NYU 29th Annual Conference on Labor*, ed. by Richard Adelman (New York: Bender, 1977); Lawrence Allen Katz, "Investigation and Conciliation of Employment Discrimination Charges Under Title VII: Employers' Rights in an Adversary Process," *IR Law Digest*, Fall 1977; Eleanor Holmes Norton, "Overhauling the EEOC," *LLJ*, Nov. 1977; Lowell W. Perry, "The Mandate and Impact of Title VII," *LLJ*, Dec. 1975; William E. Pollard, "The Need for Expanded EEOC Conciliation Efforts Under Title VII," *Proceedings of the 27th A/M, IRRA*, ed. by James Stern and Barbara Dennis (Madison: 1975); J. Clay Smith, Jr., "The EEOC Today—An Update for the 1980s: A New Creativity," *Labor Law Developments 1981*, Proceedings of the 27th Annual Institute on Labor Law, SLF (New York: Bender, 1981); J. Clay Smith, Jr., and John D. Schmelzer, "Overlapping Jurisdiction of the EEOC and NLRB," *LLJ*, July 1980; Evangeline W. Swift, "An Overview of the Equal Employment Opportunity Commission's Litigation Program: Procedural Developments; Substantial Legal Developments," *Labor Law Developments 1977*, Proceedings of the 23d Annual

Institute on Labor Law, SLF (New York: Bender, 1977); U.S. EEOC, *Laws Administered by EEOC* (Washington: 1981); U.S. GAO, *Further Improvements Needed in EEOC Enforcement Activities* (Washington: 1981); ———, *The Equal Employment Opportunity Commission Has Made Limited Progress in Eliminating Employment Discrimination* (Washington: 1976); Benjamin W. Wolkinson, *Blacks, Unions, and the EEOC: A Study of Administrative Futility* (Lexington, Mass.: Lexington Books, 1973).

See also CIVIL RIGHTS ACT OF 1964.

Equal Employment Opportunity Coordinating Council A commission created by the Equal Employment Opportunity Act of 1972 to coordinate the work of the various federal agencies responsible for the implementation and enforcement of equal employment opportunity legislation, orders, and policies. The panel was composed of the secretary of labor, the attorney general, and the chairpersons of the Equal Employment Opportunity Commission, the Civil Service Commission, and the Civil Rights Commission. The Council was abolished by Reorganization Plan No. 1 of 1978 and its functions were transferred to the EEOC.

Source reference: Civil Rights Act of 1964, as amended, Section 715, 42 U.S.C. 2000e–14 (1982).

equal employment opportunity in government Executive Order 11478, issued by President Nixon on August 8, 1969, provides federal employees with protection against discrimination by reason of race, color, religion, sex, or national origin.

Source reference: "President Nixon Issues Executive Order on Equal Employment Opportunity in Government," *Daily Labor Report,* No. 155, Aug. 12, 1969.

equal employment opportunity plan A plan required of federal agencies covered by Section 717, Title VII of the Civil Rights Act. A national and regional plan must be submitted to the EEOC by the agencies and departments. The plan must include "(1) provision for the establishment of training and education programs designed to provide a maximum opportunity for employees to advance so as to perform at their highest potential; and (2) a description of the qualifications in terms of training and experience relating to equal employment opportunity for the principal and operating officials of each such department, agency, or unit responsible for carrying out the equal opportunity program and of the allocation of personnel and resources proposed . . . to carry out . . . [the] program."

Source reference: Civil Rights Act of 1964, as amended, Section 717, 42 U.S.C. 2000e–16 (1982).

equalization pay *See* CONSUMER PRICE INDEX, COST-OF-LIVING ADJUSTMENT, ESCALATOR CLAUSE.

equal opportunity clause The seven subparagraphs requiring compliance with EEO/AA law, rules, and regulations contained in Section 202 of Executive Order 11246 and required for inclusion in all contracts covered by the Executive Order.

Source references: Executive Order 11246, 3 C.F.R. (1964–65 Comp.) 339; U.S. OFCCP, "Construction Contractors—Affirmative Action Requirements," 41 C.F.R. 60–4; ———, "Obligations of Contractors and Subcontractors," 41 C.F.R. 60–1.

Equal Pay Act of 1963 A law enacted June 10, 1963, aimed at the elimination of differentials in pay based solely on sex. It makes it unlawful for an employer to pay wages "at a rate less than the rate at which he pays wages to employees of the opposite sex in such establishment for equal work on jobs the performance of which requires equal skill, effort, and responsibility, and which are performed under similar working conditions, except where such payment is made pursuant to (i) a seniority system; (ii) a merit system; (iii) a system which measures earnings by quantity or quality of production; or (iv) a differential based on any other factor other than sex: *Provided,* that an employer who is paying a wage rate differential in violation of this subsection shall not, in order to comply with the provisions of this subsection, reduce the wage rate of any employee."

Since the Equal Pay Act took the form of an amendment to Section 6 of the Fair Labor Standards Act, its coverage is the same as that of the minimum wage provisions of the basic law. The general effective date of the equal pay standard was one year after the date of enactment, or June 11, 1964. However, in the case of employees covered by a bona fide collective bargaining agreement in effect on or before May 11, 1963, the effective date was deferred until the expiration date of the contract or June 11, 1965, whichever came first.

The administration of the Equal Pay Act was transferred to the EEOC on July 1, 1979, by Reorganization Plan No. 1 of 1978.

Source references: Fair Labor Standards Act of 1938, Fair Labor Standards Act of 1938, as amended, Section 6(d), 29 U.S.C. 206(d) (1982); Margaret Anne Bentson, "Dissonant Chords—Developments Under the Equal Pay Act of 1963," *Industrial and Labor Relations Forum,* Vol. 13, no. 2, 1979; James A. Buford, Jr. and Dwight R. Norris, "A Salary Equalization Model: Identifying and Correcting Sex-Based Salary Differences," *Employee Relations LJ,* Winter 1980/81; BNA, *Equal Pay for Equal Work* (Washington: 1963); ———, *Impact of the Equal Pay Act* (Washington: PPF Survey no. 75, 1964); John E. Burns and Catherine G. Burns, "An Analysis of the Equal Pay Act," *LLJ,* Feb. 1973; Donald Elisburg, "Equal Pay in the United States: The Development and Implementation of the Equal Pay Act of 1963," *LLJ,* April 1978; Paul S. Greenlaw and John P. Kohl, "The EEOC's New Equal Pay Act Guidelines," *PJ,* July 1982; Richard F. Richards, "Monetary Awards in Equal Pay Litigation," *IR Law Digest,* Summer 1976; Harry Sangerman, "A Look at the Equal Pay Act in Practice," *LLJ,* May 1971; Morag Macleod Simchak, "Equal Pay in the United States," *ILR,* June 1971; George R. Wendt, "Should Courts Write Your Job Descriptions?" *PJ,* Sept. 1976.

See also BENNETT AMENDMENT, EQUAL PAY FOR EQUAL WORK, FAIR LABOR STANDARDS ACT OF 1938.

equal pay for equal work A principle which seeks to establish job rates which are not dependent upon factors unrelated to quantity or quality of work, such as race, sex, and other such factors. During World War II, women replaced men on many war production jobs and frequent claims of inequitable treatment were made to the National War Labor Board. The Board developed a policy which it promulgated in General Order 16 and which it followed in its decisions.

In the *American Brass* case (Case No. 2258–D, 9 *WLR* 850) decided June 19, 1943, the Board held that: "The same rates of pay shall apply on all operations which were formerly performed by men and are now being performed by women employees unless there have been changes in job content whereby these operations require servicing by men employees, which were not required prior to such changes."

The Board also directed that questions arising out the interpretations of its equal pay for equal work policy be handled through the grievance machinery and arbitration. The *California Packing* case (Case No. 111–9228–D, 18 *WLR* 711) decided September 23, 1944, is a case in point. It provided that:

> Wage rates for women shall be set in accordance with the principle of equal pay for comparable quantity and quality of work on comparable occupations.
>
> When women take the place of men and fully perform all the tasks previously performed by men they shall be paid the same wages as the men thus replaced.
>
> Any dispute arising as to the question of quality, quantity, or comparability as herein defined shall be subject to final determination by the grievance machinery if such provides for final arbitration or, if otherwise, by an arbitrator appointed by the Twelfth Regional War Labor Board.

Source references: Alice H. Cook, "Equal Pay: Where Is It?" *IR,* May 1975; Marguerite J. Fisher, "Equal Pay for Equal Work Legislation," *ILRR,* Oct. 1948; Michael J. Klapper, "The Limitations of the Equal Pay Principle: A Critical Essay," *Industrial and Labor Relations Forum,* Spring 1975; Alice K. Leopold, "Federal Equal Pay Legislation," *LLJ,* Jan. 1955; Richard A. Lester, "The Equal Pay Boondoggle," *Change,* Sept. 1975; Morag MacLeod Simchak, "Equal Pay in the United States," *ILR,* June 1971; U.S. Dept. of Labor, Employment Standards Administration, *Equal Pay* (rev. ed., Washington: 1974).

See also EQUAL PAY ACT OF 1963.

equity A procedure and principle said to stem from the days of the king's courts in England. The regular courts which concerned themselves with statutory and common law were not equipped to mete out justice, particularly in cases involving property, and the king asked his chancellor to see that justice was done. As the equity courts developed to perform these functions, they developed their own case law and policy. They generally were concerned with problems which the regular courts could not settle by the granting of money damages. The remedy at law was inadequate to provide justice. The action complained of or to be thwarted or prevented would, if permitted to occur, lead to irreparable damage. The equity courts provided speedy justice through the equitable remedy of injunctions.

The development of the injunctive process proved timely and useful in the handling of labor disputes in the last quarter of the 19th century. It was not until the passage of the Norris-LaGuardia Act that limits were placed on the use of the injunction in labor disputes.

Source reference: Zechariah Chafee, Jr., and Sidney Simpson, *Cases on Equity* (2d ed., Chicago: Foundation Press, 1946).

See also ADEQUATE REMEDY AT LAW, NORRIS-LAGUARDIA ACT.

equivalent employment A job which in most aspects, such as wages, hours of work, opportunity for advancement, seniority, status, etc., is similar to the one held by an employee prior to discharge or separation. Under NLRB policy employees discharged or discriminated against unlawfully by the employer are ordered reinstated, and the employer is required to ". . . offer full reinstatement to his former or substantially equivalent position, without prejudice to his seniority or other rights or privileges. . . ."

See also AFFIRMATIVE ORDER, CEASE AND DESIST ORDER, MAKE WHOLE.

Erdman Act Federal law passed in 1898 which replaced the Arbitration Act of 1888. The Act provided machinery for mediation, using the good offices of the commissioner of the Bureau of Labor and the chairman of the Interstate Commerce Commission. It also provided voluntary arbitration machinery. The Act was not used effectively until 1906, when its mediation facilities were utilized in a dispute involving the Southern Pacific Railroad.

Section 10 of the Erdman Act outlawed the yellow-dog contract on railroads in interstate commerce. It was held unconstitutional in the *Adair* case in 1908.

Source references: Adair v. United States, 208 US 161 (1908); Clyde O. Fisher, *Use of Federal Power in Settlement of Railway Labor Disputes* (Washington: U.S. Dept. of Labor, BLS, Bull. no. 303, 1922); Harry D. Wolf, *The Railroad Labor Board* (Chicago: Univ. of Chicago Press, 1927).

See also ADAIR V. UNITED STATES.

escalator clause A provision found in many collective bargaining agreements which is designed to keep the "real income" of the worker reasonably stable during the term of the agreement in the face of price fluctuations. It provides for periodic wage adjustments to reflect changes in the BLS Consumer Price Index or other measure of living costs. Downward as well as upward adjustments are permitted, though there usually is a stated floor below which wages may not be reduced.

As a matter of general practice it is easier to operate escalator clauses during periods of rising prices than during periods of declining prices. In recent years, with the development of long-term contracts, escalator clauses frequently have been accompanied by so-called "improvement factor" increases, which add a fixed amount on the theory that the worker's standard of living should be steadily improved, and that such improvement is justified by the steadily increasing productivity of the American worker.

Source references: Frederick H. Harbison, "The General Motors–United Auto Workers Agreement of 1950," *Journal of Political Economy,* Oct. 1950; Eileen B. Hoffman, "Adjusting Wage to Inflation Via the Escalator Clause," *Conference Board Record,* Aug. 1974; Dudley W. Johnson, "Are Cost-of-Living Escalator Clauses Inflationary?" *LLJ,* Oct. 1960; Daniel J. B. Mitchell, "Escalators, Inflation, and Macroeconomic Policy," *Proceedings of the 31st A/M, IRRA,* ed. by Barbara Dennis (Madison: 1979); Victor J. Sheifer, "Collective Bargaining and the CPI: Escalation vs. Catch-Up," *Proceedings of the 31st A/M, IRRA,* ed. by Barbara Dennis (Madison: 1979); Jerome M. Staller and Loren

M. Solnick, "Effect of Escalators on Wages in Major Contracts Expiring in 1974," *MLR*, July 1974; ———, "Escalators and Wage Change: More Comparisons," *MLR*, Oct. 1974; George S. Stothoff, "Escalator Clauses . . . Are Escalating," *Conference Board Record*, Dec. 1973; Arnold Strasser, "Escalators and Wage Change: The Business Cycle," *MLR*, Oct. 1974; Lucretia Dewey Tanner, "Escalator Clauses Under a Voluntary Pay Program," *LLJ*, Aug. 1979; Marla Taylor, *Cost-of-Living Escalators in the Public Sector* (Berkeley: UC, Institute of IR, 1978).

See also ANNUAL IMPROVEMENT FACTOR, CONSUMER PRICE INDEX, WAGE ESCALATION.

escape clause Any provision in a contract which permits either party to be relieved of any obligation previously incurred or agreed to.

Specifically, the term has been applied to contract clauses which provide for the maintenance of union membership as a condition of employment. The escape clause is designed to give employees an opportunity to resign or to state, usually to both the union and the company, that they do not wish to be members of the union. The clause generally specifies a period of time during which the employee may "escape" the obligations of membership. Employees who fail to give proper notification are required to maintain their membership until the next escape period.

The escape clause developed out of the union security conflict during the National War Labor Board's existence. The unions sought to establish the closed shop, while employer members wanted the open-shop policy adopted in cases involving union security coming before the Board. In early cases the Board held special elections and provided security where the election indicated the employees favored union security. Later, maintenance of membership was developed as a compromise solution.

The escape period was inserted because of continued opposition from employer members of the Board. The employers sought to reverse the Board's escape concept, urging that unless an employee specifically sought membership in the union he not be covered by the maintenance of membership provisions. A 15-day period became the standard for the escape clause ordered by the Board.

A typical escape clause in National War Labor Board decisions follows:

1. Any employee properly listed as a member of the union during the expired contract periods, as extended by mutual consent of the parties during the negotiations and resolving of these disputes, who may wish to avail himself of the fifteen-day escape clause must submit his resignation to the union in writing within the period from March 23, 1944 to April 6, 1944.
2. Any member of the union as defined above may resign during the period listed above provided he has paid his initiation fee and his monthly dues to the union up to and including March 23, 1944, or has made other mutually satisfactory arrangements with the union to accomplish this purpose.
3. The maintenance-of-membership and checkoff provisions of this directive order, together with this set of rules governing the escape period, shall be posted on all company and union bulletin boards immediately upon receipt of this directive order.

Source references: Non-Ferrous Metals Cases, 18 *WLR* 215 (1944); "Union Escape Clauses and the Taft-Hartley Act," *Columbia LR*, Jan. 1948.

See also MAINTENANCE OF MEMBERSHIP, NEW ESCAPE PERIOD, UNION SECURITY CLAUSES.

Esch-Cummins Act Also known as the Transportation Act of 1920. The Act required employers and unions to exert "every reasonable effort" to avoid strikes and lockouts and to settle disputes through negotiation and collective bargaining. The Act provided for adjustment boards to resolve disputes other than wage disputes. A Railroad Labor Board was set up consisting of three members each from employers, employees and the public. The Board had authority to make decisions on all unresolved disputes and on wages. Although the Board issued orders, they were not enforceable arbitration awards. The legislative history of the Esch-Cummins Act shows that compulsory arbitration of labor disputes in the railroad industry was considered and rejected.

The Railroad Labor Board was abolished with the enactment of the Railway Labor Act of 1926.

Source references: Transportation Act (1920), as amended, Pub. L. 66–152, Feb. 28, 1920, 41 Stat. 456 (codified as amended in scattered sections of 49 U.S.C.); Railway Labor Act, as amended, 45 U.S.C. 151–188 (1982); U.S. Railroad Labor Board, *Report of the United States Railroad Labor Board, April 15, 1920 to December 31, 1925* (Washington: 1926); Harry D. Wolf, *The Railroad Labor Board* (Chicago: Univ. of Chicago Press, 1927).

See also ADAIR V. UNITED STATES, ADAMSON ACT, RAILWAY LABOR ACT.

escrow agreement An arrangement whereby two parties agree to place a sum of money or valuable documents in the hands of a third party for conditional delivery under specified circumstances.

During a strike period a union may offer to work at existing wages if the employer will put in escrow moneys equivalent to the amount asked for by the union as a wage increase. The escrow agreement may provide that at the conclusion of the strike, the employees are to receive such portions of the escrow money as are warranted on the basis of the wage increase negotiated by the parties. In other situations, sums of money may be placed in escrow where the parties are in disagreement as to its disposition subject to a decision by an arbitrator or by a court.

espionage The custom of using or hiring spies in order to thwart or break efforts at unionization. The procedure was widely used by many employers by use of "loyal" employees, local police officers, and "stooges" in the union organization who were put on the employers' payroll. In larger companies special internal organizations were set up or outside "professional" organizations were hired to do the work. The LaFollette investigation brought many of these practices to light and was instrumental in reducing their effectiveness and widespread use. The National Labor Relations Act also did much to discourage espionage activity designed to deny workers the right of self-organization and collective bargaining.

Source references: "Industrial Policing and Espionage," 52 *Harvard LR* 793 (1939); Edward Levinson, *I Break Strikes! The Techniques of Pearl L. Bergoff* (New York: McBride, 1935); U.S. Congress, House, *Employment of Pinkerton Detectives* (Washington: Report no. 2447, Feb. 7, 1893); U.S. Congress, Senate, Committee on Education and Labor, *Violations of Free Speech and Rights of Labor, Industrial Espionage* (Washington: S. Res. 266, Report no. 46, 1938); ———, *Violations of Free Speech and Rights of Labor, Industrial Policing and Espionage* (Washington: Senate Report no. 46, Part 3, 1938).

See also ANTI-UNION PRACTICES, NATIONAL LABOR RELATIONS ACT, RAILWAY AUDIT AND INSPECTION CO., SABOTAGE, SPOTTER.

essential employee Employees, generally in the public sector, so designated because the services they provide are necessary to the public health, safety, and/or welfare. They usually are prohibited from striking.

The Minnesota Public Employment Relations Act specifically designates "essential" employees as:

> firefighters, peace officers subject to licensure . . . , guards at correctional facilities, and employees of hospitals other than state hospitals; provided that (1) with respect to state employees, 'essential employee' means all employees in the law enforcement, health care professional, correctional guards, and supervisory collective bargaining units, . . . and (2) with respect to University of Minnesota employees, 'essential employee' means all employees in the law enforcement, nursing professional and supervisory units. . . .

The Hawaii Public Employment Relations Act defines "essential employee" as an employee designated by the employer to fill an "essential position" defined under the law as "any position designated by the board [Hawaii Public Employment Relations Board] as necessary to be worked in order to avoid or remove any imminent or present danger to the public health or safety, which position shall be filled by the public employer."

Source references: John F. Burton, Jr., "Can Public Employees Be Given the Right to Strike?" *LLJ*, Aug. 1970; Kurt L. Hanslowe and John L. Acierno, "The Law and Theory of Strikes by Government Employees," 67

Cornell LR 1055 (1982); Craig A. Olson, "The Use of the Legal Right to Strike in the Public Sector," *LLJ*, Aug. 1982.

See also NATIONAL EMERGENCY STRIKES.

essential occupations Jobs held by the War Manpower Commission to be vital to the effective prosecution of the war effort during World War II. They were generally skilled jobs which required six months or more training time and were needed by essential plants holding war contracts.

A "List of Essential Activities" prepared by the Department of Commerce listed 10 areas: production and maintenance of aircraft and parts; ship and boat engineering; ordnance; precision laboratory instruments, apparatus, and scientific laboratory glassware; production of electronic and communication equipment; production of chemical and allied products; water and sewage systems; health and welfare services; educational services; and research and development services. The list was used by the Selective Service System as a guide in determinations of occupational deferment requests and the selection of men for enlistment in the Ready Reserve.

See also CRITICAL OCCUPATION.

establishment The place where work is performed. An employer may have only one establishment where the work is performed, but many employers operate more than one establishment. The concept of the establishment has a bearing on the application of the Fair Labor Standards Act (Wage and Hour Law). Wage and overtime provisions under the Act are not applied to employees in certain establishments.

Section 13(a) of the Act provides, in part: "The provisions of sections 6 . . . and 7 [minimum wages and maximum hours] shall not apply with respect to . . . any employee employed by any retail or service establishment . . . if more than 50 per centum of such establishment's annual dollar volume of sales of goods or services is made within the State in which the establishment is located. . . ."

The concept of the establishment is also used in the qualification for unemployment compensation benefits.

See also FAIR LABOR STANDARDS ACT OF 1938, UNEMPLOYMENT COMPENSATION.

European Trade Union Confederation (ETUC) Established in 1973, it currently has some 30 affiliates with over 40 million members. Almost all of the labor union federations in Western Europe are members of the ETUC whose headquarters is located in Brussels. According to Windmuller, ETUC works to defend "joint trade union interests in the European Economic Community and other European-wide bodies."

Source reference: John P. Windmuller, "International Trade Union Movement," *Comparative Labour Law and Industrial Relations*, ed. by R. Blanpain (Washington: BNA, 1982).

See also INTERNATIONAL CONFEDERATION OF FREE TRADE UNIONS (ICFTU), INTERNATIONAL FEDERATION OF TRADE UNIONS (IFTU), WORLD CONFEDERATION OF LABOUR (WCL), WORLD FEDERATION OF TRADE UNIONS (WFTU).

eviction from plant The physical removal of an individual or group from the plant. It is similar to evictions for failure or inability to pay rent or for violating the terms of a rental agreement by forcible ejection, locking the tenant out, denying him access to the premises.

Evictions may occur during a strike if the employees refuse to leave the plant, or if they take possession of certain key facilities.

See also SIT-DOWN STRIKE.

evidence Materials presented to a tribunal or court for the purpose of establishing certain facts or refuting factual materials presented by the opposition. Courts of law have established certain rules of evidence designed to permit the orderly presentation of information of probative value, and keep out certain offers of proof which may prejudice the case of one of the parties.

In hearings before administrative tribunals such as the NLRB, the rules of evidence are far less stringent, although the Taft-Hartley Act requires that hearings before the Board "so far as practicable" be conducted "in accordance with the rules of evidence applicable to district courts of the United States [Section 10(b)]."

In arbitration hearings the parties may set their own standards. Some arbitrations handled by legal counsel tend to follow formal court procedures. Other arbitrations are much less formal, and the parties are permitted wide scope in the introduction of materials for the record. This may include hearsay (evidence not based on the witnesses own knowledge or observation but obtained from someone else) and other information not ordinarily accepted in a court of law.

Source references: Frank Elkouri and Edna Asper Elkouri, *How Arbitration Works* (4th ed., Washington: BNA, 1985); Marvin Hill, Jr. and Anthony V. Sinicropi, *Evidence in Arbitration* (Washington: BNA, 1980); Ronald L. Miller, "Evidence and Proof in Arbitration," *Journal of Collective Negotiations in the Public Sector*, Vol. 5, no. 4, 1976; Edmund M. Morgan and John M. Maguire, *Cases and Materials on Evidence* (2d ed., Chicago: Foundation Press, 1942).

exaction *See* FEATHERBEDDING, LEA ACT (ANTI-PETRILLO ACT).

Excelsior rule A decision by the NLRB, upheld by the Supreme Court, that an employer must file with the NLRB's regional director a list of names and addresses of all employees eligible to vote in a representation election. The rule further holds that unless the list is supplied within seven days after the regional director has approved a consent election agreement, failure to provide the list is considered grounds for setting aside the election whenever proper objections are made.

Source references: Excelsior Underwear, Inc., 156 NLRB 1236, 61 LRRM 1217 (1966); *NLRB v. British Auto Parts*, 266 FSupp 368, 64 LRRM 2641, 2786 (DC Cal 1967); *NLRB v. Wyman-Gordon Co.*, 394 US 759, 70 LRRM 3345 (1969); Bruce J. Bergman, "The NLRB's Excelsior Doctrine: A Critical View," *Industrial and Labor Relations Forum*, Nov. 1968; "The Labor Board's 'Name and Address' Rule in Action," *IR Law Digest*, April 1973.

Exchange Bakery v. Rifkin A leading case in New York, decided by the Court of Appeals in 1927, which protected the right of a union to organize employees in a company where the employer had obtained a written statement from each employee before hiring that he was not a member of a union and would not engage in any union activity during his employment with the company.

The employees of the company were organized, participated in a strike against the employer, and picketed his premises. The employer sought an injunction to restrain the union from continuing its picket line. The trial court denied the request, but it was reversed by the Appellate Division. The Court of Appeals reversed the Appellate Division. The decision written by Justice Andrews read in part:

> . . . after beginning work each waitress signed a paper stating that it was the understanding that she was not a member of any union, pledging herself not to join one or if she did to withdraw from her employment. She further promised to make no efforts to unionize the restaurant, and [said] that she [would] attempt to adjust by individual bargaining any dispute that [might] arise. This paper was not a contract. It was merely a promise based upon no consideration on the part of the plaintiff. . . .
>
> The Appellate Division has based its decision in part upon the theory that the defendants wrongfully attempted to persuade the plaintiff's employees to break this alleged contract. Even had it been a valid subsisting contract, however, it should be noticed that whatever rule we may finally adopt, there is as yet no precedent in this court for the conclusion that a union may not persuade its members or others to end [the] contract of employment where the final intent lying behind the attempt is to extend its influence. . . .

Source reference: Exchange Bakery v. Rifkin, 245 NY 260 (1927).

See also ADAIR V. UNITED STATES, YELLOW DOG CONTRACT.

exclusive bargaining agent Where a union is certified as the collective bargaining agent in a particular unit, it is the "exclusive" bargaining agent for *all* employees in the unit, nonunion as well as union.

See also BARGAINING AGENT.

exclusive bargaining rights *See* BARGAINING RIGHTS.

exclusive recognition Exclusive recognition will be granted to any organization chosen by a majority of the employees in an appropriate unit. Exclusive recognition in the federal public service gives an organization the right to enter collective negotiations with management officials with the object of reaching an agreement applicable to all employees of the unit. Such agreements must not conflict with existing federal laws or regulations, with agency regulations, with governmentwide personnel policies, or with the authority of the Congress over various personnel matters.

Under Executive Order 11491 and its successor, the Civil Service Reform Act of 1978, granting of exclusive recognition on the basis of membership, petition, and authorization cards was terminated, and a secret-ballot election is required in all cases. Exclusive recognition is accorded the organization selected by a majority of employees, without the 10 percent membership or 60 percent representative vote as previously required under Executive Order 10988.

See also FORMAL RECOGNITION, INFORMAL RECOGNITION, MINORITY REPRESENTATION, NATIONAL CONSULTATION RIGHTS, SIXTY-PERCENT RULE.

executive boards Most international unions are governed by executive boards. These boards are in control of union policy and programs in the interim between conventions, which are the final authority within the union. Occasionally reference to the entire membership is required over and beyond the action of conventions. The executive board generally consists of full-time paid union officials, and it may serve as an effective balance to prevent the concentration of too much power in the hands of the international union president.

executive compensation Since executives are in higher tax brackets, and since they are not easily replaceable, compensation is a sticky problem. To attract and retain and to provide incentives for executive performance and development, the following plans have been used in addition to high salaries: profit sharing, stock options, and performance bonuses. Many plans tend to emphasize deferred payment rather than immediate payment in order to reduce the tax burden on the recipient.

Source references: Naresh C. Agarwal, "Determinants of Executive Compensation," *IR*, Winter 1981; John C. Baker, "Are Corporate Executives Overpaid?" *Harvard BR*, July/Aug. 1977; Bruce R. Ellig, "Perquisites: The Intrinsic Form of Pay," *Personnel*, Jan./Feb. 1981; Eugene F. Finkin, "How to Figure Out Executive Compensation," *PJ*, July 1978; Harland Fox, *Top Executive Compensation (1983 Edition)* (New York: The Conference Board, Report no. 840, 1983); J. Frank Gaston, *Adjusting Executive Pay for Inflation: A Technical Report* (New York: The Conference Board, Report no. 819, 1982); David Kraus, "The 'Devaluation' of the American Executive," *Harvard BR*, May/June 1976; ———, "Executive Pay: Ripe for Reform?" *Harvard BR*, Sept./Oct. 1980; Joan Lindroth, "Inflation, Taxes and Perks: How Compensation is Changing," *PJ*, Dec. 1981; David J. McLaughlin, "Reinforcing Corporate Strategy Through Executive Compensation," *Management Review*, Oct. 1981; Arch Patton, "Executive Compensation by 1970," *Harvard BR*, Sept./Oct. 1964; ———, "Executive Compensation Here and Abroad," *Harvard BR*, Sept./Oct. 1962; Alfred Rappaport, "Executive Incentives vs. Corporate Growth," *Harvard BR*, July/Aug. 1978; Edward T. Redling, "The 1981 Tax Act: Boon to Managerial Compensation," *Personnel*, March/April 1982; Gerard R. Roche, "Compensation and the Mobile Executive," *Harvard BR*, Nov./Dec. 1975; U.S. Dept. of Labor, Employment Standards Administration, *Executive, Administrative and Professional Employees; A Study of Salaries and Hours of Work* (Washington: 1977); William L. White, "Impact of the Anti-Inflation Program on Executive Compensation," *Personnel*, July/Aug. 1979.

executive employees Certain classes of workers exempt from minimum wage and overtime hours under Section 13 of the Fair Labor Standards Act. To qualify for the exemption, they must meet standards established by the Wage and Hour Administrator.

Source references: Patricia Bonfield, *U.S. Business Leaders: A Study of Opinions and Characteristics* (New York: The Conference Board, Report no. 786, 1980); Harlan Cleveland, *The Future Executive; A Guide for Tomorrow's Managers* (New York: Harper & Row, 1972); Alfred DeMaria, Dale Tarnowieski, and Richard Gurman, *Manager Unions?* (New York: AMA, Research Report, 1972); Herman S. Jacobs and Katherine Jillson, *Executive Productivity: An AMA Survey*

Report (New York: AMA, 1974); Eugene Emerson Jennings, *Routes to the Executive Suite* (New York: McGraw-Hill, 1976); Philip Marvin, *Executive Time Management, An AMA Survey Report* (New York: AMA, 1980); Arch Patton, "The Coming Flood of Young Executives," *Harvard BR*, Sept./Oct. 1976; Robert D. Paulson, "The Chief Executive as Change Agent," *Management Review*, Feb. 1982; Ruth G. Shaeffer and Allen R. Janger, *Who is Top Management?* (New York: The Conference Board, Report no. 821, 1982); Irving S. Shapiro, "Today's Executive: Private Steward and Public Steward," *Harvard BR*, March/April 1978; Frederick D. Sturdivant and Roy D. Adler, "Executive Origins: Still a Gray Flannel World?" *Harvard BR*, Nov./Dec. 1976.

Executive Order 10988 Superseded by Executive Order 11491, Executive Order 10988 was issued by President Kennedy on January 17, 1962, dealing with employee-management cooperation in the federal service. It provided the mechanism for determining bargaining representation and forms of recognition for employees. It also established machinery in the Department of Labor and the U.S. Civil Service Commission to give technical assistance to government departments in carrying out the provisions of the order.

Source references: George W. Hardbeck and John S. Anderson, "The Impact of Executive Order 10988 on Labor-Management Relations," *LLJ*, Nov. 1969; Wilson R. Hart, "The U.S. Civil Service Learns to Live with Executive Order 10988: An Interim Appraisal," *ILRR*, Jan. 1964; John W. Macy, Jr., "The Federal Employee-Management Cooperation Program," *ILRR*, July 1966; B. V. H. Schneider, "Collective Bargaining and the Federal Civil Service," *IR*, May 1964; Cyrus F. Smythe, "Collective Bargaining Under Executive Order 10988—Trends and Prospects," *Public Personnel Review*, Oct. 1965.

See also CIVIL SERVICE REFORM ACT OF 1978, EXECUTIVE ORDER 11491, PUBLIC EMPLOYEE RELATIONS.

Executive Order 11141 Issued in 1964, it prohibits discriminatory employment practices on the basis of age by federal contractors and subcontractors.

Source reference: E.O. 11141, 3 C.F.R. (1964–65 Comp.) 179.

See also AGE DISCRIMINATION IN EMPLOYMENT ACT OF 1967.

Executive Order 11246 The Order signed by President Johnson on September 24, 1965, which dissolved the President's Committee on Equal Employment Opportunity; the OFCCP was created in October 1965 to carry out enforcement of the Order.

The Order requires every government contract to include a seven-point equal opportunity clause in which the federal contractor agrees not to discriminate against any employee or applicant because of race, color, religion, sex, or national origin. In addition, the contractor also agrees to take affirmative action to ensure that applicants and employees are employed without regard to such factors. In the event of noncompliance, a contract may be cancelled, terminated, or suspended, and the contractor may be declared ineligible for further government contracts.

The Order requires the contractor and each of its subcontractors to file compliance reports containing information on its "practices, policies, programs, and employment policies, programs, and employment statistics." A contractor or subcontractor with a collective bargaining agreement or other contract or understanding with an agency referring workers or supervising apprenticeship or training of workers may be required to obtain from such labor union or agency signed statements on its practices and policies of nondiscrimination and of cooperation to implement the policy and provisions of the Order for inclusion in the compliance report.

The Order authorizes the Secretary of Labor to issue Certificates of Merit to contractors, labor unions, or other agencies for satisfactory compliance with the Executive Order.

Executive Order 11246 was amended by Executive Order 11375 (October 13, 1967) to extend prohibition of discrimination on the basis of sex and by Executive Order 12086 (October 8, 1978) to transfer the compliance function of 11 federal agencies to the OFCCP.

Source references: E.O. 11246, 3 C.F.R. (1964–65 Comp.) 339; U.S. OFCCP, "Equal

Employment Opportunity Duties of Government Contractors," 41 C.F.R. 60–1; ———, "Revised Order No. 4," 41 C.F.R. 60–2; "Executive Order 11,246 and Reverse Discrimination Challenges: Presidential Authority to Require Affirmative Action," 54 *New York Univ. LR* 376 (1979); William J. Kilberg, "The Federal Contracts Compliance Program: Developments Under Executive Order 11,246," *Labor Law Developments 1975*, Proceedings of the 21st Annual Institute on Labor Law, SLF (New York: Bender, 1975); Marvin J. Levine, "Meeting Compliance Review Standards: The Problems of Federal Contractors," *LLJ*, Oct. 1977.

See also AFFIRMATIVE ACTION, OFFICE OF FEDERAL CONTRACT COMPLIANCE PROGRAMS (OFCCP), PLANS FOR PROGRESS, PRESIDENT'S COMMITTEE ON EQUAL EMPLOYMENT OPPORTUNITY, REVISED ORDER NO. 4.

Executive Order 11375 *See* EXECUTIVE ORDER 11246.

Executive Order 11478 A 1969 order prohibiting discrimination in federal employment because of race, color, religion, sex, national origin, handicap, or age.

Source reference: E.O. 11478, 34 F.R. 12985.

Executive Order 11491 Successor to Executive Order 10988, this order was signed by President Nixon in October 1969. It differed in outlook in a number of respects. It labeled relationships in the federal service as "Labor-Management" rather than "Employee-Management"; established supervisors as "management" and, with minor exceptions, denied them bargaining rights; and abolished "formal recognition," which had provided an organizational foothold until a union could obtain "exclusive recognition." Such changes suggested that the government felt unions of federal employees were strong enough to be on their own without help from government. In many ways (e.g., by establishing unfair labor practices for unions as well as for management), this executive order brought the relationship between the federal government and unions into one which more closely resembled those existing in private industry under the National Labor Relations Act. The Civil Service Reform Act of 1978 replaced Executive Order 11491.

Source references: Louis Aronin, "In Defense of the Executive Order in the Federal Sector," *Journal of Collective Negotiations in the Public Sector*, Fall 1974; Harriet F. Berger, "The Old Order Giveth Way to the New: A Comparison of Executive Order 10988 with Executive Order 11491," *LLJ*, Feb. 1970; M. J. Fox, Jr., Michael J. Sexton, and Jerrie C. Wells, "Executive Order 11491, Labor-Management Relations in the Federal Service, Revisited," *Journal of Collective Negotiations in the Public Sector*, Vol. 7, no. 4, 1978; Paul J. Frasser, Jr., "The Right to Union Representation Under Executive Order 11491," *LLJ*, Sept. 1974; Kenneth A. Kovach, "Executive Orders in Federal Sector Labor Relations," *Journal of Collective Negotiations in the Public Sector,"* Vol. 8, no. 3, 1979; Marvin J. Levine, "National Exclusive Recognition Under Executive Order 11491: The PATCO Case," *LLJ*, Feb. 1971; J. Joseph Loewenberg, "Development of the Federal Labor-Management Relations Program: Executive Order 10988 and Executive Order 11491," *LLJ*, Feb. 1970; Raymond McKay and Michael Petty, "The Scope of Mid-contract Bargaining Under E.O. 11491," *Journal of Collective Negotiations in the Public Sector*, Vol. 7, no. 4, 1978; John C. Shinn, "The New Federal Order and Its Proposed Administration," *NYU 23d Annual Conference on Labor*, ed. by Thomas Christensen and Andrea Christensen (New York: Bender, 1971); U.S. CSC, *Labor-Management Relations in the Federal Service, Answers to Questions About E.O. 11491* (Washington: 1976); U.S. Dept. of Labor, LMSA, *Report and Recommendations on Labor-Management Relations in the Federal Service and Executive Order 11491 of October 29, 1969* (Washington: 1969); U.S. FLRC, *Labor-Management Relations in the Federal Service, Amendments to Executive Order 11491 with Accompanying Report and Recommendations* (Washington: 1975); ———, *Labor-Management Relations in the Federal Service; Executive Order 11491, as Amended February 6, 1975, Reports and Recommendations* (Washington: 1975).

See also CIVIL SERVICE REFORM ACT OF 1978, EMPLOYEE ORGANIZATION, EXCLUSIVE

RECOGNITION, FEDERAL LABOR RELATIONS COUNCIL (FLRC), FEDERAL SERVICE IMPASSES PANEL (FSIP), FORMAL RECOGNITION, INFORMAL RECOGNITION, LABOR ORGANIZATION, NATIONAL CONSULTATION RIGHTS.

Executive Order 11616 A 1971 amendment to Executive Order 11491, limiting the scope of grievance procedures in the federal sector to disputes over interpretation and application of the collective bargaining agreement.

Source references: Council on Labor Law and Labor Relations, "Federal Bar Association Task Force I Report—E.O. 11616," *LLJ*, July 1972; Harry A. Donoian, "Recent Changes in Federal Service Labor-Management Relations," *LLJ*, March 1972; U.S. FLRC, *Labor-Management Relations in the Federal Service, Executive Order 11491 as Amended by Executive Order 11616 of August 26, 1971, Reports and Recommendations* (Washington: 1971).

Executive Order 11636 A 1971 amendment to Executive Order 11491 that removed the U.S. Foreign Service, U.S. Information Agency, and U.S. Agency for International Development from coverage under Executive Order 11491, and provided a separate labor relations system for these agencies.

Source reference: U.S. Dept. of State, *Employee-Management Relations in the Foreign Service of the United States; Text and Analysis of Executive Order 11636* (Washington: 1972).

Executive Order 11758 A 1974 order which authorizes the secretary of labor to prescribe regulations for the employment of qualified handicapped persons by federal contractors in accordance with Section 503 of the Rehabilitation Act of 1973.

Source reference: E.O. 11758, 3 C.F.R. (1971–75 Comp.) 841.

See also ACCOMMODATION, HANDICAPPED INDIVIDUAL, REHABILITATION ACT OF 1973.

Executive Order 11838 A 1975 amendment to Executive Order 11491, which among other changes provided for negotiability of the coverage and the scope of grievance procedures.

Source references: Kenneth A. Kovach, "Executive Orders in Federal Sector Labor Relations," *Journal of Collective Negotiations in the Public Sector*, Vol. 8, no. 3, 1979; James E. Martin, "Union-Management Consultation in the Federal Government: Problems and Promise," *LLJ*, Jan. 1976; "New Amendments to Executive Order 11491," *Public Personnel Management*, Nov./Dec. 1975; U.S. FLRC, *Labor-Management Relations in the Federal Service, Executive Order 11491, as Amended, February 6, 1975, Reports and Recommendations* (Washington: 1975).

Executive Order 12086 *See* EXECUTIVE ORDER 11246.

exempt class According to Stahl, positions which may be filled without examination of any kind. They usually fall into four groups: (1) laborers, (2) positions of a "confidential" or "policy-determining" character, (3) part-time or temporary positions, and (4) positions which have not been filled satisfactorily by examination methods.

Source reference: O. Glenn Stahl, *Public Personnel Administration* (7th ed., New York: Harper & Row, 1976).

exit interview A meeting between an employee who is leaving the employ of the company, voluntarily or for other reasons, and someone from the personnel office. The purpose of the meeting is to determine the reason or reasons for the separation and to get the employee's observations and comments on employment conditions or policies in the plant. Information obtained during this interview may be helpful in correcting conditions contributing to high labor turnover.

It may also be used for the purpose of maintaining good public relations and the good will of ex-employees. In some cases this interview may result in the employee's deciding to remain with the company and transfer to another operation if the reason for seeking separation is the type of work he was performing or objection to his immediate supervisor or to his fellow workers.

Source references: BNA, *Separation Procedures and Severance Benefits* (Washington: PPF Survey no. 121, 1978); "The Exit Interview: A New Interpretation," *Management Record*, Sept. 1952; Pamela Garretson and

Kenneth S. Teel, "The Exit Interview: Effective Tool or Meaningless Gesture?" *Personnel,* July/Aug. 1982; Laura Garrison and Jacqueline Ferguson, "Separation Interviews," *PJ,* Sept. 1977; Susan A. Hellweg, "The Exit Interview: A Potential Management Tool for University Administrators," *Journal of the College and University Personnel Association,* Spring 1981; Martin Hilb, "The Standardized Exit Interview," *PJ,* June 1978; John R. Hinrichs, "Employees Going and Coming: The Exit Interview," *Personnel,* Jan./Feb. 1971; Leslie This, "Exit Interviews: Do They Pay?" *PJ,* June 1955.

See also EMPLOYMENT INTERVIEW.

ex parte injunction A restraining order issued without notice to the defendant or without an opportunity for him to be heard before its issuance.

Source references: Felix Frankfurter and Nathan Greene, *The Labor Injunction* (New York: Macmillan, 1930); Duane McCracken, *Strike Injunctions in the New South* (Chapel Hill: Univ. of North Carolina Press, 1931).

See also INJUNCTION.

expected earning level A target or standard set under a piece-rate system which permits an employee to earn a fixed percentage above the base rate.

expedited arbitration *See* ARBITRATION, EXPEDITED.

expense allowances Payments made for transporation, lodging, and meals or other necessary expenses incurred by an employee and reimbursed by his employer.

See also TRAVEL ALLOWANCE.

experience Information, knowledge, and ability obtained through actual work or job performance. "Book learning" may be helpful in understanding or making a job easier to do, but it is not a substitute for actual work performance. An employee's work experience plays an important role in transfers and promotions.

experience rating A procedure or device used in connection with state unemployment compensation laws to determine the tax rate of an employer. The rate varies with the employment experience of the company. It may also be used in determining premium rates under state workers compensation laws. Employers with good safety records pay low premium rates, while those with poor safety records pay high premiums. Experience rating is sometimes referred to as "merit rating."

See also MERIT RATING.

experimental negotiating agreement (ENA) An interest arbitration plan first negotiated in 1972 by the United Steelworkers and major steel companies. The parties agreed to forego nationwide strikes and lockouts during negotiations and to authorize a three-member arbitration panel to render decisions over unresolved national bargaining issues.

The intent of the experimental plan was to prevent significant disruption of domestic steel production. An important element of the plan was to allow local plant strikes and lockouts. It was felt that permitting strikes over local issues would increase the acceptance of the national contract, result in more effective bargaining and faster resolution of local issues, and would not involve the high cost of industrywide shutdown.

Source references: I. W. Abel, *ENA, The Experimental Negotiating Agreement* (Pittsburgh: United Steelworkers of America, Pamphlet no. PR–217, 1973); ______, "Two Views on the New Basic Steel Industry Negotiating Agreement: For the Union," *Sloan Management Review,* Winter 1974; James A. Craft, "The ENA, Consent Decrees, and Cooperation in Steel Labor Relations: A Critical Appraisal," *LLJ,* Oct. 1976; Bernard Cushman, "Current Experiments in Collective Bargaining," *Proceedings of the 26th A/M, IRRA,* ed. by Gerald Somers (Madison: 1974); R. Heath Larry, "Two Views on the New Basic Steel Industry Negotiating Agreement: For the Steel Industry," *Sloan Management Review,* Winter 1974.

expiration date The formal date established in a collective bargaining agreement for the termination of the agreement or the earliest date at which the contract may be terminated.

expulsion from union Action by a union under its constitution and bylaws revoking an individual's membership in the union. Such action may stem from failure to pay dues, violation of union regulations, engaging in conduct unbecoming a union member (such as open attack upon the leadership), embezzling of funds, dual unionism, or other violations of the union's constitution or bylaws. Procedures generally are established for hearings before the local union and final appeal to the convention of the national union. It is also possible to appeal to the courts.

Under the Taft-Hartley Act the only lawful ground for discharge under a union-shop agreement is failure to pay the periodic dues required under the contract, even though the employee may no longer be a member in good standing in the union.

Source references: NLRB v. Industrial Union of Marine and Shipbuilding Workers, 309 US 1035, 68 LRRM 2257 (1968); Vincent C. De Maio, "Expulsion, Unions and the Courts," *NYU 4th Annual Conference on Labor*, ed. by Emanuel Stein (Albany: Bender, 1951).

See also UNION DISCIPLINE.

extended vacation *See* SABBATICALS.

extension of collective agreement Provisions in some contracts setting out the conditions under which the provisions of the agreement will be extended to new plants or new members of an employer association.

European practice in some countries permits extension of negotiated agreements between unions and employers to all in the industry, including plants whose employees are not organized.

Source reference: L. Hamburger, "The Extension of Collective Agreements to Cover Entire Trades and Industries," *ILR*, Aug. 1939.

extortionate picketing Tactic used to obtain funds from management for personal gain. The Labor-Management Reporting and Disclosure Act, Section 602, prohibits such picketing, punishable by a fine of $1,000 and imprisonment of up to 20 years.

Source references: R. W. Fleming, "Title VII: The Taft-Hartley Amendments," 54 *Northwestern Univ. LR* 666 (1960); Clarence M. Updegraff, "An Arbitrator's Appraisal of the New Labor Law," *The New Labor Law*, ed. by Philip Ross and Joan G. Kilpatrick (Minneapolis: Univ. of Minnesota, IRC, Research & Technical Report 18, 1960); Benjamin Wyle, "The New Law of Picketing," *LLJ*, Dec. 1959.

extras *See* TEMPORARY EMPLOYEE.

extreme provocation Grounds upon which the Public Employment Relations Board (PERB) of New York State refused to penalize members of the City of Troy Uniformed Firemen's Association for a four-hour strike against the City of Troy. Citing a number of instances in which the city manager first agreed to various proposals, then later withdrew the agreement, the PERB found these to be "acts of extreme provocation."

Source reference: City of Troy Uniformed Firemen's Association, 2 NYPERB 3077 (1969).

F

FAA *See* FOREMAN'S ASSOCIATION OF AMERICA.

FEIA *See* FLIGHT ENGINEERS' INTERNATIONAL ASSOCIATION (AFL-CIO).

FEPC *See* FAIR EMPLOYMENT PRACTICE COMMITTEE.

FEW *See* FEDERALLY EMPLOYED WOMEN (FEW).

FLRA *See* FEDERAL LABOR RELATIONS AUTHORITY (FLRA).

FLRC *See* FEDERAL LABOR RELATIONS COUNCIL (FLRC).

FLSA *See* FAIR LABOR STANDARDS ACT OF 1938.

FMCS *See* FEDERAL MEDIATION AND CONCILIATION SERVICE (FMCS).

FNHP *See* NURSES AND HEALTH PROFESSIONALS, FEDERATION OF.

FOIA *See* FREEDOM OF INFORMATION ACT (FOIA) OF 1966.

FOP *See* POLICE; FRATERNAL ORDER OF (IND).

FPA *See* ATHLETES; FEDERATION OF PROFESSIONAL (AFL-CIO).

FPSP *See* POSTAL SECURITY POLICE; FEDERATION OF (IND).

FSA *See* FEDERAL SECURITY AGENCY.

FSIP *See* FEDERAL SERVICE IMPASSES PANEL (FSIP).

Fabianism The term applied to the doctrines of a group of socialists organized in 1884 as the Fabian Society, who sought to achieve socialism through political and social reform. The Society opposed revolutionary procedures and sought instead to use educational means to produce reform through evolution. Its philosophy was not based on the class struggle as propounded by Marxian socialists.

face-to-face pay A method of determining compensation in mining operations based solely on work performed at the face where the ore actually is mined.

Source reference: Tennessee Coal, Iron and Railroad Co. v. Muscoda Local No. 123, 321 US 590 (1944).

See also PORTAL-TO-PORTAL PAY.

factfinder An individual or individuals of a factfinding panel designated to review the issues in a labor-management dispute. The factfinding procedure is generally provided by law.

Under the Taft-Hartley Act, a board of inquiry is constituted by the President to investigate disputes threatening the nation's health and safety and to report its findings to the President.

Under state and local government employees collective bargaining laws, the factfinder or factfinding panel is selected by the parties or appointed by an administrative agency and is generally required to submit nonbinding recommendations to the parties.

Source references: Joseph Adler and Donald L. Rosenthal, "Fact Finders and the Resolution of Issues at Impasse: A Survey of New York State PERB Neutrals," *Journal of Collective Negotiations in the Public Sector*, Vol. 4, no. 4, 1975; Jack Stieber and Benjamin W. Wolkinson, "Fact-Finding Viewed by Fact-Finders: The Michigan Experience," *LLJ*, Feb. 1977; Helene S. Tanimoto, *Guide to Statutory Provisions in Public Sector Collective Bargaining, Impasse Resolution Procedures* (3d issue, Honolulu: Univ. of Hawaii, IRC, 1981).

See also ARBITRATOR, CONCILIATOR, FACTFINDING, MASTER, MEDIATOR.

factfinding A dispute resolution procedure. Factfinding may be conducted by a panel of three or more members or by one person who is appointed to review the positions of labor and management in a particular dispute, with a view to focusing attention on the major issues in dispute, and resolving differences as to facts. Factfinding boards have been set up under state laws and have been used on the national level. In 1946, for example, factfinding boards or panels were established in disputes involving the automobile, bus transportation, farm equipment, meat packing, and oil industries.

Factfinding procedures may be provided by law or established by the factfinder or the factfinding panel. The parties have the prime responsibility to present data, but the factfinder or the board reserves the right to develop such additional or supplementary information as it deems proper in order to make its report or recommendations.

The factfinder or board may merely report its determination of the facts and hope that the facts are so clear as to provide the parties with an answer. More frequently, recommendations are rendered on the basis of the facts presented. If a recommendation is made, particularly where it is unanimous, it exerts pressure on the parties to accept the recommendation. It is precisely for this reason that objections have been raised and the power to make recommendations has been eliminated in some jurisdictions. The emergency boards under the Taft-Hartley Act are forbidden to make recommendations.

In the public sector, the factfinder or factfinding panel generally is required to provide recommendations for the settlement of a dispute.

Source references: Arvid Anderson, "The Use of Fact-Finding in Dispute Resolution Settlement," *Arbitration and Social Change,* Proceedings of the 22d A/M, NAA, ed. by Gerald Somers (Washington: BNA, 1970); Wayne F. Anderson, R. Theodore Clark, Jr., and John T. Weise, *Fact-Finding in the Public Sector—A Case Study* (Chicago: PPA, PERL no. 29, 1970); Tim Bornstein, *Facts About Fact-Finding* (Washington: Labor Management Relations Service, Strengthening Local Government Through Better Labor Relations Series, no. 8, 1971); Carroll R. Daugherty, *The Fact-Finding Concept in Labor Relations* (New York: AMA, Personnel Series no. 133, 1950); Daniel G. Gallagher, Peter Feuille, and Manmohan Chaubey, "Who Wins at Factfinding: Union, Management, or Factfinder?" *Proceedings of the 32d A/M, IRRA,* ed. by Barbara Dennis (Madison: 1980); Herbert L. Haber, "Factfinding with Binding Recommendations," *MLR,* Sept. 1973; Thomas J. McDermott, "Use of Fact-Finding Boards in Labor Disputes," *LLJ,* April 1960; Charles M. Rehmus, *Fact-Finding and the Public Interest* (Ithaca: Cornell Univ., NYSSILR, Institute of Public Employment, Occasional Paper no. 4, 1974); William M. Saxton, "The Use of Fact-Finding in Public-Employee Dispute Settlement, The Employer View," *Arbitration and Social Change,* Proceedings of the 22d A/M, NAA, ed. by Gerald Somers (Washington: BNA, 1970); Harold P. Seamon, "Fact Finding in the Public Sector: A Proposal to Strengthen the Fact Finder's Role," *Journal of Collective Negotiations in the Public Sector,* Spring 1974; William E. Simkin, "Fact-Finding: Its Values and Limitations," *Arbitration and the Expanding Role of Neutrals,* Proceedings of the 23d A/M, NAA, ed. by Gerald Somers and Barbara Dennis (Washington: BNA, 1970); Arthur Stark, "Fact-Finding in Labor Disputes," *NYU 5th Annual Conference on Labor,* ed. by Emanuel Stein (Albany: Matthew Bender, 1952); Bryce M. Stewart and Walter J. Couper, *Fact-Finding in Industrial Disputes* (New York: Industrial Relations Counselors, 1946); William R. Word, "Factfinding in Public Employee Negotiations," *MLR,* Feb. 1972; Arnold Zack, *Understanding Fact Finding and Arbitration in the Public Sector* (3d ed., Washington: U.S. Dept. of Labor, LMSA, 1980).

See also ARBITRATION, TRI-OFFER.

factionalism Within a union, groups of members who differ on solution of common problems, on policy, or in philosophy. When the differences grow to major proportions or the issues are of sufficient import, large segments may break from the dominant, or controlling group to form a strong opposition faction. A faction may split off and form another union. In some unions, numerous small factions work together on certain issues, divide and perhaps regroup on others.

See also DUAL UNIONISM, JURISDICTIONAL DISPUTE.

factor comparison method One of the methods used in job evaluation. (Others frequently used are: ranking method, point rating method, and classification method.) In the factor comparison method a set of key jobs is selected in the plant. The number of key jobs may vary from 10 to 30 depending on the number of different skills used in the operation and the size of the plant. After general agreement is reached on the key jobs, using the general factors such as skill, mental requirements, physical requirements, responsibility, and working conditions, other jobs are rated. Each job is then compared on the basis of the agreed factors in the key jobs. Detailed job descriptions and job specifications are needed to make this system of job evaluation effective.

Source references: Lawrence L. Epperson, "The Dynamics of Factor Comparison/Point Evaluation," *Public Personnel Management,* Jan./Feb. 1975; Edward N. Hay, "Characteristics of Factor Comparison Job Evaluation," *Personnel,* May 1946; ______, "Training the Evaluations Committee in Factor Comparison Job Evaluation," *Personnel,* Jan. 1946; Charles H. Lawshe, "An Analysis of the Factor Comparison System as It Functions in a Paper Mill," *Journal of Applied Psychology,* Oct. 1945.

See also CLASSIFICATION PLAN, JOB EVALUATION, POINT PLAN, RANKING PLAN.

factory inspection A procedure for periodic checking of facilities used for the production of goods and services to determine whether they meet health and safety standards established by law. Inspections began in England in the early part of the 19th century with the development of the factory system and the widespread exploitation of women and children which led to demands for stringent legislation to prevent sickness and epidemics resulting from the unsanitary conditions in the factories.

The factory laws in England were extended gradually beyond concern with the safety and welfare of children and women to cover male adults. Regulations from England and Europe were adopted in Massachusetts with the development of factory production on the eastern seaboard. Factory laws and inspection exist throughout the United States and are concerned with a wide variety of problems including sanitation, fire protection, safety appliances, ventilation and dust, elevator openings, payment of wages, and numerous other details designed to protect the wage earner and improve the conditions under which work is performed.

Source reference: B. L. Hutchins and A. Harrison, *A History of Factory Legislation* (3d ed., London: P. S. King & Son, 1926).

See also OCCUPATIONAL SAFETY AND HEALTH ACT (OSHA) OF 1970.

fair day's pay A wage which is regarded by workers as being just and fair for the type of work being performed and having a reasonable relationship to prevailing wages in the community. It also occasionally connotes a "living wage" sufficient to permit the worker to maintain himself and his family.

The term is generally linked with the concept of a "fair day's pay for a fair day's work." In this sense it is used to suggest that employers are willing to pay fair wages, if workers give a fair day's work in return. In the sense of this term, "fairness" is not subject to any quantitative measurement but to the particular notions and predilections of each employer and worker.

Source reference: J. J. Gracie, *A Fair Day's Pay* (London: Management Publications Trust, Ltd., 1949).

fair day's work The companion phrase to a "fair day's pay." The term is designed to describe what is reasonable and proper to expect from a worker who is not slacking on his job and is trying to give fully of his energy and ability to earn a fair day's pay.

Source references: AMA, *A Fair Day's Work for a Fair Day's Pay* (New York: 1955); Phil Carroll, Jr., "What Is the Measure of a Fair Day's Work?" *Advanced Management,* Oct./Dec. 1942; John G. Hutchinson, *Managing a Fair Day's Work: An Analysis of Work Standards in Operation* (Ann Arbor: Univ. of Michigan, Bureau of IR, 1963); Harold R. Nissley, "A Fair Day's Work," *Mill and Factory,* Aug. 1945; ______, "New Concept of a

Fair Day's Work," *Advanced Management*, Jan. 1950.

See also FAIR DAY'S PAY.

fair employment practice commission An agency created to administer and enforce state or local government fair employment practice laws. Such an agency is sometimes known as a civil rights commission, human rights bureau, or equal opportunity agency.

Source references: Robert Freiberg (ed.), *The Manager's Guide to Equal Employment Opportunity* (New York: Executive Enterprises, 1977); Malcolm H. Liggett, "The Efficacy of State Fair Employment Practices Commissions," *ILRR*, July 1969.

See also 706 AGENCY.

Fair Employment Practice Committee A committee set up by Executive Order 8802 in 1941 to "investigate complaints of discrimination" and to take the necessary steps to formulate policies to avoid discrimination because of "race, creed, color, or national origin." The executive order and the work of the Committee were confined to discrimination in defense industries. The Committee functioned within the National Office of Production Management. The Committee suspended operations in early 1943.

A second Committee was established a few months later by Executive Order 9346. The new Committee's jurisdiction was not limited to the defense industries but extended to include all government contractors and the federal government. It was also authorized to deal with discrimination complaints against labor unions. Although the Committee processed some 8,000 complaints and conducted 30 public hearings, it did not have the authority to enforce its decisions. The Committee expired in June 1946.

Source references: BNA, *The Equal Employment Opportunity Act of 1972* (Washington: 1973); Arnold Foster, "In Favor of the F.E.P.C.," *PJ*, Jan. 1952; William H. Harris, "Federal Intervention in Union Discrimination: FEPC and West Coast Shipyards During World War II," *Labor History*, Summer 1981; Chester Morgan, "An Analysis of State FEPC Legislation," *LLJ*, July 1957; "The Operation of State Fair Employment Practices Commission," *Harvard LR*, Feb. 1955.

fair employment practice laws Federal, state, and local laws which prohibit discrimination in hiring, promotion, discharge, or conditions of employment on the basis of race, color, religion, sex, or national origin.

See also CIVIL RIGHTS ACT OF 1964.

fair employment practices Those procedures in hiring and other employment practices involving wages, hours, and other working conditions which are applied without consideration of race, color, creed, sex, religion, national origin, or other features or characteristics. Many states have established agencies designed to prevent discrimination in employment based on race, color, creed, etc.

Source references: Alfred W. Blumrosen, *The Duty to Plan for Fair Employment: Plant Location in White Suburbia* (New Brunswick: Rutgers Univ., Institute of Management and Labor Relations, Reprint no. 23, 1971); Michael R. Carrell and John E. Dittrich, "Employee Perceptions of Fair Treatment," *PJ*, Oct. 1976; Peter Feuille and David Lewin, "Equal Employment Opportunity Bargaining," *IR*, Fall 1981; Russell L. Greenman and Eric J. Schmertz, *Personnel Administration and the Law* (2d ed., Washington: BNA, 1979); "Hiring and Promotion Policies Under FEP Legislation," *MLR*, Jan. 1967; IRRA, *Equal Rights and Industrial Relations* (Madison: 1977); J. Hagan James, "Guidelines for Initiating Fair Employment Practices," *Personnel*, May/June 1963; "The Job Ahead in Fair Employment Practices," *Social Action*, Dec. 1962; James E. Jones, Jr., *The Transformation of Fair Employment Practices Policies* (Madison: Univ. of Wisconsin, IRRI, Reprint 206, 1976); Kenneth A. Kovach, "Implicit Stereotyping in Personnel Decisions," *PJ*, Sept. 1981; Terry L. Leap, William H. Holley, Jr., and Hubert S. Feild, "Equal Employment Opportunity and Its Implications for Personnel Practices in the 1980s," *LLJ*, Nov. 1980; John E. Means, "Fair Employment Practices Legislation and Enforcement in the United States," *ILR*, March 1966; Mary Green Miner and John B. Miner, *Employee Selection Within the Law* (Washington: BNA, 1978); Ruth G. Shaeffer, *Nondiscrimination in Employment, 1973–1975; A Broadening and Deepening National*

Effort (New York: The Conference Board, Report no. 677, 1975); Larry E. Short, "Nondiscrimination Policies: Are they Effective?" *PJ*, Sept. 1973.

See also AGE DISCRIMINATION IN EMPLOYMENT ACT OF 1967, CIVIL RIGHTS ACT OF 1964, EXECUTIVE ORDER 11246, UNIFORM GUIDELINES ON EMPLOYEE SELECTION PROCEDURES, VIETNAM ERA VETERANS READJUSTMENT ASSISTANCE ACT OF 1974.

Fair Labor Standards Act of 1938 Statute adopted June 25, 1938, effective October 24, 1938, to regulate minimum wages, overtime pay, and child labor in interstate commerce and the production of goods for interstate commerce. Commonly known as the Wage and Hour Law, the statute established a minimum wage of 25 cents an hour during its first year, 30 cents an hour for the next six years, and 40 cents an hour at the expiration of seven years. A tripartite industry committee procedure was provided, however, for raising the minimum to the 40-cent level on an industry basis prior to expiration of the seven years. The minimum was increased by subsequent congressional action, first to 75 cents, then to $1, $1.15, $1.25, $1.40, $1.60, $2, $2.10, $2.30, $2.65, $2.90, $3.10, and to $3.35.

The law has been amended on 14 occasions, seven times substantially. The Portal-to-Portal Act of 1947 established specific standards for computing working time and provided good-faith and other defenses to liability under the Act. The 1949 amendments narrowed the law's coverage, increased the minimum wage, and established new rules for computing overtime pay. The 1961 amendments broadened coverage, modified some of the exemptions, and increased the minimum wage to $1.25. The Equal Pay Act of 1963 added provisions requiring equal pay for equal work without regard to sex. The 1966 amendments provided for escalated minimum wage increase to $1.60, modified exemptions, and extended coverage to four groups of employees: (1) schools, hospitals, and nursing homes; (2) laundries and dry cleaners; (3) hotels, motels, and restaurants; and (4) agriculture. The 1974 amendments further extended coverage of the Act to workers in public employment, household employment, and retail trade and service establishments. In 1976, however, the Supreme Court in *National League of Cities v. Usery* (426 US 833, 22 WH Cases 1064 (1976)), declared that the minimum wage and overtime coverage of state and local government employees was unconstitutional. It also overruled *Maryland v. Wirtz* (392 US 183, 18 WH Cases 445 (1968)), which had upheld the 1966 amendments of the Fair Labor Standards Act that extended coverage to include employees of public schools and hospitals. The 1974 amendments strengthened the enforcement provision of the Act and extended coverage of the Age Discrimination in Employment Act of 1967 to federal, state, and local government employees. The 1977 amendments established an independent Minimum Wage Study Commission comprised of eight members—two each appointed by the secretaries of agriculture; commerce; health, education and welfare; and labor—to conduct studies on, among other topics, the effects of minimum wages on employment, prices, and wages, and minimum wages for younger workers. The 1977 amendments also permitted the secretary of labor to waive child labor restrictions for hand harvest agricultural work paid on a piece rate basis.

The law has a complicated coverage and exemption structure. General coverage extends to an employee who is "engaged in commerce or in the production of goods for commerce, or is employed in an enterprise engaged in commerce or in the production of goods for commerce," and to most federal employees and private household domestic workers. But there are more than 40 exemptions, the most important being those applicable to executive, administrative, and professional employees, and outside salesmen.

Payment of time and one-half the employee's regular rate is required for work in excess of 40 hours a week, and employment of "oppressive" child labor is forbidden. Enforcement is by back-wage suits brought by employees or by the secretary of labor on behalf of employees, injunction actions brought by the secretary, or criminal actions brought by the Department of Justice where there are "willful" violations. The law is administered by the Wage and Hour Division in the Department of Labor.

Source references: Fair Labor Standards Act of 1938, as amended, 29 U.S.C. § 201 et seq. (1982); BNA, *Fair Labor Standards Act Amendments of 1966: Explanation of Changes, Text of Act as Amended* (Washington: 1966); ———, *The New Wage and Hour Law* (Washington: 1961); Milton C. Denbo, "The Fair Labor Standards Amendment of 1961—An Analysis," *LLJ*, Aug. 1961; Peyton Elder, "The 1974 Amendments to the Federal Minimum Wage Law," *MLR*, July 1974; ———, "The 1977 Amendments to the Federal Minimum Wage Law," *MLR*, Jan. 1978; Peyton K. Elder and Heidi D. Miller, "The Fair Labor Standards Act: Changes of Four Decades," *MLR*, July 1979; "Federal Wage-Hour Law Upheld by Supreme Court," *MLR*, Feb. 1941; G. W. Foster, Jr., "Jurisdiction, Rights, and Remedies for Group Wrongs Under the Fair Labor Standards Act: Special Federal Questions," *IR Law Digest*, Jan. 1976; Jonathan Grossman, "Fair Labor Standards Act of 1938: Maximum Struggle for a Minimum Wage," *MLR*, June 1978; Kenneth A. Kovach, "Is It Time to Amend the Overtime Provisions of the Fair Labor Standards Act?" *Human Resource Management*, Fall 1979; Mack A. Player, "Enterprise Coverage Under the Fair Labor Standards Act: An Assessment of the First Generation," *IR Law Digest*, Summer 1975; William S. Tyson, "The Fair Labor Standards Act of 1938: A Survey and Evaluation of the First Eleven Years," *LLJ*, Jan. 1950; U.S. Congress, House, Committee on Education and Labor, *Fair Labor Standards Act of 1938 (As Amended by the Fair Labor Standards Amendments of 1977) and Related Provisions of Law* (Washington: 1979); U.S. Congress, Senate, Committee on Labor and Public Welfare, *Legislative History of the Fair Labor Standards Amendments of 1974, Volumes 1 and 2* (Washington: 1976); U.S. Dept. of Labor, Employment Standards Administration, *Domestic Service Employees, A Study of the Economic Effects of the Provisions of the FLSA Submitted to Congress, 1979* (Washington: 1979); ———, *Handy Reference Guide to the Fair Labor Standards Act* (rev. ed., Washington: Pub. no. 1282, 1977); ———, *Minimum Wage and Maximum Hours Standards Under the Fair Labor Standards Act, An Economic Effects Study Submitted to Congress, 1979* (Washington: 1979); U.S. GAO, *Changes Needed to Deter Violations of Fair Labor Standards Act* (Washington: 1981).

See also MINIMUM WAGE, PORTAL-TO-PORTAL PAY ACT.

fair list The names of companies and organizations whose working conditions, including union security provisions, are acceptable to organized labor. Union members are therefore urged to patronize and support such employers. It has sometimes been referred to as the "white" list to separate it from the "black" list. A union label is also used to note that the particular product which bears the label was made under union working conditions.

See also BLACKLIST, UNION LABEL (BUG), WHITELIST.

fair representation *See* DUTY OF FAIR REPRESENTATION.

fair share agreement A form of union security defined by the Wisconsin Municipal Employment Relations Act as "an agreement between a municipal employer and a labor organization under which all or any of the employees in the collective bargaining unit are required to pay their proportionate share of the cost of the collective bargaining process and contract administration measured by the amount of dues uniformly required of all members." A similar provision is included in the Wisconsin State Employment Relations Act.

The fair share provision is also available under the laws covering government employees in New Jersey (termed "payment in lieu of dues") and Oregon.

Source reference: Wisconsin Municipal Employment Relations Act, Sec. 111.70.

See also AGENCY SHOP, SERVICE FEE.

fair wage *See* FAIR DAY'S PAY.

False Information Act Criminal statute making it a crime for an individual to make a false or fraudulent statement to any government department or agency on a matter properly within its jurisdiction. It has been utilized by the federal government in enforcing both the non-Communist affidavit provisions of the Taft-Hartley Act and the record-keeping requirements of the Fair Labor Standards Act. The penalty for violation is a fine up to $10,000, imprisonment for up to 10 years, or both.

Source reference: False Identification Crime Control Act of 1982, 18 U.S.C. §§ 1001 note, 1028, 1738 (1982); 39 U.S.C. § 3001 (1982).

See also NONCOMMUNIST AFFIDAVIT.

family allowances Wage payments, in excess of regular pay for the job, given to employees on the basis of the number of dependents. The practice, except in limited areas, is not widespread in American industry.

family budget Sometimes used synonymously with the City Worker's Family Budget issued by BLS as an aid in developing and checking the adequacy of the Consumer Price Index.

In general usage the term "family budget" applies to the actual plan of expenditure for a given period of a fixed amount of income distributed to meet the needs of the family for food, clothing, shelter, and miscellaneous expenditures.

Distinctions sometimes have been drawn between "actual" and "standard" family budgets. The standard family budget was the amount of money needed to maintain a fixed level of living such as bare subsistence (minimum of comfort), while the actual family budget was the plane at which the family actually lived—the amount spent for food, clothing, shelter, etc., even though it may have been less than needed for "subsistence."

The Family Budget series was discontinued after the issuance of the autumn 1981 data in response to a presidential directive to reduce spending.

Source references: Carolyn Shaw Bell, "Should Every Job Support a Family?" *The Public Interest,* Summer 1975; Anne Draper, "Crisis on the Family Budget," *American Federationist,* Jan. 1981; "Final Report on Family Budgets: Cost Increases Slowed, Autumn 1981," *MLR,* July 1982; Fabian Linden, "All in the Family Budget," *Across the Board,* Aug. 1977; ———, "How Three Family Budgets are Affected by Inflation—and Taxation Without Authorization," *Across the Board,* Nov. 1980; Fabian Linden and Helen Axel (ed.), *Consumer Expenditure Patterns. I: Food, Household Supplies, Personal and Health Care* (New York: The Conference Board, Report no. 745, 1978); M. Louise McCraw, "Medical Care Costs Lead Rise in 1976–77 Family Budgets," *MLR,* Nov. 1978; "Retired Couple's Budgets, Final Report, Autumn 1981," *MLR,* Nov. 1982; U.S. Dept. of Labor, BLS, *City Worker's Family Budget for a Moderate Living Standard, Autumn 1966* (Washington: Bull. 1570–1, 1967); ———, *City Worker's Family Budget, Pricing, Procedures, Specifications, and Average Prices, Autumn 1966* (Washington: Bull. 1570–3, 1968); ———, *Consumer Expenditure Survey: Interview Survey, 1972–73, Volumes 1 and 2* (Washington: Bull. 1997, 1978); ———, *Retired Couple's Budget for a Moderate Living Standard, Autumn 1966* (Washington: Bull. 1570–4, 1968); ———, *Revised Equivalence Scale for Estimating Equivalent Incomes or Budget Costs by Family Type* (Washington: Bull. no. 1570–2, 1968); ———, *Three Standards of Living for an Urban Family of Four Persons, Spring 1969* (Washington: Bull. no. 1570–5, 1970); ———, *Urban Family Budget, Autumn 1981* (Washington: 1982); Harold W. Watts, "Special Panel Suggests Changes in BLS Family Budget Program," *MLR,* Dec. 1980.

See also BARE (MINIMUM) SUBSISTENCE LEVEL, CONSUMER PRICE INDEX, STANDARD OF LIVING.

family workers Members of the immediate family, and sometimes close relatives, who usually work without compensation in the operation of an enterprise. It is frequent in certain agricultural and small family enterprises such as groceries, hand laundries, etc.

Fansteel case A decision of the Supreme Court holding that the right to strike did not extend to the use of the sitdown strike and that "sitting down" employees who were discharged had no reinstatement rights under the National Labor Relations Act. Chief Justice Hughes delivered the majority opinion; Justices Black and Reed dissented.

The Supreme Court said in part:

> This was not the exercise of "the right to strike" to which the Act referred. It was not a

mere quitting of work and statement of grievances in the exercise of pressure recognized as lawful. It was an illegal seizure of the buildings in order to prevent their use by the employer in a lawful manner and thus by acts of force and violence to compel the employer to submit. When the employees resorted to that sort of compulsion they took a position outside the protection of the statute and accepted the risk of the termination of their employment upon grounds aside from the exercise of the legal rights which the statute was designed to conserve. . . . We are unable to conclude that Congress intended to compel employers to retain persons in their employ regardless of their unlawful conduct—to invest those who go on strike with an immunity from discharge for acts of trespass or violence against the employer's property, which they would not have enjoyed had they remained at work. . . .

Source references: NLRB v. Fansteel Metallurgical Corporation, 306 US 240, 4 LRRM 515 (1939); Leon Green, "The Case for the Sit-Down Strike," *The New Republic*, March 24, 1937; Henry M. Hart, Jr. and Edward F. Pritchard, Jr., "The Fansteel Case," 52 *Harvard LR* 1275 (1939); "Sit-Down Strikes: A New Problem for Government," *Illinois LR*, March 1937; Louis Stark, "Sit-Down," *Survey Graphic*, June 1937.

Farmer-Labor Party An outgrowth of the Labor Party of Illinois which organized in 1918. It enlarged its activities in 1920 to include farmers and other liberal groups. It was active in the 1920s and 1930s but achieved little success except in Minnesota and Wisconsin, working through the Progressive Party.

Source references: Nathan Fine, *Labor and Farmer Parties in the United States, 1829–1928* (New York: Rand School of Social Science, 1928); Hayes Robbins, *The Labor Movement and the Farmer* (New York: Harcourt Brace, 1922); Murray S. Stedman, *Discontent at the Polls: A Study of Farmer and Labor Parties, 1827–1948* (New York: Columbia UP, 1949).

farming-out *See* SUBCONTRACTING.

farm labor Workers engaged on the farm or in agriculture. In highly seasonal agriculture, migratory labor is used during the peak seasonal activity.

Source references: G. Joachim Elterich, "Estimating the Cost of Extending Jobless Insurance to Farmworkers," *MLR*, May 1978; Curtis L. Gilroy, "Minimum Wages and Agricultural Employment: A Review of the Evidence," *Proceedings of the 34th A/M, IRRA*, ed. by Barbara Dennis (Madison: 1982); James S. Holt, "Extending Jobless Pay for Farmworkers," *Manpower*, Dec. 1971; Karen S. Koziara, "Agricultural Labor Relations Laws in Four States—A Comparison," *MLR*, May 1977; Jeff L. Lewin, "'Representatives of Their Own Choosing:' Practical Consideration in the Selection of Bargaining Representatives for Seasonal Farmworkers," *Industrial Relations LJ*, Spring 1976; Gary L. Lieber, "Labor-Management Relations in Agriculture: The Need for Meaningful Collective Bargaining," *IR Law Digest*, Summer 1974; H. L. Mitchell, "Farm Labour Moves Ahead," *American Federationist*, Jan. 1948; Alexander Morin, *The Organizability of Farm Labor in the United States* (Cambridge: Harvard UP, 1952); Thomas E. Murphy, "An End to American 'Serfdom'—The Need for Farm Labor Legislation," *LLJ*, Feb. 1974; Gene Rowe and Leslie Whitener Smith, *The Hired Farm Working Force of 1975* (Washington: U.S. Dept. of Agriculture, Agricultural Economic Report no. 355, 1976); H. Schwartz, *Seasonal Farm Labor in the United States* (New York: Columbia UP, 1945).

See also FARM WORKERS OF AMERICA, UNITED (AFL-CIO); MIGRATORY WORKER.

Farm Labor Panel, California *See* CALIFORNIA FARM LABOR PANEL.

Farm Labor Union; National (AFL) *See* AGRICULTURAL WORKERS UNION; NATIONAL (AFL-CIO).

Farm Workers of America; United (AFL-CIO) Formerly known as the United Farm Workers Organizing Committee, it received a charter from the AFL-CIO in February 1972. It publishes *El Malcriado*.

Address: P.O. Box 62—La Paz, Keene, Calif. 93531. Tel. (805) 822–5571

Source references: Dick Meister and Anne Loftis, *A Long Time Coming, the Struggle to Unionize America's Farm Workers* (New York: Macmillan, 1977); Thomas E. Murphy,

"An End to American 'Serfdom'—The Need for Farm Labor Legislation," *LLJ*, Feb. 1974; U.S. Congress, Senate, Committee on Labor and Human Resources, *Farmworker Collective Bargaining, 1979, Hearings* (Washington: 1979).

Farm Workers Organizing Committee; United (AFL-CIO) The successor to the Agricultural Workers Organizing Committee (AWOC), created by the AFL-CIO in 1949 to organize farm workers on the Pacific Coast, primarily in California. The National Farm Workers Association (NFWA), led by Cesar Chavez, merged with the AWOC and the name, United Farm Workers Organizing Committee, was adopted in 1966.

NFWA was recognized as bargaining representative by Schenley Industries in April 1966 and a first agreement was culminated on June 21, providing for a minimum $1.75 wage, fringe benefits, union shop, and hiring hall.

On April 1, 1967, under the terms of an arbitration award calling for a collective bargaining agreement for farm workers at three Di Giorgio Fruit Corp. ranches, the largest grape grower in California, wage increases, pensions, vacations, and health and welfare benefits were incorporated into a new agreement.

The union has been successful in organizing a substantial portion of farm laborers on the West Coast. It received a charter from the AFL-CIO in February 1972, and is now known as the United Farm Workers of America (AFL-CIO).

Source references: John G. Dunne, *Delano, The Story of the California Grape Strike* (New York: Farrar, Straus & Giroux, 1967); Donald H. Grubbs, "Prelude to Chavez: The National Farm Labor Union in California," *Labor History*, Fall 1975; Peter Matthiessen, *Sal Si Puedes, Cesar Chavez and the New American Revolution* (New York: Random House, 1969); National Advisory Committee on Farm Labor, *Farm Labor Organizing 1905–1967; A Brief History* (New York: 1967); Eugene Nelson, *Huelga: The First Hundred Days of the Great Delano Grape Strike* (Delano: Farm Workers Press, 1966); "Picking and Choosing," *Free Labour World*, June 1976; Jean Maddern Pitrone, *Chavez, Man of the Migrants* (Staten Island, N.Y.: Alba House, 1971); Ronald B. Taylor, *Chavez and the Farm Workers* (Boston: Beacon, 1975).

See also FARM WORKERS OF AMERICA, UNITED (AFL-CIO); MIGRATORY WORKER.

Farwell v. Boston & Worcester Railroad Co. A decision of the Massachusetts Supreme Court in 1842 setting out the principle that a worker assumes the ordinary risks involved in his employment. The court stated in part:

> The general rule, resulting from considerations as well of justice as of policy, is, that he who engages in the employment of another for the performance of specified duties and services, for compensation, takes upon himself the natural and ordinary risks and perils incident to the performance of such services, and in legal presumption the wage is adjusted accordingly.

Source reference: Farwell v. Boston & Worcester Railroad Co., 4 Metcalf 49 (Mass 1842).

See also CONTRIBUTORY NEGLIGENCE, WORKERS COMPENSATION.

fatigue The inability of a worker to continue the level of output or maintain efficiency due to physical or nervous exhaustion, resulting usually from long hours of work without adequate rest or relaxation. Personnel studies have shown that short rest periods have resulted in increased productive efficiency and reduction of fatigue. Modern incentive methods also take into consideration the factor of fatigue in establishing their standards.

Source references: William Gomberg, "Measuring the Fatigue Factor," *ILRR*, Oct. 1947; Gerald N. Griffith, "Fatigue and Overtime: A Myth Toppled," *Management Review*, Oct. 1969.

See also MONOTONY, OVERWORK.

fatigue allowance An amount of time added to the normal time to compensate for fatigue.

Source reference: Stephen J. Barres, "Fatigue and the Need for Work Studies," *PJ*, Dec. 1961.

fatigue costs Those costs of operation which may be directly or indirectly attributed to the effects of fatigue. Among the byproducts of industrial fatigue are: increased absenteeism, accidents, spoilage, sickness, damage to machinery, and reduced productivity. Studies of fatigue and ways to minimize its effects may result in substantial savings in cost of production.

fatigue factor *See* FATIGUE, REST PERIOD, SPEED-UP.

fatigue study Efforts to measure the causes and the extent of fatigue and its effect on the worker. Studies in setting incentive rates and establishing norms or standards must determine whether they reflect not only the ability to maintain the output for a short period of time, but over a prolonged period. Complaints of unions frequently are based on standards which can be maintained for only short periods of time and do not adequately consider the effect of fatigue if the pace is maintained over a long stretch.

Source references: Asa S. Knowles and Robert D. Thomson, *Management of Manpower* (New York: Macmillan, 1943); Richard H. Lansburgh and William R. Spriegel, *Industrial Management* (New York: Wiley, 1940).

fat work Work which pays more money without any extra effort. In the printing trades, receiving pay for blank spaces on a page or short lines of verse is considered "fat." In incentive pay, where the rates are loosely set, the rate is said to be "fat" as compared to rates which are "lean" or "tight."

Source references: Albert Barrere and Charles G. Leland (ed.), *A Dictionary of Slang, Jargon and Cant* (2 vols., London: Ballantyne Press, 1889–90); Eric Partridge, *A Dictionary of Slang and Unconventional English* (New York: Macmillan, 1950).

"favored nations" clause An agreement provision indicating that one party to the agreement (employer or union) shall have the opportunity to share in more favorable terms negotiated by the other party with another employer or union.

favoritism Action by the employer or supervisor which is based on considerations other than fairness or equity to all of the employees involved. This may be manifested in promoting a worker merely because he may bring gifts to the supervisor or is an "apple polisher," rather than using objective standards for promotion such as ability, measured production, qualification for the job, length of outstanding performance, etc.

See also APPLE POLISHING.

featherbedding Practices on the part of some unions to make work for their members through the limitation of production, the amount of work to be performed, or other make-work arrangements. Many of these practices have come about because workers have been displaced by mechanization and the union has sought some method of retaining the employees, even though there may be no work for them to perform, or their services may not be required.

The Taft-Hartley Act makes it an unfair labor practice ". . . to cause or attempt to cause an employer to pay or deliver or agree to pay or deliver any money or other thing of value in the nature of an exaction, for services which are not performed or not to be performed."

Source references: Labor Management Relations Act, Section 8(b)(6), as amended, 29 U.S.C. § 158(b)(6) (1982); *United States v. Petrillo,* 75 FSupp 176, 21 LRRM 2205 (ND Ill 1948); Benjamin Aaron, *Governmental Restraints on Featherbedding* (Los Angeles: UC, Institute of IR, 1953); Ivar Berg and James Kuhn, "The Assumptions of Featherbedding," *LLJ*, April 1962; William L. Brach, "Legislative Shackles on Featherbedding Practices," *Cornell LQ*, Winter 1948; Walter L. Daykin, "Featherbedding," *LLJ*, Nov. 1956; Morris A. Horowitz, "Featherbedding: The Specter in Future Collective Bargaining?" *LLJ*, Jan. 1960; Paul Jacobs, *Dead Horse and the Featherbird: A Report* (Santa Barbara: Center for the Study of Democratic Institutions, 1962); William R. Sherrard, "Legal Aspects of Featherbedding," *PJ*, April 1963; Norman J. Simler, "The Economics of Featherbedding," *ILRR*, Oct. 1962; Paul A. Weinstein (ed.), *Featherbedding and Technological Change* (Boston: Heath, 1965); ———, "The Featherbedding Problem," *Proceedings of the 16th A/M, IRRA*, ed. by Gerald Somers (Madison: 1964).

See also ANTI-RACKETEERING ACT (HOBBS ACT), BOGUS (TYPE) WORK, LEA ACT (ANTI-PETRILLO ACT), MAKE-WORK PRACTICES.

Federal Anti-Injunction Act *See* NORRIS-LAGUARDIA ACT.

Federal Committee on Apprenticeship Training A tripartite committee established under the Apprenticeship Act of August 16, 1937, to advise the U.S. Department of Labor in setting basic standards of apprentice training. The apprentice-training service was established as part of the U.S. Department of Labor.

Source reference: National Apprenticeship Act, as amended, 29 U.S.C. §§ 50–50b (1982).

See also APPRENTICESHIP.

Federal Corrupt Practices Act The federal act of 1925 as amended, further modified in Section 304 of the Taft-Hartley Act, designed to restrict political contributions of corporations and labor unions.

Source reference: Labor Management Relations Act of 1947, Section 304. (Currently, Section 316 of the Federal Election Campaign Act of 1972, 2 U.S.C. § 441(b), corresponds to the former Section 304 of the Labor Management Relations Act).

Federal Emergency Administration of Public Works Established following enactment of the National Industrial Recovery Act of 1933 and consolidated into the Federal Works Agency to be administered as the Public Works Administration in 1939.

See also FEDERAL WORKS AGENCY, PUBLIC WORKS ADMINISTRATION (AUTHORITY).

Federal Emergency Relief Administration (FERA) An independent agency of the federal government established in May 1933 to coordinate and subsidize relief programs of the states in relieving hardships caused by unemployment and drought. An initial appropriation of $500,000,000 was set aside for this program. One half was to be used for matching state and local funds and the other half was to be used in a discretionary manner where the problems of relief were most acute. Liquidated by the Works Progress Administration in June 1938.

Source reference: Edward Williams, *Federal Aid for Relief* (New York: Columbia UP, 1939).

See also WORKS PROGRESS ADMINISTRATION.

Federal Employees; National Federation of (Ind) Organized originally in September 1917 under charter from the American Federation of Labor. The organization withdrew from the AFL in 1932 and has been independent ever since. The AFL later chartered another organization having jurisdiction over government employees—the American Federation of Government Employees (AFL-CIO).

On March 18, 1968, the Federal Tobacco Inspectors Mutual Association (Ind) merged with the union.

Its official publications are *The Federal Employee* (monthly), *NFFE Action* (monthly), and *NFFE Outlook* (bimonthly).

Address: 1016 16th St., N.W., Washington, D.C. 20036. Tel. (202) 862–4400

Federal Employment Stabilization Board A board set up under the Federal Employment Stabilization Act of 1931. The Board was composed of the secretaries of commerce, agriculture, labor, and treasury. Its functions were to advise the President on the trend of employment and business activity and to alert the President in case of a possible business depression. The functions were subsequently transferred to the Department of Commerce and then to the National Resources Planning Board in the Executive Office of the President, under Reorganization Plan I, effective July 1, 1939.

Source reference: Employment Stabilization Act of 1931, 29 U.S.C. §§ 48–48g (1982), obsolete by act of June 26, 1943, 57 Stat. 170.

See also ECONOMIC REPORT.

Federal Labor Relations Authority (FLRA) An independent agency created by Reorganization Plan No. 2 that administers Title VII of the Civil Service Reform Act. The three members of the FLRA are appointed by the President and confirmed by the Senate. The agency determines appropriate units, supervises and conducts representation elections, resolves scope of negotiation issues, adjudicates unfair labor practices cases, prescribes criteria for compelling need, resolves exceptions to arbitration awards, and establishes policy and guidance for Title VII.

The FLRA was established to meet two Congressional objectives: (1) to assure impartial adjudication of federal labor-management disputes and (2) to eliminate the fragmentation of authority in the federal labor relations program. Two major components of the FLRA are the Office of the General Counsel and the Federal Service Impasses Panel (FSIP). The FLRA has nine regional offices.

Source references: Ronald W. Haughton, "The Role of the Federal Labor Relations Authority in the United States," *Proceedings of the 35th A/M, IRRA*, ed. by Barbara Dennis (Madison: 1983); U.S. GAO, *The Federal Labor Relations Authority: Its First Year in Operation* (Washington: 1980).

See also CIVIL SERVICE REFORM ACT OF 1978, FEDERAL SERVICE IMPASSES PANEL (FSIP), REORGANIZATION PLAN NO. 2 OF 1978.

Federal Labor Relations Council (FLRC) Established by Executive Order 11491 to administer and interpret the Order, "decide major policy issues, prescribe regulations, and report and make recommendations to the President." It determined criteria for national consultation rights and served as the final board of appeal for decisions of the assistant secretary of labor for labor-management relations. It also considered appeals on negotiability issues and exceptions to arbitration awards. The FLRC was composed of the chair of the Civil Service Commission, who also served as the chairperson of the Council, the secretary of labor, the director of the Office of Management and Budget, and other officials of the executive branch the President may have designated. The Council was dissolved with the passage of the Civil Service Reform Act of 1978.

Source references: U.S. Congress, House, Committee on Post Office and Civil Service, *Federal Service Labor-Management Relations Program, Report of the Federal Labor Relations Council* (Washington: 1977); U.S. FLRC, *Negotiability Determinations by the Federal Labor Relations Council (FLRC), January 1, 1970 to June 1, 1978* (Washington: 1978); ———, *Report of the Federal Labor Relations Council, January 1, 1970–December 31, 1976* (Washington: 1978); ———, *Rules and Regulations of the Federal Labor Relations Council and Federal Service Impasses Panel* (Washington: 1976).

federal labor unions Local unions which were affiliated with and chartered directly by the AFL. They were used largely as a method of organizing in isolated localities which included numerous crafts, or in areas where no national or international union had been chartered or claimed jurisdiction. It was expected that ultimately members of a craft in a federal labor union would join the appropriate national or international union. The federal labor union was used by the AFL as a building device for new national organizations. The federal labor union occasionally was referred to as an "industrial" union on a local scale.

Federally Employed Women (FEW) A private organization established in 1968 by women in the Washington, D.C. area employed by the federal government. It seeks to eliminate employment discrimination against women in the federal service.

The formation of FEW was prompted by the concern of the women over full implementation of Executive Order 11375 and the Federal Women's Program (FWP). Executive Order 11375 added "sex" to the other forms of discrimination prohibited within federal employment and by government contractors.

The FWP was established by the Civil Service Commission in 1967; under this program, federal agencies are required to have a full-time FWP coordinator or an FWP committee to act as the agency's contact point, source of information, and adviser to the head of the agency on matters involving the employment of women.

Unlike FWP, which operates with government funding, FEW is funded by membership dues and can engage in political action, lobby, and carry out other activities to publicize the status of women.

The first FEW chapter was chartered in January 1970, in Central Cincinnati. Allie Latimer Weeden was FEW's first president (1968–69) and Steve Harrison was the organization's first male member. FEW is now a worldwide organization with more than 200 chapters and 11 regional offices in 46 states and four foreign countries. It publishes the bimonthly *News & Views*.

Address: 1010 Vermont Ave., N.W., Suite 821, Washington, D.C. 20005. Tel. (202) 638–4404

Source references: Jennie Farley, *Affirmative Action and the Women Worker* (New York: AMACOM, 1979): Federally Employed Women, *A Brief History of FEW* (Washington: 1980).

Federal Mediation and Conciliation Service (FMCS) An independent agency created under Title II of the Taft-Hartley Act. It took over the staff and files of the U.S. Conciliation Service, and assumed the functions and duties of the Service which had operated within the U.S. Department of Labor since 1913. The director of the FMCS is appointed by the President with the advice and consent of the Senate. Title II formalized some of the practices of the U.S. Conciliation Service and gave explicit statutory sanction to FMCS.

Source references: Labor Management Relations Act, Sections 201–212, as amended, 29 U.S.C. §§ 171–182 (1982); Jerome T. Barrett and Lucretia Dewey Tanner, "The FMCS Role in Age Discrimination Complaints: New Uses of Mediation," *LLJ*, Nov. 1981; Herbert Fishgold, "Dispute Resolution in the Public Sector: The Role of FMCS," *LLJ*, Dec. 1976; Max M. Kampelman, "The United States Conciliation Service," *Minnesota LR*, June 1947; William J. Kilberg, "The FMCS and Arbitration: Problems and Prospects," *MLR*, April 1971; Harold S. Roberts, *The First Six Months Under the Taft-Hartley Act* (Honolulu: Univ. of Hawaii, Occasional Papers no. 45, 1948); ———, "The Labor-Management Relations Act of 1947," *MLR*, Oct. 1947; Jerome H. Ross, "Federal Mediation in the Public Sector," *MLR*, Feb. 1976; James F. Scearce and Lucretia Dewey Tanner, "Health Care Bargaining: The FMCS Experience," *LLJ*, July 1976; L. Lawrence Schultz, "Arbitration Trends: An Agency Perspective," *LLJ*, Aug. 1978; U.S. FMCS, *Annual Reports* (Washington: annually); U.S. GAO, *The Federal Mediation and Conciliation Service Should Strive to Avoid Mediating Minor Disputes* (Washington: 1980); Edgar L. Warren, "The Conciliation Service: V.J. Day to Taft-Hartley," *ILRR*, April 1948.

Federal Pay Comparability Act of 1970 Signed into law on January 8, 1971, the law mandates that federal white-collar employees be paid rates that are comparable with those in the private sector for the same work levels and that they receive equal pay for substantially equal work. Private sector rates are to be determined by the BLS' national survey of professional, administrative, technical, and clerical pay. The law provides for annual pay increases in amounts to be decided by the President; Congressional approval is not required.

The President is assisted by his Pay Agent (the directors of the Office of Management and Budget and the Office of Personnel Management, and the secretary of labor), the Federal Employees Pay Council (composed of five representatives from the leading federal labor unions), and the Advisory Committee on Federal Pay (a three-member body of persons not employed by the federal government). If the President decides that economic conditions do not warrant adjustments, he can prepare an alternative plan which will automatically go into effect unless a majority of either house of Congress votes its disapproval, in which case the President is required to implement comparability adjustments.

Source references: Federal Pay Comparability Act of 1970, as amended, Pub. L. 91–656, 84 Stat. 1946 (codified as amended in scattered sections of 2, 5, and 39 U.S.C.); Lily Mary David, "Experience Under the Federal Pay Comparability Act of 1970," *Proceedings of the 33d A/M, IRRA*, ed. by Barbara Dennis (Madison: 1981); U.S. Advisory Committee on Federal Pay, *A Decade of Federal White-Collar Pay Comparability 1970–1980* (Washington: 1981); U.S. CSC, *Questions and Answers Regarding the Federal Pay Comparability Act of 1970* (Washington: 1971); U.S. Dept. of Labor, BLS, *National Survey of Professional, Administrative, Technical, and Clerical Pay, March 1982* (Washington: Bull. 2145, 1982).

See also CLASSIFICATION ACT EMPLOYEES, FEDERAL WAGE SYSTEM, WAGE BOARD EMPLOYEES.

Federal Salary Act of 1967 The Salary Reform Act of 1962 established the goal of achieving salary comparability between federal and private employment. The 1967 Act authorized the necessary steps to achieve comparability with the latest available measure of pay in private industry. The Federal

Salary Act of 1967 boosted federal classified workers' pay by an average of 4.5 percent in October 1967 and provided the remaining federal-private industry pay gap be closed by July 1969 in two stages by executive order.

Source reference: Arnold Strasser, "Federal Employees' Comparability Pay Raise," *MLR,* August 1969.

Federal Security Agency An independent government agency created in 1939 under the President's first reorganization plan. The purpose was to bring under one department the major governmental agencies concerned with human welfare, education, and economic security. It included the functions of the Social Security Administration, the Office of Education (transferred from Interior), the Public Health Service (transferred from Treasury), the Food and Drug Administration (transferred from Agriculture), and a number of temporary agencies, such as the National Youth Administration and the Civilian Conservation Corps.

The functions of the Federal Security Agency were transferred to the Department of Health, Education, and Welfare when it was established in 1953.

Federal Service Impasses Panel (FSIP) Established under Executive Order 11491 as an agency within the Federal Labor Relations Council to consider negotiation impasses when voluntary efforts have failed. The Panel may recommend procedures for resolution of the impasse, or it may settle the impasse itself. The Panel originally consisted of three members appointed by the President. Under the Civil Service Reform Act of 1978, the Panel is composed of a chairperson and at least six other members who are appointed by the President.

Source references: John V. Madden, "To Strike or Not to Strike: Does the Government Already Have an Alternative?" *LLJ,* May 1970; Edward E. Potter, *Fact Finding in the Federal Sector; The Development, Experience, and Evaluation of the Federal Service Impasses Panel* (Ithaca: Cornell Univ., 1972); Harold S. Roberts, *Labor-Management Relations in the Public Service* (Honolulu: Univ. of Hawaii Press, 1970); U.S. Federal Service Impasses Panel, *Annual Report, 1974+* (Washington: 1975+); ______, *Report of the Federal Service Impasses Panel, July 1, 1970–December 31, 1973* (Washington: 1974).

federal-state jurisdiction The division of jurisdiction over labor-management relations between the federal and state governments. It has been the subject of legislation and numerous court decisions. Section 10(a) of the Taft-Hartley Act of 1947 authorized the NLRB to cede jurisdiction over labor disputes to state tribunals, but it established conditions that no state was able to meet. Then in the 1957 *Guss* case, the Supreme Court ruled that a state tribunal could act in a case within the NLRB's Taft-Hartley jurisdiction only where the Board had ceded jurisdiction to the state under Section 10(a). A refusal by NLRB to assert jurisdiction over a case, the Court said, did not vest the state tribunal with jurisdiction (*Guss v. Utah Board,* 352 US 817, 39 LRRM 2567 (1957)).

The effect of this decision was to create a legal "no-man's" land in which there was no forum to which parties could turn for relief; the NLRB would not assert jurisdiction, and the state tribunals were barred from taking jurisdiction. Congress sought to rectify the situation in the 1959 Landrum-Griffin amendments to the Taft-Hartley Act. Amendments to Section 14 provided that: (1) the NLRB, by rule of decision or by published rules, may decline to assert jurisdiction over any labor dispute involving any class or category of employers where the effect on interstate commerce is not sufficiently substantial to warrant the exercise of jurisdiction; (2) the Board, however, may not decline to assert jurisdiction over any dispute over which it would have asserted jurisdiction under the standards prevailing on August 1, 1959; and (3) cases rejected by the NLRB under its jurisdictional standards may be handled by agencies or courts of the states and territories.

Where a party to a dispute comes within the NLRB's standards for asserting jurisdiction, a state may not take jurisdiction over activities that potentially are subject to regulation under the Taft-Hartley Act except where violence or coercive conduct is involved. This is the holding of the *Garmon* case (*San Diego Building Trades Council v. Garmon,* 359 US 236, 43 LRRM 2838 (1958)).

Source references: George W. Hardbeck, "Federal-State Jurisdictional Issues and Policies Under the New Labor Law," *LLJ*, Feb. 1961; Paul R. Hays, "Federalism and the Taft-Hartley Act: Constitutional Crisis," *Proceedings of the 8th A/M, IRRA*, ed. by L. Reed Tripp (Madison: 1956); Stephen J. McGarry, "A New Federal Remedy for the Protection of Employee Rights," *LLJ*, Dec. 1980; Mozart G. Ratner, "New Developments in Federal-State Jurisdiction," *NYU 15th Annual Conference on Labor*, ed. by Emanuel Stein (Albany: Bender, 1962); ———, "Problems of Federal-State Jurisdiction in Labor Relations," *NYU 5th Annual Conference on Labor*, ed. by Emanuel Stein (Albany: Bender, 1952); Louis Sherman, "Federal-State Powers in Labor Relations," *MLR*, Feb. 1956; Carl S. Silverman, "The Case for the National Labor Relations Board's Use of Rulemaking in Asserting Jurisdiction," *LLJ*, Oct. 1974; Russell A. Smith, "The Taft-Hartley Act and State Jurisdiction Over Labor Relations," 46 *Michigan LR* 594 (1948).

See also NATIONAL LEAGUE OF CITIES V. USERY; NO-MAN'S LAND; PREEMPTION, DOCTRINE OF.

federal wage and hour law *See* FAIR LABOR STANDARDS ACT OF 1938.

Federal Wage System Includes all aspects of the policies, rules, and regulations covering prevailing rate (blue-collar) employees. Wage surveys are but one part of the entire system. It includes, for example, the job grading system.

Authorized by P.L. 92–392 (August 19, 1972), the Federal Wage System provides wage adjustments based on prevailing local rates for prevailing rate employees (also known as wage employees or wage board employees). A prevailing rate employee is defined as a "person employed in or under an agency in a recognized trade or craft, or other skilled mechanical craft, or in an unskilled, semiskilled, or skilled manual labor occupation, and any other person, including a foreman and a supervisor, in a position having trade, craft, or labor experience and knowledge as the paramount requirement. . . ." Postal employees are not included in the Federal Wage System.

Wage surveys of 135 private sector wage areas are conducted annually to determine the prevailing rates of pay. The survey includes 22 occupations; 29 other occupations are surveyed on an optional basis.

The Federal Wage System includes the three-member local wage-survey committees, the five-member agency wage committees, and the 11-member Federal Prevailing Rate Advisory Committee. The Office of Personnel Management (OPM) "is responsible for prescribing the practices and procedures governing the implementation and administration of the Federal Wage System and for consulting with appropriate labor organizations."

The local wage-survey committees are established in wage areas where labor organizations have been granted exclusive recognition. Each committee's wage survey is forwarded to the lead agency for analysis and referral to the agency wage committee. One member of the local committee is a labor organization representative. All members are federal employees.

Each agency assigned lead-agency responsibility establishes an agency wage committee. The committee recommends wage schedules upon completion of a wage survey and consideration of the recommendations of the local wage-survey committee. "The head of each executive agency is responsible, within the policies and practices of the Federal Wage System for fixing and administering rates of pay for wage employees of his/her organization." Three members of the agency committee are designated by the head of the lead agency and two members by labor organizations.

The functions of the Federal Prevailing Rate Advisory Committee are to "study the prevailing rate system, and other matters pertinent to that system and, from time to time, advise the Office of Personnel Management thereon." The Committee is required to submit an annual report to the OPM and the President for transmittal to Congress. The Committee consists of a chairperson appointed by the director of OPM for a four-year term; two members from the military departments, one member from OPM, one member from other than the Department of Defense, all designated by the OPM director; one member designated by the secretary of defense; and five labor organization representatives.

Source references: U.S. GAO, *Comparison of Collectively Bargained and Administratively Set Pay Rates for Federal Employees* (Washington: 1982); U.S. OPM, *Federal Personnel Manual,* Supplement 532–1, Dec. 30, 1982.

See also WAGE BOARD EMPLOYEES.

Federal Women's Program *See* FEDERALLY EMPLOYED WOMEN (FEW).

Federal Works Agency Created in 1939 to consolidate agencies of the federal government dealing with public works (Works Progress Administration and Public Works Administration among others) not incidental to the normal work of other departments, and which administered federal grants or loans to state and local governments or other agencies for construction purposes. Abolished in 1949 and functions transferred to the General Services Administration.

federal works program A program authorized by Congress in the early 1930s which had as a major objective employment for those idle and without funds who were receiving relief. The federal government accepted the responsibility since the problem was national in scope and beyond the control of local or state agencies. Among the agencies active in providing financial assistance were the Works Progress Administration (WPA), later known as the Works Projects Administration, and the Public Works Administration (PWA).

federation A league or alliance of national and international unions designed to provide mutual assistance on the federal level as to legislation, research, policy formation, exchange of information, etc., and at the same time provide autonomy to the units affiliated or federated with it. Both the American Federation of Labor and the Congress of Industrial Organizations were federations of this type, although the authority and the practical application of that authority by the two parent organizations were quite different. The combined AFL-CIO is also a federation of national and international unions.

Source references: Lewis L. Lorwin, *The American Federation of Labor* (Washington: Brookings Institution, 1933); J. Raymond Walsh, *C.I.O. Industrial Unionism in Action* (New York: Norton, 1937).

See also AMERICAN FEDERATION OF LABOR-CONGRESS OF INDUSTRIAL ORGANIZATIONS.

Federation of Nurses and Health Professionals *See* NURSES AND HEALTH PROFESSIONALS, FEDERATION OF.

Federation of Organized Trades and Labor Unions An organization formed in 1881 by skilled craftsmen in many trades who felt that it was important to protect the special needs of skilled workers. Samuel Gompers and Adolph Strasser were the leading spirits in the formation of the Federation. In 1886, the name of the organization was changed to the American Federation of Labor.

Feeney case A 1979 Supreme Court case which challenged the constitutionality of the Massachusetts veterans preference statute on grounds that it discriminates against women in violation of the equal protection clause of the 14th Amendment. The Court upheld the statute, which grants lifetime preference in hiring to veterans, ruling that although the law "operates overwhelmingly to the advantage of males," (1) this negative impact on women was due to their nonveteran status and not to a gender-based classification system and (2) Feeney "failed to demonstrate that the law in any way reflects a purpose to discriminate on the basis of sex." The Court stated it was meant to reward veterans, both men and women, and therefore did not violate the 14th Amendment.

Source reference: Personnel Administrator of Massachusetts v. Feeney, 442 US 256, 19 FEP Cases 1377 (1979).

fees Pay or fixed charges for specific services to be performed, or for admission to membership in an organization.

See also ASSESSMENTS, DUES, INITIATION FEE, SERVICE FEE.

fellow servant doctrine The principle or doctrine in common law which held that the employer could not be held responsible for accidents suffered by a worker and resulting from the negligence of the worker. It was assumed that the employer had explained the nature of the work, warned his workers of the hazards involved in the work, established rules designed to permit safe places of work, and hired workers with due care as to their ability.

See also ASSUMPTION OF RISK, CONTRIBUTORY NEGLIGENCE.

Fibreboard case Controversial case in which the Supreme Court held that a company was obligated under the Taft-Hartley Act to bargain with the union representing its maintenance employees about an economically motivated decision to subcontract the maintenance work. The Court also held that the NLRB had authority to order the company to resume the operation it had subcontracted without bargaining with the union and to reinstate the displaced employees with back pay. The Court stressed, however, that the holding is "on the facts of this case" and does not "encompass other forms of 'contracting out' or 'subcontracting' which arise daily in our complex economy."

Source references: Fibreboard Paper Products Corp. v. NLRB, 379 US 203, 57 LRRM 2609 (1965)); Owen Fairweather, "The 'Fibreboard' Decision and Subcontracting: Two Views," *AJ*, Vol. 19, no. 2, 1964; David E. Feller, "The 'Fibreboard' Decision and Subcontracting: Two Views," *AJ*, Vol. 19, no. 2, 1964; Arthur Mermin, "The Impact of Darlington-Fibreboard," *NYU 18th Annual Conference on Labor*, ed. by Thomas Christensen (Washington: BNA, 1966); Robert J. Rabin, "Fibreboard and the Termination of Bargaining Unit Work: The Search for Standards in Defining the Scope of the Duty to Bargain," *IR Law Digest*, Jan. 1972; ———, "The Decline and Fall of Fibreboard," *NYU 24th Annual Conference on Labor* (New York: Bender, 1972).

See also COLLECTIVE BARGAINING, SUBCONTRACTING.

fictional seniority *See* RETROACTIVE SENIORITY.

field examiners These are individuals attached to the regional offices of the NLRB, sometimes also known as labor-management relations examiners. They have two major functions to perform. One is to arrange for and to conduct elections held under the procedures prescribed in the National Labor Relations Act. Where there is no contest, this function merely involves agreement on the unit, the date of the election, and the individuals entitled to vote at the time. Where there is a contest, the field examiner may also serve as a hearing officer in the region to take testimony and submit a report to the regional director, under whose jurisdiction the field examiner is usually placed.

In dispute cases, the field examiner's job is to analyze and gather the factual materials involved in particular cases to which he is assigned. The cases usually arise when an employer or union files an unfair labor practice. Since most cases are actually settled informally, the field examiner has an important role in meeting with labor and management groups to obtain conformance with the provisions of the Taft-Hartley Act.

Source references: U.S. NLRB, *A Career in Labor-Management Relations as a Field Examiner* (Washington: 1966); ———, *A Career in Labor-Management Relations as a Field Examiner* (Washington: 1982).

See also REGIONAL DIRECTOR.

filing requirements Provisions of the Labor-Management Reporting and Disclosure Act (LMRDA) requiring labor unions, union officers and employees, employers, and labor relations consultants to file reports containing financial and other information with the Department of Labor. The provisions superseded the filing requirements of the Taft-Hartley Act under which unions had to file financial reports and their officials, non-Communist affidavits with the NLRB in order to invoke the Board's processes. The LMRDA repealed the Taft-Hartley provisions.

The term also refers to the provisions of the Employee Retirement Income Security Act of 1974 which require administrators of welfare and pension plans to file plan descriptions with the secretary of labor. The administrators are also required to submit annual reports to the Internal Revenue Service.

Source references: Employee Retirement Income Security Act of 1974, as amended, Pub. L. 93–406, 88 Stat. 829 (codified as amended in scattered sections of 5, 18, 26, 29, 31, and 42 U.S.C.); Labor-Management Reporting and Disclosure Act of 1959, as amended, 29 U.S.C. §§ 431–441, 461–466 (1982); BNA, *The Labor Reform Law* (Washington: 1959); PH, *Pension and Profit Sharing*, Vol. 1–A, 16,021 et seq.

See also EEO REPORTS, EMPLOYEE RETIREMENT INCOME SECURITY ACT (ERISA) OF 1974, LABOR-MANAGEMENT REPORTING AND DISCLOSURE ACT OF 1959, NONCOMMUNIST AFFIDAVIT.

final offer arbitration *See* ARBITRATION, FINAL OFFER.

final offer ballot *See* EMPLOYER'S FINAL OFFER.

financial condition of company *See* ABILITY TO PAY.

financial reports of unions *See* FILING REQUIREMENTS.

fines for agreement violation Some contracts provide for money penalties when the contract is violated. These fines are designed to prevent or deter either party, more frequently the union, from taking direct action in forcing a decision rather than taking the issue through the contract grievance machinery and arbitration. Title III of the Taft-Hartley Act has set up procedures for handling suits for violation of contracts.

Source reference: Labor-Management Relations Act, Section 301, as amended, 29 U.S.C. § 185 (1982).

finish-go-home basis of pay A method of wage payment which guarantees pay for the day upon completion of the task assigned for the period. The standard is set for the eight-hour day or other period, and upon completion of the operation the employee is permitted to go home and to receive full pay for the entire day. It is a form of incentive designed to expedite an operation in which time is an essential consideration.

fink A professional strikebreaker. An individual who hires out during a strike period for special bonus rates or other considerations in order to help the employer break the strike. Finks who have special qualifications and assume leadership or act as recruiters and in a supervisory capacity over other finks are sometimes referred to as "nobles."

See also ANTI-STRIKEBREAKING ACT (BYRNES ACT), SCAB.

fire To dismiss, expel, or discharge an employee from his job.

See also DISCHARGE.

Fire Fighters; International Association of (AFL-CIO) Fire fighters organized in 1901 and affiliated directly with the American Federation of Labor. In 1918, delegates from various cities who had organized fire fighters met and established a national organization known as the International Association of Fire Fighters. The official monthly publication is *The International Fire Fighter*.

Address: 1750 New York Ave., N.W., Washington, D.C. 20006. Tel. (202) 872–8484

Firemen and Oilers; International Brotherhood of (AFL-CIO) Organized originally in December 1898, in Kansas City, Missouri as the International Brotherhood of Stationary Firemen. As its jurisdiction expanded, it changed its name in 1902 to the International Brotherhood of Stationary Firemen and Oilers. Some time later the word "stationary" was eliminated.

The official publication is the *Firemen and Oilers Journal*, issued bimonthly.

Address: 122 C St., N.W., Suite 280, Washington, D.C. 20001. Tel. (202) 737–5300

First International An organization of workers of international scope which grew out of the efforts of Marx and Engels to organize workers in the 1840s. The organization was formed in 1864 as the International Working Men's Association. Somewhat socialistic in its inception, it was designed to obtain equal rights for workers and to eliminate discrimination. It became increasingly socialistic and even attracted Bakunin and a group of anarchists. Bakunin and his group were expelled and the office of the International was moved to New York. The official date of its demise is 1876.

Source references: Julius Braunthal, *History of the International, Vol. 1: 1864–1914* (New York: Praeger, 1967); E. H. Carr, *Michael Bakunin* (London: Macmillan, 1937); Morris Hillquit, *History of Socialism in the United States* (5th rev. and enl. ed., New York: Funk & Wagnalls, 1910); L. E. Mins (ed.), *Founding of the First International: A Documentary Record* (New York: 1937); Angelo S. Rappoport, Dictionary of Socialism

(London: Fisher Unwin, 1924).

first round increases Wage demands made by unions following the end of World War II, designed largely to offset the wage "stabilization" during the war. Factfinding boards in 1946 recommended 18½ cents per hour wage adjustments.

See also FOURTH ROUND INCREASE, THIRD ROUND INCREASES.

five-day workweek A goal of American labor during the 1920s which was supported by some employers, particularly in the 1930s, in part to "spread" the work and in part to provide workers with adequate leisure time so they would become consumers of more goods and services, and have increased time for educational and recreational purposes.

Source references: Lamar T. Beman, *The Five-Day Week* (New York: Wilson, 1928); "Extent of Five-Day Weeks," *MLR,* Sept. 1931; "The Five-Day Week in the Ford Plant," *MLR,* Dec. 1926; William Green, "The Five-Day Week," *Harvard BR,* April 1931; ———, *The Five Day Week* (New York: North American Review Corp., 1926); NICB, *The Five-Day Week in Manufacturing Industries* (New York: 1929); Princeton Univ., IR Section, *Five-Day Week in Industry: Statement of Fact and Opinion* (Princeton: 1929).

See also FOUR-DAY WORKWEEK, HOURS OF WORK, WORKWEEK.

fix, to To bribe or use other unscrupulous methods in order to prevent the normal application or operation of law. In labor relations, the work of an intermediary or "labor consultant" to settle a strike or bring about an agreement through bribes rather than the normal processes of collective bargaining or negotiation with representatives of unions and employers.

fixed shift Assignment of individuals or groups to the same shift on a regular basis in plants or establishments which operate more than one shift. Other plants on a continuous production basis or where multiple shifts are in use may use "rotating" shifts so that the inconvenience of night shifts may be spread among employees rather than assigned to one group.

See also SHIFT.

flags of convenience In order to escape union wages and other labor standards required by the U.S. Government or by American unions, American shipping companies often have their ships licensed by foreign countries such as Panama, Liberia, or Honduras. These U.S.-owned ships thus sail under the flag of the licensing country.

Source references: Anrico Argiroffo, "Flags of Convenience and Substandard Vessels: A Review of the ILO's Approach to the Problem," *ILR,* Nov. 1974; Joseph Curran and Paul Hall, "Modern Piracy," *American Federationist,* Jan. 1959; L. F. E. Goldie, "Flags of Convenience," *International and Comparative LQ,* July 1963; R. L. Rowan, H. R. Northrup, and M. J. Immediata, "International Enforcement of Union Standards in Ocean Transport," *BJIR,* Nov. 1977; Edward B. Shils, "The 'Flag of Necessity' Fleet and the American Economy," *LLJ,* Feb. 1962; ———, "'Flags of Necessity,' 'Flags of Convenience' or 'Runaway Ships'?" *LLJ,* Dec. 1962; Edward B. Shils and Sidney L. Miller, Jr., "Foreign Flags on U.S. Ships: Convenience or Necessity?" *IR,* May 1963.

flat rate A rate for repair work computed on the basis of a "standard" time, set in the repair manual, indicating how long it should take to make the repair.

flexible benefits *See* CAFETERIA PLANS.

flexible retirement *See* RETIREMENT, FLEXIBLE.

flexible schedule A work schedule which permits adjustment of the daily or weekly hours worked to meet the production needs of a company.

See also BELO WAGE PLAN.

flextime/flexitime A work scheduling method that allows employees to vary their arrival and departure time around a required number of work hours. Such plans may require all employees to be on the job during certain operating hours.

Source references: George W. Bohlander, *Flextime—A New Face on the Work Clock* (Los Angeles: UC, Institute of IR, Policy and Practice Publications, 1977); The Conference Board, *Company Experience with Flexible Work Schedules* (New York: Research Bull.

no. 110, 1982); Janice Neipert Hedges, "Flexible Schedules: Problems and Issues," *MLR*, Feb. 1977; Donald J. Peterson, "Flexitime in the United States: Lessons of Experience," *Personnel*, Jan./Feb. 1980; Pam Silverstein and Jozetta H. Srb, *Flexitime: Where, When, and How?* (Ithaca: Cornell Univ., NYSSILR, Key Issues Series no. 24, 1979); U.S. CSC, *Flexitime—A Guide* (Washington: 1974); U.S. GAO, *The Alternative Work Schedules Experiment; Congressional Oversight Needed to Avoid Likely Failure* (Washington: 1980); ———, *Designing Experiments in Use of Flexitime and Compressed Work Schedules; Information for State and Local Governments* (Washington: 1981).

Flight Attendants; Association of A division of the Air Line Pilots Association (AFL-CIO), formed in November 1960 to replace the International Air Line Stewards and Stewardesses Association which left the Air Line Pilots Association and merged with the Transport Workers Union of America (AFL-CIO). Its quarterly publication is *Flightlog*.

Address: 1625 Massachusetts Ave., N.W., Washington, D.C. 20036. Tel. (202) 328–5400

Flight Engineers' International Association (AFL-CIO) An organization founded in 1948.

Address: 905 16th St., N.W., Washington, D.C. 20006. Tel. (202) 347–4511

Flint Glass Workers' Union of North America; American (AFL-CIO) *See* GLASS WORKERS' UNION OF NORTH AMERICA; AMERICAN FLINT (AFL-CIO).

floater A worker who drifts from job to job; an itinerant who does not like to stay long in any one place of employment. Sometimes referred to as a "boomer."

The term may also refer to employees who are assigned to work stations or departments as help is needed.

floor under wages Generally has reference to the minimum wage provisions of the Fair Labor Standards Act, since it sets an hourly wage floor below which an employer is not permitted to pay. Collective bargaining agreements also set minimum wage levels for various labor grades and in this sense set up floors under wages. Many state minimum wage laws have been set for firms not engaged in interstate commerce.

See also FAIR LABOR STANDARDS ACT OF 1938.

Florida Association of Professional Employees A branch of the National Marine Engineers' Beneficial Association (AFL-CIO).

Address: 412 Highpoint Dr., Cocoa, Florida 32922. Tel. (305) 867–7332

flow diagram Pictorial presentation of the layout of a process showing location of all activities appearing on the flow process chart and the paths of travel of the work.

See also FLOW PROCESS CHART.

flow process chart Graphic representation of all operations, transportations, inspections, delays, and storages occurring during a process or procedure. The chart includes information considered desirable for analysis, such as time required and distance moved.

fluctuating workweeks Work schedules which vary from the statutory 40 hours under the Fair Labor Standards Act.

See also BELO WAGE PLAN, HOURS OF WORK.

flying squadron A group of specially trained employees who are familiar with all or most of the key jobs in a plant or other production unit, and are available to meet special contingencies as they arise.

These may arise when an unusual work order has to be met, when absences are unusually heavy, and in case of labor difficulties or other emergencies. The employees of the flying squadron, sometimes called a "service squad," or "shock troops," are carefully selected and trained and are eligible for executive promotion.

The term is sometimes applied to special groups used by unions during a strike to take part in special or mass picketing; they may move quickly by special truck and other vehicles to help bolster a strike, and are referred to as the union's "flying squadron."

Source reference: P. W. Litchfield, "Our Flying Squadron," *Factory*, March 1, 1920.

Food and Allied Services Trades Department One of eight trade and industrial departments of the AFL-CIO, founded as the

Food and Beverage Trades Department. It adopted its current name in 1983. Its first president, James T. Housewright, and secretary-treasurer, Daniel E. Conway, in 1977 declared that the "department will develop programs to effectively collaborate on legislation, research, public relations and public policy to protect and foster the well-being of affiliated organizations."

Affiliates of the department include: Bakery, Confectionery and Tobacco Workers; Distillery and Wine Workers; Operating Engineers; Firemen and Oilers; Glass, Pottery, Plastics Workers; Grain Millers; Hotel and Restaurant Employees; Laundry and Dry Cleaning Union; Oil, Chemical and Atomic Workers; Plumbers; Railway, Airline and Steamship Clerks; Retail, Wholesale and Department Store Union; Seafarers; Service Employees; and Food and Commercial Workers. It issues the publication, *F & B Topics.*

Address: AFL-CIO Building, 815 16th St. N.W., Washington, D.C. 20006. Tel. (202) 737–7200

See also AFL-CIO DEPARTMENTS.

Food and Commercial Workers International Union; United (AFL-CIO) On June 7, 1979, the Retail Clerks International Union (AFL-CIO) and the Amalgamated Meat Cutters and Butcher Workmen of North America (AFL-CIO) merged to form this union. The United Retail Workers Union (Ind) on November 1, 1981, and the Insurance Workers International Union (AFL-CIO) in October 1983, merged with the union. Its publication, *UFCW Action,* is issued eight times a year.

Address: 1775 K St., N.W., Washington, D.C. 20006. Tel. (202) 223–3111

Football League Players Association; National An organization formed in January 1968 made up of all the teams in the National Football League. It is affiliated with the Federation of Professional Athletes (AFL-CIO).

The Association originally outlined a six-point program for negotiation with club owners, involving

(1) major increases in minimum player salary from $5,000 to a new minimum of $15,000;
(2) payment of $500 per player for all exhibition games with a possible reduction in the number of games per club;
(3) provision that no player be required to report to camp or be fined for failure to do so, unless he has signed his contract;
(4) a $5-million contribution to the players benefit fund;
(5) revision of postseason game players shares to provide fixed equal amounts for both teams along the lines of the championship games;
(6) formal grievances and arbitration procedures so the Players Association can represent its members when the occasion is necessary.

The Association issues the *Audible* (monthly), *The Checkoff* (weekly, July to January), and *Professional Athlete* (quarterly).

Address: 1300 Connecticut Ave., N.W., Washington, D.C. 20036. Tel. (202) 463–2200

forced choice arbitration *See* ARBITRATION, FORCED CHOICE.

forced labor Labor which is required or compelled by government. In totalitarian countries political or other prisoners may be placed in labor camps and forced to perform services required by the government.

Source references: Richard Carlton, *The Economic Role of Forced Labor in Eastern Europe* (New York: Mid-European Studies Center, no. 35, 1954); David J. Dallin and Boris I. Nicolaevsky, *Forced Labor in Soviet Russia* (New Haven: Yale UP, 1947); Albert K. Herling, "Gulag: A Spotlight on Forced Labor," *American Federationist,* April 1974; Sharon V. Salinger, "Colonial Labor in Transition: The Decline of Indentured Servitude in Late Eighteenth-Century Philadelphia," *Labor History,* Spring 1981; George Stolz, *Forced Labor in Soviet Orbit* (New York: Mid-European Studies Center, 1954); U.S. Congress, Senate, Committee on Labor and Public Welfare, *Forced Labor* (Washington: 1956); Walter Wilson, *Forced Labor in the United States* (New York: International Publishers, 1933).

forced quit *See* CONSTRUCTIVE DISCHARGE.

foreman Generally the first line of management in the operation of the plant or facility. The individual who, in the eyes of the production worker, represents management and authority. He is generally the immediate supervisor of a group of workers and has the responsibility to recommend suspension, discharge, or promotion. He also has the direct responsibility to see that the work is performed and the production schedule met. He carries out management policy on the operating level and acts as an intermediary between workers and middle management.

In some industries, foremen were historically permitted to become members of the bargaining unit. These were largely working foremen, as in the building and printing trades.

Whether a supervisory employee or foreman is acting as an agent of the employer, in cases where an employer has been accused of an unfair labor practice under the Taft-Hartley Act, will be determined by the NLRB according to the extent of authority exercised by the foreman over the employees.

Source references: T. W. Bonham, "The Foreman in an Ambiguous Environment," *PJ*, Nov. 1971; Russell L. Greenman, *The Worker, the Foreman and the Wagner Act* (New York: Harper, 1939); Robert D. Leiter, *The Foreman in Industrial Relations* (New York: Columbia UP, 1948); Michael Maccoby, "A Foreman Who Taught Workers to Take Over His Job," *Across the Board*, Feb. 1982; John A. Patton, "The Foreman: Most Misused Person in Industry," *Management Review*, Nov. 1974; David F. Smith, "Developing Effective Leadership in Front-Line Supervision," *PJ*, June 1975; U.S. Dept. of Labor, Division of Labor Standards, *The Foreman's Guide to Labor Relations* (Washington: Bull. no. 66, 1944).

See also SUPERVISOR, WORKING FOREMAN.

Foreman's Association of America An independent union of foremen organized in 1941 in Detroit. The enactment of the Taft-Hartley Act contributed to the demise of the association.

Source references: Charles P. Larrowe, "A Meteor on the Industrial Relations Horizon: The Foreman's Association of America," *Labor History*, Fall 1961; Herbert R. Northrup, "The Foreman's Association of America," *Harvard BR*, Winter 1945.

foreman training Programs designed by management for supervisory employees which have for their purpose the more effective functioning of the foreman on his job. These may include broad programs designed to permit him to better understand the functions of management, or detailed programs concerned with safety, production scheduling, quality control, maintenance of equipment, grievance machinery, etc. More and more, management realizes the necessity of keeping first-line supervisors and foremen abreast of developments in technical as well as policy areas so they may better carry out the objectives of top management.

Source references: Guvec G. Alpander, "Training First-Line Supervisors to Criticize Constructively," *PJ*, March 1980; BNA, *Management Training and Development Programs* (Washington: PPF Survey no. 116, 1977); William C. Byham and James Robinson, "Building Supervisory Confidence—A Key to Transfer of Training," *PJ*, May 1977; James E. Gardner, *Training the New Supervisor* (New York: AMACOM, 1980); A. A. Imberman, "Foremen Training: The Deal and the Reality," *PJ*, April 1975; Jerry J. Jensen, "How to Get Started on Supervisory Training," *Personnel*, Sept./Oct. 1965; Donald L. Kirkpatrick, *A Practical Guide for Supervisory Training and Development* (Reading, Mass.: Addison-Wesley, 1971); Elizabeth Marting, *AMA Encyclopedia of Supervisory Training: Basic Materials from Successful Company Programs* (New York: AMA, 1961); Bernard L. Rosenbaum, "A New Approach to Changing Supervisory Behavior," *Personnel*, March/April 1975; Arthur F. Strohmer, Jr., "Labor Relations Training for Foremen: A New Approach," *PJ*, Jan. 1968; Stanley D. Truskie, "In-House Supervisory Training Programs: High Caliber, High Impact," *PJ*, June 1979; Harry L. Waddell, *How to Make Your Workers Want to Become Foremen* (New York: AMA, Personnel Series no. 145, 1952); Walter S. Wikstrom, *Supervisory Training* (New York: The Conference Board, Report no. 612, 1973).

foremen unionization Efforts of supervisory employees to organize and problems incident to such efforts.

Source references: Alan Balfour, "Rights of Collective Representation for Public Sector Supervisors," *Journal of Collective Negotiations in the Public Sector,* Vol. 4, no. 3, 1975; J. Carl Cabe, *Foremen's Unions: A New Development in Industrial Relations* (Urbana: Univ. of Illinois, Bureau of Economic & Business Research, Bull. no. 65, 1947); Phillip E. Garber, "The Role of Supervisors in Employee Unions," 40 *Univ. of Chicago LR* 185 (1972); Hawaii, Dept. of Personnel Services, *The Supervisor in the Bargaining Unit. A Good Supervisor and a Good Union Member, Symposium Proceedings* (Honolulu: 1974); ———, *The Supervisor in the Bargaining Unit. Part I: The Supervisor in Hawaii's Public Employment* (Honolulu: 1973); Stephen L. Hayford, "An Empirical Investigation of the Public Sector Supervisory Bargaining Rights Issue," *LLJ,* Oct. 1975; Stephen L. Hayford and Anthony V. Sinicropi, *Collective Bargaining and the Public Sector Supervisor* (Chicago: IPMA, PERL no. 54, 1976); I. B. Helburn and Stephen R. Zimmer, "The Federal Supervisor: A Comment on Executive Order 11491," *Public Personnel Review,* Jan. 1971; Randall G. Kesselring and Paul Brinker, "Employer Domination Under Section 8(a)(2)," *LLJ,* June 1979; Ronald L. Miller, "Professional Associations and Supervisor Members: When Does an Employer Dominate and Interfere?" *LLJ,* Jan. 1979.

forewoman A woman supervisor, generally in charge of a group of female workers. Sometimes referred to as a forelady.

See also FOREMAN.

formal notification Procedures which are occasionally required in a collective bargaining agreement which specify the form a particular type of notice is to take in order to assure the parties that the information will be properly and officially delivered. Formal notification is usually by registered mail, with return receipt requested.

formal recognition Formerly granted under Executive Order 10988 to any organization with a membership of 10 percent of the employees in a unit or activity of a government agency, where no organization had been granted exclusive recognition. It gave an organization the right to be consulted on matters of interest to its members. Terminated under Executive Order 11491.

Source reference: Harold S. Roberts, *Labor-Management Relations in the Public Service* (Honolulu: Univ. of Hawaii Press, 1970).

See also EXCLUSIVE RECOGNITION, INFORMAL RECOGNITION, NATIONAL CONSULTATION RIGHTS.

forms and records As the number of employees in a plant or company increases, it becomes more and more necessary to maintain certain information in order to permit the efficient performance of the personnel management functions. Not only wage and hour data required under state or federal laws, but also sufficient information to permit careful evaluation of staff for promotion and for salary adjustments are needed.

Much work has been done in this area and forms and records covering most needs are available.

The use of computers in the storage and retrieval of personnel records is becoming more widespread.

Source references: H. Michael Boyd, "Employment Paperwork Systems," *PJ,* Dec. 1977; Gary B. Brumback, "Consolidating Job Descriptions, Performance Appraisals, and Manpower Reports," *PJ,* Aug. 1971; BNA, *Selection Procedures and Personnel Records* (Washington: PPF Survey no. 114, 1976); William E. Fulmer, "Tailoring Employee Evaluation Forms to Your Organization's Needs," *Personnel,* Jan./Feb. 1978; Elizabeth Marting (ed.), *AMA Book of Employment Forms* (New York: AMA, 1967); NICB, *Forms and Records in Personnel Administration* (New York: Studies in Personnel Policy no. 175, 1960); Virginia E. Schein, "Privacy and Personnel: A Time for Action," *PJ,* Dec. 1976; William Swarts, "An Update on Personnel Recordkeeping and Employee Privacy," *PJ,* May 1980; Alan F. Westin, *Computer Science and Technology: Computers, Personnel Administration, and Citizen Rights* (Washington: U.S. Dept. of Commerce, 1979).

See also EMPLOYMENT HISTORY, RATING FORM.

forty-four hour week *See* ENGLISH WORKWEEK.

forty-hour week The National Industrial Recovery Act gave impetus to the acceptance of the 40-hour week as a method of spreading employment by requiring overtime payment beyond 40 hours. Most of the National Recovery Administration's codes provided for the 40-hour week. The Walsh-Healey Public Contracts Act and the Fair Labor Standards Act of 1938 (Wage and Hour Law) provided a broader base and wider acceptance of the 40-hour week as a desirable objective for manufacturing industries throughout the United States.

See also FAIR LABOR STANDARDS ACT OF 1938, FIVE-DAY WORKWEEK, HOURS OF WORK.

four-day workweek An alternative work schedule which compresses the full-time, 40-hour workweek to four 10-hour days. Initiated by management in the early 1970s, it was designed to reduce absenteeism and improve productivity. Extended weekends and reduced commuting time and cost are among the advantages for employees. The primary argument against the four-day workweek is its potential adverse effect on the health of the workers because of the long hours which, in turn, may affect productivity.

Source references: Janice Neipert Hedges, "A Look at the 4-Day Workweek," *MLR*, Oct. 1971; Eileen B. Hoffman, "The Four-Day Week Raises New Problems," *Conference Board Record*, Feb. 1972; Institute for Local Self Government, *The Four-Day Workweek: A Local Government Perspective* (Berkeley: 1972); David Mark Maklan, "How Blue-Collar Workers on 4-Day Workweeks Use Their Time," *MLR*, Aug. 1977; Stanley D. Nollen, "What is Happening to Flexitime, Flexitour, Gliding Time, the Variable Day? And Permanent Part-Time Employment? And the Four-Day Week?" *Across the Board*, April 1980; Riva Poor (ed.), *4 Days, 40 Hours and Other Forms of the Rearranged Workweek* (New York: New American Library, 1973); Carmen D. Saso, *4/40: The Four-Day Workweek* (Chicago: PPA, 1972).

See also FLEXTIME/FLEXITIME.

four-fifths rule *See* EIGHTY PERCENT (80%) RULE.

fourth round increase Wage requests made by unions in the major industries in 1949. The "first" postwar round of wage increases was in 1946.

Source reference: Jules Backman, *Economics of a Fourth Round Wage Increase, Testimony on behalf of Steel Companies before the Presidential Steel Board* (n.p., 1949).

See also FIRST ROUND INCREASES, THIRD ROUND INCREASES.

free discussion Justice Frankfurter, in delivering the majority opinion in the picketing case of *American Federation of Labor v. Swing* (312 US 321, 7 LRRM 307 (1941)), cited three illustrative cases in which the Supreme Court held that the "right to free discussion . . . is to be guarded with a jealous eye," *Herndon v. Lowry*, 301 US 242 (1936); *Schneider v. State*, 308 US 147, 5 LRRM 659 (1939); *United States v. Carolene Products Co.*, 304 US 144 (1937).

See also PICKETING.

freedom budget The freedom budget proposed a comprehensive program for the practical liquidation of poverty in the United States. To quote A. Philip Randolph, the freedom budget differed from previous efforts "because it fuses general aspirations with qualitative content, and imposes time schedules. It deals not only with where we must go, but also with how fast and in what proportions. It measures costs against resources, and thus determines feasible priorities. It is not only a call to action, but also a schedule for action."

Source reference: A. Philip Randolph Institute, *A "Freedom Budget" for All Americans* (New York: 1966).

See also GUARANTEED INCOME, NEGATIVE INCOME TAX.

"freedom now" theory One of three interpretations of Title VII and its application to discriminatory seniority systems, which argues that maintenance of the distribution of jobs established by a discriminatory system after Title VII became law constitutes an unlawful employment practice. It is distinguished from the "rightful place" approach in the following way. If the adjustment of seniority rights under the "rightful place" theory indicates that a senior black would have priority over a white worker currently holding a particular job if that job were unfilled, then under "freedom now" the black would be immediately entitled to it, even though this would require the displacement of the white incumbent. The concept of "freedom now" was rejected by the court of appeals in favor of "rightful place" as the basis of the remedy granted in *Local 189, Papermakers v. U.S.*

Source references: Local 189, United Papermakers and Paperworkers v. U.S., 416 F2d 980, 1 FEP Cases 875 (CA 5, 1969); "Title VII, Seniority Discrimination, and the Incumbent Negro," 80 *Harvard LR* 1260 (1967).

See also "RIGHTFUL PLACE," "STATUS QUO" THEORY.

freedom of association The right of people to assemble in public or private for the purpose of joining for a common cause and to associate with one another to achieve their goal. The right of association is a prerequisite to the right of organization for the purposes of collective bargaining. Denial of freedom of association by a government dooms opportunity for organization of labor unions. The International Labour Organization has sponsored conventions which seek to protect the right of both labor and employer groups to freedom of association for the purposes of mutual aid and protection.

Source references: Guy Caire, *Freedom of Association and Economic Development* (Geneva: ILO, 1977); ILO, *Freedom of Association* (Geneva: Studies and Reports, Series A (Industrial Relations), nos. 28–32, 1927–30); ———, *Freedom of Association, An International Survey* (Geneva: 1975); ———, *Freedom of Association, Digest of Decisions of the Freedom of Association Committee of the Governing Body of the ILO* (Geneva: 1972); G. von Potobsky, "Protection of Trade Union Rights: Twenty Years' Work by the Committee on Freedom of Association," *ILR*, Jan. 1972; A. J. Pouyat, "The ILO's Freedom of Association Standards and Machinery: A Summing Up," *ILR*, May/June 1982; Harold S. Roberts, "An Industrial Relations Charter for the Americas," *MLR*, June 1946; Jean-Michel Servais, "Freedom of Association and the Inviolability of Trade Union Premises and Communications," *ILR*, March/April 1980.

See also RIGHT OF ASSOCIATION.

freedom of contract A doctrine developed by the courts in many labor cases holding that certain types of legislation infringed upon the rights of employees "to contract" and therefore denied them rights protected under the 14th Amendment. Since the right to contract was held a property right, the restriction of that right ran contrary to the 14th Amendment. The 14th Amendment provides that "no state shall deprive any person of life, liberty, or property without due process of law."

The Supreme Court also relied on the Fifth Amendment to protect the freedom to contract. In the *Adair* case, Justice Harlan held that the Erdman Act (forbidding the yellow dog contract) deprived the employer of his freedom to contract. He said:

> That section (10) in the particular mentioned, is an invasion of the personal liberty, as well as the right of property, guaranteed by that (fifth) amendment. Such liberty and right embraces the right to make contracts for the purchase of the labor of others and equally the right to make contracts for the sale of one's own labor. . . .

See also ADAIR V. UNITED STATES.

freedom of discussion *See* AMERICAN FEDERATION OF LABOR V. SWING, PICKETING.

Freedom of Information Act (FOIA) of 1966 Statute establishing a process that empowers citizens to gain access to information upon which government decisions are based. Each agency is required by the Act to publish quarterly, and distribute by sale or otherwise, an index identifying information available to the public unless the agency deems by order published in the Federal Register that publication is unnecessary and impracticable. The Act also requires that each federal agency make available upon request identifiable records under the control of the agency, unless the information requested falls within one of the specific exemptions. Requests are subject to search and copying fees, which are waived or reduced if the agency determines the information would benefit the general public. Citizens denied their requests may sue in federal district court to obtain the information.

The Act does not apply to certain records, including matters which are in the interest of national defense, personnel files, internal personnel rules and practices of any agency, trade secrets, and "privileged and confidential" commercial or financial information.

In *Committee on Masonic Homes v. NLRB*, the court of appeals ruled that union authorization cards presented to the NLRB are exempt from the disclosure provisions of the Act, reasoning that the cards were similar to personnel files. On the other hand, in *Van Bourg v. NLRB*, the court of appeals ruled that a list of names and addresses of employees eligible to vote in a representation election is not exempt from disclosure.

Source references: Freedom of Information Act, 5 U.S.C. 552; *Committee on Masonic Homes v. NLRB*, 556 F2d 214, 95 LRRM 2457 (CA 3, 1977); *Van Bourg v. NLRB*, 728 F2d 1270, 115 LRRM 3374 (CA 9, 1984); Daniel Gorham Clement, "The Right of Submitters to Prevent Agency Disclosure of Confidential Business Information: The Reverse Freedom of Information Act Lawsuit," *IR Law Digest*, Fall 1977; Walter B. Connolly and John Fox, "Employer Rights and Access to Documents Under the Freedom of Information Act," *IR Law Digest*, Spring 1978; John S. Irving and Carol De Deo, "The Right to Privacy and Freedom of Information: The NLRB and Issues Under the Privacy and Freedom of Information Act," *NYU 29th Annual Conference on Labor*, ed. by Richard Adelman (New York: Bender, 1976); Kenneth A. Kovach, "A Retrospective Look at the Privacy and Freedom of Information Acts," *LLJ*, Sept. 1976; David B. Montgomery, Anne H. Peters, and Charles B. Weinberg, "The Freedom of Information Act: Strategic Opportunities and Threats," *Sloan Management Review*, Winter 1978; Guy J. Sternal, "Informational Privacy and Public Records," *IR Law Digest*, Fall 1977.

freedom of organization The right, protected by federal law, to organize for the purposes of collective bargaining. The Taft-Hartley Act states in its findings and policies:

> It is hereby declared to be the policy of the United States . . . to reduce industrial strife by encouraging the practice and procedure of collective bargaining and by protecting the exercise by workers of full freedom of association, self-organization, and designation of representatives of their own choosing, for the purpose of negotiating the terms and conditions of their employment or other mutual aid or protection.

See also RIGHT TO ORGANIZE.

freedom of speech The issue of freedom of speech arises in labor-management relations in two contexts. First, it is advanced as a defense for picketing. Second, it is a factor in determining the legality or permissibility of employer and union statements and communications during organizing campaigns or before representation elections under the Taft-Hartley Act.

The first major indication that picketing might be accorded protection as free speech under the First Amendment to the U.S. Constitution came in the Supreme Court's 1937 opinion in the *Senn* case. The Court said: "Members of a union might, without special statutory authorization by a state, make known the facts of a labor dispute, for freedom of speech is guaranteed by the Federal Constitution" (*Senn v. Tile Layers Protective Union*, 301 US 468 (1937)).

Then in the 1940 *Thornhill* decision, the Court equated peaceful picketing to protected free speech in striking down an Alabama statute that broadly prohibited the picketing of business establishments. A state may not forbid a union, the Court said, to "enlighten the public on the nature and causes of a labor dispute" (*Thornhill v. Alabama*, 310 US 88, 6 LRRM 697 (1940)).

In the later *Giboney* and *Hanke* cases, however, the Court held that the First and 14th Amendments do not bar the states from restraining peaceful picketing for reasons of state public policy (*Giboney v. Empire Storage and Ice Co.*, 336 US 490, 20 LRRM 2584 (1949); *Teamsters v. Hanke*, 339 US 470, 26 LRRM 2076 (1950)). The Court also made clear that free-speech protection does not apply to picketing that takes place in a context of violence (*Milk Wagon Drivers Union v. Meadowmoor Dairies*, 312 US 287, 7 LRRM 310 (1941)).

In the 1957 *Vogt* case, the Court reviewed its rulings on picketing as protected free speech and summarized the limits placed on the power of states to enjoin peaceful picketing as follows:

(1) Neither state legislatures nor state courts may impose blanket prohibitions against picketing. There must be an investigation into its conduct and purposes.
(2) But there is a broad field in which a state, in enforcing some public policy, constitutionally may enjoin peaceful picketing aimed at preventing effectuation of that policy. This policy may be expressed either in the criminal or the civil law, and it may be enunciated by either the legislature or the courts (*Teamsters Local 695 v. Vogt, Inc.*, 354 US 284, 40 LRRM 2208 (1957)).

These decisions permitting the states to regulate picketing that conflicts with state law or public policy are not applicable where a dispute is potentially subject to regulation under the Taft-Hartley Act and comes within the NLRB's jurisdictional standards.

During the early years of the National Labor Relations Act, the NLRB and the courts tended to require employers to maintain complete neutrality in speech, as well as action, during union organizing campaigns. In the 1941 *Virginia Electric* case, however, the Supreme Court upheld the right of an employer to speak out against unionism during an organizing drive. It held to be noncoercive and privileged an employer speech pointing out that strikes and unrest might follow unionization and pointing to the peaceful past record on an unorganized basis (*NLRB v. Virginia Electric and Power Co.*, 314 US 469, 9 LRRM 405 (1941)).

The 1947 Taft-Hartley amendments inserted a new Section 8(c), known as the free-speech proviso, specifying as follows: "The expressing of any views, arguments, or opinion, or the dissemination thereof, whether in written, printed, graphic, or visual form, shall not constitute or be evidence of an unfair labor practice under any of the provisions of this Act if such expression contains no threat of reprisal or force or promise of benefit."

The limitations of Section 8(c), however, are not necessarily applicable to representation cases in which objections to elections are filed. Thus, an employer's remarks may be privileged under Section 8(c) and yet the Board may set the election aside. "Conduct that creates an atmosphere which renders improbable a free choice will sometimes warrant invalidating an election even though the conduct may not constitute an unfair labor practice," the NLRB has said (*General Shoe Co.*, 77 NLRB 124, 21 LRRM 1337 (1948)).

Some later decisions suggested that the privilege under Section 8(c) was being extended to representation cases, but this suggestion was rejected specifically by the Board in a 1962 decision. Section 8(c) is limited to "unfair labor practice cases, and it has no application to representation cases," the Board stated. It added, however, that "the strictures of the First Amendment, to be sure, must be considered in all cases." The Board also said in the same case that it would look at the surrounding circumstances and the economic realities of the employer-employee relationship in determining whether preelection statements interfered with employee freedom of choice (*Dal-Tex Optical Co.*, 137 NLRB 1782, 50 LRRM 1489 (1962)).

There are two other significant NLRB rules that affect campaigning before an election. One is the *Peerless Plywood* doctrine under which the Board will set an election aside if either party makes a speech to the employees, even though noncoercive, in the 24-hour period preceding the election (*Peerless Plywood Co.*, 107 NLRB 427, 33 LRRM 1151 (1953)).

The other is the captive-audience rule first enunciated by the Board in the 1951 *Bonwit-Teller* case and later reaffirmed in the 1962 *May Department Stores* case. Under this rule, a department store that enforces a broad no-solicitation, no-distribution rule and then makes an anti-union speech to employees assembled in the store during working time is required to give the union an equal opportunity to reply. Failure to do so is both an unfair labor practice and ground for setting the election aside. The *May* decision was reversed by the U.S. Court of Appeals at Cincinnati, but the Board adhered to its position in the later *Montgomery Ward* case (*Bonwit Teller, Inc.*, 96 NLRB 608, 28 LRRM 1547 (1951); *May Department Stores Co.*, 136 NLRB 797, 49 LRRM 1862 (1962); *Montgomery Ward & Co., Inc.*, 145 NLRB 846, 55 LRRM 1063 (1964)).

Source references: Benjamin Aaron, "Employer Free Speech: The Search for a

Policy," *Public Policy and Collective Bargaining*, ed. by Joseph Shister, Benjamin Aaron, and Clyde W. Summers (New York: Harper, IRRA Pub. no. 27, 1962); Jack Barbash, "Employer 'Free Speech' and Employee Rights: Free Speech in Union-Management Relations and the Law," *LLJ*, April 1963; Thomas G. Field, Jr., "Representation Elections, Films and Free Speech," *LLJ*, April 1974; Cindy M. Hudson and William B. Werther, Jr., "Section 8(c) and Free Speech," *LLJ*, Sept. 1977; Staughton Lynd, "Employee Speech in the Private and Public Workplace: Two Doctrines or One?" *Industrial Relations LJ*, Winter 1977; David C. Palmer, "Free Speech and Arbitration: Implications for the Future," *LLJ*, May 1976; Melissa Patack, "Employees and Freedom of Speech," *Industrial and Labor Relations Forum*, Vol. 13, no. 1, 1978.

See also HERNDON CASE.

free labor market Theoretically, a place where an employer is free to hire workers and where there is competitive bidding by employees for available jobs. It assumes that there are no restrictions by labor unions, no minimum wage standards or other conditions of employment set by organized groups of workers, and that the employer is free to hire anyone he wishes under conditions which the employee will accept. It also assumes that the employee is free to choose his employer without limitation or restriction—that there is complete mobility and freedom between the buyers and sellers of labor.

The term also has been used to describe a locality where the "open shop" exists, and employers are free from unionization and "organized" restraints on the employers' freedom in employment.

Source references: Clark Kerr, "Labor Markets: Their Character and Consequences," *Proceedings of the 2d A/M, IRRA*, ed. by Milton Derber (Champaign: 1950); Richard A. Lester, *Hiring Practices and Labor Competition* (Princeton: Princeton Univ., IR Section, 1954); Charles A. Myers and George P. Shultz, *The Dynamics of a Labor Market* (New York: PH, 1951); Lloyd G. Reynolds, *The Structure of Labor Markets* (New York: Harper, 1951).

free riders Employees who do not belong to a contract-holding union (but who are eligible for membership), who do not pay dues or other fees and assessments to the union, but who receive the benefits of the union's activities in collective bargaining and grievance and arbitration handling. Unions generally hold this to be one of the strongest arguments for nonunion individuals to join, since nonmembers receive benefits without having to pay any of the expenses or do any of the work for the benefits which accrue to them.

See also AGENCY SHOP.

freeze The fixing or stabilizing of wages, prices, or manpower at a point desired by government during a period of emergency or war. Although technically wages, prices, or manpower may be frozen, regulations are set up to permit sufficient flexibility within established policy.

frictional unemployment A catch-all category of those unemployed because of temporary conditions in the labor market, personal desires of workers with respect to available jobs, lack of mobility in the labor market because of conditions set by employers or unions (such as age, union membership, trade requirements, etc.), minor dislocations because of financial failure of a company, and other temporary or transitional idleness between jobs. Sometimes held to be the "irreducible minimum" of unemployment, even under the most ideal economic conditions.

Source references: William Beveridge, *Full Employment in a Free Society* (New York: Norton, 1945); ———, *Unemployment: A Problem of Industry* (new ed., London: Longmans, Green, 1930); Paul H. Douglas and Aaron Director, *The Problem of Unemployment* (New York: Macmillan, 1931); Philip Klein, *The Burden of Unemployment* (New York: Russell Sage Foundation, 1923); Isadore Lubin, *The Absorption of the Unemployed by American Industry* (Washington: Brookings Institution, 1929); Wesley C. Mitchell, *Business Cycles and Unemployment* (New York: McGraw-Hill, 1923); Lester M. Pearlman, Leonard Eskin, and Edgar E. Poulton, "Nature and Extent of Frictional Unemployment," *MLR*, Jan. 1947; John H. Pierson, *Full Employment* (New Haven: Yale UP, 1941).

See also CYCLICAL UNEMPLOYMENT, FULL EMPLOYMENT, SEASONAL UNEMPLOYMENT, SECULAR UNEMPLOYMENT, STRUCTURAL UNEMPLOYMENT, TECHNOLOGICAL UNEMPLOYMENT.

fringe benefits Nonwage benefits or payments received by workers. They include such items as vacation pay, paid sick leave, paid holidays, pensions, and insurance benefits.

Although some of these benefits antedated the War Labor Board, wage controls on hourly wage rates to prevent inflation led the Board to grant minor fringe items which, although cost items, would be paid out in the future, such as pension and retirement benefits, and would not have as immediate an impact on prices as direct wage increases. After World War II, unions continued their efforts to secure a wide variety of benefits. In some cases employers encouraged granting of fringe benefits to help stabilize the work force and provide better working conditions and more satisfied employees.

According to the annual survey conducted by the Chamber of Commerce of the United States in 1981, the average fringe benefit payment was 37.3 percent of the payroll, $3.21 per hour, and $6,627 per year per employee.

Source references: Chamber of Commerce of the U.S., *Employee Benefits 1981* (Washington: 1982); ———, *Employee Benefits Historical Data: 1951–1979* (Washington: 1981); Yung-Ping Chen, "The Growth of Fringe Benefits: Implications for Social Security," *MLR*, Nov. 1981; Council of State Governments, *Fringe Benefits in State Government Employment* (Lexington: Pub. no. RM–553, 1975); Austin M. Fisher and John F. Chapman, "Big Costs of Little Fringes," *Harvard BR*, Sept./Oct. 1954; Richard B. Freeman, "The Effect of Unionism on Fringe Benefits," *ILRR*, July 1981; "Fringe Benefits: Some Neglected Considerations," *Personnel*, Jan. 1957; T. J. Gordon and R. E. LeBleu, "Employee Benefits, 1970–1985," *Harvard BR*, Jan./Feb. 1970; Donald R. Herzog, "Fringe Benefits: The Federal Government vs. Private Industry," *LLJ*, Feb. 1971; James C. Hill, "Stabilization of Fringe Benefits," *ILRR*, Jan. 1954; Geraldine Leshin, *EEO Law: Impact of Fringe Benefits* (Los Angeles: UC, Institute of IR, Policy and Practice Publication, 1979); Noel Arnold Levin, *Negotiating Fringe Benefits, An AMA Management Briefing* (New York: AMA, 1973); Bevars Mabry, "The Economics of Fringe Benefits," *IR*, Feb. 1973; Allan I. Mendelsohn, "Fringe Benefits and Our Industrial Society," *LLJ*, June 1956; Mitchell Meyer, *Profile of Employee Benefits: 1981 Edition* (New York: The Conference Board, Report no. 813, 1981); ———, *Women and Employee Benefits* (New York: The Conference Board, Report no. 752, 1978); NICB, *Computing the Cost of Fringe Benefits* (New York: 1952); Rudolph Oswald and J. Douglas Smyth, "Fringe Benefits—On the Move," *American Federationist*, June 1970; Arthur M. Ross, "Fringe Benefits Today and Tomorrow," *LLJ*, Aug. 1956; Martin E. Segal and Company, *Employee Benefits Factbook, 1970* (New York: Fleet Academic Editions, 1970); Loren M. Solnick, "Unionism and Fringe Benefit Expenditures," *IR*, Feb. 1978; Harold Stieglitz, *Fringe Benefit Packages* (New York: NICB, 1954); U.S. Congress, House, Committee on Post Office and Civil Service, *Comparisons of Major Employee Benefits Programs—April 1973* (Washington: 1973); ———, *Retirement, Life Insurance and Health Benefits Programs, December 1973, Benefit Comparisons and Cost Projections* (Washington: 1974); U.S. Dept. of Labor, BLS, *Employee Benefits in Industry, 1980* (Washington: Bull. 2107, 1981); ———, *Major Collective Bargaining Agreements: Administration of Negotiated Pension, Health and Insurance Plans* (Washington: Bull. 1425–12, 1970); Thomas E. Wahlrobe, *Aggressive Benefits Management, An AMA Management Briefing* (New York: AMA, 1976).

See also BENEFIT PLANS; CAFETERIA PLANS; CHILD CARE; DENTAL CARE, PREPAID; LEAVE OF ABSENCE; LEGAL SERVICE PLANS; TUITION AID.

front-end load Negotiated increases in wages and/or benefits that are scheduled to occur early in the term of the collective bargaining agreement.

Source reference: Allan W. Drachman, *Municipal Negotiations: From Differences to Agreement* (Washington: Labor-Management Relations Service, 1970).

front pay Defined by the OFCCP as "compensation provided an individual or group which begins when a remedy for alleged discrimination is agreed to and ends when the individual or group attains its 'rightful place.' "

Also referred to as "future pay," it may be ordered as a remedy if placement or reinstatement is not possible or practical. Front pay is monetary relief for any future loss of earnings resulting from past discrimination.

Source references: Fitzgerald v. Sirloin Stockade, Inc., 624 F2d 945, 22 FEP Cases 262 (1980); *Johnson v. Ryder Truck Lines, Inc.*, 12 FEP Cases 895 (DC NC 1975); U.S. OFCCP, *Federal Contract Compliance Manual* (Washington: 1979).

See also "RIGHTFUL PLACE."

frozen seniority The protection of a worker's length of service as of a specific time. There is no accumulation of service during a period of layoff or separation. Some contracts provide for the loss of all seniority if layoff exceeds a fixed period of time, such as one year. Greater protection may be given to employees with long company service.

full crew rule Provisions, generally in law, seeking to satisfy safety requirements by specifying a full complement of men to handle an operation. Railroad regulations might require a minimum complement of workers on each train which might include the engineer, fireman, conductor, and others.

The term may also be applied to maritime work and the number necessary to man a certain ship or operation. The term occasionally has been applied to certain practices by the Musicians Union requiring a definite "crew" for the handling of a program. Railroad contracts may specify the size of the crew. For example, a contract might provide that "All yard crews shall consist of one conductor and at least two brakemen."

full dinner pail A demand of wage earners directed to provide adequate income for the necessities of life, including sufficient income for food. The slogan is attributed to William McKinley in his campaign for the Presidency in 1896.

full employment A desired goal in a free enterprise system which provides employment opportunities (at reasonable occupational levels, compensation, and duration) for all who desire employment and are able and willing to work. The literature on the subject suggests lack of agreement on the meaning of full employment.

Arthur M. Ross in "The Role of Government in Promoting Full Employment," which was presented at a University of Illinois symposium in March 1966, raised the question of the definition of "full employment." He suggested three approaches, the first being "the classical definition of Sir William Beveridge . . . that a country has full employment when the number of job vacancies equals or exceeds the number of unemployed workers. This definition is over-simplified because it says nothing about the characteristics of the vacancies and of the unemployed."

The second concept, according to Professor Ross, is more familiar to American economists: ". . . full employment is reached when there is no lack of effective demand for labor. In such cases the residual unemployment is the result of frictional factors such as movement in and out of the job market, labor turnover and seasonal fluctuations of output. As a practical matter there would also be a residue of hardcore unemployed whose handicaps are so great that they are unacceptable to employers even when labor is scarce."

The third concept "has been the most important from an operational standpoint. In this view, full employment is attained, for practical purposes, when inflationary tendencies become so strong as to require fiscal and monetary policies which slow down the economy. The Eisenhower Administration thought the economy was overheated in 1957 when the unemployment rate fell to about 4 percent. This is now almost universally viewed as a mistake; but some conservative economists stated in February 1966 that the dangers of inflation were so great that unemployment should not be pushed below the most recently reported 4 percent rate—which had actually fallen to 3.7 percent."

"Clearly this concept of full employment is judgmental and political rather than statistical. Aside from fear of inflation, several other factors tend to stop an expansion short of providing job opportunity for all who desire it."

Source references: William H. Beveridge, *Full Employment in a Free Society* (New York: Norton, 1945); Paul Bullock (ed.), *Goals for Full Employment, the Full Employment and Balanced Growth Act of 1976, A Discussion* (Los Angeles: UC, Institute of IR, 1976); Edgar R. Fiedler, "Obstacles to Full Employment," *Conference Board Record,* Aug. 1976; Eugene Forsey, "Trade Union Policy Under Full Employment," *Insights Into Labor Issues,* ed. by R. A. Lester and J. Shister (New York: Macmillan, 1948); Alan Gartner, William Lynch, Jr., and Frank Riessman (ed.), *A Full Employment Program for the 1970s* (New York: Praeger, 1976); R. A. Gordon, *The Need to Disaggregate the Full Employment Goal* (Washington: U.S. National Commission for Manpower Policy, Special Report no. 17, 1978); Leon H. Keyserling, *Full Employment Without Inflation* (Washington: Conference on Economic Progress, 1975); Abba P. Lerner and Frank D. Graham (ed.), *Planning and Paying for Full Employment* (Princeton: Princeton UP, 1946); G. William Miller, "The Not Impossible Goal: Full Employment and Price Stability," *Across the Board,* March 1978; Walter A. Morton, "Trade Unionism, Full Employment and Inflation," *AER,* March 1950; Oxford Univ., Institute of Statistics, *The Economics of Full Employment* (Oxford: Blackwell, 1945); John H. Pierson, *Full Employment* (New Haven: Yale UP, 1941); "Planning for Full Employment," *Annals,* March 1975; Markley Roberts, "Full Employment: The Next Vital Step," *American Federationist,* Aug. 1976; Arthur M. Ross, "The Role of Government in Promoting Full Employment," *NYSSILR Report Card,* Feb. 1967; Irving H. Siegel, *Fuller Employment with Less Inflation* (Kalamazoo: Upjohn Institute for Employment Research, 1981); U.S. National Commission for Manpower Policy, *Demographic Trends and Full Employment* (Washington: Special Report no. 12, 1976); Jacob Viner, "Full Employment at Whatever Cost," *Quarterly Journal of Economics,* Aug. 1950.

Full Employment and Balanced Growth Act of 1978 Also known as the Humphrey-Hawkins Act, it establishes as national goals the reduction of unemployment to 4 percent by 1983, and an inflation rate of 3 percent by 1983 and zero percent by 1988. The Act requires the President to recommend programs and policies for achieving these goals and provides for congressional review of the recommendations. The law permits the President to alter the timetables, if necessary, to achieve the unemployment and inflation goals. The Act also seeks to promote full employment and productivity, increased real income, balanced growth, trade balance, and reasonable price stability.

Source references: Full Employment and Balanced Growth Act of 1978, Pub. L. 95–527, 92 Stat. 1887 (codified in scattered sections of 2, 12, and 15 U.S.C.); AEI, *Reducing Unemployment, The Humphrey-Hawkins and Kemp-McClure Bills* (Washington: 1976); U.S. Congressional Budget Office, *The Fiscal Policy Response to Inflation* (Washington: 1979).

full-time earnings The amount earned by a worker who has worked a full schedule of hours for a designated period of time.

full-time job A job which requires the complete attention of the employee for a set work schedule. Such a job in a large production plant may be one shift schedule of eight hours. For a busy executive, a full-time job may be 14 to 16 hours. Generally, it is a job which doesn't permit holding down another position at the same time, even on a part-time basis.

full-time worker rate The wage rate paid to a regular employee who works on a full-time basis. This is to distinguish it from wage rates paid to temporary employees and those who work only on a part-time basis.

functionalization A technical term used to describe the organization of management functions and work performance in a manner designed most effectively to achieve the basic objectives of the enterprise. It attempts to achieve this by careful allocation of work to those best able to perform it, and by dividing the work to be performed into functional groups.

functus officio A term, literally translated meaning "a task performed," applied to an officer who has fulfilled the function or purpose of his office or whose term of office has expired, and who therefore has no further official authority. It can also be applied to an instrument which has fulfilled the purpose for which it was created and which has no further effect. As applied to labor arbitration proceedings, arbitrators are functus officio when they have executed their awards and declared their decision.

Source reference: AAA, "'Functus Officio' As It Applies to Arbitration Proceedings," *Lawyers' Arbitration Letter,* Aug. 15, 1963.

funded pension plan A plan in which pension benefits are built up over a period by setting aside funds in a reserve. This reserve is accumulated during the time the employee is working for the company, and the amount of benefits is determined by actuarial experience. The plan may be set up under contract with an insurance company or as a special trust account.

See also PARTIALLY FUNDED PENSION PLAN, PENSION PLAN, SELF-ADMINISTERED (TRUSTEED) PLAN.

funeral leave pay Pay to a worker, usually for a limited period of three or four days, for time lost because of death and funeral of a member of the worker's immediate family.

Source reference: Theessa L. Ellis and Laura A. Wood, "Paid Leave on Death in Family in Major Union Contracts, 1961," *MLR,* April 1962.

Fur and Leather Workers' Union of United States and Canada; International (CIO) Founded in 1939, it was expelled by the CIO executive board on June 15, 1950. It became a department of the Amalgamated Meat Cutters and Butcher Workmen of North America (AFL) on February 22, 1955.

Source reference: Philip S. Foner, *The Fur and Leather Workers Union* (Newark: Nordan Press, 1950).

See also MEAT CUTTERS AND BUTCHER WORKMEN OF NORTH AMERICA; AMALGAMATED (AFL-CIO).

furlough A leave of absence from work or other duties usually initiated by an employee to meet some special problem. It is temporary in nature since the employee plans to return as soon as the furlough period is over.

The Civil Service Reform Act defines furlough as "the placing of an employee in a temporary status without duties and pay because of lack of work or funds or other nondisciplinary reasons."

Source reference: BNA, *White Collar Layoffs and Cutbacks* (Washington: 1982).

See also LAYOFF.

Furniture Workers of America; United (AFL-CIO) A union of workers engaged in manufacturing furniture. The official monthly publication is the *Furniture Workers Press.*

Address: 1910 Air Lane Dr., Nashville, Tenn. 37210. Tel. (615) 889–8860

future service benefits The retirement credits earned by a worker during the period of his membership in a pension plan.

G

GCIU *See* GRAPHIC COMMUNICATIONS INTERNATIONAL UNION (AFL-CIO).

GPPAW *See* GLASS, POTTERY, PLASTIC AND ALLIED WORKERS INTERNATIONAL UNION (AFL-CIO).

GUA *See* GUARDS UNION OF AMERICA; INTERNATIONAL (IND).

gaffer *See* GANG BOSS.

gag orders Executive orders issued by Presidents Theodore Roosevelt and William H. Taft, the former to stop political activities of federal employees and the latter to prohibit federal employees from acting on congressional requests for information. Executive Order 163 issued by Roosevelt on January 31, 1902, was aimed at postal organizations but was phrased to cover the entire federal service. Employees were forbidden "either directly or indirectly, individually or through associations, to solicit an increase in pay or to . . . attempt to influence in their own behalf any other legislation whatsoever . . . save through the heads of the department in or under which they serve." Taft's Executive Order 1142, issued January 25, 1909, extended these restrictions by forbidding a federal employee from responding to requests from Congress "except through or as authorized by the head of his department." Taft intended that Executive Order 1142 would lead to an orderly administrative hierarchy and a politically neutral civil service.

Source reference: Murray B. Nesbitt, *Labor Relations in the Federal Government Service* (Washington: BNA, 1976).

See also LLOYD-LAFOLLETTE ACT OF 1912.

gainful occupation Any work for which a person receives pay, or in which the person helps in the production of goods or services. For census purposes the term covers all persons who usually follow a gainful occupation, even though they may be temporarily unemployed at the time the census is taken.

gain sharing Any method whereby workers participate with management in gains due to increased productivity. It is a form of profit sharing, although it was originally tied to increased premiums for additional output as in the Halsey Gain-Sharing Plan. The term has been attributed to H. R. Towne, president of Yale and Towne Manufacturing Company of Connecticut, who had introduced such a program. "My system," he said, "consists in ascertaining the present labor cost of a given product, and in dividing equitably with those engaged in producing it the gain or benefit accruing from increased efficiency or economy on their part."

Source references: C. Canby Balderston, *Profit Sharing for Wage Earners* (New York: Industrial Relations Counselors, Inc., 1937); Z. Clark Dickinson, *Compensating Industrial Effort* (New York: Ronald Press, 1937); Daniel J. B. Mitchell, "Gain-Sharing: Anti-Inflation Reform," *Challenge*, July/Aug. 1982; Carla S. O'Dell, *Gainsharing: Involvement, Incentives, and Productivity; an AMA Management Briefing* (New York: AMA, 1981).

See also GANTT TASK AND BONUS PLAN, HALSEY PREMIUM (GAIN-SHARING) PLAN, PROFIT SHARING.

galloping overtime rate *See* COOLIE OVERTIME.

gang boss A minor supervisor in charge of a small group or gang operation.

gangsters *See* LABOR RACKETEER, RACKETEERING.

Gantt chart A graphic device, developed by H. L. Gantt, which is designed to measure the relation between actual and anticipated production records. It is designed to help work performance by finding out the reasons for deviation between estimated and actual time taken to perform the work.

Gantt task and bonus plan An incentive method which incorporates the Halsey Plan, but provides an extra bonus for employees who reach the standard or 100 percent efficiency. Substandard workers are given additional training to help them reach standard. Gang bosses and foremen also receive bonuses for the number of workers under their supervision who reach 100 percent efficiency.

Source reference: Alex W. Rathe (ed.), *Gantt on Management* (New York: AMA, 1961).

See also HALSEY PREMIUM (GAIN-SHARING) PLAN.

Gardner-Denver case *See* ALEXANDER V. GARDNER-DENVER.

Garment Workers of America; United (AFL-CIO) Organized in New York in April 1891. The Special Order Clothingmakers' Union joined the Garment Workers in 1903. In 1909, the shirt workers who were organized in the Shirtwaist and Laundry Workers' International Union were transferred to the United Garment Workers. A split occurred in the union in 1914. The delegates who withdrew formed the Amalgamated Clothing Workers.

The official publication is *The Garment Worker*, published monthly.

Address: 200 Park Ave. South, New York, N.Y. 10003. Tel. (212) 677–0573

See also CLOTHING WORKERS OF AMERICA; AMALGAMATED (AFL-CIO).

garnishment A procedure, usually by court action, whereby a portion of the employee's wages is attached to pay a creditor. Garnishment procedures are covered by state statutes.

Source references: Robert W. Fisher, "How Garnished Workers Fare Under Arbitration," *MLR*, May 1967; Robert D. Moran, "Curbing the Garnishment Grab," *American Federationist*, Sept. 1970; Stanley Morganstern, *Legal Protection in Garnishment and Attachment* (Dobbs Ferry, N.Y.: Oceana Publications, 1971).

See also ASSIGNMENT OF WAGES.

Gas, Coke and Chemical Workers of America; United (CIO) Merged with the Oil Workers International Union (CIO) to form the Oil, Chemical and Atomic Workers International Union (CIO) during March 1955.

See also OIL, CHEMICAL AND ATOMIC WORKERS INTERNATIONAL UNION (AFL-CIO).

gate interview *See* EXIT INTERVIEW.

general counsel Under the Taft-Hartley Act, the legal officer of the NLRB who has the responsibility to issue complaints in cases involving unfair labor practices under the Act.

Section 3(d) provides that:

> There shall be a General Counsel of the Board who shall be appointed by the President, by and with the advice and consent of the Senate, for a term of four years. The General Counsel of the Board shall exercise general supervision over all attorneys employed by the Board (other than trial examiners and legal assistants to Board members) and over the officers and employees in the regional offices. He shall have final authority, on behalf of the Board, in respect of the investigation of charges and issuance of complaints under section 10, and in respect of the prosecution of such complaints before the Board, and shall have such other duties as the Board may prescribe or as may be provided by law.

The Civil Rights Act of 1964 and the Civil Service Reform Act of 1978 provide for the appointment of a general counsel for the EEOC and the FLRA, respectively. The respective general counsels are appointed by the President.

General Electric case On December 14, 1964, the NLRB handed down its decision in one of the most bitterly litigated cases in the Board's history. It involved the legality of the General Electric Company's bargaining approach, known as "Boulwarism," as applied in the company's 1960 negotiations with the Electrical Workers (IUE). Over 10,000 pages of testimony were taken in the case, and NLRB Trial Examiner Arthur Leff had written a 111-page report in which he found that the company had violated its good-faith bargaining duty under the Taft-Hartley Act.

Upholding the trial examiner, the NLRB held that the company violated the good-faith bargaining duty by its conduct both at and away from the bargaining table as evidenced by the company's:

(1) Failure timely to furnish certain information requested by the union during contract negotiations.
(2) Attempts to deal separately with locals on matters properly the subject of national negotiations, and its solicitation of locals to abandon or refrain from supporting the strike.
(3) Presentation of its personal accident insurance proposal to the union on a take-it-or-leave-it basis.
(4) Overall approach to and conduct of bargaining.

In support of its holding on the overall approach to and conduct of bargaining, the Board emphasized the company's insistence on its "fair and firm" contract proposal and its employee communications campaign. On the first point, the Board said that a party who enters negotiations with a "take-it-or-leave-it" attitude violates its bargaining duty even though it goes through the forms of bargaining, does not insist on any illegal or nonmandatory bargaining proposals, and wants to sign an agreement. Good-faith bargaining, the Board added, means more than "going through the motions of negotiating"; it is essential that there be a serious intent to adjust differences and to reach an acceptable common ground.

Regarding the communications campaign, the Board said it is inconsistent with good-faith bargaining for an employer to mount a campaign to disparage and discredit the union in the eyes of the employees and to create the impression that the employer, rather than the union, is the true protector of the employees' interests. It is the employer's obligation to deal with the employees through the union and not with the union through the employees.

Source reference: General Electric Co., 150 NLRB 192, 57 LRRM 1491 (1964).

See also BOULWARISM, COLLECTIVE BARGAINING.

General Electric v. Gilbert A 1976 Supreme Court decision, in which it was held that an employer's generally comprehensive disability plan which excluded from coverage disabilities due to pregnancy was not in violation of the Title VII prohibition against sex discrimination in employment because the disability plan did not exclude anyone on the basis of gender. The Court noted that while pregnancy is confined to women, it is "significantly different" from the typical covered disease or disability; in fact, "it is not a 'disease' at all, and is often a voluntarily undertaken and desired condition." The Court found that the exclusion was not a pretext for discriminating against women and that there was no proof that the "package" of risks covered by the plan was in fact worth more to men than to women.

The Court, by so ruling, rejected the EEOC Guidelines on Sex Discrimination which held that pregnancy-related disabilities should be considered as any other disability covered by insurance or sick leave plans. The Court stated that EEOC Guidelines are subject to consideration in determining legislative intent "[b]ut it does not mean that courts properly may accord less weight to such guidelines than to administrative regulations which Congress has declared shall have the force of law. . . ."

Congress reacted to *Gilbert* and to *Nashville Gas Co. v. Satty* (434 US 136, 16 FEP Cases 136 (1977)) by adding Section 701(k)—the EEOC position on pregnancy—to Title VII in 1978. This section reverses the Supreme Court decision and specifically outlaws discrimination based on pregnancy.

Source references: General Electric v. Gilbert, 429 US 125, 13 FEP Cases 1657 (1976); Steven C. Kahn, "*General Electric Co. v. Gilbert*: Retreat from Rationality?" *Employee Relations LJ*, Summer 1977; Michael A. Mass, "Sex Discrimination Based on Pregnancy: The Post-*Gilbert* Environment," *Employee Relations LJ*, Autumn 1978.

See also PREGNANCY DISCRIMINATION ACT, SEX DISCRIMINATION.

General Electric X-Ray rule Departing from precedent, the NLRB in 1946 decided that "a mere naked assertion" of majority representation by a union did not have the same standing as a formal petition for certification. This rule took its name from the employer involved, General Electric X-Ray Corporation. The effect of the holding in the *General Electric X-Ray* case was to let stand an agreement signed by the employer and the Machinists signed by the employer and the Machinists Union (AFL) during a period when a rival CIO union had asserted by letter that it represented a majority of employees at the plant, but did not file a petition with the NLRB until after the Machinist contract had been executed. The contract thus acted as a bar to the election sought by the CIO union (United Electrical, Radio and Machine Workers).

Source reference: General Electric X-Ray Corp., 67 NLRB 997, 18 LRRM 1047 (1946).

general grievance *See* GROUP GRIEVANCE.

general labor union A term generally applied to an organization of workers which accepts into membership all those desirous of joining. It embraces all workers, from the unskilled to the skilled. It is distinguished from the craft unions, which are confined to a group with homogeneous needs and where the collective bargaining is directed toward the problems of that group.

general schedule employees *See* CLASSIFICATION ACT EMPLOYEES.

general strike The concerted and sympathetic refusal of workers throughout an entire geographic or political area to perform their normal services or activities. It is not confined to any one union, one industry, or one company. Its essential purposes are power and show of political and industrial strength to achieve its goals. Although theoretically a tool of revolution, it is rarely used since divergence of union aims as to industrial and political objectives rarely provides unanimity of action.

It differs from the general industry strike which is directed against a single industry widely scattered throughout the country. There is relatively little support among democratic labor unions for the general strike as a tool to aid in collective bargaining to achieve normal union goals.

Source references: Robert P. Arnot, *The General Strike, May 1926, Its Origin and History* (New York: Augustus M. Kelley, Reprints of Economic Classics, 1967); Wilfred H. Crook, *The General Strike* (Chapel Hill: Univ. of North Carolina Press, 1931); Ernest T. Hiller, *The Strike* (Chicago: Univ. of Chicago Press, 1928); Arthur M. Ross, "Changing Patterns of Industrial Conflict," *Proceedings of the 12th A/M, IRRA*, ed. by David Johnson (Madison: 1960).

general wage increase A wage adjustment given at one time to all or a significant group of the workers in a plant, company, or industry. The increase may be applied as a percentage or in a fixed cents-per-hour adjustment.

Source references: A. Barry Feiden, "Results of Across-the-Board Wage Increases," *PJ*, Oct. 1953; Lloyd G. Reynolds, "Bargaining Over General Wage Changes," *NYU 2d Annual Conference on Labor*, ed. by Emanuel Stein (Albany: Bender, 1949).

See also ACROSS-THE-BOARD INCREASE.

gentlemen's agreement An agreement or understanding based solely on the good will and word of the parties involved. It is unenforceable and exists only as the two parties are willing to give it weight.

geographical mobility A measure of the movement of workers in a particular labor market area. The extent to which workers move from area to area rests on many considerations, including wages, housing, and climate.

Source references: Robert L. Bunting, "A Test of the Theory of Geographic Mobility," *ILRR*, Oct. 1961; Michael J. Greenwood, "The Geographic Mobility of College Graduates," *Journal of Human Resources*, Fall 1973; John B. Lansing et al., *Geographical Mobility of Labor, 1st Report* (Ann Arbor: Univ. of Michigan, Institute for Social Research, 1963); John B. Lansing and James N. Morgan, "The Effect of Geographical Mobility on Income," *Journal of Human Resources*, Fall 1967; John B. Lansing and Eva Mueller, *The Geographic Mobility of Labor* (Ann Arbor: Univ. of Michigan, Institute for Social Research, 1967); Fabian Linden, "Geography is Destiny," *Across the Board*, May 1981; Larry D. Schroeder, "Interrelatedness of Occupational and Geographical Labor Mobility," *ILRR*, April 1976; Lewis H. Smith, *Economic, Demographic, and Sociological Factors Influencing the Geographic Mobility of Young Workers* (University: Univ. of Mississippi, Center for Manpower Studies, 1972).

See also INDUSTRIAL MOBILITY, LABOR MOBILITY, OCCUPATIONAL MOBILITY.

geographic wage differentials Variations in wages paid for similar work by companies located in different sections of the country. Union organization seeks to eliminate or reduce the spread of these differentials.

Source references: Albert F. Hinrichs and Arthur F. Beal, "Geographical Differences in Hours and Wages, 1925–1937," *MLR*, May 1940; Albert E. Schwenk and Martin E. Personick, "Analyzing Earnings Differentials in Industry Wage Surveys," *MLR*, June 1974; Sharon P. Smith, *Government Wage Differentials by Region and Sex* (Princeton: Princeton Univ., IR Section, WP no. 58, 1974); David J. Thomsen, "Geographic Differentials in Salaries Within the United States," *PJ*, Sept. 1974.

See also NORTH-SOUTH WAGE DIFFERENTIALS, REGIONAL (WAGE) DIFFERENTIAL.

Ghent plan A system, inaugurated by the city of Ghent in 1900–1901, designed to encourage private voluntary organizations to extend or establish systems of unemployment benefit payments to their members. Since labor organizations were active in this area the subsidies or grants in aid were most advantageous to trade union groups. The plan encouraged out-of-work benefit funds. Subsidies were in proportion to benefits paid by the unions or other voluntary organizations. The plan did not encompass employer participation.

ghost town A term applied to a community once active and prosperous but which has become depopulated. A community from which industry has moved and industrial buildings are vacant and inhabited by "ghosts." Many cities which went through great industrial upheaval because of unionization (such as Akron, Ohio) were heralded as future "ghost" cities or towns because of the claim that industry would move from these organized centers to other areas which were unorganized.

Source references: "The Lesson of St. Mary," *United Rubber Worker*, Oct. 1939; Nelson C. Sparks, "Why Akron Is a Ghost City," *Liberty*, Sept. 24, 1938.

G.I. bill of rights *See* SERVICEMEN'S READJUSTMENT ACT OF 1944.

gild (guild) system A system of manufacturing, prior to the industrial revolution in Europe, in which the master craftsmen, organized in a tightly knit organization called the "gild," regulated the trade. The gild was essentially monopolistic in practice. It limited the numbers admitted to the trade, established apprenticeship regulations, set the standards of quality for the product, and resolved conflicts within its own organization. Although it contributed in many ways toward high standards of workmanship and desirable regulations in its early period, it tended later to inhibit the development and growth of trade because of its monopolistic and self-centered activities.

See also GUILDS, MERCHANT GILDS.

Gissel Packing Co. case A Supreme Court decision establishing the principles that (1) the NLRB may require bargaining on the basis of authorization cards, (2) an employer is not obligated to rely on authorization cards as proof of majority status and may request a representation election, and (3) the NLRB may order bargaining where an employer rejects a union card majority while at the same time committing unfair labor practices that tend to undermine the union's majority and make a fair election among employees an unlikely possibility.

Source references: NLRB v. Gissel Packing Co., 395 US 575, 71 LRRM 2481 (1969); Daniel M. Carson, "The *Gissel* Doctrine: When a Bargaining Order Will Issue," *IR Law Digest*, April 1973; Ira Golub, "The Propriety of Issuing *Gissel* Bargaining Orders Where the Union Has Never Attained a Majority," *LLJ*, Oct. 1978; Jacqui C. Hood, "Bargaining Orders: The Effect of *Gissel Packing Company*," *LLJ*, April 1981; Andrea Svonoe and Thomas G. S. Christensen, "*Gissel Packing* and 'Good Faith Doubt': The Gestalt of Required Recognition of Unions Under the NLRA," *IR Law Digest*, April 1971; Max S. Wortman, Jr. and Nathaniel Jones, "Remedial Actions of the NLRB in Representation Cases: An Analysis of the *Gissel* Bargaining Order," *LLJ*, May 1979.

See also AUTHORIZATION CARD.

giveback *See* CONCESSION BARGAINING, EMPLOYEE GIVEBACK.

Glass and Ceramic Workers of North America; United (AFL-CIO) One of the major unions in the glass industry, once affiliated with the CIO. The union was formerly known as the Federation of Glass, Ceramic and Silica Sand Workers of America (CIO). The official monthly publication was *The Glass Workers' News*.

It merged with the Aluminum, Brick and Clay Workers of America (AFL-CIO) in September 1982 to form the Aluminum, Brick and Glass Workers International Union (AFL-CIO).

See also ALUMINUM, BRICK AND GLASS WORKERS INTERNATIONAL UNION (AFL-CIO).

Glass Bottle Blowers Association of the United States and Canada (AFL-CIO) The United Green Glass Workers' Association formed in 1890 and withdrew from the Knights of Labor in 1891. In 1896, it changed its name to the Glass Bottle Blowers Association of the United States and Canada. It affiliated with the AFL in 1899. On August 1, 1975, the Window Glass Cutters League of America (AFL-CIO) merged with the union. Its official monthly publication was the *GBBA Horizons*.

The union merged with the International Brotherhood of Pottery and Allied Workers (AFL-CIO) in August 1982, to form the Glass, Pottery, Plastic and Allied Workers International Union (AFL-CIO).

See also GLASS, POTTERY, PLASTIC AND ALLIED WORKERS INTERNATIONAL UNION (AFL-CIO).

Glass Cutters League of America; Window (AFL-CIO) Early organization of window glass cutters that dates from the time of the Knights of Labor. Local Assembly 300 of the Knights, founded in 1880 as a national trade body, covered the four major skilled crafts in window glass manufacture—gatherers, blowers, flatteners, and cutters. The cutters withdrew in 1896 and formed the Window Glass Cutters' League. The flatteners followed suit. The two groups formed the Window Glass Cutters' and Flatteners' Association of America, Inc. in 1902.

An independent union was organized in 1910 at the machine plants of the American Window Glass Co. It was known as the Window Glass Cutters' and Flatteners' Protective Association. The Libbey-Owens Company cutters formed the Cutters' League in 1917, and were chartered by the AFL in 1925. In 1930, the Cutters' League and the Window Glass Cutters' and Flatteners' amalgamated to form the Window Glass Cutters' League of America. Its official publication was *The Glass Cutter*.

On August 1, 1975, the union merged with the Glass Bottle Blowers Association of the United States and Canada (AFL-CIO).

See also GLASS BOTTLE BLOWERS ASSOCIATION OF THE UNITED STATES AND CANADA (AFL-CIO).

Glass, Pottery, Plastic and Allied Workers International Union (AFL-CIO) The Glass Bottle Blowers Association of the United States and Canada (AFL-CIO) and the International Brotherhood of Pottery and Allied Workers (AFL-CIO) merged to form this union in August 1982. Its monthly publication is the *GPPAW Horizons*.

Address: 608 E. Baltimore Pike, Media, Pa. 19063. Tel. (215) 565–5051

Glass Workers' Union of North America; American Flint (AFL-CIO) Organized in Pittsburgh, Pa., July 1878. Its official monthly publications are *Flint* and *Circular*.

Address: 1440 South Byrne Rd., Toledo, Ohio 43614. Tel. (419) 385–6687

Glidden case In 1957 the Glidden Company, which had been in Elmhurst, N.Y., since 1929, decided to relocate its plant in Bethlehem, Pa. Its union contract gave workers with a specified length of employment seniority-rehire rights for a number of years. Although the company waited until the contract term ended before moving, some workers requested that the company honor these seniority rights in the new plant. When the company refused, the workers brought suit. Prior to the lawsuit, the workers had attempted to arbitrate the matter, but the company succeeded in getting the state court to bar the arbitration on the ground that the arbitration clause was too narrow to cover the claim.

In the 1961 lawsuit, *Zdanok v. Glidden Co.* (288 F2d 99, 47 LRRM 2856 (1961)), the New York Court of Appeals for the Second Circuit, by a two-to-one vote, held that the workers had acquired vested rights which the company was required to recognize and thus that seniority rights survived the expiration of a contract and relocation of a plant. Later in 1968, in the case of *Local 1251, UAW v. Robertshaw Controls Co.* (68 LRRM 2671), the same New York Court of Appeals overruled the 1961 *Glidden* decision.

Source references: Benjamin Aaron, "Reflections on the Legal Nature and Enforceability of Seniority Rights," 75 *Harvard LR* 1532 (1962); Meyer S. Ryder, "Labor Relations Aspects of Plant Relocation: The Legal Dilemma," *MLR*, April 1963; William D. Turner, "Plant Removals and Related Problems," *LLJ*, Nov. 1962; Arnold R. Weber, "Plant Removals and Subcontracting of Work: Social and Economic Considerations," *LLJ*, April 1963; John H. Weeks, "Labor Relations Aspects of Plant Relocation: Personnel Considerations," *MLR*, April 1963.

Globe doctrine The policy, set forth by the NLRB *In the Matter of Globe Machine and Stamping Company*, in which the Board provided for special balloting to determine the representation wishes of employees. The situation involved a bargaining unit determination by the Board where a smaller craft unit and a larger industry unit were equally plausible. By permitting the employees in the smaller unit to indicate their preference, the Board was able to decide whether to leave the craft group in the smaller bargaining unit or to combine it with the larger group. Special protection for the crafts was written into the Taft-Hartley Act.

Source references: In the Matter of the Globe Machine and Stamping Co., 3 NLRB 294, 1-A LRRM 122 (1937); "The 'Globe Rule' for Units Under the Wagner Act," 6 *Univ. of Chicago LR* 673 (1939); Michael F. Mayer, "Determination of the Appropriate Bargaining Unit in Multi-Plant Enterprises," 51 *Yale LJ* 155 (1941); Benjamin Rathbun, Jr., "The Taft-Hartley Act and Craft Unit Bargaining," 59 *Yale LJ* 1023 (1950); Fred Witney, "The Appropriate Bargaining Unit Controversy," *Southern Economic Journal*, Oct. 1949; J. Albert Woll, James A. Glenn, and Herbert S. Thatcher, "Craft Unionism and the National Labor Relations Act," *LLJ*, Oct. 1949.

See also BARGAINING UNIT.

Glove Workers' Union of America; International (AFL-CIO) Organized in Washington, D.C. in December 1901. The union merged with the Amalgamated Clothing Workers of America (AFL-CIO) in December 1961.

See also CLOTHING WORKERS OF AMERICA; AMALGAMATED (AFL-CIO).

goals and timetables A component of an affirmative action program established for each job group in which underutilization exists following the completion of the contractor's underutilization analyses. Goals and timetables are established separately for minorities and women and must be designed to completely correct the underutilization. The employer must make every good faith effort to reach the goal of utilizing workers according to their availability.

Goals refer to the placement in numbers and percentages of underutilized group members in the work force; they are based on projected job openings and the availability of the persons underutilized. Timetables are the time periods calculated for meeting the goals.

OFCCP regulations require government contractors to include goals and timetables for minorities or women in their affirmative action plans. Although usually developed by the employer, goals and timetables may be issued by the OFCCP director covering federal construction contractors in specific geographic locations.

Goals should not be confused with quotas, which are temporary, mandatory court-ordered remedies for discrimination.

Source references: U.S. OFCCP, "Construction Contractors—Affirmative Action Requirements," 41 C.F.R. 60–4; ———, "Revised Order No. 4," 41 C.F.R. 60–2; Geraldine Leshin, *Equal Employment Opportunity and Affirmative Action in Labor-Management Relations, A Primer* (Los Angeles: UC, Institute of IR, 1976); U.S. OFCCP, *Federal Contract Compliance Manual* (Washington: 1979).

See also AVAILABILITY, QUOTA, UTILIZATION ANALYSIS.

going rate The predominant rate or the rate most commonly paid to workers in a specific occupation in an industry or area. The concept is usually closely tied to the "prevailing" wage, which is a rate determined by the Secretary of Labor and which must be paid to workers on government manufacturing or supply contracts subject to the Walsh-Healey Act or federally financed construction subject to the Davis-Bacon Act.

The "prevailing" rate concept has been variously applied to meet problems which arise in the setting of legal rates under the law. When a public contract is set for a locality which has no available labor supply in the immediate labor market area and when labor will have to be brought in from nearby labor markets, the geographic area for the "prevailing rate" will have to be enlarged. Statistical measures for prevailing rates may be determined by the use of the median, arithmetic mean or other measures which show frequency or cluster.

Source references: Davis-Bacon Act, as amended, 40 U.S.C. § 276a et seq. (1982); Federal-Aid Highway Act of 1956, as amended, 23 U.S.C. § 113 (1982); Federal Airport Act, as amended, 49 U.S.C. app. § 2214(b) (1982); Walsh-Healey Public Contracts Act, as amended, 41 U.S.C. §§ 35–45 (1982).

See also PREVAILING RATE.

goldbricking Giving the appearance or pretense of working. Also applied to actions by workers or unions limiting output and to loafing on the job.

See also SLOWDOWN.

Goldfinger v. Feintuch A case in which the New York Court of Appeals upheld the right of a union to engage in secondary picketing where it was peaceful and in furtherance of the union's efforts to persuade customers not to buy in stores selling products produced by nonunion labor under substandard (below union) wage conditions. The Court of Appeals reversed the Appellate Division and dissolved the injunction issued against picketing by the union.

Source reference: Goldfinger v. Feintuch, 276 NY 281, 1-A LRRM 718 (1937).

See also FREEDOM OF SPEECH, PICKETING.

goldfish bowl bargaining A procedure which focuses attention on the fact that the bargaining process is open to the public and constantly under the surveillance of the public eye. The general feeling is that bargaining with relatively few exceptions should be reasonably private, but that where public funds are involved perhaps the final actions dealing with implementation of agreement provisions should be available for public scrutiny.

Source references: Donald R. Magruder, *Bargaining in Public: Help or Hindrance?* (Washington: Labor-Management Relations Service, Special Report, 1976); Peter Schnaufer, "Representing the Teachers' Interests," *Collective Bargaining in the Public Service*, Proceedings of the 1966 Annual Spring Meeting, IRRA, ed. by Gerald Somers (Madison: 1966).

Gompersite An individual who supported the labor policies of Samuel Gompers.

Gompers' non-partisan policy The policy of the American Federation of Labor, attributed to Samuel Gompers, which sought to use the two major political parties to assist the AFL to achieve its industrial objectives without being committed to either party. The support of the AFL was for individuals who were helpful to it, and its opposition was to those who were inimical to its welfare, regardless of political affiliation.

Source references: Mollie R. Carroll, *Labor and Politics* (New York: Houghton-Mifflin, 1923); Harwood L. Childs, *Labor and Capital in National Politics* (Columbus: Ohio State UP, 1930); Henry David, "One Hundred Years of Labor in Politics," *The House of Labor*, ed. by J. B. S. Hardman and Maurice F. Neufeld (New York: PH, 1951); Nathan Fine, *Labor and Farmer Parties in the United States, 1828–1928* (New York: Rand School of Social Science, 1928); Bernard Mandel, *Samuel Gompers, A Biography* (Yellow Springs, Ohio: Antioch Press, 1963); Mark Perlman, *Labor Union Theories in America* (New York: Harper, 1958); Selig Perlman, *History of Trade Unionism in the United States* (New York: Macmillan, 1922); Norman J. Ware, *The Labor Movement in the United States, 1860–1895* (New York: Appleton, 1929).

Gompers v. Bucks' Stove and Range Company *See* BUCKS' STOVE AND RANGE CASE.

good-faith bargaining Negotiations between representatives of union and company to reach a mutually satisfactory agreement setting forth the conditions of employment under a collective bargaining contract. What constitutes "good faith" in the bargaining process is frequently difficult to determine. The Taft-Hartley Act defines it as a mutual obligation "to meet at reasonable times and confer in good faith with respect to wages, hours, and other terms and conditions of employment." Neither side, however, is required to agree to a proposal or to make a concession.

The criteria which the NLRB developed under the National Labor Relations Act and extended under the Taft-Hartley Act go to the totality of the relationship between the parties. The Board may consider, among other things: dilatory behavior, refusal to meet at convenient and reasonable times, actions designed to weaken the unions, refusal to incorporate the terms agreed upon into a written contract, and other factors that suggest that one of the parties is making a mockery of the bargaining process.

Source references: Harold W. Davey, *Contemporary Collective Bargaining* (2d ed., New York: PH, 1959); John T. Dunlop, *Collective Bargaining* (Chicago: Irwin, 1949); "Good Faith Bargaining in Labor Relations," 61 *Harvard LR* 1224 (1948); "The Good Faith Requirement in Collective Bargaining," *Virginia LR*, Jan. 1957; Frank C. Pierson, *Collective Bargaining Systems* (Washington: American Council on Public Affairs, 1942); Benjamin M. Selekman, "Varieties of Labor Relations," *Harvard BR*, March 1949; Twentieth Century Fund, *How Collective Bargaining Works* (New York: 1942).

See also COLLECTIVE BARGAINING, GENERAL ELECTRIC CASE, HEINZ CASE, REFUSAL TO BARGAIN.

good faith effort Defined by the OFCCP as "actions required by 41 CFR Chapter 60 [Revised Order No. 4], and those the contractor may voluntarily develop, to achieve compliance with the contract's equal opportunity and affirmative action clauses."

Source references: U.S. OFCCP, "Revised Order No. 4," 41 C.F.R. 60–2; ______, *Federal Contract Compliance Manual* (Washington: 1979).

See also COMPLIANCE REVIEW, EXECUTIVE ORDER 11246, GOALS AND TIMETABLES, REVISED ORDER NO. 4.

goon A slang term for a person, plug-ugly, thug, roughneck, or slugger hired by an employer or union during a labor dispute to create or resist violence. The person or persons are hired to terrorize the workers or the employer.

See also ANTI-STRIKEBREAKING ACT (BYRNES ACT).

goon squad A group of thugs or sluggers who are hired by employers or unions to create or resist violence during a labor dispute.

government employees Workers employed by an instrumentality of government. Section 305 of the Taft-Hartley Act which prohibited strikes by federal employees was repealed on August 9, 1955. The strike prohibition is currently provided under Title 5 U.S.C. Secs. 7311, 3333 and Title 18 U.S.C. Sec. 1918. A fine in the amount of not more than $1,000 or imprisonment of not more than one year and a day, or both, are penalties for participation in strike activity. Executive Order 10988, issued in 1962 by President John F. Kennedy, laid the groundwork for a system of collective bargaining within the federal service.

Source references: R. G. Davis, "Government Employees and the Right to Strike," *Social Forces*, March 1950; David Ziskind, *One Thousand Strikes of Government Employees* (New York: Columbia UP, 1940).

See also CIVIL SERVICE REFORM ACT OF 1978, CLASSIFICATION ACT EMPLOYEES, COLLECTIVE NEGOTIATION, EXECUTIVE ORDER 10988, EXECUTIVE ORDER 11491, PUBLIC EMPLOYEE RELATIONS, RIGHT TO STRIKE, WAGE BOARD EMPLOYEES.

Government Employees; American Federation of (AFL-CIO) Organized in August 1932 following the withdrawal of the National Federation of Federal Employees from the AFL. The group opposed to leaving the AFL formed the American Federation of Government Employees and affiliated with the AFL.

On April 1, 1971, the Association of Engineers and Scientists merged with the union. Its publications are *Political Action* (biweekly) and *The Government Standard* (monthly).

Address: 1325 Massachusetts Ave., N.W., Washington, D.C. 20005. Tel. (202) 737–8700

Government Employees; National Association of One of the major unions representing federal sector employees. The International Brotherhood of Police Officers and the Federal Aviation Science and Technology Association are affiliated with the union. Effective December 1, 1982, the union merged with the Service Employees' International Union (AFL-CIO). Under the merger agreement, the union retains its autonomy and its officers occupy five seats on the Service Employees' executive board. It publishes the monthly *Fednews*.

Address: 295 Dorchester Ave., Boston, Mass. 02127. Tel. (617) 268–5002

Source references: "Service Employees and NAGE Merge Forming Union of 780,000 Members," *Daily Labor Report*, No. 240, Dec. 14, 1982; U.S. OPM, *Union Recognition in the Federal Government* (Washington: OLMR 82–4, 1982).

Government Employes Council Formed in 1945 as a planning organization of AFL-CIO unions having members in government service to prepare programs for legislative and administration action. It later merged with the Public Employee Department.

See also PUBLIC EMPLOYEE DEPARTMENT.

Government Inspectors; National Association of (Ind) Founded in 1955, the union changed its name to the National Association of Government Inspectors and Quality Assurance Personnel in the 1970s.

See also GOVERNMENT INSPECTORS AND QUALITY ASSURANCE PERSONNEL; NATIONAL ASSOCIATION OF.

Government Inspectors and Quality Assurance Personnel; National Association of Formerly known as the National Association of Government Inspectors, the union adopted its present name in the 1970s. In December 1983 it affiliated with the American Federation of Government Employees (AFL-CIO).

Address: Box 31319, Jacksonville, Fla. 32230. Tel. (904) 743–7742

government seizure A procedure used by the government, usually during a war period or other emergency, to take over the operation of plants necessary to the prosecution of the war effort.

Seizure during peacetime without statutory authority was contested in the 1952 steel cases and the Supreme Court held, in *Youngstown Sheet and Tube Co. v. Sawyer*, that the seizure power by the President requires specific statutory authority.

Source references: Youngstown Sheet and Tube Co. v. Sawyer, 343 US 579, 30 LRRM 2172 (1952); John L. Blackman, Jr., *Presidential Seizure in Labor Disputes* (Cambridge: Harvard UP, 1967); Harold S. Roberts, *Seizure in Labor Disputes* (Honolulu: Univ. of Hawaii, IRC, 1949); Murray M. Rohman, "National Emergency Disputes and Seizure," *LLJ*, Jan. 1962; Ludwig Teller, "Government Seizures in Labor Disputes," 60 *Harvard LR* 1017 (1947); George C. Vietheer, "The Government Seizure Stratagem in Labor Disputes," *Public Administration Review*, Spring 1946; Bertram F. Willcox and E. S. Landis, "Government Seizures in Labor Disputes," 34 *Cornell LQ* 155 (1948); Edwin Witte, "Wartime Handling of Labor Disputes," 25 *Harvard BR* 169 (1947).

See also PRESIDENTIAL SEIZURE, WAR LABOR DISPUTES ACT, YOUNGSTOWN SHEET AND TUBE CO. V. SAWYER.

gradualism The process of achieving a goal or result through slow progression and by degrees so that wide acceptance can be achieved through education. This was the policy followed by Samuel Gompers as leader of the AFL.

graduated strike An alternative to a conventional strike in which public employees stop working during portions of their usual workweek and receive reduced wages. Bernstein believes the graduated strike offers a promising alternative because striking employees will continue to receive partial wages and public services will not be halted.

Source reference: Merton C. Bernstein, "Two Alternatives to Traditional Strikes by Public Employees," *MLR*, May 1972.

See also PARTIAL STRIKE.

graduated wage Generally has reference to wages which are adjusted on the basis of length of service with the company, or length of service coupled with certain standards of performance.

graft in unions The acquisition by union officials or employees of money, position, or profit through dishonest or questionable means, such as embezzlement of union funds, receiving bribes or kickbacks from employers, using union money for personal expenses, investing union funds for private gain, and other practices which are inimical to clean unionism. The congressional hearings in the late 1950s on "Improper Practices in the Labor-Management Field" led to the adoption of the 1959 Landrum-Griffin Act imposing a fiduciary duty on union officials, making embezzlement of union funds a federal crime, forbidding certain payments to union officials, and requiring unions to file detailed financial reports with the Labor Department. Welfare and pension funds are regulated by the Employee Retirement Income Security Act and theft or embezzlement of such funds is a federal crime.

See also EMPLOYEE RETIREMENT INCOME SECURITY ACT (ERISA) OF 1974, LABOR-MANAGEMENT REPORTING AND DISCLOSURE ACT OF 1959, MCCLELLAN COMMITTEE, WELFARE AND PENSION PLANS DISCLOSURE ACT OF 1958 (TELLER ACT).

Grain Millers; American Federation of (AFL-CIO) It publishes the quarterly *Grain Miller News*.

Address: 4949 Olson Memorial Highway, Minneapolis, Minn. 55422. Tel. (612) 545–0211

grand lodge The term applied to the head office (national or international) of a union organized along fraternal lines or using the language of fraternal societies. Local unions of the International Association of Machinists are referred to as "lodges," and the national headquarters as the "Grand Lodge."

Granite Cutters' International Association of America; The (AFL-CIO) Union organized in Rockland, Maine in March 1877 as the Granite Cutters' National Union. It adopted its present name in 1905. The official monthly publication was *The Granite Cutters' Journal*.

On January 7, 1980, the union merged with the Tile, Marble and Terrazzo Finishers and Shopmen International Union (AFL-CIO).

See also TILE, MARBLE, TERRAZZO FINISHERS, AND SHOPWORKERS AND GRANITE CUTTERS INTERNATIONAL UNION (AFL-CIO).

grapevine A term for the "underground" system of communication among employees themselves for conveying rumors about changes in factory administration and policies. One of the problems of management communication with employees is preventing the spread of untrue rumors which may unduly alarm employees.

Source references: Robert Hershey, "The Grapevine—Here to Stay But Not Beyond Control," *Personnel*, Jan./Feb. 1966; "How to Shut Down the Rumor Factory," *Supervisory Management*, Jan. 1965; Joy Larcom, "The Grapevine—How to Beat It or Join It," *Personnel Management and Methods*, July 1963; D. H. Scott, "Letting the Grapevine Take Over: Mistakes Executives Make," *Sales Management*, March 18, 1960.

Graphic Arts International Union (AFL-CIO) A union formed in September 1972, with the merger of the International Brotherhood of Bookbinders (AFL-CIO) and the Lithographers and Photoengravers International Union (AFL-CIO).

On July 1, 1983, the union merged with the International Printing and Graphic Communications Union (AFL-CIO) to form the Graphic Communications International Union (AFL-CIO).

See also GRAPHIC COMMUNICATIONS INTERNATIONAL UNION (AFL-CIO).

Graphic Communications International Union (AFL-CIO) Union formed on July 1, 1983, with the merger of the Graphic Arts International Union (AFL-CIO) and the International Printing and Graphic Communications Union (AFL-CIO). It issues the monthly *Tabloid*.

Address: 1900 L St., N.W., Washington, D.C. 20036. Tel. (202) 462–1400

graveyard shift A work schedule, usually in plants on continuous operation, which begins around midnight and ends during the early morning. It may be from 11 p.m. to 7 a.m. or 12 midnight to 8 a.m. The graveyard connotation probably relates to the quietness of the shift during the dead of night or the time when, according to myth, there is activity in the graveyard area.

See also SHIFT.

green hands Workers who are new to a job or occupation, or inexperienced in the performance of the work.

Greyhound cases Cases in which the Supreme Court in 1938 upheld orders of the NLRB disestablishing company-dominated unions *(The Employees Association of the Pennsylvania Greyhound Lines, Inc. and the Drivers' Association).* The Court held that the NLRB could require the company to dissolve an organization dominated and sponsored by the company. It also held that it was not necessary for the NLRB to direct the order against the company-dominated union or to permit it to become a party to the proceedings.

Source references: NLRB v. Pacific Greyhound Lines, Inc., 303 US 272, 2 LRRM 604 (1938); *NLRB v. Pennsylvania Greyhound Lines, Inc.*, 303 US 261, 2 LRRM 599 (1938).

See also COMPANY-DOMINATED UNION, DISESTABLISHMENT.

grievance Any complaint by an employee or by a union (sometimes by the employer or employer association), concerning any aspect of the employment relationship. The complaint may be real or fancied, arbitrable or nonarbitrable under the contract. Arbitrable grievances are usually those which arise out of the interpretation or application of the terms of the collective bargaining agreement.

Source references: John A. Lapp, *How to Handle Labor Grievances* (Deep River: National Foremen's Institute, Inc., 1945); Paul M. Muchinsky and Mounawar A. Maassarani, "Public Sector Grievances in Iowa," *Journal of Collective Negotiations in the Public Sector*, Vol. 10, no. 1, 1981; George Rose, "The Nature of a Grievance in Labor Relations," *LLJ*, Sept. 1952; William E. Simkin and Van Dusen Kennedy, *Arbitration of Grievances* (Washington: U.S. Dept. of Labor, Division of Labor Standards, Bull. no. 82, 1946); Morris Stone, *Labor Grievances and Decisions* (New York: AAA, 1970); A. K. Wnoroski, "Once You Have an Agreement (How to Avoid Grievances)," *PJ*, Oct. 1970.

See also ARBITRATION, WRITTEN GRIEVANCES.

grievance adjustment Methods of settling or adjusting a grievance vary from contract to contract. In most cases the gripe of claim of contract violation or alleged unfairness is taken up between the foreman and the employee involved, or through the shop steward speaking for the employee. If not settled it moves through one or more steps where union and company representatives of higher rank try to iron out the difficulty. The terminal step in the grievance machinery is usually arbitration.

Source references: Benjamin Aaron, *The Settlement of Disputes Over Rights: A Comparative View* (Los Angeles: UC, Institute of IR, Reprint no. 247, 1974); AMA, *How to Handle Grievances, Selected Reprints from AMA Periodicals* (New York: 1962–1969); Mollie H. Bowers, Ronald L. Seeber, and Lamont E. Stallworth, "Grievance Mediation: A Route to Resolution for the Cost-Conscious 1980s," *LLJ*, Aug. 1982; Steven Briggs, "The Steward, the Supervisor, and the Grievance Process," *Proceedings of the 34th A/M, IRRA*, ed. by Barbara Dennis (Madison: 1982); Paul F. Brissenden, *Settlement of Disputes Over Grievances in the United States* (Honolulu: Univ. of Hawaii, IRC, 1965); BNA, *Grievance Guide* (6th ed., Washington: 1982); J. H. Foegen, "An Ombudsman as Complement to the Grievance Procedure," *LLJ*, May 1972; Jeffrey Gandz and J. David Whitehead, "The Relationship Between Industrial Relations Climate and Grievance Initiation and Resolution," *Proceedings of the 34th A/M, IRRA*, ed. by Barbara Dennis (Madison: 1982); Harry Graham and Brian Heshizer, "The Effect of Contract Language on Low-Level Settlement of Grievances," *LLJ*, July 1979; Stephen L. Hayford and Richard Pegnetter, "Grievance Adjudication for Public Employees: A Comparison of Rights Arbitration and Civil Service Appeals Procedures," *AJ*, Sept. 1980; James W. Kuhn, *Bargaining in Grievance Settlement* (New York: Columbia UP, 1961); James E. Martin, "Grievance Procedures in the Federal Service: The Continuing Problem," *Public Personnel Management*, July/Aug. 1978; Joyce M. Najita, *Guide to Statutory Provisions in Public Sector Collective Bar-*

gaining—Grievance Adjustment Procedures (Honolulu: Univ. of Hawaii, IRC, 1974); John A. Spitz, *Grievance Handling and Preparing for Arbitration in the Public Sector* (Los Angeles: UC, Institute of IR, 1976); Joseph C. Ullman and James P. Begin, *Negotiated Grievance Procedures in Public Employment* (Chicago: PPA, PERL no. 25, 1970); U.S. Dept. of Labor, BLS, *Grievance and Arbitration Procedures in State and Local Agreements* (Washington: Bull. 1833, 1975); Arnold Zack, *Understanding Grievance Arbitration in the Public Sector* (3d ed., Washington: U.S. Dept. of Labor, LMSA, 1980).

See also DISPUTE ADJUSTMENT, GRIEVANCE MACHINERY, INTERIM GRIEVANCE PROCEDURE.

grievance arbitration *See* ARBITRATION, GRIEVANCE.

grievance committee The group of union and/or management representatives that reviews grievances after they have come up from the lower steps of the grievance machinery. Such committees have greater authority because they represent a broad group and are in a position to deal with policy questions. In some contracts a special joint grievance committee may be set up which acts as a review committee to see if the grievance can be resolved before being submitted to arbitration or, in case of multiplant contracts, to the central office for examination by a representative of the international union and someone from the central personnel office of the company.

Source reference: Benjamin M. Selekman, "Handling Shop Grievances," *Harvard BR*, Summer 1945.

See also SHOP COMMITTEE.

grievance machinery The provisions set up, usually in the collective bargaining agreement, to resolve problems which arise in the application and interpretation of the contract, or problems which arise out of the agreement. The contractual provisions below were ordered by the National War Labor Board for the Amalgamated Meat Cutters and the Swift and Company plant in Fontana, California:

> Should differences arise between the Company and the Union, or the Company and the employees, or between the employees of the Company, or should any local trouble of any kind arise in the plant pertaining to matters involved in this agreement or incident to the employment regulation, there shall be no strike, stoppage, slowdown, or suspension of work on the part of the Union, or its members, or lockout on the part of the Company on account of such disputes until after an earnest effort has been made to settle all such matters immediately in the following manner and order:
>
> 1. The employee should first take the question up with his department foreman. The employee may be accompanied by an employee union representative.
> 2. In the event no conclusion is reached, the employee may be accompanied by his employee union representative when presenting the question to the plant foreman.
> 3. If the case is not settled, then the employee may be accompanied by a union representative when presenting the question to the manager of the plant.
> 4. In the event that no decision is reached in the first three steps, the parties will then within ten days agree upon an arbitrator whose decision shall be final and binding upon the parties. In case the parties fail to agree upon an arbitrator within ten days, either party may request the War Labor Board to appoint an arbitrator. However, prior to the submission of the question to arbitration, the grievance issue shall be reduced to writing.
>
> When a settlement is arrived at, at any stage of the foregoing procedures, such a decision shall be final and binding.
>
> In the event it becomes necessary to have an arbitrator, then the expenses incidental to arbitration are to be shared equally by the Union and the Company.

The Supreme Court in developing the concept of labor arbitration in collective bargaining in its trilogy cases made the following observation in the *Warrior Navigation Co.* case:

> . . . the grievance machinery under a collective bargaining agreement is at the very heart of the system of industrial self government. Arbitration is the means of solving the unforeseeable by molding a system of private law for all the problems which may arise and to provide for their solution in a way which will generally accord with the variant needs and desires of the parties. The processing of disputes through the grievance machinery is actually a vehicle by which meaning and content is given to the collective bargaining agreement.

Source references: United Steelworkers v. American Manufacturing Co., 363 US 564, 46 LRRM 2414 (1960); *United Steelworkers v. Enterprise Wheel & Car Co.*, 363 US 593, 46 LRRM 2423 (1960); *United Steelworkers v. Warrior & Gulf Navigation Co.*, 363 US 574, 46 LRRM 2416 (1960); Steven Briggs, "The Grievance Procedure and Organizational Health," *PJ*, June 1977; Neil W. Chamberlain, "Grievance Proceedings and Collective Bargaining," *Insights Into Labor Issues*, ed. by Richard A. Lester and Joseph Shister (New York: Macmillan, 1948); Robert Coulson, "Justice Brennan on Wheels: *Complete Auto Transit, Best Freight* and *Clayton v. UAW*," *NYU 34th Annual National Conference on Labor*, ed. by Richard Adelman (New York: Bender, 1982); Thomas F. Gideon and Richard B. Peterson, "A Comparison of Alternate Grievance Procedures," *Employee Relations LJ*, Autumn 1979; Marvin Hill, Jr., "Grievance Procedure and Title VII Limitations," *LLJ*, June 1977; Daniel J. Julius, "A Guide for the Effective Management of Employee Grievances," *Journal of the College and University Personnel Association*, Winter 1981; Abbott Kaplan, *Making Grievance Procedure Work* (Los Angeles: UC, Institute of IR, 1950); Sid Lens, "Meaning of the Grievance Procedure," *Harvard BR*, Nov. 1948; Leonard N. Persson, "Considerations for an Institutional Grievance Procedure," *Journal of the College and University Personnel Association*, Jan./Feb. 1976; Richard B. Peterson and David Lewin, "A Model for Research and Analysis of the Grievance Process," *Proceedings of the 34th A/M, IRRA*, ed. by Barbara Dennis (Madison: 1982); Otto Pragan, "Grievance Procedures in the Federal Service," *MLR*, June 1966; Robert Repas, "Grievance Procedures Without Arbitration," *ILRR*, April 1967; Peter Seitz, "Time to Review Your Grievance and Arbitration Procedures!" *PJ*, June 1965; William Simkin, "Grievance Machinery—From an Arbitrator's Point of View," *NYU 2d Annual Conference on Labor*, ed. by Emanuel Stein (Albany: Bender, 1949); Paul D. Staudohar, "Exhaustion of Remedies in Private Industry Grievance Procedures," *Employee Relations LJ*, Winter 1981/82; Andrew W. J. Thomson, *The Grievance Procedure in the Private Sector* (Ithaca: Cornell Univ., NYSSILR, 1974); Lloyd Ulman, "American and Foreign Grievance Systems, Discussion," *Developments in American and Foreign Arbitration*, ed. by Charles M. Rehmus (Washington: BNA, 1968); U.S. Dept. of Labor, BLS, *Major Collective Bargaining Agreements: Grievance Procedures* (Washington: Bull. no. 1425–1, 1964); Rolf Valtin, "Preventive Mediation, Grievance Disputes and the Taft-Hartley Act," *LLJ*, Dec. 1956; Peter A. Veglagn, "Making the Grievance Procedure Work," *PJ*, March 1977; Janusz K. Zawodny, "Grievance Procedures in Soviet Factories," *ILRR*, July 1957.

grievance pay *See* PAY FOR GRIEVANCE TIME, PAY FOR SHOP STEWARDS.

grievance procedure *See* GRIEVANCE MACHINERY.

grievance procedure, interim *See* INTERIM GRIEVANCE PROCEDURE.

grievances, individual employee *See* INDIVIDUAL EMPLOYEE GRIEVANCES.

Griggs v. Duke Power Co. A landmark Supreme Court decision which held that employment tests or criteria operating to exclude minority groups in hiring are prohibited under Title VII of the Civil Rights Act unless the requirements are shown to be related to job performance.

Source references: Griggs v. Duke Power Co., 401 US 424, 3 FEP Cases 175 (1971); William F. Bramble, "A Study of *Griggs v. Duke Power Company*; A Landmark Decision on Employment Testing," *Industrial and Labor Relations Forum*, Dec. 1971; James C. McBrearty, "Legality of Employment Tests: The Impact of *Duke Power Co.*," *LLJ*, July 1971; Donald J. Peterson, "The Impact of Duke Power on Testing," *Personnel*, March/April 1974; James D. Portwood and Stuart M. Schmidt, "Beyond *Griggs v. Duke Power Company*: Title VII After *Washington v. Davis*," *LLJ*, March 1977; Hugh Steven Wilson, "A Second Look at Griggs v. Duke Power Company: Ruminations on Job Testing, Discrimination, and the Role of Federal Courts," *IR Law Digest*, Jan. 1973.

See also ADVERSE IMPACT, PROTECTED CLASS.

griping *See* GRIEVANCE.

gross average hourly earnings A figure computed monthly by BLS as part of its regular employment and payroll reporting program. It is a measure of hourly wages based on total compensation before payroll deductions, divided by man-hours worked and compensated.

gross average weekly earnings A figure computed monthly by BLS as part of its regular employment and payroll reporting program. It is a measure of weekly earnings based on total compensation before payroll deductions, divided by total employment. An alternate procedure is to multiply average hourly earnings by average weekly hours.

group bonus A method of wage payment based on the performance of a group of persons on the job. The bonus is in the form of an incentive for work performed beyond a norm based on time, quantity, and quality of output. The group may involve a large unit such as a plant. It may then be referred to as a plantwide incentive bonus. Although plantwide incentives generally apply to production workers, frequently the nonproduction personnel participate in the bonus or incentive payment.

Source references: C. Canby Balderston, *Group Incentives* (Philadelphia: Univ. of Pennsylvania Press, 1930); Barry D. Whelchel, "Can Individual Incentives Be as Efficient as Group Incentives?" *PJ*, June 1962.

group grievance A complaint filed by the union seeking determination of a question that is of importance to the group, has an effect on group interests, or involves a group of employees who have identical concerns and are known to the employer and the union, even though the dispute relates to particular individual rights. Remedies are granted or are available to all similarly situated employees such as members of a department, a bargaining unit, or all employees of a company.

Grievances are filed by a union on behalf of the group or class with or without identification of individual grievants. A collective bargaining agreement may mandate individual grievants to sign the grievance, but a grievance filed and signed by a union official without the signature of an "affected" employee has been deemed a proper group grievance. Also, individual employee grievances involving the same contract provisions and issues may be combined to form a group grievance.

The term is often referred to as a class grievance and sometimes as a "general" or "policy" grievance.

Source references: John Deere Tractor Co., 17 LA 330 (1951); *Jonco Aircraft Corp.*, 22 LA 887 (1954); *Trans World Air Lines, Inc.*, 47 LA 1127 (1967); Frank Elkouri and Edna Asper Elkouri, *How Arbitration Works* (4th ed., Washington: BNA, 1985); Marvin Hill, Jr. and Anthony V. Sinicropi, *Remedies in Arbitration* (Washington: BNA, 1981).

group insurance A program designed to provide low-cost protection to large groups of workers through a plan, generally negotiated with an insurance company, to cover life, accident, sickness, hospitalization, and medical and surgical benefits. The plan may be financed by the employer (noncontributory plan) or jointly by the employer and the employees (contributory). Group-insurance plans may be inaugurated unilaterally where there is no collective bargaining agent. Where there is a collective bargaining agent the plan frequently is a negotiated one.

Source references: Helen Baker and Dorothy Dahl, *Group Health Insurance and Sickness Benefit Plans in Collective Bargaining* (Princeton: Princeton Univ., IR Section, 1945); Robert D. Eilers and Robert M. Crowe, *Group Insurance Handbook* (Homewood: Irwin, 1965); Davis S. Gregg, *Group Life Insurance: An Analysis of Concepts, Contracts, Costs, and Company Practices* (3d ed., Homewood: Irwin, 1962); Louise Walters Ilse, *Group Insurance and Employee Retirement Plans* (New York: PH, 1953); NICB, *Company Group Insurance Plans* (New York: Studies in Personnel Policy nos. 107 and 112, 1950 and 1951).

group leader A worker who acts as a foreman, usually over a small group of employees. He generally performs the same work as the others in the group, and his supervisory work is only an incidental part of his job. In the agricultural field he may be known as a crew boss.

guaranteed annual wage A plan adopted by some employers to provide a stable labor force on a year-round basis. The employer agrees to pay his employees wages for each week in the year, whether work is available or not. Flexibility is provided under the Fair Labor Standards Act for companies which provide a guaranteed annual wage plan so that overtime is not computed on a fixed daily or weekly basis. This was designed to encourage the spread of guaranteed wage plans.

There is a wide variety of plans in effect, which vary in the guarantee of the wages during the year and in the category of employees to which the guarantee applies.

Source references: James L. Allen and C. Wilson Randle, "Challenge of the Guaranteed Annual Wage," *Harvard BR*, May/June 1954; Jules Backman, "Economies of the Guaranteed Wage," *LLJ*, Oct. 1956; Richard M. Bourne, "Wage Guarantees: A Re-examination," *LLJ*, Feb. 1960; George E. Bowles, "The GAW Negotiations," *LLJ*, Aug. 1955; Otis Brubaker, "Guaranteed Annual Wage," *LLJ*, June 1953; BNA, *The Guaranteed Annual Wage; Existing Plans, Employer and Union Approaches, Bargaining Strategy* (Washington: 1955); Alexander Calder and James L. Knipe, *Guaranteed Annual Wages* (Minneapolis: Univ. of Minnesota Press, 1945); Chamber of Commerce of the U.S., *The Economics of the Guaranteed Wage* (Washington: 1953); Jack Chernick, *A Guide to the Guaranteed Wage* (New Brunswick: Rutgers Univ., Institute of Management and Labor Relations, Bull. no. 4, 1955); Jack Chernick and Monroe Berkowitz, "The Guaranteed Wage—The Economics of Opulence in Collective Bargaining," *Journal of Business*, July 1955; Jack Chernick and George C. Hellickson, *Guaranteed Annual Wages, Industry's Next Step?* (Minneapolis: Univ. of Minnesota Press, 1945); Robert L. Chiaravalli, "The Guaranteed Annual Wage and the United Automobile Workers," *Industrial and Labor Relations Forum*, June 1981; Waldo E. Fisher, *The Guaranteed Annual Wage* (Pasadena: California Institute of Technology, IR Section, 1945); J. W. Garbarino, *Guaranteed Wages* (Berkeley: UC, Institute of IR, 1954); Edwin B. George, "Can the GAW Cure Seasonal Unemployment?" *Dun's Review and Modern Industry*, Dec. 1956; "Guaranteed Annual Wage," *Economic Outlook*, Oct. 1953; "Guaranteed Wages and the C.I.O.," *Economic Intelligence*, May 1953; Seymour E. Harris, "The Economics of the Guaranteed Wage," *MLR*, Feb. 1955; Thomas T. Heney, "A Guaranteed Annual Wage Plan," *NYU 8th Annual Conference on Labor*, ed. by Emanuel Stein (Albany: Bender, 1955); Werner Hochwald, "Guaranteed Wages," *AER*, June 1947; International Union of Electrical Workers, *The Guaranteed Annual Wage, Report Made to IUE-CIO Convention* (Washington: 1953); A. D. H. Kaplan, *The Guarantee of Annual Wages* (Washington: Brookings Institution, 1947); ———, "The Guaranteed Annual Wage," *NYU 5th Annual Conference on Labor*, ed. by Emanuel Stein (Albany: Bender, 1952); Wayne A. Leeman, "The Guaranteed Annual Wage, Employment and Economic Progress," *ILRR*, July 1955; Morton Levine and James Nix, "Guaranteed Employment and Wages Under Collective Agreements," *MLR*, May 1952; Thomas J. Luck, *The Guaranteed Annual Wage* (Gainesville: Univ. of Florida, Economic Leaflets, 1954); Campbell R. McConnell, "Pros and Cons of the Guaranteed Annual Wage," *LLJ*, July 1956; Philip Murray, "A Guaranteed Annual Wage for Labor?" *The New York Times Magazine*, April 8, 1945; Norma Pope and Paul A. Brinker, "Recent Developments with the Guaranteed Annual Wage: The Ford Settlement," *LLJ*, Sept. 1968; Don A. Seastone, "The History of Guaranteed Wages and Employment," *Journal of Economic History*, Vol. 15, no. 2, 1955; Helen B. Shaffer, "Guaranteed Annual Wage," *Editorial Research Report*, Jan. 1953; Robert E. Sibson, "Elements of a Guaranteed Wage Plan," *LLJ*, Jan. 1953; Henry C. Thole and Charles C. Gibbons, *Prerequisites for a Guaranteed Annual Wage* (Kalamazoo: Upjohn Institute of Community Research, 1956); U.S. Office of War Mobilization and Reconversion, Office of Temporary Contracts, *Guaranteed Wages: Report to the President by the Advisory Board* (Washington: 1947); S. Herbert Unterberger, "From Guaranteed Annual Wages to Income Security," *LLJ*, April 1955; Alan Weisenfeld, "An Alternative to the Guaranteed Annual Wage," *LLJ*, Oct. 1955; Harvey A. Young and Michael F. Dougherty, "Influence of the Guaranteed Annual Wage Upon Labor

Relations and Productivity: National Sugar Refinery's Experience," *Management of Personnel Quarterly*, Winter 1971.

See also GUARANTEED INCOME, SUPPLEMENTAL UNEMPLOYMENT BENEFITS.

guaranteed base rate The amount guaranteed per hour or other period for workers on piece rates or other incentive wage-payment plans. It is sometimes applied to the guarantee at "standard" production.

guaranteed earnings Provision under some contracts which safeguards for an employee a guaranteed minimum wage where failure to maintain production is caused by machinery breakdown or other causes beyond the employee's control.

guaranteed employment A program, instituted by an employer or by joint negotiation with a union, assuring workers a specified number of hours of work per week or number of weeks per year. Guaranteed employment plans are usually part of an overall plan which includes wage payments along with or in lieu of the employment guarantee.

Source references: "Annual Guaranteed Employment Plans in Union Agreements," *MLR*, Aug. 1940; William A. Berridge and Cedric Wolfe, *Guaranteed Employment and Wage Plans* (New York: American Enterprise Assn., 1948); Audrey Freedman, "Reexamining Income Security: SUB vs. Guaranteed Work," *Conference Board Record*, May 1976; ———, *Security Bargains Reconsidered; SUB, Severance Pay, Guaranteed Work* (New York: The Conference Board, Report no. 736, 1978); Joseph L. Snider, *The Guarantee of Work and Wages* (Cambridge: Harvard UP, 1947); Robert Zager, "Managing Guaranteed Employment," *Harvard BR*, May/June 1978.

See also GUARANTEED ANNUAL WAGE, GUARANTEED INCOME, SUPPLEMENTAL UNEMPLOYMENT BENEFITS.

guaranteed income These plans include proposals aimed at alleviating poverty through fractional guarantee of minimum income (Milton Friedman and others) to those designed to provide full guarantee of the minimum amount of income below which a unit would otherwise be in poverty (Robert Theobald, Edward E. Schwartz, and others). The various proposals are based on differing assumptions and hence offer varying mechanisms for making available the guaranteed income.

Source references: Joseph M. Becker, *Guaranteed Income for the Unemployed, The Story of SUB* (Baltimore: Johns Hopkins Press, 1968); Sheldon Danziger, Robert Plotnick, and Robert Haveman, *Two Notes on Income Support Policy* (Madison: Univ. of Wisconsin, Institute for Research on Poverty, Reprint 421, 1981); Otto Eckstein (ed.), *Studies in Economics of Income Maintenance* (Washington: Brookings Institution, 1967); Milton Friedman, *Capitalism and Freedom* (Chicago: Univ. of Chicago Press, 1962); "The Gary Income Maintenance Experiment," *Journal of Human Resources*, Fall 1979; C. Russell Hill, "Two Income Maintenance Plans, Work Incentives and the Closure of the Poverty Gap," *ILRR*, July 1972; Robinson G. Hollister, "Welfare Reform and Labor Markets: What Have We Learned from the Experiments?" *Proceedings of the 31st A/M, IRRA*, ed. by Barbara Dennis (Madison: 1979); Merrill G. Murray, *The Role of Unemployment Insurance Under Guaranteed Minimum Income Plans* (Kalamazoo: Upjohn Institute for Employment Research, 1969); Larry L. Orr, Robinson G. Hollister, and Myron J. Lefcowitz (ed.), *Income Maintenance; Interdisciplinary Approaches to Research* (Chicago: Markham Pub., 1971); Edward E. Schwartz, "An End to the Means Test," *The Guaranteed Income*, ed. by Robert Theobald (Garden City, N.Y.: Doubleday, 1966); "The Seattle and Denver Income Maintenance Experiments," *Journal of Human Resources*, Fall 1980; Timothy M. Smeeding and Irwin Garfinkel, "New Directions in Income Transfer Programs," *MLR*, Feb. 1980; Robert Theobald (ed.), *The Guaranteed Income* (Garden City, N.Y.: Doubleday, 1966); U.S. Congress, Joint Committee on Economic Policies and Practices, *Guaranteed Minimum Income Programs Used by Governments of Selected Countries* (Washington: 1968); U.S. Congress, Joint Economic Committee, *Studies in Public Welfare. Paper no. 13—How Income Supplements Can Affect Work Behavior* (Washington: 1974); U.S. GAO, *Income Maintenance Experiments: Need to Summarize Results and Communicate the Lessons Learned*

(Washington: 1981); ———, *U.S. Income Security System Needs Leadership, Policy, and Effective Management* (Washington: 1980).

See also FREEDOM BUDGET, NEGATIVE INCOME TAX, NEW CAREERS.

guarantee on trial rate A minimum rate set while trial runs are made on new work in order to set piece rates. The guarantee is usually higher than the plant base rates and generally near the average of past earnings of the worker or the group within the immediate period prior to the new trial runs.

Guards and Watchmen; International Union of (Ind) *See* SECURITY OFFICERS; INTERNATIONAL UNION OF (IND).

Guards Union of America; International (Ind) Founded in 1947, it issues the *Guards Booklet* (semiannually).

Address: 1444 Gardiner Lane, Louisville, Ky. 40213. Tel. (502) 454–0278

guerrilla unionism A term used to describe the activities of a union whose prime concern is with violence and ruthlessness in its dealings with employers.

guestworker program A temporary work program for aliens, often in lower-level manual or agricultural occupations. Ideally, it is a short-term program and implies voluntary exit or enforced departure at the end of the program. As Bohning explains, the "guestworker policy controls the *inflow* of foreigners, not their stock or return flow." Guestworker programs were started during the post-World War II period in Switzerland, Germany, and France at the behest of large employers. Literally translated from the German *Gastarbeiter*, "guestworkers" refer to legal foreign workers who are not expected to take up permanent residence. In the absence of government action to ensure the workers' return to their countries of origin, a number of guestworkers have remained in the host countries.

The guestworker program has been advocated in the U.S. as a means for dealing with illegal immigration.

Source references: W. R. Bohning, "Estimating the Propensity of Guestworkers to Leave," *MLR*, May 1981; Ayse Kudat and Mine Sabuncuoglu, "The Changing Composition of Europe's Guestworker Population," *MLR*, Oct. 1980; Ray Marshall, "Guest Workers: No Need, No Justification," *American Federationist*, Aug. 1981; Philip L. Martin, *Guestworker Programs: Lessons from Europe* (Washington: U.S. Dept. of Labor, BILA, Monograph no. 5, 1980); Philip L. Martin and Mark J. Miller, "Guestworkers: Lessons from Western Europe," *ILRR*, April 1980; ———, "Regulating Alien Labor in Industrial Societies," *Proceedings of the 32d A/M, IRRA*, ed. by Barbara Dennis (Madison: 1980).

See also ALIEN LABOR.

Guffey Coal Act A law passed by Congress in 1937 for the purpose of stabilizing the coal industry through price regulation and promotion of fair competition. It also sought to regulate wages and hours in the soft coal industry. It was terminated by joint resolution of Congress in 1943. The predecessor Act, the Bituminous Coal Conservation Act of 1935, was declared unconstitutional in 1936.

Source reference: Carter v. Carter Coal Co., 298 US 238 (1936).

guideposts *See* WAGE-PRICE POLICY.

guilds Organizations of skilled craftsmen which acted as mutual benefit societies to take care of the needs of their members. In their early development they helped set standards of training for the trade and for the quality of the product.

Source references: John A. Fitch, "The Guild Reappears in Industry," *The Survey*, Nov. 16, 1918; Samuel G. Hobson, *Guild Principles in War and Peace* (London: Bell & Sons, 1918).

See also GILD (GUILD) SYSTEM.

guild shop *See* UNION SHOP.

Gunther case First case in which the Supreme Court ruled that women bringing claims of sex-based wage discrimination are not required under Title VII of the Civil Rights Act of 1964 to satisfy the "equal work" standards of the Equal Pay Act.

Female jail guards were held to have stated a Title VII claim even though the women did not perform work equal to that of male jail guards. The case was remanded to the district court for a determination on the merits of the Title VII claim, but the parties settled before the trial was held.

Source references: County of Washington v. Gunther, 452 US 161, 25 FEP Cases 1521 (1981); BNA, *The Comparable Worth Issue: A BNA Special Report* (Washington: 1981); John B. Golper, "The Current Legal Status of 'Comparable Worth' in the Federal Courts," *LLJ*, Sept. 1983; Raymond L. Hogler, "Equal Pay, Equal Work, and the United States Supreme Court," *LLJ*, Nov. 1981.

See also BENNETT AMENDMENT, COMPARABLE WORTH, PAY EQUITY.

H

HAU *See* HEBREW ACTORS UNION, INC.

HCMW *See* HATTERS, CAP AND MILLINERY WORKERS INTERNATIONAL UNION; UNITED (AFL-CIO).

HERE *See* HOTEL EMPLOYEES AND RESTAURANT EMPLOYEES INTERNATIONAL UNION (AFL-CIO).

HFIA *See* ASBESTOS WORKERS; INTERNATIONAL ASSOCIATION OF HEAT AND FROST INSULATORS AND (AFL-CIO).

HMO *See* HEALTH MAINTENANCE ORGANIZATION (HMO).

habeas corpus, writ of An order issued by a competent court ordering the person having custody of another person to produce him at a specific time and place and to show cause to the court why the person should not be set free.

Hague case Case in which former Mayor Frank Hague and other officials of Jersey City, N.J., were enjoined from enforcing a so-called street meeting ordinance that had been invoked by the officials to forbid union members to hold meetings in streets and parks. The Supreme Court affirmed a lower court holding that the ordinance was "void upon its face" by a 5–2 vote, with two justices not participating. There was no majority opinion, the seven justices writing five opinions.

Source reference: Hague et al. v. CIO, 307 US 496, 4 LRRM 501 (1939).

halo effect A term used to describe a noticeable error among those who rate employees because of the frequency with which a single or general impression tends to permeate the rating of all other factors. The rater's own bias toward some specific quality or factor may influence his rating of the employee in other areas. The "halo" created by a single factor or general impression prevents a careful and dependable evaluation of other traits important in the job qualification.

Source reference: Clarence Brown and Edwin Ghiselli, *Personnel and Industrial Psychology* (2d ed., New York: McGraw-Hill, 1955).

See also EMPLOYMENT INTERVIEW.

Halsey premium (gain-sharing) plan Considered the first incentive wage plan which offered a guaranteed wage in addition to an extra bonus for output in excess of the standard. In the early application the standard was based on past performance (not on time and motion studies), and workers who exceeded the number of units set for standard would receive a bonus of one-fourth to one-half of the time saved. The additional money saved frequently was allotted to nonproductive and supervisory personnel.

See also GAIN SHARING, INCENTIVE WAGE.

Hammer v. Dagenhart A decision of the Supreme Court that the Federal Child Labor Law (1916) was unconstitutional and not a proper exercise of the power to regulate commerce among the states. The law was designed to prohibit shipment in interstate commerce of goods on which child labor had been employed. By a vote of 5–4, the Court held that the federal statute was in conflict with state laws and the right of the states to exercise their police power over local trade and manufacture.

Source reference: Hammer v. Dagenhart, 247 US 251 (1918).

See also CHILD LABOR, CHILD LABOR LAWS.

Handbag, Luggage, Belt and Novelty Workers' Union; International (AFL) *See* LEATHER GOODS, PLASTIC AND NOVELTY WORKERS' UNION; INTERNATIONAL (AFL-CIO).

handicapped individual Defined by the Rehabilitation Act of 1973 as "any person who

(i) has a physical or mental impairment which substantially limits one or more of such person's major life activities, (ii) has a record of such impairment or (iii) is regarded as having such an impairment. For purposes of sections 503 and 504 [of this act] as such sections relate to employment, such term does not include any individual who is an alcoholic or drug abuser whose current use of alcohol or drugs prevents such individual from performing the duties of the job in question or whose employment, by reason of such current alcohol or drug abuse, would constitute a direct threat to property or the safety of others."

Affirmative action and fair employment safeguards for the handicapped are provided by the Rehabilitation Act, Executive Order 11758, and OFCCP regulations.

Source references: Rehabilitation Act of 1973, as amended, 29 U.S.C. 701 et seq. (1982); John Jay Dystel, "The Courts and the Disabled: Tenuous First Steps Toward Equality Under the Law," *Employee Relations LJ*, Winter 1979/80; Vigdor Grossman, *Employing Handicapped Persons: Meeting EEO Obligations* (Washington: BNA, 1980); Diane P. Jackson, "Affirmative Action for the Handicapped and Veterans: Interpretative and Operational Guidelines," *LLJ*, Feb. 1978; Steven S. Tokarski et al., "Not all Illnesses are Handicaps," *Employee Relations LJ*, Summer 1976.

See also ACCOMMODATION, EXECUTIVE ORDER 11758, REHABILITATION ACT OF 1973, VIETNAM ERA VETERANS READJUSTMENT ASSISTANCE ACT OF 1974.

handicapped worker A person who has mental or physical disabilities which limit his working potential. Extensive work in rehabilitation programs by the government and proper vocational guidance has permitted many of those previously considered handicapped to perform work in special fields with equal or greater skill than those not classed as "handicapped." The rules and regulations of the Fair Labor Standards Act define a handicapped worker as "an individual whose earning capacity is impaired by age or physical or mental deficiency or injury for the work he is to perform." Handicapped workers may be paid less than the prevailing rate with the approval of the Wage-Hour Administrator.

Source references: Charles A. Burden and Russell Faulk, "The Employment Process for Rehabilitants: Two Studies of the Hiring of Emotional Rehabilitants," *PJ*, Oct. 1975; James A. Craft, Thomas J. Benecki, and Yitzchak M. Shkop, "Who Hires the Seriously Handicapped?" *IR*, Winter 1980; Lawrence D. Haber, "Social Planning for Disability," *Journal of Human Resources*, Volume VIII, Supplement, 1973; "Job Opportunities for the Handicapped," *American Federationist*, April 1977; Terry L. Leap, "State Regulation and Fair Employment of the Handicapped," *Employee Relations LJ*, Winter 1979/80; Sar A. Levitan and Robert Taggart, *Jobs for the Disabled* (Baltimore: Johns Hopkins UP, 1977); Robert B. Nathanson and Jeffrey Lambert, "Integrating Disabled Employees into the Workplace," *PJ*, Feb. 1981; Gopal C. Pati and Glenn Morrison, "Enabling the Disabled," *Harvard BR*, July/Aug. 1982; "Rules and Regulations: Part 524—Regulations Applicable to Employment of Handicapped Persons Pursuant to Section 14 of the Fair Labor Standards Act of 1938," *WHM*, 92:65 et seq.; Howard A. Rusk, *New Hope for the Handicapped* (New York: Harper, 1949); U.S. Dept. of Labor, ETA, *Project Skill: Strategies and Techniques, Project on the Employment of Handicapped Persons in State Government Positions* (Washington: R & D Monograph 54, 1978); Anne Waltz, "Integrating Disabled Workers Into Your Workforce," *Public Personnel Management*, Winter 1981; Benjamin W. Wolkinson, "Arbitration and the Employment Rights of the Physically Disadvantaged," *AJ*, March 1981; Benjamin W. Wolkinson and David Barton, "Arbitration and the Rights of Mentally Handicapped Workers," *MLR*, April 1980.

See also ACCOMMODATION, EXECUTIVE ORDER 11758, FAIR LABOR STANDARDS ACT OF 1938, HANDICAPPED INDIVIDUAL, REHABILITATION ACT OF 1973, VIETNAM ERA VETERANS READJUSTMENT ASSISTANCE ACT OF 1974.

handicapped worker rate A special rate, below the legal minimum, permitted under the Fair Labor Standards Act for workers who are physically handicapped.

handicraft economy One of the stages of economic development in which specialized handwork was performed, either in the family unit or a small productive organization. It required relatively little capital outlay and only a small number of tools. It led to development of skilled artisans and formation of the guilds and crafts as the medieval towns and cities developed. It was the precursor of the factory system and the concentration of production in large units. Major inventions, specialization, and large aggregates of capital ushered in the factory system and its attendant problems, which gave reason and direction to the development of labor unions.

Source references: Norman S. B. Gras, *Industrial Evolution* (Cambridge: Harvard UP, 1930); Melvin M. Knight, "Handicraft," *Encyclopedia of the Social Sciences*, ed. by Edwin R. A. Seligman (Vol. 7, New York: Macmillan, 1932); George M. Modlin and Frank T. DeVyver, *Development of Economic Society* (Boston: Little, Brown, 1937).

hand labor Work which requires the actual manual manipulation of materials by physical handling. The work may involve unskilled labor, or highly skilled work that cannot easily be done by machines or is done more artistically by skilled hand operators.

harassment *See* SEXUAL HARASSMENT.

hard core of unemployment That group in the labor market which is able and willing to work but which, even in periods of short labor supply, still remains unemployed. Some hold this "hard core" unemployable because of the effect of long periods of unemployment, with consequent breakdown of morale. Others hold that the hard core will remain because of lack of mobility, lack of needed skills, lack of adequate labor market information, etc.

A National Alliance of Businessmen study outlined the following as characteristics of the hard-core unemployed: unemployed for 18 months, never received intensive skill training, parents were unskilled, lives in a unit with one and a half families, needs eyeglasses and dental work, has seen a physician only once in his life, married with three children, has no means of transportation to work, lacks education beyond the sixth grade, has proficiency levels of third-grade reading and fourth-grade math, has had some contact with law enforcement officials and has spent at least 30 days in jail, and is a member of a minority group.

Source references: Eugene S. Callender, "Business and the Hard-Core Unemployed: I. The Ghetto Subculture," *Personnel*, July/Aug. 1968; Louis A. Ferman, "The Hard-Core Unemployed: Myth and Reality," *Poverty and Human Resources Abstracts*, Vol. 4, No. 6, 1969; ———, *Job Development for the Hard-to-Employ* (Ann Arbor: Univ. of Michigan-Wayne State Univ., Institute of Labor and IR, Policy Papers in Human Resources and IR no. 11, 1969); Lawrence A. Johnson, *Employing the Hard-Core Unemployed* (New York: AMA, Research Study no. 98, 1969); Holly MacNamee, "Learning the Hard Facts of Hardcore Unemployment," *Conference Board Record*, Aug. 1968; Theodore V. Purcell and Rosalind Webster, "Window on the Hard-Core World," *Harvard BR*, July/Aug. 1969; Wil J. Smith (ed.), *The Poor and the Hard-Core Unemployed, Recommendations for New Approaches* (Ann Arbor: Univ. of Michigan-Wayne State Univ., Institute of Labor and IR, 1970); U.S. National Citizens' Committee for Community Relations, *Putting the Hard-Core Unemployed Into Jobs, Part I. Conference Summary, Part II. Case Studies* (Washington: 1968).

See also DISADVANTAGED WORKERS, UNEMPLOYABLE.

hard labor Labor requiring unusual physical exertion. Generally connected with work of convict labor.

harmony clause This is a provision in a collective bargaining contract setting the "tone" of employer-union-employee relationships as cooperation in the best interests of all. Such a clause might provide as follows:

> The general purpose of this agreement is, in the mutual interest of the corporation, the union, and the employees, to set forth terms and conditions of employment, to promote orderly and peaceful labor relations, and to provide for the operation of the plants and offices at the highest levels of efficiency and output.
>
> The parties recognize that the success of the corporation rests on its ability to produce and sell quality products, and that the job security and prosperity of employees rests on the corporation's success in maintaining and increasing its

competitive strength in its highly competitive field.

To these ends, the corporation and the union encourage to the fullest degree friendly and cooperative relations between their respective representatives at all levels and among all employees.

In some contracts antedating the Taft-Hartley Act, certain clauses of this general tenor almost required union membership as a condition of employment. This is an example of such a clause:

In the interest of promoting a more harmonious relationship, the company approves of its employees becoming members of the union; and, therefore, it is further desired by the company that those of its employees who are not members of the union shall become members.

Harvil Aircraft Die Casting Corp. case A decision of the National War Labor Board which granted a union shop provision (although maintenance of membership was its standard policy) where the union had enjoyed this form of union security before the war. The decision was dated February 12, 1943.

Source reference: Harvil Aircraft Die Casting Corp., 6 WLR 334.

Hatch Act The Federal Corrupt Practices Act, Section 313 of which was amended by Section 304 of the Labor Management Relations Act of 1947, makes it unlawful for (1) national banks and corporations authorized by Congress to make a contribution or expenditure in connection with election to any political office, primary election, political convention, or caucus; and (2) any corporation whatever or any labor organization to make a contribution or expenditure in connection with any election, primary, convention, or caucus for the purpose of selecting presidential or vice presidential electors, or a senator or representative, or a delegate or resident commissioner to Congress.

The most controversial aspect of this section has been the ban on union "expenditures." In a 1948 test case, the Supreme Court held that Section 304 did not prohibit the use of general union funds for the publishing and distribution expenses of an issue of a regularly published union newspaper containing the union's endorsement of the candidacy of a candidate for the U.S. House of Representatives. The Court, however, did not pass directly on the constitutionality of Section 304 (*U.S. v. C.I.O.*, 335 US 106, 22 LRRM 2194 (1948)).

In a later case, the Court held that the ban on union expenditures applies to the use of union dues to pay for a political broadcast in support of certain candidates for Congress. But the Court again decided to bypass the issue of the constitutionality of Section 304 (*U.S. v. United Auto Workers*, 352 US 567, 39 LRRM 2508 (1957)).

Source references: Labor Management Relations Act of 1947, Section 304 (currently, Section 316 of the Federal Election Campaign Act of 1972, 2 U.S.C. 441(b), corresponds to the former Section 304 of the Labor Management Relations Act); AEI, *Hatch Act Revision* (Washington: Legislative Analysis no. 20, 1978); John R. Bolton, *The Hatch Act, A Civil Libertarian Defense* (Washington: AEI, Domestic Affairs Study no. 43, 1976); Philip L. Martin, "The Hatch Act: The Current Movement for Reform," *Public Personnel Management*, May/June 1974; U.S. GAO, *Hatch Act Reform—Unresolved Questions* (Washington: 1979).

Hatters, Cap and Millinery Workers International Union; United (AFL-CIO) The United Hatters Union was an amalgamation of the United Hatters of North America, which was organized in 1896, and the Cloth Hat, Cap, and Millinery Workers' International Union, which was organized in 1901. The combination of the two organizations took place in New York on January 19, 1934. On December 2, 1982, the Hatters merged with the Amalgamated Clothing and Textile Workers Union.

Source references: Charles H. Green, *The Headwear Workers—A Century of Trade Unionism* (New York: United Hatters, Cap and Millinery Workers International Union, 1944); Donald B. Robinson, *Spotlight on a Union, the Story of the United Hatters, Cap and Millinery Workers International Union* (New York: Dial Press, 1948).

See also CLOTHING AND TEXTILE WORKERS UNION; AMALGAMATED (AFL-CIO).

hatters' shakes A form of industrial mercury poisoning. It is due to inhalation of mercury vapor or dust. It was prevalent among workers who made felt hats and used mercury salts in the process. Symptoms usually involved tremors of the limbs or head. It is sometimes referred to as "Danbury Shakes," since the felt hat industry was located around Danbury, Conn.

Source references: William M. Gafafer (ed.), *Manual of Industrial Hygiene* (Philadelphia: Saunders, 1944); Rutherford T. Johnstone and Seward E. Miller, *Occupational Diseases and Industrial Medicine* (Philadelphia: Saunders, 1960).

Hawaiian native Defined by the Job Training Partnership Act of 1982 as "any individual any of whose ancestors were natives, prior to 1778, of the area which now comprises the State of Hawaii." Hawaiian natives are eligible for training and employment programs under the law.

Source reference: Job Training Partnership Act, as amended, 29 U.S.C. § 1503(11) (1982).

Hawes-Cooper Act A statute enacted by Congress in 1929 which permitted any state after January 1934 to regulate or limit, within its jurisdiction, the sale of goods made by prison labor. This Act did not prohibit the shipment of prison-made goods in interstate commerce, but permitted the state to limit the sale of such goods within state borders.

See also ASHURST-SUMNERS ACT, PRISON LABOR.

Hawkins v. Bleakly A decision by the Supreme Court in 1917 holding constitutional a workers compensation law of the state of Iowa. The Supreme Court found no denial of due process of law or violation of the equal protection of the laws in the Iowa statute.

Source reference: Hawkins v. Bleakly, 243 US 210 (1917).

Haymarket riot A mass meeting in Haymarket Square in Chicago, held on May 4, 1886, to listen to speeches on labor unionism and the eight-hour day that turned into a riot when someone threw a bomb at the police. This led to the death of seven policemen and the injury of about a hundred other people, including workers in the crowd. (The Knights of Labor disclaimed any connection with the affair.) Eight radicals were tried. They were found guilty and condemned to death. Only four were executed. One committed suicide and three were pardoned by Governor John P. Altgeld.

Source references: Louis Adamic, *Dynamite: The Story of Class Violence in America* (New York: Viking, 1931); Henry David, *The History of the Haymarket Affair* (New York: Farrar, Rinehart, 1936); Robert Hunter, *Violence and the Labor Movement* (New York: Macmillan, 1914); Bernard R. Kogan (ed.), *The Chicago Haymarket Riot: Anarchy on Trial, Selected Source Materials for College Research Papers* (Boston: Heath, 1959); Dyer D. Lum, *The Great Trial of the Chicago Anarchists* (New York: Arno Press and the New York Times, 1969); Lucy Parsons, *Famous Speeches of the Eight Chicago Anarchists* (New York: Arno Press and the New York Times, 1969).

Haynes "manit" wage plan A method of incentive wage payments introduced in 1921 which attempts to reduce all work to a common denominator—"manit"—or work performed in a man-minute. Extra pay is for work in excess of 60 "manits" per hour.

hazardous occupations Work which has been held dangerous to the health of women and minors by state and federal laws. These occupations are carefully regulated as to safety conditions and hours of work. Employment of minors is prohibited in some of these occupations.

Source references: Alfred Blumrosen et al., "Injunctions Against Occupational Hazards: The Right to Work Under Safe Conditions," *Industrial Relations LJ*, Spring 1976; Frank D. Ferris, "Resolving Safety Disputes: Work or Walk," *LLJ*, Nov. 1975; Robert Hershey, "Who Has a Hazardous Job?" *Personnel*, July/Aug. 1971; Herbert M. Hohn, "The Federal Role in Job Safety and Health, Research to Determine What's Dangerous," *MLR*, Aug. 1973; J. Paul Leigh, "Are Unionized Blue Collar Jobs More Hazardous Than Nonunionized Blue Collar Jobs?" *Journal of Labor Research*, Summer 1982; Norman Root and Deborah Sebastian, "BLS Develops Measures of Job Risk by Occupation," *MLR*, Oct. 1981; John J. Stote, "Employee Protection Against Abnormally Dangerous Working Conditions," *Industrial and Labor Relations Forum*, March 1969.

See also CHILD LABOR, FAIR LABOR STANDARDS ACT OF 1938.

hazard pay A premium rate or compensation paid for work under uncomfortable or unpleasant conditions or for work which endangers the life or health of the worker.

headwork Work which requires the use of brain rather than brawn. The term has no technical usage, but merely refers to aspects of a job which require a little thought before actual performance.

health and decency standard of living A term used to describe the requirements of a family, which includes low rental housing in a nice heighborhood, with private toilet facilities and adequate light and heat. Provision is also made for adequate clothing; some recreation, including a magazine, movies, stationery; some insurance, medical and dental care; but little or no savings for emergency situations. The standard is above the subsistence level, but below that of comfort.

See also FAMILY BUDGET, STANDARD OF LIVING.

Health and Human Services, Department of Established in 1979 upon the separation of the education function from the Department of Health, Education and Welfare.

The major divisions of the department include the Office of Human Development Services, Public Health Service, Health Care Financing Administration, Social Security Administration, Office of Community Services, and Office of Child Support Enforcement.

Address: 200 Independence Ave., S.W., Washington, D.C. 20201. Tel. (202) 245–6296

health and welfare funds Employee and employer contributions held in trust for the benefit of the employee and his dependents as provided by Section 302(c) of the Taft-Hartley Act. Such health and welfare funds are to provide for, among other benefits, the cost of medical and hospital care, pensions, injury or illness compensation, unemployment benefits, educational scholarships, child care, and legal services.

Source references: Labor Management Relations Act of 1947, 29 U.S.C. § 186(c) (1982); BNA, *Negotiated Health and Welfare Plans* (Washington: 1950); Thomas J. Butters, "State Regulations of Noninsured Employee Welfare Benefit Plans," *IR Law Digest*, Spring 1974; Sylvia B. Gottlieb, "Negotiation and Administration of Health and Welfare Programs," *MLR*, May 1957; Adolph Held, "Health and Welfare Funds in the Needle Trades," *ILRR*, Jan. 1948; Leonard W. Krouner, "Employee Benefit Plans: Due Process for Beneficiaries," *LLJ*, July 1972; Nathaniel M. Minkoff, "Union Health and Welfare Plans," *MLR*, Feb. 1947; Gerard Morales, "Employee Benefit Plans; Discretion of Trustees to Grant or Deny Applications for Benefits," *LLJ*, Nov. 1978; NICB, *Union Health and Welfare Funds* (New York: Studies in Business Economics no. 8, 1947); I. Philip Sipser, "Failure to Make Benefit Fund Payments: Problems and Issues," *NYU 33d Annual Conference on Labor*, ed. by Richard Adelman (New York: Bender, 1981); Robert Tilove, "Recent Trends in Health and Welfare Plans," *NYU 3d Annual Conference on Labor*, ed. by Emanuel Stein (Albany: Bender, 1950); U.S. Dept. of Labor, BLS, *Health and Insurance Benefits and Pension Plans for Salaried Employees, Early 1969* (Washington: Bull. no. 1629, 1969); John S. Welch and Hugh S. Wilson, "Applicability of Traditional Principles of Trust Law to Union and Management Representatives Administering Taft-Hartley Trusts," *LLJ*, Nov. 1972.

See also DENTAL CARE, PREPAID; DISABILITY INSURANCE; HEALTH BENEFIT PROGRAMS; HEALTH INSURANCE; HOSPITALIZATION BENEFITS; MAJOR MEDICAL EXPENSE BENEFIT; MATERNITY BENEFITS; OLD AGE, SURVIVORS, AND DISABILITY INSURANCE; SURGICAL BENEFITS.

health benefit programs Plans, generally worked out through collective bargaining, which provide for sick benefit payments and other programs conducive to maintaining a healthy workforce. Many plans include the worker's family in their coverage.

Source references: AFL, *Health Benefit Plans by Collective Bargaining* (Washington: 1946); Donald R. Bell, "Dental and Vision Care Benefits in Health Insurance Programs," *MLR*, June 1980; John M. Brumm, *Health Programs in Collective Bargaining* (Urbana: Univ. of Illinois, Institute of Labor and IR, 1949); BNA, *Employee Health & Welfare Benefits* (Washington: PPF Survey no. 122, 1978); "Health Benefit Programs Established Through Collective Bargaining," *MLR*, Aug. 1945; Dorothy R. Kittner, "Changes in Health and Insurance Plans for Salaried Employees," *MLR*, Feb. 1970; ———, "Changes in Health Plans Reflect Broader Benefit Coverage," *MLR*, Sept. 1978; Betty G. Lall, "Collective Bargaining and Health Legislation," *Proceedings of the 27th A/M, IRRA*, ed. by James Stern and Barbara Dennis (Madison: 1975); U.S. Dept. of Labor, BLS, *Digest of Selected Health and Insurance Plans, 1977–79 Edition; Vol. I: Health Benefits, Vol. II: Insurance Benefits* (Washington: 1978).

See also HEALTH INSURANCE, SURGICAL BENEFITS, SURVIVORS' BENEFITS.

health care cost containment Efforts to control the cost of health care as an employee benefit. Programs include, among others, auditing medical claims for billing errors, requiring second opinions prior to surgery, promoting health awareness and disease prevention training, and establishing health maintenance organizations.

Source references: BNA, *Controlling Health Care Costs: Crisis in Employee Benefits* (Washington: 1983); K. Per Larson, "Taking Action to Contain Health Care Costs," *PJ*, Aug. 1980 and Sept. 1980; W. Bryan Latham, *Health Care Costs; There Are Solutions*, An AMA Management Briefing (New York: AMA, 1983); C. Carl Pegels, "Health Care Cost Containment Potential for Employers," *Public Personnel Management*, Vol. 9, no. 3, 1980; Sherman G. Sass, "New Frontiers of Health Care Cost Containment," *PJ*, Feb. 1982; Kenneth L. Shellhammer and Douglas L. Nottingham, *Containing the Rising Cost of Health Services: An Examination of the Problem with Expanding Government Controls* (Morgantown: West Virginia Univ., Office of Health Services Research, Pub. no. 1, 1976); Gerard Tavernier, "An Aggressive Approach to Healthcare Cost Containment," *Management Review*, Nov. 1983.

See also HEALTH MAINTENANCE ORGANIZATION ACT OF 1973.

health center A union-sponsored or union-influenced health service enterprise providing a combination of protective, diagnostic, and treatment services, integrating professional services and hospital care, including dental care, visiting nurses, drugs, and eye glasses. The idea of the union health center emphasizes health maintenance rather than sickness care, reflecting the union's desire to influence the organization of professional services and the quality of health care.

Source reference: Jack Barbash, "The Unions and Negotiated Health and Welfare Plans," *New Dimensions in Collective Bargaining*, ed. by Harold W. Davey, Howard S. Kaltenborn, and Stanley H. Ruttenberg (New York: Harper, IRRA Pub. no. 21, 1959).

Health, Education and Welfare; Department of An executive department of government established in 1953 which took over the functions of the Federal Security Agency created in 1939. Programs, including the old-age and survivors' insurance, the public assistance program, the maternal and child health services, the services for crippled children, and the child welfare services, were administered through the Social Security Administration within the Department of Health, Education and Welfare. The other major section of the Social Security Act, the unemployment insurance program, was administered by the Bureau of Employment Security within the Department of Labor.

Among the agencies in the department were the Social Security Administration, Rehabilitation Services Administration, Office of Education, Food and Drug Administration, Environmental Control Administration, and Howard University.

The Department was reorganized in 1979 and its functions delegated to the Department of Health and Human Services and the Department of Education.

Source reference: U.S. Dept. of HEW, Office of Program Analysis, *Handbook of Programs of the U.S. Department of Health, Education and Welfare, 1961* (Washington: 1961).

See also EDUCATION, DEPARTMENT OF; HEALTH AND HUMAN SERVICES, DEPARTMENT OF.

health insurance Originally applied to employee health care services provided under prepayment plans jointly financed by employer and employees. Current programs include basic medical payments for hospitalization, surgical, and physicians' care; accidental death and dismemberment; catastrophic illness through major medical insurance; protection against temporary and long-term loss of income due to disability; and death through the provision of life insurance. Plans are usually negotiated and insured through Blue Cross, Blue Shield, or commercial insurance companies; sometimes self-insured in whole or in part. Health centers or clinics may also be provided under some plans.

Efforts to enact federal national health legislation began in the late 1960s. During the 93rd Congress it was reported that, as of July 1974, 22 national health insurance (NHI) bills had been introduced. Pauly notes that despite "repeated predictions that passage of NHI legislation was 'imminent' and 'inevitable,' Congress has still not passed an NHI bill. . . . As a result of a decade of policy-related research, there now appears to be greater willingness to question the basic concept of NHI as a grand solution to all the perceived problems in health." According to Davis, the objectives of national health care insurance consists of "ensuring access to medical care for all Americans, reducing the financial hardship of medical care bills, and improving efficiency in the provision of health care services."

Source references: AEI, *National Health Insurance Proposals* (Washington: Legislative Analysis no. 19, 1974); Odin W. Anderson, *Health Insurance* (Cambridge: Harvard UP, 1957); UC, Institute of IR, *National Health Insurance Schemes, Proceedings of a Conference on Proposed Legislation in the United States and on the British National Health Care Experience, October 7, 1971* (Los Angeles: 1972); Karen Davis, *National Health Insurance: Benefits, Costs, and Consequences* (Washington: Brookings Institution, 1975); I. S. Falk, "Health Security's Roots in the U.S. History," *American Federationist*, Nov. 1977; Judith Feder, John Holahan, and Theodore Marmor, *National Health Insurance; Conflicting Goals and Policy Choices* (Washington: Urban Institute, 1980); Herbert E. Klarman, "Major Public Initiatives in Health Care," *The Public Interest*, Winter 1974; Theodore R. Marmor, "Rethinking National Health Insurance," *The Public Interest*, Winter 1977; George Meany, "The Case for National Health Insurance," *American Federationist*, Jan. 1970; Wesley S. Mellow, "Determinants of Health Insurance and Pension Coverage," *MLR*, May 1982; Joseph P. Newhouse and Vincent Taylor, "How Shall We Pay for Hospital Care?" *The Public Interest*, Spring 1971; Mark V. Pauly (ed.), *National Health Insurance; What Now, What Later, What Never?* (Washington: AEI, 1980); Louis F. Rossiter and Amy K. Taylor, "Union Effects on the Provision of Health Insurance," *IR*, Spring 1982; Bert Seidman, "Health Security: The Complete Rx," *American Federationist*, Oct. 1975: Paul Starr, "The Undelivered Health System," *The Public Interest*, Winter 1976; U.S. Congress, House, Committee on Ways and Means, *Analysis of Health Insurance Proposals Introduced in the 92d Congress* (Washington: 1971); ———, *Comparisons and Descriptions of Selected National Health Insurance Proposals Introduced in the 93d Congress as of April 12, 1974* (Washington: 1974); ———, *National Health Insurance Resource Book* (rev. ed., Washington: 1976); U.S. Congress, House, *Resolved: That the Federal Government Should Enact a Program of Comprehensive Medical Care for all United States Citizens* (Washington: 1972); Nathan Weber (ed.), *Insurance Deregulation: Issues and Perspectives* (New York: The Conference Board, Report no. 824, 1982); David A. Weeks, *An Interim Report: National Health Insurance and Corporate Benefit Plans* (New York: The Conference Board, Report no. 633, 1974); Ronald W. Wilson, Jacob J. Feldman, and Mary Grace Kovar, "Continuing Trends in Health and Health Care," *Annals*, Jan. 1978; Robert A. Zelton, "Consequences of the Increased Third-Party Payments for Health Care Services," *Annals*, May 1979; Christopher J. Zook, Francis D. Moore, and Richard J. Zeckhauser, "'Catastrophic' Health Insurance—A Misguided Prescription?" *The Public Interest*, Winter 1981.

See also MEDICAL CARE, MEDICARE.

health maintenance organization (HMO) HMOs provide health care to members under a prepaid, fixed fee plan instead of the traditional health care delivery system which provides care on a fee-for-service basis. Supporters believe such plans will curb spiraling health care costs by (1) changing the financial incentives for health care providers, (2) curbing utilization, and (3) emphasizing cost-effective preventive care. The Kaiser Permanente Health Plan is an example of an HMO.

There are three health maintenance organizational forms: (1) group practice, in which physicians are paid on a salary or per member basis and share centrally located medical facilities and ancillary personnel; (2) staff model, in which physicians are salaried employees of the HMO; and (3) individual practice association, in which participating physicians maintain separate medical facilities and are paid on fee-for-service basis.

Source references: James F. Doherty, "HMOs: The Road to Good Health Care," *American Federationist*, June 1979; Deborah H. Harrison and John R. Kimberly, "HMOs Don't Have to Fail," *Harvard BR*, July/Aug. 1982; Gordon K. MacLeod, "Health Maintenance Organizations in the United States," *ILR*, Oct. 1974; Thomas E. Snedeker and Michael L. Kuhns, "HMOs: Regulations, Problems and Outlook," *PJ*, Aug. 1981; Ruth H. Stack, *HMOs from the Management Perspective*, An AMA Management Briefing (New York: AMA, 1979); Paul Starr, "The Undelivered Health System," *The Public Interest*, Winter 1976; Harry L. Sutton, Jr., "The HMO—Can It Help Employers Control Exploding Health Care Benefits Costs?" *Employee Relations LJ*, Spring 1977; U.S. GAO, *Health Maintenance Organizations Can Help Control Health Care Costs* (Washington: 1980).

Health Maintenance Organization Act of 1973 Legislation which mandates that employers provide their employees with the option of membership in a qualified health maintenance organization (HMO) and authorizes funds for grant and loan programs to assist in the development of HMOs. It was amended in 1976 and 1978. The 1978 amendments increased funds for HMOs to cover their initial operating losses, authorized a special construction loan fund, and established the National Health Maintenance Organization Intern Program to train HMO managers.

Source reference: Health Maintenance Organization Act of 1973, as amended, Pub. L. 93–222, 87 Stat. 914 (codified as amended in scattered sections of 5, 12, 21, and 42 U.S.C.).

hearing The proceeding in which a court or an administrative body receives evidence for the purpose of performing an adjudicatory function or, in the case of an administrative body, a factfinding or rule-making function. It also refers to the proceeding used by a congressional or legislative committee to obtain information needed in legislating. The provision in the Fifth Amendment to the U.S. Constitution specifying that no person shall be "deprived of life, liberty, or property, without due process of law" guarantees persons a "fair hearing" before courts and administrative bodies. This requires both due notice and an opportunity to present evidence, to know the claims of the opposing party, and to meet them. The Administrative Procedure Act also establishes certain standards that administrative bodies must meet in both adjudicative and rule-making proceedings. Among other things, it requires that timely notice be given of the time, place, and subject of the hearing and that persons affected be given the opportunity to appear at the hearing in person or by or with counsel. Each administrative body also has its own rules and procedures for the conduct of hearings. Hearings at the NLRB under the Taft-Hartley Act and at the Labor Department under the Fair Labor Standards and Walsh-Healey Acts are conducted by administrative law judges. Arbitrators also conduct hearings before making awards, but these are not subject to all the formalities of judicial or administrative hearings.

Source references: Administrative Procedure Act, as amended, 5 U.S.C. 551–559 (1982); U.S. Congress, Senate, *The Constitution of the United States of America—Analysis and Interpretation* (Washington: 1952).

See also ARBITRATION, FACTFINDING, NATIONAL LABOR RELATIONS BOARD.

Heat and Frost Insulators and Asbestos Workers; International Association of (AFL-CIO) *See* ASBESTOS WORKERS; INTERNATIONAL ASSOCIATION OF HEAT AND FROST INSULATORS AND (AFL-CIO).

Hebrew Actors Union, Inc. Founded in 1900, it is a branch of the Associated Actors and Artistes of America (AFL-CIO).

Address: 31 East 7th St., New York, N.Y. 10003. Tel. (212) 674–1923

Heinz case A landmark decision of the Supreme Court upholding an order of the NLRB requiring the Heinz Company to sign a collective bargaining agreement with a union, where the wages, hours, and other terms and conditions were not in dispute.

Source references: H. J. Heinz Co. v. NLRB, 311 US 514, 7 LRRM 291 (1941); U.S. NLRB, *The Written Trade Agreement in Collective Bargaining* (Washington: Bull. no. 4, 1940).

Heller Committee for Research in Social Economics A committee which did primary research in establishing standard budgets for family groups in California. Its studies were based on actual expenditures by middle class families and were sometimes referred to as the Heller budgets.

Helvering v. Davis Decision of the Supreme Court upholding the constitutionality of various provisions of the Social Security Act (old age benefit tax) and the authority of Congress to levy taxes (under Title VIII of the Act) in aid of the general welfare.

Source reference: Helvering v. Davis, 301 US 619 (1937).

Henderson v. Mayor of New York A decision of the Supreme Court holding that immigration is an area exclusively within the jurisdiction of the federal government under the clause of the Constitution which gives Congress the "right to regulate commerce with foreign nations."

Source reference: Henderson v. Mayor of New York, 92 US 259 (1875).

Herndon case Decision of the Supreme Court in 1937 involving an organizer in Atlanta who was convicted under an 1861 statute for "inciting to insurrection." The Court set aside the 18- to 20-year sentence on the chain gang given to Angelo Herndon for exercising his constitutional right of free speech and peaceable assembly.

See also DEJONGE CASE, FREEDOM OF SPEECH.

Herrin massacre Outbreak of violence during a coal strike at Herrin, Illinois. The battle, which took place in June 1922 when the company sought to operate with strikebreakers, led to the loss of 19 lives.

hidden unemployment *See* DISCOURAGED WORKER.

higgling of the market A phrase used to describe the interaction in the market between buyers and sellers. It has been contended that the individual laborer in a free and competitive market is caught in a "bind" because he cannot store his labor until he gets the price he wants. With the development of collective bargaining and the organization of workers into more effective "bargaining" units, the higgling in the market place does not force the worker to come to terms on pain of starvation.

Highlander Folk School Resident labor school located at Monteagle, Tennessee. The program was directed to the needs of trade unionists. The subject matter included: Trade Union Problems and Policies (organization, strike tactics, public relations); Personnel and Human Problems; Trade Union History; Wage and Hour Problems; Parliamentary Procedure, etc. In addition to the resident program, courses were offered during the summer to meet the needs of unions in the area. These courses were usually for two or more weeks and were designed to meet the needs of the union men and women.

Hines v. Anchor Motor Freight A 1976 case involving a claim under Section 301 of the Labor Management Relations Act for wrongful discharge in which the Supreme Court ruled that an employer is not protected from relitigation by express contractual provision declaring an arbitration committee's decision to be final and binding. The Court reasoned that the union's breach of the duty of fair representation permits the employees to pursue other forums for relief outside the contractual grievance procedure, and the breach "if it seriously undermines the integrity of the arbitral process . . . also removes the bar of the finality provisions of the contract." The

Court held that employees are entitled to appropriate remedy against the employer as well as the union if they could prove (1) an erroneous discharge and (2) the union breach of the duty of fair representation tainted the arbitration decision.

The case involved the dismissal of drivers charged with falsifying the cost of lodging which was to be reimbursed to them. An arbitration committee denied the grievance. It was later discovered that the motel clerk had inflated the lodging cost and pocketed the excess charges.

Source reference: Hines v. Anchor Motor Freight, 424 US 554, 91 LRRM 2481 (1976).

hiring The act of taking on an employee for a designated or stated period of time.

Source references: The Conference Board, *Personnel Practices I: Recruitment, Placement, Training, Communication* (New York: Information Bull. 89, 1981); "Sixty Years of Hiring Practices," *PJ*, June 1980; Harrison M. Trice and William T. Wasmuth, *Effective Hiring in Small Business Organizations* (Ithaca: Cornell Univ., NYSSILR, Bull. no. 46, 1962).

See also ABILITY, DISCRIMINATION.

hiring hall Sometimes known as the central hiring hall, or union hiring hall. It is an office, usually run by the union, which coordinates the referrals of workers to jobs. Its use was widespread when the closed shop existed, particularly in the maritime, building trades, needle trades, and other seasonal and casual industries.

Since the closed shop is illegal under the Taft-Hartley Act in industries affecting commerce, the hiring halls, where they exist, are not confined to union members only. Nonunion members must also be given the chance to register and be referred to employment opportunities.

Under Title VII of the Civil Rights Act of 1964, it is an unfair employment practice for a labor organization to deny employment opportunities to any individual on the basis of race, color, religion, sex, or national origin.

Source references: Harry H. Craig, "Hiring Hall Arrangements and Practices," *LLJ*, Dec. 1958; Jerome D. Fenton, "Union Hiring Halls Under the Taft-Hartley Act," *LLJ*, July 1958; Herbert Hammerman, "Minorities in Construction Referral Unions—Revisited," *MLR*, May 1973; Elmo P. Hohman, "Merchant Seamen in the United States, 1937–1952," *ILR*, Jan. 1953; Clark Kerr, "Collective Bargaining on the Pacific Coast," *MLR*, April 1947; Charles P. Larrowe, *Shape-Up and Hiring Hall* (Berkeley: UC Press, 1955); Malcolm H. Liggett, "Unions and Title VII: Remedies for Insiders and Outsiders," *Proceedings of the 24th A/M, IRRA*, ed. by Gerald Somers (Madison: 1972); Harry H. Rains, "Construction Trades Hiring Halls," *LLJ*, June 1959; Philip Ross, "Origin of the Hiring Hall in Construction," *IR*, Oct. 1972; U.S. Commission on Civil Rights, *The Challenge Ahead: Equal Opportunity in Referral Unions* (Washington: 1976); U.S. Dept. of Labor, LMSA, *Exclusive Union Work Referral Systems in the Building Trades* (Washington: 1970); Stanley L. Weir, *Informal Workers' Control: The West Coast Longshoremen* (Urbana: Univ. of Illinois, Institute of Labor and IR, Reprint series no. 247, 1975); James N. Wilhoit, III and Jonathan C. Gibson, "Can a State Right-to-Work Law Prohibit the Union-Operated Hiring Hall?" *LLJ*, May 1975.

See also DISPATCHERS, JOINT HIRING HALL, PREFERENTIAL HIRING, PREFERENTIAL SHOP, SHAPE-UP.

hiring policies The guides established, usually by the employer, for the personnel office to follow in taking on new employees. These policies are primarily designed to get the most capable employees, at reasonable wages, who are able to perform the work and have potential for growth and advancement in the company. The policies may involve such items as skills, attitudes, etc. Hiring practices are subject to, among others, the provisions of Title VII of the Civil Rights Act of 1964 and the Age Discrimination in Employment Act of 1967.

Source references: Robert J. Gaston, "Labor Market Conditions and Employer Hiring Standards," *IR*, May 1972; Mervin Kohn, "Hiring College Graduates Through Off-Campus Selection Interviewing," *Public Personnel Management*, Jan./Feb. 1975; E. William Noland and E. Wight Bakke, *Workers Wanted: A Study of Employers' Hiring Policies, Preferences and Practices in New Haven and Charlotte* (New York: Harper, 1949); Henry F. O'Neill, "Isn't it Time to Change Our Hiring Policies?" *PJ*, Aug. 1973;

Vernon R. Taylor, *Essentials of Effective Personnel Selection, A Guide for Appraising and Upgrading Practices* (Chicago: PPA, Personnel Report no. 721, 1972); M. Anders Tronsen, "Protecting Personnel Policy from Further Government Regulation," *PJ*, Aug. 1976; U.S. Dept. of Labor, Manpower Administration, *Hiring Standards and Job Performance* (Washington: Research Monograph no. 18, 1970).

hiring rate *See* ENTRANCE RATE.

Hispanic According to OFCCP, "A person of Mexican, Puerto Rican, Cuban, Central or South American, or other Spanish culture or origin, regardless of sex." Persons who may have adopted the Spanish culture but are not otherwise of Spanish culture are to be treated according to their racial identity. Thus, persons of Portugese ancestry would not fall into the Hispanic category, but rather would be associated with white Caucasians. Under Title VII, Hispanic is a protected class and one of the racial/ethnic categories for which data is reported to the federal government.

Source references: Alfredo F. Montoya, "Hispanic Workforce: Growth and Inequality," *American Federationist*, April 1979; Morris J. Newman, "A Profile of Hispanics in the U.S. Work Force," *MLR*, Dec. 1978; U.S. National Commission for Employment Policy, *Hispanics and Jobs: Barriers to Progress* (Washington: Report no. 14, 1982); U.S. OFCCP, *Federal Contract Compliance Manual* (Washington: 1979).

See also AFFECTED CLASS, PROTECTED CLASS.

historical wage differentials Those wage relationships in a particular industry between plants, occupations, or areas, which have continued over a long period of time. In collective bargaining or in wage disputes before the National War Labor Board during World War II, unions demanded that these differentials be given consideration in applying the wage stabilization policy.

Hitchman Coal and Coke Co. v. Mitchell A decision of the Supreme Court limiting the right of a union to induce workers under a "yellow dog contract" to join the union while still in the employ of the company. The Court held to be erroneous the union's assumption that all "peaceable" measures in which it engaged were lawful if they stopped short of physical violence or coercion. "In our opinion," said the Court, "any violation of plaintiff's legal rights contrived by defendants for the purpose of inflicting damage, or having that as its necessary effect, is as plainly inhibited by the law as if it involved a breach of the peace. A combination to procure concerted breaches of contract by plaintiff's employees constitutes such a violation."

In the *American Steel Foundries* case (257 US 184 (1921)), the Court summed up its decision in the *Hitchman* case as follows:

> There the action was by a coal mining company of West Virginia against the officers of an International Labor Union and others to enjoin them from carrying out a plan to bring the employees of the complainant company and all the West Virginia mining companies into the International Union, so that the union could control, through the union employees, the production and sale of coal in West Virginia, in competition with the mines of Ohio and other States. . . . This Court held that the purpose was not lawful and that the means were not lawful and that the defendants were thus engaged in an unlawful conspiracy which should be enjoined.

Source reference: Hitchman Coal and Coke Co. v. Mitchell 245 US 229 (1917).

See also AMERICAN STEEL FOUNDRIES V. TRI-CITY CENTRAL TRADES COUNCIL, DAMAGE SUITS.

hitting the bricks Workers who go on strike are said to "hit the bricks." The phrase has also been used to describe men who have been released from prison.

Hobbs Act *See* ANTI-RACKETEERING ACT (HOBBS ACT).

Hockey League Players' Association; National (Ind) Founded in 1967 as the National Hockey Players League (Ind), the union adopted the present name in the early 1970s.

Address: 65 Queen St., West, Toronto, Ont., Canada M5H 2M5. Tel. (416) 868–6574

Hod Carriers', Building and Common Laborers' Union of America; International (AFL-CIO) *See* LABORERS' INTERNATIONAL UNION OF NORTH AMERICA (AFL-CIO).

hold-back pay All moneys due an employee for services already performed but which have not yet been paid to him. This does not include money withheld because of legal requirements and which is not to be received by the employee.

Source references: M. Joseph Dooher and Vivienne Marquis, *The AMA Handbook of Wage and Salary Administration* (New York: AMA, 1950); Lionel B. Michael, *Wage and Salary Fundamentals and Procedures* (New York: McGraw-Hill, 1950).

Holden v. Hardy A decision of the Supreme Court which held that the state of Utah had the right to legislate on hours of work in the mining and smelting industry. The state could exercise its police power to protect the public health, the Court ruled.

Source reference: Holden v. Hardy, 169 US 336 (1898).

hold-the-line order Executive Order 9328, issued by President Roosevelt in April 1943, designed to stabilize prices and wages. The economic stabilization director was directed to place price controls on all items that entered into the cost of living index. The War Labor Board was to limit wage adjustments except those based on the Little Steel Formula. On May 12th a clarification was issued by Economic Stabilization Director Byrnes which set up a new yardstick for measuring inequities, based on "sound and tested wage brackets" for job classifications in specific labor market areas.

Source references: E.O. 9328, April 8, 1943; George Taylor, *Government Regulation of Industrial Relations* (New York: PH, 1948); U.S. National War Labor Board, *The Termination Report of the National War Labor Board* (3 vols., Washington: 1947); Fred Witney and Joseph Shister, *Government in Collective Bargaining* (Philadelphia: Lippincott, 1951).

See also SOUND AND TESTED RATES.

hold-up unionism Generally refers to corrupt unionism where employers pay tribute to the union in order to avoid violence. The general purpose seems to be to exploit the consumer by collusive practices which eliminate competition among employers. It is sometimes referred to as predatory unionism.

Source reference: Louis Adamic, "Racketeering and Organized Labor," *Harper's*, Sept. 1930.

See also MCCLELLAN COMMITTEE, RACKETEERING.

holiday pay Provisions in collective bargaining agreements which require the employer to pay workers for time not worked on a holiday. Where work is required a premium rate is set, including doubletime and a half or triple time. Holidays are usually those designated as legal through state or federal law. Contract provisions may read as follows:

> For purposes of this Agreement, the following shall be considered as holidays: New Year's Day, Memorial Day, Independence Day, Labor Day, Thanksgiving Day, Christmas Day, and two (2) year-end holidays to be designated by the Company between December 22 and January 5. In addition to the above specific holidays, an additional holiday, the day after Thanksgiving, will be observed during the first four (4) years of this Agreement. During the fifth (5th) year of this Agreement, the Company will designate the second (2nd) holiday, with the option to move the day after Thanksgiving to another date during the contract year. The Company will not designate Saturday as a holiday.
>
> For purposes of this Agreement, any of the above designated holidays which fall on Sunday shall be observed on the following Monday, and any falling on Saturday shall be observed the preceding Friday.
>
> Hourly factory workers on the active payroll on the day set aside for the celebration of New Year's Day, Good Friday, Memorial Day, Fourth of July, Labor Day, Thanksgiving Day, and Christmas Day will each receive an amount for that holiday equal to their individual hourly base rate times eight (8). . . . No payment will be made for any such holiday when the day celebrated falls on Sunday, or in a week when an entire Company plant is shut down due to the lack of work, or in a week when any strike or work stoppage occurs.

Half-holidays may also be designated such as the day before New Year's or Christmas. Holiday pay may also be granted on a worker's birthday.

Source references: BNA, *Paid Holiday and Vacation Policies* (Washington: PPF Survey no. 130, 1980); Rick Galleher, "Time Off: More Vacations and Holidays," *American Federationist*, Jan. 1974; Lester L. Peterman, "Fringe Benefits of Urban Workers," *MLR*,

Nov. 1971; James A. Socknat, "Prevalence of Holiday Provisions in Major Union Contracts, 1961," *MLR*, May 1962; U.S. Dept. of Labor, BLS, *Major Collective Bargaining Agreements: Paid Vacation and Holiday Provisions* (Washington: Bull. 1425–9, 1969); John Zalusky, "Vacations-Holidays: Tools in Cutting Work Time," *American Federationist*, Feb. 1977.

Homestead Act An Act of Congress (1861–62) which sought to provide for agrarian land reform by permitting citizens to obtain federal lands for the sum of $10 for registration, on condition that the land would be cultivated for five years. A citizen could obtain 160 acres of land for the asking.

Homestead strike A bitter strike in 1892 by workers at the Carnegie Steel Company. The strike was organized by the Amalgamated Iron and Steel Workers in dispute with the company over the wage scale and termination date of the agreement. The issue went much deeper and involved the ability of the union to survive under the pressure exerted by the company. When the company brought in strikebreakers through the Pinkerton Agency, a pitched battle resulted and a number of men were killed. The workers returned to work without gaining their objectives and unionism in the steel industry received a serious setback.

Source reference: Margaret F. Byington, *Homestead: The Households of a Mill Town* (New York: Charities Publication Committee, 1910).

homework, industrial An arrangement whereby partly processed goods are finished or made ready for further processing by persons, frequently women and children, working at home. The arrangements are generally handled by an agent who pays on a piecework basis and then resells or returns the finished goods to the manufacturer. Industrial homework is common in those industries which require handwork and where the nature of the process permits the handling of the materials away from the plant. Sewing, embroidery, the making of artificial flowers, toys, paper and leather products lend themselves to this type of operation. Many states regulate industrial homework since it tends toward "sweat shop" or bad tenant conditions and is at least potentially harmful to young children who may be working at this type of operation. The Fair Labor Standards Act of 1938 also deals with industrial homework.

Source references: Fair Labor Standards Act of 1938, Section 11(d), as amended, 29 U.S.C. § 211(d) (1982); Emily C. Brown, *Industrial Home Work* (Washington: U.S. Dept. of Labor, Women's Bureau, Bull. no. 79, 1930); Ruth Crawford, "Development and Control of Industrial Homework," *MLR*, June 1944; "Meeting of State Labor Officials, 1941; Resolution on Industrial Homework," *MLR*, Dec. 1941; Ruth E. Shallcross, *Industrial Homework* (New York: Industrial Affairs Publishing Co., 1939).

honeymoon period A phrase used rather loosely to describe the period immediately after major agreement between a union and company when both sides are anxious to please one another and try to overlook the small difficulties involved in the labor-management relationship. In many cases the honeymoon period provides the basis for setting up a mature relationship in the years that follow.

It sometimes has reference to the growth of the AFL from the late 1890s to 1902.

hooked man A worker who is engaged in espionage and surveillance, frequently without knowing that he is reporting to a detective agency or that the information he is passing along or the reports that he is writing go to the employer. Workers who know the implications of their acts may be forced to continue providing information because they are under obligation or fearful of reprisal if they should refuse to cooperate. Since the passage of the National Labor Relations Act in 1935, surveillance of this type has come under the prohibition of Section 8(1) as an unfair labor practice.

hooking The process of trapping a worker in order to have him spy on the union activities of his fellow workers. Hooking is sometimes accomplished through the pretext of hiring the worker to prepare reports (of a general nature) for an agency for a purpose which sounds legitimate, and over a period of time shifting the emphasis of the reports so that the prime purpose is to keep the agency or the employer informed about the plans and operation of the union.

See also ESPIONAGE.

horizontal movement of labor A term used to describe the shift or movement of individuals from one company or from one employer or firm to another, but continuing to perform the same type or class of work.

The term "horizontal movement of labor" has been used on occasion to describe the craft unions which bring together all workers in a particular occupation. This might apply, for example, to carpenters or electricians organized in one union regardless of the industry in which the work actually takes place.

horizontal unions Generally refers to craft unions whose organization includes all workers in a particular craft or skill across the industry, region, or country. It is distinguished from industrial unions whose organization is based on the structure of the operation and includes all workers engaged in the production of a product, including the skilled crafts. The Carpenters, Electricians, and Pattern Makers are illustrations of horizontal craft unions, while the Steelworkers, Mine Workers, and Rubber Workers are examples of industrial unions.

Organizational activity among unions during the last three decades has resulted in many craft unions organizing along industrial lines or going into industries where the industrial form of organization was the only realistic way to handle the problems of collective bargaining. "Pure" craft or horizontal unions are few in number.

See also CRAFT UNION, INDUSTRIAL UNION.

Horseshoers; International Union of Journeymen (AFL-CIO) Organized as the Journeymen Horseshoers' National Union of the United States of America in April 1874, it changed its name to the International Union of Journeymen Horseshoers of the U.S. and Canada in 1893, and to the Union of Journeymen Horseshoers of the United States in the 1970s. The union adopted its present name in the 1980s. It publishes the *U.J.H. Newsletter* (annually).

Address: 8 Berkeley Rd., Mineola, N.Y. 11501. Tel. (516) 742–4456

Hosiery Workers; American Federation of (AFL-CIO) The hosiery workers withdrew from the United Textile Workers in 1915 and remained independent until 1922 as the American Federation of Full Fashioned Hosiery Workers. It then reaffiliated with the AFL as an autonomous unit. It changed its name in 1933 after obtaining jurisdiction over the seamless hosiery workers. The Hosiery Workers merged with the Textile Workers Union of America (AFL-CIO) in April 1965.

Source references: David J. Pivar, "The Hosiery Workers and the Philadelphia Third Party Impulse, 1929–1935," *Labor History*, Winter 1964; George W. Taylor, "Hosiery," *How Collective Bargaining Works* (New York: Twentieth Century Fund, 1942).

See also TEXTILE WORKERS UNION OF AMERICA (AFL-CIO).

hospitalization benefits Provided under basic medical expense contracts to include the costs of room, board, and nursing care for a specified number of days and limited to a specific dollar maximum. Benefits also include hospital service allowances such as the use of the operating room, supplies, medication, and X-ray examinations. Maternity benefits are usually included in the hospitalization plan. Benefits may be in services rather than cash benefits. Similar benefits may also be provided under major medical expense plans.

Source references: Robert D. Eilers and Robert W. Crowe, *Group Insurance Handbook* (Homewood: Irwin, 1965); Ernest W. Saward, *The Relevance of Prepaid Group Practice to the Effective Delivery of Health Services* (Washington: U.S. Dept. of HEW, Public Health Service, 1969); Anne R. Somers, *Health Plan Administration: A Guide to the Management of Negotiated Hospital, Surgical and Medical Care Benefits* (New York: Foundation of Employee Health, Medical Care and Welfare, 1961); U.S. Dept. of Labor, BLS, *Analysis of Health and Insurance Plans Under Collective Bargaining, Late 1955* (Washington: Bull. 1221, 1959); ———, *Digest of One Hundred Selected Health and Insurance Plans Under Collective Bargaining, Early 1966* (Washington: Bull. 1502, 1966); ———, *Health and Insurance Plans Under Collective Bargaining: Hospital*

Benefits, Early 1959 (Washington: Bull. 1274, 1960).

hot cargo provisions As used by labor unions, the term "hot cargo" refers to goods produced or shipped by an "unfair" employer. In such a context, the term "unfair" may refer to a struck employer, an employer whose goods bear no union label, or an employer whose wages or working conditions are deemed substandard by the union. As a measure of self-protection, some unions negotiated contracts giving their members the right to refuse to handle or process hot cargo.

Until the 1959 Landrum-Griffin amendments, the legality of these hot-cargo provisions under the Taft-Hartley Act had to be judged under the technical language of the Section 8(b)(4)(A) secondary-boycott prohibition. Initially, the NLRB took the position that neither the signing nor the enforcement of a hot-cargo contract violated the law. But in the 1955 *Sand Door* case, the Board made these rulings: (1) There is nothing unlawful in a union's executing a hot-cargo agreement and in appealing directly to the employer to abide by it; (2) however, any appeal to the employees to strike or to refuse to handle the "unfair" goods in a situation otherwise within the secondary-boycott prohibition would be a violation, the hot-cargo provisions not providing a defense *(Local 1976, Carpenters Union and Sand Door & Plywood Co.*, 113 NLRB 1210, 36 LRRM 1478 (1955)). The decision later was upheld by the Supreme Court (*Local 1976, Carpenters v. NLRB* [Sand Door & Plywood Co.], 357 US 93, 42 LRRM 2243 (1958)).

The 1959 amendments inserted a new Section 8(e) in the Act making it an unfair labor practice for a union and an employer to enter into an agreement, express or implied, under which the employer is to stop handling, using, selling, transporting, or otherwise dealing in the products of any other employer or to stop doing business with any other person. Agreements of this type previously entered into were declared unenforceable and void. It also was made an unfair labor practice under Section 8(b)(4)(A) for a union to use secondary-boycott pressures to force an employer to enter into such an agreement.

There are two exceptions to the Section 8(e) hot-cargo prohibition. There is a limited exception permitting contract restrictions on job-site subcontracting in the construction industry. This exception, however, does not apply to the basic Section 8(b)(4) secondary-boycott ban. There is a broader exception for contracts restricting jobbing and subcontracting in the apparel and clothing industry. This exception applies to both the hot-cargo and secondary-boycott prohibitions.

Much of the litigation under Section 8(e) has been concerned with the "protection-of-rights" clauses drafted by the Teamsters union and deals with such matters as observance of picket lines, refusals to handle struck work, and subcontracting restrictions. The original clauses were largely invalidated by the NLRB, but the U.S. Court of Appeals for the District of Columbia reversed the Board and upheld some features of the clauses. After the Supreme Court refused to review the appeals court's holding, the union redrafted the clauses to meet the court's specifications. (See *Truck Drivers Local No. 413 v. NLRB* [Patton Warehouse, Inc.], *Truck Drivers Local No. 728 v. NLRB* [Brown Transport Corp.], 334 F2d 539, 55 LRRM 2878 (CA DC, 1964), *cert. denied*, 379 US 916, 57 LRRM 1352 (1964).)

There also has been considerable litigation concerning the construction industry subcontracting exception. Initially, the NLRB held that, although job-site subcontracting restrictions in the construction industry were lawful under Section 8(e), a union could not strike or picket either to obtain or to enforce such restrictions. After three U.S. courts of appeals had reversed the Board's holding on strikes or picketing to obtain the subcontracting restrictions, the Board modified its position. Both the Board and the appeals courts now appear agreed on these rules: (1) a union may strike or picket to obtain a lawful restriction on construction-site subcontracting; (2) a union may not strike or picket to enforce a subcontracting restriction even though the restricting clause itself is lawful; and (3) a union may enforce a lawful subcontracting restriction through a judicial proceeding. (See *Northeastern Indiana Building and Construction Trades Council et al.* and *Centlivre Village Apartments*, 148 NLRB 854, 57 LRRM 1081 (1964).)

Source references: Paul A. Brinker, "Hot Cargo Cases in the Construction Industry Since 1958," *LLJ*, Nov. 1971; ———, "Hot Cargo Cases Since 1958," *LLJ*, Sept. 1971; Walter L. Daykin, "Legality of the Hot Cargo Clauses," *LLJ*, Aug. 1958; Leonard S. Janofsky and Andrew C. Peterson, "The Exercise of Unreviewed Administrative Discretion to Reverse the U.S. Supreme Court: *Ponsford Brothers*," *LLJ*, Dec. 1974; David Palmer, "Restriction of the 'Hot Cargo' Clause Under the Taft-Hartley and Landrum-Griffin Acts," *Industrial and Labor Relations Forum*, Vol. 12, no. 1, 1976; I. Herbert Rothenberg, "Cooling the 'Hot Cargo' Contract," *LLJ*, April 1957; George E. Seay, Jr., "The Hot Cargo Agreement in Labor-Management Contracts—From Conway's Express to National Woodwork," *IR Law Digest*, Oct. 1968; A. Paul Victor, "'Hot Cargo' Clauses: An Examination of Developments Under Section 8(c) of the LMRDA of 1959," *LLJ*, May 1964.

Hotel and Restaurant Employees and Bartenders International Union (AFL-CIO) Organized in Detroit in December 1890 under the name of the Waiters and Bartenders' National Union of the United States. It changed its name to the Hotel and Restaurant Employees' International Alliance and Bartenders' International League of America in 1898, then to the Hotel and Restaurant Employees and Bartenders International Union in the late 1940s. Finally in August 1981, the name was changed to the Hotel Employees and Restaurant Employees International Union (AFL-CIO).

Source reference: Matthew Josephson, *Union House, Union Bar: The History of the Hotel and Restaurant Employees and Bartenders International Union, AFL-CIO* (New York: Random House, 1956).

See also HOTEL EMPLOYEES AND RESTAURANT EMPLOYEES INTERNATIONAL UNION (AFL-CIO).

Hotel Employees and Restaurant Employees International Union (AFL-CIO) Formerly known as the Hotel and Restaurant Employees and Bartenders International Union, it adopted the present name in August 1981. Its monthly publications are the *Catering Industry Employee* and *Food for Thought.*

Address: 120 East 4th St., Cincinnati, Ohio 45238. Tel. (513) 621–0300

hot goods clause Provision of the Fair Labor Standards Act which prohibits the shipment in interstate commerce of goods produced in violation of the standards of the Act. Section 15(a) provides in part:

> [I]t shall be unlawful for any person (1) to transport, offer for transportation, ship, deliver, or sell in commerce, or to ship, deliver, or sell with knowledge that shipment or delivery or sale thereof in commerce is intended, any goods in the production of which any employee was employed in violation of section 6 (minimum wages) or section 7 (maximum hours), or in violation of any regulation or order of the Secretary [of Labor] issued under section 14; . . .

Source references: Fair Labor Standards Act of 1938, as amended, 29 U.S.C. § 215(a)(1) (1982); U.S. Dept. of Labor, *Annual Reports* (Washington: annually); ———, Wage and Hour and Public Contracts Divisions, *General Coverage of the Wage and Hour Provisions of the Fair Labor Standards Act of 1938, as Amended* (Washington: 1950).

hot goods injunction The secretary of labor under the Fair Labor Standards Act may obtain an order to stop the transportation of goods produced by employees who are paid rates below those required by the Act or cases in which, 30 days prior to the removal of the goods, child labor has been employed. Goods so produced are "hot goods" and a court may restrain their movement in interstate commerce.

See also FAIR LABOR STANDARDS ACT OF 1938.

Houde Engineering case A decision by the NLRB in 1934 (under the National Industrial Recovery Act, not under the National Labor Relations Act) setting out the principle of majority rule and the importance of the collective bargaining agreement in labor relations.

hourly earnings *See* AVERAGE HOURLY EARNINGS, AVERAGE STRAIGHT-TIME HOURLY EARNINGS.

hourly earnings index The BLS index based on average hourly earnings for workers in the private nonfarm sector which reflects percent change in average hourly earnings. A summary index appears in each issue of the *Monthly Labor Review.*

Source references: Thomas W. Gavett, "Measures of Change in Real Wages and Earnings," *MLR*, Feb. 1972; Norman J. Samuels, "New Hourly Earnings Index," *MLR*, Dec. 1971.

hourly wage rate The contract or legal rate paid to time workers under a collective bargaining or other agreement. It is not the same as the amount actually earned in an hour since it does not include overtime, or other premiums and bonuses. In the context of incentive wage payments, the term is sometimes used synonymously with "earned rate per hour."

Source references: John R. Abersold, *Problems of Hourly Rate Uniformity* (Philadelphia: Wharton School of Finance and Commerce, Univ. of Pennsylvania Press, Industry-Wide Collective Bargaining Series, 1949); Lionel B. Michael, *Wage and Salary Fundamentals and Procedures* (New York: McGraw-Hill, 1950).

See also WAGE RATE.

hours, actual *See* ACTUAL HOURS WORKED.

hours, ceiling Generally refers to the maximum number of hours employees may work at regular rates. Hours in excess of this "ceiling" are prohibited, or compensated at penalty (overtime) rates.

See also FAIR LABOR STANDARDS ACT OF 1938.

hours, nominal The number of hours planned or scheduled for work during the day or week. The number of hours actually worked may be different from those scheduled for the work period.

hours, standard The hours specified in a collective bargaining agreement which constitute the workday and workweek. Work in excess of the standard is usually at premium rates.

hours of work A general phrase which applies to the many problems relating to the time that a person spends at work. This includes the efforts of unions to reduce the number of hours of work. It also applies to the host of problems in the plant relating to the scheduling of work, the problems of starting and finishing time, rest and meal periods, clean-up time, etc. Most collective bargaining agreements incorporate detailed language concerning hours of work, particularly in relation to the payment of overtime.

A typical clause dealing with hours of work may read as follows:

> The regular workweek shall consist of five eight-hour days. Work performed in excess of 40 hours in one week shall constitute overtime. Work performed in excess of eight hours in one day shall constitute overtime. Employees are to be credited with full time when they are required to be on the premises of the employer.
>
> Overtime shall be paid at the rate of time and one-half the regular rate of pay for all hours worked in excess of eight per day, or 40 per week, whichever amounts to the greater payment.

Source references: Howard Davis, "Hours and Earnings of Production or Nonsupervisory Workers, 1968–78," *MLR*, April 1980; Ronald G. Ehrenberg and Paul L. Schumann, *Longer Hours or More Jobs?, An Investigation of Amending Hours Legislation to Create Employment* (Ithaca: Cornell Univ., NYSSILR, 1982); Eli Ginzberg et al., *Work Decisions in the 1980s* (Boston: Auburn House, 1982); Janice Neipert Hedges and Stephen J. Gallogly, "Full and Part Time: A Review of Definitions," *MLR*, March 1977; Janice Neipert Hedges and Daniel E. Taylor, "Recent Trends in Worktime: Hours Edge Downward," *MLR*, March 1980; Charles Hill, "Fighting the Twelve-Hour Day in the American Steel Industry," *Labor History*, Winter 1974; D. Maric, *Adapting Working Hours to Modern Needs, The Time Factor in the New Approach to Working Conditions* (Geneva: ILO, 1977); William T. Moye, "The End of the 12-Hour Day in the Steel Industry," *MLR*, Sept. 1977; John D. Owen, "Workweeks and Leisure: An Analysis of Trends, 1948–75," *MLR*, Aug. 1976; Ronnie Steinberg Ratner, "The Paradox of Protection: Maximum Hours Legislation in the United States," *ILR*, March/April 1980; George D. Stamas, "Percent Working Long Hours Shows First Post-Recession Decline," *MLR*, May 1980; Lazare Teper, *Hours of Labor* (Baltimore: Johns Hopkins Press, 1932); U.S. National Commission for Manpower Policy, *Adjusting Hours to Increase Jobs, An Analysis of the Options* (Washington: Special Report no. 15, 1977); ———, *Work Time and*

Employment, A Conference Report (Washington: Special Report no. 28, 1978); Leo Wolman, "Hours of Work in American Industry," *NBER Bulletin*, Nov. 27, 1938.

See also ADAMSON ACT, BASIC WORKWEEK, FIVE-DAY WORKWEEK, FLEXTIME/FLEXITIME, FLUCTUATING WORKWEEKS, FORTY-HOUR WEEK, FOUR-DAY WORKWEEK, REDUCTION IN HOURS, SCHEDULED HOURS, SEVEN-HOUR DAY, SHORTER WORKWEEK, SIX-HOUR DAY, THIRTY-HOUR WEEK, WORKING TIME, WORKWEEK.

house organ A magazine, newspaper, or other publication issued periodically by a company to its employees in order to keep them informed about the company, its products and operation, and the activities of other employees. It is one of the media of communication used by a company to build or maintain morale through up-to-date information about the company, its products, and its employees.

Source references: George C. Corcoran, "Let's Hear It for the Newsletter," *PJ*, March 1969; Roger M. D'Aprix, "The Believable House Organ," *Management Review*, Feb. 1979; Jim Mann, "Is Your House Organ a Vital Organ?" *PJ*, Sept. 1977; D. G. Paterson and B. J. Walker, "Readability and Human Interest of House Organs," *Personnel*, May 1949; William Schupp, "Any Company Can," *PJ*, July 1973; Robert Stephen Silverman, "The Cross-Fertilization Concept: An Employee Publication that Communicates," *PJ*, Sept. 1973; Harold Taub, "House Organs for Employee Morale," *Personnel*, Sept. 1941; Sherman Tingey, "Six Requirements for a Successful Company Publication," *PJ*, Nov. 1967.

See also INTERNAL HOUSE ORGAN.

housing *See* UNION HOUSING.

Hudson Shore Labor School *See* BRYN MAWR SUMMER SCHOOL.

human engineering The broad area of human relations insofar as it applies to labor-management relations. The technicians in the field of human engineering view their role as scientists who can chart and compute, as do the engineers, the stresses and strains on the human structure, and design ways and means to accomplish industrial objectives through understanding and application of the scientific laws of human behavior.

Although there has been substantial progress in understanding the behavior and motivations of the human being, many industrial relations practitioners feel that the "engineering" and "scientific" tags still are somewhat premature and that much of the "new" human relations has been known and practiced without the modern labels.

Source references: George Berkwitt, "The Inevitable Science of Human Engineering," *Management Review*, Dec. 1965; Jack Dunlap, "Human Engineering: What It Is and What It Can Do for You," *Factory Management and Maintenance*, Jan. 1953; Henry Ford II, *The Challenge of Human Engineering* (Detroit: Ford Motor, 1946); Lawrence A. Hartley, *Human Engineering and Industrial Economy* (Chicago: Marshall-Jackson, 1928); Elton Mayo, *Human Problems of an Industrial Civilization* (New York: Macmillan, 1933).

human relations committees *See* CONTINUOUS BARGAINING COMMITTEES.

human resource management *See* PERSONNEL MANAGEMENT.

hunger marches Demonstrations of unemployed workers who marched to state and federal capitals to focus attention on their economic plight and to point out the need for assistance during the Great Depression of 1929 and succeeding years.

hunky A derogatory slang term for an unskilled foreign worker of Hungarian or Slavic origin.

Hutcheson case A decision by the Supreme Court in 1941 affirming dismissal of a criminal indictment charging officers of the Carpenters Union with violation of the Sherman Antitrust Act by conspiring to interfere with commerce by striking and picketing Anheuser-Busch, Inc., and others, and conducting a do-not-buy boycott campaign against Anheuser-Busch products. The majority opinion emphasized a change in national policy wrought by the Norris-LaGuardia Act, saying, "whether trade union conduct constitutes a violation of the Sherman Law is to be determined only by reading the Sherman Law and Sec. 20 of the

Clayton Act and the Norris-LaGuardia Act as a harmonizing text of outlawry of labor conduct." A dissenting opinion said of this construction:

> By a process of construction never, as I think, heretofore indulged by this Court, it is now found that, because Congress forbade the issuing of injunctions to restrain certain conduct, it intended to repeal the provisions of the Sherman Act authorizing actions at law and criminal prosecutions for the commission of torts and crimes defined by the antitrust laws. The doctrine now announced seems to be that an indication of a change of policy in an Act as respects one specific item in a general field of the law, covered by an earlier Act, justifies this Court in spelling out an implied repeal of the whole of the earlier statute as applied to conduct of the sort here involved.

The majority opinion staked out the area of union conduct exempt from prosecution under the antitrust laws thus:

> So long as a union acts in its own self-interest and does not combine with non-labor groups, the licit and the illicit under Sec. 20 [of the Clayton Act] are not to be distinguished by any judgment regarding the wisdom or the unwisdom, the rightness or wrongness, the selfishness or unselfishness of the end of which the particular union activities are the means.

Source reference: United States v. Hutcheson et al., 312 US 219, 7 LRRM 267 (1941).

See also ALLEN-BRADLEY CASE, ANTITRUST LAWS, PENNINGTON CASE.

I

IAFF *See* FIRE FIGHTERS; INTERNATIONAL ASSOCIATION OF (AFL-CIO).

IAM *See* MACHINISTS AND AEROSPACE WORKERS; INTERNATIONAL ASSOCIATION OF (AFL-CIO).

IAS *See* SIDEROGRAPHERS; INTERNATIONAL ASSOCIATION OF (AFL-CIO).

IATC *See* TOOL CRAFTSMEN; INTERNATIONAL ASSOCIATION OF (IND).

IATSE *See* THEATRICAL STAGE EMPLOYEES AND MOVING PICTURE MACHINE OPERATORS OF THE UNITED STATES AND CANADA; INTERNATIONAL ALLIANCE OF (AFL-CIO).

IAU *See* ITALIAN ACTORS UNION.

IBEW *See* ELECTRICAL WORKERS; INTERNATIONAL BROTHERHOOD OF (AFL-CIO).

IBFO *See* FIREMEN AND OILERS; INTERNATIONAL BROTHERHOOD OF (AFL-CIO).

IBT *See* TEAMSTERS, CHAUFFEURS, WAREHOUSEMEN AND HELPERS OF AMERICA; INTERNATIONAL BROTHERHOOD OF (IND).

ICFTU *See* INTERNATIONAL CONFEDERATION OF FREE TRADE UNIONS (ICFTU).

ICW *See* CHEMICAL WORKERS UNION; INTERNATIONAL (AFL-CIO).

IFTU *See* INTERNATIONAL FEDERATION OF TRADE UNIONS (IFTU).

ILA *See* LONGSHOREMEN'S ASSOCIATION; INTERNATIONAL (AFL-CIO).

ILGWU *See* LADIES' GARMENT WORKERS' UNION; INTERNATIONAL (AFL-CIO).

ILO *See* INTERNATIONAL LABOR OFFICE (ILO), INTERNATIONAL LABOR ORGANIZATION (ILO).

ILRR *See* INDUSTRIAL AND LABOR RELATIONS REVIEW.

ILWU *See* LONGSHOREMEN'S AND WAREHOUSEMEN'S UNION; INTERNATIONAL (IND).

IMAW *See* MOLDERS' AND ALLIED WORKERS' UNION; INTERNATIONAL (AFL-CIO).

IR *See* INDUSTRIAL RELATIONS; A JOURNAL OF ECONOMY AND SOCIETY.

IRRA *See* INDUSTRIAL RELATIONS RESEARCH ASSOCIATION.

IT *See* INDUSTRIAL TRADE UNIONS; NATIONAL ORGANIZATION OF (IND).

ITS *See* INTERNATIONAL TRADE SECRETARIATS (ITS).

ITU *See* TYPOGRAPHICAL UNION; INTERNATIONAL (AFL-CIO).

IUE *See* ELECTRONIC, ELECTRICAL, TECHNICAL, SALARIED AND MACHINE WORKERS; INTERNATIONAL UNION OF (AFL-CIO).

IUEC *See* ELEVATOR CONSTRUCTORS; INTERNATIONAL UNION OF (AFL-CIO).

IUMSW *See* MARINE AND SHIPBUILDING WORKERS OF AMERICA; INDUSTRIAL UNION OF (AFL-CIO).

IUOE *See* OPERATING ENGINEERS; INTERNATIONAL UNION OF (AFL-CIO).

IUP *See* INLANDBOATMEN'S UNION OF THE PACIFIC.

IUPA *See* POLICE ASSOCIATIONS; INTERNATIONAL UNION OF (AFL-CIO).

IUPW *See* PETROLEUM AND INDUSTRIAL WORKERS; INTERNATIONAL UNION OF.

IUSO *See* SECURITY OFFICERS; INTERNATIONAL UNION OF (IND).

IWA *See* INTERNATIONAL WORKINGMAN'S ASSOCIATION; WOODWORKERS OF AMERICA, INTERNATIONAL (AFL-CIO).

IWIU *See* INSURANCE WORKERS INTERNATIONAL UNION (AFL-CIO).

IWW *See* INDUSTRIAL WORKERS OF THE WORLD.

Idaho Public Employees Association (Ind) An organization affiliated with the Assembly of Governmental Employees. It issues the *I.P.E.A. News* every six weeks.

Address: 1434 West Bannock St., Boise, Idaho 83702. Tel. (208) 336–2841

identification badge A button, badge, or other identification worn by a person in the plant in order to identify him and also to prevent individuals who are not authorized on the premises from entering the plant or special areas.

High-security facilities require some form of identification to be worn by the person while in the plant or when moving from one area to another.

Collective bargaining contracts do not usually make reference to identification badges.

idleness rate *See* WORK STOPPAGE STATISTICS.

idle time Payment for time during which a worker is unable to work at his machine because of a delay in receiving material, breakdown of equipment, a power shortage, or some other factor which is not within the control of the employee. Generally, idle time is compensated at the employee's regular rate or some other guarantee.

See also DEAD TIME.

illegal aliens *See* ALIEN LABOR, UNDOCUMENTED WORKERS.

illegal purpose doctrine A principle adopted by some courts to decide whether some union activities which were not in themselves unlawful, but whose purpose or objective could be held unlawful, should be prohibited. Some writers have contended that the illegal purpose doctrine was a device used by courts to perpetuate their own economic or social concepts by determining what union objectives were proper. Since many courts were not particularly in favor of unions or union activity, the adoption of this doctrine hindered trade union development.

illegal strike Any strike which has been held unlawful under existing law. The term also has reference to a strike called in violation of the provisions of a collective bargaining agreement or a strike called without conforming to the procedures of the union constitution or bylaws.

Illinois State Employees Association (Ind) An organization affiliated with the Assembly of Governmental Employees. On August 19, 1974, the organization merged with the Service Employees' International Union (AFL-CIO). It disaffiliated with the Service Employees on May 20, 1975, and reaffiliated with AGE. Its monthly publication is *The Alerter*.

Address: 2800 South Walnut St., Springfield, Ill. 62704. Tel. (217) 525–1944

illness frequency rate A statistical measure generally computed on a monthly basis, designed to show the total number of illnesses per one thousand employees. Illnesses included in the computation are those during which an employee is away from the job for a full workday or an entire shift.

immigration The movement of persons to a country. The United States immigration laws set quotas by countries and provide regulations to assure that undesirable persons do not come to this country. The Congress occasionally passes special laws to permit persons to come to the United States outside the quota system. Special regulations permit foreign nationals to stay in the United States.

Source references: Elliott Abrams and Franklin S. Abrams, "Immigration Policy—Who Gets In and Why?" *The Public Interest*, Winter 1975; Vernon M. Briggs, Jr., "Immigration," *LLJ*, Aug. 1977; Henry Pratt Fairchild, *Immigration: A World Movement and Its American Significance* (rev. ed., New York: Macmillan, 1933); Walter Fogel, "United States Immigration Policy and Unsanctioned Migrants," *ILRR*, April 1980; Margaret S. Gordon, "Immigration and Its Effect on Labor Force Characteristics," *MLR*, May 1959; George E. Johnson, "The Labor Market Effects of Immigration," *ILRR*, April 1980; Kyle Johnson and James Orr, *Labor Short-*

ages and Immigration: A Survey and Taxonomy (Washington: U.S. Dept. of Labor, BILA, Economic Discussion Paper 13, 1981); Philip L. Martin, "Select Commission Suggests Changes in Immigration Policy—A Review Essay," *MLR*, Feb. 1982; David S. North and Philip L. Martin, "Immigration and Employment: A Need for Policy Coordination," *MLR*, Oct. 1980; Michael J. Piore, *Birds of Passage; Migrant Labor and Industrial Societies* (Cambridge, England: Cambridge UP, 1979); Ellen Sehgal and Joyce Vialet, "Documenting the Undocumented: Data Like Aliens, Are Elusive," *MLR*, Oct. 1980; Bruno Stein, "Immigration as a Social Issue," *Proceedings of the 27th A/M, IRRA*, ed. by James Stern and Barbara Dennis (Madison: 1975); U.S. Dept. of Labor, ETA, *Seven Years Later: The Experiences of the 1970 Cohort of Immigrants in the United States* (Washington: R & D Monograph 71, 1979); U.S. GAO, *Illegal Aliens: Estimating Their Impact on the United States* (Washington: 1980); U.S. National Commission for Manpower Policy, *Manpower and Immigration Policies in the United States* (Washington: Special Report no. 20, 1978); Michael L. Wachter, "The Labor Market and Illegal Immigration: The Outlook for the 1980s," *ILRR*, April 1980; Robert Warren, "Recent Immigration and Current Data Collection," *MLR*, Oct. 1977.

See also ALIEN LABOR, GUESTWORKER PROGRAM, HENDERSON V. MAYOR OF NEW YORK.

impact bargaining *See* DECISION/EFFECTS BARGAINING.

impact ratio A statistical method used to determine whether any race, sex, or ethnic group has experienced a substantially disadvantageous rate of selection in employment decisions. The impact ratio of hiring, promotion, and training decisions is the selection rate for one group divided by the selection rate of the group with the highest selection rate. For termination, disciplinary action, and layoff, it is the termination rate of the group with the lowest rate divided by the termination rate for the group in question. OFCCP sometimes compares impact ratios to the 80 percent rule in determining adverse impact.

Source reference: U.S. OFCCP, *Federal Contract Compliance Manual* (Washington: 1979).

See also ADVERSE IMPACT, EIGHTY PERCENT (80%) RULE, OFFICE OF FEDERAL CONTRACT COMPLIANCE PROGRAMS (OFCCP).

impartial chairperson The term is synonymous with impartial arbitrator or impartial umpire.

Under some agreements the third party or arbitrator may be known as the chairperson or umpire. Even though the title might imply that the individual is acting as chair of the group in reaching a decision, frequently the chair acts as an individual in arriving at the award.

The title usually is given to an arbitrator selected jointly by the parties to a contract for a definite term and for a stated salary or fee. The powers of such an impartial chairperson usually are broader in scope than those of an ad hoc arbitrator. This is primarily due to the chairperson's long-standing familiarity with and acceptance by both labor and management in the industry. Because of this acceptance, the chairperson may be consulted by and assist the parties in arriving at the terms of a new contract or resolving problems under an existing agreement which may not be subject to arbitration.

The chairperson may be asked to arbitrate some or all of the provisions of a new agreement at the expiration of the old contract and at the same time may assist the parties in administering the agreement during its term. In other respects, when handling grievances, the chairperson operates as any other arbitrator in the interpretation and application of the agreement. The contract itself may provide the chairperson with wider latitude or greater authority than those of a regular arbitrator but this depends largely on the desires of labor and management and the extent to which they depend upon the impartial chairperson or umpire to assist them in solving their problems.

Some contracts provide fairly broad latitude to a regular or permanent arbitrator which may be equal to that of an impartial chairperson. Since an arbitrator acts in the interest of both parties, they largely can determine the role they want the chairperson to play.

Source references: Gabriel N. Alexander, "Impartial Umpireships: The General Motors-UAW Experience," *Arbitration and the Law*, Proceedings of the 12th A/M, NAA, ed. by Jean McKelvey (Washington: BNA, 1959); Lois MacDonald et al., "The Impartial Chairmanship—An Institution in Labor-Management Relations," *NYU 7th Annual Conference on Labor*, ed. by Emanuel Stein (Albany: Bender, 1954); Harry Shulman, "The Role of the Impartial Umpire," *The Collective Bargaining Agreement in Action* (New York: AMA, Personnel Series no. 82, 1944); Maurice S. Trotta, "The Impartial Chairman," *Industrial Bulletin*, April 1957.

See also ARBITRATION, PERMANENT ARBITRATOR, REFEREE, UMPIRE.

impasse Deadlock in negotiations between management officials and representatives of an employee organization over the terms and conditions of employment. Whether an impasse exists "is a matter of judgment," the NLRB said in its 1967 decision in *Taft Broadcasting Co. v. AFTRA* (163 NLRB 475, 64 LRRM 1386 (1967)). "The bargaining history, the good faith of the parties in negotiations, the length of the negotiations, the importance of the issue or issues as to which there is disagreement, the contemporaneous understanding of the parties as to the state of negotiations, are all relevant factors to be considered in deciding whether an impasse in bargaining existed," the Board pointed out.

Many state laws governing labor relations in the public sector generally do not define the term "impasse." However, these laws frequently provide for the determination of impasses. The New York statute, for example, states: "an impasse may be deemed to exist if the parties fail to achieve agreement at least 120 days prior to the end of the fiscal year of the public employer." Procedures to be invoked in case an impasse is reached in negotiations are provided for under many of these laws.

No provision was made under Executive Order 10988 for resolution of negotiation disputes and impasses. Under Executive Order 11491 the Federal Mediation and Conciliation Service (FMCS) assisted parties in negotiating agreements, and services of the Federal Service Impasses Panel (FSIP) were provided to bring about final resolution of negotiation impasses if mediation were unsuccessful.

Under the Civil Service Reform Act of 1978, the FMCS provides "services and assistance to agencies and exclusive representatives in the resolution of impasses." If the FMCS or other third party mediation assistance fails to resolve an impasse, the parties may request the FSIP to consider the matter or they may adopt binding arbitration, which is subject to approval by the FSIP. When an impasse is brought before the FSIP, the FSIP may recommend procedures for settling the dispute or assist the parties in resolving the impasse. The FSIP is authorized to take whatever action is necessary to resolve an impasse.

Source references: Mollie H. Bowers, "The Dilemma of Impasse Procedures in the Public Safety Services," *AJ*, Sept. 1973; Anthony F. Campagna, Stanley Benecki, and R. Michael Montgomery, *A Strategy for Evaluating the Use of Impasse and Dispute Resolution Procedures in State and Local Government* (n.p., 1975); Peter Feuille, "Public Sector Impasses: Symposium Introduction," *IR*, Oct. 1977; James J. Gallagher, *Impasse Resolution in Public Sector Interest Disputes* (Los Angeles: UC, Institute of IR, 1976); Paul F. Gerhart and John E. Drotning, *A Six State Study of Impasse Procedures in the Public Sector* (n.p., 1980); Thomas P. Gilroy and Anthony V. Sinicropi, "Impasse Resolution in Public Employment: A Current Assessment," *ILRR*, July 1972; Thomas A. Kochan, *Evaluating the Effectiveness of Impasse Procedures: Some Conceptual and Research Design Issues* (Ithaca: Cornell Univ., NYSSILR, 1975); Paul D. Staudohar, "Some Implications of Mediation for Resolution of Bargaining Impasses in Public Employment," *Public Personnel Management*, July/Aug. 1973; Elvis C. Stephens, "Resolution of Impasses in Public Employee Bargaining," *MLR*, Jan. 1976; George T. Sulzner, "The Political Functions of Impasse Procedures," *IR*, Oct. 1977; Helene S. Tanimoto, *Guide to Statutory Provisions in Public Sector Collective Bargaining—Impasse Resolution Procedures* (3d ed., Honolulu: Univ. of Hawaii, IRC, 1981); Roy Wesley, *Impasse Resolution: An Analysis of Old and New Ways to End Deadlocks* (Washington: Labor-Management Relations Service, Special Report, 1976); Sam Zagoria, "The U.S. Cities Tackle Impasses," *Proceedings of the 25th A/M, IRRA*, ed. by Gerald Somers (Madison: 1973).

improvement factor *See* ANNUAL IMPROVEMENT FACTOR, AUTOMATIC WAGE ADJUSTMENT.

incapacity for work Relates primarily to the inability of a person to perform work and the provisions for insurance to cover that incapacity.

Source reference: ILO, *Evaluation of Permanent Incapacity for Work and Social Insurance* (Montreal: Social Insurance Report no. 14, 1937).

See also DISABILITY, DISABILITY INSURANCE.

incentive contracts Clauses in collective bargaining agreements which establish systems of incentive wage payments and specify how such systems are to be extended to new groups which may come within the bargaining unit. Examples I and II below illustrate such clauses:

I

(a) As used in this incentive plan, the 'personal rate' of an employee is his classification rate plus any applicable shift differential, holiday premium, automatic increase, and merit increase.

(b) The employer will make participation in this plan as complete as feasible. All employees whose work can be measured with reasonable accuracy will be included. During the first 30 days after an employee's job has been placed on incentive or after an employee has been transferred from another job of equal or lesser classification to a new one for the company's convenience, he will be paid his actual incentive earnings or his personal rate, whichever is higher.

(c) No limit will be placed on earnings of any person or group working on a regular production job under the incentive plan. Earnings of employees working on inspection, or special or critical jobs, may be limited to 25 percent premium. Quality of work must remain within acceptable limits at all times. . . .

(f) Rejected parts will not be counted in determining quantity produced.

(g) All standards established by the company will be available in written form and open to inspection by interested employees. Standards will be stated in terms of the number of pieces required per hour to equal incentive base rate.

(h) Except for correction of clerical or typographical errors, standards once established will not be changed by the company except where individual or accumulated changes are made in materials, methods, or machines to the extent of 5 percent of the entire operation. When standards are thus changed, they will be changed only to the extent affected by the changes in materials, methods, or machines. When a standard is changed, the affected employees and the union committeeman for that department will be advised of the changes made and how they affect the old standard.

(i) In determining a standard, the company will add time to allow for personal time, fatigue, and minor unavoidable delays which cannot be anticipated. All standards will be established so as to permit the average experienced employee, working with good skill and good effort on an incentive operation, to earn 25 percent above the incentive base rate for the operation.

(j) Any standard established or changed by the company may be challenged by an affected employee in the same way in which a grievance is processed under Article X, and may be submitted to arbitration under Article XI. The arbitrator shall not substitute his judgment for that of the company, but shall determine only whether the company has acted arbitrarily or committed a significant error of observation or calculation.

(k) Regardless of work produced, all employees are guaranteed and will receive as a minimum, payment for all hours worked at their personal rate or the incentive rate, whichever is lower. Hours worked shall include time lost, outside the employee's control, because of lack of material or machine breakdown.

II

Sec. 1. Any extension of incentive payment plans to departments or groups of employees not heretofore coming within the existing incentive program and any change in the general principles or methods governing the existing incentive program shall be mutually agreed upon between the company and the union.

Sec. 2. Any adjustment in incentive prices or standard or piece rates made necessary by technological changes may first be determined by the company and may be placed in effect but the union may take up any grievance arising from such changes through the grievance procedure, including arbitration.

Sec. 3. Any employee or group of employees assigned to incentive work under a contract shall be given a copy of the contract describing the work and establishing the price or standard prior to commencing the work, except in unusual cases where this is not feasible. There shall be no change made in the contract price during the progress of the job or after the completion of any job except when changes are made in the quantity or quality of work originally specified in the incentive work contract. Any complaint which may arise concerning a specific incentive contract may be taken up for adjustment under the grievance procedure with incentive records made available in settling any such dispute, but such dispute shall not be subject to arbitration.

incentive rate Generally applies to any type of wage rate for production above a fixed or agreed upon standard of output. This may be in the form of a piece rate, rate for production beyond or in excess of a set or fixed standard, or some other method agreed to by the parties.

Contracts may provide for the payment of special rates which may be part of the incentive plan or to take care of situations which arise when a new incentive rate has to be set or where experimental work is tried out before the new rates are established. Incentive wage systems may also provide a guaranteed rate below which the earnings may not fall.

See also RATE CUTTING, STANDARD HOUR, STANDARD TIME.

incentive wage Refers to any system of wage payment in which payment to the employee rises with increased production. Payments to individuals are based on specific results.

Incentive wage plans are designed to provide greater stimulation to the workers and to permit those with greater initiative to take home increased earnings. Some plans provide for payment to indirect employees as well as to workers directly involved in production. There are all varieties of incentive wage plans and they are usually adjusted to meet the specific problems in particular plants.

Historically workers have opposed incentive wage plans because they found that employers kept increasing the standards without corresponding compensation and thereby got greater production at the expense of the employees. At the present time many unions accept incentive wage plans with adequate safeguards.

Source references: Solomon Barkin, "Wage Incentive Problems in Arbitration," *LLJ*, Jan. 1970; Joseph C. Bush, "Incentive Pay Plans in the Steel Industry," *MLR*, Aug. 1974; Norma W. Carlson, "Time Rates Tighten Their Grip on Manufacturing Industries," *MLR*, May 1982; Samuel R. Collins, "Incentive Programs: Pros and Cons," *PJ*, July 1981; Paula Cowan, "How Blue Cross Put Pay-for-Performance to Work," *PJ*, May 1978; Mitchell Fein, "Restoring the Incentive to Wage Incentive Plans," *Conference Board Record*, Nov. 1972; Lillian Gilbreth, "Incentives in Industry," *Executive Management Seminar VI* (Madison: Univ. of Wisconsin, Industrial Management Institute, 1948); Donald L. McManis and William G. Dick, "Monetary Incentives in Today's Industrial Setting," *PJ*, May 1973; John S. Piamonte, "In Praise of Monetary Motivation," *PJ*, Sept. 1979; "Prevalence of Incentives in Major Bargaining Agreements," *MLR*, July 1979; Harold S. Roberts, "The Basis of Labor's Attitude Toward Incentives," *Labor-Management Relations in Hawaii, Part II* (Honolulu: Univ. of Hawaii, IRC, 1955); U.S. Dept. of Labor, BLS, *Major Collective Bargaining Agreements: Wage-Incentive, Production Standard, and Time-Study Provisions* (Washington: Bull. 1425–18, 1979); W. Kip Viscusi, "Strategic Behavior and the Impact of Unions on Wage Incentive Plans," *Journal of Labor Research*, Winter 1982.

See also BEDEAUX WAGE PLAN, EMERSON EFFICIENCY PLAN, FINISH-GO-HOME BASIS OF PAY, GANTT TASK AND BONUS PLAN, HALSEY PREMIUM (GAIN-SHARING) PLAN, HAYNES "MANIT" WAGE PLAN, ONE-HUNDRED-PERCENT PREMIUM PLAN, OUT-OF-LINE RATES, PREMIUM WAGE SYSTEM.

income in kind Most income received by workers is in the form of money wages. Sometimes payment for work done is a noncash payment. For example, domestic, hotel, and agricultural workers may receive payments in kind in the form of meals, lodging, or other noncash payment such as wearing apparel or other services. Payment may be partly in cash and partly in kind.

See also PERQUISITES.

income maintenance *See* GUARANTEED INCOME.

incorporation of unions During the open shop drive of the early 20th century there was a demand by antiunion forces that workers' organizations be required to incorporate. Incorporation was necessary, they said, because as unions became strong there was a need for greater responsibility on their part.

There were some union leaders who felt that incorporation might limit liability in so far as damage suits were concerned. However, the general feeling of organized labor has been against compulsory incorporation of trade unions. Some independent and so-called company unions have incorporated. Incorporation as such does not imply company domination.

Source references: James D. Hoover, *Union Incorporation and Regulation* (Madison: Univ. of Wisconsin, 1938); "Incorporation, Registration and Listing of Labor Unions," *National Lawyers' Guild Quarterly*, Jan. 1940; Louis Waldman, *Should Unions Be Incorporated?* (Washington: Social Democratic Federation, 1937).

increased compensation plan *See* EMERSON EFFICIENCY PLAN.

indentured apprenticeship A procedure whereby a worker and an employer by means of a written instrument agree on a special training program in a particular skill or occupation. Provision generally is made for the duration of the agreement, the conditions of employment, and rates of pay. The apprenticeship is designed both to train individuals and to provide employers with a skilled work force.

Source reference: W. F. Patterson, "Indentured Apprenticeship," *PJ*, Sept. 1936.

See also APPRENTICESHIP, MASTER-SERVANT RELATIONSHIP.

indentured servant A person who agrees or is required to work for another as a servant. During the early colonial period, particularly in the 17th and 18th centuries, indentured servants were quite common. Individuals abroad sold themselves into servitude in order to obtain money for ocean transportation to seek freedom and opportunity in the new world.

See also MASTER-SERVANT RELATIONSHIP.

independent American shop Sometimes called the American Plan, it was designed to call the attention of workers to their right to work in a trade or business under conditions satisfactory to them without interference on the part of any union.

See also AMERICAN PLAN, OPEN SHOP.

Independent Labor Federation of America An organization of employee associations and independent unions which organized in Hershey, Pennsylvania, following a strike by the CIO in 1937. The independent unions sought to establish an organization to compete with the AFL and the CIO. The actual organization suggested that employer support was behind this drive. The Independent Labor Federation did not get much support.

See also COMPANY UNION.

independent national union A labor organization which is not affiliated with the AFL-CIO and is not a company-dominated union. It may cover workers in an entire industry and have members throughout the country. The United Mine Workers is an independent national union. So is the International Brotherhood of Teamsters.

It should be noted that many independent national unions have at one time or another been affiliated either with the American Federation of Labor or with the Congress of Industrial Organizations.

independent unions Organizations of workers, usually in a single plant or company, which are not affiliated with any national or international organization. Independent unions frequently have been thought of as company-dominated. A union may be independent without being employer-dominated.

Source references: Gary N. Chaison and William K. Rock, "Competition Between Local Independent and National Unions," *LLJ*, May 1974; John J. Collins, *Bargaining at the Local Level* (New York: Fordham UP, 1974); Julius Rezler, "Labor Organization at DuPont: A Study in Independent Local Unionism," *Labor History*, Spring 1963; James W. Robinson, "Structural Characteristics of the Independent Union in America," *LLJ*, July 1968; Arthur B. Shostak, *America's Forgotten Labor Organization: A Survey of the Role of the Single-Firm Inde-*

pendent Union in American Industry (Princeton: Princeton Univ., IR Section, 1962); Leo Troy, "Local Independent Unions and the American Labor Movement," *ILRR*, April 1961; U.S. Dept. of Labor, BLS, *Unaffiliated Intrastate and Single-Employer Unions, 1967* (Washington: Bull. no. 1640, 1969).

Independent Unions; Allied (Ind) Affiliated with the National Independent Union Council. It joined the International Brotherhood of Teamsters, Chauffeurs, Warehousemen and Helpers of America (Ind) during January 1957.

See also TEAMSTERS, CHAUFFEURS, WAREHOUSEMEN AND HELPERS OF AMERICA; INTERNATIONAL BROTHERHOOD OF (IND).

Independent Unions; Congress of (Ind) Affiliated with the National Federation of Independent Unions. Its official monthly publication is the *Union Labor News Review*.

Address: 303 Ridge St., Alton, Ill. 62002. Tel. (618) 462–2447

Independent Unions; National Federation of *See* NATIONAL FEDERATION OF INDEPENDENT UNIONS.

index number A statistical measure for determining differences in the magnitude of a group of related variables.

The index number is useful in showing the relative changes in a particular series over a period of time. The change generally is measured from a fixed date or base period equal to 100. Subsequent changes are taken from that fixed period. The base period may be changed from time to time but when a new series is issued the base period change is noted so that a statistician may relate the old series to the new base period.

The index number is a device widely used in comparing wage and price series. The method of construction of a particular index number can be obtained by studying the technical publications made available by the agency publishing the statistical series. Most statistical textbooks provide a chapter or two on the construction and use of index numbers.

Source references: Thomas W. Gavett, "Quality and a Pure Price Index," *MLR*, March 1967; Wesley C. Mitchell, *The Making and Using of Index Numbers* (Washington: U.S. Dept. of Labor, BLS, Bull. no. 656, 1938); William A. Neiswanger, *Elementary Statistical Methods* (rev. ed., New York: Macmillan, 1956).

See also CONSUMER PRICE INDEX.

index-number wages These are wages which vary in accordance with the cost of living or some other index agreed upon to provide adjustments either upward or downward with changes in the index number.

See also CONSUMER PRICE INDEX, COST-OF-LIVING ADJUSTMENT, ESCALATOR CLAUSE.

Index to Labor Union Periodicals A monthly subject index to materials from a selected list of newspapers and journals published by major labor unions. Published by the Bureau of Industrial Relations, The University of Michigan, Graduate School of Business Administration, Ann Arbor, beginning in January 1962. It ceased publication with the February 1969 issue.

Source reference: Eleanor H. Scanlan, "A Key to the Labor Press: Michigan Index to Labor Union Periodicals," *Management of Personnel Quarterly*, Fall 1968.

Indiana State Employees Association (Ind) An organization affiliated with the Assembly of Governmental Employees. It publishes the *ISEA News* (bimonthly) and *ISEA Legislative Reporter* (weekly when the state legislature is in session).

Address: 328 Illinois Bldg., 17 West Market St., Indianapolis, Ind. 46204. Tel. (317) 632–7254

indirect labor Indirect labor includes labor cost which is not specifically charged to any operation or department but is a cost of general plant operation.

The terms indirect labor and direct labor are helpful in cost accounting to determine unit costs and to study areas in which costs might be reduced. In some incentive systems, workers not involved in production directly may receive incentive payments dependent on the total volume of output. It is possible for specific operations, depending upon the plant or departmental or operational layout, to be either direct or indirect labor.

Source reference: David B. Caminoz, *Control Over Indirect Labor and Material Expenses* (New York: AMA, Production Series 164, 1946).

See also DIRECT LABOR.

individual agreement The term is similar to the individual contract. It is an agreement by a single worker with an employer determining the conditions of employment. It is to be distinguished from the collective bargaining agreement, in which the terms and conditions of employment apply to all employees in the appropriate bargaining unit. The individual agreement is rare where collective bargaining exists.

See also AGREEMENT, COLLECTIVE.

individual bargaining This term applies to negotiations which take place between a single employee and an employer. During the period when collective bargaining was in its infancy and the employer was free to determine the conditions of employment with each individual employee, it might be said that individual bargaining prevailed. In actuality, there was not much individual bargaining unless the employee was in a particular skill or craft which was in short supply or an outstanding worker with special qualifications.

Individual bargaining sometimes has reference to the right of the individual to present a grievance without taking it up through existing grievance machinery under the collective bargaining contract. Under the provisions of the Taft-Hartley Act an individual may not settle a case with the company if (1) the settlement involved would be contrary to the terms and conditions of employment under the collective bargaining agreement and (2) the union representative is not present.

Source references: John R. Commons et al., *History of Labour in the United States* (2 vol., New York: Macmillan, c.1946, 1961); Peter J. Dekom, "Individual vs. Collective Agreements: A Study in Conflict and Union Leverage," *IR Law Digest*, Fall 1974; Robert G. Howlett, "Contract Rights of the Individual Employee Against the Employer," *LLJ*, May 1957.

See also AGREEMENT, COLLECTIVE; COLLECTIVE BARGAINING.

individual employee grievances Usually refer to the rights of an individual employee under the terms of the collective bargaining agreement. The right of the individual employee to process a grievance outside the grievance machinery was circumscribed under the National Labor Relations Act by a series of decisions. Under the Taft-Hartley Act greater latitude is provided for an individual to handle the grievance without the necessity of processing it through the union.

The settlement the employee makes may not violate the terms of the collective bargaining agreement and the union must be notified and have the opportunity to have its representative present at the time the final settlement is made with the individual employee.

Source references: Benjamin Aaron, "Employee Rights Under an Agreement: A Current Evaluation," *MLR*, Aug. 1971; Archibald Cox, "Individual Enforcement of Collective Bargaining Agreements," *LLJ*, Dec. 1957; Herman A. Gray, "The Individual Worker and the Right to Arbitrate," *LLJ*, Sept. 1961; "Individual Control Over Personal Grievances Under *Vaca v. Sipes*," *Yale LJ*, Jan. 1968; Anthony R. Marchione, "A Case for Individual Rights Under Collective Agreements," *LLJ*, Dec. 1976; Israel Ben Scheiber, "Individual Rights in Arbitration," *NYU 14th Annual Conference on Labor*, ed. by Emanuel Stein (Albany: Bender, 1961).

individual rate The wage rate actually paid to the individual employee as contrasted with the rate for the job set up in the employer's wage or rate structure. It may apply to the rate paid to the individual where no formal wage structure exists in the plant.

It also may apply to a so-called red circle rate, that is, a rate which has been received by an employee and which is retained after a job evaluation has taken place; the individual receives a rate higher than the rate actually set after the job evaluation has been completed. The red circle rate is usually retained by the individual while occupying that particular job. When the individual leaves, however, the new employee taking the job will receive the rate established for the specific job qualifications.

See also JOB RATE, RED CIRCLE RATE.

induction Following an interview and the actual selection of a worker for a job, the employee is assigned to the actual workplace, department, or operation in which he is to perform his regular functions.

Although the employee obtains information concerning the company, its background, and organization during the interview, it usually rests with the immediate supervisor to introduce the new employee to the particular job, and to those other employees with whom the employee will be in close association. The induction process may be relatively brief, at which time the supervisor informs the individual about the hours of work, the general shop rules and policies, the location of time clocks, and other routine items. The induction procedure should give the individual confidence and acceptance on his job as well as establish an easy working relationship with other workers on the job.

Source references: Laron B. Burnham, *Induction* (Ithaca: Cornell Univ., NYSSILR, 1957); John Paul Jones, "Induction Plan Makes New Workers Want to Stay," *Factory Management and Maintenance*, Jan. 1945; John P. Kotter, "Managing the Joining-Up Process," *Personnel*, July/Aug. 1972; John J. Leonard, "An Employee Induction Model," *PJ*, June 1972; NICB, *Employee Induction* (New York: Studies in Personnel Policy no. 131, 1953); Morris A. Savitt, "A Fresh Slant on the Induction Program," *PJ*, Dec. 1965.

See also ORIENTATION.

industrial accident A sudden, unforeseen, or unexpected occurrence which results in injury, disability, or death to a person while working at the job.

Source references: Monroe Berkowitz, "Occupational Safety and Health," *Annals*, May 1979; Earl F. Cheit, *Injury and Recovery in the Course of Employment* (New York: Wiley, 1961); William P. Curington, "The Impact of the Occupational Safety and Health Act of 1970 on Occupational Injuries," *Proceedings of the 32d A/M, IRRA*, ed. by Barbara Dennis (Madison: 1980); Alan E. Dillingham, "Sex Differences in Labor Market Injury Risk," *IR*, Winter 1981; John Mazor, "How Accurate are Employers' Illness and Injury Reports?" *MLR*, Sept. 1976; Norman Root and Judy R. Daley, "Are Women Safer Workers? A New Look at the Data," *MLR*, Sept. 1980; Norman Root and David McCaffrey, "Providing More Information on Work Injury and Illness," *MLR*, April 1978; Robert Stewart Smith, "The Impact of OSHA on Manufacturing Injury Rates," *Journal of Human Resources*, Spring 1979; U.S. Dept. of HEW, Public Health Service, *Time Lost From Work Among the Currently Employed Population, United States—1968* (Washington: 1972); U.S. Dept. of Labor, BLS, *Occupational Injuries and Illnesses in the United States by Industry, 1980* (Washington: Bull. 2130, 1982); ———, *State Data on Occupational Injuries and Illnesses in 1976* (Washington: Report 576, 1979); U.S. GAO, *How Can Workplace Injuries Be Prevented? The Answers May Be In OSHA Files* (Washington: 1979); Chao Ling Wang and Harvey J. Hilaski, "The Safety and Health Record in the Construction Industry," *MLR*, March 1978.

See also ACCIDENT FREQUENCY RATE, ACCIDENT PREVENTION, WORKERS COMPENSATION.

industrial action Generally refers to the economic strategy used by unions through such devices as picketing, boycotts, or strikes. The term is used to distinguish it from other types of action used by unions such as negotiation and political action.

industrial agreement The same as collective bargaining agreement.

See also AGREEMENT, COLLECTIVE; AGREEMENT, SWEETHEART; AGREEMENT COVERAGE; AGREEMENT REVISION.

Industrial and Labor Relations Review A quarterly publication of the New York State School of Industrial and Labor Relations, located at Cornell University in Ithaca, New York. The publication discusses current labor relations issues and contains book reviews and an extensive section of bibliographical references to current literature.

industrial assembly *See* COMPANY UNION.

Industrial Assembly of North America An organization established in 1864, designed to bring together on a national basis various craft unions and groups of local trade associations.

industrial classification Categories of industrial groups set up to provide a simple and workable arrangement for separating or classifying groups for statistical analysis. Classification may be on the basis of the work performed, the type of service handled, or other classification dealing with the nature of the product and its distribution.

industrial conflict A general term designed to describe the broad areas of disagreement and difficulty between labor and management. The literature covers the basis for disagreement, and the specific efforts and strategy or tactics used by labor and management in resolving those conflicts. It also deals with the machinery established by government to temper or reduce the areas of industrial disagreement or conflict.

The phases of industrial conflict with which the public is generally familiar include boycotts, picketing, strikebreaking, etc.

Source references: Carroll R. Daugherty, "The Allowable Area of Industrial Conflict," *Proceedings of the 2d A/M, IRRA*, ed. by Milton Derber (Champaign: 1950); John Ferguson, *Substitutes for the Strike—An Appraisal* (Honolulu: Univ. of Hawaii, IRC, 1953); George W. Hartmann and Theodore Newcomb (ed.), *Industrial Conflict—A Psychological Interpretation* (New York: Cordon, 1939); Everett M. Kassalow, "Industrial Conflict and Consensus in the United States and Western Europe: A Comparative Analysis," *Proceedings of the 30th A/M, IRRA*, ed. by Barbara Dennis (Madison: 1978); Clark Kerr, "Industrial Conflict and Its Mediation," *American Journal of Sociology*, Nov. 1954; Gerd Korman and Michael Klapper, "Game Theory's Wartime Connections and the Study of Industrial Conflict," *ILRR*, Oct. 1978; Arthur Kornhauser, Robert Dubin, and Arthur Ross, *Industrial Conflict* (New York: McGraw-Hill, 1954); *Management of Conflict, Implications for Community Relations and for the World of Work; Proceedings of the 15th Annual Research Conference on Industrial Relations, March 13, 1973* (Los Angeles: UC, Institute of IR, 1974); Edwin Stacey Oakes, *The Law of Organized Labor and Industrial Conflict* (Rochester: Lawyers' Cooperative Publishing, 1927); Ross Stagner, *Psychology of Industrial Conflict* (New York: Wiley, 1956); Hoyt N. Wheeler, *Roots of Industrial Conflict: Consequences for Conflict Management* (Minneapolis: Univ. of Minnesota, IRC, WP 82–02, 1980).

See also BOYCOTT, LABOR DISPUTE, LAFOLLETTE COMMITTEE, PICKETING, STRIKE, VIOLENCE IN LABOR DISPUTES.

industrial courts Essentially these are arbitration tribunals. Instead of being selected by the parties to resolve their problems, they are government tribunals whose primary functions are to arbitrate disputes under an existing statute or law.

Source references: Kurt Braun, *Labor Disputes and Their Settlement* (Baltimore: Johns Hopkins Press, 1955); Domenico Gagliardo, *The Kansas Industrial Court* (Lawrence: Univ. of Kansas, 1941); ILO, *Labor Courts: An International Survey of Judicial Systems for Settlement of Disputes* (Geneva: 1938).

See also ARBITRATION, COMPULSORY; KANSAS COURT OF INDUSTRIAL RELATIONS; LABOR COURT.

industrial democracy The term is designed to describe the relationship in a plant or industry between representatives of management and labor to provide a procedure for handling basic problems in the plant.

When employee representation plans were established in the 1920s, the procedure followed the pattern of political democracy, permitting workers to elect representatives to an assembly.

The term has also been used to describe the removal of arbitrary or autocratic procedures by management and the substitution of machinery in which the workers have an opportunity to present their problems and grievances and to receive adequate consideration by management.

The development of collective bargaining is viewed by many as providing the machinery through which industrial democracy has developed.

The provision of greater opportunity to workers to present their point of view creates a problem for both management and union because, as in the political area, it is difficult to get widespread participation of the members.

In many local unions the number of individuals who take an active part in the process is relatively small compared to the total membership.

Source references: Solomon Barkin, *Labor Participation: A Way to Industrial Democracy* (Amherst: Univ. of Massachusetts, Labor Relations and Research Center, Reprint Series no. 52, 1978); Harry Bernstein and Joanne Bernstein, *Industrial Democracy in 12 Nations* (Washington: U.S. Dept. of Labor, BILA, Monograph no. 2, 1979); Milton Derber, *Collective Bargaining: The American Approach to Industrial Democracy* (Urbana: Univ. of Illinois, Institute of Labor and IR, Reprint Series 256, 1977); ———, "Some Further Thoughts on the Historical Study of Industrial Democracy," *Labor History*, Fall 1973; Stephen J. Frenkel, *Industrial Democracy in America, Britain and Australia: A Comparative Analysis of Recent Developments* (Kensington: Univ. of New South Wales, Dept. of IR, WP 3/1978, 1978); Richard D. Lambert (ed.), "Industrial Democracy in International Perspective," *Annals*, May 1977; Russell D. Lansbury, "Industrial Democracy Under Liberal Capitalism: A Comparison of Trends in Australia, France and the USA," *Journal of IR*, Dec. 1978; Michael Poole, "Industrial Democracy: A Comparative Analysis," *IR*, Fall 1979; Benjamin C. Roberts (ed.), *Towards Industrial Democracy; Europe, Japan and the United States* (Montclair, N.J.: Allanheld, Osmun, 1979); Douglas Soutar, "Co-Determination, Industrial Democracy and the Role of Management," *Proceedings of the 26th A/M, IRRA*, ed. by Gerald Somers (Madison: 1974); Adolf F. Sturmthal, *Unions and Industrial Democracy* (Urbana: Univ. of Illinois, Institute of Labor and IR, Reprint Series 257, 1977); Sidney and Beatrice Webb, *Industrial Democracy* (London: Longmans, Green, 1920); Daniel Zwerdling, *Workplace Democracy, A Guide to Workplace Ownership, Participation and Self Management Experiments in the United States and Europe* (New York: Harper & Row, 1980).

See also DEMOCRACY, EMPLOYEE REPRESENTATION PLANS.

industrial discipline *See* UNION DISCIPLINE.

industrial disease Those incapacities which develop on the job due to unhealthy working conditions or the handling of materials which lead to incapacity.

Source references: Earl F. Cheit, "Radiation Hazards: A New Challenge to Workmen's Compensation," *The Insurance LJ*, Dec. 1957; Benjamin W. Mintz, *OSHA: History, Law, and Policy* (Washington: BNA, 1984); Henry B. Selleck and Alfred H. Whittaker, *Occupational Health in America* (Detroit: Wayne State UP, 1962).

See also ASBESTOSIS; BLACK LUNG BENEFITS REFORM ACT OF 1977; BRASS CHILLS; CAISSON DISEASE; DERMATITIS, INDUSTRIAL; HATTERS' SHAKES; INDUSTRIAL POISON; MERCURY POISONING; OCCUPATIONAL DISEASE; PHOSSY JAW; RADIATION HAZARD; RADIUM POISONING; SILICOSIS; WORKERS COMPENSATION.

industrial disputes Conflicts in the field of labor-management relations which arise from inability of the parties to resolve their differences. Very frequently they are concerned with new contract terms and the establishment of wages, hours, and working conditions. The public interest becomes apparent when an industrywide dispute arises or when a dispute affecting a large geographic area creates problems in transportation, curtails the flow of essential materials, or interferes with necessary public services.

See also CONCILIATION, LABOR DISPUTE, MEDIATION, NATIONAL EMERGENCY BOARDS, NATIONAL EMERGENCY DISPUTES, STRIKE.

industrial education Sometimes used as synonymous with industrial training. The special skills or knowledge required by the employee may be obtained either on or off the job. The training may be obtained through apprenticeship, schools, or through educational courses offered by the employer after hours at the place of employment or at some educational institution. Occasionally educational training is arranged with a local vocational school and the courses are designed to meet the special needs of a single employer or industrial group.

Source references: Curtis C. Aller and C. Daniel Vencill, "The Community College as a Neglected CETA Resource," Paper presented at the National CETA Staff Development and Training Conference, "An Edge on the 80's," sponsored by the Center for Public Affairs, Virginia Commonwealth Univ., April 2–4, 1980, Williamsburg, Virginia; Paul H. Douglas, *American Apprenticeship and Industrial Education* (New York: Columbia UP, Studies in History, Economics and Public Law no. 216, 1921); Bernice M. Fisher, *Industrial Education, American Ideals and Institutions* (Madison: Univ. of Wisconsin Press,

1967); Charles T. Schmidt, Jr., "Education: Can Business Do a Better Job?" *Management of Personnel Quarterly*, Spring 1968; U.S. Dept. of Labor, ETA, *Classroom Training—The OIC Approach: CETA Program Models* (Washington: 1978).

See also APPRENTICESHIP, LABOR EDUCATION, TRAINING, VESTIBULE SCHOOL, VOCATIONAL EDUCATION.

industrial effort The term has reference generally to an employee's motivation and desire to operate at peak or maximum efficiency. Performance or output is related to effort, but effort alone may not result in peak performance, either in output or quality.

Methods of compensation in industrial plants are generally based on actual efficiency or performance and not on the amount of effort shown by the individual employee. However, some supervisory employees consider the effort factor in making recommendations for a merit rating increase or for a promotion, even though the actual performance potential of the individual may not be as high as that of another who shows less effort or interest in his job. Other factors, such as punctuality and cooperativeness, may play a part in rating employees.

Source reference: Z. Clark Dickinson, *Compensating Industrial Effort* (New York: Ronald Press, 1937).

See also EFFICIENCY RATING, MERIT RATING.

industrial employment Generally refers to employment in productive industries such as processing and manufacturing. Service industries and agricultural labor are excluded.

Source reference: Elsie B. Solter, "Industrial Employment in War and Peace," *America's Needs and Resources* (New York: Twentieth Century Fund, 1947).

See also EMPLOYMENT STATISTICS.

industrial engineering A term designed to describe the application of engineering techniques and processes to the industrial plant. In its early application, the term was used primarily in connection with the determination of wage rates and the application of incentive systems. The term, however, now has much broader coverage and may include such things as plant layout, the flow of goods and materials, and specific processes and other engineering techniques which are designed to increase production.

Source references: Michael A. Campion and Eileen J. Phelan, "Biomechanics and the Design of Industrial Jobs," *PJ*, Dec. 1981; David A. Folker, "Does the Industrial Engineer Dehumanize Jobs?" *Personnel*, July/Aug. 1973; William Gomberg, "Union Attitudes on the Application of Industrial Engineering Techniques to Collective Bargaining," *Personnel*, May 1948; ILO, *Introduction to Work Study* (3d ed., Geneva: 1978); William Grant Ireson and Eugene L. Grant (ed.), *Handbook of Industrial Engineering and Management* (2d ed., Englewood Cliffs; PH, 1971); David Lasser, "Labor Looks at Industrial Engineering," *Advanced Management*, Jan. 1956; Richard G. Pearson and Mahmoud A. Ayoub, "Ergonomics Aids Industrial Accident and Injury Control," *Management Review*, Nov. 1975; William Penzer, "Bridging the Industrial Engineering/Behavioral Science Gap," *PJ*, Aug. 1973; Charles D. Scheips, "The Humanization of Work," *Personnel*, Sept./Oct. 1972.

industrial espionage *See* ANTI-UNION PRACTICES, ESPIONAGE, LAFOLLETTE COMMITTEE, NATIONAL LABOR RELATIONS BOARD.

industrial fatigue *See* FATIGUE, FATIGUE COSTS, FATIGUE STUDY, REST PERIOD, SPEED-UP.

industrial homework *See* HOMEWORK, INDUSTRIAL.

industrial hygiene Those aspects of medicine which apply to the environment in the plant or factory and in any way affect the well-being, health, and medical safety of workers.

Industrial disease related to the job or the working conditions surrounding the particular plant or facility has received increased attention during much of the 20th century. Factors which seek to maintain the well-being of the individual and to prevent disease or uncomfortable working conditions tend to contribute toward the safety and productivity of the employee. Most states have codes dealing with those working conditions which affect the health of workers. These codes may be supervised and enforced by the state department of labor or the state department of health.

Source references: Andrew J. J. Brennan, "How to Set Up a Corporate Wellness Program," *Management Review*, May 1983; Murray C. Brown, "Health Hazards in the Workplace," *American Federationist*, May 1966; ILO, *Hygiene in Shops and Offices* (Geneva: Conference Report no. 6(1), 1962); National Health Forum, *The Health of People Who Work*, ed. by Albert Q. Maisel (New York: National Health Council, 1960); U.S. Dept. of Labor, Manpower Administration, *Health and Safety Aspects of Automation and Technological Change* (Washington: 1964).

industrial injury *See* INDUSTRIAL ACCIDENT.

industrial insurance The variety of insurance available to industry as protection against various risks such as employer's liability insurance, workers compensation insurance, and group health insurance.

See also DISABILITY INSURANCE, EMPLOYER'S LIABILITY INSURANCE, GROUP INSURANCE, HEALTH INSURANCE, MUTUAL STRIKE AID, UNEMPLOYMENT INSURANCE, WORKERS COMPENSATION.

industrialization Refers to the changes from agricultural and domestic stages of economic development to the factory or industrial system.

Source references: John T. Dunlop et al., *Industrialism and Industrial Man Reconsidered, Some Perspectives on a Study Over Two Decades of the Problems of Labor and Management in Economic Growth* (Princeton: The Inter-University Study of Human Resources in National Development, 1975); Clark Kerr et al., "Industrialism and World Society," *Harvard BR*, Jan./Feb. 1961; ———, *Industrialization and Industrial Man* (2d ed., New York: Oxford UP, 1964); ———, "Postscript to 'Industrialism and Industrial Man,'" *ILR*, June 1971; Wilbert E. Moore, *Industrialization and Labor* (Ithaca: Cornell UP, 1951); Simon Rottenberg, "Labor's Role in Industrialization," *Annals*, Jan. 1953; Yves Sabolo, "Industrialisation, Exports and Employment," *ILR*, July/Aug. 1980.

See also TECHNOLOGICAL UNEMPLOYMENT.

industrial journalism The term generally is used to describe plant publications issued by a company dealing with general conditions in the plant and reporting on the basic operations and activities of the company and its employees.

See also HOUSE ORGAN, LABOR JOURNALISM.

industrial jurisprudence The counterpart of the judicial system in industrial relations. Slichter indicates that it is the rules labor and management fashion to define their specific rights and obligations in the workplace. It is a system which attempts to prevent arbitrary discipline, discharge, or denial of promotion or benefits. Contract terms, plant or shop rules, and informal practices establish "the law of the shop." Shop committees and grievance procedures are often instituted to apply and interpret these rules and policies.

Source reference: Sumner H. Slichter, *Union Policies and Industrial Management* (Washington: Brookings Institution, 1941).

industrial library Organized materials, including books, magazines, and other publications of a general or technical nature set up by an employer for use by his employees.

The industrial library has become increasingly useful in the educational and training program of many companies and its facilities are designed to be helpful to all in the plant. Some companies encourage employees and their families to make use of library facilities and to take a greater interest in advancement and educational opportunities as well as in technical information which ultimately will be of benefit to the company. In some plants the industrial library is an arm of the research organization and cooperates very closely with it.

Source references: Susan V. Billingsley, "Industrial Libraries—Some Personnel Problems Not in the Books," *PJ*, Sept. 1961; "How the Company Library Serves," *Conference Board Record*, May 1965; Samuel Sass, "Industrial Libraries Come of Age," *Management Review*, March 1957.

industrial Magna Carta *See* CLAYTON ACT OF 1914, MAGNA CARTA, NATIONAL LABOR RELATIONS ACT, NORRIS-LAGUARDIA ACT.

industrial medicine The extension of medical techniques to the industrial scene designed to prevent and treat illness, and rehabilitate individuals who, because of sickness or injury, are unable to continue their productive employment.

Established to meet special problems such as accidents and illness through the use of industrial nurses, many programs have developed so that their emphasis is on the prevention of illness rather than the treatment or rehabilitation of employees. The problems of industrial medicine are closely related to safety engineering and may also be a part of the education program within a plant.

Source references: Robert D. Caplan et al., *Job Demands and Worker Health; Main Effects and Occupational Differences* (Washington: U.S. Dept. of HEW, Public Health Service, 1975); N. E. Cooper, "Vocational Reintegration of Handicapped Workers with Assistive Devices," *ILR*, May/June 1977; Audrey Freedman, *Industry Response to Health Risk* (New York: The Conference Board, Report no. 811, 1981); Rhoda L. and Bernard Goldstein, *Doctors and Nurses in Industry; Social Aspects of In-Plant Medical Programs* (New Brunswick: Rutgers Univ., Institute of Management and Labor Relations, 1967); Rutherford T. Johnstone and Seward E. Miller, *Occupational Diseases and Industrial Medicine* (Philadelphia: Saunders, 1960); William A. Toomey, Jr., *Labor Relations Aspects of Industrial Medicine* (Ithaca: Cornell Univ., NYSSILR, 1960); U.S. Dept. of HEW, Public Health Service, *Man, Medicine and Work: Historic Events in Occupational Medicine* (Washington: Pub. no. 1044, 1964); Richard E. Walters, "Does Your Company Need a Doctor?" *PJ*, Nov. 1962; G. K. Warner, Jr., "An Effective Industrial Medical Department," *PJ*, Feb. 1962.

See also ABSENTEEISM, INDUSTRIAL ACCIDENT, SAFETY PROGRAMS.

industrial mobility The ability of workers to move from one job to another, usually from one geographic area to another. It may also refer to the ability of workers to adjust quickly to the needs of an expanding war economy, or their return to the normal or postwar production facility without major loss in skills or in job opportunities. The term is generally used as synonymous with labor mobility.

Source references: Leonard P. Adams and Robert L. Aronson, *Workers and Industrial Change—A Case Study of Labor Mobility* (Ithaca: NYSSILR, Cornell Univ., 1957); Thomas G. Gutteridge, "Labor Market Adaptations of Displaced Technical Professionals," *ILRR*, July 1978; Dale E. Hathaway, "The Farm Worker's Transition to Industry," *MLR*, Jan. 1966; Charles A. Myers and W. Rupert MacLaurin, *The Movement of Factory Workers: A Study of a New England Industrial Community* (New York: Wiley, 1943); Gladys L. Palmer et al., *The Reluctant Job Changer: Studies in Work Attachments and Aspirations* (Philadelphia: Univ. of Pennsylvania Press, 1962); U.S. Dept. of HEW, Social Rehabilitation Service, *Overview Study of the Dynamics of Worker Job Mobility; National Study of Social Welfare and Rehabilitation Workers, Work, and Organizational Contexts* (Washington: Research Report no. 1, 1971); U.S. Dept. of Labor, OMAT, *Mobility and Worker Adaptation to Economic Change in the United States* (Washington: Bull. no. 1, 1963).

See also GEOGRAPHICAL MOBILITY, INTERNAL MOBILITY, LABOR MOBILITY, OCCUPATIONAL MOBILITY, WAR MANPOWER COMMISSION.

industrial music *See* MUSIC AT WORK.

industrial nurse In a small plant, the person who has the primary problem of promoting the health of the workers in the plant. The functions of the nurse may include the operation of the dispensary as well as providing limited medical examinations and the handling of minor injuries and illnesses.

In a large plant with a well-organized industrial medical program the work of the nurse may be relatively routine and concerned with the handling of more specialized problems on a regular basis.

Source references: Patricia E. O'Brien, "Health, Safety and the Corporate Balance Sheet," *PJ*, Aug. 1973; Margaret L. Steele, "Person to Person—Method and Necessity of Industrial Nursing," *PJ*, Nov. 1961; U.S. Dept. of HEW, Public Health Service, *Occupational Health Nurses: Initial Survey*

(Washington: Pub. no. 1470, 1966); ———, *Public Health Nursing in Industry* (Washington: Pub. no. 1788, 1968).

industrial paternalism *See* PATERNALISM, EMPLOYER.

industrial peace The term is used to describe the relationship between labor and management in which relatively little conflict exists. The term is sometimes used synonymously with the absence of any serious conflict.

During the great industrial unrest of the 1880s and 1890s, many solutions were offered to achieve industrial peace. Compulsory arbitration was one that was widely suggested.

In recent years, emphasis has shifted to the study of those factors which contribute to industrial peace. A series of studies supported by the National Planning Association was made among some of the major industries and unions to determine the ingredients which have been found to be helpful to the parties in meeting their problems on a mature and reasonably satisfactory basis. These studies called attention to the fact that there is much more harmony and satisfactory working relationships than conflict.

The factors widely emphasized in the 13 studies as measures of mature and stable labor-management relations are: the acceptance by both parties of collective bargaining; the acceptance of private ownership and operation of the industry by unions; the acceptance by employers of the need for strong, responsible, and democratic unions; the loyalty of workers to their union; mutual trust between the parties and no serious ideological incompatibilities; the approach to the solution of problems on a nonlegalistic and problem-centered basis; a large degree of information sharing between labor and management; the prompt settlement of grievances; and substantial union-management consultation. All of these factors, of course, will not exist in every situation, but they are the main ingredients found to be conducive to industrial peace.

Source references: David L. Cole, *The Quest for Industrial Peace* (New York: McGraw-Hill, 1963); Ann Douglas, *Industrial Peacemaking* (New York: Columbia UP, 1962); NPA, *Case Studies on the Causes of Industrial Peace, No. 1—Crown Zellerbach Corp., No. 2—The Libbey-Owens-Ford Glass Co., No. 3—Dewey & Almy Chemical Co., No. 4—Hickey-Freeman Co., No. 5—Sharon Steel Corp., No. 6—Lockheed Aircraft Corp., No. 7—Nashua Gummed & Coated Paper Co., PP–71—The Development of a Policy for Industrial Peace in Atomic Energy, No. 8—Marathon Corp., No. 9—Minnequa Plant of Colorado Fuel & Iron Corp., No. 10—The LaPointe Machine Tool Co., No. 11—American Velvet Co., No. 12—Atlantic Steel Co., No. 13—Working Harmony in 18 Companies, No. 14—Fundamentals of Labor Peace: A Final Report* (Washington: 1948–1953); Harold J. Ruttenberg, "The Strategy of Industrial Peace," *Harvard BR*, Winter 1939; Hubert Somervell, *Industrial Peace in Our Time* (New York: Macmillan, 1952); U.S. National Commission for Industrial Peace, *Report and Recommendations* (Washington: 1974); William Foote Whyte, *Pattern for Industrial Peace* (New York: Harper, 1951).

See also ARBITRATION; ARBITRATION, COMPULSORY; MEDIATION; NATIONAL EMERGENCY BOARDS.

industrial physician The doctor hired by a company to handle the problems relating to the health and care of its employees.

The functions of the doctor may include any one or more of the following activities: the examination of workers either prior to employment or upon rehire or examination after a medical operation; periodic physical check-ups; the handling of occupational diseases; inspection of sanitary conditions; the prevention of infectious diseases; the supervision of general health and hygienic conditions of the plant, and the care and review of hazards which might affect the well-being of the individual.

Source references: Rhoda L. and Bernard Goldstein, *Doctors and Nurses in Industry: Social Aspects of In-Plant Medical Programs* (New Brunswick: Institute of Management and Labor Relations, Rutgers Univ., 1967); William P. Shepard, *The Physician in Industry* (New York: McGraw-Hill, 1961).

See also FACTORY INSPECTION, INDUSTRIAL HYGIENE, INDUSTRIAL MEDICINE, INDUSTRIAL NURSE, SAFETY.

industrial poison Those chemicals, materials, or other ingredients which are worked on by employees or are part of the manufacturing process which may be harmful or toxic to employees.

Federal and state departments of labor have given consideration to the problems created by the use of industrial poisons. State safety codes and company practices are designed to minimize damage from this hazard in industrial production.

Source reference: Alice Hamilton, *Industrial Poisons in the United States* (New York: Macmillan, 1925).

See also HATTERS' SHAKES, INDUSTRIAL DISEASE, MERCURY POISONING, OCCUPATIONAL SAFETY AND HEALTH ACT (OSHA) OF 1970, RADIUM POISONING.

industrial psychology Concerned with the behavior and motivation of individual employees either in their immediate or larger social groupings. The industrial psychologist seeks to study the individual in his industrial environment and his relationships with others either in the work group or the larger plant group.

Industrial psychology may concern itself with the intergroup reactions and adjustments of individuals in the plant and their behavior in relation to specific types of motivation suggested by the employer. The industrial psychologist may examine the psychological adjustments of individuals in relation to the basic attitude of supervisors, the effect of the use of music, the amount of lighting available, or other factors which may have some impact on the individual.

The industrial psychologist may also conduct testing of employees.

Source references: Bernard M. Bass and Gerald V. Barrett, *Man, Work, and Organizations; An Introduction to Industrial and Organizational Psychology* (Boston: Allyn and Bacon, 1972); Wayne F. Cascio, *Applied Psychology in Personnel Management* (Reston, Va.: Reston Pub., 1978); Eugene Louis Cass and Frederick G. Zimmer (ed.), *Man and Work in Society, A Report on the Symposium Held on the Occasion of the 50th Anniversary of the Original Hawthorne Studies, Oakbrook, Illinois, November 10–13, 1974* (New York: Van Nostrand Reinhold, 1975); Louis A. Ferman and Jeanne P. Gordus (ed.), *Mental Health and the Economy* (Kalamazoo: Upjohn Institute for Employment Research, 1979); Edwin A. Fleishman and Alan R. Bass (ed.), *Studies in Personnel and Industrial Psychology* (3d ed., Homewood: Dorsey Press, 1974); Edwin E. Ghiselli and Clarence W. Brown, *Personnel and Industrial Psychology* (2d ed., New York: McGraw-Hill, 1955); Michael E. Gordon and William J. Fitzgibbons, "Unions and Psychology—An Updated View," *American Federationist*, Sept. 1979; Harry Levinson, "The Abrasive Personality," *Harvard BR*, May/June 1978; Fred Luthans and Robert Kreitner, *Organizational Behavior Modification* (Glenview, Ill.: Scott, Foresman, 1975); Rolf E. Rogers, "Psychosomatic Aspects of Modern Organizations," *Human Resource Management*, Spring 1973; George C. Thornton, III and Philip G. Benson, "Industrial Psychologists as Expert Witnesses: Role Conflicts in Fair Employment Litigation," *LLJ*, July 1980; Joseph Tiffin and Ernest J. McCormick, *Industrial Psychology* (5th ed., Englewood Cliffs: PH, 1965); Kenneth N. Wexley and Gary A. Yukl (ed.), *Organizational Behavior and Industrial Psychology: Readings and Commentary* (New York: Oxford Univ. Press, 1975).

See also SENSITIVITY TRAINING.

industrial recreation One phase of the industrial environment of the worker. It is concerned with the types of facilities helpful to the worker in adjusting to the plant situation and to his job.

During the period when unions were less accepted than they are now, the recreation program of a company, no matter how well intentioned, was considered by the union as a block to unionization. The recreational program—the basketball team, the softball team, the bowling alleys and other facilities—was regarded as designed essentially to establish a closer bond between the worker and the company and a lesser bond between the worker and a labor organization.

Recreation programs may also include those sponsored by labor unions.

Source references: BNA, *Social, Recreational and Holiday Programs* (Washington: PPF Survey no. 109, 1975); Karen Debats, "Industrial Recreation Programs: A New

Look at an Old Benefit," *PJ*, Aug. 1981; Sidney Kraus, "Bowling as an Important Industrial Recreation Activity," *PJ*, July 1969; Howard N. Morse, "Personnel Recreation Programs—Is the Company Liable for Injuries to Employees?" *PJ*, Dec. 1961.

industrial relations The term has been defined broadly as dealing with everything that affects the relationship of the individual worker or groups of workers to the employer. It involves anything which affects the employee from the time he is interviewed until he leaves his job. In this definition all relationships including such things as recruiting, hiring, placement, training, discipline, promotion, layoff, termination, wages, salaries, overtime, bonuses, profit-sharing stock plans, education, health, safety, sanitation, recreation, housing, hours of work, rest, vacation, unemployment, sickness benefits, accidents, old age, and disability are in the industrial relations area. This definition holds the collective bargaining process to be only a part of the industrial relations process. Others take the view that industrial relations means only union-management relations.

Source references: Lee Balliet, *Survey of Labor Relations* (Washington: BNA, 1981); Jack Barbash, "Values in Industrial Relations: The Case of the Adversary Principle," *Proceedings of the 33d A/M, IRRA*, ed. by Barbara Dennis (Madison: 1981); Solomon Barkin, "Diversity in Industrial Relations Patterns," *LLJ*, Nov. 1976; John T. Dunlop, *Industrial Relations Systems* (New York: Holt, 1958); Audrey Freedman, *Managing Labor Relations* (New York: The Conference Board, Report no. 765, 1979); Julius G. Getman, *Labor Relations; Law, Practice and Policy* (Mineola, N.Y.: Foundation Press, 1978); Thomas A. Kochan, *Collective Bargaining and Industrial Relations; From Theory to Policy and Practice* (Homewood: Irwin, 1980); Richard A. Lester, *Labor and Industrial Relations* (New York: Macmillan, 1951); Benjamin Martin and Everett M. Kassalow (ed.), *Labor Relations in Advanced Industrial Societies; Issues and Problems* (Washington: Carnegie Endowment for International Peace, 1980); Daniel Quinn Mills, *Labor-Management Relations* (New York: McGraw-Hill, 1978); Richard B. Morris (ed.), *Labor and Management* (New York: New York Times, 1973); Herbert R. Northrup and Richard L. Rowan (ed.), *Employee Relations and Regulations in the '80s* (Philadelphia: Univ. of Pennsylvania, Wharton School, Industrial Research Unit, LRPP Series no. 22, 1982); Lloyd George Reynolds, *Labor Economics and Labor Relations* (7th ed., Englewood Cliffs: PH, 1978); Michael J. Shershin and W. Randy Boxx, "Building Positive Union-Management Relations," *PJ*, June 1975; Sumner H. Slichter, *The Challenge of Industrial Relations* (New York: Cornell UP, 1947); Arthur A. Sloane and Fred Witney, *Labor Relations* (3d ed., Englewood Cliffs: PH, 1977); George Strauss (ed.), *Organizational Behavior: Research and Issues* (Madison: IRRA, 1974); Arnold R. Weber and John T. Dunlop, *The Changing Environment in Industrial Relations; The Industrial Relations Agenda for the Next 20 Years* (East Lansing: Michigan State Univ., School of Labor and IR, 1976); Wesley M. Wilson, *The Labor Relations Primer* (Homewood: Dow Jones-Irwin, 1973).

See also EMPLOYER-EMPLOYEE RELATIONS, EMPLOYMENT RELATIONS.

Industrial Relations; A Journal of Economy and Society Journal published and issued three times a year by the Institute of Industrial Relations, University of California at Berkeley. It includes "articles and symposia on all aspects of the employment relationship" with particular attention to labor economics, sociology, psychology, political science, and law.

industrial relations centers Organizations, variously known as Centers, Institutes, or Labor and Management Programs, which have indicated an interest in the field of industrial relations. The specific areas of concern and specialization vary with the institutions. The list below indicates organizations interested in the labor-management relations area.

University of Alabama, Human Resources Institute, Box J, University, Ala. 35486.

Boston University, Institute on Employment Policy, Boston, Mass. 62215.

University of British Columbia, Institute of Industrial Relations, 453 Henry Angus Building, Vancouver, B.C., Canada V6T 1W5.

California Institute of Technology, Industrial Relations Center, Pasadena, Calif. 91125.

University of California, Institute of Industrial Relations, 2521 Channing Way, Berkeley, Calif. 94720.

University of California, Institute of Industrial Relations, Los Angeles, Calif. 90024.

Carnegie-Mellon University, Center for Labor Studies, School of Urban and Public Affairs, Pittsburgh, Pa. 15213.

Case Western Reserve University, Division of Industrial Relations, University Circle, Cleveland, Ohio 44106.

University of Cincinnati, Department of Management, College of Business Administration, Cincinnati, Ohio 45221.

Cleveland State University, Industrial Relations Center, 1983 East 24th St., Cleveland, Ohio 44115.

Columbia University, Graduate School of Business, 116th St. and Broadway, New York, N.Y. 10027.

Cornell University, New York State School of Industrial and Labor Relations, P.O. Box 1000, Ithaca, N.Y. 14853.

Dalhousie University, Industrial Relations Section, 1315 LeMarchant St., Halifax, N.S., Canada B3H 3J5.

University of the District of Columbia, Labor Studies Center, 724 Ninth St., N.W., Suite 210, Washington, D.C. 20001.

Georgia State University, Institute of Industrial Relations, University Plaza, Atlanta, Ga. 30303.

Harvard University, Baker Library, Graduate School of Business Administration, Soldiers Field, Boston, Mass. 02163.

Harvard University, Littauer Center, Cambridge, Mass. 02138.

University of Hawaii, Industrial Relations Center, 2425 Campus Rd., Honolulu, Hawaii 96822.

University of Illinois, Institute of Labor and Industrial Relations, 504 E. Armory Ave., Champaign, Ill. 61820.

Midwest Center for Public Sector Labor Relations, School of Public and Environmental Affairs, Indiana University, Bloomington, Ind. 47405.

Indiana University of Pennsylvania, Center for the Study of Labor Relations, Indiana, Pa. 15705.

University of Iowa, Department of Industrial Relations and Human Resources, Iowa City, Iowa 52242.

Université Laval, Département des Relations Industrielles, Ste. Foy, Quebec, Canada G1K 7P4.

London School of Economics and Political Science, Houghton St., London, England WC2A 2AE.

Loyola University of Chicago, Institute of Industrial Relations, 820 N. Michigan Ave., Chicago, Ill. 60611.

University of Maryland, Division of Organizational Behavior and Industrial Relations, College of Business and Management, College Park, Md. 20742.

Massachusetts Institute of Technology, Sloan School of Management, Cambridge, Mass. 02139.

University of Massachusetts, Labor Relations and Research Center, 102 Draper Hall, Amherst, Mass. 01002.

McGill University, Industrial Relations Centre, 1001 Sherbrooke St., West, Montreal, Quebec, Canada H3A 1G5.

Michigan State University, School of Labor and Industrial Relations, South Kedzie Hall, East Lansing, Mich. 48824.

University of Michigan, Industrial Relations Library, 330 Graduate School of Business Administration, Ann Arbor, Mich. 48109.

University of Minnesota, Industrial Relations Center, 271–19th Ave. South, Minneapolis, Minn. 55116.

Université de Montréal, Département des Relations Industrielles, P.O. Box 6128, Montreal, Quebec, Canada H3C 3J7.

University of New South Wales, Department of Industrial Relations, P.O. Box 1, Kensington, NSW, Australia 2033.

City University of New York, National Center for the Study of Collective Bargaining in Higher Education and the Professions, Baruch College, 17 Lexington Ave., Box 322, New York, N.Y. 10010.

New York Institute of Technology, Center for Labor and Industrial Relations, Old Westbury, N.Y. 11568.

New York University, Institute of Labor Relations, 70 Washington Square South, New York, N.Y. 10012.

Ohio State University, Center for Human Resource Research, 5701 North High St., Worthington, Ohio 43085.

Oklahoma State University, Manpower Research and Training Center, Stillwater, Okla. 74074.

Pennsylvania State University, Department of Labor Studies, 901 Liberal Arts Building, University Park, Pa. 16802.

University of Pennsylvania, Industrial Research Unit, Wharton School, 3733 Spruce St., Philadelphia, Pa. 19104.

Princeton University, Industrial Relations Section, P.O. Box 248, Princeton, N.J. 08540.

Purdue University, Krannert Graduate School of Management, West Lafayette, Ind. 47907.

Queen's University, Industrial Relations Centre, Kingston, Ontario, Canada K7L 3N6.

University of Rhode Island, Organizational Management and Industrial Relations, College of Business Administration, Kingston, R.I. 02881.

Rutgers University, Institute of Management and Labor Relations, Ryders Lane, New Brunswick, N.J. 08903.

St. Joseph's University, Institute of Industrial Relations, 5600 City Ave., Philadelphia, Pa. 19131.

San Diego State College, Institute of Labor Economics, San Diego, Calif. 92115.

Shippensburg State College, School of Business Administration, Shippensburg, Pa. 17257.

Temple University, Center for Labor and Human Resource Studies, Philadelphia, Pa. 19122.

University of Toronto, Centre for Industrial Relations, 123 St. George St., Toronto, Ontario, Canada M5S 1A1.

University of Utah, Institute of Industrial Relations, Salt Lake City, Utah 84112.

University of Warwick, Industrial Relations Research Unit, Coventry, Warwickshire, England CV4 7AL.

Wayne State University, Archives of Labor History and Urban Affairs, Detroit, Mich. 48202.

Wayne State University, Walter P. Reuther Library, 5401 Cass Ave., Detroit, Mich. 48202.

West Virginia University, Institute of Industrial Relations, Morgantown, W. Va. 26506.

State Historical Society of Wisconsin, 816 State St., Madison, Wisc. 53706.

University of Wisconsin-Madison, Industrial Relations Research Institute, 8432 Social Science Building, 1180 Observatory Drive, Madison, Wisc. 53706.

Industrial Relations Counselors, Inc. *See* ORGANIZATION RESOURCES COUNSELORS, INC.

industrial relations court *See* KANSAS COURT OF INDUSTRIAL RELATIONS.

industrial relations manager A term commonly used to describe the management official responsible for conduct of his company's relations with unions representing employees. He also may be responsible for the company's personnel policies, especially in smaller firms. In larger concerns, this official may be an executive officer, usually a vice president. Personnel functions, or employer-employee relations—as distinct from employer-union relations—may be under the jurisdiction of a different officer of the company.

Formerly it was not unusual for the industrial relations manager to double in brass as public relations officer also. This practice is diminishing, if not disappearing.

See also EMPLOYMENT MANAGER, PERSONNEL DIRECTOR.

industrial relations research *See* RESEARCH, INDUSTRIAL RELATIONS.

Industrial Relations Research Association A private organization, formed in 1947, to encourage and disseminate research in industrial relations. Its annual proceedings are devoted to discussions of problems and reports on current research in the field of industrial relations.

Address: 7226 Social Science Building, University of Wisconsin, Madison, Wis. 53706. Tel. (608) 262–2762

industrial revolution A term generally applied to the changes which occurred in

England roughly between the middle of the 18th century and the first 40 years of the 19th century. The period was characterized by the urbanization of population, the mechanization of agricultural processes, and the development of the factory system. These developments were made possible by use of the steam engine and other labor-saving machinery.

These changes had their origin in a much earlier period, and included such inventions as the flying shuttle and the spinning jenny, but accelerated toward the middle of the 18th and first half of the 19th century.

The misery and poverty which resulted for certain groups, particularly in factory operations, and the social and economic upheaval which accompanied these changes seemed to justify the term "revolution" rather than "evolution."

Source references: F. C. Dietz, *The Industrial Revolution* (New York: Holt, 1927); J. C. Hammond, "Industrial Revolution and Discontent," *Economic History Review*, Jan. 1930; Arnold Toynbee, *The Industrial Revolution* (Boston: Beacon Press, 1956).

industrial safety *See* SAFETY.

industrial standards The term is used to describe the actual criteria set up in the plant which are used as measures of performance. They may relate to the output or quality of the materials in the product. Standards may be modified when the material or equipment is changed or when it is possible to modify the engineering or economic processes.

See also LABOR STANDARD.

Industrial Trade Unions; National Organization of (Ind) Its quarterly publication is *Union Craft*.

Address: 148–06 Hillside Ave., Jamaica, N.Y. 11435. Tel. (212) 291–3434

industrial union A term used to describe the structure of a particular union in relation to company operation. Workers in an industrial union are organized essentially on the basis of the product. For example, workers in rubber, steel, automobile, and mining operations are essentially organized along industrial lines. Generally, all the workers in a plant or industry, unskilled, semiskilled, and skilled, are included in the industrial union. This type of structure is sometimes referred to as vertical unionism.

Craft unionism is sometimes referred to as horizontal unionism. Many of the early organizations of the AFL started as craft unions, but as industrial development progressed and greater plant integration developed, a large number of labor organizations, even though organized along craft lines, functioned as industrial unions.

In many plants which have been organized along industrial lines, there may also occasionally be small units of highly skilled employees who are able to carve out separate bargaining units under the terms of the National Labor Relations Act. For example, locals of pattern makers or other highly skilled groups may retain their craft organization and set up small bargaining units even where the majority of workers are organized on an industrial basis.

Source references: Julia E. Johnsen (comp.), *Industrial vs. Craft Unionism* (New York: Wilson, 1937); James O. Morris, *Conflict Within the AFL: A Study of Craft Versus Industrial Unionism, 1901–1938* (Ithaca: Cornell UP, 1958); Raymond J. Walsh, *C.I.O. Industrial Unionism in Action* (New York: Norton, 1937); Arnold R. Weber, "The Craft-Industrial Issue Revisited: A Study of Union Government," *ILRR*, April 1963.

See also BARGAINING UNIT, CRAFT UNION, LABOR UNION.

industrial union council CIO counterpart of the AFL central labor council; an organization of former CIO unions in a locality or city.

With the merger of the AFL and CIO, the CIO industrial union councils were combined with existing AFL central labor councils.

Source reference: Edward Levinson, *Labor on the March* (New York: University Books, 1956).

Industrial Union Department One of the departments of the AFL-CIO, concerned primarily with the interests of "industrial" as opposed to "craft" unions. The Department includes unions of both production and white collar workers. Basically, it is made up of former CIO unions. Its quarterly publication is *Viewpoint*.

The unions affiliated with the Industrial Union Department include: Aluminum,

Brick and Glass Workers; Automobile Workers; Bakery, Confectionery and Tobacco Workers; Boilermakers; Carpenters; Cement Workers; Chemical Workers; Clothing and Textile Workers; Communications Workers; Coopers; Electronic and Machine Workers; Electrical Workers; Operating Engineers; Firemen and Oilers; Food and Commercial Workers; Furniture Workers; Ladies Garment Workers; Glass, Pottery and Plastics Workers; Flint Glass Workers; American Federation of Government Employees; Grain Millers; Graphic Arts; Industrial Workers; Laborers; Marine and Shipbuilding Workers; Maritime Union; Mechanics Educational Society; Metal Polishers; Molders; Newspaper Guild; Office and Professional Employees; Oil, Chemical and Atomic Workers; Painters; Paperworkers; Plumbers; Printing and Graphic Communications Union; Federation of Professional Athletes; Professional and Technical Engineers; Railway Carmen; Retail, Wholesale and Department Store Union; Rubber Workers; Service Employees; Sheet Metal Workers; Theatrical Stage Employees; State, County and Municipal Employees; Steelworkers; Stove, Furnace and Allied Appliance Workers; American Federation of Teachers; Telegraph Workers; Textile Workers; Transit Union; Transport Workers; Upholsterers; Utility Workers; and Woodworkers.

Address: AFL-CIO Building, 815 16th St., N.W., Washington, D.C. 20006. Tel. (202) 842–7800

See also AFL-CIO DEPARTMENTS.

industrial welfare Those programs which affect the conditions of employment of the individual. The welfare program of a company may concern itself with various phases of industrial hygiene, medical programs, and the like. It may involve housing accommodations and other phases of activity which affect the well-being of the employee.

See also WELFARE PLANS.

industrial workers The general term to apply to employees engaged in modern industrial operations and to distinguish them from agricultural workers and other groups not engaged primarily in industrial operations. Other terms that apply to special groups of workers are white-collar worker, blue-collar worker, etc.

Source references: Eric G. Chambers, *Psychology and the Industrial Worker* (New York: Cambridge UP, 1951); Harvey G. Forster, *The Industrial Worker: His Quest for Meaning* (Toronto: 1966); Norman Ware, *The Industrial Worker* (Boston: Houghton-Mifflin, 1924).

Industrial Workers of America; International Union, Allied (AFL-CIO) Formerly known as the International Union, United Automobile Workers of America (AFL-CIO). Its official monthly publication is the *Allied Industrial Worker.*

This former AFL group, like the CIO group, was the outgrowth of the National Council of Automobile Workers, which had been formed in 1934 to integrate the federal labor unions that had been formed in the automobile industry. A segment of the group that went over to the CIO in 1935 withdrew in 1939 to reaffiliate with the AFL. It is now a member union of the AFL-CIO.

Address: 3520 West Oklahoma Ave., Milwaukee, Wis. 53215. Tel. (414) 645–9500

Industrial Workers of the World Sometimes known as the IWW or "Wobblies." The IWW was established in 1905 although its origin goes back to strikes in 1903 and 1904. The prime purpose of the organization of the IWW was to compete with existing conservative unions such as those of the AFL. The IWW felt that labor and management had nothing in common, that their basic objectives were divergent and always would be, and that therefore any attempt to establish collective bargaining agreements would be ineffective. They believed in direct action, the use of the general strike, and activities designed to weaken what they referred to as the "capitalist system." Their prime purpose, at least during the early days of the organization, was to eliminate the capitalist society and to substitute for it a workers' society.

The group, when it was founded, included radical socialists, Marxian socialists, syndicalists, and anarchists. When the organization split in 1908, two major groups were formed, those believing in direct action, who remained in Chicago, and those in Detroit, representing the socialist revolutionary unions, who believed in action designed ultimately to gain control of the means of production by workers.

The concept of class struggle and opposition to evolutionary changes in the working relationship between labor and management led to the decline of the organization. The IWW was not concerned with working out reasonable adjustments and methods of solving problems, but rather in abolition of the existing wage and production system.

Source references: Paul F. Brissenden, *The I.W.W., A Study in American Syndicalism* (New York: Columbia UP, 1920); ———, *The Launching of the Industrial Workers of the World* (Berkeley: UC Press, 1913); Glen J. Broyles, "The Spokane Free Speech Fight, 1909–1910: A Study in IWW Tactics," *Labor History,* Spring 1978; Cletus E. Daniel, "In Defense of the Wheatland Wobblies: A Critical Analysis of the IWW in California," *Labor History,* Fall 1978; Melvyn Dubofsky, *We Shall Be All; A History of the Industrial Workers of the World* (Chicago: Quadrangle Books, 1969); *The Founding Convention of the IWW, Proceedings* (New York: Merit Publishers, 1969); John Gambs, *The Decline of the I.W.W.* (New York: Columbia UP, 1932); Daniel T. Hobby (ed.), " 'We Have Got Results': A Document on the Organization of Domestics in the Progressive Era," *Labor History,* Winter 1976; Clayton R. Koppes, "The Kansas Trial of the IWW, 1917–1919," *Labor History,* Summer 1975; Joyce Kornbluh (ed.), *Rebel Voices, An I.W.W. Anthology* (Ann Arbor: Univ. of Michigan Press, 1964); Charles A. Madison, "The Insurgent IWW," *Labor and Nation,* July/Aug. 1949; Patrick Renshaw, *The Wobblies* (Garden City: Doubleday, 1967); Robert C. Sims, "Idaho's Criminal Syndicalism Act: One State's Response to Radical Labor," *Labor History,* Fall 1974; Philip Taft, "The Federal Trials of the IWW," *Labor History,* Winter 1962; Fred Thompson (comp.), *The I.W.W.—Its First Fifty Years (1905–1955)* (Chicago: IWW, 1955); Laura A. White, *Rise of the Industrial Workers of the World* (Lincoln: Univ. of Nebraska, 1912).

Industrial Workers Union; National (Ind) Affiliated with the National Federation of Independent Unions.

Address: 514 North Main St., P.O. Box 1893, Lima, Ohio 45802. Tel. (419) 224–1030

industry arbitrator The person designated by the parties in a labor contract to make a final and binding decision in an industry. The parties to an industrywide agreement may grant broad powers to the arbitrator or arbitration tribunal.

industrywide collective bargaining *See* COLLECTIVE BARGAINING, INDUSTRYWIDE; COLLECTIVE BARGAINING, MULTI-EMPLOYER.

industrywide strike A work stoppage which involves an entire industry or the major part of an industry.

inequities Working conditions, including wages and hours, which are so out of line with those prevailing elsewhere as to warrant adjustment. How far out of line the working conditions have to be in order to be inequities will vary from case to case. Some have suggested that they must be grossly out of line or so different as to necessitate a change. The concept is similar to the "prevailing wage" or working condition concept which seeks to compare working conditions in one plant with those prevailing in other plants or within the geographic area or industry.

During World War II many wage adjustments were predicated or justified on the basis of so-called inequities. Inequities within the plant were referred to as "intra-plant inequities;" inequities between plants in the same labor market area were referred to as "inter-plant inequities." Inequities also could be claimed between different plants of the same company or between comparable industries.

Toward the end of World War II, following specific "hold-the-line" orders, a special guide for the determination of inequities was established by the use of wage brackets. Wage brackets established for a labor market area were used as guides for companies and unions seeking wage adjustments. These wage ranges were sometimes called the "sound and tested" rates existing for particular occupations or classifications within an industry or geographic area.

See also SOUND AND TESTED RATES, STANDARD RATE.

inflation A continuous or persistent upward movement of prices which may develop from such causes as a limited supply of goods and services or an increasing supply of money or credit. Typically, inflation is characterized by a decline in the buying power of standard units of money.

Inflationary tendencies bring demands by unions for upward wage adjustments, and for wage "floors." Cost-of-living adjustments or bonuses are examples of contract provisions designed to offset upward price movements during a contract term.

Source references: David W. Callahan, "Defining the Rate of Underlying Inflation," *MLR*, Sept. 1981; Otto Eckstein and Roger Brinner, *The Inflation Process in the United States* (Washington: U.S. Congress, Joint Economic Committee, 1972); Martin Feldstein, "Inflation and the American Economy," *The Public Interest*, Spring 1982; David H. Freedman, "Inflation in the United States, 1959–1974: Its Impact on Employment, Incomes and Industrial Relations," *ILR*, Aug./Sept. 1975; Steven R. Malin, "Have We Really Whipped Inflation?" *Across the Board*, Dec. 1982; Daniel J. B. Mitchell, *Controlling Inflation* (Los Angeles: UC, Institute of IR, Reprint no. 283, 1979); Geoffrey H. Moore, *The Anatomy of Inflation* (Washington: U.S. Dept. of Labor, BLS, Report no. 373, 1969); Rudy Oswald, "Inflation: Attacking the Real Causes," *American Federationist*, Jan. 1982; Wallace C. Peterson, "Inflation: Is It Controllable?" *Sloan Management Review*, Fall 1974; Robert M. Solow, "The Intelligent Citizen's Guide to Inflation," *The Public Interest*, Winter 1975; Albert T. Sommers (ed.), *Answers to Inflation and Recession: Economic Policies for a Modern Society* (New York: The Conference Board, Report no. 666, 1975); Lester C. Thurow, "Three Perspectives on the Wage Price Freeze. I. Inflation and the Alternatives," *Sloan Management Review*, Winter 1972; U.S. Congress, Joint Economic Committee, *Incentive Anti-Inflation Plans, A Study* (Washington: 1981); ———, *Studies in Price Stability and Economic Growth. Paper no. 2—Economic Policy and Inflation in the United States: A Survey of Developments from the Enactment of the Employment Act of 1946 Through 1974* (Washington: 1975); ———, *Studies in Price Stability and Economic Growth. Papers nos. 3 and 4—International Aspects of Recent Inflation* (Washington: 1975); U.S. Congressional Budget Office, *Report of the Task Force on Inflation Together with Supplemental, Additional, and Minority Views* (Washington: 1980); Stanley S. Wallack, "Inflation Versus Unemployment: Another View of the Trade-Off," *MLR*, Nov. 1971; Murray L. Wiedenbaum, *Government-Mandated Price Increases, A Neglect Aspect of Inflation* (Washington: AEI, 1975); Marvin E. Wolfgang (ed.), "Social Effects of Inflation," *Annals*, July 1981.

See also COST-OF-LIVING ADJUSTMENT, ESCALATOR CLAUSE.

informal recognition Formerly granted under Executive Order 10988 to any organization, regardless of what status may have been extended to any other organization, it permitted an organization to be heard on matters of interest to its members, but placed an agency under no obligation to seek the organization's views. Terminated under Executive Order 11491.

Source reference: Harold S. Roberts, *Labor-Management Relations in the Public Service* (Honolulu: Univ. of Hawaii Press, 1970).

See also EXCLUSIVE RECOGNITION, FORMAL RECOGNITION, NATIONAL CONSULTATION RIGHTS.

informational picketing A form of publicity picketing which has had a rather checkered career both before the NLRB and the federal courts. A majority of the Board has held the view that the publicity proviso permits "purely informational picketing . . . which has no present object of recognition." Also in the majority view that proviso is confined "to picketing where the sole objective is dissemination of information divorced from a present object of recognition." The minority of NLRB has held that this view in effect made informational picketing ineffective and suggested that the proviso be construed to permit "dual" purpose picketing—"recognition or organization picketing which truthfully advised the public (including consumers) that the employer did not have a contract with the union."

Source references: Hotel & Restaurant Employees Local 681 (Crown Cafeteria), 135

NLRB 1183, 49 LRRM 1648 (1962), *aff'd sub nom. Smitley v. NLRB*, 327 F2d 351, 55 LRRM 2302 (CA 9, 1964); Paul A. Brinker, "Section 8(b)(4)(B) and Consumer and Informational Picketing and Publicity Other than Picketing," *LLJ*, April 1972; Morris D. Forkosch, "Informational, Representational and Organizational Picketing," *LLJ*, Dec. 1955; "Illegal Picketing Under Section (8)(b)(7)—A Reexamination," *IR Law Digest*, April 1969; William S. Ostan, "The Right of Federal Civilian Employees to Picket: Confusion and Controversy," *LLJ*, April 1978.

initial spurt The amount of effort expended at the beginning of a work period. This may be due to the fact that the employee is fresh and approaches his job without fatigue. As the work period continues the work performance may tend to level off around the general norm of operation. Toward the end of the work period, there may be another spurt of effort to complete an assignment.

initiation fee A fee charged by a union as a condition to acquiring membership in the union. Under Section 8(b)(5) of the Taft-Hartley Act, it is an unfair labor practice for a union to charge employees covered by a union shop contract an initiation fee that the NLRB finds is "excessive or discriminatory under all the circumstances."

Under the Landrum-Griffin Act, a local or international union may not raise initiation fees without meeting certain procedural safeguards. In a local, the increase must be approved by majority vote in either a special membership meeting or in a membership referendum. Both must be by secret ballot. National and international unions may increase dues, fees, and assessments by majority vote in a regular or special convention, by a secret-ballot referendum of the membership, or by majority executive board vote—to be effective until the union's next convention.

Source references: BNA, *The Labor Reform Law* (Washington: 1959); Philip Taft, "Dues and Initiation Fees in Labor Unions," *Quarterly Journal of Economics*, Feb. 1946.

See also ASSESSMENTS, DUES, FEES.

injunction A prohibitory writ issued by a court to restrain an individual or a group from committing an act that is regarded as inequitable as far as the rights of some other person are concerned. For many years, the usual response to picketing and boycotts by unions was for the employer to go into court and obtain an injunction. But in 1932, Congress adopted the Norris-LaGuardia Act, forbidding the federal courts to issue injunctions in labor disputes unless certain prior conditions are fulfilled. A number of the states then adopted "Little Norris-LaGuardia Acts" patterned after the federal law.

Among the conditions that must be fulfilled before an injunction may be issued is that the union be given an opportunity to state its case; there may be no ex parte injunction. A showing also must be made that all efforts to obtain a settlement by conciliation and other methods provided by law have been exhausted and that withholding the injunction will cause more harm to one party than granting it will cause to the other.

The adoption of the Taft-Hartley Act in 1947 established a detailed code of law governing strikes, picketing, and boycotts. Additions were made to this code by the 1959 Landrum-Griffin amendments to the law. The Taft-Hartley Act, as thus amended, provides for the issuance of injunctions in three types of situations.

Under Section 10(j), the NLRB has discretionary power to seek an injunction to restrain a person from committing an alleged unfair labor practice pending adjudication of the case by the Board. Where the alleged unfair labor practice is a secondary boycott, recognition picketing, or any of the other practices forbidden by Section 8(b)(4), Section 10(l) makes it mandatory for the Board to seek an injunction pending its adjudication of the case.

The third type of situation in which an injunction may be issued under the Taft-Hartley Act involves a national emergency strike—one that, if permitted to occur, would in the opinion of the President imperil the national health or safety. Under the procedure set up under the Act, such strikes may be postponed by injunction for up to 80 days.

Injunctions also are used in the enforcement of the Fair Labor Standards Act, the secretary of labor having the authority to bring actions in the federal district courts for injunctions to restrain violations of the Act.

Source references: Roger I. Abrams, *The Labor Injunction and the Refusal to Cross Another Union's Picket Line* (Cleveland: Case Western Reserve Univ., Reprint 1976); Paul F. Brissenden, "Campaign Against the Labor Injunction," *AER*, March 1933; ———, *The Labor Injunction in Hawaii* (Washington: Public Affairs Press, 1956); George H. Cohen, "Strikes and Injunctions: The Buffalo Forge Case," *NYU 30th Annual National Conference on Labor*, ed. by Richard Adelman (New York: Bender, 1977); William J. Curtin, "Buffalo Forge and the Union's No-Strike Commitment: A Management Perspective," *Labor Law Developments 1977*, Proceedings of the 23d Annual Institute on Labor Law, SLF (New York: Bender, 1977); Joel M. Douglas, "Injunctions Under New York's Taylor Law: An Occupational Analysis," *Journal of Collective Negotiations in the Public Sector*, Vol. 10, no. 3, 1981; ———, "The Labor Injunction: Enjoining Public Sector Strikes in New York," *LLJ*, June 1980; Guy Farmer, "The Use of Injunctions in Labor Disputes: A Management View," *NYU 30th Annual National Conference on Labor*, ed. by Richard Adelman (New York: Bender, 1977); Felix Frankfurter and Nathan Greene, *The Labor Injunction* (New York: Macmillan, 1930); Carolyn Gentile, "Injunctive Relief: An Old Remedy Rejuvenated," *NYU 25th Annual Conference on Labor* (New York: Bender, 1973); Charles O. Gregory, "Government by Injunction Again," 14 *Univ. of Chicago LR* 363 (1947); Alan I. Horowitz, "The Applicability of *Boys Markets* Injunctions to Refusals to Cross a Picket Line," *IR Law Digest*, Fall 1976; "The Labor Management Relations Act (1947) and the Revival of the Labor Injunction," *Columbia LR*, July 1948; Duane McCracken, *Strike Injunctions in the New South* (Chapel Hill: Univ. of North Carolina Press, 1931); William T. Payne, "Enjoining Employers Pending Arbitration—From *M-K-T* to *Greyhound* and Beyond," *Industrial Relations LJ*, Vol. 3, no. 1, 1979; Harry H. Rains, "*Boys Market* Injunctions: Strict Scrutiny of the Presumption of Arbitrability," *LLJ*, Jan. 1977; Bernard Samoff, "NLRB Priority and Injunctions for Discriminatory Discharges," *LLJ*, Jan. 1980; Bruce H. Simon, "Injunctive Relief to Maintain the Status Quo Pending Arbitration: A Union Practitioner's View," *NYU 29th Annual Conference on Labor*, ed. by Richard Adelman (New York: Bender, 1976); Paul D. Staudohar, "The Changing Role of the Injunction in the Public Sector," *LLJ*, May 1971; Cleon A. Swayzee, *Contempt of Court in Labor Injunction Cases* (New York: Columbia UP, 1935); U.S. Congress, Senate, Committee on Labor and Public Welfare, *State Court Injunctions* (Washington: 1951); Edwin E. Witte, "Value of Injunctions in Labor Disputes," *Journal of Political Economy*, June 1924; William C. Zifchak, "Coping with Sympathy Strikes After *Buffalo Forge*: Never Send a *Boys* to Do a Man's Job," *Employee Relations LJ*, Spring 1977.

See also ADEQUATE REMEDY AT LAW, "BLANKET" INJUNCTION, EX PARTE INJUNCTION, HOT GOODS INJUNCTION, NORRIS-LAGUARDIA ACT, PERMANENT INJUNCTION, SENN V. TILE LAYERS' PROTECTIVE UNION.

Inlandboatmen's Union of the Pacific Formerly a division of the Seafarer's International Union of North America (AFL-CIO), it merged with the Atlantic, Gulf, Lakes and Inland Waters District of the SIU in September 1976.

See also ATLANTIC, GULF, LAKES AND INLAND WATERS DISTRICT.

Inland Steel Co. v. NLRB Decision upholding the NLRB ruling that Inland Steel Company was required to bargain with the Steelworkers Union on retirement and pension matters.

Source references: Inland Steel Co. v. NLRB, 170 F2d 247, 22 LRRM 2506 (CA 7, 1948), *cert. denied*, 336 US 960, 24 LRRM 2019 (1949); Dean O. Bowman, *Public Control of Labor Relations* (New York: Macmillan, 1942); Howard S. Kaltenborn, *Governmental Adjustment of Labor Disputes* (Chicago: Foundation Press, 1943); Joseph Rosenfarb, *The National Labor Policy and How It Works* (New York: Harper, 1940).

inside operatives *See* ESPIONAGE.

inside organizer Generally a union organizer who is an employee of the company and who is seeking to organize the workers of that company. The organizer's identification with the union may or may not be known.

inside union An unaffiliated union. The term often is used synonymously with company union.

Source reference: Samuel M. Salny, *Independent Unions Under the Wagner Act* (Boston: Hildreth, 1944).

See also COMPANY UNION, EMPLOYEE REPRESENTATION PLANS.

insubordination A worker's refusal or failure to obey a management directive or to comply with an established work procedure. Under certain circumstances, use of objectionable language or abusive behavior toward supervisors may be deemed to be insubordination because it reveals disrespect of management's authority. Insubordination is considered a cardinal industrial offense since it violates management's traditional right and authority to direct the work force.

Arbitrator Joseph F. Gentile in *Kay-Brunner Steel Products* (78 LA 363) states that the proven facts of "a classical case of insubordination" include: "(1) the Grievant was given orders, (2) the Grievant refused to obey the orders, (3) the orders came from the Grievant's supervisors, who were known to him, (4) the orders were reasonably related to his job and within the language of the contract, (5) the orders were clear, direct, and understood by the Grievant, (6) the Grievant was forewarned of the possible and probable consequences of his continued actions by specific reference to the contractual guidelines . . . , and (7) the Grievant was neither insulated nor protected from possible disciplinary action by his role as a representative of the employees. . . ."

The "obey now, grieve later" rule generally governs arbitral decisions in cases involving insubordination. The leading exception to this rule is refusing to follow an order that would endanger the employee's health or safety or that of other workers. Some arbitrators have found that employees are not insubordinate if they disobey an order they consider to be illegal or which would jeopardize their position, e.g., as a union representative.

Source references: BNA, *Grievance Guide* (6th ed., Washington: 1982); Joseph C. Graham III, "Arbitration of Insubordination Disputes in the Public Sector," *AJ*, Sept. 1976; William H. Leahy, "Arbitration and Insubordination of Union Stewards," *AJ*, March 1972; W. B. Nelson, "Insubordination: Arbitral 'Law' in the Reconciliation of Conflicting Employer/Employee Interests," *LLJ*, Feb. 1984; Lawrence Stessin, *Employee Discipline* (Washington: BNA, 1960).

insurance, disability *See* DISABILITY INSURANCE.

insurance, employer's liability *See* EMPLOYER'S LIABILITY INSURANCE.

insurance, group *See* GROUP INSURANCE.

insurance, health *See* HEALTH INSURANCE.

insurance, strike *See* MUTUAL STRIKE AID.

insurance, unemployment *See* UNEMPLOYMENT INSURANCE.

insurance, workers compensation Insurance plans which are required by law whereby the employer insures his workers against industrial accidents and occupational diseases. Workers injured on the job receive medical care and financial reimbursement. Workers compensation laws are enacted by the states.

The standards for the employer's responsibility, the coverage, and the waiting period are set forth in the statute. Generally the administration of the law rests with the state agency administering other labor statutes.

See also WORKERS COMPENSATION.

insurance plan A contract generally agreed to between an insurance company and the employer (sometimes after negotiation with a union) which covers the employees of a company. The plan may provide life insurance and payments to cover accidents, sickness, surgical, and hospital expenses. Costs often are shared by the company and the employees.

Collective bargaining in recent years has resulted in a wide variety of agreements providing insurance coverage of employees.

See also HEALTH BENEFIT PROGRAMS, HEALTH INSURANCE.

Insurance Workers International Union (AFL-CIO) In May 1959 the former AFL Insurance Agents International Union and the former CIO Insurance Workers of America merged to form the Insurance Workers International Union (AFL-CIO). In October 1983 the union merged with the United Food and Commercial Workers International Union (AFL-CIO).

See also FOOD AND COMMERCIAL WORKERS INTERNATIONAL UNION; UNITED (AFL-CIO).

insured plan Generally a life or other medical or health plan which is funded through an insurance company.

insured population That part of the work force which is covered by unemployment insurance and is eligible for payments when they meet the requirements for unemployment benefits under existing law.

intelligence tests Examinations or batteries of tests which attempt to measure an individual's capacity or potential. The tests, although originally designed for use in schools in order to assist in the teaching process and the setting up of reasonably homogeneous groups for such purposes, in recent years have been extended to industrial situations. Numerous tests are used in recruiting as well as in determining possible promotional opportunities.

Because of limited job opportunities for the hard-core unemployed and the disadvantaged job applicant, other testing media have been devised and substituted for the standardized intelligence tests in the employment procedure. In 1967, for example, the U.S. Employment Service and the National Urban League began a joint demonstration and research project to learn how testing can be used to open up job opportunities for blacks, including the use of the non-reading aptitude tests, the testing of basic skills in arithmetic and reading to measure the job-readiness of educationally deficient adults, the tryout of pre-testing orientation techniques providing practice in taking tests, and the use of visual aids in taking tests. The Metropolitan Life Insurance Co. of New York in 1968 began using a culture fair intelligence test to identify capable minority group applicants who, because of culturally disadvantaged backgrounds, had not acquired the verbal and arithmetical skills necessary to pass the company's standard clerical aptitude test. The test, part of a 13-week on-the-job work and study employment qualification course, measures an individual's capacity to perceive relations and is based on "the general fluid intelligence factor" which is independent of culture and a "well-stocked memory." Picture illustrations that answer multiple-choice questions are selected by the candidate.

Source references: Charles Bahn, "Can Intelligence Tests Predict Executive Competence?" *Personnel,* July/Aug. 1979; Richard S. Gillmer, "Are You Misusing Intelligence Tests?" *Personnel,* March/April 1964.

See also GRIGGS V. DUKE POWER CO., TEST.

intent A rather commonly used term in labor-management relations, particularly in the application of the provisions of the collective bargaining agreement.

In arbitration the question may be raised about the intent of the parties with respect to certain language in the agreement, as applied to situations that arise during its term. In the absence of clear language or a record of what the parties wanted to accomplish with a particular clause, an arbitrator may ask the parties what their objectives were at the time the particular language was incorporated.

The "intent" of language in a federal labor statute may be sought in the conference or other committee reports, the congressional debate, or even in the committee hearings on the bills antecedent to the statute's adoption.

intercity differential An existing or established wage differential between cities. Comparison of wage differences may be made on the basis of average or overall wages or comparison of rates of key occupations in the industries in the cities involved.

Comparisons of intercity wage differentials may be used in negotiations, either to maintain previously established relationships, or to establish parity and remove the differential. Claims might be made in negotiations that the differential should be eliminated since the factors which led to the variations are no longer valid.

See also WAGE DIFFERENTIALS.

interdepartmental The term is often used to apply to transfers or promotions between departments or units of a company. It also may describe the method of communication between or among various departments of an organization.

interdependence of labor The extent to which, in a mechanized society with a high degree of specialization, workers are dependent on each other not only for the completion of a particular job but also for providing the basic services needed to maintain a city or community. Dependence is not only on labor or services but also on the organization needed to keep the flow of goods and services in balance and to maintain production.

interest arbitration *See* ARBITRATION, INTEREST.

interference An employer unfair labor practice under the Taft-Hartley Act. Section 8(a)(1) makes it unlawful for an employer "to interfere with, restrain, or coerce employees" in the exercise of their self-organizational rights guaranteed in Section 7. This unfair labor practice of "interference" is a broad one. It embraces the more specific unfair practices of discrimination, domination, and refusal to bargain, plus a variety of additional acts. The acts forbidden may range all the way from restraining the solicitation of union members to granting a wage increase during an organizing drive.

Coercive questioning of employees about their union membership, espionage and surveillance of employee activities, removal of privileges, and the circulation of anti-union petitions also have been held unlawful employer "interference" with employee rights.

interim agreement A collective bargaining agreement which is designed to maintain a temporary truce or to maintain conditions of employment pending the settlement of a dispute or pending the signing of a final contract. It is a contract designed to tide the parties over a difficult period or until contract negotiations are completed. For example, an interim agreement might be reached involving a pension or insurance plan pending a more detailed study by the parties to work out the cost and operation of a particular program. Or it might involve setting an incentive job rate on an interim basis pending subsequent agreement on the actual rate.

See also AGREEMENT, COLLECTIVE; COLLECTIVE BARGAINING.

interim grievance procedure A rather infrequent procedure set up prior to the negotiation of a first contract. Machinery is established for resolving grievances or other problems while the parties are establishing the terms and conditions of employment in a first contract.

See also GRIEVANCE ADJUSTMENT.

intermediate report Prior to September 3, 1963, this was the recommended order handed down by a trial examiner for the NLRB following hearings in a complaint ("C") case involving charges of unfair labor practices under the Taft-Hartley Act. These intermediate reports or recommended orders were subject to review by the Board. New NLRB regulations effective September 3, 1963, gave these reports the status of decisions, not subject to Board review unless a party to the proceedings files exceptions to the trial examiner's decision. Trial examiners in 1972 were given the title of administrative law judges.

See also TRIAL EXAMINER'S DECISION.

intermittent industry Sometimes referred to as a noncontinuous industry.

Source references: William Mitchell, *Organization and Management of Production* (New York: McGraw-Hill, 1939).

intermittent worker A person who normally works only a small number of days during a work period or season. It may be temporary employment during a seasonal period or during peak production.

internal affairs of unions Those activities which involve the relationship of the union to its members and the local union to its international organization. The relationships are generally set forth in the constitution and bylaws which deal with the procedures for elections, holding meetings, appointments of committees, and appeal procedures in case of claims of discrimination.

Unions are jealous of efforts designed to interfere with what they refer to as "internal" union affairs. This was a primary basis for union objections to the Landrum-Griffin Act.

Source references: Benjamin Aaron and Michael I. Komaroff, "Statutory Regulation of Internal Union Affairs," *Illinois LR*, Sept./Oct. 1949 and Nov./Dec. 1949; George W. Bohlander, "How the Rank and File Views

Local Union Administration—A Survey," *Employee Relations LJ*, Autumn 1982; Walter J. Gershenfeld and Stuart M. Schmidt, "Officer, Member, and Steward Priorities for Local Unions: Congruities, Differences," *Proceedings of the 34th A/M, IRRA*, ed. by Barbara Dennis (Madison: 1982); Lois S. Gray, "Unions Implementing Managerial Techniques," *MLR*, June 1981; Burton Hall (comp.), *Autocracy and Insurgency in Organized Labor* (New Brunswick: Transaction Books, 1972); J. B. S. Hardman, *Labor at the Rubicon* (New York: NYU Press, 1972); Myron Roomkin, "Union Structure, Internal Control, and Strike Activity," *ILRR*, Jan. 1976; George Strauss, "Union Government in the U.S.: Research Past and Future," *IR*, May 1977; George Strauss and Malcolm Warner, "Research on Union Government: Introduction," *IR*, May 1977; Philip Taft, "Judicial Procedure in Labor Unions," *Quarterly Journal of Economics*, May 1945.

See also REGULATION OF LABOR UNIONS.

internal disputes plan *See* NO-RAIDING AGREEMENT.

internal house organ A company publication primarily for public relations purposes and directed to employees or stockholders of the company. Occasionally a distinction is made between internal house organs and external house organs.

External house organs are company publications which seek to reach individuals outside of the company. These generally are distributed to the public to explain the company's programs and policies with the view of obtaining general public understanding and support of the company, its product, and its policies.

See also HOUSE ORGAN.

internal mobility The movement of employees within a company or units of the company. The movement may come as a result of reorganization of operations, promotions, transfer, or for other reasons. The movement of employees outside of the company is referred to as "labor turnover."

Internal Revenue Employees; National Association of (Ind) Founded in 1938 as the National Association of Collectors of Internal Revenue, the union changed its name to the National Treasury Employees Union (Ind) in the early 1970s.

See also TREASURY EMPLOYEES UNION; NATIONAL (IND).

International Association for Labor Legislation (IALL) This was an organization consisting of a number of European countries whose prime purpose was to hold meetings and to establish working conditions by agreements among the various countries. The conditions of work were to be established on the basis of certain recommendations setting forth minimum protection for workers, including children and women. The International Labor Organization, which was established in 1919, took over some of the functions of the IALL as well as the setting up of standards or conventions for member countries active in the ILO.

See also INTERNATIONAL LABOR ORGANIZATION (ILO).

International Confederation of Free Trade Unions (ICFTU) The Confederation is the largest international organization of free trade unions in the world. It has 134 affiliated unions in 94 countries and territories which cover all five continents. The claimed total membership is 85 million, an increase from the 48 million in 53 countries at the time of its formation in 1949. The ICFTU split from the World Federation of Trade Unions (WFTU) in 1949, largely on the ground that the World Federation was Communist-oriented in policies and programs. The AFL, which did not become a member of the WFTU, joined the ICFTU. The AFL-CIO withdrew from the ICFTU in 1969 primarily as the result of a dispute over the request of the then independent United Automobile Workers for membership in the ICFTU. The AFL-CIO reaffiliated with the ICFTU on January 1, 1982. The United Mine Workers of America (Ind) has maintained a separate affiliation with the ICFTU since 1949.

To assist development of trade unions in Third World countries, the ICFTU has established three regional organizations—the Asian Regional Organization with headquarters in New Delhi; the African Regional Organization in Monrovia, Liberia and Ouagadougou, Upper Volta; and the Inter-American Organization of Workers (ORIT) in Mexico City.

The ICFTU Secretariat is located in Brussels, with offices in Geneva and New York. It maintains colleges for the training of trade union leaders. *Free Labour World* is the official journal of the ICFTU.

Source references: ICFTU, *Free Trade Unions for Economic and Social Progress* (Brussels: 1966); "The ICFTU—What It Is, What It Does," *Free Labour World,* 2/1983; Adolf Sturmthal, "The International Confederation of Free Trade Unions," *ILRR,* April 1950; John P. Windmuller, "Cohesion and Disunity in the ICFTU: The 1965 Amsterdam Congress," *ILRR,* April 1966; ———, "ICFTU After Ten Years: Problems and Prospects," *ILRR,* Jan. 1961; ———, "Leadership and Administration in the ICFTU: A New Phase of Development," *BJIR,* June 1963.

See also EUROPEAN TRADE UNION CONFEDERATION (ETUC), WORLD CONFEDERATION OF LABOUR (WCL), WORLD FEDERATION OF TRADE UNIONS (WFTU).

internationale A revolutionary song adopted by the socialist movement and sometimes by labor organizations which had strong socialist leanings.

Source reference: Joel Seidman, *The Needle Trades* (New York: Farrar & Rinehart, 1942).

International Federation of Christian Trade Unions (IFCTU) *See* WORLD CONFEDERATION OF LABOUR (WCL).

International Federation of Trade Unions (IFTU) An organization of national trade union federations founded in the early 1900s to disseminate organized labor's position on numerous issues. It was originally known as the International Secretariat of Trade Union Centers and adopted the name, IFTU, in 1913. The AFL was a member from 1910–1921, withdrew, and rejoined in 1937. It remained in the IFTU until its dissolution around 1945. According to Windmuller, the IFTU membership of over 20 million was reduced to less than 10 million "after the destruction of the German unions by the Nazi regime."

Source references: Val R. Lorwin, "Labor's International Relations," *The House of Labor,* ed. by J. B. S. Hardman and Maurice F. Neufeld (New York: PH, 1951); Walter Schevenels, *Forty-Five Years, 1901–1945: International Federation of Trade Unions; A Historical Precis* (Brussels: IFTU, 1956); John P. Windmuller, "International Trade Union Movement," *Comparative Labour Law and Industrial Relations,* ed. by R. Blanpain (Washington: BNA, 1982).

See also EUROPEAN TRADE UNION CONFEDERATION (ETUC), INTERNATIONAL CONFEDERATION OF FREE TRADE UNIONS (ICFTU), WORLD CONFEDERATION OF LABOUR (WCL), WORLD FEDERATION OF TRADE UNIONS (WFTU).

International Labor Office (ILO) The Secretariat and staff of the International Labor Organization. The office includes the director and the operating and research staff which prepares reports and compiles data for the Conferences and assists the director and the ILO in carrying out the functions of the organization.

Source references: George N. Barnes, *History of the International Labor Office* (London: Williams & Norgate, 1926); Norman F. Dufty, "Technical Assistance and the International Labour Office," *Journal of IR,* Nov. 1967.

International Labor Organization (ILO) An organization founded during the peace conference following World War I and established as part of the League of Nations. One of its main purposes is to better the standards of labor throughout the world. The annual Conferences which discuss and promulgate Conventions setting out minimum working conditions and standards for their improvement are composed of delegates of governments, management, and labor from member countries.

The section of the Treaty of Versailles which sets out the objectives of the ILO reads in part as follows:

> Whereas the League of Nations has for its object the establishment of universal peace, and such a peace can be established only if it is based upon social justice;
>
> And whereas conditions of labour exist involving such injustice, hardship and privation to large numbers of people as to produce unrest so great that the peace and harmony of the world are imperiled; and an improvement of those conditions is urgently required: as, for example, by the regulation of the hours of work, including the

establishment of a maximum working day and week, the regulation of the labour supply, the prevention of unemployment, the provision of an adequate living wage, the protection of the worker against sickness, disease and injury arising out of his employment, the protection of children, young persons and women, provision for old age and injury, protection of the interests of workers when employed in countries other than their own, recognition of the principle of freedom of association, the organization of vocational and technical education and other measures; . . .

The nations signing the Treaty agreed to the establishment of the International Labor Organization. The United States joined the ILO in 1934, but withdrew for a two-year period in 1977 to protest the "politicization" of the organization.

The ILO is now a specialized agency of the United Nations.

Source references: Anthony Alcock, *History of the International Labor Organization* (New York: Octagon Books, 1971); Michael D. Boggs, "The ILO Back on the Track," *American Federationist,* Nov. 1980; Leonard J. Calhoun, *The International Labor Organization and United States Domestic Law* (New York: American Enterprise Assn., 1953); Nathalis De Bock, "More Teeth for the ILO," *Free Labour World,* Feb. 1972; J. H. E. Fried, "Relations Between the United Nations and the International Labor Organization," *American Political Science Review,* Oct. 1947; "ILO and the United Nations," *ILR,* Sept. 1947; Lane Kirkland, "A Time of Testing at the ILO," *American Federationist,* Aug. 1976; Albert LeRoy, *International Labor Organization* (Westminster, Md.: Newman Press, 1957); Spencer Miller, Jr., *What the International Labor Organization Means to America* (New York: Columbia UP, 1936); George V. Moser, "The International Labor Organization," *Harvard BR,* July/Aug. 1952; Gary B. Ostrower, "The American Decision to Join the International Labor Organization," *Labor History,* Fall 1975; George J. Pantos, "The United States and the International Labor Organization," *Employee Relations LJ,* Spring 1978; Paul Perigord, *The International Labor Organization* (New York: Appleton-Century, 1926); K. T. Samson, "The Changing Pattern of ILO Supervision," *ILR,* Sept./Oct. 1979; Bert Seidman, "The ILO—Past Accomplishments and Future Prospects," *Proceedings of the 27th A/M, IRRA,* ed. by James Stern and Barbara Dennis (Madison: 1975); Charles H. Smith, Jr., "ILO—Accomplishments, Prospects, Recommendations: The U.S. Employers' View," *Proceedings of the 27th A/M, IRRA,* ed. by James Stern and Barbara Dennis (Madison: 1975); Burton W. Teague, "I.L.O.'s World Watch on Labor Standards," *Conference Board Record,* Nov. 1975; U.S. GAO, *Need for U.S. Objectives in the International Labor Organization, Departments of State, Labor, and Commerce* (Washington: 1977); "U.S. to Rejoin International Labor Organization, President Announces," *Daily Labor Report,* No. 31, Feb. 13, 1980; Nicolas Valticos, "The Role of International Labour Standards in a Changing World," *Free Labour World,* March 1975; G. Von Potobsky, "On-the-Spot Visits: An Important Cog in the ILO's Supervisory Machinery," *ILR,* Sept./Oct. 1981; John P. Windmuller, "U.S. Participation in the ILO: The Political Dimension," *Proceedings of the 27th A/M, IRRA,* ed. by James Stern and Barbara Dennis (Madison: 1975).

International Labour Review The official monthly journal of the ILO. It contains articles, reports, and statistical series on working conditions and standards of member countries. It is somewhat similar to the *Monthly Labor Review* issued by the U.S. Department of Labor, except that it directs its emphasis toward matters of international concern.

international representative A full-time staff officer of an international union who serves as a liaison between the organizational headquarters and the local unions.

The duties of the international representative include assisting in contract negotiations, grievances, and organizing nonunion employees within the union's jurisdiction.

International Trade Secretariats (ITS) Federations of national trade unions representing workers in various industries in different countries. There are 16 such organizations with a total of between 55 and 60 million members; the largest is the International Metalworkers' Federation with over 13 million members.

The ITS was founded in 1889 with the organization of the International Federation of Boot and Shoe Operatives. The Secretariats were organized on a single occupation or industry basis. However, with ITS mergers and development of new industries, membership currently crosses occupational and industrial lines. The membership of the International Metalworkers' Federation, for example, consists of unions in auto, steel, electrical and electronic products, and shipbuilding.

The Secretariats cooperate with the ICFTU and maintain headquarters with a permanent secretary in Geneva.

Source references: ICFTU, *International Trade Secretariats* (Brussels: 1965); George C. Lodge, *Spearheads of Democracy, Labor in the Developing Countries* (New York: Harper, 1962); John P. Windmuller, "International Trade Union Movement," *Comparative Labour Law and Industrial Relations*, ed. by R. Blanpain (Washington: BNA, 1982); ———, *The Shape of Transnational Unionism: International Trade Secretariats* (Washington: U.S. Dept. of Labor, BILA, Monograph no. 3, 1979).

international union The term applied to most unions in the United States which have affiliated locals in the United States and some in other countries—mostly Canada. They also are referred to as national unions. The structure of American unions is such that substantial power rests with the officers of the international union and its staff, including organizers and research personnel.

Source references: Jack Barbash, *American Unions: Structure, Government, and Politics* (New York: Random House, 1967); ———, *Labor Unions in Action* (New York: Harper, 1948); John P. Windmuller, "International Trade Union Organizations: Structure, Functions, Limitations," *International Labor,* ed. by Solomon Barkin et al. (New York: Harper, IRRA Pub., 1967).

See also NATIONAL AND INTERNATIONAL UNIONS.

International Workingman's Association The International Workingman's Association, sometimes known as the "First International," which had been formed in Europe in 1864, moved its headquarters to New York in 1872, and dissolved in 1875.

interplant Between plants. The term occasionally is used in connection with interplant transfers or promotions. During World War II the term was applied to interplant inequities in wage rates by the War Labor Board.

interpretative bulletin An explanatory publication setting out the official interpretations of a governmental agency about the meaning of the particular statute which it has the responsibility of enforcing. Probably the best known of these bulletins are those issued by the Wage and Hour Division of the U.S. Department of Labor, interpreting provisions of the Fair Labor Standards Act of 1938 (Wage-Hour Law), as amended.

interstate commerce Refers to trade or traffic between or among the states. It is the basis for the right of the federal government to legislate in the labor-management relations field.

The Landrum-Griffin Act (Labor-Management Reporting and Disclosure Act of 1959) defines commerce as follows:

> 'Commerce' means trade, traffic, commerce, transportation, transmission, or communication among the several states or between any state and any place outside thereof. [Section 3(a)]
>
> 'Industry affecting commerce' means any activity, business, or industry in commerce or in which a labor dispute would hinder or obstruct commerce or the free flow of commerce and includes any activity or industry 'affecting commerce' within the meaning of the Labor-Management Relations Act, 1947 (Taft-Hartley Act) as amended, or the Railway Labor Act, as amended. [Section 3(c)]

See also AFFECTING COMMERCE.

Interstate Commerce Commission; Professional Association of the (Ind) 12th St. and Constitution Ave., N.W., Washington, D.C. 20423. Tel. (202) 655–4000

interunion dispute A conflict between two unions over membership of employees or over the work or job opportunities.

When the Committee for Industrial Organization was formed, it was labeled by the AFL as "dual unionism." Rival unionism is generally held to apply to disputes between two or more unions for the control of workers or certain kinds of work.

Source references: Stephen J. Cabot, "How Not to Get Caught in the Middle When Labor

Unions Start Squabbling With Each Other," *LLJ*, Sept. 1973; Walter Galenson, *Rival Unionism in the United States* (Washington: American Council on Public Affairs, 1940); Sylvester Petro, "Federal Law and Inter-union Disputes," *LLJ*, March 1952.

See also DUAL UNIONISM, JURISDICTIONAL DISPUTE, RIVAL UNIONISM.

interview (employment) *See* EMPLOYMENT INTERVIEW.

intimidation Efforts to interfere with the right of workers to self-organization by coercion or intimidation (actual or threatened violence) is prohibited under federal law. Courts occasionally prohibit economic pressure by unions, holding that they can intimidate employees through mere gestures, jeers, or congregation of large numbers of workers.

intraplant training Instruction and acquisition of skills through observation and practice within the plant. The instruction may be by a trained specialist or highly skilled employee on the job. An attempt is made through such programs to raise the level of employee performance and skill.

See also INDUSTRIAL EDUCATION, TRAINING WITHIN INDUSTRY.

intrastate commerce Trade, traffic, or communication wholly within the state and subject to regulation by the state.

See also AFFECTING COMMERCE, INTERSTATE COMMERCE.

inventory of employee skills A compilation of full data about an employee, which includes a listing of skills and occupations performed by him, not only in the organization but also in previous employment and training schools. A complete listing or inventory of skills permits the most judicious use of manpower. It also permits the company to use the highest skills of the workers.

When transfers, promotions, or new job opportunities arise, it is possible to determine available manpower sources and to place people in accordance with their highest skills.

See also EMPLOYMENT HISTORY, PERSONNEL AUDIT (OR SURVEY), SENIORITY.

inverse seniority A method under which workers are laid off in inverse order of seniority, i.e., highest seniority workers first. A number of these arrangements have been instituted in auto plants where the United Auto Workers has membership.

Source references: Sheldon Friedman, Dennis C. Bumstead, and Robert T. Lund, "Inverse Seniority as an Aid to Disadvantaged Groups," *MLR*, May 1976; ______, "The Potential of Inverse Seniority as an Approach to the Conflict Between Seniority and Equal Employment Opportunity," *Proceedings of the 28th A/M, IRRA*, ed. by James Stern and Barbara Dennis (Madison: 1976); Robert T. Lund, Dennis C. Bumstead, and Sheldon Friedman, "Inverse Seniority: Timely Answer to the Layoff Dilemma?" *Harvard BR*, Sept./Oct. 1975; "UAW Asks Shultz's Help in Getting Inverse Seniority in Chrysler Layoffs," *Daily Labor Report*, No. 32, Feb. 16, 1970.

involuntary check-off A form of dues deduction by the employer in which the employee has no choice. Section 302(c)(4) of the Taft-Hartley Act provides that an employee must give written authorization before such deduction is made:

> The provisions of this section shall not be applicable . . . (4) with respect to money deducted from the wages of employees in payment of membership dues in a labor organization: Provided, that the employer has received from each employee, on whose account such deductions are made, a written assignment which shall not be irrevocable for a period of more than one year, or beyond the termination date of the applicable collective agreement, whichever occurs sooner; . . .

See also AUTOMATIC CHECK-OFF, RAND FORMULA, VOLUNTARY CHECK-OFF.

ironclad agreement (contract) Sometimes referred to as an anti-union or yellow dog contract. The agreement signed by the employee stated that he would not join any union as long as he remained an employee of the company. Some contracts also provided that the employee would not engage in any strike activity and the employer was free to discharge him and terminate the contract at will.

See also YELLOW DOG CONTRACT.

iron law of wages According to economist David Ricardo, wages tend to remain at the subsistence level (the natural price of labor).

Where the actual or market price of labor goes beyond the natural price, economic forces (rise and fall in population) tend to bring them back to the natural level. Ricardo's theory sometimes is referred to as the subsistence theory of wages. It was developed by Ferdinand Lasalle, one of the founders of German socialism, into the Iron Law of Wages. He contended that in order to raise wages beyond the subsistence level it was essential to obtain government assistance. He suggested producer's cooperatives as one way the government could help workers achieve a higher standard of living.

Source references: James Bonar, *Malthus and His Work* (New York: Macmillan, 1924); Charles Gide and Charles Rist, *A History of Economic Doctrines* (Boston: Heath, 1915); John K. Ingram, *A History of Political Economy* (New York: Macmillan, 1915); David Ricardo, *Principles of Political Economy and Taxation* (London: Bell & Sons, 1908); Michael T. Wermel, *The Evolution of the Classical Wage Theory* (New York: Columbia UP, 1939).

Iron Workers; International Association of Bridge, Structural and Ornamental (AFL-CIO) Organized in Pittsburgh on February 4, 1896. It extended its jurisdiction in 1914 and changed its name to the International Association of Bridge, Structural and Ornamental Iron Workers and Pile Drivers. This led to a jurisdictional dispute with the Carpenters union over the pile drivers. The union refused to give up the jurisdiction and was suspended from the AFL. It was permitted to return after it dropped the claim over the pile drivers. It refused, however, to give up the ornamental iron workers although the AFL never recognized the claim in its charter.

Its monthly publication is *The Ironworker*.

Address: 1750 New York Ave., N.W., Suite 400, Washington, D.C. 20006. Tel. (202) 383–4800

Italian Actors Union Established in 1938, it is a branch of the Associated Actors and Artistes of America (AFL-CIO).

Address: 184 Fifth Ave., New York, N.Y. 10010. Tel. (212) 675–1003

itinerant worker A worker who is not attached to a specific community and moves from job to job.

IUE v. Westinghouse Electric Corp. A suit challenging the wage structure of Westinghouse, charging that rates were set on the basis of sex and not on job requirements, in violation of Title VII of the Civil Rights Act. The court of appeals found that female employees stated a Title VII claim by alleging that when the employer integrated its "men's" and "women's" jobs into one ranking system, it intentionally assigned women's jobs to grades lower than those assigned men's jobs previously of the same rank.

In January 1982, the parties agreed to an out-of-court settlement which included (1) agreement by the company to upgrade jobs and award back pay to some 600 present and past employees of the Trenton lamp manufacturing plant, (2) establishment of a $75,000 back pay fund by the company to be apportioned among female employees on its payroll from August 8, 1972, to the date of the settlement, and (3) upgrading of some 85 jobs currently held by women.

The suit was initiated in 1973 when the International Union of Electrical, Radio and Machine Workers filed a national charge against Westinghouse with the Equal Employment Opportunity Commission.

Source references: IUE v. Westinghouse Electric Corp., 631 F2d 1094, 23 FEP Cases 588 (CA 3, 1980); BNA, "Out-of-Court Settlements Are Reached in *Gunther, Westinghouse* Comparable Worth Cases," *Daily Labor Report*, No. 47, March 10, 1982; Winn Newman and Jeanne M. Vonhoff, " 'Separate but Equal'—Job Segregation and Pay Equity in the Wake of Gunther," 1981 *Univ. of Illinois LR* 269 (1981).

See also COMPARABLE WORTH, PAY EQUITY.

J

JOBS *See* JOB OPPORTUNITIES IN THE BUSINESS SECTOR (JOBS).

JTPA *See* JOB TRAINING PARTNERSHIP ACT (JTPA) OF 1982.

JWU *See* JEWELRY WORKERS' UNION; INTERNATIONAL (AFL-CIO).

jack of all trades A person who claims ability to perform a variety of jobs, but is not an expert at any of them.

Jacksonville wage agreement An agreement signed by the United Mine Workers and Union Coal Operators extending the basic $7.50 a day wage from April 1924 to April 1927. The $7.50 rate per day had been obtained in 1920 as the result of a presidential commission set up in 1919 to arbitrate the dispute arising out of the bituminous coal strike of November 1919.

Source references: Saul Alinsky, *John L. Lewis* (New York: Putnam, 1949); Morton S. Baratz, *The Union and the Coal Industry* (New Haven: Yale UP, 1955); Edmond Beame, "The Jacksonville Agreement," *ILRR*, Jan. 1955; Louis Bloch, *Coal Miners Insecurity* (New York: Russell Sage Foundation, 1922); McAlister Coleman, *Men and Coal* (New York: Farrar & Rinehart, 1943); Charles B. Fowler, *Collective Bargaining in the Bituminous Coal Industry* (New York: PH, 1927); John L. Lewis, *The Miners Fight for American Standards* (Indianapolis: Bell Publishing, 1925); David J. McDonald and Edward A. Lynch, *Coal and Unionism* (Silver Spring: Cornelius Printing, 1939).

See also MINE WORKERS OF AMERICA; UNITED (IND).

Jamestown Area Labor-Management Committee Created in 1972 through the efforts of the mayor and labor and management representatives to reverse a New York community's economic decline brought about by the loss of manufacturing jobs, people migration, the failure to attract new business, and poor labor-management relations. It was the first communitywide labor-management committee to receive federal funds under the Labor Management Cooperation Act of 1978. The committee also helped local companies set up in-plant labor management problem-solving committees.

The committee is composed of 50 members with an equal number of management and labor members; it is co-chaired by labor and management representatives. In addition to establishing and guiding plant committees, it serves as a clearinghouse for labor relations information and sponsors meetings, seminars, and conferences. The Jamestown program is frequently cited as a model in the establishment of similar committees in other communities.

Source references: Charlotte Gold, *Employer-Employee Committees and Worker Participation* (Ithaca: Cornell Univ., NYSSILR, Key Issues Series no. 20, 1976); *Labor-Management Committees in the Public Sector, A Practitioner's Guide* (Bloomington: Indiana Univ., Midwest Center for Public Sector Labor Relations, 1979); Richard D. Leone, "Area-Wide Labor-Management Committees: Where Do We Go From Here?" *Proceedings of the 35th A/M, IRRA*, ed. by Barbara Dennis (Madison: 1983); Gerald I. Susman, *A Guide to Labor-Management Committees in State and Local Government* (Washington: U.S. Department of Housing and Urban Development, 1980); Edgar Weinberg, "Labor-Management Cooperation: A Report on Recent Initiatives," *MLR*, April 1976.

See also LABOR MANAGEMENT COOPERATION ACT OF 1978, TOLEDO LABOR-MANAGEMENT-CITIZENS COMMITTEE.

Japanese labor The organization of workers and employment relations in Japan.

Source references: Iwao Ayusawa, *Organized Labor in Japan* (Tokyo: Foreign Affairs Assn. of Japan, 1962); William B. Gould, *Japan's Reshaping of American Labor Law* (Cambridge: MIT Press, 1984); Tadashi Hanami, *Labor Relations in Japan Today* (Tokyo: Kodansha International, 1979); Japan Institute of Labour, *Labor Unions and Labor-Management Relations* (Tokyo: Japanese IR series 2, 1983); Everett M. Kassalow, "Japan as an Industrial Relations Model," *Journal of IR*, June 1983; Solomon B. Levine, *Industrial Relations in Postwar Japan* (Urbana: Univ. of Illinois Press, 1958); ———, "Japanese Industrial Relations: What Can We Import?" *NYU 36th Annual National Conference on Labor*, ed. by Richard Adelman (New York: Bender, 1983); Tadashi Mitsufuji and Kiyohiko Hagisawa, "Recent Trends in Collective Bargaining in Japan," *ILR*, Feb. 1972; Ichiro Nakayama, *Industrialization and Labor-Management Relations in Japan* (Tokyo: Japan Institute of Labour, 1975); Taishiro Shirai (ed.), *Contemporary Industrial Relations in Japan* (Madison: Univ. of Wisconsin Press, 1983); Frank J. Versagi, "What American Labor/Management Can Learn From Japanese Unions," *Management Review*, June 1982.

See also ENTERPRISE UNIONISM, LIFETIME EMPLOYMENT SYSTEM, SENIORITY WAGE SYSTEM.

Jencks case Case in which the Supreme Court reversed the conviction of a union official for violating the False Information Act (18 U.S.C. 1001) by filing a false non-Communist affidavit with the NLRB pursuant to Section 9(h) of the Taft-Hartley Act. The Court ruled that the union official was entitled to inspect key reports by government witnesses to the FBI without first laying a preliminary foundation of inconsistency. The criminal proceeding must be dismissed, the Court added, when the government elects on the ground of privilege not to comply with an order to produce the reports.

Source reference: Jencks v. U.S., 353 US 657, 40 LRRM 2147 (1957).

Jewelry Workers' Union; International (AFL-CIO) Originally established in 1900, the union gave up its AFL charter in 1912. It reorganized in 1916. The Diamond Workers' Protective Union of America (AFL) merged with the union on November 1, 1954, to form the Diamond Workers Division of Local 1.

In July 1980, the union merged with the Service Employees' International Union (AFL-CIO).

See also SERVICE EMPLOYEES' INTERNATIONAL UNION (AFL-CIO).

Jim Crow laws Laws directed in some way to restrict the rights of blacks. In the political and social field, Jim Crowism involves discrimination through such means as the use of separate transportation, housing, school, and other public facilities.

Among labor unions, discrimination against black workers may be shown by the establishment of separate locals for such workers.

Source references: Brailsford R. Brazeal, *The Brotherhood of Sleeping Car Porters: Its Origin and Development* (New York: Harper, 1946); Herbert R. Northrup, *Organized Labor and the Negro* (New York: Harper, 1944); Roi Ottley, *Black Odyssey* (New York: Charles Scribners, 1948); Sterling D. Spero and Abram L. Harris, *The Black Worker* (New York: Columbia UP, 1931).

job In general usage it includes all of the factors which go into a person's activities, responsibilities, and operations in the performance of his work. The various components that go into a particular job distinguish it from other jobs. For example, the job of a salesman differs from that of a telephone operator or a pattern maker.

Sometimes the term is used to describe a group of similar positions within a company, which are identical with respect to their major tasks. The employees are performing the same type of work even though each may work at a different part of the task.

The term "job" is sometimes used as equivalent to "occupation" but its use may be broader, including other jobs in the same field of work.

Source references: Thomas Nardone, "The Job Outlook in Brief," *Occupational Outlook Quarterly*, Spring 1980; Martin Patchen, *Participation, Achievement, and Involvement on the Job* (Englewood Cliffs: PH, 1970).

See also OCCUPATION.

job action Concerted activity undertaken by employees to exert pressure on management during negotiations. Job actions include such activities as off-hour picketing, slowdowns, union meetings during work hours, "going by the rulebook," mass resignations, sickouts, or official walkouts.

The tactics are directed at affecting the quality or quantity of services provided and are used where strikes are prohibited.

Source reference: The Twentieth Century Fund, Task Force on Labor Disputes in Public Employment, *Pickets at City Hall* (New York: The Twentieth Century Fund, 1970).

See also BLUE FLU, DIRECT ACTION, "RULEBOOK" SLOWDOWN, SICKOUT, WORK TO RULE.

job analysis A complete investigation or study of a particular job or position in order to determine the facts about a job including the methods or procedures of work, tools, responsibilities, supervision, the standards of output, and other data concerning the technical nature of the work. It also involves obtaining information about the physical environment which might include such things as noise and other hazards.

The job analysis also would attempt to include the relation of the particular job to others and would include factors such as coworkers and efforts to coordinate the particular job and those assigned to help in the operation. The job analysis would include items such as wages, hours of work, opportunity for promotion, and the relative stability or permanence of employment.

Source references: Kenneth Byers, *Job Analysis* (Chicago: Civil Service Assembly, 1955); Sidney A. Fine, "Functional Job Analysis: An Approach to a Technology for Manpower Planning," *PJ*, Nov. 1974; Sidney A. Fine, Ann M. Holt, and Maret F. Hutchinson, *Functional Job Analysis, How to Standardize Task Statements* (Kalamazoo: Upjohn Institute for Employment Research, Methods for Manpower Analysis no. 9, 1974); Edwin Ghiselli and Clarence Brown, *Personnel and Industrial Psychology* (2d ed., New York: McGraw-Hill, 1955); Ollie A. Jensen, "An Analysis of Confusions and Misconceptions Surrounding Job Analysis, Job Evaluation, Position Classification, Employee Selection, and Content Validity," *Public Personnel Management*, July/Aug. 1978; D. Patrick Lacy, Jr., "EEO Implications of Job Analyses," *Employee Relations LJ*, Spring 1979; Ernest James McCormick, *Job Analysis: Methods and Applications* (New York: AMACOM, 1979); Jay L. Otis and Richard H. Leukart, *Job Evaluation* (2d ed., New York: PH, 1954); John A. Patton, *Job Analysis* (rev. ed., Homewood: Irwin, 1957); Thomasine Rendero, "Job Analysis Practices," *Personnel*, Jan./Feb. 1981; Howard W. Risher, "Job Analysis: A Management Perspective," *Employee Relations LJ*, Spring 1979; U.S. CSC, *Job Analysis, Developing and Documenting Data, A Guide for State and Local Governments* (Washington: 1973); U.S. Dept. of Labor, ETA, *Task Analysis Inventories, Series II* (Washington: 1980); U.S. Dept. of Labor, Manpower Administration, *Handbook for Analyzing Jobs* (Washington: 1972); ———, *Job Analysis for Human Resource Management: A Review of Selected Research and Development* (Washington: Research Monograph no. 36, 1974).

job analyst An individual whose function and responsibility are to prepare specifications and descriptions of specific jobs, to analyze them, and to classify and grade all jobs or occupations.

job assignment The allotting or assigning of specific duties and responsibilities to a person.

Questions occasionally arise between labor and management whether certain functions or duties fall within the scope of the job assigned to the individual. The question is sometimes raised whether the addition of certain duties and responsibilities actually results in the establishment of a *new* job that is not part of the regular or normal job functions assigned or to be assigned to a particular individual or occupation. The addition of new functions or substantially different work may result in a claim by the employee or a union that the job has been changed and therefore a new and usually higher job rate should be set. Additional compensation may be requested because of the claim of additional work responsibilities. Where the amount of work assigned is increased but not changed, the claim for additional compensation would be based on claims of increased production.

Procedures for assignment of employees to higher or lower rated jobs may be provided by collective bargaining agreement. The following clause is illustrative:

> When an employee is assigned to a higher rated job he will immediately receive the rate of that job and continue to receive such rate as long as he fulfills the job satisfactorily.
>
> When an employee's regular job is available for him for any part of a shift and he is assigned during that shift to a lower rated job, he shall receive his regular rate of pay for all time worked during that shift.
>
> When an employee's regular job is scheduled for no part of an entire shift or is available for him during no part of an entire shift and he is assigned to one or more lower rated jobs for part or all of such shift, he shall receive the rate for the job to which he has been assigned.
>
> If an employee refuses or fails to accept an assignment of a job other than his regular one, either in his own department or by transfer to some other department, he shall not lose his seniority in his own department.

job breakdown The basic elements of a particular job divided into separate units, so that a complex job can be divided and broken down into simpler operations and the less complex operations performed by a less-skilled worker. Sometimes called job splitting.

Source reference: Ralph Barnes, *Work Methods Manual* (New York: Wiley, 1944).

See also JOB ANALYSIS.

job classification A method of arranging jobs into various categories or classes in a particular company or industry. The arrangement may be based on requirements such as training, experience, or skill. The grouping is designed to bring together occupations with characteristics sufficiently clear to distinguish them from those in other classes. The wage compensation usually parallels the requirements of the job and is based on progressively higher skills, experience, training, or other factors required in the job.

When related jobs are placed into classes, they may be assigned to labor grade groups with specific single rates or rate ranges which have a minimum and maximum for each labor grade.

Source references: Bernard H. Baum and Peter F. Sorensen, Jr., "A 'Total' Approach to Job Classification," *PJ*, Jan. 1969; Kenneth M. Byers, Robert Montilla, and Elmer V. Williams, *Elements of Position Classification in Local Government* (Chicago: PPA, Personnel Report no. 554, 1955); Lawrence L. Epperson, "The Dynamics of Factor Comparison/Point Evaluation," *Public Personnel Management*, Jan./Feb. 1975; Michael S. Frank, "Position Classification: A State-of-the-Art Review and Analysis," *Public Personnel Management*, Fall 1982; Daniel F. Halloran, "Why Position Classification?" *Public Personnel Review*, April 1967; Kenneth Pearlman, *Job Families: A Review and Discussion of Their Potential Utility for Personnel Selection* (Washington: U.S. CSC, Professional Series 78–2, 1978); Gilbert A. Schulkind, "Monitoring Position Classification—Practical Problems and Possible Solutions," *Public Personnel Management*, Jan./Feb. 1975.

See also JOB EVALUATION.

job content Includes all of the functions, requirements, and duties of a given job. It is frequently assumed that the job content is the same as the job title. This may not be true since jobs with the same title may have *different* job content, duties, and responsibilities because of the type of machinery in use and different methods of production in different plants.

Source references: Milton L. Rock (ed.), *Handbook of Wage and Salary Administration* (2d ed., New York: McGraw-Hill, 1984); James G. Scoville, *The Job Content of the U.S. Economy, 1940–1970* (New York: McGraw-Hill, 1969).

job control Applies to the efforts by an organization to have the right to be consulted about employees working in an occupation, company, or industry. Occasionally the phrase is applied to the types of contract provisions which place limitations on the right of the employer to control the job, through such clauses as those on plant seniority, promotions, working conditions, and the handling of disciplinary problems through the grievance machinery.

Source references: Simon Rottenberg, "Intra-Union Disputes Over Job Control," *Quarterly Journal of Economics*, Aug. 1947;

Sumner Slichter, *Union Policies and Industrial Management* (Washington: Brookings Institution, 1941).

See also CONTROL OF JOB, JURISDICTIONAL DISPUTE, RIVAL UNIONISM.

Job Corps The Job Corps was created in 1965 as part of the Economic Opportunity Act of 1964 to prepare youths, aged 16 to 21, who are out of school and out of work "for the responsibility of citizenship and to increase [their] employability . . . by providing them . . . with education, vocational education, useful work directed toward conservation of natural resources, and other appropriate activities" (Sec. 101).

Maximum length of enrollment is two years, but Corps members can leave at any time. Besides living expenses, enrollees receive (since 1983) allowances of $65 per month for the first six months of enrollment and $110 per month thereafter. Enrollees who have served at least 90 days receive readjustment allowances of up to $110 per month of service when they leave the Corps.

Originally administered by the Office of Economic Opportunity, the Job Corps was divided into urban job training and rural conservation centers. Because most Corps members are school dropouts the program includes basic education as well as vocational training, physical education, and recreational activities. Training at urban centers concentrated on basic education and skills training for occupations in such fields as electronics, business machines repair, auto repair and maintenance, and office work. The boys also learned how to apply for a job and the functioning of a typical industrial organization. Rural conservation centers, which were geared to boys with very little conventional schooling, provided remedial education and work experience on such conservation projects as fire prevention and the construction of camp grounds, picnic sites, bridges, and hiking trails. The boys also received instruction in plumbing, woodwork, and other crafts. The initial concentration on conservation work at the rural centers later diminished in favor of more literacy and skill training, similar to that provided by the urban centers from the beginning.

Job Corps centers for girls were established in urban areas and were operated by private firms. The centers offered an educational program as well as occupational training in household service, clerical and sales work, and some types of factory work. The girls also received training in homemaking skills.

Following reorganization in fiscal 1970, responsibility for the Job Corps was transferred from the Office of Economic Opportunity to the Department of Labor. Some centers were closed and replaced by new residential centers closer to the urban homes of the enrollees. The new program also envisioned greater involvement of management, labor, and of state vocational education agencies, and closer ties with the public employment service to enable better screening and selection of enrollees and better placement services for graduates.

The Job Corps was continued under the Comprehensive Employment and Training Act of 1973 and is currently covered by Title IV of the Job Training Partnership Act of 1983.

Source references: T. C. Allen, "Achievements of an Industry-Operated Job Corps Center," *Proceedings of the 1968 Annual Spring Meeting, IRRA*, ed. by Gerald Somers (Madison: 1968); Glen G. Cain, *Benefit/Cost Estimates for Job Corps* (Madison: Institute for Research on Poverty, Univ. of Wisconsin, 1967); Stephen R. Engleman, "Job Corps: Some Factors Affecting Enrollee Earnings," *IR*, May 1972; Sar A. Levitan, "Job Corps Experience with Manpower Training," *MLR*, Oct. 1975; Sar A. Levitan and Benjamin H. Johnston, *The Job Corps, A Social Experiment that Works* (Baltimore: Johns Hopkins UP, Policy Studies in Employment and Welfare no. 22, 1975); Joseph A. Pichler, "The Job Corps Transition," *ILRR*, April 1972; U.S. Dept. of Labor, ETA, *The Noneconomic Impacts of the Job Corps* (Washington: R & D Monograph 64, 1978); Christopher Weeks, *Job Corps: Dollars and Dropouts* (Boston: Little, Brown, 1967).

job creation Refers to increasing the number of employment opportunities in the labor market. New jobs may be created through direct or indirect government policy.

According to Werneke, job creation efforts include human resource programs providing immediate employment opportunities to the disadvantaged directly from the government.

Source reference: Diane Werneke, "Job Creation Programmes: The United States Experience," *ILR*, July/Aug. 1976.

job description A written record summarizing the main features or characteristics of the job. This may include the description of the duties of the job, the responsibilities, promotional opportunities, general working conditions, the qualifications of the employee, the materials handled, the amount of responsibility of the individual, the tools required in the job performance, and occasionally the amount of time assigned to various parts of the job. The description may be based on analysis of the actual job performance of an incumbent or may be set up as a listing of the component parts of a job which would be desirable or required of a person newly assigned to its performance.

Source references: David L. Austin, "A New Approach to Position Descriptions," *PJ*, July 1977; Conrad Berenson and Henry O'Ruhnke, "Job Description: Guidelines for Personnel Management," *PJ*, Jan. 1966; ———, *Job Descriptions: How to Write and Use Them* (Swarthmore: PJ, 1967); Donald E. Britton, "Are Job Descriptions Really Necessary?" *Management Review*, April 1975; Herbert J. Chruden and Arthur W. Sherman, Jr., *Personnel Management* (3d ed., Cincinnati: South-Western, 1968); Richard I. Henderson, *Job Descriptions—Critical Documents, Versatile Tools* (New York: AMACOM, 1976); Donald E. Klingner, "When the Traditional Job Description is Not Enough," *PJ*, April 1979; Jack L. Mendleson, "Improving Executive Job Descriptions," *Management of Personnel Quarterly*, Spring 1969; Walter D. Scott, Robert C. Clothier, and William R. Spriegel, *Personnel Management* (6th ed., New York: McGraw-Hill, 1961); John W. Thompson, "Functional Job Description," *PJ*, March 1952; George R. Wendt, "Should Courts Write Your Job Descriptions?" *PJ*, Sept. 1976; Herbert Zollitsch and Adolph Langsner, *Wage and Salary Administration* (2d ed., Cincinnati: South-Western, 1970).

job dilution A procedure for subdividing the various parts or components of a highly skilled job into individual separate operations of skilled, semiskilled, and unskilled portions. Work is then assigned among the work force on the basis of the requirements of each specific operation. In this manner it is possible to reduce the need for highly skilled operators, except for portions of the work which require such skills, and to use less skilled workers for other parts of the job. This process of job dilution was accelerated during World War II when there was a scarcity of highly skilled workers. The process of job dilution was objected to by many of the crafts since it reduced the job opportunities for skilled workers and also led to mechanization of many of the subdivided operations of less skilled work.

See also JOB SPLITTING, TECHNOLOGICAL UNEMPLOYMENT.

job engineering Structuring or designing job content to fit the intellectual and psychological characteristics of the employee. Job engineering is generally utilized as part of a job enrichment program. According to Penzer, job engineering adopts both the human growth potential assumptions of behavioral scientists and the methods design principles of industrial engineers.

Job engineering involves design efforts directed toward increasing the employee's work responsibility and discretion to make certain decisions. This effort is distinguished from the assignment of additional work that is at the employee's present level.

Source reference: William N. Penzer, *Productivity and Motivation Through Job Engineering* (New York: AMACOM, 1973).

job enlargement The procedure of broadening the scope, and assigning additional responsibilities to a job in order to assure, among other things, a wider sense of the significance of the particular operation and greater satisfaction to the employee who is performing it.

Source references: J. F. Biggane and Paul A. Stewart, *Job Enlargement: A Case Study* (Iowa City: State Univ. of Iowa, Bureau of Labor and Management, Research Series no. 25, 1963); Joseph L. Delate, Jr., "The Civil Technology Program: A System of Employee Education and Vertical Job Enlargement," *Public Personnel Review*, Jan.

1968; John B. Gifford, "Job Enlargement," *Personnel Administration*, Jan./Feb. 1972; Thomas H. Patten, Jr., "Job Evaluation and Job Enlargement: A Collision Course?" *Human Resource Management*, Winter 1977; William N. Penzer, *Productivity and Motivation Through Job Engineering*, An AMA Management Briefing (New York: AMA, 1973); Richard D. Scott, "Job Enlargement—The Key to Increasing Job Satisfaction?" *PJ*, April 1973; Gerald I. Susman, "Job Enlargement: Effects of Culture on Worker Responses," *IR*, Feb. 1973.

See also JOB ENRICHMENT.

job enrichment An effort to motivate employees and to improve job satisfaction through a redesign of work content. Herzberg, who introduced the term in 1968, differentiates job enrichment from job enlargement: "Job enrichment provides the opportunity for the employee's psychological growth, while job enlargement merely makes a job structurally bigger."

A premise of job enrichment is that employees are motivated by such factors as achievement, recognition, the work itself, responsibility, and growth or advancement. A job is restructured, or enriched, according to these factors.

Source references: Antone Alber and Melvin Blumberg, "Team vs. Individual Approaches to Job Enrichment Programs," *Personnel*, Jan./Feb. 1981; Frederick Herzberg, "One More Time: How Do You Motivate Employees?" *Harvard BR*, Jan./Feb. 1968; ———, "The Wise Old Turk," *Harvard BR*, Sept./Oct. 1974; Harold L. Sheppard, "Task Enrichment and Wage Levels as Elements in Worker Attitudes," *Proceedings of the 26th A/M, IRRA*, ed. by Gerald Somers (Madison: 1974); Benjamin B. Tregoe, Jr., "Job Enrichment: How to Avoid the Pitfalls," *PJ*, June 1974; Lyle York, *Job Enrichment Revisited*, An AMA Management Briefing (New York: AMA, 1979).

See also JOB ENGINEERING, JOB SATISFACTION.

job environment Those factors which surround an employee while performing work. These may include the physical environment and involve such matters as noise, heat, dust, and the kind of material handled. Other factors in the job environment which may be either distracting or helpful are lighting, color scheme, temperature, and the physical characteristics of the work area. The job environment may also be taken to include the other employees, those working directly with the individual, those working nearby or cooperating with the individual, as well as supervisors and others with whom the individual associates in the performance of work.

job evaluation A systematic method of determining the value of each job in relation to other jobs in the plant. This may be accomplished by some rating method, frequently on the basis of a specific number of points for each of the factors involved. These factors might include education, skill, experience, and responsibility. The evaluation is designed to assist in establishing a rational wage structure and to avoid or eliminate internal inequalities. The evaluation is concerned with the nature and content of the job or jobs and not with the actual work or the qualifications of any specific individual for that job. The establishment of wage rates based on an evaluation of relationships between jobs helps to reduce the claim of favoritism or inequity within a particular wage structure.

Source references: Marsh W. Bates and Richard G. Vail, "Job Evaluation and Equal Employment Opportunity: A Tool for Compliance—A Weapon for Defense," *Employee Relations LJ*, Spring 1976; Joseph J. Beisel, "Recognition of Professional Preparation: The Key to Job Evaluation in Health Care Facilities," *PJ*, Feb. 1972; BNA, *Job Evaluation Policies and Procedures* (Washington: PPF Survey no. 113, 1976); Marvin G. Dertien, "The Accuracy of Job Evaluation Plans," *PJ*, July 1981; Arthur H. Dick, "Job Evaluation's Role in Employee Relations," *PJ*, March 1974; William Gomberg, *A Trade Union Manual of Job Evaluation* (Chicago: Roosevelt Press, 1947); International Association of Machinists, Research Dept., *What's Wrong With Job Evaluation: A Trade Union Manual* (Washington: 1954); Clark Kerr and Lloyd H. Fisher, "Effects of Environment and Administration of Job Evaluation," *Harvard BR*, May 1950; Elizabeth Lanhan, *Job Evaluation* (New York: McGraw-Hill, 1955); Bryan Livy, *Job Evaluation: A Critical Review* (New York:

Wiley, 1975); Charles W. Lytle, *Job Evaluation Methods* (2d ed., New York: Ronald Press, 1954); Jay L. Otis and Richard H. Leukart, *Job Evaluation* (2d ed., New York: PH, 1954); Thomas H. Patten, Jr., "Job Evaluation and Job Enlargement: A Collision Course?" *Human Resource Management*, Winter 1977; John A. Patton and C. L. Littlefield, *Job Evaluation, Text and Cases* (rev. ed., Homewood: Irwin, 1957); "Pitfalls in Administering Job Evaluation," *Management Review*, April 1955; Howard Risher, "Job Evaluation: Mystical or Statistical?" *Personnel*, Sept./Oct. 1978; Harold Suskin (ed.), *Job Evaluation and Pay Administration in the Public Sector* (Chicago: IPMA, 1977); David. J. Thomsen, "Eliminating Pay Discrimination Caused by Job Evaluation," *Personnel*, Sept./Oct. 1978; Donald J. Treiman, *Job Evaluation: An Analytic Review; Interim Report to the Equal Employment Opportunity Commission* (Washington: National Research Council, National Academy of Sciences, 1979); U.S. CSC, *Position Classification and Salary Setting, A Guide for Local Governments* (Chicago: 1979); John Zalusky, "Job Evaluation: An Uneven World," *American Federationist*, April 1981.

See also COMPARABLE WORTH, FACTOR COMPARISON METHOD, JOB, JOB ANALYSIS, JOB DESCRIPTION, JOB SPECIFICATION, PEG POINT, POINT PLAN.

job evaluation plans Sometimes referred to as job evaluation systems, they are the broad classifications used in establishing a job evaluation program. The two major systems of job evaluation plans are quantitative evaluation measures and qualitative evaluation measures. Treiman lists two schemes for each major system. Under the quantitative evaluation system are (1) the point system and (2) the factor-comparison system; under the qualitative evaluation measures system are (1) the ranking system and (2) the grading or classification system.

Source reference: Donald J. Treiman, *Job Evaluation: An Analytic Review,* Interim Report to the EEOC (Washington: National Academv of Sciences, 1979).

See also JOB EVALUATION, POINT PLAN, RANKING PLAN, WEIGHTED POINT METHOD.

job factor An element or characteristic of the job which has important bearing on the relative worth or value of the job among the major elements or job factors. These would usually include skill, accuracy, mental effort, practical ability or knowledge, working conditions, physical effort, responsibility, fatigue, experience, education, and similar factors.

In job evaluation the individual elements or factors used in a particular analysis are generally handled separately. After each of the elements is set up and properly rated, the sum of all of the factors in the particular job is used for the total evaluation.

job family A grouping of jobs having similar skill, experience, or other factors in common, such as training and aptitude. The factors may deal with tools and handling of machinery, or the type of materials with which an employee works. The job family usually includes a number of occupations. These occupations can be grouped since they have a number of common job or worker characteristics.

job grades Setting job grades is sometimes considered the last stage or step in job classification when the relationship of jobs, one to the other, has been established. The grade is designed to reflect the position of the particular job in the overall structure of jobs in the plant.

Jobs are ranked on the basis of wage rates to be paid rather than the wage actually received by employees on the particular job. The rates are usually assigned on the basis of rank, generally from low to high.

job grading The procedure in setting or establishing the various classes of jobs according to their relative importance. The job factors may include the qualifications for the job such as skill, knowledge, physical effort, and other factors considered in establishing the relative importance of the jobs. The grading or ranking method of job grading includes the careful analysis of the job, its job description, and the grading or ranking of the job from high to low order which shows the relative importance or requirements of the job.

Source references: Leon T. Alford and H. Russell Beatty, *Principles of Industrial Management* (New York: Ronald Press, 1951);

Charles W. Lytle, *Job Evaluation Methods* (2d ed., New York: Ronald Press, 1954).

See also RANKING PLAN.

job instruction training A program which received special attention during World War II mainly through the efforts of the Training-Within-Industry program of the War Manpower Commission designed to teach foremen and other supervisory employees the techniques of imparting information to workers. The Job Instruction Training (JIT) instructor followed a program which subsequently was used by the supervisory staff in the plant to train new workers or workers who transferred to a new department or operation.

The steps used in the War Production JIT given to new or transferred workers included the following:

(1) The preparation of the person learning the job;
(2) The presentation of the operation and the knowledge required;
(3) The performance tryout; and
(4) The subsequent follow-up to determine how the person was performing the work.

Source references: Alvin E. Dodd and James O. Rice, *How to Train Workers for War Industries* (New York: Harper, 1942); N. J. Murphy, "Job Instruction Training: One Answer to Your Dream Worker Problem," *Factory Management and Maintenance*, Jan. 1951; Vernon G. Schaefer, *Job Instruction* (New York: McGraw-Hill, 1943); Claude Thompson, *Personnel Management for Supervisors* (New York: PH, 1948); U.S. War Manpower Commission, Training Bureau, Training Within Industry Service, *The Training Within Industry Report, 1940–45* (Washington: 1945).

job instructor The individual assigned the job of showing others, particularly new or transferred workers, how to perform their jobs. The job instructor usually has the ability and know-how and is able to demonstrate how the job is to be best performed.

job methods training A job methods training program was developed and accelerated during World War II as part of the Training-Within-Industry program. The emphasis of job methods training was on the establishment of better procedures or more efficient ways of performing the work largely through simplification of job operations. The objective was not necessarily to speed up the job, but to break the job down into simpler operations and to eliminate duplication of effort. Short-cuts were devised to eliminate those operations which did not result in more efficient production. Through careful study of detailed job descriptions, it was possible to simplify and break the job down into minute parts. Each part was examined to determine whether it was necessary, and new work methods were subsequently developed.

job open for bid The phrase refers to the existence of a job opening and the opportunity for employees who feel they are qualified to perform the job to request that they be considered for the job opening.

Contract language dealing with the procedure for bidding might read as follows:

> A job is to be considered opened for bid only after an employee covered under this contract has left the job through layoff, discharge, or resignation, or transferred to another job or shift by bid. Any *new* job is to be considered an open job.
>
> A job to be considered open for bid shall have five consecutive days work on the same job before being posted for bid.
>
> However, when it is a known fact that an employee is going to leave a bid job, the management and the committee may agree to place another employee on said job temporarily, or the job may be bid if so desired.
>
> Any employee covered under this contract may bid for a job provided he has the ability and the seniority to entitle him to such job.
>
> On open jobs, the foreman shall post a list on the bulletin board and give a list of the time and the date of posting the job to the chairman of the shop committee.
>
> Any dispute that may arise shall be handled under the grievance procedure set forth in Article ——hereof.

See also BIDDING, POSTING.

job opening An available or vacant position which is to be filled through the employment or transfer of an individual. Job openings or job vacancies may be posted and employees notified of their existence under special language of the collective bargaining agreement.

See also JOB VACANCY.

Job Opportunities in the Business Sector (JOBS) A joint undertaking started in 1968 by the National Alliance of Businessmen and the Department of Labor to train and upgrade unemployed and disadvantaged persons. It was the first employment program involving the private sector. Employers were encouraged to provide jobs and training and a full range of support services to ensure satisfactory job adjustment. The program involved two types of employers—contract employers (reimbursement for extraordinary costs was funded by the Department of Labor) and noncontract employers (no reimbursement provided). The goal of the program was to place 500,000 disadvantaged persons in skilled jobs within three years. By the end of June 1970, 494,000 trainees were hired (74 percent by noncontract employers), with a retention rate of 47 percent.

According to Werneke, the JOBS programs "turned out to be quite vulnerable to the recession. Firms laid off workers and cancelled JOBS contracts, the participation of employers in new JOBS contracts fell off substantially, and funds which had been earmarked in anticipation of continued growth were reallocated to other programmes." The JOBS program was eliminated when Congress failed to authorize its $375 million budget for fiscal year 1977.

Source references: "Compromise on Public Works Bill; New Proposal for Full Employment," *Manpower Information Service*, June 23, 1976; George P. Shultz, *JOBS '70 Program* (Washington: U.S. Dept. of Labor, 1970); U.S. Congress, Joint Economic Committee, *Studies in Public Welfare, Paper No. 3—The Effectiveness of Manpower Training Programs: A Review of Research on the Impact on the Poor, A Staff Study*, by Jon H. Goldstein (Washington: 1972); Diane Werneke, "Job Creation Programmes: The United States Experience," *ILR*, July/Aug. 1976; Sterling E. Zimmerman, Jr., *The JOBS Program: An Evaluation of its Goals and Effects* (Ithaca: NYSSILR, Cornell Univ., 1968).

See also NATIONAL ALLIANCE OF BUSINESS (NAB), PUBLIC SERVICE CAREERS (PSC).

job pattern *See* MANNING TABLE.

job placement One of the major functions of the personnel office is to recruit employees and, through various methods of testing and interview, place these individuals in positions for which they are best qualified. Job placement may also involve the transfer of individuals from one position to another which the individual can perform more effectively. Efficient placement and assignment of work may lead to substantial reduction in labor turnover and consequent decrease in cost of recruiting and training new employees.

job posting *See* POSTING.

job protection A somewhat loosely used term to cover various efforts of a union to protect its members. This may include special protection in connection with procedures for discharge or layoff as a result of the application of job or shop rules, or may relate to protection under the seniority or other provisions of the collective bargaining agreement.

job questionnaire A form filled in by the employee requesting specific information about his job, on the basis of which a job analysis is made. The use of blank forms or questionnaires has not proven too satisfactory, particularly where the employee is not sufficiently familiar with his job or may be unable to describe it with sufficient detail or clarity. The job questionnaire may be used as a check or for comparative purposes to determine how the individual regards his own job and its component parts. The procedure may be useful in the examination or analysis of a job or job description.

Source reference: Richard C. Smyth and Matthew Murphy, *Job Evaluation and Employee Rating* (New York: McGraw-Hill, 1946).

job ranking *See* JOB GRADING.

job rate The lowest or minimum rate paid to a qualified or experienced worker for a particular job. The rate may be a single rate or in case of payments within a rate range it would be the minimum of the range. Job rates below the minimum rate would be those in which employees are hired as learners or probationary employees at an entrance rate below that of the experienced worker on the job.

job rating Comparison of information on each job or position against the rating scales already established. Job rating is designed to determine the position of each job compared to other jobs or positions being evaluated. The evaluation involves some rating technique. It has been held by many authors in the job evaluation field that rating in some form or another is utilized in most job evaluation methods: the factor comparison method, the point rating method, the ranking method, and the classification method.

Job rating may be done by a single individual whose judgment may be final, or it may be done by two or more raters working independently who then compare notes on the rating of the job, or it may be done by a special committee.

Source references: AMA, *Putting Job Rating to Work* (New York: Personnel Series no. 49, 1941); National Electric Manufacturers Association, IR Dept., *Job Rating Manual* (New York: 1946); National Metal Trades Association, *Job Rating Plan and Salary Rating Plan* (Chicago: 1945); M. F. Steigers, *The Theory and Practice of Job Rating* (New York: McGraw-Hill, 1944).

job relations training The training is concerned with methods of obtaining increased production by getting the supervisor to understand better the people who work for him, to appreciate their basic differences, and to establish good working relationships with the people around him. Cooperation and teamwork are key considerations in job relations training. Methods of problem-solving as well as procedures for handling grievances are also part of this program, developed by the Training-Within-Industry section of the War Manpower Commission during World War II.

job rotation A method used in some plants to provide an opportunity for employees to become familiar with a variety of operations in the company. In some situations it may help build morale and provide a greater sense of understanding of the total production picture within the plant or operation. Occasionally it may help maintain production schedules where employees in some operations are absent or ill, and where those who have had the job rotation training are able to fill in for a short period of time.

job safety training Training given to employees and supervisors to reduce the hazards in certain occupations and to provide safer working conditions. It may assist supervisors in training those under their supervision to avoid accidents.

See also SAFETY CAMPAIGNS, SAFETY PROGRAMS.

job satisfaction Those outward or inner manifestations which give the individual a sense of enjoyment or accomplishment in the performance of his work. Job satisfaction may come from the product or item produced, from the speed with which it is accomplished, or from other features relating to the job and its performance. Attitudes toward the job may be affected by such items as the pay scale, the relationship of the individual to the supervisor, the general working conditions, including safety, and many other factors which are not easily discernible on the surface.

Source references: Paul J. Andrisani, *Work Attitudes and Labor Market Experience, Evidence From the National Longitudinal Surveys* (New York: Praeger, 1978); Bonnie Carroll, *Job Satisfaction*, revised and updated by Mary B. Blumen (rev. ed., Ithaca: Cornell Univ., NYSSILR, Key Issues Series no. 3, 1973); Anthony F. Chelte, James Wright, and Curt Tausky, "Did Job Satisfaction Really Drop During the 1970's?" *MLR*, Nov. 1982; Frederick Herzberg and Alex Zautra, "Orthodox Job Enrichment: Measuring True Quality in Job Satisfaction," *Personnel*, Sept./Oct. 1976; Malcolm D. Hill, "Variations in Job Satisfaction Among Higher Education Faculty in Unionized and Nonunionized Institutions in Pennsylvania," *Journal of Collective Negotiations in the Public Sector*, Vol. 11, No. 2, 1982; Frederic Jacobs and Peter Cowden, "The Relevance of Recurrent Education to Worker Satisfaction," *MLR*, April 1977; Robert P. Quinn and Martha S. Baldi de Mandilovitch, *Education and Job Satisfaction: A Questionable Payoff* (Washington: U.S. Dept. of HEW, National Institute of Education, NIE Papers in Education and Work no. 5, 1977); Guy Roustang, "Why Study Working Conditions via Job Satisfaction? A Plea for Direct Analysis," *ILR*, May/June 1977; Harold L. Sheppard and Neal

Q. Herrick, *Where Have All the Robots Gone? Worker Dissatisfaction in the '70s* (New York: Free Press, 1972); George Strauss, *Job Satisfaction, Motivation, and Job Redesign* (Berkeley: UC, Institute of IR, Reprint no. 390, 1974); U.S. Dept. of Labor, ETA, *Work Attitudes and Work Experience, The Impact of Attitudes on Behavior* (Washington: R & D Monograph 60, 1979).

See also WORK SATISFACTION.

job scarcity A limited opportunity for employment which may be due to economic or business recession or seasonality of work or special problems in connection with production in a particular industry. Even during periods of high employment there are areas or pockets of job scarcity in certain special skills or occupations.

job security A sense or feeling that the employee is protected against job loss. This may be the result of having special skills difficult to duplicate, the nature of the work, seniority, or through some other method of job protection. Some efforts toward greater job security are directed toward stabilizing employment. Unions, for example, may try to negotiate contracts that preserve or guarantee work for unit members. Unemployment compensation and efforts to enlarge the area of guaranteed annual wages or supplemental unemployment benefit (SUB) plans are also directed toward providing greater employment stability and a sense of job security. Job security, like other forms of security, is a relative concept.

Source references: Richard N. Block, "The Impact of Union-Negotiated Employment Security Provisions on the Manufacturing Quit Rate," *Proceedings of the 29th A/M, IRRA*, ed. by James Stern and Barbara Dennis (Madison: 1977); Ted Cassman, "Deconsolidating the Work Preservation Doctrine: *Dolphin-Associated Transport*," *Industrial Relations LJ*, Vol. 4, no. 4, 1981; Rosaline Levenson, *Job Security in Public Employment: A Vanishing Myth* (Chico: California State Univ., School of Behavioral and Social Sciences, Discussion Paper 79–2, 1979); June Weisberger, *Job Security and Public Employees* (Ithaca: NYSSILR, Cornell Univ., Institute of Public Employment, Monograph no. 2, 1973); ———, *Recent Developments in Job Security: Layoffs and Discipline in the Public Sector* (Ithaca: NYSSILR, Cornell Univ., Institute of Public Employment, Monograph no. 6, 1976).

See also TENURE.

job segregation *See* OCCUPATIONAL SEGREGATION.

job selling A procedure once quite widespread in the form of kickbacks or payment of fees for obtaining employment. These payments were in the form of a partial return of wages or a special payment on a fixed basis over a period of time for either obtaining a job or staying on the payroll.

job sharing Defined by Meier as "an arrangement whereby two employees hold a position together, whether they are as a team jointly responsible for the whole or separately for each half." The arrangement is variously termed sharing, splitting, pairing, twinning, and tandem employment and "there is little agreement on terminology, even among practitioners. Job sharing is generally taken to refer to a *way to convert* full time jobs into two or more part time positions—often without regard to *how* jobs are divided." Meives suggests that "job pairing" may be the more precise term to describe the arrangement calling for joint responsibility of the total workload.

According to Meier, job sharing was initiated during the 1960s in order to increase career part-time employment opportunities. Job sharing is seen as a means of enhancing the work participation of women and young and older workers. It is also thought to promote more leisure time and greater work flexibility.

Job sharing is not work sharing. Work sharing is the temporary redistribution of work time among employees in lieu of a layoff.

Source references: Fred Best and Barry Stern, "Education, Work, and Leisure: Must They Come in That Order?" *MLR*, July 1977; Clifford E. Hutton and Joy Simon McFarlin, "Providing Better University Personnel Through Job Sharing," *Journal of the College and University Personnel Association*, Summer 1982; Gretl S. Meier, *Job Sharing, A New Pattern for Quality of Work and Life* (Kalamazoo: Upjohn Institute for Employment Research, 1979); Susan Fritch Meives "Part-Time Work: A Multiperspective Analysis" (Unpublished Ph.D. dissertation, Univ. of Wisconsin-Madison, 1979); Barney Olmstead, "Job Sharing: An Emerging Work-Style," *ILR*, May/June 1979; U.S. Dept. of Labor, ETA, *Exchanging Earnings for Leisure: Findings of an Exploratory National Survey on Work Time Preferences* (Washington: R & D Monograph 79, 1980).

See also WORK SHARING.

job specification This is sometimes referred to as a man-job specification, job description, or personnel specification. It consists of the job analysis of a particular job and the requirements of the person who most effectively would fill that position. This would include the nature of the operation, the process, the type of materials used, the machinery, equipment, time standards, the general and environmental features of the work, and its possible effect on the employee both physically and emotionally. It might include such items as vision, dexterity, physical strength, hearing, education and training, previous experience, the hours, wages, and other factors involving remuneration, the opportunities for transfers or promotion, and the relation of the particular job to other positions in the plant.

Job specifications are an important part of the personnel program in recruiting and hiring and are used to avoid the assignment of individuals to jobs for which they are not properly equipped. The job specification should contain all of the vital and basic characteristics and requirements of the job. It may not necessarily contain the maximum conditions but it should contain the minimum or standard requirements for the effective performance of the job.

job splitting The breaking up of a job into its various components so that those parts requiring the least skill can be performed by individuals who are not highly skilled and so that the specialized work can be done by skilled employees. The effort to divide work is also directed toward more efficient production as well as better quality. It is also expected that the splitting of jobs into their various components may result in reduction of fatigue and in better utilization of equipment, methods, and work materials.

See also JOB DILUTION.

jobs sent out *See* SUBCONTRACTING.

job study An attempt to collect full and complete information concerning a particular job and its content. Job study includes the study of all phases of the job and provides the basic data for job specifications and job descriptions. Many methods and procedures are utilized and a wide variety of techniques is available for job study, including not only time and motion study but also other methods of analyzing the full requirements and characteristics of the job.

See also JOB ANALYSIS.

job tenure According to BLS, "a measure of the length of time an employee has worked continuously for the same employer," although not necessarily in the same occupation. Job tenure "is *not* a measure of how long a person will stay with a single employer. Rather, it is an index of how long one has been with an employer as of a specific point in time . . . job tenure is an index of accumulated time on the job for those still working." Persons terminate their tenure "by quitting, being laid off for 30 days or more, entering the Armed Forces, or transferring to a job in a different company."

Source references: Richard Freeman, *Determinants of Job Tenure in the U.S.* (Washington: U.S. National Technical Information Service, 1977); ———, "The Effect of Unionism on Worker Attachment to Firms," *Journal of Labor Research*, Spring 1980; Robert E. Hall, *The Importance of Lifetime Jobs in the U.S. Economy* (Cambridge: NBER, WP 560, 1980); Francis W. Horvath, "Job Tenure of Workers in January 1981," *MLR*, Sept. 1982; William Merrilees, "Interindustry Variations in Job Tenure," *IR*, Spring 1978; Nancy F. Rytina, "Tenure as a Factor in the Male-Female Earnings Gap," *MLR*, April 1982; U.S. Dept. of Labor, BLS, *Job Tenure and Occupational Change, 1981* (Washington: Bull. 2162, 1983).

See also ACADEMIC TENURE, TENURE.

job title The name or other designation which is used to identify the particular work such as carpenter, painter, pipe fitter, die maker, etc. Jobs with the same job title may not always contain the same job content or include the identical type of work. This is particularly true where large machines are used in one plant and relatively small or old machines in another.

job training Various methods and procedures directed toward providing an opportunity for unskilled or semiskilled workers to qualify for jobs of a higher skill or greater complexity. Training for specialized work or for work of higher skill may require long periods of training in some positions and relatively short training periods for others.

See also TRAINING.

Job Training Partnership Act (JTPA) of 1982 The law that replaced the Comprehensive Employment and Training Act. The goal of JTPA is to train or retrain and place eligible individuals in permanent, unsubsidized employment, preferably in the private sector. The purpose of the Act is "to establish programs to prepare youth and unskilled adults for entry into the labor force and to afford job training to those economically disadvantaged individuals and other individuals facing serious barriers to employment, who are in special need of such training to obtain productive employment." Specific programs in the Act include training services for the disadvantaged, employment and training assistance for dislocated workers, and the Job Corps.

The Act establishes the National Commission for Employment Policy, which has the responsibility to examine issues on the development, coordination, and administration of employment and training programs and to advise the President and the Congress on national employment and training issues. The Act also amends the Wagner-Peyser Act. This amendment is intended to promote coordination between job training programs and the U.S. Employment Service.

Source references: Job Training Partnership Act of 1982, as amended, Pub. L. 97–300, 96 Stat. 1322 (codified as amended in scattered sections of 18, 29, and 42 U.S.C.); Robert Guttman, "Job Training Partnership Act: New Help for the Unemployed," *MLR*, March 1983.

See also APPRENTICESHIP, COMPREHENSIVE EMPLOYMENT AND TRAINING ACT (CETA) OF 1973, DEMONSTRATION PROJECT, PRIVATE INDUSTRY COUNCIL (PIC).

job vacancy A vacant position which an employer hopes to fill, including part-time and casual job openings.

According to Chavrid and Kuptzin, the following are excluded from the job vacancy category: "(1) jobs held for employees who will be recalled; (2) jobs to be filled by transfer, promotion, or demotion; (3) jobs held for workers on paid or unpaid leave; (4) jobs filled by overtime work which are not intended to be filled by new workers; (5) job openings for which new workers were already hired and scheduled to start work at a later date; and (6) jobs unoccupied because of labor-management disputes."

There is increasing interest in compiling job vacancy data to effectuate maximum utilization of manpower resources.

Source references: Edward Alban and Mark Jackson, "The Job Vacancy-Unemployment Ratio and Labor-Force Participation," *ILRR*, April 1976; Paul A. Armknecht, Jr., "Job Vacancies in Manufacturing, 1969–73," *MLR*, Aug. 1974; Vladimir D. Chavrid and Harold Kuptzin, "Employment Service Operating Data As a Measure of Job Vacancies," *The Measurement and Interpretation of Job Vacancies* (New York: NBER, 1966); Leonard A. Lecht, *Changes in Occupational Characteristics: Planning Ahead for the 1980s* (New York: The Conference Board, Report no. 691, 1976); John G. Myers, "Can You Measure Job Vacancies?" *Conference Board Record*, May 1965; ———, *Job Vacancies in the Firm and the Labor Market* (New York: NICB, Studies in Business Economics no. 109, 1969); John G. Myers and Daniel Creamer, *Measuring Job Vacancies* (New York: NICB, Studies in Business Economics no. 97, 1967); NBER, *The Measurement and Interpretation of Job Vacancies* (New York: 1966); New York State, Dept. of Labor, *Projected Annual Job Openings by Occupation and Vocational Education Region, New York State, 1974–1985* (New York: 1982); Noreen L. Preston, *The Help-Wanted Index: Technical Description and Behavioral Trends* (New York: The Conference Board, Report no. 716, 1977).

See also JOB OPENING.

job work Usually work for which an employee is paid a fixed amount after the work is completed. It differs from piecework or other methods of compensation where payment is made for completion of particular items or for a period of time rather than the completion of an entire job or project.

Johns Hopkins University Studies (in Historical and Political Science) on American Trade Unionism Some of the studies are listed below: G. E. Barnett (ed.), *A Trial Bibliography of American Trade-Union Publications*, 1904; A. M. Sakolski, *The Finances of American Trade Unions*, 1906; W. Kirk, *National Labor Federations in the United Sates*, 1906; J. M. Motley, *Apprenticeship in American Trade Unions*, 1907; J. B. Kennedy, *Beneficiary Features of American Trade Unions*, 1908; E. R. Spedden, *The Trade Union Label*, 1910; F. T. Stockton, *The Closed Shop in American Trade Unions*, 1911; D. A. McCabe, *The Standard Rate in American Trade Unions*, 1912; F. E. Wolfe, *Admission to American Trade Unions*, 1912; T. W. Glocker, *The Government of American Trade Unions*, 1913; N. R. Whitney, *Jurisdiction in American Building-Trades Unions*, 1914; J. H. Ashworth, *The Helper and American Trade Unions*, 1915; L. Wolman, *The Boycott in American Trade Unions*, 1916; G. M. James, *The Control of Strikes in American Trade Unions*, 1916; W. C. Weyforth, *The Organizability of Labor*, 1917; D. P. Smelzer, *Unemployment and American Trade Unions*, 1919; J. S. Robinson, *The Amalgamated Association of Iron, Steel and Tin Workers*, 1920; F. T. Stockton, *The International Molders Union of North America*, 1922; V. J. Wyckoff, *The Wage Policies of Labor Organizations in a Period of Industrial Depression*, 1926; D. M. Schneider, *The Workers' (Communist) Party and American Trade Unions*, 1928; A. T. Helbing, *The Departments of the American Federation of Labor*, 1931; J. I. Seidman, *Yellow Dog Contract*, 1932; L. Teper, *Hours of Labor*, 1932.

Johnstown Citizens Committee This was a special group of "citizens" organized in 1937 during the Little Steel Strike. Reports on the Committee's work in connection with the Cambria Plant of the Bethlehem Steel Corporation indicated that it was sponsored and supported by the Bethlehem company and was designed largely to undermine support of the union in its strike against Bethlehem Steel. The record showed that the company turned over in excess of $32,000 through the Committee to Mayor Shields who utilized these funds to hire special deputies and to purchase ammunition to be used during the strike.

The operation of the Johnstown Citizens Committee was similar to the strategy involved in the more well-known Mohawk Valley formula, which was utilized by the Remington Rand Company in the promotion of a back-to-work movement.

Source reference: George W. Hartmann and Theo. Newcomb (ed.), *Industrial Conflict—A Psychological Interpretation* (New York: Cordon, 1939).

See also BACK-TO-WORK MOVEMENT, MOHAWK VALLEY FORMULA.

joint agreement Sometimes used interchangeably with the term "collective bargaining agreement" or with the term "industrywide agreement." Generally, it is a contract signed by several unions with one employer, or several employers with one union, or several unions and several employers. It may cover an association of employers in the industry or in a general area.

The broader reference to a collective agreement indicates that the terms have been mutually or jointly agreed to by both unions and management. The reference to the geographic character of the agreement or the coverage of many employers or many unions is designed to reflect the common interest of a group of craft organizations in a locality or a group of employers or unions within a specific industry in a multiparty contract.

See also AGREEMENT, COLLECTIVE; AGREEMENT, INDUSTRYWIDE.

joint and survivor annuity An annual income which begins at retirement and continues for life with a provision that should the employee die while his annuitant is still living, predetermined payments or a predetermined rate will continue to be paid to the annuitant for life.

See also ANNUITY.

joint apprenticeship committee or council An employer-union panel established by agreement to administer an apprentice training program. A typical contract clause provides thus:

> Duties of Joint Apprenticeship Committee: The Local Joint Apprenticeship Committee [three employer and three union representatives] shall select a chairman and secretary and shall determine rules of procedure and set the time and place of meetings which shall be held with practical regularity.
>
> The Local Joint Apprenticeship Committee shall be responsible for the administration and supervision of the Apprenticeship Standards which among other things, include a progressive schedule of wages, on-the-job training, periodic examination, ratio, classroom instruction, and adjustment of complaints.
>
> The Local Joint Apprenticeship Committee may seek assistance from any agency interested in furthering apprenticeship and may request the designation of a representative who shall serve as an advisor and consultant.

joint bargaining *See* COLLECTIVE BARGAINING, COALITION.

Joint Congressional Committee on the Economic Report Under the terms of the Full Employment Act of 1946, a special committee of senators and representatives is required to review the President's Annual Economic Report and Report to the Congress. The Joint Congressional Committee frequently holds hearings and invites citizens and specialists to present comments and evaluate the data covered by the Economic Report. This may involve information concerning inflation, wages, prices, foreign trade, and the whole series of economic factors having some relation to the state of the economy of the country. Substantial data frequently are presented by labor and management organizations, private economists, and specialists from universities.

See also COUNCIL OF ECONOMIC ADVISERS.

joint council board An organization or group of delegates who represent a number of locals of the same national or international union in a particular locality or region. They are sometimes called District Councils. This organization attempts to review problems of mutual concern and to establish some basis for activity or policy which best meets the general interest of the group.

joint hiring hall Essentially, a central hiring or employment office which is administered by the union and employer or unions' and employers' organizations. Although the closed shop is prohibited by the Taft-Hartley Act, hiring halls are permitted.

The hiring hall procedures originally were designed to decasualize labor in the maritime and longshore industry, to provide a central pooling of employees, and to rotate job opportunities.

Prior to passage of the Taft-Hartley Act, the joint hiring halls established, for example on the Pacific Coast for longshoremen, were administered by joint committees of labor and management and the costs of administration were shared by the union and the employer association. The dispatcher who assigned the individual to the job was appointed by the union and union members were given preference. Nonmembers on the extra list were hired when no union member was available. Disputes concerning the operation of the hiring hall were subject to the arbitration machinery of the contract.

Under present federal law, there must be no discrimination because of membership or nonmembership in the union.

Source references: Paul Eliel, "Industrial Peace and Conflict: A Study of Two Pacific Coast Industries," *ILRR*, July 1949; Joseph P. Goldberg, *The Maritime Story: A Study in Labor-Management Relations* (Cambridge: Harvard UP, 1958); Vernon H. Jensen, *Hiring of Dock Workers* (Cambridge: Harvard UP, 1964); U.S. Congress, Senate, Committee on Labor and Public Welfare, *Maritime Hiring Halls* (Washington: 1950, 1951, 1952).

See also HIRING HALL.

joint industrial council Sometimes known as work councils or Whitley Councils, named after a special British parliamentary committee known as the Whitley Committee, which made recommendations in 1917 leading to the establishment of joint consultation committees. The committees or councils consisted of representatives of management and unions primarily concerned with procedures for getting greater efficiency and industrial harmony. The work of the committees was to be an adjunct to, not a substitute for, the collective bargaining procedures. The functions of these committees were largely advisory and were designed to make the actual collective bargaining process work more smoothly.

The Whitley Councils in Great Britain were organized on national, district, and local levels.

The Whitley Committee, which assumed that organization of labor and collective bargaining were desirable, held that "the essential condition of securing a permanent improvement in the relations between employers and employed is that there should be adequate organization on the part of both employers and work people." The proposals outlined for joint cooperation throughout several industries depended for their ultimate success upon there being such organization on both sides; such organization was necessary also to provide means whereby the arrangements and agreements made might be effectively carried out. The recommendations of the Whitley Committee included the following items:

(1) The extension of the trade or wage boards to industries which were not extensively or highly organized;
(2) The formation of national joint industrial councils, district councils, and works committees in industries which were highly organized—those in which at least 75 percent of the employees were in the union;
(3) The formation of a standing arbitration tribunal and the formation of ad hoc bodies to inquire into and report on disputes as well as the retention and continuation of the then existing voluntary boards of conciliation.

Source references: L. W. C. S. Barnes, *Consult and Advise* (Kingston: Queen's Univ., IRC, Research and Current Issues series no. 26, 1974); Paul H. Douglas, "Shop Committees: Substitute for, or Supplement to Trade Unions?" *Journal of Political Economy*, Feb. 1921; Walter Galenson, *Comparative Labor Movements* (New York: PH, 1952); ILO, *Conciliation and Arbitration in Industrial Disputes* (Geneva: Studies and Reports, Series A(IR) no. 34, 1933); Henry Parris, *Staff Relations in the Civil Service* (London: Allen & Unwin, 1973); Boris Stern, *Joint Industrial Councils in Great Britain* (Washington: U.S. Dept. of Labor, BLS, Bull. no. 255, 1919); ———, *Works Council Movement in Germany* (Washington: U.S. Dept. of Labor, BLS, Bull. no. 383, 1925); Albert B. Wolfe, *Works Committees and Joint Industrial Councils* (2d ed., Philadelphia: U.S. Shipping Board Emergency Fleet, IR Div., 1919).

joint label In cases where more than one union has taken part in the production of a particular commodity or product, the union label that indicates the names of these labor organizations is generally known as a joint label.

See also UNION LABEL (BUG); UNION LABEL AND SERVICE TRADES DEPARTMENT.

joint production committees These are labor-management committees concerned primarily with increasing production during periods of emergency or war. The committees in nonunion plants would be selected by the employees and by management to assist in working out various problems which might include safety, absenteeism, or other problems which retard or reduce plant efficiency. In unionized plants the selection of the committee representing the employees would be made by the union and the same type of functions would be performed except that matters are limited to those covered by the terms of the collective bargaining agreement.

Source references: W. Ellison Chalmers, "Joint Production Committees in United States War Plants," *ILR*, Jan. 1943; ILO, *Joint Production Committees in Great Britain* (Montreal: Studies and Reports, Series A, no. 42, 1943); Emil J. Lever and F. Goodell, "Organization and Conduct of the Joint Production Committee," *Advanced Management*, March 1948; Frank S. McElroy and Alexander Moros, "Joint Production Committees, January 1948," *MLR*, Aug. 1948; Clarence H. Northcott, "Joint Production Committees," *PJ*, Oct. 1942.

See also LABOR COOPERATION, LABOR-MANAGEMENT COMMITTEE, LABOR-MANAGEMENT PRODUCTION COMMITTEES.

joint rate setting A method commonly used for establishing piece rates by representatives of management and labor through joint action. The degree of participation and the functions performed will vary from situation to situation. Much of the practice will depend on how effectively labor and management find the joint process helpful rather than a hindrance, not only in the setting up of the job and the establishment of the rate, but also in settling the difficulties arising after the rate has been jointly established.

See also RATE SETTING.

joint study committees *See* CONSULTATION.

joint time study Generally refers to efforts in time and motion study where both union and company representatives take part in timing the operation or job. Frequently agreement is possible following the study; otherwise, procedures are established to work out differences between company and union representatives.

See also TIME STUDY.

joint wage review committee During World War II procedures sometimes were adopted whereby joint committees of labor and management would review the work of employees after their probationary period, or at regular time intervals, to determine the hourly wage rate of the employee in the particular department. The following provision is illustrative.

> The union and the company shall establish and maintain joint committees to review by mutual agreement hourly wage rates of employees in each department upon completion of each individual's six months period of continuous employment with the company.
>
> Each wage review committee shall consist of six members, three from the union and three from the company, who are company employees. One of the union members shall be rotated so that the union committeeman of each department can serve as a member of the committee during the time the rates of his department are being reviewed. If a wage review committee fails to reach an agreement in regard to any case brought before it, then and in that event, the matter in question shall be referred in writing within 24 hours to a general wage committee, consisting of three men from each party to the agreement. Within 5 days after the general wage committee has received a deadlocked case, a decision shall be handed down. In the event the general wage committee is unable to reach an agreement, the matter shall be submitted to arbitration as provided for in the agreement. In accordance with past practice, the company will approve interim individual increases when justified by proof of the individual involved that he has been performing work which calls for a higher rate, job, or wage classification to the satisfaction of his foreman. In all such cases, the foreman and the union committeemen shall be consulted prior to the granting of such increases.

See also WAGE REVIEW.

Jones and Laughlin Steel case *See* NLRB V. JONES AND LAUGHLIN STEEL COMPANY.

journeyman A qualified, skilled tradesman who has completed a special apprenticeship program and mastered a specific skill or craft. In the medieval period apprenticeship led to qualification as a journeyman. The journeyman in turn was ultimately admitted to the guild as a master who would be able to hire apprentices for training.

A skilled worker may be required to plan a particular job and obtain the desired results from a description of the finished product or from sketches or blueprints setting out the particular job to be performed. The journeyman must have the ability to combine various basic or fundamental operations in order to complete a particular job.

journeyman pay (rate) The wages or rate of pay given to a skilled craftsman or journeyman. Occasionally rates below the minimum for the journeyman rate may be given to handicapped employees or those unable to perform all of the functions of the job. Rates above the minimum rate may be paid depending on the length of time or seniority of the individual worker. Special rates for superannuated or handicapped journeymen are generally made by special arrangement with the particular union involved. Otherwise, the minimum rate for the trade in a particular area is the union scale for the fully qualified individual, skilled in a particular trade or craft, who has finished his apprenticeship or equivalent training.

Joyce v. Great Northern Railway A 1907 decision of the Supreme Court of Minnesota holding constitutional a law forbidding the use of the blacklist. This decision was issued during a period when the practice was widespread and when no effort was being made to prevent its use.

It was, of course, difficult to maintain any degree of supervision over blacklisting practices engaged in by some employer groups because such practices were handled unofficially. Some employers resorted to the establishment of a whitelist which consisted of employees who were *eligible* for employment rather than the so-called blacklist or group held to be undesirable. Both lists accomplished the purpose of preventing undesirable or unionized employees from obtaining employment.

Source reference: Joyce v. Great Northern Railway, 100 Minnesota 225, 110 NW 975 (1907).

See also BLACKLIST, NORRIS-LAGUARDIA ACT, WHITELIST.

Joy Silk Mills case Case in which the NLRB ordered an employer to bargain with a union even though the union lost a consent representation election conducted by the Board. The Board found that the employer had refused to bargain when the union represented a majority of the employees and that the union's loss of strength was caused by the employer's coercive activities. The order was enforced by the U.S. Court of Appeals for the District of Columbia.

Source reference: Joy Silk Mills v. NLRB, 185 F2d 732, 27 LRRM 2012 (CA DC, 1950), *cert. denied*, 341 US 914, 27 LRRM 2633 (1951).

judicial procedure of unions *See* INTERNAL AFFAIRS OF UNIONS.

jurisdiction, union The authority claimed by a union to represent certain groups of workers either in a specific type of work or occupation in a particular industry or industries or in a certain geographic area. The claim of jurisdiction may come from a grant, by AFL-CIO, of a charter giving a union the right to organize employees in a particular area, both as to work or industry. Sometimes the jurisdiction of a union in a particular area may come from a grant extended to it by the national or international union.

The term may apply to the authority of a particular union over certain employees or groups within a plant where more than one union has members. The particular union's jurisdiction would be confined to those members covered by its own collective bargaining agreement.

Sometimes the claim of jurisdiction does not rest on a charter from the parent organization or the international union, but stems entirely from the fact that employees have been organized by the union and it negotiates for them or has obtained the exclusive bargaining rights as the result of an election held by the NLRB or a state board. The jurisdictions of unions not affiliated with AFL-CIO depend almost completely on the extent to which they are able to persuade workers to join their organization.

Union jurisdiction or claim of jurisdiction will vary over a period of time as the changes in industrial technology lead to the use of new materials, new machinery, and new facilities, so that the union itself must take cognizance of these changes and seek to maintain membership in that particular area of production or extend to other areas should employment decline within its own previous jurisdiction.

See also CRAFT UNION, INDUSTRIAL UNION, JURISDICTIONAL DISPUTE.

jurisdictional agreement An understanding or pact between two or more organizations indicating some agreement as to the employees which each should have the authority to organize. The agreement may cover the type of occupation or industrial grouping or may specify a particular company or geographic area. Such an agreement between unions is, of course, not binding on other organizations, independent or otherwise, which may also seek to organize these employees and to assert jurisdiction over them.

jurisdictional dispute A disagreement, controversy, or conflict between two or more unions concerning the assignment of, or the right to perform, certain types of work. Also, a dispute over the right to represent employees in a particular company or industry. Organizational disputes involving two or more unions may be resolved by the AFL-CIO, or may be resolved by agreement of the two unions, or submitted to a third party or body for determination. With the passage of the Taft-Hartley Act holding jurisdictional strikes contrary to public policy, unions are under greater pressure to resolve their own jurisdictional problems without submission to the NLRB.

The question as to which group of employees should perform the work in a particular plant or industry creates numerous disputes, particularly when changes in operation or materials involve the use of new equipment, machinery, or work products. The substitution for wood frames of metal frames, and the question whether jobs that involve the handling of items for a short period of time must be performed by separate craftsmen, are problems which illustrate the nature of the difficulty.

Various efforts have been made by the respective federations and the combined AFL-CIO to reduce, if not completely eliminate, jurisdictional disputes harmful not only to the unions involved but also to the public and to the labor movement as a whole. Although most jurisdictional disputes are resolved without a strike, some may result in strike activity by one or the other of the unions involved.

Section 8(b)(4) of the Taft-Hartley Act holds it to be an unfair labor practice for a union to engage in certain activities which would result in a strike or other difficulty arising out of action by a union forcing or requiring an employer to assign particular work to employees in a particular trade, craft, or class rather than to another trade, craft, or class, the exception being the case when such an employer is failing to conform to an order of certification of the NLRB, determining the bargaining representative for employees performing such work.

When the union is unable to work out the problem through submission to some outside group for settlement or through negotiations, the Board is given the authority under Section 10(k) to decide which union has jurisdiction over the work. Section 704(a) of the Labor-Management Reporting and Disclosure Act of 1959 retained the language of the Taft-Hartley Act dealing with jurisdictional disputes.

The Supreme Court in *NLRB v. Radio and Television Broadcast Engineers Union, Local 1212, International Brotherhood of Electrical Workers* (364 US 573, 47 LRRM 2332 (1961)), held that the NLRB *was required* under the statute to determine the issue of jurisdiction between two unions. The Supreme Court held, in part, that the Board was required in the absence of a voluntary adjustment or agreement by the parties to decide the case on the merits and to determine which of the employee groups was entitled to the disputed work and to make an award in accordance with its decision. The Court said:

> We agree with the Second, Third and Seventh Circuits that Section 10(k) requires the Board to decide jurisdictional disputes on their merits and conclude that in this case that requirement means that the Board should affirmatively have decided whether the technicians or the stage employees were entitled to do the disputed work. The language of Section 10(k), supplementing Section 8(b)(4)(D) as it does, sets up a method adopted by Congress to try to get jurisdictional disputes settled. The words "hear and determine the dispute" convey not only the idea of hearing but also the idea of deciding a controversy.

The Supreme Court summed up as follows:

> We conclude therefore that the Board's interpretation of its duty under Section 10(k) is wrong and that under that Section it is the Board's responsibility and duty to decide which of two or more employee groups claiming the rights to perform certain work tasks is right. Having failed to meet this responsibility in this case, the Board could not properly proceed under Section 10(k) to adjudicate the unfair labor charge. The Court of Appeals was therefore correct in refusing to enforce the order which resulted from that proceeding.

Source references: Benjamin Aaron, "The Mediation of Jurisdictional Disputes," *LLJ*, Aug. 1956; Harriet Berger and Edward A. Blomstedt, "Clerk vs. Mail Handler: Jurisdictional Disputes in the Postal Service," *LLJ*, Oct. 1976; BNA, *Construction Craft Jurisdiction Agreements* (Washington: 1971); David L. Cole, "Interrelationships in the Settlement of Jurisdictional Disputes," *LLJ*, July 1959; Abraham L. Gitlow, "Technology and NLRB Decisions in Bargaining Unit and Jurisdictional Dispute Cases," *LLJ*, Dec. 1965; Richard N. Goldstein, "Electronic Journalism and Union Rivalry: Is Litigation the Answer?" *LLJ*, March 1978; Robert G. Hoffman, "The Representational Dispute," *LLJ*, June 1973; Edgar A. Jones, Jr., "An Arbitral Answer to a Jurisdictional Dilemma: The Carey Decision and Trilateral Arbitration of Jurisdictional Disputes," 11 *UCLA LR* 327 (1964); ———, "A Sequel in the Evolution of the Trilateral Arbitration of Jurisdictional Labor Disputes—The Supreme Court's Gift to Embattled Employers," 15 *UCLA LR* 877 (1968); Douglas Leslie, "The Role of the NLRB and the Courts in Resolving Union

Jurisdictional Disputes," *IR Law Digest*, Summer 1976; Philip Taft, "Jurisdictional Disputes," *Annals*, Nov. 1946.

See also DEMARCATION DISPUTE, FACTIONALISM, INTERUNION DISPUTE, RAIDING, RIVAL UNIONISM.

jurisdictional guide, NLRB A booklet once prepared by the Division of Information, NLRB, offering guidance to labor and management and other parties who may want to use the processes of the National Labor Relations Act.

The pamphlet listed the legal origins and functions of the NLRB, its jurisdiction, and standards for accepting cases. Current information on NLRB jurisdiction is available in *An Outline of Law and Procedure in Representation Elections.*

Source reference: U.S. NLRB, *An Outline of Law and Procedure in Representation Elections* (Washington: 1974).

jurisdictional strike A work stoppage resulting from a dispute over jurisdictional claims by two competing unions.

Source references: Benjamin Aaron, "The California Jurisdictional Strike Act," *Southern California LR*, April 1954; Norman Perelman, "Labor Union Court to Deal with Jurisdictional Strikes or Disputes," *Labor and the Nation*, Jan./Feb. 1948.

See also JURISDICTIONAL DISPUTE.

jury leave *See* PAID JURY LEAVE.

just cause Proper or sufficient reasons for disciplinary measures imposed on workers by management. The term is commonly used in agreement provisions to safeguard workers from disciplinary action which is unjust, arbitrary, capricious or which lacks some reasonable foundation for its support. Disciplinary action also may be held to be lacking "just cause" if the penalties bear no reasonable relationship to the degree of the alleged offense. The just cause justifying a discharge generally is related to the employee's work—any conduct, action, or inaction by, arising from, or directly connected with the work, which is inconsistent with the employee's obligations to the employer under the contract of hire, or union contract—and reflects the employee's willful disregard of the employer's interests. When defined in agreements, "just cause" for discipline usually includes such offenses as dishonesty, theft, insubordination, fighting on the job, inefficiency, repeated absence or tardiness, intoxication on the job, and destruction of company property.

Professor Carroll R. Daugherty in *Enterprise Wire Co.* has suggested seven test questions for determining "just cause" for discipline. Daugherty maintains that a "no" answer to any one of the following questions would normally indicate that just cause for discipline did not exist. His test questions are:

(1) Was the employee given advance warning of the possible or probable disciplinary consequences of the employee's conduct?
(2) Was the rule or order reasonably related to the efficient and safe operation of the business?
(3) Before administering discipline, did the employer make an effort to discover whether the employee did, in fact, violate a rule or order of management?
(4) Was the employer's investigation conducted fairly and objectively?
(5) Did the investigation produce substantial evidence or proof that the employee was guilty as charged?
(6) Had the company applied its rules, orders, and penalties without discrimination?
(7) Was the degree of discipline administered in the particular case reasonably related to (a) the seriousness of the employee's proven offense, and (b) the employee's record of company service?

Source references: Employing Lithographers Assn. of Detroit, 21 LA 671 (1953); *RCA Communications, Inc.*, 29 LA 567 (1957); *Grief Bros. Cooperage Corp.*, 42 *LA* 555 (1964); *West Virginia Pulp & Paper Co.*, 45 LA 515 (1965); *Enterprise Wire Co.*, 46 LA 359 (1966); Alfred W. Blumrosen, "Strangers No More: All Workers are Entitled to 'Just Cause' Protection Under Title VII," *Industrial Relations LJ*, Winter 1978; Frank Elkouri and Edna A. Elkouri, *How Arbitration Works* (4th ed., Washington: BNA, 1985); Marvin Hill, Jr. and Anthony V. Sinicropi, *Remedies in Arbitration* (Washington: BNA, 1981); Stephen J. Rosen, "How Arbitrators View Just Cause," *Proceedings of the 35th A/M, IRRA*, ed. by Barbara Dennis (Madison: 1983); Lawrence Stessin, *Employee Discipline* (Washington: BNA, 1960).

justice and dignity clause A contract provision which permits an employee who is "disciplined or discharged for routine or administrative reasons" to remain at work, upon filing of a grievance, until the grievance is resolved. The provision was included in the 1980 agreement between the Steelworkers and the can industry.

Source references: Elliot I. Beitner, "Justice and Dignity: A New Approach to Discipline," *LLJ*, Aug. 1984; Dee W. Gilliam, "Innocent Until Proven Guilty: The Union View," *Arbitration—Promise and Performance*, Proceedings of the 36th A/M, NAA, ed. by James Stern and Barbara Dennis (Washington: BNA, 1984); T. S. Hoffman, Jr., "Innocent Until Proven Guilty: The Management View," *Arbitration—Promise and Performance*, Proceedings of the 36th A/M, NAA, ed. by James Stern and Barbara Dennis (Washington: BNA, 1984).

just wage *See* FAIR DAY'S PAY, LIVING WAGE, STANDARD OF LIVING.

K

Kaiser Steel Long-Range Sharing Plan A plan, negotiated in 1963 by the Kaiser Steel Corp. and the United Steelworkers of America, which attempted to promote greater employee interest in an acceptance of company goals and which attempted to give the company greater flexibility in working toward its goals.

The plan guaranteed employees greater protection against loss of jobs and income because of technological change and assured them a share of the gains in any cost reduction brought about through greater efficiency. For the company, the plan meant four years of being relatively free from bargaining over wages and benefits and from the threat of strikes. It also gave the company a chance to change work practices and methods with less employee resistance to these changes.

Source references: William Aussieker, "The Decline of Union-Management Cooperation: Kaiser Long Range Sharing Plan," *Proceeding of 35th A/M, IRRA*, ed. by Barbara Dennis (Madison: 1983); Robert A. Bedolis, "The Kaiser Sharing Plan's First Year," *Conference Board Record,* July 1964; ———, "The Kaiser Sharing Plan's Second Year," *Conference Board Record,* July 1965; BNA, *The Long-Range Sharing Plan of Kaiser Steel Corp., Fontana Operations, and the United Steelworkers of America, Locals 2869 and 3677* (Washington: Special Report, 1963); "Long Range Sharing Plan for Kaiser Steel Corporation Employees," *MLR,* Feb. 1963; C. A. McIlvaine, "Appraisal of Kaiser's Sharing Plan," *MLR,* April 1964; NICB, *The Kaiser-Steel Union Sharing Plan* (New York: Studies in Personnel Policy no. 187, 1963).

See also LINCOLN ELECTRIC INCENTIVE CASH BONUS, SCANLON PLAN.

Kansas Court of Industrial Relations Until the passage of compulsory arbitration statutes by various other state legislatures in 1947, Kansas was the only state that had had prior experience with compulsory arbitration. The Kansas statute was passed during a special session in 1920. Kansas had been relatively free from labor disputes for a long period until the coal strikes of 1915 through 1919. During that time it was estimated that some 700 strikes occurred in the Kansas coal mines. The prolonged coal strike in the winter of 1919 which led to a series of shortages of coal caused the state of Kansas to apply the antitrust statutes and appoint a receiver for the mines. It was against this background of fuel shortages and the prolonged series of strikes in the coal mines that led the Kansas legislature to establish compulsory arbitration.

The Court of Industrial Relations which was established by the statute was composed of three judges appointed by the governor with the advice and consent of the Senate. Although the group was considered a court, it actually operated substantially as a public commission. The court had jurisdiction over industries affected with the public interest. These, according to the statute, included the manufacture of food and food products; the manufacture of clothing and all manner of wearing apparel in common use; mining or production of coal and production of fuel; the transportation of all food products or articles or substances entering into wearing apparel or food from place of production to place of consumption; and public utilities and common carriers.

The court acted substantially as a compulsory arbitration tribunal although it also had authority to mediate and to investigate. Its decisions or orders were subject to review by the State Supreme Court. The statute also gave the Court of Industrial Relations authority to assume control, direct, and operate industries during an emergency.

The court had the problem of determining standards in disputes involving the determination of wages. It adopted those used by the Railway Labor Board under the Esch-Cummins Act. These consisted of seven specific critieria:

(1) The scale of wages for similar kinds of work in other industries;
(2) The relation between wages and cost of living;
(3) Hazards of employment;
(4) Training and skill required;
(5) The degree of responsibility;
(6) The character and regularity of employment; and
(7) Inequalities of increases in wages or of treatment resulting from previous wage orders.

The constitutionality of the Kansas statute was raised in a number of cases involving wage reductions. The U.S. Supreme Court on review ruled that the compulsory arbitration machinery as applied to manufacturing and transportation industries was unconstitutional and that these industries could not be regarded as affected with the public interest so as to permit wage determination. The Court held that the fixing of wages, hours, rules, and regulations by such an agency was contrary to the due process clause of the 14th Amendment in that it curtailed the right of an employer on the one hand and of the employee on the other to contract about their affairs.

Source references: Kansas General Statutes, 1935, 44–601; *Dorchy v. Kansas,* 264 US 286 (1923); *Howat v. Kansas,* 258 US 181 (1921); *State v. Howat,* 116 Kan 412 (1920); *Wolff Packing Co. v. Court of Industrial Relations,* 262 US 522 (1922), 267 US 522 (1924); Herbert Feis, "The Kansas Court of Industrial Relations," *Quarterly Journal of Economics,* Aug. 1923; Domenico Gagliardo, *The Kansas Industrial Court* (Lawrence: Univ. of Kansas, 1941); NICB, *The Kansas Court of Industrial Relations* (New York: 1924); U.S. Dept. of Labor, BLS, *Kansas Court of Industrial Relations* (Washington: Bull. no. 322, 1923); Edwin E. Witte, *The Government in Labor Disputes* (New York: McGraw-Hill, 1932).

See also ARBITRATION, COMPULSORY; INDUSTRIAL COURTS; LABOR COURT.

Kemp et al. v. Division No. 241 A court case affecting employees of the Chicago Railway Company and the Amalgamated Association of Street and Electrical Railway Employees of America. A strike was called by the union in protest against eight employees of the Chicago Railway Company who were not union members. The question was raised whether an injunction could be issued to restrain the union from striking against the employer in order to force the employer to discharge the nonunion members.

The court held that the employees had the right to strike to enforce their demands against the nonunion employees and that an injunction was improper under the circumstances.

Source reference: Kemp v. Division No. 241, Amalgamated Association of Street Electric Railway Employees, 285 Ill 213, 99 NE 389 (1912).

Kennedy round *See* TRADE EXPANSION ACT OF 1962.

Kentucky Whip and Collar Co. v. Illinois Central Railway The Ashurst-Sumners Act of 1935 provided that an effort should be made to limit the shipment and sale of prison-made goods. The law provided that goods shipped in interstate commerce must be marked showing the names and addresses of the shipper and the person receiving the shipment as well as a description of the contents and the name of the institution from which the goods originally came. The Supreme Court upheld the constitutionality of the Ashurst-Sumners Act in *Kentucky Whip and Collar Company v. Illinois Central Railway Company.*

Source reference: Kentucky Whip and Collar Co. v. Illinois Central Railway, 299 US 334 (1937).

key job (or key personnel) A general term to designate individuals in the plant operation who are responsible for the overseeing of operations or whose particular jobs are such that others are dependent on them. In modern operations most jobs are interrelated, but the key personnel or key jobs are those who cannot easily be replaced and of whom substantial knowledge and training are required in the smooth functioning of the particular operation.

kickback A form of extortion which may be perpetrated either by labor leaders or by employers. The procedure is to withold or to have an employee turn back a certain portion of the individual's wages on threat of losing his job. The practice has been in existence for a long time. Many devices have been employed by employers who would pay the worker a rate less than the contract rate or receive from the individual an amount after the actual full wages are paid. In the past, failure to make this payment, or kickback, would result in the loss of employment.

Many states by statute outlaw the kickback. Congress has outlawed kickbacks on public works.

Generally speaking, a kickback includes any form of deduction from wages except those which are legitimate debts due to the employer or payments to the union.

The anti-kickback law makes it a crime, punishable by a fine of up to $5,000 or by imprisonment up to five years or both, for any individual—by force, intimidation, threat of procuring dismissal from employment, or any other means—to induce an employee on work covered by the law to give up any part of the compensation to which he has a right under his contract of employment.

Under this law—the Copeland Act—the secretary of labor is authorized to make reasonable regulations for contractors as well as subcontractors engaged in construction covered by the Act. The regulations indicate under what conditions deductions from wages are and are not permitted. They require the contractors to present evidence that proposed deductions are proper ones, and approval of the Department of Labor is required for such deductions. Among other things, the regulations require payroll records showing the information needed to determine whether required wages are actually being paid. These regulations are part of every contract for a federal or a federal-aid job.

Source references: Anti-Kickback Acts, as amended, 40 U.S.C. 276b (1982), repealed June 25, 1948, 62 Stat. 862; Act of June 25, 1948, 18 U.S.C. 874 (1982).

See also ANTI-KICKBACK LAW (COPELAND ACT).

Knights of Labor The Noble Order of the Knights of Labor had its origin in Philadelphia in 1869 through the efforts of Uriah Smith Stevens, a tailor, who organized the Garment Cutters in Phildelphia. It had a tremendous impact during the period of its rapid rise and equally rapid decline. It was quite different from earlier craft unions which limited entry into the union. The Knights of Labor appealed to all workers, skilled and unskilled, who were organized into local assemblies. These local assemblies were composed of workers from various trades. The prime objective was to bring into one big union all workers regardless of nationality, creed, race, sex, or skill. Its goals were highly idealistic, seeking social reform through worker cooperatives and through educational means. Its policy nationally was against the use of economic weapons such as the boycott or the strike, although it did engage in strike activity later, which was partly responsible for its decline.

The Knights of Labor was a highly centralized organization with fixed and absolute authority in the national organization and its offices. The mixed local assemblies which contained the membership were completely under the authority of the national organization. The operation of the mixed and polyglot group in the assemblies made it extremely difficult to focus attention on issues of common concern to the group, and substantial conflict arose between the mixed local assemblies and the national organization. The union had grown to an estimated membership of some 700,000 in 1886 and dwindled to less than 100,000 by 1890. By that time, it was competing with the newly formed organization which later became the AFL.

Source references: Henry J. Browne, *The Catholic Church and the Knights of Labor* (Washington: Catholic Univ. of America Press, 1949); Leon Fink, " 'Irrespective of Party, Color or Social Standing': The Knights of Labor and Opposition Politics in Richmond, Virginia," *Labor History,* Summer 1978; Gerald N. Grob, "Terrence V. Powderly and the Knights of Labor," *Mid-America,* Jan. 1957; Robert R. Jackaway, *The Great Question or, The Noble Mission of the Knights of Labor* (Savannah: Times Publishing, 1886); Symmes M. Jelley, *The Voice of Labor* (Philadelphia: Smith, 1891); Donald L. Kemmerer and Edward D. Wickersham, "Reasons for the Growth of the Knights of Labor in 1885–1886," *ILRR,* Jan. 1950; Douglas R.

Kennedy, *The Knights of Labor and Canada* (Ontario: Univ. of Western Ontario, 1956); *The Knights of Labor Illustrated, including the full illustrated ritual and the unwritten work as well as an historical sketch of the order* (Chicago: Cook, 1886); James M. Morris, "The Cincinnati Shoemakers' Lockout of 1888: A Case Study in the Demise of the Knights of Labor," *Labor History*, Fall 1972; Terrence V. Powderly, *The Path I Trod* (New York: Columbia UP, 1940); ———, *Thirty Years of Labor, 1859–1889* (Columbus: Excelsior, 1889); Norman J. Ware, *The Labor Movement in the United States, 1860–1895; A Study in Democracy* (New York: Appleton, 1929).

Knights of Saint Crispin An organization of skilled craftsmen in the shoe industry organized in large part to protest the introduction of shoemaking equipment which would lead to the loss of their jobs. It was founded in 1867, probably in Milwaukee, and had a tremendous rise in membership during the next few years with an estimated membership size of from 40,000 to 50,000. It became highly involved in politics, and the 1873 panic saw its demise.

Source reference: Don D. Lescohier, *The Knights of Saint Crispin, 1867–1874; A Study in the Industrial Causes of Trade Unionism* (Madison: Univ. of Wisconsin, Economics and Political Science Series, Vol. 17, no. 1, 1910).

See also DAUGHTERS OF SAINT CRISPIN.

knocked off Colloquialism for being discharged. Sometimes referred to as being "canned."

Kuder Preference Record and Interest Surveys One of the interest tests used in personnel counseling that allows individuals to select the activity which they would most like to perform and the one which they would least like to perform. The test is designed to measure the degree of interest in 10 broad job fields. These include social service, musical, literary, artistic, clerical, scientific, mechanical, outdoor, computational, and persuasive activities. These tests are helpful when used with other tests, including aptitude, intelligence, and other currently available measuring techniques. Another test frequently used is the Strong Vocational Interest Blank.

Source references: Joseph J. Famularo (ed.), *Handbook of Modern Personnel Administration* (New York: McGraw-Hill, 1972); G. Frederic Kuder, *Kuder Preference Record, Vocational Form C* (Chicago: Science Research Associates, 1948); J. Tiffen and R. F. Phelin, "Use of Kuder Preference Record to Predict Turnover in an Industrial Plant," *Personnel Psychology*, Summer 1953; Dale Yoder and Herbert G. Heneman, Jr. (ed.), *Staffing Policies and Strategies, ASPA Handbook of Personnel and Industrial Relations, Volume I* (Washington: BNA, 1979); Donald G. Zytowski, *The Predictive Validity of the Kuder Preference Record Over a 25 Year Span* (Ames: Iowa State Univ., IRC, WP no. 1974–04, 1974).

L

LAIRS *See* LABOR AGREEMENT INFORMATION RETRIEVAL SYSTEMS (LAIRS).

LDC *See* LAUNDRY AND DRY CLEANING INTERNATIONAL UNION (AFL-CIO).

LGPN *See* LEATHER GOODS, PLASTIC AND NOVELTY WORKERS' UNION; INTERNATIONAL (AFL-CIO).

LIUNA *See* LABORERS' INTERNATIONAL UNION OF NORTH AMERICA (AFL-CIO).

LMRA *See* LABOR MANAGEMENT RELATIONS ACT OF 1947.

LMRDA *See* LABOR-MANAGEMENT REPORTING AND DISCLOSURE ACT OF 1959.

LMSA *See* LABOR-MANAGEMENT SERVICES ADMINISTRATION (LMSA).

LPN *See* LICENSED PRACTICAL NURSES; NATIONAL FEDERATION OF (IND).

LSIA *See* LOG SCALERS INTERNATIONAL UNION (IND).

LWU *See* LEATHER WORKERS INTERNATIONAL UNION OF AMERICA (AFL-CIO).

label trades Those occupations, crafts or trades which generally use the union label on their products.

See also UNION LABEL AND SERVICE TRADES DEPARTMENT.

labor This is a generic term which refers to the human effort or exertion applied to the production and distribution of goods and services toward an economic end and for which some compensation or payment is received. It is generally recognized that when exertion or effort is undertaken for its own sake it is not usually classified as coming within the general term "labor."

Some have defined labor as human energy which has been expended "for the purpose of acquiring income." Some have defined it as exertion as a means of "acquiring wealth or income." Some define it as "all human activity involved in production." In its general usage, however, the term "labor" or "labor problem" has been directed essentially toward the industrial worker and the conditions under which the worker makes a living. It is now more generally accepted that labor is exerted in many forms and it does not have to manifest itself primarily in the form of manual effort. As our economy automates more and more, the nature of the "labor" exerted by individuals who watch dials and push buttons will still be classified as labor even though the exertion is far from what it was in earlier generations.

The classical analysis of production and the major factors in production, including land, labor, and capital and the later addition of entrepreneur, have undergone substantial change, and the term "labor" itself will probably undergo even more serious change as our techniques and methods of production make it necessary to assign to the term "labor" a much more inclusive connotation.

It is not unlikely that in the 21st century work in the fields of art or music or some of the other humanities and pursuits, which might not presently be classified as productive and within the present usage of the term "labor force," would still provide for reasonable and adequate compensation under our general social and economic scheme to assure those individuals engaged in these pursuits that their work contributes toward the well-being and welfare of the total community. This new concept of labor and a redefinition of the labor force is something which is presently in the making, but which is not yet an accepted concept.

Source references: Charles Gamba, "The Making of Industrial Workers," *Journal of IR*, Dec. 1973; Eli Ginzberg et al., *Work Decisions in the 1980s* (Boston: Auburn House, 1982); Herbert Harris, *American Labor* (New

Haven: Yale UP, 1939); Melvin Kranzberg and Joseph Gies, *By the Sweat of Thy Brow: Work in the Western World* (New York: Putnam, 1975); Richard A. Lester, *Labor and Industrial Relations* (New York: Macmillan, 1951); Sar A. Levitan and William B. Johnston, *Work is Here to Stay, Alas* (Salt Lake City: Olympus, 1973); Richard B. Morris, "A Bicentennial Look at the Early Days of American Labor," *MLR*, May 1976; Richard B. Morris (ed.), *The U.S. Department of Labor Bicentennial History of the American Worker* (Washington: U.S. Dept. of Labor, 1976); NPA, *Upgrading Low-Level Employment: A Major National Challenge* (Washington: Report no. 141, 1975); James J. O'Toole "Dystopia: The Irresponsible Society," *Management Review*, Oct. 1979; Charlton R. Price, *New Directions in the World of Work, A Conference Report* (Kalamazoo: Upjohn Institute for Employment Research, 1972); Robert Schrank, *Ten Thousand Working Days* (Cambridge: The MIT Press, 1978); Louis Terkel, *Working: People Talk About What They Do All Day and How They Feel About What They Do* (New York: Pantheon Books, 1974); Hermann Wellenreuther, "Labor in the Era of the American Revolution: A Discussion of Recent Concepts and Theories," *Labor History*, Fall 1981.

labor, common The term refers to individuals who usually perform unskilled, manual work which involves relatively simple duties and which can be learned within a short period of time and also does not require substantial judgment or special skills.

See also COMMON LABOR RATE.

labor, horizontal movement of *See* HORIZONTAL MOVEMENT OF LABOR.

labor, indirect *See* INDIRECT LABOR.

labor, noncompeting groups of The term "noncompeting labor groups" suggests that in the total labor supply of a country the units within that labor supply consist of many nonhomogeneous groups, namely, groups that do not because of skill, training, or for other reasons, compete with one another in the labor market. The usual division is given as among unskilled, semiskilled, and highly skilled. However, it is quite apparent that with changing technology and the necessity of training for different skills it is possible to have individuals move from one category to another, and hence, in this sense are competitive. The purpose of the division, according to economists, is to provide a better explanation and understanding of the competitive functioning of labor groups and the existence of groups which are not competitive with one another.

labor agreement The phrase is generally used as the equivalent of the collective bargaining agreement, the collective agreement, the union contract, or the labor-management contract.

See also AGREEMENT, COLLECTIVE; LABOR CONTRACT.

Labor Agreement Information Retrieval System (LAIRS) An automated data file of federal service labor agreements and arbitration awards. Established by the U.S. Civil Service Commission pursuant to Section 25 of Executive Order 11491, it first began operating on a trial basis in May 1974; it is currently maintained by the Office of Personnel Management (OPM).

LAIRS is used by the Office of Employee, Labor and Agency Relations (formerly Office of Labor-Management Relations), OPM, to produce reports identifying current trends in federal collective bargaining in such areas as grievance procedures and arbitration, merit promotion, safety and health, labor agreement expirations, reduction in force, union representation. One of its first publications, *Productivity Clauses in Federal Agreements* is a survey of 35 provisions on productivity found in the LAIRS file. LAIRS also issues *Digest of Arbitration Awards*.

Address: U.S. Office of Personnel Management, LAIRS Section, Room 7H29, 1900 E St., N.W., Washington, D.C. 20415. Tel. (202) 655–4000

Source references: "Spotlight on Labor Relations," *Civil Service Journal*, April/June 1974; U.S. CSC, *Productivity Clauses in Federal Agreements* (Washington: 1974).

labor arbitration *See* ARBITRATION, LABOR.

laboratory training Refers to all training in which people learn about their own behavior and that of others through examination of actual experience of group life under laboratory conditions. Patterns of behavior are discovered and analyzed in a climate supporting change and protected for the time from the practical consequences of customary associations. The participant is provided with an opportunity to re-examine his self-image, and the training group offers the climate to permit this. Laboratory training combines traditional training practices, such as lectures, group problem-solving sessions, role-playing, and skill development questionnaires, with the encounter and self-awareness techniques of T-Groups and sensitivity training sessions. The first planned laboratory training program, The National Training Laboratory in Group Development, was held in the summer of 1947 under the joint sponsorship of the National Education Association and the Research Center for Group Dynamics at M.I.T.

Source references: Chris Argyris, "Issues in Evaluating Laboratory Education," *IR,* Oct. 1968; Marvin D. Dunnette and John P. Campbell, "Laboratory Education: Impact on People and Organizations," *IR,* Oct. 1968; Thomas H. Patten, Jr., "Relating Learning Theory to Behavior Change in Organizations," *Human Resource Management,* Winter 1974; Albert R. Roberts, "Training Programs for Treatment Specialists in Corrections: A University-Based Model," *Public Personnel Management,* March/April 1974; E. H. Schein and W. G. Bennis, *Personal and Organizational Changes Through Group Methods: The Laboratory Approach* (New York: Wiley, 1965); Henry P. Sims, Jr. and Charles C. Manz, "Modeling Influences on Employee Behavior," *PJ,* Jan. 1982; Alexander Winn, "Laboratory Training in Industry," *Personnel Administration,* May/June 1964.

See also SENSITIVITY TRAINING, T-GROUP.

labor attachés These are special agents of the State Department whose functions parallel in part those of the commercial attachés. Their prime function, however, is to keep abreast of labor developments in the country to which they are assigned and to report to Washington on those developments. The labor attachés also attempt to keep individuals in the country to which they are assigned familiar and informed about the role of the free labor unions in our own country.

The labor attaché as a special agent of the State Department or the Department of External Affairs as in Great Britain was first introduced in England around 1944. The policy was subsequently adopted by the United States State Department and has developed over the years into a useful organization for information about foreign labor relations.

labor attorney The term generally applied to a lawyer who specializes in industrial and labor legislation and who works for either a union or an employer in the handling of cases before the various labor agencies, such as the NLRB or state labor agencies.

The labor lawyer has been a feature in the United States since the 1930s with the development of major labor legislation, both on a national and state level.

labor audit A term which is not used widely today, but in the early part of the century referred to the general review of the personnel policy of a particular company or organization. Its purpose was to determine whether or not the policies and actual practices were being carried out in line with the policies and objectives of the organization.

Source reference: U.S. Federal Board for Vocational Education, *The Labor Audit, A Method of Industrial Investigation* (Washington: Bull. no. 43, Employment Management Series no. 8, 1920).

See also PERSONNEL AUDIT (OR SURVEY).

labor banking During the early 1920s, more specifically from 1920 to 1926, there was widespread interest in the establishment of labor banks, that is, banks owned or controlled by a union or cooperating unions. The first such bank was opened in Washington, D.C., in May 1920 by the International Association of Machinists and another in November 1920, the Cooperative National Bank in Cleveland, Ohio, by the Brotherhood of Locomotive Engineers.

Among other labor unions which sponsored banks during this period were the Amalgamated Clothing Workers, the International Printing Pressmen's Union, and the International Ladies' Garment Workers' Union.

The Brotherhood of Locomotive Engineers sponsored some 11 banks, and the failure of some of their enterprises in June 1927 was responsible in large part for discrediting the labor banking movement.

Source references: Edward W. Morehouse, "Labor Institutionalism: Banking," *American Labor Dynamics,* ed. by J. B. S. Hardman (New York: Harcourt, Brace, 1928); Jacob S. Potofsky, "The Pioneering of Workers' Banks," *American Federationist,* May 1963; Princeton Univ., IR Section, *The Labor Banking Movement in the United States* (Princeton: 1929); H. Bruce Throckmorton, "A Note on Labor Banks," *Labor History,* Fall 1979; U.S. Dept. of Labor, BLS, *Beneficial Activities of American Trade Unions* (Washington: Bull. no. 465, 1928); "Why Workers' Banks?" *Free Labour World,* Oct. 1968.

labor budget The estimate of the amount a business will spend for labor within a certain period of time. The labor budget indicates not only the cost of labor required to operate the business but also the number of workers, and in manufacturing industry, the man-hours or machine-hours that will be required during the period for which the budget is made. From the number of workers or man-hours estimated in the budget the production or personnel departments estimate how many new workers will have to be hired.

See also LABOR COSTS.

labor bureau Essentially an agency designed to reduce unnecessary unemployment resulting essentially from lack of information about the labor market. The purpose of the agency is to bring the worker and the job together.

The labor agency has developed in large part as a result of the system of unemployment compensation and the necessity to attempt to place employees who are able and willing to obtain a job. These agencies also attempt to sort the requirements and to keep the various labor markets informed of workers available in various skills, as well as the needs of employers for individuals requiring certain special abilities.

See also EMPLOYMENT AGENCIES, U.S. EMPLOYMENT SERVICE.

labor bureaucracy Refers to the administrative organization which runs the everyday affairs of the union. Many union administrators are union officials who no longer work in industry but hold office jobs.

labor camp In current usage applies to those facilities made available by some labor unions where labor union officials, union members, and their families can take vacations, and where it frequently is possible for them to get together to discuss various problems.

Historically, however, the term "labor camp" was applied in the early 19th century to organizations for vagrants who were brought together in labor colonies where they occasionally were taught a trade or were provided an opportunity to perform work of a useful nature. Occasionally, these individuals were trained in specific skills in order to make them useful in the community. Quite frequently, they were the unemployables in a community who were brought together in the hope that they ultimately would return to the community in some useful job occupation.

labor code The term is generally applied to the total collection of laws on the statute books as well as administrative regulations dealing with industrial relations. This body of laws and regulations as well as executive orders, administrative orders, and interpretations apply to the total area of wages, hours, and working conditions.

In the United States there is no cohesive labor code as such but there are numerous statutes covering minimum wages, hours, and other regulations as well as the Welfare and Pensions Plans Act, the Taft-Hartley and Landrum-Griffin laws dealing with the areas of collective bargaining, picketing, national emergency disputes, union security, and other general areas. We have no code of labor such as has been developed in some countries, which in effect results from a periodic review of all existing laws, which are then brought together into one code covering the various areas of social and labor laws.

labor colleges A number of labor colleges were organized by city centrals in various parts of the country between 1919 and 1921. The most popular one was Brookwood Labor College in Katonah, N.Y., which was founded in 1921 and remained in operation until 1937. Its prime function was the training of union leadership and the offering of various courses in social problems, labor history, trade union methods, journalism, and public speaking. The Commonwealth College in Mena, Ark., founded in 1925, was another popular college. The oldest resident labor college was the Work People's College in Smithville, Minn. Formerly a Lutheran theological seminary, it was transformed into a socialist school and became an I.W.W. school in 1916. Courses were offered in history, sociology, English, economics, arithmetic, and public speaking.

Source reference: Carroll R. Daugherty, *Labor Problems in American Industry* (Boston: Houghton Mifflin, 1948).

See also BROOKWOOD LABOR COLLEGE, LABOR EDUCATION.

labor combinations Groups of workers acting in concert to improve their work and economic situation. In England such workers' organizations were formed in the 18th century in response to the early effects of the industrial revolution as most workers ceased to be independent producers. Initially these organizations were merely trade clubs and were composed of skilled craftsmen rather than the large mass of displaced, unskilled workers suffering oppression. The doctrine of *laissez faire* determined the government's attitude toward the workers' early appeals; and after a series of rebuffs, the workers began to form more forceful and better managed organizations. The Combination Acts of 1799 and 1800, which were in effect until 1824 and 1825, placed stringent restrictions on any sort of organization. Although the acts applied to employers as well as to workers, they did not greatly inconvenience the formation of employers' associations.

In the United States there had been some concerted protest among workers in colonial days. However, such worker organizations as did exist were fraternal or benevolent associations. Organized combinations of workers were first formed late in the 18th century. These early labor combinations were organized along skilled craft lines and confined to local areas, rarely operating beyond the confines of a city. They were weak in making demands, engaged in individual rather than collective bargaining, and concerned themselves mainly with social uplift matters rather than giving attention to basic questions of wages, hours of labor, and working conditions. Employers opposed such concerted labor action and most court decisions dealing with labor disputes considered the labor organizations as illegal conspiracies. In the early 1800s the locally based organizations expanded to citywide unions and then national unions. The unions, still organized along craft lines, became more political and supported such measures as free public education, tax reform, abolition of debt imprisonment, and monopoly regulation. In 1842, the *Commonwealth v. Hunt* decision of the Massachusetts Supreme Court limited the use of the conspiracy doctrine in labor disputes and supported the right of labor organizations to carry out legitimate functions. Labor organizations were still viewed by employers and courts with suspicion into the 20th century; but the unions became larger, better organized, and more effective in pressing their demands.

Source references: Marjorie S. Turner, *The Early American Labor Conspiracy Cases; Their Place in Labor Law; A Reinterpretation* (San Diego: Social Science Monograph Series, Vol. 1, no. 3, San Diego State College Press, 1967); Sidney and Beatrice Webb, *The History of Trade Unionism* (New York: Kelley, c.1894, 1965).

See also COMMONWEALTH V. HUNT, CONSPIRACY DOCTRINE, LABOR ORGANIZATION, LAW OF LABOR COMBINATIONS.

labor conscription Generally refers to an action or law which requires compulsory labor service. In the United States this is not possible under the Constitution, which prevents involuntary servitude.

During periods of war or special emergency, national service laws might achieve the same purpose through some form of civilian conscription in order to protect the country during that particular emergency. Occasionally, efforts have been made to conscript labor during a strike period by placing the individuals in the government service. Such action, however, has not been supported except during war periods.

labor content A measure designed to determine the relative amount of the cost of the product which is allocable to labor as between overhead plant costs of machinery and equipment and the costs actually allocated for the payment of labor.

See also LABOR COSTS.

labor contract Sometimes referred to as a labor or collective bargaining agreement, which results from the negotiation or collective bargaining process.

There has been a long history of legal controversy concerning the interpretation of the labor agreement, distinguishing it from other legal contracts which require performance. A labor contract of necessity implies that the individual worker will perform, but to mandate such performance would be contrary to the rights of an individual to withhold his labor. On the other hand, courts are holding the collective bargaining or labor contract enforceable at law and have applied this in varying situations even in contracts involving the so-called runaway shop.

With the passage of the Taft-Hartley law and Section 301 in 1947, specific provision was made for the enforcement of the collective bargaining agreement by both labor and management under that provision of the statute.

All agreements, including the labor contracts, require the mutual acceptance of rights and obligations agreed to. This was true even in individual contracts which in the past created a master-servant relationship.

Source references: Neil W. Chamberlain, "Collective Bargaining and the Concept of Contract," *Columbia LR*, Sept. 1948; Ralph F. Fuchs, "Labor Contract," *Encyclopedia of the Social Sciences*, ed. by Edwin R. A. Seligman (New York: Macmillan, 1932); David A. McCabe and Richard A. Lester, *Labor and Social Organizations* (Boston: Little, Brown, 1938); Harry H. Wellington, "Judge Magruder and the Labor Contract," *Harvard LR*, May 1959.

See also AGREEMENT, COLLECTIVE; ENFORCEMENT OF AGREEMENT; LABOR MANAGEMENT RELATIONS ACT OF 1947; RUNAWAY SHOP.

labor convention This is generally a meeting of the elected delegates of local unions of a national union throughout the country held annually or biennially to determine the policy of the union for the ensuing year or years. The convention will frequently pass resolutions and adopt policy as well as modify the provisions of its constitution and bylaws. Frequently, the convention also acts as the final authority on review of policy matters and elects the officials and the executive officers for the following year or years.

For example, the former constitutions of the AFL and CIO had articles dealing with the conventions of those organizations. The CIO constitution adopted in 1944, provided in Article 7, Section 1: "The convention shall be the supreme authority of the organization and except as otherwise provided in the constitution, its decisions shall be by a majority vote."

The constitution of the AFL also set out in detail in Article 3 the functions of the conventions, and Article 9, Section 13 provided: "The Executive Council shall be authorized and empowered to take such action and render such decisions as may be necessary to carry out fully and adequately all provisions contained in the constitution and general laws, as well as declarations and decisions of the conventions, and it shall be authorized and empowered to take such further action and render such further decisions during the interim of conventions as may become necessary to safeguard and promote the best interest of the Federation and of all its affiliated unions."

It is clear from these quotes that the ultimate authority of the parent organizations rests in the convention. The same thing is true of the national or international union conventions in relation to the local unions of the particular trade or industry.

A second use of the term "labor convention" relates to the International Labor Organization. Under its provisions there is an arrangement for agreement at the annual meetings of the ILO for the establishment of certain standards which are to have the force of international treaties under the ILO Charter and presently under the UN Charter. These are known as "conventions." They constitute something similar to an international agreement entered into voluntarily by the participating countries and effectuated under the terms of the convention itself.

See also INTERNATIONAL LABOR ORGANIZATION (ILO).

labor cooperation This generally refers to efforts by labor and management to cooperate in meeting various problems within the plant. This may involve questions of safety, production, and other factors of mutual concern to the parties. These may also be known as joint labor-management committees.

During World War II, the National War Labor Board on occasion required the parties to establish joint committees. For example, in the case of the Celanese Corporation of America, Newark Plastics Division, the board provided for a section in the contract for a joint committee with the United Mine Workers, District 50. The contract language read in part: "The parties shall establish a committee consisting of representatives of the union and the company for the purpose of discussing and eliminating problems that arise in the productive process. The parties shall resume negotiations upon the scope of the functions of the committee and upon the precise terms of this provision."

Source reference: "Celanese Corp. of America—Decision of Regional Board II (New York)," 17 *WLR* 510.

See also JOINT PRODUCTION COMMITTEES, LABOR-MANAGEMENT COOPERATION.

labor costs This term generally applies to the total labor bill, sometimes divided between direct labor costs, wages and other payments, and indirect costs which apply throughout the plant but which may not be specifically allocable.

It is interesting that on occasion the actual wage bill or labor cost may be reduced when the hours of work are reduced, although this would normally result in increased labor costs. The Commonwealth Steel Company shift from a 12 to an 8 hour day in the open hearth department resulted in more economical production and in a lower wage bill per day.

Source references: Patricia Capdevielle and Donato Alvarez, "International Comparisons of Trends in Productivity and Labor Costs," *MLR*, Dec. 1981; N. Ellen Cook, Dennis R. Briscoe, and Robert F. O'Neil, "Fixed vs. Variable Labor Costs: The *Nenko* Path to Higher Profits," *Personnel*, Jan./Feb. 1982; Richard D. Gustely, *A Comparison of Changes in City Government Labor Costs Among the Ten Largest U.S. Cities; 1966–1971* (Syracuse: Syracuse Univ., Maxwell School of Citizenship and Public Affairs, Internal WP no. 11, 1972); ———, *The Components of Expenditure Change: An Analysis of the Technique and An Application to Changes in City Government Labor Costs* (Syracuse: Syracuse Univ., Maxwell School of Citizenship and Public Affairs, WP no. 16, 1973); Marshall F. Howes and Bennie D. Yates, "How to Control Personnel Costs in Overhead Functions," *Personnel*, July/Aug. 1976; Investors Management Sciences, Inc., *Corporate Manpower Analysis 1977, A Study of Labor Costs and Income* (New York: Standard & Poor's Corp., 1977); Stephen Nickell, *Unemployment and the Structure of Labour Costs* (Princeton: Princeton Univ., IR Section, WP no. 118, 1979); Robert V. Penfield, "A Guide to the Computation and Evaluation of Direct Labor Costs," *PJ*, June 1976; Carl J. Schramm, "Containing Hospital Labor Costs—A Separate-Industries Approach," *Employee Relations LJ*, Summer 1978; Frederick L. Sullivan, *How to Calculate the Manufacturer's Costs in Collective Bargaining*, An AMA Management Briefing (New York: AMA, 1980); Marc J. Wallace, Jr. and M. Lynn Spruill, "How to Minimize Labor Costs During Peak Demand Periods," *Personnel*, July/Aug. 1975.

See also EMPLOYMENT COST INDEX (ECI).

labor coupon A form of exchange designed for certain socialist communities which would utilize it instead of the normal gold or other monetary exchange. The value of the labor coupon would be the actual equivalent of the amount of labor performed. The value of the product presumably would be based on the number of hours of work performed.

See also LABOR EXCHANGE NOTES.

labor court This essentially is a tribunal established by law which acts as a decision-making body for disputes which are submitted to it or which are presented to it under the particular laws of the country. It is sometimes referred to as an industrial relations court or a court of permanent arbitration. The only parallel in this country to those which are in effect in some European countries and in use under the Australian and New Zealand statutes was the Kansas Court of Industrial Relations, which in effect operated as a labor court although the body itself was more in the nature of a commission rather than a court of law.

Source references: Kurt Braun, *Labor Disputes and Their Settlement* (Baltimore: Johns Hopkins Press, 1955); J. De Givry, "Labour Courts as Channels for the Settlement of Labour Disputes: An International Review," *BJIR*, Nov. 1968; Robben W. Fleming, "The Presidential Address: The Labor Court Idea," *The Arbitrator, the NLRB and the Courts*, Proceedings of the 20th A/M, NAA, ed. by Dallas Jones (Washington: BNA, 1967); Thomas E. Harris, "The Choice Before Us: Labor Board, Labor Court, or District Court," *Labor Law Developments 1971*, Proceedings of the 17th Annual Institute on Labor Law, SLF (New York: Bender, 1971); ILO, *Labour Courts* (Geneva: 1938); Marvin J. Levine, "Compulsory Dispute Settlement Via Litigation: The Rhodes Labor Court Proposal," *AJ*, Sept. 1972; William H. McPherson, "Basic Issues in German Labor Courts Structure," *LLJ*, June 1954; William H. McPherson and Frederic Meyers, *The French Labor Courts: Judgment by Peers* (Urbana: Univ. of Illinois, 1966); Charles J. Morris, "Labor Court: A New Perspective," *NYU 24th Annual Conference on Labor* (New York: Bender, 1972); Steve M. Slaby, *The Labor Court in Norway* (Oslo: Norwegian Academic Press, 1952).

See also ARBITRATION, COMPULSORY; INDUSTRIAL COURTS; KANSAS COURT OF INDUSTRIAL RELATIONS.

Labor Day This is a legal holiday celebrated the first Monday in September in almost all of the states of the United States in the honor and interest of working men and women.

The major move in this country to set aside a day for the celebration of working men was inaugurated by the Knights of Labor in 1882. It was not, however, until June 1894 that Congress passed a bill providing for such a holiday throughout the nation. Implementing legislation was necessitated by passage of state laws. There is some question in the literature whether Colorado was the first state to enact such a law (March 15, 1887) or whether it was Oregon which first passed a law recognizing that day (February 21, 1887). The various encyclopedias differ on which of these states had the honor of claiming the right to be the first in the Union to pass such a law.

labor demand The total of unfilled positions and manpower requirements in a particular area, industry, or enterprise at one specific point of time. In a business the labor demand depends upon three things: (1) the technological conditions of producing the firm's product; (2) the supply conditions, such as machines and raw materials, affecting other factors of production; and (3) the conditions affecting the demand for the firm's product.

Labor Department, U.S. One of the executive departments of the U.S. government headed by a secretary who is a member of the President's Cabinet. It was established by federal law on March 4, 1913. A similar unit as part of the Department of Commerce and Labor existed from 1903 to 1913, until a separate and independent Department of Labor was established.

The prime functions of the department are to promote employment and to improve the working conditions and general welfare of the wage earners.

The responsibilities of the department have varied throughout its period of existence. It is reponsible for the collection of major labor statistics including wages, hours and other working conditions, data involving collective bargaining agreements, and strike data. It has within its ambit the work of the Bureau of Labor Statistics, Women's Bureau, Bureau of International Labor Affairs, Labor-Management Services Administration, Employment Standards Administration, Occupational Safety and Health Administration, the Mine Safety and Health Administration, and divisions involving welfare and pension programs and the reporting requirements under the Landrum-Griffin Act.

From its origin in 1913, it was responsible for the mediation and conciliation functions until they were separated from the department in 1947 under the Taft-Hartley Act. The mediation and conciliation functions were established in the FMCS, a separate and independent agency. As a matter of public policy and operation, however, the department is still responsible for the problems involved in labor relations as a result of the President's responsibility, particularly in issues involving the public interest or a national emergency. The department is also concerned with the general problems of employment and through the Employment and Training Administration, operates and cooperates in the program with the respective states.

Source references: Margaret R. Brickett, "Labor History Resources in the U.S. Department of Labor Library," *Labor History*, Spring 1961; U.S. Dept. of Labor, *The Anvil and the Plow: A History of the United States Department of Labor, 1913–1963* (Washington: 1963); W. Willard Wirtz, "U.S. Department of Labor—The Worker's Agency," *American Federationist*, Feb. 1963.

See also FEDERAL MEDIATION AND CONCILIATION SERVICE (FMCS).

labor deportation During and following war the workers of a defeated country are sometimes forced to leave their home country to work in the victorious country or in another country determined by the victor. For example, during World War II, workers from Belgium and France were sent to Germany to work.

labor dispute The term generally involves any controversy dealing with the terms, tenure, or conditions of employment, or those concerning the association or representation of persons in negotiating, fixing, maintaining, or changing the terms and conditions of employment, regardless of "whether the disputants stand in the proximate relation of employer and employee." The term has frequently been used to cover in its broader connotations all disagreements or any evidence of disagreement between employer and employees. Generally, it is applied to a dispute which directly affects the employer-employee relationship, and even though a strike may occur the employer-employee relationship is retained. A labor or industrial dispute may not involve all of the employees in a company; it may involve a small group or a small class or a craft within that particular group.

The Norris-LaGuardia Act has had to define the term in its many ramifications, and the courts frequently have had to examine with great particularity the extent to which a controversy constitutes a labor dispute within the meaning of the Act. The coverage of labor disputes under the Norris-LaGuardia Act is to be found in Sections 13(a), (b), and (c). Section 13(c) states that "the term 'labor dispute' includes any controversy concerning terms or conditions of employment, or concerning the association or representation of persons in negotiating, fixing, maintaining, changing, or seeking to arrange terms or conditions of employment, regardless of whether or not the disputants stand in the proximate relation of employer and employee."

Section 13(a) reads in part, "a case shall be held to involve or to grow out of a labor dispute when the case involves persons who are engaged in the same industry, trade, craft, or occupation; or have a direct or indirect interest therein, or who are employees of the same employers; or who are members of the same or/and affiliated organization of employers or employees; whether such dispute is (1) between one or more employers or association of employers and one or more employees or association of employees; . . ." The definition continues on into two other categories, and in Section (b) provides that, "a person or association shall be held to be a person participating or interested in a labor dispute if relief is sought against him or it, and if he or it is engaged in the same industry, trade . . ."

Section 2(9) of Title I of the National Labor Relations Act, as amended, defines the term "labor dispute" in the same manner as it is defined under the Norris-LaGuardia Act.

Source references: Benjamin Aaron, "Emergency Dispute Settlement," *Labor Law Developments, 1967*, Proceedings of 13th Annual Institute on Labor Law, SLF (New York: Bender, 1967); David L. Cole, "Major Labor Disputes—Re-examination and Recommendations," *The Profession of Labor Arbitration*, Selected papers from the First Seven Annual Meetings, NAA, ed. by Jean McKelvey (Washington: BNA, 1957); Archibald Cox, "The Role of Law in Labor Disputes," 39 *Cornell LQ* 592 (1954); Howard S. Kaltenborn, *Governmental Adjustment of Labor Disputes* (Chicago: Foundation Press, 1943); OECD, *Labour Disputes, a Perspective* (Paris: 1979); Clinton L. Rossiter, "The President and Labor Disputes," *Journal of Politics*, Feb. 1949; Edwin E. Witte, "Wartime Handling of Labor Disputes," *Harvard BR*, Winter 1947.

See also GRIEVANCE, INDUSTRIAL DISPUTES, JURISDICTIONAL DISPUTE, LAUF V. E.G. SHINNER & CO., INC., NATIONAL EMERGENCY DISPUTES, NORRIS-LAGUARDIA ACT, STRIKE.

labor disunity A general term which seeks to describe the difficulties within the labor union movement leading to discord and difficulty. During the period when the CIO was a dissident element and broke away from the AFL, labor disunity referred to the failure in reuniting the AFL and the CIO. In most periods of American labor history there have been areas of discord and disunity. At no time has there been a complete unanimity of position in policy and action throughout the labor movement, nor is it likely that there ever will be.

With the merger of the AFL-CIO a greater opportunity was provided for the resolution of difficulties within the organization itself, both in areas of jurisdiction and the problems arising between the industrial and craft structure of the organizations as well as other problems which tended to divide the two major parent labor organizations.

See also AMERICAN FEDERATION OF LABOR-CONGRESS OF INDUSTRIAL ORGANIZATIONS, DUAL UNIONISM, NO-RAIDING AGREEMENT, RIVAL UNIONISM.

labor economics A division of the general area of economics which is concerned primarily with the employment situation and the relation of the worker to his job. The areas covered include the labor market, the general problems of real wages, hours, and working conditions, as well as many aspects of social security. It is a division of economics similar to the area of banking economics, transportation economics, or marketing economics.

Some indication of the scope of the field of labor economics may be had from an examination of a general current text in this area which may cover, among other things, labor in the industrial society; population and migration; the labor force; the theories of the labor movement; labor union government; the scope, objectives, and legal context of collective bargaining; wage theories; the labor market; wages and employment; the wage structure and wage supplements; wages and the national income; unemployment; technological change and unemployment; hours of work; workers compensation; old-age benefits; and the general area of public assistance. The field of labor economics is a dynamic one and the scope and substance of the field have been enlarged to a great extent in the past few decades.

Source references: Jack Barbash, *The Legal Foundations of Capitalism and the Labor Problem* (Madison: Univ. of Wisconsin, IRRI, Reprint 205, 1976); Gordon F. Bloom and Herbert R. Northrup, *Economics of Labor Relations* (9th ed., Homewood: Irwin, 1981); Richard B. Freemen, *Labor Economics* (2d ed., Englewood Cliffs: PH, 1979); Abraham L. Gitlow, *Labor and Manpower Economics* (3d ed., Homewood: Irwin, 1971); ———, *Labor Economics and Industrial Society* (rev. ed., Homewood: Irwin, 1963); R. A. Gordon, "Wages, Prices, and Unemployment, 1900–1970," *IR*, Oct. 1975; Daniel S. Hamermesh, "Potential Problems in Human Capital Theory," *Proceedings of the 26th A/M, IRRA*, ed. by Gerald Somers (Madison: 1974); Juanita M. Kreps, Gerald G. Somers, and Richard Perlman, *Contemporary Labor Economics: Issues, Analysis, and Policies* (Belmont, Calif.: Wadsworth, 1974); Ray Marshall, "Understanding the 'Supply-Side' Fallacy," *American Federationist*, June 1981; F. Ray Marshall, Allan M. Cartter, and Allan G. King, *Labor Economics; Wages, Employment, and Trade Unionism* (4th ed., Homewood: Irwin, 1980); Paul J. McNulty, *Labor Economics in the History of Economic Thought* (New York: Columbia Univ., Graduate School of Business, Research Paper no. 11, 1973); Daniel J. B. Mitchell, *Unions and Wages, What We've Learned Since the '50s* (Los Angeles: UC, Institute of IR, Reprint no. 295, 1980); Orme W. Phelps, *Introduction to Labor Economics* (4th ed., New York: McGraw-Hill, 1967); Albert Rees, *The Economics of Work and Pay* (2d ed., New York: Harper & Row, 1979); Lloyd G. Reynolds, *Labor Economics and Labor Relations* (4th ed., Englewood Cliffs: PH, 1964); Philip Taft, *Economics and Problems of Labor* (3d ed., Harrisburg: Stackpole, 1955); Lloyd Ulman, *Unionism, Inflation, and Consensus* (Berkeley: UC, Institute of IR, Reprint no. 411,

1977); Finis Welch, "Labor Supply and Labor Demand Over Business and Life Cycles," *Proceedings of the 26th A/M, IRRA*, ed. by Gerald Somers (Madison, 1974).

labor education This term is generally applied to the area of worker education which in its early application was designed to provide the worker with knowledge and additional skills which might be directed toward a particular vocational program or in the development of an apprenticeship program, or in immigrant or foreign communities, directed toward citizenship programs and greater understanding of American political and social institutions.

Worker education is viewed by Barbash as "any planned educational activity which a union undertakes; or an educational activity undertaken by any agency other than a union, where a major objective is to build more effective union citizenship." Labor education includes training in collective bargaining and the more complex provisions in contracts dealing with pension plans, insurance, and training union staff on such topics as job evaluation and wage setting, health and safety administration, equal employment opportunity, and technological changes. Many programs have been directed toward labor leaders, shop stewards, and union officers. These programs deal with, among other areas, union administration, public speaking, parliamentary law, preparation of a union newspaper, the background and preparation for negotiations, and grievance handling. Programs have also been directed toward a better understanding of the national economy dealing with basic governmental policies, including foreign trade.

Sponsorship of labor education programs has come from the labor movement itself and from higher education. Among programs currently operating are the George Meany Center for Labor Studies and the Wisconsin School for Workers.

Source references: Frances K. Barasch, "Learning in the Workplace: Stronger Support from the Union," *Change,* April 1981; Jack Barbash, *Universities and Unions in Workers' Education* (New York: Harper, 1955); Mark L. Brown, "A Pilot Project in Labor Education," *American Federationist,* Dec. 1966; Edward Cohen-Rosenthal, "Enriching Workers' Lives," *Change,* July/Aug. 1979; Alice H. Cook and Agnes M. Douty, *Labor Education Outside the Unions: A Review of Postwar Programs in Western Europe and the United States* (Ithaca: Cornell Univ., NYSSILR, 1958); *Educational Advancement and Manpower Development for Wage Earners* (New Brunswick: Rutgers Univ., Institute of Management and Labor Relations, 1972); *Educational Advancement and Manpower Development Manual* (New Brunswick: Rutgers Univ., Institute of Management and Labor Relations, 1972); Lois Gray, "Academic Degrees for Labor Studies—A New Goal for Unions," *MLR,* June 1977; ———, "The American Way in Labor Education," *IR,* Feb. 1966; ———, *Labor Studies Credit and Degree Programs: A Growth Sector of Higher Education* (Ithaca: Cornell Univ., NYSSILR, Reprint Series no. 399, 1976); Arthur Levine, "An Unheralded Educational Experience—Brookwood Remembered," *Change,* Nov./Dec. 1981; Stan Luxenberg, "Labor Studies Blossom in Community Colleges," *Change,* July/Aug. 1979; Al Nash, *Ruskin College, A Challenge to Adult and Labor Education* (Ithaca: NYSSILR, Cornell Univ., 1981); ———, "The University Labor Educator: A Marginal Occupation," *ILRR,* Oct. 1978; Ronald J. Peters and Jeanne M. McCarrick, *Roots of Public Support for Labor Education 1900–1945* (Urbana: Univ. of Illinois, Institute of Labor and IR, Reprint Series no. 254, 1976); Hal Stack and Carroll M. Hutton (ed.), *Building New Alliances: Labor Unions and Higher Education* (San Francisco: Jossey-Bass, 1980); Gus Tyler, "The University and the Labor Union Educating the Proletariat," *Change,* Feb. 1979; Barbara Mayer Wertheimer (ed.), *Labor Education for Women Workers* (Philadelphia: Temple UP, 1981); Edwin E. Witte, "Labor Education and the Changing Labor Movement," *Thirty-Fifth Anniversary Papers* (Madison: Univ. of Wisconsin, School for Workers, Extension Division, 1960).

See also BROOKWOOD LABOR COLLEGE, BRYN MAWR SUMMER SCHOOL, HIGHLANDER FOLK SCHOOL, INDUSTRIAL EDUCATION, MEANY (GEORGE) CENTER FOR LABOR STUDIES, WISCONSIN SCHOOL FOR WORKERS.

labor efficiency *See* EFFICIENCY OF LABOR.

Laborers' International Union of North America (AFL-CIO) Until October 1965 was known as the International Hod Carriers', Building and Common Laborers' Union of North America (AFL-CIO). It was organized in Washington, D.C. in April 1903 by directly affiliated local unions of hod carriers and building workers. First known as the International Hod Carriers and Building Laborers' Union of America, it was concerned primarily with workers in the building trades. It enlarged its jurisdiction to include common laborers from other industries. When the American Brotherhood of Cement Workers dissolved in 1916, the hod carriers took over the membership. The Compressed Air and Foundation Workers' International Union merged with the Hod Carriers in 1918, and the Tunnel and Subway Constructors' International Union joined in 1929.

In 1968, the Journeymen Stone Cutters Association of North America (AFL-CIO) and the National Association of Post Office Mail Handlers (AFL-CIO) merged with the Laborers.

The official monthly publication is *The Laborer*.

Address: 905 16th St., N.W., Washington, D.C. 20006. Tel. (202) 737–8320

labor espionage *See* ANTI-UNION PRACTICES, ESPIONAGE, LAFOLLETTE COMMITTEE, PINKERTON DETECTIVE AGENCY.

labor exchange This is sometimes known as the employment exchange or an employment agency. Under the Wagner-Peyser Act the Congress in 1933 established the Employment Service in the U.S. Department of Labor. This established a procedure for assisting state employment agencies to coordinate public employment offices throughout the country. Private employment agencies also exist and provide service to individuals for a fee. The prime function of an employment exchange or an employment agency is to serve as a clearinghouse to bring together the individual seeking employment and the individual seeking an employee and to provide the information for the proper utilization of the skills available in the labor market.

See also EMPLOYMENT AGENCIES, U.S. EMPLOYMENT SERVICE.

labor exchange notes These are sometimes referred to as labor coupons. They were designed as a form of currency in cooperative societies and were suggested, by Robert Owen, among others, in 1829. The exchange notes were the equivalent of currency, and goods were to be exchanged on the basis of the number of labor hours worked. Apparently no distinction was set up between skilled and unskilled work but primarily on the basis of the equivalent labor hours that the product was worth. This was a simple way in which to establish the value of a commodity quite apart from its market and the effect of supply or demand. The equivalent labor hours of work also became part of the theory of value developed by the socialists and by Karl Marx.

labor exit permit In some countries a permit must be obtained before a worker can leave his home country to work in another country. During World War II the system was used in many belligerent countries to avoid a loss of manpower.

labor flux This term is the equivalent of the term more frequently used in American parlance, namely, labor turnover. It is designed to show the fluctuations of employees in the company or on the payroll during a particular period of time, usually in the form of a ratio between accessions and separations.

See also ACCESSION, ACCESSION RATE, LABOR TURNOVER, SEPARATION.

labor flux rate This is the same as the labor turnover rate and is measured by the addition of accessions plus separations divided by the full-time working force. It is expressed in formula form as: (labor turnover) is equal to A plus S divided by WF where WF is the full-time working force, or

$$LT = \frac{A + S}{WF}$$

See also ACCESSION RATE, LABOR TURNOVER.

labor force This term is the one generally used by the Census Bureau and defined by it for each of the censuses taken. The term has varied from census to census. It is, therefore, important in comparing the data of the labor force in various periods to check the definitions, particularly the changes which were in effect prior to 1940. In the censuses held prior to 1940 the terms "gainful workers" or "gainfully occupied" were the equivalents of the present term "labor force." The term, as defined by the census, includes persons who have jobs or who are actively seeking employment. This includes not only the employed, but also those unemployed. The term "employment" is generally held to include occupations in which money is earned, or some equivalent of money is earned, or which results in production of some good or service.

The labor force as currently defined includes all persons in the population 16 years of age and over who report any of the following activities during the survey week: (1) worked "as paid employees, in their own business, profession, or farm," including unpaid family workers, (2) with a job but not at work because of illness, bad weather, vacation, labor-management dispute, or personal reasons, (3) not at work, but made specific efforts to find a job within the past four weeks, and were available for work; including those who did not work at all, were available for work, and were waiting to be called back to a job from which they had been laid off or were waiting to report to a new job within 30 days. Members of the armed forces stationed in the United States have been included in the labor force count since January 1983.

Individuals in categories (1) and (2) and resident armed forces personnel comprise the "employed persons" of the labor force; those in category (3) comprise the "unemployed persons" of the labor force. All other persons 16 years and older are classified as "not in the labor force," and are further classified as "engaged in own home housework," "in school," "unable to work" because of long-term physical or mental illness, retired, or "other," composed of the voluntarily idle, seasonal workers for whom the survey week fell in an "off" season and who were not reported as unemployed, or discouraged workers.

The "full-time" labor force consists of persons working on full-time schedules (35 hours or more), persons involuntarily working part-time because full-time work is not available, and unemployed persons seeking full-time jobs. The "part-time" labor force consists of persons working part time voluntarily (one to 34 hours) and unemployed persons seeking part-time work.

The term is sometimes very tersely defined as the total number of people actually in the labor market at any given time.

The distinction is sometimes made between the civilian labor force and the total labor force. The total labor force includes military personnel.

Source references: Arvil V. Adams, "The American Work Force in the Eighties: New Problems and Policy Interests Require Improved Labor Force Data," *Annals*, Jan. 1981; Nancy S. Barrett, *Labor Force Data Needs for Macroeconomic Planning and Projections* (Washington: U.S. National Commission on Employment and Unemployment Statistics, Background Paper no. 25, 1979); John E. Bregger, "Labor Force Data from the CPS to Undergo Revision in January 1983," *MLR*, Nov. 1982; Glen G. Cain, *Labor Force Concepts and Definitions in View of Their Purposes* (Washington: U.S. National Commission on Employment and Unemployment Statistics, Background Paper no. 13, 1978); Louis J. Ducoff and Margaret J. Hagood, *Labor Force Definition and Measurement* (New York: Social Science Research Council, Bull. no. 56, 1947); John D. Durand, *The Labor Force in the United States, 1890–1960* (New York: Gordon & Breach, 1968); Paul O. Flaim and Howard N. Fullerton, Jr., "Labor Force Projections to 1990: Three Possible Paths," *Proceedings of the 31st A/M, IRRA*, ed. by Barbara Dennis (Madison: 1979); Howard N. Fullerton, "How Accurate Were Projections of the 1980 Labor Force?" *MLR*, July 1982; Howard N. Fullerton, Jr., "The 1995 Labor Force: A First Look," *MLR*, Dec. 1980; Joseph L. Gastwirth, "Estimating the Demographic Mix of the Available Labor Force," *MLR*, April 1981; Harold Goldstein, *State and Local Labor Force Statistics* (Washington: U.S. National Commission on Employment and Unemployment Statistics, Background Paper no. 1, 1978); Juanita Morris Kreps and Robert Clark, *Sex, Age, and Work: The Changing Composition of the Labor Force* (Baltimore: Johns Hopkins UP, Policy Studies in Employment and Welfare no. 23, 1975); Deborah Pisetzner, "Labor Force Data: The Impact of the 1980 Census,"

MLR, July 1982; Paul M. Ryscavage, "BLS Labor Force Projections: A Review of Methods and Results," *MLR*, April 1979; U.S. Dept. of Labor, BLS, *BLS Handbook of Methods, Volume 1* (Washington: 1982); ———, *A Guide to Seasonal Adjustment of Labor Force Data* (Washington: Bull. 2114, 1982); ———, *Questions and Answers on Popular Labor Force Topics* (Washington: Report 522, 1978); U.S. National Commission on Employment and Unemployment Statistics, *Concepts and Data Needs; Counting the Labor Force, Appendix Volume 1* (Washington: 1980); ———, *Counting the Labor Force* (Washington: 1979); ———, *Data Collection, Processing and Presentation: National and Local; Counting the Labor Force, Appendix Volume II* (Washington: 1980); ———, *Some Sources of Error in Labor Force Estimates from the Current Population Survey* (Washington: Background Paper no. 15, 1978); Arnold R. Weber, "In the 1980s: A Dramatically Different Labor Force," *Across the Board*, Dec. 1979; Diane Werneke (ed.), *Counting the Labor Force: Readings in Labor Force Statistics, Appendix Volume III*. (Washington: U.S. National Commission on Employment and Unemployment Statistics, 1980).

See also CIVILIAN LABOR FORCE, LABOR SUPPLY.

labor force availability *See* AVAILABILITY.

labor force participation rate It is the ratio of persons 16 years of age and older in the labor force (which includes members of the armed forces stationed in the United States) to the noninstitutional population. BLS defines noninstitutional population as those persons 16 years and older "who are not inmates of penal or mental institutions, sanitariums, or homes for the aged, infirm, or needy, and members of the Armed Forces stationed in the United States."

Source references: Belton M. Fleisher, "The Economics of Labor Force Participation: A Review Article," *Journal of Human Resources*, Spring 1971; Joseph L. Gastwirth, "On the Decline of Male Labor Force Participation," *MLR*, Oct. 1972; Morley Gunderson, "Probit and Logit Estimates of Labor Force Participation," *IR*, Spring 1980; Ann R. Miller, "Changing Work Life Patterns: A Twenty-Five Year Review," *Annals*, Jan. 1978; Paul Offner, "Labor Force Participation in the Ghetto," *Journal of Human Resources*, Fall 1972; Frederic B. Siskind, "Labor Force Participation of Men, 25–54, by Race," *MLR*, July 1975.

See also LABOR FORCE.

labor force time lost An attempt to measure the man-hours not used or utilized because of unemployment and involuntary part-time work. It is expressed as a percent of the total man-hours which are potentially available to the civilian labor force. A 37½ hour workweek is assumed as the standard workweek.

Source reference: Gertrude Bancroft, "Some Alternative Indexes of Employment and Unemployment," *MLR*, Feb. 1962.

See also EMPLOYMENT STATISTICS.

labor government A reference generally to a labor party which is broadly representative of the labor movement or trade union movement in the country which has obtained political control of the government. Labor governments have been in power in various times in such countries as Australia, Great Britain, New Zealand, and Sweden.

Although the labor movement in some countries may be separately organized and distinct from the political arm of the labor party, quite frequently the working relationship is rather close and frequently they are jointly financed and basic policies are coordinated.

labor grade As a result of wage rate negotiations or in a job evaluation or wage analysis procedure, it is generally necessary after reviewing the job content, skill, experience, education, and other job requirements to place occupations or groups which have an approximately equal value into the same labor grade or job class. Jobs within a single job class command the same rate of pay. Quite frequently the wage rate structure of a particular company will contain a series of labor grades, perhaps as many as 10 or 12, and within each of these labor grades there will be a series of jobs or job groups which fall within the general requirements of skill, experience, training, and other working conditions established for the job class.

labor history The term generally applied to any systematic recording of developments which have taken place during the history of the labor movement. These labor histories may be very broad and general in scope, covering the major developments of trade union organization as well as the achievements of that period. They may also cover individual industries where an effort is made to develop, over a period of time in some organized fashion, the characteristics of labor organization and collective bargaining history in that particular industry.

Studies have also been made of important individuals who played a crucial role in the growth and development, not only of individual unions, but also in the overall development of trade unionism.

Recent developments in research suggest the greater utilization of sources of materials coming not only from government archives but also from labor unions, employer associations, university research centers, court transcripts, oral histories and interviews, and private libraries to permit a more careful study and evaluation of labor history. In terms of substance, according to Brody, there seems to be change in the focus of study to include interest in study of workers, ethnic history, and shop-floor history. Other scholars not known as labor historians are also found to be adding information on work and workers.

Source references: Stanley Aronowitz, *False Promises, the Shaping of American Working Class Consciousness* (New York: McGraw-Hill, 1973); David Brody, "The Old Labor History and the New: In Search of an American Working Class," *Labor History*, Winter 1979; John R. Commons et al., *History of Labour in the United States* (2 vols., New York: Macmillan, 1946); Foster Rhea Dulles, *Labor in America: A History* (3d ed., New York: Crowell, 1966); Albert Fried (ed.), *Except to Walk Free; Documents and Notes in the History of American Labor* (Garden City, N.Y.: Anchor Books, 1974); George H. Hildebrand, *American Unionism: An Historical and Analytical Survey* (Reading, Mass.: Addison-Wesley, 1979); Gerd Korman (comp.), *Labor History Documents,* Volumes I–III (Ithaca: NYSSILR, Cornell Univ., 1974); Bertram McNamara, "A Labor Leader Looks at Labor History," *Proceedings of the 30th A/M, IRRA*, ed. by Barbara Dennis (Madison: 1978); Robert Ozanne, "Trends in American Labor History," *Labor History,* Fall 1980; Morris Bartel Schnapper, *American Labor; A Pictorial Social History* (Washington: Public Affairs Press, 1972); U.S. Dept. of Labor, *Important Events in American Labor History, 1778–1968* (Washington: 1969); ———, *Labor Firsts in America* (Washington: 1977); U.S. Dept. of Labor, BLS, *Brief History of the American Labor Movement* (Washington: Bull. no. 1000, 1970); U.S. Dept. of Labor, ETA, *200 Years of American Worklife* (Washington: 1977).

labor hour A term designed to describe the amount of work actually performed by an individual during a one-hour period. Occasionally, such data are developed for the purpose of determining unit labor costs.

labor immobility This is an attempt to explain the lack of mobility or the unwillingness and sometimes inability of an individual to move from one labor market area to another which might possibly provide better terms and conditions of employment. Some of the reasons for immobility in the past have been the ownership of a home, attachment to a particular locality, the customs and habits of a particular group of workers as well as other restrictions on mobility.

More and more, the problem of mobility is being considered in the total labor market picture and efforts are being made, particularly because of the dynamic technological revolution which is going on, to provide for a greater degree of mobility by use of various incentives, including retraining programs, the payment of transportation costs and other expenses involved in moving, and occasionally protection of seniority and other rights built up under a particular collective bargaining agreement or within a particular firm.

See also LABOR MOBILITY, VOCATIONAL GUIDANCE, VOCATIONAL TRAINING.

labor injunction *See* INJUNCTION, NORRIS-LAGUARDIA ACT.

labor inspection A procedure in which individuals, usually attached to a labor enforcement agency within a state or elsewhere, determine whether or not certain conditions established under state safety or other laws are being carried out. The individuals are generally referred to as labor inspectors.

labor inspector Generally, the individual who has the responsibility for determining whether or not provisions of a particular statute or regulation are being properly enforced in a plant or other place of work.

labor institute A term frequently used to describe a particular center where industrial relations programs are carried out or directed in large part toward the trade unions and toward labor leadership. Individual institutes may be set up for a summer session or for a number of days or weeks to carry out a particular program, sometimes in cooperation with labor leaders in a locality or with the international unions.

Occasionally the industrial relations centers themselves may be called institutes of labor and industrial relations to convey the idea that they are educational organizations concerned with the various problems of prime concern to labor. Some of these labor institutes also provide training for management groups.

labor institutionalism Welfare activities conducted by labor unions for the benefit of their members. Such activities sometimes compete with commercial enterprises which provide similar services. Such welfare institutions include labor banks; insurance against sickness, accidents, old age; credit unions; and building and loan associations.

laboristic economy The term designed to describe the economic features and philosophy of an economy which is directed and organized by a labor party. Professor Slichter spoke of it as an economy in which the conditions were primarily determined by the labor organizations or were attuned to their interests and ideals.

Source reference: Fels Rendig, "An Ideology For a Laboristic Economy," *Southern Economic Journal,* Jan. 1950.

laborites A term generally applied to members of the British Labor Party. It may also be applied to any group which advocates a political philosophy based on labor's position.

labor journalism Refers generally to the labor press and the program of individual unions concerned with procedures for presenting their stories to the community. The American labor press also consists of the major journals issued by the parent organizations. Thus far the major efforts have been embodied in the programs of the international unions and the parent labor organizations.

Source references: Gordon H. Cole (ed.), *Labor's Story as Reported by the American Labor Press* (New York: Community Publishers, 1961); James C. Duram, "The Labor Union Journals and the Constitutional Issues of the New Deal: The Case for Court Restriction," *Labor History,* Spring 1974; N. H. Hedges, "Why a Labor Press?" *House of Labor,* ed. by J. B. S. Hardman and Maurice F. Neufeld (New York: PH, 1951); International Labor Press Assn., *Collective Bargaining and the Labor Press—A Closer Look, A Forum* (Washington: 1978); Louis A. Jacobs and Gary W. Spring, "Fair Coverage in Internal Union Periodicals," *Industrial Relations LJ,* Vol. 4, no. 2, 1981; Samuel Jacobs, "How to Write for the Labor Press," *Labor and the Nation,* March/April 1947; Frank Kabela, Jr., "The Labor Press: Its History, Nature and Influence," *LLJ,* May 1960; Donald James Myers, *The Birth and Establishment of the Labor Press in the United States* (Madison: Dane County Title Co., 1967); Martin M. Perline, "The Trade Union Press: An Historical Analysis," *Labor History,* Winter 1969; R. E. Porter, "The Growth and Influence of the Labor Press," *Machinists Monthly Journal,* Aug. 1948; R. Vicker, "The Labor Press," *Wall Street Journal,* Dec. 22, 1951.

See also TRADE UNION PUBLICATIONS.

labor law The term is used generally to cover all federal or state legislation designed to protect or improve the conditions of workers as well as the rights of labor unions, employers, and the public. Protection may deal with such diverse areas as collective bargaining, wage and hour regulation, the employment of children and women, safety, and a wide variety of other areas directly or indirectly related to conditions of employment.

In dealing with the term "law" or "labor law" it is frequently important to note that there are two important aspects of the law. One refers to the statutory law which consists of legislation passed by individual state legislatures or by the Congress, and the other, common law or case law, which may be said to arise from interpretations of issues by the courts. Occasionally in the field of industrial relations a third facet is suggested, namely, "industrial jurisprudence," which may consist of the actions arising out of the day-to-day collective bargaining relationship of the parties and the administration of the contract. This may also be thought of as the common law of industrial relations. These may be given substance in arbitration awards or are accepted by the parties themselves as a base for working out their relationships.

In our federal-state relations it is also important to note the jurisdiction of our 50 states. The division of authority between the state and federal law is not fixed. Over the years, Supreme Court decisions have changed the boundaries between state and federal jurisdiction.

Source references: John B. Andrews, *Labor Laws in Action* (New York: Harper, 1938); Duane Beeler, *Labor Law for the Union Officer* (Chicago: Union Representative, 1975); Leo C. Brown, *The Impact of the New Labor Law on Union-Management Relations* (St. Louis: St. Louis Univ., Institute of Social Order, 1948); Alvin L. Goldman, *The Supreme Court and Labor-Management Relations Law* (Lexington, Mass.: Lexington Books, 1976); William B. Gould, *A Primer on American Labor Law* (Cambridge: MIT Press, 1982); Russell L. Greenman and Eric J. Schmertz, *Personnel Administration and the Law* (2d ed., Washington: BNA, 1979); Charles O. Gregory, *Labor and the Law* (2d rev. ed., New York: Norton, 1961); Harvard Law Review Assn., *Selected Essays on Labor Law* (Cambridge: Gannet House, 1959); George Meany, "Common Sense in Labor Law," *LLJ*, Oct. 1976; Aaron Howard Myers and David P. Twomey, *Labor Law and Legislation* (5th ed., Cincinnati: South-Western, 1975); Peter G. Nash, "Jurisdictional Overlap," *Labor Law Developments 1982*, Proceedings of 28th Annual Institute on Labor Law, SLF (New York: Bender, 1982); Russell A. Smith, "Significant Developments in Labor Law During the Last Half Century," *Michigan LR*, June 1952; Benjamin J. Taylor and Fred Witney, *Labor Relations Law* (4th ed., Englewood Cliffs: PH, 1983); U.S. Congress, House, *Compilation of Laws Relating to Mediation, Conciliation, and Arbitration Between Employers and Employees* (2 vols., Washington: 1981); U.S. Congress, Senate, Committee on Labor and Public Welfare, *Compilation of Selected Labor Laws Pertaining to Labor Relations* (3 vol., Washington: 1974); ———, *Compilation of Selected Federal Laws Relating to Employment and Training* (Washington: 1976); W. J. Usery, Jr., "The Impact of Legislation on Collective Bargaining," *LLJ*, July 1974.

See also INTERSTATE COMMERCE; INTRASTATE COMMERCE; PREEMPTION, DOCTRINE OF; PROTECTIVE LABOR LEGISLATION.

labor law case books To provide convenient reference material for students, lawyers, and practitioners who need to refer to provisions (or in many cases the full text) of important laws and court decisions influencing labor relations, a number of case books have been published. Among them are: American Bar Association, Section of Labor Relations Law, *The Developing Labor Law: The Board, The Courts, and the NLRA* (2 vols., 2d ed., Washington: Bureau of National Affairs, 1983); Archibald Cox, Derek C. Bok, and Robert A. Gorman, *Cases and Materials on Labor Law* (9th ed., Mineola, N.Y.: Foundation Press, 1981); Charles Gregory and Harold Katz, *Labor and the Law* (3d ed., New York: Norton, 1979); Milton Handler and Paul R. Hays, *Cases and Materials on Labor Law* (2d ed., St. Paul: West Pub., 1953); Labor Law Group Trust, *Labor Relations and Social Problems: A Course Book, Units 1–10, Reference Supplement* (Washington: Bureau of National Affairs, 1971+); Russell A. Smith, Harry T. Edwards, and R. Theodore Clark, Jr., *Labor Relations in the Public Sector, Cases and Materials* (Indianapolis: Bobbs-Merrill, 1974); Russell A. Smith, Leroy S. Merrifield, and Harry T. Edwards, *Collective Bargaining and Labor Arbitration, Materials on Collective Bargaining, Labor Arbitration and Discrimination in Employment* (2d ed., Indianapolis: Bobbs-Merrill, 1979).

Labor Law Journal A monthly publication issued by the Commerce Clearing House, which is devoted entirely to articles dealing with the developing problems in labor law and legislation. It also has a section on recent publications and information on other current developments of interest to labor law practitioners, including materials dealing with the subject of arbitration.

labor law reform bills of 1977–1978 Federal legislation intended to aid union organization efforts. According to Mills, the bills sought to:

(1) Set time limts for NLRB representation elections; (2) Permit unions to address employees at representation meetings on company property called by employer; (3) Increase the NLRB from five to seven members to expedite cases before the Board; (4) Expedite review of decisions of administrative law judges appealed to the NLRB; (5) Prohibit federal contract awards for three years to any person or corporation found coercing employees; (6) Provide double back-pay awards to employees illegally discharged because of a union organizational drive; and (7) Permit the NLRB to order compensation to bargaining unit employees for an employer's refusal to bargain over an initial contract.

The nation's employers formed a lobbying group, the National Action Committee on Labor Law Reform, and also a national organization, the Council on a Union-Free Environment, to oppose the legislation. The leading proponent was the AFL-CIO. H.R. 8410 was passed on October 6, 1977, but the companion bill, S. 2467, died in the Senate in June 1978.

Source references: Vincent Apruzzese, "The Proposed Labor Reform Legislation—A Management View of the Most Controversial Labor Reform Proposals in Decades: An Analysis of the Provisions—And Where We Go From Here," *Labor Law Developments 1979*, Proceedings of 25th Annual Institute on Labor Law, SLF (New York: Bender, 1979); Elliot Bredhoff, "Labor Law Reform: A Labor Perspective," *Boston College LR*, Nov. 1978; Andrew M. Kramer, "Labor Law Reform: A Management Perspective," *Boston College LR*, Nov. 1978; "Labor Law Reform: Continuing the Fight," *American Federationist*, Nov. 1977; George Meany, "The Case for Labor Law Reform," *American Federationist*, Sept. 1977; D. Quinn Mills, "Flawed Victory in Labor Law Reform," *Harvard BR*, May/June 1979; Peter G. Nash, "The Labor Reform Act of 1977: A Detailed Analysis," *Employee Relations LJ*, Summer 1978; Bernard Samoff, "NLRB Priority and Injunctions for Discriminatory Discharges," *LLJ*, Jan. 1980; Howard Schulman, "The Proposed Labor Reform Legislation—Its Frustrations and Suggested Consequences," *Labor Law Developments 1979*, Proceedings of 25th Annual Institute on Labor Law, SLF (New York: Bender, 1979).

labor leader A designation usually assigned to an individual who is devoting his full time to the labor movement, or one who has achieved prominence as a person active in leading a major local union, a national union, or a person active as a leader of a parent organization.

Leadership ranges, of course, from those active in local and regional areas to those who play important roles not only in major policy of the labor movement but also in the national arena.

The components of labor leadership do not vary substantially from those of leadership in other areas of democratic life, except that the individuals are essentially devoted to the prime objectives of the labor union movement and are frequently drawn from the middle class, the labor union movement itself, or from among the intellectuals (particularly in the early history of American trade unionism).

Source references: Jack Barbash, "The Leadership Factor in Union Growth," *MLR*, Feb. 1963; ——— (ed.), *Unions and Union Leadership, Their Human Meaning* (New York: Harper, 1959); Thomas R. Brooks, *Clint: A Biography of a Labor Intellectual, Clinton S. Golden* (New York: Atheneum, 1979); Gary M. Fink (ed.), *Biographical Dictionary of American Labor Leaders* (Westport, Conn.: Greenwood Press, 1974); Eli Ginzberg, "American Labor Leaders: Time in Office," *ILRR*, Jan. 1948; ———, *The Labor Leader* (New York: Macmillan, 1948); A. A. Imberman, "Labor Leaders and Society," *Harvard BR*, Jan. 1950; Clark Kerr, *Unions and Union Leaders of Their Own Choosing* (New York: Fund for the Republic, 1957); Lois MacDonald, *Leadership Dynamics and the Trade Union Leader* (New York: NYU Press, 1959); Charles A. Madison, *American Labor Leaders: Personalities and Forces in the Labor Movement* (2d ed., New York: Ungar, 1962); C. Wright Mills, *The New Men of*

Power (New York: Harcourt, Brace, 1948); James O. Morris, "The Acquisitive Spirit of John Mitchell, UMW President (1899–1908)," *Labor History*, Winter 1979.

See also LABOR HISTORY, UNION LEADERSHIP, UNION OFFICERS.

labor lobby A term applied to those groups of trade unionists or individuals assigned to the state or federal legislatures to attempt to influence action and support of special labor legislation or legislation designed to protect or assist members of their organizations.

The effectiveness of labor lobbies varies from state to state depending upon their organization and their labor support in the area. They may be more effective during certain administrations or with groups whose programs are sympathetic with their own.

See also POLITICAL ACTION, UNION.

labor lobbying The activities by those assigned to state and federal legislatures to work with legislators, or attempts to obtain legislation favorable to the welfare of labor unions or their members.

labor maintenance A term generally applied to procedures or policies designed to maintain a stable labor force. Among those activities toward which programs are directed are absenteeism, turnover, and other factors which might lead to an unstable labor force, and, hence, result in greater costs of retraining.

labor management This term is sometimes used as the equivalent of personnel management or the activity involved in the operation of a personnel department which generally covers the areas of selection, assignment, training, and the most efficient utilization of the labor force. In many companies the personnel management program includes the determination of wages and the handling of the major problems in personnel policy.

See also PERSONNEL ADMINISTRATION, PERSONNEL MANAGEMENT.

labor-management-citizens committee This usually refers to a tripartite group consisting of public representatives and representatives of labor and management whose prime function is directed toward the handling of labor-management disputes. In some areas, they also may act to bring to the community additional business and to promote greater stability in labor-management relations.

See also NEW YORK CITY OFFICE OF COLLECTIVE BARGAINING, TOLEDO INDUSTRIAL PEACE BOARD (TOLEDO PLAN), TOLEDO LABOR-MANAGEMENT-CITIZENS COMMITTEE.

labor-management committee The committee which generally consists of representatives of management and employees whose prime concern is with the most effective use of materials and manpower in the plant. In many plants the labor-management committees will concern themselves with those conditions in the plant which need particular attention and in which there is a substantial amount of mutual interest. They are not usually concerned with labor-management negotiations, although some of their activities may flow from the needs shown in collective bargaining or problems which may arise out of the administration of the collective bargaining agreement. They were fairly important in the movement to accelerate production during World War II.

Source references: W. Ellison Chalmers and Herman Wolf, "Labor-Management Committees Speed Production," *Public Opinion Quarterly*, Fall 1943; Laurence P. Corbett, "Specific Experiences of Labor-Management Committees; The Health Care Experience," *Proceedings of the 34th A/M, IRRA*, ed. by Barbara Dennis (Madison: 1982); Indiana Univ., Midwest Center for Public Sector Labor Relations, *Labor-Management Committees in the Public Sector, A Practitioner's Guide* (Bloomington: 1979); Phillip E. Ray, "Specific Experiences of Labor-Management Committees; The Retail Food Industry," *Proceedings of the 34th A/M, IRRA*, ed. by Barbara Dennis (Madison: 1982); Charles E. Shaw, "Management-Labor Committees," *ILRR*, Jan. 1950; Gerald I. Susman, *A Guide to Labor-Management Committees in State and Local Government* (Washington: U.S. Dept. of Housing and Urban Development, 1980); U.S. National Center for Productivity and Quality of Working Life, *Recent Initiative in Labor-Management Cooperation* (Washington: 1976); ———, *Starting a Labor-Management*

Committee in Your Organization; Some Pointers for Action (Washington: 1978); U.S. National Commission on Productivity and Work Quality, *Labor-Management Committees in the Public Sector, Experiences of Eight Committees* (Washington: 1975); ———, *Labor-Management Productivity Committees in American Industry* (Washington: 1975).

See also JOINT PRODUCTION COMMITTEES, LABOR COOPERATION, LABOR-MANAGEMENT COOPERATION, LABOR-MANAGEMENT PRODUCTION COMMITTEES.

Labor-Management Conference (1945) Although other conferences have been held involving labor and management, the one which is generally known as the Labor-Management Conference applies to the one convened in November 1945 by President Truman, following the end of the National War Labor Board. It was thought that the close relationship between industry and labor during the war period might be continued in the postwar period with an attempt to find some common areas of agreement.

The conference lasted from November 5 to November 30, 1945. The work of the conference was distributed among six major committees. Only three committees submitted reports which were adopted by the conference. These dealt with the work of the conciliation service and the mediation and voluntary arbitration functions; the handling of collective bargaining and the negotiation of first agreements; and the general procedures and standards for the handling of grievances and voluntary arbitration.

Judge Walter P. Stacy was the conference chairman and George W. Taylor, the conference secretary. The labor members included for the AFL, William Green, Harry C. Bates, William L. Hutcheson, George Meany, Daniel J. Tobin, David Dubinsky, George Harrison, and Matthew Woll. The CIO was represented by Philip Murray, Sidney Hillman, R. J. Thomas, Emil Rieve, Reid Robinson, John Green, Albert J. Fitzgerald, and Lee Pressman. The United Mine Workers was represented by John L. Lewis, and the Railroad Brotherhoods by T. C. Cashen. The employer members included Ira Mosher, Edward N. Allen, M. W. Clement, Clifford W. Gaylord, John Holmes, C. R. Hook, George H. Love, T. O. Moore, Edward P. Palmer, Eric A. Johnston, Harry Woodhead, Charles E. Wilson, E. J. Thomas, H. W. Steinkraus, David Sarnoff, Louis Ruthenberg, W. M. Rand, H. W. Prentis, Jr.

Source references: U.S. Dept. of Labor, *A Brief History of Labor-Management Conferences* (Washington: 1962); U.S. Dept. of Labor, Division of Labor Standards, *The President's National Labor-Management Conference, November 5–30, 1945, Summary and Committee Reports* (Washington: Bull. no. 77, 1946).

See also PRESIDENT'S ADVISORY COMMITTEE ON LABOR-MANAGEMENT POLICY.

labor-management cooperation Joint efforts by labor and management to enlarge the scope of the areas of argreement and to work toward common objectives in the production effort. This involves complete employer acceptance of the union and the acceptance of the basic principles of management by the employees. Both are concerned with the efficiency of plant operations and seek methods of improving production, through safer working conditions, improved quality, and greater utilization of manpower in the plant. Sometimes referred to as union-management cooperation.

Source references: William L. Batt, Jr. and Edgar Weinberg, "Labor-Management Cooperation Today," *Harvard BR,* Jan./Feb. 1978; David L. Cole, "Improving Labor-Management Cooperation: A Proposed Program of Action for the ILO," *ILR,* May 1956; James W. Driscoll, "Labor Management Panels: Three Case Studies," *MLR,* June 1980; Lee Dyer, David B. Lipsky, and Thomas A. Kochan, "Union Attitudes Toward Management Cooperation," *IR,* May 1977; David A. Gray, Anthony V. Sinicropi, and Paula Ann Hughes, "From Conflict to Cooperation: A Joint Union-Management Goal-Setting and Problem-Solving Program," *Proceedings of the 34th A/M, IRRA,* ed. by Barbara Dennis (Madison: 1982); Kenneth E. Moffett, *Labor Management Cooperation: A Response to an Economy in Crisis* (Washington: SPIDR, Occasional Paper no. 81–1, 1981); Richard P. Nielsen, "Stages in Moving Toward Cooperative Problem Solving Labor Relations Projects and a Case Study," *Human Resource Management,* Fall 1979; A. H. Raskin, "Can Management and Labor Really Become Partners?" *Across the Board,* July/Aug. 1982; Donald N. Scobel, "Business and Labor—From Adversaries to Allies," *Harvard BR,* Nov./Dec. 1982; Twentieth Century Fund, *Partners in Production: A Basis for Labor-Management Understanding* (New York: 1949); U.S. Dept. of Labor, LMSA, *Labor-Management Cooperation: Recent Efforts and Results; Readings from the Monthly Labor Review* (Washington: LMSA Pub. 6, BLS Bull. 2153, 1982); Edgar Weinberg, "Labor-Management Cooperation: A Report on Recent Initiatives," *MLR,* April 1976.

See also JOINT PRODUCTION COMMITTEES, LABOR COOPERATION, LABOR-MANAGEMENT PRODUCTION COMMITTEES.

Labor Management Cooperation Act of 1978 Law which authorizes and directs the FMCS to provide grants and assist in the establishment and operation of labor-management committees. The law seeks through these committees to improve organizational effectiveness, working conditions, and working relationships; to provide mechanisms to resolve problems; to enhance employee decision making and participation in workplace matters; and to encourage free collective bargaining. The legislation was introduced by Congressman Lundine, who earlier as mayor of Jamestown, New York, was instrumental in establishing the Jamestown Area Labor-Management Committee.

The statute was implemented in 1981, when a $1.2 million appropriation was approved. By 1983, 21 programs had been approved for funding, 14 of which were established in November 1981.

Source references: Labor Management Cooperation Act of 1978, 29 U.S.C. 173, 175a, 186 (1982); BNA, "Federal Aid to Labor-Management Panels Justified by Results, Participants Say," *Daily Labor Report,* No. 108, June 3, 1983; Richard D. Leone and Michael F. Eleey, "The Origin and Operations of Area Labor-Management Committees," *MLR,* May 1983.

See also JAMESTOWN AREA LABOR-MANAGEMENT COMMITTEE.

labor-management production committees Production was one of the key contributing factors in the winning of World War II. A large part of the credit for the unprecedented production record of American labor and management during the war period is given to the work of the labor-management production committees which were established in approximately 5,000 war plants. These committees were extremely effective in devising techniques and methods and in creating ways of improving the efficiency of operations, reducing hazards, and utilizing ideas for the most efficient use of plant equipment and personnel.

Although the War Production Board provided the stimulus and assistance, the labor-management production committees are credited with the accomplishment of production during the difficult days of the wartime economy.

See also JOINT PRODUCTION COMMITTEES, LABOR COOPERATION, LABOR-MANAGEMENT COMMITTEE.

labor-management relations *See* INDUSTRIAL RELATIONS.

Labor Management Relations Act of 1947 This is the formal title of the Act that is popularly known as the Taft-Hartley Act.

It was the first major successful effort to revise the National Labor Relations Act of 1935.

The law was passed following the serious outbreak of labor disputes at the end of World War II and the great concern of Congress as well as many state legislatures about the inequality of power created under the provisions of the National Labor Relations Act. The law attempted to equalize the bargaining power by providing a series of union unfair labor practices to parallel the employer unfair labor practices under the National Labor Relations Act. The Taft-Hartley Act also limited the union security provisions of the National Labor Relations Act by outlawing the closed shop and the automatic check-off, and substituting therefor a form of union shop under certain circumstances.

The law also provided special machinery for the handling of national emergency disputes, including the use of an injunction for approximately 80 days during which time a board of inquiry would attempt to provide information on the basic issues, elections would be held on the company's last offer, and, presumably, mediation efforts would be made to assist the parties in reaching agreement. The statute also provided methods of enforcing the collective bargaining agreement through suits in the federal courts.

The mediation and conciliation functions of the U.S. Conciliation Service in the U.S. Department of Labor were set up in a separate and independent agency known as the Federal Mediation and Concilation Service. Other provisions of the law dealt with the non-Communist affidavit, the filing of certain financial statements with the Department of Labor, and limitations on certain types of strike activity.

The name Taft-Hartley comes from the chairmen of the respective committees in the House and Senate. Fred A. Hartley, Jr., Republican of New Jersey, was the chairman of the House Labor Committee; and Senator Robert A. Taft, Republican of Ohio, was the chairman of the Senate Labor and Public Welfare Committee. The Act was passed by both houses and on June 20, 1947, President Truman vetoed the bill and sent his message of disapproval to the Congress. The House overrode the veto by a vote of 331 to 83 and on June 23, the Senate overrode the veto by a vote of 68 to 25.

Source references: American Bar Association, Section of Labor Relations Law, *The Developing Labor Law; The Board, the Courts, and the National Labor Relations Act* (Washington: BNA, 1971); Archibald Cox, "Some Aspects of the Labor-Management Relations Act of 1947," *Harvard LR,* Nov. 1947 and Jan. 1948; Harold W. Davey, "The Operational Impact of the Taft-Hartley Act Upon Collective Bargaining Relationships," *New Dimensions in Collective Bargaining,* ed. by Harold W. Davey, Howard S. Kaltenborn, and Stanley H. Ruttenberg (New York: Harper, IRRA Pub. no. 21, 1959); Emil C. Farkas, "The National Labor Relations Act: The Health Care Amendments," *LLJ,* May 1978; Harry A. Millis and Emily C. Brown, *From the Wagner to the Taft-Hartley* (Chicago: Univ. of Chicago Press, 1965); Stephen P. Pepe and Calvin L. Keith, "Health Care Labor Relations Law—Understanding the Issues," *Employee Relations LJ,* Autumn 1981; Harold S. Roberts, *The Taft-Hartley Act in Review* (Honolulu: Univ. of Hawaii, IRC, 1948); Joseph Shister, "The Impact of the Taft-Hartley Act on Union Strength and Collective Bargaining," *ILRR,* April 1958; Clyde W. Summers, "A Summary Evaluation of the Taft-Hartley Act," *ILRR,* April 1958; U.S. Dept. of Labor, LMSA, *Impact of the 1974 Health Care Amendments to the NLRA on Collective Bargaining in the Health Care Industry* (Washington: 1979); Peter D. Walther and Robert R. LeGros, "The Health Care Industry Under the 1974 Amendments to the National Labor Relations Act," *Labor Law Developments 1976,* Proceedings of the 22d Annual Institute on Labor Law, SLF (New York: Bender, 1976).

See also CLOSED SHOP, LABOR-MANAGEMENT REPORTING AND DISCLOSURE ACT OF 1959, NATIONAL LABOR RELATIONS ACT, NON-COMMUNIST AFFIDAVIT.

labor-management relations committee The term is generally applied to the committee provided by the Labor Management Relations Act of 1947, known as the Congressional Joint Committee on Labor-Management Relations. The committee was required to study and report upon developments in the field of labor-management relations and was sometimes referred to as the "watch-dog committee."

Labor-Management Reporting and Disclosure Act of 1959 This statute also is known as the Landrum-Griffin Act. Designed as a labor reform act, Congress held this to be an act "to provide for the reporting and disclosure of certain financial transactions and administrative practices of labor organizations and employers, to prevent abuses in the administration of trusteeships by labor organizations, to provide standards with respect to the election of officers of labor organizations and for other purposes."

The Act was drafted in part to provide greater internal union democracy through establishment of a Bill of Rights, the regulation of trusteeships, and formulation of standards for holding elections of union officers and for the fiscal obligations of union officers. Among the other purposes of the statute were amendments to the Taft-Hartley Act relating to the hot cargo clauses, the handling of various types of picketing and secondary boycotts, and the ceding of jurisdiction to the states in those controversies where the NLRB had failed to handle a dispute. The Taft-Hartley Act was amended also by elimination of the non-Communist affidavit and provision for certain other limitations on the holding of office by Communists or former Communists.

The findings, purposes, and policies of the Act are set out in Section 2(a), (b), and (c), and they read in part as follows:

> Sec. 2. (a) The Congress finds that, in the public interest, it continues to be the responsibility of the federal government to protect employees' rights to organize, choose their own representatives, bargain collectively, and otherwise engage in concerted activities for their mutual aid or protection; that the relations between employers and labor organizations and the millions of workers they represent have a substantial impact on the commerce of the nation; and that in order to accomplish the objective of a free flow of commerce it is essential that labor organizations, employers, and their officials adhere to the highest standards of responsibility and ethical conduct in administering the affairs of their organizations, particularly as they affect labor-management relations.
>
> (b) The Congress further finds, from recent investigations in the labor and management fields, that there have been a number of instances of breach of trust, corruption, disregard of the rights of individual employees, and other failures to observe high standards of responsibility and ethical conduct which require further and supplementary legislation that will afford necessary protection of the rights and interests of employees and the public generally as they relate to the activities of labor organizations, employers, labor relations consultants, and their officers and representatives.
>
> (c) The Congress therefore further finds and declares that the enactment of this Act is necessary, to eliminate or prevent improper practices on the part of labor organizations, employers, labor relations consultants, and their officers and representatives which distort and defeat the policies of the Labor-Management Relations Act of 1947, as amended, and the Railway Labor Act, as amended. . . .

Source references: Benjamin Aaron, "The Labor-Management Reporting and Disclosure Act of 1959," 73 *Harvard LR* 851, 1086 (1960); ———, "The Union Member's 'Bill of Rights': First Two Years," *IR*, Feb. 1962; Janice R. Bellace and Alan D. Berkowitz, *The Landrum-Griffin Act, Twenty Years of Federal Protection of Union Members' Rights* (Philadelphia: Univ. of Pennsylvania, Wharton School, Industrial Research Unit, LRRP Series no. 19, 1979); George W. Bohlander and William D. Werther, Jr., "The Labor-Management Reporting and Disclosure Act Revisited," *LLJ*, Sept. 1979; BNA, *The Labor Reform Law* (Washington: 1959); Ronald I. Gilardi, "Counsel Fees and Title I of the Landrum-Griffin Act," *LLJ*, April 1977; Arthur J. Goldberg and Kenneth Meiklejohn, *Analysis of Labor-Management Reporting and Disclosure Act of 1959* (Washington: AFL-CIO, 1959); Eric Heyden, "Landrum-Griffin Section 101(a)(4)—Its Impact on Employee Rights," *Employee Relations LJ*, Spring 1982; William P. Hobgood, "Reporting Requirements for Consultants Under the Labor-Management Reporting and Disclosure Act," *NYU 33d Annual National Conference on Labor*, ed. by Richard Adelman (New York: Bender, 1981); John L. Holcombe, *The Landrum-Griffin Act: Some Problems of Its Administration* (Honolulu: Univ. of Hawaii, IRC, 1962); "The Labor-Management Reporting and Disclosure Act of 1959, Interpretation and Implications," *Georgetown LR*, Winter 1959; Doris B. McLaughlin and Anita L. W. Schoomaker, *The Landrum-Griffin Act and Union Democracy* (Ann Arbor: Univ. of Michigan Press, 1979); Baker Armstrong Smith, "Landrum-Griffin After Twenty-One Years: Mature Legislation or Childish Fantasy?" *LLJ*, May 1980; Russell A. Smith, "The Labor-Management Reporting and Disclosure Act of 1959," 46 *Virginia LR* 195 (1960); U.S. Dept. of Labor, LMSA, *Compliance, Enforcement and Reporting in 1978* (Washington: 1981); ———, *Reports Required Under the LMRDA and the CSRA* (rev. ed., Washington: 1980); ———, *Union Officer Elections and Trusteeships Case Digest* (Washington: 1980); U.S. Dept. of Labor, Office of Labor-Management and Welfare-Pension Reports, *Legislative History of the Labor-Management Reporting and Disclosure Act of 1959, Titles I–VI* (Washington: 1964); U.S. GAO, *Laws Protecting Union Members and Their Pension and Welfare Benefits Should be Better Enforced* (Washington: 1978); U.S. NLRB, *Legislative History of the*

Labor-Management Reporting and Disclosure Act of 1959 (2 vols., Washington: 1959); J. Albert Woll, *Landrum-Griffin* (Washington: AFL-CIO, Pub. no. 111, 1960).

See also REGULATION OF LABOR UNIONS, U.S. V. ARCHIE BROWN.

Labor-Management Services Administration (LMSA) A division of the U.S. Department of Labor established on August 21, 1963. The LMSA has administrative responsibilities of the Employee Retirement Income Security Act of 1974, the Labor-Management Reporting and Disclosure Act of 1959, and Section 7120 of the Civil Service Reform Act of 1978.

The major subdivisions of the LMSA are: Division of Cooperative Labor-Management Programs, Office of Labor-Management Relations Service, Office of Labor-Management Standards Enforcement, Pension and Welfare Benefit Programs, and Office of Veterans' Reemployment Rights.

See also OFFICE OF LABOR-MANAGEMENT STANDARDS ENFORCEMENT, PENSION AND WELFARE BENEFIT PROGRAMS.

labor-management understanding *See* LABOR-MANAGEMENT COOPERATION.

labor manager The labor manager or personnel director generally has the prime responsibility for the organization and direction of the working force. This may include the selection, allocation, and utilization of employees as well as the handling of the policies involved in the wages, hours, and working conditions in the plant.

See also EMPLOYMENT MANAGER, LABOR MANAGEMENT, PERSONNEL ADMINISTRATION, PERSONNEL DIRECTOR.

labor market A concept used in labor economics to indicate the relation or interplay between the supply and demand for labor in a particular area. It may also concern itself with the behavior of the individual in a local area, a larger geographic area, or throughout the entire country. It may also concern itself with the special features of the labor force, the character of the supply and demand, as well as the category and skill of the group, and the methods designed for providing employment and the general features of turnover and labor mobility.

Source references: Orley Ashenfelter and Gary Solon, *Longitudinal Labor Market Data: Source, Uses, and Limitations* (Princeton: Princeton Univ., IR Section, WP no. 155, 1982); Ross E. Azevedo, *Labor Market Adjustments During Periods of Unemployment* (Minneapolis: Univ. of Minnesota, IRC, WP 77–08, 1977); Martin Neil Baily, *The Labor Market in the 1930s: Implications for Policy Today* (Washington: U.S. Dept. of Labor, 1981); E. Wight Bakke, *A Positive Labor Market Policy* (Columbus: Merrill Books, 1963); Barbara R. Bergmann, *Labor Market Data Needs Relating to Antidiscrimination Activity* (Washington: U.S. National Commission on Employment and Unemployment Statistics, Background Paper no. 26, 1979); Bennett Harrison and Andrew Sum, *Labor Market Data Needs From the Perspective of 'Dual' or 'Segmented' Labor Market Research* (Washington: U.S. National Commission on Employment and Unemployment Statistics, Background Paper no. 29, 1979); Edward Kalachek, "Longitudinal Labor Market Surveys: Asking 'How Come,' Not 'How Many,'" *MLR*, Sept. 1978; ______, *Longitudinal Surveys and Labor Market Analysis* (Washington: U.S. National Commission on Employment and Unemployment Statistics, Background Paper no. 6, 1978); Clark Kerr, "Labor Markets: Their Character and Consequences," *Proceedings of the 2d A/M, IRRA*, ed. by Milton Derber (Champaign: 1950); Don D. Lescohier, *The Labor Market* (New York: Macmillan, 1919); Herbert R. Northrup, "Labor Market Trends and Policies in the 1980s," *Employee Relations LJ*, Summer 1981; Lloyd G. Reynolds, *Structure of Labor Markets* (New York: Harper, 1951); George P. Shultz and Charles A. Myers, *The Dynamics of a Labor Market* (New York: PH, 1951); U.S. Dept. of Labor, BLS, *Employment Projections for the 1980's* (Washington: Bull. 2030, 1979); Harold Wool, *The Adequacy of Occupational Data on Employed and Unemployed Workers for Analyzing Labor Market Behavior* (Washington: U.S. National Commission on Employment and Unemployment Statistics, Background Paper no. 18, 1978).

labor market area The "market" is generally considered to be an area or region where the supply and demand for a particular commodity or for a given grade of commodity prevail.

A labor market area is similarly one in which the supply and demand for labor are brought together. It is also frequently assumed that in such a labor market area the supply and demand are presumably in equilibrium, in other words, a certain price for a particular grade of labor would clear the market or provide for its maximum return depending on the operation of perfect competition in a free labor market.

Sometimes the term refers to the prevailing wage structure which is common to a particular geographic area. Frequently, the labor market situation refers to the then prevailing employment opportunities, for example, whether it is a "tight labor market" or one which is in oversupply considering the total demand for a certain type of labor. Occasionally the supply may be large with regard to certain unskilled occupations and tight with regard to certain skilled occupations.

The concept of perfect competition within a labor market area sets certain conditions which may never actually be met, but it is contended that it provides a model to be used for understanding and attempting to recognize certain variants and conditions which may actually prevail. Depending upon the type of labor and its mobility, the labor market area may be a relatively small location or it may be a substantially large geographic area.

Source references: Leonard A. Lecht, *Occupational Projections for National, State, and Local Areas* (Washington: U.S. National Commission on Employment and Unemployment Statistics, Background Paper no. 20, 1978); Juan de Torres, *Metropolitan America: The Development of Its Major Markets* (New York: The Conference Board, Report no. 692, 1976); U.S. Dept. of Labor, BES, *Directory of Important Labor Areas* (6th ed., Washington: 1968); ———, *Handbook on Defining Labor Market Areas* (Washington: 1960).

See also RELEVANT LABOR MARKET AREA.

labor member of parliament The representative of a labor group or party in the legislative body of a country with a parliamentary form of government. The term is used in Great Britain, New Zealand, Australia, and in other members of the Commonwealth where the labor movement has an organized political party.

labor mobility Labor mobility is occasionally referred to as "labor flux" or "labor turnover." It is concerned with the general movement of labor into and out of industrial establishments or in particular geographic areas or even in industries. The mobility of labor may be related to the organization of the job market, the particular attachment of an individual to an industrial or geographic community, the social ties and values which may prevent his movement, as well as major financial considerations and economics involved in retraining or utilizing skills in other communities.

Source references: Ann Bartel, *Wages, Nonwage Job Characteristics and Labor Mobility* (Cambridge: NBER, WP 552, 1980); Robert E. Cole, *Work, Mobility, and Participation; A Comparative Study of American and Japanese Industry* (Berkeley: UC Press, 1979); Charles K. Fairchild, "Rural Disadvantaged Mobility," *LLJ*, Aug. 1969; Louis A. Ferman and Michael Aiken, "Mobility and Situational Factors in the Adjustment of Older Workers to Job Displacement," *Human Organization*, Winter 1967; Sheldon E. Haber, "The Mobility of Professional Workers and Fair Hiring," *ILRR*, Jan. 1981; Sanford M. Jacoby, "Industrial Labor Mobility in Historical Perspective," *IR*, Spring 1983; Seymour Martin Lipset, "Social Mobility and Equal Opportunity," *The Public Interest*, Fall 1972; Howard D. Marshall, "The Impact of Unions on Labor Mobility" (Unpublished Ph.D. dissertation, Columbia Univ., 1954); Olivia S. Mitchell, "Fringe Benefits and Labor Mobility," *Journal of Human Resources*, Spring 1982; J. Wilson Mixon, Jr., "The Minimum Wage and Voluntary Labor Mobility," *ILRR*, Oct. 1978; Lloyd Ulman, "Labor Mobility and the Industrial Wage Structure in the Postwar United States," *Quarterly Journal of Economics*, Feb. 1965; Harold L. Wilensky, "Measures and Effects of Social Mobility," *Social Structure and Mobility in Economic Development*, ed. by Neil J. Smelser and Seymour Martin Lipset (Chicago: Aldine Publishing, 1966).

See also GEOGRAPHICAL MOBILITY, INDUSTRIAL MOBILITY, INTERNAL MOBILITY, LABOR IMMOBILITY, OCCUPATIONAL MOBILITY.

labor monopoly The term is applied to the control which labor unions have over the supply of labor and the labor market in order to obtain wages and working conditions favorable to a particular group of employees. Sometimes the claim of monopoly control applies to individual craft groups; occasionally, it may apply to an entire industry as, for example, the claim that a stoppage of work by the United Steelworkers constituted monopolistic control over all labor in the steel industry.

Occasionally the term is used to describe a union which had a closed shop as well as a closed union which denied entry into a particular trade and thus controlled the supply of potential labor to the labor market. The term in recent discussions has been applied to the total power which labor unions have in our industrial society.

The May 1962 report on *Free Collective Bargaining* issued by the President's Advisory Committee on Labor-Management Policy contains statements by two industry members with regard to the claim of monopoly power and the comments by the labor members of the committee refuting that contention.

Source references: AFL-CIO, *Camouflage: The Myth of Labor Monopoly* (Washington: Pub. no. 33, 1960); Edward Berman, *Labor and the Sherman Act* (New York: Harper, 1930); Patrick M. Boarman, *Union Monopolies and Antitrust Restraints* (Washington: Labor Policy Association, 1963); Edward H. Chamberlain, *The Economic Analysis of Labor Union Power* (Washington: American Enterprise Association, 1958); John A. Copps, "On the Meaning of Monopoly Power in Labor Relations," *LLJ*, May 1956; Archibald Cox, "Labor and the Antitrust Laws—A Preliminary Analysis," *Univ. of Pennsylvania LR*, Nov. 1955; Arthur J. Goldberg, "Labor and Antitrust," *IUD Digest*, Winter 1958; Arthur M. Goldberg, "Antitrust: The Union as Plaintiff," *Labor Law Developments 1980*, Proceedings of the 26th Annual Institute on Labor Law, SLF (New York: Bender, 1980); "Interface of National Labor and Antitrust Policies: When Antitrust Liability Attaches," *LLJ*, Feb. 1982; Andrew R. Laidlaw, "Labor Antitrust Problems: Trap for the Unwary," *Employee Relations LJ*, Spring 1978; John Landon and William Peirce, "Discrimination, Monopsony, and Union Power in the Building Trades: A Cross Sectional Analysis," *Proceedings of the 24th A/M, IRRA*, ed. by Gerald Somers (Madison: 1972); Richard A. Lester, "Some Reflections on the Labor Monopoly Issue," *Journal of Political Economy*, Dec. 1947; Richard A. Mann, Brian Powers, and Barry S. Roberts, "The Accommodation Between Antitrust and Labor Law: The Antitrust Labor Exemption," *LLJ*, May 1979; Donald R. Richberg, *Labor Union Monopoly* (Chicago: Regnery, 1957); Harold S. Roberts (ed.), *Labor and Anti-Trust Legislation* (Honolulu: Univ. of Hawaii, IRC, 1961); Simon Rottenberg, "Labor Monopoly Policy Reconsidered," *MLR*, Feb. 1963; Jerre S. Williams, "Labor and the Antitrust Laws," *Labor Law Developments*, Proceedings of the 12th Annual Institute on Labor Law, SLF (Washington: BNA, 1966); Leo Wolman, *Industry-Wide Bargaining* (Irvington-on-Hudson: Foundation for Economic Education, 1948).

See also CLAYTON ACT OF 1914, SHERMAN ACT OF 1890, UNION SECURITY CLAUSES.

labor motivation Those factors or incentives which have the capacity to bring out the greatest production effort or the greatest service from those engaged in production or service. The incentive or motivation may be the wage, it may be the nature and character of the job, it may be the particular product produced or there may be a host of other factors which motivate the individual under particular and specific circumstances.

Those studying motivation and industrial psychology have found a variety of factors which help explain the motivations necessary to achieve certain levels of production or those which tend to retard or hinder production. Constant research is necessary in this field since the types of motivations or incentives vary, not only among industrial groups, but also among various societal arrangements.

See also INCENTIVE RATE, INCENTIVE WAGE, MOTIVATION.

labor movement This is a generally inclusive term designed to bring within its scope the variety of organized group action, essentially economic in its nature but which may also include political activity. It encompasses the sum total of unions and their activities in the field of collective bargaining or in areas of social welfare. Although generally applied to organized workers and wage earners and concerned with their growth, structure, and activities, it is sometimes also conceived to encompass the total mass movement of a working population and their families and not merely those organized into labor unions.

John A. Fitch in his book, *The Causes of Industrial Unrest,* carries this broad concept much further and conceives the labor movement to be "an instinctive movement, and it is a movement for something more than the possession of a larger portion of the world's goods. Just as the politically disfranchised have pressed forward and secured for themselves a share in the control of government, so the industrially disfranchised are moving toward the securing of a share in the control of industry. The movement, therefore, is in its fundamental aspects a demand for a changed status for the people who toil with their hands."

Some conceive the term "labor movement" to cover not only the structure, growth, and activities, but also the attitudes of unity and cooperation among workers which go beyond the concern with their own specific vocations to encompass a much broader scope in the total program of political, social, and economic action in a country or a community.

Source references: AFL-CIO, *One Hundred Years of American Labor, 1881–1981* (Washington: Pub. no. 157, 1982); Jack Barbash, "The American Labor Movement," *Oberlin Alumni Magazine,* Dec. 1962; Solomon Barkin, *The Decline of the Labor Movement and What Can be Done About It* (Santa Barbara: Center for the Study of Democratic Institutions, 1961); ______ (ed.), *Worker Militancy and its Consequences, 1965–75; New Directions in Western Industrial Relations* (New York: Praeger, Special Studies in International Economics and Development, 1975); David Brody (comp.), *The American Labor Movement* (New York: Harper & Row, 1971); Marjorie R. Clark and S. Fanny Simon, *The Labor Movement in America* (New York: Norton, 1938); John R. Commons and Associates, *History of Labour in the United States* (4 vols., New York: Macmillan, 1918, 1935, 1946); Melvyn Dubofsky (ed.), *American Labor Since the New Deal* (Chicago: Quadrangle Books, 1971); John A. Fitch, *The Causes of Industrial Unrest* (New York: Harper, 1924); Herbert Harris, *American Labor* (New Haven: Yale UP, 1938); Leon Litwack, *The American Labor Movement* (Englewood Cliffs, PH, 1962); Alice Lynd and Staughton Lynd, *Rank and File; Personal Histories by Working-Class Organizers* (Boston: Beacon Press, 1973); David Montgomery, "American Labor, 1865–1902: The Early Industrial Era," *MLR,* July 1976; Maurice F. Neufeld, "The Persistance of Ideas in the American Labor Movement: The Heritage of the 1830s," *ILRR,* Jan. 1982; Selig Perlman, *A Theory of the Labor Movement* (New York: Augustus Kelley, 1949); A. H. Raskin, "From Sitdowns to 'Solidarity,' Passages in the Life of American Labor," *Across the Board,* Dec. 1981; David J. Saposs, "The Labor Movement: A Look Backward and Forward," *The Labor Movement: A Reexamination,* A Conference in Honor of David J. Saposs (Madison: Univ. of Wisconsin, IRRI & State Historical Society of Wisconsin, 1967); Alvin Schwartz, *The Unions: What They Are: How They Came to Be, How They Affect Each of Us* (New York: Viking Press, 1972); "A Short History of American Labor," *American Federationist,* March 1981; James L. Stern and Barbara D. Dennis (ed.), *Trade Unionism in the United States: A Symposium in Honor of Jack Barbash, April 24–26, 1981* (Madison: Univ. of Wisconsin, IRRI, 1981); Philip Taft, "A Labor Historian Views Changes in the Trade Union Movement," *MLR,* Sept. 1969; ______, "Theories of the Labor Movement," *Interpreting the Labor Movement,* ed. by George W. Brooks et al. (Madison: IRRA Pub. no. 9, 1952); U.S. Dept. of Labor, *Important Events in American Labor History, 1778–1978* (Washington: 1979); U.S. Dept. of Labor, BLS, *Brief History of the American Labor Movement* (Washington: Bull. 1000, 1976).

labor notes *See* LABOR COUPON.

labor offices Refers to the U.S. Employment Standards Administration publication,

Labor Offices in the United States and Canada, which lists federal, state, and provincial offices and agencies "responsible for the performance of labor and labor-related functions."

Labor offices are defined as "primary labor agencies such as departments or bureaus of labor, as well as other separate commissions, boards, or agencies with functional responsibility for such programs as employment services, including employment offices and unemployment compensation; regulation of private employment agencies; equal employment opportunity and civil rights; labor-management relations; mediation and arbitration; occupational safety and health; mine safety; workers' compensation; and vocational rehabilitation."

Source reference: U.S. Dept. of Labor, Employment Standards Administration, *Labor Offices in the United States and Canada* (Washington: Bull. 177, 1979).

labor organization A group of workers in a voluntary association combined for the common purpose of protecting or advancing the wages, hours, and working conditions of their members. Although these organizations are concerned with matters of social and political concern, this is not their primary aim, but a function which is made necessary by the common interest in protecting and advancing the welfare of their members. Political activity frequently is directed toward that end rather than toward the political arena as such.

The National Labor Relations Act defines the term "labor organization" as "any organization of any kind, or any agency or employee representation committee or plan, in which employees participate and which exists for the purpose, in whole or in part, of dealing with employers concerning grievances, labor disputes, wages, rates of pay, hours of employment or conditions of work." Definitions under a statute, however, apply only to the purpose of that statute and for purposes of coverage within the meaning of that statute.

Executive Order 11491 defined the term as:

'Labor organization' means a lawful organization of any kind in which employees participate and which exists for the purpose, in whole or in part, of dealing with agencies concerning grievances, personnel policies and practices, or other matters, affecting the working conditions of their employees; but does not include any organization which—

(1) consists of management officials or supervisors, except as provided in section 24 of this Order;
(2) asserts the right to strike against the Government of the United States or any agency thereof, or to assist or participate in such a strike, or imposes a duty or obligation to conduct, assist or participate in such a strike;
(3) advocates the overthrow of the constitutional form of government in the United States; or
(4) discriminates with regard to the terms or conditions of membership because of race, color, creed, sex, age, or national origin; . . .

Labor organization, under the Civil Service Reform Act of 1978, is defined as:

. . . an organization composed in whole or in part of employees, in which employees participate and pay dues, and which has as a purpose the dealing with an agency concerning grievances and conditions of employment, but does not include—

(A) an organization which, by its constitution, bylaws, tacit agreement among its members, or otherwise, denies membership because of race, color, creed, national origin, sex, age, preferential or nonpreferential civil service status, political affiliation, marital status, or handicapping condition;
(B) an organization which advocates the overthrow of the constitutional form of government of the United States;
(C) an organization sponsored by an agency; or
(D) an organization which participates in the conduct of a strike against the Government or any agency thereof or imposes a duty or obligation to conduct, assist, or participate in such a strike. . . .

Source references: John T. Dunlop, "The Development of Labor Organization: A Theoretical Framework," *Insights into Labor,* ed. by Richard A. Lester and Joseph Shister (New York: Macmillan, 1948); David A. McCabe and Richard A. Lester, *Labor and Social Organization* (Boston: Little, Brown, 1938).

See also LABOR UNION.

labor organizer A person generally on the payroll of a union, usually the international union, who is assigned to a particular plant or region to attempt to bring the employees of a particular company or region into a labor union. Organization takes place in many places and by many people. Among the most successful organizers are individuals in the plant who are union members who inform others about the importance of the union.

The labor organizer is a specialist in this area who is able to bring together the particular talents and abilities available in a plant or community to present the aims, purposes, and ideals of the organization, and to bring individuals into the union. Organization may be for a new local, or it may be for the preparation of an election which involves competing unions. The labor organizer's job is to promote organizational efforts in his assigned area and generally to have the members and local unions take an active part in his international union.

See also BUSINESS AGENT, ORGANIZERS.

labor peace *See* INDUSTRIAL PEACE.

labor piracy Sometimes referred to as labor pirating. This is a procedure followed by some employers who steal from other employers, generally in the same field of work, highly skilled individuals and technical staff. The techniques and procedures used for pirating will vary with the kind of individual involved, his particular skills, and how vital it is that the person be obtained by a competitor. The usual incentives are higher wages or salaries, better working conditions, or better hours and surroundings. Sometimes particular fringe benefits may be important. These may include welfare or medical plans and various types of pensions. For pirating of executive skills, the incentives are more frequently in the area of participation in compnay profits or in some stock or other bonus plan.

During manpower shortages, generally in periods of war, pirating will take place in many occupations and trades and not necessarily in those of the highly technical and skilled employees.

See also SNOWBALLING.

labor policy This is a general term which sets out the objectives, the goals, the aims, and principles of a particular organization, or principles designed to act as a guide to the particular organization. It may deal with matters of labor-management policy, or it may deal with long-range goals in the area of wage payments, or it may be concerned with the wide range or problems in a particular field which affect labor relations.

Although the term is generally applied to the labor policy of a union or labor organization, it may be equally applicable to the labor policy of a particular company or corporation, or to the labor policy of the nation as a whole.

When it concerns the labor policy of a company, it sets out the principles and policies which a company establishes for itself or for the guidance of management in its relations with its employees. These may apply to manpower management or to other internal affairs of the company.

Source references: Jack Barbash, *Rationalization in the American Union* (Madison: Univ. of Wisconsin, IRRI, Reprint no. 119, 1970); Douglass V. Brown and Charles A. Myers, "Public Policy and Collective Bargaining, Historical Evolution," *Public Policy and Collective Bargaining,* ed. by Joseph Shister, Benjamin Aaron, and Clyde W. Summers (New York: Harper, IRRA Pub. no. 27, 1962); CED, Labor Study Group, *The Public Interest in National Labor Policy* (New York: 1961); Gary M. Fink, "The Rejection of Voluntarism," *ILRR,* Jan. 1973; Richard Lester, "Labor Policy in a Changing World," *IR,* Oct. 1962; Harold W. Metz, *Labor Policy of the Federal Government* (Washington: Brookings Institution, 1945); Georges Minet, "Trade Unions, Employers' Associations and Protection of the Environment," *ILR,* Nov. 1975; R. Tchobanian, "Trade Unions and the Humanisation of Work," *ILR,* March 1975; Ludwig Teller, *A Labor Policy for America* (New York: Baker, Voorhis, 1945); U.S. National Commission for Manpower Policy, *Labor's Views on Employment Policy* (Washington: Special Report no. 25, 1978); ———, *Proceedings of a Conference on Labor's Views on Manpower Policy* (Washington: Special Report no. 6, 1976).

labor pool plan The term describes the procedure adopted by the NLRB for conducting elections in the building trades, particularly those elections involving the union shop authorization.

Since the union shop authorization elections have been eliminated by amendments to the Taft-Hartley Act, no such elections need be held for an employer and union desirous of negotiating a union shop agreement.

labor press *See* LABOR JOURNALISM.

labor priority The term generally applies to the procedures adopted during a war period when controls are necessary in the allocation of manpower to various programs and industries. In the establishment of essential operations the labor priority system attempts to determine which of the particular grades or levels of skills or occupations are more important to the handling of certain operations.

labor problem A term widely used toward the turn of the century which applied to all of the major labor issues of the times.

In actuality the handling of the labor problem involves the specific determination and handling of numerous problems. It is a composite of many problems involving wages, hours, working conditions, employment, political action, and others which constitute in their entirety the labor problem. The labor problem frequently becomes the problem of the entire nation as, for example, a concern with the problem of unemployment. This in turn involves the area of technological change and the necessity for government involvement in legislation dealing with manpower training and various other programs. It also relates to the tax program designed to provide additional income to enable workers to purchase additional goods and services to stimulate the economy.

Source references: Carroll R. Daugherty and John P. Parrish, *Labor Problems of American Society* (New York: Houghton Mifflin, 1952); Albion G. Taylor, *Labor Problems and Labor Law* (New York: PH, 1938).

labor productivity *See* OUTPUT PER HOUR (LABOR PRODUCTIVITY), PRODUCTIVITY.

labor racketeer The term applies to a dishonest or unethical labor leader who engages in bribery, the use of threats or force, or who attempts through the use of violence to obtain funds from employers as the price of maintaining peace.

George Soule in his book, *A Planned Society*, defined the term "labor racketeer" rather broadly and perhaps not inaccurately. He wrote, "The racketeer has, in this respect, merely taken a leaf from the practices of government. He collects tribute (taxes) by virtue of his control of gunmen and thugs (policemen). His powers of violence can be turned to the task of annoying or even murdering the citizen if he does not come across. . . . Racketeers thrive on the need for profit-seeking businessmen to hold all competitors in an association for price maintenance, on need of employers to avoid strikes, and the need of unions to hold employers in line. They are a volunteer, unofficial police force in the business of maintaining whatever kind of order is most required by anyone who can pay."

The parallel of course is not a very good one. It does, however, point up some of the essential features which encourage or support labor racketeers.

Source references: John Hutchison, "The Anatomy of Corruption in Trade Unions," *IR*, Feb. 1969; Simon Rottenberg, "A Theory of Corruption in Trade Unions," *Symposia Studies Series of June 1960* (Washington: National Institute of Social and Behavioral Science, 1960); David J. Saposs, "Labor Racketeering: Evolution and Solutions," *Social Research*, Autumn 1958; Harold Seidman, *Labor Czars: A History of Labor Racketeering* (New York: Liveright Publishing, 1938); George Soule, *A Planned Society* (New York: Macmillan, 1932); Edward D. Sullivan, *This Labor Union Racket* (New York: Hillman, Curl, 1936); Paul A. Weinstein, "Racketeering and Labor: An Economic Analysis," *ILRR*, April 1966.

See also RACKETEERING.

labor racketeering *See* MCCLELLAN COMMITTEE, RACKETEERING.

labor reformer This term is applied to any person who attempts to promote and improve the conditions of workers through legislation, political action, or other activity. The labor reformer may seek to obtain objectives through peaceful means or through more revolutionary practices. Generally the term "labor reformer" does not apply to those involved in revolutionary tactics or anarchistic tactics or those involved in the encouragement of sabotage or violence or other forms of forceful intimidation.

Labor Reform Party *See* NATIONAL LABOR AND REFORM PARTY.

labor registration The term refers to the registration of labor unions in order to qualify for certain benefits.

Under the New Zealand and Australian industrial arbitration laws, unions seeking access to the arbitration tribunals as well as special union security provisions are required to register.

Efforts by some states to require the registration of labor unions, or their incorporation, or to obtain a license for organizers and business agents in order to engage in union activity, have been set aside by decisions of the Supreme Court. For example, in the state of Florida, a statute which required a union to register with the secretary of the state and to provide certain information was held invalid in the case of *Hill v. State of Florida.*

Not directly parallel, and to be distinguished from labor registration, are the laws to provide a greater degree of disclosure of certain basic information from labor unions. The major statute requiring such information is the Labor-Management Reporting and Disclosure Act of 1959.

Source references: Commonwealth of Australia Conciliation and Arbitration Act, 1904–1961; *Hill Watson, Ex Rel. State of Florida,* 325 US 538, 16 LRRM 734 (1945).

See also LABOR-MANAGEMENT REPORTING AND DISCLOSURE ACT OF 1959, WELFARE AND PENSION PLANS DISCLOSURE ACT OF 1958 (TELLER ACT).

labor relations boards The term applied to the group of boards set up under the National Industrial Recovery Act (NIRA), under Section 7(a) dealing with the right of employees to organize into labor unions. Among the boards in this group were those established under various industry codes—the Auto Board, the Steel Board, as well as the main board, the National Labor Board.

A Maritime Labor Board was established at one time, and this would also be considered a labor relations board. Among the current labor relations boards, one might include the NLRB, which administers the National Labor Relations Act, as amended by Taft-Hartley and Landrum-Griffin; the National Mediation Board and the National Railroad Adjustment Board under the Railway Labor Act.

A labor relations board may concern itself with the handling of unfair union and employer practices, may supervise elections, and may handle a whole series of policy matters which are incorporated into the statutes.

Labor relations boards are also established on the state level, both in the private and public sectors. Such boards concern themselves with problems similar to those handled by the NLRB. Some also concern themselves with mediation functions and arbitration.

Source references: Robert D. Helsby, *Development of Professional Personnel for Public Employment Labor Relations Boards and Commissions in State and Local Governments of the United States* (n.p., Carnegie Foundation and Association of American Colleges, 1977); Robert G. Howlett, "State Labor Relations Board and Arbitrators," *LLJ*, Jan. 1966; Jay Kramer, "Law and Policy in State Labor Relations Acts: The New York Board as Innovator," *Annals*, Jan. 1961; Lewis L. Lorwin and Arthur Wubnig, *Labor Relations Boards* (Washington: Brookings Institution, 1935); Joyce M. Najita and Helene S. Tanimoto, *Guide to Statutory Provisions in Public Sector Collective Bargaining—Characteristics, Functions, and Powers of Administering Agencies* (Honolulu: Univ. of Hawaii, IRC, 1981); Hyman Parker, "The Role of the Michigan Labor Mediation Board in Public Employee Labor Disputes," *LLJ*, Sept. 1959; Public Employment Relations Services, *Portrait of a Process—Collective Negotiations in Public Employment*, ed. by Muriel K. Gibbons et al. (Fort Washington, Pa.: Labor Relations Press, 1979); Arthur Stark, "An Administrative Appraisal of the New York State Board of Mediation," *ILRR*, April 1952.

See also MARITIME LABOR BOARD; NATIONAL INDUSTRIAL RECOVERY ACT, SECTION 7(A); NATIONAL LABOR RELATIONS BOARD; NATIONAL MEDIATION BOARD; NATIONAL RAILROAD ADJUSTMENT BOARD.

Labor Relations Expediter The title of a volume which is part of the Labor Relations Reporter service published by the Bureau of National Affairs, Inc., Washington, D.C.

Its main substance consists of articles organized on a subject basis dealing with issues in the field of industrial relations. Among these are arbitration, collective bargaining, hours of work, strikes and picketing, and unemployment. The articles contain cross references to other parts of the Labor Relations Reporter service, including the Labor Relations Reference Manual, Labor Arbitration Reports, Wage and Hour Cases, and Fair Employment Practice Cases.

The *Expediter* also contains major texts of laws, regulations, forms and a directory of labor agencies.

See also BUREAU OF NATIONAL AFFAIRS, INC.; THE

Labor Relations Reference Manual One of the parts of the Labor Relations Reporter service published by The Bureau of National Affairs, Inc., Washington, D.C. The Labor Relations Reference Manual is published three times a year, putting in permanent form decisions of courts, NLRB, state agencies, and other material of permanent reference value. The series of volumes has been published continuously since 1937.

labor research The term generally is applied to organized and carefully prepared studies in the field of labor economics or labor relations. Work in this field, although concerned primarily with the subject matter of labor-management relations, has been done by governmental agencies, by independent agencies both privately owned and for profit, by union and management agencies, and by private individuals.

Among the earliest of these agencies was the Bureau of Labor, established in 1884 in the Department of Interior. Its major functions were developed and are presently carried out by BLS.

One of the developments in labor unions has been the establishment of research units and research departments in the international unions. Most of the major international unions have research departments under a director of research responsible for coordinating research activities and providing economic and collective bargaining data to the national union as well as to the locals. These studies may include the analysis of agreements of the particular union as compared with other negotiated agreements; they may be concerned with the problems of the profits of the company, technological change, or other matters of importance to the union in its negotiations and collective bargaining, as well as with state and federal political activities.

Source references: Robert L. Aronson, "Research and Writing in Industrial Relations—Are They Intellectually Respectable?" *Essays on Industrial Relations Research—Problems and Prospects* (Ann Arbor: Univ. of Michigan Press, 1961); Milton Derber, "Divergent Tendencies in Industrial Relations Research," *ILRR*, July 1964; Rudy A. Oswald, "Labor's Agenda for 1980's Research," *Proceedings of the 33d A/M, IRRA*, ed. by Barbara Dennis (Madison: 1981); William F. Whyte, "Needs and Opportunities for Industrial Relations Research," *Essays on Industrial Relations Research—Problems and Prospects* (Ann Arbor: Univ. of Michigan Press, 1961); ———, "Toward an Integrated Approach for Industrial Relations Research," *MLR*, Feb. 1964.

See also RESEARCH, INDUSTRIAL RELATIONS.

labor reserve The term generally describes a reservoir of workers whose services are required more or less irregularly. Although the services of these workers are not continuously required, they do find employment from time to time. Most of this group tends to be in the unskilled and semiskilled categories, although occasionally some may be in the skilled group. H. Patterson held that the labor reserve "extends across the twilight zone between the unemployed and the unemployable."

Some have defined the labor reserve as consisting of all persons who are potential but not present members of the work force. Among these would be those with physical handicaps, those regarded as too old, housewives, and students. They may be available to perform work but not on full-time regular jobs.

Source reference: H. Patterson, *Social Aspects of Industry* (3d ed., New York: McGraw-Hill, 1943).

labor-saving machinery Any mechanical device or machine the prime purpose of which is to reduce or eliminate the need for hand labor and to curtail the time spent by individuals in the production of a commodity.

The machinery is generally semiautomatic in nature, or more recently in the changing technological field, completely automatic and performs many of the processes which required hand labor and skills of individuals.

One of the major problems in our changing technology is the task of adjusting to these technological changes and providing other employment and retraining for individuals displaced by labor-saving machines.

There is general agreement about the necessity for utilizing these machines to their best advantage in order to increase the productivity of a country, as well as of the world, but at the same time it is equally important to see that the human adjustments are also taken into account, either by the employer utilizing these labor-saving machines or by government, when it is impossible for employers or unions to assist, either on a company or industry basis.

labor secretaries The secretaries of labor of the U.S. Department of Labor are listed below in order of their appointment and the period for which they served.

(1) William B. Wilson, March 4, 1913 to March 4, 1921;
(2) James J. Davis, March 5, 1921 to November 30, 1930;
(3) William N. Doak, December 9, 1930 to March 4, 1933;
(4) Frances Perkins, March 4, 1933 to June 30, 1945;
(5) Louis B. Schwellenbach, July 1, 1945 to June 10, 1948;
(6) Maurice J. Tobin, August 13, 1948 to January 20, 1953;
(7) Martin P. Durkin, January 21, 1953 to September 10, 1953;
(8) James P. Mitchell, October 9, 1953 to January 20, 1961;
(9) Arthur J. Goldberg, January 21, 1961 to September 20, 1962 (appointed Justice of the Supreme Court);
(10) W. Willard Wirtz, September 25, 1962 to January 20, 1969;
(11) George P. Shultz, January 21, 1969 to June 30, 1970;
(12) James P. Hodgson, July 2, 1970 to February 1, 1973;
(13) Peter J. Brennan, February 2, 1973 to March 15, 1975;
(14) John T. Dunlop, March 18, 1975 to January 31, 1976;
(15) W. J. Usery, Jr., February 10, 1976 to January 20, 1977;
(16) Ray Marshall, January 27, 1977 to February 2, 1981;
(17) Raymond J. Donovan, February 3, 1981 to March 15, 1985;
(18) William E. Brock, III, April 26, 1985—

labor shortage This term is applied to a situation where there is a shortage or scarcity of workers to perform certain types of work. The labor scarcity may be in an industry, in a region, or it may be and this is unlikely, in an entire country during periods of war.

The factors which create labor shortages are those normally at work in the total labor market picture. Shortages may be due to lack of labor mobility, they may be due to lack of adequate training of employees in particular jobs, or they may be due to lack of incentive or unsatifactory conditions of employment in a particular industry or region.

See also LABOR SURPLUS AREA.

labor skate The term generally has been used to describe an individual as an official of a union or labor organization. It is a colloquialism which only occasionally has an overtone of friendliness.

Labor's League for Political Education (LLPE) Formed by the AFL in 1948 in order to avoid Taft-Hartley Act restrictions on union expenditures for political purposes, the LLPE was supported by voluntary contributions. It was the AFL's equivalent of the CIO's Political Action Committee, the Independent International Association of Machinsts' Non-Partisan Political League, and the railroad unions' Railway Labor's Political League.

Labor's Non-Partisan League This was an organization essentially under CIO leadership but widely supported by AFL organizations, established in Washington, D.C., on August 10, 1936, with George L. Berry as President, Sidney Hillman, treasurer, and John L. Lewis, chairman of the Executive Board.

The prime function, apparently, of the Labor's Non-Partisan League was to re-elect Franklin D. Roosevelt as President. Its program, although not directed toward establishing a third party, still was contrary to the normal position of the AFL, which was bipartisan in its general policy.

When in April 1938 William Green, president of the AFL, urged that AFL unions leave the group, he was reported as stating that the League was "nothing more than a CIO agency, a ventriloquist dummy for the CIO leaders."

The American Labor Party in New York, one of the offshoots of the Labor's Non-Partisan League, was held responsible for the reelection of Mayor LaGuardia in New York City.

See also AFL-CIO COPE.

labor solidarity Applied to the efforts on the part of groups combined into labor organizations to work together toward major common objectives. The solidarity may be among labor unions in similar groups or among labor unions in competing industries.

It is a term much used in socialist literature, pointing to the need to maintain a united front and the need to maintain a combined working force to show unity or solidarity of position of a particular group on major social and economic issues. Sometimes it was designed to express the concern and need for a single bond, the so-called universal brotherhood of workers.

Occasionally the term has been used to describe the solidarity, or working together of labor unions in a particular country. For example, the quest for labor solidarity was made when the AFL and CIO were separate organizations. A sense of labor solidarity was achieved when the two organizations merged as the AFL-CIO in 1955.

labor spy An individual hired by the employer or by a person for an employer, such as a detective agency, who becomes a member of a union to spy on union activities and frequently to create confusion and suspicion for the purpose of defeating unionization. Although the terms "spy" and "stool pigeon" have pretty much the same meaning, one distinction has been drawn in part, namely, that the stool pigeon is a person who normally works his way into the union and obtains information from the inside, whereas the spy may perform his work in peripheral areas to obtain his results.

Source references: Clinch Calkins, *Spy Overhead* (New York: Harcourt, Brace, 1937); GT–99 (pseud.), *Labor Spy* (Indianapolis: Bobbs-Merrill, 1937); Sidney Howard, *The Labor Spy* (New York: Republic Publishing, 1924); Leo Huberman, *The Labor Spy Racket* (New York: Modern Age Books, 1937); New York State Legislature, Joint Committee on Industrial and Labor Conditions, *The American Story of Industrial and Labor Relations* (New York: Williams Press, 1944).

See also ANTI-UNION PRACTICES, COMPANY SPY, ESPIONAGE, LAFOLLETTE COMMITTEE, MISSIONARY, STOOL PIGEON.

labor stage The term is generally applied to efforts by American unions to present plays dealing with labor activities and trade union programs. The International Ladies' Garment Workers' Union presented a play called "Pins and Needles" which received wide public attention in the 1940s. Another play which was on the legitimate stage, but dealt with some of the labor stage problems, was a play called "Waiting for Lefty."

labor standard Basic criteria or conditions of wages, hours or employment conditions, safety, etc., designed to protect, as much as possible, minimum conditions for a decent standard for workers and their families.

One parallel in the international field is the effort by the International Labor Organization to establish labor standards through the media of ILO Conventions which set forth minimum working conditions for member countries of the ILO. By their nature, standards are not fixed; they continue to be modified as changing technology, physical surroundings, and other conditions make necessary.

See also INTERNATIONAL LABOR ORGANIZATION (ILO).

Labor Standards, Bureau of *See* BUREAU OF LABOR STANDARDS.

Labor Statistics, Bureau of *See* BUREAU OF LABOR STATISTICS.

labor studies *See* LABOR EDUCATION.

labor supply Criticism has been leveled against the concept of the classical economist who held that the supply of labor was synonymous with the total population. This has been criticized by, among others, Paul Douglas, former professor and senator from the state of Illinois, in a study on the theory of wages. Professor Douglas notes in his study that "Because two countries have equal populations, it does not follow that they have equal supplies of labor. . . . The supply of labor may differ appreciably between two countries which have equal population and identical age distribution. . . ." This, he says, was pointed out by Long in 1866 when he sought to refute the wage-fund theory. Long stated that "a supply of labor is a supply of potential work, and every practical man knows that the quantity of work to be got from the laborers is no more determined by their number than the quantity of apples to be got from an orchard."

Professor D. D. Lescohier in his study on the labor market during the turn of the century devoted some attention to labor supply. He noted that there were five essential facts with regard to the labor supply in the United States which had to be taken into account in coping with the American labor problem. These, of course, have changed quite considerably but they are of historic interest. The five he noted are:

(1) The fluctuating but unceasing flow of immigrant laborers,
(2) An ever-present labor reserve,
(3) The centralized character of that reserve,
(4) Excessive labor turnover, and
(5) A defective system of labor distribution.

He said "these five are closely related. Each is both a cause and a result of the other. Taken together, they furnish a picture of the labor supply side of our labor market."

The labor supply then is determined not only by the size of the labor force and age distribution, but also by skill and geographic location, as well as by individual willingness and ability to be productive.

Source references: Orley Ashenfelter and James Heckman, *Estimating Labor Supply Functions* (Princeton: Princeton Univ., IR Section, WP 34, 1972); George J. Borjas and James J. Heckman, "Labor Supply Estimates for Public Policy Evaluation," *Proceedings of the 31st A/M, IRRA*, ed. by Barbara Dennis (Madison: 1979); Paul H. Douglas, *The Theory of Wages* (New York: Macmillan, 1934); John C. Ham, *Rationing and the Supply of Labor: An Econometric Approach* (rev. ed., Princeton: Princeton Univ., IR Section, WP 103A, 1979); Edward Kalachek, Wesley Mellow, and Fredric Raines, "The Male Labor Supply Function Reconsidered," *ILRR*, April 1978; Edward D. Kalachek, Fredric Q. Raines, and Donald Larson, "The Determination of Labor Supply: A Dynamic Model," *ILRR*, April 1979; Mark R. Killingsworth, *Wage Data and Estimation of the Labor Supply Function* (Princeton: Princeton Univ., IR Section, WP no. 83, 1976); Robert J. Lampman, *Labor Supply and Social Welfare Benefits in the United States* (Washington: U.S. National Commission on Employment and Unemployment Statistics, Background Paper no. 14, 1978); Donald A. Larson, "Labor Supply Adjustment Over the Business Cycle," *ILRR*, July 1981; Don D. Lescohier, *The Labor Market* (New York: Macmillan, 1919); Joan Lindroth, "How to Beat the Coming Labor Shortage," *PJ*, April 1982; Francis D. Longe, *A Refutation of the Wage-Fund Theory of Modern Political Economy* (London: Longmans, Green, 1866); Michael Ransom, *Estimating Family Labor Supply Models Under Quantity Constraints* (Princeton: Princeton Univ., IR Section, WP no. 150, 1982); Richard M. Scheffler and George Iden, "The Effect of Disability on Labor Supply," *ILRR*, Oct. 1974; Harold Wool, "Future Labor Supply for Lower Level Occupations," *MLR*, March 1976.

See also LABOR FORCE.

labor surplus area A labor market area in which the supply of labor exceeds the need of industry in that particular area. It is sometimes referred to as a depressed area.

The Department of Labor has the responsibility of designating labor surplus areas in order to give preference to employers in these areas to bid on federal contracts. An unemployment rate exceeding by at least 1.20 times the national rate during a two-year period is a criterion used by the Department of Labor to designate a labor surplus area. Such areas are designated according to civil jurisdictions, such as a county, county equivalents, or cities with a population of at least 50,000.

The concept was introduced in February 1952 when the Office of Defense Mobilization issued Defense Manpower Policy Number Four (DMP–4). The labor surplus area program was strengthened with the enactment of an amendment to the Small Business Act in August 1977 (P.L. 95–89). Executive Order 12073, signed on August 16, 1978, directed the General Services Administration "to work with each Federal agency to set targets for labor surplus area contracts, monitor agency performance, and report to the President every 6 months on the progress of each agency."

There were 1,374 labor surplus areas as of July 1, 1983.

Source references: "Eligible Labor Surplus Areas for Bidding on Federal Contracts," *Area Trends in Employment and Unemployment,* July 1983; L. G. Reynolds, "Wages and Employment in a Labor-Surplus Economy," *AER,* March 1965; U.S. GAO, *The Labor Surplus Area Policy: Is It Effective in Providing Government Contracts to High Unemployment Areas and Jobs for the Disadvantaged? Departments of Defense and Labor, General Services Administration* (Washington: 1977).

See also AREA REDEVELOPMENT ACT OF 1961, DEPRESSED AREA, PUBLIC WORKS AND ECONOMIC DEVELOPMENT ACT OF 1965.

labor temple Usually applied to a building owned by labor unions in a locality or large city which becomes the center of workers' social activities in that area. Frequently these labor temples house the offices of the union and are also used for union meetings.

In addition to these labor temples, most unions now have established centers for union activity which include housing for union staff facilities, for workshops, the showing of motion pictures, assembly halls, and other facilities to make the union office a center for more than the normal activities involved in negotiating a contract, handling grievances, and assigning workers to jobs.

labor theory of property A theory developed by John Locke in 1690 which held that private property is the reward for the amount of labor expended in creating that property. His argument and theory questioned the divine right of kings to take property without adequate compensation to those who worked for it.

labor theory of value The labor theory of value was part of the system which Karl Marx developed indicating the exploitation of labor in capitalist society. He stated that the exchange value of any commodity was measured by the amount of labor required for its production, that is, labor which was socially necessary to make it. Since labor, according to Marx, was not only the measure but also the source of all value, every commodity ultimately could be traced back to human work or the amount of labor involved in its production.

The theory of surplus value which is explicit in Marx's theory attempted to prove that the amount of return for the sale of a product was in excess of the labor expended on it and therefore created a surplus value which went to the capitalist over and above the subsistence value or the amount produced by the laborer. This surplus value was expropriated by the capitalist society. The capitalist presumably paid the worker the subsistence necessary to produce the commodity but the amount actually put in by the worker was in excess of the subsistence value. The industrialist's claim of the excess was regarded by the Marxists as a form of exploitation.

Source reference: Walter W. Jennings, *A History of the Economic and Social Progress of European Peoples* (Cincinnati: South-Western, 1936).

labor time standard A measurement of the average or reasonable time required to perform an operation by an average worker without undue fatigue, that is, with allowance for rest and other time out. The studies are usually based on motion and time study or they may be based on previous or past performance records.

Source reference: Herbert G. Zollitsch and Adolph Langsner, *Wage and Salary Administration* (2d ed., Cincinnati: South-Western, 1970).

labor transference A procedure, usually of a compulsory nature, of shifting large groups of workers from one enterprise to another more essential enterprise during a particular emergency effort, generally in time of war.

labor treaty A term occasionally applied to the International Labor Organization Conventions which set out standards to be adopted by the participating countries. Conventions become effective after acceptance of the treaty by a certain number of countries and by subsequent ratification by each country wishing to be covered by the proposed treaty or convention.

See also CONVENTION, INTERNATIONAL LABOR ORGANIZATION (ILO).

labor turnover Generally applied to the change or mobility in the labor force of a plant or company or possibly an industry. It is an attempt to measure the changes in the work force which would include the accessions, quits, discharges, and layoffs. The general measure of turnover in a particular plant or industry is a percentage which is derived from a fraction, the numerator being the number of separations from the plant and the denominator the average number on the payroll. Thus if 10,000 employees left the payroll in a particular plant during a year and the average work force in the plant during that same period was 5,000, the turnover rate would be 200 percent.

A great deal of attention is given to this problem in the personnel functions of any company since it is expensive to train individuals for a job. A high turnover rate generally involves additional costs to the company in training programs. It might also indicate certain personnel problems which needed attention. This can be obtained through separation interviews to find out the causes for the separation from the particular plant. These interviews may be helpful in correcting those situations in the plant which lead to a high turnover and thereby provide for a more stable labor force and a lower turnover rate.

Source references: Paul F. Brissenden and Emil Frankel, *Labor Turnover in Industry: A Statistical Analysis* (New York: Macmillan, 1922); BNA, *Job Absence and Turnover Control* (Washington: PPF Survey no. 132, 1981); Grant W. Canfield, "How to Compute Your Labor Turnover Cost," *PJ*, April 1959; Malcolm S. Cohen and Arthur R. Schwartz, "U.S. Labor Turnover: Analysis of a New Measure," *MLR*, Nov. 1980; William N. Cooke, "Turnover and Earnings: Some Empirical Evidence," *IR*, Spring 1979; Richard B. Freeman, "The Effects of Unionism on Worker Attachment to Firms," *Journal of Labor Research*, Spring 1980; Frederick J. Gaudet, *Labor Turnover* (New York: AMA, 1960); ———, "Turnover: It Costs More Than You Think," *Supervisory Management*, Jan. 1959; Robert E. Hall and David M. Lilien, *The Measurement and Significance of Labor Turnover* (Washington: U.S. National Commission on Employment and Unemployment Statistics, Background Paper no. 27, 1979); Kenneth L. Kahl, "What's Behind Employee Turnover?" *Personnel*, Sept./Oct. 1968; Stephen A. Laser, "Dealing with the Problem of Employee Turnover," *Human Resource Management*, Winter 1980; William Merrilees, "Interindustry Variations in Job Turnover," *IR*, Spring 1981; Edward Roseman, *Managing Employee Turnover, A Positive Approach* (New York: AMACOM, 1981); Dixie Sommers and Carin Cohen, "New Occupational Rates of Labor Force Separation," *MLR*, March 1980; Clair Vickery, *The Impact of Turnover on Group Unemployment Rates* (Berkeley: UC, Institute of IR, Reprint no. 419, 1978).

See also ACCESSION, DISCHARGE, LAYOFF, NET LABOR TURNOVER RATE, QUIT.

labor union In its widest and broadest use a labor union in the words of Professor Webb is a "continuous association of wage earners for the purpose of maintaining or improving the conditions of their working lives." In current parlance this would involve the responsibility of acting as the collective bargaining agent for its members and negotiating the wages, hours, and terms of conditions of employment for them. Unions constitute groups with a common interest and are established to further that interest.

Historically, and in a more strict sense, the term "labor union" was applied to the type of structure which was best typified by the Knights of Labor. This organization welcomed into its organization (labor union) all classes of workers. Its function essentially was idealistic, and its reliance was on education and social reform rather than on the use of the economic weapons of the strike or boycott.

The three generally recognized structural types for purposes of definition are the trade union, the industrial union, and the labor union. The trade union consists of an association of workers in a particular trade or craft, whereas the industrial union cuts across craft lines and seeks to unite those individuals in the industry into a coherent central organization. The labor union in a historical sense included all workers regardless of craft, industry, profession, and without regard to differences, suggesting the concept of the solidarity of the working class and the "brotherhood of man."

Another division of labor unions may be made on the basis of their location. These include (1) the local union, (2) the national union, and (3) the international union.

Source references: Jack Barbash, *American Unions, Structure, Government, and Politics* (New York: Random House, 1967); ———, *Labor Unions in Action* (New York: Harper, 1948); ———, "The Union as a Bargaining Organization: Some Implications for Organizational Behavior," *Proceedings of the 28th A/M, IRRA*, ed. by James Stern and Barbara Dennis (Madison: 1976); George W. Cassidy and Abraham J. Simon, "A Public Goods Approach to the Analysis of Public and Private Sector Unions," *Journal of Collective Negotiations in the Public Sector*, Vol. 6, no. 4, 1977; The Conference Board, *Labor Unions: Where Are They Heading?* (New York: Information Bull. 93, 1981); N. E. Coward, "The Work of Central Labor Unions," *American Federationist*, March 1955; Marten Estey, *The Unions: Structure, Development, and Management* (2d ed., New York: Harcourt Brace Jovanovich, 1976); Kenneth A. Kovach, "Do We Still Need Labor Unions?" *PJ*, Dec. 1979; Florence Peterson, *American Labor Unions* (2d ed., New York: Harper, 1963); Leonard R. Sayles and George Strauss, *The Local Union* (rev. ed., New York: Harcourt, Brace, 1967); Alvin Schwartz, *The Union: What they Are, How they Came to Be, How they Affect Each of Us* (New York: Viking Press, 1972); Joseph Shister, "The Direction of Unionism 1947–1967: Thrust or Drift?" *ILRR*, July 1967; Gus Tyler, *The Labor Revolution; Trade Unions in a New America* (New York: Viking Press, 1967); B. J. Widick, *Labor Today, The Triumphs and Failures of Unionism in the United States* (Boston: Houghton Mifflin, 1964).

See also CRAFT UNION, GENERAL LABOR UNION, HORIZONTAL UNIONS, INDEPENDENT NATIONAL UNION, INDUSTRIAL UNION, INTERNATIONAL UNION, LABOR ORGANIZATION, LOCAL UNION, NATIONAL AND INTERNATIONAL UNIONS, NATIONAL UNION, PARENT UNION, TRADE UNION.

Labour Gazette The official publication of the Canadian Department of Labour published since 1900. The *Gazette* is roughly equivalent to the *Monthly Labor Review* issued by the U.S. Department of Labor.

Labour Progressive Party The Communist Party of Canada which was formed in 1924 and changed its name in 1943 to the Labour Progressive Party.

Lace Operatives of America; Amalgamated (Ind) A labor organization formed in Philadelphia in 1892. Its full title at that time was The Chartered Society of Amalgamated Lace Curtain Operatives of America. When it enlarged its jurisdiction to the entire lace industry, the word "curtain" was eliminated from its official title. Although originally a member of the AFL, it had its charter revoked in 1919 when it refused to merge with the newly formed United Textile Workers.

Address: 4013 Glendale St., Philadelphia, Pa. 19124. Tel. (215) 743–9358

Ladies' Garment Workers' Union; International (AFL-CIO) Organized in New York City in 1900, largely from members of the United Brotherhood of Cloak Makers of New York. The ILGWU is well-known for its efforts in workers' education, recreation, and health and welfare programs.

The official publication is *Justice*, issued monthly.

Address: 1710 Broadway, New York, N.Y. 10019. Tel. (212) 265–7000

Source references: Jack Barbash, "The ILGWU as an Organization in the Age of Dubinsky," *Labor History* (Special Supplement), Spring 1968; Abraham Bisno, *Abraham Bisno—Union Pioneer* (Madison: Univ. of Wisconsin Press, 1967); David Dubinsky, "The I.L.G.W.U. and the American Labor Movement," *Labor History*, Spring 1968; Louis Levine, *The Women's Garment Workers: A History of the International Ladies' Garment Workers' Union* (New York: Viking Press, 1924); Raymond Munts and Mary Louise Munts, "Welfare History of the I.L.G.W.U.," *Labor History*, Spring 1968; Theresa Wolfson, "The Role of the ILGWU in

Stabilizing the Women's Garment Industry," *ILRR*, Oct. 1950.

LaFollette Committee The LaFollette Committee was more generally known as the LaFollette Civil Liberties Committee since the prime concern in its investigations was the denial of the civil liberties of American workers. Its major investigation dealt with the operation of some of the leading detective agencies which were servicing major corporations. Among these were the Railway Audit and Inspection Company, the Pinkerton Company, the Corporation Auxiliary Company, the International Corporation Service, and the William J. Burns International Detective Agency.

It was the most thorough of any of the investigations into labor's rights to organize and the denial of civil liberties. The LaFollette Committee began its work in 1936 and continued publications of its materials until May 1942. In all, some 75 volumes were published, including a number of detailed reports covering such items as: strikebreaking services, private police systems, industrial munitions, labor policies of employer associations, the National Metal Trades Association, the Associated Industries of Cleveland, the Little Steel Strike and Citizens' Committees, and employers associations and collective bargaining in California. The official title of the published volumes is "Violations of Free Speech and Rights of Labor, Hearings before a subcommittee of the Committee on Education and Labor, United States Senate . . . pursuant to S.Res. 266 (74th Congress)."

Source reference: Jerold S. Averbach, *Labor and Liberty; The LaFollette Committee and the New Deal* (Indianapolis: Bobbs Merrill, 1966).

See also ANTI-UNION PRACTICES, BACK ROOM BOYS, BOYCOTT, ESPIONAGE, INDUSTRIAL CONFLICT, LABOR SPY, PICKETING, STRIKE, VIOLENCE IN LABOR DISPUTES.

laissez-faire doctrine A term generally attributed to the French Physiocrats and intended to denote that things are to be permitted to continue without interference. It is a doctrine which followed the rather strict economic control philosophy known as Mercantilism.

Probably the best exponent of the laissez-faire doctrine as applied to economic life was Adam Smith, in his book entitled *An Inquiry into the Nature and Causes of the Wealth of Nations.* Smith has been described as the father of free enterprise economics and developed the concept that enlightened self-interest ultimately would lead to the best interest of the community as a whole.

Landrum-Griffin Act *See* LABOR-MANAGEMENT REPORTING AND DISCLOSURE ACT OF 1959.

lapsed member A term generally applied to the termination of certain benefits of membership due to the failure of the member to comply with the provisions of a union constitution and bylaws; more specifically, when he no longer is in good standing because of failure to pay dues, assessments, fines, or some other commitment required by the union's constitution and bylaws.

last best offer *See* ARBITRATION, FINAL OFFER.

last offer ballot A procedure in the Taft-Hartley Act authorizing the FMCS to hold elections to determine whether employees will accept the employer's last offer.

In theory, the last offer ballot has been proposed on the assumption that employees of a company would accept the company's last offer if they had the free choice in a government-supervised election, rather than support their own leaders and, if necessary, go on strike or continue on strike for demands greater than those offered by the employer.

See also EMPLOYER'S FINAL OFFER.

lates A popular term which applies to workers who have not reported for work on time and are, therefore, tardy or late.

late ticket A term used to describe the card or slip on which an employee who reports late for work explains the reason for his lateness.

Lathers International Union; The Wood, Wire and Metal (AFL-CIO) A union organized in December 1899 in Detroit, Michigan, with jurisdiction among other things of "directing and installing of all light iron construction; furring, making and erecting of brackets, clips, and hangers; wood, wire and metal lath, plaster board or other material which takes the place of same to which plaster material is adhered.

The union merged with the United Brotherhood of Carpenters and Joiners of America (AFL-CIO) on August 31, 1979.

See also CARPENTERS AND JOINERS OF AMERICA; UNITED BROTHERHOOD OF (AFL-CIO).

Lauf v. E. G. Shinner & Co., Inc. A decision of the Supreme Court (setting aside a district court decision) holding that picketing by the Amalgamated Meat Cutters of the Shinner meat markets in Milwaukee, Wis., was a "labor dispute" within the meaning of the Norris-LaGuardia Act, even though the picketing was for purposes of union organization.

Justice Roberts, delivering the opinion of the Court, said in part:

> The District Court erred in granting an injunction in the absence of findings which the Norris-LaGuardia Act makes prerequisites to the exercise of jurisdiction.
>
> Section 13(c) of the Act is: "The term 'labor dispute' includes any controversy concerning terms or conditions of employment, or concerning the association or representation of the persons negotiating, fixing, maintaining, changing, or seeking to arrange terms or conditions of employment, regardless of whether the disputants stand in the proximate relation of employer and employe."
>
> This definition does not differ materially from that (of) the Wisconsin Labor Code, and the facts of the instant case bring it within both.

Source references: Edward Lauf v. E. G. Shinner & Co., Inc., 303 US 323, 2 LRRM 585 (1938); Orval Etter, "Statutory Definitions of Labor Dispute," 19 *Oregon LR* 81 (1940).

Laundry and Dry Cleaning International Union (AFL-CIO) Chartered by the AFL-CIO to replace the Laundry, Cleaning and Dye House Workers International Union, which was expelled at the AFL-CIO convention in December 1957.

Address: 1603 Statler Building, 107 Delaware Ave., Buffalo, N.Y. 14202. Tel. (716) 853–1880

Laundry, Cleaning and Dye House Workers International Union (Ind) *See* TEXTILE PROCESSORS, SERVICE TRADES, HEALTH CARE, PROFESSIONAL AND TECHNICAL EMPLOYEES INTERNATIONAL UNION.

Laundry, Dry Cleaning and Dye House Workers International Union (Ind) *See* TEXTILE PROCESSORS, SERVICE TRADES, HEALTH CARE, PROFESSIONAL AND TECHNICAL EMPLOYEES INTERNATIONAL UNION.

Laundry Workers' International Union (AFL-CIO) *See* TEXTILE PROCESSORS, SERVICE TRADES, HEALTH CARE, PROFESSIONAL AND TECHNICAL EMPLOYEES INTERNATIONAL UNION.

Lawlor v. Loewe A famous labor case frequently referred to as the *Danbury Hatters'* case. It arose under the provisions of the Sherman Anti-Trust Law and resulted essentially from the efforts of the United Hatters of North America to organize the then unorganized manufacturers of men's hats. At the time of the union's action against Loewe, a manufacturer at Danbury, Connecticut, the union had organized 70 of the manufacturers into union shops and there were only 12 additional manufacturers of men's hats in the United States which the union had not organized.

The effort to organize Loewe at Danbury resulted in a strike which was ineffective. The union then resorted to a boycott with the assistance of other affiliates of the AFL. The boycott apparently was effective. The company held that its listing by the union as an unfair firm resulted in an injury of some $80,000. It sought a restraining order and damages in the amount of $80,000 which was tripled under the Sherman Act to $240,000. The Supreme Court held that the Sherman Act applied to the union and that the union was in violation of the law. It said in part, "the combination described in the declaration is a combination in restraint of trade or commerce among the several states in the sense in which those words were used in the Act. . . . The Act prohibits any combination whatever to secure action which essentially obstructs the free flow of commerce between the states, or restricts in that regard, the liberty of a trader to engage in business."

A judgment was issued against the members of the union for $240,000. The subsequent reaction of the trade unions ultimately led to the passage of the Clayton Act.

Source references: Clayton Act, Pub. L. 212 (ch. 323), Oct. 15, 1914, 38 Stat. 730 (codified as amended in scattered sections of 15, 18, 29 U.S.C.); Sherman Antitrust Act, as amended, 15 U.S.C. 1–7 (1982); *Lawlor v. Loewe,* 235 US 522 (1915); *Loewe v. Lawlor,* 208 US 274 (1908); Edward Berman, *Labor and the Sherman Act* (New York: Harper, 1930); Milton Handler, *Cases and Materials on Labor Law* (St. Paul: West, 1944); George W. Terborgh, "The Application of the Sherman Law to Tarde-Union Activities," *Journal of Political Economy,* April 1929.

See also CLAYTON ACT OF 1914, SHERMAN ACT OF 1890.

law of diminishing returns A general economic law which has been applied to all of the factors in production. The law states generally that any increase of one of the factors of production applied beyond a certain point will not provide a proportionate increase in production from the additional unit of labor, capital, or other productive factor. In its application to labor, it merely states that beyond a certain point the additional application of labor will not provide a proportionate increase in the output of work.

law of labor combinations The law of labor combinations has the same meaning as the conspiracy doctrine and probably comes from the combination laws in England passed by the Eighth Parliament in the 14th century. As defined in American law, the term is probably best expressed by Justice Shaw in the *Commonwealth v. Hunt* case in which he stated that a conspiracy is a combination of two or more persons, by some concerted actions, to accomplish some purpose not in itself criminal or unlawful by criminal or unlawful means.

See also COMMONWEALTH V. HUNT, LABOR COMBINATIONS.

law of the shop *See* INDUSTRIAL JURISPRUDENCE.

layoff A term generally applied to a temporary or indefinite separation from employment.

Employees in layoff status usually retain certain seniority rights and other protection under contract or company practice. The term occasionally is confused with "discharge." On occasion the layoff is used as a disciplinary penalty, in which case it is for a specific period of time and it is a penalty for the specific abuse of company rule or regulation. The employee is generally re-employed.

Source references: L. D. Belzung, John P. Owen, and John F. MacNaughton, *The Anatomy of a Workforce Reduction* (Houston: Center for Research in Business and Economics, Univ. of Houston, 1966); Francine D. Blau and Lawrence M. Kahn, *Causes and Consequences of Layoffs* (Urbana: Univ. of Illinois, Institute of Labor and IR, Reprint Series no. 292, 1981); Farrell E. Bloch, *An Analysis of Quit and Layoff Rates in U.S. Manufacturing Industries* (Princeton: Princeton Univ., IR Section, WP no. 76, 1975); Joseph W. Bloch and Robert Platt, "Layoff, Recall and Work Sharing Procedures," *MLR,* Feb. 1957; BNA, *Layoff and Unemployment Compensation Policies* (Washington: PPF Survey no. 128, 1980); ———, *White Collar Layoff and Cutbacks, A BNA Special Report* (Washington: 1982); William N. Cooke, "Permanent Layoffs: What's Implicit in the Contract?" *IR,* Spring 1981; Alan V. Friedman and Allen M. Katz, "Retroactive Seniority for the Identifiable Victim Under Title VII—Must Last Hired, First Fired Give Way," *NYU 28th Annual Conference on Labor,* ed. by Richard Adelman (New York: Bender, 1976); "Last Hired, First Fired Layoffs and Title VII," *IR Law Digest,* Fall 1975; Rose Theodore, "Layoff, Recall and Work Sharing Procedures," *MLR,* March 1957; U.S. Commission on Civil Rights, *Last Hired, First Fired: Layoffs and Civil Rights, A Report of the United States Commission on Civil Rights* (Washington: 1977); U.S. Congressional Budget Office, *Dislocated Workers: Issues and Federal Options* (Washington: Background Paper, 1982); U.S. Dept. of Labor, BLS, *Major Collective Bargaining Agreements: Severance Pay and Layoff Benefit Plans* (Washington: Bull. no. 1425–2, 1965); U.S. Dept. of Labor, ETA, *A Guide for Communities Facing Major Layoffs or Plant Shutdowns* (Washington: 1980).

See also DISCHARGE, DISCIPLINARY LAYOFF, REDUCTION IN FORCE, REDUNDANCY, RETRENCHMENT, SEPARATION, TEMPORARY LAYOFF.

layoff notice The form and procedure usually under the labor contract, of notifying the employee in cases of layoff and occasionally providing for some pay in lieu of such notice.

A National War Labor Board decision in one important case ordered the following clause into a contract:

> The company shall notify an employee of its intention to lay him off two working days in advance of such layoff or in lieu of notice, shall compensate the laid off employee at the rate of 12 hours' pay at his average rate including bonuses. This provision shall apply only to layoffs in excess of two weeks that are due to the company's scheduling and not to forces beyond the company's control.

layoff pay This is a payment either in a lump sum amount or in weekly or other instalments to individuals who leave the service of a company without fault of their own. It is not dismissal pay or complete severance pay, but generally payment to a person who is temporarily terminated from employment.

Some layoffs may be for a period longer than what is normally referred to as a temporary layoff, in which case the layoff comes fairly close to being a severance. It is distinguished from dismissal, since a dismissal is frequently based on "cause."

In recent years there has been increased interest in severance pay and in supplementary unemployment benefits received by employees in addition to their unemployment benefits while temporarily laid off.

See also DISMISSAL COMPENSATION, SUPPLEMENTAL UNEMPLOYMENT BENEFITS.

layoff policies Normally, provisions in a contract found in the seniority sections which indicate the procedures to be followed in a layoff. Protection is frequently set up on the basis of length of service, on a companywide or departmentwide basis, and in some areas on a craft basis. The procedure is designed to provide a reasonable practice fair to the employees and to the continued efficient operation of the company when layoffs are made necessary either by a decline in need for the product or occasionally for retooling or design of new products.

Source references: Robert L. Aronson, *Layoff Policies and Practices: Recent Experience Under Collective Bargaining* (Princeton: Princeton Univ., IR Section, 1950); Paul Kull, "Seniority and Layoff Procedures" (Masters thesis, New York Univ., 1957); Joyanna Moy and Constance Sorrentino, "Unemployment, Labor Force Trends, and Layoff Practices in 10 Countries," *MLR*, Dec. 1981; U.S. Dept. of Labor, BLS, *Major Collective Bargaining Agreements: Layoff, Recall, and Worksharing Procedures* (Washington: Bull. no. 1425–13, 1972).

See also SENIORITY.

layoff rate A computation designed to measure the percent of employees laid off as against the employees on the payroll for a specific period of time or averaged over a one-year period.

See also NET LABOR TURNOVER RATE.

layoff slip A form generally used by employers to inform the individual that he is to be laid off as of a specific date. In situations where the layoff is temporary, the layoff slip might indicate the date on which the employee is to return to work.

layover The term is applied to practices in railroad transportation and in intracity or bus transportation where a worker will receive payment or compensation for a layover which is required because of the nature of his run. Frequently payment will also be made for the cost of returning to his home base when his particular run or trip terminates at a distant stop from his home town or home office.

Lea Act (Anti-Petrillo Act) A federal law designed to outlaw certain "featherbedding" practices of the Musicians Union, such as the use of "stand-ins" when nonlive (canned) music was used. The law makes it unlawful to require radio broadcasters to pay for services not to be performed, or to hire more persons than actually needed on the job.

Source reference: United States v. Petrillo, 332 US 1, 20 LRRM 2254 (1947).

See also CANNED MUSIC, FEATHERBEDDING.

leaders The term occasionally is applied to individuals who are hired to establish performance standards and individuals unions claim are "speeders" used by employers to increase the rate at which average workers are required to perform.

See also LEADMAN.

leadership A term which is somewhat vague but is generally applied to qualities and forces existing within an organization (usually centered in the top executives) which motivate, guide, and direct individuals as well as groups within the organization to achieve its broad objectives and goals.

Work in the personnel field in private industry and in government services has attempted to develop and attract outstanding individuals so that the organization will have a continuing flow of young persons of high competence who will assume leadership roles in their respective organizations. Advanced management programs are frequently concerned with the development of leadership. In addition to encouraging those qualities essential to leadership, a large amount of substantive factual material has been built into these programs, including a broad background in the social sciences, accounting, finance, business organization, industrial relations, and other areas.

Source references: James J. Cribbin, *Leadership; Strategies for Organizational Effectiveness* (New York: AMACOM, 1981); Vincent S. Flowers and Charles L. Hughes, "Choosing a Leadership Style," *Personnel,* Jan./Feb. 1978; Robert T. Golembiewski, "Three Styles of Leadership and Their Uses," *Personnel,* July/Aug. 1961; Larry E. Greiner, "What Managers Think of Participative Leadership," *Harvard BR,* March/April 1973; Eugene E. Jennings, "Autonomy of Leadership," *Management of Personnel Quarterly,* Autumn 1961; John P. Jones, "Changing Patterns of Leadership," *Personnel,* March/April 1967; Richard I. Lester, "Leadership: Some Principles and Concepts," *PJ,* Nov. 1981; Harry Levinson, *The Great Jackass Fallacy* (Boston: Division of Research, Graduate School of Business Administration, Harvard Univ., 1973); Thomas J. Peters, "Leadership: Sad Facts and Silver Linings," *Harvard BR,* Nov./Dec. 1979; Roger J. Plachy, "Leading vs. Managing: A Guide to Some Crucial Distinctions," *Management Review,* Sept. 1981; Burt K. Scanlan, "Managerial Leadership in Perspective: Getting Back to Basics," *PJ,* March 1979; Robert Tannenbaum and Warren H. Schmidt, "How to Choose a Leadership Pattern," *Harvard BR,* May/June 1973; Ordway Tead, *The Art of Leadership* (New York: McGraw-Hill, 1935); Carl E. Welte, "Management and Leadership: Concepts with an Important Difference," *PJ,* Nov. 1978; Abraham Zaleznik, "The Human Dilemmas of Leadership," *Harvard BR,* July/Aug. 1963; ———, "Managers and Leaders: Are They Different?" *Harvard BR,* May/June 1977.

leadership training Programs designed to provide the basic understanding of the function and characteristics of leadership and to provide a broad base of information to assist those either in leadership roles or who are to assume leadership responsibility. In recent years efforts have been directed in the field of labor education to train leaders in the labor movement, not only for organizational purposes, but also for research and other top offices.

Source references: Raymond A. Gumport and Ronald K. Hambleton, "Situational Leadership: How Xerox Managers Fine-Tune Managerial Styles to Employee Maturity and Task Needs," *Management Review,* Dec. 1979; Verne J. Kallejian, Irving R. Weschler, and Robert Tannenbaum, "Training Managers for Leadership," *Personnel,* Jan. 1954; L. F. McCollum, "Developing Managers Who Make Things Happen," *Management Review,* May 1967; Raymond E. Miles and Lyman W. Porter, "Leadership Training—Back to the Classroom?" *Personnel,* July/Aug. 1966; Marsha Sinetar, "Developing Leadership Potential," *PJ,* March 1981; Maynard N. Toussaint and Fred C. Munson, "How Not to Conduct a Management Training Program," *Personnel Administration,* Sept./Oct. 1963.

See also MANAGEMENT DEVELOPMENT.

leadman A term applied usually to the individual who sets the pace for a group or a team working on a particular operation. This individual may sometimes be the working foreman. It also refers to an individual who has responsibility for new workers in a particular occupation and who is completely familiar with the requirements of the job and is able not only to direct the activities of those in this group but also to maintain maximum production.

Source reference: U.S. Dept. of Labor, BES, *Dictionary of Occupational Titles* (3d ed., Washington: 1965).

leaf-raking Sometimes used as the equivalent of the term "boondoggling." This is a form of busy work and the performance of activities which give the appearance of functional use but which may actually be designed only to keep the person occupied.

See also BOONDOGGLING.

League for Industrial Democracy Founded as the Inter-Collegiate Socialist Society in 1905 by Upton Sinclair, Jack London, Clarence Darrow, and other writers and civic leaders to encourage and develop progressive (socialistic) thought in the United States. The current name was adopted in 1921.

The League is an American educational organization dedicated to increasing democracy in economic, political, and cultural life. "League members are devoted to the struggle for full racial equality, the abolition of poverty, the strengthening of trade unions and cooperatives, the expansion of civil liberties, the extension of public ownership and democratic economic planning, and the realignment of our political organizations with a view toward making them more responsive to the will of the people."

The League issues pamphlets and conducts institutes and conferences.

Address: 275 Seventh Avenue, New York, N.Y. 10001. Tel. (212) 989–8130

Source references: Thomas R. Brooks, *Tragedy at Ocean Hill* (New York: League for Industrial Democracy, Occasional Paper no. 13, 1969); B. Bruce-Briggs, *The Minimum Wage Muddle* (New York: League for Industrial Democracy, Labor Issues Papers, 1981); Steve Lagerfeld, *The Ideology of Union Busting* (New York: League for Industrial Democracy, Labor Issues Papers, 1981).

League for Industrial Rights An organization established in 1902 whose prime concern was the organization of employers and others to fight unions in the courts, particularly in the handling of economic sanctions, such as the boycott. It was active in helping employers finance the famous *Danbury Hatters* case. The League was originally known as the American Anti-Boycott Association.

See also AMERICAN ANTI-BOYCOTT ASSOCIATION, LAWLOR V. LOEWE.

leap-frogging A term applied to a collective bargaining situation in which an employer dealing with several unions bargains with each union separately and signs an agreement with each union separately. The last union with which the employer bargains may decide that it will break the agreement pattern reached by all the other unions and hold out and even strike to gain an advantage. If the other unions refuse to cross the picket lines, the plant will of course remain shut down. When the employer finally reaches an agreement with the hold-out union on more favorable terms, the other unions which have already signed agreements may demand that they receive the same terms as the hold-out union and the bargaining issue will be opened again. The hold-out union has thus leap-frogged over the agreement pattern already set by the other unions, and the other unions leap-frog when they insist upon parity of treatment with the original hold-out union. In such a situation it would actually be to the employer's advantage if the unions involved would bargain in a coalition.

learner The term is generally applied to a beginner in an occupation or trade which requires less skill than an apprentice and which frequently takes a relatively short period of time to learn. In general contract provisions learners may be described as individuals with no previous experience in the industry, individuals who have not worked in the industry for a fixed total period of time, or an individual who has not performed work of the type for which he is hired.

Source references: John V. L. Morris, *Employee Training* (New York: McGraw-Hill, 1921); Stewart Scrimshaw, *Apprenticeship, Principles, Relationships, Procedures* (New York: McGraw-Hill, 1932).

See also APPRENTICESHIP.

learner rate The rate of pay which is generally applied to a worker who is inexperienced in the job for the period during which he receives his training. When the individual is sufficiently competent to meet the job requirements, he is generally given the minimum job rate.

Under the Fair Labor Standards Act, it is possible for an employer to hire learners at a rate lower than the legal minimum under certain conditions. Students receiving instruction and employed by the educational institution on a part-time basis may qualify as learners. If it is believed that such rates are necessary to prevent the curtailment of employment opportunities in a plant or area, the Wage and Hour Administrator will hold hearings and determine the nature of the limitations as to wages, time, number, and length of service, and special certificates authorizing the employment of learners to be issued to an employer for specific occupations in a particular plant.

See also FAIR LABOR STANDARDS ACT OF 1938, JOB RATE.

learner's certificate Certificates issued by the Wage and Hour Division of the U.S. Department of Labor under the Fair Labor Standards Act which permit employers to pay less than the minimum wage to persons who are in the process of learning a skill. Once the individual is competent in the job requirements, he is generally given the statutory minimum wage rate.

learner training A procedure and scheduled program for workers in a trade which requires skills less than those necessary for the apprenticeship program.

See also APPRENTICESHIP.

learning period The time it takes for a learner to obtain the skills necessary in a particular job. This period is less than the apprenticeship time for a highly skilled job.

Leather Goods, Plastic and Novelty Workers' Union; International (AFL-CIO) A union organized in 1923, as the International Pocketbook Workers' Union. It was affiliated with the United Leather Workers' International Union until 1937 when it withdrew and affiliated with the AFL as an international union taking the name International Ladies' Handbag, Pocketbook and Novelty Workers Union. It adopted its present name in the 1950s.

Address: 265 West 14th St., New York, N.Y. 10011. Tel. (212) 675–9240

Leather Workers International Union; United (AFL) The United Leather Workers' International Union, the forerunner of this organization, was organized in Indianapolis in April 1917. Its predecessors were the United Brotherhood of Leather Workers on Horse Goods, which was an amalgamation of two previous organizations, the United Brotherhood of Harness and Saddle Workers and the National Association of Saddle and Harness Makers of America. Another section of the leather union consisted of the Trunk and Bag Makers and was organized in Kentucky as the Trunk and Bag Workers' International Union of America. It affiliated with the AFL in 1896. In 1903 it became the Travelers' Goods and Leather Novelty Workers' International Union of America. Still another segment of the leather workers was the Amalgamated Leather Workers of America, which consisted primarily of tannery workers and was in the AFL from 1901 to 1912 when it surrendered its charter. The United Leather Workers' International Union was an amalgamation of all of these organizations which took place in 1917.

The union merged with the Amalgamated Meat Cutters and Butcher Workmen of North America (AFL-CIO) in the early 1950s.

See also MEAT CUTTERS AND BUTCHER WORKMEN OF NORTH AMERICA; AMALGAMATED (AFL-CIO).

Leather Workers International Union of America (AFL-CIO) 11 Peabody Square, Peabody, Mass. 01960. Tel. (617) 531–5605

leave of absence A grant to an employee of time off from his job, generally without loss of seniority and with the right to reinstatement. Many collective bargaining agreements permit an individual to remain away from his job for a limited period of time without jeopardizing his status. The leave of absence may be for a short period of time in case of family difficulty, deaths, short illness, or jury duty. It may be for longer periods but generally is not given for more than a year. The areas which leaves of absence most normally cover in collective bargaining are long illness, the filling of public offices, jury duty of a more than short duration, military duty, maternity leaves, and union business, generally the holding of an official union position.

In general, leaves of absence for long periods of time are without pay, although some leaves in cases of illness may provide for full or part payment.

Some clauses ordered in War Labor Board decisions illustrate the nature of contract provisions for leaves of absence. The following represents a leave of absence granted to a union representative:

An employee selected to fill a full time union position shall be entitled to leave of absence for the period of such service not exceeding one year provided that during the preceding six months he has not been on similar leave. A leave of absence for a period in excess of one year or for an employee who has recently enjoyed such leave may be arranged by agreement between the company and the union. The employee's seniority shall accumulate throughout the period of such leave.

A maternity leave of absence clause provides as follows:

A maternity leave of absence without pay will be granted to an employee for a period of one (1) year. Seniority shall accumulate during an approved maternity leave. Unless medical considerations dictate otherwise, the employee shall advise the company at least two (2) weeks in advance of the date she wishes to begin maternity leave. At any time during the leave period the employee may give notice to the company of her intention to return to work, but must do so at least five (5) days prior to her return.

A provision for leave of absence for an employee to enter the armed services reads as follows:

Any employee who enters into active service of the armed forces of the United States or the American Merchant Marine will be given a leave of absence for, and will accumulate seniority during, such period of service and upon the termination of such service shall be offered reemployment at his previous position or a position of like seniority status in pay, unless the circumstances have so changed as to make it impossible or unreasonable to do so, in which event he will be offered such employment as may be available, which he is capable of doing, at the common rate of such work, provided he has not been dishonorably discharged, is physically able to work, and reports for work within sixty days from the date of such discharge.

See also ADOPTION LEAVE, EDUCATIONAL LEAVE, FUNERAL LEAVE PAY, FURLOUGH, MATERNITY LEAVE, MILITARY LEAVE, PAID JURY LEAVE, PAID LEAVE, PAID SICK LEAVE, PATERNITY LEAVE, SABBATICALS.

leaver A person who takes the initiative and voluntarily leaves his employment.

leave without pay *See* LEAVE OF ABSENCE.

left wing Generally that segment of an organization whose ideas are considered by the majority to be at the radical extreme. This frequently describes the social, economic, and political outlook of the group; sometimes these include the socialist wing and almost invariably include the groups that are held to be in sympathy with the Communist position.

Source references: Daniel Aaron, *Writers on the Left, Episodes in American Literary Communism* (New York: Harcourt, Brace, 1961); David J. Saposs, *Communism in American Unions* (New York: McGraw-Hill, 1959); ———, *Left Wing Unionism in the United States* (New York: Int. Publishers, 1926).

legal aid society Generally an organziation private in nature, occasionally sponsored or encouraged by a semipublic organization, to provide advice and counsel on legal matters to those who are in poverty or who cannot afford the services of an attorney. In some situations, legal aid societies also handle wage claims.

legal dispute This term occasionally is applied to a grievance arising under a collective bargaining agreement. The term "justiciable dispute" or a grievance involving interpretation or application of an agreement, or "rights dispute," is used more frequently than "legal dispute."

See also ARBITRATION, RIGHTS.

legal periodicals The following is a selected listing of law journals and law reviews issued in the United States. The list contains many of the major journals which frequently contain notes and articles affecting labor-management relations.

American Bar Association Journal (monthly), American Bar Association, 1155 E. 60th St., Chicago, Ill. 60637; *Arizona Law Review* (four times a year), College of Law, University of Arizona, Tucson, Ariz. 85721; *Boston College Industrial and Commercial Law Review* (quarterly), Boston College Law School, Brighton, Mass. 02135; *Boston University Law Review* (five times a year), Boston University Law School, 765 Commonwealth Ave., Boston, Mass. 02215; *Buffalo Law Review* (four times a year), University of Buffalo Law School, 77 W. Eagle St., Buffalo, N.Y. 14202; *California Law Review* (six times a year), School of Law, University of California, Berkeley, Calif. 94720; *Case Western Reserve Law Review* (four times a year), School of Law, Case Western Reserve University, Cleveland, Ohio 44106; *Catholic University Law Review* (quarterly), Catholic University of America Press, Washington, D.C. 20064; *Columbia Law Review* (eight times a year), Columbia University, 435 W. 116th St., New York, N.Y. 10027; *Cornell Law Review* (bimonthly), Law School, Cornell University, Myron Taylor Hall, Ithaca, N.Y. 14853; *Duke Law Journal* (bimonthly), School of Law, Duke University, Durham, N.C. 27706; *Fordham Law Review* (six times a year), School of Law, Fordham University, 140 W. 62nd St., New York, N.Y. 10023; *Georgetown Law Journal* (six times a year), Georgetown Law Journal Association, 600 New Jersey Ave., N.W., Washington, D.C. 20001; *Harvard Law Review* (eight times a year), Harvard Law Review Association, Gannett House, Cambridge, Mass. 02138; *Hastings Law Journal* (six times a year), Hastings College of Law, University of California, San Francisco, 305 Golden Gate Ave., San Francisco, Calif. 94102; *Iowa Law Review* (five times a year), College of Law, University of Iowa, Iowa City, Iowa 52240; *Law and Contemporary Problems* (quarterly), School of Law, Duke University, Duke Station, Durham, N.C. 27706; *Minnesota Law Review* (six times a year), Law School, University of Minnesota, Minneapolis, Minn. 55455; *Nebraska Law Review* (quarterly), College of Law, University of Nebraska, Lincoln, Neb. 68508; *New York University Law Review* (six times a year), Law Review, New York University, 249 Sullivan St., New York, N.Y. 10012; *North Carolina Law Review* (six times a year), School of Law, University of North Carolina at Chapel Hill, Chapel Hill, N.C. 27514; *Northwestern University Law Review* (bimonthly), School of Law, Northwestern University, 357 E. Chicago Ave., Chicago, Ill. 60611; *Ohio State Law Journal* (quarterly), College of Law, Ohio State University, 1659 N. High St., Columbus, Ohio 43210; *Oregon Law Review* (four times a year), School of Law, University of Oregon, Eugene, Ore. 97403; *Rutgers University Law Review* (five times a year), Rutgers University School of Law, 180 University Ave., Newark, N.J. 07102; *Southern California Law Review* (six times a year), Law Center, University of Southern California, University Park, Room 314, Los Angeles, Calif. 90007; *Stanford Law Review* (six times a year), Stanford School of Law, Stanford University, Stanford, Calif. 94305; *Temple Law Quarterly*, Temple University School of Law, 1715 N. Broad St., Philadelphia, Pa. 19122; *UCLA Law Review* (six times a year), School of Law, University of California, Los Angeles, 405 Hilgard Ave., Los Angeles, Calif. 90024; *University of Chicago Law Review* (quarterly), University of Chicago Law School, 1111 E. 60th St., Chicago, Ill. 60637; *University of Illinois Law Forum* (quarterly), College of Law, University of Illinois at Urbana–Champaign, Champaign, Ill. 61820; *University of Michigan Journal of Law Reform* (three times a year), University of Michigan Law School, 731 Legal Research Bldg., Ann Arbor, Mich. 48104; *University of Pennsylvania Law Review* (six times a year), University of Pennsylvania Law School, 3400 Chestnut St., Philadelphia, Pa. 19174; *University of Pittsburgh Law Review* (four times a year), School of Law, University of Pittsburgh, 1417 Cathedral of Learning, Pittsburgh, Pa. 15213; *University of San Francisco Law Review* (four times a year), School of Law, University of San Francisco, Kendrick Hall, 2130 Fulton St., San Francisco, Calif. 94117; *Vanderbilt University Law Review* (six times a year), Vanderbilt University School of Law, Nashville, Tenn. 37240; *Virginia Law Review* (bimonthly), School of Law, University of Virginia, Charlottesville, Va. 22901; *Washington Law Review* (four times a year), School of Law, University of Washington, Condon Hall, Seattle, Wash. 98105; *West Virginia Law Review* (quarterly), West Virginia University Law Center, Morgantown, W. Va. 26505; *Wisconsin Law Review* (four times a year), Law School, University of Wisconsin–Madison, Bascon Hall, Madison, Wisc. 53706; *Yale Law Journal* (eight times a year), Yale Law Journal Co., Inc., 401-A Yale Station, New Haven, Conn. 06520.

Source reference: Ulrich's International Periodical Directory (20th ed., New York: Bowker, 1981).

legal sanction Remedies or penalties available to employers, unions, or individuals under Section 301 of the Taft-Hartley Act or under the provisions of a state labor relations law.

Source reference: Labor-Management Relations Act of 1947 as amended, Section 301, 29 U.S.C. 185 (1982).

See also ECONOMIC SANCTION, PROFESSIONAL SANCTION.

legal service plans An employee benefit plan similar in operation to a health plan.

Plans vary in terms of the delivery system—open panel plans permit the subscriber to select any attorney (or at least to select the lawyer from a larger pool), while partially open panel and closed panel plans limit the choice to a group of participating attorneys.

An example of a negotiated legal service plan is the General Motors/United Auto Workers plan which is funded by employer contributions of 3 cents per hour worked and is administered by a joint labor-management committee. The plan provides legal services for, among other items, social security claims, traffic violations, misdemeanors, personal bankruptcies, consumer complaints, tax audits, landlord-tenant disputes, divorces, and child custody cases.

Source references: Florian Bartosic and Jules Bernstein, "Group Legal Services as a Fringe Benefit: Lawyers for Forgotten Clients Through Collective Bargaining," *IR Law Digest*, Spring 1974; Sandy DeMent, "A New Bargaining Focus on Legal Services," *American Federationist*, May 1978; ———, "Prepaid Legal Services: Now in the Middle Phase," *Employee Relations LJ*, Spring 1976; Richard F. Kahle, Jr., *Prepaid Legal Services and Hawaii* (Honolulu: Hawaii, Legislative Reference Bureau, Report no. 4, 1975); Susan T. MacKenzie, *Group Legal Services* (Ithaca: Cornell Univ., NYSSILR, Key Issues series no. 18, 1975); Theodore J. St. Antoine, "Growth Patterns in Legal Services," *American Federationist*, Feb. 1976; Sheldon N. Sandler, "Negotiated Prepaid Legal Services Plans: Past, Present and Future," *LLJ*, May 1976; Neil T. Shayne, *Prepaid Legal Services*, An AMA Management Briefing (New York: AMA, 1974).

leisure Defined by Moore and Hedges as "time free of the necessity to earn a living." They state that "current definitions of leisure use work as the reference point. That is, leisure time or leisure activities are contrasted, implicitly or directly, with worktime or productive activities. . . . To some they [the perimeters of modern leisure] encompass nonworking time, to others, only time that is free of all commitments."

Henle finds that "leisure time is not defined simply as time away from work because, in an economic sense, leisure has little meaning unless it represents paid time taken voluntarily."

Leisure has been increased by reductions in the average workweek, longer vacations, more holidays, and greater opportunities for part-time work, educational activity, and early retirement.

Source references: Fred Best, "Preferences on Worklife Scheduling and Work-Leisure Tradeoffs," *MLR*, June 1978; Peter Henle, "Leisure and the Long Workweek," *MLR*, July 1966; David M. Maklan, *The Four-Day Workweek; Blue Collar Adjustment to a Nonconventional Arrangement of Work and Leisure Time* (New York: Praeger, 1977); Margaret Mead, *The Changing Cultural Patterns of Work and Leisure* (Washington: U.S. Dept. of Labor, Manpower Admin., Seminar on Manpower Policy and Program, 1966); Geoffrey H. Moore and Janice Neipert Hedges, "Trends in Labor and Leisure," *MLR*, Feb. 1971; John D. Owen, "Workweeks and Leisure: An Analysis of Trends, 1948–75," *MLR*, Aug. 1976; Harold L. Wilensky, "Impact on Change on Work and Leisure," *MLR*, Sept. 1967.

Leisy v. Hardin A decision of the Supreme Court in 1890 holding that a state may not prevent the shipment in or exclusion of legitimate articles of commerce under the guise of an inspection law or under the cover of police power in order to regulate commerce.

Source reference: Leisy v. Hardin, 135 US 100 (1890).

Leitch plan A form of representative government designed to establish industrial democracy. It was developed by John Leitch and discussed in his book, *Man to Man: The Story of Industrial Democracy*, published by Forbes in New York in 1919. The plan is designed to approximate the three representative bodies of the United States, namely a house, a senate, and a cabinet. Presumably the cabinet would be the equivalent of the executive. In actuality the only elected group was the house since the senate was appointed by the management and consisted of minor executives, department heads, and foremen; and the cabinet consisted of the executive officers of the company, with the company president as the chairman. Although there were many variations of the Leitch Plan, in essence, the plans provided the senate as well as the cabinet with veto power, since it required passage by both houses and approval by the cabinet before any action could be put into effect. There was no possibility under the Leitch Plan for overruling the veto of the cabinet.

Some refer to the Leitch Plan as another form of company unionism, which appeared particularly in the 1920s.

John Leitch in his own book claimed a number of contributions which this plan made to industrial democracy in plants with which he was familiar. Among these were a decline in cost of production, increase in the volume of production, a decrease in labor turnover, a reputation in the community that the company was a good company to work for, which made hiring easier, and also an immunity from strikes and other labor troubles. At the time Section 7(a) of the National Labor Relations Act was put into effect in 1933, only seven such plans were reported in existence and by the time the Act was held constitutional in 1937, most of these had been discontinued.

Source references: Paul F. Gemmill, *Present Day Labor Relations: A Critical Examination of Methods of Collective Negotiations Between Employer and Employees* (New York: Wiley, 1929); John Leitch, *Man to Man: The Story of Industrial Democracy* (New York: Forbes & Sons Publishing, 1919).

length of service The period of a person's continuous service with a particular company. Its computation usually runs from the date the individual is placed on the payroll to the time the actual length of service is computed. Computation usually is for the purpose of determining the individual's benefits and rights under the terms of the collective bargaining contract, where such an agreement exists between the employer and the union, or where such benefits accrue to the individual because of the company's policy or practices.

Length of service may be determined for various purposes and on a companywide, plantwide, departmental, or occupational basis. It will depend upon agreement between the company and union, or on practice.

Some agreements provide for breaks in service resulting from absenteeism without reasonable excuse or other violation of company policy or agreement.

Length of service or seniority consideration has been developed for various reasons; among the ones generally listed are elimination of favoritism and bias in determining layoffs, hiring, or promotion. It is also designed to prevent discrimination against union members as well as to afford greater security and protection for individuals who have been with a company for a long time.

Source references: Frederic Meyers, "The Analytic Meaning of Seniority," *Proceedings of the 18th A/M, IRRA*, ed. by Gerald Somers (Madison: 1966); C. Wilson Randle, "The Pros and Cons of Seniority," *Unions, Management and the Public*, ed. by E. Wight Bakke, Clark Kerr, and Charles W. Anrod (3d ed., New York: Harcourt, Brace, 1967).

See also LAYOFF, PROMOTION, SENIORITY, TRANSFER.

length-of-service increases These generally are automatic adjustments in wages given periodically for satisfactory performance. They may be in the form of a graduated wage rate, an extra bonus, or a percentage added to the base or to the regular earnings. The wage or bonus is determined by and based on longevity in actual service.

The term is also applied occasionally to automatic wage increases given to apprentices, trainees, or learners.

Letter Carriers; National Association of (AFL-CIO) Union organized in Boston in 1889. During the early years of its existence there was widespread conflict between letter carriers in the Knights of Labor and those not in the Knights.

With the decline of the Knights of Labor most of the letter carrier groups joined ranks and were incorporated into the National Association of Letter Carriers. The organization stayed independent until 1907, when it joined the AFL. The pressure for joining was due to the chartering of the National Federation of Postal Employees by the AFL, which also gave them jurisdiction over the postal service. This jurisdiction was turned over to the National Association of Letter Carriers once it joined the AFL. The union was once known as the National Association of Letter Carriers of the United States of America.

Its official publications are *The Postal Record* (monthly), *NALC Bulletin* (biweekly), and *Capitol Notes* (quarterly).

Address: 100 Indiana Ave., N.W., Washington, D.C. 20001. Tel. (202) 393–4695

Source references: William C. Doherty, *Mailman, U.S.A.* (New York: David McKay Co., 1960); Miles E. Hoffman, *National Association of Letter Carriers of the United States of America, AFL-CIO: Development, Structure, Functions* (Philadelphia: National Assn. of Letter Carriers, 1963); Sterling D. Spero, *Government as Employer* (New York: Remsen Press, 1948); ———, *The Labor Movement in a Government Industry: A Study of Employee Organization in the Postal Service* (New York: Durand, 1924).

Letter Carriers' Association; National Rural (Ind) Organized in Chicago in 1903. At one time it contained more than 60 percent of all of the rural mail carriers. With the sale of the *R.F.D. News* its key publication, dissension set in and in 1920 led to the formation of the National Federation of Rural Letter Carriers, which affiliated with the AFL.

Its official weekly publication is the *National Rural Letter Carrier.*

Address: Suite 100, 1448 Duke St., Alexandria, Va. 22314. Tel. (703) 684–5545

leveling Sometimes referred to as performance rating. A procedure in motion and time study used to evaluate an individual operator's or worker's time, to determine expected output. The output, however, should be that of an average qualified worker. Stopwatch studies are made of the actual time it takes an individual worker to perform the specific operational elements. The actual time readings in motion and time study do not indicate whether the worker is producing more or less than an average worker. It is therefore necessary to make adjustments to determine the time required by an average worker. The technique of adjusting these individual differences is called performance rating or leveling. This time, not the actual time, is a theoretical time during which a qualified worker completes a job under standardized conditions.

There are many methods of performance rating but one which is frequently used consists of four leveling factors. These are (1) skill, (2) effort, (3) physical conditions, and (4) consistency.

In addition, some time is allowed for factors which may not be involved in the actual job performance. These allowances may include (1) delay, (2) fatigue, and (3) personal allowances.

Source references: Stuart M. Lowry, Harold B. Maynard, and G. J. Stegmerton, *Time and Motion Study and Formulas for Wage Incentives* (3d ed., New York: McGraw-Hill, 1940); United Automobile Workers, *The UAW–CIO Looks at Time Study* (Detroit: Pub. no. 146, 1947); *U.E. Guide to Wage Payment Plans, Time Study, and Job Evaluation* (New York: The Workers, 1943); Herbert G. Zollitsch and Adolph Langsner, *Wage and Salary Administration* (2d ed., Cincinnati: South-Western, 1970).

See also ALLOWED TIME, TIME AND MOTION STUDY.

level premium funding A procedure whereby all or part of pension costs are funded by equal payments during the worker's or the individual's working years under a retirement plan. It may be level as to the number of dollars or level as to the percentage of the worker's earnings.

See also FUNDED PENSION PLAN, PENSION PLAN.

Levering and Garriques Co. v. Morrin A case which upheld the constitutionality of the Norris-LaGuardia Act. Paul Morrin and others, who were members of the International Association of Bridge, Structural and Ornamental Iron Workers, attempted to establish a closed shop by notifying general contractors and architects of the intention of the members of the union to refuse to work. An injunction was obtained, the decree which granted the injunction was reversed, and when the case came up on appeal to the circuit court, the Norris-LaGuardia Act was held valid.

When the case came before the Supreme Court, the Court refused certiorari, which left the circuit court decision standing.

Source references: Levering and Garriques Co. v. Morrin, 287 US 590 (1932); 289 US 103 (1933); 293 US 595 (1934).

Libbey-Owens-Ford case A decision of the NLRB in April 1941, in which the Board in a bargaining unit decision approved a plant unit. The Board held in favor of a bargaining unit of a single plant unless all the plants of the company were unionized.

Prior to the *Libbey-Owens-Ford* decision, the Board most frequently chose the employer unit, if the union had majorities in most of the plants of the company. This policy was best illustrated in the *Pittsburgh Plate Glass* decision.

Source reference: In the Matter of Libbey-Owens-Ford Glass Co., 31 NLRB 243, 8 LRRM 135 (1941).

See also PITTSBURGH PLATE GLASS CASE.

Licensed Practical Nurses; National Federation of (Ind) Established in 1949. It issues the monthly *Journal of Nursing Care.*

Address: Box 11038, 214 S. Driver St., Durham, N.C. 27703. Tel. (919) 596–9609

life annuity An insurance policy which provides an annual income for the individual beginning at his retirement and continuing for the duration of the individual's life.

See also ANNUITY.

life expectancy An actuarial computation used in the determination of insurance costs which sets out the average number of years a group of individuals is likely to survive after a given age.

See also ACTUARY, MORTALITY TABLE.

lifetime employment system Japanese employment practice, also known as permanent employment, lifetime commitment, and career employment, under which the employer provides workers with security throughout their working lives; in turn, the workers offer unlimited commitment and loyalty to their employer. Employees are recruited upon graduation from high school and qualify as regular or permanent employees after a period of probation. They are expected to stay with the company until they reach company retirement age, usually between 55 and 60 years of age. There is no legal obligation for an employee to stay with a company for more than a year, and the company is not obligated to keep an employee. There are no written contracts guaranteeing lifetime employment. However, employers are not expected to dismiss regular employees, except for grave misconduct or for unusual decline in business.

Approximately one-third of the total non-agricultural employment in Japan is covered by lifetime employment practice according to Levine.

Source references: Robert E. Cole, *Japanese Blue Collar* (Berkeley: UC Press, 1971); Tadashi Hanami, *Labor Relations in Japan Today* (Tokyo: Kodansha Int., 1979); Solomon Levine, "Japanese Industrial Relations: What Can We Import?" *NYU 36th Annual National Conference on Labor,* ed. by Richard Adelman (New York: Bender, 1983); Kazuo Okochi, Bernard Karsh, and Solomon B. Levine (ed.), *Workers and Employers in Japan* (Princeton: Princeton UP and Univ. of Tokyo Press, 1974); Taishiro Shirai (ed.), *Contemporary Industrial Relations in Japan* (Madison: Univ. of Wisconsin Press, 1983).

See also ENTERPRISE UNIONISM, SENIORITY WAGE SYSTEM.

limitation of apprentices A procedure much utilized prior to 1900 as a method of limiting union membership by requiring the individual to receive a prolonged training in order to qualify for the trade. In addition the union, frequently by agreement with employers, would set a fixed ratio of apprentices to journeymen, and thereby create a scarcity of workers in the particular trade. This secured, for some, high wages and reasonably secure employment.

With increasing mechanization, however, this procedure has been greatly reduced, although many trades still place limits on the number of apprentices in order to satisfy or protect the unions' rights. The most frequently used methods of restricting the number of apprentices are (1) requiring a minimum number of years for apprenticeship,

(2) restricting the number of apprentices to be admitted into the trade, and (3) controlling actual wages paid to apprentices.

Source reference: Sumner H. Slichter, *Union Policies and Industrial Management* (Washington: Brookings Institution, 1941).

See also APPRENTICESHIP, APPRENTICESHIP COMMITTEE.

limitation of membership A procedure used by some unions to keep the number of union members relatively small. This was particularly true of unions which had in addition to a closed shop, a closed union. The effect of this was to provide a highly restricted number of individuals to perform the particular work and automatically bar newcomers. Since the Taft-Hartley Act, the closed shop is illegal in interstate commerce, and the practice of limiting union membership through excessive initiation fees has substantially declined.

See also RESTRICTION OF MEMBERSHIP.

limitation of output The phrase generally is applied to actions by unions limiting the number of items produced in a particular period of time by maintaining a standard substantially lower than is normally possible. It may be accomplished through the use of various types of tools which limit the actual amount to be produced, for example, the limitation on the width of a paint brush or the imposition of a fixed standard of production, as by limiting the number of bricks an individual is permitted to set in a particular period of time.

Union objectives, among others, may be to provide a maximum number of job opportunities for the individual in the plant or for the union; it may be designed also to protect the job rates of the organized employees; and it also may be set up to protect the individual's health and safety by prohibition of unnecessary speed-up and health or safety hazards that might arise in the handling of certain types of materials.

The criticism of limitations of output has been largely aimed at the practices where no social purpose is attained and where an individual is soldiering on the job.

See also FEATHERBEDDING, RESTRICTION OF OUTPUT, SLOWDOWN, SOLDIERING, WORK RULES.

limited union recognition A form of recognition which encompasses recognition for members only. Under the provisions of the National Labor Relations Act, a union which represents a majority of the employees is recognized as the bargaining agent for all the employees and cannot be limited to recognition for members only. On the other hand, it is possible in intrastate commerce, where there is no state labor relations act providing for majority rule, to have a form of union recognition which is limited in nature. It is, of course, also possible for unions to accept limited recognition in those areas where they have not sought the representation machinery of the National Labor Relations Act.

Under Executive Order 11491 and subsequently under the Civil Service Reform Act of 1978, in setting up procedures for representation of government employees, formal and informal recognition were abolished. Elections are required in all cases to determine exclusive recognition of a bargaining agent.

See also CIVIL SERVICE REFORM ACT OF 1978, EXECUTIVE ORDER 10988, EXECUTIVE ORDER 11491.

Lincoln Electric incentive cash bonus One of the most famous incentive profit sharing distribution plans is that of the Lincoln Electric Company of Cleveland, Ohio. The Lincoln Incentive System, which has been in operation since 1935, is used by the company in addition to a standard hour-type incentive plan and has provided year-end bonuses ranging from a total of 20 percent to 128 percent of the employees' annual wages.

At the end of the year, a percentage of the company's profits is paid to stockholders as a dividend. After the dividend is provided for, the directors of the company determine an amount of money to be reinvested in the company. After these deductions have been made, the remaining balance of profits is divided as a bonus among workers and management. The amount of the bonus distributed to each employee, plus employee promotion, is based upon each employee's contribution to the success of the company during the year. That individual contribution is determined by performance appraisals made three times per year.

Source references: James F. Lincoln, *Incentive Management* (Cleveland: Lincoln Electric Company, 1951); ———, *Incentive Management: A New Approach to Human Relations in Industry and Business* (Cleveland: Lincoln Electric Company, 1957); ———, *Lincoln's Incentive System* (Cleveland: Lincoln Electric Company, 1951).

See also KAISER STEEL LONG-RANGE SHARING PLAN, SCANLON PLAN.

Lincoln Mills case A major decision of the Supreme Court dealing with the question of arbitration and its importance in national labor policy. In this case the Supreme Court held that the arbitration clause is the quid pro quo given by the employer in return for the no-strike clause agreed to by the union.

Source references: Textile Workers v. Lincoln Mills, 353 US 448, 40 LRRM 2113 (1957); Benjamin Aaron, "On First Looking Into the Lincoln Mills Decision," *Arbitration and the Law,* Proceedings of the 12th A/M, NAA, ed. by Jean McKelvey (Washington: BNA, 1959); Archibald Cox, "Reflections Upon Labor Arbitration in the Light of the Lincoln Mills Case," *Arbitration and the Law,* Proceedings of the 12th A/M, NAA, ed. by Jean McKelvey (Washington: BNA, 1959); William J. Isaacson, "Lincoln Mills Revisited: Caution, Judges Inventing," *NYU 12th Annual Conference on Labor,* ed. by Emanuel Stein (Albany: Bender, 1959); Saul G. Kramer, "In the Wake of Lincoln Mills," *LLJ,* Nov. 1958; Doug Riggs, "Lincoln Mills; Its Impact on Labor Arbitration," *Industrial and Labor Relations Forum,* Nov. 1967.

See also SUITS FOR CONTRACT VIOLATION.

line organization Applies to the section or portions of the structure of a company in which there is a definite sequence of rank or authority which flows from the president or head of the company through the various levels of responsibility down to department heads, foremen, and rank and file employees. The form of the line organization structure is usually that of a pyramid, with the president at the apex and various layers of subordinates down to the basic unit of workers.

Staff organization on the other hand is generally a delegated authority, of a limited nature, to service, advise, audit, and occasionally to control the actions of the line organization in the performance of specific functions.

See also MIDDLE MANAGEMENT, MULTIPLE MANAGEMENT.

liquidated damages Damages, agreed to in advance, in respect to their amount in the event of a breach of agreement. This in effect constitutes a predetermined estimate and covenant as to the extent of the damages and also avoids the necessity of taking the issue to a court or to a third party for subsequent determination. Liquidated damages, in effect, constitute payment in lieu of actual performance.

Lithographers and Photoengravers International Union (AFL-CIO) The merged organization of the Amalgamated Lithographers of America (Ind) and the International Photo-Engravers' Union of North America (AFL-CIO). The merger became effective September 7, 1964.

In September 1972, the union merged with the International Brotherhood of Bookbinders (AFL-CIO) to form the Graphic Arts International Union (AFL-CIO).

See also GRAPHIC ARTS INTERNATIONAL UNION (AFL-CIO).

Lithographers of America; Amalgamated (Ind) The union was organized in 1883 as the Lithographers' Protective and Insurance Association. In 1896, the name was changed to the Lithographers' International Protective and Beneficial Association under which name it received its charter from the AFL in 1906.

In 1915, the Lithographers' International Protective and Beneficial Association, the International Union of Lithographic Workmen, and the Lithographic Stone and Plate Preparers amalgamated into one organization, the Amalgamated Lithographers of America. With development of the offset press, a serious jurisdictional dispute arose within the AFL which involved the Lithographers, the International Printing Pressmen and Assistants' Union, and the International Photo-Engravers' Union. The Printing Pressmen claimed that their jurisdiction covered all press work and that pressmen in the Lithographers Union running offset presses should be transferred to the Pressmen's Union. The International Photo-

Engravers' Union claimed that the lithographers making offset plates were doing the work which was within its jurisdiction.

In 1918, the AFL Executive Council brought in a report giving the Pressmen's Union full jurisdiction over the offset press and the lithographic pressmen, and giving the International Photo-Engravers' Union jurisdiction over other workers in lithographic processes. In 1918, the Lithographers absorbed the Lithographic Press Feeders and Apprentices' Association, which had been suspended from the AFL in 1914.

On September 7, 1964, the Lithographers and Photoengravers voted to merge and formed the Lithographers and Photoengravers International Union (AFL-CIO).

Source references: Henry E. Hoagland, *Collective Bargaining in the Lithographic Industry* (New York: Columbia UP, 1917); Fred C. Munson, *Labor Relations in the Lithographic Industry* (Cambridge: Harvard UP, 1963).

See also LITHOGRAPHERS AND PHOTOENGRAVERS INTERNATIONAL UNION (AFL-CIO).

little steel The phrase is used to distinguish such smaller companies as Bethlehem, Republic, Inland, Youngstown Sheet and Tube, Jones & Laughlin, and others from the U.S. Steel Corporation.

When U.S. Steel recognized the Steel Workers Organizing Committee (CIO), the union still had to obtain recognition from the "little steel" companies and a major strike occurred in 1937.

Source references: Robert R. Brooks, *As Steel Goes—Unionism in a Basic Industry* (New Haven: Yale UP, 1940); Vincent D. Sweeney, *United Steel Workers of America—The First Ten Years* (Pittsburgh: United Steelworkers, 1946); ———, *United Steelworkers of America: Twenty Years Later, 1936–1956* (Pittsburgh: United Steelworkers, 1956).

See also MOHAWK VALLEY FORMULA.

little steel formula The little steel formula was a statement of wage policy adopted by the National War Labor Board on July 16, 1942, which applied to the companies known as the little steel companies. The formula attempted to establish the wage stabilization policy of the National War Labor Board and at the same time to correct inequalities. President Roosevelt in his message to Congress of April 27, 1942, stated in part, "Wages in general can and should be kept at existing scales . . . giving due consideration to inequalities and the elimination of substandards of living."

George W. Taylor wrote the majority opinion of the Board on the wage issue involving the "formula," which he stated as follows:

> (1) For the period from January 1, 1941 to May 1942 which followed a long period of relative stability, the cost of living increased by about 15 percent. If any group of workers averaged less than a 15 percent increase in hourly wage rates during, or immediately preceding or following, this period, their established peacetime standards have been broken. If any group of workers averaged a 15 percent wage increase or more their established peacetime standards have been preserved.
>
> (2) Any claims for wage adjustments for the groups whose peacetime standards have been preserved can only be considered in terms of the inequalities or of the substandard conditions specifically referred to in the President's message of April 27, 1942.
>
> (3) Those groups whose peacetime standards have been broken are entitled to have these standards reestablished as a stabilization factor. . . .
>
> We are convinced that the yardsticks of wage stabilization thus applied are fair and equitable and at the same time sufficient to prevent the cost of living from spiraling upward because of wage adjustments. We think they lead to a "terminal" for the tragic race between wages and prices.

Source references: "Little Steel Companies," 1 *WLR* 325; U.S. National War Labor Board, *Wage Report to the President on the Wartime Relationship of Wages to the Cost of Living* (Washington: 1945).

See also HOLD-THE-LINE ORDER, SOUND AND TESTED RATES.

little Wagner acts *See* BABY WAGNER ACTS.

little War Labor Board The phrase occasionally applied to the regional War Labor Boards which were established by the National War Labor Board in decentralizing and providing greater opportunity for the handling of both wage adjustments and disputes under the National War Labor Board.

Provision was made for appeal to the national board. The national board also retained jurisdiction over those cases which involved broad national policy.

living wage The concept of a living wage appears regularly in labor literature and also in the determination of wage policy. This was true of the War Labor Board during World War I. It is also a central concept in the handling of wage problems in countries which have compulsory arbitration. The term originally was defined as equivalent to the "subsistence wage" or a wage barely sufficient to permit the individual to stay alive.

The broadening of the concept of a living wage to incorporate more than subsistence developed over a period of time on the insistence of workers as well as the public toward the concept of living standards which began to include reasonable needs and comforts. It is now generally considered to be a wage which will provide the basic minimum needs, such as food, clothing, and shelter, as well as a reasonable income to take care of minimum health, recreation, education, and similar factors which have become common in the general community.

The concept of a wage sufficient to take care of minimum health, recreational, and educational needs will tend to be flexible, since there is a constant development in standards.

See also SUBSISTENCE WAGE.

Lloyd-LaFollette Act of 1912 Federal law enacted to nullify the Roosevelt and Taft gag orders by affirming "the right of persons employed in the civil service of the United States either individually or collectively to petition Congress or any member thereof or to furnish information to either House of Congress, or to any committee or member thereof. . . ." The Act specifically guaranteed the right of postal employees to belong to labor organizations. It also established safeguards against removals for organization activity.

Source reference: Murray B. Nesbitt, *Labor Relations in the Federal Government Service* (Washington: BNA, 1976).

See also GAG ORDERS.

lobster shift Sometimes referred to as the "graveyard shift," the "midnight shift," or the "third shift" (night shift). On a three-shift operation, the regular morning or day shift is known as the first shift; the afternoon, the second shift; and the night, graveyard, or lobster shift is the third shift. Although the time is not fixed it generally begins somewhere around midnight and ends in the early morning hours. It may, for example, be a shift from 11 p.m. to 7 a.m. or from 12 midnight to 8 a.m.

See also GRAVEYARD SHIFT, SHIFT DIFFERENTIAL.

local *See* LOCAL UNION.

local independent union Applies generally to a local union, that is, one which is confined to a single plant or to a small geographic area and which is not affiliated with a national or international union.

See also INDEPENDENT UNIONS.

local industrial union A local union which was directly affiliated with the CIO. These industrial unions were the building blocks for additional organization, particularly where no national or international union covering those employees had been chartered or was in existence. The structure of the local industrial union was similar to the federal labor unions which were not part of or attached to any of the national or international unions within the AFL but chartered by the AFL.

See also FEDERAL LABOR UNIONS.

local lodge This is the same as the "local union." In some unions, such as the Machinists and some railway unions, the term "lodge" is used.

See also SISTER LODGE (LOCAL).

local strike A term not in general use which refers to the existence of a strike which is limited to a single community, to a single plant, or to a small locality.

local union The basic unit of labor organization in the United States. The term generally applies to a single plant unit or a small geographical unit. The craft locals, such as those of electricians, plumbers, and carpenters, may be consolidated by locality or region, whereas the industrial locals may be established within a company or plant. In either case, the local union is generally the basic unit for all of the national and international unions, and it is chartered by the international and affiliated with it. Although local unions have their own structure, including the officers, a constitution and bylaws, and in large locals a newspaper and other services, in most industries they are reasonably well integrated within the national organization, which provides research and other leadership facilities to permit the locals to function more effectively. Where bargaining takes place on a regional or national level, the local unions operate through various coordinating committees in order to have a part in the process and a close relationship with the international union.

In some organizations, the large locals have a fairly important role to play in the international and because of their large membership may be able to control a large bloc of votes during the national conventions.

One of the major problems in labor union development has been the difficulty in maintaining adequate interest in the operation of the local union since there is a tendency to centralize authority and responsibility at regional and national levels. A great deal of the work of the national union obviously must take place in the local union. This is particularly true in the handling of grievances, the election of shop stewards, and the day-to-day operation in the plant.

Source references: William Isaacson, Jr., "The Local Union and the International," *NYU 3d Annual Conference on Labor,* ed. by Emanuel Stein (Albany: Bender, 1950); Florence Peterson, *American Labor Unions, What They Are and How They Work* (2d ed., New York: Harper, 1963); Leonard Sayles and George Strauss, *The Local Union: Its Place in the Industrial Plant* (rev. ed., New York: Harcourt, Brace, 1967); ———, "The Local Union Meeting," *ILRR,* Jan. 1953; Joel Seidman, Jack London, and Bernard Karsh, "Leadership in a Local Union," *American Journal of Sociology,* Nov. 1950; Leo Troy, *Management and the Local Independent Union* (New York: Industrial Relations Counselors, Inc., IR Memo no. 145, 1966).

local union election appeals The Labor-Management Reporting and Disclosure Act (LMRDA) sets the standards for handling of union elections. The law provides machinery to permit a union member to file a complaint with the secretary of labor for violation of union procedures or minimum standards of the LMRDA. The law requires that a complainant exhaust remedies available within the union prior to filing a complaint with the secretary of labor. The law also provides that if no final decision is given by the national union under the existing regulations and constitution within a three-month period, the individual may appeal directly to the secretary of labor.

Section 402 provides:

(a) A member of a labor organization—
(1) who has exhausted the remedies available under the constitution and bylaws of such organization and of any parent body, or
(2) who has invoked such available remedies without obtaining a final decision within three calendar months after their invocation, may file a complaint with the Secretary within one calendar month thereafter alleging the violation of any provision of section 401 (including violation of the constitution and bylaws of the labor organization pertaining to the election and removal of officers).

The Office of Labor-Management Standards Enforcement reported that 293 criminal and civil investigations involving union elections were completed during fiscal year 1982.

Source references: U.S. Dept. of Labor, *United States Department of Labor Seventieth Annual Report, Fiscal Year 1982* (Washington: 1983); U.S. Dept. of Labor, LMSA, *Electing Union Officers* (Washington: 1980); ———, *Local Union Election Appeals* (Washington: 1966); ———, *Union Officer Election and Trusteeships Case Digest* (Washington: 1980).

location of industry A company's decision of where to locate a new plant depends upon many factors including availability and cost of land; tax considerations; transportation facilities; proximity of the new plant to the markets it will serve; acceptance by the community; facilities provided by the community; availability of labor in the location community in terms of age, education, skills possessed; and the balance in the community between the cost of living and the cost of labor. In the United States between 1947 and 1958, there was a substantial decline in the percentage share of manufacturing firms located in the principal cities and a rise in the firms located in the suburbs. In recent years, the South and Southwest have become attractive regions for industrial location.

Source references: Robert J. Atkins and Richard H. Shriver, "New Approach to Facilities Location," *Harvard BR*, May/June 1968; The Conference Board, *Factors in Corporate Locational Decisions* (New York: Information Bull no. 66, 1979); ———, *Urban Plant Siting* (New York: Research Bull no. 123, 1982); William C. Freund, "Business and the North: Whose Responsibility to Stem Decline?" *Management Review*, March 1978; Victor R. Fuchs, *Changes in the Location of Manufacturing in the United States Since 1929* (New Haven: Yale UP, 1962); Maurice Fulton, "New Factors in Plant Location," *Harvard BR*, May/June 1971; Michael F. McCormick, "Locating New Plants in Rural Communities," *LLJ*, Aug. 1969; Laurence G. O'Donnell, "Why Companies Move Back to Town," *Management Review*, Oct. 1961; J. Roger O'Meara, *Corporate Moves to the Suburbs: Problems and Opportunities* (New York: The Conference Board, Report no. 564, 1972); Roger W. Schmenner, "Looking Beyond the Obvious in Plant Location," *Harvard BR*, Jan./Feb. 1969; Robert B. Stobaugh, Jr., "Where in the World Should We Put That Plant?" *Harvard BR*, Jan./Feb. 1969; Keith Wheelock, "Office Relocations in the 1980s," *Personnel*, Sept./Oct. 1979.

Lochner v. New York A case in which the Supreme Court reviewed Article 8, Chapter 415 of the Laws of 1897 of New York state. The statute provided that "no employee (in a bakery) shall be required or permitted to work in excess of 60 hours during a week or 10 hours in any day." Justice Peckham in his opinion said that in the Court's judgment there was no reasonable foundation for holding that this legislation was necessary or appropriate as a health measure, to safeguard the public health or the health of individuals following the occupation of baker.

The Court regarded the action of New York as a meddlesome interference in the protection of the rights of individuals to earn a living. The Court said, in part:

> The statute necessarily interferes with the right of contract between the employer and employees concerning the number of hours in which the latter may labor in the bakery of the employer. The general right to make a contract in relation to his business is part of the liberty of the individual protected by the Fourteenth Amendment. . . . Under that provision no state can deprive any person of life, liberty, or property without due process of law. The right to purchase or to sell labor is part of the liberty protected by this amendment, unless there are circumstances which exclude the right.

On the question of the police powers and the extent to which these are in conflict with the federal powers, the Court said no specific showing was made by the statute or by New York state as to the necessity for such protection under the police powers. The Court said:

> There is no contention that bakers as a class are not equal in intelligence and capacity to men in other trades or manual occupations, or that they are not able to assert their rights and care for themselves without the protecting arm of the state interfering with their independence of judgment and of action. They are in no sense wards of the State. . . . It seems to us that the real object and purpose were simply to regulate the hours of labor between the master and his employees . . . in a private business, not dangerous in any degree to morals or in any real and substantial degree, to the health of the employees. Under such circumstances the freedom of master and employee to contract with each other in relation to their employment, and in defining the same, cannot be prohibited or interfered with, without violating the Federal Constitution. The judgment of the Court of Appeals of New York . . . must be reversed. . . .

Source references: Lochner v. New York, 198 US 45 (1905); *United States v. Hirsch*, 25 US 539 (1879); 49 *Law Edition* 937.

lockout The lockout is the employer's side of the economic pressure when the parties are unable to resolve their problems in negotiations or agree on the terms or conditions of employment. The strike is the union's last resort; the lockout is the employer's. The lockout generally implies the temporary withholding of work, by means of shutting down the operation or plant, from a group of workers in order to bring pressure on them to accept the employer's terms. There is great difficulty in classifying a situation as a strike or lockout since it depends upon determination of who, the union or the employer, is the initiator of the work stoppage.

In the strike statistics maintained by the U.S. Department of Labor, the term "work stoppages" brings both strikes and lockouts into the picture. In current disputes, strikes occur more frequently.

Provocation by the employer is also extremely difficult to determine. The union frequently argues the existence of a lockout to place responsibility for the work stoppage on the employer themselves. The public frequently sees only the union doing the picketing and taking the overt action and so places the responsibility for the work stoppage on the union.

Source references: American Shipbuilding Co. v. NLRB, 380 US 300, 58 LRRM 2672 (1965); *Delhi-Taylor Refining Division and the Oil, Chemical and Atomic Workers International Union (AFL-CIO)*, 167 NLRB No. 8, 65 LRRM 1744 (1967); Milton C. Denbo, "Is the Lockout the Corollary of the Strike?" *LLJ*, May 1963; Frederic Freilichter, "The Supportive Lockout," *Syracuse LR*, Spring 1968; Robert F. Koretz, "Legality of the Lockout," *Syracuse LR*, Spring 1953; Willard A. Lewis, "The 'Lockout as Corollary of Strike' Controversy Reexamined," *LLJ*, Nov. 1972; ———, "Lockout—The Other Dimension," *MLR*, August 1967; Robert S. Musa, "Lockouts and Replacements in Bargaining—Management on the Offensive," *IR Law Digest*, Summer 1976; Sylvester Petro, "The National Labor Relations Act and Lockouts," *LLJ*, Oct. 1952; N. M. Spindelman and W. K. Davenport, "Legality of Employers Use of Lockout," *Michigan LR*, Jan. 1953.

See also NATIONAL EMERGENCY DISPUTES, NO-LOCKOUT CLAUSE, STRIKE, WORK STOPPAGE STATISTICS.

Lockwood Committee inquiry An investigation in New York in the early 1920s disclosing collusion between business agents and employers in the building trades.

Source reference: New York State Legislature, Joint Committee on Housing, *Final Report of the Joint Legislative Committee on Housing*, Legislative Document, No. 48 (Albany: J. B. Lyon, Printers, 1923).

Locomotive Engineers; Brotherhood of (Ind) The earliest organization of railroad engineers was convened in Baltimore, Maryland, on November 6, 1855. The convention was attended by 70 delegates representing 14 states and 55 railroads. The association formed at that convention was known as the National Protective Association of the United States and remained in existence for only one year. Another organization was established at a meeting held in March 1862 when 12 engineers established Division No. 1 of the Brotherhood of the Footboard in Detroit. There were 54 divisions at the time of its second annual meeting in August 1864. At this convention held in Indianapolis the name was changed to the Brotherhood of Locomotive Engineers. Its semimonthly publication is *The Locomotive Engineer*.

Address: Engineers Building, 1365 Ontario St., Room 1108, Cleveland, Ohio 44114. Tel. (216) 241–2630

Source references: William Z. Foster, *Wrecking the Labor Banks: The Collapse of the Labor Banks and Investment Companies of the Brotherhood of Locomotive Engineers* (Chicago: Trade Union Educational League, 1927); Reed C. Richardson, *The Locomotive Engineer, 1863–1963* (Ann Arbor: Univ. of Michigan, Bureau of IR, 1963).

Locomotive Firemen and Enginemen; Brotherhood of (AFL-CIO) The Brotherhood of Locomotive Firemen and Enginemen grew out of a meeting in Port Jervis, New York, on December 1, 1873. It arose following the accidental death of a fireman employed by the Erie Railroad. Joshua A. Leach, the founder of the Brotherhood, organized the friends of the dead man into a fraternal society which became Deer Park Lodge, No. 1, of the Brotherhood of Locomotive Firemen (now known as the Joshua A. Leach Lodge).

On December 15, 1874, the Grand Lodge Convention was held with delegates representing 12 lodges in the five states of New York, New Jersey, Pennsylvania, Ohio, and Indiana. The 1877 railroad strike had a very serious effect on the Brotherhood although it was not involved in the strike. The blacklisting techniques of the railroad companies against union sympathizers resulted in large losses of membership. A second organization of firemen appeared under the name of the

International Firemen's Union, whose approach was more militant than the Brotherhood. A merger was effected in 1878.

Eugene V. Debs, later to leave the Brotherhood to form the American Railway Union, was elected general secretary-treasurer and editor of the Union's first official publication in 1881.

In 1906, the words "and Enginemen" were added to the name of the Brotherhood in recognition of those members who retained their membership in the Firemen's organization after becoming engineers. It affiliated with the AFL-CIO in 1956.

On January 1, 1969, the Locomotive Firemen and Enginemen and three other railroad unions—the Brotherhood of Railroad Trainmen, the Order of Railway Conductors and Brakemen, and the Switchmen's Union of North America—merged to form the United Transportation Union.

Source references: Brotherhood of Locomotive Firemen and Enginemen, *Twenty-Sixth Convention (First Triennial), Fortieth Anniversary, Wash., D.C., 1913* (Indianapolis: Brotherhood of Locomotive Firemen and Enginemen's Magazine, 1913); John A. Hall, *The Great Strike on the "Q," With a History of the Organization and Growth of the Brotherhood of Locomotive Firemen and Switchmen's Mutual Aid Association of North America* (Chicago: Elliot, Beezley, 1889).

See also TRANSPORTATION UNION; UNITED (AFL-CIO).

lodge *See* LOCAL LODGE.

Log Scalers International Union (Ind) Formerly known as the Pacific Log Scalers Association (Ind).

Address: 2300 Cherry St., P.O. Box 292, Aberdeen, Wash. 98520. Tel. (206) 532–3212

longevity pay Wage adjustments based on length of service or seniority. They are frequently made at specified intervals, particularly where the adjustment is in a wage rate range, that is, where a minimum and maximum exist and where the longevity pay is adjusted periodically until the maximum rate for the job is reached. Contracts frequently spell out the procedures for automatic progression and will contain the criteria or consideration for their movements. In some contracts, they may be automatic from the minimum to the mid-point and then based on work performance from the mid-point to the maximum.

See also AUTOMATIC PROGRESSION, MERIT INCREASE.

Longshoremen; International Brotherhood of (AFL-CIO) Established on September 24, 1953, following expulsion of the International Longshoremen's Association by the AFL convention on September 22, 1953. When the ILA affiliated with the AFL-CIO on November 17, 1959, the Brotherhood of Longshoremen merged with the ILA.

See also LONGSHOREMEN'S ASSOCIATION; INTERNATIONAL (AFL-CIO).

Longshoremen's and Harbor Workers' Compensation Act The Act of March 4, 1927, later amended, provides workers compensation benefits for persons in marine employment (except masters and crews of vessels) in U.S. navigable waters. Longshoremen and ship repairmen are the principal employees who receive benefits for accidental injuries and occupational disease arising out of the employment.

Longshoremen's and Warehousemen's Union; International (Ind) Once a semi-autonomous branch of the International Longshoremen's Association (AFL) on the Pacific Coast, the ILWU broke off in 1937 and affiliated with the CIO. The ILWU was later expelled by the CIO for alleged left-wing leadership.

The union represents longshore and warehouse workers on the west coast, and in Hawaii, where it also represents, among others, the workers in sugar, pineapple, and hotel industries. It has 76 locals and a membership of 64,000. It publishes the monthly *The Dispatcher*.

Address: 1188 Franklin St., San Francisco, Calif. 94109. Tel. (415) 775–0533

Source references: William F. Dunne, *The Great San Francisco General Strike; The Story of the West Coast Strike—The Bay Counties' General Strike and the Maritime Workers' Strike* (New York: Workers Library Publishers, 1934); Paul Eliel, *The Waterfront and General Strikes, San Francisco, 1934*

(San Francisco: Hooper Printing, 1934); International Longshoremen's and Warehousemen's Union, *The ILWU Story: Three Decades of Militant Unionism* (2d ed., San Francisco: ILWU Book Club, 1963); Charles P. Larrowe, *Harry Bridges; The Rise and Fall of Radical Labor in the United States* (New York: L. Hill, 1972); Herman Phleger, *Pacific Coast Longshoremen's Strike of 1934* (San Francisco: Waterfront Employers Union of San Francisco, 1934); Philip Ross, "Two Views of the Longshore Situation: Distribution of Power Within the ILWU and the ILA," *MLR*, Jan. 1968; Paul W. Ryan, *The Big Strike* (Olema: Olema Publishing, 1949); ———, *On the Drumhead; A Selection From the Writings of Mike Quin*, ed. by Harry Carlisle (San Francisco: Pacific Publishing Foundation, 1948); Harvey Schwartz, *The March Inland: Origins of the ILWU Warehouse Division, 1934–1938* (Los Angeles: UC, Institute of IR, Monograph Series 19, 1978); Sanford Zalburg, *A Spark is Struck! Jack Hall and the ILWU in Hawaii* (Honolulu: Univ. Press of Hawaii, 1979).

See also WEST COAST LONGSHORE MECHANIZATION AGREEMENT.

Longshoremen's Association; International (AFL-CIO) The International Longshoremen's Association was organized in Detroit, Michigan, in August 1892, as the Lumber Handlers of the Great Lakes. It changed its name in 1893 to the National Longshoremen's Association of the United States, and following its extension and jurisdiction to Canada in 1893 changed its name to the present one.

In 1902 it attempted to extend its jurisdiction to include all marine workers and transport workers. The move ran into difficulty since it was in conflict with the jurisdiction of the International Seamen's Union. The AFL did not recognize the extended jurisdiction and the Longshoremen's Association subsequently reverted to its old jurisdiction. It was expelled by the AFL in 1953 on charges of domination by corrupt influences. In October 1959 it was permitted to affiliate with AFL-CIO, but ILA was put on probation until 1961, subject to expulsion by the AFL-CIO Executive Council if it failed to comply with the federation's directives.

On November 17, 1959, the International Brotherhood of Longshoremen (AFL-CIO) merged with the union. In July 1971, the International Organization of Masters, Mates, and Pilots became the Marine Division of the union.

Its official publication is the *ILA Newsletter*, issued every six weeks.

Address: 17 Battery Pl., Room 1530, New York, N.Y. 10004. Tel. (212) 425–1200

Source references: Charles B. Barnes, *The Longshoremen* (New York: Russell Sage Foundation, 1915); Daniel Bell, "Some Aspects of the New York Longshore Situation," *Proceedings of the 7th A/M, IRRA*, ed. by L. Reed Tripp (Madison: 1955); Malcolm M. Johnson, *Crime on the Labor Front* (New York: McGraw-Hill, 1950); Charles P. Larrowe, *Shape Up and Hiring Hall: A Comparison of Hiring Methods and Labor Relations on the New York and Seattle Waterfronts* (Berkeley: UC Press, 1955); Allen Raymond, *Waterfront Priest (Reverend John M. Corridan)* (New York: Holt, 1955); Philip Ross, "Waterfront Labor Response to Technological Change: A Tale of Two Unions," *LLJ*, July 1970; Edward E. Swanstrom, *The Waterfront Labor Problem* (New York: Fordham UP, 1938).

long-term contract Generally applies to collective bargaining agreements which are negotiated for periods in excess of a year. Many contracts now in effect have duration periods of three to five years. The move toward longer-term contracts in order to establish greater industrial relations stability was recognized by the NLRB in its general ruling extending the contract-bar rule to a three-year period.

Source references: Joseph W. Garbarino, *Wage Policy and Long-Term Contracts* (Washington: Brookings Institution, 1962); James D. Hodgson, "Stretching Out the Duration of Labor Contracts," *MLR*, Sept. 1973; Edward Reighard, *The Long Term Contract in Labor-Management Relations* (Stanford: Stanford Univ., Division of IR, 1954); Jack Stieber, "Evaluation of Long-Term Contracts," *New Dimensions in Collective Bargaining*, ed. by Harold W. Davey, Howard S. Kaltenborn, and Stanley H. Ruttenberg (New York: Harper, IRRA Pub. no. 21, 1959);

Milton C. Taylor, "Representation Proceedings and the New Long-Term Contracts," *LLJ*, July 1952.

See also CONTRACT-BAR RULE.

loose rate Generally applied to incentive or piece rates where the earnings for the employee are not in line with earnings for similar jobs of like requirements. A loose rate may be established as a result of the change in method of work without corresponding adjustment in the incentive, or it may be the result of faulty or improper rate setting, or a rate set with a view to providing a wage adjustment which would not otherwise have been possible. This was true during periods of governmental wage control. Some companies utilized the incentive rate system and timing procedures to permit higher earnings. This was not costly to employers who were on cost-plus contracts. Serious problems, however, arose when the incentive rates were tightened following the end of the war. Adjustments were extremely difficult since employees expected to maintain the earnings which they had obtained under the then existing incentive rates.

Source reference: Van Dusen Kennedy, *Union Policy and Incentive Wage Methods* (New York: Columbia UP, 1945).

See also AUTOMATIC PROGRESSION, INCENTIVE WAGE, RUNAWAY RATE, SENIORITY.

lost time *See* WAITING PERIOD (TIME).

lost time accidents Disabling injuries which result in loss of time beyond the shift or day during which they occur.

See also INDUSTRIAL ACCIDENT.

Lovell case A case involving freedom of the press decided by the Supreme Court in 1938. The Court held that freedom of the press was infringed by a local ordinance of Griffin County, Georgia. The ordinance required permits for the distribution of union organizing leaflets. The Court held that the ordinance could not be held constitutional because it merely related to distribution and not to the publication of the leaflet. It said, in part, "Liberty of circulating is as essential to that freedom as liberty of publishing; indeed, without the circulation, the publication would be of little value."

Source reference: Lovell v. City of Griffin, 303 US 444 (1938).

See also FREEDOM OF SPEECH, HAGUE CASE.

loyal workers The term has been used in industrial relations to describe individuals whose sympathies are more with the employer than with the union. In some cases loyalty is measured by the willingness of the individual to work during a strike period or to assist the employer in combating union organizing efforts.

In its broader sense, loyal workers are those who have the interest of the company at heart. This, however, does not imply that they have less loyalty for their union, which is concerned with obtaining better conditions, wages, hours, and working conditions.

See also ANTI-UNION PRACTICES, DUAL ALLEGIANCE, ESPIONAGE.

Luddites A group of workers in England in the early part of the 19th century who fought the introduction of labor-saving machinery in factories. The origin of the term is attributed to an English workman by the name of Lud, who destroyed a number of special machines known as stocking frames in 1779. Harsh measures were taken by the English government leading to the arrest, imprisonment, and hanging of those guilty for some of the violence and destruction of the machinery.

Poor working conditions, low wages, and mass unemployment led to the outbreaks because the workers felt that the machines were responsible for those conditions.

See also MECHANIZATION, TECHNOLOGICAL UNEMPLOYMENT, WORK RULES.

Ludlow massacre During a coal strike of the United Mine Workers against the Colorado Fuel and Iron Corporation, one of the Rockefeller companies, strikers were evicted from their homes and settled in a tent colony on land adjacent to their homes. Strikebreakers were hired and many were deputized to protect the property. The militia occupied a hill overlooking the tents and on April 20, 1913, fired on one of those colonies. The tents were set on fire, leading to a number of deaths.

Source references: Samuel Yellen, *American Labor Struggles* (New York: Harcourt, Brace, 1936); J. B. S. Hardman, *American*

Labor Dynamics in the Light of Post-War Developments (New York: Harcourt, Brace, 1928).

lump of labor theory A theory which had support at various times, holding that there is just so much labor and work available in any particular period and that in order to protect this amount of labor and to get the benefits from it, workers should reduce the hours of work, set limits on output, and restrict production in such a way that the amount of labor available would be adequately divided to provide for regular employment of the workers. Theoretically, if the amount of work available or to be done is fixed, regardless of the cost of production, workers would be able to obtain more labor income by reducing the number of hours of work, or in other ways reducing or restricting production.

There is not much current interest in or support for the lump of labor theory as such. Union policy is directed so that individuals will have an opportunity to work and receive a wage adequate to maintain a reasonable standard of living. A reduction in the number of hours is one way the unions feel additional employment opportunities can be provided.

See also HOURS OF WORK, SABBATICALS, UNEMPLOYMENT.

lunch period The time generally set aside, frequently by terms of a contract, to give employees the opportunity to have their noonday meal. There are substantial variations in the amount of time allowed and in the practices which provide for overtime compensation when, because of emergency needs, lunch periods are skipped or passed.

See also MEALTIME.

M

MBO *See* MANAGEMENT BY OBJECTIVES (MBO).

MDTA *See* MANPOWER DEVELOPMENT AND TRAINING ACT OF 1962.

MEBA *See* MARINE ENGINEERS' BENEFICIAL ASSOCIATION; NATIONAL (AFL-CIO).

MESA *See* MECHANICS EDUCATIONAL SOCIETY OF AMERICA (AFL-CIO).

MFOW *See* PACIFIC COAST MARINE FIREMEN, OILERS, WATERTENDERS AND WIPERS ASSOCIATION.

MLBPA *See* BASEBALL PLAYERS ASSOCIATION; MAJOR LEAGUE (IND).

MLU *See* UMPIRES ASSOCIATION; MAJOR LEAGUE (IND):

MMP *See* MASTERS, MATES AND PILOTS; INTERNATIONAL ORGANIZATION OF.

MPBP *See* METAL POLISHERS, BUFFERS, PLATERS AND ALLIED WORKERS INTERNATIONAL UNION (AFL-CIO).

MPEA *See* MACHINE PRINTERS AND ENGRAVERS ASSOCIATION OF THE UNITED STATES (IND).

MPPAA *See* MULTIEMPLOYER PENSION PLAN AMENDMENTS ACT (MPPAA) OF 1980.

MSA *See* METROPOLITAN STATISTICAL AREA (MSA).

MSPB *See* MERIT SYSTEMS PROTECTION BOARD (MSPB).

Machine Printers and Engravers Association of the United States (Ind) Formerly known as the Machine Printers' Beneficial Association of the United States (Ind).

Address: 690 Warren Ave., East Providence, R.I. 02914. Tel. (401) 438–5849

Machinists and Aerospace Workers; International Association of (AFL-CIO) The Machinists grew out of an organization originally formed in Atlanta, Georgia, on May 5, 1888, and which was known as the United Machinists and Mechanical Engineers of America. In 1889, a convention was held in Atlanta and the name was changed to the National Association of Machinists with headquarters in Atlanta, Georgia. In 1891, the union assumed the name International Association of Machinists, since it had organized workers in Canada. In 1904 the Machinists absorbed the International Association of Allied Metal Mechanics. Later it brought in the U.S. and Canadian membership of the Amalgamated Society of Engineers, a British union. The union was suspended by the AFL in December 1945, but reaffiliated in 1951.

On September 1, 1956, the International Metal Engravers and Marking Device Workers Union (AFL-CIO) merged with the union.

In November 1964, the membership voted to adopt its present name. Its monthly publication is *The Machinist.*

Address: 1300 Connecticut Ave., N.W., Washington, D.C. 20036. Tel. (202) 857–5200

Source references: Douglas Caddy, *The Hundred Million Dollar Payoff* (New Rochelle, N.Y.: Arlington House, 1974); Fred H. Colvin, *Sixty Years With Men and Machines: An Autobiography in Collaboration with D. J. Duffin* (New York: McGraw-Hill, 1947); George T. Kotrotsios, "IAM Training for Active Participation in Local Lodges," *MLR*, June 1952; John Laslett, *Labor and the Left: A Study of Socialist and Radical Influences in the American Labor Movement, 1881–1924* (New York: Basic Books, 1970); Mark Perlman, *Democracy in the International Association of Machinists* (New York: Wiley, Studies of Comparative Union Governments, 1962); ———, *The*

Machinists: A New Study in American Trade Unionism (Cambridge: Harvard UP, 1961).

MacNamaras During the early part of the 20th century, the relations between the Bridge and Structural Iron Workers and the American Bridge Company became strained. The National Erectors Association, the employer organization, attempted to undermine the union, at least according to the union's position. Sam Parks, John J. MacNamara, the secretary of the union, and his brother J. B. MacNamara, engaged in terrorizing campaigns and dynamiting which ultimately led to the bombing of the Times Building in Los Angeles.

The dynamiting of the Los Angeles Times Building resulted in the loss of some 21 lives. Thirty labor leaders were sentenced to prison. The AFL attempted to exonerate the MacNamaras and the union through a thorough investigation and retained Clarence J. Darrow as chief counsel. Ultimately the blame for the violence rested on the trade union movement when the MacNamaras confessed their guilt.

Source references: William J. Burns, *The Mask War: The Story of a Peril That Threatened the United States by a Man Who Uncovered the Dynamite Conspirators and Sent Them to Jail* (New York: Doran, 1913); Lewis L. Lorwin, *The American Federation of Labor* (Washington: Brookings Institution, 1933); Ortie E. McManigal, *The National Dynamite Plot* (Los Angeles: Neal, 1913).

See also VIOLENCE IN LABOR DISPUTES.

made work Applied generally to attempts by government to provide employment for individuals, who are unemployed or on relief rolls, for the purpose not only of retaining their skills but also to maintain their self respect through the performance of work and services useful to the community.

Among the programs developed in the Depression period, during the Roosevelt administration, were the Works Progress Administration (WPA), the Civilian Conservation Corps (CCC), the Civil Works Administration (CWA), and the Public Works Administration (PWA). The programs of the Civilian Conservation Corps included employment opportunities for young men and helped develop facilities for communities not only for immediate use, but also for long-range public conservation.

Such an approach was deemed preferable to the dole in that such individuals were given an opportunity to utilize their skills. The work, although "made" in the sense that it would normally not have been available, still had substantial usefulness.

See also CIVILIAN CONSERVATION CORPS, DOLE, MAKE-WORK PRACTICES, PUBLIC WORKS ADMINISTRATION (AUTHORITY), WORKS PROGRESS ADMINISTRATION.

Magna Carta A code, document, or other pronouncement which is designed to provide security and protection for the freedoms of groups. The Clayton Anti-trust Act of 1914 was regarded by American labor as a "Magna Carta."

See also CLAYTON ACT OF 1914, NATIONAL LABOR RELATIONS ACT, NORRIS-LAGUARDIA ACT.

mail ballots A procedure for conducting an election by governmental or private (Honest Ballot Association) agencies such as the NLRB or state labor relations boards where the membership of the union is not in a single plant but is geographically distributed.

The procedure for holding such balloting may vary, but generally notice is given to the parties prior to the mailing of the ballots. Ballots are mailed to those individuals legally entitled to vote, with a return envelope setting the date by which the ballot must be returned. Procedures also may be set up whereby the envelopes are checked against the official voting list prepared by the state or federal board, and an opportunity is provided for observers to check the returns. The mail ballots are then counted as any other ballots.

Mailers Union; International (Ind) Formerly located in Denver, Colorado, the union merged with the International Typographical Union (AFL-CIO) on January 1, 1979. It published the monthly *International Mailer* and annual *Convention Review*.

See also TYPOGRAPHICAL UNION; INTERNATIONAL (AFL-CIO).

Maine State Employees Association (Ind) An organization affiliated with the Assembly of Governmental Employees. It issues the monthly *Maine Stater*.

Address: 65 State St., Augusta, Maine 04330. Tel. (207) 622–3151

maintenance of dues A proviso in a union contract which requires the check-off of union dues during the entire period of the agreement. In some cases prior to enactment of the Taft-Hartley law, the maintenance-of-dues proviso would continue the check-off even though the union member withdrew or was expelled from the union. Occasionally the phrase also refers to contracts which provide merely for the individual to maintain dues and does not require actual union membership or good standing in the union during the contract period. (See Section 8(a)(3)(B) of the Taft-Hartley Act.)

See also AGENCY SHOP, CHECK-OFF, MAINTENANCE OF MEMBERSHIP, UNION SECURITY CLAUSES.

maintenance of membership A form of union security devised by the public members of the National War Labor Board during World War II to resolve the conflict between the opposing positions of the labor and industry members of the Board. The labor members urged the extension of the union and closed shop during the war period while the employers sought to limit union security to existing forms, including the open shop. The compromise was designed to protect the security of the union by providing that individuals who were members of the union or who subsequently joined the union would continue to maintain their membership for the duration of the contract. In order to protect the employer position, qualifying language was incorporated providing a 15-day escape period during which time employees were free to decide whether they wanted to remain in the union or to withdraw. This, in part, protected the freedom of choice of the individual employees.

There were many variations to this proviso in National War Labor Board decisions and also many variations following the demise of the War Labor Board.

A maintenance-of-membership clause under a National War Labor Board order might read as follows:

> All employees who, 15 days after the date of the mailing of the regional War Labor Board's directive order in this matter, are members of the union in good standing in accordance with the constitution and bylaws of the union and all employees who thereafter become members shall, as a condition of employment, remain members of the union in good standing for the duration of this contract.

A clause which provided for maintenance of membership for regular employees and a union shop for new employees might read something like this:

> All employees who are now or may hereafter become members of the union shall remain members in good standing during the life of this agreement. New employees must become members of the union within one month from the date of employment.

Following the passage of the Taft-Hartley Act and the outlawing of the closed shop, the union shop became much more frequent for companies engaged in interstate commerce. Maintenance-of-membership clauses also were popular. In actual practice, however, the provisos frequently resulted in the maintenance of union dues because of the language of section 8(a)(3)(B) of the Taft-Hartley Act.

Source references: Frank P. Graham, "Maintenance of Membership: A Historical Note," *LLJ*, August 1955; Bryce M. Stewart and Walter J. Couper, *Maintenance of Union Membership: A Study of Official Cases and Company Experience* (New York: Industrial Relations Counselors, Inc., 1943).

See also ESCAPE CLAUSE, NEW ESCAPE PERIOD, OPEN SHOP, PERCENTAGE SHOP, UNION SECURITY CLAUSES, UNION SHOP.

Maintenance of Way Employes; Brotherhood of (AFL-CIO) The union organized first as the Brotherhood of Railway Section Foremen of North America at LaPorte City, Iowa, in 1886. A southern organization in the same field was formed at Demopolis, Alabama, in 1887. In 1891 these two organizations met in St. Louis, Missouri, and formed the International Brotherhood of Railway Track Foremen of America. The organization was essentially a benevolent society but when it extended its jurisdiction to track laborers in 1896, it became a labor organization and changed its name to the Brotherhood of Railway Trackmen of America.

In 1899, the United Brotherhood of Railroad Trackmen, a Canadian organization founded in 1892, became part of the organization and in 1902 the name of the union was changed to the International Brotherhood of Maintenance of Way Employes. In 1914 a segment of the organization seceded and established a rival union in the southeastern part of the United States. This group reaffiliated in 1918 and the organization adopted the combined name of The United Brotherhood of Maintenance of Way Employes and Railroad Shop Laborers. The 1925 convention of the union shortened the name to the Brotherhood of Maintenance of Way Employes.

Its publications include the monthly *Brotherhood of Maintenance of Way Employes Railway Journal*, the *Scoreboard*, and the biweekly *Labor*.

Address: 12050 Woodward Ave., Detroit, Mich. 48203. Tel. (313) 868–0490

Source references: Brotherhood of Maintenance of Way Employes, *Pictorial History 1877–1951* (Detroit: The Brotherhood, 1952); William Haber et al., *Maintenance of Way Employment on United States Railroads, An Analysis of the Sources of Instability and Remedial Measures* (Ann Arbor: Univ. of Michigan–Wayne State Univ., 1957); Denver W. Hertel, *History of the Brotherhood of Maintenance of Way Employes: Its Birth and Growth, 1887–1955* (Washington: Ransdell, 1955).

major disputes These are disputes under the Railway Labor Act which have to do with new or revised contract provisions. They deal with the substantive terms of contract provisions, such as wages, hours, and working conditions. Grievance disputes sometimes are referred to as minor disputes.

See also MINOR DISPUTES, RAILWAY LABOR ACT.

majority rule The National Labor Relations Act, state labor relations acts, and the Civil Service Reform Act provide for holding elections to determine who should represent employees of a particular employer or group of employers for the purpose of collective bargaining. The rules developed under previous statutes, including the Railway Labor Act and various boards under Section 7(a) of the National Labor Relations Act, provided that a majority of the employees voting in the appropriate bargaining unit would determine and constitute the agency for all of the employees in the unit.

This rule follows the policy generally established in political elections where a majority also determines who should represent the citizens in a particular locality.

The provisions of the National Labor Relations Act are specific with regard to the exclusive bargaining rights of a majority of the employees. Section 9(a) provides as follows:

> Representatives designated or selected for the purposes of collective bargaining by the majority of the employees in a unit appropriate for such purposes, shall be the exclusive representative of all the employees in such unit for the purposes of collective bargaining in respect to rates of pay, wages, hours of employment, or other conditions of employment.

Such a proviso is designed to avoid the possibility of having more than one group act as bargaining agent. It also provides that the conditions of employment negotiated by the exclusive agent representing the majority of employees shall apply to all of the employees in the unit, union and nonunion alike.

The Taft-Hartley amendments under Section 9(a) provide for the handling of individual grievances. However, certain provisos are incorporated to protect the collective bargaining contract and to assure that the representative of the union has an opportunity to be present when the adjustment of the individual grievance is made.

Source references: ILGWU v. NLRB, 366 US 731, 48 LRRM 2251 (1961); Gerard Morales, "Presumptions of Union's Majority Status in NLRB Cases," *LLJ*, May 1978; George Schatzki, "Majority Rule, Exclusive Representation, and the Interests of Individual Workers: Should Exclusivity Be Abolished?" *IR Law Digest*, Fall 1975; Ruth Weyand, "Majority Rule in Collective Bargaining," 45 *Columbia LR* 556 (1945).

See also HOUDE ENGINEERING CASE, WEINGARTEN CASE.

major medical expense benefit A plan insuring workers against medical expenses resulting from serious injury or prolonged illness. Sometimes these plans are supplementary to other health insurance plans (hospital, medical, or surgical), and sometimes they are comprehensive protection plans.

See also HEALTH INSURANCE.

major union contracts The phrase applies to the list of important contracts, generally covering a thousand or more employees each, which are of prime interest in determining important changes in wages, hours, and working conditions in the United States. The phrase may also be applied to those contracts within a particular industry which serve as key barometers of change or policy or set the pattern in the determination of wages, hours, and working conditions.

Source references: "Characteristics of Major Union Contracts," *MLR*, July 1956; U.S. Dept. of Labor, BLS, *Characteristics of Major Collective Bargaining Agreements, January 1, 1980* (Washington: Bull. 2095, 1981).

See also AGREEMENT, COLLECTIVE.

make-ready activities Preliminary or preparatory activities of employees prior to the performance of the actual job. They may include the cleaning, preparation, and sharpening of tools, putting on special clothing, or other preparations which are essential before the actual work is begun.

It is also one of the three main steps in the operation of any job, the so-called "get ready" operation referred to in motion and time study; the other two steps being the "do," the actual work being performed, and the third part, the "put away" or the "cleaning up" following the actual performance.

Source references: Ralph N. Barnes, *Motion and Time Study* (5th ed., New York: Wiley, 1949); Robert L. Morrow, *Time Study and Motion Economy* (New York: Ronald Press, 1946).

See also CLEAN-UP PERIOD, DRESSING TIME.

make-up pay Generally applies to the procedure by which an employer pays a piece worker the difference between the amount he actually earned on piecework and the actual earnings to which he is entitled either under a statutory minimum or a contractual or other guarantee for the job. The difference is the make-up pay.

Occasionally the phrase is applied to the actual pay given to an employee when he makes up time because of absences or other time lost on his regular job. The wages paid for this time are in a sense make-up pay for time which the employee was not able to perform during the regularly scheduled workweek. The make-up pay may be at regular or overtime rates, depending on the language of the contract, past practice, or other conditions.

make-up time Provisions under collective bargaining agreements which permit an employee to make up time during which he is unable to work on the regularly scheduled hours. Such a loss of time may be due to personal reasons, family illness, jury duty, or other reasons not specifically spelled out in the contract.

The individual is permitted to make up the time either after hours or during times when he would not normally have been scheduled to work. Arrangements to make up time and its compensation vary among contracts. It may be paid at straight time rates when it is for the personal convenience of the individual, or at special or overtime rates if the time lost is because of equipment breakdown or for the convenience of the employer, or on the responsibility of the employer.

make whole The process of undoing a wrong against an individual who has been discriminated against by an employer, as through an unfair labor practice, such as a discharge because of union membership. The employee is made whole by reinstatement with back pay to his job in the same status that he would have been had there been no discrimination. Making whole may also involve adjustments in seniority, wage status, promotions, etc. Since changes take place in the plant during an absence (period of discrimination) the requirement to place a person in the spot he would have been in calls for delicate judgment and requires reconstructing and projecting the situation to achieve equity, since frequently it is not possible actually to determine where the individual would have been.

The policy of the NLRB in unfair labor practice cases is to require the undoing of the damage done, that is, to establish the situation as though the violation of law had not occurred. To accomplish this, the Board seeks a remedy which will return to the employee those things which he may have been deprived of—such as wages, seniority, and other rights. The Board in its affirmative order seeks to "make whole" and as far as possible undo the effects of the unfair labor practice. The same principle may be applied by arbitrators in the handling of contract grievances.

See also AFFIRMATIVE ORDER, BACK PAY, CEASE AND DESIST ORDER, NATIONAL LABOR RELATIONS ACT, NET EARNINGS.

make-work practices Generally applies to those activities of unions or individual workers who either limit their production or create unnecessary work or jobs, frequently in order to take up a slack in employment or to spread available work. The practices are designed to spread the available work so that more workers are employed.

The phrase also applies to limits on output or the use of excess numbers of workers in order to perform the job. Make-work practices are sometimes referred to as "soft jobs" or "featherbedding jobs" or "observers."

Source references: John R. Van de Water, "Influences of the Common Law on Make-Work Practices in Industry," *LLJ*, Feb. 1955; ———, "Legal and Managerial Control of Work Restrictions in Industry," *LLJ*, Sept. 1963.

See also BOGUS (TYPE) WORK, CA' CANNY, DEAD-HORSE RULE, DOUBLE EMPLOYMENT, FEATHERBEDDING, LEA ACT (ANTI-PETRILLO ACT), RESTRICTION OF OUTPUT, WORK RULES.

malice in law Justice Holmes in his article, "Privilege, Malice and Intent" (8 *Harvard Law Review* 1–2, 1894) said, "I mean by malice a malevolent motive for action, without reference to any hope of a remoter benefit to oneself to be accomplished by the intended harm to another."

Ames, however, in his article, "How Far an Act May be a Tort Because of the Wrongful Motive of the Actor" (18 *Harvard Law Review* 411, 422 note 1, 1905) says, "Malice as used in the books, means sometimes malevolence, sometimes absence of excuse, and sometimes absence of motive for the public good. If so 'slippery' a word . . . were eliminated from legal arguments and opinions, only good would result."

Perhaps the best explanation of the use of malice in law is presented by John R. Commons and John B. Andrews in their *Principles of Labor Legislation* (New York: Harper & Bros., 1920). They say in part, "[Courts] start with the proposition that the employer has a right of free access to the labor market and to the commodity market. Intentional interference with this right to do business is *prima facie* wrongful. Only when the injury done to the employer is the result of the exercise of equal or superior rights by the workingmen is it justified. These courts distinguish between *malice in fact* and *malice in law*. Where the personal ill-will and spite, for malice in fact, actuates the workingmen, they hold to be of no importance. Malice in law determines the legality of their actions, and malice in law is merely the intentional infliction of an injury without justification."

But as Millis and Montgomery point out in *Organized Labor* (New York: McGraw-Hill, 1945), "If intentional infliction of injury without justification is unlawful, everything turns upon the question of what is sufficient justification—of whether the workers have just cause for their action. Accordingly, the courts must evaluate the rights of the parties, and this evaluation once more has to be in part a subjective thing."

Malthusianism This refers to the theory of the political economist T. R. Malthus that population tends to increase more rapidly than its means of subsistence can be made to do. According to Malthus, population increase must be checked or poverty becomes inevitable.

management The term when used as a noun applies to an employer or to executives of a corporation who are accountable and responsible for the administration and direction of an enterprise and the functions of leadership.

The term also concerns itself with the general management or administrative functions, which include planning, organizing, and motivation of the activities of a corporation or other business enterprise so that it may achieve its objectives most efficiently and economically.

Source references: Geoffrey Barraclough, *Management in a Changing Economy*, An AMA Survey Report (New York: AMA, 1976); Hyler J. Bracey and Aubrey Sanford, *Basic Management: An Experience-Based Approach* (Dallas: Business Pub., 1977); Gene W. Dalton, Louis B. Barnes, and Abraham Zaleznik, *The Distribution of Authority in Formal Organizations* (Boston: Harvard Univ., 1968); Peter F. Drucker, *Management: Tasks, Responsibilities, Practices* (New York: Harper & Row, 1974); ———, *The Practice of Management* (New York: Harper, 1954); Eli Ginzberg and Ivar E. Berg, *Democratic Values and the Rights of Management* (New York: Columbia UP, 1963); Theo Haimann, William G. Scott, and Patrick E. Connor, *Managing the Modern Organization* (Boston: Houghton Mifflin, 1978); Frederick Harbison and Charles A. Myers, *Management in the Industrial World* (New York: McGraw-Hill, 1959); Lee H. Hill and Charles R. Hook, Jr., *Management at the Bargaining Table* (New York: McGraw-Hill, 1945); Alfred J. Marrow (ed.), *The Failure of Success* (New York: AMACOM, 1972); Harwood E. Merrill (ed.), *Classics in Management* (New York: AMA, 1960); Richard Tanner Pascale, "Zen and the Art of Management," *Harvard BR*, March/April 1978; Richard Tanner Pascale and Anthony G. Athos, *The Art of Japanese Management; Applications for American Executives* (New York: Simon and Schuster, 1981); Stanley Peterfreund, *Mind-to-Mind Management, How to Meet the New Breed on its Own Ground*, An AMA Management Briefing (New York: AMA, 1977); F. J. Roethlisberger, *Man-in-Organization* (Cambridge: Harvard Univ., 1968); David Rogers, "Managing in the Public and Private Sectors: Similarities and Differences," *Management Review*, May 1981; Benjamin M. Selekman, *A Moral Philosophy for Management* (New York: McGraw-Hill, 1959); Peter B. Vail, "Management as a Performing Art," *Personnel*, July/Aug. 1976; Max S. Wortman and Fred Luthans (ed.), *Emerging Concepts in Management; Process, Behavioral, Quantitative, and Systems* (New York: Macmillan, 1975).

See also EMPLOYER.

management by objectives (MBO) System of management in which (1) the common goals of an organization are identified mutually by both organizational superior and subordinate, (2) the areas of responsibility are defined in terms of expected results, and (3) the achieved results are used to assess individual and organizational performance.

Drucker, credited with first use of the term, describes MBO as a management philosophy which gives "full scope to individual strength and responsibility and at the same time give[s] common direction of vision and effort, establish[es] team work and harmonize[s] the goals of the individual with the common weal."

Odiorne defines MBO as a "process whereby the superior and subordinate managers of an organization jointly identify its common goals, define each individual's major areas of responsibilities in terms of the results expected of him, and use these measures as guides for operating the unit and assessing the contribution of each of its members." He explains further that it produces such results as improved profit, more growth, lower costs, increased revenues, better morale, more promotable people, improved quality of service, and improved delegation of decision making.

Source references: Richard Babcock and Peter F. Sorensen, Jr., "An MBO Checklist: Are Conditions Right for Implementation?" *Management Review*, June 1979; Gerard F. Carvalho, "Installing Management by Objectives: A New Perspective on Organization Change," *Human Resource Management*, Spring 1972; Peter F. Drucker, *The Practice of Management* (New York: Harper & Row, 1954); Paul Mali, *Managing by Objectives; An Operating Guide to Faster and More Profitable Results* (New York: Wiley-Interscience, 1972); Dale D. McConkey, "20 Ways to Kill Management by Objectives," *Management Review*, Oct. 1972; George S. Odiorne, "How to Succeed in MBO Goal Setting," *PJ*, Aug. 1978; ———, *Management by Objectives* (New York: Pitman, 1965); Peter P. Schoderbek and Donald L. Plambeck, "The Missing Link in Management by Objectives—Continuing Responsibilities," *Public Personnel Management*, Jan./Feb. 1978.

management clause A provision in the collective bargaining agreement which sets out the scope of management rights, functions, and responsibilities. The clause sets forth those functions of management which are not subject to contractual limitations. Union rights are protected in the grievance machinery and in particular contract provisions which modify the management rights clause.

There is a great deal of discussion whether a management clause preserves to management all the residual rights not specifically extended or shared with the union in the contract, or whether the management clause limits management rights specifically to the items enumerated in it.

An illustrative management clause might read as follows:

> The management of the company and the direction of the working force, including the right to plan, direct, curtail, determine, and control plant operations, hire, suspend, discipline, or discharge for proper cause, layoff, transfer, or relieve employees from duties because of lack of work, to promote efficiency or for other legitimate reasons, and all rights and powers customarily exercised by an employer, except as may be specifically limited by this agreement, are vested exclusively in the company.

Source references: Richard F. Groner and Leon E. Lunden, "Management Rights Provisions in Major Agreements," *MLR*, Feb. 1966; Jules L. Justin, "How to Preserve Management Rights Under the Labor Contract," *LLJ*, March 1960; "The Union Challenge to Management Control," *ILRR*, Jan. 1963; Max S. Wortman, Jr., Craig E. Overton, and Robin Johnson, "The Structure of Management Rights Clauses in Major Metropolitan Firefighter Contracts," *LLJ*, Oct. 1978; Frank Zeidler, *Management's Rights Under Public Sector Collective Bargaining Agreements* (Chicago: IPMA, PERL no. 59, 1980).

See also MANAGEMENT RIGHTS.

management development An organized program for management personnel, usually at the top or middle level for the purpose of developing and improving managerial functions, including planning, organizing, motivating, and controlling the activities of an organization. Management development programs concern themselves not only with specific knowledge and skills, but also with the basic attitudes which permit management to function effectively.

Source references: Chris Argyris, *Management and Organizational Development; The Path From XA to YB* (New York: McGraw-Hill, 1971); Willard E. Bennett, "Master Plan for Management Development," *Harvard BR*, May/June 1956; Charles P. Bowen, Jr., "Let's Put Realism Into Management Development," *Harvard BR*, July/Aug. 1973; Robert E. Boynton, "Executive Development Programs: What Should They Teach?" *Personnel*, March/April 1981; BNA, *Management Training and Development Programs* (Washington: PPF Survey no. 116, 1977); Lester A. Digman, "Management Development: Needs and Practices," *Personnel*, July/Aug. 1980; Francis W. Dinsmore, *Developing Tomorrow's Managers Today* (New York: AMACOM, 1975); William G. Dyer, "What Makes Sense in Management Training?" *Management Review*, June 1978; G. David Garson, "The Institute Model for Public-Sector Management Development," *Public Personnel Management*, July/Aug. 1979; Harvard BR, *Executive Development Series, Part I, Reprints from Harvard Business Review* (Cambridge: 1955–1964); ———, *Executive Development Series, Part II, Reprints from Harvard Business Review* (Cambridge: 1965–1967); W. D. Heisel, "A Non-Bureaucratic View of Management Development," *Public Personnel Management*, March/April 1980; Henry D. Meyer, Bruce L. Margolis, and William M. Fifield, *The Manager's Guide to Developing Subordinate Managers*, An AMA Management Briefing (New York: AMA, 1980); Robert F. Pearse, *Manager to Manager: What Managers Think of Management Development*, An AMA Survey Report (New York: AMA, 1974).

management rights Sometimes referred to as management or employer prerogatives or functions. They encompass those aspects of the employer's operations which do not require discussion with or concurrence by the union, or rights reserved to management which are not subject to collective bargaining. Such rights or prerogatives may include matters of hiring, production, scheduling, price fixing, and the maintenance of order and efficiency, as well as the processes of manufacturing and sales.

This area is one of substantial conflict between labor and management because the scope of collective bargaining tends to be modified as economic and social conditions change. It was impossible for the labor and management representatives at the Labor-Management Conference in 1945 to agree on the broad areas which constitute areas of management rights or management prerogatives.

Management contends that because of its responsibility for maintaining the operation of a company and the control of the business for the benefit of stockholders, it must of necessity be vested with adequate authority to carry out those functions. The unions on the other hand insist that these management functions are reasonable and proper only where they do not impinge on the specific needs or concerns which affect the individual in relation to the job. Thus the field is an open one and judging from decisions not only of the employers and unions in collective bargaining but also of the NLRB, the scope of collective bargaining will continue to be a changing one. What was a management right a few years ago may now be a joint concern of labor and management.

Source references: James Baird, *Management Rights: Little Understood, Little Used, Quickly Lost* (2d ed., Washington: Labor-Management Relations Service, Strengthening Local Government Through Better Labor Relations Series, 1978); Charles G. Bakaly, Jr., "Management Prerogatives: The Limits of Mandatory Bargaining," *Labor Law Developments 1971*, Proceedings of the 17th Annual Institute on Labor Law, SLF (New York: Bender, 1971); Neil W. Chamberlain, "The Union Challenge to Management Control," *ILRR*, Jan. 1963; Margaret Chandler, *Management Rights and Union Interests* (New York: McGraw-Hill, 1964); Donald E. Cullen and Marcia L. Greenbaum, *Management Rights and Collective Bargaining: Can Both Survive?* (Ithaca: Cornell Univ., NYSSILR, Bull. no. 58, 1966); I. B. Helburn, "The Scope of Bargaining in Public Sector Negotiations: Sovereignty Reviewed," *Journal of Collective Negotiations in the Public Sector*, Spring 1974; Richard L. Higginbotham, "The Protection of Management Rights Through Contract Language," *Journal of Collective Negotiations in the Public Sector*, May 1972; Walter P. Loomis, Jr. and Joseph Herman, "Management Reserved Rights and the NLRB—An Employer's View," *LLJ*, Nov. 1968; Elihu Platt, "The Duty to Bargain as Applied to Management Decisions," *LLJ*, Nov. 1968; Jacob Sheinkman, "Management Prerogatives: The Limits of Mandatory Bargaining," *Labor Law Developments 1971*, Proceedings of the 17th Annual Institute on Labor Law, SLF (New York: Bender, 1971); Robert A. Swift, *NLRB and Management Decision Making* (Philadelphia: Univ. of Pennsylvania, Wharton School, Industrial Research Unit, LRPP Series no. 9, 1974); George W. Torrence, *Management's Right to Manage* (rev. ed., Washington: BNA, 1968); Arnold M. Zack, "Mandatory Management Rights: Help or Hindrance?" *Public Personnel Management*, Nov./Dec. 1975.

See also LABOR-MANAGEMENT CONFERENCE (1945).

managerial employee Employees who "formulate and effectuate management policies by expressing and making operative the decisions of their employer." This definition, developed by the NLRB in *Palace Laundry Dry Cleaning Corp.* has been accepted by the courts in the absence of specific mention of the term in both the National Labor Relations Act and the Taft-Hartley Act. The Supreme Court in *NLRB v. Yeshiva University* recites previous court decisions which state that "managerial employees must exercise discretion within or even independently of established employer policy and must be aligned with management. . . . [n]ormally an employee may be excluded as managerial only if he represents management interests by taking or recommending discretionary actions that effectively control or implement employer policy."

Title VII of the Civil Service Reform Act defines "management official" as "an individual employed by an agency in a position the duties and responsibilities of which require or authorize the individual to formulate, determine, or influence the policies of the agency." Management officials may form bargaining units separate from nonmanagement employees and be "represented by labor organizations which historically or traditionally represent management officials or supervisors in private industry and which hold exclusive recognition for units of such officials or supervisors in any agency on the effective date of this chapter."

Under state and local government employee laws, managerial employees do not generally enjoy bargaining rights. While they vary, the statutes can be found to define managerial or management employees as those who:

(1) Have significant responsibilities in the formulation, determination, or administration of policies and programs,
(2) May reasonably be required on behalf of the public employer to assist in the preparation for or conduct of collective bargaining negotiations,
(3) Have a major role in administration of agreements,
(4) Have a significant role in personnel administration or in employee relations,
(5) Have budget preparation and administration responsibilities, or
(6) Are required to exercise independent judgment. The New York Taylor Law defines managerial employees as "persons (i) who formulate policy or (ii) who may reasonably be required on behalf of the public employer to assist directly in the preparation for and conduct of collective negotiations or to have a major role in the administration of agreements or in personnel administration provided that such role is not of a routine or clerical nature and requires the exercise of independent judgment."

Source references: Civil Service Reform Act of 1978, 5 U.S.C. 7101 et seq. (1982); *Ford Motor Company and United Office and Professional Workers of America*, 66 NLRB 1317, 17 LRRM 394 (1946); *Palace Laundry Dry Cleaning Corp.*, 75 NLRB 320, 21 LRRM 1039 (1947); Daniel Rhodes Barney, "*Bell Aerospace* and the Status of Managerial Employees Under the NLRA, A Comment," *Industrial Relations LJ*, Summer 1976; Melvin K. Bers, *The Status of Managerial, Supervisory and Confidential Employees in Government Employment Relations* (Albany: New York Public Employment Relations Board, 1970); Joyce M. Najita and Helene S. Tanimoto, *Guide to Statutory Provisions in Public Sector Collective Bargaining: Unit Determination* (4th issue, Honolulu: Univ. of Hawaii, IRC, 1981); Bonnie Siber Weinstock, "Section 8(a)(1) Protection for Managerial, Confidential, and Supervisory Personnel," *LLJ*, Sept. 1982.

See also YESHIVA UNIVERSITY CASE.

mandatory retirement *See* RETIREMENT, COMPULSORY.

mandatory subjects for bargaining Items which are by agreement, law, court or administrative ruling subject to negotiations and required to be bargained in good faith by both parties.

Under the National Labor Relations Act, mandatory subjects of bargaining include any topic that falls under the category of wages, hours, and working conditions. Mandatory subjects of bargaining may be taken to impasse. In the private sector this means the union has the right to strike and management has the right to take a strike over the issue.

Since much of the collective bargaining process depends on a consideration of changing economic and social conditions, subjects which had not been considered matters for mandatory or required bargaining may over a period of time move from the permissive to the required category.

Source references: Arvid Anderson, "Public Employees and Collective Bargaining: Comparative and Local Experience," *NYU 21st Annual Conference on Labor*, ed. by Thomas Christensen (New York: Bender, 1969); I. B. Helburn, "The Scope of Bargaining in Public Sector Negotiations: Sovereignty Reviewed," *Journal of Collective Negotiations in the Public Sector*, Spring 1974; Jules J. Justin, *How to Manage With a Union* (2 vols., New York: IR Workshop Seminars, 1969); Myron Lieberman, "Impact of Proposed Federal Public Employee Bargaining on State Legislation; the Potential Legislation on Mandatory Subjects of Bargaining," *Journal of Collective Negotiations in the Public Sector*, Vol. 4, no. 2, 1975; New York State, Public Employment Relations Board, *Mandatory/Non-Mandatory Subjects of Negotiations* (Albany: 1978); Murray L. Sackman, "Redefining the Scope of Bargaining in Public Employment," 19 *Boston College LR* 155 (1977); "The Scope of Required Collective Bargaining Under the Labor-Management Relations Act," *Columbia LR*, March 1950; Deborah Tussey, "Bargainable or Negotiable Issues in State Public Employment Labor Relations," 84 *ALR*3d 242 (1978); Joan

Weitzman, *The Scope of Bargaining in Public Employment* (New York: Praeger, 1975).

See also BORG-WARNER CASE, PERMISSIVE SUBJECTS FOR BARGAINING, PROHIBITED SUBJECTS FOR BARGAINING, SCOPE OF BARGAINING.

man-day The term applies to the amount of work performed by an individual in one day. The phrase is also used in strike or work stoppage statistics dealing with man-days of idleness.

man-days idle A term used in work stoppage statistics and applied to workers who are made idle for one shift or longer in the establishment or plant directly involved in a work stoppage. It should be noted that idleness resulting in stoppages in other establishments as a result of material or service shortages are not included in these figures.

See also WORK STOPPAGE STATISTICS.

Manhart case A Supreme Court decision holding that an employer who required female employees to contribute larger premiums than male employees to the pension plan violated Section 703(a)(1) of Title VII of the Civil Rights Act of 1964. The pension plan used sex-segregated actuarial tables which estimated longer life expectancy for women and thus required them to contribute 14.84 percent more per month.

Source references: City of Los Angeles, Dept. of Water and Power v. Manhart, 435 US 702, 17 FEP Cases 395 (1978); Roger B. Jacobs, "The *Manhart* Case: Sex-Based Differentials and the Application of Title VII to Pensions," *LLJ*, April 1980; Linda H. Kistler and Richard C. Healy, "Sex Discrimination in Pension Plans Since *Manhart*," *LLJ*, April 1981.

See also NORRIS CASE.

man-hour This is a standard unit utilized quite widely in labor statistics and is equal to one person working for one hour. Man-hour data may be applied to any series which involves actual work time and also has been used in industrial accident statistics and other types of cost determination.

See also OUTPUT PER HOUR (LABOR PRODUCTIVITY), PRODUCTIVITY.

manit A contraction of "man minutes" which has been applied to various incentive systems.

The manit system is a wage or incentive plan in which a bonus is paid for the man-minutes or minutes over and above a set standard. The manit under the Haynes system is defined as "⅘'s of the amount of work that a normal worker can turn out in a minute of time without over-exertion." Production in excess of 75 manits receives additional compensation whereas production below 60 manits receives a minimum guarantee rate.

Source reference: U.S. War Production Board, Management Consultant Division, *A Handbook on Wage Incentive Plans* (Washington: 1945).

See also HAYNES "MANIT" WAGE PLAN.

manning scale The system for determining the number of officers and men to be assigned to a ship. The complement may be established by statute. It is based on the specific tonnage of the ship and the nature of the operation. Where changes in the conditions or service make it necessary, the manning scales may be modified. On government-subsidized ships, the Maritime Administration of the Department of Commerce is empowered by law to establish minimum manning scales that are "fair and reasonable." As a practical matter, the issue is subject to collective bargaining.

Some of the ILO Maritime Conventions deal with the problem of the manning scales or manning tables in order to set conditions on board ship which would provide minimum safety, security, and other conditions of employment for maritime workers.

Source reference: Rudolph W. Wissman, *The Maritime Industry, Federal Regulation in Establishing Labor and Safety Standards* (New York: Cornell Maritime Press, 1942).

See also CREW ASSIGNMENT, MANNING TABLE.

manning table The manning table concept was developed by the War Manpower Commission during World War II. The concept involves setting up a personnel inventory or staffing schedule which covers the jobs within a particular organization, plant, or smaller departmental unit. The information may include such items as age, sex, marital status, experience, handicaps, and other pertinent data of employees which would be helpful in determining manpower requirements for a particular job or a particular set of functions.

During the war more than 8,000 establishments developed manning tables which set up job patterns as well as other information to permit the proper utilization of manpower facilities, as well as to determine whether particular individuals would be available for the armed services.

The manning table concept has been utilized in the military service as well as in shipping operations. It sets out an ideal structure, listing the requirements of the task as well as a plan or schedule for best performing a particular function.

manpower The term is generally applied to the human resources and skills of a people.

By the 1960s it became apparent that the manpower utilization of the country had a major impact on its economic growth and development. The improvement, additional training, and employment opportunities of the manpower of a country play an important role in the growth of the gross national product. This factor, as well as concern with the major problem of unemployment and underemployment, led the Kennedy administration to develop a number of manpower proposals for Congress.

The opening statement of findings and purpose of the Manpower Development and Training Act of 1962 reflected the concern over manpower needs:

> The Congress finds that there is critical need for more and better trained personnel in many vital occupational categories, including professional, scientific, technical and apprenticeable categories; that even in periods of high unemployment, many employment opportunities remain unfilled because of the shortages of qualified personnel; and that it is in the national interest that current and prospective manpower shortages be identified and that persons who can be qualified for these positions through education and training be sought out and trained, in order that the nation may meet the staffing requirements of the struggle for freedom.

Source references: Manpower Development and Training Act of 1962, as amended, 42 U.S.C. 2571 et seq. (1982), repealed, 87 Stat. 883 (1973) (matters formerly covered by the Manpower Development and Training Act of 1962 are now covered by the Job Training Partnership Act, 29 U.S.C. 1501 et seq. (1982)); Michael E. Borus, *Measuring the Impact of Employment-Related Social Programs, A Primer on the Evaluation of Employment and Training, Vocational Education, Vocational Rehabilitation, and Other Job-Oriented Programs* (Kalamazoo: Upjohn Institute for Employment Research, 1979); Vernon Briggs, Charles Killingsworth, and Garth Mangum, *An Employment Policy to Fight Recession and Inflation, A Policy Statement* (Washington: National Council of Employment Policy, 1980); Eli Ginzberg, *National Commission for Manpower Policy, The First Five Years: 1974–1979* (Washington: U.S. National Commission for Employment Policy, Special Report no. 36, 1979); Stanley Lebergott, *Manpower in Economic Growth: The American Record Since 1800* (New York: McGraw-Hill, 1964); Sar A. Levitan, "Human Resource Implications of Reaganomics," *Proceedings of the 34th A/M, IRRA*, ed. by Barbara Dennis (Madison: 1982); Garth L. Mangum, "Evaluating Federal Manpower Programs," *Proceedings of the 20th A/M, IRRA*, ed. by Gerald Somers (Madison: 1968); ———, "Twenty Years of Employment and Training Programs: Whatever Happened to the Consensus?" *LLJ*, Aug. 1981; Ray Marshall, *Some Reflections on Employment and Training Policies* (University: Univ. of Alabama, Human Resources Institute, 1982); Laurence S. Seidman, *The Design of Federal Employment Programs* (Lexington, Mass.: Lexington Books, 1975); Teresa A. Sullivan and Philip M. Hauser, *The Labor Utilization Framework: Assumptions, Data, and Policy Implications* (Washington: U.S. National Commission on Employment and Unemployment Statistics, Background Paper no. 19, 1978); U.S. National Commission for Employment Policy, *The Federal Interest in Employment and Training, Seventh Annual Report to the President and the Congress* (Washington: Report no. 13, 1981); U.S. National Commission for Manpower Policy, *Directions for a Manpower Policy: A Collection of Policy Papers Prepared for Three Regional Conferences* (Washington: Special Report no. 14, 1976); ———, *Directions for a National Manpower Policy: A Report on the Proceedings of*

Three Regional Conferences (Washington: Special Report no. 13, 1976); ———, *Labor's View on Employment Policy* (Washington: Special Report no. 25, 1978).

See also EMPLOYMENT AND TRAINING ADMINISTRATION (ETA); LABOR FORCE; MANPOWER ADMINISTRATION, DEPARTMENT OF LABOR.

Manpower Administration, Department of Labor Secretary of Labor W. Willard Wirtz on February 19, 1963, issued an administrative order creating a Manpower Administration within the Department of Labor.

The Manpower Administration underwent a major reorganization, effective March 17, 1969, which established the separate offices of the Manpower Administrator, who headed the Manpower Administration, and the Assistant Secretary of Labor for Manpower. The Manpower Administrator was responsible to the Assistant Secretary. In addition, the reorganization abolished both the Bureau of Employment Security and the Bureau of Work-Training Programs and combined the major functions of these bureaus into the newly established U.S. Training and Employment Service.

The program structure of the Manpower Administration consisted of: the Bureau of Apprenticeship and Training, U.S. Training and Employment Service, and the Unemployment Insurance Service.

The responsibilities of the Assistant Secretary for Manpower were to be found, among others, in the following pieces of legislation: Wagner-Peyser Act of 1933; Social Security Act of 1935, as amended; Federal Unemployment Tax Act; Servicemen's Readjustment Act of 1944; Farm Labor Contractor Registration Act of 1963; Immigration and Nationality Act; Manpower Development and Training Act of 1962, as amended; Trade Expansion Act of 1962; Public Works and Economic Development Act of 1965; Public Works Acceleration Act of 1962; National Apprenticeship Act of 1937; Appalachian Regional Development Act of 1965; Economic Opportunity Act of 1964; and Civil Rights Act of 1964.

The name of the agency was changed to the Employment and Training Administration on November 12, 1975.

Source references: Manpower Development and Training Act of 1962, as amended, 42 U.S.C. 2571 et seq. (1982), repealed, 87 Stat. 883 (1973) (matters formerly covered by the Manpower Development and Training Act of 1962 are now covered by the Job Training Partnership Act, 29 U.S.C. 1501 et seq. (1982)); *Federal Register,* April 15, 1969; U.S. Congress, House, Committee on Education and Labor, *Manpower Development and Training Act Amendments of 1966* (Washington: 1966); U.S. Dept. of Labor, *News,* Release 5627, Feb. 20, 1963; U.S. Dept. of Labor, Manpower Administration, *Amendments to the Manpower Development and Training Act: More Effective Training Program for Young Workers* (Washington: Preprint no. 4, 1964); ———, *The Manpower Act of 1965* (Washington: Preprint no. 7, 1965); ———, *Manpower Training Facts* (Washington: 1965); U.S. Dept. of Labor, OMAT, *An Explanation of the Manpower Development and Training Act* (Washington, 1962).

See also EMPLOYMENT AND TRAINING ADMINISTRATION (ETA), MANPOWER DEVELOPMENT AND TRAINING ACT OF 1962.

Manpower Commission *See* WAR MANPOWER COMMISSION.

manpower control The control of the labor force may be achieved through limitations on emigration, freezing of employees to jobs, or requiring individuals to take only certain jobs. In countries which have a planned or dictatorial society, manpower allocations are used in order to carry out the general plans of the country. In a democracy, manpower controls are generally applied only during war periods.

During World War II, the War Manpower Commission had the responsibility of planning the most effective use of the nation's manpower.

Source references: Avery Craven and Walter Johnson, *The United States, Experiment Democracy* (Boston: Ginn, 1950); Irwin Gray, "Impact of Defense Expenditures on Job Opportunities and Manpower Requirements," *Proceedings of the 19th A/M, IRRA,* ed. by Gerald Somers (Madison: 1967).

Manpower Development and Training Act of 1962 The Act, as amended, basically provided training programs to combat unemployment, underemployment, and manpower shortages, to meet technological changes brought on by automation, and to provide employment opportunities to the rising number of young people entering the labor force. The Act also directed the secretary of labor to conduct manpower studies, research, and projects, and required the secretaries of labor and of health, education, and welfare and the President to present annual reports to Congress.

The provisions of the Act were grouped in the following five sections:

Title I Manpower Requirements, Development, and Utilization
Title II Training and Skill Development Programs
Title III Miscellaneous
Title IV Seasonal Unemployment in the Construction Industry
Title V Supplementary State Programs.

The law was repealed with the enactment of the Comprehensive Employment and Training Act of 1973.

Source references: Daniel S. Hamermesh, *Economic Aspects of Manpower Training Programs: Theory and Policy* (Lexington, Mass.: Heath, 1971); Garth L. Mangum, *Contributions and Costs of Manpower Development and Training* (Ann Arbor: Univ. of Michigan–Wayne State Univ., Institute of Labor and IR, Policy Papers in Human Resources and IR, no. 5, 1967); ———, *MDTA, Foundation of Federal Manpower Policy* (Baltimore: Johns Hopkins Press, 1968); Garth L. Mangum and John Walsh, *A Decade of Manpower Development and Training* (Salt Lake City: Olympus Pub. Co., 1973); Charles R. Perry et al., *The Impact of Government Manpower Programs in General, and on Minorities and Women* (Philadelphia: Industrial Research Unit, Wharton School, Univ. of Pennsylvania, 1975); U.S. Congress, House, Committee on Education and Labor, *Manpower Development and Training Act Amendments of 1966* (Washington: 1966); U.S. Dept. of Labor, Manpower Administration, *An Explanation of the Manpower Development and Training Act* (Washington: 1962); ———, *The Manpower Development and Training Act: A Review of Training Activities* (Washington: 1967); ———, *MDTA, A Summary of the Manpower Development and Training Act of 1962, As Amended* (Washington: 1965); ———, *Methods of Assessing the Disadvantaged in Manpower Programs: A Review and Analysis* (Washington: Research and Development Findings no. 14, 1973); ———, *Trade Unions and the MDTA* (Washington: 1966); Seymour L. Wolfbein (ed.), *Manpower Policy: Perspectives and Prospects; Papers on the Occasion of the Tenth Anniversary of the Manpower Development and Training Act of 1962* (Philadelphia: Temple Univ., School of Business Administration, 1973).

manpower projections A distinction is sometimes drawn by technicians between a projection and a forecast. Manpower projectionists usually note that a forecast constitutes "an unconditional prophecy or prediction." Since many unforeseen events can modify a projection, those who are projectors use the word "projection" to distinguish "the conditional prediction from the unconditional prediction." A United Nations report notes: "Economic life is much too complicated to permit unconditional forecasts. The best that can be achieved is to form a judgment as to the most probable course of certain variables based upon certain assumptions, both explicit and implicit, concerning their relationships to other determining or explanatory variables. The probable future course of these explanatory variables, however, can also be known only with some margin of uncertainty. All projections, therefore, inevitably include a large element of judgment and—also inevitably—all are subject to some margin of error. . . ."

Source references: Glenn A. Bassett, "Elements of Manpower Forecasting and Scheduling," *Human Resource Management*, Fall 1973; S. C. Kelley, Thomas N. Chirikos, and Michael G. Finn, *Manpower Forecasting in the United States: An Evaluation of the State of the Art* (Columbus: Ohio State Univ., Center for Human Resources, 1975); United Nations, Economic and Social Council, *World Economic Situation: Evaluation of Long-Term Economic Projections, A preliminary report by the Secretary-General, Thirtieth Session* (New York: 1960); U.S. Dept. of Labor, BLS, *Tomorrow's Manpower Needs. Research Report on Manpower Projection*

Methods (Washington: Bull. 1769, 1973); ———, *Tomorrow's Manpower Needs, Vol. I–IV* (Washington: Bull. 1606, 1969); ———, *Tomorrow's Manpower Needs, Vol. IV—The National Industry-Occupational Matrix and Other Manpower Data* (rev. ed., Washington: Bull. 1737, 1972); U.S. Dept. of Labor, Manpower Administration, *Manpower Projections: An Appraisal and a Plan of Action, Report of the Working Group on Manpower Projections to the President's Committee on Manpower* (Washington: 1967).

man rating *See* LEVELING, MERIT RATING.

manual and motor skill tests Special aptitude tests which are designed to measure an individual's dexterity, his ability to coordinate, his speed of reaction, and other muscular skills.

See also TEST.

manual dexterity The ability to perform work with the hands.

manual worker Applies generally to semiskilled and unskilled workers who use their physical rather than their mental ability in the performance of certain jobs. In actuality, of course, it is difficult to separate the manual and the intellectual, since almost all activity requires intellectual ability. The term essentially indicates that more physical dexterity and ability than mental manipulation are required.

See also BLUE-COLLAR WORKER.

Marble, Slate and Stone Polishers, Rubbers and Sawyers, Tile and Marble Setters' Helpers and Marble Mosaic and Terrazzo Workers' Helpers; International Association of (AFL-CIO) This union was first organized in 1901 as the International Association of Marble Workers in Detroit. In 1916, the name of the organization was changed to the International Association of Marble, Slate and Stone Polishers, Rubbers and Sawyers when the union gave up its jurisdiction of marble setters to the Bricklayers, Masons and Plasterers' International Union. In 1918, provision was made for the admission of the Tilesetters Helpers and in 1921 such jurisdiction was granted by the AFL. The Terrazzo Workers' Helpers entered later and the name incorporated all the organizations covered within the union.

The union adopted the name Tile, Marble and Terrazzo Finishers and Shopmen International Union (AFL-CIO) in the early 1970s.

See also TILE, MARBLE, TERRAZZO FINISHERS AND SHOPWORKERS AND GRANITE CUTTERS INTERNATIONAL UNION (AFL-CIO).

marginal productivity theory of wages Part of the general theory of value applied to the four factors of production: land, labor, capital, and business enterprise. As applied to wages, the theory attempts to measure the share of each of the factors in production in relation to labor's share or labor's value in production. The theory claims that wages tend to be fixed at the point that represents the employer's estimate of the contribution of the last unit of labor employed. This unit becomes the marginal unit. The actual number of units of labor he employs will be determined by what he pays for the marginal unit of labor as compared to the marginal units of land, capital, and the risk of possible profit.

The theory holds that each worker will actually receive in wages an amount equal to the value of the marginal product of his particular labor group. The marginal product is determined by supply and demand and its actual measurement can be determined by the loss in production due to the withdrawal of one worker from a specific combination of capital, labor, land, and business enterprise.

Marginal productivity analysis has been popular in this country in the field of economics. The theory leaves many unanswered questions—What specific knowledge does the employer have of the labor market? What is the actual mobility of the factors in production under certain circumstances? Is it correct to assume that in the actual marketplace the employer is familiar with the marginal productivity of any of the units of production? Marginal productivity is a useful tool of analysis and has been helpful in focusing attention on the general theory of value.

Source reference: Nathan Belfer and Gordon F. Bloom, "Unionism and the Marginal Productivity Theory," *Insights Into Labor Issues,* ed. by Richard Lester and Joseph Shister (New York: Macmillan, 1948).

marginal worker A worker the value of whose production equals his actual wage.

Marine and Shipbuilding Workers of America; Industrial Union of (AFL-CIO) The organization started in September 1934, when six locals which had organized in the previous year met in Quincy, Massachusetts, and established the Industrial Union of Marine and Shipbuilding Workers of America.

Its quarterly publication is *The Shipbuilder.*

Address: 8121 Georgia Ave., Silver Spring, Md. 20910. Tel. (301) 589–8820

Marine Cooks and Stewards' Union Formerly a division of the Seafarers' International Union of North America (AFL-CIO), the union merged with the Seafarers' Atlantic, Gulf, Lakes and Inland Waters District in June 1978.

See also ATLANTIC, GULF, LAKES AND INLAND WATERS DISTRICT.

Marine Engineers' Beneficial Association; National (AFL-CIO) This union represents licensed engineers employed on ships. Unions affiliated with it include the Engineers and Scientists of California, Florida Association of Professional Employees, Brotherhood of Marine Officers, and National Weather Service Employees Organization. Its official monthly publication is *The American Marine Engineer.*

Address: 444 North Capitol St., Washington, D.C. 20001. Tel. (202) 347–8585

See also ENGINEERS AND SCIENTISTS OF CALIFORNIA; FLORIDA ASSOCIATION OF PROFESSIONAL EMPLOYEES; MARINE OFFICERS, BROTHERHOOD OF; WEATHER SERVICE EMPLOYEES ORGANIZATION; NATIONAL.

Marine Firemen, Oilers, Watertenders and Wipers Association; Pacific Coast *See* PACIFIC COAST MARINE FIREMEN, OILERS, WATERTENDERS AND WIPERS ASSOCIATION.

Marine Officers; Brotherhood of A branch of the National Marine Engineers' Beneficial Association (AFL-CIO).

Address: 95 River St., Hoboken, N.J. 07030. Tel. (201) 659–2015

Maritime Labor Board An agency established by Congress in 1938 to mediate labor disputes between companies and organized seamen and longshoremen, as well as to develop a general maritime labor policy.

During its three years of operation, it was considered generally effective as a mediation body. It handled some 195 cases involving 200,000 employees, 79 of which were strike cases.

Source references: Joseph P. Goldberg, *The Maritime Story: A Study in Labor-Management Relations* (Cambridge: Harvard UP, 1958); Charles P. Larrowe, *Maritime Labor Relations on the Great Lakes* (East Lansing: Michigan State Univ., Labor and IRC, 1959); U.S. Maritime Labor Board, *Report to the President and to the Congress, March 1, 1940* (Washington: 1940); ———, *Supplemental Report to the President and to the Congress* (Washington: 1942).

Maritime Trades Department One of the AFL-CIO trade and industrial union departments. The biennial convention is held prior to the regular AFL-CIO convention. Its official quarterly publication is *Maritime.*

The following unions are affiliated with the Department: Air Line Pilots; Aluminum, Brick and Glass Workers; Variety Artists; Federation of Professional Athletes; Boilermakers; Carpenters; Cement Workers; Chemical Workers; Communications Workers; Distillery and Wine Workers; Electrical Workers; Elevator Constructors; Operating Engineers; Fire Fighters; Firemen and Oilers; Food and Commercial Workers; Glass, Pottery, Plastics Workers; Grain Millers; Graphic Arts; Hotel and Restaurant Employees; Iron Workers; Laborers; Laundry and Dry Cleaning Union; Leather Goods Union; Longshoremen; Machinists; Marine and Shipbuilding Workers; Marine Engineers; Allied, Novelty and Production Workers; Office and Professional Employees; Oil, Chemical, and Atomic Workers; Painters; Paperworkers; Plasterers; Plumbers; Railway, Airline and Steamship Clerks; Retail, Wholesale and Department Store Union; Rubber Workers; Seafarers; Sheet Metal Workers; State, County and Municipal Employees; Telegraph Workers; and Textile Workers.

Address: AFL-CIO Building, 815 16th St., N.W., Washington, D.C. 20006. Tel. (202) 628–6300

See also AFL-CIO DEPARTMENTS.

Maritime Union of America; National (AFL-CIO) This union represents unlicensed ship personnel, basically "deck" workers. Its official monthly publications are *The NMU Pilot, ITPE News*, and *NMU Government Operations News.*

Address: 346 West 17th St., New York, N.Y. 10011. Tel. (212) 620–5700

market basket A term for that part of the family budget assigned to the purchase of food. Frequently it refers to a method for determining consumer prices by pricing predetermined or specific items that go into a normal market basket. The items in that market basket are priced at different times to determine the change in prices over a period of time.

See also CONSUMER PRICE INDEX.

Marxism The doctrine or system developed around the theories of Karl Marx.

Maryland Classified Employees Association, Inc. (Ind) An organization affiliated with the Assembly of Governmental Employees. Its official monthly publications are *MCEA News* and *BALCO News.*

Address: 7127 Rutherford Rd., Baltimore, MD. 21207. Tel. (301) 298–8800

Massachusetts choice of procedures Refers to legislation adopted in the state of Massachusetts to handle labor-management disputes. A wide variety of procedures is available to the state, including intervention by the governor, to prevent and settle major disputes affecting the public interest.

Source reference: G. P. Schultz, "The Massachusetts Choice of Procedures Approach to Emergency Disputes," *ILRR*, April 1957.

See also ARBITRATION, COMPULSORY; BOARD OF INQUIRY; GOVERNMENT SEIZURE; MEDIATION; NATIONAL EMERGENCY BOARDS; NATIONAL EMERGENCY PROVISIONS.

mass picketing Picketing is the procedure generally followed by workers during a strike. It involves patrolling, frequently with placards or banners, the entrances of a plant or, during a boycott, patrolling in front of the store or facility which is presumably unfair to the union.

Mass picketing occurs when an effort is made by the union to indicate broad support from its own striking members or from other supporters, and a desire to have the picketing so effective as to prevent other individuals, "strikebreakers" or "scabs," from taking the jobs which the employees left to go on strike.

Occasionally, mass picketing involves a column of strikers who by locking arms and walking in close file may prevent any person or other moving object from passing into the plant or facilities being struck.

In examining the nature of picketing at a particular operation, the courts have concerned themselves with the range of pressure exerted by the strikers from peaceful persuasion to coercive practices and unlawful intimidation.

Source references: American Steel Foundries v. Tri-City Central Trades Council, 257 US 184 (1921); Robert R. R. Brooks, *When Labor Organizes* (New Haven: Yale UP, 1937); David Ziskind, *Strikes and Lockout* (New York: Columbia UP, 1940).

See also AMERICAN STEEL FOUNDRIES V. TRI-CITY CENTRAL TRADES COUNCIL, PICKETING.

mass production Modern production methods which require a highly developed use of machine technology and permit production of standardized products at low cost. These methods utilize large concentrations of capital and substantial divisions of labor. Mass production is considered one of the major keys to modern industrial development and has led to the increased use of management development to achieve a high degree of coordination of operations. All these measures are designed to reduce costs, to standardize products, and to obtain volume production through economy, speed, repetition, and accuracy in design and performance.

Source reference: Dexter S. Kimball, *Principles of Industrial Organization* (New York: McGraw-Hill, 1947).

master A master, whether a master mechanic, master electrician, or master plumber, is a worker who has completed a full apprenticeship program. Technically the individual has achieved the highest skill of the trade and is a skilled artisan who is able to act as an instructor or teacher to apprentices.

Under the guild system, an individual who completed apprenticeship became a journeyman, generally working for a master worker or a craftsworker. Upon completion of the journeyman period, the individual became eligible to set up a private business as a master worker.

Under some of the guild rules, the individual had to satisfy the other masters with a display of the individual's ability and competence as a skilled worker. This involved some demonstration either by examination or by the actual creation of an item which incorporated the individual's work. This was known as the "masterpiece."

The term may also apply to the relationship which exists between a servant and "master," or may simply refer to an employer.

A master may also be an officer of a court, or of a labor relations agency as under the Florida state and local government employees law. The Florida law provides for the appointment of a "special master" by the Public Employees Relations Commission in the impasse resolution procedure. The "special master" holds hearings and renders a recommended decision for settlement of each issue in dispute.

See also GUILDS, MASTER-SERVANT RELATIONSHIP.

master agreement *See* AGREEMENT, MASTER.

masterpiece A piece of work submitted by a journeyman who wanted to qualify as a master under the guild system during the Middle Ages. The masterpiece was supposed to represent the individual's highest skills as a workman in the trade. This was the examination for entrance and qualification as a master.

See also MASTER.

master-servant relationship A form of relationship between employers and employees developed during the industrial period, generally between an apprentice and the master or between an indentured servant and the master. The arrangement was established by contract, and the stipulations of the relationship were set out by agreement and established by law, or through common law practice. The rights and duties of each party were known. The worker was required to perform for a period of time for certain payment and perquisites and the employer was responsible for the acts of his servant and was required to provide proper care and the payment of certain wages.

This was a major step forward from the earlier medieval period which provided for outright ownership of individuals—slaves who were the property of the landowner or serfs who were bound to the land.

The modern employer-employee relationships and free contract arrangements developed from the master-servant relationship.

See also APPRENTICESHIP, INDENTURED APPRENTICESHIP, INDENTURED SERVANT.

Masters, Mates and Pilots; International Organization of The organization was established in New York City in 1887 and was known as the American Brotherhood of Steamboat Pilots. The jurisdiction of the union was broadened to include captains in 1891 and the union was reincorporated on April 3, 1891, under the New York State laws as the American Association of Masters and Pilots of Steam Vessels. The mates were subsequently included and in 1916 the organization became known as the National Organization of Masters, Mates and Pilots of America.

In July 1971, the union became the Marine Division of the International Longshoremen's Association (AFL-CIO). The American Radio Association (AFL-CIO) merged with the union on January 5, 1981. Its monthly publication is *The Master, Mate and Pilot*.

Address: 700 Maritime Blvd., Linthicum Heights, Md. 21090. Tel. (301) 850–8700

Match Workers Council (AFL-CIO) One of the organizing committees of the AFL-CIO which did not attain full-fledged status as an affiliated national or international union. It was disbanded by the AFL-CIO Executive Council.

maternity benefits Benefits generally available through health and insurance plans payable to women workers during pregnancy and childbirth, including hospital, surgical, and medical benefits related to these conditions, and to workers' wives under plans providing for such dependents' benefits. These benefits also include job security against dismissal because of pregnancy and against dismissal during the leave of absence, accumulation of seniority during the leave of absence, and compensation (usually for a limited period of time) during the leave of absence.

Source references: William K. Cooper, "Maternity Disability Benefits: Why Not Compromise?" *Personnel,* March/April 1977; Sheila B. Kamerman, "Child Care and Family Benefits: Policies of Six Industrialized Countries," *MLR,* Nov. 1980; Dorothy R. Kittner, "Maternity Benefits Available to Most Health Plan Participants," *MLR,* May 1978; Michael A. Mass, "Sex Discrimination Based on Pregnancy: The Post-*Gilbert* Environment," *Employee Relations LJ,* Autumn 1978; Frank B. Miller and Mary S. Zitwer, "Women Workers Win One in New York," *LLJ,* Nov. 1977; Robert C. Tilmann, "Teacher Pregnancy: Care to Look at Your Contract?" *Journal of Collective Negotiations in the Public Sector,* Fall 1973; U.S. Dept. of Labor, Women's Bureau, *Maternity Benefit Provisions for Employed Women* (Washington: Bull. no. 272, 1960).

See also MATERNITY LEAVE, PREGNANCY DISCRIMINATION ACT.

maternity leave Applies to the period of time generally granted by an employer for employees to undergo and recuperate from childbirth. The period of time varies under provisions of state laws and in collective bargaining agreements.

With the increase in the number of women in industry, provisions in collective bargaining agreements to safeguard the health and care of the workers as well as the welfare of the child have become more prevalent. The period of leave, before and after confinement, may vary from four months to a year.

Under provisions of the agreement, the worker generally retains her status as an employee with reemployment rights. Provision may also be made for the accumulation of seniority during maternity leave.

Source references: Anna M. Baetjer, *Women in Industry* (Philadelphia: Saunders, 1946); Joe H. Danziger, "Mandatory Maternity Leave of Absence Policies—An Equal Protection Analysis," *IR Law Digest,* Jan. 1973; Dartnell Corporation, *Policies and Allowances for Pregnancy in 140 Companies* (Chicago: Dartnell File P-2: Compensation, 1958); L. Bruce Fryburger, "Maternity Leave Policies Under Title VII," *LLJ,* March 1975; Linda H. Kistler and Carol C. McDonough, "Maternity Leave: Sharing the Costs of Motherhood," *Personnel,* Nov./Dec. 1975; ———, "Paid Maternity Leave—Benefits May Justify the Cost," *LLJ,* Dec. 1975; Mitchell Meyer, *Women and Employee Benefits* (New York: The Conference Board, Report no. 752, 1978); Harry H. Rains, "Problems and Legalities of Maternity Leave, Child Care Leave, and Paid Sick Leave Application," *Journal of Collective Negotiations in the Public Sector,* Fall 1974; Margaret Ann Sipser, "Maternity Leave: Judicial and Arbitral Interpretation, 1970–1972," *LLJ,* March 1973; U.S. CSC, *Maternity/Sick Leave Provisions in Federal Agreements* (Washington: 1975).

maximum wage laws This phrase has little current usage. During the early colonial period, provision was found in some of the Massachusetts laws which prohibited excessive rates for workers.

Occasionally the term is applied to wage restrictions during a war period, such as the limitations during World War II under the Wage Stabilization Act. Such restrictions do not constitute maximum wage laws, but rather set up standards for stabilizing levels of wages under regulations established by Executive Order and the administering agency of government.

See also NATIONAL WAR LABOR BOARD, WAGE STABILIZATION.

McClellan Committee The popular name for the special Senate Select Committee on Improper Activities in the Labor or Management Field under the chairmanship of Senator John L. McClellan (D-Ark).

The committee's hearings, held in 1957, were largely responsible for the passage of the Landrum-Griffin Act, concerned with eliminating some of the activities uncovered by the committee.

Source references: BNA, *The McClellan Hearings, 1957* (Washington: 1958); "Findings From the Second Report of the McClellan Committee," *MLR,* Sept. 1959; John L. McClellan, *Crime Without Punishment* (New

York: Duell, Sloan & Pearce, 1962); Joel Seidman, "Emergence of Concern with Union Government and Administration," *Regulating Union Government*, ed. by Marten S. Estey, Philip Taft, and Martin Wagner (New York: Harper, IRRA Pub. no. 31, 1964); U.S. Congress, Senate, Select Committee on Improper Activities, *Investigation of Improper Activities in the Labor or Management Field, Hearings* (Washington: 1957).

See also LABOR-MANAGEMENT REPORTING AND DISCLOSURE ACT OF 1959.

mealtime The time set aside, frequently by contract, during which the employee is to take his food, whether lunch or dinner.

Some contracts make provision for meal periods when a person is required to work a certain number of hours beyond the regular scheduled workday. The following clause suggests one procedure:

> No employee shall be required to work longer than five consecutive hours without a meal period except by mutual agreement between the union and the company. Meal periods shall be for one hour unless changed to a lesser period by mutual agreement.

See also LUNCH PERIOD.

means test *See* NEEDS TEST.

Meany (George) Center for Labor Studies Established by the AFL-CIO in 1969 as a national school for labor leaders. Course offerings are available to all full-time officers, representatives, and staff members of AFL-CIO affiliates without charge. Classes are limited to 25 participants.

The Center's core programs are, in general, one week in length. Institute topics include, among others, collective bargaining, new staff training, labor law, psychology for union leaders, computers, economics, grant writing, public speaking, union publications, organizing, arbitration, and issues for working women.

The Center and Antioch University have established a college degree program which confers a Bachelor of Arts degree with a major in labor studies. The curriculum covers three major areas: general education, labor studies, and work study. At least 70 union officers and staff members have earned degrees as of 1983.

The Center was first known as the National Labor Studies Center and then as the AFL-CIO Labor Studies Center. It adopted its present name in 1975.

Address: 10000 New Hampshire Ave., Silver Spring, Md. 20903. Tel. (301) 431–6400

Source references: AFL-CIO, *Proceedings of the Twelfth Constitutional Convention* (Washington: 1978); *George Meany Center for Labor Studies, 1984–1985 Catalogue, Our 15th Year* (Silver Spring, Md.: 1984).

measured day work This is sometimes referred to as measured day rate. It is a wage system, somewhat complex in nature, which was established primarily because of union opposition to the use of incentive plans. The system first establishes specific standards of performance through detailed and careful use of time study and establishes a basic hourly or day wage for each job classification. The individual, in addition to the base wage rate, receives added compensation based on his dependability, versatility on the job, quality of output, punctuality, length of service, and sometimes even the cost of living. This added inducement is designed to take into consideration any factors which the employer feels are likely to increase production.

The measured day rate is based upon an examination of the person's previous job performance, generally for a period of a month or more. It is considered successful in operations where the base rate varies from an accepted percentage (75–90) of the total measured day rate. This in a way, of course, is also an incentive plan but is sufficiently broad in its application to mitigate some of the opposition of workers opposed to the introduction of wage incentives.

Source references: Allan Flanders, "Measured Daywork and Collective Bargaining," *BJIR*, Nov. 1973; Dexter S. Kimball, *Principles of Industrial Organization* (New York: McGraw-Hill, 1947); Richard Martin, "How Companies Are Using Office Work Measurement," *Management Review*, July 1966; William R. Spriegel, *Industrial Management* (New York: Wiley, 1947); Andrew J. Waring, "The Case for the Measured Day Rate Plan," *PJ*, Oct. 1961.

See also INCENTIVE CONTRACTS, INCENTIVE RATE, INCENTIVE WAGE.

Meat Cutters and Butcher Workmen of North America; Amalgamated (AFL-

CIO) The meat cutters and butchers started as directly affiliated locals of the AFL in 1897.

Unions which have merged with the Meat Cutters include: Leather Workers International Union (AFL) in the early 1950s, the Stockyard Workers Association of America (Ind) in July 1954, International Fur and Leather Workers' Union of United States and Canada (Ind) on February 22, 1955, National Agricultural Workers Union (AFL-CIO) in August 1960, and the United Packinghouse, Food and Allied Workers (AFL-CIO) on July 1, 1968.

On June 7, 1979, the union merged with the Retail Clerks International Union and formed the United Food and Commercial Workers International Union (AFL-CIO).

Source references: David Brody, *The Butcher Workmen: A Study of Unionization* (Cambridge: Harvard UP, 1964); Lewis Corey, *Meat and Man: A Study of Monopoly, Unionism and Food Policy* (New York: Viking Press, 1950); Thomas B. Ewers, "A Comparative Study of Grievances in the Meat Packing Industry" (Master's thesis, Loyola Univ., 1957); Hilton E. Hanna (ed.), *50 Golden Years, The Amalgamated Meat Cutters and Butcher Workmen of North America* (Chicago: 1947); Hilton E. Hanna and Joseph Belsky, *Picket and the Pen: The "Pat Gorman" Story* (Yonkers: American Institute of Social Science, 1960).

See also FOOD AND COMMERCIAL WORKERS INTERNATIONAL UNION; UNITED (AFL-CIO).

mechanical aptitude tests Examinations for the purpose of measuring an individual's mechanical ability.

See also APTITUDE TESTS.

mechanical pacing Usually refers to the operations of an assembly line, where the speed at which the machine is set determines the pace at which the individual operates. Although the pacing is done by the machine and by the mechanical time set, as a practical matter, the employees have the opportunity to discuss with the company through collective bargaining the speed at which the machine is to operate. Adjustments are worked out so that the individual produces a fair amount, depending upon the flow of material and the movement of the assembly, and at the same time the employers receive a fair day's work.

Negotiations for rates depend in part on the setting of the pace of the machine. This may be considered as part of the wage arrangement since under a paced operation, it is impossible for the individual to increase his productivity beyond the speed of the machine. The machine automatically sets the maximum production rate.

Mechanics and Foremen of Naval Shore Establishments; National Association of Master Disaffiliated from the AFL-CIO in April 1964; no longer functions as trade union.

Mechanics Educational Society of America (AFL-CIO) A union of skilled tool and die makers in the automobile industry. Its official monthly publication is the *MESA Educator*.

Address: 15300 East Seven Mile Rd., Detroit, Mich. 48205. Tel. (313) 372–5700

Source reference: Harry Dahlheimer, *A History of the Mechanics Educational Society of America in Detroit From Its Inception in 1933 Through 1937* (Detroit: Wayne UP, 1951).

mechanization A term of very broad meaning, but essentially dealing with changes in the processes of production which result in the displacement of human labor or human skills by machine operations. Mechanization may achieve a better flow of materials and increase output through the introduction of new and better machinery.

Although a great boon in the ability of man to increase production, mechanization has over periods of time created much unrest and economic disorganization when it resulted in mass layoffs of employees and has come without adequate protection and planning to take care of the needs of individual workers whose jobs are threatened or have been displaced. A similar movement is sometimes referred to as the "Automation Revolution."

Source references: John T. Dunlop (ed.), *Automation and Technological Change* (Englewood Cliffs: PH, 1962); Lincoln Fairley, "The ILWU-PMA Mechanization and Modernization Agreement," *LLJ*, July 1961; Bradley T. Gale, "Can More Capital Buy Higher Productivity?" *Harvard BR*, July/Aug. 1980; Roy B. Helfgott, "Easing the

Impact of Technological Change on Employees: A Conspectus of United States Experience," *ILR*, June 1965; Harry Jerome, *Mechanization in Industry* (New York: NBER, 1934); Charles C. Killingsworth, "Cooperative Approaches to Problems of Technological Change," *Adjusting to Technological Change* (New York: Harper, IRRA Pub. no. 29, 1963); "Mechanization Clause in New United States Dockworkers' Agreement," *ILR*, July 1962; Morris Philipson (ed.), *Automation—Implications for the Future* (New York: Random House, Vintage Books, 1962); B. A. Stout and C. M. Downing, "Agricultural Mechanisation Policy," *ILR*, March/April 1976.

See also AUTOMATION, INDUSTRIAL REVOLUTION, ROBOTICS, TECHNOLOGICAL UNEMPLOYMENT, WEST COAST LONGSHORE MECHANIZATION AGREEMENT.

Mechanization and Modernization Agreement *See* WEST COAST LONGSHORE MECHANIZATION AGREEMENT.

med-arb An impasse procedure in which a neutral third party serves as a mediator and arbitrator. Items not resolved in mediation are subject to an arbitration decision by the mediator-arbitrator. Recourse to med-arb requires giving up the right to strike or to lockout.

Source references: Karen Dunlap, "Mediation-Arbitration: Reactions From the Rank and File," *MLR*, Sept. 1973; Sam Kagel, "Combining Mediation and Arbitration," *MLR*, Sept. 1973; Sam Kagel and John Kagel, "Using Two New Arbitration Techniques," *MLR*, Nov. 1972; Harry Polland, "Mediation-Arbitration: A Trade Union View," *MLR*, Sept. 1973; Jerome H. Ross, *The Med-Arb Process in Labor Agreement Negotiations* (Washington: SPIDR, Occasional Paper no. 82–1, 1982).

mediation In current usage, the terms "conciliation" and "mediation" are often used interchangeably. For example, the former U.S. Conciliation Service is now known as the Federal Mediation and Conciliation Service.

The distinction between mediation and conciliation is primarily in the nature of the activity of the person who is acting as conciliator or mediator. In conciliation generally, the person acting as the conciliator merely attempts to bring the parties together and permits them to act by themselves in resolving their problems. In mediation, on the other hand, the involvement of the third party is more active and the mediator attempts to suggest to the parties various proposals and methods for the actual resolution of the problem.

In neither conciliation nor mediation does the conciliator or mediator make decisions. In the most active role, possible areas for compromise and additional points of view to the situation are suggested, but fundamentally, it is the parties who have to resolve the dispute. If the parties are unwilling to help find a solution, the role of the conciliator or mediator is of relatively little value.

Under previous usage, the term "mediation" applied to a third party intervention and "conciliation" was merely the device designed to bring the two parties together without the presence of a third party. That usage is not presently accepted.

As a practical matter, however, there is relatively little need to draw any sharp distinction between conciliation and mediation. The roles of the intermediaries can shift from one to the other depending on which technique is most effective and best designed to bring the parties to the point where they themselves can find solutions.

One of the key ingredients in the mediation process is the attempt to sense or determine the actual needs of the parties. Through the interchange of ideas and concepts and a clarification of the particular issues of prime concern, as against those which are peripheral, the mediator is able to bring the parties to the point where a solution is advanced either by the mediator or by the parties themselves. The mediator rarely acts to pressure either party to accept a solution which the mediator has placed on the table for discussion and rarely takes part in debate concerning the merits of a particular issue except where it comes to a matter of fact which can be determined either by reference to statistical or other data or to court decisions or the actual language of a statute.

Source references: Mollie H. Bowers, Ronald L. Seeber, and Lamont E. Stallworth, "Grievance Mediation: A Route to Resolution for the Cost-Conscious 1980s,"

LLJ, Aug. 1982; Jeanne M. Brett, Stephen B. Goldberg, and William Ury, "Mediation and Organizational Development: Models for Conflict Management," *Proceedings of the 33d A/M, IRRA*, ed. by Barbara Dennis (Madison: 1981); Harold W. Davey, *Third Parties in Labor Relations—Negotiation, Mediation, Arbitration* (Ames: Iowa State Univ., IRC, WP no. 1973–04, 1973); Ann Douglas, "What Can Research Tell Us About Mediation," *LLJ*, Aug. 1955; Paul F. Gerhart and John E. Drotning, "Dispute Settlement and the Intensity of Mediation," *IR*, Fall 1980; Gordon A. Gregory and Robert E. Rooney, Jr., "Grievance Mediation: A Trend in the Cost-Conscious Eighties," *LLJ*, Aug. 1980; Clark Kerr, "Industrial Conflict and Its Mediation," *American Journal of Sociology*, Nov. 1954; Thomas A. Kochan and Todd Jick, *The Public Sector Mediation Process, A Theory and Empirical Examination* (Ithaca: Cornell Univ., NYSSILR Reprint Series no. 440, 1978); Joseph Krislov, "Mediation Under the Railway Labor Act: A Process in Search of a Name," *LLJ*, May 1976; Henry Landsberger, "Final Report of a Research Project," *LLJ*, Aug. 1956; ———, "Interim Report of a Research Project in Mediation," *LLJ*, Aug. 1955; William M. Leiserson, "The Function of Mediation in Labor Relations," *Proceedings of the 4th A/M, IRRA*, ed. by L. Reed Tripp (Madison: 1952); James A. Mackraz, "General Role of Mediation in Collective Bargaining," *LLJ*, June 1960; Walter A. Maggiolo, *Techniques of Mediation in Labor Disputes* (Dobbs Ferry, N.Y.: Oceana Publications, 1971); William McPherson, "European Variation on the Mediation Theme," *LLJ*, Aug. 1955; ———, "Grievance Mediation Under Collective Bargaining," *ILRR*, Jan. 1956; William E. Simkin, *Mediation and the Dynamics of Collective Bargaining* (Washington: BNA, 1971).

See also CONCILIATION, DISPUTE ADJUSTMENT, FEDERAL MEDIATION AND CONCILIATION SERVICE (FMCS), INDUSTRIAL DISPUTES, LABOR DISPUTE, MED-ARB, NATIONAL EMERGENCY BOARDS, STRIKE, WAGE MEDIATION.

mediation, preventive A mediation procedure primarily used to maintain a continuing dialogue between labor and management and to explore avenues and procedures for effective problem solving away from crisis bargaining with deadlines and strike threats at the expiration of the contract. The neutral mediators work with labor and management between contract negotiations to seek ways to alleviate future difficulties; to establish more cooperative working relationships between unions and management, and in other ways to give professional advice on technical matters so that the parties have adequate factual knowledge in addition to proper attitudes in getting along with one another.

The National Labor-Management Panel in its second report issued on December 30, 1964, to the Director of the Federal Mediation and Conciliation Service (FMCS), following review of various procedures used in problem solving by management and labor, recommended the expansion of the FMCS preventive mediation program.

Among the types of activities which fall into the preventive mediation category are: consultation, pre-negotiation conferences and study activity, continuing liaison, post-negotiation contract review, labor-management committees, training programs, and the Relations by Objectives (RBO) program. The RBO program developed by the FMCS in 1973, involves a team of mediators who "spend three-four days with local union and management leadership helping them to thoroughly analyze their troubled relationship and jointly determine goals, with a timetable, through which they believe they can move their relationship from what it is to what they want it to be."

Source references: Paul Prasow, "Preventive Mediation, A Technique to Improve Industrial Relations," *LLJ*, Aug. 1950; Carl Sallade, "Preventive Mediation: What It Is and What It Has Been," *Industrial and Labor Relations Forum*, Dec. 1973; John R. Stepp, Robert P. Baker, and Jerome T. Barrett, "Helping Labor and Management See and Solve Problems," *MLR*, Sept. 1982; U.S. FMCS, *Annual Report 1981* (Washington: 1982).

See also FEDERAL MEDIATION AND CONCILIATION SERVICE (FMCS), JOINT PRODUCTION COMMITTEES, NATIONAL EMERGENCY BOARDS, NATIONAL LABOR-MANAGEMENT PANEL, TOLEDO INDUSTRIAL PEACE BOARD (TOLEDO PLAN).

mediation board A group generally established to effect a settlement between labor and management in a particular dispute. A mediation board under some state statutes may be a tripartite board or an all-public board, either ad hoc, or on a continuing basis. Sometimes a mediation board may consist of a single person.

See also NATIONAL DEFENSE MEDIATION BOARD, NATIONAL MEDIATION BOARD, NEW YORK CITY OFFICE OF COLLECTIVE BARGAINING, TOLEDO INDUSTRIAL PEACE BOARD (TOLEDO PLAN), TOLEDO LABOR-MANAGEMENT-CITIZENS COMMITTEE.

mediation with finality President Lyndon B. Johnson, following the 20-day extension granted for negotiation in the 1966–1967 railroad dispute, requested Congress on May 4, 1967, to enact legislation to delay a threatened work stoppage until January 1, 1969.

Public Law 90–54, passed by Congress and signed by the President on July 17, 1967, provided for a 90-day period consisting of 30 days of mediation, 30 days of factfinding, and another 30 days for the recommendations of a five-man board appointed to seek a settlement between the railroads and the six shop craft unions. If no settlement were reached within the 90-day period, Congress was authorized to effectuate the board's recommendation, while both sides continued to negotiate. The board's recommendations were to remain in effect until January 1, 1969 (or until an agreement was reached, whichever occurred earlier).

Source references: Emergency Settlements of Railway Labor Disputes-Shopcraft Dispute (1967)—Joint Resolution of July 17, 1967, P.L. 90–54, 81 Stat. 122; "Report of the Special Railroad Board," *MLR*, Nov. 1967; "Special Message to the Congress Recommending Procedure to Complete Collective Bargaining in the Railway Labor Dispute, May 4, 1967, to the Congress of the United States," *Public Papers of the Presidents of the United States, Lyndon B. Johnson, Book I* (Washington: 1968).

mediator The person who is a conciliator or mediator. An impartial third party or public official, or, rarely, a person chosen by both parties, who, under federal or state law, meets with the parties, acts as a go-between, and suggests possible avenues for resolving the particular issue in dispute. Some refer to the mediator as an industrial diplomat or catalytic agent who is able to effect solutions to particular problems by working with the parties but is not permitted to use force or pressure to effect a settlement. In attempting to find a common basis for agreement, the mediator does not attempt to impose any particular solution, but tries to find some solution which would be acceptable to the parties and which they would feel helped resolve their problems. The mediator's powers are essentially powers of persuasion and conviction rather than force.

Source references: Samuel E. Angoff, "Impartial Opinion and Constructive Criticism of Mediators, Mediation Agencies and Conciliators," *LLJ*, Jan. 1961; Joseph F. Byrnes, "Mediator-Generated Pressure Tactics," *Journal of Collective Negotiations in the Public Sector*, Vol. 7, no. 2, 1978; David C. Haman, Arthur P. Brief, and Richard Pegnetter, "Studies in Mediation and the Training of Public Sector Mediators," *Journal of Collective Negotiations in the Public Sector*, Vol. 7, no. 4, 1978; Bernard P. Indik et al., *The Mediator: Background, Self-Image and Attitudes* (New Brunswick: Rutgers Univ., Institute of Management and Labor Relations, 1966); Deborah M. Kolb, "Roles and Strategies of Labor Mediators," *Proceedings of the 32d A/M, IRRA*, ed. by Barbara Dennis (Madison: 1980); ———, "Roles Mediators Play: State and Federal Practice," *IR*, Winter 1981; Arthur S. Meyer, "Function of the Mediator in Collective Bargaining," *ILRR*, Jan. 1960; Harold R. Newman, "Mediator Pressures—High and Low," *Journal of Collective Negotiations in the Public Sector*, Vol. 8, no. 1, 1979; Charles A. Odewahn, "The Mediator in the Public Sector—A New Breed," *LLJ*, Oct. 1972; Eva Robins, *A Guide for Labor Mediators* (Honolulu: Univ. of Hawaii, IRC, 1976); William E. Simkin, "Code of Professional Conduct for Labor Mediators," *LLJ*, Oct. 1964; Damon Stetson, "Focus on Bargaining: Improving News Coverage, The Mediator's Role," *American Federationist*, May 1974; Allan Weisenfeld, "Profile of a Labor Mediator," *LLJ*, Oct. 1962; Perry A. Zirkel and J. Gary Lutz, "Characteristics and Functions of Mediators: A Pilot Study," *AJ*, June 1981.

See also ARBITRATOR, CONCILIATION, CONCILIATOR, FACTFINDER, MEDIATION.

medical benefits *See* HEALTH INSURANCE.

medical care Refers to particular plans in or subject to a collective bargaining agreement or in a statement of company policy in nonunion plants setting forth the specific health insurance or service program for the individuals covered under a plan.

Source references: Caldwell B. Esselstyn, "Changing Patterns of Medical Care," *American Federationist,* Oct. 1967; C. Wayne Higgins and Billy U. Philips, "Keeping Employees Well: How Company-Sponsored Fitness Programs Keep Employees on the Job," *Management Review,* Dec. 1979; Seymour Lusterman, *Industry Roles in Health Care* (New York: The Conference Board, Report no. 610, 1974); Raymond Munts, *Bargaining for Health: Labor Unions, Health Insurance, and Medical Care* (Madison: Univ. of Wisconsin Press, 1967); Thomas H. Paine and Richard G. Woods, "Evaluating the Medical Care Program," *Personnel,* Jan./Feb. 1960; E. R. Plunkett and Aaron Levenstein, "Setting Up a Company Medical Program," *Management Review,* April 1976; Rosalind M. Schwartz (ed.), *Health Care and Industrial Relations: Costs, Conflicts and Controversy* (Los Angeles: UC, Institute of IR, Monograph and Research series 28, 1981); Herman M. and Anne R. Somers, *Doctors, Patients, and Health Insurance: The Organization and Financing of Medical Care* (Washington: Brookings Institution, 1961); William M. Timmins, "Public Employee Physical Fitness Programs," *Public Personnel Management,* Summer 1981.

See also HEALTH INSURANCE.

medical care plans Group insurance or service plans which generally provide hospital, surgical, and medical benefits on a group basis. Some of these plans are prepaid medical care plans, such as those of Group Health in Washington, D.C., and the Kaiser-Permanente in California and Hawaii. Others are indemnity plans.

Source references: Isidore S. Falk, "Labor's Interests in Medical Care Plans," *MLR,* Feb. 1960; Dennis F. Quigley, "Changes in Selected Health Care Programs," *MLR,* Dec. 1975; Quentin I. Smith, "Health Care Coverage and Costs: A Major Challenge for Innovative Managers," *Management Review,* Dec. 1980; Kevin G. Wetmore, "Improvements in Employee Health Care Benefits," *MLR,* Aug. 1972; Sander W. Wirpel, "Management's Interests in Medical Care Plans," *MLR,* Feb. 1960.

See also HEALTH MAINTENANCE ORGANIZATION (HMO), SURGICAL BENEFITS.

medical examination An evaluation of the medical condition of an individual. Some employers require physical or medical examinations prior to employment and/or prior to coverage by the company's insurance program. In some situations, medical examinations are set up for individuals who have been on leave for medical reasons to assure that the individual is physically qualified to perform the job when he returns to the plant.

In some plants medical examinations are provided periodically for the staff of the company in order to assure that adequate protection and care are provided for individuals who are important members of the management team.

medicare The term now generally applies to the Social Security Act amendments of 1965 which provide broad programs dealing with medical care for the aged. The program provides benefits which are divided into two sections—the basic plan, which covers hospitalization and related costs and for which practically all persons 65 and over are eligible; and the voluntary supplemental plan, for which persons 65 and over must apply and which helps pay for certain physicians' and dentists' services, home health services, and additional medical services.

Source references: Robert J. Myers, *Medicare* (Homewood: Irwin, 1970); Milton I. Roemer, *The Organisation and Medical Care Under Social Security* (Geneva: ILO, Studies and Reports New Series no. 73, 1969); Herman M. and Anne Ramsay Somers, *Medicare and the Hospitals, Issues and Prospects* (Washington: Brookings Institution, 1967); U.S. GAO, *History of the Rising Costs of the Medicare and Medicaid Programs and Attempts to Control These Costs: 1966–1975, Department of Health, Education, and Welfare* (Washington: 1976); ———, *Perfor-*

mance of the Social Security Administration Compared with that of Private Fiscal Intermediaries in Dealing with Institutional Providers of Medicare Services (Washington: 1975); Erwin Witkin, *The Impact of Medicare* (Springfield, Ill.: Thomas, 1971).

See also HEALTH INSURANCE.

medicine, industrial *See* INDUSTRIAL MEDICINE.

meet and confer A procedure in which an employer and an employee organization exchange information, views, concerns, and proposals to endeavor to reach agreement on such matters as salaries, terms, and conditions of employment.

Kenneth Warner makes the following distinction between "meet and confer" and collective bargaining: "Under a comprehensive bargaining system, the negotiated settlement is put in writing in the form of a mutually binding agreement. The settlement has been reached through bilateral decisions of both management and the employee organization. Under a meet and confer system, the results of meetings may or may not be reduced to writing and are seldom binding on either party. Management gives serious consideration to employees' proposals, but the final settlement is a unilateral decision of management."

Source reference: Richard Salik (ed.), *The Right to Meet and Confer—Laws and Policies* (Chicago: PPA, PERL no. 10, 1968).

membership in good standing The term generally applies to persons who are members or have applied for membership in the union or have come into the union through a union security provision in the collective bargaining agreement.

The term is an important part of union security, particularly under maintenance-of-membership clauses which require the employer to discharge individuals who are not in good standing. Generally, individuals who pay their dues and normal assessments under the union's constitution and bylaws retain their membership in good standing. Provision is also found under the constitutions and bylaws of some trade unions where membership in a union may be lost because of conduct unbecoming a union member or as a result of objectionable activities of a union member, such as crossing a bona fide picket line.

Since the individual's good standing in a union is important in relation to his employment and qualification to run for union office, safeguards have been set up not only in union constitutions and bylaws, but also by the courts in their reviews of union expulsions.

See also LABOR-MANAGEMENT REPORTING AND DISCLOSURE ACT OF 1959, MAINTENANCE OF MEMBERSHIP, UNION SECURITY CLAUSES, UNION SHOP.

membership limitations *See* LIMITATION OF MEMBERSHIP.

members only contract *See* BARGAINING AGENT, FOR MEMBERS ONLY.

memorandum of understanding A written agreement prepared jointly by management and an employee organization reached through meet and confer procedures and concerning wages, hours, or working conditions. The agreement may be submitted to the appropriate determining body or a government official for ratification and implementation.

Source references: Los Angeles Administrative Code, Ch. 8, Div. 4, Ordinance no. 141,527, Sec. 4.801; *San Francisco Administrative Code*, Art. XI.A, Ch. 16, Sec. 16.202(11).

Memphis Fire Department v. Stotts A 1984 Supreme Court decision holding that bona fide seniority systems are protected by Title VII of the 1964 Civil Rights Act and that federal judges lack the authority to modify consent decrees that require white employees to be laid off before black employees with less seniority.

The case stemmed from planned citywide layoffs based on the "last hired, first fired" rule. Black firefighters obtained court orders protecting hiring and promotion gains made under a previous consent decree, with the result that senior nonminority employees were laid off or demoted. Although the lower courts held that the discriminatory effect of the seniority rule would justify modifying the consent decree to prevent minority layoffs, the Court, relying on *Teamsters v. U.S.*, held that seniority could only be awarded in cases in which the beneficiary had been an actual victim of discrimination.

Source reference: Firefighters Local Union No. 1784 v. Stotts and *Memphis Fire Department v. Stotts,* U.S. Sup.Ct. Nos. 82–206, 82–229, 34 FEP Cases 1702 (1984).

See also BONA FIDE SENIORITY SYSTEM, TEAMSTERS V. U.S.

men's jobs Certain jobs which are either traditionally or frequently performed only by men.

The specific qualifications of a job may in part eliminate the likelihood of it being performed by a woman or conversely a job may have certain requirements which are not normally filled by a man. Work requirements, not the sex of the employee, determine who gets the job. Under the Equal Pay Act (an amendment to the Fair Labor Standards Act) and the Civil Rights Act of 1964, job discrimination on the basis of sex is forbidden.

See also EQUAL PAY ACT OF 1963, EQUAL PAY FOR EQUAL WORK, OCCUPATIONAL SEGREGATION.

mentor A person who guides, supports, and challenges an employee or student in order to help the individual realize career or educational potential. A mentor may serve as a teacher and a coach for an individual during a transition period such as, for example, following a promotion.

Source references: Laurent A. Daloz, "Mentors, Teachers Who Make a Difference," *Change,* Sept. 1983; Daniel J. Levinson, *The Seasons of a Man's Life* (New York: Knopf, 1978); Michael M. Lombardo and Morgan W. McCall, Jr., "Management Homilies: Do They Hold Up Under Close Examination," *Management Review,* July 1983; Barbara M. Wertheimer and Anne H. Nelson, *Education for Social Change: Two Routes* (Ithaca: NYSSILR, Cornell Univ., Reprint no. 526, 1982).

merchant gilds Trade groups active in the Middle Ages which attempted to control trade through regulations limiting the number of individuals entering the trade and keeping the group to a small but effective regulatory trade agency.

See also GILD (GUILD) SYSTEM, GUILDS.

mercury poisoning A form of industrial disease which was common among workers handling chemical compounds in the period of early industrial development. It was one of the factors leading to increased state legislation for the protection of employees.

See also INDUSTRIAL DISEASE, INDUSTRIAL POISON, OCCUPATIONAL SAFETY AND HEALTH ACT (OSHA) OF 1970, WORKERS COMPENSATION.

merit A term to reflect and measure the effectiveness of an individual's work performance on the job. It may include the worker's attitude toward the job. It may also refer to ability to show improvement in quality of work as well as dependability. The term is of substantial importance in the handling of promotions. The term is frequently considered together with ability.

See also ABILITY, EFFICIENCY RATING.

merit increase A voluntary pay increase to an individual employee because of the quality of the work, improved efficiency, or as a reward for increased production, improvement in attitude, or quality of performance.

Merit increases are distinguishable from increases due primarily to length of service, which are sometimes referred to as longevity adjustments. These are generally given to the employee because of length of service with reasonable performance, but are not based on merit except as they go to the mere adequacy of the performance.

Source references: C. Richard Farmer, "Merit Pay: Viable?" *Personnel,* Sept./Oct. 1978; Douglas L. Fleuter, "A Different Approach to Merit Increases," *PJ,* April 1979; James G. Goodale and Michael W. Mouser, "Developing and Auditing a Merit Pay System," *PJ,* May 1981; Edward E. Lawler, "Merit Pay: Fact or Fiction?" *Management Review,* April 1981; James R. Miller and Jon I. Young, "Merit Pay: An Unexamined Concept in Higher Education," *Journal of the College and University Personnel Association,* Winter 1979; William H. Mobley, "The Link Between MBO and Merit Compensation," *PJ,* June 1974; Thomas H. Patten, Jr., "Merit Increase and the Facts of Organizational Life," *Management of Personnel Quarterly,* Summer 1968; Charles A. Peck, *Compensating Salaried Employees During Inflation:*

General vs. Merit Increases (New York: The Conference Board, Report 796, 1981); Jeffrey D. Schwartz, "Maintaining Merit Compensation in a High Inflationary Economy," *PJ*, Feb. 1982; George W. Torrence, "Administering Merit Increases for Salaried Personnel," *Management Record*, Nov. 1961.

See also LONGEVITY PAY.

merit principle The concept that the selection and retention of employees are based on qualification, ability, and performance. It serves as the basis for the merit system, which is also referred to as a civil service system.

The National Governors' Conference in 1967 defined it as "the concept that public employees should be selected and retained solely on the basis of merit. Political, religious, or racial considerations should play no part in such employment practices as selection, promotion, wages, career progression, assignment, and discharge."

Section 4701 of the Intergovernmental Personnel Act of 1970 calls for the development of personnel administration consistent with the following merit principles:

(1) Recruiting, selecting, and advancing employees on the basis of their relative ability, knowledge, and skills, including open consideration of qualified applicants for initial appointment;
(2) Providing equitable and adequate compensation;
(3) Training employees, as needed, to assure high-quality performance;
(4) Retaining employees on the basis of the adequacy of their performance, correcting inadequate performance, and separating employees whose inadequate performance cannot be corrected;
(5) Assuring fair treatment of applicants and employees in all aspects of personnel administration without regard to political affiliation, race, color, national origin, sex, or religious creed and with proper regard for their privacy and constitutional rights as citizens; and
(6) Assuring that employees are protected against coercion for partisan political purposes and are prohibited from using their official authority for the purpose of interfering with or affecting the result of an election or a nomination for office.

Source references: Intergovernmental Personnel Act of 1970, Pub. L. 91–648, Jan. 5, 1971, 84 Stat. 1909 (codified as amended in scattered sections of 5 and 42 U.S.C.); *Report of the Task Force on State and Local Government Labor Relations, 1967 Executive Committee, National Governors' Conference* (Chicago: PPA, 1967); Joel Seidman and Joyce M. Najita, *The Merit Principle and Collective Bargaining in Hawaii* (Honolulu: Hawaii, Dept. of Personnel Services, 1976); U.S. Dept. of Labor, LMSA, *Collective Bargaining in Public Employment and the Merit System* (Washington: 1972).

See also CIVIL SERVICE, CIVIL SERVICE ACT OF 1883.

merit progression *See* WAGE PROGRESSION.

merit rating A system used to measure periodically the relative work performance of employees. The appraisal is generally used to determine which employees are eligible for wage adjustments or promotions. It may also be utilized for other personnel purposes, including transfer, as well as to assess the individual's potential for new or advanced positions.

The term "merit rating" also has application to certain types of state unemployment tax. The merit rating system in unemployment insurance statutes evaluates the actual experience of individual companies in providing steady employment, that is, showing a relatively low rate of unemployment. The unemployment compensation tax is adjusted accordingly on a scale, for example, from 0 to 3 percent, based on the actual rating or experience of the particular employer. The steadier the employment, the lower the tax rate.

The term "merit rating" is sometimes used as the equivalent of the term "efficiency rating" or "performance rating."

Source references: Joseph M. Becker, *Experience Rating in Unemployment Insurance: Virtue or Vice* (Kalamazoo: Upjohn Institute for Employment Research, 1972); I. F. Denny, "How to (Mis-) Use Merit Assessment," *Personnel Administration*, July/Aug. 1964; William M. Fox, "Consentient Merit Rating: A Critical Incident Approach," *Personnel*, July/Aug. 1981; James G. Goodale and Michael W. Mouser, "Developing and Auditing a Merit Pay System," *PJ*, May 1981;

Richard N. Schowengerdt, "How Reliable are Merit Rating Techniques?" *PJ*, July 1975 and Sept. 1975; William R. Spriegel and Edwin W. Mumma, *Merit Rating of Supervisors and Executives* (Austin: Bureau of Business Research, Univ. of Texas, Personnel Study no. 14, 1961); Joseph Tiffin, "Six Merit Rating Systems," *PJ*, Jan. 1959.

See also EFFICIENCY RATING, EXPERIENCE RATING, INDUSTRIAL EFFORT, PERFORMANCE APPRAISAL, RATING.

merit review The procedure set up unilaterally by the employer or under the terms of a contract to provide for an examination at regular intervals of the rating of individual employees. The review may provide for appeal through the regular grievance machinery, where it occurs under a contract with a union, or by some other means to assure that any individual who feels that the ratings are improperly set will have an opportunity to present the case.

Source reference: Philip M. Oliver, "Mechanics of Conducting a Merit Review Program," *PJ*, Nov. 1960.

merit system The mechanism established to measure the efficient performance of individuals, usually for the purpose of effecting an appointment, promotion, or transfer. In promotions, conflict sometimes develops because of the relative weight to be accorded length of service and the ability and competence of the individual.

The merit system is also known as the civil service system, in which personnel actions are based on merit and examinations, as distinguished from the "spoils system" or the political system. According to Stahl, early application of the merit system concerned only entrance into government service. The term today "is commonly used not only to convey a form of selection for entrance to the service but also to embrace other aspects of the personnel system—advancement on merit, pay related to the nature of the job and to quality of performance, and desirable working conditions. In its broadest sense a merit system in modern government means a personnel system in which comparative merit or achievement governs each individual's selection and progress in the service and in which the conditions and rewards of performance contribute to the competency and continuity of the service."

Source references: Joel Seidman and Joyce M. Najita, *The Merit Principle and Collective Bargaining in Hawaii* (Honolulu: Hawaii, Dept. of Personnel Services, 1976); O. Glenn Stahl, *Public Personnel Administration* (7th ed., New York: Harper & Row, 1976).

See also CIVIL SERVICE, MERIT PRINCIPLE.

Merit Systems Protection Board (MSPB) An independent federal agency created by Title II of the Civil Service Reform Act of 1978. The three members of the Board are appointed to seven-year terms by the President with Senate approval. The Board is authorized to review regulations and programs of OPM and actions of other agencies to ensure adherence to the merit system and to guard against prohibited personnel actions. The Board hears appeals from federal employees and orders corrective and/or disciplinary action against an employee or agency when appropriate. It is also empowered to hear cases involving adverse personnel actions, including allegations of discrimination. Employees, however, may appeal such MSPB decisions to the EEOC.

The independent special counsel within the MSPB is authorized to investigate charges of prohibited personnel practices, including reprisals against whistleblowers. The special counsel may request the MSPB to enjoin prohibited practices and prosecute violations of the merit system.

Source references: Civil Service Reform Act of 1978, 5 U.S.C. 1201 et seq. (1982): U.S. OPM, *Civil Service Reform, A Report on the First Year* (Washington: 1980).

merit wage adjustment The adjustment following a merit review which shows that subject employees have increased their efficiency or increased the quality of their performances.

Merrick multiple-piece rate plan An incentive plan similar to that used by Frederick W. Taylor, known as the Taylor Differential Piece Rate Plan, which was established at the Midvale Steel Company, Philadelphia, Pennsylvania, in 1884.

Under the Taylor Plan, those working at or below the standard received the normal piece rate, whereas those performing above the standard received special earnings under the incentive plan.

The Merrick Multiple Piece Rate Plan provides an additional scale for workers who are below the standard.

Source references: Charles W. Lytle, *Wage Incentive Plans* (New York: Ronald Press, 1942); F. W. Taylor, "A Piece Rate System," *Transactions,* Vol. 16, 1895.

See also DIFFERENTIAL PIECE-RATE PLAN.

Messengers; The National Association of Special Delivery (AFL-CIO) On July 1, 1971, the union merged with the National Association of Post Office and General Services Maintenance Employees (AFL-CIO), National Federation of Post Office Motor Vehicle Employees (AFL-CIO), National Postal Union (Ind), and United Federation of Postal Clerks (AFL-CIO) to form the American Postal Workers Union (AFL-CIO).

See also POSTAL WORKERS UNION; AMERICAN (AFL-CIO).

Metal Engravers and Marking Device Workers Union; International (AFL-CIO) Formerly an independent union, it received a charter from the AFL in 1951. The union merged with the International Association of Machinists (AFL-CIO) on September 1, 1956.

See also MACHINISTS AND AEROSPACE WORKERS; INTERNATIONAL ASSOCIATION OF (AFL-CIO).

Metal Engravers Union; International (Ind) An organization at one time affiliated with the AFL. It was organized in Buffalo, New York, in September 1920, by a group of independent locals known as the "Gravers and Chisel Clubs."

The union changed its name to the International Metal Engravers and Marking Device Workers Union in 1948.

See also METAL ENGRAVERS AND MARKING DEVICE WORKERS UNION; INTERNATIONAL (AFL-CIO).

Metal Polishers, Buffers, Platers and Allied Workers International Union (AFL-CIO) Metal polishers and brass workers were organized originally under the Knights of Labor and in October 1888 became the National Trade Assembly, No. 252, of the Knights of Labor. After a number of separations and reaffiliations, the Knights of Labor Trades Assembly No. 252 and the composition metal workers and polishers combined and organized in Syracuse, New York, on July 2, 1896, and affiliated with the AFL. The merged organization was known as the Metal Polishers, Buffers, Platers and Brass Workers' Union of North America. In 1911, the Brass Molders were transferred to the International Molders' Union of North America; the union was later known as the Metal Polishers, Buffers, Platers and Helpers International Union (AFL-CIO). It adopted its present name in the early 1970s.

Address: 5578 Montgomery Rd., Cincinnati, Ohio 45212. Tel. (513) 531–2500

Metal Trades Department An AFL-CIO Department chartered in 1908 "to coordinate negotiating, organizing and legislative efforts of affiliated metal working and related crafts and labor unions." Its monthly publication is the *Metaletter.*

Among the affiliated organizations of the Metal Trades Department are the following: Asbestos Workers; Boilermakers; Carpenters; Chemical Workers; Electrical Workers; Elevator Constructors; Operating Engineers; Firemen and Oilers; Iron Workers; Laborers; Machinists; Molders; Office and Professional Employees; Painters; Pattern Makers; Plasterers; Plumbers; Professional and Technical Engineers; Service Employees; Sheet Metal Workers; Stove, Furnace and Allied Appliance Workers; and Upholsterers.

Address: AFL-CIO Building, 815 16th St., N.W., Washington, D.C. 20006. Tel. (202) 347–7255

Source references: Otto S. Beyer et al., *Wertheim Lectures on Industrial Relations, 1928* (Cambridge: Harvard UP, 1929); Mildred Fairchild, *Skill and Specialization: A Study in the Metal Trades* (Baltimore: 1930); Metal Trades Department, AFL-CIO, *What It Is—What It Does* (Washington: n.d.).

See also AFL-CIO DEPARTMENTS.

methods analysis Essentially this is the same as motion and time study, being concerned with the various techniques and methods for increasing production through the proper and economic use of motion, thereby saving time, either by the organization of work or by the breaking down of the process so that the job can be performed more efficiently.

See also METHODS STUDY, TIME AND MOTION STUDY.

methods study The term is occasionally used interchangeably with motion study. It is concerned primarily with the analysis of a job or manufacturing process or method in order to break it down into its component elements with the purpose of improving job performance, increasing production per unit of time, and consequently reducing the unit cost. Essentially, this is also the basic purpose of motion and time study. Ralph N. Barnes, in his volume on *Motion and Time Study*, published in 1953, summarizes motion and time study as follows:

> Motion and time study is the analysis of the methods, of the materials, and of the tools and equipment used, or to be used, in the performance of a piece of work—an analysis carried on with the purpose of (1) finding the most economical way of doing this work; (2) standardizing the methods, materials, tools, and equipment; (3) accurately determining the time required by a qualified person working at a normal pace to do the task; and (4) assisting in training the worker in the new method.

Source references: Charles W. Lytle, *Job Evaluation Methods* (2d ed., New York: Ronald Press, 1954); Ben Miller, *Gaining Acceptance for Major Methods Changes* (New York: AMA, Research Study no. 44, 1960).

See also TIME AND MOTION STUDY.

Metropolitan Statistical Area (MSA) A geographic classification used for the purposes of collecting and reporting government data, including labor market information. Formerly known as the "Standard Metropolitan Statistical Area," an MSA is designated by the Office of Management and Budget through the Federal Committee on Standard Metropolitan Statistical Areas.

An MSA generally consists of at least one central county or city containing the area's main population concentration and adjacent communities which have a high degree of economic and social integration with the population center. Under specified conditions, two adjacent areas may be combined into a single MSA.

Areas qualifying for recognition as an MSA have either a city with a population of at least 50,000 or a Bureau of Census urbanized area of at least 50,000 and a total MSA population of at least 100,000.

Each MSA is categorized in one of the following levels based on total population:

Level A. MSAs of 1 million or more.
Level B. MSAs of 250,000 to 1 million.
Level C. MSAs of 100,000 to 250,000.
Level D. MSAs of less than 100,000.

Source reference: U.S. Dept. of Labor, BLS, *BLS Handbook of Methods Vol. 1* (Washington: 1982).

Michigan State Employees Association (Ind) An organization affiliated with the Assembly of Governmental Employees. It issues *MSEA News* every three weeks.

Address: 5929 Executive Dr., Lansing, Mich. 48901. Tel. (517) 394–5900

micromotion study A refinement of time and motion study which utilizes the facilities of a motion picture camera which is able to show very small or microscopic motion. It permits careful recording and permanent records of minute operations for stricter analysis than is possible through the use of a stop watch.

A procedure utilized to eliminate unnecessary movements and to simplify the necessary movements.

middle management A term used to describe a group of company officers whose position is between top management and the front line supervisors. Their job is to carry out the programs and policies of the organization as set down by top management and at the same time coordinate those functions through the operating branches.

See also LINE ORGANIZATION.

migratory worker The term is used almost exclusively to describe an individual engaged in agricultural or related food processing work who moves or "migrates" to areas where job opportunities are available. Typically, this involves following a series of crop harvesting seasons through a particular area of the country. The work almost necessarily is temporary, thus raising questions about the application of certain protective legislation. In 1965 the migratory farm worker came into some prominence as the federal government ended the "bracero" program, under which

Mexican agricultural laborers were brought into the United States to "follow the crops." Serious efforts have been started to bring migratory workers under broadly protective federal law. For the most part, attempts to unionize these workers have not been successful. By mid-1970, however, it was reported that a substantial portion of the grape growers in California had signed collective bargaining agreements with the United Farm Workers Organizing Committee (now the United Farm Workers of America (AFL-CIO)).

Source references: Vernon M. Briggs, Jr., "Mexican Workers in the United States Labour Market: A Contemporary Dilemma," *ILR*, Nov. 1975; Melvin S. Brooks, *The Social Problems of Migrant Farm Laborers* (Carbondale: Southern Illinois Univ., Dept. of Sociology, 1960); Herrington J. Bryce, "The Measurement and Interpretation of the Earnings of Migratory Farm Workers," *Poverty and Human Resources Abstract*, June 1973; Franz Daniel, "Problems of Union Organization for Migratory Workers," *LLJ*, July 1961; James A. Hefner, "Adjustment Patterns of Black and White Migrants in a Southern Labor Market," *LLJ*, Aug. 1974; George Iden, "Factors Affecting Earnings of Southern Immigrants," *IR*, May 1974; Louis Levine, "The Migratory Worker in the Farm Economy," *LLJ*, July 1961; John W. Livingston, "On-the-Move Migrant Workers and Trade Unions," *American Federationist*, Feb. 1960; Michael J. Piore, *Birds of Passage; Migrant Labor and Industrial Societies* (Cambridge, Eng.: Cambridge UP, 1979); Louise R. Shotwell, *The Harvesters: The Story of the Migrant People* (New York: Doubleday, 1961); U.S. Congress, House, Committee on Education and Labor, *Hearings on Migratory Labor* (Washington: 1961); U.S. Congress, Senate, Committee on Labor and Human Resources, *Oversight on Issues Affecting Hispanic and Migrant and Seasonal Farmworkers, Hearing* (Washington: 1981); U.S. Dept. of Labor, Bureau of Labor Standards, *Housing for Migrant Agricultural Workers, Labor Camp Standards* (Washington: Bull. no. 235, 1962); Sidney Weintraub and Stanley R. Ross, "'Poor United States, So Close to Mexico,'" *Across the Board*, March 1982; Harrison A. Williams, Jr., "Proposed Legislation for Migratory Workers," *LLJ*, July 1961.

See also FARM LABOR.

military leave A provision incorporated into a collective bargaining agreement or statement of company personnel policy protecting an employee's seniority and other rights while in military service and providing for reinstatement upon return from the service.

An illustrative clause reads:

> Regular employees who leave the service of the Employer to enter that of the United States Armed Forces, or the service of the U.S. Maritime Commission, or who are drafted by the United States Government for civilian service, will upon their return, within ninety (90) days from release from such service, be granted all seniority rights including vacation rights as if continuously employed by the Employer during such service. Such persons will be rehired by the Employer to take the place of other persons employed by the Employer who have less seniority. All rights under this Section shall cease in the event an employee voluntarily reenlists.

Source references: "Additional Job Protection for Reservists and Guardsmen," *MLR*, Sept. 1960; BNA, *Military Leave Practices* (Washington: PPF Survey no. 65, 1962); "Company Bonuses for Military Service," *Conference Board Record*, Sept. 1965; David A. Weeks, "Company Pay Practices for Riot Control, Military Duty, and Summer Training," *Conference Board Record*, May 1968; "What a Call-Up of Reserves Would Mean to Industry," *Management Review*, Aug. 1968.

Milk Wagon Drivers' case A case involving the milk wagon drivers and the Meadow-Moor Dairies, Inc. of Illinois. According to Professor Charles O. Gregory, "a Milk Wagon Drivers Union had combined a little bombing, hijacking and hatchet work with the picketing of companies organized by a rival union." An injunction, granted by a trial court in Illinois, prohibited violent picketing but permitted peaceful picketing. The Supreme Court of the State of Illinois reversed the trial court and prohibited all picketing for the duration of the strike because of the violence which previously had been committed. The union appealed the case to the U.S. Supreme Court and the Supreme Court upheld the decision of the state supreme court. The

Court held in part that "acts of picketing when blended with violence may have a significance which neutralizes the constitutional immunity which such acts would have in isolation."

Source references: Milk Wagon Drivers' Union v. Meadow-Moor Dairies, Inc., 312 US 287, 7 LRRM 310 (1941); Robert Feinberg, "Picketing, Free Speech and Labor Disputes," 17 *NYU Law Review Quarterly* 385 (1940); Charles O. Gregory, "Peaceful Picketing and Freedom of Speech," 26 *American Bar Association Journal* 709 (1940); William K. Sherwood, "The Picketing Cases and How They Grew," 10 *George Washington LR* 763 (1942).

Miller Act A statute passed in August 1935 which applies to contracts over $25,000 for the construction, alteration, or repair of any public building or public work of the United States. The Act provides that prior to the execution of any contract and the award of such contract, the contractor must execute a performance bond and a payment bond with surety to protect persons supplying labor and material.

If a worker does not receive full payment of wages within 90 days after the date on which the last labor was performed, the worker has the right to sue on the contractor's bond.

Source reference: Miller Act, as amended, 40 U.S.C. 270a–270d (1982).

Miller v. Wilson A decision of the Supreme Court in 1915 which upheld the constitutionality of the eight-hour day for women. This decision reviewed the California statute which limited the employment of working women to eight hours a day and 48 hours a week. The Supreme Court stated in part that "the liberty of contract guaranteed by the constitution is freedom from arbitrary restraint—not immunity from reasonable legislation to safeguard the public interest."

Source reference: Miller v. Wilson, 236 US 373 (1915).

Mine, Mill and Smelter Workers; International Union of (Ind) The Western Federation of Miners developed from the metal strikes in Idaho in 1892. Although it began as a craft union of miners, it took in the mechanical crafts and became an industrial organization of workers "in and about the mines." The Federation was independent from the time it was organized in May 1893 until 1896, when it became a part of the AFL. This affiliation was short-lived since in 1898 the Western Federation became the sponsor of the Western Labor Union and from 1905 to 1907 was part of the Industrial Workers of the World. It did not reaffiliate with the AFL until 1911. Following its reaffiliation and expansion of its jurisdiction, it changed its name to the International Union of Mine, Mill and Smelter Workers.

During the formation of the CIO, it affiliated with the CIO but was expelled on February 15, 1950.

At the January 14, 1967, convention of the Mine, Mill and Smelter Workers held at Tucson, Arizona, the 28,000 members of the union in the nonferrous metal industry voted to merge with the United Steelworkers of America. Under the plan of procedure, the 65 locals of the union received temporary charters, which became permanent on July 1, 1967, in the United Steelworkers of America organization.

Source references: Lallah S. Davidson, *South of Joplin: Story of a Tri-State Diggin's* (New York: Norton, 1939); Vernon H. Jensen, *Heritage of Conflict: Labor Relations in the Nonferrous Metal Industry Up to 1930* (Ithaca: Cornell UP, 1950); ———, *Nonferrous Metals Industry Unionism, 1932–1954: A Story of Leadership Controversy* (Ithaca: NYSSILR, Cornell Univ., 1954); Robert S. Keitel, "The Merger of the International Union of Mine, Mill and Smelter Workers Into the United Steelworkers of America," *Labor History,* Winter 1974; Malcolm H. Ross, *Death of a Yale Man* (New York: Farrar & Rinehart, 1939); Earl Bruce White, "A Note of the Archives of the Western Federation of Miners and International Union of Mine, Mill and Smelter Workers," *Labor History,* Fall 1976.

See also AMERICAN FEDERATION OF LABOR; COMMUNISM IN AMERICAN LABOR UNIONS; CONGRESS OF INDUSTRIAL ORGANIZATIONS; STEELWORKERS OF AMERICA, UNITED (AFL-CIO).

Mine Workers of America; International Union of District 50, United (Ind) *See* DISTRICT 50, UNITED MINE WORKERS OF AMERICA (IND).

Mine Workers of America; Progressive (Ind) *See* PROGRESSIVE MINE WORKERS OF AMERICA (IND).

Mine Workers of America; United (Ind) The United Mine Workers was organized in Columbus, Ohio, in January 1890.

Local organizations of miners go back as far as 1849 in the Pennsylvania anthracite area. The American Miners Association had been formed in the bituminous coal area in Illinois. Depression and the Civil War frustrated most of these organizational efforts; it was not until 1869 that an organization known as the Miners' and Laborers' Benevolent Association was formed. The organization was reasonably successful until the panic of 1873 and a general strike of miners in 1875.

The secret organization of Irish mine workers known as the Molly Maguires and the infiltration efforts by the Pinkerton Detective Agency and subsequent punishment of the Molly Maguires had a deleterious effect and ultimately resulted in the decline of the Miners' and Laborers' Benevolent Association.

Organization in the bituminous coal area developed in 1885 with the formation of the National Federation of Miners and Mine Laborers, and in 1888 with the formation of the National Progressive Union. In January 1890, these two organizations and a number of the Knights of Labor assemblies joined together to form the United Mine Workers of America.

The first interstate agreement followed a strike called by bituminous coal workers in 1897. This agreement resulted in recognition of the union and the establishment of grievance and negotiating machinery.

Efforts to organize anthracite workers followed around 1899. The organization was strong enough to engage in a major strike in 1902. The strike received nationwide attention and President Theodore Roosevelt intervened and established the Anthracite Coal Commission, which investigated the conditions in the industry and effectuated settlement of the dispute. The story of the role of the United Mine Workers in the formation of the CIO is well known. It is presently independent. Its official monthly publication is *United Mine Workers Journal.*

Address: 900 15th Street, N.W., Washington, D.C. 20005. Tel. (202) 842–7200

Source references: Harold W. Aurand, *From the Molly Maguires to the United Mine Workers; The Social Ecology of an Industrial Union, 1869–1897* (Philadelphia: Temple UP, 1971); Louis Bloch, *Labor Agreements in Coal Mines* (New York: Russell Sage Foundation, 1931); John Brophy, *A Miner's Life* (Madison: Univ. of Wisconsin Press, 1964); Robert C. Benedict, "The UMW Perspective on Industrial Relations," *LLJ*, Aug. 1981; McAlister Coleman, *Men and Coal* (New York: Farrar & Rinehart, 1943); Melvyn Dubofsky and Warren Van Tine, *John Lewis, A Biography* (New York: Quadrangle/The New York Times Book Co., 1977); Joseph E. Finley, *The Corrupt Kingdom; Rise and Fall of the United Mine Workers* (New York: Simon and Shuster, 1972); Brit Hume, *Death and the Mines; Rebellion and Murder in the United Mine Workers* (New York: Grossman, 1971); Joseph J. Klock, Jr. and Doris Plazer, "Democracy in the UMW?" *LLJ*, Oct. 1974; William H. Miernyk, "The 1981 Coal Strike: A View from the Outside," *LLJ*, Aug. 1981; Arnold R. Miller, "The Coal Industry," *Arbitration—1976*, Proceedings of the 29th A/M, NAA, ed. by Barbara Dennis and Gerald Somers (Washington: BNA, 1976); James O. Morris, "The Acquisitive Spirit of John Mitchell UMW President (1899–1908)," *Labor History*, Winter 1979; Joseph Rauh, "Internal Union Problems: A Study of the United Mine Workers Union," *NYU 26th Annual Conference on Labor*, ed. by Emanuel Stein and S. Theodore Reiner (New York: Bender, 1974); C. L. Sulzberger, *Sit Down with John L. Lewis* (New York: Random House, 1938); Frank W. Warne, *The Coal Mine Workers: A Study in Labor Organization* (New York: Longmans, Green, 1905); Edward A. Wieck, *The American Miners Association: A Record of the Origin of Coal Miners Unions in the United States* (New York: Russell Sage Foundation, 1940); ———, *The Miners Case of the Public Interest: A Documentary Chronology* (New York: Russell Sage Foundation, 1947).

minimum plant rate The lowest hourly rate paid for unskilled work at a plant. It is usually the same as the common labor rate or the lowest labor grade.

minimum rates The two most frequently used minimum rates are those which apply to the job and those that apply to the plant. There are also minimum rates or guarantees which are applied to specific jobs under a wage incentive system.

The minimum plant rate has already been noted as the lowest rate for an unskilled experienced worker in the lowest paid job in the plant or establishment. This may be a single rate or the minimum of a rate range where a range exists for the particular job. The use of the term may vary with individual plants and companies. Some employers have had separate minimum rates for men and women, and for probationary employees. Learner rates may be set below the minimum plant rate or the minimum job rate.

See also EQUAL PAY ACT OF 1963.

minimum wage The term generally applies to the wage rate set under the Fair Labor Standards Act of 1938, although minimum wages are established also through the collective bargaining process. It is the rate below which no employee may be paid. Where a state establishes a minimum wage in excess of the rate established by the Fair Labor Standards Act, which applies to interstate commerce, the state act would apply. Provisions are made under the Fair Labor Standards Act establishing minima below those set for the United States in Puerto Rico and the Virgin Islands where minimum rates are established through recommendations of industry committees composed of labor, management, and the public. American Samoa, which was included in these minimum standard determinations, has been dealt with similarly since 1956.

Efforts by the states and the federal government to establish minimum wage legislation is an interesting chapter in American labor history. Note particularly the early minimum wage cases to come before the Supreme Court, such as *Adkins v. Children's Hospital.* The Court held that a minimum wage law of the District of Columbia set an uncertain yardstick and discriminated arbitrarily against employers, and under the due process provisions of the Fifth Amendment of the Constitution was held to be an unreasonable interference with liberty and the rights of contract protected by those provisions.

Source references: AEI, *Proposals for a Subminimum Wage for Youth* (Washington: Legislative Analysis no. 28, 1981); Farrell E. Bloch, "Political Support for Minimum Wage Legislation," *Journal of Labor Research,* Fall 1980; Charles Brown, Curtis Gilroy, and Andrew Kohen, *The Effect of the Minimum Wage on Employment and Unemployment: Survey* (Cambridge: NBER, WP no. 846, 1982); Donald E. Cullen, *Minimum Wage Laws* (Ithaca: Cornell Univ., NYSSILR, 1960); Richard B. Freeman, Wayne Gray, and Casey Ichniowski, *Low Cost Student Labor: The Use and Effects of the Subminimum Wage Provisions for Full-Time Students* (Cambridge: NBER, WP no. 765, 1981); Robert S. Goldfarb, "The Policy Content of Quantitative Minimum Wage Research," *Proceedings of the 27th A/M, IRRA,* ed. by James Stern and Barbara Dennis (Madison: 1975); Robert S. Goldfarb and John S. Heywood, "An Economic Evaluation of the Service Contract Act," *ILRR,* Oct. 1982; ILO, *Minimum Wage Fixing and Economic Development* (Geneva: Studies & Report New Series no. 72, 1968); Richard Lester and John M. Peterson, "Employment Effects of Minimum Wages," *ILRR,* Jan. 1960; Sar A. Levitan and Richard S. Belous, "The Minimum Wage Today: How Well Does It Work?" *MLR,* July 1979; "Life at the Bottom, Alias the Minimum Wage," *American Federationist,* Feb. 1981; J. Peter Mattila, "Youth Labor Markets, Enrollments, and Minimum Wages," *Proceedings of the 31st A/M, IRRA,* ed. by Barbara Dennis (Madison: 1979); Richard B. McKenzie, "The Labor Market Effects of Minimum Wage Laws: A New Perspective," *Journal of Labor Research,* Fall 1980; George Meany, "The Working Poor Cannot Wait," *American Federationist,* Aug. 1977; C. St. J. O'Herlihy, *Measuring Minimum Wage Effects in the United States* (Geneva: ILO, 1969); John M. Peterson, *Minimum Wages; Measures and Industry Effects* (Washington: AEI, Studies 331, 1981); Brigitte Sellekaerts, "The Case for Indexing the Minimum Wage," *Proceedings of the 34th A/M, IRRA,* ed. by Barbara Dennis (Madison: 1982); N. Arnold Tolles, "The Purposes and

Results of U.S. Minimum Wage Laws," *MLR*, March 1960; U.S. Minimum Wage Study Commission, *Report of the Minimum Wage Study Commission, Volume I–VII* (Washington: 1981); Finis Welch, "The Trouble With the Minimum Wage," *Across the Board*, Aug. 1979; Walter J. Wessels, *Minimum Wages, Fringe Benefits, and Working Conditions* (Washington: AEI, Studies 304, 1980).

See also ADKINS V. CHILDREN'S HOSPITAL; FAIR LABOR STANDARDS ACT OF 1938; WALSH-HEALEY ACT OF 1936.

minimum wage determination The secretary of labor is authorized under the Walsh-Healey Public Contracts Act to determine prevailing minimum wages in an industry on the basis of standards provided in the Act. The Act sets basic labor standards for work done on U.S. government contracts exceeding $10,000 in value for materials, articles, supplies, equipment, or naval vessels. Minimum wage determinations generally are issued by the secretary of labor after public hearings. All employees engaged in the performance of a contract which is let under the provisions of the Walsh-Healey Act must be paid not less than the minimum established by the secretary of labor.

Source references: Walsh-Healey Public Contracts Act, as amended, 41 U.S.C. 35–45 (1982); Portal to Portal Act of 1947, as amended, 29 U.S.C. 216, 251–262 (1982); Abraham L. Gitlow, *Wage Determination Under National Boards* (Englewood Cliffs: PH, 1953); Gerald Starr, *Minimum Wage Fixing, An International Review of Practices and Problems* (Geneva: ILO, 1981); ______, "Minimum Wage Fixing: International Experience With Alternative Roles," *ILR*, Sept./Oct. 1981.

minimum wage law *See* FAIR LABOR STANDARDS ACT OF 1938, WALSH-HEALEY ACT OF 1936.

minimum work Generally referred to as minimum call-in pay. A contract clause covering this might read as follows:

> Any employee who shall be called for work, who is ready, willing, and able to work, shall be given an opportunity to work at least five hours and in any event shall be paid for not less than five hours, unless the normal shift of such employees is less than five hours work, and in any event shall be paid for at least four hours work.

See also CALL-IN PAY.

Minnesota plan In 1933 during the height of the Depression, most unemployment benefit plans were depleted. The Minnesota Plan, so-called, was the result of a study by a Minnesota commission which reported in 1933 that the unemployment benefit plans were designed to handle seasonal rather than cyclical unemployment and suggested that the way to relieve the pressure on the unemployment benefit funds was either by larger joint contributions, smaller benefit payments, or a longer waiting period for employees before becoming eligible to receive the benefits.

See also UNEMPLOYMENT COMPENSATION.

minor disputes Disputes involving the interpretation or application of existing contract provisions. They are generally referred to as "grievance disputes." Under the Railway Labor Act they are handled by the National Railroad Adjustment Board at the last appeal step.

Source reference: "Settlement of Minor Labor Disputes in Australia," *LLJ*, Feb. 1961.

See also ARBITRATION, RIGHTS; MAJOR DISPUTES; NATIONAL RAILROAD ADJUSTMENT BOARD.

minority groups Those persons of ethnic and/or racial background different from that of the majority population of the country and who constitute a smaller proportion of the country's population. In the United States, before World War I, the groups regarded as minorities were the European immigrants who were concentrated in the large cities in the East (such as the Irish, Slavs, Italians, and Jews) and the Orientals who were mainly situated on the Pacific coast.

At present, major attention is being focused on specific minority groups, including two which have been in the United States for hundreds of years—American Indians and blacks—and the Hispanics and Orientals who came as immigrants in the 20th century. In the 1980 Census, these groups together comprised about 20 percent of the total U.S. population. Increased attention is being focused on the problems of these minority groups in terms of education, income, health, housing, and employment. In regard to employment, efforts are being made to gain fuller representation for these groups in existing unions and to organize previously unorganized minority workers, such as farm laborers. Labor unions, industry, and government are establishing programs to deal with the hiring, training, and civil rights problems of minority workers.

Under Revised Order No. 4, the term "minority" includes blacks, Spanish-surnamed Americans, American Indians, and Orientals.

Minority group members under the Minority Business Enterprises program include "Negroes, Spanish-speaking American persons, American-Orientals, American-Indians, American-Eskimos, and American-Aleuts."

Source references: "Federal Procurement Regulations," 41 C.F.R. Part 1–1, General, Subpart 1–1.13, Minority Business Enterprises; Elizabeth McTaggart Almquist, *Minorities, Gender, and Work* (Lexington, Mass.: Lexington Books, 1979); Richard F. America, "How Minority Business Can Build on Its Stength," *Harvard BR,* May/June 1980; Paul Bullock (ed.), *Minorities in the Labor Market, Proceedings of a Conference* (Los Angeles: UC, Institute of IR, 1978); Stephen L. Cohen, "Issues in the Selection of Minority Group Employees," *Human Resource Management,* Spring 1974; Nathan Glazer, *Beyond the Melting Pot: The Negroes, Puerto Ricans, Jews, Italians and Irish of New York City* (Cambridge: MIT Press, 1963); James D. Gwartney and James E. Long, "The Relative Earnings of Blacks and Other Minorities," *ILRR,* April 1978; Grace Hall and Allan Saltzstein, "Equal Employment in Urban Governments: The Potential Problem of Interminority Competition," *Public Personnel Management,* Nov./Dec. 1975; Joseph Herman, "Private Arrangements and Agreements for Employment of Minority Groups," *NYU 24th Annual Conference on Labor* (New York: Bender, 1972); Roberson L. King, "Protecting Rights of Minority Employees," *LLJ,* Feb. 1960; Sar A. Levitan, William B. Johnson, and Robert Taggart, *Minorities in the United States: Problems, Progress, and Prospects* (Washington: Public Affairs Press, 1975); Alex Maurizi, "Minority Membership in Apprenticeship Programs in the Construction Trades," *ILRR,* Jan. 1972; David H. Rosenbloom, "A Note on Interminority Group Competition for Federal Positions," *Public Personnel Management,* Jan./Feb. 1973; Bayard Rustin, "Ethnics: A New Separatism," *American Federationist,* Dec. 1974; Paula Singer-Sandler, "Mandate: Minority Business Utilization," *Proceedings of the 31st A/M, IRRA,* ed. by Barbara Dennis (Madison: 1979); Clarence Thomas, "Minorities, Youth, and Education," *Journal of Labor Research,* Fall 1982; U.S. Bureau of the Census, *Statistical Abstract of the United States 1981* (Washington: 1981); U.S. Commission on Civil Rights, *Social Indicators of Equality for Minorities and Women* (Washington: 1978); U.S. Dept. of Labor, Women's Bureau, *Minority Women Workers: A Statistical Overview* (Washington: 1977); U.S. GAO, *Federal Efforts to Increase Minority Opportunities in Skilled Construction Craft Unions Have Had Little Success* (Washington: 1979).

See also CIVIL RIGHTS ACT OF 1964, NATIONAL ORIGIN DISCRIMINATION, RACIAL DISCRIMINATION, REVISED ORDER NO. 4.

minority representation In the political field this term applies to various forms of proportional representation in which efforts are made to provide representation of all points of view in roughly the proportion of the number of supporters which each group has in the community.

In collective bargaining, minority representation has no real place under federal law, which provides for "exclusive" bargaining rights following the certification of a union. However, it is possible in a company which is engaged in *intra*state commerce, where no state law provides for "exclusive" representation, for a union to establish its position and obtain minority representation or, sometimes, to bargain "for members only." Most states which have labor relations laws also provide for exclusive bargaining rights. Occasionally minority representation may be recognized in a plant where the union has organized but has not yet presented a petition requesting an election or certification as exclusive bargaining representative to the state or federal agency authorized to make a determination of majority status in the particular bargaining unit.

Problems occasionally arise where an employer recognizes a union which does not represent a majority of the employees. Under such conditions, if a competing union claims to represent a majority and petitions the agency, elections will be held to determine which union represents the majority of the employees and is entitled to exclusive recognition by the employer.

Executive Order 10988 dealing with bargaining rights of public employees provided for minority representation (under certain conditions) through the informal and formal recognition procedures. Under Executive Order 11491, and then the Civil Service Reform Act of 1978, informal and formal recognition are terminated and replaced by national consultation rights. The latter, however, may not be granted to an agency where a union already holds exclusive recognition in the unit.

Source references: Harriet F. Berger, "The Old Order Giveth Way to the New: A Comparison of Executive Order 10988 with Executive Order 11491," *LLJ*, Feb. 1970; Harold S. Roberts, *Labor-Management Relations in the Public Service* (Honolulu: Univ. of Hawaii Press, 1970).

See also BARGAINING AGENT, EXCLUSIVE BARGAINING AGENT, EXCLUSIVE RECOGNITION, NATIONAL CONSULTATION RIGHTS, PUBLIC EMPLOYEE RELATIONS.

minority union By definition, a union which does not enjoy exclusive bargaining or majority status. Frequently it is an organization which has been unable to obtain a majority of the employees in the appropriate unit for certification but still retains its identity as a group within the plant and possibly may be recognized by the employer as representative of such group.

See also NATIONAL CONSULTATION RIGHTS, PUBLIC EMPLOYEE RELATIONS.

Missile Sites Labor Commission A tripartite commission established in 1961 by Executive Order 10946, chaired by the secretary of labor with the director of the Federal Mediation and Conciliation Service (FMCS) serving as vice-chair. The prime purpose of the Commission was to maintain uninterrupted and economical operation of the missile and space sites.

Labor and management gave the Commission a no-strike, no-lockout pledge and agreed to maintain production at a high level and to operate as economically as possible. The Commission established a special tripartite advisory committee at each missile site, which was headed by a mediator from the FMCS. Overall policy and special problems were handled by the Commission in Washington.

Among the policy recommendations made by the Commission included its directions to those negotiating contracts to avoid the pyramiding of premium pay, excessive travel and subsistence allowances, and unusual premiums for various types of work operations.

In October 1967, by Executive Order 11374, the Commission was abolished and its functions and responsibilities were transferred to the FMCS.

Source references: Wayne E. Howard, *The Missile Sites Labor Commission, 1961 Thru 1967* (Washington: 1969); W. S. Price and Armin Behr, "Control of Uneconomic Practices at Government Sites: A Comparative Study of Two Government Panels," *LLJ*, Aug. 1964; P. L. Siemiller, "Special Government Dispute Settlement Panels," *LLJ*, July 1964; William E. Simkin, "Aerospace Bargaining: Collective Bargaining Does Work," *LLJ*, Oct. 1963; U.S. Senate, Committee on Government Operations, *Work Stoppages at Missile Bases* (Washington: Report no. 1312, 1962); John R. Van de Water, "Growth of Third-Party Power in the Settlement of Industrial Disputes," *LLJ*, Dec. 1961.

missionary A term in the labor relations field assigned to a "spy" whose primary work is to spread anti-union propaganda or to lay the foundation for anti-strike action. The individual works in the general neighborhood of a plant or facility, creating dissension among the wives of workers. A missionary is not generally employed in the plant or the facility toward which the activities are directed.

mixed motive cases Also known as dual motive cases, where an employer's decision to discipline or discharge involves both a legitimate business reason and the employer's reaction to its employees' union activity. In these cases, the NLRB applies a two-part test developed in *Wright Line:* first the NLRB General Counsel is required to make a prima facie showing that the protected activity was a motivating factor for the employer's action, then the employer has the burden of showing that the same action would have been taken in the absence of the protected conduct. The Supreme Court in *NLRB v. Transportation Management*, upheld the NLRB *Wright Line* burden of proof approach in mixed motive cases.

Source references: NLRB v. Transportation Management Corp., 462 US 393, 113 LRRM 2857 (1983); *Wright Line,* 251 NLRB 1083, 105 LRRM 1169 (1980); Peyton T. Hairston, Jr., "Mixed Motive Cases: How to Meet the Burden of Proof Under *Wright Line,*" *LLJ*, Oct. 1983; Peter G. Kilgore, "The Proper Test for Determining Violations in Mixed Motive Cases," *LLJ*, May 1983.

mobility, industrial *See* INDUSTRIAL MOBILITY.

mobility, labor *See* LABOR MOBILITY.

mobility, occupational *See* OCCUPATIONAL MOBILITY.

model agreement A collective bargaining agreement sometimes recommended or initiated by an employer organization or an international union to serve as a standard or pattern for a geographic area or industry. Its main functions are to obtain a degree of uniformity and to avoid having each of the individual local unions in a particular industry attempt to set its own standards or to incur expenditures for drafting special language, where such work has already been done by the national or international union.

See also AGREEMENT, MASTER; PENNINGTON CASE.

moderate family budget *See* FAMILY BUDGET.

modified cash refund annuity A contract which provides that an individual will receive an annual income which begins at retirement and continues for life. If the employee should die before receiving pension payments equal to his own contributions and interest, the balance will be paid to the person whom he designates as his beneficiary.

Source reference: BNA, *Pensions and Profit Sharing* (3d ed., Washington: 1964).

See also ANNUITY.

modified closed shop Any contract which requires a closed shop but exempts certain groups of employees from the union membership requirement, such as present employees who are not members or employees who have been with the company for a minimum period of time. All new employees would be required to become members of the union *before* employment, and all individuals who were members would be required to retain their membership in the union. The closed shop is illegal under the Taft-Hartley Act.

See also CLOSED SHOP, RIGHT TO WORK LAW, UNION SECURITY CLAUSES.

modified union shop Any union-shop agreement which deviates from the general standard requiring that all employees become members of the union after a certain period of time following their employment. One frequent variation of the union shop is designed to take care of employees who have been with the company for a long number of years, but who for some reason, occasionally religious, do not feel they should join any organization. The modified union-shop contract in those circumstances would exempt these employees under the contract, but would require that all new employees become union members within the specified period of time. All individuals who are members must retain their membership in order to remain in good standing.

See also MAINTENANCE OF MEMBERSHIP, UNION SHOP.

Mohawk Valley formula An elaborate plan developed by the Remington Rand Corporation and its then president, James H. Rand, Jr., to combat union organizational efforts in a number of plants. The "formula" is sometimes referred to as the Rand Formula or the Johnston Plan, which was adopted by the steel industry in 1937. The Mohawk Valley Formula was applied in 1936 during a strike in a number of Remington Rand plants.

The formula is broadly conceived and examines the role of employees in the community and utilizes all of the devices known in public relations to put the union in a bad light and to create the conditions for a back-to-work movement. Professor Fred Witney has summarized the process in nine steps. These are

(1) When a strike is threatened, label the union leaders as agitators and attempt to discredit them with their own followers as well as with the public;
(2) When a strike is called, raise the banner of law and order, thereby causing the community to institute legal and police weapons against alleged or imaginary violence and forget that these employees are members of the community who have equal rights with other members in that community;
(3) Call a mass meeting of citizens to coordinate public sentiment against the strikers and establish and strengthen citizens' committees to exert pressure upon the local political and other authorities as well as sponsor vigilante activities;
(4) Help establish a large armed police force to intimidate the strikers and to exert psychological pressure upon citizens;
(5) Heighten the demoralizing effect of the above steps by convincing the strikers that their cause is hopeless, and create a back-to-work movement either by a puppet organization or by so-called loyal employees secretly organized by the employer;
(6) When a sufficient number of applications is available, set a date for the opening of the plant through a device which uses the back-to-work association as the agency requesting that the company open the plant;
(7) Stage the opening theatrically, throwing open the gates at an auspicious time and having employees march into the plant in a mass group protected by armed squads of police, so as to give a dramatic and exaggerated quality to the back-to-work movement and thereby further demoralize the strikers;
(8) Capitalize on this demoralization and continue to show police force and pressure of citizens' committees to insure that those employees who have returned will stay on the job and force the remaining strikers to give in and return to work;
(9) Close the publicity barrage, which has continued on a daily basis, to increase the demoralization by stating that the plant is in full operation and that the strikers are only a small minority attempting to interfere with the right of individuals to work, and thus put a public stamp of moral disapproval upon the action of the strikers and a stamp of approval on the behavior of the employer.

Source references: In the Matter of Remington Rand, Inc., 2 NLRB 626, 1 LRRM 88 (1937); Fred Witney, *Government and Collective Bargaining* (Philadelphia: Lippincott, 1951).

See also BACK-TO-WORK MOVEMENT, STRIKEBREAKER.

Molders' and Allied Workers' Union; International (AFL-CIO) An early society of Molders got together in 1849 in New York City and joined with others in July 1859 in Philadelphia to form the National Union of Iron Molders. With representation of Canadian unions at the 1861 and 1863 conventions, the organization changed its name to the Iron Molders' International Union. This is believed to be the first instance of the extension of territorial jurisdiction of a labor organization from one country to another.

In 1911, the Brass Molders, which had left the Knights of Labor and formed the International Brotherhood of Brass Molders in 1890 and later amalgamated with the Metal Polishers in 1896 to form the Metal Polishers, Buffers, Platers, Brass Molders, Brass and Silver Workers' Union of North America, transferred to the Molders' International Union. The Coremakers' International Union, chartered by the AFL, proved difficult because of jurisdictional trouble with the molders, but by agreement in 1903 the Coremakers became part of the International Molders' Union. The union formerly was known as the International Molders and Foundry Workers Union of North America (AFL-CIO). Official publication is the *Molders Journal*, published bimonthly.

Address: 1225 East McMillan Street, Cincinnati, Ohio 45206. Tel. (513) 221–1525

Source references: Jonathan P. Grossman, *William Sylvis: Pioneer of American Labor* (New York: Columbia UP, 1945); Frank T. Stockton, *International Molders Union of North America* (Baltimore: Johns Hopkins UP, 1921); James C. Sylvis, *The Life, Speeches, Labors and Essays of William H. Sylvis, Late President of the Iron Molders International Union and Also of the National Labor Union* (Philadelphia: Claxton, 1872); Charlotte Todes, *William H. Sylvis and the National Labor Union* (New York: International Publishers, 1942).

Molders and Foundry Workers Union of North America; International (AFL-CIO) *See* MOLDERS' AND ALLIED WORKERS' UNION; INTERNATIONAL (AFL-CIO).

Molly Maguires A secret ring of workers which flourished in the anthracite coal fields during the 1860s and 1870s. They appeared as early as 1852 as the Ancient Order of Hibernians. They have been considered by some to be the first labor racketeers. Their practices included wrecking trains, blowing up collieries; they resorted to the calculated and deliberate murder of supervisors or employers who were not cooperative with them. Their reign of terror came to an end in 1876 when 10 of their ringleaders were executed and 14 others were jailed. Actually the group was not a labor organization, but a group of individuals who utilized their own power and terrorist tactics to gain their ends in the anthracite coal fields.

Source references: Charles Albright, *The Great Molly Maguire Trials in Carbon and Schuylkill Counties, Pennsylvania, 1876* (Pottsville: Chronicle Book, Job Rooms, 1876); Anthony Bimba, *The Molly Maguires* (New York: International Publishers, 1932); Wayne G. Broehl, Jr., *The Molly Maguires* (Cambridge: Harvard UP, 1964); James W. Coleman, *The Molly Maguire Riots: Industrial Conflict in the Pennsylvania Coal Region* (Richmond, Va.: Garrett, Massie, 1936); Francis P. Dewees, *The Molly Maguires: The Origin, Growth and Character of the Organization* (Philadelphia: Lippincott, 1877); James D. McCabe, *The History of the Great Riots* (Philadelphia: National Publishing, 1877); Larry A. Webb, "An Analysis of the Economic Conditions That Gave Rise to the Molly Maguires as a Protest Movement" (M.A. thesis, Univ. of Florida, 1957).

money-purchase plan *See* PENSION PLAN.

money wage Same as nominal wage. The amount of actual cash or money received by the employee as distinguished from the purchasing power of his money or real wages.

See also REAL WAGES, TAKE-HOME PAY.

monitorship A device for "equitable intervention in and supervision of private organizations" employed by the U.S. District Court for the District of Columbia in a consent decree involving the International Brotherhood of Teamsters union.

Monitorship is utilized primarily "to investigate the affairs of the association and to recommend curative measures." Unlike receivers, monitors do not manage the organization, and its officers remain provisionally in power. Unlike the master who makes recommendations to the court, monitors are required to make recommendations to the defendant. These recommendations can be enforced by the courts if the incumbent officers choose not to accept them.

The three-member Teamsters Board of Monitors appointed by Judge F. Dickinson Letts served from 1958 to 1961.

Source references: George R. Ittel, "The Role of the Court-Appointed Board of Monitors for the Teamsters Union, 1957–1961" (M.A. thesis, Univ. of Illinois, 1963); Leonard B. Mandelbaum, "The Teamster Monitorship: A Lesson for the Future," *Federal Bar Journal,* Spring 1960; "Monitors: A New Equitable Remedy?" *Yale LJ,* Nov. 1960; Sam Romer, "The Teamster Monitors and the Administration of the International Union," *Proceedings of the 1961 Annual Spring Meeting, IRRA,* ed. by Gerald Somers (Madison: 1961).

See also TRUSTEESHIP, UNION.

monopoly of labor unions *See* LABOR MONOPOLY.

monopsony A technical term used by economists to designate a situation in which buyers monopolize the demand for a product or where one employer has an absolute monopoly in the recruitment of labor in an area or obtaining materials in an area—for example, a situation in which a single smelter exists and is the only market for ores mined in a particular geographic district.

Economists distinguish this buyer monopoly (monopsony) from one in which there are a few buyers (oligopsony).

Source references: Lewis Froman, *Principles of Economics* (Chicago: Irwin, 1946); John Ise, *Economics* (New York: Harper, 1950); Richard A. Lester, *Economics of Labor* (2d ed., New York: Macmillan, 1964); Vernon Mund, *Government and Business* (New York: Harper, 1950).

monotony A state during work in which the employee's interest is low and listlessness and boredom are manifested. This may be due to the nature of the job being performed, the lack of opportunity for the individual to be creative, or the job may be so routine that it requires no special attention or concern and the degree of attention needed has been reduced to a minimum.

Monotony is important because of its effect on production as well as on the maintenance of safety and morale in the plant. Studies have been made and are continuing to be made to determine ways in which monotony and boredom may be reduced.

Source references: Amos Drory, "Individual Differences in Boredom Proneness and Task Effectiveness at Work," *Personnel Psychology*, Spring 1982; Saul W. Gellerman, "Doing Dull Work Well," *Conference Board Record*, Sept. 1974; William McBain, "What Can Be Done About Job Monotony?" *Personnel Administration*, May/June 1963; Ross Stagner, *Boredom on the Assembly Line: Age and Personality Variables* (Ann Arbor: Univ. of Michigan–Wayne State Univ., Institute of Labor and IR, Reprint Series no. 65, 1975).

See also INDUSTRIAL PSYCHOLOGY, MUSIC AT WORK.

Montana Public Employees Association (Ind) An organization affiliated with the Assembly of Governmental Employees. Its bimonthly publication is the *Public Employee*.

Address: 1426 Cedar St., Helena, Mont. 59601. Tel. (406) 442–4600

Monthly Labor Review The official publication of the Bureau of Labor Statistics, U.S. Department of Labor. It was in part the outgrowth of an earlier publication, *The Bi-Monthly Bulletin*, first published in 1895 by the U.S. Bureau of Labor, the forerunner of the Bureau of Labor Statistics.

This monthly journal publishes the results of original investigation and summarizes reports which are subsequently issued in separate volumes or in bulletin form. It contains a brief review of the month's activities in the field of labor as well as changes in legislation and court decisions. It contains a list of current publications and major statistical series. The statistical series entitled "Current Labor Statistics" includes data on employment, hours, earnings, unemployment insurance, prices, productivity, and work stoppages (involving establishments with 1,000 or more workers). This very useful source of current information on labor economics and labor relations is published by the U.S. Government Printing Office. A detailed index of articles and authors is published from time to time. A typical Table of Contents (May 1984) illustrates the scope of the publication:

Contents

Inflation remained low in 1983 in face of strong recovery

Workers' purchasing power rises even as wage and salary gains lag

How social security payments affect private pensions

Recessionary impacts on the unemployment of men and women

Industrial democracy: made in the U.S.A.

IRRA Papers

Most U.S. workers still may be fired under employment-at-will

Easing the worker's transition from job loss to employment

What do unions get in return for concessions?

Reports

A comparison of pension benefit increases and inflation, 1973–79

Departments

Labor month in review

Conference papers

Research summaries

Research notes

Technical note

Major agreements expiring next month

Developments in industrial relations
Book reviews
Current labor statistics

Monthly Report on the Labor Force The labor force data program started in 1940 and currently called the Current Population Survey. It was also the title of a monthly publication issued by BLS which was discontinued in 1966 and retained as part of *Employment and Earnings, Monthly Report on the Labor Force.* The subtitle, "Monthly Report on the Labor Force," was dropped in 1969.

Source references: John E. Bregger, "The Current Population Survey: A Historical Perspective and BLS' Role," *MLR,* June 1984; U.S. President's Committee to Appraise Employment and Unemployment Statistics, *Measuring Employment and Unemployment* (Washington: 1962).

See also CURRENT POPULATION SURVEY (CPS).

Mooney-Billings case A famous case in the history of labor warfare which resulted from the 1916 San Francisco Preparedness Day bombings. Thomas J. Mooney and Warren K. Billings were sentenced to life imprisonment as the result of these bombings. It long was alleged that Mooney and Billings were the victims of a frame-up. They were pardoned by Governor Culbert L. Olsen of California in 1939.

Source references: Ernest J. Hopkins, *What Happened in the Mooney Case?* (New York: Harcourt, Brace, 1932); U.S. National Commission on Law Observance and Enforcement, Section on Lawless Enforcement of Law, *The Mooney-Billings Report: Suppressed by the Wickersham Commission* (New York: Gotham House, 1932).

moonlighting *See* DOUBLE EMPLOYMENT, SECONDARY EMPLOYMENT.

morale survey A procedure used by some companies, sometimes with the assistance of qualified industrial psychologists or personnel specialists, to determine the morale within a particular group of employees in the plant, the attitudes of individuals toward supervision, company policies and procedures, and the company itself. The survey is carried on ideally through a series of questionnaires to a large sample of employees and through fairly intensive interviews of a more carefully selected group to help clarify and obtain, in more depth, information brought out by the general questionnaires.

Source references: Ellen Joy Bernstein, "Employee Attitude Surveys: Perception vs. Reality," *PJ,* April 1981; William B. Cash, Jr., "How to Calculate an Employee Relations Index," *PJ,* March 1979; Bonnie Goldberg and George G. Gordon, "Designing Attitude Surveys for Management Action," *PJ,* Oct. 1978; Donald L. Hawk, "Effective Attitude Surveys," *PJ,* July 1978; Sandra L. Holmes, "What to Expect From Your First Survey of Employee Morale," *Personnel,* March/April 1979; Martin Patchen, *Some Questionnaire Measures of Employee Motivation and Morale* (Ann Arbor: Univ. of Michigan, Institute for Social Research, Monograph no. 41, 1965); David Sirota and Alan D. Wolfson, "Adequate Grievance Channels: Overcoming the Negative Effects of Work Measurement on Employee Morale," *Human Resource Management,* Summer 1972; Ronald Paul Yuzuk, *The Assessment of Employee Morale* (Columbus: Ohio State Univ., Bureau of Business Research, Monograph no. 99, 1961).

See also OPINION SURVEY, SHOP MORALE.

"more favorable terms" agreements These are collective bargaining agreements generally with employer associations where the union agrees that it will not sign contracts with other employers under more favorable terms. This is designed to keep working conditions reasonably uniform within the group and not give one employer a competitive advantage over another.

Sometimes the language of the agreement may be automatic, that is, if conditions more favorable are granted to a competitor, then the more favorable conditions automatically apply to the signatory company. Other cases may involve renegotiation. Sometimes these agreements are called "most favored nation" contracts, a term borrowed from the lexicon of diplomacy.

See also "FAVORED NATIONS" CLAUSE.

Morehead v. Tipaldo A case involving the New York minimum wage statute passed in 1933. Tipaldo, the owner and manager of a Brooklyn laundry, was convicted of paying women employees less than the minimum that had been established. The New York Court of Appeals on March 3, 1936, held the state statute to be unconstitutional on the basis of the *Adkins* decision. The case was appealed to the U.S. Supreme Court and the Court on June 1, 1936, upheld the New York court by a 5-4 vote. Justice Butler wrote the majority opinion with Justices Sutherland, McReynolds, Van Devanter, and Roberts concurring. The dissenters included Chief Justice Hughes and Justices Stone, Brandeis, and Cardozo.

The decision of the court in effect rested on the ground that the statute deprived employers of their property without due process of law. Justice Butler stated in part, "The decision and the reasoning upon which it [the lower court decision] rests clearly show that the State is without power by any form of legislation to prohibit, change, or nullify contracts between employers and adult women workers as to the amount of wages paid." The statute was held to be contrary to the due process provisions of the 14th Amendment.

Source reference: Morehead v. New York Ex Rel Tipaldo, 298 US 587 (1936).

See also ADKINS V. CHILDREN'S HOSPITAL.

mortality table A listing of the mortality experience of individuals at each age. There are hundreds of mortality tables and the mortality rates shown by different tables may not agree because the statistics upon which they are based differ. The tables are used in setting premiums (rates) for life insurance and pensions.

Source references: American Compensation Association, *Glossary of Compensation Terms* (Scottsdale: 1984); Allen L. Mayerson, *Introduction to Insurance* (New York: Macmillan, 1962).

See also LIFE EXPECTANCY, MANHART CASE, NORRIS CASE.

most favored nation clause *See* "FAVORED NATIONS" CLAUSE.

Mother Jones A very colorful campaigner for social justice and an active and frequent participant in numerous strikes in the United States. Emma Langdon, in her book *The Cripple Creek Strike* (Great Western, 1905), wrote of Mother Jones:

> "Mother" is the workers' refuge and inspiration . . . "Mother" again is the cry when the troops, re-inforced by hunger, are beating them into the earth; often she has changed defeat into victory. . . .

Mother Jones died in November 1930, at the age of 99.

Source references: Archie Green, "The Death of Mother Jones," *Labor History,* Winter 1960; Emma F. Langdon, *The Cripple Creek Strike, A History of Industrial Wars in Colorado* (New York: Arno Press and The New York Times, 1969); Mary F. Parton (ed.), *Autobiography of Mother Jones* (Chicago: Charles H. Kerr, 1925).

motion economy A technique used in motion study to obtain increases in output through reduction of the number of motions required to perform any single task. Unproductive motions do not assist the productive operation and motion economy is designed to eliminate them.

In developing the basic principles for micromotion study, it was felt that not only was it necessary to relate motion economy to the actual use of various parts of the body, but also the saving of motion as it is related to the actual arrangement at the place of work, and the proper designing of tools and equipment to reduce the number of motions necessary to handle a particular product.

See also METHODS STUDY.

motion study The study and observation of the movements of machinery and materials as they relate to the actual motion of the individual worker. The analysis of these movements in the performance of any particular operation is studied so unnecessary and uneconomical movements can be eliminated and the proper sequence arranged to standardize performance and obtain greater productivity. The purpose is to make performance easier, economize motion, and increase productive time.

Source references: Ralph M. Barnes, *Motion and Time Study* (6th ed., New York: Wiley, 1968); Stewart M. Lowry, Harold B. Maynard, and G. J. Stegemerten, *Time and Motion Study Formulas for Wage Incentives* (3d ed., New York: McGraw-Hill, 1940); Robert L. Morrow, *Time and Motion Economy* (New York: Ronald Press, 1946); Benjamin W. Niebel, *Motion and Time Study* (4th ed., Homewood: Irwin, 1967).

See also MICROMOTION STUDY, TIME AND MOTION STUDY, TIME STUDY.

motivation In the positive sense, those factors or forces, whether physical, psychological, or other, which influence or encourage individuals to act, to undergo hardship, or to choose more difficult tasks which permit them to achieve their particular goals or objectives. Motivation may be obtained through wage incentives, praise, or other forms of stimulation sufficient to appeal to the individual or group.

Source references: AMA, *Motivation, Key to Good Management, Selected Reprints from AMA Periodicals* (New York: 1957–1967); Clement J. Berwitz, "Beyond Motivation," *Harvard BR,* May/June 1960; Albert A. Blum and Michael L. Moore, "The Effect of Motivational Programs on Collective Bargaining," *PJ,* July 1973; Robert K. Burns, "Management and Employee Motivation," *Public Personnel Review,* April 1959; David Caldwell, "Employee Motivation Under Merit Systems," *Public Personnel Management,* Jan./Feb. 1978; B. A. Emery, "Managerial Leadership Through Motivation by Objectives," *Personnel Psychology,* Spring 1959; Saul W. Gellerman, *Motivation and Productivity* (New York: AMA, 1963); John M. Greiner et al., *Productivity and Motivation; A Review of State and Local Government Initiatives* (Washington: Urban Institute Press, 1981); Frederick Herzberg et al., *The Motivation to Work* (New York: Wiley, 1959); John R. Hinrichs, *The Motivation Crisis; Winding Down and Turning Off* (New York: AMA, 1974); Harry Levinson, *The Great Jackass Fallacy* (Boston: Harvard Univ., Graduate School of Business Adm., 1973); Rensis Likert, "Motivational Approach to Management Development," *Harvard BR,* July/Aug. 1959; Mitchell Lokiec, "Motivating the Worker," *PJ,* Nov. 1973; Douglas McGregor, *Leadership and Motivation* (Cambridge: MIT Press, 1966); John S. Piamonte, "An Employee Motivational System that Leads to Excellent Performance," *Personnel,* Sept./Oct. 1980; Thomas C. Rodney, "Can Money Motivate Better Job Performance," *Personnel Administration,* March/April 1967; Donald P. Schwab, "Conflicting Impacts of Pay on Employee Motivation and Satisfaction," *PJ,* March 1974; Max B. Shousen, "Increasing Individual Productivity Through Motivation Controls," *Meeting the Productivity Challenge* (New York: AMA, Management Report no. 40, 1960); David E. Terpstra, "Theories of Motivation—Borrowing the Best," *PJ,* June 1979; A. Zaleznik, C. R. Christensen, and F. J. Roethlisberger, *The Motivation, Productivity, and Satisfaction of Workers* (Boston: Harvard Univ., Grad. School of Business Adm., 1958).

See also LABOR MOTIVATION.

Motor Carrier Act A statute passed by Congress in 1935 which brings commercial motor vehicles operating in interstate and foreign commerce within the scope of the Interstate Commerce Commission's jurisdiction. The administration of the Act was transferred to the secretary of transportation in 1966. The law subjects the rate structure and the services of these companies to the regulations of the transportation secretary. Among other things, it gives the secretary power to determine maximum hours of service for certain employees of motor vehicle carriers. The determination of maximum number of hours of service which may be required from employees is designed to establish the safe operation of passenger, freight, and motor vehicles in interstate commerce.

Source reference: Motor Carrier Act, Aug. 9, 1935, 49 U.S.C. 304, 49 Stat. 543.

Mountain Pacific case A decision of the Supreme Court involving Local 357 of the Teamsters Union and the Los Angeles-Seattle Motor Express which set aside the National Labor Relations Board *Mountain Pacific* case rule of 1958 on hiring hall agreements which do not contain the Board prescribed safeguards. The Supreme Court held that since Congress did not ban hiring halls as such in the Taft-Hartley Act, the Board's establishment of safeguards amounted to a legislative act which it had no power to effect.

The majority opinion was delivered by Justice Douglas, who summed up the position of the Court as follows: "There being no express ban of hiring halls in any provisions of the [Taft] Act, those who add one, whether it be the Board or courts, engage in a legislative act. The Act deals with discrimination either by the employers or unions that encourages or discourages union membership."

The majority opinion also stated that ". . . it may be that hiring halls need more regulation than the Act presently affords. Perhaps the conditions which the Board attaches to hiring hall arrangements will in time appeal to the Congress . . . where, as here, Congress has aimed its sanctions only at specific discriminatory practices, the Board cannot go farther and establish a broader, more pervasive regulatory scheme."

Source references: Local 357, IBT v. NLRB, 365 US 667, 47 LRRM 2906 (1961); *Mountain Pacific Chapter, Associated General Contractors, Inc.*, 119 NLRB 883, 41 LRRM 1460 (1958); Richard H. Siegel, "The Demise of the Mountain Pacific Doctrine: Teamsters Local No. 357 vs. NLRB," *LLJ*, June 1961; "Supreme Court Knocks Down NLRB's Standards for Legal Hiring Halls," *Daily Labor Report*, April 17, 1961.

See also DISPATCHERS, HIRING HALL.

Mountain Timber Company v. Washington A decision in 1917 by the Supreme Court which upheld the prevailing types of workers compensation laws passed by the states. The Court held in part, "The Act cannot be deemed oppressive to any class or occupation, provided the scale of compensation is reasonable, unless the loss of human life and limb is found in experience to be so great that if charged to the industry it leaves no sufficient margin for reasonable profits. But certainly if any industry involves so great a human wastage as to leave no fair profit beyond it, the State is at liberty in the interest of the safety and welfare of its people, to prohibit such an industry altogether."

Source reference: Mountain Timber Co. v. Washington, 343 US 238 (1917).

See also WORKERS COMPENSATION.

moving allowances Provisions in collective bargaining agreements or company policy which provide funds to permit employees to offset some or all of their costs of transportation, either to a new company site or to another facility when a particular plant is shut down. Relocation allowance is a synonym.

Source references: The Conference Board, *Personnel Practices II: Hours of Work, Pay Practices, Relocation* (New York: Information Bull. 92, 1981); Karen E. Debats, "The Current State of Corporate Relocation," *PJ*, Sept. 1982; Harriet Gorlin, *Elements of Corporate Relocation Assistance Policies* (New York: The Conference Board, Report no. 715, 1977); Edward C. and Karen S. Koziara, "Development of Relocation Allowances as Manpower Policy," *ILRR*, Oct. 1966; Margaret Magnus and John Dodd, "Relocation: Changing Attitudes and Company Policies," *PJ*, July 1981; Gaylord F. Milbrandt, "Relocation Strategies, Parts I and II," *PJ*, July 1981 and Aug. 1981; John M. Moore, "Employee Relocation: Expanded Responsibilities for the Personnel Department," *Personnel*, Sept./Oct. 1981; J. Roger O'Meara, "Relocation Allowances for Employees Transferred Overseas," *Conference Board Record*, April 1969; Rudolph Oswald, "The Transfer Rights of Displaced Workers," *American Federationist*, July 1966; U.S. Dept. of Labor, BLS, *Major Collective Bargaining Agreements: Plant Movement, Interplant Transfer, and Relocation Allowances* (Washington: Bull. 1425–20, 1981); K. K. White, *Reimbursing Personnel for Transfer and Relocation Costs* (New York: AMA, Research Study no. 67, 1964).

mucker A worker who is engaged either in common labor or mining which involves the moving of muck, which is generally regarded to be anything offensive, dripping, or filthy, or any moist material.

muckraker A general term applied to writers and other publicists who call attention to social and economic conditions which are offensive and unsocial in order to bring about social change or legislation. Exposure of and publicizing the conditions in the Chicago stockyards is one illustration of muckraking activity which led to the passage of the Pure Food and Drug Act.

Source reference: Arthur M. and Lila Weinberg (ed.), *The Muckrakers: The Era in Journalism That Moved America to Reform* (New York: Simon & Schuster, 1961).

Muller v. Oregon A decision of the Supreme Court in 1908 which upheld the constitutionality of the Oregon Ten-Hour Law as a health measure. The Oregon law limited the employment of women in manufacturing and mechanical establishments and laundries to

10 hours in one day. It was claimed that the statute violated liberty of contract, was class legislation, and was not a valid exercise of police powers. The Court, however, said in part, "As healthy mothers are essential to vigorous offspring, the physical well-being of women becomes an object of public interest and care in order to preserve the strength and vigor of the race. . . . The limitations which this statute places upon her contractual powers, upon her right to agree with her employer as to the time she shall labor, are not imposed solely for her benefit, but also for the benefit of all."

Source references: Muller v. Oregon, 208 US 412 (1908); John R. Commons and John B. Andrews, *Principles of Labor Legislation* (4th rev. ed., New York: Harper, 1936).

multicraft union A labor organization which has within its jurisdiction more than one craft or occupation.

multi-employer bargaining *See* COLLECTIVE BARGAINING, MULTI-EMPLOYER.

Multiemployer Pension Plan Amendments Act (MPPAA) of 1980 An amendment to the Employee Retirement Income Security Act of 1974, the law extends Pension Benefit Guaranty Corporation (PBGC) benefit guarantees to multi-employer pension plans and requires an employer who chooses to withdraw from a multi-employer pension plan to pay a fair share of the plan's unfunded vested liability. Prior to the enactment of MPPAA, an employer withdrawing from a multi-employer plan incurred no liability unless the plan terminated within five years after the withdrawal with insufficient assets to provide benefits at the levels guaranteed by the PBGC.

The Act also provides for arbitration of disputes involving the amount of withdrawal liability assessed by the plan sponsor. It allows financially insecure plans to undergo reorganization, and establishes rules for mergers and transfers of assets and liabilities between multi-employer plans and for transfers from a multi-employer plan to a single-employer plan.

Source references: Multiemployer Pension Plan Amendments Act of 1980, Pub. L. 96–364, Sept. 26, 1980, 94 Stat. 1208 (codified as amended in scattered sections of 5, 26, and 29 U.S.C.); Joseph A. LoCicero, "Multiemployer Pension Plans: A Time Bomb for Employers?" *PJ*, Nov. 1980; Richard S. Soble, "Bankruptcy Claims of Multiemployer Pension Plans," *LLJ*, Jan. 1982.

multi-employer units Collective bargaining units in which a single union deals with a number of employer units.

Source reference: "NLRB and Multi-Employer Units in a Competitive Economy," *Illinois LR*, Jan./Feb. 1949.

multilateral bargaining Participation of more than two parties in the bargaining process.

Kochan defines it "as a process of negotiation in which more than two distinct parties are involved in such a way that a clear dichotomy between the employee and management organizations does not exist." In his study of city governments, he found that multilateral bargaining occurred with the participation of, among others, city officials, interest groups, and elected officials.

Source references: Tim L. Bornstein, "Taxpayer and Other Third-Party Collective Bargaining in City Governments," *ILRR*, July 1974; Thomas A. Kochan, "City Government Bargaining: A Path Analysis," *IR*, Feb. 1975; ———, "A Theory of Multilateral Collective Bargaining in City Governments," *ILRR*, July 1974; J. Joseph Loewenberg, "Multilateral Bargaining: Variation on a Theme," *LLJ*, Feb. 1975; Kenneth McLennan and Michael H. Moskow, "Multilateral Bargaining in the Public Sector," *Proceedings of the 21st A/M, IRRA*, ed. by Gerald Somers (Madison: 1969).

multinational bargaining Coordinated or centralized collective bargaining between an employer or employers of an industry with a union or group of unions representing employees in facilities located in two or more nations. Coordinated bargaining implies bargaining between a labor union and all or most subsidiaries of a multinational corporation. Centralized or transnational bargaining is collective bargaining between the parent company and a union representing workers in several countries. Northrup and Rowan state that multinational bargaining is "virtually nonexistent today." According to Cordova, there are a few cases of "true" multinational bargaining such as that between the International Transport Workers and the shipping industry and in the European recording, radio, and television industries.

Multinationals are defined by the OECD as "companies or other entities whose ownership is private, state or mixed, established in different countries and so linked that one or more of them may be able to exercise a significant influence over the activities of others and, in particular, to share knowledge and resources with the others." The Commission of the European Communities defines multinationals as "all enterprises with at least one subsidiary in a foreign country." The Commission found in a 1973 survey that nearly 46 million workers were employed by some 5,000 multinational corporations.

Source references: R. Blanpain (ed.), *Comparative Labour Law and Industrial Relations* (Washington: BNA, 1982); Robert F. Banks and Jack Stieber (ed.), *Multinationals, Unions, and Labor Relations in Industrialized Countries* (Ithaca: Cornell Univ., NYSSILR, 1977); Robert Copp, "The Labor Affairs Function in a Multinational Firm," *LLJ*, Aug. 1973; Robert J. Flanagan and Arnold R. Weber (ed.), *Bargaining Without Boundaries: The Multinational Corporation and International Labor Relations* (Chicago: Univ. of Chicago Press, 1974); David C. Hershfield, *The Multinational Union Challenges the Multinational Company* (New York: The Conference Board, Report no. 658, 1975); "Industrial Relations in a Multinational Framework," *ILR*, June 1973; ILO, *Employment Effects of Multinational Enterprises in Industrialised Countries* (Geneva: 1981); Everett M. Kassalow, *Regulation and Control of Multinational Corporations: The Labor Aspects* (Madison: Univ. of Wisconsin, IRRI, Reprint 216, 1978); Betty Southard Murphy, "Multinational Corporations and Free Coordinated Transnational Bargaining: An Alternative to Protectionism?" *LLJ*, Oct. 1977; Herbert R. Northrup and Richard L. Rowan, *Multinational Collective Bargaining Attempts; The Record, the Cases, and the Prospects* (Philadelphia: Univ. of Pennsylvania, Wharton School, Industrial Research Unit, 1979); Lloyd Ulman, "Multinational Unionism: Incentives, Barriers, and Alternatives," *IR*, Feb. 1975.

multiplant bargaining Collective bargaining between an employer and a union representing workers in more than one of the plants of that employer.

See also COLLECTIVE BARGAINING, COMPANYWIDE.

multiplant unit A bargaining unit which includes a number of plants of a single employer.

Source reference: George W. Brooks and Mark Thompson, "Multiplant Units: The NLRB's Withdrawal of Free Choice," *ILRR*, April 1967.

multiple jobholders *See* DOUBLE EMPLOYMENT; SECONDARY EMPLOYMENT.

multiple management A technique developed in the early 1930s as a means of strengthening communication between middle management and top management through the establishment of various junior boards of directors. In the case of the McCormick Company, the plan utilized three boards of junior executives—the first, a Junior Board of Directors; the second, a Factory Board; and third, a Sales Board. These boards actually functioned as committees of the Senior Board of Directors and were permitted to initiate proposals and study company problems. It was designed not only to provide good material for the development of senior executives, but also an opportunity to permit free exchange, greater communication, and strengthening of middle management.

Sometimes the phrase has reference to utilizing worker organizations in this multiple management program by giving the leaders of the employees an opportunity to discuss programs and activities with the employer in order to minimize misinformation and to provide a common ground for understanding.

Source references: Charles P. McCormick, *The Power of the People: Multiple Management Up to Date* (New York: Harper, 1949); K. Brantley Watson, "The Maturing of Multiple Management," *Management Review*, July 1974.

multiple piecework plan *See* DIFFERENTIAL PIECE-RATE PLAN.

multiple shift A working arrangement or schedule which utilizes more than one shift or tour in the plant or establishment.

See also SINGLE-SHIFT SYSTEM.

multiplied strike A labor dispute which involves individuals who walk out in sympathy with the individuals on strike and thereby multiply the number of individuals actually engaged in striking. It is basically a sympathetic strike. The term is not widely used.

See also SYMPATHETIC (SYMPATHY) STRIKE.

multiplier, theory of A theory of economic analysis which attempts to establish a relationship between changes in investment and changes in total production. It is designed to support those who feel that money or credit can have an effect on income and employment far greater than the initial expenditure, hence, the term "multiplier effect."

As John Maynard Keynes, the person to whom this theory is attributed, stated in his book, *The General Theory of Employment, Interest and Money,* "for in a given circumstance a definite ratio, to be called the multiplier, can be established between income and investment and subject to certain simplification between the total employment and employment directly employed on investment (which we shall call the primary employment). This further step is an integral part of our theory of employment, since it establishes a precise relationship, given the propensity to consume between aggregate employment and income and the rate of investments."

This was also expressed by Beveridge in his book, *Full Employment in a Free Society.* He said in part, "Every act has an infinite chain of consequences, therefore, the act of employing an unemployed man and paying him wages does not stop there. The man who is taken on and gets wages which are more than he was getting as unemployment benefits or assistance, will spend most or all of his additional income on goods and services supplied by others, and bring others into employment. They in turn will have more income; they spend some of it giving fresh employment and so on. So long as there are unemployed men in the community, employing one of the unemployed for wages will increase the number employed by more than one and will add to the national output more than what he himself produces. The primary effect will be multiplied owing to secondary and tertiary effects."

multi-union bargaining Collective bargaining in which the employer negotiates and bargains with more than one union.

Source reference: Lynn E. Wagner, "Multi-Union Bargaining: A Legal Analysis," *LLJ*, Dec. 1968.

See also COLLECTIVE BARGAINING, COALITION.

Murgia case A Supreme Court decision upholding a Massachusetts statute requiring retirement of state uniformed police officers at age 50. The law was challenged as a violation of the equal protection clause of the 14th Amendment. The Court held that the statute met the "rational basis" standard for judging the equal protection challenge because the age requirement is related to furthering the state interest to protect the public by assuring physical preparedness of uniformed police.

Source reference: Massachusetts Board of Retirement v. Murgia, 427 US 307, 12 FEP Cases 1569 (1976).

Murphy v. Sardell A decision of the Supreme Court in which the Arizona minimum wage statute was held unconstitutional.

Source reference: Murphy v. Sardell, 269 US 530 (1925).

Musical Artists, Inc.; American Guild of A branch of the Associated Actors and Artistes of America (AFL-CIO). Its bimonthly publication is the *Agmazine.*

Address: 1841 Broadway, New York, N.Y. 10023. Tel. (212) 265–3687

music at work A phrase which describes the efforts by some employers to introduce a degree of relaxation and variety at the plant, particularly where the work is monotonous or where relaxing music might assist in either establishing greater morale or reducing fatigue.

Perhaps an adaptation of the old practice of cigar makers to pay a person to read to them while they "rolled" cigars by hand.

Source references: Jacob Jacoby, "Work Music and Morale: A Neglected But Important Relationship," *PJ*, Dec. 1968; Donald M. O'Neill, "Music to Enhance the Work Environment," *Management of Personnel Quarterly*, Fall 1966; R. S. Uhrbrook, "Music on the Job: Its Influence on Worker Morale and Production," *Personnel Psychology*, Spring 1961.

See also FATIGUE, MONOTONY.

Musicians; American Federation of (AFL-CIO) The American Federation of Musicians was founded at a convention held in Indianapolis on October 19, 1896. Although it competed for a while with another organization, the National League of Musicians of America, which was primarily a professional society, most of the members of the League were absorbed into the American Federation of Musicians.

The name of James C. Petrillo, its president for many years, is prominent in the history of the union. Its official monthly publication is the *International Musician.*

Address: 1500 Broadway, New York, N.Y. 10036. Tel. (212) 869–1330

Source references: Oscar Ameringer, *If You Don't Weaken: The Autobiography of Oscar Ameringer* (New York: Holt, 1940); Robert D. Leiter, *The Musicians and Petrillo* (New York: Bookman Associates, 1953).

See also LEA ACT (ANTI-PETRILLO ACT).

mutual benefit associations Associations frequently sponsored by employers in which both employer and employees seek to set up a fraternal organization to provide relief for disability, death, or sickness not protected under state laws.

These organizations have been extremely helpful in eliminating some of the risks which are not protected by federal or state law, and where joint administration has been established, it has eliminated the criticism first leveled against such programs because of their paternalistic approach. These associations have become less prevalent with the growth of unions and the extension of health and welfare programs.

Source references: Henry Bruere and Grace Pugh, *Profitable Personnel Practice* (New York: Harper, 1929); Abraham Epstein, *Insecurity: A Challenge to America* (New York: Random House, 1938).

mutualism A social theory which advocates the organization of groups based on common ownership and effort and designed to support mutual help and brotherhood. To a large extent such mutualism is found in integrated family groups but has not been developed except in theory in socialist countries.

mutual rating An evaluating system in which employees rate all the other employees in their particular unit. This may be a division or a department in which the employees work. Generally, the individuals are given a scale and asked to evaluate and rate all of the others on the same scale with the understanding that the rating is to be considered confidential.

A rating device used during World War I, known as the Scott Man-to-Man Scale, required individuals not only to rate themselves, but also a number of their colleagues as to general characteristics, such as leadership, intelligence, etc. Then each individual who was rated was asked to list the ratees in order, from least promising to the most promising. Generally, mutual rating scales do not involve comparisons from a low to high scale, but merely rate each of the individuals on a scale.

The mutual rating scale differs from so-called vertical rating, in which individuals are rated by their superiors. This involves rating of employees by supervisors and foremen, foremen by department heads, etc.

mutual strike aid Sometimes referred to as employer strike insurance. A procedure developed by a number of industries, mostly in the public service area, including the airlines, in which efforts are made to share the impact of a strike. The employers who benefit from the strike return some of their additional earnings to the particular company which has had to bear the brunt of the strike.

Source references: John Barry, "Strike Insurance: A Threat to Collective Bargaining," *American Federationist,* March 1961; Eugene Cronin, "Employers' Mutual Aid: No Antitrust Laws Need Apply and Almost All's Fair in Industrial War," *IR Law Digest,* Winter 1977; Thomas P. Gilroy, "The Long-Range Impact of Strike Insurance Plans," *Personnel,* Sept./Oct. 1963; Mark L. Kahn, "Mutual Strike Aid in the Airlines," *LLJ,* July 1960; Marvin J. Levine and L. W. Helly, "The Airlines' Mutual Aid Pact: A Deterrent to Collective Bargaining," *LLJ,* Jan. 1977; Sam Marshall, "Curbing Mutual Aid Pacts," *American Federationist,* Feb. 1979; Benjamin R. Miller, *New Developments in Labor Relations: A Discussion of Service Interruption Insurance* (Washington: American Trucking

Assn., IR Dept., 1960); Frank M. Tuerkheimer, "Strike Insurance: An Analysis of the Legality of Inter-Employer Economic Aid Under the Present Federal Legislation," *NYU LR*, Jan. 1963; S. Herbert Unterberger and Edward C. Koziara, "Airline Strike Insurance: A Study in Escalation," *ILRR*, Oct. 1975; ———, "The Demise of Airline Strike Insurance," *ILRR*, Oct. 1980.

mutual survival A theory developed by Dr. E. Wight Bakke which holds that in the long run industrial relations will be more highly developed when parties recognize the need to understand and respect each other's survival needs. He contends in his studies that the attempt by each side, labor and management, to retain its own sovereignty will not provide any basis for understanding but that their sovereignty will be best protected through mutual understanding and a need to recognize the concern for mutual survival rather than individual sovereignty.

Source reference: E. Wight Bakke, *Mutual Survival: The Goal of Unions and Management* (2d ed., Hamden: Archon Books, 1966).

mysteries of the craft The ancient craft guilds were frequently known as "mysteries." A member of the guild while going through his apprenticeship obtained skills which were not known except to those within the mystery. This was a vested property right which he maintained and was able to use as long as he maintained his position within the craft.

N

NAAE *See* AGRICULTURE EMPLOYEES; NATIONAL ASSOCIATION OF (IND).

NAATS *See* AIR TRAFFIC SPECIALISTS; NATIONAL ASSOCIATION OF (IND).

NAB *See* NATIONAL ALLIANCE OF BUSINESS (NAB).

NABET *See* BROADCAST EMPLOYEES AND TECHNICIANS; NATIONAL ASSOCIATION OF (AFL-CIO).

NAGE *See* GOVERNMENT EMPLOYEES; NATIONAL ASSOCIATION OF (AFL-CIO).

NAGI *See* GOVERNMENT INSPECTORS AND QUALITY ASSURANCE PERSONNEL; NATIONAL ASSOCIATION OF (IND).

NALC *See* LETTER CARRIERS; NATIONAL ASSOCIATION OF (AFL-CIO).

NAPEP *See* PLANNERS, ESTIMATORS, AND PROGRESSMEN; NATIONAL ASSOCIATION OF (IND).

NAPFE *See* POSTAL AND FEDERAL EMPLOYEES; NATIONAL ALLIANCE OF (IND).

NAPS *See* POSTAL SUPERVISORS; NATIONAL ASSOCIATION OF (IND).

NBPA *See* BASKETBALL PLAYERS ASSOCIATION; NATIONAL (IND).

NBPW *See* PACKINGHOUSE AND INDUSTRIAL WORKERS; NATIONAL BROTHERHOOD OF (IND).

NEA *See* NATIONAL EDUCATION ASSOCIATION (IND).

NFFE *See* FEDERAL EMPLOYEES; NATIONAL FEDERATION OF (IND).

NFI *See* NATIONAL FOREMAN'S INSTITUTE, INC.

NFIU *See* NATIONAL FEDERATION OF INDEPENDENT UNIONS.

NFLPA *See* FOOTBALL LEAGUE PLAYERS ASSOCIATION; NATIONAL.

NHLPA *See* HOCKEY LEAGUE PLAYERS' ASSOCIATION; NATIONAL (IND).

NILE *See* NATIONAL INSTITUTE OF LABOR EDUCATION (NILE).

NIRA *See* NATIONAL INDUSTRIAL RECOVERY ACT.

NIW *See* INDUSTRIAL WORKERS UNION; NATIONAL (IND).

NLP *See* POSTMASTERS OF THE UNITED STATES; NATIONAL LEAGUE OF (IND).

NLRA *See* NATIONAL LABOR RELATIONS ACT.

NLRB *See* NATIONAL LABOR RELATIONS BOARD.

NLRBP *See* NATIONAL LABOR RELATIONS BOARD PROFESSIONAL ASSOCIATION (IND).

NLRBU *See* NATIONAL LABOR RELATIONS BOARD UNION (IND).

NMB *See* NATIONAL MEDIATION BOARD.

NMD *See* NEWSPAPER AND MAIL DELIVERERS' UNION OF NEW YORK AND VICINITY (IND).

NMU *See* MARITIME UNION OF AMERICA; NATIONAL (AFL-CIO).

NOW *See* NATIONAL ORGANIZATION FOR WOMEN (NOW).

NPW *See* NOVELTY AND PRODUCTION WORKERS; INTERNATIONAL UNION OF ALLIED (AFL-CIO).

NRA *See* NATIONAL RECOVERY ADMINISTRATION.

NTE *See* TREASURY EMPLOYEES UNION; NATIONAL (IND).

NWLB *See* NATIONAL WAR LABOR BOARD.

NWSB *See* NATIONAL WAGE STABILIZATION BOARD.

NYA *See* NATIONAL YOUTH ADMINISTRATION.

NYC *See* NEIGHBORHOOD YOUTH CORPS (NYC).

narcotic effect The tendency of parties to rely or become dependent on impasse procedures instead of resolving issues at the bargaining table. It has been suggested, for example, that arbitration may have a narcotic effect because the parties view it as an easier process than reaching a bilateral settlement.

Source references: Richard J. Butler and Ronald G. Ehrenberg, "Estimating the Narcotic Effect of Public Sector Impasse Procedures," *ILRR*, Oct. 1981; Thomas A. Kochan and Jean Baderschneider, "Estimating the Narcotic Effect: Choosing Techniques that Fit the Problem," *ILRR*, Oct. 1981; Hoyt N. Wheeler, "Compulsory Arbitration: A 'Narcotic Effect'?" *IR*, Feb. 1975.

See also CHILLING EFFECT.

Nash "golden rule" For many years the A. Nash Clothing Company of Cincinnati maintained a form of unionization similar to the company union. The company used stock distribution, bonuses, and other devices to develop a form of labor-management relations which could take the place of the trade union. The head of the company spoke at numerous places on the "Golden Rule" as the solution to labor-management problems.

In 1925 the company voluntarily requested a union, the Amalgamated Clothing Workers, to organize its employees. The company felt that the Amalgamated would be a constructive influence among employees. Such a voluntary proposal in the 1920s was unusual and attracted a great deal of attention. Apparently the action of the head of the company in developing the "Golden Rule" was not motivated by antipathy toward trade unions, but was an attempt to find some substitute which would provide all of the values of a union and avoid any of its limitations. Nash finally concluded that the relationship with the Amalgamated Clothing Workers Union would create harmonious relations as well as increase the efficiency of the company.

National Academy of Arbitrators A private organization consisting of individuals actively engaged in the arbitration process and supporting the use of arbitration in the field of labor-management relations.

The organization is concerned with establishing higher standards within the profession, and works with the American Arbitration Association and the Federal Mediation and Conciliation Service for utilization of the arbitration process as a useful and helpful device in labor-management relations. It was organized in September 1947 and holds annual meetings to discuss current issues in the field of arbitration.

The presidents of the organization since 1947 follow:

Ralph T. Seward	1947–1949
William E. Simkin	1950
David L. Cole	1951
David A. Wolff	1952
Edgar L. Warren	1953
Saul Wallen	1954
Aaron Horvitz	1955
John Day Larkin	1956
Paul N. Guthrie	1957
Harry H. Platt	1958
G. Allan Dash, Jr.	1959
Leo C. Brown, S.J.	1960
Gabriel N. Alexander	1961
Benjamin Aaron	1962
Sylvester Garrett	1963
Peter M. Keilliher	1964
Russell A. Smith	1965
Robben W. Fleming	1966
Bert L. Luskin	1967
Charles C. Killingsworth	1968
James C. Hill	1969
Jean T. McKelvey	1970
Lewis M. Gill	1971
Gerald A. Barrett	1972
Eli Rock	1973
David P. Miller	1974
Rolf Valtin	1975
H. D. Woods	1976
Arthur Stark	1977
Richard Mittenthal	1978
Clare B. McDermott	1979
Eva Robins	1980
Edgar A. Jones, Jr.	1981

Byron Abernethy 1982
Mark Kahn 1983

Address: 4335 Cathedral Ave., N.W., Washington, D.C. 20016. Tel. (202) 362–8316

Source references: The annual proceedings of the National Academy of Arbitrators, published by The Bureau of National Affairs, Inc. include: *The Profession of Labor Arbitration* (1948–1954); *Arbitration Today* (1955); *Management Rights and the Arbitration Process* (1956); *Critical Issues in Labor Arbitration* (1957); *The Arbitrator and the Parties* (1958); *Arbitration and the Law* (1959); *Challenges to Arbitration* (1960); *Arbitration and Public Policy* (1961); *Collective Bargaining and the Arbitrator's Role* (1962); *Labor Arbitration and Industrial Change* (1963); *Labor Arbitration: Perspectives and Problems* (1964); *Proceedings of the 18th Annual Meeting* (1965); *Problems of Proof in Arbitration* (1966); *The Arbitrator, the NLRB and the Courts* (1967); *Developments in American and Foreign Arbitration* (1968); *Arbitration and Social Change* (1969); *Arbitration and the Expanding Role of Neutrals* (1970); *Arbitration and the Public Interest* (1971); *Labor Arbitration at the Quarter-Century Mark* (1972); *Arbitration of Interest Disputes* (1973); *Arbitration—1974* (1974); *Arbitration—1975* (1975); *Arbitration—1976* (1976); *Arbitration—1977* (1977); *Truth, Lie Detectors, and Other Problems in Labor Arbitration* (1978); *Arbitration of Subcontracting and Wage Incentive Disputes* (1979); *Decisional Thinking of Arbitrators and Judges* (1980); *Arbitration Issues for the 1980s* (1981); *Arbitration 1982; Conduct of the Hearing* (1982); *Arbitration—Promise and Performance* (1983); *Arbitration 1984: Absenteeism, Recent Law, Panels, and Published Decisions* (1984).

National Air Transport Adjustment Board Section 205 of the Railway Labor Act authorizes the National Mediation Board to constitute the Adjustment Board for "the prompt and orderly settlement of disputes" between air carriers and their employees "growing out of grievances or out of the interpretation or application of agreements between said carriers . . . and any class or classes of . . . their employees, covering rates of pay, rules, or working conditions. . . ."

The National Mediation Board, as of 1981, has not considered such a national board necessary. The airlines and unions have instead established their own grievance procedures with final decisions issued by a system board of adjustment.

Source references: Railway Labor Act of 1926, as amended, 45 U.S.C. 151–163, 181–188 (1982); Mark L. Kahn, "Labor-Management Relations in the Airlines Industry," *The Railway Labor Act at Fifty* (Washington: U.S. NMB, 1976); U.S. NMB, *Forty-Seventh Annual Report* (Washington: 1982).

See also NATIONAL MEDIATION BOARD.

National Alliance of Business (NAB) An association of business leaders formed as the National Alliance of Businessmen in 1968 to work with the federal government to provide the necessary program promotion and to enlist the resources of private industry to develop training programs and job pledges for hard-core unemployed workers identified under the Job Opportunities in the Business Sector (JOBS) program.

In the late autumn of 1969, a new contract campaign called Jobs '70 was instituted by the Department of Labor, expanding the NAB-JOBS project to include hospitals, schools, and other nonprofit institutions.

NAB local offices in some 150 major cities are staffed with local business executives on loan from their companies. The local NAB representatives ask private employers for signed pledges to hire disadvantaged workers. Costs of recruiting, training, and counseling are borne by the employers, except for extraordinary costs which are defrayed by the Department of Labor.

With the passage of the 1978 Comprehensive Employment and Training Act, the NAB and the federal government developed the Private Sector Initiative Program (PSIP). The program, through the Private Industry Councils (PICs) encouraged business to provide training and employment opportunities for the economically disadvantaged. It continues to coordinate and offer technical assistance in developing training programs under the Job Training Partnership Act of 1982.

The NAB was first chaired by Henry Ford II; its current chair is David M. Roderick of United States Steel.

The Alliance adopted its current name in 1978. It issues various publications including the monthly *WorkAmerica* and held its 16th annual conference in 1984.

Address: 1015 15th St., N.W., Washington, D.C. 20005. Tel. (202) 457–0040

Source references: "Hard-Core Jobless Get a Friend at the Top," *Business Week*, March 8, 1969; Kenneth B. Hoyt, *National Alliance of Business and Career Education* (Washington: U.S. Dept. of HEW, Office of Education, Monographs on Career Education, 1978); Allen R. Janger, "What's Been Learned About Managing the Disadvantaged," *Conference Board Record*, Dec. 1969; "LBJ Expands War on Job Barriers," *Business Week*, Jan. 27, 1968; Sar A. Levitan, Garth L. Mangum, and Robert Taggart III, *Economic Opportunity in the Ghetto: The Partnership of Government and Business* (Baltimore: Johns Hopkins Press, Policy Studies in Employment and Welfare no. 3, 1970); National Alliance of Business, *The PSIP Clearinghouse* (Washington: n.d.); Jules Pagano, "Union-Management Adaptation to Needs of Disadvantaged New Employees," *Proceedings of the 21st A/M, IRRA*, ed. by Gerald Somers (Madison: 1969); E. F. Shelly and Co., *Private Industry and the Disadvantaged*, Prepared for the Urban Coalition (New York: 1969); U.S. Dept. of Labor, Manpower Administration, *JOBS Entry Program, National Alliance of Businessmen* (rev. ed., Washington: 1972); Robert E. Van Brunt, "Unexpected Results When Training the Handicapped," *Training and Development Journal*, Oct. 1969.

See also JOB OPPORTUNITIES IN THE BUSINESS SECTOR (JOBS), PRIVATE INDUSTRY COUNCIL (PIC), PRIVATE SECTOR INITIATIVE PROGRAM (PSIP).

national and international unions A listing of the unions to be found in the Dictionary follows. The unions are listed here *alphabetically* according to their official names. Individual entries of these unions in the Dictionary, however, are to be found according to industry or trade designation which is noted in *italics* in this listing. The word in italics is generally the one used to identify the industry or craft and wherever possible this practice has been followed. For example, the Amalgamated *Clothing* and Textile Workers Union (AFL-CIO) will not be entered under Amalgamated, but under *Clothing* and Textile Workers Union; Amalgamated (AFL-CIO). Similarly, the American Federation of *Grain Millers* (AFL-CIO) is listed under *Grain Millers*, not American Federation of.

The individual entry will contain some information on each of the national and international unions, including the official publication issued by the organization. In most cases, the current address and telephone number of the organization also are given.

For more detailed information, it is suggested that copies of the *Directory of U.S. Labor Organizations, 1984–85 Edition* be obtained from the Bureau of National Affairs. The 1984–85 edition is the second of the series published to continue the *Directory of National and International Labor Unions in the United States*, once issued by the Bureau of Labor Statistics. This publication shows the structure and membership of trade unions as well as developments in the trade union movement over a period of years.

Actors' Equity Association.

Airline Communications Employees Association (Ind).

Air Line Dispatchers Association (AFL-CIO).

Air Line Employees Association; International.

Air Line Pilots Association; International (AFL-CIO).

Alliance of Independent *Telephone* Unions (Ind).

Allied *Independent* Union (Ind).

Aluminum, Brick and Clay Workers International Union (AFL-CIO).

Aluminum, Brick and Glass Workers International Union (AFL-CIO).

Aluminum Workers International Union (AFL-CIO).

Amalgamated Association of *Street*, Electric Railway and Motor Coach Employes of America (AFL-CIO).

Amalgamated *Clothing* and Textile Workers Union (AFL-CIO).

Amalgamated *Clothing Workers* of America (AFL-CIO).

Amalgamated *Lace Operatives* of America (Ind).

Amalgamated *Lithographers* of America (Ind).

Amalgamated *Meat Cutters* and Butcher Workmen of North America (AFL-CIO).
Amalgamated *Transit* Union (AFL-CIO).
American Association of *Classified School Employees* (Ind).
American Association of University Professors (AAUP) (Ind).
American *Bakery* and Confectionery Workers' International Union (AFL-CIO).
American *Communications* Association (Ind).
American Federation of *Government Employees* (AFL-CIO).
American Federation of *Grain Millers* (AFL-CIO).
American Federation of *Hosiery Workers* (AFL-CIO).
American Federation of *Musicians* (AFL-CIO).
American Federation of *School Administrators* (AFL-CIO).
American Federation of *State*, County and Municipal Employees (AFL-CIO).
American Federation of *Teachers* (AFL-CIO).
American Federation of *Technical Engineers* (AFL-CIO).
American Federation of *Television* and Radio Artists.
American Flint *Glass Workers'* Union of North America (AFL-CIO).
American Guild of *Musical Artists*, Inc.
American Guild of *Variety Artists*.
American *Nurses'* Association (Ind).
American *Postal Workers* Union (AFL-CIO).
American *Radio* Association (AFL-CIO).
American *Train Dispatchers* Association (AFL-CIO).
American *Watch Workers* Union (Ind).
American *Wire Weavers* Protective Association (AFL-CIO).
Associated *Actors and Artistes* of America (AFL-CIO).
Associated Unions of America (Ind).
Association of *Civilian Technicians* (Ind).
Association of *Engineers* and Scientists (Ind).
Association of *Flight Attendants*.
Association of *Railway Trainmen* and Locomotive Firemen (Ind).
Association of Western *Pulp* and Paper Workers (Ind).
Atlantic, Gulf, Lakes and Inland Waters District.
Atlantic Independent Union (Ind).
Bakery and Confectionery Workers' International Union of America (AFL-CIO).
Bakery, Confectionery and Tobacco Workers International Union (AFL-CIO).
Barbers and Beauty Culturists Union of America (AFL-CIO).
Barbers, Beauticians, and Allied Industries International Association (AFL-CIO).
Boot and *Shoe Workers'* Union (AFL-CIO).
Bricklayers, Masons and Plasterers' International Union of America (AFL-CIO).
Brotherhood of *Locomotive Engineers* (Ind).
Brotherhood of *Locomotive Firemen* and Enginemen (AFL-CIO).
Brotherhood of *Maintenance* of Way Employes (AFL-CIO).
Brotherhood of *Marine Officers*.
Brotherhood of *Railroad Signalmen* (AFL-CIO).
Brotherhood of *Railroad Trainmen* (AFL-CIO).
Brotherhood of *Railway*, Airline and Steamship Clerks, Freight Handlers, Express and Station Employes (AFL-CIO).
Brotherhood of *Railway Carmen* of America (AFL-CIO).
Brotherhood of *Railway Carmen* of the United States and Canada (AFL-CIO).
Brotherhood of *Shoe* and Allied Craftsmen (Ind).
Brotherhood of Sleeping Car *Porters* (AFL-CIO).
Brotherhood of *Utility Workers* of New England, Inc. (Ind).
Building Service Employees' International Union (AFL-CIO).
Burlesque Artists Association.
Christian Labor Association of the United States of America (Ind).
Cigar Makers' International Union of America (AFL-CIO).
Civil Service Employees Association, Inc. (New York).
Communications Workers of America (AFL-CIO).
Composers and Lyricists Guild of America (Ind).
Congress of *Independent Unions* (Ind).
Coopers' International Union of North America (AFL-CIO).
Diamond Workers' Protective Union of America (AFL).
Directors Guild of America, Inc. (Ind).

Distillery, Rectifying, Wine and Allied Workers' International Union of America (AFL-CIO).

Distillery, Wine and Allied Workers' International Union (AFL-CIO).

Distributive, Processing and Office Workers of America (Ind).

Distributive Workers of America (Ind).

District 50, United Mine Workers of America (Ind).

Eighth Region *NLRB* Association (Ind).

Engineers and Scientists of California.

Federal Plant *Quarantine Inspectors* National Association (Ind).

Federal *Tobacco Inspectors* Mutual Association (Ind).

Federated Council of the International Association of *Railway Employees* and Association of Railway Trainmen and Locomotive Firemen (Ind).

Federation of *Nurses* and Health Professionals.

Federation of *Postal Security Police* (Ind).

Federation of Professional *Athletes* (AFL-CIO).

Federation of *Westinghouse* Independent Salaried Unions (Ind).

Flight Engineers' International Association (AFL-CIO).

Fraternal Order of *Police* (Ind).

Friendly Society of *Engravers* and Sketchmakers, Inc. (Ind).

Glass Bottle Blowers Association of the United States and Canada (AFL-CIO).

Glass, Pottery, Plastic and Allied Workers International Union (AFL-CIO).

Graphic Arts International Union (AFL-CIO).

Graphic Communications International Union (AFL-CIO).

Hebrew Actors Union, Inc.

Hotel and Restaurant Employees and Bartenders International Union (AFL-CIO).

Hotel Employees and Restaurant Employees International Union (AFL-CIO).

Independent *Bakery Employees* Union (Ind).

Independent Union of Plant *Protection Employees* (Ind).

Independent *Watchmen's* Association (Ind).

Industrial Union of *Marine* and Shipbuilding Workers of America (AFL-CIO).

Inlandboatmen's Union of the Pacific.

Insurance Workers International Union (AFL-CIO).

International *Air Line Stewards* and Stewardesses Association.

International Alliance of *Bill Posters*, Billers and Distributors of the United States and Canada (AFL-CIO).

International Alliance of *Theatrical* Stage Employees and Moving Picture Machine Operators of the United States and Canada (AFL-CIO).

International Association of Bridge, Structural and Ornamental *Iron Workers* (AFL-CIO).

International Association of *Cleaning* and Dye House Workers (AFL-CIO).

International Association of *Fire Fighters* (AFL-CIO).

International Association of Heat and Frost Insulators and *Asbestos Workers* (AFL-CIO).

International Association of *Machinists* and Aerospace Workers (AFL-CIO).

International Association of *Marble*, Slate and Stone Polishers, Rubbers and Sawyers, Tile and Marble Setters' Helpers and Marble Mosaic and Terrazzo Workers' Helpers (AFL-CIO).

International Association of *Siderographers* (AFL-CIO).

International Association of *Tool Craftsmen* (Ind).

International *Broom* and Wisk Makers' Union of America (AFL-CIO).

International Brotherhood of *Boilermakers*, Iron Ship Builders, Blacksmiths, Forgers and Helpers (AFL-CIO).

International Brotherhood of *Bookbinders* (AFL-CIO).

International Brotherhood of *Electrical Workers* (AFL-CIO).

International Brotherhood of *Firemen* and Oilers (AFL-CIO).

International Brotherhood of *Longshoremen* (AFL-CIO).

International Brotherhood of *Painters* and Allied Trades of the United States and Canada (AFL-CIO).

International Brotherhood of *Paper Makers* (AFL-CIO).

International Brotherhood of *Pottery* and Allied Workers (AFL-CIO).

International Brotherhood of *Pulp*, Sulphite and Paper Mill Workers (AFL-CIO).
International Brotherhood of *Teamsters*, Chauffeurs, Warehousemen and Helpers of America (Ind).
International *Chemical Workers* Union (AFL-CIO).
International *Die Sinkers'* Conference (Ind).
International Federation of *Professional* and Technical Engineers (AFL-CIO).
International Federation of Technical Engineers, *Architects'* and Draftsmen's Union (AFL).
International *Fur* and Leather Workers' Union of the United States and Canada (CIO).
International *Glove Workers'* Union of America (AFL-CIO).
International *Guards* Union of America (Ind).
International *Jewelry Workers'* Union (AFL-CIO).
International *Ladies' Garment* Workers Union (AFL-CIO).
International *Leather* Goods, Plastic and Novelty Workers' Union (AFL-CIO).
International *Longshoremen's* and Warehousemen's Union (Ind).
International *Longshoremen's* Association (AFL-CIO).
International *Mailers* Union (Ind).
International *Metal Engravers* and Marking Device Workers Union (AFL-CIO).
International *Metal Engravers* Union (Ind).
International *Molders'* and Allied Workers' Union (AFL-CIO).
International Organization of *Masters*, Mates and Pilots.
International *Photo-Engravers'* Union of North America (AFL-CIO).
International *Plate Printers'*, Die Stampers' and Engravers' Union of North America (AFL-CIO).
International *Printing* and Graphic Communications Union (AFL-CIO).
International *Printing Pressmen* and Assistants Union of North America (AFL-CIO).
International *Production*, Service and Sales Union (Ind).
International *Spinners* Union (Ind).
International *Stereotypers'* and Electrotypers' Union of North America (AFL-CIO).
International *Typographical* Union (AFL-CIO).
International Union, Allied *Industrial Workers* of America (AFL-CIO).
International Union of Allied *Novelty* and Production Workers (AFL-CIO).
International Union of *Bricklayers* and Allied Craftsmen (AFL-CIO).
International Union of *District 50*, Allied and Technical Workers of the United States and Canada (Ind).
International Union of Dolls, *Toys*, Playthings, Novelties and Allied Products of the United States and Canada (AFL-CIO).
International Union of *Electrical*, Radio and Machine Workers (AFL-CIO).
International Union of *Electronic*, Electrical, Technical, Salaried and Machine Workers (AFL-CIO).
International Union of *Elevator Constructors* (AFL-CIO).
International Union of Journeymen *Horseshoers* (AFL-CIO).
International Union of *Mine*, Mill and Smelter Workers (Ind).
International Union of *Operating Engineers* (AFL-CIO).
International Union of *Petroleum* and Industrial Workers.
International Union of *Petroleum Workers*, Inc. (Ind).
International Union of *Police* Associations (AFL-CIO).
International Union of *Security Officers* (Ind).
International Union of *Tool*, Die and Mold Makers (Ind).
International Union of United *Brewery*, Flour, Cereal, Soft Drink and Distillery Workers of America (AFL-CIO).
International Union, United *Automobile*, Aerospace and Agricultural Implement Workers of America (AFL-CIO).
International Union, United *Automobile Workers* of America (AFL-CIO).
International Union, United *Plant Guard* Workers of America (Ind).
International Union, United *Weldors* (Ind).
International *Woodworkers* of America (AFL-CIO).
Italian Actors Union.
Journeymen *Barbers*, Hairdressers, Cosmetologists and Proprietors' International Union of America (AFL-CIO).

Journeymen *Stone Cutters* Association of North America (AFL-CIO).
Laborers' International Union of North America (AFL-CIO).
Laundry and Dry Cleaning International Union (AFL-CIO).
Leather Workers International Union of America (AFL-CIO).
Lithographers and Photoengravers International Union (AFL-CIO).
Log Scalers International Union (Ind).
Machine Printers and Engravers Association of the United States (Ind).
Major Indoor *Soccer League Players* Association.
Major League *Baseball Players* Association (Ind).
Major League *Umpires* Association (Ind).
Marine Cooks and Stewards' Union.
Match Workers Council (AFL-CIO).
Mechanics Educational Society of America (AFL-CIO).
Metal Polishers, Buffers, Platers and Allied Workers International Union (AFL-CIO).
National *Agricultural Workers* Union (AFL-CIO).
National Alliance of *Postal and Federal* Employees (Ind).
National Association of *Aeronautical Examiners* (Ind).
National Association of *Aeronautical Production Controllers* (Ind).
National Association of *Agriculture Employees* (Ind).
National Association of *Air Traffic Specialists* (Ind).
National Association of *ASCS* County Office Employees (Ind).
National Association of *Broadcast Employees* and Technicians (AFL-CIO).
National Association of *Government Employees* (AFL-CIO).
National Association of *Government Inspectors* (Ind).
National Association of *Government Inspectors* and Quality Assurance Personnel.
National Association of *Internal Revenue* Employees (Ind).
National Association of *Letter Carriers* (AFL-CIO).
National Association of Master *Mechanics* and Foremen of Naval Shore Establishments.
National Association of *Planners*, Estimators and Progressmen (Ind).
National Association of *Postal Supervisors* (Ind).
National Association of *Post Office* and General Service Maintenance Employees (AFL-CIO).
National Association of *Post Office Mail Handlers*, Watchmen, Messengers and Group Leaders (AFL-CIO).
National *Basketball Players* Association (Ind).
National Brotherhood of *Packinghouse* and Dairy Workers (Ind).
National Brotherhood of *Packinghouse* and Industrial Workers (Ind).
National Council of *Distributive Workers* of America (Ind).
National Education Association (Ind).
National Federation of *Federal Employees* (Ind).
National Federation of *Licensed Practical Nurses* (Ind).
National Federation of *Post Office Clerks* (AFL-CIO).
National Federation of *Post Office Motor Vehicle* Employees (AFL-CIO).
National *Football League* Players Association.
National *Hockey League* Players' Association (Ind).
National *Industrial Workers* Union (Ind).
National Labor Relations Board Professional Association (Ind).
National Labor Relations Board Union (Ind).
National League of *Postmasters* of the United States (Ind).
National *Marine Engineers'* Beneficial Association (AFL-CIO).
National *Maritime* Union of America (AFL-CIO).
National Organization of *Industrial* Trade Unions (Ind).
National *Plant Protection* Association (Ind).
National *Postal Transport* Association (AFL-CIO).
National *Postal* Union (Ind).
National Rural *Letter Carriers'* Association (Ind).
National *Treasury Employees* Union (Ind).
National *Weather Service* Employees Organization.
Newspaper and Mail Deliverers' Union of New York and Vicinity (Ind).

North American *Soccer League Players* Association.

Office and Professional Employees International Union (AFL-CIO).

Oil, Chemical and Atomic Workers International Union (AFL-CIO).

Operative *Plasterers'* and Cement Masons' International Association of the United States and Canada (AFL-CIO).

Order of *Railway Conductors* and Brakemen (Ind).

Overseas Education Association, Inc.

Pacific Coast Marine Firemen, Oilers, Watertenders and Wipers Association.

Patent Office Professional Association (Ind).

Pattern Makers' League of North America (AFL-CIO).

Playthings, Jewelry and Novelty Workers International Union (CIO).

Professional Air Traffic Controllers Organization.

Professional Association of the *Interstate Commerce* Commission (Ind).

Progressive Mine Workers of America (Ind).

Railroad Yardmasters of America (AFL-CIO).

Railroad Yardmasters of North America, Inc. (Ind).

Railway Patrolmen's International Union (AFL-CIO).

Retail Clerks International Association (AFL-CIO).

Retail Clerks International Union (AFL-CIO).

Retail, Wholesale and Department Store Union (AFL-CIO).

Sailors' Union of the Pacific.

Screen Actors Guild.

Screen Extras Guild.

Seafarers' International Union of North America (AFL-CIO).

Service Employees' International Union (AFL-CIO).

Sheet Metal Workers' International Association (AFL-CIO).

Southern Labor Union (Ind).

Stockyard Workers Association of America (Ind).

Stove, Furnace and Allied Appliance Workers' International Union of North America (AFL-CIO).

Switchmen's Union of North America (AFL-CIO).

Telecommunications International Union (Ind).

Textile Processors, Service Trades, Health Care, Professional and Technical Employees International Union.

Textile Workers Union of America (AFL-CIO).

The American *Railway* and Airline Supervisors Association (AFL-CIO).

The American *Railway* and Airway Supervisors Association (AFL-CIO).

The Commercial *Telegraphers'* Union (AFL-CIO).

The *Granite Cutters'* International Association of America (AFL-CIO).

The National Association of Special Delivery *Messengers* (AFL-CIO).

The *Newspaper* Guild (AFL-CIO).

The Order of *Railroad Telegraphers* (AFL-CIO).

The United *Brick and Clay Workers* of America (AFL-CIO).

The Wood, Wire and Metal *Lathers* International Union (AFL-CIO).

Tile, Marble, Terrazzo Finishers and Shopworkers and Granite Cutters International Union (AFL-CIO).

Tobacco Workers International Union (AFL-CIO).

Trademark Society, Inc. (Ind).

Transportation-Communication Employees Union (AFL-CIO).

Transport Workers Union of America (AFL-CIO).

Union of American *Physicians* and Dentists (Ind).

United *Allied Workers* International Union (Ind).

United Association of Journeymen and Apprentices of the *Plumbing* and Pipe Fitting Industry of the United States and Canada (AFL-CIO).

United Brotherhood of *Carpenters* and Joiners of America (AFL-CIO).

United *Cement*, Lime and Gypsum Workers International Union (AFL-CIO).

United *Cement*, Lime, Gypsum, and Allied Workers International Union (AFL-CIO).

United *Department Store* Workers of America (CIO).

United *Electrical*, Radio and Machine Workers of America (Ind).

United *Farm Workers* of America (AFL-CIO).
United *Farm Workers* Organizing Committee (AFL-CIO).
United Federation of *Postal Clerks* (AFL-CIO).
United *Food* and Commercial Workers International Union (AFL-CIO).
United *Furniture Workers* of America (AFL-CIO).
United *Garment Workers* of America (AFL-CIO).
United *Gas*, Coke and Chemical Workers of America (CIO).
United *Glass and Ceramic Workers* of North America (AFL-CIO).
United *Hatters*, Cap and Millinery Workers International Union (AFL-CIO).
United *Leather Workers* International Union (AFL).
United *Mine Workers* of America (Ind).
United National Association of *Post Office Craftsmen* (Ind).
United *Optical* and Instrument Workers of America (CIO).
United *Packinghouse*, Food and Allied Workers (AFL-CIO).
United *Papermakers* and Paperworkers (AFL-CIO).
United *Paperworkers* International Union (AFL-CIO).
United *Railroad Workers* of America (CIO).
United *Rubber*, Cork, Linoleum and Plastic Workers of America (AFL-CIO).
United *Shoe Workers* of America (AFL-CIO).
United Slate, Tile and Composition *Roofers*, Damp and Waterproof Workers Association (AFL-CIO).
United *Steelworkers* of America (AFL-CIO).
United *Stone* and Allied Products Workers of America (AFL-CIO).
United *Telegraph* Workers (AFL-CIO).
United *Textile Workers* of America (AFL-CIO).
United *Transportation* Union (AFL-CIO).
United *Transport Service* Employees (AFL-CIO).
United Union of *Roofers*, Waterproofers and Allied Workers (AFL-CIO).
United *Wall Paper* Craftsmen and Workers of North America (AFL-CIO).
Upholsterers' International Union of North America (AFL-CIO).
Utility Workers Union of America (AFL-CIO).
Window *Glass Cutters* League of America (AFL-CIO).
Writers Guild of America (Ind).

National Association of Manufacturers (NAM) An organization of employers, originally organized in 1895, which has remained in existence since that time. Its major work is performed by its trade, law, publicity, and industrial relations departments.

As early as 1903 the association formed the Citizens Industrial Association of America, whose major concern was opposition to organized labor. In 1907 it established a National Council for Industrial Defense which later changed its name to the National Industrial Council, whose major purpose was to oppose federal and state labor legislation friendly toward unionism.

According to one of the writers in the field of labor problems, Professor C. R. Daugherty, the NAM is "anti-union in three main ways: (1) cooperation with other belligerent associations; (2) effecting this cooperation through the National Industrial Council created in 1907 for the purpose of blocking labor legislation by lobbying in all legislative halls; (3) continuous propaganda by means of bulletins issued by the open shop or industrial-relations division."

When Warner P. Gullander became NAM's first full-time president in 1962, his basic mandate was to change "not just the image but the character of NAM." He held that a negative position is of little value. What he wanted was to convert the NAM into a "problem-solving organization."

Among the programs launched by the new leadership were STEP (Solutions to Employment Problems) and MIND (Methods of Intellectual Development). As one vice president of the NAM put it, "our present approach is one of working on a constructive, responsible and problem-solving basis to improve the industrial climate in this country."

Membership in 1983 was estimated at 12,000 companies. It publishes the monthly *Enterprise*.

Address: 1776 F St., N.W., Washington, D.C. 20006. Tel. (202) 626–3700

Source references: Carroll R. Daugherty, *Labor Problems in American Industry* (Boston: Houghton Mifflin, 1941); Albion G. Taylor, *Labor Practices of the National Association of Manufacturers* (Urbana: Univ. of Illinois Press, 1938).

National Board of Jurisdictional Awards An organization established in 1918–1919 by the Building Trades Department of the AFL, contractors, and architects to resolve jurisdictional disputes. Although the tribunal functioned effectively for a number of years, it was unable to withstand the refusal of the Carpenters Union to abide by a decision unfavorable to it. The tribunal was dissolved in 1927. The problem of enforcing arbitration awards within the building trades was almost insoluble until the passage of the Taft-Hartley Act which placed the responsibility for making determinations of jurisdictional disputes in the hands of the NLRB.

Professor John Dunlop was responsible for organizing and heading the tribunal to handle jurisdictional disputes in the building trades industry after the enactment of the Taft-Hartley Act. The board, known as the National Joint Board for the Settlement of Jurisdictional Disputes, was established in 1948 by the leaders of the AFL Building and Construction Trades Department and the major national contractor associations with the support of the NLRB chairperson and General Counsel. An equal number of labor and contractor representatives constituted the board's membership and during its first 10 years Professor Dunlop served as chair. The board was dissolved in September 1969 and re-established in April 1970. It was reorganized in 1973 as the Impartial Jurisdictional Disputes Board, a three-member board comprised of neutrals knowledgeable and experienced in construction.

Source references: BNA, *Labor Relations Expediter*; John T. Dunlop, *Dispute Resolution, Negotiation and Consensus Building* (Dover, Mass.: Auburn House, 1984); Herbert Harris, *Labor's Civil War* (New York: Knopf, 1940); Edwin C. Pendleton, "Comments on Jurisdictional Disputes," *Symposium on Labor Relations Law*, ed. by Ralph Slovenko (Baton Rouge: Claitor's Bookstore, 1961).

See also JURISDICTIONAL DISPUTE, WORK ASSIGNMENT.

National Child Labor Committee Following the growth of trade unions toward the end of the 19th century and the public concern over labor by children below the age of 14, substantial public opinion was mobilized for federal and state legislation. This sentiment was focused in the National Child Labor Committee, established in New York in 1904. Its prime concern was the abolition of child labor. In order to accomplish this, it studied conditions of work of children in various states, proposed legislation, and took an active part in obtaining legislation, both state and federal. The committee was largely responsible for establishment of the federal Children's Bureau, set up by Congress in 1912, whose prime responsibility was to investigate and report on all matters pertaining to children, including their employment.

Source references: Tom Ireland, *Child Labor as a Relic of the Dark Ages* (New York: Putnam's Sons, 1937); Katherine D. Lumpkin and Dorothy W. Douglas, *Child Workers in America* (New York: McBride, 1937); Lois MacDonald, *Labor Problems and the American Scene* (New York: Harper, 1938).

National Commission for Employment Policy Established in 1974 as the National Commission for Manpower Policy by Title VI of the Comprehensive Employment and Training Act. The commission changed its name in 1978 and currently functions under Title IV of the Job Training Partnership Act. It is responsible for "examining broad issues of development, coordination, and administration of employment and training programs, and for advising the President and the Congress on national employment and training issues." The commission is composed of 15 members who are appointed by the President.

Source references: Job Training Partnership Act, 29 U.S.C. 1771–1775 (1982); U.S. National Commission for Employment Policy, *The First Five Years: 1974–1979*, a Report by Eli Ginzberg (Washington: Special Report 36, 1980).

National Commission on Social Security Reform Established by Executive Order 12335, on December 16, 1981, to "review relevant analyses of the current and long-term financial condition of the Social Security trust funds; identify problems that may threaten the long-term solvency of such funds; analyze potential solutions to such problems that will both assure the financial integrity of the Social Security System and the provision of appropriate benefits; and provide appropriate recommendations to the Secretary of Health and Human Services, the President, and the Congress." The President, the majority leader of the Senate, and the speaker of the House each selected five members of the commission.

The recommendations of the commission, which were submitted on January 20, 1983, were implemented by the Social Security Act Amendments of 1983. Among other provisions, the amendments increased the social security tax to provide an estimated $168 billion in additional financial resources to the social security program, reduced benefits, extended coverage to employees of nonprofit organizations and federal employees hired after 1983, and disallowed state and local governments from terminating participation in the social security program.

In accordance with the terms of the executive order, the commission was dissolved 30 days following submission of its report.

Source reference: U.S. National Commission on Social Security Reform, *Report of the National Commission on Social Security Reform* (Washington: 1983).

National Commission on Technology, Automation, and Economic Progress A 14-member public body, established by P.L. 88–444 in August 1964, to study the pace and the effects of technological change in the United States. The commission concerned itself with the question of technology as it applies to unmet human and community needs and made recommendations for public and private action to facilitate adjustment to technological changes. The commission was terminated in 1966 as provided by the statute establishing it.

Source references: U.S. National Commission on Technology, Automation, and Economic Progress, *Technology and the American Economy* (Washington: 1966); ———, *Technology and the American Economy, Appendix I–VI* (Washington: 1966).

National Commission on Working Women Organization created in 1977 to focus on needs of working women "who are concentrated in lower-paying, dead-end clerical, service, sales, plant and factory jobs." Its secretariat, the Center for Women and Work, implements the commission's programs and serves as a clearinghouse for information and research related to working women. The commission explores problems and needs of working women, designs programs to help solve problems, and develops policy recommendations to improve conditions of women in the work force. The four areas of primary concern include wages and benefits, support systems, child care, and education and training. The commission is supported by funds received from the National Institute of Education, private foundations, corporations, and unions.

Address: 2000 P St., N.W., #508, Washington, D.C. 20036. Tel. (202) 872–1782

Source reference: National Commission on Working Women, *Women at Work* (Washington: 1983).

National Committee on Pay Equity Established in 1979 by a group of individuals dedicated to achieving pay equity for women. The committee has over 175 organizational and individual members including international labor unions, women's and civil rights groups, and educational and legal associations.

The purposes of the committee are (1) to provide leadership, coordination, and strategy directions to members and pay equity advocates; (2) to provide assistance and information to public officials, labor unions, women's groups, and other organizations and individuals pursuing pay equity; (3) to stimulate new comparable worth activities; and (4) to bring national and local attention to this issue.

Address: 1201 16th St., N.W., Suite 422, Washington, D.C. 20036. Tel. (202) 822–7304

Source references: Comparable Worth Project, National Committee on Pay Equity, and National Women's Political Caucus, *Who's Working for Working Women?* (Washington: 1984); Joy Ann Grune and Nancy Reder, "Addendum—Pay Equity: An Innovative Public Policy Approach to Eliminating Sex-Based Wage Discrimination," *Public Per-*

sonnel Management, Spring 1984; Nancy D. Perlman, *Testimony of the National Committee on Pay Equity . . . Before the U.S. House of Representatives, Subcommittee on Civil Service . . .* (Washington: 1982).

national consultation rights A form of recognition established under Section 9 of Executive Order 11491 and substituted for formal and informal recognition which were eliminated under Executive Order 11491. A union accorded national consultation rights by an agency as the representative of a substantial number of employees may confer with the agency concerning personnel policy matters. They are not accorded where another union holds exclusive recognition.

Criteria for national consultation rights are currently set by the Federal Labor Relations Authority under Title VII of the Civil Service Reform Act of 1978.

Source references: Civil Service Reform Act of 1978, 5 U.S.C. 7113 (1982); Harold S. Roberts, *Labor-Management Relations in the Public Service* (Honolulu: Univ. of Hawaii Press, 1970).

National Consumers League An organization which was largely responsible for obtaining the first minimum wage law in the United States, in the state of Massachusetts in 1912. The National Consumers League attempted to get public support against the practice of "sweating" and to obtain support through legislation to get manufacturers to observe factory laws and to prevent the exploitation of women and children ("sweat labor").

Address: 600 Maryland Ave., S.W., Washington, D.C. 20024. Tel. (202) 554–1600

See also SWEATSHOP.

National Defense Mediation Board By executive order President Roosevelt on March 19, 1941, created a National Defense Mediation Board whose prime concern was the resolution of disputes in defense industries. The board had no authority to enforce its decisions but relied entirely on public opinion. The President noted in his executive order that he had declared a state of emergency on September 8, 1939, and it was therefore essential that labor and management in defense industries exert every effort to avoid interruption of production.

The board had no original jurisdiction to take cases. It could hear only those cases certified to it by the secretary of labor following failure by the U.S. Conciliation Service to resolve the dispute. Under the terms of the executive order it was authorized (1) to make every reasonable effort to adjust any controversy or dispute by assisting the parties thereto to negotiate agreements, (2) to afford means for voluntary arbitration with an agreement by the parties to abide by the decision arrived at by such arbitration, (3) to assist in establishing, when desired by the parties, procedures for resolving future controversies, (4) to investigate issues between employers and employees, conduct hearings, take testimony, make findings of fact, and formulate recommendations for the settlement of any dispute, and (5) to request the NLRB to settle any controversy or dispute relating to the appropriate unit or appropriate representative to be designated for purposes of collective bargaining.

The board was successful in resolving a number of major disputes in defense industries, but was dissolved after the CIO representatives withdrew from the board because of its failure to settle the United Mine Workers dispute in November 1941. The board consisted of 11 members—three representing the public, four from labor, and four from industry.

Source references: "Establishment of the National Defense Mediation Board," *MLR*, May 1941; Louis L. Jaffe and William G. Rice, Jr., *Report of the Work of the National Defense Mediation Board, March 19, 1941–January 12, 1942* (Washington: U.S. Dept. of Labor, BLS, Bull no. 714, 1942); Howard S. Kaltenborn, *Government Adjustment of Labor Disputes* (Chicago: Foundation Press, 1943).

National Education Association (Ind) Founded on August 26, 1857, in Philadelphia by 43 educators from a dozen states and the District of Columbia as the National Teachers Association. In 1870, it joined with the National Association of School Superintendents and the American Normal School Association to form the National Education Association (NEA).

By a special act of Congress on June 30, 1906, the NEA was incorporated as a nonprofit, charitable, tax-exempt association. It has subsequently been declared a labor organization and in 1979 the NEA was made subject to the provisions of the Labor-Management Reporting and Disclosure Act.

According to West, the NEA's loss in a representation election of New York City teachers in 1961 "speeded up the development of a workable policy of organizing and negotiating with school boards."

The NEA is one of the largest independent labor organizations with some 1.6 million members. Its publications include *Today's Education* (quarterly), *NEA Today* (issued eight times a year), and *NEA Advocate*.

Address: 1201 16th St., N.W., Washington, D.C. 20036. Tel. (202) 822–7000

Source references: Edgar B. Wesley, *NEA: The First Hundred Years* (New York: Harper, 1957); Allan M. West, *The National Education Association: The Power Base for Education* (New York: Free Press, 1980).

See also OVERSEAS EDUCATION ASSOCIATION, INC. (IND).

national emergency boards A board established under Section 10 of the Railway Labor Act after the procedures of the Act have been followed without agreement between the carrier and the employees. The Act provides in part:

> If a dispute between a carrier and its employees be not adjusted under the foregoing provisions of this Act and should, in the judgment of the Board of Mediation, threaten substantially to interrupt interstate commerce to a degree such as to deprive any section of the country of essential transportation service, the Board of Mediation shall notify the President, who may thereupon, in his discretion, create a board to investigate and report respecting such dispute. . . . Such board shall be created separately in each instance and it shall investigate promptly the facts as to the dispute and make a report thereon to the President within thirty days from the date of its creation. . . .
>
> After the creation of such board and for 30 days after such Board has made its report to the President, no change, except by agreement, shall be made by the parties to the controversy in the conditions out of which the dispute arose.

The national emergency provisions of the Taft-Hartley Act provide for the appointment of boards of inquiry which perform functions similar to those of an emergency board.

Some states have used emergency boards in the handling of disputes in the public utility field. The right of states to legislate in this field has been subject of much litigation. The Supreme Court in the so-called preemption cases has confined the jurisdiction of the states in the field of labor-management relations to a very narrow area.

Source references: Jacob J. Kaufman, "Emergency Boards Under the Railway Labor Act," *LLJ*, Dec. 1958; Harold S. Roberts, *The Doctrine of Preemption* (Honolulu: Univ. of Hawaii, IRC, 1957); Arthur A. Sloane, "Presidential Boards of Inquiry in National Emergency Disputes—An Assessment After 20 Years of Performance," *LLJ*, Nov. 1967; U.S. Congress, Senate, Special Committee on National Emergencies and Delegated Emergency Powers, *A Brief History of Emergency Powers in the United States, A Working Paper* (Washington: 1974).

See also BOARD OF INQUIRY; PREEMPTION, DOCTRINE OF.

national emergency disputes National emergency disputes are major disputes that are not settled through collective bargaining. Special emergency provisions of the Railway Labor Act, or the emergency provisions of Title II, Section 206, of the Taft-Hartley Act, may be invoked in such cases.

A distinction should be made between disputes and strikes. Disputes are difficulties or problems subject to negotiation and mediation and other forms of voluntary settlement. A strike takes place when all of these efforts have failed and the parties resort to direct action.

As used in the Taft-Hartley Act, national emergency designates an actual or threatened strike or lockout which may imperil the national health or safety.

Source references: Benjamin Aaron, "Emergency Disputes: Recent British and American Experiences," *Proceedings of the 25th A/M, IRRA*, ed. by Gerald Somers (Madison: 1973); ———, "How Other Nations Deal With Emergency Disputes," *MLR*, May 1972; ———, "National Emergency Disputes: Some Current Proposals," *Proceedings of the 1971 Annual Spring Meet-*

ing, IRRA, ed. by Gerald Somers (Madison: 1971); Howard R. Bloch, "Emergency Disputes," *Personnel Administration*, Jan./Feb. 1971; Robert C. Crawford, "Government Intervention in Emergency Labor Disputes in Atomic Energy," *LLJ*, June 1959; Howard G. Foster, "Final Offer Selection in National Emergency Disputes," *AJ*, June 1972; David C. Hershfield, "An End to Emergency Labor Disputes?" *Conference Board Record*, Dec. 1972; Industrial Relations Counselors, Inc., *Emergency Disputes—A National Labor Policy Problem* (New York: IR Memo no. 138, 1961); James E. Jones, Jr., *Toward a Definition of "National Emergency Dispute"* (Madison: Univ. of Wisconsin, IRRI, Reprint no. 153, 1971); Thomas Kennedy, "The Handling of Emergency Disputes," *Proceedings of the 2d A/M, IRRA*, ed. by Milton Derber (Champaign: 1950); Charles C. Killingsworth, "Emergency Disputes and Public Policy," *MLR*, Aug. 1971; Labor Study Group, *The Public Interest in National Labor Policy* (New York: CED, 1961); Richard A. Levin, "National Emergency Disputes Under Taft-Hartley: A Legal Definition," *LLJ*, Jan. 1971; A. Pankert, "Settlement of Labour Disputes in Essential Services," *ILR*, Nov./Dec. 1980; I. Herbert Rothenberg, "National Emergency Disputes," *LLJ*, Feb. 1961; Stuart Rothman, "National Emergency Disputes Under the LMRA and RLA," *LLJ*, April 1964; Benjamin J. Taylor, "Emergency Disputes Involving Privately Owned Local Level Services," *LLJ*, Aug. 1971; U.S. Congress, Senate, Committee on Labor and Public Welfare, *National Emergency Disputes, 1971–72, Hearings, Parts 1–4* (Washington: 1972); Thomas A. Woodley, "Emergency Labor Disputes and the Public Interest: The Proposals for Legislative Reform," *IR Law Digest*, Oct. 1973.

See also CONCILIATION, LABOR DISPUTE, MEDIATION, STRIKE.

national emergency provisions Refers to the language in the Railway Labor Act and the Taft-Hartley Act which established the procedures to be followed when an emergency is deemed to exist under either of the statutes.

Source reference: Irving Bernstein, Harold Enarson, and R. W. Fleming (ed.), *Emergency Disputes and National Policy* (New York: Harper, IRRA Pub. no. 15, 1955).

national emergency strikes What constitutes a national emergency strike depends on the determination of a court in its application of Sections 206–210 of the Taft-Hartley Act. Section 206 provides, "Whenever in the opinion of the President of the United States, a threatened or actual strike or lockout affecting an entire industry or a substantial part thereof engaged in trade, commerce, transportation, transmission, or communication among the several states or with foreign nations, or engaged in the production of goods for commerce, will, if permitted to occur or to continue, imperil the national health or safety, he may appoint a board of inquiry to inquire into the issues involved in the dispute and to make a written report to him within such time as he shall prescribe." An injunction to restrain a strike or lockout requires action by the attorney general in any district court of the United States which has jurisdiction of the parties.

The court has to establish on the basis of the evidence before it that a threatened or actual strike or lockout would affect an entire industry or a substantial part and if permitted to occur or to continue "will imperil the national health or safety."

The procedure essentially is a cooling-off process with a requirement that the attorney general petition the court for the dissolution of the injuction at the end of 80 days.

Probably the most thorough review of any district court on the question of what constitutes a national emergency was in a 1959 steel case (*Steelworkers v. United States*, 361 US 39, 45 LRRM 2209 (1959)). The Supreme Court on November 7, 1959, affirmed the decision of the circuit court but narrowed the scope of its findings and concluded essentially that it was not examining the over-all terms "national health" and "safety" but specifically was limiting its findings to the fact that the strike "imperiled the national safety." The Court said in part, "Here we rely upon the evidence of the strike's effect on specific defense projects; we need not pass on the government's contention that 'national safety' in this context should be given a broader construction and application."

Source references: Donald E. Cullen, *National Emergency Strikes* (Ithaca: Cornell Univ., NYSSILR, ILR Paperback no. 7, 1968); Robben W. Fleming, "Emergency Strikes and National Policy," *LLJ*, April 1960; Jeffrey L. Gottlieb, "The Application of Title II of the Taft-Hartley Act to the Coal Strike of 1978," *Industrial and Labor Relations Forum*, June 1980; Michael H. Moskow, "National Emergency Strikes: The Final Offer, Selection, Procedure and Other Options," *NYU 24th Annual Conference on Labor* (New York: Bender, 1972); George W. Taylor, "The Adequacy of Taft-Hartley in Public Emergency Disputes," *Annals*, Jan. 1961; U.S. Congress, Senate, Committee on Labor and Public Welfare," *Federal Legislation to End Strikes: A Documentary History, Parts 1 and 2* (Washington: 1967); Edgar L. Warren, "Thirty-Six Years of National Emergency Strikes," *ILRR*, Oct. 1951.

National Employment Service Act *See* U.S. EMPLOYMENT SERVICE; WAGNER-PEYSER ACT.

National Erectors' Association An organization formed in 1903 which has been considered one of the belligerent employers associations because of its campaigns in opposition to organized labor. It was one of the major organizations advocating the open shop. It was supported by the American Bridge Company, a subsidiary of the U.S. Steel Corporation.

National Federation of Independent Unions A independent labor federation formed in March 1963 with the merger of the Confederated Unions of America and the National Independent Union Council. Its affiliates include the Congress of Independent Unions, National Industrial Workers Union, National Brotherhood of Packinghouse and Industrial Workers, and the International Association of Tool Craftsmen. The Federation issues the quarterly *News for Independent Unions.*

Address: 1111 19th St., N.W., Washington, D.C. 20036. Tel. (202) 659–1490

National Foremen's Institute, Inc. A private labor information service located in Deep River, Connecticut.

National Founders' Association An employer organization established in the machine foundry industry whose major function was to eliminate strikes or, where they occurred, to assist the employers in dealing with them.

The Association had a number of programs designed to assist its members during a strike, either by providing up to 70 percent of the average number of workers employed or having the work of the employer done elsewhere up to 70 perent or by providing some form of compensation up to a certain number of dollars per day.

national income An index developed and published by the U.S. Department of Commerce to assist in business forecasting and budgeting. The index represents the value of goods and services produced in both public and private sectors of the economy. It has been defined for statistical purposes as "the incomes that originate in the production of goods and services attributable to the labor and property supplied by residents of the United States. Incomes are recorded in the forms in which they accrue to residents, and are measured before deduction of taxes on those incomes. They consist of compensation of employees, proprietors' income, net interest, corporate profits, and the rental income of persons."

Source references: Arnold Collery, *National Income and Employment Analysis* (New York: Wiley, 1966); Jacques Lecaillon and Dimitrios Germidis, "Economic Development and the Wage Share in National Income," *ILR*, May 1975; Sam Rosen, *National Income, Its Measurement, Determination and Relation to Public Policy* (New York: Holt, Rinehart & Winston, 1963); Anthony P. Thirlwall, *Changes in Industrial Composition in the UK and US and Labour's Share of National Income, 1948–1969* (Princeton: Princeton Univ., IR Section, Reprint, 1973); U.S. Dept. of Commerce, *1979 Business Statistics, 22nd Biennial Edition* (Washington: 1980).

National Industrial Conference Board *See* CONFERENCE BOARD, THE.

National Industrial Recovery Act A major piece of legislation under the Roosevelt administration, designed to establish self-government of industry through codes of fair competition. These codes were to eliminate in part competitive practices and to protect employers under the Sherman Act. They also established procedures for minimum wages and maximum hours of work. Industries which had established codes of fair practice and companies which adopted those codes were permitted to display a "Blue Eagle" insigne to indicate that they were in conformity with those codes.

Section 7(a) of the Act was incorporated into the codes. This protected the right of employees to organize, and although there was some disagreement on whether it permitted company unions, Section 7(a) served as a springboard for organizational efforts during the early periods of the Roosevelt administration.

The National Industrial Recovery Act was declared unconstitutional in 1935 by the Supreme Court in the *Schechter* case.

Source reference: National Industrial Recovery Act, Pub. L. 67 (ch. 90), June 16, 1933, 48 Stat. 195, repealed E.O. 7252, Dec. 21, 1935, and E.O. 7323, Mar. 26, 1936 (see 15 U.S.C. 701 note).

See also SCHECHTER POULTRY CORPORATION V. UNITED STATES.

National Industrial Recovery Act, Section 7(a) Section 7(a) was an afterthought to the National Industrial Recovery Act but had a tremendous impact on the organizational efforts of workers. It gave trade unions the basis for organizing and declared the right of employees to form unions of their own choosing. It also provided the basis for the various industry boards under the respective codes to enforce the provision of Section 7(a) and, later, Public Resolution No. 44.

The section provided as follows:

> Every code of fair competition, agreement, and license approved, prescribed, or issued under this title shall contain the following conditions: (1) that employees shall have the right to organize and bargain collectively through representatives of their own choosing, and shall be free from the interference, restraint, or coercion of employers of labor, or their agents, in the designation of such representatives or in self organization or in other concerted activities for the purpose of collective bargaining or other mutual aid or protection; (2) that no employee and no one seeking employment shall be required as a condition of employment to join any company union or to refrain from joining, organizing, or assisting a labor organization of his own choosing; and (3) that employers shall comply with the maximum hours of labor, minimum rates of pay, and other conditions of employment, approved or prescribed by the President.

Source reference: Paul F. Brissenden, "Genesis and Import of the Collective-Bargaining Provisions of the Recovery Act," *Economic Essays in Honor of Wesley Clair Mitchell* (New York: Columbia UP, 1935).

National Institute for Occupational Safety and Health *See* OCCUPATIONAL SAFETY AND HEALTH ACT (OSHA) OF 1970.

National Institute of Labor Education (NILE) A private organization concerned with labor education, including off-campus programs with an emphasis on a liberal education. It was privately financed through grants from foundations, labor organizations, and other groups.

National Labor and Reform Party The National Labor and Reform Party was established in 1872 with the following goals: (1) exclusive use of greenbacks for currency; (2) abolition of the contract systems of convict labor; (3) exclusion of Chinese immigrants; (4) eight-hour work day.

Richard F. Trevellick, who became president of the National Labor Union in 1870, was interested in political reform activities rather than trade unionism and in 1870 appointed a committee to form a labor party. At the convention of the National Labor Union on February 21, 1872, nominations for the President of the United States were made. Judge David Davis of Illinois was nominated, and the platform of the National Labor Union was adopted as the platform of the National Labor and Reform Party. Judge Davis later withdrew his name, and the political movement and the National Labor Union collapsed.

Source references: John R. Commons and Associates, *History of Labour in the United States, Volume II* (New York: Macmillan, 1946); Florence Peterson, *American Labor Unions* (2d rev. ed., New York: Harper, 1963).

National Labor Board An agency established by Presidential order in August 1933 to interpret and apply Section 7(a) of the

National Industrial Recovery Act. Its first chairman was Senator Robert Wagner of New York. The board also included three labor and three employer members. This number later was increased to six employer and six labor members.

The board performed many functions, including mediation. It established rules and principles with regard to the meaning of collective bargaining and majority rule. These decisions formed the basis for decisions and policy developed later by the National Labor Relations Board.

Source references: Lewis L. Lorwin and Arthur Wubnig. *Labor Relations Boards, The Regulation of Collective Bargaining Under the National Industrial Recovery Act* (Washington: Brookings Institution, 1935); Joseph Rosenfarb, *The National Labor Policy and How it Works* (New York: Harper, 1940).

See also PUBLIC RESOLUTION NO. 44.

National Labor-Management Panel A panel of 12 members appointed by the President, six from management and six from labor, with three year terms, whose function is to advise the director of the FMCS on the voluntary adjustment of controversies affecting the general welfare of the country. Its general authority is defined in Section 205(a) and 205(b) of the Taft-Hartley Act.

National Labor Relations Act This statute, also known as the Wagner-Connery Act, but generally as the Wagner Act, was passed on July 5, 1935, approximately two months after the Supreme Court declared unconstitutional the National Industrial Recovery Act and Section 7(a), which protected the rights of employees to organize without employer interference.

The Act established not only the right of employees to self-organization but also the machinery for holding elections to determine the union preference of the majority of employees and provided exclusive bargaining rights for that union.

The statute also set out five unfair labor practices of employers, *viz*, those considered harmful to employees in the preservation of their right to organize. The National Labor Relations Board was established to assure that employers would not engage in those practices. The most important of these unfair labor practices were dealt with in Section 8(3), which prevented discrimination because of union membership, and Section 8(5), which required collective bargaining by employers. Section 8(2) prevented establishment and support of company-dominated unions.

The law was designed to reduce industrial strife and unrest by encouraging collective bargaining. The findings and policies stated that Congress felt there was an "inequality of bargaining power between employees who do not possess full freedom of association . . . and employers who are organized in the corporate or other forms of ownership association . . ." This situation, according to Congress, "substantially burdens and affects the flow of commerce, and tends to aggravate business depressions, by depressing wage rates and the purchasing power of wage earners in industry and by preventing the stabilization of competitive wage rates and working conditions within and between industries."

The statement of findings and policies of the Act in Section 1 concludes as follows: "It is hereby declared to be the policy of the United States to eliminate the causes of certain substantial obstructions to the free flow of commerce and to mitigate and eliminate these obstructions when they have occurred by encouraging the practice and procedure of collective bargaining and by protecting the exercise by workers of full freedom of association, self-organization, and designation of representatives of their own choosing, for the purpose of negotiating the terms and conditions of their employment or other mutual aid or protection."

Major amendments to the National Labor Relations Act were made in 1947 and they became collectively known as the Taft-Hartley Act. In addition to defining union unfair labor practices, the amendments added a substantial number of other provisions to the statute to equalize collective bargaining power between employers and unions.

Source references: National Labor Relations Act, as amended, 29 U.S.C. 141–144, 151–187 (1982); Labor Management Relations Act of 1947, as amended, 29 U.S.C. 141–144, 151–187 (1982); Cletus E. Daniel, *The ACLU and the Wagner Act; An Inquiry Into the Depression-Era Crisis of American Liber-*

alism (Ithaca: NYSSILR, Cornell Univ., 1980); Nathan P. Feinsinger, "The National Labor Relations Act and Collective Bargaining," *Michigan LR*, April 1959; Charles O. Gregory, *Labor and the Law* (2d rev. ed., New York: Norton, 1961); Richard U. Miller, "The Enigma of Section 8(5) of the Wagner Act," *ILRR*, Jan. 1965; Harry A. Millis and Emily C. Brown, *From the Wagner Act to Taft-Hartley* (Chicago: Univ. of Chicago Press, 1950); Charles J. Morris (ed.), *The Developing Labor Law: The Board, the Courts, and the National Labor Relations Act* (2d ed., Washington: BNA, 1983); Arnold Ordman, "The National Labor Relations Act: Current Developments," *NYU 24th Annual Conference on Labor* (New York: Bender, 1972); Dennis Dale Pointer and Norman Metzger, *The National Labor Relations Act; A Guidebook for Health Care Facility Administrators* (New York: Spectrum Pub., 1975); Louis Silverberg (ed.), *The Wagner Act—After 10 Years* (Washington: BNA, 1945); U.S. Congress, House, Committee on Education and Labor, *Extension of NLRA to Nonprofit Hospital Employees, Hearings* (Washington: 1972); U.S. NLRB, *Legislative History of the Labor-Management Relations Act 1947* (2 vol., Washington: 1948).

See also BARGAINING UNIT, CERTIFICATION, COMPANY UNION, LABOR MANAGEMENT RELATIONS ACT OF 1947, NLRB V. JONES AND LAUGHLIN STEEL COMPANY, UNFAIR LABOR PRACTICES.

National Labor Relations Board The tribunal provided for under the National Labor Relations Act whose members are appointed by the President with the consent of the Senate. The Board has the responsibility for determining the appropriate bargaining units, for certifying unions which represent the majority of employees, for establishing policy with regard to unfair labor practices, and for general administration of the Act. The Board acts as a quasi-judicial agency and its decisions are binding on the parties subject to review by the courts. The original Board consisted of three members, but the Act has since been amended to provide for a five-member Board. The Board maintains 33 regional offices and a number of subregional and resident offices.

Address: 1717 Pennsylvania Ave., N.W., Washington, D.C. 20570. Tel. (202) 655–4000

Source references: Robert R. R. Brooks, *Unions of Their Own Choosing: An Account of the NLRB* (New Haven: Yale UP, 1939); Owen Fairweather and Andrew R. Laidlaw, "The NLRB *Must* Change! A Proposal for Reform," *Employee Relations LJ*, Autumn 1975; John H. Fanning, "Labor Relations in a Period of Inflation and Recession: Policies of the NLRB," *LLJ*, Aug. 1975; Felicia A. Finston, "The Board's Role in the Arbitral Process," *LLJ*, Dec. 1981; William Gomberg and Bernard Samoff, "Improving Administrative Effectiveness of the NLRB," *LLJ*, April 1973; James A. Gross, *The Making of the National Labor Relations Board; A Study in Economics, Politics, and the Law, Volume I (1933–1937)* (Albany: State Univ. of New York Press, 1974); ———, *The Reshaping of the National Labor Relations Board; National Policy in Transition, 1937–1947* (Albany: State Univ. of New York Press, 1981); John S. Irving, Jr., "The Crisis at the NLRB: A Call for Reordering Priorities," *Employee Relations LJ*, Summer 1981; ———, "NLRB: Master of Its Own Destiny (Fate?)" *Labor Law Developments 1982*, Proceedings of the 28th Annual Institute on Labor Law, SLF (New York: Bender, 1982); Frank W. McCulloch and Tim Bornstein, *The National Labor Relations Board* (New York: Praeger, 1974); Edward B. Miller, *An Administrative Appraisal of the NLRB* (3d ed., Philadelphia: Univ. of Pennsylvania, Wharton School, Industrial Research Unit, LRPP Series no. 16, 1980); Betty Southard Murphy, "NLRB, the EEOC, and Baby Makes Three: Today's Concerns—or Solutions for Tomorrow," *NYU 32d Annual National Conference on Labor*, ed. by Richard Adelman (New York: Bender, 1980); ———, "The NLRB in Its Fortieth Year," *LLJ*, Sept. 1975; Peter G. Nash, "Labor Law Practice in the NLRB General Counsel's Office," *Labor Law Developments 1976*, Proceedings of 22d Annual Institute on Labor Law, SLF (New York: Bender, 1976); Robert J. Rabin, "New Directions in NLRB Policies—The View of a Neutral," *NYU 34th Annual National Conference on Labor*, ed. by Richard Adelman (New York: Bender, 1982); Mozart G. Ratner, "The Quasi-Judicial NLRB Revisited," *LLJ*, Aug.

1961; John C. Truesdale, "Impact of the NLRB on Labor-Management Relations: The Tie that Binds," *Labor Law Developments 1980*, Proceedings of 26th Annual Institute on Labor Law, SLF (New York: Bender, 1980); Peter D. Walther, "The Board's Place at the Bargaining Table," *LLJ*, March 1977; Robert E. Williams, Peter A. Janus, and Kenneth C. Huhn, *NLRB Regulation of Election Conduct* (Philadelphia: Univ. of Pennsylvania, Wharton School, Industrial Research Unit, LRPP Series Report no. 8, 1974); Don A. Zimmerman and David Dunn, "Relations Between the NLRB and the Courts of Appeals: A Tale of Acrimony and Accommodation," *Employee Relations LJ*, Summer 1982.

See also PUBLIC RESOLUTION NO. 44.

National Labor Relations Board Professional Association (Ind) Founded in 1962.

Address: 1717 Pennsylvania Ave., N.W., Washington, D.C. 20006. Tel. (202) 254–9238

National Labor Relations Board Union (Ind) Founded in 1963, it publishes the bimonthly *Remedy*.

Address: c/o NLRB Region 19, 2948 Federal Bldg., 915 Second Ave., Seattle, Wash. 98174. Tel. (206) 442–4532

National Labor Union An organization formed in 1866. Its subsidiary groups consisted of local unions, trade assemblies, eight-hour leagues, national unions, farmers societies, and other political groups. The National Labor Union (NLU) was formed to centralize the support of these various organizations and their individual programs.

The NLU, however, failed to bring together these various groups. By 1870, most of the national unions had left the NLU because of internal dissension and because of NLU's emphasis on a political program. Lacking strong leadership and failing to establish a Presidential ticket, the NLU collapsed in 1872.

Source reference: James C. Sylvis, *The Life, Speeches, Labors and Essays of William H. Sylvis* (New York: Augustus M. Kelley, Reprints of Economic Classics, 1968).

See also NATIONAL LABOR AND REFORM PARTY.

National League of Cities v. Usery A 1976 Supreme Court decision which invalidated the Fair Labor Standards Act amendments of 1974 extending minimum wage and overtime pay requirements to state and local governments. The Court found that the amendments "operated to directly displace the States' freedom to structure integral operations in areas of traditional governmental functions." The decision thus overturned *Maryland v. Wirtz* which extended the 1966 Fair Labor Standards Act amendments to employees of state hospitals, institutions, and schools.

Source references: National League of Cities v. Usery, 426 US 833, 22 WH Cases 1064 (1976); *Maryland v. Wirtz*, 393 US 183, 18 WH Cases 445 (1968); Richard Kiss, "The Effect of *National League of Cities* on the Political Subdivision Exemption of the NLRA," *LLJ*, Dec. 1981; William S. Rhyne, "Federal Powers of Regulation," *LLJ*, Sept. 1979; Laurence H. Tribe, "Unraveling National League of Cities: The New Federalism and Affirmative Rights to Essential Government Services," *IR Law Digest*, Fall 1977.

National Mediation Board An independent agency of the executive branch of the federal government, established in June 1934, to implement the Railway Labor Act amendments which abolished the Board of Mediation, assigned those functions to the National Mediation Board, and established the responsibilities of the National Mediation Board.

The three members of the board are appointed by the President, subject to Senate confirmation.

The functions of the board are set out in Section 5 (for railways) and in Section 203 (for air carriers) of the Railway Labor Act. The board is empowered to handle disputes concerning changes in rates of pay, rules, or working conditions not adjusted by the parties in conference; any other dispute not referable to the National Railroad Adjustment Board and not adjusted in conference between the parties; cases in which a controversy arises over the meaning or application of any agreement reached through mediation under the provisions of this Act; and, where the parties are unable to agree, the Act provides for the board to name the arbitrator or arbitrators. The board also determines rights of representation under Section 2(g) of the statute. For air carrier disputes, the National Mediation Board may establish a four-member board known as the National Air Transport Adjustment Board to resolve disputes.

The board has the responsibility, where an unresolved dispute may result in a substantial interruption of interstate commerce, to notify the President "who may thereupon, in his discretion, create a board to investigate and report respecting such dispute." These are the emergency boards under Section 10 which hold hearings and make findings that have come to be recommendations to the parties for disposition of the dispute.

Address: 1425 K St., N.W., Washington, D.C. 20572. Tel. (202) 523–5920

Source references: Act of May 20, 1926, Ch. 347, 69th Cong., 1st Sess., 44 Stat. 577, as amended; 45 U.S.C., 151–163, 181–188; Howard S. Kaltenborn, "The Adjustment of Labor Disputes in the Railroad Industry," *Governmental Adjustment of Labor Disputes* (Chicago: Foundation Press, 1943); U.S. NMB, *Fifteen Years Under the Railway Labor Act* (Washington: 1950); ———, *Forty-Seventh Annual Report . . . for the Fiscal Year Ended September 30, 1981* (Washington: 1982); ———, *The Railway Labor Act at Fifty; Collective Bargaining in the Railroad and Airlines Industries*, ed. by Charles M. Rehmus (Washington: 1977).

See also NATIONAL AIR TRANSPORT ADJUSTMENT BOARD, NATIONAL RAILROAD ADJUSTMENT BOARD, RAILWAY LABOR ACT.

National Organization for Women (NOW) Established on June 30, 1966, by 28 women attending the Third National Conference of Commissions on the Status of Women in Washington, D.C., as a separate civil rights organization dedicated to achieving full equality for women. Betty Friedan, a guest at the conference, invited a group of women to her hotel room to discuss strategies to combat discrimination against women. The decision was to form a separate organization, which Friedan christened NOW.

NOW's statement of purpose provides: "To take action to bring women into full participation in the mainstream of American society *now*, assuming all the privileges and responsibilities thereof in full equal partnership with men."

Over 300 women and men attended the first organizing conference on October 29–30, 1966, in Washington, D.C. Kathryn Clarenbach, head of the Wisconsin Commission on the Status of Women, was elected chair of the NOW board; Betty Friedan, president; Richard Graham, a former EEOC commissioner, vice president; and Caroline Davis of the United Auto Workers, secretary-treasurer. NOW was incorporated on February 10, 1967.

The organization has established task forces to deal with problems of women in employment, education, religion, poverty, law, and politics.

NOW currently has 260,000 members with 9 regional, 50 state, and 800 local chapters. It publishes the monthly *National NOW Times*.

Address: 425 13th St., N.W., Suite 1048, Washington, D.C. 20004. Tel. (202) 347–2279

Source reference: NOW Origins (Washington: n.d.).

national origin discrimination The EEOC defines it broadly as "including, but not limited to, the denial of equal employment opportunity because of an individual's, or his or her ancestor's, place of origin; or because an individual has the physical, cultural or linguistic characteristics of a national origin group." It may also include denial of employment opportunity because "of (a) marriage to or association with persons of a national origin group; (b) membership in, or association with an organization identified with or seeking to promote the interests of national origin groups; (c) attendance or participation in schools, churches, temples, or mosques, generally used by persons of a national origin group; and (d) because an individual's name or spouse's name is associated with a national origin group."

Employment discrimination on the basis of national origin is prohibited by Title VII of the Civil Rights Act of 1964 and Executive Order 11246. Harassment on the basis of national origin is also a violation of Title VII.

The Supreme Court in *Espinoza v. Farah Mfg. Co.* stated that an employer's refusal to hire a Spanish-surnamed applicant on the basis of noncitizenship did not violate Title VII of the Civil Rights Act of 1964.

Source references: Espinoza v. Farah Mfg. Co., 414 US 86, 6 FEP Cases 933 (1973); U.S. EEOC, "Guidelines on Discrimination Because of National Origin," 29 C.F.R. 1606; ———, "Uniform Guidelines on Employee Selection Procedures," 29 C.F.R. 1607; Daniel J. Hoffheimer, "Employment Discrimination Against Resident Aliens by Private Employers," *LLJ*, March 1984; Charles J. Hollon and Thomas L. Bright, "National Origin Harassment in the Work Place: Recent Guideline Developments from the EEOC," *Employee Relations LJ*, Autumn 1982; Oscar A. Ornati, "Arbitrators and National Origin Discrimination," *AJ*, June 1981.

National Railroad Adjustment Board Established in 1934, this agency, under the Railway Labor Act, has the responsibility to decide grievances arising out of interpretation or application of agreements entered into between employers and unions in so-called minor disputes. The carriers or employers and the unions each designate 17 representatives. These bipartite groups are divided into four separate divisions, each having jurisdiction over a distinct class of employees, known as Divisions 1, 2, 3, and 4 of NRAB.

Any grievance which remains unsettled by bargaining or mediation automatically is submitted to NRAB. Where NRAB is unable to reach agreement on the dispute, it will appoint a referee to make a final and binding decision. Where the group is unable to agree on a referee, the National Mediation Board makes the appointment and the referee then makes an award. This in effect is a form of compulsory arbitration of grievances under the terms of the contract applicable to railroad employees within the jurisdiction of the Railway Labor Act.

Source references: Elgin, Joliet & Eastern Ry. Co. v. Burley, 325 US 711, 16 LRRM 749 (1945), *aff'd on rehearing*, 327 US 661, 17 LRRM 899 (1946); *Bro. of Railroad Trainmen et al. v. Toledo, Peoria and Western Railroad*, 321 US 50, 13 LRRM 725 (1944); *Steele v. Louisville and Nashville Railroad Co.*, 323 US 192, 15 LRRM 708 (1944); Lloyd K. Garrison, "The National Railroad Adjustment Board: A Unique Administrative Agency," *Yale LJ*, Feb. 1937; Joseph Lazar, *Due Process in Disciplinary Hearings, Decisions of the National Railroad Adjustment Board* (Los Angeles: UC, Institute of IR, Monograph Series 25, 1980); ———, "'Individual' and 'Outside Union' Grievances Before the National Railway Adjustment Board First Division," *LLJ*, April 1964; William H. Spencer, *The National Railroad Adjustment Board* (Chicago: Univ. of Chicago Press, 1938); J. N. Willemin, "Actions to Secure Compliance with Awards of the National Railroad Adjustment Board," *St. Louis Univ. LJ*, Fall 1958.

See also NATIONAL MEDIATION BOARD.

National Recovery Administration The administrative agency established under the National Industrial Recovery Act.

See also NATIONAL INDUSTRIAL RECOVERY ACT.

National Research Project The National Research Project was organized in December 1935, as part of the Works Progress Administration's National Research Program to study various aspects of technological change and industrial techniques and their effects on employment and unemployment. With the cooperation of industry, labor, and governmental and private agencies, the National Research Project studies covered such topics as types and rates of technological change, production, productivity and employment, and effects of industrial change on labor markets. The project's full title was The National Research Project on Reemployment Opportunities and Recent Changes in Industrial Techniques.

National Right to Work Committee A nonprofit corporation without capital stock organized under the laws of the commonwealth of Virginia. Its stated purpose is to "help make the public aware of the fact that American citizens are being required, against their will, to join and pay dues to labor organizations in order to earn a living. . . ." The committee thus was active in promoting state "right-to-work" laws under the sanction of Section 14(b) of the Taft-Hartley Act and vigorously opposed the drive to repeal this section of the statute in the 89th Congress (1965). Its ultimate goal is the enactment of a national right-to-work law. It issues the monthly *National Right to Work Newsletter*.

Address: 8001 Braddock Rd., Springfield, Virginia 22160. Tel. (703) 321–9820

Source reference: Federal Election Commission v. National Right to Work Committee, U.S. Sup. Ct. No. 81–1506 (1982).

National Safety Council A private cooperative association of employers established prior to World War I to promote safety procedures and the dissemination of safety information, not only in the plant, but also in the home.

The Council is a nonpartisan and nonprofit organization which has done much work throughout the country in the safety field. It not only issues a monthly safety news publication, but also prepares motion pictures and slides, sets up community surveys, and provides special lessons and materials to show the techniques in which safety can be encouraged throughout American industrial and home life. It sponsors an annual safety congress and has established numerous industrial sections within its own organization to carry out major accident prevention programs.

Address: 425 North Michigan Ave., Chicago, Ill. 60611. Tel. (312) 527–4800

National Steel Labor Relations Board A board established by Executive Order 6751 on June 28, 1934, to avert a strike by the Amalgamated Association of Iron, Steel and Tin Workers (AFL).

The board had authority to hear complaints of discrimination, to mediate and arbitrate disputes, and to conduct elections.

Source reference: E.O. 6751, June 28, 1934.

See also NATIONAL LABOR BOARD.

national union Generally, the organization which brings together many local unions within an industry or craft. These unions have varying degrees of authority over local unions, frequently in the right to declare a strike and the review of the terms of agreements. In many other ways they play an important role in bargaining and general policy and strategy of the organization. The local unions generally elect delegates to periodic conventions. The conventions in turn elect the officers of the union and the executive board which has authority to act between conventions. The authority of the national union and the executive board generally is spelled out in the union constitution and bylaws.

A distinction occasionally is made between a national and an international union. National unions presumably do not have local unions or members in a foreign country. Actually not much distinction is made between a national and an international union. The term "international union" does not signify international interest or scope of organizational potential or activity. Most of the so-called international unions are "international" through the fact that they have locals in Canada or occasionally in such jurisdictions as Puerto Rico.

Source reference: Lloyd Ulman, *The Rise of the National Trade Union* (Cambridge: Harvard UP, 1955).

See also INTERNATIONAL UNION, NATIONAL AND INTERNATIONAL UNIONS, PARENT UNION.

National Urban League An organization started in 1918 which is interested primarily in finding solutions to problems of the black worker. The organization contains many prominent white citizens who have joined with black leaders in order to provide long-range and effective programs to meet the problems of black people. Its programs include those designed to secure vocational opportunities, to assist and advise young workers, and to eliminate various barriers that interfere with the freedom of blacks, including union constitutional provisions or practices which deny equal opportunity within trades and occupations controlled by the unions.

Its broad goal is to provide educational and publicity materials to point out practices that interfere with the rights of blacks and measures to eliminate discrimination against them.

Address: 500 East 62nd St., New York, N.Y. 10021. Tel. (212) 310–9000

Source reference: Herman Feldman, *Racial Factors in American Industry* (New York: Harper, 1931).

See also CIVIL RIGHTS ACT OF 1964.

National Wage Stabilization Board During the period of the Korean War, 1950–1952, Congress provided for the control of wages and salaries through the Defense Production

Act. The National Wage Stabilization Board was established to provide administratively for the stabilization of wages and salaries to achieve the general objectives specified in the Act. The jurisdiction of the board excluded persons employed in bona fide executive, administrative, professional, or outside salesmen capacities.

The Wage Stabilization Board was tripartite in make-up. The members represented in equal numbers the public, labor, and employers, an arrangement considered essential to obtain maximum acceptance of its policies, regulations, and official actions by employers and labor. The board's general authority to stabilize wages and salaries was delegated to it by the Economic Stabilization Agency which, in turn, was created by executive order of the President pursuant to the Act.

The authority in the Act for stabilization of wages and salaries was based on certain broad purposes, among them: to prevent inflation, to promote industrial stability and to preserve collective bargaining to the fullest extent possible, to foster maximum defense production, and to correct and prevent hardships and inequities.

A general but temporary freeze of the movement of all wages and salaries was imposed by the Economic Stabilization administrator on January 26, 1951, effective as of January 25, 1951. The Wage Stabilization Board undertook to unfreeze wages and salaries through the issuance of certain policies and general wage regulations to insure the orderly movement of wages and salaries consistent with the general objectives Congress included in the Defense Production Act.

To accomplish this purpose, the board developed and issued more than a score of General Wage Regulations to provide a flexible program of stabilization, taking into consideration the variety of conditions under which changes in wage and salary rates are made in business and industry. Certain General Wage Regulations were self-administering to reduce the need for petitioning the board for approval. Other regulations required prior approval of the board before wage or salary changes could be put into effect. When prior approval was required, petitions were submitted to the board either by the employer or by the employer and union jointly.

Board statistics showed at one point that only about 14 percent of the petitions were denied or modified.

The board also undertook to handle labor disputes involving both economic and noneconomic issues if certified to the board by the President or voluntarily submitted by the parties. In mid-1952, Congress amended the Defense Production Act to strip the board of authority to handle dispute cases. The board finally dissolved as a tripartite agency and became the Wage Stabilization Committee, composed of all public members. With the fighting in Korea at an end, all stabilization orders and regulations issued under the Defense Production Act were suspended by Presidential order on February 6, 1953.

An earlier agency of the same name was established by executive order in 1944 to take over wage stabilization activities following dissolution of the National War Labor Board, which had functioned during World War II. This board was tripartite in character.

Source references: E.O. 9672, *Federal Register*, Jan. 4, 1946; U.S. Dept. of Labor, *The National Wage Stabilization Board, January 1, 1946–February 24, 1947; A Documentary History of the Board Together with Brief Explanations of Its Formation, Organization, and Activities* (Washington: 1948).

See also NATIONAL WAR LABOR BOARD.

National War Labor Board The title applies both to the agency established in 1918 during World War I and the one established in January 1942 during World War II. Both agencies concerned themselves with handling labor-management disputes and wage stabilization during the war periods.

The first National War Labor Board had an agreed-upon statement of principles which served as a guide in both wage policy and dispute settlement.

The National War Labor Board during World War II merely established machinery for the resolution of disputes following an agreement by representatives of labor and management convened by President Roosevelt that there would be no strike or lockout during the war and that all disputes which remained unresolved, and which affected the war effort, would be determined by the National War Labor Board.

The second National War Labor Board in a sense was a voluntary arbitration tribunal. For those who claimed that the agency did not represent them and that they did not voluntarily agree to it, as John L. Lewis stated during one dispute, the board constituted in effect a compulsory arbitration tribunal. The board not only handled disputes of a nonwage character but also had responsibility for carrying out the World War II wage stabilization program. Prices, however, were regulated through the Office of Price Administration.

It is estimated that the board during its three years of operation handled in excess of 20,000 labor disputes and many more applications involving wage adjustments.

Many of the policies established by the National War Labor Board served as a guide during the postwar period and many of the contracts which it wrote during the war period remained in effect during the postwar era. The union security issue, one of the most difficult nonwage issues, was resolved through a compromise proposal known as "maintenance of union membership." The board also played an important role in the establishment of fringe benefits, such as vacations, which it was assumed would have no immediate effect on the cost of production and hence, on prices. The board was instrumental in establishing grievance machinery in labor contracts and in promoting the use of arbitration as a terminal point in the grievance machinery. This feature has become commonplace.

Apart from these areas and the development of numerous types of incentive plans, the board established a major precedent in working relationships through the use of tripartite agencies, not only in decision making, but also in mediation. It has been conceded generally that the board was effective both in wage stabilization and dispute settlement. The major criticism of the board resulted from the fact that in many situations labor and management avoided the collective bargaining process and placed their problems before the board rather than attempting to resolve them themselves. This was in part due to the war and the attempt to limit wage increases to avoid inflation.

Source references: Leonard B. Boudin, "The Authority of the National War Labor Board Over Labor Disputes," *Michigan LR*, Oct. 1944; BNA, *Key to War Labor Reports Covering Vol. 1–28 and Wartime Wage Control and Dispute Settlement, Regulations Cumulated From War Labor Reports* (Washington: 1945); ———, *The War Labor Reports, Verbatim Decisions and Orders, Vol. 1–28* (Washington: 1942–1946); Valeries J. Conner, "'The Mothers of the Race' in World War I: The National War Labor Board and Women in Industry," *Labor History*, Winter 1979/80; Milton Derber, "Labor-Management in World War II," *Current History*, June 1965; Paul Fisher, "The NWLB and Postwar Industrial Relations," *Quarterly Journal of Economics*, Aug. 1945; Jesse Freidin and F. J. Ullman, "Arbitration and the National War Labor Board," *Harvard LR*, Feb. 1945; Paul R. Hays, "National War Labor Board, and Collective Bargaining," *Columbia LR*, May 1944; Dexter N. Keezer, "The National War Labor Board," *AER*, June 1946; Nelson Lichenstein, "Industrial Democracy, Contract Unionism, and the National War Labor Board," *LLJ*, Aug. 1982; George Meany, "The War Labor Board: A Plan that Worked," *American Federationist*, Oct. 1971; Harold S. Roberts, *Seizure in Labor Disputes* (Honolulu: Univ. of Hawaii, 1949); Joseph Shister, "The National War Labor Board: Its Significance," *Journal of Political Economy*, March 1945; U.S. Dept. of Labor, BLS, *The National War Labor Board: A History of Its Formation and Activities Together With Its Awards and Documents of Importance in the Record of Its Development* (Washington: Bull. 287, 1922); U.S. National War Labor Board, *The Termination Report—National War Labor Board* (Washington: 1947–1948); Edwin E. Witte, "Wartime Handling of Labor Disputes," *Harvard BR*, Winter 1947.

See also LITTLE STEEL FORMULA, MAINTENANCE OF MEMBERSHIP, WAGE STABILIZATION, WAR LABOR DISPUTES ACT.

National Women's Trade Union League An organization developed prior to World War I, which as early as 1914 created leadership schools for women workers. It was helpful in organizing (with the help of a group of teachers and trade unionists) the Workers Education Bureau of America in 1921. The League also assisted in curriculum planning and the preparation of appropriate teaching materials for courses in labor.

National Youth Administration An agency established in June 1935 in the Works Progress Administration (WPA) and later put under the jurisdiction of the Federal Security Agency. Its purpose was to provide funds for young students, both at the secondary and college levels, so that they might either continue their education or to provide part-time employment for those students out of school between the ages of 18 and 24 who might contribute to projects in their own communities. The program also provided for job training, counseling, and placement services.

Native American The Job Training Partnership Act (JTPA) of 1982 includes as Native American grantees, members of an Indian tribe, band, or group; Alaskan natives; and Hawaiian natives. The Native American programs of JTPA provide for the establishment of comprehensive training and employment programs for these people.

Source reference: Job Training Partnership Act of 1982, 29 U.S.C. 1671 (1982).

See also AMERICAN INDIAN OR ALASKAN NATIVE, HAWAIIAN NATIVE.

natural wages *See* WAGE, NATURAL.

Nebraska Association of Public Employees (Ind) An organization affiliated with the Assembly of Governmental Employees. Its quarterly publication is the *Advocate*.

Address: 1302 J St., Lincoln, Neb. 68508. Tel. (402) 475–5221

needs test A determination, by welfare officials, that the person or family does not have adequate private resources to meet his needs or the needs of his family.

The term "means test" is also used instead of "needs test." The needs test received prominence in Great Britain when, in November 1931, it placed a limit on individuals who had drawn 26 weeks of unemployment insurance benefits in any one year. Provision was made that, prior to payment of additional benefits, the individual had to convince the public assistance committee that he had insufficient funds and no adequate private source of income to take care of his family's needs. This was a reversion, according to those opposed to the system, to charity and the old-fashioned poor relief system.

The U.S. system of unemployment insurance is based on the qualification of the individual to receive benefits after he has been out of work and has indicated his availability for work.

Source references: E. Wight Bakke, *The Unemployed Man* (New York: Dutton, 1934); Harry Millis and Royal Montgomery, *Labor's Risks and Social Insurance* (New York: McGraw-Hill, 1938).

See also UNEMPLOYMENT INSURANCE.

negative income tax Any form of income maintenance and supplementation based on the mechanism of the personal income tax. Payments are made as an integral part of the income tax rather than as social insurance benefits or public assistance payments. The negative income tax operates on the principle that the poverty level should mark the zero-point in taxation and that those who receive less should have supplementary income. Money would be paid out of the federal treasury to families according to a schedule based on actual income received and family size, without the use of the means test common in public assistance or social insurance programs.

Source references: John F. Cogan, *Negative Income Taxation and Labor Supply: New Evidence from the New Jersey–Pennsylvania Experiment* (Santa Monica: Rand Corp., 1978); Peter T. Gottschalk, "Principles of Tax Transfer Integration and Carter's Welfare-Reform Proposal," *Journal of Human Resources*, Summer 1978; Christopher Green, *Negative Taxes and the Poverty Problem* (Washington: Brookings Instituion, 1967); W. Joseph Heffernan, Jr., "Variations in Negative Tax Rates in Current Public Assistance Programs: An Example of Administrative Discretion," *Journal of Human Resources*, Vol. 8, Supplement, 1973; George H. Hildebrand, *Poverty, Income Maintenance, and the Negative Income Tax* (Ithaca: NYSSILR, Cornell Univ., ILR Paperback no. 1, 1967); Terry R. Johnson and John H. Pencavel, "Forecasting the Effects of a

Negative Income Tax Program," *ILRR*, Jan. 1982; Michael C. Keeley, "The Effect of a Negative Income Tax on Migration," *Journal of Human Resources*, Fall 1980; Mark R. Killingsworth, "Must a Negative Income Tax Reduce Labor Supply? A Study of the Family's Allocation of Time," *Journal of Human Resources*, Summer 1976; Robert A. Moffitt, "The Negative Income Tax: Would it Discourage Work?" *MLR*, April 1981; Albert Rees, "An Overview of the Labor-Supply Results," *Journal of Human Resources*, Spring 1974; Earl R. Rolph, "The Case for a Negative Income Tax Device," *IR*, Feb. 1967; Alvin L. Schorr, "Against a Negative Income Tax," *The Public Interest*, Fall 1966; Alfred Tella, Dorothy Tella, and Christopher Green, *The Hours of Work and Family Income Response to Negative Income Tax Plans, The Impact on the Working Poor* (Kalamazoo: Upjohn Institute for Employment Research, 1971); James Tobin, "Against a Negative Income Tax: A Rejoinder," *The Public Interest*, Fall 1966.

See also GUARANTEED INCOME.

negative strike A strike to maintain standards, wages, hours, or working conditions, where the employer is attempting to have employees give up conditions which previously they have enjoyed. Positive strikes are those in which employees seek changes or new conditions that improve wages, hours, or working conditions.

A "negative strike" sometimes is referred to as a "defense strike."

Source reference: S. Howard Patterson and W. H. Scholz, *Economic Problems of Modern Life* (New York: McGraw-Hill, 1931).

See also POSITIVE STRIKE.

negotiability *See* SCOPE OF BARGAINING.

negotiating ranges The negotiating range is the minimum and maximum set by the bargainers and within which the bargaining takes place. It is the range within which they plan to reach a settlement on any one particular issue.

Where some demands are subsidiary and either side gives up these demands, the range of settlement may be modified. This is particularly true in the wage area, where the wage range may be lowered to meet particular and specific costs on a vacation or insurance plan. In such situations the negotiators may have a total cost figure in mind as the maximum they will fix in any particular year.

In many situations the bargaining process will not include a negotiating range fixed by the parties, but their goals may be definite and specific with no room for haggling or bargaining. These particular issues are usually matters of principle, and each side claims that it has no room to negotiate since neither will accede to the demands of the other.

Source references: C. Wilson Randle and Max S. Wortman, Jr., *Collective Bargaining: Principles and Practices* (2d ed., Boston: Houghton Mifflin, 1966); Richard C. Smyth and Matthew J. Murphy, *Bargaining With Organized Labor* (New York: Funk & Wagnalls, 1948).

See also BOULWARISM, COLLECTIVE BARGAINING.

negotiation The process whereby the representatives of employees and the employer meet for the purpose of reaching agreement on wages, hours and conditions of employment for those in the appropriate bargaining unit, and methods for administering the agreement.

Source references: Donald E. Cullen, *Negotiating Labor-Management Contracts* (Ithaca: Cornell Univ., NYSSILR, Bull. 56, 1965); Richard J. Fritz, *Employers Handbook for Labor Negotiations* (Detroit: Management Labor Relations Service, 1961); Warren J. King, "Communications During Negotiations," *PJ*, Jan. 1962; Irving Paster, "When You Delegate Your Labor Contract Negotiations," *PJ*, Aug. 1968; Edward Peters, *Strategy and Tactics in Labor Negotiations* (New London: NFI, 1955); Carl M. Stevens, *Strategy and Collective Bargaining* (New York: McGraw-Hill, 1963); Selwyn H. Torff, *Collective Bargaining: Negotiations and Agreements* (New York: McGraw-Hill, 1953).

See also COLLECTIVE BARGAINING.

negotiator A person who has the responsibility to represent an employer or union in reaching a collective bargaining agreement. Where committees represent union and employer, it is customary for each side to appoint one of its members as the chief negotiator or spokesman for the group. He usually is the most experienced individual, has the major responsibility, and coordinates the activities of his group.

negro worker *See* BLACK EMPLOYMENT.

Neighborhood Youth Corps (NYC) Program authorized under the Economic Opportunity Act of 1964 to enable disadvantaged youth to remain in school, to return to school, to gain useful work experience, to earn an income, and to receive career-related services to help them develop their maximum occupational potential. Eligibility for in-school enrollees (students in grades 9 through 12, those who attended elementary school and were at least 14 years of age, and recent dropouts who were at least 14 years of age) was based on annual family income—those below the poverty line and in need of earnings to permit them to resume or maintain attendance in school. In-school enrollees were eligible for summer projects which encouraged potential dropouts to remain in school. Out-of-school enrollees to qualify had to have come from families with annual incomes below the poverty line, have dropped out of school at least 3 months prior to enrollment, have no immediate plans to return to school, be unemployed or underemployed, and be 16 years of age or over. Work assignments in both the public and private sector were provided, including education, conservation, health, food service, community and public service, and recreation.

Source references: Michael E. Borus, John P. Brennan, and Sidney Rosen, "A Benefit-Cost Analysis of the Neighborhood Youth Corps: The Out-of-School Program in Indiana," *Journal of Human Resources*, Spring 1970; Juliet F. Brudney, *Strengthening the Neighborhood Youth Corps* (New York: United Neighborhood Houses, 1969); Leonard Goodman and Thelma D. Myint, *The Economic Needs of Neighborhood Youth Corps Enrollees* (Washington: Bureau of Social Science Research, 1969); Sar A. Levitan, *Antipoverty Work and Training Efforts: Goals and Reality* (Ann Arbor: Institute of Labor and IR, Univ. of Michigan-Wayne State Univ., Policy Papers in Human Resources and IR, no. 3, 1967); Wallace Mandell, Sheldon Blackman, Clyde E. Sullivan, *Disadvantaged Youth Approaches the World of Work: A Study of NYC Enrollees in New York City* (Staten Island: Wakoff Research Center, 1969); Richard E. Sykes, *A Pilot Study in Observational Measurement of Behavioral Factors Associated With Increased Employability of Out-of-School Neighborhood Youth Corps Enrollees* (Washington: U.S. Dept. of Labor, Manpower Administration, 1969); James F. Trucker, "The First 50,000 Neighborhood Youth Corps Enrollees," *MLR*, Dec. 1965; U.S. Dept. of Labor, Manpower Administration, *The Neighborhood Youth Corps: A Review of Research* (Washington: Research Monograph no. 13, 1970); Diane Werneke, "Job Creation Programmes: The United States Experience," *ILR*, July/Aug. 1976.

"neither" vote The National Labor Relations Act establishes procedures for workers to determine the organization they want to represent them. In order to provide an opportunity for the employee to indicate opposition to any organization where two organizations are listed, provision is made for a "neither" vote where the employee may reject both of the organizations. Where more than two organizations are listed, a provision is made to vote for "none" of the organizations listed on the ballot.

See also BARGAINING UNIT, REPRESENTATION ELECTIONS.

nepotism An employment practice whereby relatives are hired in preference to other job applicants and receive special favors because of their familial connections.

net earnings In determining back pay awards to employees discriminatorily discharged, the NLRB seeks to make the employees "whole." The procedure currently in practice is to determine how much the employee would have earned had there been no discrimination and to deduct from that total what the individual actuallly earned by working elsewhere during this period. The NLRB after many years of operation instituted a procedure for assessing interest against monies which the employee would have earned and adding this to the employee's total in the back pay award.

See also BACK PAY, MAKE WHOLE.

net labor turnover rate The net turnover rate is considered as the number of replacements per 100 workers in the average working force. The labor turnover rate would be the number of separations plus the number of accessions divided by the total number working during a specified period.

$$\text{Net Labor Turnover} = \frac{\text{Total Replacements}}{\text{Av. Working Force}} \times 100$$

See also ACCESSION RATE.

net spendable earnings *See* SPENDABLE EARNINGS.

neutrals A third party who functions as a factfinder, mediator, conciliator, or arbitrator to help parties resolve a labor-management dispute.

Source references: Herbert Benar, "Woes of a Newcomer Neutral," *AJ*, Sept. 1972; Ralph S. Berger, "Training Programs for Neutrals," *Journal of Collective Negotiations in the Public Sector*, Vol. 6, no. 2, 1977; James C. Hill, "The Academy and the Expanding Role of Neutrals," *Arbitration and the Expanding Role of Neutrals*, Proceedings of the 23d A/M, NAA, ed. by Gerald Somers and Barbara Dennis (Washington: BNA, 1970); Barbara M. Wertheimer and Anne H. Nelson (ed.), *Women as Third-Party Neutrals: Gaining Acceptability, Proceedings from a Conference* (Ithaca: Cornell Univ., NYSSILR, 1978).

See also ARBITRATOR, CONCILIATOR, FACTFINDER, MEDIATOR, PUBLIC MEMBER.

Nevada Classified School Employees Association (Ind) An organization affiliated with the American Association of Classified School Employees (Ind). Its monthly publication is the *Classified Times*.

Address: 3100 Mill St., Reno, Nev. 89502. Tel. (702) 329–5413

Nevada Employees Association; State of (Ind) An organization affiliated with the Assembly of Governmental Employees. It publishes the *State Employee News* (eight issues per year) and the *SNEA Update* (weekly).

Address: 1100 East William St., Suite 102, P.O. Box 1016, Carson City, Nev. 89702. Tel. (702) 882–3910

New Careers Besides being an anti-poverty strategy, the New Careers concept is a new approach to education, training, and manpower development calling for a revolutionary reorganization of professional practice.

Basic to the New Careers theory is the distinction between a job and a career. It is noted that careers imply (1) permanence and (2) opportunity for upward mobility. The New Careers proposal argues that every person has the virtual assurance of at least horizontal mobility (increments of salary that come with years of service) and the opportunity for vertical mobility (advancement to the next station and thereon to the terminal position).

Source references: Robert Cohen, *"New Careers" Grows Older; A Perspective on the Paraprofessional Experience, 1965–1975* (Baltimore: Johns Hopkins UP, 1976); Alan Gartner and Frank Riessman, *Changing the Professions: The New Careers Strategy* (New York: NYU, New Careers Development Center, 1971); Arthur Pearl, "New Careers: One Solution to Poverty," *Poverty and Human Resources Abstracts*, Sept./Oct. 1967; Frank Riessman and Arthur Pearl, *New Careers for the Poor* (New York: Free Press, 1965); Brendan Sexton, *The New Careers Movement: A Useful Weapon in the War Against Poverty* (Washington: Citizens' Crusade Against Poverty, Training Porgram, n.d.); U.S. Dept. of Labor, Manpower Administration, *New Careers Handbook* (Washington: 1973).

new contract arbitration *See* ARBITRATION, INTEREST; ARBITRATION, NONJUSTICIABLE.

New Deal A phrase generally applied to the first and second administrations of Franklin D. Roosevelt with their broad legislative programs and the provision for the rights of employees to bargain collectively, first under Section 7(a) of the National Industrial Recovery Act and later under the National Labor Relations Act.

The phrase "New Deal" presumably was designed to incorporate the idea that a new deck of cards had been brought out and a new deal made which did not stack the cards.

New England Protective Union *See* WORKINGMEN'S PROTECTIVE UNION.

new escape period Provisions incorporated into awards issued by the National War Labor Board to provide the opportunity for employees covered under maintenance-of-membership agreements to have a period following contract expiration during which they could withdraw from membership. This generally provided that the individual had to be paid up in his dues before he had the opportunity to avail himself of the new escape period. A contract clause to illustrate the board's policy might read as follows:

> Any employee properly listed as a member of the union during the contract period ending July 1 ________, which the parties consider still in effect, who may wish to avail himself of the 15-day escape clause must submit his resignation to the union in writing within the period from March 24 ________ to April 10 ________.
>
> Any member of the union as defined above may resign during the period March 24 ________ to April 10 ________, provided that he has paid his initiation fee and his monthly dues to the union up to and including March 24 ________ or has made other mutually satisfactory arrangements with the union to accomplish this purpose.

See also ESCAPE CLAUSE.

New Hampshire State Employees Association (Ind) An organization affiliated with the Assembly of Governmental Employees. It issues the *SEA News* (monthly).

Address: 163 Manchester St., Concord, N.H. 03301. Tel. (603) 271-3411

New Harmony A colony founded by the wealthy English manufacturer Robert Owen, about 1825 at New Harmony, Indiana, where he attempted to carry out his plan for a cooperative industrial society. He urged the joint control of production by workers and the sharing of all of the profits of their labor. Dissension within the colony resulted in its dissolution after a few years. However some of its basic ideas, which included free education for all, shorter hours of work, higher wages, and a just sharing of the products of the workers' efforts have had long-term influence.

Source references: Mary Beard, *Short History of the American Labor Movement* (New York: Macmillan, 1927); New York (State) Legislature, Joint Committee on Industrial and Labor Conditions, *The American Story of Industrial and Labor Relations* (Albany: Williams Press, 1943); Marguerite Young, *Angel in the Forest, A Fairy Tale of Two Utopias* (New York: Reynal & Hitchcock, 1945).

New Lanark A textile town located north of Glasgow, Scotland, where Robert Owen established his cotton mills. It was considered at that time a model community in that wages and working conditions were much superior to those elsewhere in England, the employer received a moderate return on his capital, and the remaining profits were set aside for the benefit of those working in the mills and in the town.

Source references: Nicholas P. Gilman, *A Dividend to Labor* (Boston: Houghton Mifflin, 1899); Herbert Harris, *American Labor* (New Haven: Yale UP, 1938).

Newlands Act A statute passed by Congress July 15, 1913, after the repeal of the Erdman Act. It was designed to deal with labor problems in the railroad industry and, unlike the Erdman Act, provided a permanent procedure for mediation. Section 11 established a commissioner and an assistant commissioner of conciliation on a full-time basis to provide mediatory and conciliative functions. These functions did not have to be requested by either labor or management but could be proffered by the commissioners. In addition, the statute spelled out in great detail the form in which the parties were to draw up their agreement.

The statute provided for voluntary arbitration and the unions, after some experience under the law in major crises, refused to arbitrate. In 1916, following the Railway Brotherhoods' refusal to arbitrate the dispute on the eight-hour day, Congress passed the Adamson Act, establishing a basic eight-hour day for interstate railroad employees. The Newlands Act was replaced by the Railway Labor Act of 1926.

Source references: Newlands Act, 45 U.S.C. 101–125 (1982), repealed, 44 Stat. 587 (1926); Howard Kaltenborn, *Government Adjustment of Labor Disputes* (Chicago: Foundation Press, 1943); Harold W. Metz, *Labor Policy in the Federal Government* (Washington: Brookings Institution, 1945).

New Negro Alliance v. Sanitary Grocery Company A case decided by the Supreme Court March 28, 1938, which related to the definition of the term "labor dispute" under the Norris-LaGuardia Act. The dispute involved action by black clerks in certain stores of the Sanitary Grocery Company requesting the company to employ black clerks. When the company ignored the union's request, the union began picketing. One person patrolled the front of the store—there was no physical obstruction and there was no attempt to harass persons wishing to enter the store. The trial judge held that this was not a labor dispute and granted a decree enjoining the union from picketing and this was upheld by the Court of Appeals for the District of Columbia which did not regard this as a "labor dispute" within the meaning of the Norris-LaGuardia Act because it apparently did not involve terms and conditions of employment. The court held, therefore, that the trial court did have jurisdiction to issue the injunction.

The Supreme Court, with Justice Roberts writing the majority opinion, overruled the lower courts, and interpreted Section 13 of the Norris-LaGuardia Act in part as follows:

> [The] definitions [of the term 'labor dispute'] plainly embrace the controversy which gave rise to the instant suit and classify it as one arising out of a dispute defined as a labor dispute. They leave no doubt that the New Negro Alliance and the individual petitioners are, in contemplation of the Act, persons interested in the dispute . . . There is no justification in the apparent purposes or the express terms of the Act for limiting its definition of labor disputes and cases arising therefrom by excluding those which arise with respect to discrimination in terms and conditions of employment based upon differences of race or color.

Source reference: New Negro Alliance v. Sanitary Grocery Company, 303 US 552, 2 LRRM 592 (1938).

See also LABOR DISPUTE.

Newport News Shipbuilding and Dry Dock Company v. Schauffler A decision of the Supreme Court in January 1938, which held that the NLRB had the authority to conduct an investigation and that a federal district court did not have jurisdiction to enjoin the NLRB from conducting the investigation pursuant to the provisions of the National Labor Relations Act.

The case involved a request by the Newport News Shipbuilding Company for an injunction to restrain Bennett F. Schauffler, regional director for the fifth region of the NLRB, who had filed a complaint against the company for violations of Sections 8(1), (2), and (3) of the National Labor Relations Act. The company claimed that it was not engaged in interstate commerce, that it had not committed any unfair labor practices, and that it would be irreparably damaged if the NLRB held a hearing.

The NLRB held that the request for the injunction should be dismissed because the company had not exhausted its administrative remedies and that the granting of an injunction would usurp the authority vested by the Act in the court of appeals.

The Supreme Court found no threat of irreparable damage "and that [the District] Court has no jurisdiction of the controversy. . . ." The court of appeals had found that the company had adequate remedy under the statute and could not apply for relief until it exhaused the administrative remedy. The Supreme Court declared that to allow the district court to "entertain a suit to prevent the Board from conducting a public investigation. . . . would, in large measure, defeat the purpose of the legislation. There is no basis in the Act for such a contention."

Source reference: Newport News Shipbuilding and Dry Dock Co. v. Schauffler et al., 303 US 54, 1–A LRRM 580 (1938).

Newspaper and Mail Deliverers' Union of New York and Vicinity (Ind) Its official publication is the *Bulletin* (10 issues per year).

Address: 41–18 27th St., Long Island City, N.Y. 11101. Tel. (718) 392–8368

Newspaper Guild; The (AFL-CIO) The Newspaper Guild was the outgrowth of the establishment of a National Recovery Administration code for the publishing industry. The code provided that employees on the editorial staff were to be classified as professionals and excluded from the application of the wage and hour provisions of the code. On December 15, 1933, the American Newspaper Guild was organized to cover such employees. At the annual convention in Boston, the name was changed officially to The Newspaper Guild on July 15, 1971. The official publication issued semimonthly is *The Guild Reporter*.

Address: 1125 15th St., N.W., Washington, D.C. 20005. Tel. (202) 296–2990

new unionism A term variously used but generally applied to efforts by labor for a more cooperative working relationship with management and the development of such programs as workers education, labor housing, insurance plans, etc., rather than constant emphasis on the building up of militant and political aims of trade unions.

Professor Selig Perlman described this as follows: "The contribution of this so-called 'new unionism' resides chiefly, first in that it has rationalized and developed industrial government by collective bargaining in trade agreements as no other unionism, and second, in that it has applied a spirit of broad-minded all-inclusiveness to all workers in the industry. . . . First successful application of the 'new unionism' in the clothing industry was in 1910 by the workers on cloaks and suits in the International Ladies' Garment Workers' Union of America. . . ." On the other hand, Millis has referred to the new unionism as "the feeling of brotherhood and the desire for equal opportunity so strong in what has been called new unionism."

Source references: Jacob M. Budish and George Soule, *The New Unionism in the Clothing Industry* (New York: Harcourt, Brace & Howe, 1920); Edgar Furniss, *Labor Problems* (Boston: Houghton Mifflin, 1925); Harry Millis and Royal Montgomery, *Organized Labor* (New York: McGraw-Hill, 1945); Selig Perlman, *A History of Trade Unionism in the United States* (New York: Macmillan, 1922).

New York Central Railway Company v. White A major decision of the Supreme Court in 1917 which upheld the constitutionality of the New York Compulsory Workmen's Compensation law. The law provided compensation for disability or death of an employee resulting from an accidental personal injury arising out of and in the course of employment. Except where willful misconduct of the employee could be shown, the law provided compensation regardless of the probable cause. The Supreme Court held that the law was constitutional and regarded it as a reasonable attempt on the part of the state of New York to provide a more equitable distribution of the risks of industry, within the scope of its power to promote the public welfare, and within the police power of the state.

Source reference: New York Central Railway Co. v. White, 243 US 188 (1917).

New York City Office of Collective Bargaining An independent agency created by the city of New York pursuant to a written agreement between it and the major unions with which it deals (Executive Order No. 52; the New York City Collective Bargaining Law, Chapter 54 of the Administrative Code of The City of New York; and Local Law 53, § 1173.9.0 (1967)). Through its Board of Collective Bargaining and Board of Certification, the Office of Collective Bargaining supervises representation elections among city employees, assists in the mediation of disputes, and sets up the machinery for factfinding with nonbinding recommendations. The Board of Collective Bargaining is composed of two city representatives, two labor representatives, and three impartial members selected by the city and labor representatives. The labor representatives are nominated by the Municipal Labor Committee, membership to which is open to all certified public employee unions. The salary and expenses of the impartial members are paid for jointly by the city and the Municipal Labor Committee. The Board of Certification consists of the impartial members of the Board of Collective Bargaining.

The office is under the directorship of Arvid Anderson, who also serves as chairman of the Board of Collective Bargaining.

Address: 110 Church St., New York, N.Y. 10007. Tel. (212) 618–8200

Source references: Arvid Anderson, "Public Employees and Collective Bargaining: Comparative State and Local Experience," *NYU 21st Annual Conference on Labor*, ed. by Thomas Christensen (New York: Bender, 1969); *Office of Collective Bargaining* (New York: Office of Collective Bargaining, 1968).

New York Transit Labor Board A three-person board established by Mayor Robert F. Wagner on December 20, 1960, to assist the Transportation Workers Union and the New York Transit Authority in their 1961 collective bargaining negotiations so as to prevent "a recurring threat in the lifeline of the city's economy . . . to eliminate the threat of service when collective bargaining on new contracts has come to a stalemate."

The board was authorized to assist the negotiating parties only if agreement were not reached by December 1, 1961. Further, if by December 23, the board had failed to assist the parties in reaching an agreement, it was to submit a report on the dispute and its findings and recommendations to the mayor, the union, the Transit Authority, and the public. Negotiations failed and a four-day strike followed. David L. Cole, George W. Taylor, and Theodore W. Kheel made up the three-person board.

nibbling In situations where an employer has shifted to the incentive wage system and has subsequently found that his employees are earning 50 percent more than their regular hourly rates, nibbling refers to efforts by the employer to reduce some of the increased wage payments by reducing piece rates.

night premium A wage differential or bonus paid to employees working on other than the regular day shift. So-called night shifts are those which have a substantial number of hours of work after sundown. These hours may be included in both the second and third shifts.

The differential may be higher for the third shift than for the second. Premium pay reflects the feeling that the work is less desirable because it curtails the normal social life of the individual and also because of other inconveniences, related to transportation, shopping hours, etc.

See also PREMIUM PAY.

night shift Generally defined as either the second or the third shift which works a substantial part or all of its time after sundown. There is actually no clear demarcation of the time when a night, second, or third shift would normally start or the number of hours which an employee would have to work after sundown to be considered on the night shift.

See also GRAVEYARD SHIFT, SHIFT.

night work Early efforts by states to provide protective legislation for women and children led to legislation forbidding night work for women in factories as far back as 1890 in the state of Massachusetts. New York and other states similarly placed limitations on night work. The Supreme Court upheld the right of states to legislate in this area in 1924 in its decision *Radice v. New York*, 264 US 292 (1924).

9 to 5, National Association of Working Women An organization of women clerical workers founded by 10 women in Boston in November 1972, as 9 to 5. The Boston group developed the Bill of Rights of Women Office Workers which reads:

The right to respect as women and as workers.

The right to fair and adequate compensation, based on performance and length of service; regular salary reviews; and cost-of-living increases.

The right to written, accurate job descriptions specifying all job duties, and the right to choose whether to do the personal work of employers.

The right to fair and equal access to promotion opportunities, including a job-posting program announcing all openings and training programs that give each employee an opportunity for job growth.

The right to a say over office policies, and the right to participate in organizing to improve our status.

The right to an effective, systematic grievance procedure.

The right to fair treatment in every aspect of employment without regard to sex, age, race, or sexual preference.

In 1977, a national organization was formed and today, 9 to 5, National Association of Working Women, has affiliated groups in 25 major cities, including the original 9 to 5 in Boston. Prior to adopting its current name, it was known as Working Women, National Association of Office Workers.

9 to 5 has a membership of 12,000. The organization has a national speakers bureau, provides training, resource materials, technical support, and publications on a variety of topics including automation of the office, pay equity, health and safety issues, and the office of the future.

Address: 1224 Huron Road, Cleveland, Ohio 44118. Tel. (216) 566–9308

Source references: Ellen Cassedy and Karen Nussbaum, *9 to 5, The Working Woman's Guide to Office Survival* (New York:

Penguin Books, 1983); "Interest in Unionizing Increases Among Female Office Workers," *New York Times*, July 9, 1979.

See also DISTRICT 925, SERVICE EMPLOYEES' INTERNATIONAL UNION.

NLRB Association; Eighth Region (Ind) Formerly located at 720 Burkley Bldg., 1501 Euclid Avenue, Cleveland, Ohio 44115, the union was subsequently dissolved.

NLRB procedure The term may apply to the procedure involving the holding of employee elections and the determination of bargaining units under NLRB rules and regulations. It may also apply to other sections of the Taft-Hartley Act dealing with unfair union and employer practices as well as with the procedures used in the holding of hearings and the determination of the rights of the parties. The procedure may include the filing of a charge, its subsequent review in the field office, the issuance of a complaint, the holding of a hearing before an administrative law judge, the submission of the administrative law judge's report and briefs on his findings, all arguments before the Board, and the Board's subsequent decision. The procedure may then involve appeals in the courts.

Finally, compliance with a Board order when upheld by the courts may itself become a basis for additional NLRB procedural handling and contempt action.

Source references: Walter Gellhorn and Seymour L. Linfield, "Politics and Labor Relations—An Appraisal of Criticism of NLRB Procedure," 39 *Columbia LR* 339; U.S. NLRB, *Rules and Regulations* (Washington: various).

See also VOTING PROCEDURE, NLRB.

NLRB v. Federbush A decision by the U.S. Court of Appeals for the Second Circuit enforcing an order of the NLRB against The Federbush Co., Inc., in July 1941. The court ruled that while an employer is free to state his arguments against unions, this freedom is not absolute under the National Labor Relations Act. Hence, the Board did not encroach on the employer's constitutional right of freedom of speech by barring interference with employee organizational activities in the form of employer statements that the union involved was "just a bunch of racketeers . . . trying to collect dues and it won't get you anywhere in the end."

The court said in part: "Arguments by an employer directed to his employees . . . have an ambivalent character; they are legitimate enough as such, and *pro tanto* the privilege of 'free speech' protects them; but, so far as they also disclose his wishes, as they generally do, they have a force independent of persuasion. The Board is vested with power to measure these two factors against each other, a power whose exercise does not trench upon the First Amendment."

Source references: NLRB v. Federbush, 121 F2d 954, 8 LRRM 531 (CA 2, 1941).

See also FREEDOM OF SPEECH, PICKETING.

NLRB v. Jones and Laughlin Steel Company One of the major decisions of the Supreme Court in 1937 which upheld the constitutionality of the National Labor Relations Act.

Following the passage of the Act in 1935, a special national lawyers' committee of the American Liberty League issued a report which declared that the Act was unconstitutional on numerous grounds. This, and other advice by employer associations to companies, resulted in the refusal of many employers to abide by the provisions of the Wagner Act. It was not until the Supreme Court decisions in the *Jones & Laughlin* case, and a number of others, including *Fruehauf*, *Friedman-Harry Marks*, and the *Associated Press* cases, that greater compliance with the Act was established.

The Court held in these decisions that Congress had the right to regulate labor relations and to protect the right of employees to self-organization. It also found that the companies involved were engaged in interstate commerce within the meaning of the Constitution and that the area was within the scope of congressional authority. The Court stated in part: "Employees have as clear a right to organize and select their representatives for lawful purposes as the respondent to organize its business and select its own officers and agents. Discrimination and coercion to prevent the free exercise of the right of employees to self-organization and representation is a proper subject for condemnation by competent legislative authority . . ."

Chief Justice Hughes, who wrote the opinion, also said: "When industries organize themselves on a national scale, making their relation to interstate commerce the dominant factor in their activities, how can it be maintained that their industrial labor relations constitute a forbidden field into which Congress may not enter when it is necessary to protect interstate commerce from the paralyzing consequences of industrial war?"

Source references: NLRB v. Jones and Laughlin Steel Company, 301 US 1, 1 LRRM 703 (1937); National Lawyers Committee of the American Liberty League, *Report on the Constitutionality of the National Labor Relations Act* (Pittsburgh: Smith Bros. Law Printers, 1935); Joseph Rosenfarb, *The National Labor Policy and How It Works* (New York: Harper, 1940); Louis Silverberg (ed.), *The Wagner Act After Ten Years* (Washington: BNA, 1945).

NLRB v. Mackay Radio & Telegraph Co. An early and typically complicated case under the National Labor Relations Act decided by the Supreme Court in May 1938. The Court, enforcing an NLRB order, held that employees who go on strike do not thereby lose their status as "employees." The Court also held, however, that strikers for whom replacements have been hired in order to continue the employer's business need not be reinstated. The theory of "economic" strikers stems from this ruling, since the strike was not called because of the employer's unfair labor practices but because of failure to agree on terms of a collective bargaining agreement. (Subsequently, such "economic" strikers were distinguished from "unfair labor practice" strikers, that is, employees who go on strike because of or in consequence of an employer's unfair labor practices.)

The employer's unfair labor practice (discrimination) in this case, the NLRB found, was in refusing reinstatement to certain strikers because of their strike and/or union activity.

The case also involved procedural matters, the employer claiming, among other things, that he was denied due process because the Board took over the case without permitting its trial examiner to issue an intermediate report. The Court held that the Fifth Amendment does not guarantee an employer any particular form of procedure so long as the procedure afforded protects his substantive rights. The Court held that the employer had an adequate and appropriate hearing before the Board in this case.

Source references: NLRB v. Mackay Radio & Telegraph Co., 304 US 33, 2 LRRM 610 (1938).

NLRB v. Pennsylvania Greyhound Lines, Inc. A decision by the Supreme Court in February 1938 which affirmed an order of the NLRB requiring Pennsylvania Greyhound and an affiliated company to withdraw recognition from ("disestablish") an organization of employees found by the Board to be company-dominated in violation of the National Labor Relations Act. The Court held that the Board's order was within the contemplation of Congress in adopting the terms of the statute. The Court refused to consider the issue moot because since issuance of the Board's order the Brotherhood of Railroad Trainmen had been certified as representative of the employees, saying, "an order of the character made by the Board, lawful when made, does not become moot because it is obeyed or because changing circumstances indicate that the need for it may be less than when made."

Source reference: NLRB v. Pennsylvania Greyhound Lines, Inc., 303 US 261, 2 LRRM 599 (1938).

See also COMPANY-DOMINATED UNION, DISESTABLISHMENT, RECOGNITION.

noble An employer lieutenant of strike operations, usually in charge of a detachment of guards or sluggers.

Some have defined "nobles" as armed guards who are hired for the purpose of protecting strikebreakers. Actually, however, the nobles have a higher status since usually they are in charge of other strikebearers.

See also ANTI-STRIKEBREAKING ACT (BYRNES ACT), FINK, SCAB.

no-lockout clause A proviso in a collective bargaining contract in which the employer agrees that he will not withhold work from individuals or close down his plant or operation in order to force the employees to accept his terms.

A no-lockout clause is almost invariably joined with a no-strike clause in which the employees agree that they will not take any action to stop work for the duration of the collective bargaining agreement.

Source references: U.S. Dept. of Labor, BLS, *Labor-Management Contract Provisions, 1950–51* (Washington: Bull. no. 1091, 1952).

See also LOCKOUT, STRIKE.

no-man's land A phrase used to express the lack of clearly defined jurisdiction in industrial relations between the federal and state governments. The condition has been cleared up in large part by a series of decisions by the courts affirming the NLRB's primacy in labor disputes in which interstate commerce is involved.

Source references: Automobile Workers v. O'Brien, 339 US 454, 26 LRRM 2082 (1950); *Bethlehem Steel Co. v. New York State Labor Relations Board*, 330 US 767, 19 LRRM 2449 (1947); *LaCrosse Telephone Co. v. Wisconsin Employment Relations Board*, 336 US 18, 23 LRRM 2236 (1949); *Plankington Packing Co. v. WERB*, 338 US 953, 25 LRRM 2395 (1950); Elvis C. Stevens, "The No Man's Land of Labor Relations Remains Unoccupied," *LLJ*, Feb. 1963.

See also FEDERAL-STATE JURISDICTION; PREEMPTION, DOCTRINE OF.

nominal hours *See* HOURS, NOMINAL.

nominal workweek The total number of hours scheduled for a department or a plant for a one-week period. This also includes regularly scheduled overtime during the week.

nonappropriated fund employee An employee of a federal agency who is paid with funds generated by the activity rather than with funds appropriated by Congress. Service clubs, post exchanges, bowling alleys, and theaters on military bases are examples of nonappropriated fund facilities. These employees are covered by Title VII of the Civil Service Reform Act.

noncommunist affidavit The affidavit formerly required under Sections 9(f), (g), and (h) of the Taft-Hartley Act which provided for statements that union officers were not members of the Communist Party or affiliated with it. Provision also was made for filing certain financial and other data before the union could avail itself of the election procedure of the Act or the privilege of filing unfair labor practice charges.

The Supreme Court upheld the constitutionality of the non-Communist affidavit in the case of *National Maritime Union v. Herzog*, ruling that the Congress could condition the granting of exclusive bargaining rights and other protections of the National Labor Relation Act on the provisos set forth in Sections 9(f), (g), and (h). The Court held that the presence of communist officers in unions had been responsible for much industrial strife, and had interfered with interstate commerce. The requirements of the law were not unconstitutional even though membership in or affiliation with the Communist Party was not in and of itself illegal. Congress repealed Sections 9(f), (g), and (h) effective September 14, 1959.

Source references: National Maritime Union v. Herzog, 334 US 854, 22 LRRM 2215 (1948); "Checking on Non-Communist Oath," *Business Week*, Nov. 8, 1952; John A. Morgan, Jr., "The Supreme Court and the Non-Communist Affidavit," *LLJ*, Jan. 1959; David I. Shair, "How Effective Is the Non-Communist Affidavit," *LLJ*, Sept. 1950; "Significant Decisions in Labor Cases: False Non-Communist Affidavits," *MLR*, April 1955.

See also FALSE INFORMATION ACT.

noncompeting groups of labor *See* LABOR, NONCOMPETING GROUPS OF.

noncomplying union An organization which failed to meet the filing requirements of the Taft-Hartley Act, Sections 9(f), (g), and (h), when those sections were in effect.

Source reference: Harry A. Millis and Emily C. Brown, *From the Wagner Act to Taft-Hartley* (Chicago: Univ. of Chicago Press, 1950).

See also LABOR-MANAGEMENT REPORTING AND DISCLOSURE ACT OF 1959, NONCOMMUNIST AFFIDAVIT.

noncontinuous process Plant operations or production where the service or process may be interrupted and where it is not scheduled on a continuous or round-the-clock basis. Noncontinuous process industries usually operate on a single shift and occasionally utilize overtime procedures. They are not generally on a two or three shift schedule.

See also CONTINUOUS PROCESS.

noncontributory pension plan Pension plan which is entirely financed by employer contributions. The employees to whom the benefits accrue do not directly pay any of the costs of the plan.

Source references: BNA, *Pensions and Profit Sharing* (3d ed., Washington: 1964); Walter J. Couper and Roger Vaughan, *Pension Planning* (New York: Industrial Relations Counselors, Inc., 1954); Murray W. Latimer, *Industrial Pension Systems in the United States and Canada* (New York: Industrial Relations Counselors, Inc., 1932).

See also CONTRIBUTORY PENSION PLAN, EMPLOYEE RETIREMENT INCOME SECURITY ACT (ERISA) OF 1974.

nondisabling injury An injury which does not result in the loss of working time or in the disability of the employee.

See also INDUSTRIAL ACCIDENT, SAFETY.

nonfinancial incentives Benefits accruing to individuals which are not measured in terms of dollars and cents. These benefits are sometimes referred to as "psychic income" and the work involved may be highly pleasant, where a substantial amount of recognition is achieved by the nature of the responsibility and by the kind of work performed, and where prestige and other factors not measured in terms of money enter into the picture.

See also FRINGE BENEFITS, INCENTIVE WAGE.

nonjusticiable arbitration *See* ARBITRATION, NONJUSTICIABLE.

nonmonetary additions to wages *See* PERQUISITES.

nonoccupational injury An injury or accident incurred by a worker that results in loss of working time but which does not occur on the employer's premises, during the course of employment, or as a result of employment. Hence, the employer generally is not responsible for industrial or workers compensation.

nonoperating union A railroad union made up of workers who are not directly engaged in engine service or in the operation of the train. These "non-ops" include porters, telegraphers, maintenance of way employees, and others.

As a practical matter, all work related to the functioning of a railway transportation system contributes to operation of the industry. For technical reasons, however, the distinction is made between operating and nonoperating unions. A similar distinction occasionally is made in plants between direct and indirect labor.

See also OPERATING UNION.

nonproduction bonus Compensation or money paid to individual workers which does not depend on the production or output of the individual worker or the group. Bonuses of this type include Christmas bonuses, cost of living bonuses, certain family allowances, safety and attendance bonuses, and others. Profit-sharing could be considered a nonproduction bonus if sharing the profits does not depend directly on production output.

See also BONUS, CHRISTMAS BONUS.

nonresident employee An individual who does not reside within the geographic unit or area wherein his employer's plant is located. For employment and other benefits in a locality, the definition of nonresidency may be established by statute, ordinance, or regulation. For qualification for certain types of federal low-income housing or unemployment benefits, nonresidency may have specific consequences for an individual.

See also RESIDENCY REQUIREMENT.

nonstoppage strike The idea of the nonstoppage strike essentially provides labor and management with an alternative to the traditional strike and lockout. Recognizing that the essence of strikes and lockouts is to do economic injury to the other party, proponents of the nonstoppage strike seek to substitute financial penalties against both bargaining parties for strike and lockout tactics, thereby allowing continued production of goods and services while negotiations are in progress. This procedure in theory would protect the public interest, insure the relative bargaining power of management and labor, and remove the pressure on government to step in and speed a settlement.

Source references: Neil W. Chamberlain, *Social Responsibility and Strikes* (New York: Harper, 1953); Murray Edelman, "The Non-Stoppage Strike Plan," *Current Economic Comment*, Nov. 1950; George Goble, "An Alternative to the Strike," *LLJ*, Feb. 1955; ———, "The Non-Stoppage Strike," *LLJ*, Feb. 1951; LeRoy Marceau and Richard A. Musgrave, "Strikes in Essential Industries: A Way Out," *Harvard BR*, May 1949; Howard D. Marshall and Natalie J. Marshall, "Non-stoppage Strike Proposals—A Critique," *LLJ*, May 1956; "A No Strike-Strike Agreement," *Conference Board Record*, Aug. 1964; S. L. Stokes, Jr., "Nonstoppage Strikes: Rationale and Review," *LLJ*, Feb. 1969; Allan Weisenfeld, "Public Opinion and Strikes," *LLJ*, July 1953.

nonunion employee Generally an individual who does not belong to the particular union which exists at his place of work.

Under (unlawful) closed-shop conditions, all individuals who are eligible for membership in the appropriate bargaining unit technically are members of the union. The union constitution and bylaws may specify the conditions for membership and the conditions under which membership might be lost.

Under other types of union security, it is possible for both union and nonunion members to be within the bargaining unit and for the nonunion employees to receive the benefits of the union's negotiating activities and grievance machinery. This is one of the main reasons for union opposition to employer policies and/or legislation which keep individuals from being required to join a union under the union shop or, prior to Taft-Hartley, the closed shop. Unions claim that these individuals are "free riders" and that they should at least share the costs for benefits which accrue to nonunion employees. The agency shop is designed in part to meet this particular problem.

See also AGENCY SHOP, FREE RIDERS, RIGHT TO WORK LAW, UNION SECURITY CLAUSES.

nonunion goods or material Products or services which are produced or performed by nonunion workers or under nonunion conditions. In the past, the term was applied to goods produced in sweatshops or substandard (wage, hour, and working condition) plants. The union label is used by many companies to indicate that the particular goods were produced under union working conditions.

See also BEDFORD CUT STONE CO. V. JOURNEYMEN STONE CUTTERS' ASSOCIATION, BLACKLIST, BOYCOTT, HOT CARGO PROVISIONS, SWEATSHOP, UNION LABEL (BUG).

nonunion shops In general usage, a place of employment without a recognized collective bargaining agent.

Some authors make reference to the open nonunion shop which exists where both union and nonunion employees work without discrimination, but in which the union is not recognized as the bargaining agency. This kind of arrangement is not widespread.

Professor C. R. Daugherty designates three kinds of nonunion-shop relationships: one, the closed anti-union shop in which union members never are allowed to work; second, a preferential anti-union shop in which union members are tolerated on occasion; and third, the true open nonunion shop where the union is not recognized but individual members of the union are permitted to work with nonunion employees without discrimination.

nonworkers A term which has relatively little meaning, but may be used for classification purposes to distinguish between certain *work* classifications and *nonwork* classifications. For example, nonworkers in the census classification will include self-employed, farmers, professional persons and enterprises, executives, managers, foremen, supervisors, salesmen, and unpaid family workers on farms. Although many entrepreneurs obviously work for a living, they are not regarded as "workers" for purposes of classification. The same is true of the millions of housewives, who are "nonworkers" for classification purposes.

no-raiding agreement A pact signed by the American Federation of Labor and the Congress of Industrial Organizations on June 9, 1954, in which they pledged they would not attempt to organize or represent employees where "an established bargaining relationship" existed between the employer and another union. David L. Cole was named impartial umpire under the AFL-CIO No-

Raiding Pact and during the first five years of its existence handed down more than 70 decisions. Subsequent to the AFL-CIO merger, the substance of the No-Raiding Pact became a part of the AFL-CIO Constitution.

Effective January 1, 1962, Article XX of the AFL-CIO Constitution instituted the Internal Disputes Plan. This plan was the result of a major overhaul of the No-Raiding Agreement undertaken by the 1961 convention. The provisions of the plan, made binding on all affiliates of the federation, seek to protect established work relationships as well as established bargaining relationships by imposing certain sanctions on noncomplying affiliates. Article XX also makes it clear that disputes concerning general work or trade jurisdiction which formerly caused so much trouble are not to be raised or considered.

Source references: David L. Cole, "Arbitration of Jurisdictional Disputes, The AFL-CIO No-Raiding Agreement," *Arbitration Today*, Proceedings of the 8th A/M, NAA, ed. by Jean McKelvey (Washington: BNA, 1955); ———, "The Internal Disputes Plan: A Working Reality," *American Federationist*, June 1969; Joseph Krislov and John Mead, "Arbitrating Union Conflicts: An Analysis of the AFL-CIO Internal Disputes Plan," *AJ*, June 1981; Seymour L. Lehrer, "Some Jurisdictional Problems Confronting the AFL-CIO," *ILR Research*, Summer 1957; "Test of No-Raiding Pact," 32 *LRRM* 41.

See also JURISDICTIONAL DISPUTE, RAIDING.

norm *See* TASK.

normal retirement age Generally the specific age established in any pension or retirement plan of a company which is used as a guide for the regular retirement program. It is the age generally associated with receipt of pension benefits. When exceptions are made under special circumstances, these may be set forth in the agreement and are subject to review.

Source references: BNA, *Pensions and Profit Sharing* (3d ed., Washington: 1964); Walter W. Kolodrubetz, "Normal Retirement Provisions Under Collective Bargaining," *MLR*, Oct. 1960; Jack W. Rhode, "Fixed or Variable Retirement Ages?" *Personnel Administration*, Jan./Feb. 1961; James W. Walker, "Why Stop at 65?" *Management Review*, Sept. 1977.

See also AGE DISCRIMINATION IN EMPLOYMENT ACT OF 1967, EARLY RETIREMENT, RETIREMENT AGE.

normal unemployment A phrase to describe that amount of unemployment (the difference between the supply of and the demand for labor), which is presumed to be normal during any economic period. It suggests that there are individuals "normally" without employment even during periods of economic well-being or prosperity. Some of this unemployment may be due to temporary conditions in the labor market and to the inability of work seekers to find the right jobs because of lack of labor mobility or because of other dislocations.

See also CYCLICAL UNEMPLOYMENT, FRICTIONAL UNEMPLOYMENT, FULL EMPLOYMENT, SEASONAL UNEMPLOYMENT, TECHNOLOGICAL UNEMPLOYMENT.

normal work area A term generally used in the field of motion and time study to designate the limited area which is within easy access or reach by the worker while he is standing or seated at his normal job, performing his work. The space area generally within reach of the worker's hand is the one presumably conducive to efficient operation. When an employee has to strain and reach beyond that area, greater fatigue may result. This is unsatisfactory from the point of view of efficient industrial engineering.

normal workweek The established number of hours for the general operation of a plant, shift, or department for a one-week period. The number of hours generally would be scheduled at regular, not overtime, rates. In some operations, the normal workweek for special schedules or during peak or rush seasons may include hours scheduled at overtime rates.

Some writers have defined the normal workweek as hours actually worked at regular rates. By definition, all work performed at overtime rates would be outside the normal workweek.

See also HOURS OF WORK, WORKWEEK.

Norris case A Supreme Court decision which held that a smaller monthly pension benefit to women because women generally live longer than men was in violation of Section 703(a) of the 1964 Civil Rights Act. Contributions of both sexes to the plan had been equal. The Court based its decision on *Los Angeles Dept. of Water v. Manhart*, which held that an employer violated Title VII by requiring female employees to make larger contributions than male employees to a pension fund for the same retirement benefit.

Source reference: Arizona Governing Committee et al. v. Norris, U.S. Sup.Ct. No. 82–52, 32 FEP Cases 233 (1983).

See also MANHART CASE.

Norris-LaGuardia Act Passed by Congress in March 1932. Its purpose was to limit the use of the injunction in labor disputes as well as to make unenforceable the provisions of yellow dog contracts. In addition, it sets out a statement of public policy to protect the freedom of association and collective bargaining and limit the use and jurisdiction of the federal courts in labor disputes. The Act also holds that a union officer shall not be held responsible for acts committed during a labor dispute unless he has specifically authorized such an act. It also provides for a trial by jury of any individual charged with contempt of court, except for contempt committed in or near the presence of the court.

Section 1 of the Act provides that:

> No court of the United States, as herein defined, shall have jurisdiction to issue any restraining order or temporary or permanent injunction in a case involving or growing out of a labor dispute, except in strict conformity with the provisions of this Act; nor shall any such restraining order or temporary or permanent injunction be issued contrary to the public policy declared in this Act.

The public policy declared in the Act is set out in Section 2 as follows:

> Whereas under prevailing economic conditions, developed with the aid of governmental authority for owners of property to organize in the corporate and other forms of ownership association, the individual unorganized worker is commonly helpless to exercise actual liberty of contract and to protect his freedom of labor, and thereby to obtain acceptable terms and conditions of employment, wherefore, though he should be free to decline to associate with his fellows, it is necessary that he have full freedom of association, self-organization, and designation of representatives of his own choosing, to negotiate the terms and conditions of his employment, and that he shall be free from the interference, restraint, or coercion of employers of labor, or their agents, in the designation of such representatives or in self-organization or in other concerted activities for the purpose of collective bargaining or other mutual aid or protection; therefore, the following definitions of, and limitations upon, the jurisdiction and authority of the courts of the United States are hereby enacted.

This language in 1932 is reminiscent of the actual language subsequently incorporated into the National Labor Relations Act in 1935.

Section 4 provides that no court of the United States shall have jurisdiction to issue any restraining order or temporary or permanent injunction in any case involving or growing out of any labor dispute to prohibit any person or persons participating or interested in such a dispute from doing, whether singly or in concert, any of the following acts:

> (a) Ceasing or refusing to perform any work or to remain in any relation of employment;
> (b) Becoming or remaining a member of any labor organization or of any employer organization, regardless of any such undertaking or promise as is described in Section 3 of this Act;
> (c) Paying or giving to, or withholding from, any person participating or interested in such labor dispute, any strike or unemployment benefits or insurance, or other moneys or things of value;
> (d) By all lawful means aiding any person participating or interested in any labor dispute who is being proceeded against in, or is prosecuting, any action or suit in any court of the United States or of any state;
> (e) Giving publicity to the existence of, or the facts involved in, any labor dispute, whether by advertising, speaking, patrolling, or by any other method not involving fraud or violence;
> (f) Assembling peaceably to act or to organize to act in promotion of their interests in a labor dispute;
> (g) Advising or notifying any person of an intention to do any of the acts heretofore specified;
> (h) Agreeing with other persons to do or not to do any of the acts heretofore specified; and
> (i) Advising, urging, or otherwise causing or inducing without fraud or violence the acts heretofore specified, regardless of any such undertaking or promise as is described in Section 3 of this Act.

Source references: Norris-LaGuardia Anti-Injunction Act, as amended, 29 U.S.C. 101–110, 113–115 (1982) (sections 111–112 were repealed by 62 Stat. 862 (1948); matters formerly covered by section 11 of the Norris-LaGuardia Anti-Injunction Act are now covered by 18 U.S.C. 3692; matters formerly covered by section 12 of the Norris-LaGuardia Anti-Injunction Act are now covered by Rule 12 of the Federal Rules of Criminal Procedure); Paul F. Brissenden, "Campaign Against the Labor Injunction," *AER*, March 1933; Emanuel Dannett, "Norris-LaGuardia and Injunctions in Labor Arbitration Cases," *NYU 16th Annual Conference on Labor*, ed. by Thomas Christensen (Albany: Bender, 1963); Carroll R. Daugherty, "Anti-Union Contracts," 9 *Harvard BR* 191 (1931); O. K. Frankel, "Recent Statutes Affecting Labor Injunctions and Yellow-Dog Contracts," 30 *Illinois LR* 854 (1936); Felix Frankfurter and Nathan Greene, *The Labor Injunction* (New York: Macmillan, 1930); Ronald N. Loeb, "Accommodation of the Norris-LaGuardia Act to Other Federal Statutes," *LLJ*, June 1960; Edwin E. Witte, "The Federal Anti-Injunction Act," 16 *Minnesota LR* 638 (1932); ———, "Yellow-Dog Contracts," 6 *Wisconsin LR* 21 (1930).

See also ADEQUATE REMEDY AT LAW, "BLANKET" INJUNCTION, BOYCOTT, EX PARTE INJUNCTION, INJUNCTION, PICKETING, YELLOW DOG CONTRACT.

North Carolina; State Employees Association of (Ind) The North Carolina State Employees Association and the North Carolina State Government Employees Association merged to form this organization on July 1, 1984. It is affiliated with the Assembly of Governmental Employees.

The organization publishes the monthly *State Employees Reporter.*

Address: 413–419 N. Harrington St., Raleigh, N.C. 27603. Tel. (919) 821–2287

North Dakota Public Employees Association (Ind) An organization affiliated with the Assembly of Governmental Employees. Formerly known as the North Dakota State Employees Association (Ind). It issues the bimonthly publication, *Association Advocate.*

Address: 810 East Divide Ave., Bismarck, N.D. 58501. Tel. (701) 223–1964

north-south wage differentials Differences in wage rates, both by industry and job classification, which show variations by region and geography. For a long time the North-South wage differential was large. With passage of the Wage and Hour Act and more unionization in the South, these wage differentials have lessened.

Source references: Wilfrid Crook, "Recent Developments in the North-South Wage Differential," *ILRR*, Oct. 1952; Richard A. Lester, "Diversity in North-South Wage Differentials," *Southern Economic Journal*, Jan. 1946; J. W. Markham, "Some Comments Upon the North-South Differentials," *Southern Economic Journal*, Jan. 1950.

See also GEOGRAPHIC WAGE DIFFERENTIALS, REGIONAL (WAGE) DIFFERENTIAL, WAGE DIFFERENTIALS.

no-solicitation rule A rule or regulation adopted by employers which forbids solicitation of union membership or dues on company time or premises.

no-strike clause A provision in collective bargaining agreements in which the union gives its promise that during the term of the contract the employees will not engage in activities that will result in a stoppage of work at the employer's plant.

The no-strike clause is paralleled with a no-lockout clause.

Source references: Drake Bakeries v. Local 50, American Bakery & Confectionery Workers International, AFL-CIO, 370 US 274, 50 LRRM 2440 (1962); *Needham Packing Co. v. Local 721, United Packinghouse, Food & Allied Workers, AFL-CIO*, 376 US 247, 55 LRRM 2580 (1964); *John Wiley & Sons v. Livingston*, 376 US 543, 55 LRRM 2769 (1964); Thomas P. Gies, "Employer Remedies for Work Stoppages that Violate No-Strike Provisions," *Employee Relations LJ*, Autumn 1982; Richard A. Givens, "Responsibility of Individual Employees for Breaches of No-Strike Clauses," *ILRR*, July 1961; ———, "Section 301, Arbitration and the No-Strike Clause," *LLJ*, Nov. 1960; Thomas J. McDermott, "Enforcing No-Strike Provisions Via Arbitration," *LLJ*, Oct. 1967; Evan J. Spelfogel, "Enforcement of No-Strike Clause by Injunction, Damage Action and Discipline," *LLJ*, Feb. 1966.

no-strike pledge *See* NO-STRIKE CLAUSE.

no-suit clause A provision in a contract whereby the employer agrees not to file suit against the union for actions which occur, particularly those which are subject to resolution under the terms of the agreement. Usually the contract also contains a no-strike, no-lockout clause.

Following the passage of the Taft-Hartley Act in 1947, many unions were concerned about the provisions of the Taft-Hartley Act dealing with suits for violation of contract. Union efforts to obtain no-suit clauses were designed in part to prevent any serious damage to their financial position.

Novelty and Production Workers; International Union of Allied (AFL-CIO) Formerly known as the International Union of Doll and Toy Workers of the United States and Canada (AFL-CIO) and the International Union of Dolls, Toys, Playthings, Novelties and Allied Products of the United States and Canada (AFL-CIO).

Address: 147–149 East 26th St., New York, N.Y. 10010. Tel. (212) 889–1212

nullification of agreement Setting aside or abrogating the terms of an agreement. This may be accomplished by a new settlement which holds all prior agreements and understandings null and void. More frequently the claim may be made that the terms of a collective bargaining agreement have been voided or nullified by the failure of one party to perform under its terms. Generally, alleged violations or breaches of the agreement in labor relations are subject to established grievance machinery.

See also ABROGATION OF AGREEMENT, SUITS FOR CONTRACT VIOLATION.

nurse, industrial *See* INDUSTRIAL NURSE.

Nurses and Health Professionals, Federation of A division of the American Federation of Teachers (AFL-CIO). Founded in 1978.

Address: 11 Dupont Circle, N.W., Washington, D.C. 20036. Tel. (202) 797–4491

Nurses' Association; American (Ind) *See* AMERICAN NURSES' ASSOCIATION (IND).

O

OASDI *See* OLD AGE, SURVIVORS, AND DISABILITY INSURANCE.

OCAW *See* OIL, CHEMICAL AND ATOMIC WORKERS INTERNATIONAL UNION (AFL-CIO).

OEA *See* OVERSEAS EDUCATION ASSOCIATION, INC.

OECD *See* ORGANIZATION FOR ECONOMIC CO-OPERATION AND DEVELOPMENT (OECD).

OFCCP *See* OFFICE OF FEDERAL CONTRACT COMPLIANCE PROGRAMS (OFCCP).

OJT *See* ON-THE-JOB TRAINING (OJT).

OPA *See* OFFICE OF PRICE ADMINISTRATION.

OPCM *See* PLASTERERS' AND CEMENT MASONS' INTERNATIONAL ASSOCIATION OF THE UNITED STATES AND CANADA; OPERATIVE (AFL-CIO).

OPEIU *See* OFFICE AND PROFESSIONAL EMPLOYEES INTERNATIONAL UNION (AFL-CIO).

OPM *See* OFFICE OF PERSONNEL MANAGEMENT (OPM).

OSHA *See* OCCUPATIONAL SAFETY AND HEALTH ACT (OSHA) OF 1970.

objective standards (NWLB) During World War II the National War Labor Board had numerous cases involving plants which had rate ranges for particular jobs. A major issue concerned the methods by which employees were to be placed and to progress within the rate ranges for these jobs.

The board in its directive order in a major decision involving the W. L. Maxson Corporation ruled as follows:

> The parties by negotiation [shall] define objective standards of performance for various rates within each range. At specified periods, also to be negotiated by the parties, each employee's performance shall be reviewed by the company for the purpose of determining whether the employee has met the agreed standards for moving up to a higher rate within the range. The company shall have discretion to make more frequent reviews than those at the specified periods. Any claim that the company has exercised discrimination or has improperly measured the employee's performance with reference to the agreed upon standards may be submitted to the grievance and arbitration procedure of the contract.

In the *Rane Tool Company* case decided by NWLB on May 22, 1945, the board modified a decision of the New York regional board which provided for the negotiation of objective standards of performance but set out a procedure for arbitration at the end of 30 days if the parties were unable to agree through negotiation on the objective standards. The national board modified the New York regional board's order by setting aside the procedure for arbitration, if there is no agreement at the end of 30 days.

Source references: Rane Tool Company, 111-7546-D, Release B 2098; "W. L. Maxson Corporation," 21 *WLR* 269.

occupation The term usually is applied to a person's trade or vocation. For example, a teacher's or accountant's employment or principal way of making a living is generally considered to be an occupation.

The term also is used to indicate a grouping of jobs which are closely related and have many features in common, or which may also be common to many companies and many areas. This, for example, would be true of such occupations as carpenter, electrician, or plumber.

Source references: Robert L. Aronson, *Components of Occupational Change in the United States, 1950–1960* (Ithaca: NYSSILR,

Cornell Univ., Technical Manpower Series no. 1, 1969); Max L. Carey and Kevin Kasunic, "Evaluating the 1980 Projections of Occupational Employment," *MLR*, July 1982; Joan M. Costello and Reita Parsont Wolfson (ed.), *Concise Handbook of Occupations* (Chicago: Ferguson Pub., 1971); "Emerging Occupations: Not Every Acorn Becomes an Oak," *Occupational Outlook Quarterly*, Fall 1982; Horace N. Goodson, "Occupational Data Program Yielding Big Dividends," *MLR*, Oct. 1977; Allan G. King, "Occupational Choice, Risk Aversion, and Wealth," *ILRR*, July 1974; Carol Boyd Leon, "Occupational Winners and Losers: Who They Were During 1972–80," *MLR*, June 1982; Sigmund Nosow and William H. Form (ed.), *Man, Work, and Society: A Reader in the Sociology of Occupations* (New York: Basic Books, 1962); Dixie Sommers, "Occupational Rankings for Men and Women by Earnings," *MLR*, Aug. 1974; U.S. Dept. of Commerce, Bureau of the Census, *1980 Census of Population, Alphabetical Index of Industries and Occupations* (Washington: 1980); U.S. Dept. of Labor, BLS, *Exploring Careers* (Washington: Bull. 2001, 1979); ———, *National Survey of Professional, Administrative, Technical, and Clerical Pay, March 1982* (Washington: Bull. 2145, 1982); ———, *Occupational Projections and Training Data, 1982 Edition* (Washington: Bull. 2202, 1982); Patrick D. Wash, "Comparing Occupations: Four Measures," *Occupational Outlook Quarterly*, Fall 1982; Harold Wool, "Future Labor Supply for Lower Level Occupations," *MLR*, March 1976.

See also JOB.

occupational deferment Deferment of—in some cases, literally exemption from—compulsory military service on the ground that an individual's continued pursuit of the civilian occupation contributes more to the country than the military service would. During periods of war or great military need it is necessary to defer certain individuals with special skills, or in certain occupations, not only to produce munitions and other materials of war but also to maintain the civilian economy upon which the war effort is based.

occupational disability *See* DISABILITY.

occupational disease A disease or illness which is due primarily and directly to or arises from employment in an industry. It may be traceable to conditions of employment such as dampness, dust, obnoxious conditions, poisons, etc. The term is used synonymously with industrial disease.

Some occupational diseases are associated immediately with certain working conditions while others develop over many years and may lead to disability and death but may not be associated immediately with the nature of the occupation or industry. Many of the industrial or occupational diseases occur among workers in so-called hazardous occupations.

The Occupational Safety and Health Administration has categorized illnesses and disorders for reporting purposes as:

(1) Occupational skin diseases or disorders,
(2) Dust diseases of the lungs (pneumoconioses),
(3) Respiratory conditions due to toxic agents,
(4) Poisoning (systemic effects of toxic materials),
(5) Disorders due to physical agents (other than toxic materials),
(6) Disorders due to repeated trauma, and
(7) All other occupational illness.

Source references: Audrey Freedman, *Industry Response to Health Risk* (New York: The Conference Board, Report no. 811, 1981); Mary Lee Gosney, "Whatever Happened to Brown Lung? Compensation for Difficult to Diagnose Occupational Diseases," *Industrial Relations LJ*, Vol. 3, no. 1, 1979; H. W. Heinrich, *Industrial Accident Prevention* (4th ed., New York: McGraw-Hill, 1959); Harvey J. Hilaski and Chao Ling Wang, "How Valid are Estimates of Occupational Illness," *MLR*, Aug. 1982; Marilyn K. Hutchison, *A Guide to the Work-Relatedness of Disease* (Washington: U.S. Dept. of HEW, Public Health Service, 1976); Marvin J. Levine, "Legal Questions Regarding the Causation of Occupational Disease," *LLJ*, Feb. 1975; Joseph A. Page and Mary-Win O'Brien, *Bitter Wages: Ralph Nader's Study Group Report on Disease and Injury on the Job* (New York: Grossman Pub., 1973); Charles R. Perry, "Safe and Healthful Working Conditions: The Case of

Vinyl Chloride," *Proceedings of the 32d A/M, IRRA*, ed. by Barbara Dennis (Madison: 1980); Hiroyuki Sakabe, "Some Reflections on the Limits of Exposure to Dangerous Airborne Substances," *ILR*, Sept./Oct. 1978; W. Edward Stead and Jean G. Stead, "Cancer in the Workplace: A Neglected Problem," *PJ*, Oct. 1980; U.S. Dept. of Labor, *An Interim Report to Congress on Occupational Diseases* (Washington: 1980); Chao Ling Wang, "Occupational Skin Disease Continues to Plague Industry," *MLR*, Feb. 1979; Matt Witt, "Dangerous Substances and the U.S. Worker: Current Practice and Viewpoints," *ILR*, March/April 1979; Norman J. Wood, "Environmental Law and Occupational Health," *LLJ*, March 1976.

See also HAZARDOUS OCCUPATIONS, INDUSTRIAL DISEASE, INDUSTRIAL HYGIENE.

occupational group Analyses of labor force data as well as detailed classifications of occupations attempt to slot occupations into groups or subgroups which are closely related. Occupations may be broken down into closely related groups or into major, and more inclusive, occupational groups. The major groups would include such categories as the following: professional, technical, and managerial; clerical and sales; service work, agricultural, marine and forestry; mechanical work; manual work. Other occupational groupings might be either listings of professional workers such as teachers, lawyers, doctors, accountants, etc., or skilled craftsmen, such as machinists, carpenters, bakers, etc.

occupational history *See* EMPLOYMENT HISTORY.

occupational immobility *See* LABOR IMMOBILITY, LABOR MOBILITY.

occupational information Data and descriptive material usually prepared as a result of job analyses, questionnaires, and other methods of evaluation, which describe the salient features and characteristics of particular occupations, their requirements, and the industries in which they are found. These sources may describe how training may best be obtained or how to choose a vocation.

Source references: Trevor Bain and Myron D. Fottler, "Sources of Occupational Information Among High School Seniors," *Proceedings of the 30th A/M, IRRA*, ed. by Barbara Dennis (Madison: 1978); "Career Information: What's Available in Schools?" *Occupational Outlook Quarterly*, Summer 1982; Max L. Carey, "Occupational Employment Growth Through 1990," *MLR*, Aug. 1981; ———, "Three Paths to the Future: Occupational Projections, 1980–90," *Occupational Outlook Quarterly*, Winter 1981; Russell B. Flanders, "NOICC: A Coordinator for Occupational Information," *Occupational Outlook Quarterly*, Winter 1980; Russell B. Flanders and Neale Baxter, "The Sweat of Their Brows: A Look Back Over Occupational Information and Career Counseling," *Occupational Outlook Quarterly*, Fall 1981; Leonard A. Lecht, *Occupational Choices and Training Needs; Prospects for the 1980s* (New York: Praeger, 1977); Carroll L. Shartle, *Occupational Information: Its Development and Application* (3d ed., Englewood Cliffs: PH, 1965); John Thompson, "BLS Job Cross-Classification System Relates Information From Six Sources," *MLR*, Nov. 1981; U.S. Dept. of Labor, BLS, *A Counselor's Guide to Occupational Information* (Washington: Bull. 2042, 1980); ———, *Jobs for Which a College Education is Usually Required* (Washington: 1976); ———, *Jobs for Which a High School Education is Preferred, But Not Essential* (Washington: 1976); ———, *Jobs for Which You Can Qualify If You're a High School Graduate* (Washington: 1979); ———, *Jobs for Which You Can Qualify If You're Not a High School Graduate* (Washington: 1979); ———, *Jobs for Which You Can Train Through Apprenticeship* (Washington: 1979); ———, *Jobs for Which You Probably Will Need Some College or Specialized Training* (Washington: 1979); ———, *The National Industry-Occupation Employment Matrix, 1970, 1978, and Projected 1990, Volumes I, II* (Washington: Bull. 2086, 1981); ———, *Occupational Employment Statistics, 1960–70* (Washington: Bull. 1738, 1972); U.S. Dept. of Labor, ETA, *Guide for Occupational Exploration* (Washington: 1979); ———, *Health Careers Guidebook* (4th ed., Washington: 1979); Roswell Ward, *Out of School Vocational Guidance* (New York: PH, 1956).

See also VOCATIONAL GUIDANCE.

occupational injury An accident or injury which is work-connected.

See also INDUSTRIAL ACCIDENT.

occupational mobility The extent to which individuals in a particular occupation move into work other than that for which they were specially trained. Occupational mobility is fairly common where job training is not so highly specialized and where there may be a carry-over in the training.

The study of occupational mobility includes efforts to determine how individuals move from one occupational group to another and the factors which make such mobility possible.

Source references: George J. Borjas, "Job Mobility and Earnings Over the Life Cycle," *ILRR*, April 1981; James J. Byrne, "Occupational Mobility of Workers," *MLR*, Feb. 1975; Barry R. Chiswick, "A Longitudinal Analysis of the Occupational Mobility of Immigrants," *Proceedings of the 30th A/M, IRRA*, ed. by Barbara Dennis (Madison: 1978); Gregory E. DeFreitas, "Occupational Mobility Among Recent Black Immigrants," *Proceedings of the 33d A/M, IRRA*, ed. by Barbara Dennis (Madison: 1981); H. M. Gitelman, "Occupational Mobility Within the Firm," *ILRR*, Oct. 1966; Timothy J. Keaveny and John H. Jackson, "Propensity for Career Change Among Supervisors," *Human Resource Management*, Fall 1977; Duane E. Leigh, "The Occupational Mobility of Young Men, 1965–1970," *ILRR*, Oct. 1976; Anthony H. Pascal, *An Evaluation of Policy Related Research on Programs for Mid-Life Career Redirection: Vol. I—Executive Summary; Vol. II—Major Findings* (Santa Monica: Rand Corp., 1975); Martine M. Perline and Ronald M. Presley, "Mobility of Unemployed Engineers: A Case Study," *MLR*, May 1972; Nancy F. Rytina, "Occupational Changes and Tenure, 1981," *MLR*, Sept. 1982; Carl J. Schramm, "Education, Job Training, and the Process of Occupational Mobility," *Proceedings of the 27th A/M, IRRA*, ed. by James Stern and Barbara Dennis (Madison: 1975); Lawrence Slifman, "Job Mobility and Labor Demand," *IR*, May 1976; Dixie Sommers and Alan Eck, "Occupational Mobility in the American Labor Force," *MLR*, Jan. 1977; Damon Stetson, *Starting Over* (New York: Macmillan, 1971); Yoav Vardi and Tove Helland Hammer, *Intraorganizational Mobility and Career Perceptions Among Rank and File Employed in Different Technologies* (Ithaca: Cornell Univ., NYSSILR, Reprint Series no. 433, 1977); Helen Wood, "Occupational Mobility of Scientific and Technical Personnel," *Vocational Guidance Journal*, May 1950.

See also GEOGRAPHICAL MOBILITY, INDUSTRIAL MOBILITY.

Occupational Outlook Handbook A biennial publication issued by BLS, U.S. Department of Labor since 1949, originally in cooperation with the Veterans Administration to meet the needs for occupational information in the counseling and training program for World War II veterans. Widely used by counselors, it currently covers more than 250 occupations. The information included in the handbook covers employment outlook, training, qualifications, earnings, and working conditions in major industries.

Source references: Maxine G. Stewart, "Occupational Outlook Handbook in Brief," *Occupational Outlook Quarterly*, May 1968; U.S. Dept. of Labor, BLS, *Occupational Outlook for College Graduates, 1980–81 Edition* (Washington: Bull. 2076, 1980); ———, *Occupational Outlook Handbook, 1982–83 Edition* (Washington: Bull. 2200, 1982).

Occupational Outlook Quarterly A publication of BLS, U.S. Department of Labor, which deals with current developments in employment opportunities in the various occupations and industries.

occupational prescription A term used in occupational therapy, either in the treatment of handicapped workers or those with other types of illness, including mental illness. The occupational prescription is designed to suggest appropriate activities and environment for treatment of the handicapped or ill employee.

Source reference: Carroll L. Shartle, *Occupational Information* (3d ed., Englewood Cliffs: PH, 1965).

occupational pyramid A phrase used in the social sciences, particularly in sociology, to indicate the structure of the working force. It is applicable not only to a nation but also to a state, city or industry. It arrays occupations in a scale from the least desirable, from the point of view of social prestige, skill, salary, and other standards of value, to those which have the highest prestige or status. At the bottom of the occupational pyramid are the common laborers and other unskilled workers and at the top the highly skilled professional and managerial workers and others whose prestige status by whatever scale is high.

There is, of course, much argument as to the factors which should be considered in determining status and prestige, but the occupational pyramid is simply a device to set up some rough approximation of status at any particular time and within a particular social and economic environment.

Source reference: Donald Super, *Dynamics of Vocational Adjustment* (New York: Harper, 1942).

occupational rate A wage rate which is assigned to a specific occupation, either in a single plant, a geographic area, or an industry. Rates may be single rates or a range of rates from minimum to maximum. Individual workers who have the background and qualifications to perform the work of a particular occupation would receive the scheduled occupational rate. Same as job rate.

Occupational Safety and Health Act (OSHA) of 1970 Federal law which authorizes the Department of Labor to prescribe and enforce safety and health standards upon enterprises affecting commerce.

The Occupational Safety and Health Administration, directed by the assistant secretary of labor for occupational safety and health, is responsible for enforcement and administration of the Act. Compliance officers have primary responsibility for direct enforcement of the Act and may make unannounced workplace inspections; citations are issued by compliance officers with the approval of the area director.

The Occupational Safety and Health Review Commission is the independent body established by the Act to hear and rule on appeals by employers cited for violations. It is composed of three members appointed for six-year terms by the President, with advice and consent of the Senate. The commission assigns cases to administrative law judges, whose rulings may be reviewed by the commission. Decisions of the commission may be appealed to the U.S. courts of appeals.

The Act also established the National Institute for Occupational Safety and Health in the Department of Health and Human Services to "develop and establish recommended occupational safety and health standards." The director of the institute, appointed for a six-year term by the secretary of health and human services, is authorized to conduct research and experimental programs for new and improved safety and health standards and to make recommendations to the secretaries of labor and health and human services for the implementation of such standards.

Source references: Occupational Safety and Health Act of 1970, Pub. L. 91–596, Dec. 29, 1970, 84 Stat. 1590 (codified as amended in scattered sections of 5, 15, 18, 29, 42, and 49 U.S.C.); Nicholas A. Ashford and Judith I. Katz, "Unsafe Working Conditions: Employee Rights Under the Labor Management Relations Act and the Occupational Safety and Health Act," *IR Law Digest*, Winter 1978; Frank R. Barnako, "An Assessment of Three Years of OSHA: Management View," *Proceedings of the 27th A/M, IRRA*, ed. by James Stern and Barbara Dennis (Madison: 1975); Peter S. Barth, "OSHA and Workers' Compensation: Some Thoughts on Fatalities," *LLJ*, Aug. 1975; Charles M. Binford, Cecil S. Fleming, and Z. A. Prust, *Loss Control in the OSHA Era* (New York: McGraw-Hill, 1975); Frederick D. Braid, "OSHA and the NLRA: New Wrinkles on Old Issues," *LLJ*, Dec. 1978; BNA, *Safety Policies and the Impact of OSHA* (Washington: PPF Survey no. 117, 1977); William N. Cooke and Frederick H. Gautschi III, "OSHA, Plant Safety Programs, and Injury Reduction," *IR*, Fall 1981; Donald R. Crowell II and David A. Copus, "Safety and Equality at Odds: OSHA and Title VII Clash Over Health Hazards in the Workplace," *Industrial Relations LJ*, Winter 1978; Nancy K. Frank, "A Question of Equity: Workers' 'Right to Refuse' Under OSHA Compared to the Criminal Necessity Defense," *LLJ*, Oct. 1980; Gregory J. Kamer, "Employee Participation in Settlement Negotiations and Proceedings Before the OSHRC," *LLJ*, April 1980; Joel M. Kushnir and Uma R. Kastury, "How to Self-Police for Regulatory Compliance," *Management Review*, July 1982; Michael F. Marino III, "The Occupational Safety and Health Act and the

Federal Workplace: Implementation of OSHA by the Departments of Defense and the Navy," *LLJ*, Nov. 1977; John Mendeloff, *Regulating Safety: An Economic and Political Analysis of Occupational Safety and Health Policy* (Cambridge, Mass.: MIT Press, 1979); Benjamin W. Mintz, *OSHA: History, Law, and Policy* (Washington: BNA, 1984); Rollin H. Simonds, "OSHA Compliance: 'Safety is Good Business'," *Personnel*, July/Aug. 1973; U.S. Dept. of Labor, Occupational Safety and Health Administration, *Training Requirements in OSHA Standards* (rev. ed., Washington: 1980); John Zalusky, "The Worker Views the Enforcement of Safety Laws," *LLJ*, April 1975; William Zisko, "The Seventh Amendment and Employee Safety—Conflicting Values? A Review of *Atlas Roofing Co. v. Occupational Safety and Health Review Commission*," *Industrial Relations LJ*, Winter 1978.

See also INDUSTRIAL DISEASE, SAFETY, WHIRLPOOL CORP. V. MARSHALL.

occupational segregation A term used to describe the concentration of women and minorities in certain types of jobs. It is frequently used to refer to sex segregation. For example, discussions of occupational segregation usually note that women are typically employed in service-producing industries and that the largest single occupational group among women workers is clerical.

The Women's Bureau of the Department of Labor finds that there has been no appreciable change in the employment patterns of women since 1950. It states: "Of the 420-odd occupations listed by the 1950 census of occupations, women were employed primarily in 20. The fact was virtually unchanged by 1970. In 1978, only 9.9 percent of women employees held traditionally male jobs, 21.6 percent held jobs that are not sex-stereotyped, and 68.5 percent held traditionally female jobs. Predominantly male occupations are defined as those with 25 percent or fewer women holding them whereas predominantly female occupations are those with 55 percent or more women. Occupations having between 25 and 55 percent women are considered fairly well integrated." Such segregation is usually associated with lower wages being paid in predominantly female occupations.

Source references: Andrea Beller, "Occupational Segregation by Sex: Determinants and Changes," *Journal of Human Resources*, Summer 1982; Francine D. Blau and Carol L. Jusenius, *Economists' Approaches to Sex Segregation in the Labor Market: An Appraisal* (Urbana: Univ. of Illinois, Institute of Labor and IR, Reprint Series no. 253, 1976); Ruth G. Blumrosen, "Wage Discrimination, Job Segregation, and Title VII of the Civil Rights Act of 1964," 12 *Univ. of Michigan Journal of Law Reform* 397 (1979); Randall S. Brown, Marilyn Moon, and Barbara S. Zoloth, "Occupational Attainment and Segregation by Sex," *ILRR*, July 1980; Donald E. Lewis, "The Measurement of the Occupational and Industrial Segregation of Women," *Journal of IR*, Sept. 1982; Peter J. Meyer and Patricia L. Maes, "The Reproduction of Occupational Segregation Among Young Women," *IR*, Winter 1983; Valerie Kincade Oppenheimer, "The Sex-Labeling of Jobs," *IR*, May 1968; Nancy F. Rytina, "Occupational Segregation and Earnings Differences by Sex," *MLR*, Jan. 1981; JoAnn M. Steiger and Sue H. Schlesinger, *Fostering Sex Fairness in Vocational Education: Strategies for Administrators* (Washington: U.S. Dept. of HEW, Office of Education, Information Series no. 147, 1979); U.S. Commission on Civil Rights, *Social Indicators of Equality for Minorities and Women* (Washington: 1978); U.S. Dept. of Labor, Women's Bureau, *The Employment of Women: General Diagnosis of Developments and Issues*, U.S. Report for OECD High Level Conference on the Employment of Women (Washington: 1980).

See also PAY EQUITY, PINK COLLAR WORK.

occupational seniority A form of seniority whereby transfers or layoffs under a contract are based on the actual length of service of the individual in his occupation. Occupational seniority may be applied in promotions, as well as transfers and layoffs.

See also DEPARTMENTAL SENIORITY, PROMOTION, TRANSFER.

occupational shift Changes in the technology of industry as well as changes resulting from special circumstances, such as the shift from a peacetime to a wartime economy or the reconversion from a wartime to a peacetime economy, which requires major shifts of the labor force and frequently also changes in the occupational patterns of the economy. Frequently, occupational shifts will occur as a result of changing methods of production, and changes in the nature of materials used in industrial processes.

See also INDUSTRIAL MOBILITY, LABOR FORCE.

occupational stratification The phrase may apply to the actual arrangement of various occupations in the order of their status level. The phrase also has reference to the actual stratification or rigidity within particular occupations and the lack of opportunity for mobility among various occupational groups.

Source references: Andre L. Delbecq and James Vigen, "Prestige Ratings of Business and Other Occupations," *PJ*, Feb. 1970; William A. Faunce and Donald A. Clelland, "Professionalization and Stratification Patterns in an Industrial Community," *American Journal of Sociology*, Jan. 1967; Thomas V. Greer and Robert C. Maddox, "An Exploration into Occupational Prestige," *PJ*, April 1965; Milton D. Hakel, Thomas D. Hollmann, and Marvin D. Dunnette, "Stability and Change in the Social Status of Occupations Over 21 and 42 Year Periods," *Personnel and Guidance Journal*, April 1968; Albert J. Reiss, Jr. et al., *Occupations and Social Status* (New York: Free Press of Glencoe, 1961).

occupational structure The attempt to classify and code, frequently by the use of numerical arrangements, the various occupations within a particular economy or in a particular industry, or within a plant, from the highest to the lowest labor grade.

Source references: Peter M. Blau and Otis D. Duncan, *The American Occupational Structure* (New York: Wiley, 1967); Constance Bogh DiCesare, "Changes in the Occupational Structure of U.S. Jobs," *MLR*, March 1975; Norval D. Glenn, "Changes in the American Occupational Structure and Occupational Gains of Negroes During the 1940's," *Social Forces*, Dec. 1962; Max Rutzick and Sol Swerdloff, "The Occupational Structure of U.S. Employment, 1940–60," *MLR*, Nov. 1962; U.S. Dept. of Labor, ETA, *Dictionary of Occupational Titles* (4th ed., Washington: 1977); Emanuel Weinstein, "On the Way: A Standard Occupational Classification System," *Occupational Outlook Quarterly*, Fall 1975.

occupational survey A procedure for studying the occupational groupings of a country, state or locality, plant, or industry. Effort is made in the study, either by means of a questionnaire or personal interview, to determine the characteristics of the various occupations, and depending on the scope of the study, information to indicate how shifts in the occupation might be obtained or how the qualifications of the individuals within the occupations might be better utilized. Frequently, the survey provides related information normally tabulated in statistical surveys, such as age, sex, geographical location, and training.

occupational therapy A program to facilitate rehabilitation of mentally, physically, or emotionally handicapped individuals through education, recreation, or social activities. An occupational therapy program seeks to help individuals to attain independence, to prepare them to return to employment, to restore physical functions, and to aid them in adjusting to the disability.

Source references: David Hinshaw, *Take Up Thy Bed and Walk* (New York: Putnam's Sons, 1948); U.S. Dept. of Labor, ETA, *Dictionary of Occupational Titles* (4th ed., Washington: 1977); Edna Yost and Lillian Gilbreth, *Normal Lives for the Disabled* (New York: Macmillan, 1944).

occupational wage relationship An attempt to show the interrelation of occupational wage rates in occupations which in themselves show a range of responsibilities and skills. Studies of occupational wage relationships are possible on a broad industry basis as well as in individual plants.

occupation analysis The study of the content and requirements of specific occupations or occupational groups to determine whether similar job titles or occupation names or titles actually have the same content. Efforts to analyze individual occupations require more than the listing of jobs with similar titles or designations. The real analysis flows from the actual content and requirements of the occupation or job.

Job evaluation concerns itself with the efforts to rationalize a wage and salary structure insofar as the occupations or jobs relate to one another; that is, in relation to the entire range of jobs and occupations within the plant.

Source references: Glen Cain, W. Lee Hansen and Burton A. Weisbrod, "Occupational Classification: An Economic Approach," *MLR*, Feb. 1967; Richard A. Morano, "A New Concept in Personnel Development and Employee Relations," *PJ*, Aug. 1974; Carroll Shartle, *Occupational Information* (3d ed., Englewood Cliffs: PH, 1965); U.S. Office of Federal Statistical Policy and Standards, *Standard Occupational Classification Manual, 1980* (Washington: 1980); Kathy Wilson, "Matching Personal and Job Characteristics," *Occupational Outlook Quarterly*, Fall 1978.

See also JOB ANALYSIS, JOB EVALUATION.

Office and Professional Employees International Union (AFL-CIO) Formerly known as the Office Employees International Union (AFL-CIO). On April 27, 1972, the Associated Unions of America (Ind) merged with the union. Its official quarterly publication is *White Collar*.

Address: 256 West 14th St., Suite 610, New York, N.Y. 10011. Tel. (212) 675–3210

Office of Education First created in 1867, the Office of Education became part of the Department of Health, Education, and Welfare when that department was established in 1953.

The statutory functions of the Office of Education were to collect statistics on the condition and progress of education, to diffuse such information in order to aid in the establishment and maintenance of efficient school systems, and in general to promote the cause of education. The office also managed federal financial assistance to education, maintained programs of student exchange and financial assistance, conducted special studies and research projects, and issued numerous publications on its research and on the state of education.

The Office of Education was headed by the commissioner of education, who was usually a distinguished American educator, and consisted of various staff offices and program bureaus. Among these offices and program bureaus were the following: the Office of Programs for the Disadvantaged, the Institute of International Studies, the Bureau of Adult, Vocational and Library Programs, the Bureau of Education for the Handicapped, and the Bureau of Educational Personnel Development.

The programs are currently administered by the Department of Education.

See also EDUCATION, DEPARTMENT OF.

Office of Federal Contract Compliance Programs (OFCCP) Established in October 1965 by the secretary of labor to carry out the enforcement activities of Executive Order 11246. Originally called the Office of Federal Contract Compliance, the name was changed to the Office of Federal Contract Compliance Programs when it was merged with two other equal employment programs within the Employment Standards Administration in June 1975. The EEO/AA responsibility of 11 federal agencies was transferred to the OFCCP in 1978.

The OFCCP is responsible for the implementation of equal employment opportunity practices of federal government contractors to eliminate discrimination on the basis of race, religion, color, sex, handicap, and veteran status.

In the enforcement of Executive Order 11246, OFCCP is authorized to conduct compliance reviews; to investigate complaints of discrimination; to conduct hearings to obtain compliance; to conduct hearings prior to imposition of penalties and sanctions or referral to the solicitor of labor, the appropriate solicitor, or the attorney of the Department of Labor; to recommend appropriate proceedings under Title VII of the Civil Rights Act of 1964 to the Equal Employment Opportunity Commission; and to attempt compliance through conference, conciliation, or persuasion prior to recommending action by the Department of Justice for compliance or for judicial proceedings.

The OFCCP also monitors federal contract compliance with Section 503 of the Rehabilitation Act of 1973 which requires affirmative action and reasonable accommodation in the employment of qualified physically and mentally handicapped persons, and with Section 2012 of the Vietnam Era Veterans Readjustment Assistance Act of

1974 which mandates affirmative employment of Vietnam veterans and disabled veterans.

The OFCCP has promulgated the following rules and regulations to carry out its responsibilities: "Equal Employment Opportunity Duties of Government Contractors," 41 C.F.R. 60–1; "Revised Order No. 4," 41 C.F.R. 60–2; "Affirmative Action Programs of Government Construction Contractors," 41 C.F.R. 60–4; "Sex Discrimination Guidelines for Government Contractors," 41 C.F.R. 60–20; "Hearing Rules for Sanction Proceedings," 41 C.F.R. 60–30; "Examination and Copying of OFCCP Documents," 41 C.F.R. 60–40; "Guidelines on Discrimination Because of Religion or National Origin," 41 C.F.R. 60–50; "Revised Order No. 14," 41 C.F.R. 60–60; "Affirmative Action Program for Disabled Veterans and Veterans of the Vietnam Era," 41 C.F.R. 60–250; and "Affirmative Action Program for Handicapped Persons," 41 C.F.R. 60–741.

Source references: E.O. 11246, 3 C.F.R. (1964–65 Comp.) 339; U.S. OFCCP, "Equal Employment Opportunity Duties of Government Contractors," 41 C.F.R. 60–1; Donald Elisburg, "Office of Federal Contract Compliance Programs—New Directions," *NYU 33d Annual National Conference on Labor*, ed. by Richard Adelman (New York: Bender, 1981); Malcolm R. Lovell, Jr., "New Directions for OFCCP," *LLJ*, Dec. 1981; Weldon J. Rougeau, "The Office of Federal Contract Compliance Programs: Its Expanding Role and New Directions," *Labor Law Developments 1979*, Proceedings of 25th Annual Institute on Labor Law, SLF (New York: Bender, 1979); U.S. Dept. of Labor, Employment Standards Administration, *OFCCP: Making EEO and Affirmative Action Work* (Washington: 1979).

See also EXECUTIVE ORDER 11246, REHABILITATION ACT OF 1973, REVISED ORDER NO. 4, REVISED ORDER NO. 14, VIETNAM ERA VETERANS READJUSTMENT ASSISTANCE ACT OF 1974.

Office of Labor-Management and Welfare-Pension Reports A division within the Labor-Management Services Administration of the U.S. Department of Labor, assigned to administer the Labor-Management Reporting and Disclosure Act of 1959 and the Welfare and Pension Plans Disclosure Act (WPPDA) of 1958.

Prior to August 21, 1963, these laws were separately administered by the Bureau of Labor-Management Reports and the Office of Welfare and Pension Plans. The merger of these two offices was effected "to minimize the potential for duplication of effort, while assuring coordination of technical assistance and investigative activities." The Employee Retirement Income Security Act of 1974 repealed the WPPDA.

The Office is now known as the Office of Labor-Management Standards Enforcement.

Source references: Marten S. Estey, "Some Comments on the First Four Years of BLMR Research and Statistics," *Regulating Union Government*, ed. by Marten S. Estey, Philip Taft, and Martin Wagner (New York: Harper, IRRA pub. no. 31, 1964); John D. Stewart, "The Bureau of Labor-Management Reports: Its Organization, Functions, and Activities," *Regulating Union Government*, ed. by Marten S. Estey, Philip Taft, and Martin Wagner (New York: Harper, IRRA Pub. no. 31, 1964).

See also OFFICE OF LABOR-MANAGEMENT STANDARDS ENFORCEMENT.

Office of Labor-Management Standards Enforcement A division within the Labor-Management Services Administration of the U.S. Department of Labor, assigned to administer the Labor-Management Reporting and Disclosure Act (LMRDA) of 1959 and the Employee Retirement Income Security Act (ERISA) of 1974. ERISA repealed the Welfare and Pension Plans Disclosure Act.

Following enactment of ERISA, the Office of Labor-Management and Welfare-Pension Reports was redesignated the Office of Labor-Management Standards Enforcement.

Address: 200 Constitution Ave., N.W., Washington, D.C. 20216.

Source reference: U.S. Dept. of Labor, LMSA, *Compliance, Enforcement and Reporting in 1975 Under the Labor-Management Reporting and Disclosure Act* (Washington: 1978).

See also LABOR-MANAGEMENT REPORTING AND DISCLOSURE ACT OF 1959, WELFARE AND PENSION PLANS DISCLOSURE ACT OF 1958 (TELLER ACT).

Office of Manpower, Automation and Training (OMAT) *See* MANPOWER ADMINISTRATION, DEPARTMENT OF LABOR.

Office of Personnel Management (OPM) The central personnel management agency administering the merit system of the federal government. OPM was created by Reorganization Plan No. 2 of 1978, which abolished the U.S. Civil Service Commission.

The OPM seeks "to develop personnel programs which will improve government management and efficiency." The OPM is responsible for the nationwide recruiting and examination of applicants for general schedule and wage board positions, coordinating government affirmative action programs, carrying out training and development of federal employees, and assisting federal agencies in the administration of incentive awards. It has 10 regional offices.

Address: 1900 E St., N.W., Washington, D.C. 20415.

Source reference: U.S. OPM, *Civil Service Reform—A Report on the First Year* (Washington: 1980).

Office of Price Administration The agency that administered the Price Control Act during World War II, and paralleled efforts at wage stabilization and dispute settlement under the National War Labor Board. The Price Control Act was designed to limit advances in prices and to maintain a stable economy, thereby reducing the pressure for wage and salary adjustments.

Office of Vocational Rehabilitation A division within the U.S. Department of Health, Education, and Welfare concerned with the problem of vocational rehabilitation. The federal-state vocational rehabilitation program was first administered by the Vocational Education Board. In 1943 the Office of Vocational Rehabilitation was created to manage the expanded vocational rehabilitation program, and in 1953 the Office was placed under the newly established Department of Health, Education, and Welfare. In 1963 the Office of Vocational Rehabilitation was redesignated the Vocational Rehabilitation Administration, and when HEW was reorganized in 1967 the latter became a component of the new Social and Rehabilitation Service known as the Rehabilitation Services Administration.

See also REHABILITATION SERVICES ADMINISTRATION, VOCATIONAL REHABILITATION.

office worker An individual generally engaged in work which involves such jobs as typing, secretarial work, filing, and other related clerical jobs in and around an office. With the increasing responsibility of control in the centralized offices, more and more jobs are becoming office jobs. The office worker is referred to also as a "white-collar worker."

The term is used to distinguish individuals who work in an office from those who work in the field or in a plant.

See also CLERICAL WORK.

official time Time granted to federal employees to participate in negotiation and impasse proceedings during working time without loss of pay. Section 7131 of the Civil Service Reform Act of 1978 provides for official time. In *Bureau of Alcohol, Tobacco and Firearms v. FLRA* (no. 82–799, November 29, 1983), the Supreme Court ruled that official time does not include payment for travel time and per diem allowances. The Federal Labor Relations Authority (FLRA) determines whether official time shall be authorized for employee representatives participating in FLRA proceedings. The parties have the right to negotiate official time for other appropriate purposes which may include charity drives, employee organization, and agency-related activities.

EEOC regulations provide official time to federal employees for the presenting of complaints of discrimination on the basis of race, color, religion, sex, national origin, and age to the respective federal agency. Section 1613.214(b) of the regulations provides, in part: "If the complainant is an employee of an agency, he shall have a reasonable amount of official time to present his complaint if he is otherwise in an active duty status. If the complainant is an employee of the agency and he designates another employee of the agency as his representative, the representative shall have a reasonable amount of official time, if he is otherwise in an active duty status, to present the complaint."

Source references: Civil Service Reform Act of 1978, 5 U.S.C. 7131 (1982); U.S. EEOC,

"Equal Employment Opportunity in the Federal Government," 29 C.F.R. 1613, *FEP* 401: 291; AFL-CIO, *The AFL-CIO Manual for Federal Employees* (Washington: Pub. no. 138, 1983); Barry S. Jackson, "Is Too Much Official Time Spent on Labor Relations and EEOC?" *Public Personnel Management*, Summer 1981.

See also PAY FOR GRIEVANCE TIME, PAY FOR SHOP STEWARDS, RELEASED TIME, TIME LOST ON GRIEVANCES.

off-shift Generally any shift other than the regular day shift. When there is shift rotation, it might be any shift other than those regularly scheduled.

off-shift differential A premium that is paid for hours of work other than those of the regular shift. This payment may be for work during a night shift, a graveyard shift, or any other shift hours that are inconvenient to work.

See also GRAVEYARD SHIFT, NIGHT SHIFT, WAGE DIFFERENTIALS.

Ohio Association of Public School Employees An organization once affiliated with the American Association of Classified School Employees, it merged with the American Federation of State, County and Municipal Employees (AFL-CIO) on February 11, 1984. Its publication, the *Advocate*, is issued bimonthly.

Address: 6805 Oak Creek Dr., Columbus, Ohio 43229. Tel. (614) 890–4770

Ohio Civil Service Employees Association, Inc. An organization once affiliated with the Assembly of Governmental Employees, it merged with the American Federation of State, County and Municipal Employees (AFL-CIO) on May 25, 1983. Its monthly publication is the *Public Employee News*.

Address: 995 Goodale Blvd., Columbus, Ohio 43212. Tel. (614) 221–2409

Oil, Chemical and Atomic Workers International Union (AFL-CIO) In March 1955 the Oil Workers International Union (CIO) merged with the United Gas, Coke and Chemical Workers of America (CIO) to form the organization. Its official publication is *OCAW News*, issued bimonthly.

Address: 255 Union Blvd., Lakewood, Colo. 80228. Tel. (303) 987–2229

Source references: Harvey O'Conner, *History of Oil Workers International Union (CIO)* (Denver: Oil Workers International Union, 1950); Melvin Rothbaum, *The Government of the Oil, Chemical and Atomic Workers Union* (New York: Wiley, Trade Unions Monograph Series, 1962); Harry Seligson, *Oil Chemical and Atomic Workers: A Labor Union in Action* (Denver: Univ. of Denver, 1960).

"Oil Workers" Refers to the Oil Workers International Union (CIO) which, after its merger with the United Gas, Coke and Chemical Workers (CIO), adopted the name of Oil, Chemical and Atomic Workers International Union (AFL-CIO).

old age A term which is undergoing redefinition because of great advances in medical and other technology which have increased the life span of individuals.

Although a chronological age such as 65, 75, or 85 could be set for old age, various provisions of law, particularly those dealing with retirement and old-age insurance, set a specific age for the purpose of administrative handling. The process of aging varies with individuals and the setting of a particular chronological age for the determination of old age would be misleading as applied to all individuals.

Source references: Alan Anderson, Jr., "'Old' is Not a Four-Letter Word," *Across the Board*, May 1978; James E. Birren (ed.), *Handbook of Aging and the Individual: Psychological and Biological Aspects* (Chicago: Univ. of Chicago Press, 1960); Marilyn Moon, "The Incidence of Poverty Among the Aged," *Journal of Human Resources*, Spring 1979; National Council on the Aging, *Aging in North America: Projections and Policies, The Report of the North American Regional Technical Meeting on Aging, June 15–19, 1981* (Washington: 1982); Shirley H. Rhine, *America's Aging Population: Issues Facing Business and Society* (New York: The Conference Board, Report no. 785, 1980); Bert Seidman and Lyndon Drew, "The Injustices of Aging," *American Federationist*, July 1978; U.S. Congress, Senate, Committee on Labor and Public Welfare, *Studies of the Aged and Aging: Selected Documents* (12 vols., Washington: 1956–57); U.S. Dept. of HHS, SSA, *Income and Resources of the Aged, 1978* (Washington: 1981); Marvin E. Wolfgang, "Planning for the Elderly," *Annals*, July 1978.

See also OLDER WORKER.

old age assistance A form of public assistance under the Social Security Act designed to assist individuals in need who through the years have not built up social insurance rights or where their needs are greater than those presently provided by social insurance benefits.

Source references: E. Wight Bakke, *Insurance or Dole?* (New Haven: Yale UP, 1935); Eveline M. Burns, *Toward Social Security* (New York: Whittlesey House, 1936); Lenore A. Epstein, *Income Security Standards in Old-Age* (Washington: U.S. Dept. of HEW, SSA, Research Report no. 3, 1963); Margaret S. Gordon, "Aging and Income Security," *Aging and Society: A Handbook of Social Gerontology*, ed. by Clark Tibbitts (Chicago: Univ. of Chicago Press, 1960); ———, *Aging and Income Security in the U.S.: 35 Years After the Social Security Act* (Berkeley: UC, Institute of IR, Reprint 350, 1971); Lewis Merriam, *Relief and Social Security* (Washington: Brookings Institution, 1946); U.S. Congress, House, Select Committee on Aging, *Retirement: The Broken Promise, A Report (with Supplemental Views)* (Washington: 1981); Jennifer L. Warlick, "Participation of the Aged in SSI," *Journal of Human Resources*, Spring 1982; Walter Williams, "The Supplemental Security Income Program: Guaranteed Income for the Aged and Disabled," *Proceedings of the 25th A/M, IRRA*, ed. by Gerald Somers (Madison: 1973).

See also SOCIAL SECURITY ACT.

old age benefit taxes Levies under the Federal Insurance Contributions Act which apply both to employers and employees, based on wages paid in certain covered employments. These are generally referred to as social security taxes, since the Social Security Act was the statute originally setting the tax. Taxes which are levied on individual employees are withheld by the employer, and these withholdings and the taxes levied on employers are collected by the Internal Revenue Service.

old age insurance Generally refers to the provisions of the Social Security Act of 1935, which established a federal old-age insurance system. The Act also made provision for federal cooperation with the states in administering unemployment insurance systems, as well as the establishment of financial assistance to needy individuals, the aged, the dependent children and the blind. The Social Security Act was held constitutional by the Supreme Court on May 24, 1937. The Court upheld the state unemployment insurance laws and the provisions for the payment of federal old age benefits and taxes which were set up under the Social Security Act of 1935.

The old age insurance provisions of the Social Security Act, as originally enacted, provided retirement incomes after the age of 65 for workers insured under the system. Amendments to the Act have increased the amount of benefits and expanded the type of benefits, and insured wage earners are now permitted to receive benefits at age 62, but with permanently reduced benefits.

Source references: J. Douglas Brown, "Concepts in Old-Age and Survivors' Insurance," *Proceedings of the 1st A/M, IRRA*, ed. by Milton Derber (Champaign: 1949); ———, *Philosophical Basis of the National Old Age Insurance Program* (Princeton: Princeton Univ., IR Section, Reprint, 1977); John J. Carroll, *Alternative Methods of Financing Old-Age, Survivors' and Disability Insurance* (Ann Arbor: Univ. of Michigan, Institute of Public Adm., 1960); John J. Corson, "Old-Age and Survivors' Insurance," *Social Worker Yearbook 1945* (New York: Russell Sage Foundation, 1945); Alvin M. David, "Old-Age, Survivors' and Disability Insurance: 25 Years of Progress," *ILRR*, Oct. 1960; "Secure Retirement: Sorting Out the Myths," *American Federationist*, April 1975; Bruno Stein, "Pensions and Social Security: The Changing Relationship," *Proceedings of the 32d A/M, IRRA*, ed. by Barbara Dennis (Madison: 1980); ———, *Social Security and Pensions in Transition; Understanding the American Retirement System* (New York: Free Press, 1980); U.S. Congress, House, Select Committee on Aging, *Social Security: A Critique of Recommendations to Tax Benefits and to Raise the Eligibility Age for Retirement Benefits, A Report* (Washington: 1980);

U.S. Congress, Joint Economic Committee, *Old-Age Income Assurance: An Outline of Issues and Alternatives* (Washington: 1966); ———, *Social Security and Pensions: Programs of Equity and Security, A Staff Study* (Washington: 1980); U.S. Congress, Senate, Special Committee on Aging, *Termination of Social Security Coverage: The Impact on State and Local Government Employees, A Working Paper* (Washington: 1976).

See also SOCIAL SECURITY ACT.

old age, survivors, and disability insurance Refers to income and benefit payments provided under Title II of the Social Security Act. The OASDI program covers the retired and their dependents, the disabled and their dependents, and the dependents of the insured worker who dies.

Source references: William G. Bowen et al., *The Princeton Symposium on the American System of Social Insurance, Its Philosophy, Impact, and Future Development; In Honor of J. Douglas Brown* (New York: McGraw-Hill, 1968); Eveline M. Burns, "Social Security in Evolution: Towards What?" *Proceedings of the 17th A/M, IRRA*, ed. by Gerald Somers (Madison: 1965); Earl F. Cheit, "Survivors' Benefits—A Plan to Make Them Equitable," *MLR*, Oct. 1961; ———, "Workmen's Compensation, OASDI, The Overlap Issue," *IR*, Feb. 1964; Yung-Ping Chen and Kwang-Wen Chu, *Tax-Benefit Ratios and Rates of Return Under OASI: 1974 Retirees and Entrants* (Los Angeles: UC, Institute of IR, Reprint no. 243, 1974); Wilbur J. Cohen, "Economic Security for the Aged, Sick and Disabled: Some Issues and Implications," *Towards Freedom From Want*, ed. by Sar A. Levitan, Wilbur J. Cohen, and Robert J. Lampman (Madison: IRRA, 1968); Margaret S. Gordon, *The Economics of Welfare Policies* (New York: Columbia UP, 1963); Jacob Perlman, "Changing Trends Under Old-Age and Survivors Insurance, 1935–1950," *ILRR*, Jan. 1951; U.S. Dept. of HHS, SSA, *Effects of OASDI Benefit Increase, June 1980* (Washington: Research and Statistics Note no. 11, 1980); ———, *History of the Provisions of Old Age, Survivors, Disability, and Health Insurance, 1935–1981* (Washington: 1982); ———, *Preliminary Findings From the 1978 Survey of Survivor Families With Children* (Washington: Research and Statistics Note no. 12, 1980); U.S. GAO, *Social Security Administration Should Improve Its Recovery of Overpayments Made to Retirement, Survivors, and Disability Insurance Beneficiaries* (Washington: 1979); ———, *The Social Security Administration Should Provide More Management and Leadership in Determining Who is Eligible for Disability Benefits, Department of Health, Education, and Welfare* (Washington: 1976); Alanson W. Wilcox, "The Contributory Principle and the Integrity of Old-Age and Survivors Insurance: A Functional Evaluation," *ILRR*, April 1955; Clair Wilcox, *Toward Social Welfare, An Analysis of Programs and Proposals Attacking Poverty, Insecurity, and Inequality of Opportunity* (Homewood: Irwin, 1969).

See also OLD AGE ASSISTANCE, OLD AGE INSURANCE, SURVIVORS' BENEFITS.

older worker A term somewhat nebulous in meaning. From the employer's point of view it may imply that the individuals have reached the age at which they are no longer sufficiently alert and able to shoulder the responsibilities and duties of the job. In some operations and industries, employer hiring practices have rested on the assumption that persons as young as 40 or 45 are too old for certain occupations. Morrison defines older workers as those age 65 and older.

The federal government and many states have enacted legislation to prevent discrimination against workers because of age.

Source references: Ewan Clague, Balraj Palli, and Leo Kramer, *The Aging Worker and the Union; Employment and Retirement of Middle-Aged and Older Workers* (New York: Praeger, 1971); Gordon H. Cole, "The Rich Resource of Older Workers," *American Federationist*, March 1982; Lois Farrer Copperman and Fred D. Keast, "Older Workers: A Challenge for Today and Tomorrow," *Human Resource Management*, Summer 1981; Hamilton Crook and Martin Heinstein, *The Older Worker in Industry: A Study of the Attitudes of Industrial Workers Toward Aging and Retirement* (Berkeley: UC, Institute of IR, 1958); Jack F. Culley and Fred Slavick, *Employment Problems of Older Workers* (Iowa City: State Univ. of Iowa,

Bureau of Labor and Management, Information Series no. 1, 1959); H. L. Douse, "Discrimination Against Older Workers," *ILR*, April 1961; Victor R. Fuchs, "Self-Employment and Labor Force Participation of Older Males," *Journal of Human Resources*, Summer 1982; Margaret Gordon, "The Older Worker and Hiring Practices," *MLR*, Nov. 1959; Edward J. Harrick and Paul E. Sultan, "Workforce of the Future: The Problems and Opportunities of Maturity," *Personnel*, July/Aug. 1982; Elizabeth L. Meier, *Employment of Older Workers, Disincentives and Incentives* (Washington: U.S. President's Commission on Pension Policy, Working Papers, 1980); Malcolm H. Morrison, "The Aging of the U.S. Population: Human Resource Implications," *MLR*, May 1983; Dean Morse, *The Utilization of Older Workers* (Washington: U.S. National Commission for Manpower Policy, Special Report no. 33, 1979); Joseph F. Quinn, "Wage Differentials Among Older Workers in the Public and Private Sectors," *Journal of Human Resources*, Winter 1979; Shirley H. Rhine, *Older Workers and Retirement* (New York: The Conference Board, Report no. 738, 1978); Philip L. Rones, "The Aging of the Older Population and the Effect on its Labor Force Rates," *MLR*, Sept. 1982; ———, "Older Men—The Choice Between Work and Retirement," *MLR*, Nov. 1978; Norman Root, "Injuries at Work are Fewer Among Older Employees," *MLR*, March 1981; Carl Rosenfeld and Scott Campbell Brown, "The Labor Force Status of Older Workers," *MLR*, Nov. 1979; Arthur M. and Jane N. Ross, *Employment Problems of Older Workers* (Berkeley: UC, Institute of IR, Reprint no. 140, 1960); Betty V. H. Schneider, *The Older Worker*, ed. by Irving Bernstein (Berkeley: UC, Institute of IR, 1962); Harold L. Sheppard, *New Perspectives on Older Workers* (Kalamazoo: W. E. Upjohn Institute for Employment Research, 1971); Jeffrey Sonnenfeld, "Dealing With the Aging Work Force," *Harvard BR*, Nov./Dec. 1978; U.S. Congress, Senate, Special Committee on Aging, *Emerging Options for Work and Retirement Policy (An Analysis of Major Income and Employment Issues With an Agenda for Research Priorities), An Information Paper* (Washington: 1980); U.S. Dept. of Labor, ETA, *Employment-Related Problems of Older Workers: A Research Strategy* (Washington: R & D Monograph 73, 1979); United Steelworkers of America, *Older and Retired Workers: Plans, Programs and Services in the Field of Aging* (Washington: n.d.).

See also AGE DISCRIMINATION IN EMPLOYMENT ACT OF 1967, PRERETIREMENT EDUCATION, SUPERANNUATED RATE.

oldest local union in the country This honor apparently should be given to the Columbia Typographical Union of Washington, D.C., which has been in continuous existence since 1815.

Source reference: "D.C. Union 130 Years Old," *American Federationist*, Feb. 1945.

oligopsony A form of monopoly or control by a small number of buyers who are in a position to influence the demand for a particular commodity. In the labor market, a group of employers (a few buyers) who have a partial control or monopoly in obtaining labor in a particular labor market area.

Olsen v. Nebraska A decision of the Supreme Court in 1941 which upheld the right of the state of Nebraska to withhold a license from a private employment agency which had failed to limit fees for its services in line with the provisions of state law.

The Supreme Court in this case reversed its previous decision in *Ribink v. McBride*.

Source reference: Olsen v. Nebraska, 61 S.Ct. 862 (1941).

ombudsman The ombudsman is an official of a government or agent of other entities who receives and may investigate grievances of the constituency. The office originated in Sweden in the 1800s. Ombudsman in Swedish means agent or representative.

Hawaii was the first state to implement an ombudsman's office.

Source references: The Ombudsman: A Bibliography (San Francisco: Northern California Friends Committee on Legislation, 1965); Henry S. Reuss and Stanley V. Anderson, "The Ombudsman: Tribune of the People," *Annals*, Jan. 1966.

on-call time pay A method of compensation whereby individuals are paid for the time during which they are "on call" or on standby, ready and able to go to work. Some jobs require individuals to be available and "on call" to take care of various types of emergencies. These individuals are paid on a call time plan rather than for the actual time worked.

one big union Refers to the movement started about 1903 by the Western Federation of Miners which attempted to join all workers of the United States and perhaps of the whole world into a single revolutionary organization. As Louis Adamic put it, the purpose was to create "one big union—formed upon industrial rather than trade lines. It was a typically western idea—big: the sky was the limit."

Its concept was the brotherhood of man. The "one big union" in western Canada has been considered the best illustration. The organization was formed in March 1919 when a western labor conference consisting of some 237 delegates from four Canadian provinces met at Calgary and adopted a resolution asking the organized segments of labor to withdraw from the old-line unions and to form an industrial union of all workers whose ultimate purpose would be to abolish the "profit system." The movement was launched as the "One Big Union" which reached its climax in the general strike in Winnipeg in May 1919.

Source references: Louis Adamic, *Dynamite* (New York: Viking Press, 1931); Carroll Daugherty, *Labor Problems in American Industry* (5th ed., Boston: Houghton Mifflin, 1941); Harold Logan, *The History of Trade-Union Organization in Canada* (Chicago: Univ. of Chicago Press, 1928); Lewis L. Lorwin, *The American Federation of Labor* (Washington: Brookings Institution, 1933).

one-hundred-percent premium plan An incentive plan which is also referred to as a "standard hour" plan. The worker is paid in direct proportion to his output. The plan provides a guaranteed day rate for production up to a 100 percent measured production standard. The bonus payment is additional to the guaranteed rate and is based on the "standard hours" earned. The incentive provides an increase of one percent of the wage-base-rate earnings for every one percent of increased production. In effect, the line drawn on a standard chart shows that it is identical with the straight piece rate.

Source references: J. Keith Louden, *Wage Incentives* (New York: Wiley, 1944); Charles W. Lytle, *Wage Incentive Plans* (New York: Ronald Press, 1942); Herbert G. Zollitsch and Adolph Langsner, *Wage and Salary Administration* (2d ed., Cincinnati: Southwestern Publishing, 1970).

See also INCENTIVE WAGE.

one-man town The term generally is used as the equivalent of a company town where a single company, corporation, or a large industrialist owns the plant facilities, the company store, the housing, and other facilities primarily because the plant is located in an isolated community.

The company town became objectionable because it led in effect to the domination and exploitation of the workers in a particular community. Company ownership of the property and frequently company police made protection of the rights of individuals a real concern. In many areas civil rights were denied, particularly when efforts were made by the employees to protest conditions which they felt were objectionable or when they sought to bring about changes through unionization.

Source references: Marquis W. Childs, *This Is Democracy* (New Haven: Yale UP, 1938); Robert W. Dunn, *Company Unions: Employers' Industrial Democracy* (New York: Vanguard, 1927); Leifur Magnusson, *Housing by Employers in the United States* (Washington: U.S. Dept. of Labor, BLS, Bull. no. 263, 1920).

See also CIVIL LIBERTIES; COMPANY TOWN; PATERNALISM, EMPLOYER.

one-thousand-hour clause A provision in Section 7(b)(1) of the original Fair Labor Standards Act (Wage and Hour Law) which allowed unions to negotiate up to 12 hours a day and 56 hours a week at regular rather than overtime rates provided the contract or collective bargaining agreement specified that individuals covered under the agreement would not be required to work more than 1,000 hours in any consecutive 26 weeks. This exception permitted work schedules which did not apply the overtime rates up to 12 hours a day and 56 hours a week.

See also FAIR LABOR STANDARDS ACT OF 1938, GUARANTEED ANNUAL WAGE, TWO-THOUSAND-HOUR CLAUSE.

one-to-one organization A form of personnel structure in which supervision is direct supervision of one employee over the work of another employee. Possible only in very small shops.

one-year rule A policy adopted by the NLRB allowing a union certified as the exclusive bargaining agent for employees to establish its collective bargaining relationship within a reasonable period of time. This period was set at one year and acted as a bar to other unions which sought to obtain an election to challenge the representation of that union. The Taft-Hartley amendments provided that only one election can be ordered within the 12-month period immediately following the last valid election.

The Board under exceptional circumstances may set what it considers to be an appropriate time quite apart from its general rule.

Source reference: General Cable Corporation, 139 NLRB 1123, 51 LRRM 1444 (1962).

See also CERTIFICATION, CONTRACT-BAR RULE, DECERTIFICATION, TWO-YEAR RULE.

on-site labor Labor employed at the actual site of a construction project as distinguished from labor indirectly associated with the activities of the project, as in the production and delivery of materials and equipment.

on-the-job training (OJT) A procedure which utilizes the actual job or work site as the place at which an individual receives instruction while at the same time engaging in productive work.

Training on the job is the most commonly used method of training. The training can be performed by having the individual work with an experienced worker, using the same tools, equipment, and material as the experienced employee. Another form of instruction may be through a specially trained instructor who devotes time to tutoring the trainee while performing on the job. The training may be performed by the trainee's immediate supervisor who is familiar with the job.

Other forms of instruction may be supplemental to on-the-job training. These may involve classroom study or special reading to help the individual perform the job more effectively. The major training, however, is done on the job site under actual working conditions.

The on-the-job training program, authorized by the Manpower Development and Training Act of 1962, was designed to give job skills to the unemployed and the underemployed, and workers whose jobs were endangered by changing technology. Trainees were selected by the employer either from a panel of unemployed persons tested and referred by the local state employment service, or from the employer's own sources for new help. Groups sponsoring OJT programs were reimbursed for such costs as wages and salaries of instructors, instructional materials, damaged or spoiled production material, and rented equipment or space, when necessary. The on-the-job training concept has been incorporated into many of the federally sponsored programs, including Job Corps, Neighborhood Youth Corps, Operation Mainstream, the Comprehensive Employment and Training Act (CETA), and the Job Training Partnership Act (JTPA). JTPA, the successor to CETA, continues the provisions allowing for reimbursement to OJT program providers to aid economically disadvantaged and hard-to-employ individuals.

Source references: AMA, *On-the-Job Training* (New York: 1965); ———, *On the Job Training: Making the Most of Manpower, Selected Reprints from AMA Periodicals* (New York: 1962–1968); Delbert W. Fisher, "Educational Psychology Involved in On-the-Job Training," *PJ*, Oct. 1977; Thomas F. Gilbert, "The High Cost of Knowledge," *Personnel*, March/April 1976; Morley Gunderson, "Determinants of Individual Success in On-the-Job Training," *Journal of Human Resources*, Fall 1973; Saul D. Hoffman, "On-the-Job Training: Differences by Race and Sex," *MLR*, July 1981; Arthur D. Kellner, On-Job-Training—Fertile Ground for Managers," *PJ*, Dec. 1961; Jacob Mincer, "On-the-Job Training: Costs, Returns and Some Implications," *Journal of Political Economy*, Oct. 1962; Michael L. Moore and C. George Johnson, "Bona Fide Training Programs: The Legal Basis," *LLJ*, Feb. 1977; Paul Ryan, "The Costs of Job Training for a Transferable Skill," *BJIR*, Nov. 1980; U.S. Dept. of Labor, ETA, *On-the-Job Training and the Private Industry Council: A Technical Assistance Guide*

(Washington: 1980); ———, *On-the-Job Training: CETA Program Models* (Washington: 1977); Robert E. Wenig and William D. Wolansky, *Review and Synthesis of Literature on Job Training in Industry* (Columbus: Ohio State Univ., Center for Vocational and Technical Education, 1972); William D. White and Anthony Robbins, "Role of On-the-Job Training in a Clinical Laboratory," *MLR*, March 1971.

See also TRAINING, TRAINING WITHIN INDUSTRY.

open door principle The principle that it should be possible for any employee to speak to any of the employer's executives, including the chief executive or president, on any matter which is of concern to the employee, including the handling of personal grievances.

Although such a principle is laudatory, it is impossible to administer it in plants of any size or companies which have thousands of employees on the payroll. It also creates difficulties because it may suggest bypassing existing channels of communication and under normal circumstances would create substantial difficulty. On the other hand, it is desirable that there be an opportunity to reach the chief executive or the person in authority after reviews at lower levels.

The Taft-Hartley Act made provision for the right of individual employees or groups of employees to present grievances to their employer and to have those grievances adjusted without the intervention of the collective bargaining representative. It provided that any adjustment made must be consistent with the collective bargaining agreement negotiated by the union which is the exclusive bargaining representative and also that the union agent be present when disposition is made of the personal grievance.

See also GRIEVANCE, GRIEVANCE COMMITTEE, GRIEVANCE MACHINERY, INDIVIDUAL BARGAINING.

open-end agreement A collective bargaining contract with no termination or expiration date. A duration during which the contract is binding is set forth in the agreement with the understanding that negotiations may be reopened or the agreement terminated at any time by either party with advance notice.

Source reference: CCH, *Union Contract Clauses* (Chicago: 1954).

open-end clause (open-end wage clause) A provision in a collective bargaining agreement which, although fixed for a period of time, is still open for adjustments of wages under certain conditions. The most frequent type of open-end clause is the so-called escalator or cost-of-living clause, which provides for upward adjustment in case of rising prices, or an established ratio related to rising prices, so the actual monetary income will be equivalent to the real income. (Some writers hold that an escalator clause is not an "open-end" clause since there is a fixed relationship between wage adjustments and the consumer price index.)

The open-end clause is not limited merely to adjustments due to changes in prices, but may permit the reopening of the contract on the wage issue under certain other circumstances.

The phrase is sometimes applied to the entire agreement, for example, when the contract has no set expiration date.

Source references: Lee H. Hill and Charles R. Hook, Jr., *Management at the Bargaining Table* (New York: McGraw-Hill, 1945); Twentieth Century Fund, *How Collective Bargaining Works* (New York: 1942); Benjamin Werne, *The Law of Labor Relations* (New York: Macmillan, 1951).

See also CONSUMER PRICE INDEX, ESCALATOR CLAUSE.

open house A procedure used by companies to provide an opportunity for the community, patrons, family, and friends of the worker to become familiar with the company and to establish a sense of pride in the company, its products, and programs. It is a combination of a conducted tour, a reception, and a party.

In many areas, it has the role of a social function in which many people in the community get together. In addition it induces individuals from other areas to become familiar with the company, the various jobs in the plant, the individuals who actually do the work, and the kind of products being produced.

Source references: M. B. Andrews, "Open House: The Way to an Open Heart," *Textile World*, July 1952; Robert Newcomb and Marg

Sammons, "Modern Look for the Open House," *Personnel*, March/April 1968; "Open House That Opens Eyes," *Mill and Factory*, Nov. 1950; "Ten Practical Tips on Running Open House," *Factory Management*, Dec. 1952.

open shop A plant in which, in theory, workers are employed regardless of union affiliation. However, in American labor history, it appears that as a practical matter shops which were "open shops" generally were open to nonunion workers but not open to union members. Many unions felt that the open shop in effect was closed to union members.

The open shop drives during 1903–1916 and during the 1920s were basically anti-union and the conditions of employment established in open shops were designed primarily to eliminate unions in those places or to prevent their entrance. William M. Leiserson, in his article on the "Closed Shop and Open Shop" in *Unions, Management and the Public*, said in part: "An open shop, according to its formal definition, is a place where workers are employed regardless of union affiliation and where unionists and non-unionists may work without discrimination. This formal definition is intended to imply a certain ethical superiority for the open shop over the closed shop, and employers who are opposed to labor unions attempt to press this advantage still further by presenting the use of the term 'American Plan' as a synonym for open shop. It is to be noted that a place that is closed to union members, where none but non-unionists may work, is commonly called an open shop."

A rather popular quotation taken from an article by F. P. Dunne, entitled "Mr. Dooley on the Open Shop" in *Unions, Management and the Public*, reads as follows:

> "What's all this that's in the papers about the open shop?" asked Mr. Hennessey.
>
> "Why, don't ye know?" said Mr. Dooley. "Really, I'm surprised at yer ignorance, Hinnissey. What is th' open shop? Sure, 'tis where they kape the doors open to accomodate th' constant stream av' min comin' in t' take jobs cheaper than th' min what has th' jobs. 'Tis like this, Hinnissey: Suppose wan av these freeborn citizens is workin' in an open shop f'r th' princely wage av wan large iron dollar a day av tin hours. Along comes anither son-av-gun and he sez t' th' boss, 'Oi think Oi could handle th' job nicely f'r ninety cints.' 'Sure,' sez th' boss, and th' wan dollar man gets out into th' crool woruld t' exercise hiz inalienable roights as a freeborn American citizen an' scab on some other poor devil. An' so it goes on Hinnissey. An' who gits th' benefit? Thrue, it saves th' boss money, but he don't care no more f'r money thin he does his right eye.
>
> "It's all principle wid him. He hates t' see men robbed av their indipindence. They must have their indipindence, regardless av anything else."
>
> "But," said Mr. Hennessey, "these open-shop min ye menshun say they are f'r unions if properly conducted."
>
> "Shure," said Mr. Dooley, "if properly conducted. An' there we are: an' how would they have them conducted? No strikes, no rules, no contracts, no scales, hardly iny wages, an' dam' few mimbers."

Source references: E. Wight Bakke, Clark Kerr, and Charles W. Anrod (ed.), *Unions, Management and the Public* (3d ed., New York: Harcourt, Brace, 1967); "The Employer's Stake in the Open Shop," *American Federationist*, May 1976; Harold U. Faulkner and Mark Starr, *Labor in America* (New York: Harper, 1944); Norman Hill, "The Double-Speak of Right-to-Work," *American Federationist*, Oct. 1980; Julia E. Johnsen (comp.), *The Closed Shop* (New York: Wilson, 1942); Richard Lester, *Economics of Labor* (2d ed., New York: Macmillan, 1964); Ernest F. Lloyd, *The Closed Union Shop v. The Open Shop: Their Social and Economic Values Compared* (New York: NICB, 1920); Edwin C. Robbins (comp.), *Selected Articles on the Open Shop v. Closed Shop* (Minneapolis: Wilson, Debaters Handbook Series, 1911); Jean E. Spielman, *The Stool Pigeon and the Open Shop Movement* (Minneapolis: American Publishing, 1923).

See also AMERICAN PLAN, AMERICAN SHOP, CLOSED SHOP, INDEPENDENT AMERICAN SHOP, UNION SECURITY CLAUSES.

open shop drive A campaign spearheaded by various major national employer associations to reduce union activity and to install the so-called "American Plan" which in effect was to keep the unions from obtaining any measure of strength within the plants. The two major open shop drives occurred from 1903 to

1916 and during the 1920s following World War I.

The following quotation from Philip Taft describing the open shop drive in the early part of the century is of interest.

> The tocsin of revolt against the encroachment of organized labor was sounded by David N. Parry, president of the National Association of Manufacturers, in 1903. Under his leadership, the Association became the most vociferous opponent of unionism in the United States. A "declaration of principles," affirming a belief in the open shop as the most desirable and efficient type of employment, was issued by the Convention of 1903.
>
> Since that time the N.A.M. has been a steadfast opponent of unionism. It played an important role in the organizing of the Citizens' Industrial Association of America which, after its inception in 1903, became the spearhead of the first extensive open shop drive. In 1907 the N.A.M. sponsored another and more inclusive anti-union group, the National Council of Industrial Defense. . . . In a later statement on employment relations, the N.A.M. emphasized its opposition to the closed shop on the grounds that it regarded the closed shop as a denial of freedom and equality of opportunity. Instead, the Association advocated the true open shop which discriminates neither against members or nonmembers of labor unions.

Source references: Marjorie Clark and Fanny Simon, *The Labor Movement in America* (New York: Norton, 1938); Edward Levinson, *Labor on the March* (New York: Harper, 1938); Philip Taft, *Economics and Problems of Labor* (3d ed., Harrisburg: Stackpole, 1955).

open trade A condition in a particular job area or occupation or trade which does not limit entry.

See also APPRENTICESHIP.

open union A labor organization that grants membership to all qualified employees. It also contemplates that membership not be limited by either high or prohibitive initiation fees or special membership requirements which are impossible or unreasonable and that there be no discrimination because of race, sex, national origin, and any other prohibitive rule or regulation.

Source references: John R. Commons, *History of Labor in the United States* (New York: Macmillan, 1935); "The Extension of Collective Agreements to Cover Entire Trades and Industries," *ILR*, Aug. 1939; Philip S. Foner, *History of the Labor Movement in the United States* (4 vol., New York: International Publishers, 1947, 1955, 1964, 1965); Robert F. Hoxie, *Trade Unionism in the United States* (New York: Appleton-Century, 1920); Julia E. Johnsen (ed.), *Industrial Versus Craft Unionism* (New York: Wilson, 1937); L. E. Lasch, "The Validity of Agreements to Employ Union Labor Exclusively," 3 *Temple LQ* 421 (1929); Joel Seidman, *Union Rights and Union Duties* (New York: Harcourt, Brace, 1943); Sumner H. Slichter, *The Challenge of Industrial Relations—Trade Unions, Management, and the Public Interest* (Ithaca: Cornell UP, 1947); Jerome T. Toner, *The Closed Shop* (Washington: American Council on Public Affairs, 1942).

See also CLOSED UNION, LABOR-MANAGEMENT REPORTING AND DISCLOSURE ACT OF 1959.

Operating Engineers; International Union of (AFL-CIO) Organized in St. Louis, Mo., in 1896 as the National Steam Engineers' Union. The name was changed to the International Union of Steam Engineers in 1905 and to the International Union of Steam and Operating Engineers in 1915. In 1915 the American Federation of Labor granted a charter to steamshovel and dredge men. The Engineers opposed this as a dual organization. Following objection by the Engineers, the AFL ordered the steamshovel men to join the Engineers. When they failed to obey the order they were expelled. In 1927 an amalgamation of the two organizations (Brotherhood of Steam Shovel and Dredge Men and the International Union of Steam and Operating Engineers) took place and it adopted its new name, the International Union of Operating Engineers, in 1928.

On March 1, 1969, the International Union, United Weldors (Ind) merged with the Engineers. The union's monthly publication is *The International Operating Engineer.*

Address: 1125 17th St., N.W., Washington, D.C. 20006. Tel. (202) 429–9100

Source references: Garth L. Mangum, "The Development of Local Union Jurisdiction in the International Union of Operating Engineers," *Labor History*, Fall 1963; ———, *The Operating Engineers: The Eco-*

nomic History of a Trade Union (Cambridge: Harvard UP, 1964).

operating union Refers to those unions representing railroad workers "engaged in the actual physical movement of trains and cars," as contrasted to the nonoperating unions. These unions were sometimes referred to as the "Big Five."

Source reference: Jacob J. Kaufman, *Collective Bargaining in the Railroad Industry* (New York: King's Crown Press, 1954).

See also NONOPERATING UNION, RAILROAD BROTHERHOODS.

Operation Mainstream Program authorized by the 1965 amendments to the Economic Opportunity Act to provide permanent jobs at decent wages for older and chronically unemployed workers. Designed for rural areas and towns, the projects concentrated on work experience and training activities. The program also sought to improve communities and low-income areas by rehabilitation of slum housing, air and water pollution control, improvement of parks, protection of wildlife, and extension of education, health, and social services. To be eligible for the program, individuals had to be at least 22 years of age with an annual family income below the poverty level.

Under the administration of the Office of Economic Opportunity, the program was known as the "Nelson Programs." It was transferred to the Department of Labor in 1967. The Economic Opportunity Act was repealed with the enactment of the Comprehensive Employment and Training Act in 1973.

Source references: Pat Thompson, "Operation Mainstream: Franklin County, Washington," *American County Government*, Feb. 1969; U.S. Dept. of HEW, Office of Education, *Federal Programs in Job Training and Retraining* (Washington: 1967); U.S. Dept. of Labor, *Manpower Report of the President, 1969* (Washington: 1969).

operative A spy employed by an agency who may be either a "hooked man" or a professional spy.

opinion survey A method of inquiry used by personnel managers to obtain information about the basic attitudes of various groups of employees within the organization. The purpose of the opinion survey is to give the executives a better understanding of the attitudes of individual employees toward particular programs and policies. In addition, it supplies the supervision or executive group with some indication of the extent to which the company's policies are being accepted, rejected, or merely not implemented. The opinion-attitude survey, if it properly reflects the concern of individual employees, can serve a very positive function for management in promoting its policies, programs, and objectives.

Source references: Michael R. Cooper, "Warning: Traditional Employee Attitude Surveys Don't Work," *Management Review*, Aug. 1982; Robyn M. Dawes, *Fundamentals of Attitude Measurement* (New York: Wiley, 1972); William H. Fonvielle, "Making Employee Surveys Work for *Your* Organization," *Management Review*, April 1982; Mitchell Lee Marks, "Conducting an Employee Attitude Survey," *PJ*, Sept. 1982; John McCollum, "Union-Management Sponsored Employee Attitude Survey: Some Implications and Results of a Case Study," *Proceedings of the 8th A/M, IRRA*, ed. by L. Reed Tripp (Madison: 1956); C. R. McPherson, "That Employee Opinion Survey," *PJ*, Nov. 1959; William Penzer, "Employee Attitudes Toward Attitude Surveys," *Personnel*, May/June 1973; U.S. OPM, *Federal Employee Attitudes. Phase 1: Baseline Survey 1979 Government-Wide Report* (Washington: 1980); Leland G. Verheyen and Louis Olivas, "Attitude Survey Supports Training Needs," *Public Personnel Management*, Jan./Feb. 1980; Alfred Vogel, "Employee Surveys: The Risks, the Benefits," *Personnel*, Jan./Feb. 1982; John H. Wakeley, "One Way to Get Meaningful Results from Attitude Surveys," *Personnel*, Nov./Dec. 1964; Bruce C. Wheatley and William B. Cash, "The Employee Survey: Correcting Its Basic Weakness," *PJ*, June 1973.

See also ATTITUDE MEASUREMENT, MORALE SURVEY.

oppressive child labor This has generally been defined under the Fair Labor Standards Act as work by children under 16 years of age in "nonexcepted occupations" or work by minors under 18 years of age in "hazardous occupations."

Source references: Fair Labor Standards Act of 1938, as amended, 29 U.S.C. 212 (1982); Paul T. David, *Barriers to Youth Employment* (Washington: American Council of Education, 1942).

See also CHILD LABOR, FAIR LABOR STANDARDS ACT OF 1938.

oppressive labor practices Activities of trade unions which, in cases of early organization and frequently during periods of serious strikes, involve violence, sabotage, and other coercive activities which go beyond the persuasion and peaceful picketing allowed by law. The term also refers to those strong arm or pressure tactics of trade unions which are sufficient to force compliance by employers, or practices of some unions which border on racketeering.

See also LABOR-MANAGEMENT REPORTING AND DISCLOSURE ACT OF 1959, MCCLELLAN COMMITTEE.

Optical and Instrument Workers of America; United (CIO) The union requested that its CIO charter be withdrawn in March 1954. Some of the locals joined the International Union of Electrical, Radio and Machine Workers (CIO) and the United Glass and Ceramic Workers of North America (CIO).

Oregon Anti-Picketing Act A law passed by Oregon in 1938 which was an extremely rigid and severe anti-picketing statute. It was held invalid by the Oregon Supreme Court in 1940.

The U.S. Supreme Court has, in a number of instances, held ordinances prohibiting picketing to be unconstitutional.

See also NORRIS-LAGUARDIA ACT.

Oregon Public Employees Association A former affiliate of the Assembly of Governmental Employees. It was previously known as the Oregon State Employees Association (Ind), and issued the monthly *Oregon State Employee News*. In November 1980, the Association merged with the Service Employees' International Union (AFL-CIO).

Oregon School Employees Association (Ind) An organization affiliated with the American Association of Classified School Employees (Ind). Its official monthly publication is the *Journal*.

Address: 821 Saginau South, P.O. Box 3011, Salem, Ore. 97302. Tel. (503) 588–0121

organizational picketing A form of picketing engaged in by a union whose purpose is to persuade the employer or employer organization to accept it as the bargaining agent for employees. The Landrum-Griffin Act of 1959 amended the National Labor Relations Act and placed certain restrictions on organizational picketing.

Source references: William J. Isaacson, "Organizational Picketing: What Is the Law?—Ought the Law to Be Changed?" 8 *Buffalo LR* 345 (1959); Bernard D. Meltzer, "Organizational Picketing and the NLRB: Five on a See-saw," *Univ. of Chicago LR*, Autumn 1962; " 'Recognitional' Picketing in the Garment Industry—Garment Unions Granted Protected Status Under Section 8(b)(7)(C) of the National Labor Relations Act—*Danielson v. Joint Board of Coat, Suit & Allied Garment Workers' Union, ILGWU*, 494. F.2d 1230 (2d Cir. 1974)," *IR Law Digest*, April 1976.

See also LAUF V. E. G. SHINNER & CO., INC.

Organization for Economic Co-Operation and Development (OECD) Established under the Marshall Plan in 1948 as the Organization for European Economic Cooperation (OEEC) "to ensure that the war-ravaged countries would work together toward their economic recovery." With the achievement of economic recovery, the United States and Canada joined the 18 OEEC nations and formed the Organization for Economic Co-Operation and Development (OECD) on December 14, 1960. Japan, Finland, Australia, New Zealand, and Yugoslavia later joined the OECD. The body seeks to promote economic growth of all nations and to contribute to expansion of world trade. The OECD provides for the international exchange of information through conferences and research studies.

Address: 2, rue Andre-Pascal, 75775 Paris Cedex 16, France.

Source references: Roger Blanpain (ed.), *Comparative Labour Law and Industrial Relations* (Washington: BNA, 1982); Duncan C. Campbell and Richard L. Rowan, *Multina-*

tional Enterprises and the OECD Industrial Relations Guidelines (Philadelphia: Univ. of Pennsylvania, Wharton School, Industrial Research Unit, Multinational IR Series no. 11, 1983).

Organization Resources Counselors, Inc. "A nonprofit research and educational organization established in 1926 and dedicated by its charter 'to advance the knowledge and practice of human relationships in industry, commerce, education and government.' " It issues occasional publications and for many years published a weekly digest of news and developments in the field of industrial relations, entitled *Current News*, which was discontinued in 1968. In February 1969 it began the publication of *I.R. Concepts*. Prior to 1970 the organization was known as Industrial Relations Counselors, Inc.

Address: 1211 Avenue of the Americas, New York, N.Y. 10036. Tel. (212) 719–3400

organization structure The organization structure is the general framework through which work is organized, responsibilities established, lines of communication, responsibility, and direction determined, and coordination of activities so established as to permit the particular organization to accomplish its purposes.

organized labor A term frequently used to distinguish that segment of labor that is unionized rather than nonunionized. The term also is used generically to describe the structure of labor organizations or the labor movement in a particular country.

Source references: Morris L. Cooke and Philip Murray, *Organized Labor and Production* (New York: Harper, 1946); Henry Mayer, "Organized Labor's Dilemma," *LLJ*, Aug. 1962; Katherine B. Shippen, *This Union Cause: The Growth of Organized Labor in America* (New York: Harper, 1958).

See also LABOR MOVEMENT, LABOR ORGANIZATION.

organizers In union parlance, organizers are individuals active in signing up employees for union membership and in getting workers in a plant to assist in informing other workers of union goals and objectives and the long-range, and sometimes immediate, benefits that may be obtained through union organization and membership.

The term "organizers" of course applies equally to management individuals except that the term there is essentially applied to individuals who have skill in utilizing manpower, materials, equipment, and financial and other resources for the purpose of production or for the advancement of a particular objective of the organization.

Source references: AFL-CIO, *A Guidebook for Union Organizers* (Washington: Industrial Union Department, Pub. no. 42, 1961); Robert R. R. Brooks, *When Labor Organizes* (New Haven: Yale UP, 1937); Ernest Dale, *The Great Organizers* (New York: McGraw-Hill, 1960); Philip S. Foner, "Journal of an Early Labor Organizer," *Labor History*, Spring 1969; George W. Hartmann and Theodore Newcomb (ed.), "An Employer and an Organizer View the Same Series of Conflicts," *Industrial Conflict: A Psychological Interpretation* (New York: Cordon, 1939); Howard M. Leftwich, "Organizing in the Eighties: A Human Resources Perspective," *LLJ*, Aug. 1981; Max Zimny, "Access of Union Organizers to 'Private' Property," *LLJ*, Oct. 1974.

See also LABOR ORGANIZER.

organizing In union parlance, organizing refers to the actual efforts made by organizers and their superiors in achieving union objectives.

In management usage, it refers to the process of assembling all the needed resources incidental to the achievement of the organization's objectives.

Source references: Richard N. Block, "Union Organizing and the Allocation of Union Resources," *ILRR*, Oct. 1980; Harry A. Donoian, "Organization Problems of Government Employee Unions," *LLJ*, March 1967; Edward S. Haines and Alan Kistler, "The Techniques of Organizing," *American Federationist*, July 1967; Alan Kistler and Charles McDonald, "The Continuing Challenge of Organizing," *American Federationist*, Nov. 1976; Joseph Krislov, "Union Organizing of New Units, 1955–1966," *ILRR*, Oct. 1967; Joseph Al Latham, Jr., "Susceptibility to a Successful Union Organizing Campaign—The Seven Warning Signals," *Employee Relations LJ*, Autumn 1980; John

W. Livingston, "Organizing—Labor's First Mission," *American Federationist*, April 1959; Richard Prosten, "The Longest Season: Union Organizing in the Last Decade, a/k/a How Come One Team Has to Play With Its Shoelaces Tied Together?" *Proceedings of the 31st A/M, IRRA*, ed. by Barbara Dennis (Madison: 1979); Stephen I. Schlossberg and Frederick E. Sherman, *Organizing and the Law* (3d ed., Washington: BNA, 1983); Ron Shumsky, "Incentive Systems in Union Organizing," *Industrial and Labor Relations Forum*, Jan. 1981.

orientation Orientation refers to the efforts and procedures adopted by an organization to acquaint and integrate a new employee into the work environment. It may be a very complex process for certain jobs, or it may be relatively simple where the person's responsibilities are minor or where the job is reasonably simple.

Source references: BNA, *Orientation of New Employees* (Washington: PPF Survey no. 60, 1961); Daniel C. Feldman, "A Socialization Process That Helps New Recruits Succeed," *Personnel*, March/April 1980; George B. Graen, J. Burdeane Orris, and Thomas W. Johnson, *Role Assimilation Processes in a Complex Organization* (Champaign: Univ. of Illinois, Institute of Labor and IR, Reprint Series no. 231, 1973); Robert W. Hollmann, "Let's Not Forget About New Employee Orientation," *PJ*, May 1976; Murray Lubliner, "Employee Orientation," *PJ*, April 1978; William Penzer, "Employee Orientation: Does It Relieve Pain or Create It?" *Management Review*, July 1973; Walter D. St. John, "The Complete Employee Orientation Program," *PJ*, May 1980.

See also INDUCTION.

outlaw strike A work stoppage or strike which has been forbidden by law or which has been called without union authorization.

In common usage, an outlaw strike is generally regarded as a work stoppage by union members not properly authorized by the union.

The outlaw strike is sometimes referred to as an illegal strike, although the term "illegal strike" is more frequently applied to strikes that are forbidden by law, whereas the "wildcat strike" is one that has not been authorized by the union and one that has not received proper sanction under the union's constitution or bylaws.

Source reference: Arthur Kornhauser, Robert Dubin, and Arthur M. Ross, *Industrial Conflict* (New York: McGraw-Hill, 1954).

See also ILLEGAL STRIKE, WILDCAT STRIKE.

out-of-line rates In operations which bear incentive or piece rates, it is possible for an individual rate to allow more than normal earnings for the particular job. This can be due to changing technology or improper or faulty rate setting. During the wage stabilization period of World War II incentive rates often were set loosely and tended to result in earnings far beyond normal expectations. An out-of-line rate, however, generally applies to a single or related rate rather than to loose rate setting, which applies to an entire department or plant and is designed in part to provide greater earnings. It is generally expected that jobs with similar requirements and similar rates established through time and motion study will yield similar earnings.

The term is also sometimes used to refer to rates which are "out-of-line" with rates for comparable jobs in a locality or other plants performing similar work.

See also RED CIRCLE RATE.

out-of-work benefits Prior to the development of unemployment insurance, it was a common practice for unions to try to establish benefit funds to assist members during periods of high unemployment. Such union attempts often involved special exemptions from regular dues payments and, whenever union treasuries permitted, the extension of special loans.

In most cases, however, out-of-work benefits when provided were relatively meager and in major unemployment cases, the union's financial situation was such as to make prohibitive any really effective assistance to its members.

See also UNEMPLOYMENT INSURANCE.

outplacement Employer assistance to aid employees in job search and relocation due to layoff or discharge. An outplacement program may include formal classroom training in resumé preparation, interviewing and job search techniques, and career change counseling. It may include the services of a professional outplacement or executive search firm.

Source references: William J. Broussard and Robert J. DeLargey, "The Dynamics of the Group Outplacement Workshop," *PJ*, Dec. 1979; Judson Gooding, "Out-Placement . . . How it Eases the Shock on an Executive Who is Being Fired," *Across the Board*, April 1979; Deborah Meyers and Lee M. Abrahamson, "Firing with Finesse: A Rationale for Outplacement," *PJ*, Aug. 1975; John Scherba, "Outplacement as a Personnel Responsibility," *Personnel*, May/June 1973; Donald H. Sweet, "Something New in Personnel: 'Out-Placement'," *PJ*, July 1971.

output A term generally applied to the amount of production measured either in the form of physical units or in the form of the dollar value of the product.

In recent years, efforts have been made to measure income and wealth through the use of input and output measurements, and to establish models that accurately measure the effectiveness of the economy.

Source reference: NBER, *Output, Input and Productivity Measurement* (New York: Studies in Income and Wealth, Vol. 25, Princeton UP, 1961).

See also RESTRICTION OF OUTPUT.

output, restriction of *See* RESTRICTION OF OUTPUT.

output per hour (labor productivity) A measure of productivity established primarily by the federal government and compiled regularly by BLS, U.S. Department of Labor. Agricultural estimates of productivity are compiled by the Economic Research Service of the Department of Agriculture. Annual indexes have been compiled by selected industries and industry groups since 1941 and figures for the private economy as a whole have been issued since 1909.

According to the *BLS Handbook of Methods*, "output per hour measures are constructed as the ratio between gross domestic product—GDP—originating in the private business economy and its subsectors, and the corresponding hours of all persons engaged in each sector. The changes through time in these major indexes reflect efficiency in the use of labor, and indirectly, the effect of other input factors in the domestic production of goods and services."

Source references: Sylvia B. Gottlieb, "Output Per Man-Hour in the Private Economy, 1947–63," *MLR*, April 1964; U.S. Dept. of Labor, BLS, *BLS Handbook of Methods, Volume 1* (Washington: Bull. 2134–1, 1982).

See also PRODUCTIVE CAPACITY, MEASURES OF; PRODUCTIVITY.

outside agitators During organizational campaigns in the early history of American labor, this term was frequently used as a label for union organizers by members of anti-union or strongly nonunion communities.

See also AGITATOR.

Overseas Education Association, Inc. A branch of the National Education Association (Ind). Its monthly publication is *OEA Washington Journal.*

Address: 1201 16th St., N.W., Room 210, Washington, D.C. 20036. Tel. (202) 822–7850

overtime The hours worked by an employee in excess of the standard established by law, by the collective bargaining agreement, or by company policy. Hours in excess of the standard are generally paid for in "penalty" or overtime rates. Frequently, the rate is one and one-half times the actual rate.

The Fair Labor Standards Act established basic weekly hours and set premium or overtime rates beyond those hours, except in exempted industries, or where other conditions are met under the provisions of the law.

Source references: Ronald G. Ehrenberg, *Fringe Benefits and Overtime Behavior; Theoretical and Econometric Analysis* (Lexington, Mass.: Lexington Books, 1971); Robert D. Leiter, "The Principle of Overtime," *LLJ*, Jan. 1951; Joseph Mathewson, "How Companies Are Cutting Overtime," *Management Review*, Aug. 1965; Frederic Meyers, "The Economics of Overtime," *Hours of Work*, ed. by Clyde E. Dankert et al. (New York: Harper, IRRA pub. no. 32, 1965); Diane N. Westcott, "Trends in Overtime Hours and Pay, 1969–74," *MLR*, Feb. 1975.

See also COMPENSATORY TIME OFF, COOLIE OVERTIME, DOUBLETIME, FAIR LABOR STANDARDS ACT OF 1938, ONE-THOUSAND-HOUR CLAUSE, PREMIUM PAY, PYRAMIDING, TWO-THOUSAND-HOUR CLAUSE.

overtime-on-overtime Under the provisions of the Fair Labor Standards Act employees were entitled to receive overtime pay for hours in excess of 40 in one week. Under some procedures and collective bargaining agreements, employees received premium rates for night work, weekends, holidays, meal periods, and so on. They argued that these special rates, which were essentially for undesirable hours or other conditions, should be considered as part of the "regular rate of pay" and that the overtime premium should be on top of this regular rate of pay. Employers objected and argued that this would be payment of overtime on overtime. When the issue came before the Supreme Court in 1948 in the *Bay Ridge* case, the Court upheld the position of the union that these special premiums for undesirable work and night work should be considered as part of the regular rate of pay for the regular hours, and that the premium must be additional.

As the result of the opposition of employers and their claim that many suits were being instituted for pay for previous years, the Congress in July 1949 amended the Fair Labor Standards Act to avoid the impact of the Supreme Court's overtime-on-overtime interpretation.

Source reference: John S. Bugas, *Double Overtime Pay, Statement Before Committee on Labor and Public Welfare, U.S. Senate, July 8, 1965* (Detroit: Auto Manufacturers Association, 1965).

See also BAY RIDGE CASE, FAIR LABOR STANDARDS ACT OF 1938.

overtime pay The payment of a premium for hours generally worked in excess of eight in one day or 40 in one week. Many contracts also provide for premium pay or overtime pay for holidays, Saturdays, and Sundays, regardless of the number of hours worked during the week. This is a form of premium pay but not actually overtime pay, although presumably the hours actually worked on the Saturdays, Sundays, or holidays would be in excess of those worked during the regular week.

Source references: "Doubletime Pay to Spread Employment," *American Federationist*, July 1965; Ronald G. Ehrenberg and Paul L. Schumann, *Compensating Wage Differentials for Mandatory Overtime* (Cambridge: NBER, WP no. 805, 1981); John Fenlon, "Patterns in Overtime Hours and Premium Pay," *MLR*, Oct. 1969; J. Carroll Swart and Robert A. Quakenbush, "Unions' Views Concerning Alternative Work Schedules and Proposals to Alter Federal Overtime Pay Legislation," *Proceedings of the 30th A/M, IRRA*, ed. by Barbara Dennis (Madison: 1978); Burton W. Teague, *Overtime Pay Practices for Exempt Employees* (New York: The Conference Board, Report 797, 1981); U.S. Dept. of Labor, Employment Standards Administration, *Overtime Compensation Under the Fair Labor Standards Act* (Washington: WH Pub. 1325, 1978); David A. Weeks, *Overtime Pay for Exempt Employees* (New York: NICB, Studies in Personnel Policy no. 208, 1967); James R. Wetzel, "Overtime Hours and Premium Pay," *MLR*, May 1967; ———, "Overtime Hours and Premium Pay, May 1965," *MLR*, Sept. 1966.

See also COOLIE OVERTIME, PREMIUM PAY.

overtime premium pay The term is synonymous with the phrase "actual overtime rate"; it denotes the payment of wages at a premium rate for hours worked beyond or outside the regular hours in the establishment—a rate set either by law, industry practice, collective bargaining agreement, or employer policy. Premium rates generally are one and one-half times the regular rate of pay, although some premiums may be set at double time.

overtime rate The wage rates actually set by contract, by statute, or by company policy for hours worked in excess of or outside the regularly scheduled workday, workweek, shift, etc.

overtime work The actual hours put in by an employee in excess of the regularly scheduled work time.

overwork A situation in which workers, in the performance of their jobs, exceed the limits of physical and mental endurance. Overwork may result from excessive hours of work, from the unusual speed or pace required of a job, or from inadequate rest periods. It may also be due to working conditions incidental to the nature of the work, to pressures exerted by supervision, and to other factors some of which may simply cause an employee to feel overworked.

Concern with excessive strain has led to efforts by unions to safeguard working conditions, particularly in the use of machines and automatic belt conveyors. Unions have negotiated safeguards to prevent employees from being worked beyond their normal limitations.

See also FATIGUE, STRESS.

P

PAICC *See* INTERSTATE COMMERCE COMMISSION; PROFESSIONAL ASSOCIATION OF THE (IND).

PAT *See* PAINTERS AND ALLIED TRADES OF THE UNITED STATES AND CANADA; INTERNATIONAL BROTHERHOOD OF (AFL-CIO).

PATCO *See* PROFESSIONAL AIR TRAFFIC CONTROLLERS ORGANIZATION.

PAYSOP *See* PAYROLL-BASED EMPLOYEE STOCK OWNERSHIP PLAN (PAYSOP).

PBGC *See* PENSION BENEFIT GUARANTY CORP. (PBGC).

PERT *See* PROGRAM EVALUATION AND REVIEW TECHNIQUE (PERT).

PGW *See* PLANT GUARD WORKERS OF AMERICA; INTERNATIONAL UNION, UNITED (IND).

PH *See* PRENTICE-HALL, INC.

PIC *See* PRIVATE INDUSTRY COUNCIL (PIC).

PML *See* PATTERN MAKERS' LEAGUE OF NORTH AMERICA (AFL-CIO).

PMW *See* PROGRESSIVE MINE WORKERS OF AMERICA (IND).

POPA *See* PATENT OFFICE PROFESSIONAL ASSOCIATION (IND).

PPA *See* PLANT PROTECTION ASSOCIATION; NATIONAL (IND).

PPDSE *See* PLATE PRINTERS', DIE STAMPERS' AND ENGRAVERS' UNION OF NORTH AMERICA; INTERNATIONAL (AFL-CIO).

PPE *See* PROTECTION EMPLOYEES; INDEPENDENT UNION OF PLANT (IND).

PPF *See* PLUMBING AND PIPE FITTING INDUSTRY OF THE UNITED STATES AND CANADA; UNITED ASSOCIATION OF JOURNEYMEN AND APPRENTICES OF THE (AFL-CIO).

PSC *See* PUBLIC SERVICE CAREERS (PSC).

PSE *See* PUBLIC SERVICE EMPLOYMENT (PSE).

PSIP *See* PRIVATE SECTOR INITIATIVE PROGRAM (PSIP).

PSS *See* PRODUCTION, SERVICE AND SALES UNION; INTERNATIONAL (IND).

PTE *See* PROFESSIONAL AND TECHNICAL ENGINEERS; INTERNATIONAL FEDERATION OF (AFL-CIO).

PWA *See* PUBLIC WORKS ADMINISTRATION (AUTHORITY).

pacers Employees who are exceptionally fast workers and are used by the employer to set norms or production standards in incentive or piece rate systems. Unions object to the use of exceptionally fast workers and insist on the use of average or "normal" workers when a job is to be timed for the purpose of setting standards or rates. In Canadian usage, pacers are sometimes referred to as speeders or bell-horses.

See also RUSHERS.

Pacific Coast Marine Firemen, Oilers, Watertenders and Wipers Association A division of the Seafarers' International Union of North America (AFL-CIO). Its monthly publication is the *The Marine Fireman.*

Address: 240 Second St., San Francisco, Calif. 94105. Tel. (415) 362–4592

Pacific Islander *See* ASIAN OR PACIFIC ISLANDER.

package The term "package" is designed to describe the total benefits which the parties agree to in collective bargaining, including wages and other cost or monetary items in the form of fringe benefits such as insurance, paid vacations, and sick leave.

Occasionally in negotiations the employer may set a maximum ceiling on the total cost which he is willing to consider and will request the union to suggest how the total cost might be distributed between wage adjustments and other benefits.

The package may include items other than monetary or cost items in which case the total package has both a dollar and cents value and a nonmoney value.

The package is sometimes referred to after settlement as the "package deal."

Packinghouse and Dairy Workers; National Brotherhood of (Ind) Formerly known as the National Brotherhood of Packinghouse Workers, the union changed its name to the National Brotherhood of Packinghouse and Industrial Workers in the early 1970s.

See also PACKINGHOUSE AND INDUSTRIAL WORKERS; NATIONAL BROTHERHOOD OF (IND).

Packinghouse and Industrial Workers; National Brotherhood of (Ind) Formerly known as the National Brotherhood of Packinghouse and Dairy Workers, the union is affiliated with the National Federation of Independent Unions. Its monthly publication is the *Union Labor News Review.*

Address: 3855 Bell Crossing Dr., Kansas City, Kan. 66104. Tel. (913) 371–5538

Packinghouse, Food and Allied Workers; United (AFL-CIO) The organization was previously known as the United Packinghouse Workers of America. It merged with the Amalgamated Meat Cutters and Butcher Workmen of North America (AFL-CIO) on July 1, 1968.

Source references: Arthur E. Carver, *Personnel and Labor Relations in the Packing Industry* (Chicago: Institute of Meat Packing, 1928); Lewis Corey, *Meat and Man: A Study of Monopoly, Unionism and Food Policy* (New York: Viking Press, 1950); Leslie F. Orear and Stephen H. Diamond, *Out of the Jungle: The Packinghouse Workers Fight for Justice and Equality* (Chicago: Hyde Park Press, 1968).

See also MEAT CUTTERS AND BUTCHER WORKMEN OF NORTH AMERICA; AMALGAMATED (AFL-CIO).

Packinghouse Workers; National Brotherhood of (Ind) *See* PACKINGHOUSE AND DAIRY WORKERS; NATIONAL BROTHERHOOD OF (IND).

Packinghouse Workers of America; United (AFL-CIO) *See* PACKINGHOUSE, FOOD AND ALLIED WORKERS; UNITED (AFL-CIO).

padrone system This system operated substantially as a contract labor arrangement. The leader, who did the recruiting, was known as the padrone. He provided emigrants with transportation, and supplied food and accommodations. Many workers from Italy were brought to the United States under these arrangements. The padrone contracted with employers for the workers' labor for periods of one or more years, or until the worker had repaid the padrone for transportation and other expenses.

Legislation in the 1880s made unenforceable any contracts which required the performance of labor, such as that under the padrone system.

See also PEONAGE.

paid holidays *See* HOLIDAY PAY.

paid jury leave Leave with pay granted to an employee to perform jury service during normal or regular working hours.

A sample contract provision follows:

Section 1.

(a) An employee shall be excused from work on a work day on which he performs jury service, provided he gives prior notice to his supervisor.

(b) An employee shall be permitted to work part time outside his regular jury service if the nature of his work is such as will permit this practice.

Section 2.

An employee who is excused for jury service and who furnishes the company with a statement from the court with regard to jury pay received and time spent on jury service on a regularly scheduled work day, will be reimbursed by the company as follows:

(a) An employee absent for his entire shift will be paid the difference between jury pay and his regular wages for his regular shift.

(b) An employee who performs jury service and works on the same work day will be paid the difference, if any, between his actual earnings for the day plus the jury pay and his regular wages for his regular shift.

(c) An employee who is called for jury service, responds to the call and loses time from work, but is not accepted for jury service, will receive an amount equal to his regular wages for such time lost on his regular shift, provided he returns to his job promptly.

(d) For purposes of this section, regular wages shall be the employee's straight-time earnings for the shift, using the employee's hourly rate in the case of the day worker and the employee's average piecework earning rate in the case of the piece worker. In addition, night shift bonus will be paid, if applicable.

Source references: Robert L. Aronson, "Compensation of Industrial Workers for Jury Service," *LLJ*, Feb. 1957; BNA, *Paid Leave and Leave of Absence Policies* (Washington: PPF Survey no. 111, 1975); Dena G. Weiss, "Union Contract Provisions for Paid Jury Leave," *MLR*, May 1955; Dena G. Weiss and Ernestine M. Moore, "Paid Jury Leave in Major Union Contracts, 1961," *MLR*, April 1962.

paid leave A provision in contracts which provides for leave with pay for the individual employee for a stipulated period of time. Among the most frequent paid leave provisions are those which involve vacations, holidays, jury duty, funeral, and sick leave. Innovations in paid leave practices include personal leave, paternity leave, adoption leave, maternity leave, and an employee's birthday.

Source references: BNA, *Policies on Leave from Work* (Washington: PPF Survey no. 136, 1983); NICB, *Time Off With Pay*, (New York: Studies in Personnel Policy no. 196, 1965); Patrick M. Towle, "Calculating Sick Leave and Vacation With an Hourly Accrual System," *PJ*, May 1979; U.S. CSC, *A Survey of Leave Provisions in Federal Sector Agreements* (Washington: 1977); U.S. Dept. of Labor, BLS, *Paid Leave Provisions in Major Contracts, 1961* (Washington: Bull. no. 1342, 1962).

See also ADOPTION LEAVE, FUNERAL LEAVE PAY, HOLIDAY PAY, LEAVE OF ABSENCE, PAID JURY LEAVE, PAID SICK LEAVE, PAID VACATION PLAN, PATERNITY LEAVE, PAY FOR TIME SPENT ON UNION BUSINESS.

paid sick leave A provision in an agreement or company policy which permits employees to take leave without loss of seniority or employment rights, and with pay, for periods of illness.

In recent years concern over expenses of illness and health care has been evidenced by various internal company programs, including annual physical check-ups and broader health programs. In addition, employers and unions have negotiated medical and health plans to meet some of the costs resulting from illness.

Alternative forms of sick leave plans provide partial payment (e.g., 60 percent of regular pay) for additional sick leave after employees exhaust the alloted paid sick leave or employees may be granted an advance of sick leave under some plans.

Paid sick leave plans may provide employees compensation for unused sick leave upon their retirement, at the end of the year, after a certain amount of leave is accrued, or upon termination of employment.

Other sick leave plans offer incentives by permitting employees to use unused sick leave time for vacations, personal leaves, monetary awards, or salary increases.

Source references: BNA, *Policies on Leave From Work* (Washington: PPF Survey no. 136, 1983); Maureen Heneghan and Sigmund G. Ginsburg, "Use of Sick Leave," *Personnel Administration*, Sept./Oct. 1970; Kenneth J. Hoffman, "Provisions for Paid Sick Leave in Metropolitan Areas," *MLR*, Feb. 1966; Edgar H. Johnson, Jr., "Control of Sick Leave," *Personnel Administration*, Jan./Feb. 1969; U.S. Dept. of Labor, BLS, *Paid Sick Leave Provisions in Major Union Contracts, 1959* (Washington: Bull. no. 1282, 1960).

paid vacation plan Prior to unionization many companies had established vacation plans for their clerical and supervisory employees. With unionization the employees in production operations sought to obtain similar benefits. Over a period of time this has been substantially accomplished.

One of the major fringe benefit programs supported by the National War Labor Board was the standard vacation plan of one week for one year and two weeks for five years' service. Since World War II, the length of the vacation period has been increased from the two weeks prevalent in 1949 to the three to four weeks commonly found in 1983. The trend also indicates a reduction in the length of service requirements. According to a survey of sample contracts, the five-week vacation which constituted 2 percent of the contracts in 1966 is currently included in 58 percent of the sample contracts. Twenty percent of these contracts provide for six-week vacations. The aluminum and steel companies have negotiated a special "sabbatical" vacation plan which provides a 13-week vacation period for senior employees once every five years.

Source reference: BNA, *Collective Bargaining Negotiations and Contracts*, Vol. 2, 91:1.

See also SABBATICALS, VACATION PAY.

Painters and Allied Trades of the United States and Canada; International Brotherhood of (AFL-CIO) The organization of painters was established at a meeting called by the Baltimore, Maryland, painters in March 1887. This conference was attended by representatives of various Knights of Labor assemblies and independent craft unions. The Brotherhood of Painters and Decorators resulted from this meeting. The name of the union was changed in 1890 to include the paperhangers.

Composed originally of house painters and decorators, the Brotherhood has enlarged its jurisdiction to the entire field of painting, paperhanging, and the decorative arts. At various times it has absorbed the following organizations into its own membership: The United Scenic Artists, the National Paperhangers Association, the National Union of Sign Painters, and the Amalgamated Glass Workers International Union, which includes glass workers handling stained and decorative glass.

Formerly known as the Brotherhood of Painters, Decorators and Paperhangers of America, the name was changed to the International Brotherhood of Painters and Allied Trades in 1969. The present name was adopted in the early 1970s.

The union's official monthly publication is the *Painters and Allied Trades Journal.*

Address: 1750 New York Ave., N.W., Washington, D.C. 20006. Tel. (202) 637–0700

Painters, Decorators and Paperhangers of America; Brotherhood of (AFL-CIO) *See* PAINTERS AND ALLIED TRADES OF THE UNITED STATES AND CANADA; INTERNATIONAL BROTHERHOOD OF (AFL-CIO).

panel of arbitrators The American Arbitration Association and the Federal Mediation and Conciliation Service both maintain lists or panels of qualified arbitrators who have been screened by the two organizations to serve as arbitrators.

A procedure generally followed by the AAA is to submit a list of names to the parties requesting arbitration and to permit each of the parties to eliminate a certain number of names on the list. If a list of 10 is submitted, each side is permitted to cross out five names. If the list when returned contains names not crossed out, these individuals presumably are acceptable to both sides. If all of the names have been crossed out, the parties may request an additional roster of names.

Some state agencies have lists of individuals who are qualified to serve as arbitrators and on request of parties may submit a panel of names.

Source references: Steven Stambaugh Briggs and John C. Anderson, "An Empirical Investigation of Arbitrator Acceptability," *IR*, Spring 1980; Robert Coulson, "Labor Arbitration: The Insecure Profession," *NYU 20th Annual Conference on Labor*, ed. by Thomas Christensen (New York: Bender, 1968); Joseph Krislov, "The Supply of Arbitrators: Prospects for the 1980's," *MLR*, Oct. 1976; Frederick R. Livingston et al., "The Development of Qualified New Arbitrators: Workshop," *Collective Bargaining and the Arbitrator's Role*, Proceedings of the 15th A/M, NAA, ed. by Mark Kahn (Washington: BNA, 1962); Thomas J. McDermott, "Activities Directed at Advancing the Acceptability of New Arbitrators," *Labor Arbitration at the Quarter-Century Mark*, Proceedings of the 25th A/M, NAA, ed. by Barbara Dennis and Gerald Somers (Washington: BNA, 1973); Morris L. Myers, "Arbitrators: The Chosen Few," *NYU 20th Annual Conference on Labor*, ed. by Thomas Christensen (New York: Bender, 1968); Walter J. Primeaux, Jr. and Dalton E. Brannen, "Why Few Arbitrators are Deemed Acceptable," *MLR*, Sept. 1975.

See also ARBITRATOR.

paper locals Local unions which frequently obtain charters, or are self-chartered or established, for the purpose primarily of obtaining payoffs from employers. Such organizations are opposed by legitimate trade unions.

See also AGREEMENT, SWEETHEART; CODES OF ETHICS.

Paper Makers; International Brotherhood of (AFL-CIO) The union was organized in May 1893 in Holyoke, Massachusetts, and was chartered by the AFL as the United Brotherhood of Paper Makers. With the establishment of a competing organization, the International Paper Machine Tenders Union, the Paper Makers lost much of their membership and by 1897 had only three local unions in existence. The Paper Makers and the Tenders merged in 1902 and was known as the International Brotherhood of Paper Makers, which was changed to the International Brotherhood of Paper and Pulp Makers later that same year. A secession movement of the pulp and sulphite workers started in 1906, led to the formation of the International Brotherhood of Pulp, Sulphite and Paper Mill Workers.

Its present name was adopted in 1909. The Paper Makers and the United Paperworkers of America merged in March 1957 to form the United Papermakers and Paperworkers (AFL-CIO).

Source references: James A. Gross, "The Making and Shaping of Unionism in the Pulp and Paper Industry," *Labor History*, Spring 1964; Clark Kerr and Roger Randall, *Causes of Industrial Peace Under Collective Bargaining: A Study of Crown Zellerbach and the Pacific Coast Pulp and Paper Industry* (Washington: NPA, Case Study no. 1, 1948); Harold M. Levinson, *Determining Forces in Collective Wage Bargaining* (New York: Wiley, 1966).

See also PAPERMAKERS AND PAPERWORKERS; UNITED (AFL-CIO).

Papermakers and Paperworkers; United (AFL-CIO) The union made up of the former International Brotherhood of Paper Makers and the United Paperworkers of America. In February 1959, the union absorbed the American Wire Weavers Protective Association.

In May 1964, a faction withdrew from the union to join a dissatisfied faction of the International Brotherhood of Pulp, Sulphite and Paper Mill Workers to form a new organization, the Association of Western Pulp and Paper Workers (Ind).

On August 9, 1972, the union merged with the International Brotherhood of Pulp, Sulphite and Paper Mill Workers (AFL-CIO) to form the United Paperworkers International Union (AFL-CIO).

See also PAPERWORKERS INTERNATIONAL UNION; UNITED (AFL-CIO).

Paperworkers International Union; United (AFL-CIO) The United Papermakers and Paperworkers (AFL-CIO) and the International Brotherhood of Pulp, Sulphite and Paper Mill Workers (AFL-CIO) merged to form this union on August 9, 1972. Its official monthly publication is *The Paperworker*.

Address: 702 Church St., P.O. Box 1475, Nashville, Tenn. 37202. Tel. (615) 834–8590

parent union The union organization which has prime responsibility for its affiliates. Generally the parent union is the international union to which the individual local union belongs.

Occasionally reference is made to a federation, such as the old AFL or CIO or the present AFL-CIO, as the parent union or parent federation to which the international unions belong. Such use is not general, and reference to the parent union usually is to the international union.

See also NATIONAL UNION.

parity Equivalence established between wage schedules of two or more groups of workers commonly termed wage parity. In the public sector, for example, wage parity issues commonly arise in negotiations involving police and fire fighters.

In EEO/AA efforts involving the employment of women or minorities, two measures of parity are used: (1) population parity, which compares the percentage of protected class members in the work force of an employer to the relevant labor market area, and (2) occupational parity, which compares the rate of employed protected class members in the various job groups with the rate of qualified protected class members in the relevant labor pool. No federal law or regulation requires parity although the goal of affirmative action programs is to bring about occupational parity.

Source references: Joseph Adler, Marjorie Bird, and Tallien Robinson, *Pay Parity for Police and Fire Fighters* (Ithaca: Cornell Univ., NYSSILR, Institute for Public Employment, Occasional Paper no. 7, 1975); James C. Amar, "Pay Parity Between Police and Fire Fighters," *Journal of Collective Negotiations in the Public Sector*, Vol. 7, no. 3, 1978; G. W. Cassidy, "Legal, Institutional and Economic Implications of Police/Fire-Fighter Parity," *Journal of Collective Negotiations in the Public Sector*, Vol. 9, no. 2, 1980; Robert Freiberg (ed.), *The Manager's Guide to Equal Employment Opportunity* (New York: Executive Enterprises, 1977); Paul A. Lafranchise and Michael T. Leibig, "Collective Bargaining for Parity in the Public Sector," *LLJ*, Sept. 1981; Geraldine Leshin, *Equal Employment Opportunity and Affirmative Action in Labor-Management Relations, A Primer* (Los Angeles: UC, Institute of IR, 1976); David Lewin, "Wage Parity and the Supply of Police and Firemen," *IR*, Feb. 1973; Hoyt N. Wheeler, Richard Berger, and Stephen McGarry, "Parity: An Evaluation of Recent Court and Board Decisions," *LLJ*, March 1978.

See also GOALS AND TIMETABLES, RELEVANT LABOR MARKET AREA.

parliamentary procedure General rules or procedures which have been established to maintain order and to assist the normal and routine organization and conduct of the business of deliberative bodies.

Parliamentary procedure is a rather popular area of trade union interest and many labor education programs provide training in the normal procedures for conducting a meeting.

Since many trade union groups function through large membership meetings, it is necessary that opportunity be provided for the members to present their points of view and to reflect the needs of the membership. Additionally, under recent laws, it is necessary that unions handle their meetings in the prescribed manner and provide for appropriate voting procedures not only for collective agreements resulting from negotiations but also in the election of officers.

Source references: AFL-CIO, Dept. of Education, *How to Run a Union Meeting* (Washington: 1959); Frederick C. Jonas, *Rules of Order, Simplified; For Use By Members of Union, Business, Fraternal, Social, Parent-Teacher and Other Service Organizations* (Chicago: National Labor-Management Foundation, 1960); Henry M. Robert, *Robert's Rules of Order Revised for Deliberative Assemblies* (Chicago: Scott, Foresman, 1943); Byrl Albert Whitney, *Please Come to Order! A New and Unique Approach to Efficient Group Decision-Making Based on Illustrative Parliamentary Situations and Presiding Officers' Rulings, Incorporating Whitney's Chart of Parliamentary Motions* (Annandale, Va.: Turnpike Press, 1966).

partially funded pension plan A pension plan which does not set up sufficient actuarial reserve during the employees' working period to fund the pension completely upon retirement.

See also FUNDED PENSION PLAN.

partial strike A cessation of work by a small group of the total organized group in a plant or industry. The purpose of a partial strike is to limit the individuals directly involved in strike activity and yet put as much economic pressure on the employer as though a full-fledged strike of all of his employees were involved. Partial strikes are generally not announced and are directed toward key or vulnerable segments of the organization.

A partial strike may also be useful where the union is not sure of the success of a strike involving all of the employees in the organization but has fair assurance that those in key operations will strike.

participative management A means of more actively involving the individual employees in determining management goals related to their work to secure reduction of costs, increased production, job enlargement, improved communication within the company, and greater worker understanding of company goals and company welfare. Workers' participation is sometimes viewed as a solution to labor-management relations problems and sometimes as a synonym for industrial democracy. Workers' participation can be as indirect as the use of suggestion boxes or as direct as conferences between employees and management and committees of employee representatives which meet periodically with company executives.

Source references: Robert C. Albrook, "Participative Management: Time for a Second Look," *Management Review*, June 1967; Irving Bluestone, "Creating a New World of Work," *ILR*, Jan./Feb. 1977; R. J. Coleman, "Employee Participation in the U.S. Enterprise," *BJIR*, July 1978; E. Cordova, "Workers' Participation in Decisions Within Enterprises: Recent Trends and Problems," *ILR*, March/April 1982; Milton Derber, "Crosscurrents in Workers Participation," *IR*, Feb. 1970; John F. Donnelly, "Participative Management at Work," *Harvard BR*, Jan./Feb. 1977; Nancy Foy and Herman Gadon, "Worker Participation: Contrasts in Three Countries," *Harvard BR*, May/June 1976; Charlotte Gold, *Employer-Employee Committees and Worker Participation* (Ithaca: Cornell Univ., NYSSILR, Key Issues Series no. 20, 1976); Larry E. Greiner, "What Managers Think of Participative Leadership," *Harvard BR*, March/April 1973; ILO, *Workers' Participation in Decisions Within Undertakings* (Geneva: Labour-Management Relations Series no. 48, 1976); W. Matthew Juechter, "The Pros and Cons of Participative Management," *Management Review*, Sept. 1982; Michael E. Murphy, "Workers on the Board: Borrowing a European Idea," *LLJ*, Dec. 1976; M. Gene Newport, "Participative Management: Some Caution," *PJ*, Oct. 1966; John M. Roach, *Worker Participation: New Voices in Management* (New York: The Conference Board, Report no. 594, 1973); Joel M. Rosenfeld and Matthew J. Smith, "Participative Management: An Overview," *PJ*, Feb. 1967; Joyce Rothschild-Whitt, *Conditions Facilitating Participatory-Democratic Organizations* (Ithaca: Cornell Univ., NYSSILR, Reprint Series no. 446, 1978); Raymond Russell, Arthur Hocher, and Stewart E. Perry, "Participation, Influence, and Worker-Ownership," *IR*, Fall 1979; Marshall Sashkin, *A Manager's Guide to Participative Management*, An AMA Management Briefing (New York: AMA, 1982); Johannes Schregle, "Forms of Participation in Management," *IR*, Feb. 1970; Paul F. Shaw, "Worker Participation—American Style," *Employee Relations LJ*, Summer 1977; George Strauss and Eliezer Rosenstein, "Workers Participation: A Critical View," *IR*, Feb. 1970; John R. Turney and Stanley L. Cohen, "Participative Management: What is the Right Level?" *Management Review*, Oct. 1980.

See also CODETERMINATION, MULTIPLE MANAGEMENT, QUALITY CIRCLES, WORKERS' COUNCILS.

parties to agreement Collective bargaining agreements generally provide, at the end of the contract, space for the signatures of the representatives of the company and the union. The individuals who sign presumably are responsible under the terms of the contract and speak for those they represent, on both the company and union sides.

Occasionally signatories may include not only those directly negotiating the agreement, the representatives of the employees and the company in a particular plant, but may also include in the case of a local union which is a member of an international organization, a member of the international union which indicates that it accepts responsibility in connection with the contract. In some instances, signature by an international union official is required on local union contracts.

part-time employment The term may apply to part-time work, in which case it indicates that the individual may be employed for only a few hours during the day. This may be true of women who accept part-time employment during periods when their young children are in school, but are not generally able to accept full-time employment. Part-time work may also apply to the schedule of an employer when work is provided for only part of the total scheduled work day or workweek, or when the plant is not fully operative and the operation is on a part-time basis.

Part-time employees are those who do not work a full schedule or are not considered full-time employees of the company. They may work only part of a schedule or perform only certain limited work.

Source references: Amy Hewes, "Women Part-Time Workers in the United States," *ILR*, Nov. 1962; "An International Survey of Part-Time Employment," *ILR*, Oct. and Nov.

1963; Carol Leon and Robert W. Bednarzik, "A Profile of Women on Part-Time Schedules," *MLR*, Oct. 1978; James E. Long and Ethel B. Jones, "Married Women in Part-Time Employment," *ILRR*, April 1981; Susan Fritch Meives, "Part-Time Work: A Multi-perspective Analysis" (Unpublished Ph.D. dissertation, Univ. of Wisconsin-Madison, 1979); Judith A. Mintz, *Part-Time Work: The Effect of Fragmentation on Employees* (Springfield, Va.: U.S. National Technical Information Service, 1978); Stanley D. Nollen and Virginia H. Martin, *Alternative Work Schedules. Part 2: Permanent Part-Time Employment, Part 3: The Compressed Work-week; An AMA Survey Report* (New York: AMA, 1978); James Parson, "Brainpower Wanted—But No Part-Time Workers Need Apply," *Personnel*, May/June 1963; Robert L. Stein and Jane L. Meredith, "Growth and Characteristics of the Part-Time Work Force,"*MLR*, Nov. 1960; Allen K. Trueman, "How Companies Are Using Temporary Workers," *Management Review*, Sept. 1964; U.S. CSC, *Flexibility Through Part-Time Employment of Career Workers in the Public Service* (Washington: Professional Series no. 75–3, 1975); U.S. GAO, *Part-Time and Other Federal Employment: Compensation and Personnel Management Reforms Needed* (Washington: 1979).

See also JOB SHARING.

part-time labor force *See* LABOR FORCE.

part timer A worker who is employed only part of the time in an establishment which also schedules employees on a full-time basis, or a domestic household employee who may work only part of the day and whose time may be divided among several households, either during the day or during the week.

Source references: William E. Clark, *What Part-Timers Think About Their Job, Vol. II—Part-Time Employees, Their Relationships and Motivations* (New York: National Retail Merchants Association, Retail Research Institute, 1962); William V. Deutermann, Jr. and Scott Campbell Brown, "Voluntary Part-Time Workers: A Growing Part of the Labor Force," *MLR*, June 1978; David W. Leslie and D. Jane Ikenberry, "Collective Bargaining and Part-Time Faculty: Contract Content," *Journal of the College and University Personnel Association*, Fall 1979; John D. Owen, "Why Part-Time Workers Tend to Be in Low-Wage Jobs," *MLR*, June 1978; Sylvia Lazos Terry, "Involuntary Part-Time Work: New Information from the CPS," *MLR*, Feb. 1981; Howard P. Tuckman and Jaime Caldwell, "The Reward Structure for Part-Timers in Academe," *Journal of Higher Education*, Nov./Dec. 1979; Howard P. Tuckman and William D. Vogler, "The Fringes of a Fringe Group: Part-Timers in Academe," *MLR*, Nov. 1979; U.S. Dept. of Labor, BES, *Dictionary of Occupational Titles* (4th ed., Washington: 1977).

part-time worker rate A rate received by temporary or contingent employees. These rates may be equivalent to those received by regular full-time employees or may be either lower or higher, depending on the industry or market conditions. Part-time workers are frequently found in department stores and other retail establishments as well as in hotels and restaurants because of the unusual hours and peak periods of activity.

past practice A term found in collective bargaining agreements and one which has been the basis for many arbitration awards. The question, "What constitutes a past practice" generally means how long does the particular practice have to be in existence and how deeply ingrained, to be considered by the parties as a past practice which should be continued by the employer or which should not be changed except by mutual agreement.

Past practice provisos occasionally are incorporated into agreements when the employer does not desire to spell out in detail all of the items which constitute previous practice and the union does not want to limit the number of items which it believes might come within the broad framework of past practice. As a result, contracts will provide that past practices will be continued and then leave the matter for joint resolution by the parties. In the absence of such resolution, it falls to an arbitrator, under the grievance procedure, to determine whether the particular item was or was not part of the company's past practices, within the meaning of the contract.

Source references: Jules J. Justin, *How to Manage With a Union, Book Two* (New York: IR Workshop Seminars, 1969); Richard P.

McLaughlin, "Custom and Past Practices in Labor Arbitration," *AJ*, Vol. 18, no. 4, 1963; Richard Mittenthal, "Past Practice and the Administration of Collective Bargaining Agreements," *Arbitration and Public Policy*, Proceedings of the 14th A/M, NAA, ed. by Spencer Pollard (Washington: BNA, 1961); Lawrence A. Nurse, "Custom and Practice in Labour Relations in the United States: A Review of the Evidence," *LLJ*, Jan. 1979.

past service benefits Retirement credits which are granted to employees for service in the company prior to the installation of a particular pension plan.

Source reference: BNA, *Pensions and Profit Sharing* (3d ed., Washington: 1964).

past service funding A procedure for paying the cost of past service liabilities. Internal Revenue Service regulations limit the maximum amount that may be allocated in any one year for funding past service if it is to be used as a tax deduction.

Source reference: BNA, *Pensions and Profit Sharing* (3d ed., Washington: 1964).

past service liability When a pension plan is funded it frequently is necessary to determine actuarially the amount necessary to pay for the cost of past service (prior to the inception of a funded plan) of employees to be covered. The fund for such past service may be accumulated (through contributions) over a period of years.

Source reference: BNA, *Pensions and Profit Sharing* (3d ed., Washington: 1964).

patent assignment An agreement between workers and their employer, where employees are engaged in research and development or highly specialized engineering or chemical or other research, that if new inventions are developed as a result of their research and development, the patent rights on the development will accrue to the company, not to the employee.

Source references: Naveed Alam, "Employers' Obligations Regarding Employee Inventions—A New Perspective," *Employee Relations LJ*, Winter 1982/83; Sally C. Cornwell, "Employee Rights in Innovative Works," *ILR*, May/June 1980; Francis J. Lavoie, "Is the Corporate Inventor Getting a Fair Shake?" *Management Review*, Dec. 1972; NICB, *Employee Patent and Secrecy Agreements* (New York: Studies in Personnel Policy no. 199, 1965); ———, *Patent Counsel in Industry* (New York: Studies in Business Policy no. 112, 1964); Fredrik Neumeyer, "Employees' Rights in Their Invention: A Comparison of National Laws," *ILR*, Jan. 1961; J. Roger O'Meara, "Company Patent Practices Challenged," *Conference Board Record*, June 1964; ———, "Should Inventor-Employees Get Royalties?" *Conference Board Record*, April 1966; Worth Wade, *Business and the Professional Unions, With a Survey of Patent Clauses in Union Contracts* (Ardmore, Pa.: Advance House, 1961).

Patent Office Professional Association (Ind) Founded in 1960, it publishes the monthly *POPA Newsletter*.

Address: Crystal City, Arlington, Va. 22202. Tel. (703) 557–3107

paternalism, employer A term, generally used in a derogatory sense, describing the "fatherly" interest of an employer in his workers. Unions have held that the paternalistic attitude of the employer, which sometimes led to minute regulation of the affairs of the employee, is designed to frustrate unionization and keep the worker dependent on the good will of the employer. Housing, medical care, company stores, and recreation, designed for the well-being of the worker, were resented by unions and frequently by workers as an indication of a too-close reliance on the "fatherliness" of the boss. Many of the benefits of paternalism now are found in negotiated health and welfare plans.

Historically, much of the concern of so-called paternalistic employers was genuine and stemmed from the isolation of communities in many areas. The employer had to plan housing, medical, and other facilities to attract workers. This brought regulation of worker activities outside the plant.

Some writers indicate the difficulty in programs of employers designed to win the loyalty of the worker by taking a pervasive and unilateral interest in his well-being and frequently encouraging the employee to become more dependent on the employer and his benefits. Clinton Golden and Harold Ruttenberg in their *Dynamics of Industrial Democracy* have this comment to make: "Paternalism is no solution for the dissatisfaction of workers. They do not want anything given to them. The pleasure that management derives from giving things away should be confined to the members of the immediate family and friends. Workers want to earn their livelihoods; they want only what they feel they deserve, and their pride and adult dignity are hurt when management plays the part of father and gives them as gifts a paid vacation, wage raises, Christmas bonus, or something else which, in the first instance, workers feel they have justly earned."

Norman J. Ware in his *Labor in Modern Industrial Society* says: "Paternalism is always despotic, but it may be either benevolent or malicious; there are occasions when its malignity is clothed in terms of benevolence." Ware states that "by paternalism is meant that system of government which assumes the superior wisdom of the governor in matters of all sorts and the equal inability of all the governed to think or act for themselves. In its second stage, paternalism becomes indignant, though possibly still benevolent despotism, and in its third, it becomes despotism robbed of benevolence and even of indignation and clothed in cold, calculating power."

Albert Walton comments as follows: ". . . the management must avoid the appearance of paternalism, of granting something as out of the good of their hearts. What is done must be done as a matter of right and justice, not as a favor or charity."

Source references: Albert A. Blum, "Paternalism and Collective Bargaining," *Personnel Administration*, Jan./Feb. 1963; Edwin C. Pendleton, *Reversal of Roles: The Case of Paternalism in Hawaiian Labor-Management Relations* (Honolulu: Univ. of Hawaii, IRC, 1962); John D. Rockefeller, Jr., *The Colorado Industrial Plan* (New York: The Author, 1916); ———, *The Personal Relation in Industry* (New York: Boni, Liverright, 1923); U.S. Dept. of Labor, BLS, *Welfare Work for Employees in Industrial Establishments in the United States* (Washington: Bull. no. 250, 1919); Albert Walton, *The Fundamentals of Industrial Psychology* (New York: McGraw-Hill, 1941); Norman J. Ware, *Labor in Modern Industrial Society* (Boston: Heath, 1935).

See also COMPANY TOWN, COMPANY UNION, PERQUISITES.

paternity leave Paid or unpaid time off from work granted to male employees for the care of children. The 1980 contract negotiated by the U.S. Department of Labor and the American Federation of Government Employees provided up to two years of child rearing leave to men and women.

Source reference: J. H. Foegen, "The Next Employee Benefit—Grand Paternity Leave?" *Human Resource Management*, Fall 1980.

pattern bargaining A procedure in collective bargaining whereby a union seeks to obtain equal or identical terms from a group of employers in a particular industry based on an agreement already obtained from an important company. The particular agreement or the particular terms serve as a model for imitation by other employers and unions.

The terms obtained from a pattern setting company or industry, such as steel or the electrical or automobile industry, may set the style not only for others within that particular industry but also may fan out to other industries in related fields.

The pattern may also be established at the request of an international union for a model contract for a particular group of employees in an industry. This standard contract then is considered the pattern to be followed by local unions and companies throughout the country.

Source references: Jerry D. Anker, "Pattern Bargaining, Antitrust Laws and the National Labor Relations Act," *NYU 19th Annual Conference on Labor*, ed. by Thomas Christensen (Washington: BNA, 1967); Walter H. Carpenter, Jr. and Edward Handler, *Small Business and Pattern Bargaining* (Babson Park: Babson Institute Press, 1961); Audrey Freedman and William E. Fulmer, "Last Rites for Pattern Bargaining," *Harvard BR*, March/April 1982; Harold M. Levinson, "Pattern Bargaining: A Case Study of the Automobile Workers," *LLJ*, Sept. 1958.

See also COLLECTIVE BARGAINING, MULTI-EMPLOYER; WAGE PATTERNS.

Pattern Makers' League of North America (AFL-CIO) The Pattern Makers' League was organized in Philadelphia, Pennsylvania, in May 1887. Its official bimonthly publication is the *Pattern Makers' Journal.*

Address: 1925 North Lynn St., Arlington, Va. 22209. Tel. (703) 525–9234

pay day The day on which employees receive their wages or salaries. It may be weekly, bimonthly, or on the basis of any other arrangement which the employer and employees jointly agree upon.

Some states regulate the minimum frequency of pay days.

pay equity Generally concerns the issue of earnings differentials of men and women performing different jobs and attempts to obtain comparability (pay equity) for women workers on the basis of the value or worth of the jobs. The concept of pay equity may also be termed "comparable worth" or "sex-based wage discrimination."

According to the Census Bureau, women workers in 1980 earned on the average 60 percent of men's earnings. The disparity in earnings has persisted despite passage of the Equal Pay Act, leading to examination of the kinds of jobs women hold and how women are compensated. Studies find that (1) women tend to be concentrated in certain jobs, and (2) based on skill, effort, responsibility, and working conditions, women tend to be underpaid for their work. Race is also a factor in the pay equity issue according to organizations such as the National Institute for Women of Color (NIWC) and the NAACP Legal Defense Fund. The NIWC states that while the wage gap between white women and women of color has been reduced over the past 20 years, the latter group still earns less than any other group.

Nancy Perlman, chair of the National Committee on Pay Equity, says "pay equity involves correcting the practice of paying women less than men for work that requires comparable skill, effort, responsibility and working conditions."

Source references: AFSCME, *Breaking the Pattern of Injustice: AFSCME's Blueprint for Pay Equity* (Washington: 1983); ———, *Pay Equity on Trial* (Washington: 1983); BNA, *Pay Equity and Comparable Worth* (Washington: 1984); Joy Ann Grune (ed.), *Manual on Pay Equity, Raising Wages for Women's Work* (Washington: Conference on Alternative State and Local Policies, 1980); George T. Milkovich, "Pay Inequities and Comparable Worth," *Proceedings of the 33d A/M, IRRA*, ed. by Barbara Dennis (Madison: 1981); Winn Newman, "Pay Equity: An Emerging Labor Issue," *Proceedings of the 34th A/M, IRRA*, ed. by Barbara Dennis (Madison: 1982); Nancy Rytina, "Earnings of Men and Women: A Look at Specific Occupations," *MLR*, April 1982; U.S. Dept. of Commerce, Bureau of the Census, *Money Income of Households, Families, and Persons in the United States: 1982* (Washington: Current Population Reports, Consumer Income Series P–60, no. 142, 1984).

See also COMPARABLE WORTH, EQUAL PAY FOR EQUAL WORK, OCCUPATIONAL SEGREGATION.

pay for grievance time Provisions in collective bargaining agreements in which the employer agrees to compensate certain union officers for time spent in handling grievances. Generally the time is limited to a specific number of union officers for a specific limited number of hours, to be put in during reasonable periods so as not to disrupt operations.

During National War Labor Board days, provisions frequently were put in contracts for grievance time without loss of pay to the union representatives. However, where such time was excessive or used for purposes other than handling grievances, (for example, campaigning for union office), adjustments were made and the time limited. Some large companies now pay what amounts to full-time wages to members of the union grievance committees whose activities are considered a necessary part of effective plant management.

Source references: J. J. Bambrick, Jr., "Pay for Union-Management Meetings," *Management Record*, June 1948; U.S. Dept. of Labor, BLS, *Major Collective Bargaining Agreements: Employer Pay and Leave for Union Business* (Washington: Bull. 1425–19, 1980).

See also GRIEVANCE ADJUSTMENT, GRIEVANCE COMMITTEE, OFFICIAL TIME, RELEASED TIME, TIME LOST ON GRIEVANCES.

pay for shop stewards This is the same as pay for grievance time but may make particular reference to shop stewards and other members of the executive staff of the union. A contract may provide as follows:

Company to pay stewards for time lost on grievances.

(a) It will be the policy of the company to continue the past practice of paying stewards, chief stewards, and committeemen for time lost on grievances during working hours.

(b) The company agrees to pay the union bargaining committee for all time spent on settling grievances in meetings with the company during the hours from 9:00 a.m. to 3:00 p.m.

(c) Additional bargaining time may be allowed and paid for if approved by the chairman of the company labor relations committee.

(d) In the above cases, employees will be paid at the rate of their average hourly earnings for the last two pay periods.

See also OFFICIAL TIME, PAY FOR GRIEVANCE TIME, RELEASED TIME, TIME LOST ON GRIEVANCES.

pay for time spent on union business Provisions in agreements which go beyond the handling of grievances may make provision for time spent on other union business which relates to general plant operations for which the employer is willing to compensate.

Source references: John N. Gentry, "Company Pay for Time Off on Union Business," *MLR*, Oct. 1969; James C. Hill, G. Allan Dash, and Thomas G. S. Christensen, "Arbitration: Three Arbitrators View One Case," *NYU 23d Annual Conference on Labor*, ed. by Thomas Christensen and Andrea Christensen (New York: Bender, 1971); William H. Leahy, "Grievances Over Union Business on Company Time and Premises," *AJ*, Sept. 1975; U.S. Dept. of Labor, BLS, *Collective Bargaining Clauses: Company Pay for Time Spent on Union Business* (Washington: Bull. No. 1266, 1959); ———, *Major Collective Bargaining Agreements: Employer Pay and Leave for Union Business* (Washington: Bull. 1425–19, 1980).

See also OFFICIAL TIME, RELEASED TIME.

payment-by-result Any method of wage payment which relates earnings of workers to the amount of output. It may apply to piecework or other forms of incentive systems. Such earnings may be based on the output of the individual or the group.

payment in kind *See* INCOME IN KIND.

payment in lieu of dues *See* FAIR SHARE AGREEMENT.

pay period The time between the beginning and end of a particular period for the purpose of computing the employee's pay. It may be a weekly, bimonthly, or other period set up to permit routine computation of the payroll.

payroll Generally the total wages earned by all of the named employees in a particular plant or establishment for a given payroll period.

The payroll may be used by agencies of government, such as the NLRB or state labor board, in holding elections to determine the employees eligible to vote as of a specific date.

The payroll may show not only gross wages or salaries, but also various tax and other deductions as well as contributions for various types of savings by employees. It may be on a weekly, semimonthly, or monthly basis.

payroll-based employee stock ownership plan (PAYSOP) A plan to provide employees with shares of company stock by allowing corporate tax credit based on a percentage of covered payroll. PAYSOPs are authorized by the Economic Recovery Tax Act of 1981 and provide a participating employer with a tax credit of one-half of one percent of the covered payroll for 1983 and 1984, and three-fourths of one percent of the payroll from 1985 through 1987, for contributions to the plans.

Prior to passage of the Economic Recovery Tax Act, employee stock ownership plans based on capital investment (TRASOP) were permitted under the Tax Reduction Act of 1975.

Source references: John J. Miller, "ESOPs, TRASOPs, and PAYSOPs: A Guide for the Perplexed," *Management Review*, Sept. 1983; Howard V. Sontag and Gary G. Quintiere, "PAYSOPs: ERTA's Revised TRASOPs," *Compensation Review*, Second Quarter 1982.

See also TAX REDUCTION ACT STOCK OWNERSHIP PLAN (TRASOP).

payroll deductions Amounts withheld or deducted from an individual's gross earnings by his employer. These withholdings or deductions may include social security, income taxes, group insurance premiums, local payroll taxes, union dues or other voluntary wage assignments, savings set aside for the purchase of government bonds, retirement, stock purchase, etc.

See also CHECK-OFF, DEDUCTIONS.

payroll tax Taxes levied or imposed by the government. Taxes under the Social Security Act for the financing of unemployment insurance and old age and survivors' insurance are examples.

peaceful persuasion A term used in the legal literature of industrial relations and particularly with reference to union activities on the picket line.

The term also is used in the field of mediation and conciliation where peaceful persuasion is stressed as the only effective and sensible approach to labor relations. In this area it is sought to have the parties through reason and understanding reach a common agreement while the third party merely uses his good offices to suggest through peaceful persuasion that alternative methods of settlement are more appropriate than economic force and coercion.

In labor disputes, the conduct which is legally permitted is generally that which avoids the use of force, violence, coercion, or intimidation. Where peaceful persuasion is permitted, the question as to what constitutes peaceful persuasion is difficult. As one authority has put it, "Peaceful persuasion . . . is commonly designated as lawful and allowable. Yet with the possible exception of 'violence,' each of these terms (violence, force, coercion, etc.) is so vague that in actual application to specific cases liberal and conservative courts have differed widely in interpretation and definition. To take but one example from among many, liberal courts have said that 'intimidation' results only from actual violence or threats of physical violence, while conservative courts have held that looks, gestures, and even mere force of numbers are enough to produce intimidation."

Source references: American Steel Foundries v. Tri-City Central Trades Council, 257 US 184 (1921); Carroll R. Daugherty, *Labor Problems in American Industry* (5th ed., Boston: Houghton, Mifflin, 1941); Milton Handler, *Cases and Materials on Labor Law* (St. Paul: West Publishing, 1944).

See also PICKETING.

peaceful picketing A form of picketing or marching to inform employees, or the public, that there is a labor dispute in existence or that a firm purchases or uses nonunion materials or services. Whether the picketing is peaceful is frequently a matter for decision and evaluation by a court. Generally it is peaceful when there is an absence of violence or when the actions of the pickets do not threaten those who seek free access to the place picketed.

Source references: American Steel Foundries v. Tri-City Central Trades Council, 257 US 184 (1921); Manuelo Albuquerque Scott, "The Invisible Hand and the Clenched Fist: Is There a Safe Way to Picket Under the First Amendment?" *IR Law Digest*, Summer 1975.

See also ATCHISON TOPEKA & SANTA FE R.R. V. GEE.

peg point Applies to a specific occupational rate for a key job in any of the major groupings within the wage structure—unskilled, semiskilled or skilled job. The peg or anchor points are designed to provide check points for the rest of the wage structure. When the peg points are accepted, union and employer build the rest of the wage structure through collective bargaining using the key jobs or occupations as the critical points for the establishment of the wage rates for other jobs and occupations.

Peg points may be used in setting up a wage structure under job evaluation.

Source references: John T. Dunlop, *Wage Determination Under Trade Unionism* (New York: Augustus M. Kelley, 1950); Herbert G. Zollitsch and Adolph Langsner, *Wage and Salary Administration* (2d ed., Cincinnati: South-Western Publishing, 1970).

penalty cargo Cargoes in the shipping and longshoring industry which because of their obnoxious, disagreeable, or dangerous character are loaded at a premium (higher) rate of pay.

Source reference: Hobart S. Perry, *Ship Management and Operation* (New York: Simmons-Boardman Publishing, 1931).

penalty rates A term used interchangeably with premium rate or rates for overtime, Sunday, and holiday work, or for unpleasant, obnoxious, or hazardous work. The rates may be at time and one-half the regular rate for actual hours of work, or double time, or at a specified monetary amount greater than the straight-time rate when the hours fall on a holiday or on Sunday.

See also HAZARDOUS OCCUPATIONS, OVERTIME RATE, PREMIUM PAY.

Pendleton Act of 1883 *See* CIVIL SERVICE ACT OF 1883.

Pennington case Case in which the United Mine Workers Union was held potentially subject to heavy treble damage claims under the Sherman Anti-Trust Act. It grew out of an attempt by the union to collect welfare fund contributions from a small coal company. The company filed a counter suit alleging that the UMW and the major coal companies had been engaged in a conspiracy since 1950 under which the UMW agreed not to oppose rapid mechanization of the mines in exchange for an agreement by the companies not to protest wage increases demanded by the union as long as the increases were matched by increased productivity through mechanization. A federal district court ruled in favor of the company and awarded treble damages of $270,000, plus attorneys' fees of $55,000; the U.S. Court of Appeals at Cincinnati upheld the award, and the case went to the Supreme Court.

The Supreme Court made these rulings:

(1) A union may make wage agreements with a multi-employer bargaining unit and, in pursuance of its own union interests, may seek to obtain the same terms from other employers.

(2) But a union forfeits its exemption from the antitrust laws when it clearly is shown that the union has agreed with one set of employers to impose a certain wage scale on other bargaining units. One group of employers may not conspire to eliminate competitors from the industry, and the union is liable, along with the employers, if it becomes a party to the conspiracy.

The Supreme Court, however, reversed the decision and remanded the case for a new trial because it found that the trial court erroneously admitted evidence concerning the efforts of the UMW and the companies to get the secretary of labor to set a high Walsh-Healey minimum wage and also because the trial court told the jury that it could include damages resulting from this action in its verdict.

Source reference: United Mine Workers v. Pennington, 381 US 657, 59 LRRM 2369 (1965).

See also ALLEN-BRADLEY CASE, HUTCHESON CASE, SHERMAN ACT OF 1890.

Pennsylvania Greyhound Lines case *See* NLRB V. PENNSYLVANIA GREYHOUND LINES, INC.

pension Periodic payments of money, usually on a monthly basis, to individuals who have been retired from the employ of a company after reaching a specified age, or period of service, or because of accident, illness, or some other reason.

Industrial pensions are those developed by private industry for individuals who have worked continuously over a period of time. Trade union pensions are those systems adopted by the trade unions to provide for older members who have been in continuous membership and are in good standing at the time of their retirement. Beginning in 1950, pension plans were negotiated between labor and management and covered by collective bargaining contracts.

Among the classifications of pensions, those of formal or informal plans may be noted. Informal plans are generally found in smaller companies without fixed rules or any regular plan. Formal plans are well developed, stating in detail the procedures concerning the age of retirement, length of service, administration of the plan, and the amounts to which employees are entitled, as well as other specifications.

Plans also may be classified as contributory or noncontributory. Noncontributory plans are financed entirely by the employer; contributory plans are financed by employer and employees.

Plans may also be classified as contractual or noncontractual. The noncontractual give the employer greater option to abandon or modify the plan, whereas the contractual plans set forth the conditions for maintenance and procedures for modification.

Source references: BNA, *Pensions and Other Retirement Benefit Plans* (Washington:

PPF Survey no. 134, 1982); ———, *Pensions and Profit Sharing* (3d ed., Washington: 1964); Gary Burtless and Jerry A. Hausman, *"Double Dipping": The Combined Effects of Social Security and Civil Service Pensions on Employee Retirement* (Cambridge: NBER, WP no. 800, 1981); Charles L. Dearing, *Industrial Pensions* (Washington: Brookings Institution, 1954); William Goldner, *Pensions Under Collective Bargaining* (Berkeley: UC, Institute of IR, 1950); Daniel I. Halperin and Gaby E. Gross, "Sex Discrimination and Pensions: Are We Moving Toward Unisex Tables?" *NYU 30th Annual National Conference on Labor*, ed. by Richard Adelman (New York: Bender, 1977); James A. Hamilton and Dorrance C. Bronson, *Pensions* (New York: McGraw-Hill, 1958); Daniel M. Holland, "What Can We Expect from Pensions?" *Harvard BR*, July/Aug. 1959; Dan M. McGill, *Fulfilling Pension Expectations* (Homewood: Irwin, 1962); Marianna M. Perkins, "Pension Claims in Bankruptcy," *LLJ*, June 1981; Dallas L. Salisbury, "Toward a National Retirement Income Policy: Priorities for the Eighties," *LLJ*, May 1981; Thomas C. Sassman, "Postretirement Increase Plans: Why You Need Them and How to Pick the Right One," *PJ*, April 1980; Bert Seidman, "Pensions: The Public-Private Interplay," *American Federationist*, July 1976; Kenneth P. Shapiro, "An Ideal Pension System," *PJ*, April 1981; Jozetta H. Srb, *Portable Pensions, A Review of the Issues* (Ithaca: NYSSILR, Cornell Univ., Key Issues Series no.4, 1969); Tax Foundation, Inc., *Employee Pension Systems in State and Local Government* (New York: Research Pub. no. 33, 1976); U.S. Congress, House, Select Committee on Aging, *Women and Retirement Income Programs: Current Issues of Equity and Adequacy, A Report* (Washington: 1979); U.S. Dept. of Justice, *The Pension Game: American Pension System from the Viewpoint of the Average Woman*; Report of the Task Force on Sex Discimination (Washington: 1979); Gerard P. Walsh, Jr. (comp.), *Pension Laws* (Washignton: U.S. Congress, House, 1981); "Will You Ever Collect a Pension?" *Across the Board*, Sept. 1982; Burton A. Zorn, "Bargaining Over Pensions," *NYU 3d Annual Conference on Labor*, ed. by Emanuel Stein (Albany: Bender, 1950).

See also BRIDGING, EMPLOYEE RETIREMENT INCOME SECURITY ACT (ERISA) OF 1974, INLAND STEEL CO. V. NLRB, MANHART CASE, NORRIS CASE, PRIVATE PENSION PLAN, RETIREMENT EQUITY ACT OF 1984, VESTED RIGHTS.

pensionable age The age specified under a particular pension program at which the employee either becomes eligible to receive retirement benefits on a voluntary basis, or is required to retire and accept the pension under plans that have a fixed or automatic age for retirement.

Some pension plans set a "normal" retirement age but defer "compulsory" retirement to a later age (i.e., permissive retirement at 65 and compulsory at 70).

See also RETIREMENT AGE.

Pension and Welfare Benefit Programs Office established in April 1975 within the Labor-Management Services Administration to oversee the Department of Labor's responsibilities under the Employee Retirement Income Security Act (ERISA). It investigates potential ERISA violations; it also conducts research and provides information and technical assistance to plan administrators and the public.

Source references: U.S. Dept. of Labor, *Seventieth Annual Report* (Washington: 1982); U.S. Dept. of Labor, LMSA, *Administration of the Employee Retirement Income Security Act through December 31, 1975, Report of the Secretary of Labor to the Congress* (Washington: 1976).

Pension Benefit Guaranty Corp. (PBGC) Established by Title IV of ERISA, the PBGC insures the retirement income of participants and beneficiaries covered by "defined benefit plans." According to PBGC, defined benefit plans refer to "plans which promise a specific benefit determinable in advance and payable to plan participants when they retire." Coverage is limited to private sector plans.

The PBGC insurance program requires each plan to:

(1) Proffer annual insurance premium payments to the PBGC,
(2) Notify PBGC of termination of multiemployer plans or intent to terminate single-employer plans,

(3) Follow procedures in terminating plans and in the allocation and distribution of assets, and
(4) Apply to PBGC for financial assistance needed by multi-employer plans to pay the guaranteed benefits.

The secretaries of labor, commerce, and treasury comprise the PBGC board of directors.

Address: 2020 K St., N.W., Washington, D.C. 20006. Tel. (202) 254–4817

Source references: Edwin M. Jones, "PBGC at the Crossroads," *LLJ*, June 1983; ———, "PBGC's Critical Needs," *LLJ*, Nov. 1982; U.S. Pension Benefit Guaranty Corp., *Annual Report to the Congress FY 82* (Washington: 1983); ———, *Plan Coverage Under PBGC's Pension Insurance* (Washington: 1982).

See also EMPLOYEE RETIREMENT INCOME SECURITY ACT (ERISA) OF 1974, MULTI-EMPLOYER PENSION PLAN AMENDMENTS ACT (MPPAA) OF 1980.

pensioner An individual who has retired and receives a pension from his employer for the performance of past services.

pension fund A fund set aside to cover the costs of the particular pension plan established and maintained by an employer to provide retirement payments of fixed and determinable amounts to employees over a period of years. The retirement benefits of the individual to be taken from the fund are based upon years of service, earnings, and similar factors which relate to the employee's time with the company and contribution (if a contributory plan) in terms of income.

Pension plans may be funded plans which provide a fixed amount of money so the amount the employee is to receive on retirement will not depend on the position of future management toward the pension or on the question whether the fund will have sufficient money to meet the obligations of the plan. The established fund is fixed as part of the regular expense of operation and the money not only has been written off as an expense of the business, but has been placed in a fund set aside for the particular purpose for which the plan was established.

Source references: Victor L. Andrews, "Interests at Stake in the Investment of Pension Funds," *MLR*, July 1959; James R. Barth and Joseph J. Cordes, "Nontraditional Criteria for Investing Pension Assets: An Economic Appraisal," *Journal of Labor Research*, Fall 1981; The Conference Board, *Current Directions in Pension Fund Management* (New York: Information Bull. 39, 1978); Patrick J. Davey, *Financial Management of Company Pension Plans* (New York: The Conference Board, Report no. 611, 1973); Frank L. Griffin, Jr. and Charles L. Trowbridge, *Status of Funding Under Private Pension Plans* (Homewood: Irwin, 1969); Paul P. Harbrecht, *Pension Funds and Economic Power* (New York: Twentieth Century Fund, 1959); ———, "Union Participation in the Investment of Pension Funds," *NYU 14th Annual Conference on Labor*, ed. by Emanuel Stein (Albany: Bender, 1961); Joseph Krislov, "A Study of Pension Funding," *MLR*, June 1966; Roger F. Murray, *Economic Aspects of Pensions, A Summary Report* (New York: NBER, General Studies no. 85, 1968); James P. Northrup and Herbert R. Northrup, "Union Divergent Investing of Pensions: A Power, Non-Employee Relations Issue," *Journal of Labor Research*, Fall 1981; Roy A. Schotland, "Have Pension Investment Managers Over-Emphasized the Needs of Retirees?" *Journal of Labor Research*, Fall 1981; Robert Tilove, *Public Employee Pension Funds, A Twentieth Century Fund Report* (New York: Columbia UP, 1976); U.S. GAO, *Funding of State and Local Government Pension Plans: A National Problem* (Washington: 1979).

See also EMPLOYEE RETIREMENT INCOME SECURITY ACT (ERISA) OF 1974, SELF-ADMINISTERED (TRUSTEED) PLAN.

pension plan An organized program maintained by an employer, the purpose of which is to provide specific and determinable benefits to his employees to be paid over a period of years following the retirement of the employees. The payment generally extends throughout the life of the individual pensioned.

The Employee Retirement Income Security Act (ERISA) of 1974 defines pension plan as "any plan, fund, or program . . . established or maintained by an employer or by an employee organization, or by both, . . . [which] (i) provides retirement income to employees, or (ii) results in a deferral of income by employees for periods extending to the termination of covered employment or beyond. . . ." In 1981, approximately 650,000 pension plans with 50 million participants and $560 billion in assets came under the purview of the ERISA.

Source references: American Council of Life Insurance, *Pension Facts, 1982* (Washington: 1982); AFL-CIO, *Pension Plans Under Collective Bargaining* (Washington: Pub. no. 132, 1964); Philip M. Doyle, "Municipal Pension Plans: Provisions and Payments," *MLR*, Nov. 1977; Raymond Goetz, "Pension Plans and Labor Law," *IR Law Digest*, Jan. 1969; John V. Harper, "Fiduciary Obligations and Sex Discrimination," *Employee Relations LJ*, Autumn 1979; Robert C. Joiner, "Changes in Pension Plans for Salaried Employees," *MLR*, April 1966; Dorothy R. Kittner, "Health Insurance and Pension Plan Coverage in Union Contracts," *MLR*, March 1962; Walter W. Kolodrubetz, "Multiemployer Pension Plans Under Collective Bargaining—Parts I, II and III," *MLR*, Oct. 1961, Feb. 1962, and April 1962; Marianna M. Perkins, "Pension Claims in Bankruptcy," *LLJ*, June 1981; Richard S. Soble, "Bankruptcy Claims of Multiemployer Pension Plans," *LLJ*, Jan. 1982; Jozetta H. Srb, *Communicating With Employees About Pension and Welfare Benefits* (Ithaca: Cornell Univ., NYSSILR, Key Issues Series no. 8, 1971); U.S. Dept. of Labor, LMSA, *Employee Retirement Income Security Act, 1981 Report to Congress* (Washington: 1982); U.S. President's Commission on Pension Policy, *Coming of Age: Toward a National Retirement Income Policy* (Washington: 1981); _______, *An Interim Report* (Washington: 1980); _______, *Retirement Income Goals* (Washington: 1980); Ernest J. White, "Pension Plans in Labor Agreements v. Older Workers," *LLJ*, Jan. 1961.

See also CONTRIBUTORY PENSION PLAN, EMPLOYEE RETIREMENT INCOME SECURITY ACT (ERISA) OF 1974, FUNDED PENSION PLAN, FUTURE SERVICE BENEFITS, NONCONTRIBUTORY PENSION PLAN, PORTABLE PENSION, PRIVATE PENSION PLAN.

pension planning Procedures adopted by those concerned with the problems of pensions and the study of various assumptions so that a pension plan will meet the objectives for which the particular pension is established.

Source references: AMA, *Pension Planning: A Data Book* (New York: Research Study no. 43, 1960); BNA, *Pensions and Profit Sharing* (3d ed., Washington: 1964); Robert D. Collins, "Looking Forward in Pension Planning," *NYU 15th Annual Conference on Labor*, ed. by Emanuel Stein (Albany: Bender, 1962); Richmond M. Corbett, *Pension Trends and the Self-Employed* (New Brunswick: Rutgers UP, 1961); Walter J. Couper and Roger Vaughan, *Pension Planning: Experience and Trends* (New York: Industrial Relations Counselors, Inc., 1954); George H. Foote and David J. McLaughlin, "The President's Stake in Pension Planning," *Harvard BR*, Sept./Oct. 1965; A. J. Meuche, *Successful Pension Planning* (New York: PH, 1949); Robert E. Sibson, *A Survey of Pension Planning* (Chicago: CCH, 1952); Robert Tilove, "Developments in Pension Planning and Administration," *NYU 14th Annual Conference on Labor*, ed. by Emanuel Stein (Albany: Bender, 1961).

peon Generally a common laborer or one who performs work which is relatively unskilled. In some areas it may refer to a person who is held in servitude to pay off a debt.

peonage A form of involuntary service, generally under contract. Although peonage is somewhat removed from slavery, it is so only because in peonage there is a contractual relationship between the individual and the master. The involuntary servitude results from indebtedness of the individual who accepts employment in return for which the employer may provide advances for food, clothing, housing, or transportation to the area in which the individual is going to work.

See also PADRONE SYSTEM.

People Ex Rel Tipaldo v. Morehead *See* MOREHEAD V. TIPALDO.

People v. Merlin A decision of the Court of General Sessions in New York City in 1810, which indicted a group of striking shoemakers for engaging in a conspiracy. The court held that a combination "to do an act, unlawful in itself, to the prejudice of other persons, or to accomplish a lawful end by unlawful means is to be deemed a criminal conspiracy; the common law of England . . . must be deemed to be applicable."

Source reference: People v. Merlin, New York 262 (1810).

People v. United Mine Workers An important decision in Colorado in 1921 which upheld the right of the state to require publicity and the use of legislative investigations and mediation in handling disputes in essential industries, including coal mining. The Colorado statute was passed in 1916, following the bitter strike known as the "Ludlow Massacre" of 1913–1914.

Although the state court upheld the right of the state to so regulate in the area of public utilities, it held in another case involving a theatre that theatres were not "affected with a public interest."

Source references: People v. United Mine Workers, 70 Colo. 269 (1921); *People ex rel Industrial Commission v. Aladdin Theatre Corp.*, 96 Colo. 527 (1935); Carl Raushenbush and Emanuel Stein, *Labor Cases and Materials* (New York: Crofts, 1941).

See also LUDLOW MASSACRE.

People v. Wilzig A case in New York which involved the application of the common-law doctrine of conspiracy. The doctrine holds that an act of an individual which may be lawful may become unlawful when it is the object of concerted action or action by groups. The court in *Wilzig* held that "a combination of men is a very serious matter . . . no man can stand up against a combination: he may successfully defend himself against a single adversary, but when his foes are combined and numerous, he must fall."

Source reference: People v. Wilzig, New York crim. 403 (1886).

per capita income Per capita means "for each person," so the per capita income in the United States would be the total income divided by the number of individuals. Per capita income within a state would be determined by the income of the state divided by the individuals within the state. Per capita income is frequently used as a measure of the well-being of a country or community. If it is measured merely in terms of money, it reflects the per capita money income but may not reflect the actual real income. Per capita income may be adjusted to reflect changes in prices or purchasing power, over a period of time, to show real per capita income.

Source references: Edwin J. Coleman, "Personal Income by States in 1961," *Survey of Current Business*, Aug. 1962; ———, "Regional Income Developments in 1962," *Survey of Current Business*, April 1963; William F. Ogburn and Francis R. Allen, "Technological Development and Per Capita Income," *American Journal of Sociology*, Sept. 1959; Melvin W. Reder, "Trends in Wages, Earnings, and Per Capita Income," *MLR*, May 1959.

per capita tax The dues payment made by a local union to the international union to which it is affiliated, or by an international union to its parent federation, based on the number of members in the local union. The per capita tax is an assessment made by the national or international union for service to the local union. It may also be a tax assessed by the parent organization, AFL-CIO, to its national or international unions for services which the federation performs for them.

percentage shop A procedure developed by the National War Labor Board during World War II in which a company was required to maintain a fixed percentage of union employees in relation to the total work force employed. The procedure was designed in part to maintain the union's security by not permitting the dilution of union strength in the plant with nonunion employees. This was a modification of the general policy of maintenance of union membership widely used by the War Labor Board.

performance appraisal A systematic review of an individual employee's job performance to evaluate the effectiveness or adequacy of the work.

Performance appraisals are designed for rating or evaluating the individual during his training and development and as a basis for possible promotion where the appraisal indicates outstanding performance of the individual, or to reward the employee with a wage adjustment.

Source references: BNA, *Performance Appraisal Programs* (Washington: PPF Survey no. 135, 1983); Frank D. Ferris, "Grieving Performance Evaluations in Federal Promotion Actions," *Journal of Collective Negotiations in the Public Sector*, Vol. 8, no. 2, 1979; Elaine F. Gruenfeld, *Performance Appraisal: Promise and Peril* (Ithaca: Cornell Univ., NYSSILR, Key Issues Series no. 25, 1981); Robert Hoppock, "Ground Rules for Appraisal Interviewers," *Personnel*, May/June 1961; S. L. Johnson and W. W. Ronan, "An Exploratory Study of Bias in Job Performance Evaluation," *Public Personnel Management*, Sept./Oct. 1979; Marion S. Kellogg, *What to Do About Performance Appraisal* (rev. ed., New York: AMACOM, 1975); E. Bruce Kirk, "Performance Appraisals: Formal vs. Informal," *PJ*, April 1963; Donald L. Kirkpatrick, *How to Improve Performance Through Appraisal and Coaching* (New York: AMACOM, 1982); Lawrence S. Kleiman and Richard L. Durham, "Performance Appraisal, Promotion and the Courts: A Critical Review," *Personnel Psychology*, Spring 1981; Kenneth J. Lacho, G. Kent Stearns, and Maurice F. Villere, "A Study of Employee Appraisal Systems of Major Cities in the United States," *Public Personnel Management*, March/April 1979; Gary P. Latham and Kenneth N. Wexley, *Increasing Productivity Through Performance Appraisal* (Reading, Mass.: Addison-Wesley, 1981); Robert I. Lazer, "The 'Discrimination' Danger in Performance Appraisal," *Conference Board Record*, March 1976; Priscilla Levinson, *A Guide for Improving Performance Evaluation, A Handbook* (Washington: U.S. CSC, Personnel Management Series no. 28, 1977); Joseph A. Litterer, "Pitfalls in Performance Appraisal," *PJ*, July/Aug. 1960; Felix M. Lopez, Jr., *Evaluating Employee Performance* (Chicago: PPA, 1968); Gary L. Lubben, Duane E. Thompson, and Charles R. Klasson, "Performance Appraisal: The Legal Implications of Title VII," *Personnel*, May/June 1980; Harold Mayfield, "In Defense of Performance Appraisal," *Harvard BR*, March/April 1960; Douglas McGregor, "An Uneasy Look at Performance Appraisal," *Harvard BR*, May/June 1957; Richard F. Olson, *Performance Appraisal; A Guide to Greater Productivity* (New York: Wiley, 1981); Terry L. Talbert, Kathleen I. Carroll, and William W. Ronan, "Measuring Clerical Job Performance," *PJ*, Nov. 1976; Kenneth S. Teel, "Performance Appraisal: Current Trends, Persistent Progress," *PJ*, April 1980; Washington Local Government Personnel Institute, *Evaluating Employee Performance, A Manual for Local Governments* (Seattle: 1979); Thomas L. Whisler and Shirley F. Harper (ed.), *Performance Appraisal: Research and Practice* (New York: Holt, Rinehart, Winston, 1962); Robert White, "Performance Enhancement by Reciprocal Accountability," *Public Personnel Management*, July/Aug. 1979.

See also ASSESSMENT CENTER, EFFICIENCY RATING, INDUSTRIAL EFFORT, MERIT RATING, RATING.

performance rating *See* EFFICIENCY RATING, MERIT RATING.

performance tests Measures or tests which determine an individual's performance or proficiency in doing the job. Tests of this type should have some measure of standardization, and should cover work which is typical and normally would be required of the employee in the actual performance of the job. Methods should be devised to validate and check the actual performance as measured in output, tolerance, or by whatever other standards set up to measure the performance.

See also TEST.

periodic review This term may apply to regular merit reviews of individual employees under company or collectively bargained programs for adjustments of individual rates within a rate range or possibly for promotion. It may refer to a personnel audit which involves the regular review or appraisal of the individual employee and the impact of the company's personnel program or policies upon the individual.

permanent arbitrator An arbitrator who is appointed under the terms of a collective bargaining agreement for a specific period of time, generally the duration of the contract, which may be for a period of one, two, or three years. If the parties become dissatisfied with the arbitrator, even when appointed for a term, it is often the practice to obtain a new arbitrator and to provide reimbursement to the original arbitrator for the remainder of the contract. The term "permanent" does not have much significance in the arbitration process since the arbitrator has no tenure and serves at the convenience of the parties.

Paul Douglas makes reference to the impartial umpire machinery in which the individual permanent arbitrator performs a role not only in the interpretation and application of the agreement, but may be of assistance to the parties in trying to resolve problems of long range effect on the union, the employer, and the industry. He cites the need in *The Worker in Modern Economic Society*: ". . . for a permanent arbitrator to act judicially in interpreting and analyzing the agreement and, what is fully as important, to maintain as a living process, the central idea of a joint interest in the . . . conditions of the industry. To a degree as yet undetermined this 'impartial machinery' also takes account of a 'public interest' as distinct from the interests of the contracting parties."

Source references: Marion Beatty, *Labor-Management Arbitration Manual* (New York: Eppler, 1960); Domingo P. Disini, Jr., "The Permanent Impartial Arbitration System of the B. F. Goodrich Company and the United Rubber, Cork, Linoleum and Plastic Workers of America, AFL-CIO" (M.S. thesis, Cornell Univ., 1966); Paul H. Douglas, Curtice N. Hitchcock, and Willard E. Atkins, *The Worker in Modern Economic Society* (Chicago: Univ. of Chicago Press, 1923).

See also ARBITRATION; ARBITRATION, AD HOC; IMPARTIAL CHAIRPERSON; REFEREE; UMPIRE.

permanent disability The inability of an individual, as the result of an injury or accident, to perform regular or normal work, or, in extreme cases, any kind of gainful employment. The disability may be partial or total. Pension plans frequently provide benefits to employees retiring because of disability. Such employees have to meet certain length-of-service requirements.

Source references: Earl F. Chiet, "Work Injuries and Recovery: II—Permanent Disability—A Policy Proposal," *MLR*, Nov. 1961; U.S. Dept. of HEW, SSA, *The Disabled Worker Under OASDI* (Washington: Research Report no. 6, 1964).

See also DISABILITY, DISABILITY INSURANCE, PERMANENT PARTIAL DISABILITY, PERMANENT TOTAL DISABILITY.

permanent employee An employee who has met the requirements of the probationary period. This will vary in individual plants. The permanent-status conditions may be set out in the collective bargaining agreement. A permanent employee has benefits which do not accrue to a temporary employee. Individuals on permanent status acquire seniority and receive the general benefits established by collective bargaining agreements or the personnel policies of the company.

Permanent status does not mean that the employer is required to retain the employee regardless of economic conditions or changes in company policy or operation. The authority to discharge an individual because of inefficiency or other shortcomings remains with the employer, provided it conforms with the terms of the collective bargaining contract, where a contract exists. Employees have status within a company and a relative position based on their qualifications and seniority, but not tenure. Permanence in employment does not exist except where by contract a form of guaranteed employment is set up, and these generally are limited to duration of the agreement.

See also JOB TENURE.

permanent injunction Injunctions granted by courts are generally of three categories: (1) restraining orders, (2) temporary injunctions, and (3) permanent injunctions. The procedures established by various statutes, particularly the Norris-LaGuardia Act, are designed to assure that appropriate hearing and opportunity for review are given by the court before any injunction is granted. The Norris-LaGuardia Act sets forth the conditions under which federal courts may grant injunctive relief.

Source reference: Norris-LaGuardia Anti-Injunction Act, as amended, 29 U.S.C. §§ 101–110, 113–115 (1982) (29 U.S.C. §§ 111–112 were repealed by 62 Stat. 862 (1948); matters formerly covered by section 11 of the Norris-LaGuardia Anti-Injunction Act are now covered by 18 U.S.C. § 3692; matters formerly covered by section 12 of the Norris-LaGuardia Anti-

Injunction Act are now covered by Rule 12 of the Federal Rules of Criminal Procedure).

See also INJUNCTION, NORRIS-LAGUARDIA ACT.

permanent partial disability Permanent partial disability is a disability which generally permits partial use of the affected member, such as a limb. Accident and health insurance policies often establish a schedule of fees or monies to be paid to an insured employee when the inability to perform the duties has been brought about as the result of illness or accident.

See also PERMANENT DISABILITY.

permanent piece rate A piece rate which is established after preliminary or temporary trial rates have been applied to a particular job or operation, and after conditions under which the job is to be run have been standardized. They are presumed to remain in effect for a substantial period of time or until the basic job conditions, content, or materials change.

permanent total disability A phrase used with reference to employees who are considered permanently unable to perform their regular work. Walter Dodd, in *Administration of Workmen's Compensation*, considers that the loss of both hands, or both arms, or both feet, or both legs, or both eyes, or any two thereof shall, "in the absence of conclusive proof to the contrary, constitute permanent total disability. In all other cases, permanent total disability shall be determined in accordance with the facts." The existence of the impairment must be certified by a physician, under the Social Security Act and under most private pension plans, in order for the worker to qualify for benefits.

Source reference: Walter F. Dodd, *Administration of Workmen's Compensation* (New York: Commonwealth Fund, 1936).

See also PERMANENT DISABILITY.

permissive subjects for bargaining Topics that are neither illegal nor mandatory subjects of bargaining, sometimes termed voluntary subjects.

The NLRB with approval of the Supreme Court has created three categories of bargaining topics. The first category consists of illegal subjects, such as the closed shop or hot cargo clauses. The second category consists of subjects made mandatory by law: wages, hours, and terms and conditions of employment. The third category consists of topics outside the first two categories that the parties may bargain over "at their joint pleasure."

Either party may refuse to bargain over a permissive subject. Permissive subjects may not be taken to impasse and strikes may not occur over such issues.

Source reference: Walter J. Gershenfeld, J. Joseph Lowenberg, and Bernard Ingster, *Scope of Public-Sector Bargaining* (Lexington, Mass.: Lexington Books, 1977).

See also BORG-WARNER CASE, MANDATORY SUBJECTS FOR BARGAINING, PROHIBITED SUBJECTS FOR BARGAINING.

permissive wage adjustment Any provision or procedure which permits the reopening of wage negotiations during the life of the contract when certain conditions take place which require a review of the wages of the particular company. The conditions for wage reopening may result from upward adjustments of prices or changes in the consumer price index, major changes in general economic conditions, the introduction of new methods of work, or other factors which the parties feel are of such importance that a review of the wages becomes urgent.

As a matter of general policy, any collective bargaining agreement may be reopened at any time by consent of both parties and provide for wage adjustments. It is the practice, however, to sign contracts for a fixed term in order to obtain general stability not only of working conditions, but of labor costs.

See also WAGE ADJUSTMENT PLANS.

permit card A certificate or similar document issued by a union, for a fee, which allows or "permits" an individual who is not a member of the union (in some cases he may be in the process of becoming a member) to work on a job covered by the issuing union's contract. In the past, "permit cards" usually were associated with closed-shop contracts; now, in work covered by the Taft-Hartley Amendments to the National Labor Relations Act—in interstate commerce, that is—such cards may be issued where union-shop contracts are in effect.

Permit cards are well known among the building trades unions. They may appear almost anywhere that periodical, or seasonal, factors cause an "unusual" demand for workers. Theoretically but not always in practice, a permit or permit card allows employment of "permit men" for only a limited period.

In some situations a union may grant a permit card to an apprentice who has almost completed apprenticeship and qualified as a journeyman, thus allowing work at journeymen rates before formally achieving the status of a journeyman or qualified craftsman.

Source reference: Kurt Braun, *The Right to Organize and Its Limits* (Washington: Brookings Institution, 1950).

See also APPRENTICESHIP.

permit fee The charge made by a union for a permit card.

perquisites Additional compensation furnished by an employer, usually in goods or services over and above the general payment of wages or salaries. The perquisites may consist of food, lodging, and payments in kind, particularly where the employee is working on agricultural products and the payments in kind may include special food. In case of employees working in restaurants, it may consist of meals and other items which are in fact additional compensation but not in the form of direct wage payments.

See also INCOME IN KIND; PATERNALISM, EMPLOYER.

persistent unemployment A general description of a prolonged and sustained rate of unemployment which has continued even during periods of high employment and upward movement of the business cycle.

Source references: Robert Aronson et al., "The Incidence of Persistent Unemployment, Discussion," *Proceedings of the 12th A/M, IRRA*, ed. by David Johnson (Madison: 1960); William H. Miernyk, "The Incidence of Persistent Unemployment," *Proceedings of the 12th A/M, IRRA*, ed. by David Johnson (Madison: 1960).

personality inventory A test or tests designed to measure personality traits particularly those traits which have a bearing on the person's effectiveness in handling a particular job.

The Bernreuter "Personality Inventory" is a widely used test which attempts to measure (1) sociability, (2) self-confidence, (3) dominance-submission, (4) introversion-extroversion, (5) self-sufficiency, and (6) neurotic tendency. A criticism is that the person being tested may guess the answers that are desired.

A personality inventory designed by Leonard G. Gordon makes it difficult for a person to anticipate the kind of answer which would put the individual in the best light. This provides a set of multiple choices, usually four, and the individual taking the test indicates which feature or characteristic is most like and the one least like the individual. This "forced-choice" type of inventory avoids some of the problems which arise when the employee being tested attempts to select the "correct" response. Gordon also developed a personal inventory which attempts to measure (1) cautiousness, (2) original thinking, (3) personal relations, and (4) vigor. This system also uses the "forced-choice" procedure.

Source references: Solomon Barkin, "Personality Profile of Seven Textile Workers," *LLJ*, June 1960; Robert G. Bernreuter, *The Personality Inventory* (Stanford: Stanford UP, 1935); Warren S. Blumenfeld, "Effects of Various Instructions on Personality Inventory Scores," *Personnel Administration/Public Personnel Review*, Sept./Oct. 1972; Leonard G. Gordon, *Gordon Personal Profile* (New York: World Book, 1953); Herbert Myer and Joseph N. Bertotti, "Uses and Misuses of Tests in Selecting Key Personnel," *Personnel*, Nov. 1956; Christopher Orpen, "The 'Correct' Use of Personality Tests: A View From Industrial Psychology," *Public Personnel Management*, May/June 1974; C. Harold Stone and William E. Kendall, *Effective Personnel Selection Procedures* (New York: PH, 1956); Robert L. Thorndike, *Personnel Selection* (New York: Wiley, 1949); William H. White, Jr., "The Fallacies of Personality Testing," *Fortune*, Sept. 1954; Ronald C. Winkler and Theodore W. Mathews, "How Employees Feel About Personality Tests," *PJ*, Sept. 1967.

See also INVENTORY OF EMPLOYEE SKILLS, PERSONNEL AUDIT (OR SURVEY), PSYCHOLOGICAL TESTING, TEST.

personality profile The broad summary picture which results from personality inventory testing and interviews. It is designed to give a broad view of the individual's personality.

personality testing *See* PERSONALITY INVENTORY.

personalized rate *See* RED CIRCLE RATE.

personal problems consultant A counselor attached to the personnel department staff of a company. The functions may include review of conditions in the plant and their impact on the employee. The consultant may provide personal counseling guidance to employees. This may involve an interview and discussion with the employees to make them aware of the problems and alternative paths available to them for their solution. Where problems are persistent or deeply rooted, they may involve more intensive and more highly specialized consultation outside of the personnel office.

Source reference: Harry K. Tootle, *Employees Are People* (New York: McGraw-Hill, 1947).

See also COUNSELING.

personnel A term applied to all of the individuals engaged in any enterprise toward whom a personnel administration program is directed.

personnel administration The broad structure of a personnel program designed to obtain most effective utilization of manpower, not only for more efficient production, but also for better utilization of facilities and equipment.

The personnel program in private industry concerns itself with at least four major areas. The first and most important is the objectives to be achieved by the program; second, the policies established and directed toward achieving the goals; third, the procedures set up to carry out the policies; and fourth, the budgets designed both to carry out the procedures and to measure the results of particular programs and activities as a factor of cost.

The control process is directed primarily toward evaluation of the performance of the organization to assure that its basic plans are being accomplished.

Source references: Joseph J. Famularo (ed.), *Handbook of Modern Personnel Administration* (New York: McGraw-Hill, 1972); Edwin E. Ghiselli and Clarence W. Brown, *Personnel and Industrial Psychology* (2d ed., New York: McGraw-Hill, 1955); Russell L. Greenman and Eric J. Schmertz, *Personnel Administration and the Law* (2d ed., Washington: BNA, 1979); Allen R. Janger, *The Personnel Function: Changing Objectives and Organization* (New York: The Conference Board, Report 712, 1977); Rossall J. Johnson, *Personnel and Industrial Relations: A Text Book With Cases, Problems and Role Playing* (Homewood: Irwin, 1960); Alva F. Kindall, *Personnel Administration, Principles and Cases* (Homewood: Irwin, 1961); John J. Leach, "Merging the Two Faces of Personnel: A Challenge of the 1980s," *Personnel*, Jan./Feb. 1980; Dalton E. McFarland, *Cooperation and Conflict in Personnel Administration* (New York: American Foundation for Management Research, 1962); John B. Miner and Mary Green Miner, *Personnel and Industrial Relations; A Managerial Approach* (3d ed., New York: Macmillan, 1977); NICB, *Personnel Administration: Changing Scope and Organization* (New York: Studies in Personnel Policy no. 203, 1966); Paul Pigors and Charles A. Myers, *Personnel Administration; A Point of View and a Method* (9th ed., New York: McGraw-Hill, 1981); Sidney H. Simon, "The Total Personnel System," *PJ*, Dec. 1979; George Strauss and Leonard R. Sayles, *Personnel: The Human Problems of Management* (4th ed., Englewood Cliffs: PH, 1980); William B. Wolf, *Cases and Exercises in the Management of Personnel* (Belmont: Wadsworth, 1961).

See also PERSONNEL MANAGEMENT.

personnel audit (or survey) An annual personnel administration inventory which is an analysis and measurement of a company's personnel policies and practices to determine their effectiveness. The purpose of the audit is to develop ways in which the program may be improved and to determine whether existing policies and practices are effective.

The term sometimes denotes an annual review of individuals within an enterprise to determine their potential for promotion or transfer and the potential of employees in their particular areas of competence.

Source references: Ross E. Azevedo, *Missing Ingredient in Skills Inventories* (Minneapolis: Univ. of Minnesota, IRC, Reprint 124, 1977); R. T. Heiser, "Auditing the Personnel Function in a Decentralized, Multi-Unit Organization," *PJ*, March 1968; H. G. Heneman, Jr., *Personnel Audits and Manpower Assets* (Minneapolis: Univ. of Minnesota, IRC, Special Release no. 5, 1967); Ernest C. Miller, "The Personnel Audit—Gateway to the Future," *PJ*, Sept. 1961; NICB, *Personnel Audits and Reports to Top Management* (New York: Studies in Personnel Policy no. 191, 1964); George S. Odiorne, "Of Profits and the Personnel Department," *Personnel*, July/Aug. 1958; Eugene Schmuckler, "The Personnel Audit: Management's Forgotten Tool," *PJ*, Nov. 1973; James S. Westbrook, "Auditing Personnel Program Follow-Through," *Personnel*, Nov./Dec. 1967; Max S. Wortman, Jr., "Evaluation of the Personnel Function Through the Audit," *PJ*, Feb. 1968; Dale Yoder et al., *Handbook of Personnel Management and Labor Relations* (New York: McGraw-Hill, 1958).

See also INVENTORY OF EMPLOYEE SKILLS, LABOR AUDIT, PERIODIC REVIEW.

personnel department The department of a company charged with responsibility for coordinating personnel activities and assisting managers and supervisors in the management of their personnel.

The scope of the personnel department will vary with the extent to which management relies on it to carry out the functions of personnel management, including recruitment, hiring, testing, training, promotion, job analysis, and, perhaps, collective bargaining.

Source references: AMA, *Company Officers Assess the Personnel Function* (New York: Research Study no. 79, 1967); Edwin H. Burack and Edwin L. Miller, "The Personnel Function in Transition," *Management Review*, March 1977; BNA, *The Personnel Department* (Washington: PPF Survey no. 73, 1964); T. F. Cawsey, "Why Line Managers Don't Listen to Their Personnel Departments," *Personnel*, Jan./Feb. 1980; Charles J. Coleman and Joseph M. Rich, "Why Not Fire the Personnel Manager?" *Human Resource Management*, Summer 1975; Fred K. Foulkes and Henry M. Morgan, "Organizing and Staffing the Personnel Function," *Harvard BR*, May/June 1977; Edward Gross, "Sources of Lateral Authority in Personnel Departments," *IR*, May 1964; Allen R. Janger, *The Personnel Function: Changing Objectives and Organization* (New York: The Conference Board, Report 712, 1977); Steven Langer, "The Personnel and Industrial Relations Report, Part I: Personnel Salaries," and "Part II: Budgets and Staffing," *PJ*, June 1982 and July 1982; R. Bruce McAfee, "Evaluating the Personnel Department's Internal Functioning," *Personnel*, May/June 1980; Oscar A. Ornati, Edward J. Giblin, and Richard R. Floersch, *The Personnel Department, Its Staffing and Budgeting;* An AMA Research Study (New York: AMA, 1982); Alfred J. Walker, "The Newest Job in Personnel: Human Resources Data Administrator," *PJ*, Dec. 1982.

See also SERVICE DIVISION.

personnel director In general, the manager of the personnel department and the chief officer administering personnel policies. In some cases the personnel director also is responsible for the conduct of relations between company management and one or more unions.

Source references: Steven H. Applebaum, "Contemporary Personnel Administrators: Agents of Change?" *PJ*, Nov. 1974; BNA, *Aspects of the Personnel Function: Structure, Use of Electronic Data Processing and Professional Activities* (Washington: PPF Survey no. 127, 1979); Charles J. Coleman, "The Personnel Director: A Cautious Hero Indeed," *Human Resource Management*, Winter 1979; Malcolm L. Denise, "The Personnel Manager and His Educational Preparation," *ILRR*, Oct. 1962; Robert E. Finley (ed.), *The Personnel Man and His Job* (New York: AMA, 1962); Myron D. Fottler and Norman A. Townsend, "Characteristics of Public and Private Personnel Directors," *Public Personnel Management*, July/Aug. 1977; William L. Grey, "The Modern Role of the Industrial Relations Manager," *Personnel*, July/Aug. 1969; James L. Kennedy, "The Personnel Director's Changing Charter," *PJ*, Sept. 1962; Steven Langer, "The Personnel and Industrial Relations Report, Part I: Personnel Salaries, Part II: Budgets and Staffing," *PJ*, June 1982, July 1982; Willard A. Lewis, "The Personnel Manager-as-Compliance-Officer," *PJ*, Dec. 1971; Harvey F. Marriner, "RX for the Personnel Man with Too Many Hats," *Personnel*, March/April 1961; George Ritzer and Harrison M. Trice, *An Occupation in Conflict, A Study of the Personnal Manager* (Ithaca: NYSSILR, Cornell Univ., 1969); Andrew F. Sikula, "The Values and Value Systems of Industrial Personnel Managers," *Public Personnel Management*, July/Aug. 1973; Harrison Trice and George Ritzer, "The Personnel Manager and His Self-Image," *Personnel Administration*, Jan./Feb. 1972; Lawrence A. Wangler, "The Intensification of the Personnel Role," *PJ*, Feb. 1979.

See also EMPLOYMENT MANAGER, INDUSTRIAL RELATIONS MANAGER.

personnel inventory *See* PERSONNEL AUDIT (OR SURVEY).

personnel management The function primarily concerned with utilization of the human resources in a particular company or organization in such a way that the individual employee is given an opportunity to make maximum contribution under safe and congenial working conditions. Its purpose also is to create and maintain confidence between management and employees and to carry on all the activities necessary to achieve that purpose.

Source references: Lewis R. Benton, *A Guide to Creative Personnel Management* (Englewood Cliffs, PH, 1962); Herbert J. Chruden and Arthur W. Sherman, Jr., *Personnel Management* (3d ed., Cincinnati: South-Western, 1968); Gary Dessler, *Personnel Management, Modern Concepts and Techniques* (Reston, Va.: Reston, 1978); Edwin B. Flippo, *Principles of Personnel Management* (5th ed., New York: McGraw-Hill, 1980); Fred K. Foulkes, "How Top Nonunion Companies Manage Employees," *Harvard BR*, Sept./Oct. 1981; Wendell French, *The Personnel Management Process* (3d ed., Boston: Houghton Mifflin, 1974); Michael J. Jucius, *Personnel Management* (7th ed., Homewood: Irwin, 1971); Henry A. Landsberger, *Hawthorne Revisited* (Ithaca: NYSSILR, Cornell Univ., 1962); Mary Green Miner and John B. Miner, *A Guide to Personnel Management* (Washington: BNA, 1973); Thomas H. Patten, Jr. (ed.), *Classics of Personnel Management* (Oak Park, Ill.: Moore, 1979); Leonard R. Sayles and George Strauss, *Managing Human Resources* (Englewood Cliffs: PH, 1981); Walter D. Scott, Robert C. Clothier and William R. Spriegel, *Personnel Management* (6th ed., New York: McGraw-Hill, 1961); Wickham Skinner, "Big Hat, No Cattle: Managing Human Resources," *Harvard BR*, Sept./Oct. 1981; Dale Yoder and Herbert G. Heneman, Jr. (ed.), *ASPA Handbook of Personnel and Industrial Relations* (8 vol., Washington: BNA, 1974 +).

See also PERSONNEL ADMINISTRATION.

Personnel Policies Forum The Bureau of National Affairs panel of personnel and industrial relations executives who are surveyed periodically on current or major personnel and industrial relations problems. The results of these surveys are analyzed, edited, and published in a format that makes them usable for long-term reference. The surveys are distributed to subscribers to BNA labor services.

personnel policy An organization's guiding principles with respect to employees, very often embodied in a statement (or in statements) by management which in varying degree specifies what actions are to be taken and the principles upon which these directions rest. Purpose is to state the philosophy of the enterprise or organization and the means, in terms of employee well-being, by which the goals of the organization are to be attained.

Source references: BNA, *Personnel Policies for Unorganized Employees* (Washington: PPF Survey no. 84, 1968); Harriet Gorlin, "An Overview of Corporate Personnel Practices," *PJ*, Feb. 1982; Mason Haire, "Approach to an Integrated Personnel Policy," *IR*, Feb. 1968; Hawaii Employers Council, *Personnel Practices in Hawaii* (Honolulu: 1977); J. W. Lawson II and B. Smith, *How to Develop a Company Personnel Policy Manual* (3d ed., Chicago: Dartnell Corp., 1978); James M. Miles, "How to Establish a Good Industrial Relations Climate," *Management Review*, Aug. 1980; Ernest C. Miller, "Personnel Policy in a Decentralized Organization," *PJ*, Dec. 1959; George S. Odiorne, "Why Personnel Policy Is Important to Managers," *Personnel Management—New Perspectives*, ed. by Albert W. Schrader and

George S. Odiorne (Ann Arbor: Univ. of Michigan, Bureau of IR, Bull. no. 29, 1961); Terry W. Smith, "Developing a Policy Manual," *PJ*, June 1982.

personnel records *See* EMPLOYMENT HISTORY.

personnel relations The activities of an employer in communicating or otherwise dealing with individual employees most effectively to utilize their qualifications and to develop their potentialities, as well as to promote their well-being.

The term is used also to distinguish personnel relations functions from industrial relations functions.

See also PERSONNEL ADMINISTRATION, PERSONNEL MANAGEMENT.

personnel services A variety of facilities provided on a service basis by a company which may range from cafeteria and food services to recreational programs, or first aid and educational and training facilities.

See also COUNSELING; PATERNALISM, EMPLOYER.

Petrillo Act *See* LEA ACT (ANTI-PETRILLO ACT).

Petroleum and Industrial Workers; International Union of Formerly known as the International Union of Petroleum Workers, Inc., it is an affiliate of the Seafarers' International Union of North America (AFL-CIO). The union adopted its present name in the early 1970s. The bimonthly publication is the *IUPIW Views*.

Address: 8131 East Rosecrans Blvd., Paramount, Calif. 90723. Tel. (213) 630–6232

Petroleum Labor Policy Board One of the boards established during the National Recovery Administration and similar in function to those established in the textile, auto, and steel industries. The Petroleum Board, however, differed in part from these boards in being an autonomous body within the Petroleum Administration and directly responsible to Secretary of the Interior Harold Ickes. The petroleum code had been removed from the National Recovery Administration to the Petroleum Administration in the Department of Interior. The board was established in October 1933 and its prime function was the settlement of labor disputes within the industry. However, the administrator decided that the board might have broader functions and in November 1933 asked it to study and recommend wage differentials for skilled and unskilled labor, and to look "into any employer-employee difficulties that might arise."

Source reference: Lewis Lorwin and Arthur Wubnig, *Labor Relations Boards* (Washington: Brookings Institution, 1935).

Petroleum Workers; Independent Union of (Ind) *See* PETROLEUM WORKERS, INC.; INTERNATIONAL UNION OF (IND).

Petroleum Workers, Inc.; International Union of (Ind) This union was formerly known as the Independent Union of Petroleum Workers (Ind). It affiliated with the Seafarers' International Union of North America (AFL-CIO) in August 1962. The name was changed to the International Union of Petroleum and Industrial Workers in the early 1970s.

See also PETROLEUM AND INDUSTRIAL WORKERS; INTERNATIONAL UNION OF.

Philadelphia Plan Originally issued in the fall of 1967 by the federal Executive Board pursuant to Executive Order 11246. It required government contractors in the Philadelphia area to submit an "acceptable" affirmative action program for the employment of minorities in the construction industry prior to the award of federal or federally assisted construction contracts. Such a requirement was later ruled to be in violation of the principles of competitive bidding.

The plan was revised in 1969, setting forth ranges for minority manpower utilization on federally involved construction projects and requiring contractors to make a "good faith" effort to meet the goals.

In 1970, the Contractors Association of Eastern Pennsylvania filed suit to challenge the constitutionality of the plan and sought an injunction to prevent its implementation. The district court found that the plan did not violate the equal protection clause of the U.S. Constitution and was not in conflict with Title VII of the Civil Rights Act of 1964 because it did "not require the contractors to hire a definite percentage of a minority group." The decision was upheld by the court of appeals in 1971 and the Supreme Court denied certiorari the same year.

The OFCCP has largely replaced "imposed" plans, "hometown" plans, and "special bid conditions" with a system that sets goals and timetables for all covered construction contractors on a uniform basis.

Source references: Contractors Assn. of Eastern Pennsylvania v. Shultz, 311 FSupp 1002, 2 FEP Cases 472 (DC Pa, 1970), *aff'g,* 442 F2d 159, 3 FEP Cases 395 (CA 3, 1971), *cert. denied sub nom. v. Hodgson,* 404 US 854, 3 FEP Cases 1050 (1971); U.S. Congress, Senate, Committee on the Judiciary, *Philadelphia Plan, Hearings* (Washington: 1970); U.S. Dept. of Labor, *Philadelphia Plan: Questions and Answers* (Washington: 1969).

See also EXECUTIVE ORDER 11246, GOALS AND TIMETABLES, OFFICE OF FEDERAL CONTRACT COMPLIANCE PROGRAMS (OFCCP).

Phillips v. Rainey A decision of the New York Court of Appeals which held that the law requiring prison goods to be labeled was invalid since it was in conflict with the commerce clause of the U.S. Constitution.

Source reference: Phillips v. Rainey, 198 New York 539 (1910).

phossy jaw An industrial disease in which there is an eating away of the bones. It occurred in plants where phosphorus was a major element in producing goods.

See also INDUSTRIAL DISEASE.

Photo-Engravers' Union of North America; International (AFL-CIO) An organization of workers which broke away from the International Typographical Union in 1900 and was chartered by the AFL in 1904. On September 7, 1964, the union merged with the Amalgamated Lithographers of America (Ind) to form the Lithographers and Photoengravers International Union (AFL-CIO).

Source references: Wilfrid T. Connell, "The Photo Engravers," *American Federationist,* Aug. 1959; International Photo Engravers' Union of North America, *Fifty Years of Progress* (St. Louis: 1952); Charles Leese, *Collective Bargaining Among Photo Engravers in Philadelphia* (Philadelphia: Wharton School, Industrial Research Study no. 2, Univ. of Pennsylvania Press, 1929).

See also LITHOGRAPHERS AND PHOTOENGRAVERS INTERNATIONAL UNION (AFL-CIO).

physically handicapped Individuals who have some physical incapacity or have limited use of their limbs which creates difficulty in the performance of work. Frequently the specific handicaps do not interfere with the performance of other activities. Physical therapy has enabled many individuals to handle tasks in spite of their limitations.

See also HANDICAPPED WORKER.

Physically Handicapped, Office of President's Committee on Employment of *See* PRESIDENT'S COMMITTEE ON EMPLOYMENT OF THE HANDICAPPED.

Physicians and Dentists; Union of American (Ind) Founded in 1972, its official monthly publication is *UAPD Leadership News.*

Address: 1730 Franklin St., Suite 200, Oakland, Calif. 94612. Tel. (415) 839–0193

pick Generally refers to the selection or choice of work assignments in the transportation industry. The assignment is usually on the basis of seniority. The pick sometimes is referred to as a "run" since it covers the assignment of an entire day's trip or the working schedule for an entire week or other period.

The term "pick" is thought to have become popular since in some areas it was customary for the employees to "pick" or choose their runs on the basis of their seniority rights.

See also RUN.

picket An individual or person generally assigned by a union, and almost always a member of that organization, to stand or walk near the approaches to a place of work or the exits from which the employees leave the plant. The purpose is to persuade and influence the employees not to enter the plant or, if they are already in it, to join the union. A picket is not, of course, limited to an industrial dispute, but may be used in any demonstration of protest by a show of signs or banners against the policies of those in authority.

The attitude of courts toward the picket has varied widely. As one authority put it in the 1940s, "The thought behind such laws [to limit picketing] and judicial decisions is that effective picketing involves coercion." Another authority has pointed out that the purpose of a picket line is to exercise "a moral and physical deterrent on those who want to get into the plant in order to carry on production. A picket line, like other mass and crowd phenomena, generates its own tensions." Still another has stated that "It is the task of the picket to dissuade or prevent by intimidation or force . . . workers from entering the shop or mill. Persuasion may be all that is necessary. The picket attempts to substitute the idea of loyalty to the group for loyalty to the employer."

The picket may seek through peaceful persuasion to achieve the objectives of the union or may extend activities in such a manner that they approximate intimidation or coercion or lead to violence.

See also PICKETING.

picketing The actual patrolling at or near the employer's place of business during a strike or other dispute to give notice of the existence of a labor dispute, to publicize it, or to persuade workers to join the union and to discourage or prevent persons from entering or going to work. The picketing may be for the purpose of informing the public at large of the existence of a labor dispute at the particular company or it may be to inform the employees or those seeking employment in the plant that a work stoppage or dispute is in progress, or for the purpose of informing customers or suppliers of the existence of a dispute.

Picketing takes many forms and the process has varied as conditions change and as legislation limits the economic behavior of unions. This is particularly true of the Taft-Hartley and Landrum-Griffin Acts, which limit certain types of organizational or recognition picketing.

The line between posting information on placards held by individuals to inform the public and situations in which cards perform the basic functions of the picket line depends almost entirely on the particular circumstances of the case.

As one labor service put the problem, "Lack of a standard definition of the word 'picketing' in the Taft Act, its legislative history, dictionaries, or elsewhere long has been a problem for the Labor Board, and it appears that this will continue with respect to the proviso of Section 8(b)(4), which allows union publicity in a dispute with an employer, so long as this does not include picketing."

By recognition picketing a union seeks to hurt the employer sufficiently through economic pressure to persuade the employer to recognize the union for bargaining purposes. This also is referred to as "organizational picketing."

Mass picketing occurs when large numbers of workers congregate at entrances or exits of a struck plant or where a labor dispute exists in order to demonstrate strength and thereby limit or try to prevent the entrance of individuals into the struck plant or to prevent shipping or receipt of raw or finished materials or products. Mass picketing may be stationary in front of exit or entrance gates or there may be a solid moving line of pickets which makes it impossible for employees to enter the struck plant.

Cross picketing applies to situations where there are two or more rival unions, each of which claims to represent the employees.

Secondary picketing is the picketing of those places which are not directly involved in the labor dispute. Because of related ownership or business dealing with the employer directly involved, the union feels that pressure exerted on the secondary firm can help win the primary dispute.

Source references: David L. Benetar and Robert C. Isaacs, "Pickets or Ballots? The New Trend in Labor Law," *American Bar Association Journal*, Oct. 1957; Paul A. Brinker, "Secondary Strikes and Picketing," *LLJ*, Nov. 1972; Herbert Burstein, "Picketing—A Management Point of View," *NYU 14th Annual Conference on Labor*, ed. by Emanuel Stein (Albany: Bender, 1961); Robert C. Castle and Richard Pegnetter, "Secondary Picketing: The Supreme Court Limits the *Tree Fruits* Exception," *LLJ*, Jan. 1982; Jerome A. Cooper, "Picketing and Boycott: A Functional Analysis—Labor Viewpoint," *NYU 15th Annual Conference on Labor*, ed. by Emanuel Stein (Albany: Bender, 1962); Emanuel Dannett, "Picketing in Breach of a No-Strike Clause," *LLJ*, May 1960; Walter L. Daykin, "Picketing," *LLJ*, Sept. 1959; Patrick T. Duerr, "Developing a Standard for Secondary Consumer Picketing," *LLJ*, Sept. 1975; Guy Farmer and Charles G. Williamson, Jr., "Picketing and the Injunctive Power of State Courts—From Thornhill to Vogt," *Univ. of Detroit LJ*, April 1958; William Feldesman, "Restrictions on Picketing and Boycotts 'Proviso, and Proviso, and Proviso,—'," *LLJ*, April 1963; Morris D. Forkosch, "An Analysis and Reevaluation of Picketing in Labor Relations," *Fordham LR*, Autumn 1957; Richard B. Huss and Richard J. Simmons, "Hudgens v. NLRB: Protection of Shopping Center Picketing Under the Constitution or NLRA?" *Industrial Relations LJ*, Fall 1976; John E. Jay, "Shopping Centers as Battlegrounds Under the National Labor Relations Act," *Employee Relations LJ*, Autumn 1976; Robert Lewis, "Free Speech and Property Rights Re-Equated: The Supreme Court Ascends from *Logan Valley*," *LLJ*, April 1973; Charles H. Livengood, Jr., "Picketing Revisited—Rights and Obligations of the Employee, the Employer, and the Union," *Labor Law Developments, 1974*, Proceedings of the 20th Annual Institute on Labor Law, SLF (New York: Bender, 1974); "Lloyd Corp. v. Tanner: The Demise of Logan Valley and the Disguise of Marsh," *IR Law Digest*, Oct. 1973; W. C. Owen, "Plazas, Parking Lots, and Picketing: *Logan Valley Plaza* is Put to the Test," *LLJ*, Dec. 1972; Jane Rigler, "The Status of Area Standards Picketing as Protected Conduct Under Section 7," *LLJ*, Dec. 1981; Samuel D. Rosen, "Area Standards Picketing," *LLJ*, Feb. 1972; Bernard L. Samoff, "Picketing and the First Amendment: 'Full Circle' and 'Formal Surrender,'" *LLJ*, Dec. 1958; Victor Schachter, "Regulating Union Trespasses on Private Property: State Injunctive Relief is the Answer," *LLJ*, April 1977; Evan J. Spelfogel, "Private Property Picketing," *LLJ*, Oct. 1982; Paul D. Staudohar, "Rights and Limitations of Picketing by Public Employees," *LLJ*, Oct. 1974; Stephen C. Vladeck, "Some Thoughts on Picketing in View of the Landrum-Griffin Amendments," *NYU 14th Annual Conference on Labor*, ed. by Emanuel Stein (Albany: Bender, 1961); Donald H. Wollett, "The Weapons of Conflict: Picketing and Boycotts," *Public Policy and Collective Bargaining*, ed. by Joseph Shister, Benjamin Aaron, and Clyde W. Summers (New York: Harper, IRRA Pub. no. 27, 1962); Benjamin Wyle, "The New Law of Picketing," *LLJ*, Dec. 1959.

See also AMERICAN FEDERATION OF LABOR V. SWING, ATCHISON TOPEKA & SANTA FE R.R. V. GEE, CLEAR AND PRESENT DANGER DOCTRINE, FREEDOM OF SPEECH, LAFOLLETTE COMMITTEE, MILK WAGON DRIVERS' CASE, PEACEFUL PERSUASION, SECONDARY BOYCOTT.

picketing, chain *See* CHAIN PICKETING.

picketing, circular *See* CIRCULAR PICKETING.

picketing, cross *See* CROSS PICKETING.

picketing, dry-run *See* DRY-RUN PICKETING.

picketing, extortionate *See* EXTORTIONATE PICKETING.

picketing, informational *See* INFORMATIONAL PICKETING.

picketing, mass *See* MASS PICKETING.

picketing, organizational *See* ORGANIZATIONAL PICKETING.

picketing, peaceful *See* PEACEFUL PICKETING.

picketing, publicity *See* INFORMATIONAL PICKETING.

picketing, recognition *See* RECOGNITION PICKETING.

picketing, secondary *See* SECONDARY PICKETING.

picketing, stranger *See* STRANGER PICKETING.

picketing at common site (situs) The most difficult cases under the Taft-Hartley Act's secondary-boycott provisions have been those in which a union has picketed a so-called common site or situs—one at which employees of both a struck employer and neutral employers are working. This is the usual situation in the picketing of a construction project.

The basic rules governing picketing in such common-situs situations were laid down in the *Denver Building Trades* and *Moore Dry Dock* cases. In its 1951 decision in the *Denver Building Trades* case, the Supreme Court rejected the contention that the general contractor and its subcontractors on a construction project were "allies" for the purpose of the secondary-boycott prohibition. In applying the boycott provisions, the Court said, the contractor and the subcontractors must be treated as separate employers. So the picketing of a construction project in support of a strike against a subcontractor was considered a violation of the secondary-boycott ban if it had the effect of inducing the employees of the general contractor or other subcontractors to stop work.

The NLRB previously had evolved a series of standards for determining the legality of common-situs picketing. The tests used in the 1950 *Moore Dry Dock* case stated:

(1) Picketing must be limited to times when the primary (struck) employer's employees actually are present at the common site;
(2) Picketing must be limited to places "reasonably close" to the operations of the primary employer's workers;
(3) The pickets must show clearly that their dispute is with the primary employer alone; and
(4) The primary employer's workers must be engaged in the employer's normal business at the common site.

In 1953, the NLRB added another condition to the permissibility of common-situs picketing. It held that a union engaging in such picketing must show that the struck employer has no permanent place of business in the area that can be picketed. Enunciated in the *Washington Coca Cola* case, this rule later was rejected as too "rigid" or "mechanical" by the U.S. Courts of Appeals at New Orleans and the District of Columbia in the *Otis Massey* and *Campbell Coal* cases. Then in 1962, the NLRB itself abandoned the rule, stating in the *Plauche Electric* case that henceforth the availability of an establishment of the struck employer in the area, along with the place of picketing, would merely be one circumstance to be considered in determining the legality of the picketing.

A year later, the Board said that the *Moore Dry Dock* standards themselves are not to be applied on an indiscriminate *per se* basis, but are to be regarded merely as aids in determining the underlying question of statutory violations. On this basis, the Board held in a case involving New Power Wire & Electric Corporation that a union did not violate the Act by picketing the premises of neutral employers at which employees of a struck employer were working, even though the employees of the struck employer were absent from some of the picketed premises for substantial periods of time.

Closely related to the common-situs picketing cases are those involving the picketing of gates at manufacturing plants that have been "reserved" for the sole use of employees of independent contractors who are working on the plant's premises. In a case involving General Electric and the Electrical Workers (IUE), the NLRB held that the picketing of such a reserved gate violated the secondary-boycott ban. In reviewing the Board's holding, the Supreme Court agreed that the picketing of such a reserved gate would appear to come within the prohibition. But it added the qualification that the contractors must be doing work that is "unrelated to the normal operations of the plant" for the picketing to be unlawful. The NLRB later reconsidered its initial decision in the light of this test and held for the union, the work being performed by the contractors having been found to be related to General Electric's normal operations at the plant.

Source references: Electrical Workers Union (IBEW), Local 3 (New Power Wire and Electric Corp.), 144 NLRB 1089, 54 LRRM 1178 (1963); *Electrical Workers (IBEW), Local 861 (Plauche Electric, Inc.),* 135 NLRB 250, 49 LRRM 1446 (1962); *Electrical Workers (IUE), Local 761,* 138 NLRB 342, 51 LRRM 1028 (1962); *Electrical Workers (IUE), Local 761 (General Electric Co.),* 123 NLRB 1547, 44 LRRM 1173 (1959); *Electrical Workers (IUE), Local 761 v. NLRB,* 366 US 667, 48 LRRM 2210 (1961); *NLRB v. Denver Building & Construction Trades Council (Gould & Priesner),* 341 US 675, 28 LRRM 2108 (1951); *NLRB v. Teamsters Local 968 (Otis Massey Co.),* 350 US 914, 37 LRRM 2142 (1955); *Sailors' Union of the Pacific and Moore Dry Dock Co.,* 92 NLRB 547, 27 LRRM 1108 (1950); *Truck Drivers Local 728 v. NLRB (Campbell Coal Co.),* 229 F2d 514, 37 LRRM 2166 (CA DC, 1955); *Washington Coca-Cola Bottling Co. (Brewery & Beverage Drivers &*

Workers, Local 67, IBT), 107 NLRB 299, 33 LRRM 1122 (1953); Richard N. Block, Benjamin W. Wolkinson, and David E. Mitchell, "The NLRB and Alternative Situs Picketing: The Search for the Elusive Standard," *Industrial Relations LJ*, Winter 1979; Paul A. Brinker, "Common Situs Picketing by Construction Unions Since 1958," *LLJ*, June 1972; Stephen J. Cabot and Robert J. Simmons, "The Future of Common Situs Picketing," *LLJ*, Dec. 1976; Peter G. Nash, "Common Situs Picketing—Why the Uproar?" *Employee Relations LJ*, Summer 1976; Warren C. Ogden, "Common Situs Picketing and the 'Observer' Phenomenon," *LLJ*, Oct. 1982; U.S. Congress, House, Committee on Education and Labor, *Veto of the Common Situs Picketing Act, Message from the President of the United States* (Washington: 1976).

picket line The group of pickets posted at plant entrances and gates or marching near the entrances and gates to notify employees of the existence of a labor dispute.

Source references: James T. Carney and Mark J. Florsheim, "The Treatment of Refusals to Cross Picket Lines: 'By-Paths and Indirect Crookt Ways,'" *IR Law Digest*, April 1971; Arthur M. Marshall, "Carrier Service and the Picket Line: A Dilemma," *LLJ*, April 1962; "Picket Line Observance: The Board and the Balance of Interest," *IR Law Digest*, April 1971; Mori Rubin, "To Cross or Not to Cross: Picket Lines and Employee Rights," *Industrial Relations LJ*, Summer 1981; Carl A. Warns, Jr., "Right of Management to Discipline for Refusal to Cross a Picket Line," *Arbitration of Interest Disputes*, Proceedings of the 26th A/M, NAA, ed. by Barbara Dennis and Gerald Somers (Washington: BNA, 1974).

See also PICKETING.

piece rate A predetermined amount paid to an employee under a wage incentive system for each unit of output. Determination of the rates may be based either on individual or group output.

Source references: Jules Backman, *Railroad Mileage Pay and Piece Rates in Other Industries, A Report Prepared for the Carriers' Conference Committee* (n.p., 1961); Marcel Bolle de Bal, "The Psycho-Sociology of Wage Incentives," *BJIR*, Nov. 1969; Peter B. Doeringer, "Piece Rate Wage Structures in the Pittsburgh Iron and Steel Industry—1880–1900," *Labor History*, Spring 1968; J. A. Greenwood, "Payments by Results Systems: A Case Study in Control at the Workplace with a National Piecework Price List," *BJIR*, Nov. 1969; Richard A. Peterson and Michael J. Rath, "Structural Determinants of Piecework Rates," *IR*, Oct. 1964; B. R. Skelton and Bruce Yandle, "Piece Rate Pay," *Journal of Labor Research*, Spring 1982.

See also DIFFERENTIAL PIECE-RATE PLAN, PERMANENT PIECE RATE.

piecework *See* INCENTIVE WAGE, PIECE RATE, WAGE PAYMENT PLANS.

"piggy-back" trucking A procedure for moving loaded truck trailers to various places on railroad flat cars rather than hauling them over the highway by trucks.

pink collar work Jobs performed predominantly by women. Louise Howe states that "[w]hile it has become commonplace to discuss how the lines between so-called blue collar and white collar work have been fading . . . it has been barely observed that the most dramatic distinctions continue between what can most descriptively be termed pink collar work and work in the male and integrated markets." Among the occupations she refers to as "the pinkest of pink collar occupations" are registered nurses, typists, secretaries, hairdressers, sewers and stitchers, private household workers, and homemakers. The socialization process that determines the occupational choices of women, Howe says, "is largely a class matter as well as a matter of gender," which she terms the "pink blanket theory."

Source references: Louise Kapp Howe, *Pink Collar Workers, Inside the World of Women's Work* (New York: Putnam, 1977); Martin F. Payson, "Wooing the Pink Collar Work Force," *PJ*, Jan. 1984.

See also OCCUPATIONAL SEGREGATION.

Pinkerton Detective Agency An organization established in the 1870s, best known in past years for espionage on union activities and for strikebreaking services performed for employers. Pinkerton was a major supplier of guards or plant police to protect industrial property and maintain plant security. Pinkerton operatives in some instances were union members.

Source references: Allan Pinkerton, *Strikers, Communists, Tramps and Detectives* (New York: Arno Press and The New York Times, 1969); U.S. Congress, Senate, Subcommittee of the Committee on Education and Labor, *Violations of Free Speech and Rights of Labor, Hearings* (Washington: 1936–1940).

See also ANTI-STRIKEBREAKING ACT (BYRNES ACT), ANTI-UNION PRACTICES, ESPIONAGE, LAFOLLETTE COMMITTEE.

Pittsburgh Plate Glass case A decision in which the NLRB determined that six plants of the Pittsburgh Plate Glass Company constituted the appropriate bargaining unit despite the fact that employees in one plant overwhelmingly rejected representation by the majority union.

The NLRB accepted the union argument that such a unit would promote harmony among all employees in the six plants with the establishment of uniform working conditions, including comparable wages and hours. The NLRB also considered the historical efforts of the union to organize employees on a companywide basis. The existence of unfair labor practices and the dissolution of an independent union in the one plant also contributed to the NLRB decision.

Normally no appeal is permitted on representation petitions. Only after an employer has been required to bargain and has refused to bargain would a case come to the courts for review. The Supreme Court, however, granted review because an NLRB decision "is subject to challenge when . . . a complaint of unfair practices is made predicated upon the ruling." The Court in April 1941 ruled that the NLRB had the authority to make such determination.

Source references: Pittsburgh Plate Glass Co. and Federation of Flat Glass Workers of America (CIO), 15 NLRB 515, 5 LRRM 144 (1939); *Pittsburgh Plate Glass Company v. NLRB*, 313 US 146, 8 LRRM 425 (1941); Dean O. Bowman, *Public Control of Labor Relations: A Study of the National Labor Relations Board* (New York: Macmillan, 1942).

Planners, Estimators, and Progressmen; National Association of (Ind) Founded in 1942. It issues the *N.A.P.E.E.P. Quarterly News Letter*.

Address: 310 West M St., Benicia, Calif. 94510. Tel. (707) 745–3554

Plans for Progress A program to reduce discrimination in employment, primarily discrimination against blacks, particularly by companies holding large government contracts. The program included plans developed jointly by the President's Committee on Equal Employment Opportunity and individual companies which received government contracts. One such statement, agreed to jointly by W. M. Allen of the Boeing Company and Lyndon B. Johnson, then Vice President of the United States, follows:

> The President of the United States has stated a national policy that all persons are entitled to equal employment opportunity, regardless of their race, creed, color, or national origin. He has established and charged the President's Committee on Equal Employment Opportunity with responsibility to assist in carrying out this policy.
>
> The Boeing Company intends, to the best of its ability, to follow the President's policy as set forth herein and has voluntarily embarked on a companywide program to expand and strengthen its efforts to promote equal employment opportunity.
>
> Boeing has, on forms submitted to it by the President's Committee, attached statistical data on its personnel and responded to questions with regard to its employment policies and practices. All such information was furnished on a completely confidential basis and is only for the official use of the Committee. This information will be used by the Committee as one of the measures of Boeing's achievements under this Plan for Progress.
>
> The President's Committee is aware that there are many basic factors over which Boeing has no direct control and which may materially hamper the Company's achievement of the Plan for Progress, such as training programs and referral facilities. Boeing will seek the assistance of public and private agencies in carrying forward its efforts to provide equal employment opportunities, calling on the Committee when it believes the services of that group can be materially constructive in obtaining such assistance.
>
> Boeing and the President's Committee recognize that this Plan for Progress is a long-range undertaking. In this regard, Boeing will periodically review (at least once a year) this Plan with the President's Committee. These reviews

will be aimed at measuring Boeing's progress under the Plan. Boeing also recognizes that circumstances may prompt amendments to this Plan in order to better and more rapidly attain the goal of equal employment opportunity.

Administrative support for the implementation of the Plans for Progress program is covered under Executive Order 11246.

See also PRESIDENT'S COMMITTEE ON EQUAL EMPLOYMENT OPPORTUNITY.

plant closing Termination of operations as employer relocates or goes out of business. Economic considerations, which may include the availability of a lower-paid labor force in another region or country, are primary causes of plant shutdowns.

Source references: Audrey Freedman, " 'Plant Closed—No Jobs'," *Across the Board*, Aug. 1980; Jeanne Prial Gordus, Paul Jarley, and Louis A. Ferman, *Plant Closings and Economic Dislocation* (Kalamazoo: Upjohn Institute for Employment Research, 1981); Robert McKersie, " 'Plant Closed—No Jobs'," *Across the Board*, Nov. 1980; Arthur Shostak, "The Human Cost of Plant Closings," *American Federationist*, Aug. 1980; James L. Stern, Kenneth A. Root, and Stephen M. Hills, "The Influence of Social-Psychological Traits and Job Search Patterns on the Earnings of Workers Affected by a Plant Closure," *ILRR*, Oct. 1974.

See also DECISION/EFFECTS BARGAINING, PLANT MIGRATION, SUCCESSOR EMPLOYER.

Plant Guard Workers of America; International Union, United (Ind) Formerly known as the United Plant Guard Workers of America (Ind). It issues the quarterly publication *The Guard News*.

Address: 22510 Kelly Rd., Roseville, Mich. 48066. Tel. (313) 772–7250

Source reference: Int. Union, United Plant Guard Workers of America, *UPGWA* (Detroit: 1970).

plant migration The movement of factories to a new location. The purpose may be to effect economies made possible by new equipment and plant layout, better access to transportation, tax benefits, raw materials, or labor supply. It also may reflect the desire of the employer to get away from a union or a highly organized community.

Source references: Everett J. Burtt, Jr., "Workers Adapt to Plant Relocation in Suburbia," *MLR*, April 1968; Gary J. Felsten, "Current Considerations in Plant Shutdowns and Relocations," *PJ*, May 1981; Morris P. Glushien, "Plant Removal," *NYU 15th Annual Conference on Labor*, ed. by Emanuel Stein (Albany: Bender, 1962); Morris P. Glushien et al., "Plant Removals and Related Problems: A Panel Discussion," *LLJ*, Nov. 1962; Jeanne Prial Gordus, Paul Jarley, and Louis A. Ferman, *Plant Closings and Economic Dislocation* (Kalamazoo: Upjohn Institute for Employment Research, 1981); Industrial Relations Counselors, *Plant Relocation—Industrial Relations Implications, A Review Based on the Glidden Case* (New York: IR Memo no. 142, 1962); Richard Van M. Krotseng, "Plant Relocations and Consolidations: Employers' Obligations Regarding Employee Transfer and Union Recognition," *LLJ*, Sept. 1982; Edgar R. Lehman, "Corporate Relocation: How One Company Paved the Road," *Management Review*, June 1972; Richard B. McKenzie and Bruce Yandle, "State Plant Closing Laws: Their Union Support," *Journal of Labor Research*, Winter 1982; Stephen S. Mick, "Social and Personal Costs of Plant Shutdowns," *IR*, May 1975; M. S. Ryder, "Plant Relocation: Management's Collective Bargaining Legal Dilemma," *Michigan Business Review*, July 1963; Lee C. Shaw, "Plant Removals and Subcontracting of Work," *LLJ*, April 1963; William D. Turner, "Plant Removals and Related Problems," *LLJ*, Nov. 1962; U.S. Dept. of Labor, BLS, *Major Collective Bargaining Agreements: Plant Movement, Transfer, and Relocation Allowances* (Washington: Bull. no. 1425–10, 1969); Edmund S. Whitman and W. James Schmidt, *Plant Relocation* (New York: AMA, 1966).

See also DARLINGTON CASE, DECISION/EFFECTS BARGAINING, GLIDDEN CASE, PLANT CLOSING, RUNAWAY SHOP.

Plant Protection Association; National (Ind)

Address: 2204 North Wayne Rd., P.O. Box 181, Westland, Mich. 48185. Tel. (313) 728–7345

plant relocation *See* PLANT MIGRATION.

plant rules Generally the detailed working rules of an establishment. In a unionized plant they may be incorporated into the collective bargaining agreement by reference. The employer may be granted the authority in the contract to establish fair and reasonable working rules for the operation and maintenance of the plant. Occasionally these rules are established only after joint negotiation and consultation; in some cases plant rules may be required by union contract to be based on mutual agreement. It may be provided that working rules are not to conflict with terms of the collective bargaining agreement.

Where agreements are negotiated on a regional or industry basis, the agreement may set out the general conditions of employment but allow individual local unions and plant managers to work out the details of so-called plant rules.

Source references: Fremont A. Shull, Jr., and L. L. Cummings, "Enforcing the Rules: How Do Managers Differ?" *Personnel*, March/April 1966; Joseph B. Wollenberger, "Acceptable Work Rules and Penalties: A Company Guide," *Personnel*, July/Aug. 1963.

plant tours *See* OPEN HOUSE.

plant union Generally refers to an organization of employees within a single plant. It may be an unaffiliated independent union or, as was frequent prior to adoption of the National Labor Relations Act, a company union. Some plant unions have affiliated with federations of independent unions.

See also COMPANY UNION, INDEPENDENT UNIONS.

plant unit A bargaining unit which consists of the employees within a single plant.

See also APPROPRIATE UNIT, BARGAINING UNIT.

plantwide collective bargaining *See* COLLECTIVE BARGAINING, PLANTWIDE.

Plasterers' and Cement Finishers' International Association of the U.S. and Canada; Operative (AFL) *See* PLASTERERS' AND CEMENT MASONS' INTERNATIONAL ASSOCIATION OF THE UNITED STATES AND CANADA; OPERATIVE (AFL-CIO).

Plasterers' and Cement Masons' International Association of the United States and Canada; Operative (AFL-CIO) Established in 1864 as the National Plasterers' Organization of the United States, in 1889 it changed its name to the Operative Plasterers' International Association of the United States and Canada. With dissolution of the American Brotherhood of Cement Workers in 1916, the cement finishers who belonged to that organization were transferred to the Plasterers' Union. The official monthly publication is *The Plasterer and Cement Mason.*

Address: 1125 17th Street, N.W., Washington, D.C. 20036. Tel. (202) 393–6569

Plate Printers', Die Stampers' and Engravers' Union of North America; International (AFL-CIO) Formed in Boston, Massachusetts, in 1892. The union's jurisdiction was extended over die stampers in 1920. The International Steel and Copper Plate Engravers' League amalgamated with the organization in 1925.

Address: 2023 Muliner Ave., Bronx, N.Y. 10462. Tel. (212) 792–1086

Playthings, Jewelry and Novelty Workers International Union (CIO) The union in May 1954 became part of the Retail, Wholesale and Department Store Union (CIO).

See also RETAIL, WHOLESALE AND DEPARTMENT STORE UNION (AFL-CIO).

Plumbing and Pipe Fitting Industry of the United States and Canada; United Association of Journeymen and Apprentices of the (AFL-CIO) First organized in October 1889 and known as the International Association of Plumbers, Steam Fitters and Gas Fitters, which consisted of Knights of Labor locals and a few independent craft unions. A dual organization was established in 1899 known as the International Union of Steam and Hot Water Fitters, chartered by the AFL. Both organizations functioned independently until 1912, when the Federation ordered amalgamation of the two organizations. The International Union of Steam and Hot Water Fitters failed to comply with the order and was expelled. It soon dissolved and some of the local unions joined the International Association of Plumbers, Steam Fitters and Gas Fitters, and the union of Steam and Hot Water Fitters went out of existence. The official publications are the *United Association Journal* (monthly) and the *General Officers' Washington Report* (weekly).

Address: 901 Massachusetts Ave., N.W., Washington, D.C. 20001. Tel. (202) 628–5823

Plumb Plan A program named after Glenn E. Plumb, general counsel of the organized railroad workers in 1919. The program provided for nationalization of the railroads and establishment of joint operating control through a 15-member board of directors. The plan called for the President to name five members to represent the public on the board, the employers were to elect five to represent industry, and the classified employees of the Railroad Brotherhoods were to elect five. It was proposed that the government issue bonds to secure the funds for the purchase of the railroads, after proper appraisal by the courts, and that the railroads were to operate as a national nonprofit corporation. The earnings were to be used to pay interest and operating expenses and to retire the bonds within a period of 50 years. Savings over and above expenditures were to be divided between the government and employees in accordance with a detailed schedule proposed in the plan.

Following hearings before the House Committee on Interstate and Foreign Commerce in 1920, the plan was held to be unfeasible and never was reported for action by Congress.

Source references: Alfred L. Bernheim and Dorothy Vandoren (ed.), *Labor and the Government* (New York: McGraw-Hill, 1935); Mollie R. Carroll, *Labor and Politics* (New York: Houghton Mifflin, 1923); Herbert Harris, *American Labor* (New Haven: Yale UP, 1938); Harry W. Laidler, *A Program for Modern America* (New York: Crowell, 1936).

point plan The point plan or point system requires the use of a point manual which contains a scale against which the job specifications are compared, factor by factor, in actual determination of the point values of a job. The values established in this way provide the basis for "slotting" the job into the appropriate wage classification.

Among the known and widely used point manuals are those of the National Office Management Associations, National Metal Trades, and the National Electrical Manufacturers.

Source references: Keith W. Bennett, "Accounting for the Value of Your Manpower," *Management Review,* Dec. 1973; Herbert J. Chruden and Arthur W. Sherman, Jr., *Personnel Management* (3d ed., Cincinnati: South-Western, 1968); Joseph Dooher and Vivienne Marquis, *The AMA Handbook of Wage and Salary Administration* (New York: AMA, 1950); Elizabeth Lanhan, *Job Evaluation* (New York: McGraw-Hill, 1955); John A. Patton and Cleatice L. Littlefield, *Job Evaluation* (Homewood: Irwin, 1957); Douglas S. Sherwin, "The Job of Job Evaluation," *Harvard BR,* May/June 1957.

See also JOB EVALUATION, WEIGHTED POINT METHOD.

poison, industrial *See* INDUSTRIAL DISEASE, INDUSTRIAL POISON.

Police; Fraternal Order of (Ind) Founded in 1915, it is the largest national police employee organization, claiming some 150,000 members. It invites police officers of all ranks to membership, and associate memberships are made available to the general public. Its quarterly publication is *The Journal.*

Address: 5613 Belair Rd., Baltimore, Md. 21206. Tel. (301) 488–6880

Source reference: Michael H. Moskow, J. Joseph Loewenberg, and Edward C. Koziara, *Collective Bargaining in Public Employment* (New York: Random House, 1970).

Police Associations; International Union of (AFL-CIO) Established by former members of the International Conference of Police Associations after that organization dissolved over the issue of AFL-CIO affiliation. The union was chartered by the AFL-CIO on February 20, 1979. It issues *The Law Officer* (bimonthly), *Newsletter* (quarterly), and *Legislative Update* (quarterly).

Address: 815 16th St., N.W., Washington, D.C. 20006. Tel. (202) 628–2740

Source reference: U.S. Dept. of Labor, BLS, *Directory of National Unions and Employee Associations, 1979* (Washington: Bull. 2079, 1980).

Police Officers; International Brotherhood of (Ind) *See* GOVERNMENT EMPLOYEES; NATIONAL ASSOCIATION OF.

policy grievance *See* GROUP GRIEVANCE.

political action, union Activities of a union directed to electing pro-union individuals to political office—federal, state, or local—and to effect the adoption of legislation favored by unions and defeat legislation opposed by unions.

Historically, organized labor has blown hot and cold on direct participation in political campaigns. Forerunner of labor's present intensive political activity was the Labor's Non-Partisan League (LNPL), formed in the 1930s by the Congress of Industrial Organizations (CIO) when it was headed by John L. Lewis, president of the United Mine Workers. In 1941, Lewis pulled the UMW out of the CIO, and took the LNPL with him. Sidney Hillman, president of the Amalgamated Clothing Workers (CIO), who had been a top official of the LNPL, in 1943 worked up a CIO political organization called CIO Political Action Committee, or CIO-PAC. The organization was active in the 1944 Roosevelt campaign, the "fourth term" year. Its work was advertised as "educational."

The AFL subsequently changed its mind about politicking and formed the Labor's League for Political Education (LLPE). Following the AFL-CIO merger in 1955, the present COPE, or Committee on Political Education, took over the functions of the former PAC and LLPE. Its activities are modeled on those of the CIO-PAC.

Source references: AFL-CIO, *The AFL-CIO Platform Proposals Presented to the Democratic and Republican National Conventions 1980* (Washington: 1980); Jack Barbash, "The Architecture of Union Political Action," *MLR*, June 1965; ———, *The Politics of American Labor* (Madison: Univ. of Wisconsin, IRRI, Reprint 200, 1976); Andrew J. Biemiller, "The Dangerous Way to Regulate Lobbying," *American Federationist*, June 1975; R. Theodore Clark, Jr., "Politics and Public Employee Unionism: Some Recommendations for an Emerging Problem," 44 *Cincinnati LR* 680 (1975); Kenneth Cloke, "Mandatory Political Contributions and Union Democracy," *Industrial Relations LJ*, Vol. 4, no. 4, 1981; Edwin M. Epstein, "Labor and Federal Elections: The New Legal Framework," *IR*, Oct. 1976; Richard F. Hamilton, "Trends in Labor Union Voting Behavior, 1948–1968," *IR*, Feb. 1973; James B. Kau and Paul H. Rubin, "The Impact of Labor Unions on the Passage of Economic Legislation," *Journal of Labor Research*, Spring 1981; Lane Kirkland, "Labor and Politics After 1980," *American Federationist*, Jan. 1981; Michael J. Klapper, "The Response of Organized Labor to the Socialist Party Campaign of 1920," *Industrial and Labor Relations Forum*, March 1974; Arthur S. Leonard, "The AFL-CIO's First National Campaign," *Industrial and Labor Relations Forum*, Nov. 1972; Marick F. Masters and John Thomas Delaney, "The AFL-CIO's Political Record, 1974–1980," *Proceedings of the 34th A/M, IRRA*, ed. by Barbara Dennis (Madison: 1982); Nels E. Nelson, "Union Dues and Political Spending," *LLJ*, Feb. 1977; Frederick H. Nesbitt, "Endorsing Candidates—A Case History," *American Federationist*, Sept. 1975; Jong Oh Ra, *Labor at the Polls; Union Voting on Presidential Elections, 1952–1976* (Amherst: Univ. of Massachusetts Press, 1978); Charles M. Rehmus, Doris B. McLaughlin, and Frederick H. Nesbitt (ed.), *Labor and American Politics; A Book of Readings* (rev. ed., Ann Arbor: Univ. of Michigan Press, 1978); Joel Seidman and B. Karsh, "Political Consciousness in a Local Union," *Public Opinion Quarterly*, Winter 1951/52.

See also AFL-CIO COPE, LABOR LOBBY.

political education, union Basically, a term of art. It does involve "educating" union members in the mechanics of using their franchise, that is, how to register and how to vote, but the thrust of such education is the election of political candidates who will support legislation desired by organized labor (or its leaders) and oppose legislation that labor opposes. The kernel of this so-called political education is education in self-interest as this is conceived to be for the benefit of union members and, by extension, of the country as a whole.

Source references: AFL-CIO, *Labor and Politics* (Washington: COPE Pub. no. 59, 1959); James T. Crown, "Organized Labor in American Politics: A Look Ahead," *NYU 14th Annual Conference on Labor*, ed. by Emanuel Stein (Albany: Bender, 1961); Marc Karson, *American Labor Unions and Politics*,

1900–1918 (Carbondale: Southern Illinois UP, 1958); William O. Kuhl, "A Study of the Political Methods of the American Labor Movement Since the '80's," (Unpublished Ph.D. thesis, Univ. of Wisconsin, 1957); James L. McDevitt, "Politics and You," *American Federationist*, Jan. 1960; George Meany, "Political Education Is an AFL Tradition," *American Federationist*, May 1962; Mitchell Sviridoff, "Political Participation by Unions: The 1960 Situation," *LLJ*, July 1960.

See also AFL-CIO COPE; POLITICAL ACTION, UNION.

poor The Office of Management and Budget has established a schedule of income levels to help determine eligibility of disadvantaged individuals for participation in the Job Training Partnership Act programs. The poverty guideline for "poor" families relative to annual income levels as of June 1983 are:

Family Size	Poverty Guidelines
1	$ 4,860
2	6,540
3	8,220
4	9,900
5	11,580
6	13,260
7	14,940
8	16,620

For larger families, $1,680 is added for each additional member. The guideline for a family of four in Alaska and Hawaii is set at a higher level—$12,380 for Alaska and $11,390 for Hawaii. In addition, the lower living standard income level (LLSIL) is also used as a criterion to qualify for training programs. The LLSIL was developed by BLS for 475 cities, counties, and consortia of cities and counties operating employment and training programs with federal funds and has been in effect since May 1981. LLSIL is defined by the Job Training Partnership Act as "that income level (adjusted for regional, metropolitan, urban, and rural differences and family size) determined annually by the Secretary [of Labor] based on the most recent 'lower living family budget' issued by the Secretary." Thus, eligibility is based on the poverty guideline or the LLSIL, whichever is higher.

The Act defines "economically disadvantaged" as "an individual who (A) receives, or is a member of a family which receives, cash welfare payments under a Federal, State, or local welfare program; (B) has, or is a member of a family which has, received a total family income for the six-month period prior to application for the program involved (exclusive of unemployment compensation, child support payments, and welfare payments) which, in relation to family size, was not in excess of the higher of (i) the poverty level determined in accordance with criteria established by the Director of the Office of Management and Budget, or (ii) 70 percent of the lower living standard income level; (C) is receiving food stamps. . . ; (D) is a foster child on behalf of whom State or local government payments are made; or (E) in cases permitted by regulations of the Secretary [of Labor], is an adult handicapped individual whose own income meets the requirements of clause (A) or (B), but who is a member of a family whose income does not meet such requirements."

Source references: Job Training Partnership Act, 29 U.S.C. §§ 1771–1775 (1982); Arnold E. Chase, "Income and Expenditures of Low-Income Families," *MLR*, Aug. 1964; Laurie D. Cummings, "The Employed Poor: Their Characteristics and Occupations," *MLR*, July 1965; Camille Jeffers, *Living Poor, A Participant Observer Study of Priorities and Choices* (Ann Arbor: Ann Arbor Publishers, 1967); Elizabeth Herzog, "Perspectives on Poverty: Facts and Fictions About the Poor," *MLR*, Feb. 1969; Robert J. Lampman, "What Does It Do for the Poor?—A New Test for National Policy," *The Public Interest*, Winter 1974; Sar A. Levitan, *Programs in Aid of the Poor for the 1980s* (4th ed., Baltimore: Johns Hopkins UP, 1980); Sar A. Levitan and Robert Taggart, "The Hardship Index," *Across the Board*, Nov. 1976; Herman P. Miller, *Rich Man, Poor Man* (New York: Crowell, 1971); Paul Offner, "Labor Force Participation in the Ghetto," *Journal of Human Resources*, Fall 1972; Albert Rees, *Low-Wage Workers in Metropolitan Labor Markets* (Princeton: Princeton Univ., IR Section, Reprint, 1974); Theodore W. Schultz, *Investment in Poor People* (Washington: U.S. Dept. of Labor, Manpower Administration, Seminar on Manpower Policy and Programs, 1966); D. O. Sewell, *Training the Poor; A Benefit-Cost*

Analysis of Manpower Programs in the U.S. Antipoverty Program (Kingston, Ont.: Queen's Univ., IRC, 1971); U.S. Dept. of Labor, *News*, June 6, 1983; U.S. Dept. of Labor, BLS, *Linking Employment Problems to Economic Status* (Washington: Bull. 2123, 1982); U.S. National Commission for Manpower Policy, *Proceedings of a Conference on Employment Problems of Low Income Groups* (Washington: Special Report no. 5, 1976).

See also GUARANTEED INCOME, NEGATIVE INCOME TAX, POVERTY, PUBLIC ASSISTANCE, SOCIAL INSURANCE, WORKING POOR.

pork chopper An old term, now used mostly in good-humored banter. Originally, it may have been limited to a union organizer, or a union staff member who had organizing as one of his duties, since in pointing out the benefits of unionization he emphasized that tangible results included more money to buy food (pork chops).

Since the 1930s, the term has come to be interchangeable with "payroller," meaning a person whose salary is paid by the union he organizes for, or represents in other respects. In this sense, the term means that the union-paid representative has his own "pork chops" guaranteed.

Often the term is used as scathing denunciation of a person whose only reason for being union connected is deemed to be his regular pay and the perquisites of his job ("pork chops"). It is far from uncommon to hear rank-and-file union members refer to their union's business agent as a "pork chopper."

See also BUSINESS AGENT.

portable pension Refers to an arrangement under which employee pension credits are transferred from one pension plan to another, just as Social Security credits accumulate for the employee regardless of the number of times job changes occur. Portability may be achieved in part by a variety of means currently incorporated in various pension plans. Multi-employer plans involve employees of financially unrelated employers who have established a common pension fund. Multi-plant plans are those in which financially related companies or large corporations have pension plans which cover workers if they move from one branch or region to another or change status within the same organization. Reciprocity agreements are arrangements between pension plans which permit employees to change jobs without losing pension credits. Often, however, these are instituted along lines of collective bargaining units and credits are transferable only within these structural limits. Vesting, a procedure often confused with portability, refers to a terminating qualified employee's right to a pension based on his service credits in a plan. Vesting does not involve a transfer of credits; benefits are left in "cold storage" and paid in the form of an annuity which starts when the former employee reaches retirement age. Vesting, however, may enable portability of pension plans because an employee is entitled to the pension benefits while changing employment. Vesting rights are covered under the Employee Retirement Income Security Act of 1974. Section 402(a)(5) of the Internal Revenue Code provides for partial portability through "tax-free rollovers."

Source references: Walter W. Kolodrubetz, "Reciprocity and Pension Portability," *MLR*, Sept. 1968; Sir Leslie Melville, "Vesting and Portability," *Pension and Welfare News*, March 1969; Susan Meredith Phillips and Linda Pickthorne Fletcher, "The Future of the Portable Pension Concept," *ILRR*, Jan. 1977; Martin E. Segal, "Portable Pensions and Early Retirement: Are They Partial Solutions?" *Jobs, Men and Machines*, ed. by Charles Markham (New York: Praeger, 1964); Jozetta H. Srb, *Portable Pensions, A Review of the Issues* (Ithaca: NYSSILR, Cornell Univ., Key Issues Series no. 4, 1969); U.S. Dept. of Labor, BLS, *Labor Mobility and Private Pension Plans: A Study of Vesting, Early Retirement, and Portability Provisions* (Washington: Bull. no. 1407, 1964).

See also PENSION, PRIVATE PENSION PLAN, VESTED RIGHTS.

portal-to-portal pay Payments for time actually spent by an employee—originally on coal mine company premises—from the time of entrance at the gate to the time of return to the gate, which therefore included the time it took to reach the face of the mine and return as well as the time actually worked at the face.

Under the Wage and Hour law, it was held that portal-to-portal pay constituted an appropriate standard and that the employer was liable to payment of wages for all time spent by the employee on his premises, in preparation for work, as well as in activities following the completion of his work, until he left the plant. On appeal to the courts, the Supreme Court held on June 10, 1946, in the *Mount Clemens Pottery Company* case, that employers were liable for portal-to-portal pay under the provisions of the Fair Labor Standards Act. Following the decision many claims were filed under the Act and Congress in 1947 passed the Portal-to-Portal Act, which limited such claims.

Source references: U.S. v. Mount Clemens Pottery Co., 331 US 784 (1946); BNA, *The Portal-to-Portal Act of 1947* (Washington: 1947); Simeon Gold, "An Analysis of the Coal Dispute of 1943," *Industrial and Labor Relations Forum*, June 1968.

See also FACE-TO-FACE PAY.

Portal-to-Portal Pay Act The statute passed by the Congress in 1947 to limit the liabilities under the Wage and Hour law based on portal-to-portal pay claims.

The term "portal-to-portal" sometimes is rendered as "collar-to-collar" pay.

Porters; Brotherhood of Sleeping Car (AFL-CIO) Organized in 1925, it affiliated with the AFL in 1936. In April 1978, the union merged with the Brotherhood of Railway, Airline and Steamship Clerks, Freight Handlers, Express and Station Employes (AFL-CIO).

Source references: Brailsford R. Brazeal, *The Brotherhood of Sleeping Car Porters: Its Origin and Development* (New York: Harper, 1946); Jacob Kaufman, *Collective Bargaining in the Railroad Industry* (New York: Columbia UP, 1954); Herbert Northrup, "Industrial Relations on the Railroads," *Labor in Postwar America*, ed. by Colston E. Warne (Brooklyn: Remsen Press, 1949); Harry D. Wolf, "Railroads," *How Collective Bargaining Works* (New York: Twentieth Century Fund, 1945).

See also RAILWAY, AIRLINE AND STEAMSHIP CLERKS, FREIGHT HANDLERS, EXPRESS AND STATION EMPLOYES; BROTHERHOOD OF (AFL-CIO).

position A specific office or job.

positive strike A work stoppage which takes place on the basis of specific desires and demands of the employees for change. A positive strike is one designed to improve conditions, whereas a negative strike is one in which workers seek to prevent the reduction or loss or conditions they have achieved.

See also NEGATIVE STRIKE.

Postal and Federal Employees; National Alliance of (Ind) Formerly known as the National Alliance of Postal Employees (Ind). The union issues a monthly publication, *National Alliance*.

Address: 1628 11th St., N.W., Washington, D.C. 20001. Tel. (202) 939–6325

Postal Clerks; United Federation of (AFL-CIO) The consolidated organization which included the former National Federation of Post Office Clerks (AFL-CIO), the United National Association of Post Office Craftsmen (Ind), the United Federation of Post Office Clerks (AFL-CIO), and the National Postal Transport Association (AFL-CIO). The unions merged to form the United Federation of Postal Clerks (AFL-CIO) in 1961.

On July 1, 1971, it merged with the National Association of Special Delivery Messengers (AFL-CIO), National Association of Post Office and General Services Maintenance Employees (AFL-CIO), National Federation of Post Office Motor Vehicle Employees (AFL-CIO) and National Postal Union (Ind) to form the American Postal Workers Union (AFL-CIO).

See also POSTAL WORKERS UNION; AMERICAN (AFL-CIO).

Postal Clerks Union; National (Ind) *See* POSTAL UNION; NATIONAL (IND).

Postal Employees; National Alliance of (Ind) *See* POSTAL AND FEDERAL EMPLOYEES; NATIONAL ALLIANCE OF (IND).

Postal Reorganization Act Enacted in 1970, it abolished the Post Office Department and replaced it with the independent U.S. Postal Service.

Postal employees are accorded collective bargaining and organizing rights under the jurisdiction of the Taft-Hartley Act to the extent that such rights are not inconsistent with provisions of the Postal Reorganization Act. The NLRB is authorized to determine bargaining units, conduct elections, and adjudicate unfair practices. Postal employees, however, do not have the right to strike and are excluded from coverage of the union shop provisions of the Taft-Hartley Act.

Reporting and disclosure provisions of the Landrum-Griffin Act apply to postal unions.

Source references: Frederick C. Cohen, "Labor Features of the Postal Reorganization Act," *LLJ*, Jan. 1971; Milden J. Fox, Jr. and Donald A. Heinz, "Postal Reorganization Act: Postal Service Collective Bargaining Enters a New Era," *Journal of Collective Negotiations in the Public Sector*, Fall 1973; Stuart R. Wolk, "Postal Reform—A Year of Failure," *LLJ*, Oct. 1972.

Postal Security Police; Federation of (Ind) Founded in 1975, the union issues the quarterly *Federation News*.

Address: Box 1804, Pittsburgh, Pa. 15230. Tel. (412) 784–1943

Postal Supervisors; National Association of (Ind) Founded in 1908, it publishes *The Postal Supervisor* (monthly) and the *NAPSletter* (biweekly).

Address: 490 L'Enfant Plaza, S.W., #3200, Washington, D.C. 20004. Tel. (202) 484–6070

Postal Transport Association; National (AFL-CIO) One of the organizations which merged in 1961 to form the United Federation of Postal Clerks (AFL-CIO). The official monthly publication was known as the *Postal Transport Journal*.

See also POSTAL CLERKS; UNITED FEDERATION OF (AFL-CIO).

Postal Union; National (Ind) Formerly called the National Postal Clerks Union (Ind). On July 1, 1971, it merged with the National Association of Special Delivery Messengers (AFL-CIO), National Association of Post Office and General Services Maintenance Employees (AFL-CIO), National Federation of Post Office Motor Vehicle Employees (AFL-CIO), and United Federation of Postal Clerks (AFL-CIO) to form the American Postal Workers Union (AFL-CIO).

See also POSTAL WORKERS UNION; AMERICAN (AFL-CIO).

Postal Workers Union; American (AFL-CIO) On July 1, 1971, the National Association of Special Delivery Messengers (AFL-CIO), National Association of Post Office and General Services Maintenance Employees (AFL-CIO), National Federation of Post Office Motor Vehicle Employees (AFL-CIO), National Postal Union (Ind), and United Federation of Postal Clerks (AFL-CIO) merged to form this union. Its official monthly publication is *The American Postal Worker*.

Address: 817 14th St., N.W., Washington, D.C. 20005. Tel. (202) 842–4200

post-employment questionnaire An employee questionnaire used at any time subsequent to actual hiring of the individual. It is designed to obtain additional information regarding education, experience, and avocational interests which may assist the employee to make better use of his powers and resources. It may serve as a continuing check on individuals to see what progress they have made, not only on the job, but in other activities, including educational and other experience away from the job.

See also EXIT INTERVIEW, FAIR EMPLOYMENT PRACTICES.

posting The practice of calling attention to jobs which may be vacant or to which transfers or promotions may be available. The employer frequently is required by contract to announce the availability of such jobs on bulletin boards or through some other means, so that individuals may know of the availability of the positions.

The term also has application to the requirement that employers post notices giving effect to decisions of the NLRB. These notices are required to be posted in appropriate places to inform the employees that the company has taken the necessary action to comply with the Board's decisions. Unions may also be required to post or publish similar notices in their publications.

See also BIDDING, CEASE AND DESIST ORDER, NATIONAL LABOR RELATIONS BOARD, PROMOTION, SENIORITY.

posting of notices *See* BULLETIN BOARDS, POSTING.

Postmasters of the United States; National League of (Ind) An organization of independent postmasters, formerly known as the National League of District Postmasters of the United States (Ind). Its publications are *The*

Advocate issued monthly and *The Advocate Biweekly*.

Address: 1023 North Royal St., Alexandria, Va. 22314. Tel. (703) 548–5922

Post Office and General Services Maintenance Employees; National Association of (AFL-CIO) Formerly known as the National Association of Post Office Maintenance Employees (Ind). It affiliated with the AFL-CIO in March 1966. On July 1, 1971, it merged with the National Association of Special Delivery Messengers (AFL-CIO), National Federation of Post Office Motor Vehicle Employees (AFL-CIO), National Postal Union (Ind), and United Federation of Postal Clerks (AFL-CIO) to form the American Postal Workers Union (AFL-CIO).

See also POSTAL WORKERS UNION; AMERICAN (AFL-CIO).

Post Office Clerks; National Federation of (AFL-CIO) Organized in Chicago in August 1906 and chartered by the AFL. On April 17, 1961, the Post Office Clerks merged with the United National Association of Post Office Craftsmen (Ind) to form the United Federation of Post Office Clerks (AFL-CIO). On July 1, 1961, the National Postal Transport Association (AFL-CIO) and the newly formed United Federation of Post Office Clerks (AFL-CIO) merged to form the United Federation of Postal Clerks (AFL-CIO).

See also POSTAL CLERKS; UNITED FEDERATION OF (AFL-CIO).

Post Office Clerks; United National Association of (Ind) *See* POST OFFICE CRAFTSMEN; UNITED NATIONAL ASSOCIATION OF (IND).

Post Office Craftsmen; United National Association of (Ind) The organization merged with the National Federation of Post Office Clerks (AFL-CIO) to form the United Federation of Post Office Clerks (AFL-CIO). It was formerly known as the United National Association of Post Office Clerks. The official bimonthly publication was *The Post Office Employee*.

See also POSTAL CLERKS; UNITED FEDERATION OF (AFL-CIO).

Post Office Mail Handlers, Watchmen, Messengers and Group Leaders; National Association of (AFL-CIO) Formerly known as the National Association of Post Office and Railway Mail Service Handlers (AFL), the union became a division of the Laborers' International Union (AFL-CIO) on April 20, 1968, and later merged with the union.

See also LABORERS' INTERNATIONAL UNION OF NORTH AMERICA (AFL-CIO).

Post Office Maintenance Employees; National Association of (Ind) *See* POST OFFICE AND GENERAL SERVICES MAINTENANCE EMPLOYEES; NATIONAL ASSOCIATION OF (AFL-CIO).

Post Office Motor Vehicle Employees; National Federation of (AFL-CIO) Formerly unaffiliated, the union received its AFL-CIO charter in June 1958. On July 1, 1971, it merged with the National Association of Special Delivery Messengers (AFL-CIO), National Association of Post Office and General Services Maintenance Employees (AFL-CIO), National Postal Union (Ind), and the United Federation of Postal Clerks (AFL-CIO) to form the American Postal Workers Union (AFL-CIO).

See also POSTAL WORKERS UNION; AMERICAN (AFL-CIO).

Pottery and Allied Workers; International Brotherhood of (AFL-CIO) First organized in East Liverpool, Ohio, in December 1890, the union was formerly known as the National Brotherhood of Operative Potters (AFL) and later as the International Brotherhood of Operative Potters (AFL-CIO). It joined the Seafarers' International Union of North America (AFL-CIO) on June 21, 1976, but disaffiliated in January 1978. In August 1982, the union merged with the Glass Bottle Blowers Association (AFL-CIO) to form the Glass, Pottery, Plastics and Allied Workers International Union (AFL-CIO).

See also GLASS, POTTERY, PLASTIC AND ALLIED WORKERS INTERNATIONAL UNION (AFL-CIO).

poverty Various criteria have been established over the years by the Department of Labor, the Office of Economic Opportunity, and others to distinguish the poor from the nonpoor. Several possible criteria are: the presence of hunger; a nutritionally inadequate diet; expenditures for food, clothing, shelter, and other services below those currently required for minimum-decency standards of living; and an income or level of consumption expenditure which puts the family in the bottom percentiles of the population. The term poverty is frequently applicable to the sick, the disabled, the disadvantaged, the aged, and the unemployed.

Source references: Arthur I. Blaustein and Roger R. Woock, *Man Against Poverty: World War III* (New York: Vintage Books, 1968); Rose D. Friedman, *Poverty Definition and Perspective* (Washington: AEI, 1965); Irwin Garfinkel and Robert Haveman, "Earnings Capacity, Economic Status, and Poverty," *Journal of Human Resources,* Winter 1977; Margaret S. Gordon (ed.), *Poverty in America* (San Francisco: Chandler Pub., 1965); Peter Gottschalk, "Transfer Scenarios and Projections of Poverty into the 1980s," *Journal of Human Resources,* Winter 1981; M. J. D. Hopkins, "A Global Forecast of Absolute Poverty and Employment," *ILR,* Sept./Oct. 1980; C. Hsieh, "Fiscal Measures to Combat Poverty in the United States," *ILR,* May 1975; Deborah Pisetzner Klein, "Gathering Data on Residents of Poverty Areas," *MLR,* Feb. 1975; Sar A. Levitan, *The Great Society's Poor Law, A New Approach to Poverty* (Baltimore: Johns Hopkins Press, 1969); Herman P. Miller (ed.), *Poverty American Style* (Belmont: Wadsworth, 1968); Charles A. Murray, "The Two Wars Against Poverty: Economic Growth and the Great Society," *The Public Interest,* Fall 1982; Kathleen Patterson, *That Other War; A 12-Part Series on the War on Poverty from the Kansas City Star/Times* (Washington: U.S. Community Services Administration, 1976[?]); Samuel Rosenthal, "Poverty, Urban Renewal and Zoning," *Industrial and Labor Relations Forum,* March 1972; Paul M. Ryscavage, "Employment Problems and Poverty: Examining the Linkages," *MLR,* June 1982; Bruno Stein, *On Relief: The Economics of Poverty and Public Welfare* (New York: Basic Books, 1971); Robert Taggart, *Hardship; The Welfare Consequences of Labor Market Problems, A Policy Discussion Paper* (Kalamazoo: Upjohn Institute for Employment Research, 1982); U.S. Congressional Budget Office, *Poverty Status of Families Under Alternative Definitions of Income* (rev. ed., Washington: Background Paper no. 17, 1977); U.S. Dept. of HEW, *The Measure of Poverty, A Report to Congress Mandated by the Education Amendments of 1974* (Washington: 1976); U.S. Dept. of Labor, BLS, *Linking Employment Problems to Economic Status* (Washington: Bull. 2123, 1982); Clair Wilcox, *Toward Social Welfare: An Analysis of Programs and Proposals Attacking Poverty, Insecurity, and Inequality of Opportunity* (Homewood: Irwin, 1969).

See also GUARANTEED INCOME, NEGATIVE INCOME TAX, POOR, PUBLIC ASSISTANCE, UNEMPLOYMENT.

preamble clause A section of a collective bargaining agreement which precedes the substantive terms and which suggests that the parties, in consideration of the mutual promises made, will maintain certain basic attitudes and conditions in order to carry out the terms of the agreement. It is a sort of introductory section which in some cases sets the tone for continued cooperation between the parties.

precedent value In courts of law, the precedent value of a decision is measured by the degree to which it is followed or sanctioned in subsequent cases involving the same or similar issues. Under the principle of *stare decisis,* it is a general maxim that when a point of law has been settled by decision, it forms a precedent that is not to be departed from in subsequent cases.

Although the courts follow this principle, arbitrators generally do not regard themselves as bound by precedent in resolving labor-management disputes. As more lawyers have entered the field of labor arbitration, however, the tendency to follow precedent has increased.

Source references: Fred W. Catlett, "The Development of the Doctrine of Stare Decisis and the Extent to Which It Should Be Applied," 21 *Washington LR* 158 (1946); Charles T. Doyle, "Precedent Values of Labor Arbitration Awards," *PJ,* Feb. 1963; Philip Harris, "The Use of Precedent in Labor Arbitration," *AJ,* March 1977; Ken Jennings and Cindy Martin, "The Role of Prior Arbitration Awards in Arbitral Decisions," *LLJ,* Feb. 1978; Steven Kane, "Arbitrator Use of Bench

Decisions," *Industrial and Labor Relations Forum,* March 1973.

predatory unionism *See* HOLD-UP UNIONISM.

pre-employment contacts Procedures used by employers to recruit applicants such as printed or published job advertisements, word-of-mouth advertisements, and referrals. EEO laws require that such procedures be free of preferences or limitations based on race, color, religion, sex, national origin, age, disability, or veterans status. In addition, the job description must reflect the requirements of the position being advertised.

Source reference: Stephen Sahlein, *The Affirmative Action Handbook* (New York: Executive Enterprises, 1978).

pre-employment training Activities or training programs for individuals prior to their starting work, or work in a new area, or in a more highly skilled segment of an area with which they are familiar. Pre-employment training does not assume that the individual has little or no training in this field. In many cases, it builds on the skills and abilities the individual already possesses.

preemption, doctrine of The doctrine of federal preemption in the regulation of labor-management relations affecting interstate commerce has been spelled out in a series of more than 20 decisions handed down by the Supreme Court since the passage of the Taft-Hartley Act in 1947. As summarized by the Court in its 1959 *Garmon* opinion, the principles comprising the doctrine are as follows:

(1) State jurisdiction must yield when conduct is "arguably" or "potentially" subject to the Taft-Hartley Act, either as protected activity under Section 7 or as an unfair labor practice under Section 8.

(2) The initial determination of whether a particular activity is subject to the Act is exclusively the responsibility of the NLRB.

(3) Failure of the NLRB to determine the status of the disputed activity does not necessarily give the state the power to act, except as permitted by the 1959 amendments to the Act, as discussed below.

(4) If conduct is potentially subject to the Taft-Hartley Act, state regulation is precluded regardless of the remedy sought. The preemption doctrine applies to damage awards as well as injunctions, to state court proceedings as well as to regulation by a state labor agency, and to actions based on general statutory or common law as well as to proceedings under a state labor relations statute.

One effect of these holdings was to create a legal "no-man's land" in which the NLRB declined to assert jurisdiction and the states were forbidden to take jurisdiction. An amendment adopted in 1959 sought to remedy this situation. Under the amendment, state courts or agencies may assume jurisdiction over cases rejected by the NLRB under its dollar-volume jurisdictional standards. But the NLRB may not decline to assert jurisdiction over any dispute over which it would have asserted jursidiction under the standards prevailing on August 1, 1959. Furthermore, the states still are precluded from taking cases where the NLRB's failure to make a determination stems from the refusal of the general counsel to issue a complaint on grounds other than jurisdiction or from the NLRB's dismissal of a case because no Taft-Hartley violation was found.

Source references: Allen-Bradley v. WERB, 315 US 740, 10 LRRM 520 (1942); *Amalgamated Association [Electric Ry. Employees] v. Wisconsin Employment Relations Board,* 340 US 383, 27 LRRM 2385 (1951); *Automobile Workers v. O'Brien,* 339 US 454, 26 LRRM 2082 (1950); *Guss v. Utah Labor Board,* 352 US 817, 39 LRRM 2567 (1957); *La Crosse Telephone Co. v. Wisconsin Employment Relations Board,* 336 US 18, 23 LRRM 2236 (1949); *San Diego Building Trades Council v. Garmon,* 359 US 957, 43 LRRM 2838 (1959); Norton J. Come, "Federal Preemption Since *Garmon,*" *LLJ,* April 1966; ———, "Preemption: The Future of *Garmon,*" *NYU 23d Annual Conference on Labor,* ed. by Thomas Christensen and Andrea Christensen (New York: Bender, 1971); Robert Evans, Jr., "'Render Unto Caesar': Federal District Courts and Unfair Labor Practice Jurisdiction," *Journal of Business,* July 1966; Hugh Hafer, "A Pragmatic

Article Concerning Federal Preemption and Labor Law," *Wisconsin LR*, March 1960; Michael E. Hooton, "The Exceptional *Garmon* Doctrine," *LLJ*, Jan. 1975; William F. Isaacson, "Federal Pre-emption Under the Taft-Hartley Act," *ILRR*, April 1958; Howard Lesnick, "The Apparent Reaffirmation of *Garmon*," *Labor Law Developments 1972*, Proceedings of the 18th Annual Institute on Labor Law, SLF (New York: Bender, 1972); Thomas C. Newhouse, "The Cry From Within: Who Can I Turn To?" *Labor Law Developments 1972*, Proceedings of the 18th Annual Institute on Labor Law, SLF (New York: Bender, 1972); Jon E. Pettibone, "Preemption and Derivative Discovery in Unfair Labor Practice Proceedings," *LLJ*, Nov. 1979; Harold S. Roberts, *The Doctrine of Preemption, Federal-State Jurisdiction* (Honolulu: Univ. of Hawaii, IRC, 1957); George Rose, "The Labor Management Relations Act and the State's Power to Grant Relief," 39 *Virginia LR* 765 (1953); Russell A. Smith, "The Taft-Hartley Act and State Jurisdiction Over Labor Relations," 46 *Michigan LR* 594 (1948); Clarence M. Updegraff, *Preemption, Predictability and Progress in Labor Law* (Iowa City: Univ. of Iowa, Center for Labor and Management, Monograph series no. 5, 1967).

See also FEDERAL-STATE JURISDICTION, NO-MAN'S LAND.

preferential hiring A form of union security under which the employer agrees to give first preference to individuals who are members of the union or made available by the union, so long as the union is able to supply the necessary employees, both as to number and quality. Nonunionists are hired after all of the qualified union members have been placed.

The preferential hiring list establishes a waiting list of individuals who are eligible for employment, arranged in order of priority.

See also HIRING HALL, UNION SECURITY CLAUSES.

preferential shop A company or shop which by agreement with the union gives preference in hiring to union members as against equally qualified or competent nonunion members.

The preferential shop has been utilized widely in the clothing industry.

preferential treatment More favorable consideration accorded to individuals, for example, in selection and promotion, because of race, color, religion, sex, national origin, disability, age, veterans status, or other factors such as union membership, which are not related to job performance.

Title VII of the Civil Rights Act of 1964 does not require an employer to grant preferential treatment to individuals because of an imbalance of minorities or women in the employer's work force. The courts, however, have ruled that preferential treatment may be applied in some cases to correct the effects of past discrimination.

American Indians may receive special employment consideration under Indian preference laws. In addition, the OFCCP regulations allow federal contractors to give preferential treatment to Indians.

Title VII allows for preferential treatment to be granted to veterans in public sector jobs if such rights are created by federal, state, or local law.

Source references: Rios v. Enterprise Association Steamfitters, Local 638, 501 F2d 622, 8 FEP Cases 293 (1974); *U.S. v. N. L. Industries*, 479 F2d 354, 5 FEP Cases 823 (1973); U.S. OFCCP, "Obligations of Contractors and Subcontractors," 41 C.F.R. 60–1.5; Harry T. Edwards and Barry L. Zaretsky, "Preferential Remedies for Employment Discrimination," *IR Law Digest*, Summer 1976; Robert Freiberg (ed.), *The Manager's Guide to Equal Employment Opportunity* (New York: Executive Enterprises, 1977); Herbert Garfinkel and Michael D. Cahn, "Racial-Religious Designations, Preferential Hiring and Fair Employment Practices Commissions," *LLJ*, June 1969; Kenneth C. McGuiness (ed.), *Preferential Treatment in Employment—Affirmative Action or Reverse Discrimination?* (Washington: Equal Employment Advisory Council, 1977); James J. Mittermiller, "Preferential Treatment Remedies in Employment Discrimination Cases: An Analysis of Institutional Limitations," *Industrial Relations LJ*, Summer 1979.

See also VETERAN'S PREFERENCE.

Pregnancy Discrimination Act A 1978 amendment to Title VII of the Civil Rights Act of 1964, it expands the prohibition against employment discrimination "because of sex" or "on the basis of sex" to cover "pregnancy, childbirth or related medical conditions." The law states that "women affected by pregnancy, childbirth, or related medical conditions shall be treated the same for all employment-related purposes, as other persons not so affected but similar in their ability or inability to work. . . ." The amendment was prompted by *General Electric v. Gilbert*, in which the Supreme Court allowed the exclusion of pregnancy from an employer's disability plan.

Source references: Civil Rights Act of 1964, as amended, 42 U.S.C. 2000e et seq. (1982); U.S. EEOC, "Questions and Answers on Pregnancy Discrimination Act," 29 C.F.R. 1604, *FEP* 401:186; BNA, *Pregnancy Disability Amendment to Title VII of Civil Rights Act of 1964* (Washington: 1978); Paul S. Greenlaw and Diana L. Foderaro, "Some Further Implications of the Pregnancy Discrimination Act," *PJ*, Jan. 1980; ———, "Some Practical Implications of the Pregnancy Discrimination Act," *PJ*, Oct. 1979; Patricia M. Lines, "Update: New Rights for Pregnant Employees," *PJ*, Jan. 1979.

See also GENERAL ELECTRIC V. GILBERT.

prehearing conferences Administrative law judges (formerly trial examiners) of the NLRB may, on their own initiative or at the request of both parties, hold a prehearing conference as authorized by the Administrative Procedure Act of 1946. The purpose is to shorten and improve hearings by sharpening the issues, complaints, and defense theories before the formal hearing of evidence by the administrative law judge. "The intent is to avoid surprise and obfuscation by having the issues and respective theories of the complaint and answer spelled out and to achieve a record which is shorter and uncluttered by obtaining stipulations and agreements which simplify the issues and eliminate the taking of evidence on relevant matters about which there is no real dispute."

Source reference: Frank W. McCulloch, "NLRB Announces New Emphasis in Prehearing Conferences in Unfair Labor Practice Cases," *NLRB Release*, R–1089, Sept. 21, 1967.

prehire contract A contract agreed to by an employer and a union before the workers to be covered by the contract have been hired. The Labor-Management Reporting and Disclosure Act of 1959 (Landrum-Griffin) amended Sec. 8(f) of the Taft-Hartley Act to permit prehire and seven-day union-security contracts in the building and construction industry, subject to a number of specific restrictions.

premium money (push money) A form of incentive payment to sales people in the retail trades. The purpose is to move or sell those items which have a large profit margin or items which are slow-moving and must be disposed of prior to establishment of new lines.

premium pay Sometimes referred to as penalty pay. An extra rate which is paid to the individual for holiday and Sunday work, for work on late shifts, for overtime, or for specially hazardous, dangerous, or unpleasant work. It is an amount in excess of the regular compensation paid because of the special effort required or because of the unpleasantness of the work or for the inconvenience of the time during which the work takes place.

The term is applied occasionally to out-size rates paid to employees because of their special skills or their exceptional ability in their particular occupations.

Source references: Earl F. Mellor, "Working a Long Week and Getting Premium Pay," *MLR*, April 1978; George D. Stamas, "Long Hours and Premium Pay, May 1978," *MLR*, May 1979; Rose Theodore, "Premium Pay for Weekend Work in Major Contracts," *MLR*, April 1959; U.S. Dept. of Labor, BLS, *Premium Pay for Night, Weekend, and Overtime Work in Major Union Contracts* (Washington: Bull. no. 1251, 1959).

See also ACCELERATING PREMIUM PAY, NIGHT PREMIUM, OVERTIME PAY, PENALTY CARGO, PENALTY RATES, SHIFT DIFFERENTIAL.

premium wage system Any incentive wage system which provides a bonus or premium for work in excess of the norm and for extra exertion and effort.

Source reference: Michael J. Jucius, *Personnel Management* (6th ed., Homewood: Irwin, 1967).

See also BEDEAUX WAGE PLAN, GANTT TASK AND BONUS PLAN, HALSEY PREMIUM (GAINSHARING) PLAN, INCENTIVE WAGE, ONE-HUNDRED-PERCENT PREMIUM PLAN.

pre-negotiation A collective bargaining procedure proposed by General Electric Co. in which union and management representatives meet prior to contract reopening date based on the understanding that they are "to analyze assigned subject areas, to exchange ideas and to discuss alternative courses of action which might be profitably considered later by the full negotiating committees" when formal negotiations commence. Neither side is authorized to make commitments regarding later negotiations.

See also CONTINUOUS BARGAINING COMMITTEES.

Prentice-Hall, Inc. One of the major private labor information services in the United States. It is located in Englewood Cliffs, New Jersey. It provides weekly labor services covering major developments in industrial relations, wage and hour changes, etc.

prepayment plan A plan developed by an employer to compensate, in advance, earnings to an employee. The plan may be developed to keep an employee's earnings constant based on anticipated overtime compensation.

Source reference: CCH, *Wages-Hours*, 25,520.81.

See also MEDICAL CARE PLANS.

preretirement education Programs established for workers who are close to retirement or who are anticipating early retirement. The programs are designed to help the individual to adjust to the prospect of retirement.

The programs concern themselves not only with the financial aspects of the older worker, but also with the actual programming of time and activities in order to provide a satisfactory adjustment to the new way of life. The programs are carried out by employers, by university industrial relations centers in cooperation with unions, or directly by unions which have special departments to provide such activity.

One major program sponsored jointly by the Institute of Labor and Industrial Relations, University of Michigan–Wayne State University and the Division of Gerontology of the University of Michigan included the following areas of discussion:

(1) The social aspects of aging,
(2) The psychological aspects of aging,
(3) The physical aspects of aging,
(4) Preretirement education programs (content and method),
(5) work and retirement in a changing world,
(6) Money and retirement,
(7) Leisure activity and work,
(8) Health and happiness in retirement,
(9) Family, friends, and living arrangements,
(10) The union, the community, and the older worker.

Source references: William Arnone, "Preretirement Planning: An Employee Benefit that Has Come of Age," *PJ*, Oct. 1982; Douglas M. Bartlett, "Retirement Counseling: Making Sure Employees Aren't Dropouts," *Personnel*, Nov./Dec. 1974; Herbert T. Brenner and Robert H. Linnell, "Preretirement Planning Programs," *Journal of the College and University Personnel Association*, July/Aug. 1976; Walter H. Franke, *Preparing Workers for Retirement* (Urbana: Univ. of Illinois, Institute of Labor and IR, Bull. no. 27, 1962); William H. Holley, Jr. and Hubert S. Feild, Jr., "The Design of a Retirement Preparation Program: A Case History," *PJ*, July 1974; Woodrow H. Hunter, *Leadership Training for Preretirement Education* (Ann Arbor: Univ. of Michigan–Wayne State Univ., Institute of Labor and IR, 1960); ______, "Pre-Retirement Education," *Geriatrics*, Nov. 1960; Charles R. Naef, *Pre-Retirement Programs in New Jersey* (New Brunswick: Rutgers Univ., Institute of Management and Labor Relations, 1960); Charles E. Odell, "An Urgent Need: Education for Retirement," *American Federationist*, Sept. 1966; John F. O'Rourke and Harvey L. Friedman, *An Inter-Union Pre-Retirement Training Program: Results and Commentary* (Amherst: Univ. of Massachusetts, Labor Relations and Research Center, Reprint 34, 1972); Judith Raffel, "Combating Employee Resistance to Retirement-Planning Seminars," *PJ*, Oct. 1980; E. B. Shultz, "Selective Retirement and Pre-Retirement Counseling in the TVA," *ILRR*, Jan. 1959; Univ. of Wisconsin, Bureau of Government, *Planning Conference on State Pre-Retirement System* (Madison: 1961).

See also RETIREMENT.

Presidential Railroad Commission The 15-man commission appointed by President Eisenhower to study the general problem of the need for rule changes and the efficient operation of the railroads. The commission, after a study of almost two years, in 1962 submitted recommendations in a number of areas which would reduce the number of employees engaged as firemen working on diesel engines, make provision for basic changes in wages, and other economies. The unions opposed the recommendations and subsequently obtained a temporary injunction to restrain the railroads from putting the changes into effect. In November 1962, the case came up in the U.S. Court of Appeals for the Seventh Circuit which, on review of the claims of the employers, upheld the right of the railroads to put the necessary changes into effect. The decision supported the claim by the railroad companies that featherbedding had cost them close to $590 million in 1961. It stated in part, "Wage costs (included) unneeded employees occupying redundant positions, pay for time not worked, and the cost of owning and maintaining equipment and facilities that would not be required, apart from the restrictions placed upon the efficiency and the economy of operations by existing rules."

The circuit court also held that the railroad brotherhoods and the employers had allegedly negotiated but that these negotiations were "mere . . . discussions of differences, thus placing the carriers in a position to exercise their prerogatives . . ." The court also noted that the attempt to bargain with the union was futile and frustrated. Concerning the insistence of the unions that they would strike if the rules were put into effect, the court said: "We should like to believe that this unnecessary threat of a strike of such magnitude as to amount to a national transportation paralysis was ill-advised . . . we shall remind the persons responsible that they are dealing with railroad properties which are impaled with a public interest, which is paramount to that of all the litigants in this case."

The case was appealed to the Supreme Court which arrived at the same conclusions as the Seventh Circuit. The union subsequently ordered a strike, and President Kennedy appointed a special study commission of three whose recommendations were not accepted. The case came before Congress, which in August 1963 acted to create a commission to arbitrate the rules issue. Its decision was made public in November 1963. The arbitration award was appealed to the courts by the unions but the Supreme Court denied certiorari on April 27, 1964. Basic issues, however, continued to be in controversy. Finally on July 19, 1972, agreement was reached when the United Transportation Union and the National Railway Labor Conference signed two agreements to settle the diesel fireman dispute.

Source references: Locomotive Engineers v. B & O Railroad, 310 F2d 503, 51 LRRM 2572 (1962); Jacob J. Kaufman, "The Railroad Labor Dispute: A Marathon of Maneuver and Improvisation," *ILRR*, Jan. 1965; U.S. Dept. of Labor, BLS, *Handling of Rail Disputes Under the Railway Labor Act, 1950–69* (Washington: Bull. 1753, 1972); U.S. NMB, *The Railway Labor Act at Fifty—Collective Bargaining in the Railroad and Airline Industries,* ed. by Charles M. Rehmus (Washington: 1976); U.S. Presidential Railroad Commission, *Studies Relating to Collective Bargaining Agreements and Practices Outside the Railroad Industry Appendix, Vol. 4* (Washington: 1962); ———, *Report of the Presidential Railroad Commission* (Washington: 1962).

presidential seizure The authority of the President as commander in chief to seize certain properties when necessary to protect the national interest.

During World War II, the War Labor Disputes Act (Smith-Connally Act) made provision for seizure by the President in order to carry on the war effort.

Source reference: John L. Blackman, Jr., *Presidential Seizure in Labor Disputes* (Cambridge: Harvard UP, 1967).

See also GOVERNMENT SEIZURE, WAR LABOR DISPUTES ACT.

President's Advisory Committee on Labor-Management Policy By Executive Order 10918 issued February 16, 1961, President Kennedy established the Presidential Advisory Committee on Labor-Management Policy. The order stated that the advisory committee will study, advise, and recommend policies for labor and management to promote "free and responsible collective bargaining, industrial peace, sound wage and price policies, higher standards of living, and increased productivity."

The committee was composed of 21 members representing management, labor, and the public. The secretaries of labor and commerce alternated as chairman of the committee, with the labor secretary serving as chairman in the odd years and the commerce secretary in the even years.

The committee issued various findings on automation, collective bargaining, unemployment, foreign trade, and fiscal and monetary policy. It was abolished by Executive Order 11710 on April 4, 1973.

Source references: E.O. 10918, February 16, 1961; Jack Stieber, "The President's Committee on Labor-Management Policy," *IR*, Feb. 1966; U.S. President's Advisory Committee on Labor-Management Policy, *Automation* (Washington: 1962); ———, *Collective Bargaining* (Washington: 1962); ———, *Fiscal and Monetary Policy* (Washington: 1963); ———, *Methods of Adjusting to Automation and Technological Change* (Washington: 1964); ———, *Seminars on Private Adjustment to Automation and Technological Change* (Washington: 1965).

President's Committee on Employment of the Handicapped Committee established by Executive Order 10994 of February 14, 1962, as amended, to facilitate the development of maximum employment opportunities for the handicapped. It superseded the President's Committee on Employment of the Physically Handicapped, which was established by Executive Order 10640, October 10, 1955.

President's Committee on Equal Employment Opportunity A committee established by Executive Order 10925 issued on March 6, 1961, by President Kennedy. The committee was charged with the responsibility of effectuating equal employment opportunity both in government and in employment on government contracts. It required government and government contractors not to discriminate in employment on the basis of race, creed, color, or national origin. A subsequent order, Executive Order 11141 issued on February 13, 1964, by President Johnson, enunciated a government policy against employment discrimination based on age. The coverage of the first executive order had been extended to federally assisted construction by Executive Order 11114 issued by President Kennedy on June 22, 1963.

Similar committees had been established by executive orders issued under the Roosevelt, Truman, and Eisenhower administrations. There was an important difference, however, between the order issued by President Kennedy and those issued by his predecessors. In addition to imposing an obligation on contractors not to discriminate on the basis of race, creed, color, or national origin, the Kennedy order also required contractors to take affirmative action to make the policy effective. This was the authorization for the "Plans for Progress" program established by the committee.

In 1965, after Title VII of the Civil Rights Act with its ban on employment discrimination based on race, color, religion, sex, or national origin had become effective, the Committee on Equal Employment Opportunity was abolished by Executive Order 11246. Its functions with respect to government employment were transferred to the Civil Service Commission, while those with respect to employment on government contracts were transferred to the Labor Department, Office of Federal Contract Compliance Programs.

Reorganization Plan No. 1 of 1978 transferred the Civil Service Commission enforcement function to the Equal Employment Opportunity Commission.

Source references: E.O. 10925, 26 F.R. 1977 (1961); E.O. 11114, 28 F.R. 6485 (1963); E.O. 11141, 29 F.R. 2477 (1964); BNA, *The Civil Rights Act of 1964* (Washington: 1964); Theodore W. Kheel, *Report to Vice President*

Johnson on the Structure and Operations of the President's Committee on Equal Employment Opportunity (Washington: 1962); U.S. President, Committee on Equal Employment Opportunity, *Guide for Investigations and Compliance Reviews in Equal Employment Opportunity* (Washington: 1962); ———, *Rules and Regulations of the President's Committee on Equal Employment Opportunity—Government Contract Employment* (Washington: 1963).

See also CIVIL RIGHTS ACT OF 1964, EQUAL EMPLOYMENT OPPORTUNITY COMMISSION, EXECUTIVE ORDER 11246, OFFICE OF FEDERAL CONTRACT COMPLIANCE PROGRAMS (OFCCP), PLANS FOR PROGRESS, REORGANIZATION PLAN NO. 1 OF 1978.

President's Committee on Youth Employment On November 15, 1961, President Kennedy appointed this special committee for the purpose of formulating policies for education, training, and guidance, with particular reference to enlargement of employment opportunities for young people. The committee in its report to the President, dated April 24, 1963, made some 15 recommendations dealing with immediate as well as long-range programs to meet vocational and employment problems.

Source reference: U.S. President's Committee on Youth Employment, *The Challenge of Jobless Youth* (Washington: 1963).

President's Committee to Appraise Employment and Unemployment Statistics *See* UNEMPLOYMENT.

President's Council of Economic Advisers *See* COUNCIL OF ECONOMIC ADVISERS.

President's Missile Sites Labor Commission *See* MISSILE SITES LABOR COMMISSION.

President's National Labor-Management Conference *See* LABOR-MANAGEMENT CONFERENCE (1945).

President's Task Force on Employee-Management Relations in the Federal Service *See* EXECUTIVE ORDER 10988, PUBLIC EMPLOYEE RELATIONS.

prevailing rate The common or predominant rate paid to a group of workers, generally with reference to a specific occupation in an industry or in a specific labor market area. There are, however, many variations which are due in part to variations in usage in particular industries or under particular circumstances. Thus, the U.S. Department of Labor notes many variations in the use of the prevailing rate concept and suggests, in view of these variations, that when the term "prevailing rate" is used, it should make "specific mention of the area, occupation, industry, rate, and type of quantitative measure involved to have definite meaning."

See also GOING RATE.

prevailing rate employees *See* FEDERAL WAGE SYSTEM.

prevailing wages The actual wage rates for particular classes of work in a given geographic area; used also as a basis for the minimum rates which are established for work on public construction. Certain payments for fringe benefits are also considered as being part of the prevailing rate.

See also DAVIS-BACON ACT.

preventive mediation *See* MEDIATION, PREVENTIVE.

price list The listing of rates or piece prices paid by a single company or by a group of companies producing a similar product. Where there is a union in the plant, the price lists are established by agreement between the union and the employer.

The term frequently may refer to the piece rates set under incentive programs. During the early days of labor organization, the price list or the price scale was actually the equivalent of the present collective bargaining agreement as far as wages were concerned.

prices The actual cost of particular items. For statistical purposes the U.S. Department of Labor makes available data showing in aggregate form the variations in prices over a period of time. The Department of Labor also constructs and publishes the Consumer Price Index.

Source references: "Action by Governments to Stabilize Primary Commodity Prices," *ILR*, March 1962; Earl L. Bailey (ed.), *Pricing Practices and Strategies* (New York: The Conference Board, Report no. 751,

1978); C. Daniel Bergfeld, *Strategic Pricing, Protecting Profit Margins from Inflation*, An AMA Management Briefing (New York: AMA, 1981); John F. Early, "The Producer Price Index Revision: Overview and Pilot Survey Results," *MLR*, Dec. 1979; Abraham Freidman, *Information Sources and Beliefs About Knowledge of Prices in High Inflation, An Empirical Study* (Minneapolis: Univ. of Minnesota, IRC, WP 81–06, 1981); John Kenneth Galbraith, *A Theory of Price Control* (Cambridge: Harvard UP, 1980); Craig Howell and Jesse Thomas, "Price Changes in 1981: Widespread Slowing of Inflation," *MLR*, April 1982; John Q. Lawyer, "How to Conspire to Fix Prices," *Harvard BR*, March/April 1963; Fabian Linden, "Consumer Prices Under Inflation," *Conference Board Record*, June 1975; Gardiner C. Means, *Pricing Power and the Public Interest: A Study Based on Steel* (New York: Harper, 1962); G. William Miller, "The Not Impossible Goal: Full Employment and Price Stability," *Across the Board*, March 1978; Dereck J. Moeller, "Users Find Industrial Price Data Satisfactory But Urge Some Changes," *MLR*, Dec. 1977; Geoffrey H. Moore, "Cost-Price Signals: A New Stage in the Business Cycle?" *Management Review*, Nov. 1977; Thomas R. Tibbetts, "Improvements in the Industrial Price Program," *MLR*, May 1975; U.S. Congress, Joint Economic Committee, *Studies in Price Stability and Economic Growth. Paper no. 1—Inflation and the Consumer in 1974* (Washington: 1975); U.S. Dept. of Agriculture, *Food Prices in Perspective* (Washington: Agriculture Information Bull. no. 427, 1979); U.S. Dept. of Labor, BLS, *Comparisons of United States, German, and Japanese Export Price Indexes* (Washington: Bull. 2046, 1980); ———, *The Cyclical Behavior of Prices* (Washington: Report 384, 1971).

See also CONSUMER PRICE INDEX.

Priestly v. Fowler A decision of an English court in 1837 which was the basis for the fellow-servant rule. The decision relieved employers or masters of liability for injury sustained by an employee on account of the carelessness of a fellow servant provided only that the employer or master had exercised reasonable care in the selection of the employees.

Source reference: Albion G. Taylor, *Labor Problems and Labor Laws* (New York: PH, 1944).

See also CONTRIBUTORY NEGLIGENCE, WORKERS COMPENSATION.

prima facie evidence Evidence in the field of law which is considered to be sufficient on its face to establish a fact unless it is disputed. The establishment of a prima facie case is one in which there is no room left for doubt or where it appears on its face that the evidence is as claimed.

primary activities Those economic actions by a union against an employer designed to achieve its bargaining objectives. These might include concerted activity of various types, including picketing and strikes against the primary employer.

See also PICKETING.

primary boycott A boycott or concerted action by the union in which it seeks to prevent the use, purchase, or handling of an employer's product or service, and no effort is made to involve or to persuade or coerce those related to the dispute, but who are not the prime individuals in the dispute.

See also BOYCOTT.

Printing and Graphic Communications Union; International (AFL-CIO) Union formed on October 2, 1973, with the merger of the International Printing Pressmen and Assistants Union of North America (AFL-CIO) and the International Stereotypers' and Electrotypers' Union of North America (AFL-CIO).

On July 1, 1983, the union merged with the Graphic Arts International Union (AFL-CIO) to form the Graphic Communications International Union (AFL-CIO).

See also GRAPHIC COMMUNICATIONS INTERNATIONAL UNION (AFL-CIO).

Printing Pressmen and Assistants Union of North America; International (AFL-CIO) Organized in New York in 1889 by a group of pressmen's locals which had left the International Typographical Union. It was chartered by the AFL.

On October 2, 1973, the union merged with the International Stereotypers' and Electrotypers' Union of North America (AFL-

CIO) to form the International Printing and Graphic Communications Union (AFL-CIO).

See also PRINTING AND GRAPHIC COMMUNICATIONS UNION; INTERNATIONAL (AFL-CIO).

priority rights A term which generally was used as the equivalent of seniority in the printing trades and in the railroad industry.

In business phraseology, the term applies to the rights of an individual creditor to have a claim against a debtor met before the claims of others are considered.

priority unemployment A term that had some usage during the World War II period to describe unemployment caused by the unavailability to an employer of parts or materials that were preempted by government order for war-supporting activities, hence had a high "priority" and limited distribution.

prison labor Work done by convicts in penitentiaries or other penal institutions.

Source references: Lyle W. Branchflower, "Work Release," *Conference Board Record,* May 1971; Martin Dewey, "Prisoners Who Work for Private Companies," *Across the Board,* Sept. 1981; Jeffrey K. Ross, "Collective Bargaining in the Prison Sector," *Industrial and Labor Relations Forum,* March 1972; U.S. Dept. of Labor, BLS, *Laws Relating to Prison Labor in the United States as of July 1, 1933* (Washington: Bull. no. 596, 1933); ———, *Prison Labor in the United States, 1932* (Washington: Bull. no. 595, 1933); Walter Wilson, *Forced Labor in the United States* (New York: International Publishers, 1933).

See also ALABAMA V. ARIZONA, ASHURST-SUMNERS ACT, HAWES-COOPER ACT, PHILLIPS V. RAINEY.

private industry council (PIC) Established by Title VII of the Comprehensive Employment and Training Act (CETA) to coordinate employment and training efforts of prime sponsors and private employers under the Private Sector Initiative Program (PSIP).

Under the Job Training Partnership Act (JTPA) of 1982, PICs guide job training activities for state and local areas (service delivery areas) to increase the involvement of the business community in federally funded employment and training programs.

The chief elected official of a service delivery area appoints PIC members from among individuals nominated or recommended. Members include representatives of the private sector, educational agencies, organized labor, rehabilitation agencies, community-based organizations, economic development agencies, and the public employment service. The Act mandates that individuals representing the private sector constitute the majority of PIC membership; the chair of the PIC is selected by the council members from among representatives of the private sector.

In addition to providing policy guidance, each PIC determines procedures for the development of a job training plan, designates the entity to administer the plan, and selects grant recipients. Programs conducted under the job training plan are subject to review and evaluation by the PIC.

Source references: Comprehensive Employment and Training Act, as amended, 29 U.S.C. 801 et seq. (1982) (repealed, 96 Stat. 1357 (1982); matters formerly covered by the Comprehensive Employment and Training Act are now covered by the Job Training Partnership Act, 29 U.S.C. 1501 et seq. (1982)); Job Training Partnership Act, as amended, 29 U.S.C. 1501 et seq. (1982); Royal S. Dellinger, "Implementing the Job Training Partnership Act," *LLJ,* April 1984; Robert Guttman, "Job Training Partnership Act: New Help for the Unemployed," *MLR,* March 1983; William Mirengoff et al., *CETA; Accomplishments, Problems, Solutions* (Kalamazoo: Upjohn Institute for Employment Research, 1982); U.S. Dept. of Labor, ETA, *The PIC is the Keystone* (Washington: 1980).

See also COMPREHENSIVE EMPLOYMENT AND TRAINING ACT (CETA) OF 1973, JOB TRAINING PARTNERSHIP ACT (JTPA) OF 1982, PRIVATE SECTOR INITIATIVE PROGRAM (PSIP).

private pension plan Retirement plan which is established outside of government programs and provides regular payments to employees upon retirement. Some private pension plans also provide payments to individuals for permanent or total disability.

Source references: Benjamin Aaron, *Legal Status of Employee Benefit Rights Under Private Pension Plans* (Homewood: Irwin, 1961); Merton C. Bernstein, *The Future of Private*

Pensions (New York: Free Press, 1964); Harry E. Davis, "Pension Provisions Affecting the Employment of Older Workers," *MLR*, April 1973; Daniel M. Holland, *Private Pension Funds: Projected Growth* (New York: NBER, 1966); Joseph Krislov, "Beneficiaries and Benefit Payments from Private Pension Plans—An Untapped Source of Data," *LLJ*, Nov. 1966; Mario Leo, Preston C. Bassett, and Ernest S. Kachline, *Financial Aspects of Private Pension Plans: A Research Study and Report*, Prepared for the Financial Executives Research Foundation (New York: Financial Executives Research Foundation, 1975); Matthew M. Lind, "Alternatives to CELI: Strengthening and Preserving the U.S. Private Pension System," *LLJ*, Dec. 1978; Olivia S. Mitchell and Emily S. Andrews, "Scale Economies in Private Multi-Employer Pension Systems," *ILRR*, July 1981; Edwin W. Patterson, *Legal Protection of Private Pension Expectations* (Homewood: Irwin, 1960); Robert D. Paul, "Can Private Pension Plans Deliver?" *Harvard BR*, Sept./Oct. 1974; James H. Schulz, Thomas D. Leavitt, and Leslie Kelly, "Private Pensions Fall Far Short of Preretirement Income Levels," *MLR*, Feb. 1979; Donald J. Staats, "Normal Benefits Under Private Pension Plans," *MLR*, July 1965; ———, "Private Pension Plans: How Benefits Are Computed," *MLR*, Oct. 1965; Robert Tilove, "The Adequacy of Private Pension Plans—Another View," *NYU 18th Annual Conference on Labor*, ed. by Thomas Christensen (Washington: BNA, 1966); Norman B. Ture and Barbara A. Fields, *The Future of Private Pension Plans* (Washington: AEI, 1976); U.S. Congress, Joint Economic Committee, *Studies in Public Welfare. Paper no. 11—The Labor Market Impacts of the Private Retirement System* (Washington: 1973); U.S. Congress, Senate, Committee on Labor and Public Welfare, *Statistical Analysis of Major Characteristics of Private Pension Plans* (Washington: 1972).

See also EMPLOYEE RETIREMENT INCOME SECURITY ACT (ERISA) OF 1974, PENSION PLAN, RETIREMENT.

Private Sector Initiative Program (PSIP) Program authorized by Title VII of the Comprehensive Employment and Training Act of 1978, establishing the private industry council (PIC). Working through the PIC, prime sponsors carried out private sector–related activities coordinating programs of jobs, training, and education designed to increase private sector employment opportunities for the unemployed and underemployed.

Source references: Comprehensive Employment and Training Act of 1973, as amended, 29 U.S.C. 801 et seq. (1982) (repealed, 96 Stat. 1357 (1982); matters formerly covered by the Comprehensive Employment and Training Act are now covered by the Job Training Partnership Act, 29 U.S.C. 1501 et seq. (1982)); Job Training Partnership Act, as amended, 29 U.S.C. 1501 et seq. (1982); U.S. Dept. of Labor, *In Partnership With Business, White Paper on the Private Sector Initiative Program* (Washington: 1979); U.S. Dept. of Labor, ETA, *Private Sector Initiative Program (PSIP), The PIC is the Keystone* (Washington: 1980).

See also NATIONAL ALLIANCE OF BUSINESS (NAB), PRIVATE INDUSTRY COUNCIL (PIC).

privatization *See* SUBCONTRACTING.

probable cause *See* REASONABLE CAUSE.

probationary employee Generally a new employee who is on trial and attempting to establish a right to permanent status. During the probationary period, the individual usually does not have seniority rights and may be discharged without cause, except where the discharge discriminates against an individual because of union membership or activity. The probationary period is designed to give the company an opportunity to find out whether the employee is qualified to carry on the work for which the individual was hired.

See also TRIAL PERIOD.

probationary rate A wage rate below the minimum for the job. It frequently is used when new employees are hired and the company wishes to determine whether the employee will qualify. It is also used on occasion when an employee is transferred or promoted to a new job.

producers' cooperation Any cooperative effort on the part of a group of workers to eliminate the middleman. This effort, if successful, eliminates not only the middleman but also makes for a closer working relationship and the possibility of a lower price.

See also COOPERATIVES (CO-OPS).

production bonus Any extra monetary compensation directly related to the production turned out by an individual or group. It generally is paid for output in excess of a stipulated standard or quota, or (in the case of an hourly-rated job) where the job is completed in less than the standard time set for the task. The amount of the actual bonus may be a fixed amount or it may fluctuate on a percentage basis.

Source references: Thomas Q. Gilson and Myron L. Lefcowitz, "A Plant-Wide Productivity Bonus in a Small Factory: A Study of an Unsuccessful Case," *ILRR,* Jan. 1957; J. Keith Louden, *Wage Incentives* (2d ed., New York: Wiley, 1959); George L. Stelluto, "Report on Incentive Pay in Manufacturing Industries," *MLR,* July 1969.

See also BONUS, INCENTIVE WAGE.

Production, Service and Sales Union; International (Ind) 100 Livingston St., Brooklyn, N.Y. 11201. Tel. (718) 858–4900

production transfer The shifting or transfer of an individual from one position to another within the plant, thus permitting broader utilization of staff without the necessity for new hires or additional training.

See also TRANSFER.

production workers A term applied to the major group of employees whose work is in direct production, as contrasted with the "indirect labor" of office and clerical staff, supervisory and professional staff, and (possibly) maintenance and security employees. Production workers generally include those actually engaged in the processing, fabricating, assembling, receiving, inspection, handling, and storage of the product, as well as those concerned with warehousing, packing, shipping and maintenance, and repair. Janitorial help and those engaged in record-keeping may be directly associated with the production workers.

It is frequently important that the community of interest of these groups be kept in mind, not only in matters which relate to the determination of the appropriate bargaining unit for collective bargaining purposes, but also in connection with the establishment of incentive programs. This is particularly true of overall plant incentives, which frequently attempt to separate production from so-called nonproduction workers.

See also DIRECT LABOR.

productive capacity, measures of The difficulties inherent in the concept of productive capacity led the Joint Economic Committee of the House and Senate to establish a Subcommittee on Economic Statistics, and to conduct hearings on that concept. The hearings were held in May 1962 and the Subcommittee on Economic Statistics submitted its report to the Congress on July 24, 1962.

The committee stated in part:

> Productive capacity is among the oldest, most used, and most important concepts in economic analysis. Nevertheless, productive capacity continues to be an illusive concept. A considerable range of meanings has been attached to the concept, depending in part on the use to which it is to be put, and in part on whether the problem is approached from a strictly engineering or from some economic point of view. Almost all of the many definitions of capacity have in common these elements: 1) capacity refers to a quantity of output that can be produced per unit of time, making use of a given stock or plant and equipment. 2) Capacity estimates usually, though not always, assume that raw materials and labor will be available in the required quantities and qualities. 3) Allowance is usually made for "normal" down time, operating speed, number of shifts per day, and other usual operating conditions in each particular industry or process. 4) Either explicitly or implicitly, the various estimates assume that the capacity output can be produced either at the lowest average total cost, or at less than some "high" marginal cost. 5) In some capacity measures for individual industries and in almost all aggregate measures which cover broad segments of the economy, some allowance is made for the effect on capacity of possible bottlenecks, including limits on labor or materials, and for changes in product mix.

The Joint Committee gave particular attention to the following:

(1) The McGraw-Hill Book Company's measures of manufacturing capacity,
(2) The National Industrial Conference Board's measures of capacity,
(3) The Wharton School capacity utilization data,

(4) Fortune Magazine's capacity measure, and
(5) The two measures of capacity developed by the Federal Reserve Board: (a) the capacity and output indexes for major materials and (b) the index of manufacturing capacity.

Source references: Kenneth A. Charon and James B. Schlumpf, "IBM's Common Staffing System: How to Measure Productivity of the Indirect Workforce," *Management Review,* Aug. 1981; Leon Greenberg, *A Practical Guide to Productivity Measurement* (Washington: BNA, 1973); David V. Mollenhoff, "How to Measure Work by Professionals," *Management Review,* Nov. 1977; National Research Council, Panel to Review Productivity Statistics, *Measurement and Interpretation of Productivity* (Washington: National Academy of Sciences, 1979); Albert Rees, "Improving the Concepts and Techniques of Productivity Measurement," *MLR,* Sept. 1979; Peter R. Richardson and John R. M. Gordon, "Measuring Total Manufacturing Performance," *Sloan Management Review,* Winter 1980; David L. Rowe, "How Westinghouse Measures White Collar Productivity," *Management Review,* Nov. 1981; Irving H. Siegel, *Company Productivity, Measurement for Improvement* (Kalamazoo: Upjohn Institute for Employment Research, 1980); U.S. Congress, Joint Economic Committee, *Measures of Productive Capacity, Hearings* (Washington: 1962); ———, *Measures of Productive Capacity, Report* (Washington: 1962); U.S. Dept. of Labor, BLS, *The Meaning and Measurement of Productivity* (Washington: Bull. no. 1714, 1972); ———, *Productivity Measures for Selected Industries, 1954–80* (Washington: Bull. 2128, 1982); U.S. GAO, *Government Measures of Private-Sector Productivity: Users Recommend Changes* (Washington: 1980); U.S. National Center for Productivity and Quality of Working Life, *Improving Productivity Through Industry and Company Measurement, Series 2* (Washington: 1976); Urban Institute, *The Status of Productivity Measurement in State Government: An Initial Examination;* Prepared for the National Center for Productivity and Quality of Working Life, U.S. Dept. of Health, Education, and Welfare and U.S. Dept. of Transportation (Washington: 1976).

See also OUTPUT PER HOUR (LABOR PRODUCTIVITY).

productive labor *See* DIRECT LABOR.

productive life The period of time during which, over a normal life span, the individual actually engages in work for pay. This period generally has ranged from 40 to 50 years, depending upon the occupation, profession, or trade.

The total productive period varies also with the climate as well as with the political and economic institutions of a country. In industrialized countries, the length of productive life has been reduced because of the extension of the period of education, elimination of child labor, and lowering of retirement age. Productive life, however, will be substantially affected with the enactment of age discrimination laws and the extension of retirement age.

What obviously will be needed in the generations ahead is a redefinition of the concept of production as well as the concept of work. Provision will have to be made for compensation of individuals who will be engaging in activities which are presently not considered productive in the financial sense.

See also AGE DISCRIMINATION IN EMPLOYMENT ACT OF 1967.

productivity An index to measure the efficiency of a plant or the ability to utilize manpower and plant equipment. There are many measures of productivity. They may deal with physical output based on horsepower units, units of material consumed, units of capital used, or labor units employed. The most frequent measure of productivity is that expressed in terms of output per worker or the output per man-hour (payroll hour). Efficiency is measured on the basis of comparison of input and output over a period of time and the effective utilization of the various factors of production.

As one authority puts it, it is extremely difficult to set up or establish statistical measures to determine the flow of output because there are so many interrelated factors. He says in part, ". . . in modern industry it is not possible to isolate the influence of a single element in a complex process, to ascertain the exact contribution of each factor to the combined result. An increase in productivity presumably means more efficient utilization of one or more of the various factors of production: more efficient management, improvement in technical knowledge and tools, more effective use of existing plants and other overhead items, better supplies of materials and parts, and more ability, experience, and effort on the part of the work force."

Many measures of productivity have been devised and are being used. They have a definite value in the collective bargaining process and it is important that these measures and their limits and values be understood.

Source references: Walter L. Balk, *Improving Government Productivity: Some Policy Perspectives* (Beverly Hills: Sage, 1975); Richard A. Beaumont, *Productivity and Policy Decisions* (New York: Industrial Relations Counselors, Research Monograph no. 18, 1959); Francis Bello, "The Technology Behind Productivity," *MLR,* Aug. 1962; Paul T. Christy and Karen J. Horowitz, "An Evaluation of BLS Projections of 1975 Production and Employment," *MLR,* Aug. 1979; Kim B. Clark, "The Impact of Unionization on Productivity: A Case Study," *ILRR,* July 1980; Bill Cunningham, "Bringing Productivity into Focus," *American Federationist,* May 1979; Thomas R. Donahue, "The Human Factor in Productivity," *American Federationist,* Dec. 1980; James B. Dworkin and Dennis A. Ahlburg, *Research on Unions and Productivity* (Minneapolis: Univ. of Minnesota, IRC, WP 82–17, 1982); Solomon Fabricant, *Basic Facts on Productivity Change* (New York: NBER, 1959); ———, *A Primer on Productivity* (New York: Random House, 1969); Eric G. Flamholtz (ed.), *Human Resource Productivity in the 1980s* (Los Angeles: UC, Institute of IR, Monograph and Research Series no. 31, 1982); Saul W. Gellerman, *Motivation and Productivity* (New York: AMA, 1963); John H. Hoffman and Orry Y. Shackney, "Assessing the Productivity of Corporate Staff Services," *Management Review,* Nov./Dec. 1982; IRRA, *Collective Bargaining and Productivity,* ed. by Gerald Somers et al. (Madison: 1975); Arnold S. Judson, "The Awkward Truth About Productivity," *Harvard BR,* Sept./Oct. 1982; John W. Kendrick and Daniel Creamer, *Measuring Company Productivity: Handbook With Case Studies* (New York: NICB, Studies in Business Economics no. 89, 1965); Campbell R. McConnell, "Why is U.S. Productivity Slowing Down?" *Harvard BR,* March/April 1979; James L. Medoff and Katharine G. Abraham, "Are Those Paid More Really More Productive? The Case of Experience," *Journal of Human Resources,* Spring 1981; Jerome Rosow (ed.), *Productivity; Prospects for Growth* (New York: Van Nostrand Reinhold, 1981); U.S. Congressional Budget Office, *The Productivity Problem: Alternatives for Action* (Washington: 1981); U.S. GAO, *Productivity Sharing Programs: Can They Contribute to Productivity Improvement?* (Washington: 1981); ———, *State and Local Government Productivity Improvement: What is the Federal Role?* (Washington: 1978); U.S. National Center for Productivity and Quality of Working Life, *The Future of Productivity* (Washington: 1977).

See also ANNUAL IMPROVEMENT FACTOR, OUTPUT, OUTPUT PER HOUR (LABOR PRODUCTIVITY), PRODUCTIVITY BARGAINING.

productivity bargaining Union-management negotiations which concern changes in work rules to increase productivity or eliminate inefficiencies and to reward employees for productivity gains. Productivity bargaining may involve the elimination of outmoded work practices or the introduction of new technology in exchange for job security protections.

Source references: Ross E. Azevedo, *Productivity Bargaining: A Promising Challenge to the Public Sector* (Minneapolis: Univ. of Minnesota, IRC, WP 79–04, 1979); Michael L. Brookshire and Michael D. Rogers, "Productivity and Collective Bargaining in the Public Sector," *LLJ,* Aug. 1981; Walter J. Gershenfeld, "Work Enrichment and Productivity Bargaining: A Critique of the Issues," *NYU 27th Annual Conference on Labor,* ed. by David Raff (New York: Bender, 1975); Robert McKersie, Lawrence Hunter, and Werner Sengenberger, *Productivity Bargaining: The British and American Experience* (Washington: U.S. National Commission on Productivity, 1972); Jerome M. Rosow, "Now is the Time for Productivity Bargaining," *Harvard BR,* Jan./Feb. 1972; Ralph R. Smith, "Productivity Bargaining—Patterned for the Future?" *Employee Relations LJ*, Winter 1977.

productivity factor *See* ANNUAL IMPROVEMENT FACTOR.

productivity increase *See* ANNUAL IMPROVEMENT FACTOR.

productivity trends The general movement and direction as well as the magnitude of change in productivity.

See also PRODUCTIVITY.

Professional Airmen; Union of (AFL-CIO) *See* AIR LINE PILOTS ASSOCIATION; INTERNATIONAL (AFL-CIO).

Professional Air Traffic Controllers Organization Originally known as the Professional Association of Air Traffic Controllers, PATCO was organized in 1968, led by attorney F. Lee Bailey.

In 1970, the PATCO leadership was turned over to rank-and-file members and the union affiliated with the Marine Engineers' Beneficial Association (AFL-CIO). PATCO was chosen as the national exclusive representative of federal civilian air traffic controllers in 1972.

On August 3, 1981, PATCO began a nationwide strike. Subsequently, the Federal Labor Relations Authority (FLRA) decertified PATCO for its failure to call off the strike as directed by the FLRA in its order of October 22, 1981. The fines and damages assessed against the union following the strike forced PATCO into bankruptcy in 1982. Shortly after PATCO was liquidated, a new union, the United States Air Traffic Controllers Organization (USATCO), was formed with a number of former PATCO officers in leadership positions.

Source references: Professional Air Traffic Controllers Organization, Affiliated with MEBA, AFL-CIO and Federal Aviation Administration, Department of Transportation, Case No. 3–CO–105, 7 *FLRA* No. 10 (October 22, 1981); "Analysis: Controllers Prepared Thirteen Years for This Moment," *Government Employee Relations Report*, no. 925, Aug. 17, 1981; M. J. Fox and E. G. Lambert, "Air Traffic Controllers: Struggle for Recognition and Second Careers," *Public Personnel Management*, May/June 1974; Marvin J. Levine, "National Exclusive Recognition Under Executive Order 11491: The PATCO Case," *LLJ*, Feb. 1971; Murray B. Nesbitt, *Labor Relations in the Federal Government Service* (Washington: BNA, 1976).

Professional and Technical Engineers; International Federation of (AFL-CIO) Formerly known as the American Federation of Technical Engineers (AFL-CIO), it adopted the present name in the early 1970s. Its bimonthly publication is *The Outlook.*

Address: 818 Roeder Rd., Suite 702, Silver Spring, Md. 20910. Tel. (301) 565–9016

professional employees Individuals whose work is predominantly nonroutine and intellectual in character. They generally exercise a substantial degree of discretion and judgment in the performance of their work. The professional status frequently comes both from extensive education and training as well as from specific experience in the application of professional skills. Among professional occupations are those of doctors, lawyers, professors, engineers, actors, and so on. It is generally accepted that the status and performance of the professional are measured against standards established by those in the same profession.

Under various statutes, including the Fair Labor Standards Act and the National Labor Relations Act, special treatment is accorded individuals who are considered to be "professional employees."

Source references: Marina Angel, "Professionals and Unionization," 66 *Minnesota LR* 383 (1982); ———, "White Collar and Professional Unionization," *LLJ*, Feb. 1982; Frances Bairstow, "New Dimensions in Public-Sector Grievance Arbitration. I. Management Rights and the Professional Employee," *Truth, Lie Detectors, and Other Problems in Labor Arbitration*, Proceedings of the 31st A/M, NAA, ed. by James Stern and Barbara Dennis (Washington: BNA, 1979); L. W. C. S. Barnes, *The Changing Stance of the Professional Employee* (Kingston: Queen's Univ., IRC, Research Series no. 29, 1975); Elizabeth Bartholet, "Application of Title VII to Jobs in High Places," 95 *Harvard LR* 945 (1982); Dean E. Beachler, David C. Joswick, and R. J. Shubert, "Are Your Professionals Staying Professional?" *PJ*, Sept. 1978;

Dennis Chamot, "Professional Employees Turn to Unions," *Harvard BR*, May/June 1976; James A. Dalton and E. J. Ford, Jr., "Concentration and Professional Earnings in Manufacturing," *ILRR*, April 1978; Matthew W. Finkin, "The Supervisory Status of Professional Employees," *IR Law Digest*, Summer 1977; M. J. Fox, Jr., and Edgar E. Johnson, Jr., "Unionization of Professionals: What Can We Expect?" *Journal of Collective Negotiations in the Public Sector*, Vol. 4, no. 4, 1975; Jack Golodner, "Professionals Go Union," *American Federationist*, Oct. 1973; Sheldon E. Haber, "The Mobility of Professional Workers and Fair Hiring," *ILRR*, Jan. 1981; Felicitas Hinman (ed.), *Professional Workers and Collective Bargaining, Selected Papers* (Los Angeles: UC, Institute of IR, 1977); Eileen B. Hoffman, *Unionization of Professional Societies* (New York: The Conference Board, Report no. 690, 1976); Univ. of Illinois, Institute of Labor and IR, *Collective Bargaining for Professional and Technical Employees, Conference Report* (Urbana: 1965); William Kornhauser and Warren O. Hagstrom, *Scientists in Industry: Conflict and Accommodation* (Berkeley: UC Press, 1962); Don LeBell, "Managing Professionals: The Quiet Conflict," *PJ*, July 1980; V. Alan Mode, "Salary and the Unionization of Professionals," *Human Resource Management*, Winter 1980; Eugene Raudsepp, *Managing Creative Scientists and Engineers* (New York: Macmillan, 1963); George Strauss, "Professionalism and Occupational Associations," *IR*, May 1963; U.S. Dept. of Labor, BES, *Placement of Professional Personnel* (Washington: 1963); U.S. Dept. of Labor, BLS, *National Survey of Professional, Administrative, Technical and Clerical Pay, March 1983* (Washington: Bull. 2181, 1983); U.S. Dept. of Labor, Employment Standards Admin., *Executive, Administrative and Professional Employees; A Study of Salaries and Hours of Work* (Washington: 1977); Irene Unterberger and S. Herbert Unterberger, "Disciplining Professional Employees," *IR*, Oct. 1978.

Professional Employees, Department for The AFL-CIO department established in 1967 as the Scientific, Professional and Cultural Employees Council. The name was later changed to the Professional Employees Council. In December 1977 it was granted departmental status and adopted its present name.

Unions affiliated with the department include: Actors Equity; American Federation of Government Employees; Musicians; State, County and Municipal Employees; American Federation of Teachers; Television and Radio Artists; Musical Artists; Theatrical Press Agents and Managers; Railway and Airline Clerks; Communications Workers; Federation of Professional Athletes; Theatrical Stage Employes; Machinists; Electrical Workers; Professional and Technical Engineers; Electronic and Machine Workers; Operating Engineers; Automobile Workers; Broadcast Employees and Technicians; Office and Professional Employees; Retail, Wholesale and Department Store Union; Screen Actors Guild; Seafarers; Service Employees; Plumbers; and Food and Commercial Workers.

The program of the department includes four major functions: "mutual cooperation among members of scientific, professional, and cultural unions; encouragement of all professionals to become union members; participation in legislative activities that are of interest to professionals; and promotion of greater public interest in scientific, educational, and cultural activities."

The department issues the quarterly *Interface*.

Address: AFL-CIO Building, 815 16th St., N.W., Washington, D.C. 20006. Tel. (202) 638–0320

See also AFL-CIO DEPARTMENTS.

professional negotiation A process proposed by the National Education Association as "designed to serve the unique needs of the teaching profession" as opposed to the concept of collective bargaining in the labor context as developed in private industry fostered by the American Federation of Teachers (AFL-CIO). The National Education Association defines the term as "a set of procedures, written and officially adopted by the local staff organization and the school board, which provides an orderly method for the school board and staff organization to negotiate on matters of mutual concern, to reach agreement on these matters, and to establish educational channels for mediation and appeal in the event of an impasse. . . . [It] means much more than the simple right to be heard; . . . It means, specifically, that boards of education must be prepared to engage in give-and-take negotiations over policy matters with staff organizations. . . ."

Source references: Robert H. Chanin, "Hard Times in the Public and Nonprofit Sectors: An Employee View," *NYU 29th Annual Conference on Labor*, ed. by Richard Adelman (New York: Bender, 1977); Charles W. Cheng, *Altering Collective Bargaining; Citizen Participation in Educational Decision Making* (New York: Praeger, 1976); *Collective Bargaining and the Classroom* (Honolulu: Univ. of Hawaii, IRC, Reprint no. 7, 1972); Bruce S. Cooper, *Collective Bargaining, Strikes, and Financial Costs in Public Education: A Comparative View* (Eugene: ERIC Clearinghouse on Educational Management, Univ. of Oregon, 1982); Robert E. Doherty (ed.), *Public Access: Citizens and Collective Bargaining in the Public Schools* (Ithaca: Cornell Univ., NYSSILR, 1979); Matthew W. Finkin, "Bargaining and Professionalism," *Labor Law Developments 1974*, Proceedings of the 20th Annual Institute on Labor Law, SLF (New York: Bender, 1974); Raymond L. Hogler, "Collective Bargaining in Education and the Student," *LLJ*, Nov. 1976; Margaret A. Lareau, "The Issue of Collective Bargaining for School Supervisors and Administrators," *LLJ*, March 1980; Marvin J. Levine and Katherine G. Lewis, "The Status of Collective Bargaining in Public Education: An Overview," *LLJ*, March 1982; Myron Lieberman, "The Role and Responsibilities of the Parties in School District Bargaining," *Journal of Collective Negotiations in the Public Sector*, Vol. 10, no. 1, 1981; Myron Lieberman and Michael H. Moskow, *Collective Negotiations for Teachers* (Chicago: Rand McNally, 1966); Donald A. Myers, *Teacher Power—Professionalization and Collective Bargaining* (Lexington, Mass.: Lexington Books, 1973); National Education Assn., *Professional Negotiation: Selected Statements of School Board, Administrator, Teacher Relationships* (Washington: 1965); ———, *Professional Negotiation With School Boards: A Legal Analysis and Review* (Washington: 1965); Jane Wandel Nelson, "State Court Interpretation of Teacher Collective Bargaining Statutes: Four Approaches to the Scope of Bargaining Issue," *Industrial Relations LJ*, Fall 1977; Charles R. Perry, "Teacher Bargaining: The Experiences in Nine Systems," *ILRR*, Oct. 1979; Gregory M. Saltzman, "The Growth of Teacher Bargaining and the Enactment of Teacher Bargaining Laws," *Proceedings of the 34th A/M, IRRA*, ed. by Barbara Dennis (Madison: 1982); Martha Ware, "There Are Some Real Important Differences Between Collective Bargaining and Professional Negotiation," *NEA Journal*, Nov. 1962; Allan M. West, "Professional Negotiations or Collective Bargaining," *National Elementary Principal*, February 1963; Jacqueline A. Young (ed.), *Proceedings of the National Conference on the Impact of Collective Bargaining on the Quality of Education Today* (Amherst: Univ. of Massachusetts, Center for the Study of Collective Bargaining in Education, 1980).

See also COLLECTIVE NEGOTIATION.

professional sanction A tactic used by the American Association of University Professors (AAUP) and the National Education Association to pressure administration or governing bodies for changes.

The sanctions generally point out unsatisfactory working conditions and urge teachers not to accept employment with a particular employer. Censure, the AAUP's strongest sanction, informs AAUP members, the teaching profession at large, and the public that unsatisfactory conditions of academic freedom and tenure have been found to prevail at censured institutions.

Source references: AAUP, *Policy Documents and Reports* (Washington: 1971); Jordan E. Kurland, "Implementing AAUP Standards," *Academe*, Dec. 1980; J. Douglas Muir, "The Strike as a Professional Sanction," *LLJ*, Oct. 1968; National Education Association, *Addresses and Proceedings* (Washington: 1968).

profit sharing A system or procedure whereby an employer pays compensation or benefits to employees in addition to their regular wages, based upon the profits of the company. Payments may be made either on a current or cash plan which gives employees a share of the profits on a regular basis, or it may be on a deferred basis in which a trust fund is established and payments are made at regularly set times. The funds are accumulated under the plan and paid to the individual after a stipulated number of years or at the attainment of a specific age or upon the occurrence of some event such as disability, retirement, death, illness, or severance of employment. The payments are made to the individual who participates or to his beneficiary. The profit-sharing plan generally is based on a definite, determined formula specifying how much of the profit is to be distributed and how the profit is to be computed.

Source references: BNA, *Pensions and Profit Sharing* (3d ed., Washington: 1964); Paul E. Burke, "TRASOPs: The Beautiful Benefit," *PJ*, March 1978; Bernard A. Diekman and Bert L. Metzger (ed.), *Profit Sharing: The Industrial Adrenalin* (Evanston: Profit Sharing Research Foundation and Institute of Profit Sharing, 1975); Peter F. Drucker, "Profit-Sharing: Profit or Loss?" *NY Times Magazine*, October 15, 1961; Peter S. Hearst, "Employee Stock Ownership Trusts and Their Uses," *PJ*, Feb. 1975; I. B. Helburn, "Trade Union Response to Profit-Sharing Plans: 1886–1966," *Labor History*, Winter 1971; John J. Jehring, *The Investment and Administration of Profit Sharing Trust Funds* (Evanston: Profit Sharing Research Foundation, 1957); John J. Jehring and Bertram L. Metzger, *The Stockholder and Employee Profit Sharing* (Evanston: Profit Sharing Research Foundation, 1960); Benjamin J. Klebaner, "U.S. Labor and Profit Sharing in the Late 1800's," *MLR*, Aug. 1962; Herbert F. Lloyd, "Profit Center Incentives: Stimulants or Depressants?" *Management Review*, April 1979; Bertram L. Metzger, *Employee Investment Choice in Deferred Profit Sharing* (Evanston: Profit Sharing Research Foundation, 1975); ———, (ed.), *Pension, Profit Sharing, or Both?* (Evanston: Profit Sharing Research Foundation, 1975); Ephriam P. Smith, "Stock as a Means of Executive Compensation," *PJ*, Aug. 1974; Randy G. Swad, "Stock Ownership Plans: A New Employee Benefit," *PJ*, June 1981.

See also EMPLOYEE STOCK OWNERSHIP PLAN, GAIN SHARING, KAISER STEEL LONG-RANGE SHARING PLAN, PROGRESS SHARING PLAN, SAVINGS PLAN, SCANLON PLAN.

program evaluation and review technique (PERT) A system designed to facilitate planning and to provide management with tools for the control of specific programs.

Source references: Bruce N. Baker and Rene L. Eris, *An Introduction to PERT-CPM* (Homewood: Irwin, 1964); K. R. MacCrimmon and C. A. Ryavec, "An Analytical Study of the PERT Assumptions," *Rand Report*, No. RM–34–08–PR, Dec. 1962; Norman C. Miller, "PERT and Critical Path—Management by Chart," *Management Review*, Nov. 1961; Robert W. Miller, "How to Plan and Control With PERT," *Harvard BR*, March/April 1962; ———, "Program Cost Uncertainty: Prediction and Control Using PERT Techniques," *Industrial Management Review*, Spring 1963; Peter P. Schoderbek, "PERT in College Recruiting," *Management of Personnel Quarterly*, Winter 1965; ———, "PERT/Cost: Its Values and Limitations," *Management Review*, March 1966; Peter P. Schoderbek and Lester A. Digman, "Third Generation, PERT/LOB," *Harvard BR*, Sept./Oct. 1967; Lawrence L. Steinmetz, "PERT Personnel Practices," *PJ*, Sept. 1965; Gabriel N. Stilian et al., *PERT, A New Management Planning and Control Technique* (New York: AMA, Management Report no. 74, 1962); Glenn H. Varney and Gerard F. Carvalho, "PERT in the Personnel Department," *Personnel*, Jan./Feb. 1968.

programmed instruction or learning Machines which incorporate information in series of steps in the learning process which by means of self-instruction and automatic check of items (which have been learned), permit the individual to progress as quickly as possible once the necessary previous information has been absorbed. Programmed learning is utilized as a training method.

The instruction does not have to be handled on mechanical equipment. It can be utilized in general teaching for groups. However, the system is designed primarily for individuals working at their own speed. Programmed teaching materials can be used for learning information or particular skills.

Source references: AMA, *How to Train on the Job: A Programmed Instruction Course for Hospital Supervisors* (New York: 1969); ———, *Programmed Instruction in Indus-*

try (New York: Management Bull. no. 22, 1962); Albert B. Chalupsky and David D. Nelsen, "Programmed Learning—Better Than Regular Textbooks?" *PJ*, Nov. 1964; R. W. Christian, "Guides to Programmed Learning," *Harvard BR*, Nov./Dec. 1962; William A. Deterline, *An Introduction to Programmed Instruction* (Englewood Cliffs: PH, 1962); Theodore B. Dolmatch, "Programmed Instruction—The Managerial Perspective," *Personnel*, Jan./Feb. 1962; Theodore B. Dolmatch et al. (ed.), *Revolution in Training: Programmed Instruction in Industry* (New York: AMA, Management Report Series no. 72, 1962); James D. Finn and D. G. Perrin, *Teaching Machines and Programmed Learning, 1962: A Survey of the Industry*, A report prepared for the Technological Development Project of the National Education Association of the United States (Washington: U.S. Dept. of HEW, Office of Education, 1962); John B. Furr, "How Programmed Instruction Can Speed Plant Training," *Management Review*, Sept. 1968; David E. Hennessy, "Getting Results from Programmed Instruction," *Personnel*, Sept./Oct. 1967; Jerome P. Lysaught and C. M. Williams, *A Guide to Programmed Instruction* (New York: Wiley, 1963); Stuart Margulies and Lewis D. Eigen, *Applied Programmed Instruction* (New York: Wiley, 1962); John R. Murphy and Irving A. Goldberg, "Strategies for Using Programmed Instruction," *Harvard BR*, May/June 1964; R. David Niebler, "Programmed Instruction Saves Time—and Grows," *PJ*, May 1963; Leo E. Persselin, "Programmed Learning in a Systems Approach to Corporate Communication," *PJ*, Sept. 1964; Ernest M. Schuttenberg, "Misconceptions About Programmed Learning," *Personnel*, May/June 1965; Helen V. Shaffer, "Teaching by Machine," *Editorial Research Reports*, Jan. 25, 1961; Wendell I. Smith (ed.), *Programmed Learning: Theory and Research* (Princeton: Van Nostrand, 1962); Lawrence M. Stolurow, *Teaching by Machine* (Washington: U.S. Dept. of HEW, Office of Education, 1961).

progression *See* AUTOMATIC PROGRESSION.

progression schedule *See* AUTOMATIC PROGRESSION, MERIT RATING.

Progressive Mine Workers of America (Ind) A former AFL affiliate, it has remained independent since 1945.

Address: 120 East Scarritt St., Springfield, Ill. 62704. Tel. (217) 522–8891

progressive wage system *See* MERIT INCREASE.

progress sharing plan Concepts which have been incorporated into a number of contracts which suggest that the employer and union share in the progress made by the company in some tangible way. One such agreement is that between the United Automobile Workers and the American Motors Corporation. Another in which the parties agreed to share the "fruits of progress" is the contract between the United Steelworkers and Kaiser Steel.

Source reference: Univ. of Wisconsin, Center for Productivity Motivation, *A New Approach to Collective Bargaining? Progress Sharing at American Motors* (Madison: 1962).

See also KAISER STEEL LONG-RANGE SHARING PLAN, PROFIT SHARING.

prohibited subjects for bargaining Sometimes termed illegal items which may not be subject to negotiations as specified by agreement, statute, or court and administrative rulings. Prohibited subjects for bargaining include the demand for a closed shop and the demand for preferential treatment based on sex, race, color, religion, or national origin. In the public sector, items commonly excluded from negotiations and reserved for management authority include the right to hire, promote, discharge, or discipline employees for cause; the supervision, management, and control of the organization; and the methods, processes, and means of production.

See also BORG-WARNER CASE, MANDATORY SUBJECTS FOR BARGAINING, PERMISSIVE SUBJECTS FOR BARGAINING, SCOPE OF BARGAINING.

project method A procedure of training through the actual performance of a particular activity unit. This provides a practical experience in which the action is guided and in which there is a specific application of the particular materials to be learned.

Source reference: Eric Harlow, "Project Work in Supervisory Studies," *Industrial Training International,* Oct. 1966.

proletariat A term used in Marxist literature to designate the large masses of workers who have nothing to sell but their labor. They do not own their tools or the instruments of production. They are not serfs or slaves since they have the economic ability to dispose of their labor power.

See also WORKING CLASS.

promotability Generally those qualities of an employee which indicate the inherent potential for performing more complex and more responsible activities either because of intellectual competence, greater motivation, or potential in the particular skills required for promotion.

promotion The advancement of employees among the departments of a company or within a department in order to make the most efficient use of manpower as well as to increase morale. The advancement generally is to positions which entail greater responsibility, more prestige, greater skill, higher pay, or several of these factors.

Where the advancement is in the same general classification, it is referred to as a horizontal promotion. The vertical promotion is one in which the employee moves to a different or higher classification.

Most collective bargaining agreements establish procedures for handling transfers and promotions on the basis of ability, length of service, or a combination of these. Seniority, of course, applies in many areas, particularly in handling layoffs, reinstatement, opportunity for overtime work, in addition to transfer and promotion.

Source references: BNA, *Employee Promotion and Transfer Policies* (Washington: PPF Survey no. 120, 1978); Peter B. Doeringer, "Discriminatory Promotion Systems," *MLR,* March 1967; ———, "Promotion Systems and Equal Employment Opportunity," *Proceedings of the 19th A/M, IRRA,* ed. by Gerald Somers (Madison: 1967); Frank D. Ferris, "Remedies in Federal Sector Promotion Grievances," *AJ,* June 1979; Robert M. Fulmer and William E. Fulmer, "Providing Equal Opportunities for Promotion," *PJ,* July 1974; Eli Ginzberg, "EEO's Next Frontier: Assignments, Training, and Promotion," *Employee Relations LJ,* Summer 1978; Elaine F. Gruenfeld, *Promotion: Practices, Policies, and Affirmative Action* (Ithaca: NYSSILR, Cornell Univ., Key Issues Series no. 17, 1975); Carl Hoffmann and John Shelton Reed, "The Strange Case of the XYZ Corporation," *Across the Board,* April 1981; "Job Hunting for Promotion," *Supervisory Management,* Aug. 1956; Roy C. Kern, "Selection for Promotion," *PJ,* July/Aug. 1967; Jerome B. Kernan, William P. Dommermuth, and Montrose S. Sommers, *Promotion, An Introductory Analysis* (New York: McGraw-Hill, 1970); Harry Levinson, "The Problems of Promotion," *Management Review,* April 1965; New York State, Commission on Management and Productivity in the Public Sector, *Job Promotion Under New York State's Civil Service System, A Case Study of the Office of General Services* (Albany: 1977); ———, *The Promotion Process: Innovations in Merit System Administration* (Albany: 1978); U.S. CSC, *Fair and Effective Employee Advancement: A Guide for State and Local Government Managers* (Washington: 1976); U.S. OPM, *A Survey of Merit Promotion Provisions in Federal Post Civil Service Reform Act Agreements* (Washington: 1980); Jacobo A. Varela, "Why Promotions Cause Trouble—And How to Avoid It," *Personnel,* Nov./Dec. 1964; James W. Walker, Fred Luthans, and Richard M. Hodgetts, "Who Really Are the Promotables?" *PJ,* Feb. 1970; Andrew Young, "Models for Planning Recruitment and Promotion of Staff," *BJIR,* Nov. 1965.

See also ABILITY, LENGTH OF SERVICE, SENIORITY.

promotion chart Any graphic presentation which shows the lines of progression or promotion and the opportunities for individual movement within a particular company, among departments and in particular classifications of work.

promotion increase Any wage or salary adjustment given to an employee either incident to a change of classification or as a result of more efficient or effective work performance.

Source reference: Charles D. Stewart, "Promotional Increases—A Formula Approach," *PJ*, Sept. 1964.

proportional representation A system of voting which is designed to provide representation for minority groups. The general purpose is to give each of the groups the representation to which it is entitled on the basis of its representative strength within the overall group. There are many systems designed to accomplish this.

In general, majority representation applies to elections and certifications in labor relations in the United States. Occasionally, however, in larger units, a system of proportional representation may be adopted to protect the rights of minority groups.

proposal Generally applies to the specific offer made by either management or labor during collective bargaining. The proposal may be on the record or off the record; it may be the basis for discussion; or it may be submitted as the only offer one side is willing to accept.

In general, under the National Labor Relations Act some proposals are "mandatory" subjects of bargaining, others are permissive. Wages, hours, and conditions of employment fall within the "mandatory" concept, which means that the party advancing such proposals may insist that the opposite party bargain in good faith on these proposals (although coming to an agreement is not required).

See also COLLECTIVE BARGAINING, REFUSAL TO BARGAIN.

protected class A generic term with no precise legal meaning which describes individuals who, according to Congress and the courts, have suffered the effects of employment discrimination; it usually refers to women and minorities.

Persons between 40 and 69 years of age, Vietnam veterans, and handicapped persons are also protected classes under other legislation.

Source references: Robert Freiberg (ed.), *The Manager's Guide to Equal Employment Opportunity* (New York: Executive Enterprises, 1977); Geraldine Leshin, *Equal Employment Opportunity and Affirmative Action in Labor-Management Relations, A Primer* (Los Angeles: UC, Institute of IR, 1976).

See also AFFECTED CLASS, MINORITY GROUPS.

Protection Employees; Independent Union of Plant (Ind) An independent organization, formerly known as the Independent Union of Plant Protection Employees in the Electrical and Machine Industry (Ind).

Address: 243 Western Ave., West Lynn, Mass. 01904. Tel. (617) 581–0461

Protection Employees in the Electrical and Machine Industry; Independent Union of Plant (Ind) *See* PROTECTION EMPLOYEES; INDEPENDENT UNION OF PLANT (IND).

protective labor legislation Any legislation of a federal, state, or municipal body which reduces the dangers or threats to the safety of employees or is concerned with the protection of their general welfare. These laws are designed to protect workers from exploitation by their employers and also to reduce the effects of various types of economic and other forms of insecurity generated by the industrial system.

The scope of protective labor legislation is broad and deals not only with conditions applying to special groups. It also comprehends laws which establish minimum conditions of work and wages. Laws concerned with various types of insecurity are generally those in the area of unemployment compensation, accidents, and workers compensation.

See also ANTI-LABOR LEGISLATION, CHILD LABOR, FAIR LABOR STANDARDS ACT OF 1938, OCCUPATIONAL SAFETY AND HEALTH ACT (OSHA) OF 1970, PREGNANCY DISCRIMINATION ACT, SAFETY MOVEMENT, WORKERS COMPENSATION.

protest price In some industries which use incentive systems, piece rates for new work are established on the basis of previously set time factors. In order for the individual to earn at least as much as under the previous system, a trial production run is necessary to determine average earnings under the new rate. The worker may protest the proposed rate but continue to work under the so-called "protest price" until such time as a rate actually is set after a trial period and review.

The review may be made jointly by the union and company or the issue may be submitted to an arbitrator who is familiar with motion and time study. Whatever adjustments are made in the final establishment of the rate generally are made retroactive, so the employee will not lose as the result of working under the protest price while the rate is being reviewed. The procedure for protesting while at the same time continuing to work permits a reasonable review of the rate and, in addition, does not interfere with the normal production schedule of the company.

psychic income Income which is not measured in dollars and cents, but is assumed to provide satisfaction to the employee. This satisfaction may be due to the conditions of work, the status allotted to a particular title, or some other form of recognition.

psychological testing A variety of measures and tests developed by educational and industrial psychologists to assist those participating in the personnel function to obtain employees best suited for the job needs of the company. Selection and hiring procedures have many facets and psychological tests are designed in part to assist the personnel department not only to obtain the best qualified employees, but also recruit those most likely to adjust and do an effective job within the plant.

Source references: Merle E. Ace, "Psychological Testing: Unfair Discrimination?" *IR,* Oct. 1971; Richard S. Barrett, "Guide to Using Psychological Tests," *Harvard BR,* Sept./Oct. 1963; Stanley G. Dulsky and M. H. Krout, "Predicting Promotion Potential on the Basis of Psychological Tests," *Personnel Psychology,* Autumn 1950; Randall K. Filer, *The Validity and Feasibility of a Psychological Testing Program for Female Bank Managers* (Princeton: Princeton Univ., IR Section, WP no. 100, 1977); Wendell L. French, "Psychological Testing: Some Problems and Solutions," *Personnel Administration,* March/April 1966; ———, "What Every Executive Should Know About Psychological Testing," *PJ,* Feb. 1961; Kermit R. Hasler, "Importance of Descriptive Validity in Psychological Measurement," *PJ,* Jan. 1972; Donald H. J. Hermann III, "Privacy, the Prospective Employee, and Employment Testing: The Need to Restrict Polygraph and Personality Testing," *IR Law Digest,* April 1972; Milton G. Holmen and Richard Docter, *Educational and Psychological Testing: A Study of the Industry and Its Practices* (New York: Russell Sage Foundation, 1972); Andrew Kahn, "The Intimidation of Job Tests," *American Federationist,* Jan. 1979; Doris B. Rosen, *Personality Testing in Industry: A Review of Recent Literature* (Ithaca: Cornell Univ., NYSSILR, Technical Reports Series, 1966); Stanley Stark, "Executive Personality and Psychological Testing," *Current Economic Comment,* May 1958.

See also PERSONALITY INVENTORY, TEST.

psychology, industrial *See* INDUSTRIAL PSYCHOLOGY.

public assistance Aid, generally financial, provided by communities within a state to those in need. Under the federal social security system a number of programs have been devised which provide for state administration coordinated under the social security system. Among the public assistance programs are those involving aid to the needy, blind, to families with dependent children, to the permanently and totally disabled, and the aged and aging. Although the federal government sets certain standards for the programs and shares the costs with the states, the states alone decide eligibility and amount of allowances.

Source references: Margaret K. Adams, "State Public Assistance Legislation, 1962," *Social Security Bulletin,* April 1963; Jules H. Berman, "Public Assistance Under the Social Security Act," *ILRR,* Oct. 1960; Michael E. Borus, *Employment and Earnings Data Needed to Measure the Impact of Public Programs and Policies* (Washington: U.S. National Commission on Employment and Unemployment Statistics, Background Paper no. 21, 1978); Karen Davis and Cathy Schoen, *Health and the War on Poverty: A Ten Year Appraisal* (Washington: Brookings Institution, 1978); Rebecca H. Hayes, "Sources of Revenue for the State Share of Public Assistance Payments," *Social Security Bulletin,* Sept. 1962; Robert M. Hutchens, "Entry and Exit Transitions in a Government Transfer Program: The Case of Aid to Families with Dependent Children," *Journal of Human Resources,* Spring 1981; William G.

Johnson, William P. Curington, and Paul R. Cullinan, "Income Security for the Disabled," *IR*, Spring 1979; Sar A. Levitan (ed.), *The Federal Social Dollar in its Own Back Yard* (Washington: BNA, 1973); ———, *Programs in Aid of the Poor for the 1980s* (4th ed., Baltimore: Johns Hopkins UP, 1980); Duncan M. MacIntyre, *Public Assistance—Too Much or Too Little?* (Ithaca: Cornell Univ., NYSSILR, Bull. no. 53–1, 1964); Ida C. Merriam and Alfred M. Skolnik, *Social Welfare and Expenditures Under Public Programs in the United States, 1929–1966* (Washington: U.S. Dept. of HEW, SSA, Research Report no. 25, 1968); Robert D. Reischauer, *The Impact of Social Welfare Policies in the United States* (New York: The Conference Board, Report 823, 1982); Georgina M. Smith, *On the Welfare* (New Brunswick: Rutgers Univ., Institute of Management and Labor Relations, 1967); Bruno Stein, *On Relief: The Economics of Poverty and Public Welfare* (New York: Basic Books, 1971); U.S. Congress, Joint Economic Committee, *Income Security for Americans: Recommendations of the Public Welfare Study, Report* (Washington: 1974); ———, *Studies in Public Welfare*, Paper nos. 1–20 (Washington: 1972–1974); U.S. Congress, Senate, *What Should Be the Role of the Federal Government in Extending Public Assistance to All Americans Living in Poverty? A Collection of Excerpts and Bibliography Relating to the High School Debate Topic, 1973–74* (Washington: 1973); U.S. Dept. of HEW, Social and Rehabilitation Service, *Characteristics of State Public Assistance Plans Under Social Security Act* (Washington: Public Assistance Report no. 50, 1969).

See also GUARANTEED INCOME, NEGATIVE INCOME TAX, SOCIAL INSURANCE.

public employee Generally an individual who is working for a federal, state, county, or municipal government. Frequently public employees are those covered under civil service, special regulations, or collective bargaining law.

There are, of course, many individuals working for the federal, state, county, and municipal governments who perform public functions, but these individuals may be either elected officials or political appointees. In many jurisdictions, certain positions are exempt from civil service, particularly those which are professional in character, including those of lawyers, doctors, and other categories, the qualifications for which presumably are passed on by official boards.

See also CIVIL SERVICE REFORM ACT OF 1978, CLASSIFICATION ACT EMPLOYEES, CLASSIFIED SERVICE, ESSENTIAL EMPLOYEE, EXEMPT CLASS, EXECUTIVE ORDER 10988, EXECUTIVE ORDER 11491, GOVERNMENT EMPLOYEES, NONAPPROPRIATED FUND EMPLOYEE, PUBLIC EMPLOYEE RELATIONS, UNCLASSIFIED SERVICE, UNIFORMED SERVICES, WAGE BOARD EMPLOYEES.

public employee bargaining *See* COLLECTIVE NEGOTIATION, PROFESSIONAL NEGOTIATION, PUBLIC EMPLOYEE RELATIONS.

Public Employee Department The department was chartered by the AFL-CIO on November 6, 1974. The department seeks to promote the welfare of public employees through legislative activities, to improve working conditions through collective bargaining, to resolve jurisdictional disputes among affiliated unions, and to establish research, legal, safety, and public relations activities. The Government Employes Council merged with the department in 1974.

Unions affiliated with the department include: Automobile Workers; Boilermakers; Chemical Workers; Communications Workers; Fire Fighters; Firemen and Oilers; American Federation of Government Employees; Graphic Arts; Hotel and Restaurant Employees; Iron Workers; Laborers; Laundry and Dry Cleaning; Letter Carriers; Marine Engineers; Masters, Mates and Pilots, ILA; Office and Professional Employees; Operating Engineers; Painters; Plate Printers; Plumbers; International Union of Police Associations; Postal Workers; Printing and Graphic Communications; Professional and Technical Engineers; School Administrators; Seafarers; Service Employees; Sheet Metal Workers; American Federation of Teachers; Transit Union; Transportation Union; Typographical Union; and Utility Workers. Its quarterly publication is *In Public Service*.

Address: AFL-CIO Building, 815 16th St., N.W., Washington, D.C. 20006. Tel. (202) 393–2820

See also AFL-CIO DEPARTMENTS.

public employee relations The labor relations procedures for public employees at the federal, state, and municipal levels. Although in many areas, employee-management relations formerly were treated as matters established by the governmental agency through its personnel office, more states are now enacting new legislation or revising existing laws dealing with public employee organizations.

In a number of governmental agencies, federal, state, and local, substantial unionization has taken place. This is particularly true in the postal service, among blue-collar workers in the Navy yards, and other government repair shops. Where unionization has taken place, the employee-relations procedures have resulted in the establishment of more formal machinery for representation of the employees.

In 1961, President Kennedy established a special task force to study employee-management relations in the federal service. Following a report by that committee, headed by then-Secretary of Labor Arthur Goldberg, Executive Order 10988 was issued in January 1962 setting up more formalized procedures in employee-management relations for public employees in the federal service.

The executive order not only protected the right of federal employees to organize, but established procedures for recognition in three degrees—formal, informal, and exclusive. It also suggested the greater utilization of employee organizations in handling various aspects of government employee-management relations.

Employee relations in the federal service is now governed by the Civil Service Reform Act of 1978 (superseding Executive Order 11491).

Source references: Arvid Anderson, "Labor Relations in the Public Service," *Wisconsin LR,* July 1961; Mollie H. Bowers, *Labor Relations in the Public Safety Services* (Chicago: IPMA, PERL no. 46, 1974); Richard J. Carlson and Thomas Sedwick, *State Employee Labor Relations* (Lexington, Ky.: Council of State Governments, 1977); D. S. Chauhan, "The Judiciary's Impact on Public Labor Relations: Policy Development by the Courts," *Public Personnel Management,* Sept./Oct. 1977; R. Theodore Clark, Jr., "Problems in Public Sector Bargaining: A Management View," *NYU 32d Annual National Conference on Labor,* ed. by Richard Adelman (New York: Bender, 1980); Paul F. Gerhart, "The Emergence of Collective Bargaining in Local Government," *Public Personnel Management,* Vol. 9, no. 4, 1980; Robert D. Helsby, "A Political System for a Political World—in Public Sector Labor Relations," *LLJ,* Aug. 1973; Louis V. Imundo, Jr., "Federal Government Sovereignty and Its Effects on Labor-Management Relations," *LLJ,* March 1975; Andria S. Knapp (ed.), *Labor Relations Law in the Public Sector* (Chicago: American Bar Assn., Section of Labor Relations Law, 1977); Labor-Management Relations Service, *Three Neighboring States—Three Different Approaches to Local Labor Relations; A Special Report on New York, Pennsylvania, Maryland* (Washington: 1979); "Labor Relations in the Public Service: The Right to Organize: Collective Bargaining and Organizational Security: The Right to Strike and Its Alternatives," *Harvard LR,* Dec. 1961; David Lewin, "Mayoral Power and Municipal Labor Relations: A Three-City Study," *Employee Relations LJ,* Spring 1981; David Lewin, Peter Feuille, and Thomas Kochan, *Public Sector Labor Relations: Analysis and Readings* (2d ed., Sun Lakes, Ariz.: Thomas Horton & Daughters, 1981); Joyce M. Najita, *Article XII: Organization; Collective Bargaining* (Honolulu: Univ. of Hawaii, IRC, 1978); National Governors' Conference, *1968 Supplement to Report of Task Force on State and Local Government Labor Relations* (Chicago: PPA, 1969); ———, *1969 Supplement to Report of Task Force on State and Local Government Labor Relations* (Chicago: PPA, 1969); ———, *Report of Task Force on State and Local Government Labor Relations* (Chicago: PPA, 1967); Charles Redenius, "Public Employees: A Survey of Some Critical Problems on the Frontier of Collective Bargaining," *LLJ,* Sept. 1976; Charles M. Rehmus, "Labour Relations in the Public Sector in the United States," *ILR,* March 1974; Charles S. Rhyne and Robert H. Drummer, *The Law of*

Municipal Labor Relations (Washington: National Institute of Municipal Law Officers, 1979); Harold S. Roberts, *Labor-Management Relations in the Public Service* (Honolulu: Univ. of Hawaii Press, 1970); Richard P. Schick and Jean J. Couturier, *The Public Interest in Government Labor Relations* (Cambridge: Ballinger, 1977); Sterling Spero and John M. Capozzola, *The Urban Community and Its Unionized Bureaucracies; Pressure Politics in Local Government Labor Relations* (New York: Dunellen, 1973); David T. Stanley and Carole L. Cooper, *Managing Local Government Under Union Pressure* (Washington: Brookings Institution, 1972); U.S. Advisory Commission on Intergovernmental Relations, *Labor-Management Policies for State and Local Government* (Washington: 1970); U.S. Dept. of Commerce, Bureau of the Census, *Labor-Management Relations in State and Local Governments: 1980* (Washington: State and Local Government Special Studies no. 102, 1981); U.S. Dept. of Labor, LMSA, *Public Management's Internal Organizational Response to the Demands of Collective Bargaining in the Twelve Midwestern States* (Washington: 1977); Donald S. Wasserman, "Problems in Public Sector Bargaining: A Union View," *NYU 32d Annual National Conference on Labor,* ed. by Richard Adelman (New York: Bender, 1980); Arnold R. Weber, "Federal Labor Relations: Problems and Prospects," *Arbitration and the Public Interest,* Proceedings of the 24th A/M, NAA, ed. by Gerald Somers and Barbara Dennis (Washington: BNA, 1971); John M. Wynne, Jr., *Prison Employee Unionism: The Impact on Correctional Administration and Programs* (Washington: U.S. Dept. of Justice, LEAA, 1978); David R. Zimmerman, "The Impact of Public Service Employment on Public Sector Labor Relations," *Proceedings of the 28th A/M, IRRA,* ed. by James Stern and Barbara Dennis (Madison: 1976).

See also COLLECTIVE NEGOTIATION, EXECUTIVE ORDER 10988, EXECUTIVE ORDER 11491, PROFESSIONAL NEGOTIATION.

public employer An agency, the executive, the legislative body, or the officers of a state, county, municipality, or town subject to the provisions of a statute. A statute may define the public employer for purposes of negotiations, just as it may define a public employee.

Source reference: Harold S. Roberts, *Labor-Management Relations in the Public Service* (Honolulu: Univ. of Hawaii Press, 1970).

See also CORPORATE AUTHORITY.

public employment exchange *See* PUBLIC EMPLOYMENT OFFICE.

public employment office An agency of government, either federal or state, whose prime function is to assist employees to find jobs and employers to obtain qualified employees. The public employment offices came into being largely as a result of abuse by private placement agencies.

Although the system of public employment offices dates back to 1907, when their functions were concerned with the flood of immigrants and the need to divert large segments of the immigrant population from the major cities to rural or agricultural areas, it was not until 1933 with the passage of the Wagner-Peyser Act that the U.S. Employment Service was established as a major function of government within the U.S. Department of Labor. It was considered one of the main tools to assist in matching workers and jobs to facilitate the employment process and to provide the machinery for better utilization of human resources.

Source references: Leonard P. Adams, "The Public Employment Service," *In Aid of the Unemployed*, ed. by Joseph M. Becker (Baltimore: Johns Hopkins Press, 1965); James M. Carter, "The Role of the Job Bank in the Placement Process," *MLR*, Dec. 1972; Dave Evans, "New State and Local Job Outlook Information," *Occupational Outlook Quarterly*, Summer 1975; William S. Hubbartt, "The State Employment Service: An Aid to Affirmative Action Implementation,"*PJ*, June 1977; Arnold Katz, "Evaluating Contributions of the Employment Service to Applicant Earnings," *LLJ*, Aug. 1977; Arnold L. Nemore and Garth L. Mangum, *Reorienting the Federal-State Employment Service* (Ann Arbor: Univ. of Michigan–Wayne State Univ., Institute of Labor and IR, Policy Papers in Human Resources and IR no. 8, 1968); Willis J. Nordlund, "Employment Service Placement in the Sixties," *IR*, May 1974;

David W. Stevens, *Assisted Job Search for the Insured Unemployed* (Kalamazoo: Upjohn Institute for Employment Research, 1974); Joseph C. Ullman and George P. Huber, "Are Job Banks Improving the Labor Market Information System?" *ILRR*, Jan. 1974; U.S. Dept. of Labor, ETA, *The Employment Service: An Institutional Analysis* (Washington: R & D Monograph 51, 1977); ———, *The Public Employment Service and Help Wanted Ads, A Bifocal View of the Labor Market* (Washington: R & D Monograph 59, 1978); U.S. GAO, *Employment Service Needs to Emphasize Equal Opportunity in Job Referrals* (Washington: 1980); ———, *The Employment Service—Problems and Opportunities for Improvement, Department of Labor* (Washington: 1977).

See also U.S. EMPLOYMENT SERVICE, WAGNER-PEYSER ACT.

public interest The term "public interest" is widely used, not only by government officials but by labor and management representatives, to describe what they conceive to be actions which are generally helpful to the community at large.

Efforts by political scientists, economists and others to define the public interest have thus far proven to be somewhat unsuccessful. One political scientist stated, "The public interest is so vague and ambiguous that it is useless for scientific purposes and dangerous for practical purposes . . . it may be somewhat difficult for some readers to accept the conclusion that there is no public interest theory worthy of the name, and thus the concept itself is significant, primarily as a datum of politics. As such, it may at times fulfill a 'hair-shirt' function . . . it may also be nothing more than a label attached indiscriminately to a miscellany of particular compromises of the moment."

On the other hand, there are administrators in the field of labor relations who have a more definite view of the nature of the public interest. One of them stated that, "In a democracy such as ours, the public interest is of primary and paramount importance. And while it may be true that labor and management have the public welfare in mind when presenting their respective demands to each other, their conceptions of its nature and content are necessarily colored by their naturally greater and far more immediate concern with the attainments of their own private, local objectives. The government alone, therefore, as representative of the people, can be expected adequately to identify and properly to protect the public interest."

Source references: E. Wight Bakke, "Labor, Management and the Public Interest," *ILRR*, July 1963; George Bennett, "The Elusive Public Interest in Labor Disputes," *LLJ*, Nov. 1974; Frank E. Cooper, "Protecting the Public Interest in Labor Disputes," *Michigan LR*, April 1960; Kurt L. Hanslowe, "Labor Law and the Public Interest," *Journal of Public Law*, Vol. 2, no. 1, 1962; Raymond D. Horton, "Arbitration, Arbitrators, and the Public Interest," *ILRR*, July 1975; Labor Study Group, *The Public Interest in National Labor Policy* (New York: CED, 1961); John F. Kennedy, "Labor is a Stalwart Guardian of the Public Interest," *American Federationist*, Jan. 1961; Bernard D. Nossiter, "Management, Labor, and the Public Interest," *The Reporter*, May 24, 1962; Joseph A. Raffaele, "Collective Bargaining and the National Interest," *LLJ*, June 1963; James J. Reynolds, "The Role of Government in Collective Bargaining Negotiations: The Public Interest," *LLJ*, Nov. 1962; Glendon A. Schubert, *The Public Interest: A Critique of a Political Concept* (Glencoe: Free Press, 1960); George W. Taylor, "The Public Interest: Variations on an Old Theme," *Proceedings of the 18th A/M, NAA*, ed. by Dallas Jones (Washington: BNA, 1965); ———, "The Recognition of National Economic Interests in Bargaining," *MLR*, Jan. 1960; W. Willard Wirtz, *Labor and the Public Interest* (New York: Harper, 1964); Thomas A. Woodley, "Emergency Labor Disputes and the Public Interest: The Proposals for Legislative Reform," *IR Law Digest*, Oct. 1973.

publicity picketing *See* INFORMATIONAL PICKETING.

public member Applies generally to individuals on various public commissions and government agencies who do not represent partisan interest. For example, all of the members of the NLRB are public members.

The term frequently is meant to apply to individuals on various boards or commissions where there is representation also for other groups, such as labor and management, in which case the term "public member" applies to the individuals appointed to represent the public who presumably are the "neutral" members of the particular board.

In some arbitration proceedings, individuals who may be appointed as arbitrators are selected directly by the parties in interest (the labor and management members), and they subsequently appoint a third party or group to represent a neutral or public position. In actuality in most public bodies, all members who participate do in fact have some public responsibility. However, the designation "public member" normally distinguishes between those representing specific interests, such as labor and management, and those who do not have any particular direct interest.

See also NEUTRALS.

public policy The official position, in regard to matters of national concern or public interest, set in constitutions and by legislative bodies with regard to a particular question, such as, for example, the union shop or the right of employees to organize as guaranteed in the National Labor Relations Act.

It is frequently difficult to establish what the public policy is in a particular field. However, it is generally a little easier to discern a policy which has been formulated and established in law than it is to deal with a concept which has not been so formulated. The public policy question in legislation frequently also involves its administration. The administrative agency develops the public policy as it sees it in the provisions and intent of the law.

The courts may examine the statute and the administrative agency's interpretation of the public policy and find that the agency has not carried out the policy envisioned in the law. For example, the Supreme Court did not see eye to eye with the NLRB's concept of public policy in the handling of jurisdictional disputes—the problem of assignment of work where there is a conflict between two or more unions as to who should perform the work. The Court found that public policy required the NLRB to take positive action in such cases. In this case, although Congress established a policy, the administrative agency did not view the policy in the same way.

Source references: NLRB v. Radio and Television Broadcast Engineers Union, 364 US 573, 47 LRRM 2332 (1961); Jack Barbash, *Trade Unionism and the General Interest: A Theory of Positive Public Policy Toward Labor* (Madison: Univ. of Wisconsin, IRRI, Reprint 143, 1971); Irving Bernstein, "Public Policy and the American Worker, 1933–45," *MLR*, Oct. 1976; Gerald A. Brown, "The National Labor Policy, the NLRB, and Arbitration," *IR Law Digest*, April 1968; Lawrence J. Cohen, "The NLRB and Section 10(k): A Study of the Reluctant Dragon," *LLJ*, Nov. 1963; IRRA, *Federal Policies and Worker Status Since the Thirties*, ed. by Joseph P. Goldberg et al. (Madison: 1976); James L. McGuigan, "Our National Labor Policy: Collective Bargaining or Authoritarianism?" *LLJ*, June 1963; Harold W. Metz and Myer Jacobstein, *A National Labor Policy* (Washington: Brookings Institution, 1947); OECD, *Collective Bargaining and Government Policies*, Conference Papers Presented and Report of the General Rapportuer (Paris: 1979); ———, *Collective Bargaining and Government Policies in Ten OECD Countries: Austria, Canada, France, Germany, Italy, Japan, New Zealand, Sweden, United Kingdom, United States* (Paris: 1979); Butler D. Shaffer, "Some Alternatives to Existing Labor Policies," *LLJ*, June 1976; Joseph Shister, Benjamin Aaron, and Clyde W. Summers (ed.), *Public Policy and Collective Bargaining* (New York: Harper, IRRA Pub. no. 27, 1962).

Public Resolution No. 44 A compromise adopted by Congress on June 16, 1934, which gave the President the authority to establish, independently of the National Recovery Administration, a system of labor boards with full and exclusive authority to adjudicate controversies arising under Section 7(a) of the National Recovery Act. Under its authority the National Labor Relations Board was established on July 9, 1934, and began to function as the successor of the National Labor Board. It was given the authority to investigate labor disputes, hold hearings on Section 7(a) violations, and conduct elections for employee representatives. It also had the authority to study the structure and operation of existing labor boards, and to recommend the establishment of regional labor relations boards or of special boards for particular industries, and was vested with the power that the President was authorized to confer under Public Resolution No. 44. The prime purpose was to provide an integrated system of labor boards for the formulation of national policy.

The National Labor Relations Act (the Wagner Act) was passed the following year and the agencies created under Public Resolution No. 44 ceased to exist.

Source references: Lewis L. Lorwin and Arthur Wubnig, *Labor Relations Boards* (2d ed., Washington: Brookings, 1937); Leverett S. Lyon et al., *The National Recovery Administration* (Washington: Brookings Institution, 1935).

See also NATIONAL RECOVERY ADMINISTRATION.

public responsibility Those responsibilities of individuals and groups which are presumed to reflect the broader and more pervasive needs of the entire community.

Source references: George W. Taylor, "Labor's Public Responsibility: The Recognition of National Economic Interests in Bargaining," *MLR*, Jan. 1960; Univ. of Wisconsin, *Conference on Labor's Public Responsibility: A Symposium*, sponsored by the National Institute of Labor Education (Madison: 1960).

Public Review Board (AFT) An independent tribunal of three members not connected with the union to act as a court of final resort for members with grievances against "any local, state, or national AFT body or official." Procedures for setting up the board were adopted by the Executive Council in February 1967.

Source references: David Y. Klein, "AFT's New Public Review Board: Lessons from Another Union," *Changing Education*, Winter 1967; "Public Review Board Established by AFT," *American Teacher*, March 1967.

Public Review Board (UAW) An organization created by the UAW 16th Constitutional Convention in April 1957, establishing a seven-member public review board as a permanent part of the union's structure. In a public statement, Walter P. Reuther, late president of the UAW, said of the board, "The UAW Public Review Board, composed of seven prominent citizens not connected with the union, will act as a court of final resort for members with grievances against their local or the International, and is also empowered to insure that officers at all levels continue to observe the highest ethical and democratic practices within the UAW."

Source references: United Automobile, Aircraft and Agricultural Implement Workers of America, *A More Perfect Union—The UAW Public Review Board—Why, What, How* (Detroit: 1957); Harry R. Blaine and Frederick A. Zeller, "Who Uses the UAW Public Review Board?" *IR*, May 1965; Leonard Krouner, "Arbitration and a New Frontier—The Public Review Board of the United Automobile Workers," *Industrial and Labor Relations Forum*, March 1969; Jack Stieber, *Democracy and Public Review: An Analysis of the UAW Public Review Board* (Santa Barbara: Center for the Study of Democratic Institutions, 1960); Steven Wechsler, "Union Discipline and Public Review," *Industrial and Labor Relations Forum*, Feb. 1967.

Public Service Careers (PSC) The Department of Labor's Public Service Careers program established in early 1970 operated in the public sector much as JOBS functions in the private sector, providing jobs in government service agencies for disadvantaged workers and also assisting in upgrading employees in dead-end, low-paid positions.

The Public Service Careers program had four operating plans to implement its goals:

(1) Employment and upgrading in state and local governments,
(2) Employment and upgrading in federal grant-in-aid programs,
(3) New Careers in human service to incorporate existing New Careers projects, and
(4) Entry employment and upgrading in the federal civil service.

The PSC program reimbursed part of the costs of on-the-job training and also assisted in financing job upgrading activities. MDTA (Manpower Development and Training Act) centers provided various job-related training for PSC enrollees. Concentrated employment programs and other federal job training programs, such as the Job Corps, WIN, and Neighborhood Youth Corps, directed applicants to the Public Service Careers program.

Source references: Herbert M. Franklin, "Public Services—City Jobs for City Needs," *Manpower*, Sept. 1969; "Hard-Core Hiring Is Going Public," *Business Week*, May 16, 1970; U.S. President, *Manpower Report of the President, 1970* (Washington: 1970).

See also JOB OPPORTUNITIES IN THE BUSINESS SECTOR (JOBS), NATIONAL ALLIANCE OF BUSINESS (NAB).

public service employment (PSE) A major program of the Comprehensive Employment and Training Act (CETA) of 1973 which was intended to provide the unemployed and underemployed with temporary employment in public service jobs. Title II of the Act created additional public sector jobs in areas of "substantial unemployment." Title VI, which was added to CETA by the Emergency Jobs and Unemployment Assistance Act of 1974, authorized an emergency public service employment program in response to the unemployment created by the recession of 1974.

CETA defined public service to include work in such fields as environmental quality; health care; education; public safety; crime prevention and control; prison rehabilitation; transportation; recreation; maintenance of parks, streets, and other public facilities; solid waste removal; pollution control; housing and neighborhood improvements; rural development; conservation; beautification; veterans outreach; "and other fields of human betterment and community improvement."

Source references: Comprehensive Employment and Training Act of 1973, as amended, 29 U.S.C. 801 et seq. (1982) (repealed, 96 Stat. 1357 (1982); matters formerly covered by the Comprehensive Employment and Training Act are now covered by the Job Training Partnership Act, 29 U.S.C. 1501 et seq. (1982)); Robert Guttman, "Job Training Partnership Act: New Help for the Unemployed," *MLR*, March 1983; William Mirengoff et al., *CETA; Accomplishments, Problems, Solutions* (Kalamazoo: Upjohn Institute for Employment Research, 1982); U.S. President, *Manpower Report of the President* (Washington: 1974).

See also COMPREHENSIVE EMPLOYMENT AND TRAINING ACT (CETA) OF 1973.

Public Service Staff Relations Act Canadian legislation enacted in March 1967 granting collective bargaining rights to federal employees. The law provides for certification of exclusive representatives, dispute resolution procedures, and requires good faith bargaining. Strikes are prohibited during the term of an agreement and disputes over the interpretation or application of an agreement must be submitted to binding arbitration.

The law is administered by the Public Service Staff Relations Board.

Source references: H. W. Arthurs, *Collective Bargaining by Public Employees in Canada: Five Models* (Ann Arbor: Univ. of Michigan–Wayne State Univ., Institute of Labor and IR, 1971); John G. Bryden, "Public Employee Collective Bargaining—The Canadian Experience," *Labor Law Developments 1974*, Proceedings of 20th Annual Institute on Labor Law, SLF (New York: Bender, 1974); A. Kruger, "Bargaining in the Public Sector: Some Canadian Experiments," *ILR*, April 1974; Helene LeBel, "Collective Bargaining for Professionals Under the Public Service Staff Relations Act of Canada," *Proceedings of the 25th A/M, IRRA*, ed. by Gerald Somers (Madison: 1973).

public utility labor disputes Those disputes which affect operations within the states of companies providing public services—transportation, electricity or other power, and other public services which presumably are affected with the public interest.

Efforts have been made at various times to provide special procedures for dispute handling in order to avoid creating public panic or distress in case of a strike.

Source references: Harold S. Roberts, *Compulsory Arbitration in Public Utility Disputes* (Honolulu: Univ. of Hawaii, IRC, 1949); Max Rosen, "State Intervention in Public Utility Labor Disputes," *LLJ*, May 1961; Edward Sussna, "State Intervention in Public Utility Labor-Management Relations," *LLJ*, Jan. 1958.

See also ARBITRATION, COMPULSORY; NATIONAL EMERGENCY DISPUTES.

public works Refers generally to major projects undertaken by federal or state government for the convenience and welfare of the entire community or for controlling seasonal or cyclical fluctuations, to minimize the effects of a depression, or to accelerate programs in order to prevent a depression.

It is generally believed that construction projects or large public works probably create more job opportunities, directly as well as indirectly, than do other expedients, and that it is for the general or public good that such programs be undertaken to provide employment when the economy is sluggish or when there is high unemployment. The projects usually involve the construction of bridges, power plants, navigation projects, various types of irrigation, roads, public buildings, and other items of major interest to the public at large.

Source references: Arthur D. Gayer, *Public Works in Prosperity and Depression* (New York: NBER, 1935); Harold C. Taylor, *Public Works Policies for Boom or Bust* (Kalamazoo: Upjohn Institute, 1955); U.S. Congress, Senate, Committee on Public Works, *Public Works and Economic Development Act of 1965* (Washington: Report no. 193, 1965); ———, *Public Works Acceleration, Hearings* (Washington: 1962); U.S. GAO, *Changes Proposed for the Funding of Public Works Project Would Expedite Economic Development and Job Opportunities, Department of Commerce* (Washington: 1977).

See also CYCLICAL UNEMPLOYMENT, UNEMPLOYMENT.

Public Works Administration (Authority) Title 2 of the National Industrial Recovery Act of June 16, 1933, provided for a Public Works Administration (PWA) in the Department of the Interior with an appropriation in excess of $3 billion for public works construction projects. It was hoped that a few million workers would obtain employment as the result of the various projects, including highways, waterways, public buildings, hospitals, slum clearance, and public housing projects. Loans were to be granted to states and other localities, except for purely national projects, and efforts were made particularly in the area of slum clearance and low rent housing.

Unlike Works Progress Administration (WPA) projects, Public Works Administration projects employed persons not on relief rolls, although consideration was given to qualified individuals in greatest need. Also unlike the WPA, which employed persons directly, most of the PWA projects were let out on a competitive basis to private contractors who selected their own crews and paid prevailing wages for a standard 40-hour week.

See also FEDERAL EMERGENCY ADMINISTRATION OF PUBLIC WORKS, FEDERAL WORKS AGENCY.

Public Works and Economic Development Act of 1965 Law (79 Stat. 552, 42 U.S.C. 3121) focusing on the development of public facilities and private enterprise to directly or indirectly improve employment opportunities in depressed areas. It combines features of two major pieces of legislation enacted in previous years: the Area Redevelopment Act of 1961 and the Accelerated Public Works program passed in 1962. Under the law, the Economic Development Administration operates a program of public works grants and loans, loans for industrial or commercial facilities, working capital loan guarantees, and technical, planning, and research assistance for areas designated as redevelopment areas by the assistant secretary for economic development, head of the EDA responsible to the secretary of commerce.

Areas classified by the Department of Labor as areas of persistent unemployment are recommended to the Department of Commerce for designation as redevelopment areas provided that other conditions required by the Act and related regulations are met. Such areas are potentially eligible for all of the types of federal assistance provided under that Act.

Upon request, an area with an unusual and abrupt rise in unemployment due to the loss, removal, curtailment, or closing of a major source of employment may be designated as a redevelopment area by the secretary of commerce. To be eligible under this provision the area's rate of unemployment must have risen to a level 50 percent or more above the national average within three years prior to the date of the request, or be expected to rise to that level within three years following the date of request, unless assistance is provided.

Areas which are not classified as areas of persistent unemployment may nevertheless be eligible for federal grants for public works and development facilities under Title I of that Act if such areas experienced substantial unemployment (annual average unemployment rate of at least 6 percent) during the preceding calendar year.

Designated Economic Development Districts are eligible for bonus grants for public works projects.

The eligibility of all redevelopment areas, including those that are eligible for reasons other than unemployment, is reviewed annually.

Source reference: Sar A. Levitan, *Programs in Aid of the Poor for the 1980s* (4th ed., Baltimore: Johns Hopkins UP, 1980).

See also AREA REDEVELOPMENT ACT OF 1961, DEPRESSED AREA, LABOR SURPLUS AREA.

pull An American slang term which is the equivalent of the word "influence." It suggests or implies that a person has been able to utilize influence (pull) and has obtained a job or special consideration, not because of ability or competence, but because of connections. The influence may be due to personal acquaintance or friendship or repayment for some previous favor.

Pullman strike A major strike by the workers at the Pullman Car Company in Pullman, Illinois in 1894. The strike was the result of action by the company, which, following a depression, laid off approximately one-third of its employees and cut the wages of the rest of the employees from 20 to 40 percent. The employees joined forces with the American Railway Union, which was organized by Eugene V. Debs. A sympathetic strike was called by the American Railway Union and members were asked not to handle the Pullman cars. The federal government intervened when President Cleveland sent troops to Chicago over the protest of Governor Altgeld of Illinois.

The government obtained an injunction against the union for interfering with the mails and for refusing to obey the injunction. Debs and other leaders were found guilty of contempt of court and sent to jail.

Source references: Louis Adamic, *Dynamite* (New York: Viking Press, 1931); Edward Berman, *Labor and the Sherman Act* (New York: Harper, 1930); W. F. Burns, *The Pullman Boycott* (St. Paul: McGill, 1894); William H. Carwardine, *The Pullman Strike* (Chicago: Kerr, 1894); Grover Cleveland, *The Government in the Chicago Strike of 1894* (Princeton: Princeton UP, 1913); Harold U. Faulkner and Mark Starr, *Labor in America* (New York: Harper, 1944); Almont Lindsey, *The Pullman Strike: The Story of a Unique Experiment and of a Great Labor Upheaval* (Chicago: Univ. of Chicago Press, 1942); Lois MacDonald, *Labor Problems and the American Scene* (New York: Harper, 1938); W. T. Stead, *Chicago To-Day, The Labour War in America* (New York: Arno Press & The New York Times, 1969); U.S. Strike Commission, *Report of the Chicago Strike, 1894* (Washington: Senate Executive Document no. 7, 1894); Colston E. Warne, *The Pullman Boycott of 1894, The Problem of Federal Intervention, Problems in American Civilization* (Boston: Heath, 1967).

Pulp and Paper Workers; Association of Western (Ind) In May 1964, a faction of dissatisfied members of the United Papermakers and Paperworkers joined a group from the International Brotherhood of Pulp, Sulphite and Paper Mill Workers to form this organization. The official semimonthly journal is *The Rebel.* As of 1981, the union claimed a membership of 19,400 in 56 local unions.

Address: 1430 Southwest Clay St., Portland, Ore. 97208. Tel. (503) 228–7486

Source reference: Paul L. Kleinsorge and William C. Kerby, "The Pulp and Paper Rebellion: A New Pacific Coast Union," *IR*, Oct. 1966.

Pulp, Sulphite and Paper Mill Workers; International Brotherhood of (AFL-CIO) Organized in January 1906 at Burlington, Vt. It was a secession movement from the International Brotherhood of Paper Makers. The organization remained independent until 1909 when an agreement was reached with the Paper Makers on the general question of jurisdiction and the Pulp and Sulphite Workers joined the AFL. The United Paper

Craftsmen and Workers of North America (AFL-CIO) merged with the union on April 29, 1958.

A faction of the International Brotherhood of Pulp, Sulphite and Paper Mill Workers seceded from the union and in May 1964 joined with a faction of United Papermakers and Paperworkers to form the Association of Western Pulp and Paper Workers (Ind).

On August 9, 1972, the union merged with the United Papermakers and Paperworkers (AFL-CIO) to form the United Paperworkers International Union (AFL-CIO).

Source reference: Harold M. Levinson, *Determining Forces in Collective Wage Bargaining* (New York: Wiley, 1966).

See also PAPERWORKERS INTERNATIONAL UNION; UNITED (AFL-CIO).

purchasing power The amount of goods and services which may be purchased by a dollar. It is the ability of the dollar to command goods and services in relation to the changing price level. During periods of rising prices, the purchasing power of the dollar is relatively low; whereas during periods of declining prices, the purchasing power of a dollar is relatively high.

See also CONSUMER PRICE INDEX, REAL WAGES.

pushers Individuals who may be used by the employer to set the pace for others. They are generally highly efficient, rapid workers.

See also PACERS.

push money *See* PREMIUM MONEY (PUSH MONEY).

putting-out system *See* DOMESTIC SYSTEM.

pyramiding The payment of overtime on overtime. It may result from payment of both daily and weekly overtime for the same hours of work.

See also OVERTIME.

Q

QWL *See* QUALITY OF WORK LIFE (QWL).

quadragesimo anno The title of an encyclical letter of Pope Pius XI dealing with the reconstruction of the social order. The encyclical dealt not only with the criticism of socialism by the church but also condemned laissez faire capitalism.

qualifications Fitness, educational background, ability, or endowments a person has, or demonstrates, for a particular office or job.
See also ABILITY, HIRING, PROMOTION.

quality bonus A bonus or reward paid to individuals based on the quality of their work.
See also BONUS.

quality circles A problem-solving technique involving a group of employees who meet regularly to solve workplace problems. Quality circles are established on a permanent basis and are not ad hoc bodies created to solve specific problems. Circle members decide the problem areas to be studied, which may include productivity, cost, safety, and product quality. Recommendations are presented to management, and circle members assist in implementing recommendations accepted by management.

Source references: Keith Bradley and Stephen Hill, " 'After Japan': The Quality Circle Transplant and Productive Efficiency," *BJIR*, Nov. 1983; Robert E. Cole, "Made in Japan—Quality-Control Circles," *Across the Board*, Nov. 1979; Pat Eva Crisci, "Problems in Education and Quality Circles," *Government Union Review*, Summer 1983; Donald L. Dewar, *Quality Circles: Answers to 100 Frequently Asked Questions* (Red Buff, Calif.: Quality Circle Institute, 1979); Frank M. Gryna, Jr., *Quality Circles, A Team Approach to Problem Solving*, An AMA Research Study (New York: AMA, 1981); Gerald D. Klein, "Implementing Quality Circles: A Hard Look at Some of the Realities," *Personnel*, Nov./Dec. 1981; Philip C. Thompson, *Quality Circles, How to Make Them Work in America* (New York: Amacom, 1982).
See also THEORY Z.

quality of work life (QWL) A broad term usually associated with labor and management efforts to improve bargaining relationships in order to better organizational effectiveness and to provide the worker with psychological rewards of the job. Katz et al. state that the "common thread running through these efforts is their attempt to establish practical relationships outside such traditional union-management activities as arms-length negotiations, formal and informal grievance handling, and union-management committees."

QWL programs typically include one or more of the following elements: job redesign, quality circles, flexitime, autonomous work groups, job enlargement, and participative management.

Source references: Irving Bluestone, "How Quality of Worklife Projects Work for the United Auto Workers," *MLR*, July 1980; Thomas G. Cummings and Edmond S. Molloy, *Improving Productivity and the Quality of Work Life* (New York: Praeger, 1977); Louis E. Davis, "Enhancing the Quality of Working Life: Developments in the United States," *ILR*, July/Aug. 1977; Louis E. Davis, Albert B. Cherns and Associates, *The Quality of Working Life* (New York: Free Press, 1975); Thomas R. Donahue, *Labor Looks at Quality of Worklife Programs* (Amherst: Univ. of Massachusetts, Labor Relations and Research Center, 1982); Stephen H. Fuller, "How Quality-of-Worklife Projects Work for General Motors," *MLR*, July 1980; Paul S. Goodman, *Assessing Organizational Change, The Rushton Quality of Work Experiment* (New York: Wiley, 1979); Paul D. Greenberg and

Edward M. Glaser, *Some Issues in Joint Union-Management Quality of Worklife Improvement Efforts* (Kalamazoo: Upjohn Institute for Employment Research, 1980); Robert H. Guest, "Quality of Work Life—Learning from Tarrytown," *Harvard BR*, July/Aug. 1979; Harry C. Katz, Thomas A. Kochan, and Kenneth R. Gobeille, "Industrial Relations Performance, Economic Performance, and QWL Programs: An Interplant Analysis," *ILRR*, Oct. 1983; Thomas A. Kochan, *Collective Bargaining and Industrial Relations* (Homewood: Irwin, 1980); Barry A. Macy, "The Bolivar Quality of Work Life Program: A Longitudinal Behavioral and Performance Assessment," *Proceedings of the 32d A/M, IRRA*, ed. by Barbara Dennis (Madison: 1980); John F. Runcie, "Dynamic Systems and the Quality of Work Life," *Personnel*, Nov./Dec. 1980; George Strauss, *Quality of Worklife and Participation as Bargaining Issues* (Berkeley: UC, Institute of IR, Reprint 434, 1980); Richard E. Walton, "Quality of Working Life: What Is It?" *Sloan Management Review*, Fall 1973.

Quarantine Inspectors National Association; Federal Plant (Ind) Established in 1954, the name of the union was changed to the National Association of Agriculture Employees (Ind) in the early 1980s.

See also AGRICULTURE EMPLOYEES; NATIONAL ASSOCIATION OF (IND).

quickie stoppage or strike Generally a spontaneous and short-lived work stoppage with no advance notice to the employer or, possibly, even to the officials of the union. It frequently results from some local resentment or is in response to action by the employer which creates an emotional situation. For example, a sudden stoppage may occur in sympathy with an employee who has been disciplined. It is generally not authorized or sanctioned by the national or international union, or by the local union.

See also ILLEGAL STRIKE, SIT-DOWN STRIKE, STRIKE.

quid pro quo Literally, something in return; an equivalent. A labor union, for example, will agree not to strike for the duration of the agreement and the employer, in return, will agree to submit contract disputes to arbitration. Thus, the no-strike obligation is termed the quid pro quo for the employer to submit grievance disputes to arbitration.

Source reference: Boys Markets, Inc. v. Retail Clerks, Local 770, 389 US 235, 74 LRRM 2257 (1970).

See also LINCOLN MILLS CASE.

quit The voluntary termination or resignation from employment which is initiated by the employee.

Source references: Paul A. Armknecht and John F. Early, "Manufacturing Quit Rates Revisited: Secular Changes and Women's Quits," *MLR*, Dec. 1973; William F. Barnes and Ethel B. Jones, "Differences in Male and Female Quitting," *Journal of Human Resources*, Fall 1974; ______, "Manufacturing Quit Rates Revisited: A Cyclical View of Women's Quits," *MLR*, Dec. 1973; Francine Blau and Lawrence M. Kahn, "Race and Sex Differences in Quits by Young Workers," *ILRR*, July 1981; Farrell E. Bloch, *An Analysis of Quit and Layoff Rates in U.S. Manufacturing Industries* (Princeton: Princeton Univ., IR Section, WP no. 76, 1975); Richard N. Block, "The Impact of Seniority Provisions on the Manufacturing Quit Rate," *ILRR*, July 1978; ______, "The Impact of Union-Negotiated Employment Security Provisions on the Manufacturing Quit Rate," *Proceedings of the 29th A/M, IRRA*, ed. by James Stern and Barbara Dennis (Madison: 1977); Walter L. Daykin, *The Distinction Between Quit and Discharge* (Iowa City: Bureau of Labor and Management, State Univ. of Iowa, Research Series no. 21, 1959); John F. Early and Paul A. Armknecht, *The Manufacturing Quit Rate: Trends, Cycles, and Interindustry Variations* (Washington: U.S. Dept. of Labor, BLS, Staff Paper 7, 1973); Fred L. Fry, "More on the Causes of Quits in Manufacturing," *MLR*, June 1973; Robert E. Hall and Edward P. Lazear, *The Excess Sensitivity of Layoffs and Quits to Demand* (Cambridge: NBER, WP no. 864, 1982); Ken Jennings, "When a Quit is Not a Quit," *PJ*, Dec. 1971; Mark A. Lutz, "Quit Rates and the Quality of the Industrial Wage Structure," *IR*, Feb. 1977; T. W. Muldrow, *Voluntary and Involuntary Separations from the Work Force* (Washington: U.S. CSC, Personnel Research Report 75–2, 1975); Dixie Sommers and Carin Cohen,

"New Occupational Rates of Labor Force Separation," *MLR,* March 1980.

See also DISCHARGE, RESIGNATION, SEPARATION.

quit rate A statistical term indicating the number of quits per hundred employees computed on a monthly or other periodic basis. Occasionally, a company may compute the quit rate as the number of quits or resignations divided by the average work force, which then is multiplied by 100 in order to get a percentage figure.

quitting time The hour or hours at which employees generally leave their shift to go home.

See also HOURS OF WORK.

quorum The number of individuals, or the percent of a group, who must be present at a meeting in order to transact business. Without a quorum the action may not have legal validity or force. In most bodies, including trade unions, the constitution or bylaws include a procedure for establishing a quorum.

See also LABOR-MANAGEMENT REPORTING AND DISCLOSURE ACT OF 1959.

quota The amount of production or work which an individual employee of average ability must turn out in a specified period of time in order to earn base pay. It is sometimes referred to as standard time or the job standard.

In EEO/AA usage, it is a temporary remedy imposed by the courts to correct past discrimination through the selection of a specific number or percentage of individuals from a protected group until a prescribed goal is reached.

Source references: Rios v. Steamfitters Local 638, 501 F2d 622, 8 FEP Cases 293 (1974); Kenneth B. Clark, "Racial Justice via Quota Employment," *Conference Board Record,* Aug. 1973; Carl F. Goodman, "Equal Employment Opportunity: Preferential Quotas and Unrepresented Third Parties," *Public Personnel Management,* Nov./Dec. 1977; R. Randall Hoffman, "MJS: Management by Job Standards," *PJ*, Aug. 1979; Richard A Lester, *The Fallacies of Numerical Goals* (Princeton: Princeton Univ., IR Section, 1976); K. A. Lewis and A. P. Schinnar, *The Game of Quotas for Equal Opportunity Employers* (New York: Columbia Univ., Graduate School of Business, Research WP no. 153A, 1978); Rosalind B. Marimont, Kennedy P. Maize, and Ernest Harley, "Using FAIR to Set Numerical EEO Goals," *Public Personnel Management,* May/June 1976; John De J. Pemberton, Jr., "Quotas: Will Merit Be Lost in a Numbers Game?" *Employee Relations LJ*, Summer 1975; Jose A. Rivera, "Quotas in the Courts: Is Fair Foul?" *Employee Relations LJ*, Spring 1977; Butler D. Shaffer and J. Brad Chapman, "Hiring Quotas—Will They Work?" *LLJ*, March 1975; U.S. Dept. of Labor, BLS, *Major Collective Bargaining Agreements: Wage-Incentive, Production Standard, and Time-Study Provisions* (Washington: Bull. 1425–18, 1979).

quota-bonus plan A method of wage payment for sales personnel, which requires the employee to go beyond a fixed sales volume before special commissions or bonuses are earned.

Source references: Jacob Gonik, "Tie Salesmen's Bonuses to their Forecasts," *Harvard BR,* May/June 1978; William Spriegal and Joseph Towle, *Retail Personnel Management* (New York: McGraw-Hill, 1951).

See also COMMISSION EARNINGS.

quota rules The regulations of a union which establish the number of workers who are to be employed on a particular job within the union's jurisdiction. In the longshore operation this might be equivalent to the gang size in handling certain types of cargo.

See also MANNING SCALE.

R

RIF *See* REDUCTION IN FORCE.

RILU *See* RED INTERNATIONAL OF LABOR UNIONS (RILU).

RLCA *See* LETTER CARRIERS' ASSOCIATION; NATIONAL RURAL (IND).

RWAW *See* ROOFERS, WATERPROOFERS AND ALLIED WORKERS; UNITED UNION OF (AFL-CIO).

RWDSU *See* RETAIL, WHOLESALE AND DEPARTMENT STORE UNION (AFL-CIO).

RYA *See* RAILROAD YARDMASTERS OF AMERICA (AFL-CIO).

race differential Differences in rates of pay to workers of different races even though all of the employees are doing similar or identical work. Such discrimination is forbidden both by federal and state anti-discrimination laws, by executive orders dealing with work standards under federal contract, and in many cases by collective bargaining agreements. Such discrimination also does violence to the principle of equal pay for equal work.

See also CIVIL RIGHTS ACT OF 1964, DISCRIMINATION, EQUAL PAY FOR EQUAL WORK, FAIR EMPLOYMENT PRACTICES.

racial discrimination Any policy or procedure which discriminates in hiring, promotion, layoff, etc., because of the race or color of the employee. Like race differentials in pay, such discrimination is banned by federal and state law, executive order, and in many cases by collective bargaining agreements.

Source references: Alfred W. Blumrosen, "Craft Unions and Blacks: The View from Newark—The Need for Result Oriented Research," *Proceedings of the 24th A/M, IRRA*, ed. by Gerald Somers (Madison: 1972); Irwin Dubinsky, *Reform in Trade Union Discrimination in the Construction Industry; Operation Dig and Its Legacy* (New York: Praeger, 1975); Robert J. Flanagan, "Discrimination Theory, Labor Turnover, and Racial Unemployment Differentials," *Journal of Human Resources*, Spring 1978; William B. Gould, *Black Workers in White Unions; Job Discrimination in the United States* (Ithaca: Cornell UP, 1977); ———, "Racial Discrimination, the Courts, and Construction," *IR*, Oct. 1972; George D. Haller, "Racial Discrimination in Unions," *LLJ*, July 1957; Herbert Hill, "Black Labor, the NLRB, and the Developing Law of Equal Employment Opportunity," *LLJ*, April 1975; ———, "Racial Inequality in Employment: The Patterns of Discrimination," *Annals*, Jan. 1965; James E. Jones, Jr., "Disestablishment of Labor Unions for Engaging in Racial Discrimination—A New Use for an Old Remedy," *IR Law Digest*, April 1973; G. Donald Jud and James L. Walker, "Class and Race Discrimination: Estimates Based Upon a Sample of Young Men," *Proceedings of the 29th A/M, IRRA*, ed. by James Stern and Barbara Dennis (Madison: 1977); Alice E. Kidder, "Federal Compliance Efforts in the Carolina Textile Industry: A Summary," *Proceedings of the 25th A/M, IRRA*, ed. by Gerald Somers (Madison: 1973); William J. Kilberg and Stephen E. Tallent, "From *Bakke* to *Fullilove*: The Use of Racial and Ethnic Preferences in Employment," *Employee Relations LJ*, Winter 1980/81; Irving Kovarsky, "Racial Discrimination in Employment and the Federal Law," *Oregon LR*, Dec. 1958; Ray Marshall, "Union Racial Practices and the Labor Market," *MLR*, March 1962; Daniel M. Seifer, "Continuing Hard Problems: The 'Hard Core' and Racial Discrimination," *Public Personnel Management*, May/June 1974; Linda J. Shaffer and R. Mark Wilson, "Racial Discrimination in Occupational Choice," *IR*, Spring 1980; Michael I. Sovern, *Legal Restraints on Racial Discrimination in Employment* (New York: Twentieth Century Fund, 1966); Joseph Tussman (ed.), *The Supreme*

Court on Racial Discrimination (New York: Oxford UP, 1963).

See also BAKKE CASE, CIVIL RIGHTS ACT OF 1866, CIVIL RIGHTS ACT OF 1871, CIVIL RIGHTS ACT OF 1964, COLOR DISCRIMINATION, EXECUTIVE ORDER 11246, FAIR EMPLOYMENT PRACTICES, GRIGGS V. DUKE POWER CO., JIM CROW LAWS, MEMPHIS FIRE DEPARTMENT V. STOTTS, MINORITY GROUPS, TEAMSTERS V. U.S., WEBER CASE.

racketeering Labor racketeering, like other forms of racketeering, is the practice of unethical and extortionate use of power or the threat of violence to obtain money, either from employers, for protection presumably against labor unions and labor violence, or from employees, who are presumably to be protected by the strong-arm men. "Paper unions" have been established purely for the purpose of providing a legitimate front. As Professor Barbash points out, "racketeers who have established themselves in labor unions organize workers and even employers as a quid-pro-quo for protection against violence."

Professor Robert R. Brooks in *When Labor Organizes* provides an interesting definition of the use of the term "racketeering" as viewed by the employer, the public, and the union. He says in part:

> To an antiunion employer all unionism is racketeering if it results in the extraction from him of more money or power than he would otherwise surrender. To the consumer who is not primarily a wage receiver unionism may appear as a racket if it takes from him in the form of higher prices more than would be taken in the absence of a labor movement. To the organized worker, however, his union is a racket only if it delivers gains to him which are small in relation to the income received by the organizers and leaders of the union. This is admittedly a loose definition, but it is more real from the worker's point of view than those offered by the employer and the nonunionized consumer.

Source references: Jack Barbash, *Labor Unions in Action* (New York: Harper, 1948); Robert R. R. Brooks, *When Labor Organizes* (New Haven: Yale UP, 1937); Burton Hall (comp.), *Autocracy and Insurgency in Organized Labor* (New Brunswick: Transaction Books, 1972); John Hutchinson, "The Anatomy of Corruption in Trade Unions," *IR*, Feb. 1969; James Myers, *Do You Know Labor?* (rev. ed., New York: John Day, 1946); Harold Seidman, *Labor Czars* (New York: Liveright, 1938); Edward D. Sullivan, *This Labor Union Racket* (New York: Hillman-Curl, 1936); Philip Taft, *Corruption and Racketeering in the Labor Movement* (2d ed., Ithaca: Cornell Univ., NYSSILR, 1970); U.S. Congress, Senate, Committee on Government Operations, *Gambling and Organized Crime, Parts I and II, Hearings, before Permanent Subcommittee on Investigations* (Washington: 1961).

See also HOLD-UP UNIONISM, LABOR RACKETEER, MCCLELLAN COMMITTEE, PAPER LOCALS.

radiation hazard Exposure to radiation which may result in injury or disease such as burns or cancer.

Under the Occupational Safety and Health Act of 1970, employers are responsible for proper controls to prevent employees from being exposed to radiation, either ionizing or electromagnetic, in excess of acceptable limits. Employers are also required to post each radiation area with appropriate signs and/or barriers and to maintain records of the radiation exposure of all employees for whom monitoring is required.

Source references: "Occupational Safety and Health Standards," 29 C.F.R. 1910; A. J. Biemiller, "Atomic Radiation and Workmen's Compensation," *MLR*, June 1958; Earl F. Cheit, "Radiation Hazards: A New Challenge to Workmen's Compensation," *The Insurance LJ*, Dec. 1957.

radical unionism Although the term "radical" is itself a changing and flexible concept, depending upon the position of the person who examines the ideas of others, it nevertheless does suggest as of any specific time individuals who desire sweeping or drastic changes in the social and economic structure. The "radical" moves toward the revolutionary approach. The phrase also suggests efforts directed toward the systematic destruction of established social, political, and economic institutions. The term "revolutionary" suggests action which may involve the use of physical force and violence.

Source references: Henry P. Fairchild, *Dictionary of Sociology* (New York: Philosophical Library, 1944); William Z. Foster, *The Bankruptcy of the American Labor*

Movement (Chicago: Trade Union Educ. League, 1922); Sidney Lens, *Radicalism in America* (Philadelphia: Crowell, 1966); Mark Perlman, "Unionism as a Revolutionary Institution," *Labor Union Theories in America: Background and Development* (Evanston: Row, Peterson, 1958); David J. Saposs, *Left-Wing Unionism: A Study of Radical Policies and Tactics* (New York: International Pub., 1926); Harvey Swados, *A Radical's America* (Boston: Little, Brown, 1962); Wilber White, *White's Political Dictionary* (Cleveland: World Pub., 1947).

See also CLASS STRUGGLE, INDUSTRIAL WORKERS OF THE WORLD, REVOLUTIONARY UNIONISM.

Radice v. New York *See* NIGHT WORK.

Radio and Television Directors Guild (AFL-CIO) *See* DIRECTORS GUILD OF AMERICA, INC. (IND).

Radio Association; American (AFL-CIO) A union which represented radio operators aboard ships. It merged with the International Organization of Masters, Mates and Pilots on January 5, 1981.

See also MASTERS, MATES AND PILOTS; INTERNATIONAL ORGANIZATION OF.

radium poisoning An industrial disease which results from the use of radium in materials handled by employees. A dramatic illustration of this disease was in the painting of luminous watch dials and alarm clocks. Employees who were not careful contracted the disease which attacked the bone structure as well as the skin and was responsible for serious illness and, occasionally, death.

See also INDUSTRIAL DISEASE, INDUSTRIAL POISON, WORKERS COMPENSATION.

radius clause A provision occasionally to be found in training programs whereby an individual employee agrees that he will not seek employment, particularly with a competitor or join a competitive organization, for a specified period of time and within a specified geographic area. The purpose is to make sure that the investment which the company puts into the training of the individual will be utilized for the benefit of the company and not for the benefit of competing companies in the area.

raiding A term which describes the efforts of a union to bring into its organization individuals who are already members of another union. Raiding does not exist where a union seeks to enroll unorganized employees who may be in another union's jurisdiction.

The reasons for raiding are numerous. Among the most frequent may be the desire of a union to bring within its jurisdiction employees who have been organized by another union which does not technically have jurisdiction over them; or to strengthen its own membership for bargaining purposes by bringing within its scope a large number of employees; or to attempt to harass or retaliate against another labor organization where that organization has refused to work with it or has attempted to organize employees which it claims.

See also JURISDICTIONAL DISPUTE, NO-RAIDING AGREEMENT.

Railroad Adjustment Board *See* NATIONAL RAILROAD ADJUSTMENT BOARD.

railroad brotherhoods This term encompasses the major labor units in the railroad industry. Early organizations were established primarily for mutual benefit and insurance protection, because in the early days the work was so hazardous that private insurance companies refused to issue insurance to railroad workers. The "Big Four," so-called, were the International Brotherhood of Locomotive Engineers, organized in 1863; the Order of Railway Conductors and Brakemen, organized in 1868; the Brotherhood of Locomotive Firemen and Enginemen, organized in 1873; and the Brotherhood of Railroad Trainmen, organized in 1883. The "Big Five" included these four and the Order of Railroad Telegraphers, organized in 1886. Other organizations which were actually part of the brotherhoods include the Railway Carmen and the Railway, Airline and Steamship Clerks, Freight Handlers, Express and Station Employes.

The railroad brotherhoods generally were within the so-called independent group. The railroad employees within the AFL-CIO at the present time include the following: Railroad Yardmasters of America; Brotherhood of Railway Carmen; Brotherhood of Railway, Airline and Steamship Clerks, Freight Handlers, Express and Station Employes; Brotherhood of Maintenance of Way Employes; Brotherhood of Railroad Signalmen; and American Train Dispatchers Association.

A new union, the United Transportation Union, was formed on January 1, 1969, with the merger of the Brotherhood of Locomotive Firemen and Enginemen, the Brotherhood of Railroad Trainmen, the Order of Railway Conductors and Brakemen, and the Switchmen's Union of North America.

See also RAILROAD TELEGRAPHERS; THE ORDER OF (AFL-CIO); RAILWAY, AIRLINE AND STEAMSHIP CLERKS, FREIGHT HANDLERS, EXPRESS AND STATION EMPLOYES; BROTHERHOOD OF (AFL-CIO); RAILWAY PATROLMEN'S INTERNATIONAL UNION (AFL-CIO); TRANSPORTATION UNION; UNITED (AFL-CIO).

Railroad Labor Board The board set up under Title III of the Transportation Act of 1920, which was authorized to hear and decide disputes involving grievances, rules, or working conditions. The board had the authority to take original jurisdiction of a case or to decide disputes which the adjustment boards failed to decide. The board had no authority to enforce its decisions, except through public opinion. The board consisted of nine members appointed by the President—three public members, three from a group of nominees submitted by the railroads, and three from a group nominated by railway labor unions.

According to Professor Albion G. Taylor, "The Railroad Labor Board proved to be unsatisfactory for various reasons. From the beginning it was under a handicap in that Title III of the Transportation Act, which authorized its existence, was enacted over labor's opposition. The chairman of the board was openly critical of labor. Instead of functioning as a court of appeals in dealing with cases handed down from regional boards of adjustment, as was the original plan, the regional boards did not materialize and the Railroad Labor Board was swamped with original jurisdiction duties, with consequent delays. The so-called impartial members of the Board proved to be partisan, thus destroying the confidence of both parties as well as the public."

The board was abolished and replaced by a Board of Mediation with the enactment of the Railway Labor Act of 1926.

Source references: Carroll R. Daugherty, *Labor Problems in American Industry* (rev. ed., Boston: Houghton Mifflin, 1938); Albion Guilford Taylor, *Labor Problems and Labor Law* (2d ed., New York: PH, 1950).

See also NATIONAL MEDIATION BOARD, RAILWAY LABOR ACT.

Railroad Retirement Act A federal act which provides benefits to railroad employees who retire because of age or disability. The first such act was established in 1934 and declared unconstitutional by the Supreme Court in *Railroad Retirement Board v. Alton Railroad Company*. A second act was passed in 1935 (45 U.S.C. 215–228), which was succeeded by the Act of 1974 (45 U.S.C. 231–231t).

The Railroad Retirement Act of 1974 provides a broad program of benefits to employees and their survivors based on earnings and length of service of individual workers and is vested after 10 years of service. Workers and employers share the costs of retirement, survivor benefits, and Medicare through a special payroll tax.

Workers or survivors file claims for benefits with the Railroad Retirement Board or at any of its regional offices.

Address: Railroad Retirement Board, 844 Rush St., Chicago, Ill. 60611. Tel. (312) 751–4500

Source references: U.S. Dept. of HEW, SSA, *1976 Technical Amendments to the Railroad Retirement Act* (Washington: Research and Statistics Note no. 3, 1977); U.S. Dept. of HHS, SSA, *Social Security Handbook* (7th ed., Washington: 1982).

Railroad Retirement Board v. Alton Railroad Co. A 5–4 decision of the Supreme Court which held unconstitutional the Railroad Retirement Act of June 1934.

The majority held that the law was unconstitutional because it deprived the railroads of due process in that the statute provided pensions for persons who were at one time but are not currently in railroad service, and that the provisions for pensions had nothing to do with the safety and efficiency of the railroads.

Source reference: Railroad Retirement Board v. Alton, 295 US 330 (1935).

Railroad Signalmen; Brotherhood of (AFL-CIO) The Brotherhood was organized in 1901 as an independent organization and in 1908 was able to effect a merger with a number of other existing organizations of railroad signalmen. These included the Railway Interlockers of North America, the Independent Order of Signalmen, and the Interlockers, Switch and Signalmen's Union, Nos. 11786 and 11867 of the AFL. The Grand Lodge convention was first held in 1908 when the Brotherhood incorporated.

The Brotherhood affiliated with the AFL in 1914 and withdrew in 1928 because of jurisdictional claims of other unions. It subsequently affiliated with the Trades and Labor Congress of Canada, the Railway Labor Executives' Association, and the AFL-CIO.

The official publication is *The Signalman's Journal* (10 issues annually).

Address: 601 West Golf Rd., Mt. Prospect, Ill. 60056. Tel. (312) 439–3732

Railroad Telegraphers; The Order of (AFL-CIO) The Brotherhood of Telegraphers of the United States was known originally as District 45 of the Knights of Labor and was organized in 1882. In June 1886, a secret organization, the Order of Railway Telegraphers of North America, was formed at a convention at Cedar Rapids, Iowa. The organization was purely fraternal and adopted an anti-strike policy. Because of competition from other more militant labor organizations, the union in 1891 adopted a full-fledged labor union program and changed its name to The Order of Railroad Telegraphers.

The convention of 1909 voted to affiliate with the then newly organized Railroad Employees Department of the AFL and, since the founding in 1926 of the Railway Labor Executives Association, took an active part in that agency.

Its name was changed to the Transportation-Communication Employees Union (AFL-CIO) in 1964.

Source references: How Collective Bargaining Works: A Survey of Experience in Leading American Industries (New York: Twentieth Century Fund, 1942); Leo Wolman, *The Growth of American Trade Unions 1880–1923* (New York: NBER, 1924).

See also TELEGRAPHERS' UNION; THE COMMERCIAL (AFL-CIO); TRANSPORTATION-COMMUNICATION EMPLOYEES UNION (AFL-CIO).

Railroad Trainmen; Brotherhood of (AFL-CIO) The organization was established as the Brotherhood of Railroad Brakemen of the Western Hemisphere in September 1883 at Oneonta, New York. In 1886 the organization changed its name to the Brotherhood of Railroad Brakemen which was changed in 1899 to the Brotherhood of Railroad Trainmen.

The organization initially devoted itself to establishment of a sick benefit program and other insurance enterprises. Emphasis on insurance resulted in some measure from the difficulty the trainmen experienced in obtaining commercial insurance, because of the hazards of the occupation.

Membership of the Brotherhood included railroad operating employees in Canada and bus drivers. The union affiliated with the AFL-CIO in 1957.

On January 1, 1969, the union and three other railroad unions—the Brotherhood of Locomotive Firemen and Enginemen, the Order of Railway Conductors and Brakemen, and the Switchmen's Union of North America—merged to form the United Transportation Union.

Source references: Brotherhood of Railroad Trainmen, *The Pros and Cons of Compulsory Arbitration, A Debate Manual* (Cleveland: 1965); Walter F. McCaleb, *Brotherhood of Railroad Trainmen: With Special Reference to the Life of Alexander F. Whitney* (New York: Boni, Liveright, 1936); Joel Seidman, *The Brotherhood of Railroad Trainmen: The Internal Political Life of a National Union* (New York: Wiley, Trade Unions Monograph Series, 1962).

See also TRANSPORTATION UNION; UNITED (AFL-CIO).

Railroad Unemployment Insurance Act A statute passed in June 1938 which provides for the payment of unemployment and sickness benefits to qualified railroad employees under a uniform nationwide system. Also established under the Act are free employment offices, whose prime activities are directed toward the reemployment of individuals who apply for unemployment benefits. The Act is administered by the Railroad Retirement Board.

The financing of both the unemployment and sickness benefits is handled through a payroll tax on carriers scaled to the pay of employees. Contributions vary depending on the available balance in the railroad unemployment insurance account.

Additional information may be obtained from the Railroad Retirement Board by writing to the board at 844 Rush Street, Chicago, Ill. 60611.

Railroad Workers of America; United (CIO) Merged to become part of the Transport Workers Union of America (CIO) in October 1954.

See also TRANSPORT WORKERS UNION OF AMERICA (AFL-CIO).

Railroad Yardmasters of America (AFL-CIO) Organized in December 1918 when various groups of yardmasters met at Cincinnati, Ohio. The Railroad Yardmasters of America, Inc. (Ind) and the Railroad Yardmasters of North America (Ind) merged with the union on July 1, 1965, and July 1, 1969, respectively. Its official publication is *Railroad Yardmaster* (8 issues annually).

Address: 1411 Peterson Ave., Park Ridge, Ill. 60068. Tel. (312) 696–2510

Railroad Yardmasters of North America, Inc. (Ind) A group organized and incorporated in Buffalo, New York, in January 1925, primarily by the yardmasters on the New York Central lines who had seceded from the parent organization, the Railroad Yardmasters of America.

The union reaffiliated and merged with the Railroad Yardmasters of America (AFL-CIO) on July 1, 1969.

See also RAILROAD YARDMASTERS OF AMERICA (AFL-CIO).

Railway, Airline and Steamship Clerks, Freight Handlers, Express and Station Employes; Brotherhood of (AFL-CIO) The organization was established at Sedalia, Mo., in 1898 and was known as the Order of Railway Clerks of America. It affiliated with the AFL but withdrew in a short time and functioned independently until 1909 as the Brotherhood of Railway Clerks. It reentered the AFL in 1909, and 10 years later as its jurisdiction and organization extended, it took the name Brotherhood of Railway and Steamship Clerks, Freight Handlers, Express and Station Employes. Its present name was adopted at the union's 1967 convention to stress its role in the airline industry.

Unions which have merged with the Brotherhood include: the Railway Patrolmen's International Union (AFL-CIO) on January 1, 1969; Transportation-Communication Employees Union (AFL-CIO) on February 20, 1969; United Transport Service Employees (AFL-CIO) on September 26, 1972; Brotherhood of Sleeping Car Porters (AFL-CIO) in April 1978; and The American Railway and Airway Supervisors Association (AFL-CIO) on August 6, 1980.

Publications issued by the union include *Railway Clerk Interchange* (10 issues annually); *International President's Bulletin* (quarterly); *Air Transport Interchange* (10 issues annually); and *Supervisors' Journal* (bimonthly).

Address: 3 Research Pl., Rockville, Md. 20850. Tel. (301) 948–4910

Source reference: Harry Henig, *The Brotherhood of Railway Clerks* (New York: Columbia UP, 1937).

Railway and Airline Supervisors Association; The American (AFL-CIO) Formerly known as the American Railway Supervisors Association (AFL-CIO), the union changed its name to The American Railway and Airway Supervisors Association in the early 1970s.

See also RAILWAY AND AIRWAY SUPERVISORS ASSOCIATION; THE AMERICAN (AFL-CIO).

Railway and Airway Supervisors Association; The American (AFL-CIO) Formerly known as The American Railway and Airline Supervisors Association (AFL-CIO), it merged with the Brotherhood of Railway, Airline and Steamship Clerks, Freight Handlers, Express and Station Employes (AFL-CIO) on August 6, 1980.

See also RAILWAY, AIRLINE AND STEAMSHIP CLERKS, FREIGHT HANDLERS, EXPRESS AND STATION EMPLOYES; BROTHERHOOD OF (AFL-CIO).

Railway Audit and Inspection Co. One of a group of agencies which at various times during labor organizational drives provided professional espionage services to employers throughout the country. Essentially their job was to inform the employing railroad company about labor activities to permit it to take appropriate action to prevent organization.

Descriptions of some of the procedures of these agencies are on record in the LaFollette Commission hearings and in some labor history textbooks. Sections from one description are included below:

> The widespread use of the "stool pigeon" system in American industry may or may not be testimony to its success as an anti-union device. A somewhat more formal method of achieving the same result is the employment of professional spy agencies. Such institutions as Pinkerton, W. J. Burns, Railway Audit and Inspection . . . usually maintain one department of activity which is expressly dedicated to this form of service to the employer. . . . The employer who suspects that trouble is developing in his plant and who is himself entirely out of touch with his workers, calls a professional spy agency and asks that operatives be assigned to his plant. The operatives are taken on with other recently hired workers. . . . The operatives . . . record their findings in reports which are usually sent direct to the spy agency. There they are "edited" and sent on to the employer. Instructions are sent to the operative via the general delivery of the local post office. The operative is more or less carefully trained in methods of avoiding suspicion. If he successfully spots the troublemakers in the plant, a large part of his task is accomplished. If he cannot discover the source of agitation, he may begin fictionalizing his reports, or decide that the time has come for him to start his own agitation. If the operative himself becomes the agitator, he may be able to discover from the responses . . . who the interested workers are. If he secures no responses, then he may have to imagine enough enthusiasm to keep his reports well filled out. After this has gone on for some time, the agency may decide that the time has come to deliver the goods by eliminating the employer's labor troubles. This is accomplished . . . simply by recalling the operative and presenting a bill for services rendered.
>
> . . . The operative receives instructions to join the union and work his way up. His dues and assessments are paid by the agency and, incidentally, by the employer. He rises fast in the union and enters its inner councils. He reports the union's plans, financial condition and membership rolls. Or he may prefer to remain in the rank and file. There he does his best to stimulate factionalism, suspicion of the leaders and ill-considered action.

Source reference: Robert R. R. Brooks, *When Labor Organizes* (New Haven: Yale UP, 1937).

See also ANTI-UNION PRACTICES, ESPIONAGE, LABOR SPY, LAFOLLETTE COMMITTEE, STOOL PIGEON.

Railway Carmen of America; Brotherhood of (AFL-CIO) Organized in 1891 in Colorado, absorbing the Brotherhood of Railway Car Repairers, the Carmen's Mutual Aid Association, and the Brotherhood of Railway Carmen. The union remained independent until it affiliated with the AFL in 1909. It is basically an industrial union. The name was changed to the Brotherhood of Railway Carmen of the United States and Canada in the late 1960s.

Source reference: Leonard Painter, *Through 50 Years with the Brotherhood of Railway Carmen of America* (Kansas City, Mo.: The Union, 1941).

See also RAILWAY CARMEN OF THE UNITED STATES AND CANADA; BROTHERHOOD OF (AFL-CIO).

Railway Carmen of the United States and Canada; Brotherhood of (AFL-CIO) Formerly known as the Brotherhood of Railway Carmen of America, the union adopted the present name in the late 1960s. The official monthly publication is the *Railway Carmen's Journal.*

Address: 4929 Main St., Kansas City, Mo. 64112. Tel. (816) 561–1112

Railway Conductors and Brakemen; Order of (Ind) Organized in 1868 at Amboy, Ill. With the amalgamation of the first two divisions of conductors, the union became the Conductor's Brotherhood in July 1868. It adopted a constitution and bylaws and elected its first grand officers. In November 1868, the first international convention of the Brotherhood was held in Columbus, Ohio.

The union's name was changed to the Order of Railway Conductors of America in 1878.

Its primary purposes in organization were fraternal benefits, temperance, and opposition to economic action and strikes. Participation in strikes was a basis for expulsion from the Order until that policy was changed in 1890.

In 1942, the Order of Sleeping Car Conductors merged with the Railway Conductors. The name, Order of Railway Conductors and Brakemen, was adopted in 1954.

On January 1, 1969, the Conductors and three other railroad unions—the Brotherhood of Locomotive Firemen and Enginemen, the Brotherhood of Railroad Trainmen, and the Switchmen's Union of North America—merged to form the United Transportation Union.

Source references: Edwin C. Robbins, *The Railway Conductors: A Study in Organized Labor* (New York: Columbia UP, Studies in History, Economics and Public Law no. 148, 1914); Leo Wolman, *The Growth of American Trade Unions* (New York: NBER, 1924); Samuel Yellen, *American Labor Struggles* (New York: Russell, 1956).

See also TRANSPORTATION UNION; UNITED (AFL-CIO).

Railway Employees and Association of Railway Trainmen and Locomotive Firemen; Federated Council of the International Association of (Ind) Union formed on January 1, 1962, with the merger of the International Association of Railway Employees (Ind) and the Association of Railway Trainmen and Locomotive Firemen (Ind). On September 1, 1970, the union merged with the United Transportation Union (AFL-CIO).

See also TRANSPORTATION UNION; UNITED (AFL-CIO).

Railway Employes' Department One of the AFL-CIO trade and industrial departments. It was organized tentatively in 1908 and reorganized in 1912 to incorporate the "system federations" which are composed of all its members in the various craft unions working for the same carrier or railroad company.

The organizations affiliated with the department included: Boilermakers; Electrical Workers; Firemen and Oilers; Machinists; Railway Carmen; and Sheet Metal Workers.

The department ceased operations in 1980.

Railway Labor Act A federal statute enacted in 1926, based on a proposal by representatives of labor and management, to resolve labor disputes on the railroads by mediation and voluntary arbitration, with special provisions for emergency disputes. Coverage of the law was extended to the airlines by amendment in 1934, and a further amendment in 1951 made union-shop and check-off agreements lawful.

The Act protects the rights of employees in collective bargaining and provides for the establishment of, and requirement of the filing of written agreements with, the National Mediation Board. The board has the responsibility to certify employee representatives, to assist in the mediation of disputes, and to make recommendations in the handling of major disputes under the emergency provisions of the Act. The Act also established a National Railroad Adjustment Board which has responsibility for making final decisions on grievances arising under the terms of contracts entered into between employers and employees. The National Air Transport Adjustment Board may also be established under the law.

Source references: Railway Labor Act, as amended, 45 U.S.C. 151–163, 181–188 (1982); *Joliet Elgin & Eastern Railway Co. v. Burley*, 325 US 711, 16 LRRM 749 (1945); *Virginian Railway Co. v. System Federation No. 40*, 300 US 515, 1 LRRM 743 (1937); Edward Berman, "The Supreme Court Interprets the Railway Labor Act," *AER*, Dec. 1930; Attilio DiPasquale, "The Railway Labor Act and the Airlines," *NYU 12th Annual Conference on Labor*, ed. by Emanuel Stein (Albany: Bender, 1959); C. O. Fisher, *Use of Federal Power in the Settlement of Railway Labor Disputes* (Washington: U.S. Dept. of Labor, BLS, Bull. no. 303, 1922); Jacob J. Kaufman, *Collective Bargaining in the Railroad Industry* (New York: King's Crown Press, 1954); ———, "Procedures Versus Collective Bargaining in Railroad Labor Disputes," *ILRR*, Oct. 1971; John G. Kilgour, "Alternatives to the Railway Labor Act: An Appraisal," *ILRR*, Oct. 1971; Joseph Krislov, "Mediation Under the Railway Labor Act: A Process in Search of a Name," *LLJ*, May 1976; Fred J. Kroll, "The Railway Labor Act: An Effective Law to Avoid Strikes Without Eliminating Them," *Journal of Collective Negotiations in the Public Sector*, Vol. 11, no. 1, 1982; Leonard A. Lecht, *Experience Under Railway Labor Legislation* (New York:

Columbia UP, 1955); Herbert R. Northrup, "The Railway Labor Act: A Critical Reappraisal," *ILRR*, Oct. 1971; Charles M. Rehmus (ed.), *The Railway Labor Act at Fifty; Collective Bargaining in the Railroad and Airline Industry* (Washington: U.S. NMB, 1977); ———, "Railway Labor Act Modifications: Helpful or Harmful?" *ILRR*, Oct. 1971; Asher W. Schwartz, "The Railway Labor Act and the Airlines," *NYU 12th Annual Conference on Labor*, ed. by Emanuel Stein (Albany: Bender, 1959); U.S. Congress, Senate, Committee on Labor and Public Welfare, *Legislative History of the Railway Labor Act, as Amended (1926 through 1966)* (Washington: 1974); U.S. Dept. of Labor, BLS, *Airline Experience Under the Railway Labor Act* (Washington: Bull. no. 1683, 1971); ———, *Handling of Rail Disputes Under the Railway Labor Act, 1950–69* (Washington: Bull. no. 1753, 1972); Gary Young, "Working on the Railroad/IV. Birth of the Railway Labor Act. The Railway Brotherhoods and the Railway Labor Act: A Study in Progressive Political Action in the 1920's," *Industrial and Labor Relations Forum*, Oct. 1973; Arthur M. Wisehart, "The Airlines' Recent Experience Under the Railway Labor Act," *Law and Contemporary Problems*, Winter 1960; Harry D. Wolf, *The Railway Labor Board* (Chicago: Univ. of Chicago Press, 1927).

See also NATIONAL AIR TRANSPORT ADJUSTMENT BOARD, NATIONAL EMERGENCY BOARDS, NATIONAL RAILROAD ADJUSTMENT BOARD.

Railway Labor Executives' Association The prime objective of this organization, established following the passage of the 1926 Railway Labor Act, was to achieve cooperative action "to develop constant interpretations and utilization of all the privileges of the (Railway Labor) Act." The organization consists of the chief executive officers of all of the organizations who are members of the association. In December 1969, five unions withdrew their membership from the association to form the Congress of Railway Unions.

The association consists of 20 organizations, all but one of which are affiliated with the AFL-CIO. Nine have most of their membership in the railroad industry. The Railway Labor Executives' Association is not a labor organization or a federation of unions, but exists primarily to coordinate policy of mutual interest to railroad workers and to make legislative and other proposals.

Address: 400 First St., N.W., Washington, D.C. 20001. Tel. (202) 737–1541

Railway Patrolmen's International Union (AFL-CIO) Chartered by the AFL in July 1949. The union merged with the Brotherhood of Railway, Airline and Steamship Clerks, Freight Handlers, Express and Station Employes (AFL-CIO), effective January 1, 1969.

See also RAILWAY, AIRLINE AND STEAMSHIP CLERKS, FREIGHT HANDLERS, EXPRESS AND STATION EMPLOYES; BROTHERHOOD OF (AFL-CIO).

railway pension act *See* RAILROAD RETIREMENT ACT.

railway retirement act *See* RAILROAD RETIREMENT ACT.

Railway Supervisors Association; The American (AFL-CIO) *See* RAILWAY AND AIRLINE SUPERVISORS ASSOCIATION; THE AMERICAN (AFL-CIO).

Railway Trainmen and Locomotive Firemen; Association of (Ind) Organized in 1912 and changed its name to the Association of Colored Railway Trainmen and Locomotive Firemen in 1936. It later changed its name to the Association of Railway Trainmen and Locomotive Firemen.

On January 1, 1962, the union merged with the International Association of Railway Employees (Ind) to form the Federated Council of the International Association of Railway Employees and Association of Railway Trainmen and Locomotive Firemen (Ind).

See also RAILWAY EMPLOYEES AND ASSOCIATION OF RAILWAY TRAINMEN AND LOCOMOTIVE FIREMEN; FEDERATED COUNCIL OF THE INTERNATIONAL ASSOCIATION OF (IND).

Railway Unions, Congress of A labor executives' organization formed by United Transportation Union President Charles Luna and officials of the Railway Clerks, Maintenance of Way Employes, Dining Car Stewards, and Seafarers, following their withdrawal from the Railway Labor Executives' Association in

1969. Claiming roughly 80 percent of the workers employed on the railroads, the organization advocated working together on matters of "mutual concern to our members in the economic and legislative fields." The organization aimed to protect and promote the interests of their respective memberships. In 1975, the affiliated unions agreed to dissolve the organization and reaffiliated with the Railway Labor Executives' Association.

See also RAILWAY LABOR EXECUTIVES' ASSOCIATION.

Rand award The arbitration award handed down in 1946 by Justice I. C. Rand of the Canadian Supreme Court in a dispute between the Ford Motor Company and its employees. Although the award had many features, the one which is most frequently referred to relates to union security and was the forerunner of what is presently known as the "agency shop."

The award required all employees, union and nonunion alike, to pay dues as a condition of employment. Workers were not required to become members; nonunion members did not take part in the everyday activity of the organization, but had the right to take part in strike votes. If the union was not able to obtain a majority when it called for a strike vote, it forfeited the check-off privilege for a number of months. Another part of the award required the union to repudiate wildcat and unauthorized strikes within 72 hours of their occurrence. Justice Rand's award said in part:

> I consider it entirely equitable then that all employees should be required to shoulder their portion of the burden of expense of administering the law of their employment, the union contract; that they must take the burden along with the benefit.
>
> The obligation to pay dues should tend to induce membership, and this in turn to promote that wider interest and control within the union which is the condition of progressive responsibility. If that should prove to be the case, the device employed will have justified itself.

See also RAND FORMULA.

Rand formula The "Rand formula" applies to two different and unrelated situations. It refers to the Rand award, the arbitration decision handed down by Supreme Court Justice I. C. Rand of Canada, relating to union security. It also refers to the formula established by President J. H. Rand, Jr., of the Remington Rand Company, which deals primarily with the methods of combating unionism and is sometimes referred to as the Mohawk Valley formula.

Source references: "Award of Justice Rand in Case of Ford Motor Company of Canada," *Daily Labor Report*, No. 32, Feb. 13, 1946; Harold J. Clawson, "The Rand Formula: Subsidiary and Quasi-Legal Aspects," *Canadian Bar Review*, Dec. 1946; "The Rand Labor-Relations Formula at Work," *Factory Management and Maintenance*, March 1947.

See also AGENCY SHOP, AUTOMATIC CHECK-OFF, MOHAWK VALLEY FORMULA, RAND AWARD, VOLUNTARY CHECK-OFF.

random rates Individualized or personalized rates of pay. Different rates are paid for the same job or job classification and the pay rates have no relation to any established system of payment.

Frequently such a random rate structure is established because no system has been set up within the plant, and as individuals show their ability, rates are adjusted either by the supervisor or other person in charge and no attempt is made to obtain a consistent internal arrangement. The random rate structure may result from favoritism or may develop merely because the operations of the plant require the hiring of new employees, and different employees come in at different rates even though they may be performing the same job. The justification might be that the person has either a better background or that he is a more skilled and more able operator, hence, is entitled to a higher individual rate.

See also INDIVIDUAL RATE, RATE RANGE.

Rand School of Social Science Social studies school with labor orientation located in New York. The school was founded in 1906 by a number of socialist leaders and the majority of the original instructors were also socialist oriented. Later, teachers in the field of social reform and other areas were invited to lecture and broader programs in the field of social development and in trade union education were developed.

rank and file The term in the vernacular means "the working people." Actually the term applies to individual union members who have no special status either as officers or shop stewards in the plant. They are the persons presumably for whom the union exists and to whom the union hierarchy is ultimately responsible.

A union run by the rank and file frequently is referred to as one which is democratic, since its base is in the membership.

ranking plan A system of job evaluation which some claim to be the easiest and simplest way to classify jobs within a plant. The procedure generally involves listing the jobs in each department in their order or rank of importance. This is done by those in the department who are best able to make such an evaluation, including the top supervisory staff. Jobs of comparable importance in the various departments then are grouped together into wage and salary classes in order to provide relatively equal compensation for those of comparable importance.

One of the difficulties frequently encountered in this system is that the individuals who do the judging and the ranking may be influenced by the actual wage rates being received by the individual employee and which may have no real bearing on the actual importance of the job. The ranking plan, however, provides a simple approach in an establishment where there is no established job-evaluation plan.

See also JOB EVALUATION, JOB GRADING.

rat A derogatory and derisive slang expression frequently applied to individuals who were members of the union but who become strikebreakers and turn on their working "brothers." The term sometimes is applied to an individual who will accept a lower wage rate than those established by the union scale.

rate cutting Generally applies to the arbitrary reduction by an employer of an incentive rate where there has been no change in the job content.

Opposition by trade unions to incentives springs from two major objections. One is the speed-up and the other, experience with rate cutting. Rate cutting frequently took place after employees had acquired sufficient skill, had increased their output and thereby their incentive earnings.

Occasionally the term "rate cutting" may apply to situations where the incentive rate originally had been set too high compared to the level of earnings of other employees in the industry or area in similar operations.

Source references: Z. Clark Dickinson, *Collective Wage Determination* (New York: Ronald Press, 1941); Herbert G. Zollitsch and Adolph Langsner, *Wage and Salary Administration* (2d ed., Cincinnati: South-Western, 1970).

See also INCENTIVE RATE.

ratee The individual whose work or abilities are being rated.

rate for the job Generally the same as the standard or basic rate which has been established in a particular plant for a particular occupation. It may apply to the minimum rate of pay for an experienced worker on a given job. This may be the single rate where there is no rate range, the union rate, or the minimum job rate.

See also BASE RATE, BASIC RATE OF PAY, BEGINNER'S RATE, COMMON LABOR RATE, ENTRANCE RATE, JOB RATE, MINIMUM RATES.

rate of wages The compensation or amounts of money paid to an individual per hour, per week, per month or, if on a piece or incentive rate, per unit of output. It is generally used synonymously with the wage rate. It is to be distinguished, however, from (wage) earnings. The two major categories of wage payments are piece rate and time rate.

See also EARNINGS.

rater The individual who actually determines the competence or qualification of the individual, either in a merit rating plan or through some other plan which requires an evaluation of a person's competence and performance.

rate range The spread between the predetermined minimum and maximum rate for individuals performing a specific job. The rate range is designed to provide a flexible method of compensation for employees performing the same work. It is less rigid than the single rates often used in compensating employees.

The rate range provides an opportunity for the employer to advance individuals on the basis of merit or length of service or a combination of the two. It also is useful when transferring individuals from one job to another to give the employer greater freedom, considering the qualifications of the individuals transferred, to place them within the ranges of rates appropriate to their abilities.

See also AUTOMATIC PROGRESSION, LENGTH OF SERVICE, MERIT RATING, SINGLE RATE.

rate setting The process or procedure used by management or jointly by management and labor to set the rates for jobs in a particular plant or company. The procedures may involve job evaluation, time and motion study, the comparison of wage rates for similar work in the labor market, or other criteria designed to establish not only the equitable rate for the job insofar as the employees are concerned, but one that will permit the employer to operate economically in the face of competition.

See also JOINT RATE SETTING, WAGE DETERMINATION.

ratification *See* AGREEMENT RATIFICATION.

rating The actual numerical report, if based on a percentage, or the designation of a level of performance, such as excellent through unsatisfactory, achieved by an individual following a review of his ability and performance.

Source references: Wallace Burch, "Annual Employee Reviews," *PJ*, June 1963; William J. Kearney, "Behaviorally Anchored Rating Scales—MBO's Missing Ingredient," *PJ*, Jan. 1979; Wayne K. Kirchner, "Extra-Alternative Rating Technique," *PJ*, Sept. 1961; John D. McMillian and Hoyt W. Doyel, "Performance Appraisal: Match the Tool to the Task," *Personnel*, July/Aug. 1980; Robert S. Minor, *Appraisal, Performance and Rating* (Chicago: Dartnell, 1966); Chester A. Newland, "Performance Appraisal of Public Administrators: According to Which Criteria?" *Public Personnel Management*, Sept./Oct. 1979; PPA, *A Rating System to Improve Job Performance* (Chicago: Personnel Report no. 651, 1965); U.S. GAO, *Federal Employee Rating Systems Need Fundamental Changes* (Washington: 1978).

See also EFFICIENCY RATING, MERIT RATING, PERFORMANCE APPRAISAL, PERFORMANCE TESTS, PERIODIC REVIEW.

rating, efficiency *See* EFFICIENCY RATING.

rating, experience *See* EXPERIENCE RATING.

rating, job *See* JOB RATING.

rating, merit *See* MERIT RATING.

rating, mutual *See* MUTUAL RATING.

rating form The sheet or form used to summarize the evaluation made by the individual who does the rating. The qualities which are involved will vary with the type of job being rated and with the particular factors which are considered important. The scale may range from outstanding to good, average, weak, poor, or a continuing scale within that particular set of adjectives.

The particular items may include the quality of work, the amount of work, the attitude toward the job, knowledge of the present job, the person's individual or personal qualities, the ability to plan the work, and similar factors.

See also FORMS AND RECORDS.

rating scale A method of presenting a person's qualification by means of a graphic chart or other form. The scale will measure the individual's ability, personality, performance, and potential compared to a standard which previously has been set.

rating service *See* EFFICIENCY RATING.

ratio hiring A quota system. It is usually a court-ordered temporary relief measure in cases of proven discrimination in which members of affected groups—minorities or women—are selected in a prescribed proportion to majority groups to bring about parity in a given employer's workforce. Unions may be ordered to admit to membership minorities and women on a ratio basis.

Source references: Carter v. Gallagher, 9 FEP Cases 1191 (DMinn 1972), *on remand from* 452 F2d 315, 4 FEP Cases 121 (CA 8, 1972); *Crockett v. Green*, 534 F2d 715, 12 FEP Cases 1078 (1976), *aff'g* 388 FSupp 912, 10 FEP Cases 165 (CA 7, 1975); *Rios v. Enterprise Assn. Steamfitters, Local 638*, 501 F2d 622, 8 FEP Cases 293 (1974).

See also AFFECTED CLASS, QUOTA, WEBER CASE.

rationalization A term much more popular in the 1930s than at present. It described the techniques and methods of scientific management with a view to the reduction of waste of either manpower or materials. It also involved the careful organization of production, including standardization of materials and products, and simplification and improvement not only of production, but also of transportation and marketing. To Professor Carlton, it in general "represented an attempt to apply scientific planning to a nation as a whole or finally to the world." Rationalization, he says, "implies the belief that a more rational control of world economic life through the application of scientific methods is possible and desirable."

Source references: Frank T. Carlton, *Labor Problems* (Boston: Heath, 1933); Morris L. Cooke, *Organized Labor and Production* (New York: Harper, 1946); George Halm, *Economic Systems* (New York: Rinehart, 1951).

See also SCIENTIFIC MANAGEMENT.

"R" cases Cases coming before the NLRB which involve representation questions.

Under the Taft-Hartley Act, several kinds of representation cases are possible. These include "RC" cases, which are petitions filed by an individual, a group, or a union; "RM" cases, petitions filed by an employer; and "RD" cases, which involve petitions for decertification of representatives filed by an individual, a group, or a labor organization.

Source references: Gloria Busman, *Union Representatives' Guide to NLRB RC and CA Cases* (Los Angeles: UC, Institute of IR, Policy and Practice Publication, 1977); Joseph Krislov, "Employer Petitions for NLRB Representation Elections," *LLJ*, April 1961; Kenneth C. McGuiness and Jeffrey A. Norris, *How to Take a Case Before the NLRB* (5th ed., Washington: BNA, 1986); U.S. NLRB, *A Guide to Basic Law and Procedures Under the National Labor Relations Act* (Washington: 1978).

See also "AC" CASES, CERTIFICATION, DECERTIFICATION, EXCLUSIVE BARGAINING AGENT, REPRESENTATION ELECTIONS, "U" CASES.

real earnings Generally the same as "real wages," the purchasing power of the worker's earnings. It comprises the actual goods and services which his money earnings will be able to purchase in the market place.

Source references: Gordon Bloom and Nathan Belfer, "Unions and Real Labor Income," *Southern Economic Journal*, Jan. 1948; Janice Neipert Hedges and Earl F. Mellor, "Weekly and Hourly Earnings of U.S. Workers, 1967–78," *MLR*, Aug. 1979; Joseph Rabianski, "Real Earnings and Human Migration," *Journal of Human Resources*, Spring 1971; George D. Stamas, "Real After-Tax Annual Earnings From the Current Population Survey," *MLR*, Aug. 1979.

See also EARNINGS, MONEY WAGE.

real wages The actual goods and services which can be purchased with money wages. Real wages express the purchasing power of the dollar income earned by individuals. The purchasing power of wages is generally computed by dividing money wages by some index which measures changes in prices over a period of time, such as the Consumer Price Index.

The concern of wage earners is not for money wages but the goods and services which those wages can command. Real wages will increase when prices fall and wages do not change, where wages increase and prices remain unchanged, or where both wages and prices rise but wages rise at a faster rate than prices.

Source references: Joan D. Borum, "Wage Increases in 1980 Outpaced by Inflation," *MLR*, May 1981; CED, *How to Raise Real Wages* (New York: 1950); Paul H. Douglas, *Real Wages in the United States, 1890–1926* (Boston: Houghton Mifflin, 1930); H. M. Douty, "The Slowdown of Real Wages: A Postwar Perspective," *MLR*, Aug. 1977; ———, *The Wage Bargain and the Labor Market* (Baltimore: Johns Hopkins UP, 1980); Robert H. Ferguson, *Wages, Earnings, and Incomes: Definitions of Terms and Sources of Data* (Ithaca: Cornell Univ., NYSSILR, Bull. no. 63, 1971); Thomas W. Gavett, "Measures of Change in Real Wages and Earnings," *MLR*, Feb. 1972; Abraham L. Gitlow, *Labor and Manpower Economics* (3d ed., Homewood, Ill.: Irwin, 1971); ILO, *International Comparisons of Real Wages* (Geneva: Studies and Reports, New Series no. 45, 1956); John M. Keynes, "Relative Movements of Real

Wages and Output," *Economic Journal*, March 1939; John H. Pencavel, *Constant-Utility Index Numbers of Real Wages* (Princeton: Princeton Univ., IR Section, Reprint, 1977); Albert Rees, *Real Wages in Manufacturing, 1890–1914* (Princeton: Princeton UP and NBER, 1961); Lloyd G. Reynolds, *Labor Economics and Labor Relations* (7th ed., Englewood Cliffs: PH, 1978).

See also CONSUMER PRICE INDEX, PURCHASING POWER.

reasonable accommodation *See* ACCOMMODATION.

reasonable cause A determination required of the EEOC upon receipt of an employment discrimination complaint that there is a basis for the charge, i.e., that there is "reasonable cause" to believe that the charge is true. The EEOC, following such finding, attempts to obtain agreement to correct the unlawful practice and provides assistance through conciliation efforts. If the EEOC is unable to obtain voluntary compliance, it will issue a right to sue notice.

A determination that there is no reasonable cause does not preclude an individual from seeking redress in the courts.

Sometimes referred to as probable cause.

Source references: U.S. EEOC, "Procedural Regulations," 29 C.F.R. 1601; Robert Freiberg (ed.), *The Manager's Guide to Equal Employment Opportunity* (New York: Executive Enterprises, 1977); Roger W. Sayers, "Equal Employment Compliance—The Concept of Probable Cause or Reasonable Cause," *PJ*, May 1974.

See also RIGHT TO SUE NOTICE.

reasonable cost formula The Wage and Hour Division's rules for determining the value of goods or services which are provided workers as part of their compensation under the Fair Labor Standards Act.

rebate plan Procedures under agency shop or fair share agreements for refund of certain union fees to nonmembers. For example, the Ohio public employees collective bargaining law (S.B. 133, L. 1983) requires unions to provide for rebates of "expenditures in support of partisan politics or ideological causes not germane to the work of employee organizations in the realm of collective bargaining."

In *Machinists v. Street*, the Supreme Court suggested "restitution" as a remedy for union fees expended for political causes to which the individual is opposed. However, in *Ellis v. Brotherhood of Railway and Airline Clerks*, the Court decided that a "pure rebate approach" was inadequate, and that a "union cannot be allowed to commit dissenters' funds to improper uses even temporarily."

Source references: Ellis v. Brotherhood of Railway and Airline Clerks, U.S. Sup.Ct. No. 82–1150, 116 LRRM 2001 (1984); *Machinists v. Street*, 367 US 740, 48 LRRM 2345 (1961).

See also FAIR SHARE AGREEMENT.

Rebnick v. McBride A decision of the Supreme Court in 1928 which held that activities of employment offices were subject to state regulation. The Court also held that the state of New Jersey could not set the price for such services to be offered by a private employment office.

Source reference: Rebnick v. McBride, 277 US 350 (1928).

See also EMPLOYMENT AGENCIES.

recall The procedure followed by employers for the return of individuals who have been laid off. Recall provisions usually are covered in the contract and usually follow the seniority provisions of the contract.

It may also refer to the procedure for removing (disciplining) an officer by means of a membership vote.

recession A polite term for what used to be called a depression. Sometimes a mild depression.

Source reference: Peter Henle, "Can We Learn from the Recessions?" *American Federationist*, July 1959.

See also DEPRESSION, UNEMPLOYMENT.

recognition One of the basic and essential elements of collective bargaining. A reading of American labor history will indicate that one of the prime objectives of early organizational efforts was to have the employer recognize the union as the bargaining agent and representative of the employees. Frequently employers insisted that they would deal with their own employees but would not deal with a union. Failure to accord recognition to the union was one of the most prolific causes of industrial conflict.

With passage of the National Labor Relations Act in 1935, Congress held that such strikes could be eliminated through the use of election machinery, whereby the NLRB would determine the majority status of employees, determine the appropriate bargaining unit, and then certify the union which had received a majority. The certified organization would become the exclusive bargaining agent of the employees in the appropriate unit, and the employer was required under the law to *recognize* that union for bargaining purposes.

Executive Order 10988, which established basic labor policy for the federal service, provided for the use of two additional types of recognition—informal and formal. These types of recognition were set up to assist units with relatively small membership to operate on an informal basis until such time as those units achieved majority status and subsequent exclusive recognition.

The informal and formal recognition procedures were eliminated by Executive Order 11491 and its successor, the Civil Service Reform Act of 1978.

Source references: E. Wight Bakke, Clark Kerr, and Charles W. Anrod, *Unions, Management and the Public* (3d ed., New York: Harcourt, Brace, 1967); Duane B. Beeson, "Recognition Without Election," *Labor Law Developments 1970*, Proceedings of 16th Annual Institute on Labor Law, SLF (New York: Bender, 1970); Alexander Feller and Jacob E. Hurwitz, *How to Deal With Organized Labor* (New York: Alexander Publishing, 1937); Twentieth Century Fund, *How Collective Bargaining Works* (New York: 1942).

See also CERTIFICATION, EXCLUSIVE BARGAINING AGENT, LIMITED UNION RECOGNITION, UNION SECURITY CLAUSES.

recognition, exclusive *See* EXCLUSIVE RECOGNITION.

recognition, formal *See* FORMAL RECOGNITION.

recognition, informal *See* INFORMAL RECOGNITION.

recognition picketing Picketing with the basic or prime purpose to persuade or convince the employer, through economic pressure, to recognize the union as bargaining agent. The 1959 amendments of the Labor Management Relations Act placed certain restrictions on recognition or organizational picketing under Section 8(b)(7) of the National Labor Relations Act.

Section 8(b)(7) reads as follows:

> It shall be an unfair labor practice for a labor organization or its agents . . . (7) to picket or cause to be picketed, or threaten to picket or cause to be picketed, any employer where an object thereof is forcing or requiring an employer to recognize or bargain with a labor organization as the representative of his employees, or forcing or requiring the employees of an employer to accept or select such labor organization as their collective bargaining representative, unless such labor organization is currently certified as the representative of such employees: (A) where the employer has lawfully recognized in accordance with this Act any other labor organization and a question concerning representation may not appropriately be raised under section 9(c) of this Act, (B) where within the preceding twelve months a valid election under section 9(c) of this Act has been conducted, or (C) where such picketing has been conducted without a petition under section 9(c) being filed within a reasonable period of time not to exceed thirty days from the commencement of such picketing: *Provided*, That when such a petition has been filed the Board shall forthwith, without regard to the provisions of Section 9(c)(1) or the absence of a showing of a substantial interest on the part of the labor organization, direct an election in such unit as the Board finds to be appropriate and shall certify the results thereof: *Provided further*, That nothing in this subparagraph (C) shall be construed to prohibit any picketing or other publicity for the purpose of truthfully advising the public (including consumers) that an employer does not employ members of, or have a contract with, a labor organization, unless an effect of such picketing is to induce any individual employed by any other person in the course of his employment, not to pick up, deliver or transport any goods or not to perform any services.
>
> Nothing in this paragraph (7) shall be construed to permit any act which would otherwise be an unfair labor practice under this section 8(b).

Source references: David L. Benetar, "Picketing for Recognition," *LLJ*, Jan. 1960; Herbert Burstein, "Recent Developments in Representation Proceedings and Recognitional and Organization Picketing," *LLJ*, Jan.

1963; Thomas J. McDermott, "Recognition and Organizational Picketing Under Amendments to the Taft-Hartley Act," *LLJ*, Aug. 1960; Bernard D. Meltzer, "Recognition—Organizational Picketing and Right-to-Work Laws," *LLJ*, Jan. 1958; " 'Recognitional' Picketing in the Garment Industry—Garment Unions Granted Protected Status Under Section 8(b)(7)(C) of the National Labor Relations Act—*Danielson v. Joint Board of Coat, Suit & Allied Garment Workers' Union, ILGWU, 494 F.2d 1230 (2d Cir. 1974),*" *IR Law Digest*, April 1976; Stuart Rothman, *Current Developments in Law of Recognition and Organizational Picketing*, Remarks before the Labor Law Institute of the Missouri State Bar, St. Louis, Missouri, September 28, 1960 (Washington: U.S. NLRB, 1960); Bernard Samoff, "Recognition and Organizational Picketing—A Wider Angle of Vision," *LLJ*, Nov. 1963; Fred Witney, "NLRB Membership Cleavage: Recognition and Organizational Picketing," *LLJ*, May 1963.

recommended order *See* INTERMEDIATE REPORT.

recruiting A function of the personnel office which involves the search for individuals for the special needs of a particular company.

Source references: AMA, *Making a Recruitment Program Work: Selected Reprints from AMA Periodicals* (New York: 1965–1967); Richard L. Brecker, "10 Common Mistakes in College Recruiting—Or How to Try Without Really Succeeding," *Personnel*, March/April 1975; BNA, *Recruiting Policies and Practices* (Washington: PPF Survey no. 126, 1979); David L. Chicci and Carl L. Knapp, "College Recruitment from Start to Finish," *PJ*, Aug. 1980; William A. Douglass and Julian S. Stein, Jr., "As You Were Saying—Ban Convention Recruiting?" *PJ*, July/Aug. 1962; Paul W. Maloney, *Management's Talent Search: Recruiting Professional Personnel* (New York: AMA, 1961); F. Arnold McDermott, *The Recruitment of Manpower: A Guide for Practitioners* (Chicago: PPA, Personnel Brief no. 25, 1962); Bonnie Nunke, "The Components of Successful College Recruitment," *PJ*, Nov. 1981; George S. Odiorne and Arthur S. Hann, *Effective College Recruiting* (Ann Arbor: Univ. of Michigan, Bureau of IR, 1961); Erwin Schoenfeld Stanton, *Successful Personnel Recruiting and Selection* (New York: AMACOM, 1977); Stephen J. Wilhelm, "Is On-Campus Recruiting on Its Way Out?" *PJ*, April 1980.

See also SCOUT.

recruiting agent An agent of a company who seeks persons having special abilities and who recruits them for employment. Recruiting may be done at universities, high schools, or other centers where personnel may be available for the positions open with the particular company.

See also SCOUT.

red circle rate Generally a rate which an individual received prior to a job evaluation or other adjusted wage schedules within the plant. The red circle rate is one where the wage for the particular job is higher than the rate which is called for in the job evaluation. In order to avoid having individuals oppose job classification and evaluation, it is generally agreed prior to the job evaluation that no employee's rate will be reduced as a result of the survey. Those below the rate move up to the job evaluation rate, those above are red circled (so-called "ringed" rates).

It is assumed that when these employees move to other jobs, are transferred, or are retired, the new employee hired will receive the proper rate for the job and not the "red circle" rate.

redevelopment area A geographic area which has been hard hit by unemployment and shows a precipitous decline in the particular industry for which the area traditionally is known. This might be illustrated by certain coal mining and textile regions. Congress has passed special legislation such as the Area Redevelopment Act to aid such communities in establishing economic programs to offset the decline.

Source references: Solomon Barkin, "Principles for Area Redevelopment Legislation," *LLJ*, Aug. 1959; Carroll L. Christenson, *Economic Redevelopment in Bituminous Coal: The Special Case of Technological Advance in the United States Coal Mines, 1930–1960* (Cambridge: Harvard UP, 1962); Sar A. Levitan, "Area Redevelopment: An Analysis of the Program," *IR*, May 1964; ———, "Characteristics of Urban Depressed Areas," *MLR*,

Jan. 1964; ———, *Federal Aid to Depressed Areas* (Baltimore: Johns Hopkins Press, 1964); U.S. Dept. of Labor, OMAT, *Training for Jobs in Redevelopment Areas* (Washington: 1962).

See also AREA REDEVELOPMENT ACT OF 1961, DEPRESSED AREA, PUBLIC WORKS AND ECONOMIC DEVELOPMENT ACT OF 1965.

red flu *See* BLUE FLU.

Red International of Labor Unions (RILU) An organization formed in 1920 which consisted of the Russian unions, the socialist and syndicalist unions in various countries, and small minorities of left-wing unions in the social democratic countries. It was set up when union members from some 17 nations gathered in Moscow to establish a radical and revolutionary trade union movement which would work with the political arm of the Communist world movement, the Third International.

Source references: Julius Braunthal, *History of the International, Volume I: 1864–1914* (New York: Praeger, 1967); William Z. Foster, *From Bryan to Stalin* (New York: International Publishers, 1937); David J. Saposs, *Communism in American Unions* (New York: McGraw-Hill, 1959); Joel Seidman, *The Needle Trades* (New York: Farrar, Rinehart, 1942).

See also TRADE UNION UNITY LEAGUE, WORLD FEDERATION OF TRADE UNIONS (WFTU).

red time It generally refers to the time allowed away from work for which the company compensates the employees. The phrase is not widely used.

reduction in force Synonymous with layoff, the term is commonly used in the public sector. A federal sector collective bargaining agreement defines it as "the abolition of a position or positions, necessitated by reductions in workload, reorganization, or changes in the numbers of employees caused by a reduction in funds or other similar reasons."

Source references: Harry C. Dennis, Jr., "Reduction in Force: The Federal Experience," *Public Personnel Management*, Spring 1983; U.S. OPM, *A Survey of Reduction in Force Provisions in Federal Labor Agreements* (Washington: 1981).

reduction in hours Proposal to meet the high level of unemployment and the feeling on the part of labor particularly that increasing automation will result in a continued high level of unemployment. Many union officials feel that a substantial reduction in hours of work is the only immediate approach available to labor organizations to provide additional employment opportunities. In addition, the unions have argued that with the retention of existing earnings and the spreading of hours, additional purchasing power will be made available which will indirectly result in a spurt in production to meet the increased purchasing potential.

See also HOURS OF WORK, UNEMPLOYMENT.

redundancy A British term which is defined as dismissal or termination of employment as a result of the closing or removal of the place of work or of a reduction in the requirements for certain categories of employees.

Voluntary redundancy refers to the methods by which the individuals to be dismissed are selected. A predetermined reduction in the number of employees may be obtained by calling for volunteers who may choose redundancy in order to obtain a lump sum redundancy payment. The amount of the redundancy payment is determined either by statutory provision, according to length of service and average earnings, or, in circumstances not covered by legislation, by the employer who can provide an amount higher than that specified by law. Accepted seniority criteria to determine which individuals are to become redundant may be set aside with voluntary redundancy to enable more senior workers to leave with higher lump sum payments.

Source reference: Bob Hepple, "Individual Labour Law," *Industrial Relations in Britain*, ed. by George Sayers Bain (Oxford: Basil Blackwell, 1983).

red union Applies generally to a union dominated by Communists or to a union with revolutionary policies.

Source references: "AFL President on What Labor Wants," 33 *LRRM* 75; "General Electric Policy on Disloyal Employees," 33 *LRRM* 35; "1953 Meeting of Labor Relations Research Group," 33 *LRRM* 47.

See also COMMUNISM IN AMERICAN LABOR UNIONS, COMMUNIST CONTROL ACT OF 1954, NONCOMMUNIST AFFIDAVIT.

reemployment The act of bringing back an employee who previously had been employed by the company but had been laid off. Generally, reemployment rights are established under the seniority provisions of the contract. Employees who are reemployed are considered as "rehires" rather than new hires for statistical and reporting purposes.

Provision usually is made for reemployment rights of individuals who leave for military service. Individuals normally would be reemployed after their military service in the position which they previously held and given accrued service credits as well as adjustments in pay put in effect during the interim period.

Source references: Bruce J. Cogan, "Veterans' Reemployment Rights Reexamined—New Labels or a New Approach," *IR Law Digest*, Oct. 1971; Frederick C. Klein, "Former Employees—Back to the Fold?" *Management Review*, Jan. 1969; J. John Palen and Frank J. Fahey, "Unemployment and Reemployment Success: An Analysis of the Studebaker Shutdown," *ILRR*, Jan. 1968; S. O. Schweitzer, "New Evidence on Problems of Reemployment," *MLR*, Aug. 1967; U.S. Dept. of Labor, BLS, *Major Collective Bargaining Agreements: Layoff, Recall, and Worksharing Procedures* (Washington: Bull. no. 1425–13, 1972).

See also MILITARY LEAVE, REINSTATEMENT.

referee In court procedures, an individual who is appointed by the court to take testimony, hear evidence, and to report the findings to the court. They may be referees in bankruptcy, or they may be appointed by the court in contempt proceedings involving enforcement of a statute, such as under the National Labor Relations Act.

The term referee also has been used in connection with the arbitration process where the parties by mutual consent agree to submit a dispute to a third person for final and binding settlement. (Sometimes such person may be asked to act in a mediatory capacity.) These individuals act in the same manner as an impartial chairman of an arbitration tribunal or a permanent umpire under some systems. If a distinction is drawn between these designations, namely, impartial chairman, permanent umpire, referee, and arbitrator, it would be that the first three are used in a much broader capacity, with greater jurisdiction and responsibility, whereas the arbitrator is frequently conceived of as an ad hoc third party to decide a particular dispute for the parties. Actually there is no appreciable distinction except where a distinction needs to be drawn for some particular purpose.

See also ARBITRATION; ARBITRATION, AD HOC; IMPARTIAL CHAIRPERSON; MASTER; PERMANENT ARBITRATOR; UMPIRE.

referendum Votes required by provisions of some union constitutions and bylaws, and possibly under certain provisions of the Landrum-Griffin Act, which necessitate a vote of the full membership to elect officers, to amend the union constitution and bylaws, or to call a strike.

See also LABOR-MANAGEMENT REPORTING AND DISCLOSURE ACT OF 1959.

referral The procedure used by an employment office to direct an applicant to a particular employer as a potential candidate for a job. Referral may be made by one company's employment office to another company where a job is available.

The term occasionally is used to describe intracompany referral of a particular individual from the personnel office to the department or division which is seeking candidates for employment.

reformist unionism A term occasionally applied to business unionism or uplift unionism, the primary function of which is to obtain better wages, hours and working conditions, and other educational and cultural opportunities rather than to promote ideological and revolutionary political and social aims.

See also BUSINESS UNIONISM, REVOLUTIONARY UNIONISM, UPLIFT UNIONISM.

refusal to bargain Findings made by the NLRB under Sections 8(a)(5) or 8(b)(3) of the Taft-Hartley Act that either the employer or the union has not fulfilled collective bargaining requirements of the statute. What constitutes a refusal to bargain may depend upon specific circumstances or the total behavior of the union or the company.

With more sophisticated behavior on the part of both labor and management, instances of refusal to bargain such as failure to sign an agreement to which both parties have agreed or refusal of the employer to meet for the purpose of discussing the terms of the contract after a union has been certified very rarely occur at the present time. The Board is concerned about the relationships between the parties which are conducive to reaching a settlement and the establishment of a collective bargaining agreement. Behavior seeking to thwart such an accomplishment, whether by obvious or devious means, would be considered by the Board as indicative of a refusal to bargain.

See also COLLECTIVE BARGAINING, GOOD-FAITH BARGAINING, HEINZ CASE.

regional bargaining *See* COLLECTIVE BARGAINING, INDUSTRYWIDE.

regional director The term applied to the person in charge of a regional office of the NLRB who carries out certain duties and responsibilities under the provisions of the Taft-Hartley Act particularly with regard to the holding of elections.

The term "regional director" may of course apply to officers under different organizational arrangements where a national office exists and regional divisions have been established, such as, for example, under the Wage and Hour Law. The term often is the title given a union official who has more than local, but less than national, responsibilities.

regional labor agreements Collective bargaining agreements which establish conditions on a regional basis. Generally these are so-called industrywide agreements which are not actually industrywide but encompass broad geographic or regional areas.

Source reference: Kenneth M. McCaffree, "Regional Labor Agreements in the Construction Industry," *ILRR*, July 1956.

See also AGREEMENT, INDUSTRYWIDE.

regional (wage) differential Generally recognized differences in wage levels among broad geographic subdivisions of the country. The best known is the regional differential between the North and South. Regional differentials have been recognized over long periods of time in collective bargaining by companies with plants in various geographic regions. Where possible, attempts have been made to narrow these regional wage differentials.

Source references: Stephen E. Baldwin and Robert S. Daski, "Occupational Pay Differences Among Metropolitan Areas," *MLR*, May 1976; Sara Behman, "Interstate Differentials in Wages and Unemployment," *IR*, May 1978; Victor R. Fuchs, *Differentials in Hourly Earnings by Region and City Size* (New York: NBER, Occasional Paper no. 101, 1967); George E. Johnson, "Wage Theory and Interregional Variation," *IR*, May 1967; Nicholas M. Kiefer and Sharon P. Smith, *Wage and Wage Discrimination Across Regions* (Princeton: Princeton Univ., IR Section, WP 79, 1975); Sigurd R. Nilsen, "How Occupational Mix Inflates Regional Pay Differentials," *MLR*, Feb. 1978; Ronald L. Oaxaca, "Estimation of Union/Nonunion Wage Differentials Within Occupational/Regional Subgroups," *Journal of Human Resources*, Fall 1975; "Trends in Regional Wage Differentials in Manufacturing, 1907–46," *MLR*, April 1948.

See also DIFFERENTIAL PIECE-RATE PLAN, WAGE DIFFERENTIALS.

registration requirements Refer generally to provisions under federal statutes such as the Labor-Management Reporting and Disclosure Act of 1959 which require unions and employers to register and file certain information under the provisions of the statute.

See also FALSE INFORMATION ACT, NON-COMMUNIST AFFIDAVIT.

regular employee A term which usually refers to a full-time employee employed throughout the year who has completed the formal or informal probationary period, as distinguished from seasonal, probationary, and temporary employees.

regularization of employment Efforts and programs adopted by companies and unions to establish a stable employment situation in a particular plant or company.

See also EMPLOYMENT ACT OF 1946, EMPLOYMENT STABILIZATION, FULL EMPLOYMENT, GUARANTEED EMPLOYMENT.

regular rate The basic rate of pay of the individual, used to compute overtime pay under the provisions of the Wage and Hour Act. It is established by dividing compensation received by an employee for work done in a certain period of time, usually the workweek (with certain exclusions), by the total number of hours worked during the week. This approximates the straight-time rate of the individual. Hours over 40 are paid at overtime rates, one and one-half times the regular rate.

The term may be used to designate the rate which employees take with them from job to job as they move to jobs which carry different rates.

See also BASIC RATE OF PAY.

regulation of labor unions Those statutes and administrative regulations which relate to the operation and functioning of trade unions. Most labor laws in some way affect labor unions and indirectly involve some regulation. With the passage of the Labor-Management Reporting and Disclosure Act, the government began to take a much more active part in the supervision and regulation of the internal affairs of trade unions.

Source references: James E. Anderson, *The Emergence of the Modern Regulatory State* (Washington: Public Affairs Press, 1962); Laurence J. Cohen, "Labor and the Antitrust Laws: A New Look at a Recurring Issue," *Labor Law Developments 1976*, Proceedings of 22d Annual Institute on Labor Law, SLF (New York: Bender, 1976); Frank Traver De Vyver, "Government Control of the Internal Affairs of Trade Unions—Australia and the United States," *Journal of IR*, Sept. 1973; Joseph R. Grodin, "Legal Regulation of Internal Union Affairs," *Public Policy and Collective Bargaining*, ed. by Joseph Shister, Benjamin Aaron, and Clyde W. Summers (New York: Harper, IRRA Pub. no. 27, 1962); Doris B. McLaughlin and Anita L. W. Schoomaker, *The Landrum-Griffin Act and Union Democracy* (Ann Arbor: Univ. of Michigan Press, 1979); Benjamin B. Naumoff, "Landrum-Griffin and Regulation of Internal Union Affairs," *LLJ*, July 1967; Benson Soffer, "Collective Bargaining and Federal Regulation of Union Government," *Regulating Union Government*, ed. by Marten S. Estey, Philip Taft, and Martin Wagner (New York: Harper, IRRA Pub. no. 31, 1964); Alexander Uhl, "The Regulatory Agencies," *American Federationist*, Oct. 1960; U.S. Dept. of Labor, LMSA, *Reports Required Under the LMRDA and CSRA* (rev. ed., Washington: 1980); ———, *Rights and Responsibilities Under the LMRDA and CSRA* (rev. ed., Washington: 1979); ———, *Union Election Cases Under the Labor-Management Reporting and Disclosure Act, 1966–1970* (Washington: 1972); ———, *Union Officer Elections and Trusteeships Case Digest* (Washington: 1980).

See also INTERNAL AFFAIRS OF UNIONS, LABOR-MANAGEMENT REPORTING AND DISCLOSURE ACT OF 1959.

Rehabilitation Act of 1973 The Act prohibits discrimination based on a person's handicap by federal agencies and departments and by private employers, individuals, and organizations working under federal contracts or receiving federal grants and assistance. The law also provides funding to states for vocational rehabilitation services, expands federal responsibility and research and training programs for handicapped individuals, and promotes affirmative action and nondiscrimination.

Section 503 of the Act requires federal contractors "to take affirmative action to employ and advance in employment qualified handicapped individuals"; it is administered by the OFCCP. The rules and regulations of OFCCP specify that every government contractor or subcontractor holding a contract of $50,000 or more and having 50 or more employees, is required to prepare and maintain an affirmative action program at each establishment. Moreover, all covered contractors must include an affirmative action clause in each covered contract and reasonably accommodate the physical and mental limitations of employees or applicants unless it can be demonstrated that such accommodation would impose an undue hardship on the conduct of business.

Source references: Rehabilitation Act of 1973, as amended, 29 U.S.C. 701 et seq. (1982); U.S. OFCCP, "Affirmative Action Obligations of Contractors and Subcontractors for Handicapped Workers," 41 C.F.R. 60–741; Jana H. Guy, "The Rehabilitation Act of 1973—Its Impact on Employee Selection Practices," *Employee Relations LJ*, Summer

1978; Terry Leap and Irving Kovarsky, "The Age Discrimination in Employment Act and the Vocational Rehabilitation Act: A Proposed Consolidation," *LLJ*, Jan. 1980; Gopal C. Pati and John I. Adkins, Jr., "Hire The Handicapped—Compliance is Good Business," *Harvard BR*, Jan./Feb. 1980.

See also ACCOMMODATION, EXECUTIVE ORDER 11758, HANDICAPPED INDIVIDUAL, OFFICE OF FEDERAL CONTRACT COMPLIANCE PROGRAMS (OFCCP).

Rehabilitation Services Administration Formerly the Office of Vocational Rehabilitation of the Department of Health, Education, and Welfare, it was redesignated the Vocational Rehabilitation Administration in 1963. In a reorganization of HEW in August 1967, the Vocational Rehabilitation Administration became a component of the newly created Social and Rehabilitation Service with the title of Rehabilitation Services Administration.

On May 4, 1980, the functions were transferred to the Office of Special Education and Rehabilitative Services, Department of Education, which has, among other duties, responsibility for the development of rehabilitation programs to reduce human dependency, increase self-reliance, and fully utilize the productive capabilities of all handicapped persons.

Address: 400 Maryland Ave., S.W., Washington, D.C. 20202. Tel. (202) 732–1723

See also SOCIAL AND REHABILITATION SERVICE, VOCATIONAL REHABILITATION.

rehire *See* REEMPLOYMENT.

reinstatement Generally the restoration of employees to their former positions without the loss of seniority or other benefits.

The nature and circumstances of reinstatement may vary. It may be a reinstatement under an arbitration award, where an employee has been improperly discharged. The arbitrator may order reinstatement without loss of any prior rights, or reinstatement without loss of seniority and other rights, but without back pay.

Another form of reinstatement may be that under the National Labor Relations Act, where the employer has engaged in discriminatory practices because of union activity—one category of unfair labor practice under the statute. The Board in giving effect to the provisions of the law might order reinstatement of the employee without loss of benefits and require back pay for the period of the discrimination in order to make the employee whole. The nature of the Board's affirmative order will depend on the nature of the discrimination. Another type of reinstatement is one arising under the provisions of the statute for the return of war veterans to their previous positions following the cessation of hostilities, or the completion of the term of enlistment with the armed forces.

Reinstatement also may mean return of an individual to union membership following disqualification which may have resulted from various offenses, including failure to pay dues. When a former union member is reinstated in the union, the individual frequently may have to pay previous assessments and dues or an initiation fee prior to reinstatement.

Source references: Lee Aspin, "Job Reinstatement Rights Under Section 8(a)(3) of the NLRA," *MLR*, March 1971; ———, "Reinstatement Isn't Enough," *American Federationist*, Sept. 1971; Warren H. Chaney, "The Reinstatement Remedy Revisited," *LLJ*, June 1981; John E. Drotning and David B. Lipsky, "The Effectiveness of Reinstatement as a Public Policy Remedy: The Kohler Case," *ILRR*, Jan. 1969; John R. Erickson, "Forfeiture of Reinstatement Rights through Strike Misconduct," *LLJ*, Oct. 1980; Matthew W. Finkin, "The Truncation of *Laidlaw* Rights by Collective Agreements," *IR Law Digest*, Winter 1979; Charlotte Gold, Rodney E. Dennis, and Joseph Graham, III, "Reinstatement After Termination: Public School Teachers," *ILRR*, April 1978; Arthur Anthony Malinowski, "An Empirical Analysis of Discharge Cases and the Work History of Employees Reinstated by Labor Arbitrators," *AJ*, March 1981; Boe W. Martin, "The Rights of Economic Strikers to Reinstatement: A Search for Certainty," *IR Law Digest*, July 1971; Thomas J. McDermott and Thomas H. Newhams, "Discharge-Reinstatement: What Happens Thereafter," *ILRR*, July 1971; Elvis C. Stephens and Warren Chaney, "A Study of the Reinstatement Remedy Under the National Labor Relations Act," *LLJ*, Jan. 1974.

See also AFFIRMATIVE ORDER, BACK PAY, DUES, INTERNAL AFFAIRS OF UNIONS, MAKE WHOLE, REPUBLIC STEEL CORP. V. NLRB.

related wage practices Benefits received by employees in addition to regular wages, for example, vacations, paid holidays, pensions, etc.

See also FRINGE BENEFITS, HOLIDAY PAY, INSURANCE PLAN, SUPPLEMENTAL UNEMPLOYMENT BENEFITS, VACATIONS.

relations by objectives *See* MEDIATION, PREVENTIVE.

release The involuntary dismissal of an individual for cause. The individual released, unlike the employee who has been laid off, loses seniority and other rights. It is similar to a discharge with prejudice because of some infraction on the part of the employee.

The release terminates the employment relationship and generally is consummated by the employer.

See also DISCHARGE, DISMISSAL.

released time Releasing an employee from work duties to participate in negotiations, grievance processing, other duties related to contract administration or professional improvement and service. Released time may also refer to the reduction of a normal full-time workload for the same purposes.

Source references: Leonard Bierman, "'Released Time': California-Style," *LLJ*, Dec. 1980; University of Hawaii, IRC, *Higher Education Contract Clause Finder: Four and Two-Year Colleges and Universities* (8th issue, Honolulu: 1982).

See also EDUCATIONAL LEAVE, OFFICIAL TIME, PAY FOR GRIEVANCE TIME, PAY FOR SHOP STEWARDS, TIME LOST ON GRIEVANCES.

release slip The statement, usually in writing, received by the employee informing the individual of the termination of employment.

relevant labor market area The geographic area from which the employer recruits or can reasonably recruit employees for certain jobs. It may be a Standard Metropolitan Statistical Area (SMSA), county, city, or other area. In determining the relevant labor market for a job, consideration is given to commuting patterns, availability of public transportation, and automobile ownership. The determination of a relevant labor market area will usually vary on a case by case basis. The relevant labor market area is important in establishing labor force availability of women and minorities in the utilization analysis for an affirmative action plan.

Source references: Howard R. Bloch and Robert L. Pennington, "Measuring Discrimination: What is a Relevant Labor Market?" *Personnel*, July/Aug. 1980; U.S. OFCCP, *Federal Contract Compliance Manual* (Washington: 1979); U.S. OPM, *Assessing the Distribution of Minorities and Women in Relevant Labor Markets; Information for State and Local Government Employers* (Washington: 1981).

See also AVAILABILITY, UTILIZATION ANALYSIS.

relevant labor pool The number of qualified or trainable persons available in the applicable labor area. The relevant labor pool can be influenced by many different factors and usually depends on the particular circumstances in each case. The assessment of the relevant labor pool is usually part of the determination of availability for the utilization analysis of women and minorities in an affirmative action program.

Source references: U.S. OFCCP, "Affirmative Action Programs of Government Nonconstruction Contractors," 41 C.F.R. 60–2.11; Howard C. Hay, "The Use of Statistics to Disprove Employment Discrimination," *LLJ*, July 1978.

See also AVAILABILITY, UTILIZATION ANALYSIS.

relief Assistance provided to individuals because of their need and inability to take care of themselves or their families. It may be in the form of public welfare funds.

Source reference: Josephine C. Brown, *Public Relief, 1929–1939* (New York: Holt, 1940).

See also PUBLIC ASSISTANCE, WORK RELIEF.

relief period A short recess or rest period of from 10 to 15 minutes during the shift to give employees, particularly those on monotonous and tiring work, an opportunity for a break, or period of relaxation. It has been found that these rest or recess periods, although they are taken on work time, actually result in increased output and a decrease in the accident rate as well as in a reduction in labor turnover.

Sometimes referred to as "spell-out time."

See also REST PERIOD.

relief shift When two or more shifts are worked in a plant, the shifts are rotated to relieve one another. The purpose is to equalize or distribute the day work and the night work among all of the employees. In some operations or industries which work on a seven-day week, relief arrangements may be so set that individual workers are given different days off in each week.

More frequently the term has reference to an extra shift which is made necessary at periodic intervals because of shift rotation. The relief shift in that case may be scheduled to overlap regular plant shifts, either the afternoon shift or the swing shift.

See also ROTATING SHIFT.

religious discrimination Practices, policies, or procedures that deny equal employment opportunity on the basis of religion. Under Title VII of the Civil Rights Act of 1964, employers must make reasonable efforts to accommodate religious observance or practices of employees or job applicants unless it is demonstrated that the accommodation would impose "undue hardship" on the conduct of business.

In terms of membership in a union, the Taft-Hartley Act amendments of 1980 provide that employees whose religious convictions prevent them from joining or supporting a union are not required to join a union as a condition of employment. Such employees, however, may be required by the collective bargaining agreement to contribute a sum equal to the union dues and fees "to a nonreligious, nonlabor organization charitable fund."

Source references: Labor Management Relations Act of 1947, as amended, Section 19, 29 U.S.C. 169 (1982); Civil Rights Act of 1964, as amended, 42 U.S.C. 2000e(j) (1982); *Trans World Airlines v. Hardison*, 432 US 63, 14 FEP Cases 1697 (1977); U.S. OFCCP, "Guidelines on Discrimination Because of Religion or National Origin," 41 C.F.R. 60–50.

See also ACCOMMODATION.

relocation allowances *See* MOVING ALLOWANCES.

relocation of industry *See* PLANT MIGRATION, RUNAWAY SHOP.

renewal clause The section in a collective bargaining agreement which provides for the automatic extension or renewal of the contract until a fixed date or until the expiration of another year. Provision is made for the continuation of the agreement unless adequate notice is given by either side to terminate the agreement or to negotiate proposed changes.

An agreement clause might read as follows: "This agreement shall be effective as of (_______ date) and shall remain in effect for a period of three years, and from year to year thereafter unless notice is given by either party 60 days prior to the expiration of any such year."

reopening clause A provision in a collective bargaining agreement which permits either side to reopen the contract during its term, generally under specified circumstances or at specified periods of time prior to the actual expiration of the agreement.

These clauses provide primarily for wage reopenings at fixed periods of time, particularly where the contract is of long duration, such as a four- or five-year period. The clause may be inserted where economic conditions are changing rapidly, as during a war period or a period of rapidly changing prices, to permit the employer and the union to review economic conditions and make necessary adjustments.

A clause used during World War II read as follows:

> If, at any time during the term of this contract, a significant change occurs in governmental wage policy, either party shall have the right to request negotiations on general change rates. If the parties are in disagreement as to whether a significant change has occurred, such dispute may be submitted to the National War Labor Board for decision.

A broader contract provision might read as follows:

> In the event of changes in economic conditions, national wage policy, cost of living, or competitive conditions in the industry, either party may give 60 days' notice of its desire to negotiate changes in the wage structure.

Generally reopening clauses are not quite so broad as the one above since one of the purposes of the contract is to stabilize terms and conditions for a fixed period.

See also WAGE REOPENING CLAUSE.

Reorganization Plan No. 1 of 1978 Issued by President Carter and approved by the Congress, the plan transferred the following responsibilities to the EEOC:

(1) Administration of the Age Discrimination in Employment Act of 1967 from the secretary of labor and the Civil Service Commission;
(2) Administration of the Equal Pay Act from the secretary of labor, the wage and hour administrator, and the Civil Service Commisson; and
(3) Enforcement of equal opportunity programs in federal employment from the Civil Service Commission.

The authority to bring suits against state or local governments under Section 707 of Title VII of the Civil Rights Act of 1964 was assumed by the U.S. attorney general. The Equal Employment Opportunity Coordinating Council was abolished and its functions transferred to the EEOC. The organizational changes under this plan and Reorganization Plan No. 2 were later incorporated into the Civil Service Reform Act of 1978.

Source references: Reorganization Plan No. 1, 43 F.R. 19807, 3 C.F.R. 321; Laurence E. Rosoff, "Reorganization Plan No. 1 Under Title VII," *LLJ*, May 1979.

See also CIVIL SERVICE REFORM ACT OF 1978.

Reorganization Plan No. 2 of 1978 Abolished the Civil Service Commission and established in its place the Office of Personnel Management and the Merit Systems Protection Board and the MSPB Special Counsel. It also established the Federal Labor Relations Authority and abolished the Federal Labor Relations Council.

Source references: Reorganization Plan No. 2, 43 F.R. 36037, 5 U.S.C. 3301, 7301; U.S. GAO, *Civil Service Reform—Where It Stands Today, Report to the Congress* (Washington: 1980).

See also CIVIL SERVICE REFORM ACT OF 1978.

replacement (1) The filling of a vacancy created by a separation. (A separation generally is a termination of employment resulting from a quit, layoff, or discharge.) (2) A person who fills a vacancy created by a separation.

The term "replacement" also is used to describe workers who have been hired to replace individuals who are on strike.

See also ACCESSION, LABOR TURNOVER, NET LABOR TURNOVER RATE, SEPARATION, STRIKEBREAKER.

replacement rate The term used synonymously with net labor turnover rate. It means the number of replacements per 100 workers in the average work force of an employer.

See also NET LABOR TURNOVER RATE.

reporting pay *See* CALL-IN PAY.

representation, minority *See* MINORITY REPRESENTATION.

representation cases *See* "R" CASES.

representation elections Procedures established by federal and state statutes to determine the organizations properly representative of employees for the purpose of collective bargaining. Federal and state machinery is designed to permit employees to designate their bargaining agent without restraint, interference, or domination.

The Labor Management Relations Act of 1947, as amended in 1959, provides for three general types of election:

(1) "Representation," as described above,
(2) "Decertification," to determine if employees wish to withdraw bargaining rights from a previously certified union, and
(3) "Deauthorization," to determine if employees wish to rescind a union shop agreement.

Ordinarily only one election may be held in a bargaining unit within any 12-month period.

State election procedures tend to follow those developed by the NLRB, though this is not required.

Source references: David Black, "Election Behavior and Union Representation Elections," *LLJ*, Oct. 1980; Julius G. Getman, Stephen B. Goldberg, and Jeanne B. Herman, "NLRB Regulation of Campaign Tactics: The Behavioral Assumptions on Which the

Board Regulates," *IR Law Digest*, Jan. 1976; _______, *Union Representation Elections: Law and Reality* (New York: Russell Sage Foundation, 1976); Louis Jackson and Robert Lewis, *Winning NLRB Elections; Management's Strategy and Preventive Programs* (New York: Practising Law Institute, 1972); Leonard J. Lurie, "Union Elections—Some Unresolved Problems," *NYU 15th Annual Conference on Labor*, ed. by Emanuel Stein (Albany: Bender, 1962); Martha F. Riche, "Union Election Challenges Under the LMRDA," *MLR*, Jan. 1965; Joseph B. Rose, "What Factors Influence Union Representation Elections?" *MLR*, Oct. 1972; James P. Swann, Jr., *NLRB Elections: A Guidebook for Employers* (Washington: BNA, 1980); Robert E. Williams, Peter A. Janus, and Kenneth C. Huhn, *NLRB Regulation of Election Conduct* (Philadelphia: Univ. of Pennsylvania, Wharton School, Industrial Research Unit, LRPP Series Report no. 8, 1974).

See also APPROPRIATE UNIT, BARGAINING UNIT, CERTIFICATION, DECERTIFICATION, ELIGIBILITY OF STRIKERS TO VOTE, "NEITHER" VOTE, "R" CASES, RUN-OFF ELECTION, SELF-DETERMINATION ELECTION, UNION ELECTIONS, UNION-SHOP ELECTIONS.

representation hearing The procedures followed under the National Labor Relations Act to determine whether or not a particular union represents employees for collective bargaining purposes and whether, therefore, the employer will be required to recognize a particular union for purposes of bargaining.

Source reference: Benjamin B. Naumoff, "A Procedural-Law Guide to an NLRB Representation Hearing," *LLJ*, May 1957.

See also BARGAINING UNIT, DECERTIFICATION, "R" CASES, REPRESENTATION ELECTIONS.

representative actions Procedures involving suits brought by representatives of employees who sought recovery under the Wage and Hour Law prior to the Portal-to-Portal Pay Act.

See also COLLECTIVE ACTIONS, PORTAL-TO-PORTAL PAY ACT.

representatives of their own choosing A phrase in the Taft-Hartley Act which gives employees the right to choose their representatives without interference by the employer.

Source references: Louis B. Boudin, "Representatives of Their Own Choosing," 37 *Illinois LR* 385 (1934), 38 *Illinois LR* 41 (1934); Robert R. R. Brooks, *Unions of Their Own Choosing: An Account of the NLRB* (New Haven: Yale UP, 1939).

See also REPRESENTATION ELECTIONS.

reprimand A form of disciplinary action, it is an oral or written warning served on an employee for corrective action. The written reprimand is placed in the employee's personnel file; the employee is given the right to comment and prepare a reply.

Source references: Carmen D. Saso and Earl Tanis, *Disciplinary Policies and Practices* (Chicago: IPMA, PERL no. 40, 1973); Rosalind Schwartz and Erin-Aine Miller, *Employee Discipline* (Los Angeles: UC, Institute of IR, 1977).

Republic Steel Corp. v. Maddox A 1965 decision of the Supreme Court which reversed an Alabama court's award of severance pay to a terminated employee and ruled that an employee must submit his grievance to arbitration provided under a union contract before taking a claim to court. The terminated employee waited three years before filing a claim without going through the three-step grievance procedure with binding arbitration as the terminal point, provided under the contract. The state court awarded the pay on the reasoning that when an employment relationship ends, no further danger of industrial strife exists and the application of federal law is not warranted.

The Supreme Court in its opinion referred to the "logical extension" of the *Lincoln Mills* case, which held that an agreement to arbitrate is enforceable in court. Unless the contract provides otherwise, "there can be no doubt that the employee must afford the union the opportunity to act on his behalf. Congress has expressly approved contract grievance procedures as a preferred method for settling disputes and stabilizing the 'common law' of the plant."

Source reference: Republic Steel Corp. v. Maddox, 379 US 650, 58 LRRM 2193 (1965).

See also ARBITRATION, GRIEVANCE; DISMISSAL COMPENSATION.

Republic Steel Corp. v. NLRB A decision of the U.S. Court of Appeals for the Third Circuit in 1939 (the Supreme Court denied certiorari), in which the court rejected the company's contention that the NLRB was without power to order reinstatement of strikers who had been guilty of criminal conduct in connection with the strike.

The contention by the company that none of the strikers should be reinstated since they were all members of the same organization and hence responsible for the violence, was set aside primarily under the provisions of Section 6 of the Norris-LaGuardia Act, which, as construed, prohibits courts of the United States from holding members of a union participating in a labor dispute responsible "for the unlawful acts of individual officers, members, or agents, except upon clear proof of actual participation in, or actual authorization of, such acts, or of ratification of such acts after actual knowledge thereof." The court also said: "Equally untenable is the contention that the strikers are not entitled to reinstatement because they have not come into court with clean hands. This principle is not applicable to a proceeding in which a governmental agency is seeking enforcement of its order in the public interest. . . ."

The court distinguished this case from the *Fansteel* case in the following language:

> In the Fansteel case the court was dealing with a case which involved a sitdown strike in which the strikers forcibly and unlawfully deprived their employer of possession of his plant. The court made it clear that unlawful conduct of that character deprived the participant of the right of reinstatement. We think it must be conceded, however, that some disorder is unfortunately quite usual in any extensive or long drawn out strike. A strike is essentially a battle waged with economic weapons. Engaged in it are human beings whose feelings are stirred to the depths. Rising passions call forth hot words. Hot words lead to blows on the picket line. The transformation from economic to physical combat by those engaged in the contest is difficult to prevent even when cool heads direct the fight. Violence of this nature, however much it is to be regretted, must have been in the contemplation of the Congress when it provided in Sec. 13 of the Act, 29 U.S.C.A. Sections 163, that nothing therein should be construed so as to interfere with or impede or diminish in any way the right to strike. If this were not so the rights afforded to employees by the Act would be indeed illusory. We accordingly recently held that it was not intended by the Act that minor disorders of this nature should deprive a striker of the possibility of reinstatement. In the present case there was evidence of violence and disorder on the part of many strikers. Numbers of them were convicted of crimes in the state courts. The Board accordingly undertook to determine which of these were sufficiently serious to bar reinstatement. This it did without the benefit of the *Fansteel* opinion, which was not handed down until four months later. In making its determination the Board confined itself to evidence of convictions and properly refused to try accusations of violence which had not resulted in convictions in the criminal courts. It decided that all strikers who had been convicted of possession and use of explosives, malicious destruction of property to the value of $300, and possession of a bomb, all felonies, should be denied reinstatement, but that all others who had been convicted of less serious offenses should be reinstated. Among these others were nine convicted of unlawfully obstructing and retarding the passage of the United States mail, three of discharging firearms, seven of malicious destruction of property to the value of less than $300, one of unlawfully interfering with telegraph or telephone messages, one of transporting explosives, five of interfering with and obstructing railway tracks, 13 of carrying concealed weapons, and one of assault and battery sufficiently serious to call for the imposition of a fine of $200 and costs, and a suspended sentence of six months.

Source references: Republic Steel v. NLRB, 107 F2d 472, 5 LRRM 740 (CA3 1939); *cert. denied*, 309 US 684.

required collective bargaining *See* MANDATORY SUBJECTS FOR BARGAINING.

rerum novarum An encyclical issued by Pope Leo XIII on May 15, 1891. The title of the encyclical is taken from the opening phrase of the statement which described the conditions of labor and the attitude and principles of the church in the area of employer-employee relations.

research, industrial relations The development of organized inquiries in the field of industrial relations. The investigatory programs in some subject areas also seek to establish broad general principles and policies as a guide to future development, as well as an understanding of the past.

Source references: L. Vaughn Blankenship, "The National Science Foundation's Role in Labor-Management Research," *Proceedings of the 33d A/M, IRRA*, ed. by Barbara Dennis (Madison: 1981); Neil W. Chamberlain, Frank C. Pierson, and Theresa Wolfson (ed.), *A Decade of Industrial Relations Research 1946–1956* (New York: Harper, IRRA Pub. no. 19, 1958); James L. Cochrane, *Industrialism and Industrial Man in Retrospect, A Critical Review of the Ford Foundation's Support for the Inter-University Study of Labor* (New York: Ford Foundation, 1979); Milton Derber et al., "Union-Management Relations Research," *ILRR*, April 1961; John T. Dunlop, "Policy Decisions and Research in Economics and Industrial Relations," *ILRR*, April 1977; IRRA, *A Review of Industrial Relations Research* (2 vols., Madison: 1970–71); Clark Kerr, "Industrial Relations Research: A Personal Perspective," *IR*, May 1978; ———, "A Perspective on Industrial Relations Research—Thirty-Six Years Later," *Proceedings of the 36th A/M, IRRA*, ed. by Barbara Dennis (Madison: 1984); Thomas A. Kochan, "Industrial Relations Research: An Agenda for the 1980's," *MLR*, Sept. 1980; George P. Shultz, "Priorities in Policy and Research for Industrial Relations," *Proceedings of the 21st A/M, IRRA*, ed. by Gerald Somers (Madison: 1969); Gerald G. Somers, *Industrial Relations Centres: Their Role and Functions* (Madison: Univ. of Wisconsin, IRRI, Reprint no. 152, 1971); George Strauss, "Directions in Industrial Relations Research," *LLJ*, Aug. 1978; George Strauss and Peter Feuille, "Industrial Relations Research: A Critical Analysis," *IR*, Oct. 1978; U.S. Dept. of Labor, *Labor Management Relations Research Priorities for the 1980's, Final Report to the Secretary of Labor* (Washington: 1980); Max S. Wortman, Jr., "The Role of Collective Bargaining Research in Industrial Relations," *LLJ*, Sept. 1961.

See also LABOR RESEARCH.

research, labor *See* LABOR RESEARCH.

research methods The procedural techniques utilized in carrying through research projects. These techniques also may be used for evaluations of programs and to determine the validity of new hypotheses or to test old ones.

By and large the methods of research in the field of industrial relations are similar to those in other fields except that the materials with which the social scientists deal are not as susceptible to close experimentation or the use of mathematical techniques. There may also be a larger number of variables in the area of social behavior than in the physical and natural sciences.

Research methods concern themselves not only with problems of the establishment of a research design, and the application of scientific methodology, but also with the understanding of the sampling procedure, and the use and understanding of probability, as well as the ability to analyze factual data (compact or loose) and to summarize and interpret them clearly and accurately.

Source references: Jacques Barzun and Henry F. Graff, *The Modern Researcher* (New York: Harcourt, Brace, 1957); John Dewey, *Logic: The Theory of Inquiry* (New York: Holt, 1938); Robert Ferber and P. J. Verdoorn, *Research Methods in Economics and Business* (New York: Macmillan, 1962); William J. Goode and Paul K. Hatt, *Methods in Social Research* (New York: McGraw-Hill, 1952); Homer C. Hockett, *The Critical Method in Historical Research and Writing* (New York: Macmillan, 1955); James B. Quinn, "How to Evaluate Research Output," *Harvard BR*, March/April 1960; James B. Quinn and James A. Mueller, "Transferring Research Results to Operations," *Harvard BR*, Jan./Feb. 1963.

reserved gate *See* PICKETING AT COMMON SITE (SITUS).

residency requirement A condition, generally established by a municipality, that employees must make their home in a particular jurisdiction in order to maintain employment.

According to Rubin there are two types of residency requirements—durational and continuous. "A durational residency requirement requires an individual to reside in a municipality or county for a designated period of time before he or she may be considered for employment by that municipality. . . . Continuous residency requirements allow nonresidents to be hired as long as they move within designated boundaries during a specified period after hire and maintain residency there for as long as they hold their public job."

Residency requirements have been challenged in a number of court cases as a violation of an employee's constitutional right to travel. Although the courts have ruled that an employer may not require job applicants to be residents *before* being considered for employment, they have held that an employer may require applicants to move to a jurisdiction and maintain residency as a condition of continued employment.

Source references: United Building and Construction Trades Council of Camden County and Vicinity v. Mayor and Council of the City of Camden et al., U.S. Sup.Ct. No. 81–2110 (1984); Michael Hacker, "Locked in the City: Residency Requirements for Municipal Employees," *Industrial and Labor Relations Forum*, Summer 1975; Stephen L. Hayford and William A. Durkee, "Residency Requirements in Local Government Employment: The Impact of the Public Employer's Duty to Bargain," *LLJ*, June 1978; Richard E. Kroopnick, "Municipal Residency Requirements: Constitutional and Collective Bargaining Aspects," *IR Law Digest*, Fall 1975; Thomas J. Lynch, "Public Employment Residency Requirements and the Duty to Bargain," *Journal of Collective Negotiations in the Public Sector*, Vol. 9, no. 3, 1980; Charles S. Rhyne, William S. Rhyne, and Stephen P. Elmendorf, *The Constitutionality of Residency Requirements for Municipal Officials and Employees* (Washington: National Institute of Municipal Law Officers, Research Report 160, 1977); Richard S. Rubin, "The Battle Over Residency Requirements: New Approaches by Public Employees," *Employee Relations LJ*, Autumn 1978.

residual claimant theory (wages) A theory in economics which postulated that labor is the residual claimant of the products of industry. Under this theory it was contended that wages equal the product of industry less the rent, interest, and profit (preferred claimants), and that the laborer is the residual claimant. It also was held that if the total amount of production of a community increased, the benefit would accrue to the laboring class in the form of increased wages.

Henry George and Francis Walker denied the existence of a rigid wages fund which did not permit any increase in the amount of wages. The residual claimant theory implied the possibility that workers stood to receive benefit from increases in the productivity of a community.

Source references: Lewis H. Haney, *History of Economic Thought* (4th ed., New York: Macmillan, 1953); Henry Higgs (ed.), *Palgrave's Dictionary of Political Economy* (new ed., 3 vol., London: Macmillan, 1926); Broadus Mitchell, *A Preface to Economics* (New York: Holt, 1932).

resignation A term connoting the (usually permanent) severance, on the employee's initiative, of the employment relationship. In the event of resignation the employee generally gives notice to the employer and frequently will set the time when the resignation is to take effect.

Resignation differs from the "quit" in which the employee also severs his employment relationship on a permanent basis, in that generally a "quit" does not involve giving notice.

See also QUIT.

res judicata Literally means a matter settled by judgment. It is a legal principle which holds that once a case has been properly determined, the issues may not be relitigated. The courts normally will accord res judicata to an arbitrator's decision. The Supreme Court, however, in *Alexander v. Gardner-Denver Co.* indicated in a footnote that res judicata may not be applied to arbitration if the case also involves a challenge under Title VII of the Civil Rights Act of 1964.

Source references: Alexander v. Gardner-Denver Co., 415 US 36, 7 FEP Cases 81 (1974); Henry Campbell Black, *Black's Law Dictionary* (abridged 5th ed., St. Paul: West Pub., 1983); Katharine Seide, *A Dictionary of Arbitration and Its Terms* (Dobbs Ferry, N.Y.: Oceana Publications, 1970).

responsibility of unions *See* UNION RESPONSIBILITY.

rest period A short interruption during the work period. There generally is no loss of pay during the rest period.

Source references: Richard N. Butler, "How Our Company Answered the Coffee

Break Question," *PJ*, March 1955; R. Lund, "Rest Periods: Equivalent to Two Weeks With Pay," *Management Review*, May 1953; U.S. Dept. of Labor, BLS, *Rest Periods, Washup, Work Clothing, and Military Leave Provisions in Major Union Contracts* (Washington: Bull. no. 1279, 1961); Dena G. Weiss and Ernestine M. Moore, "Paid Rest Periods in Major Union Contracts, 1959," *MLR*, Sept. 1960.

See also FATIGUE, RELIEF PERIOD.

restraining order *See* INJUNCTION.

restraint of trade A concept developed through the common law in England and the United States which has played an important part in labor-management relations. The Sherman Anti-Trust Act was designed to limit or prohibit action in restraint of trade.

Professor Daugherty in 1941 discussed the doctrine with respect to labor thus:

> The doctrine of restraint of trade has also been important in the settlement of labor disputes. It has long been part of the common law in England and America. Briefly, the substance of the doctrine is this: Trade or commerce within a state or among states is said to be restrained under three sets of circumstances—when the public is injured by being cut off from normal access to the commodity market; when freedom of competition is hampered by employers; and when employers are prevented from the usual access to the labor market. A great variety of acts performed by labor and other combinations have the effect of restraining trade in one or more of these ways, yet such acts are not all necessarily unlawful. There are two main tests of legality. First, the trade of certain employers or groups is always restrained by competitive acts of others, and such restraint is illegal only if it is unreasonable and unjustifiable; that is to say, only if the restrainers cause harm or inconvenience to the public or are not exercising equal or superior rights of their own in their interference with the rights of others. Second, any restraint of trade is illegal if accomplished by coercion, fraud, violence, or other unlawful methods.
>
> If trade is illegally restrained under either of these two counts, it follows that any combination, labor or otherwise, which has been formed to effect the restraint is also illegal and a conspiracy. As a matter of fact, in labor disputes the common law doctrines of conspiracy and restraint of trade have often been employed together; the phrase "conspiracy in restraint of trade" has a familiar ring. Thus, the purpose of the labor combination may be to restrain trade illegally. The restraint of trade doctrine is, nevertheless, a broader thing than the conspiracy doctrine. According to the conspiracy principles a combination's motives are bad only if they unjustifiably prejudice the rights of two groups—employers and nonunionists. But the restraint of trade doctrine includes a third, much larger group—the public. If the public's rights are unjustifiably interfered with, a strike or a boycott may be declared an illegal restraint of trade for that reason alone.

Professor C. O. Gregory considered that the phrase "restraint of trade" is much too vague and one which provides no real guide for its interpretation by the courts. Professor Gregory said in part:

> . . . this phrase has the delusive exactness of a good many other well-known words and phrases of general import current in our language . . . Justice Holmes is said to have thought . . . they [the words "restraint of trade"] were almost meaningless, amounting to little, if anything, more than a fiat from Congress to the federal courts to do right by the consuming public in protecting it from the depredations of big enterprise. It set forth no economic program at all and took no position, implying at most what English and American courts had thought as a matter of common law to be the meaning of the phrase "restraint of trade." This invitation to the courts to exploit their own economic philosophy in controlling big enterprises of all sort Holmes is said to have considered so vague and irresponsible as to merit being declared unconstitutional.

Source references: Carroll R. Daugherty, *Labor Problems in American Industry* (New York: Houghton Mifflin, 1941); Charles O. Gregory, *Labor and the Law* (2d rev. ed., New York: Norton, 1961); Bruce F. Kennedy, "Labor-Antitrust: Collective Bargaining and the Competitive Economy," *IR Law Digest*, Jan. 1969; Theodore J. St. Antoine, "The Rational Regulation of Union Restrictive Practices," *Labor Law Developments 1968*, Proceedings of 14th Annual Institute on Labor Law, SLF (New York: Bender, 1968).

See also APEX HOSIERY CO. V. LEADER; BEDFORD CUT STONE CO. V. JOURNEYMEN STONE CUTTERS' ASSOCIATION; CONSPIRACY DOCTRINE; HUTCHESON CASE; PENNINGTON CASE; SHERMAN ACT OF 1890.

restriction of membership Limitation of their membership by unions to keep it from outrunning job opportunities. A variety of practices has been utilized and these have been summarized by Professor Albion G. Taylor, who says in part: "The apprenticeship system has afforded trade unions a means of limiting the supply of skilled labor and maintaining desirable standards. So long as skill was required for trade operations, the period of training supplied a practical barrier to entrance. . . . Other methods employed by unionists in their attempt to restrict the supply of labor include (1) high initiation fees, (2) the maintenance of a closed shop with a closed union, (3) the establishment of jurisdictional restrictions, and (4) the restriction of eligibility for membership."

Source references: Jerome A. Cooper, "Trade Union Compliance With Presidential Directives; Membership Acceptance; Seniority; Etc.," *NYU 17th Annual Conference on Labor*, ed. by Thomas Christensen (Washington: BNA, 1964); R. W. Rideout, "The Content of Trade Union Rules Regulating Admission," *BJIR*, March 1966; Bonnie L. Siber, "The Security of Unions and Equal Employment Opportunity: Can the Two Exist?" *Industrial and Labor Relations Forum*, Oct. 1974; Albion G. Taylor, *Labor Problems and Labor Law* (2d ed., New York: PH, 1950); U.S. Dept. of Labor, LMSA, *Admission and Apprenticeship in the Building Trades Unions* (Washington: 1971).

See also APPRENTICESHIP, CLOSED UNION, INITIATION FEE, LIMITATION OF MEMBERSHIP, UNION MEMBERSHIP.

restriction of output Actual or tacit agreement among workers to limit output below a standard of efficiency which could be maintained without risk to either the health or safety of the individual. Restrictive practices include slowdowns, featherbedding, make-work rules, or limitations which result from job standards so set to prevent unemployment or to "make" work. It may involve the use of equipment which is not the most productive or other limitations agreed to by employers and unions, but which over a period become outmoded and restrictive.

The theory upon which limitations of output are justified apparently is that there is a limited amount of work available and that efforts to speed up the work will result normally in the loss of jobs or in reduction of paid work hours. In addition, it has been maintained that a degree of uniformity in output keyed to average production may help standardize work opportunities and eliminate "speedup."

It should be noted that restrictions of output are not limited to efforts on the part of labor or for that matter even organized labor. Employers and manufacturers frequently will restrict output by limiting the number of produced units or in other ways, in order to increase the value of their product or service and not necessarily to increase its volume. Manufacturers as well as workers have had to view their particular actions in the light of what they conceive to be stabilizing and desirable for themselves and not in light of the interests of the total economy.

Source references: Chamber of Commerce of the U.S., *The Menace of Restrictive Work Practices* (Washington: 1963); Harry Cohen, "Dimensions of Restriction of Output," *PJ*, Dec. 1971; Richard P. Maher, "Union Contract Restrictions on Productivity," *LLJ*, May 1983; Stanley B. Matthewson, *Restriction of Output Among Unorganized Workers* (New York: Viking Press, 1931); C. Wilson Randle, "Restrictive Practices of Unionism," *Southern Economic Journal*, Oct. 1948; Theodore J. St. Antoine, "The Rational Regulation of Union Restrictive Practices," *Labor Law Developments 1968*, Proceedings of the 14th Annual Institute on Labor Law, SLF (New York: Bender, 1968); Sumner H. Slichter, "Make Work Rules and Policies," *Union Policies and Industrial Management* (Washington: Brookings Institution, 1941); John R. Van de Water, "Legal and Managerial Control of Work Restrictions in Industry," *LLJ*, Sept. 1963.

See also BOGEY, CA' CANNY, FEATHERBEDDING, LIMITATION OF OUTPUT, MAKE-WORK PRACTICES, SLOWDOWN, SPEED-UP.

Retail Clerks International Association (AFL-CIO) An international union organized in Detroit, Michigan, in December 1890 which extended its jurisdiction to Canada in 1899 and took the name of Retail Clerks International Protective Association. The union changed its name to the Retail Clerks International Association in 1947, then to the

Retail Clerks International Union in the mid-1970s.

Source references: Michael Harrington, *The Retail Clerks* (New York: Wiley, 1962); George C. Kirstin, *Stores and Unions: A Study of the Growth of Unionism in Drygoods and Department Stores* (New York: Fairchild, 1950); Jess P. Lacklen, Jr. and Miriam B. Wise, *Unionization in the Retail Field* (New York: NY School of Retailing, 1940); Mary LaDame, *The Filene Store; A Study of Employees' Relation to Management in a Retail Store* (New York: Russell Sage Foundation, 1930).

See also RETAIL CLERKS INTERNATIONAL UNION (AFL-CIO).

Retail Clerks International Union (AFL-CIO) Formerly known as the Retail Clerks International Association, the name was changed to the Retail Clerks International Union in the mid-1970s. The Boot and Shoe Workers' Union (AFL-CIO) merged with the union on September 1, 1977.

On June 7, 1979, the union merged with the Amalgamated Meat Cutters and Butcher Workmen of North America (AFL-CIO) to form the United Food and Commercial Workers International Union (AFL-CIO).

See also FOOD AND COMMERCIAL WORKERS INTERNATIONAL UNION; UNITED (AFL-CIO).

Retail, Wholesale and Department Store Union (AFL-CIO) The organization first was set up by a group of locals in 1937 who had been expelled from the Retail Clerks International Protective Association.

Over the years a number of unions have merged with the Retail Union: the Distributive, Processing and Office Workers of America (Ind) and the Playthings, Jewelry and the Novelty Workers International Union (CIO) in May 1954; the United Department Store Workers of America (CIO) in March 1955; and the Cigar Makers' International Union of America (AFL-CIO) on June 1, 1974.

On March 28, 1969, District 65 disaffiliated itself from the union and formed the National Council of Distributive Workers of America (Ind).

Its monthly publication is *The Record.*

Address: 30 East 29th St., New York, N.Y. 10016. Tel. (212) 684–5300

Source reference: Max Greenberg, "The Retail, Wholesale and Department Store Union," *American Federationist,* July 1959.

See also DISTRIBUTIVE WORKERS OF AMERICA; NATIONAL COUNCIL OF (IND).

retirement A voluntary or forced severance of employment because of age, disability, or illness. Generally the individual withdraws permanently from gainful work and lives on retirement allowance or a pension.

Source references: Robert C. Atchley, "Retirement: Leaving the World of Work," *Annals,* Nov. 1982; Leland P. Bradford, "Can You Survive Your Retirement?" *Harvard BR,* Nov./Dec. 1979; Joseph C. Buckley, *The Retirement Handbook: A Complete Guide to Your Future* (2d rev. ed., New York: Harper, 1962); John Clewis, "The Gray Panthers Are Coming: Is Your Institution Ready?" *Journal of the College and University Personnel Association,* Summer 1981; Peter D. Couch and Earl F. Lundgren, "Making Voluntary Retirement Programs Work," *PJ,* March 1963; J. H. Foegen, "Time to Be Honest—With Older Employees," *Public Personnel Management,* Sept./Oct. 1973; Lowell E. Gallaway, *The Retirement Decision: An Exploratory Essay* (Washington: U.S. Dept. of HEW, SSA, Research Report no. 9, 1965); Margaret S. Gordon, "Work and Patterns of Retirement," *Aging and Leisure,* ed. by Robert W. Kleemeier (New York: Oxford UP, 1961); Jeanne Prial Gordus, *Leaving Early, Perspectives and Problems in Current Retirement Practice and Policy* (Kalamazoo: Upjohn Institute for Employment Research, 1980); Lola M. Irelan et al., *Almost 65: Baseline Data From the Retirement History Study* (Washington: U.S. Dept. of HEW, SSA, Research Report 49, 1977); Juanita M. Kreps, "A Case Study of Variables in Retirement Policy," *MLR,* June 1961; Elon H. Moore, *The Nature of Retirement,* ed. by Gordon F. Streib (New York: Macmillan, 1959); J. Roger O'Meara, *Retirement: Reward or Rejection?* (New York: The Conference Board, Report 713, 1977); ———, "Retirement—The Eighth Age of Man," *Conference Board Record,* Oct. 1974; Clarence B. Randall, "The Myth of Retirement," *Dun's Review,* Dec. 1960; Shirley H. Rhine, *American's Aging Population: Issues Facing Business and Society* (New York: The

Conference Board, Report 785, 1980); Philip L. Rones, "The Retirement Decision: A Question of Opportunity?" *MLR*, Nov. 1980; Yitzchak M. Shkop, "The Impact of Job Modification Options on Retirement Plans," *IR*, Spring 1982; Yitzchak M. Shkop and Ester M. Shkop, "Job Modification as an Alternative to Retirement," *PJ*, July 1982; Gordon F. Streib and Clement J. Schneider, *Retirement in American Society: Impact and Process* (Ithaca: Cornell UP, 1971); U.S. Dept. of Labor, BLS, *Pension Plans Under Collective Bargaining: Normal Retirement, Early and Disability Retirement, Fall 1959* (Washington: Bull. no. 1284, 1961); James W. Walker and Harriet L. Lazar, *The End of Mandatory Retirement; Implications for Management* (New York: Wiley, 1978).

See also DEFERRED RETIREMENT DATE; EARLY RETIREMENT; NORMAL RETIREMENT AGE; OLDER WORKER; PRERETIREMENT EDUCATION; RETIREMENT, COMPULSORY; RETIREMENT, TRANSITIONAL.

retirement, compulsory Provision in collective bargaining agreements, company policy, or law which compels retirement of employees at a fixed age. Where contractual provisions are made for retirement of employees, arrangements usually are made for retirement benefits depending on length of service and earnings with the company.

A distinction is usually made between compulsory and automatic retirement under the terms of the pension plan. An employee may work beyond the compulsory retirement age if the employer consents, but automatic retirement rules out this option on both sides.

Source references: Douglas L. Bartley, "Compulsory Retirement: A Reevaluation," *Personnel*, March/April 1977; Michael D. Batten, "Legal Challenges to Mandatory and Involuntary Retirement: Policy Considerations," *Journal of the College and University Personnel Association*, Winter 1978; "Compulsory Retirement of Superannuated Workers Under Collective Bargaining Agreements," *Illinois LR*, March/April 1950; Dorothy R. Kittner, "Forced Retirement: How Common Is It?" *MLR*, Dec. 1977; Harmon K. Murphey, "Against Compulsory Retirement," *PJ*, July/Aug. 1956; Karl M. Ruppenthal, "Compulsory Retirement of Airline Pilots," *ILRR*, July 1961; Anne R. Somers, *Social, Economic, and Health Aspects of Mandatory Retirement* (Princeton: Princeton Univ., IR Section, Reprint, 1981); U.S. Congress, House, Select Committee on Aging, *Abolishing Mandatory Retirement (Implications for America and Social Security of Eliminating Age Discrimination in Employment)*, An Interim Report Prepared by the U.S. Dept. of Labor as Required by the Age Discrimination in Employment Act (Washington: 1981); ———, *Mandatory Retirement: The Social and Human Cost of Enforced Idleness, Report* (Washington: 1977); Jonathan A. Weiss and Jay P. Warren, "Mandatory Retirement is Unethical and Inefficient," *Employee Relations LJ*, Spring 1977; Norman J. Wood, "The Challenge to Mandatory Retirement," *LLJ*, July 1976.

See also AGE DISCRIMINATION IN EMPLOYMENT ACT OF 1967, MURGIA CASE.

retirement, flexible A plan which does not require retirement at a fixed or compulsory age, or combines features of voluntary and compulsory retirement plans. The employee may continue working at his job as long as it is performed in a satisfactory manner and there is use for his services, or until he attains a later compulsory retirement age. For example, no upper age limit may be set for some categories of employees but retirement is compulsory at normal retirement age (usually 65) or at a later than normal age for other employees. Or, retirement may be required at normal retirement age for some categories, and compulsory at an age later than normal retirement age for other employees.

Source references: Malcolm H. Morrison, "The Future of Flexible Retirement," *Journal of the College and University Personnel Association*, Winter 1978; Fred Slavick, *Compulsory and Flexible Retirement in the American Economy* (Ithaca: Cornell Univ., NYSSILR, 1966).

See also PENSION PLAN; RETIREMENT, COMPULSORY; RETIREMENT, VOLUNTARY.

retirement, transitional Programs to help employees adjust from full-time employment to retirement. Such programs may include (1) extended vacations with pay to take place some time before the retirement year, and

(2) allowing older employees to reduce their work year, workweek, or workday.

Source references: "Gradual Retirement: Three Programs That Can Ease the Transition," *Management Review*, Oct. 1967; Gloria W. White, "Bridge Over Troubled Waters: An Approach to Early Retirement," *Journal of the College and University Personnel Association*, Summer 1981.

See also BRIDGING.

retirement, voluntary Company policy of setting no formal age for retirement, but which permits employees to work so long as they are physically and mentally capable of performing their work.

See also PENSION PLAN; RETIREMENT, COMPULSORY; RETIREMENT, FLEXIBLE.

retirement age Generally set between 60 or 65 years, when a person becomes eligible for retirement or for a pension if one is provided by collective bargaining agreement. A different approach to the retirement age is to assess the individual's productive capacity. The retirement age in this approach is based primarily upon the ability of the individual to make a productive contribution to the work of his employer, usually in his own line of work.

Source references: Arden Hall and Terry R. Johnson, "The Determinants of Planned Retirement Age," *ILRR*, Jan. 1980; Thomas S. Litras, "The Battle Over Retirement Policies and Practices," *PJ*, Feb. 1979; Thomas F. Lundy, "Is the Inflexible, Compulsory Retirement Age of Sixty-Five Out-Moded?" (Unpublished M.B.A. Thesis, NYU, 1957); Elizabeth L. Meier and Cynthia C. Dittmar, *Varieties of Retirement Ages* (Washington: U.S. President's Commission on Pension Policy, Working Papers, 1980); Jack F. Rhode, "Fixed or Variable Retirement Age?" *Personnel Administration*, Jan./Feb. 1961; Sara E. Rix, "Rethinking Retirement-Age Policy in the United States and Canada," *PJ*, Nov. 1979; Sumner H. Slichter, "Retirement Age and Social Policy," *The Aged and Society*, ed. by J. Douglas Brown, Clark Kerr, and Edwin W. Witte (Champaign: IRRA Pub. no. 5, 1950).

See also AGE DISCRIMINATION IN EMPLOYMENT ACT OF 1967; EARLY RETIREMENT; MURGIA CASE; NORMAL RETIREMENT AGE; PENSIONABLE AGE; RETIREMENT, COMPULSORY.

retirement allowances *See* PENSION.

retirement annuity A general term to describe the income available to an individual upon retirement. There are many forms of annuities.

See also ANNUITY.

Retirement Equity Act of 1984 Amendment to the Employee Retirement Income Security Act (ERISA) of 1974 which, among other provisions, lowers the maximum age for participation in a pension plan from 25 to 21 and for vesting from 21 to 18, permits an individual to be absent for five consecutive years from the labor force and still remain eligible for pension benefits, and treats a one-year maternity or paternity leave as no break in service for pension benefits. The law also eliminates the prior ERISA requirement that participants must affirmatively elect to receive survivor coverage for the years the participant is employed by his or her employer. The Act replaces this election with automatic survivor coverage for vested participants whether or not they have reached the earliest retirement age.

The law is effective December 31, 1984, for existing pension plans. For collectively bargained plans, it becomes effective upon expiration of such plans, or January 1, 1987, whichever occurs first.

Source references: Retirement Equity Act of 1984, Pub. L. 98–397, Aug. 23, 1984, 98 Stat. 1426; CCH, *Retirement Equity Act of 1984, Law and Explanation* (Chicago: 1984).

retirement fund *See* PENSION FUND.

retirement plans *See* PENSION PLAN.

retirement procedures The mechanics of dealing with retirement in a business enterprise or in the public service. This involves not only creation of a fund, its financing, and so forth, but also the eligibility of the individual for retirement, the payments to be made, and all of the procedural details which have to be worked out under trust arrangements.

Source references: Helen Baker, *Retirement Procedures Under Compulsory and Flexible Retirement Policies* (Princeton:

Princeton Univ., IR Section, Research Report Series no. 86, 1952); Lenore Epstein Bixby, "Retirement Age Policy and Employment," *Journal of the College and University Personnel Association*, Summer 1979; Robert W. Hartman, "Retirement for Federal Civil Servants: Down from the Incomparable," *Proceedings of the 33d A/M, IRRA*, ed. by Barbara Dennis (Madison: 1981); Tax Foundation, Inc., *Employee Pension Systems in State and Local Government* (New York: Research Pub. 3, 1976); U.S. Congressional Budget Office, *Civil Service Retirement: Financing and Costs* (Washington: 1981).

See also PENSION PLAN.

retirement system *See* PENSION PLAN.

retraining The efforts by labor and management, or government, to utilize the existing work force and skills and to establish programs and training activities to fit individuals into new skills or change of skills made necessary by changing technology.

Source references: Fred A. Auman, "Retraining—How Much of an Answer to Technological Unemployment?" *PJ*, Nov. 1962; Michael E. Borus, "The Cost of Retraining the Hard-Core Unemployed," *LLJ*, Sept. 1965; Nelson H. Cruikshank, "Retraining the Unemployed," *American Federationist*, March 1962; Rennard Davis, "Retraining the Unemployed: III—Skill Improvement Training for Electricians and Plumbers," *MLR*, Oct. 1961; Phyllis Groom, "Retraining the Unemployed: I—European Government Programs," *MLR*, Aug. 1961; ———, "Retraining the Unemployed: II—Federal and State Legislation on Retraining," *MLR*, Sept. 1961; ———, "Retraining the Unemployed: IV—The Bridgeport Program," *MLR*, Jan. 1962; Einar Hardin and Michael E. Borus, "Benefits and Costs of MDTA–ARA Retraining," *IR*, May 1972; Ida R. Hoos, "Retraining in the United States: Problems and Progress," *ILR*, Nov. 1965; Raymond D. Larson and Max Horten, "The Retraining Issue," *The Labor Market and Social Security*, Proceedings of the 14th Annual Social Security Conference, January 23–24, 1962 (Kalamazoo: Upjohn Institute, 1962); Robert W. Scull, "Planned Renewal—Preparing Workers for Competitive Jobs," *Sloan Management Review*, Summer 1981; Gerald G. Somers (ed.), *Retraining the Unemployed* (Madison: Univ. of Wisconsin Press, 1968); U.S. Dept. of Labor, BLS, *Improving Productivity: Labor and Management Approaches* (Washington: Bull. 1715, 1971); ———, *Major Collective Bargaining Agreements: Training and Retraining Provisions* (Washington: Bull. no. 1425–7, 1969); U.S. National Center for Productivity and Quality of Working Life, *Productivity and Job Security: Retraining to Adapt to Technological Change* (Washington: 1977); Lawrence Williams, "Training Older Workers in New Skills: Some Guides for the Supervisor," *Supervisory Management*, March 1963.

See also TECHNOLOGICAL UNEMPLOYMENT, TRAINING.

retraining program Any basic, planned program designed primarily for experienced employees who because of changing technology, work rotation, reassignment, etc., need to develop new skills and direct their abilities toward different objectives.

retrenchment Adoption of a smaller scale of operations in an organization. Retrenchment may result in layoffs as part of the effort to reduce the work force.

The term is frequently used in referring to reduction in programs and faculty of higher education institutions. Retrenchment in higher education usually occurs as a result of financial exigency and declining enrollment. During severe fiscal conditions, it may require the dismissal of tenured faculty.

Source references: James R. Mingle and Associates, *Challenges of Retrenchment* (San Francisco: Jossey-Bass, 1981); George Spiro, "Facing Reductions in Force in Higher Education," *Journal of the College and University Personnel Association*, Summer 1980; "Tenure and Retrenchment Practices in Higher Education—A Technical Report," *Journal of the College and University Personnel Association*, Fall/Winter 1980.

retroactive pay Wages or other payments which are due an employee either because of an agreement between the union and the company to pay such wages pending the outcome of an arbitration award on wages, or pending the determination of a particular incentive wage. The employee receives current wages but will receive retroactive pay if the rate being earned is less than the rate the worker is entitled to receive.

In cases involving the NLRB or a state board reinstating an employee to remedy an unfair labor practice discharge, the employee may be made whole and receive retroactive pay from the time of the discharge less earnings during that period. For most purposes, "retroactive pay" and "back pay" are used interchangeably.

See also BACK PAY, MAKE WHOLE.

retroactive seniority Remedy granted by courts in Title VII actions to victims of discrimination in the form of seniority they would have had if there had been no discrimination. The granting of so-called "remedial," "fictional," "constructive," or "phantom" seniority has engendered a great deal of controversy and litigation.

Source references: EEOC v. Detroit Edison Co., 515 F2d 301, 10 FEP Cases 239 (1975); *Franks v. Bowman Transportation Co.*, 424 US 747, 12 FEP Cases 549 (1976); *Local 189, United Papermakers and Paperworkers v. U.S.*, 416 F2d 980, 1 FEP Cases 875 (1969); *Watkins v. United Steelworkers of America, Local 2369*, 516 F2d 41, 10 FEP Cases 1297 (1975); Vincent J. Apruzzese, "Seniority and its Place in Equal Employment Opportunity—An Analysis of Current Problems," *Labor Law Developments 1977*, Proceedings of 23d Annual Institute on Labor Law, SLF (New York: Bender, 1977); Thomas R. Bagby, "The Supreme Court Reaffirms Broad Immunity for Seniority Systems," *LLJ*, July 1982; Alan V. Friedman and Allen M. Katz, "Retroactive Seniority for the Identifiable Victim Under Title VII—Must Last Hired, First Fired Give Way," *NYU 28th Annual Conference on Labor*, ed. by Richard Adelman (New York: Bender, 1976); Susan C. Ross, "Reconciling Plant Seniority with Affirmative Action and Anti-Discrimination," *NYU 28th Annual Conference on Labor*, ed. by Richard Adelman (New York: Bender, 1976); "Title VII, Seniority Discrimination, and the Incumbent Negro," 80 *Harvard LR* 1260 (1967).

See also SENIORITY, TEAMSTERS V. U.S.

retroactive wage payment *See* BACK PAY.

retrogression A procedure in some contracts which permits individuals (who because of accident, physical impairment, and occasionally because of incapacity due to age have become less productive) to move back to a job which makes less onerous demands on the individual and still permits the individual to keep a job and his seniority and other rights.

reverse discrimination The claim that affirmative action measures undertaken by employers, labor organizations, and other persons in compliance with Title VII of the Civil Rights Act of 1964 accord preferential treatment to individuals on the basis of race or sex and thereby discriminate against nonminority individuals, i.e., whites and/or males. Two major Supreme Court decisions on claims of reverse discrimination are *Regents of University of California v. Bakke* and *Steelworkers v. Weber*.

Source references: U.S. EEOC, "Affirmative Action Appropriate Under Title VII of the Civil Rights Act of 1964, as amended," 29 C.F.R. 1608; Robert Mauldin Elliot, "Reverse Discrimination: The Balancing of Human Rights," *IR Law Digest*, Spring 1977; Nathan Glazer, *Affirmative Discrimination: Ethnic Inequality and Public Policy* (New York: Basic Books, 1975); Deborah Greenberg, "Reverse Discrimination in Employment," *NYU 30th Annual National Conference on Labor*, ed. by Richard Adelman (New York: Bender, 1977); Barry R. Gross (ed.), *Reverse Discrimination* (Buffalo: Prometheus Books, 1977); Sidney Hook and Miro Todorovich, "The Tyranny of Reverse Discrimination," *Change*, Winter 1975/76; Gopal C. Pati and Charles W. Reilly, "Reversing Discrimination: A Perspective," *LLJ*, Jan. 1978; "Reverse Discrimination," *FEP* 421:945; David E. Robertson and Ronald D. Johnson, "Reverse Discrimination: Did *Weber* Decide the Issue?" *LLJ*, Nov. 1980; Dennis H. Vaughn, "Employment Quotas—Discrimination or Affirmative Action?" *Employee Relations LJ*, Spring 1982.

See also BAKKE CASE, WEBER CASE.

Revised Order No. 4 Regulations covering federal nonconstruction contractors issued by the OFCCP to implement provisions of Executive Order 11246. It sets out the required contents of affirmative action plans, utilization analysis, projections of goals and timetables, and other actions related to development or reaffirmation of equal employment opportunity policy.

Source reference: U.S. OFCCP, "Revised Order No. 4," 41 C.F.R. 60–2.

See also COMPLIANCE REVIEW, EXECUTIVE ORDER 11246, GOALS AND TIMETABLES, OFFICE OF FEDERAL CONTRACT COMPLIANCE PROGRAMS (OFCCP), UTILIZATION ANALYSIS.

Revised Order No. 14 OFCCP regulation issued in 1972 establishing "standardized contractor evaluation procedures for conducting compliance reviews" of nonconstruction federal contractors.

Source reference: U.S. OFCCP, "Revised Order No. 14," 41 C.F.R. 60–60.

See also COMPLIANCE REVIEW, OFFICE OF FEDERAL CONTRACT COMPLIANCE PROGRAMS (OFCCP).

revision of agreement *See* AGREEMENT REVISION.

revolutionary unionism "Revolutionary unionism" has been considered to be primarily a form of trade unionism which is "radical" in philosophy and in policy, and has as its prime desire the overthrow of modern capitalism and the substitution of some new and different form of society.

Some historians of the trade union movement, like Professor R. F. Hoxie, say that "Revolutionary unionism is in essence a spiritual something, a group viewpoint, a theory and interpretation of society and social relationships held by groups of militant wage workers, and an attempt to realize this theory and interpretation by means of a program of action."

A carefully considered classification of revolutionary unionism is one set out by Professor Albion Taylor. He describes three main groups—the first, Socialistic; the second, quasi-anarchistic, and the third, Communistic.

Source references: John G. Brooks, *American Syndicalism: The IWW* (New York: Macmillan, 1913); ———, *Labor's Challenge to the Social Order: Democracy, Its Own Critic and Education* (New York: Macmillan, 1920); Paul K. Crosser, *Ideologies and American Labor* (New York: Oxford UP, 1941); Daniel DeLeon, *Socialist Landmarks* (New York: Labor News, 1952); Chester M. Destler, *American Radicalism, 1865–1901* (New London: Connecticut College, 1946); Theodore Draper, *The Roots of American Communism* (New York: Viking, 1957); William Z. Foster, *Pages From a Worker's Life* (New York: International Pub., 1939); Emma Goldman, *Anarchism and Other Essays* (New York: Mother Earth Pub., 1910); Robert F. Hoxie, *Trade Unionism in the United States* (New York: Appleton, 1931); Sydney Lens, *Left, Right and Center: Conflicting Forces in American Labor* (Hinsdale: Regnery, 1949); Austin Lewis, *The Militant Proletariat* (Chicago: Kerr, 1911); David J. Saposs, *Left-Wing Unionism* (New York: International Pub., 1926); Sylvia K. Selekman, *Rebellion in Labor Unions* (New York: Boni, Liveright, 1924); John Spargo, *Syndicalism, Industrial Unionism, and Socialism* (New York: Huebsch, 1913); Albion Guilford Taylor, *Labor Problems and Labor Law* (New York: PH, 1939).

See also COMMUNISM IN AMERICAN LABOR UNIONS, RADICAL UNIONISM, SYNDICALISM, TRADE UNION UNITY LEAGUE.

"rightful place" According to the OFCCP, "the job an affected-class member would now hold had there been no discrimination."

One of three interpretations of Title VII and its application to discriminatory seniority systems, this approach holds that the continued maintenance of the relative competitive disadvantage imposed on blacks by the past operation of a discriminatory system violates Title VII, just as the continued use of the discriminatory rules which created the differential would violate it. To eliminate the differential, this approach would allow an incumbent black to bid for openings in white jobs comparable to those held by whites of equal tenure (based on their full length of service with the employer). Under this approach, adjustments in competitive standing are required in future job movements as opposed to displacement of white incumbents.

Source references: EEOC v. Detroit Edison Co., 515 F2d 301, 10 FEP Cases 239 (1975); *Local 189, United Papermakers and Paperworkers v. U.S.*, 416 F2d 980, 1 FEP Cases 875 (1969); "Title VII, Seniority Discrimination, and the Incumbent Negro," 80 *Harvard*

LR 1260 (1967); U.S. OFCCP, *Federal Contract Compliance Manual* (Washington: 1979).

See also "FREEDOM NOW" THEORY, "STATUS QUO" THEORY.

right of assembly The freedom in democratic countries of individuals to assemble for the purpose of discussing matters of public interest and also to petition the authorities for changes or modifications.

The right of assembly applies essentially to the peaceful assembly of individuals, not to assembly for the purpose of committing an illegal act or a breach of public peace. The right is set forth in the First Amendment to the Constitution restricting the powers of Congress. It reads: "Congress shall make no law respecting an establishment of religion, or prohibiting the free exercise thereof; or abridging the freedom of speech, or the press; or the right of the people peaceably to assemble, and to petition the government for a redress of grievances."

right of association The term has been used as the equivalent of the right to organize, but historically the right of persons to get together and act for a common purpose or seek a common objective is far broader than the right of organization for purposes of collective bargaining. The right of association permits joint action of groups to do so without the necessity of obtaining a prior public grant of authority.

See also FREEDOM OF ASSOCIATION, RIGHT TO ORGANIZE.

rights arbitration *See* ARBITRATION, RIGHTS.

rights of union members Protection which may be available to union members both in relation to employers and their union.

Source references: Benjamin Aaron, "Employee Rights Under an Agreement: A Current Evaluation," *MLR*, Aug. 1971; ———, "Individual Employee Rights and Union Democracy," *Proceedings of the 21st A/M, IRRA*, ed. by Gerald Somers (Madison: 1969); Dee Edwards, "Rights of Individual Employee as a Member of or Against the Union," *LLJ*, May 1957; Paul N. Erickson, Jr. and Clifford E. Smith, "The Right of Union Representation During Investigatory Interviews," *AJ*, June 1978; Arthur J. Goldberg, "The Rights and Responsibilities of Union Members," *American Federationist*, Feb. 1958; Michael C. Harper, "Union Waiver of Employee Rights Under the NLRA: Part I," *Industrial Relations LJ*, Summer 1981; ———, "Union Waiver of Employee Rights Under the NLRA: Part II—A Fresh Approach to Board Deferral to Arbitration," *Industrial Relations LJ*, Vol. 4, no. 4, 1981; Eric Heyden, "Landrum-Griffin Section 101(a)(4)—Its Impact on Employee Rights," *Employee Relations LJ*, Spring 1982; Sar A. Levitan, "A Federal Assist to Guarantee the Rights of Union Members," *LLJ*, Feb. 1959; Anthony R. Marchione, "A Case for Individual Rights Under Collective Agreements," *LLJ*, Dec. 1976.

See also DUTY OF FAIR REPRESENTATION, LABOR-MANAGEMENT REPORTING AND DISCLOSURE ACT OF 1959, PUBLIC REVIEW BOARD (AFT), PUBLIC REVIEW BOARD (UAW), UNION MEMBERSHIP.

right to a job A claim made in some areas that once an individual has been employed and has satisfactorily met the job requirements, the right to have the job exists for the employee until the job becomes unavailable because of changes in economic conditions or dissolution of the company.

A more philosophic concept urges that in a democratic society every individual who is able and willing to work has a right to a job. This position is taken by unions particularly during periods of high unemployment when few job opportunities exist.

Source references: Frederic Meyers, *Ownership of Jobs: A Comparative Study* (Los Angeles: UC, Institute of IR, 1964); J. H. G. Pierson, *Full Employment* (New Haven: Yale UP, 1941): "Protecting Job Rights Through Attrition Clauses," *American Federationist*, June 1965.

See also FULL EMPLOYMENT.

right to bargain This phrase has to do with the collective bargaining rights of organizations under the provisions of federal and state laws, particularly when they have been certified as the collective bargaining agents of the employees in the appropriate bargaining unit. The right to bargain is retained as long as the unions are properly certified and have a majority in an appropriate unit.

See also CERTIFICATION, COLLECTIVE BARGAINING.

right to fire Prior to the advent of unions and the enactment of federal and state legislation, employers had the right to discharge an employee for any reason or for no reason. (The employee also had the right to leave employment with or without reason.)

Under the provisions of the National Labor Relations Act, the right to fire is limited. Employers are not permitted to discharge employees because of their efforts at organization, or to discriminate in respect "to hire and tenure of employment" because of union activity. Under the provisions of collective bargaining agreements, the employer still has the right to discharge employees for cause, but the contract generally will provide an opportunity to review the employer's action to determine whether adequate cause for such action exists in particular cases.

See also DISCHARGE, DISCIPLINE, EMPLOYMENT AT WILL, MANAGEMENT RIGHTS.

right to join a union Union rules may restrict membership to persons engaged in, or qualified to perform, the tasks of a specific occupation. Most of the older restrictions, such as closed shop conditions, eligibility only of offspring or other relatives of members, race, and the like, have been declared unlawful by statute. A good number of union constitutions bar membership to employers, "Fascists," Communists, and other groups.

Source references: R. W. Rideout, *The Right to Membership of a Trade Union* (London: Univ. of London, Athlone Press, 1963); Clyde Summers, "The Right to Join a Union," 47 *Columbia LR* 33 (1947).

See also CLOSED UNION, INITIATION FEE, LIMITATION OF MEMBERSHIP.

right to manage A phrase used synonymously with management rights or management prerogatives.

See also MANAGEMENT RIGHTS.

right to organize A protection necessary if employees are to engage in collective bargaining. This right is basic to national labor policy in the United States.

Source reference: Kurt Braun, *The Right to Organize and Its Limit* (Washington: Brookings Institution, 1950).

See also FREEDOM OF ORGANIZATION, NATIONAL LABOR RELATIONS ACT.

right to strike Generally, the right to strike is available to employees in the private sector under federal and state laws except that in some situations certain procedural steps must be taken before a strike may occur. This is particularly true in the case of the cooling-off procedures of the "national emergency disputes" section of the Taft-Hartley and Railway Labor Acts.

Public employment strikes are almost uniformly prohibited and laws usually provide for alternative methods of settling disputes. However, a few laws provide for the limited right to strike in the public sector.

Source references: Antone Aboud and Grace Sterrett Aboud, *The Right to Strike in Public Employment* (2d ed., Ithaca: Cornell Univ., NYSSILR, Key Issues Series no. 15, 1982); Jerome T. Barrett and Ira B. Lobel, "Public Sector Strikes—Legislative and Court Treatment," *MLR*, Sept. 1974; John F. Burton, Jr., *Public Sector Strikes: Legal, Ethical and Practical Considerations* (Ithaca: Cornell Univ., NYSSILR, Reprint 448, 1978); John T. Coughlin and Dennis W. Rader, "Right to Strike and Compulsory Arbitration: Panacea or Placebo?" 58 *Marquette LR* 205 (1975); J. H. Foegen, "A Qualified Right to Strike—In the Public Interest," *LLJ*, Feb. 1967; Louis V. Imundo, Jr., "Strikes and the Strike Issue in Federal Government Labor-Management Relations," *PJ*, May 1973; National Council of the Churches of Christ in the U.S.A., *The Right to Strike and the General Welfare* (New York: Council Press, 1967); Craig A. Olson, "The Use of the Legal Right to Strike in the Public Sector," *LLJ*, Aug. 1982; LeRoy H. Schramm, "The Job Rights of Strikers in the Public Sector," *ILRR*, April 1978; William J. Smith, *A Reasonable Restraint on the Right to Strike* (Jersey City: St. Paul's Institute of IR, 1962); Helene S. Tanimoto and Joyce M. Najita, *Guide to Statutory Provisions in Public Sector Collective Bargaining—Strike Rights and Prohibitions* (3d issue, Honolulu: Univ. of Hawaii, IRC, 1981); George W. Taylor, "Public Employment: Strikes or Procedures?" *ILRR*, July 1967; William W. Winpisinger, "There is no Alternative to the Right to Strike," *MLR*, Sept.

1973; Dallas M. Young and James Douglas Brown, Jr., "Two Views on the Right to Strike," *Personnel*, July/Aug. 1967.

See also NO-STRIKE CLAUSE, STRIKE, STRIKE PENALTY.

right to sue notice A notice issued by the EEOC to aggrieved persons under Title VII of the Civil Rights Act of 1964. The notice authorizes individuals to bring a civil action within 90 days from receipt of the notice. The right to sue notice will be issued under conditions, including the following instances:

(1) The EEOC has dismissed the charge,
(2) The aggrieved person requests that a notice of right to sue be issued and 180 days have passed after the date of filing of the charge, or
(3) The EEOC has been unable to obtain voluntary compliance.

Generally, the notice is issued by the attorney general in cases involving a government, governmental agency, or political subdivision.

Source reference: U.S. EEOC, "Procedural Regulations," 29 C.F.R. 1601.

Right to Work Committee *See* NATIONAL RIGHT TO WORK COMMITTEE.

right to work law Provisions in state laws which prohibit or make illegal arrangements between an employer and union (for union shop, closed shop, maintenance of membership, preferential hiring, or other union security provisions) which require membership in a union as a condition of obtaining or retaining employment.

State legislatures have the authority under the provisions of the Taft-Hartley Act to pass legislation more restrictive than the union security provisions of the federal law. The courts have upheld the right not only of the states to pass such legislation but also to enforce it.

Some of the states have also amended their constitutions to prohibit enactment of union security provisions within their respective jurisdictions.

Source references: Lincoln Union v. Northwestern I & M Company, 335 US 525, 23 LRRM 2199 (1949); AFL-CIO, *The Truth About Right to Work Laws: Facts vs. Propaganda* (Washington: 1966); Joseph A. Beirne, "The 'Right-to-Work' Issue," *American Federationist*, Oct. 1960; James T. Bennett and Manuel H. Johnson, "The Impact of Right-to-Work Laws on the Economic Behavior of Local Unions: A Property Rights Perspective," *Journal of Labor Research*, Spring 1980; Andrew J. Biemiller, "R-T-W Forces Try 'Back Door,'" *American Federationist*, Aug. 1961; Mary Ann Coghill, *Efforts to Repeal 14(B): A Review of Legislative Action by the 89th Congress on the Controversial Taft-Hartley Section* (Ithaca: Cornell Univ., NYSSILR, 1966); Joseph R. Dempsey, *The Operation of the Right-to-Work Laws* (Milwaukee: Marquette UP, 1961); J. C. Gibson, *The Legal and Moral Basis of Right to Work Laws* (Washington: National Right to Work Comm., 1960); Norman Hill, "The Double-Speak of Right-to-Work," *American Federationist*, Oct. 1980; Kenneth A. Kovach, "National Right to Work Law: An Affirmative Position," *LLJ*, May 1977; James W. Kuhn, "Right-to-Work Laws—Symbols or Substance?" *ILRR*, July 1961; William J. Lee, *Right-to-Work Laws: Some Economic and Ethical Aspects* (Washington: Catholic Univ. of America Press, 1961); Herbert H. Lehman, "'Right to Work' Laws Sow the Seeds of Depression," *American Federationist*, July 1959; Frederic Meyers, *"Right to Work" in Practice* (New York: Fund for the Republic, 1959); Ronald L. Miller, "Right-to-Work Laws and Compulsory Union Membership in the United States," *BJIR*, July 1976; William J. Moore, "Membership and Wage Impact of Right-to-Work Laws," *Journal of Labor Research*, Fall 1980; "The Moral Case Against Right-to-Work," *American Federationist*, Aug. 1976; Milton J. Nadworny, "'Right-to-Work' Laws Hamper South's Industrial Growth," *American Federationist*, April 1960; C. George Niebank, Jr., "In Defense of Right-to-Work Laws," *LLJ*, July 1957; Eleanor Roosevelt, "Why I Am Opposed to 'Right to Work' Laws," *American Federationist*, Feb. 1959; Bernard Schub, "'Right-to-Work'—A Colossal Fraud," *American Federationist*, Jan. 1960; Paul Sultan, *Right-to-Work Laws: A Study in Conflict* (Los Angeles: UC, Institute of IR, 1958); Jerome Toner, "Right-to-Work Laws and Union Security Contracts," *LLJ*, April 1977; ———, "Right-to-Work Laws: Public

Frauds," *LLJ*, March 1957; Ron Waggener, "Right-to-Work—The Missouri Decision," *American Federationist*, Jan. 1979; James N. Wilhoit, III and Jonathan C. Gibson, "Can a State Right-to-Work Law Prohibit the Union Operated Hiring Hall?" *LLJ*, May 1975.

See also AGENCY SHOP; FREE RIDERS; PREEMPTION, DOCTRINE OF; UNION SHOP.

ringed rate *See* RED CIRCLE RATE.

ripple effect Frequently used to describe the impact of wages and benefits negotiated for one bargaining unit on the wages and benefits provided by the employer to other employees.

Source reference: Allan W. Drachman, *Municipal Negotiations: From Differences to Agreement* (Washington: Labor-Management Relations Service, Strengthening Local Government Through Better Labor Relations series 5, 1970).

See also BARGAINING STRUCTURE, WAGE SPILLOVER.

rival union dispute Disputes in which two or more unions seek to organize the same employees. Procedures are available under federal and state laws to determine which organization has the right to represent the employees. Determination generally is made on the basis of an employee election.

See also JURISDICTIONAL DISPUTE, RIVAL UNIONISM.

rival unionism According to Professor Walter Galenson, "Rival unionism is the coexistence of two or more unrelated labor organizations actively competing for the control of the workers employed or the work habitually performed within a particular trade or occupation. A situation of this nature should not be confused with dual unionism, which merely implies coexistence without the further fact of competition. . . . Although there is a clearly marked distinction between the two terms, they are widely employed as synonyms."

Professor Philip Taft defines rival unionism as "the existence of two rival central labor organizations, each seeking to gain dominance over the economic movement. . . . Rival unions are ready to welcome dissatisfied groups affiliated with their competitors."

Professor Florence Peterson distinguishes rival union and jurisdictional disputes in the following way: "A rival union dispute differs from a jurisdictional dispute in that the latter is concerned with claims to jobs or kinds of work, whereas in a rival union dispute the unions acknowledge no jurisdictional boundaries between them but each is contending for the right to represent the workers on the various jobs. In other words, rival union disputes are conflicts between unions of different or no affiliation; that is, between AFL and CIO unions, one of these and an independent union, or between two independent unions."

Source references: Gary N. Chaison, "Toward a Cost-Benefit Analysis of Union Rivalry," *PJ*, Aug. 1972; Walter Galenson, *Rival Unionism in the United States* (New York: American Council on Public Affairs, 1940); Florence Peterson, *American Labor Unions* (2d ed., New York: Harper, 1963); Philip Taft, *Economics and Problems of Labor* (3d ed., Harrisburg: Stackpole, 1955).

See also DUAL UNIONISM, INTERUNION DISPUTE, JURISDICTIONAL DISPUTE.

robotics Popular term used to refer to the technology and use of robots in industry. The word robot is derived from the Czech word "robota," meaning work, first used in the United States when Karl Capek's play *R.U.R.* was presented in New York in 1922.

George C. Devol, Jr., is credited as the inventor of the first industrial robots. Joseph F. Engelberger established Unimation, Inc. of Danbury, Connecticut, which installed the first robots in the General Motors plant in Lordstown, Ohio, in 1961.

Robot is defined by the Robot Institute of America as "a reprogrammable, multifunctional manipulator designed to move material, parts, tools or specialized devices through variable programmed motions for the performance of a variety of tasks."

Robots excel in repetitive tasks and currently are used to perform dangerous and physically demanding work and are generally limited to simple operations.

Source references: Carnegie-Mellon University, Dept. of Engineering and Public Policy, *The Impacts of Robotics on the Workforce and Workplace* (Pittsburgh: 1981); Dennis Chamot and Joan M. Baggett (ed.), *Silicon, Satellites and Robots, The Impacts of Technological Change on the Workplace* (Washington: AFL-CIO, Dept. for Professional Employees, 1979); John Dodd, "Robots: The New 'Steel Collar' Workers," *PJ*, Sept. 1981; Lee Edson, "Slaves of Industry," *Across the Board*, July/Aug. 1981; Joseph F. Engelberger, *Robotics in Practice* (New York: AMACOM, 1981); Patti Hagan, "Once and Future Robots, An Interview with Joseph F. Engelberger," *Across the Board*, June 1984; Terry L. Leap and Allayne Barrilleaux Pizzolatto, "Robotics Technology: The Implications for Collective Bargaining and Labor Law," *LLJ*, Nov. 1983; Sar A. Levitan and Clifford M. Johnson, "The Future of Work: Does it Belong to Us or to the Robots?" *MLR*, Sept. 1982; Gail M. Martin, "Industrial Robots Join the Work Force," *Occupational Outlook Quarterly*, Fall 1982; Robert J. Miller (ed.), "Robotics: Future Factories, Future Workers," *Annals*, Nov. 1981; Carl Remick, "Robots: New Faces on the Production Lines," *Management Review*, May 1979; U.S. Congress, Joint Economic Committee, *Robotics and the Economy, A Staff Study* (Washington: 1982).

Rockefeller plan *See* COLORADO PLAN.

rolling *See* BUMPING.

Roofers, Damp and Waterproof Workers Association; United Slate, Tile and Composition (AFL-CIO) Organized in Pittsburgh in September 1919 by amalgamation of the International Slate and Tile Roofers Union of America (organized in 1903) and the International Brotherhood of Composition Roofers, Damp and Waterproof Workers (organized in 1907). The union changed its name to the United Union of Roofers, Waterproofers and Allied Workers in October 1978.

See also ROOFERS, WATERPROOFERS AND ALLIED WORKERS; UNITED UNION OF (AFL-CIO).

Roofers, Waterproofers and Allied Workers; United Union of (AFL-CIO) Formerly known as the United Slate, Tile and Composition Roofers, Damp and Waterproof Workers Association, it adopted its present name in October 1978.

The official quarterly publication is the *Roofers, Waterproofers and Allied Workers.*

Address: 1125 17th St., N.W., Washington, D.C. 20036. Tel. (202) 638–3228

roping A procedure whereby a worker through favors is brought into a group of labor spies and gives information about union activities. The individual "roped" generally is an active union member with easy access to union information.

rotating shift A practice, in plants which operate multiple shifts, of changing shift schedules periodically. It is designed to equalize the distribution of day and night work.

Source reference: Paul and Faith Pigors, *Human Aspects of Multiple Shift Operations* (Boston: MIT, Dept. of Economics and Social Science, Publications in Social Science, Series 2, no. 13, 1944).

See also SHIFT.

Roth case A Supreme Court decision holding that nonrenewal of an untenured assistant professor's first year contract without explanation did not deprive the professor of liberty and property rights provided by the 14th Amendment. The institution, Wisconsin State University–Oshkosh, under Wisconsin law may confer tenure following four years of year-to-year employment. A new teacher under the law is entitled to nothing beyond the one-year contract.

The Court ruled that it "stretches the concept too far to suggest that a person is deprived of 'liberty' when he simply is not rehired in one job but remains as free as before to seek another." The property interest of employment, the Court said, was created and defined by the terms of the employment contract, which "specifically provided that the respondent's employment was to terminate on June 30. They did not provide for contract renewal absent 'sufficient cause.' Indeed, they made no provision for renewal whatsoever. . . . They supported absolutely no possible claim of entitlement to re-employment. . . . In these circumstances, the respondent surely had an abstract concern in being rehired, but he did not have a *property* interest sufficient to require the University authorities to give him a hearing when they declined to renew his contract of employment."

Source references: Board of Regents, et al. v. Roth, 408 US 564 (1972); Commission on Academic Tenure in Higher Education, *Faculty Tenure; A Report and Recommendations*

(San Francisco: Jossey-Bass, 1973); Walter S. Griggs and Harvey W. Rubin, "Legal Ramifications of the Tenure Crisis," *Journal of Collective Negotiations in the Public Sector*, Vol. 6, no. 2, 1977; Carol Herrnstadt Shulman, *Employment of Nontenured Faculty: Some Implications of Roth and Sindermann* (Washington: American Association for Higher Education, ERIC/Higher Education Research Report no. 8, 1973).

See also ACADEMIC TENURE, SINDERMANN CASE.

rough shadowing To keep a man under surveillance in such a manner that he knows that he is being followed and thereby is intimidated.

round of wage increases A derivative term describing the successive wage increases obtained annually by union after union following the end of World War II, each of which affected broad segments of the economy, generally on the basis of industry classifications (oil, steel, etc.). Thus, the "first round" of postwar wage increases came in the period following the surrender of Japan in the autumn of 1946; the "second round" came in 1947, and so on.

See also FIRST ROUND INCREASES.

round-the-clock operation A production schedule which keeps the plant in operation throughout the entire 24 hours of a day and generally involves the use of three shifts.

royalty A term adopted by the United Mine Workers of America to describe the cents-per-ton of coal mined which employers are required by contract to contribute to the UMW Welfare and Retirement Fund.

Rubber, Cork, Linoleum and Plastic Workers of America; United (AFL-CIO) Organized in Akron, Ohio in September 1935, and received its AFL charter in September 1935. The organization subsequently joined the CIO and organized on an industrial basis. The official bimonthly publication is the *United Rubber Worker*.

Address: URWA Bldg., 87 South High St., Akron, Ohio 44308. Tel. (216) 376–6181

Source references: Harold S. Roberts, *The Rubber Workers* (New York: Harper, 1944); United Rubber Workers of America, *Five Years: The Story of the United Rubber Workers of America* (Akron: 1940).

"rulebook" slowdown A deliberate effort by employees aimed at slowing operations by the meticulous observation of administrative rules and regulations that are otherwise routinely ignored in the interest of efficiency.

Source reference: The Twentieth Century Fund, Task Force on Labor Disputes in Public Employment, *Pickets at City Hall* (New York: 1970).

See also JOB ACTION, WORK TO RULE.

rule of reason A principle enunciated by the Supreme Court in 1911 with respect to application of the Sherman Antitrust Act of 1890. The Court held that only those agreements which are in "undue or unreasonable" restraint of interstate trade are prohibited by that statute.

Professor Richard Lester has stated that the courts would have done well to apply the rule of reason to labor cases in evaluating the role of unions. He says in part: "In the decisions of various antitrust cases, the economic sympathies of the judges seem to have played an important part, for the 'rule of reason' has generally been applied to employer restraints of interstate trade, whereas in the cases of labor restraints the judges have based their decisions largely on the presumed 'intent' of the accused labor organization. . . . It would seem as though the social consequences of labor's restraints of interstate trade are as observable as the social effects of similar restraint by employers, so that the 'rule of reason' could be applied to labor combinations as well as to business combinations. Certainly the stabilizing effects of unions upon prices and working conditions have as much economic and social merit as stabilization achieved through trade association action or the formation of giant corporations by mergers."

Source references: James T. Adams (ed.), *Dictionary of American History* (5 vol., New York: Scribner's, 1940); Edward Berman, *Labor and the Sherman Act* (New York: Harper, 1930); Richard Lester, *Economics of Labor* (2d ed., New York: Macmillan, 1964).

See also SHERMAN ACT OF 1890.

rule of three A practice of the U.S. Office of Personnel Management and other state and local personnel agencies in certifying the top three candidates for jobs on a particular list; the employing department chooses the one believed best qualified from the list. The "rule of three" sometimes has been modified to the "rule of five."

run A term frequently used in the transportation industry for a work assignment. The "run" may apply to an entire day or week's working schedule of the individual, rather than a single trip.

The word "pick" sometimes is used, since in the transportation industry the run actually is available to employees on the basis of seniority.

See also PICK.

runaway rate An incentive or other piece rate which yields earnings that are out of line and not comparable with earnings for work of similar difficulty. A runaway rate is sometimes referred to as a "loose rate."

See also LOOSE RATE.

runaway shop A company or plant, or an operating unit of a company, which moves its operations to another state or geographic area in order, among other things, to escape subjection to existing state labor laws, to avoid an existing union, or to divest itself of bargaining obligations to a particular union. This may occur during a contract period or, more frequently, at the expiration of a collective bargaining agreement.

Where the movement is due to basic economic conditions and special incentives which have no relation to "running away" from a union or union obligations or protective labor legislation, it is referred to usually as a plant migration or relocation.

Source references: Lawrence Barker, "There is a Better Way," *LLJ*, Aug. 1981; E. Walter Bowman, "Plant Relocation: Viewed After Denial of Board's 'Runaway Shop' Remedy in *Garwin*," *IR Law Digest*, July 1968; Walter L. Daykin, "Runaway Shops: The Problem and Treatment," *LLJ*, Nov. 1961; Gary J. Felsten, "Current Considerations in Plant Shutdowns and Relocations," *PJ*, May 1981; Charles J. Morris et al., "Employers' Defensive Tactics—Lockouts, Replacements, Plant Closings and Relocations," *Labor Law Developments*, Proceedings of the 12th Annual Institute on Labor Law, SLF (Washington: BNA, 1966); Lawrence R. Schneider, "Vested Rights in the Runaway Shop," *Western Reserve LR*, March 1962; John B. Taulane, Jr., "Labor Law: The National Labor Relations Board's Pursuit of the Runaway Shop," *Villanova LR*, Spring 1962.

See also DARLINGTON CASE, PLANT MIGRATION, SUBCONTRACTING.

run-off election A procedure of the NLRB and other agencies which conduct employee representation elections. Under NLRB rules and regulations, "A runoff election is conducted only where: (a) the ballot in the original election contained three or more choices [i.e., two labor organizations and a 'neither' choice]; and (b) no single choice received a majority of the valid votes cast. Thus there can be no runoff where the original ballot provided for: (1) a 'yes' and 'no' choice in a one-union election; or (2) a 'severance' election." The ballot in the run-off election provides for a selection between the two choices receiving the largest and second largest number of votes in the original election.

Source references: Kenneth C. McGuiness and Jeffrey A. Norris, *How to Take a Case Before the NLRB* (5th ed., Washington: BNA, 1986); Harvey M. Wagner, "The Run-Off Election Paradox," *LLJ*, Feb. 1957.

See also REPRESENTATION ELECTIONS.

rushers Speedy and highly efficient employees who may be used to establish performance standards. Unions have objected to such pace-makers on the ground that they do not actually represent the performance of the average worker, hence the rates and standards so established are improper.

Professor Robert Hoxie, in *Trade Unionism in the United States*, says in part: ". . . long experience with the average employer has ground into their [unions'] soul the belief that employers as a class are constantly seeking to lower the wage rate, and at the same time to increase the speed and exertion of the workers of the group through driving or bribing individuals of the group to greater speed and longer hours; and then are setting up the work and pay of these men (rushers) as evidence to prove that the others are soldiering on the job and must increase their exertions or suffer a reduction of wage rate or a lengthening of hours of work."

See also PACERS, SOLDIERING, SPEED-UP.

Russell Sage Foundation An organization established in memory of the philanthropist, Russell Sage, by his widow and by his attorney Robert M. DeForest in 1907, with the prime purpose to improve social conditions in the United States. This was to be accomplished primarily by provision of research facilities and the publication of materials indicating the conditions of work and the necessity for their improvement.

Address: 112 E. 64th St., New York, N.Y. 10021. Tel. (212) 750–6000

Source reference: Charles J. Hicks, *My Life in Industrial Relations* (New York: Harper, 1941).

S

SAG *See* SCREEN ACTORS GUILD.

SEG *See* SCREEN EXTRAS GUILD.

SEIU *See* SERVICE EMPLOYEES' INTERNATIONAL UNION (AFL-CIO).

SES *See* SENIOR EXECUTIVE SERVICE (SES).

SFAAW *See* STOVE, FURNACE AND ALLIED APPLIANCE WORKERS' INTERNATIONAL UNION OF NORTH AMERICA (AFL-CIO).

SIU *See* SEAFARERS' INTERNATIONAL UNION OF NORTH AMERICA (AFL-CIO).

SLU *See* SOUTHERN LABOR UNION (IND).

SMSA *See* METROPOLITAN STATISTICAL AREA (MSA).

SMW *See* SHEET METAL WORKERS' INTERNATIONAL ASSOCIATION (AFL-CIO).

SPIDR *See* SOCIETY OF PROFESSIONALS IN DISPUTE RESOLUTION (SPIDR).

SUB *See* SUPPLEMENTAL UNEMPLOYMENT BENEFITS.

SUP *See* SAILORS' UNION OF THE PACIFIC.

sabbaticals A term referring to the periodic time off for research or study granted to professional people, especially university teachers.

The term also has been applied to the extended vacations provided in contracts first negotiated by the Steelworkers Union in 1963. Although these vacations may be referred to as sabbaticals, they are actually extended vacations for employees with specified seniority within the plant.

Source references: Robert A. Bedolis, "The Steel Labor Agreement, 1963," *Business Management Record,* Dec. 1963; Eli Goldston, "Executive Sabbaticals: About to Take Off?" *Harvard BR,* Sept./Oct. 1973; Richard B. McAdoo, "Sabbaticals for Businessmen," *Harper's,* May 1962; "Steel Men Thrive on Sabbaticals," *Business Week,* Nov. 26, 1966; Angelos A. Tsaklanganos, "Sabbaticals for Executives," *PJ,* May 1973.

See also VACATIONS.

sabotage Direct action by employees to injure or destroy an employer's income or property. It is a form of striking on the job, slowing down, or the actual destruction of tangible property. It has been suggested that the term derives from "sabot," the wooden shoe of French peasants, which when tossed into machinery produced the same result as that, in the American phrase, of "dropping a monkey wrench into the machine."

Professor Albion Taylor has described the use of sabotage in connection with the development of syndicalism and revolutionary unionism. He writes in part:

> The Industrial Workers of the World, organized in Chicago in 1905, was such a body, its chief ambition being to unite all the workers of the country into a labor union committed to bitter opposition to the present economic and political order. . . . The Chicago group is an example of quasi-anarchistic revolutionary unionism, whose ultimate aim is freedom in industrial association, the organization of one big union in possession of all factories, mines, farms, transportation facilities, and other organizations, together with the elimination of governmental interference in industry. It condemns not only collective bargaining but political action, and advocated direct forms of industrial action, such as the general strike, boycotts, and sabotage. Sabotage may consist merely of "soldiering" on the job, or it may involve the violent practice of burning wheat, soaping tracks, slitting lacing on belts in factories, putting sand in machine boxes, and even more destructive acts. . . .

The authorities do not necessarily agree that the destructive acts of sabotage go as far as to include action which involves danger to human life. The description and definition of sabotage set out in the *Encyclopedia of Social Sciences* runs in part:

> Sabotage, in the parlance of the labor movement, refers to the strategy of obstruction of or interference with the processes of industry by employees in order to reduce the profits of the employer and so compel him to accede to their demands. It is one of the forms of direct action, a means of exerting economic rather than political pressure. Sabotage may assume a variety of forms, ranging from the peaceful practices of restriction of output and "taking things easy" to the disabling of machinery and the dynamiting of plants. The leading advocates of sabotage, however, have opposed the permanent disabling of machinery and personal violence, and it is generally agreed that sabotage does not include acts directly involving danger to human life.

Source references: Marjorie R. Clark and S. Fanny Simon, *The Labor Movement in America* (New York: Norton, 1938); Edwin R. A. Seligman (ed.), *Encyclopedia of Social Sciences* (New York: Macmillan, 1934); Albion G. Taylor, *Labor Problems and Labor Law* (2d ed., New York: PH, 1950).

See also CA' CANNY, ESPIONAGE.

safety Efforts by management, labor, and government to prevent, and eliminate the causes of accidents.

Source references: Nicholas A. Ashford, "Worker Health and Safety: An Area of Conflict," *MLR*, Sept. 1975; James B. Atleson, "Threats to Health and Safety: Employee Self-Help Under the NLRA," *IR Law Digest*, Jan. 1976; Frank R. Barnako, "Enforcing Job Safety: A Managerial View," *MLR*, March 1975; Roland P. Blake (ed.), *Industrial Safety* (3d ed., Englewood Cliffs: PH, 1963); George T. Brown, "Labor's Stake in Safety," *American Federationist*, Jan. 1959; D. Keith Denton, "Effective Safety Management: Focus on the Human Element," *Management Review*, Dec. 1980; Richard L. Frenkel, W. Curtiss Priest, and Nicholas A. Ashford, "Occupational Safety and Health: A Report on Worker Perceptions," *MLR*, Sept. 1980; Robert D. Moran, "How to Obtain Job Safety Justice," *LLJ*, July 1973; National Safety Council, *Safety Guide for Unions* (Chicago: 1962); Charles W. Newcom, "Employee Health and Safety Rights Under the LMRA and Federal Safety Laws," *LLJ*, July 1981; John R. Oravec, "The Continuing Fight for Job Safety," *American Federationist*, June 1974; Margaret Seminario, "Women Workers: Hazards on the Job," *American Federationist*, Aug. 1978; Sally Seymour, "The Federal Role in Job Safety and Health, Forging a Partnership with the States," *MLR*, Aug. 1973; U.S. CSC, *Health and Safety Provisions in Federal Agreements* (Washington: 1975); U.S. Dept. of Labor, *Protecting the People at Work, A Reader in Occupational Safety and Health* (Washington: 1980); U.S. Dept. of Labor, Manpower Administration, *Health and Safety Aspects of Automation and Technological Change* (Washington: 1964).

See also INDUSTRIAL ACCIDENT, JOB SAFETY TRAINING, NATIONAL SAFETY COUNCIL, OCCUPATIONAL SAFETY AND HEALTH ACT (OSHA) OF 1970.

safety appliance A safeguarding device or other means of protection designed to cover the dangerous parts of industrial machinery and equipment, particularly the moving parts. One of the main purposes of a safety appliance is to reduce the chances of persons becoming entangled in operative machinery.

See also ACCIDENT PREVENTION, INDUSTRIAL ACCIDENT.

safety campaigns Organized programs instituted by companies or by the joint efforts of companies and unions to promote a positive attitude toward safety practices. The importance of maintaining safety measures is brought to the attention of employees through the use of financial incentives and appeals through posters, house organs, films, and other means. Many companies have safety engineeers to organize their safety campaigns.

In 1912 a group of safety engineers established the National Safety Council in Milwaukee, which over the years has been engaged in a continuous campaign in the area of accident prevention and in the institution of safety practices in industrial plants and in the community as a whole.

Source references: AFL-CIO, *We're Promoting Safety in Your Local* (Washington: Pub. no. 117, 1961); AMA, *Ideas for Promoting Safety*, Selected Reprints from AMA Periodicals (New York: 1965–67).

safety clause A clause found in some collective bargaining agreements which provides for safety committees, either joint committees or union committees working with the company, for the purpose of investigating, discussing, and recommending solutions to situations which are unsafe.

Source references: George T. Brown, "The Union Contract and Safety," *American Federationist*, June 1960; Winston Tillery, "Safety and Health Provisions Before and After OSHA," *MLR*, Sept. 1975; U.S. Dept. of Labor, BLS, *Major Collective Bargaining Agreements: Safety and Health Provisions* (Washington: Bull. no. 1425–16, 1976); Wayne Wendling, "Industrial Safety and Collective Bargaining," *Proceedings of the 30th A/M, IRRA*, ed. by Barbara Dennis (Madison: 1978).

safety clothing Protective apparel or equipment worn by a worker as a precaution against on-the-job hazards and accidents. Among the items frequently provided are goggles, safety gloves, certain types of headgear, safety shoes, and other items, depending on the nature of the job and the kind of protection needed.

safety committee A group generally designated by labor and management which has as its prime function the review and encouragement of safety practices within the plant.

safety department That unit in the plant responsible for the prevention of accidents, and the administration of safety in the establishment. This may involve training, checking equipment, and the general safety education of employees within the plant.

Source reference: Walter A. Cutter, *Organization and Functions of the Safety Department: Responsibility, Authority, Training of Personnel* (New York: AMA, Research Report no. 18, 1951).

safety device *See* SAFETY APPLIANCE.

safety education All of the activities which in any way relate to the prevention of accidents and safe operation on the job. This may include the preliminary instruction of the employee on the right way to perform job tasks, and procedures for maintaining safety equipment or the condition of machinery. It may also involve attending classes or participating in training programs.

It may also involve the review and examination of local, state, and federal safety codes which apply to a particular industry or occupation. Safety education concerns itself not only with the understanding of the conditions which lead to hazardous or unsafe practices and the means of preventing them, but also the establishment of a sound attitude and concern for the health and safety of employees on the job.

Source references: ILO, *Accident Prevention: A Workers' Education Manual* (Geneva: 1961); U.S. Dept. of Labor, Bureau of Labor Standards, *Housekeeping for Safety, Instructor Outline* (Washington: Safety in Industry Series, Bull. no. 295, 1967).

safety engineer An individual who may be a member of the personnel department, with the responsibility of seeing that the plant operates with a minimum of accidents and with optimum conditions for safe operations. Safety programs of many companies provide for a safety committee composed of management and employee representatives, including the safety engineer.

Source reference: U.S. Dept. of Labor, BLS, *Major Collective Bargaining Agreements: Safety and Health Provisions* (Washington: Bull. 1425–16, 1976).

safety measure Any policy, action, or device for the purpose of safeguarding the welfare of the individual in reducing accidents or protecting and remedying health and safety conditions.

Source references: Roland P. Blake (ed.), *Industrial Safety* (3d ed., Englewood Cliffs: PH, 1963); Alexander L. Dickie, *Production with Safety* (New York: McGraw-Hill, 1947); Roderick A. Forsgren, "A Model of Supportive Work Conditions Through Safety Management,"*PJ*, May 1969; R. H. Magee, "How to Build Motivation Into Safety Rules," *PJ*, Feb. 1967; James C. McHugh and Edward W. Sutton, "A Neglected Aid in Safety Management," *Personnel*, Jan./Feb. 1966.

See also SAFETY EDUCATION.

safety movement A broad program, generally of an educational nature or sometimes dealing with legislation, to convince employers and employees as well as legislators about the importance of protecting the security and safety of individuals on the job.

See also NATIONAL SAFETY COUNCIL.

safety programs Any organized set of plans designed to meet safety problems in a plant. The programs may be educational in nature, they may involve the training of individuals on the job, or they may involve an examination of the particular equipment and machinery to establish better safety conditions in the plant.

Source references: Georges Alacchi and Constantin Todradze, "Safety in Mines and the Role of Training," *ILR*, Sept./Oct. 1981; Allan J. Harrison, "Managing Safety and Health," *LLJ*, Sept. 1981, Oct. 1981; Univ. of Iowa, Bureau of Labor and Management, *Effective Safety Programs* (Iowa City: 1953); Mark E. Lichty, "A Prescription for Improving the Work Environment," *Employee Relations LJ*, Summer 1982; Svenn A. Lindskold, "The Heart of a Successful Safety Program," *Public Personnel Review*, July 1967; Robert E. McClay, "Professionalizing the Safety Function," *PJ*, Feb. 1977; Norman Root and David McCaffrey, "Targeting Worker Safety Programs: Weighing Incidence Against Expense," *MLR*, Jan. 1980; "Safety Audits Make Safety Programs Work," *Management Review*, Oct. 1969; Henry M. Taylor, "Occupational Health Management—By Objectives," *Personnel*, Jan./Feb. 1980; Philip A. Workman, "Using Statistics to Manage a State Safety and Health Program," *MLR*, March 1981.

See also JOB SAFETY TRAINING, SAFETY EDUCATION.

safety regulations Those state laws and regulations dealing specifically with the health and safety conditions of employees engaged in work such as mining, manufacturing, quarrying, etc.

With the establishment of workers compensation statutes, campaigns for safety regulation and safety practices became more widespread because it became extremely costly for employers to pay for workers compensation. Many safety measures were proposed by the insurance companies which carried the insurance for employers.

Source reference: ILO, *Prohibition of the Sale, Hire and Use of Inadequately Guarded Machinery* (Geneva: Conference Report no. 4 (1–2), 1962).

See also INDUSTRIAL ACCIDENT, OCCUPATIONAL SAFETY AND HEALTH ACT (OSHA) OF 1970, WORKERS COMPENSATION.

Sailors' Union of the Pacific A division of the Seafarers' International Union of North America (AFL-CIO). The official semimonthly publication is the *West Coast Sailors*.

Address: 450 Harrison St., San Francisco, Calif. 94105. Tel. (415) 362–8363

salami tactics A term used in political parlance; a method which Matyas Rakosi, the dictator of Hungary, advocated in order to attain objectives. It is a procedure designed to achieve long-range objectives through the slow process of small and perhaps not too noticeable demands.

Source reference: Cyrus L. Sulzberger, "How Long Can the Salami Last?" *The New York Times*, Sept. 1, 1962.

salaried employee Generally a worker who is not on an hourly or an incentive rate. The salaried employee, whether executive or white-collar worker, generally is hired on a continuing basis, usually on a monthly basis. Salary payment may be weekly, biweekly, or monthly. The individual does not receive compensation on the basis of the number of hours worked, although generally white-collar employees are expected to work a definite number of hours.

Source references: Charles W. Bartells, "Why Change Hourly Employees to Salary?" *PJ*, June 1972; Robert D. Hulme and Richard V. Bevan, "The Blue-Collar Worker Goes on Salary," *Harvard BR*, March/April 1975; Paul G. Kaponya, "Salary for All Workers," *Harvard BR*, May/June 1962; James W. Steele, *Paying for Performance and Position, Dilemmas in Salary Compression and Merit Pay;* An AMA Survey Report (New York: AMA, 1982).

salary The compensation actually received by an employee, white-collar or executive, for a period of time rather than for the actual hours of work.

salary administration The policies and procedures established for the compensation of white-collar workers and executives.

Source references: James E. Brennan, "The Problem with Salary Ranges (and a Realistic Solution)," *PJ*, March 1980; Leonard M. Lewis, "Recycle Your Salary Administration Program," *Management Review*, Oct. 1973; John D. McMillan and Valerie C. Williams, "The Elements of Effective Salary Administration," *PJ*, Nov. 1982; Jay L. Otis, "A Psychologist Looks At Salary Administration," *Management of Personnel Quarterly*, Summer 1963; Thomas H. Patten, Jr., "Open Communication Systems and Effective Salary Administration," *Human Resource Management*, Winter 1978; G. K. Warner, Jr., "Using Salary Administration Committees Effectively," *PJ*, July/Aug. 1961; David A. Weeks (ed.), *Compensation Strategies During an Uncertain Recovery, Excerpted from a Conference* (New York: The Conference Board, Report 709, 1977); Nathan B. Winstanley, "The Use of Performance Appraisal in Compensation Administration," *Conference Board Record*, March 1975; Allan K. Worrell, "Salary Administration Simplified," *Management Review*, March 1979.

See also WAGE AND SALARY ADMINISTRATION.

salary and commission Personnel engaged in sales frequently receive compensation on the basis of a percentage of total sales. They may also receive a guaranteed salary and a percentage in addition to the minimum guarantee. Occasionally the minimum guarantee is paid even though the percentage on the sales does not equal the guaranteed salary and sales in excess of the guarantee are intended to serve as an incentive to the individual. Some sales people receive both a fixed guarantee and a percentage on total sales.

salary compression A narrowing of an established pay differential which may have been based upon tenure, skill, or performance. Salary compression may result from (1) escalation of entry-level salaries to recruit new personnel in certain high demand occupations without a comparable adjustment in wages for experienced employees already employed by the firm, or (2) a greater percentage increase in pay in lower salary ranges as compared to higher salary ranges.

Source reference: Thomas A. Mahoney, *Compensation for Work* (Minneapolis: Univ. of Minnesota, IRC, WP 80–04, 1980).

salary rate The actual annual, monthly, or weekly rate for a particular type of salaried employment. There may be a range of rates just as among hourly employees.

salesperson's compensation Procedures used by various companies to compensate salespersons for their effort. These may involve travel allowances, basic salary, percentage on sales, or other types of compensation designed to encourage the employee to increase his sales.

Source references: R. E. Busher, "Why Friden Pays Commissions Only," *Sales Management*, Nov. 18, 1960; James F. Carey, "Cost and Value in Salesmen's Pay," *Management Review*, Sept. 1975; ———, "Paying the Sales Trainee," *Management Review*, Jan. 1977; Robert C. Ferber, "Designing Your Sales Compensation Plan for Improved Return on Invested Capital," *Management Review*, Nov. 1975; Jacob Gonik, "Tie Salesmen's Bonuses to Their Forecasts," *Harvard BR*, May/June 1978; Marvin A. Jolson, "Minimum Wage Laws: A New Challenge for Sales Administrators," *PJ*, April 1973; M. A. Patrick, "Are Sales Incentives Immoral?" *Industrial Marketing*, March 1962; Charles A. Peck, *Compensating Field Sales Representatives* (New York: The Conference Board, Report no. 828, 1982); D. H. Scott, "Ignoring the Human Factor in Pay Plans," *Sales Management*, May 20, 1960; Richard C. Smyth, "Financial Incentives for Salesmen," *Harvard BR*, Jan./Feb. 1968; ———, "How Industry Pay Its Salesmen," *Management Review*, Dec. 1959; John P. Steinbrink, "How to Pay Your Sales Force," *Harvard BR*, July/Aug. 1978; Aaron Sternfield, "Gearing Sales Pay to Today's Markets," *Dun's Review and Modern Industry*, Dec. 1958; C. M. Weld, "Salesmen's Compensation Survey Uncovers New Trends, Higher Earnings," *American Business*, Nov. 1959; William L. White, "Incentives for Salesmen: Designing a Plan that Works," *Management Review*, Feb. 1977.

salesperson's training The procedures used by companies to supervise and train their salespersons in order to increase their effectiveness and to analyze and improve the marketing procedures of the company.

Source references: AMA, *Evaluating Sales Training Needs and Methods* (New York: Marketing Series no. 88, 1953); ———, *Making Better Use of the Human Factor in Selling* (New York: Marketing Series no. 93, 1954); William J. Borsock, "Inside Story on Training Salesmen Overseas," *Management Review*, Aug. 1974; Harry L. David and Alvin J. Silk, "Interaction and Influence Processes in Personal Selling," *Sloan Management Review*, Winter 1972; Stephen X. Doyle and Benson P. Shapiro, "What Counts Most in Motivating Your Sales Force?" *Harvard BR* May/June 1980; J. M. Hickerson, "Successful Sales Techniques," *Harvard BR* Sept./Oct. 1952; Charles L. Lapp, *Personal Supervision of Outside Salesmen* (Columbus: Ohio State Univ., Bureau of Business Research, 1951); ———, *Training and Supervising Salesmen* (Englewood Cliffs: PH, 1960); Larry McMahon, "Taking the Sting Out of Selling!" *Sloan Management Review*, Fall 1981.

salt tablets Sodium chloride which is administered in tablet form or in solution as a means of preventing heat exhaustion, particularly in plants where there are high temperatures, or where employees work outdoors in the sun.

Source references: William B. Gafafer (ed.), *Manual of Industrial Hygiene and Medical Services in War Industries* (Philadelphia: Saunders, 1943); Rutherford T. Johnstone and Seward E. Miller, *Occupational Diseases and Industrial Medicine* (Philadelphia: Saunders, 1960).

sample survey of employers This survey by BLS provides estimates of the number of employees on the payroll in nonagricultural establishments by industry. The figures are based on reports from a sample of establishments which employ approximately 36 million workers.

See also EMPLOYMENT STATISTICS.

sample survey of households Information collected and tabulated by the Bureau of the Census, U.S. Department of Commerce, for BLS which provides a comprehensive measure of the labor force.

See also EMPLOYMENT STATISTICS.

sampling A procedure for obtaining reliable estimates where it is either impossible or too costly to make a complete count or census. This is done by obtaining data from a limited sample to achieve as exact and careful information as would have been obtained if a complete tabulation or census could be made. A large volume of statistical information of necessity is based on samples and not on actual count of the universe involved.

Source references: Raymond A. Bauer, "Exploring the Exploratory Sample," *Harvard BR*, March/April 1963; William J. Goode and Paul K. Hatt, *Methods in Social Research* (New York: McGraw-Hill, 1952); Mildred Parten, *Surveys, Polls and Samples: Practical Procedures* (New York: Harper, 1950); Frederick F. Stephan, "History of the Uses of Modern Sampling Procedures," *Journal of the American Statistical Assn.*, March 1948; Frederick F. Stephan and Philip J. McCarthy, *Sampling Opinions: An Analysis of Survey Procedure* (New York: Wiley, 1958); Chester R. Wasson, "Common Sense in Sampling," *Harvard BR*, Jan./Feb. 1963.

sanction A form of economic and social pressure exerted by organizations to obtain their objectives through means other than resorting to the picket line and the strike. On the international level, sanctions have also been considered by the United Nations.

Source reference: Harold S. Roberts, *Labor-Management Relations in the Public Service* (Honolulu: Univ. of Hawaii Press, 1970).

See also ECONOMIC SANCTION, LEGAL SANCTION, PROFESSIONAL SANCTION.

sandhogs Generally applies to persons who work in tunnels, or to those who work either in the construction industry or under compressed air as in a caisson.

Source reference: U.S. Dept. of Labor, ETA, *Dictionary of Occupational Titles* (4th ed., Washington: 1977).

Saturday work Work or activity generally performed on Saturday. In the past, when employment was on a six-day basis Saturday work was part of the week's schedule. With reduction in the total number of hours worked, Saturday work frequently was reduced to one-half day to permit the employee an additional half-day holiday in addition to the Sunday day of rest. George Westinghouse, one of the pioneers of the half-holiday on Saturday, instituted the practice in 1881.

Saturday work frequently is discussed in connection with overtime computation and its relation to the regularly scheduled workweek. During the wage stabilization period in World War II, there was a prohibition under Executive Order 92040 of payment of premium pay for Saturday or Sunday work *as such.* It was possible to pay overtime rates for the sixth consecutive day if it met the provisions of the general orders under the Wage Stabilization Act.

See also OVERTIME.

savings bank insurance Life insurance written by the insurance departments of savings banks in some states, at lower premium rates than ordinary life insurance.

Source reference: Chamber of Commerce of the U.S., *Dictionary of Insurance Terms* (Washington: 1949).

savings clause The separability clause within a law which permits sections of the law to remain in effect although other provisions are held invalid by decisions of the courts. A typical clause is the separability clause in the Taft-Hartley Act, Section 503 which reads as follows:

> If any provision of this Act, or the application of such provision to any person or circumstance, shall be held invalid, the remainder of this Act, or the application of such provision to persons or circumstances other than those as to which it is held invalid, shall not be affected thereby.

A collective bargaining agreement may also incorporate a savings or separability clause on the assumption that it might be claimed by either party, if part of the agreement is held to be legally invalid or unenforceable, that the rest of the contract would be invalid. A clause of this type might read as follows:

> This agreement is made in the full belief by both parties hereto that it is in every respect legal. If any section, clause, or sentence or part of this agreement is, for any reason, held to be invalid or unenforceable in any respect, such a decision shall not affect the remaining provisions of this agreement.

Source references: J. A. Ballentine, *Law Dictionary with Pronunciations* (Rochester: Lawyers Coop. Pub., 1930); Henry C. Black, *Black's Law Dictionary* (rev. 4th ed., St. Paul: West Pub., 1968).

See also SEPARABILITY CLAUSE.

savings plan Programs established either by employers or unions to promote saving among workers. For companies, this might lead to stock purchases, profit sharing, and savings bonds. For unions, it might result in assistance in savings through credit unions, or in housing or other plans financed by the union.

According to Fox and Mayer: "The fundamental mechanism of an employee savings plan is quite simple: (1) a participant voluntarily contributes, through payroll deductions, some part of his salary; (2) the company matches all or part of the participant's savings; (3) company and employee contributions are put into a 'qualified' employee trust fund for 'deferred' distributions; (4) these contributions in the trust fund are invested (in most cases, some or all of the funds go into company stock)." They exclude from this definition three types of benefit plans: (1) the "standard" stock purchase plan, (2) the "standard" stock bonus plan, and (3) the deferred profit sharing plan.

Source references: Harland Fox and Mitchell Meyer, *Employee Savings Plans in the United States* (New York: NICB, Studies in Personnel Policy no. 184, 1962); Edward C. Katz, "The Unsung Benefits of Employee Savings Plans," *PJ*, Jan. 1979.

See also PROFIT SHARING, THRIFT PLANS.

scab A term used quite broadly to refer to an individual who continues to work for a company while a strike is in progress, or who accepts employment during the strike. It also is applied to individuals who are not on strike or to nonunion workers who go through a union picket line. The term may be applied to an individual who will accept lower wages or poorer working conditions than those which the union has established or seeks. This is particularly true when individuals accept jobs during a period of intensive organization.

An individual who does not support a strike but stays on the job is to be distinguished from one who is a professional strikebreaker brought in for the purpose of breaking the strike. This individual generally is referred to as a "fink" and he usually leaves the job when the strike is over. He is not a person whose purpose is to stay on the job as a regular employee.

Samuel Gompers, president of the American Federation of Labor from 1884 until his death (except the year 1894), in his *Seventy Years of Life and Labor* (New York: E. P. Dutton & Co., 1925, Vol. I), says in part:

> A "scab" is to his trade what a traitor is to his country. He is first to take advantage of any benefit secured by united action, and never contributes anything toward its achievement. He is used during a struggle to defeat his fellow-workmen, and though coddled for the time being by the employer he serves, when peace is restored he is cast out, shunned by his employers, his fellow-workmen, and the whole human family.

Professor Philip Taft compares the uses of the terms "fink," "scab," and "rat." He says in part:

> Strikebreakers are recruited for jobs through well-established channels. In the terminology of the trade they are called "finks," a term first used by members of the Industrial Workers of the World to describe a strikebreaker. Some refer to them as "scabs" and union printers are inclined to use the still less elegant "rat" when referring to a strikebreaker. While all of the terms may be used interchangeably, there is a very important distinction between the "fink" and the "scab." The latter is a worker who refuses to go out on strike and who will not support the union during a labor controversy, while the "fink" is a professional whose sole purpose is to help defeat a strike. . . . While there is a class known in the trade as "hunger scabs," workers driven to take a strike job because of need and lack of work, the majority of "finks" have accepted this type of work as a career.

Source references: Samuel Gompers, *Seventy Years of Life and Labor* (New York: Dutton, 1925); Philip Taft, *Economics and Problems of Labor* (3d ed., Harrisburg: Stackpole, 1955).

See also BLACKLEG, FINK, SLUGGER.

Scanlon Plan An incentive plan which was developed by Joseph Scanlon, at one time research director of the United Steelworkers, and who later was on the staff of the Massachusetts Institute of Technology. The plan is designed to achieve greater production through increased efficiency with the opportunity for the accrued savings achieved to be distributed among the workers.

Source references: R. W. Davenport, "Enterprise for Everyman, Case History of Scanlon Plan as Applied to LaPointe Machine Tool," *Fortune*, Jan. 1950; Robert K. Goodman, J. H. Wakeley, and R. H. Ruh, "What Employees Think About the Scanlon Plan," *Personnel*, Sept./Oct. 1972; Industrial Relations Counselors, Inc., *Group Wage Incentives: Experience With the Scanlon Plan* (New York: IR Memo no. 141, 1962); Frederick G. Lesieur, *The Scanlon Plan: A Frontier of Labor-Management Cooperation* (Cambridge: Technology Press of MIT, 1958); Kent F. Murrmann, "The Scanlon Plan Joint Committee and Section 8(a)(2)," *LLJ*, May 1980; Judith Ramquist, "Labor-Management Cooperation—The Scanlon Plan at Work," *Sloan Management Review*, Spring 1982; Robert A. Ruh, Roger L. Wallace, and Carl F. Frost, "Management Attitudes and the Scanlon Plan," *IR*, Oct. 1973; Elizabeth A. Smith and Gerald F. Gude, "Reevaluation of the Scanlon Plan as a Motivational Technique," *PJ*, Dec. 1971; U.S. National Commission on Productivity and Work Quality, *A Plant-Wide Productivity Plan in Action: Three Years of Experience With the Scanlon Plan* (Washington: 1975).

See also KAISER STEEL LONG-RANGE SHARING PLAN, LINCOLN ELECTRIC INCENTIVE CASH BONUS, PROFIT SHARING.

scarcity wages A phrase which describes an upward adjustment in salaries and wages due to the temporary shortage of specially trained employees. The rate is paid because an emergency demands such employees and, in order to obtain them, wages must be raised. In addition, those employers who actually have individuals on their payroll must raise their rates in order to avoid a high turnover and loss of their employees to other employers willing to pay the scarcity wages.

Source references: John W. Riegel, *Salary Determination* (Ann Arbor: Univ. of Michigan Press, 1940); Marquis F. Stigers and E. G. Reed, *The Theory and Practice of Job Rating* (2d ed., New York: McGraw-Hill, 1944).

Schechter Poultry Corporation v. United States A decision of the Supreme Court handed down on May 27, 1935, which set aside the National Industrial Recovery Act and held that the Codes of Fair Competition established under that Act were unenforceable, that Congress did not have the right to delegate to the President power to make such codes, and that the efforts to regulate such businesses (including hours and wages of employees under the codes) were unconstitutional. Professors Millis and Montgomery summarized the main points of the decision handed down by Chief Justice Hughes as follows:

> (1) Extraordinary conditions, such as an economic crisis, may call for extraordinary remedies, but they cannot create or enlarge constitutional power. (2) Congress is not permitted by the Constitution to abdicate, or to transfer to others, the essential legislative functions with which it is vested. (3) While Congress may leave to be selected the instrumentalities for making subordinate rules within prescribed limits and determination of facts to which declared policy is to apply, it must itself lay down the policies and establish the standards. (4) Section 3 unconstitutionally delegated legislative power, and the Act was also unconstitutional in the instant case because it exceeded the power of Congress to regulate interstate commerce and invaded power reserved exclusively to the states. (5) When the poultry had reached the defendants' slaughterhouses, the interstate commerce had ended; decisions dealing with a stream in interstate commerce and with the regulation of transactions involved in that practical continuity of movement were inapplicable in this case.

Source references: Schechter Corporation v. United States, 295 US 495 (1935); Dean O. Bowman, *Public Control of Labor Relations* (New York: Macmillan, 1942); Kurt Braun, *Labor Disputes and Their Settlement* (Baltimore: Johns Hopkins Press, 1955); Lewis Lorwin and Arthur Wubnig, *Labor Relations Boards* (Washington: Brookings Institution, 1935); Harry A. Millis and Royal E. Montgomery, *Labor's Progress and Some Basic Labor Problems* (New York: McGraw-Hill, 1938); Gordon S. Watkins and Paul A. Dodd, *Labor Problems* (3d ed., New York: Crowell, 1940).

scheduled hours The number of hours planned for the day or week. The hours actually worked may differ from the plan or schedule established.

See also HOURS, NOMINAL.

School Administrators; American Federation of (AFL-CIO) Formed in 1971 as the School Administrators and Supervisors Organizing Committee, the union received its AFL-CIO charter in 1976 and adopted the present name. It publishes the monthly *American Federation of School Administrators.*

Address: 110 East 42nd St., New York, N.Y. 10017. Tel. (212) 697–5111

scientific management A term which was largely popularized by Frederick W. Taylor, the father of scientific management.

According to L. P. Alford, the three essentials or principles set out by Frederick W. Taylor were: "(1) the substitution of a science for the individual judgment of the workman; (2) the scientific selection and development of the workman, after each man has been studied, taught, and trained, and one may say experimented with, instead of allowing the workmen to select themselves and develop in a haphazard way; and (3) the intimate cooperation of the management with the workmen, so that they together do the work in accordance with the scientific laws which have been developed, instead of leaving the solution of each problem in the hands of the individual workman."

The term "scientific management" has broadened and now includes the general philosophy, methods, and principles which are concerned with the improvement of efficiency, reduction of operating costs, and the maximum utilization of human and material resources in the operation of a company, in the production of a product, or the development of a particular service.

Source references: Leon P. Alford, *Principles of Industrial Management* (New York: Ronald Press, 1940); Peter F. Drucker, "The Coming Rediscovery of Scientific Management," *Conference Board Record*, June 1976; Robert F. Hoxie, *Scientific Management and Labor* (New York: Augustus M. Kelley, Reprints on Economic Classics, 1966); Dalton McFarland, "What Ever Happened to the Efficiency Movement?" *Conference Board Record*, June 1976; William Penzer, "Bridging the Industrial Engineering/Behavioral Science Gap," *PJ*, Aug. 1973; C. P. Snow, *The Two Cultures and the Scientific Revolu-*

tion (New York: Cambridge UP, 1959); Frederick W. Taylor, *The Principles of Scientific Management* (New York: Harper, 1947).

See also RATIONALIZATION.

Scientific, Professional and Cultural Employees Council On March 15, 1967, 18 AFL-CIO unions representing about 400,000 scientific, professional, and cultural employees created this organization of professional and other white-collar workers. The name was later changed to the Professional Employees Council.

In December 1977, it was granted departmental status and adopted the name Department for Professional Employees.

Source references: "AFL-CIO Council of Scientific, Professional and Cultural Employees Formed at Washington" *Daily Labor Report*, No. 51, March 15, 1967; U.S. Dept. of Labor, BLS, *Directory of National and International Labor Unions in the United States 1969* (Washington: Bull. no. 1665, 1970).

See also PROFESSIONAL EMPLOYEES, DEPARTMENT FOR.

scope of bargaining The actual scope or subject matter which management and unions bring within the area of the collective bargaining contract. An examination of the subjects which labor and management have discussed at the bargaining table and which have been incorporated into contracts indicates that the scope of bargaining depends in large part on the kind of problems the economic and social conditions create.

Source references: Reginald Alleyne, *Statutory Restraints on the Bargaining Obligation in Public Employment* (Los Angeles: UC, Institute of IR, Reprint 268, 1977); Solomon Barkin, "It Is Impractical to Limit Scope of Collective Bargaining," *Labor and Nation*, April/May 1946; Neil W. Chamberlain, "The Nature and Scope of Collective Bargaining," *Quarterly Journal of Economics*, May 1944; Charles A. Edwards, "Employers' Liability for Union Unfair Representation: Fiduciary Duty or Bargaining Reality?" *LLJ*, Nov. 1976; Stanley A. Gacek, "The Employer's Duty to Bargain on Termination of Unit Work," *LLJ*, Nov. 1981; Walter J. Gershenfeld, J. Joseph Loewenberg, and Bernard Ingster (comp.), *Scope of Public-Sector Bargaining, First George W. Taylor Memorial Conference on Public Sector Labor Relations* (Lexington, Mass.: Lexington Books, 1977); I. B. Helburn, "The Scope of Bargaining in Public Sector Negotiations: Sovereignty Reviewed," *Journal of Collective Negotiations in the Public Sector*, Spring 1974; Robert D. Helsby, "Scope of Bargaining Issues with Professional Units," *NYU 31st Annual National Conference on Labor*, ed. by Richard Adelman (New York: Bender, 1978); Lawrence T. Holden, Jr., "The Clash Over What is Bargainable in the Public Schools and Its Consequences for the Arbitrator," *Truth, Lie Detectors, and Other Problems in Labor Arbitration*, Proceedings of the 31st A/M, NAA, ed. by James Stern and Barbara Dennis (Washington: BNA, 1979); Helen F. Humphrey, "The Scope of Collective Bargaining Under the Taft-Hartley Act," *NYU 2d Annual Conference on Labor*, ed. by Emanuel Stein (Albany: Bender, 1949); Thomas R. Jones, *The Scope of Collective Bargaining* (New York: AMA, Personnel Series no. 81, 1944); Steven C. Kahn, "The Scope of Collective Bargaining in the Public Sector: Quest for an Elusive Standard," *Employee Relations LJ*, Spring 1979; Raymond McKay and Michael Petty, "The Scope of Midcontract Bargaining Under E.O. 11491," *Journal of Collective Negotiations in the Public Sector*, Vol. 7, no. 4, 1978; James F. Morton, "Limitations Upon the Scope of Collective Bargaining,"*LLJ*, Oct. 1956; Joyce M. Najita, *Guide to Statutory Provisions in Public Sector Collective Bargaining—Scope of Negotiations* (3d issue, Honolulu: Univ. of Hawaii, IRC, 1981); Paul Prasow et al., *Scope of Bargaining in the Public Sector—Concepts and Problems, Report* (Washington: U.S. Dept. of Labor, LMSA, 1972); Paul Prasow and Edward Peters, *A Theoretical Framework for Scope of Negotiation in the Public Sector* (Los Angeles: UC, Institute of IR, Reprint no. 231, 1972); Henry H. Robinson, *Negotiability in the Federal Sector* (Ithaca: Cornell Univ., NYSSILR and AAA, 1981); Irving H. Sabghir, *The Scope of Bargaining in Public Sector Collective Bargaining (With Special Reference to Experience Under the Taylor Law)* (New York: N.Y. State Public Employment Relations Board, 1970); Murray L. Sackman, "Redefining the Scope of Bargaining in Public

Employment," 19 *Boston College LR* 155 (1977); Deborah Tussey, "Bargainable or Negotiable Issues in State Public Employment Labor Relations," 84 *American Law Report 3d* 242 (1978); U.S. CSC, *Negotiability Determinations by Federal Labor Relations Council (FLRC), January 1, 1970 to January 1, 1976* (Washington: 1976); Joan Weitzman, *The Scope of Bargaining in Public Employment* (New York: Praeger, 1975); Ruth Weyand, "Scope of Collective Bargaining Under the Taft-Hartley Act," *NYU 1st Annual Conference on Labor*, ed. by Emanuel Stein (Albany: Bender, 1948).

See also INLAND STEEL CO. V. NLRB, LABOR-MANAGEMENT CONFERENCE (1945), MANAGEMENT RIGHTS, MANDATORY SUBJECTS FOR BARGAINING, PERMISSIVE SUBJECTS FOR BARGAINING, PROHIBITED SUBJECTS FOR BARGAINING.

SCO Service The Special Contract Operative Service associated with the former National Metal Trades Association. The term has been used to denote or indicate labor espionage.

Scott man-to-man scale A rating scale developed by Dr. Walter D. Scott during World War I to enable army officers to judge and rate draftees for promotion and placement. It subsequently was known as the "man-to-man rating scale" or the "Scott" scale.

The original method used in the Army included the rating of draftees in accordance with five factors:

(1) Physical qualities,
(2) Intelligence,
(3) Leadership,
(4) Personal qualities,
(5) General value to the service.

Each factor then was subdivided into five grading areas: (a) the highest, (b) high, (c) middle, (d) low, (e) lowest. The number of points for each grade was a maximum of 100 and a minimum of 20 points. The system involved obtaining so-called standard or key men in each of the five basic factors and distribution of these men from the highest to the lowest in an attempt to provide anchor men or benchmarks. The individuals to be rated then were compared to these five anchor men.

Source reference: Walter D. Scott, Robert C. Clothier, and William R. Spriegel, *Personnel Management* (6th ed., New York: McGraw-Hill, 1961).

scout An individual working out of the personnel office of a company who seeks to recruit well qualified individuals for employment. These scouts or recruiters travel to various parts of the country interviewing and informing individuals of the special opportunities provided by the company and the kind of competence needed by the company employees. Their operations have become commonplace on college and university campuses.

See also RECRUITING AGENT.

scouting A recruiting procedure which is used by companies to obtain the best qualified individuals throughout the country, including recruitment in the colleges and universities. Scouting is utilized especially during a tight labor market.

Screen Actors Guild Founded in 1933, it is a branch of the Associated Actors and Artistes of America (AFL-CIO). It issues the *Screen Actor Magazine* (3 issues annually), *Screen Actor Newsletter* (monthly), *Newsreel Magazine* (semiannually), and *New York Newsletter* (semiannually).

Address: 7750 Sunset Blvd., Los Angeles, Calif. 90046. Tel. (213) 876–3030

Screen Directors' Guild of America, Inc. (Ind) *See* DIRECTORS GUILD OF AMERICA, INC. (IND).

Screen Extras Guild Established in 1945, it is a branch of the Associated Actors and Artistes of America (AFL-CIO). Its quarterly publication is *Background Action.*

Address: 3629 Cahuenga Blvd., West, Los Angeles, Calif. 90068. Tel. (213) 851–4301

scrip A form of token money which was used in isolated communities such as the coal and lumber towns and railroad terminals that were not near urban centers. Such wages in lieu of money wages could be redeemed only at the company store. This frequently involved paying higher prices than might normally be paid in stores where there was competition.

In areas where the scrip was accepted in other stores and purchases could be made in independent stores in larger communities, the owners of the stores took the scrip only at a substantial discount. This in effect led to a lower actual income for the employees than would have been warranted if payment had been made in legal tender.

A number of states have made illegal the use of scrip and require payment in legal tender. With the decline of the company store and company towns, scrip practice has all but disappeared.

During periods of depression and in situations where legal tender has been hard to come by because of runs on banks or their closing, communities frequently have relied on scrip payment for government employees which was generally redeemable within the community.

See also COMPANY STORE.

Seafarers' International Union of North America (AFL-CIO) The Seafarers' International Union of North America (AFL-CIO) includes:

(1) Atlantic, Gulf, Lakes and Inland Waters District;
(2) International Union of Petroleum and Industrial Workers;
(3) Pacific Coast Marine Firemen, Oilers, Watertenders and Wipers Association; and
(4) Sailors' Union of the Pacific.

The Transportation Services and Allied Workers, another union affiliated with the Seafarers was dissolved in July 1967.

Address: 5201 Auth Way, Camp Springs, Md. 20746. Tel. (301) 899–0675

See also ATLANTIC, GULF, LAKES AND INLAND WATERS DISTRICT; PACIFIC COAST MARINE FIREMEN, OILERS, WATERTENDERS AND WIPERS ASSOCIATION; PETROLEUM AND INDUSTRIAL WORKERS, INTERNATIONAL UNION OF; SAILORS' UNION OF THE PACIFIC.

seasonal employee An individual who is taken on for work for short periods of activity or during peak periods to handle a particular service or product. Clerical employees, for example, may be hired seasonally for specific holidays, such as the Christmas rush or the Easter season. This is also true of certain agricultural employment either at planting or harvest time. One of the major problems of migratory employees is the fact that their employment is highly seasonal.

See also MIGRATORY WORKER.

seasonal employment Work opportunities which are available to individuals only during certain seasons. This is true in certain types of industries such as the canning of fruit or the handling of products as in logging or in industries like the garment industry, which respond to changes in styles and season. Seasonal employment may be due to climatic influences, market conditions, or the nature of the product.

seasonal industry An industry which has high peaks of employment at certain times of the year and troughs during other seasons.

Few, if any, industries maintain uniform levels of employment throughout the year. Some industries periodically go through substantial troughs and peaks and there is relatively little evenness in the pattern of their employment opportunities.

The term is specially defined in the Fair Labor Standards Act as an industry that is forced to curtail or cease production periodically during the year.

The Act grants relief from statutory overtime pay standards to seasonal industries qualifying for these exemptions, limited to a fixed number of weeks per year.

Source references: Mary Van Kleeck, *A Seasonal Industry* (New York: Russell Sage Foundation, 1917); Wladimir S. Woytinsky, *Seasonal Variations in Employment in the United States* (New York: Social Science Research Council, 1939).

See also FAIR LABOR STANDARDS ACT OF 1938.

seasonal tolerance clause A provision in a collective bargaining agreement or statute which waives the overtime pay provisions for extra hours of work during peak seasonal periods.

See also FAIR LABOR STANDARDS ACT OF 1938, TWO-THOUSAND-HOUR CLAUSE.

seasonal unemployment Unemployment due to the seasonal nature of the industry and its operations. Agriculture, lumbering, construction, and other similar industries show variations in employment because of weather conditions. Industries such as clothing and millinery show variations in seasonal employment as the result of consumption patterns which lead to production peaks and valleys.

Source references: Merrill G. Murray, *The Treatment of Seasonal Unemployment Under Unemployment Insurance* (Kalamazoo: Upjohn Institute for Employment Research, 1972); Morris J. Newman, "Seasonal Variations in Employment and Unemployment During 1951–75," *MLR*, Jan. 1980; James O'Conner, "Seasonal Unemployment and Insurance," *AER*, June 1962; "Reducing Seasonal Unemployment," *MLR*, Sept. 1966; David C. Smith, "Seasonal Unemployment and Economic Conditions," *Employment Policy and the Labor Market*, ed. by Arthur M. Ross (Berkeley: UC Press, 1965); U.S. Joint Labor-Commerce Study of Construction Seasonality, *Seasonal Unemployment in the Construction Industry* (Washington: 1969); U.S. National Commission on Employment and Unemployment Statistics, *A Comparison and Assessment of Seasonal Adjustment Methods for Employment and Unemployment Statistics*, by Estela Bee Dagum (Washington: Background Paper 5, 1978).

See also CYCLICAL UNEMPLOYMENT, EMPLOYMENT STABILIZATION, FRICTIONAL UNEMPLOYMENT, FULL EMPLOYMENT, TECHNOLOGICAL UNEMPLOYMENT.

secession The voluntary breaking away or withdrawal of an organization from a larger one which is in existence. There have been many secession movements in labor history, the most notable in the United States being the split within the AFL which led to development of the Congress of Industrial Organizations.

secondary activities Tactics such as picketing, boycotts, or other economic action against an employer with whom the union is not directly involved in a dispute, in order to bring the pressure of that employer to bear on the employer with whom the union has a dispute, and to assist the union in winning its objectives.

secondary arbitration *See* ARBITRATION, SECONDARY.

secondary boycott Pressure exerted by a union indirectly on a neutral party who then exerts pressure against the person who is the actual adversary. It may involve the refusal to handle, purchase, or work on products of a company which is dealing with an employer who is unfair to the union or with whom the union has a dispute.

Professor Robert E. Mathews states that the core of the elusive term secondary boycott "is probably the bringing of pressure against a neutral in order to exert pressure indirectly against the real adversary. The immediate objective is to induce the neutral to bring pressure against another which becomes the means of bringing pressure against the other from whom the economic concessions are sought."

Ludwig Teller states that the secondary boycott exists "where many combine to injure one in his business by coercing third persons against their will to cease patronizing him by threats of similar injury."

Professor Lloyd Reynolds explains why the secondary boycott has been a useful device in obtaining recognition from nonunion employers. He says in part:

> The secondary boycott . . . has been used mainly as a device for winning recognition from non-union employers. It involves putting pressure on one employer so that he will exert pressure on another employer whom the union is really after. The carpenters' union, for example, has jurisdiction over factories making millwork and other lumber products. These plants are numerous, small, and often difficult to organize. One way to organize them is for the union carpenters on construction jobs to refuse to install millwork from non-union factories. This refusal forces the building contractors to buy from union plants only. The non-union plants find their market reduced or even destroyed, and are forced to recognize the union. Similarly, members of the meatcutters' union are employed both in butcher shops and in meatpacking plants. Union members in the stores may refuse to handle meat from non-union plants. Union stone masons may refuse to lay stone cut in non-union plants which the union wishes to organize.

Source references: Paul A. Brinker and William E. Cullison, "Secondary Boycotts in the United States Since 1947," *LLJ*, May 1961; Paul A. Brinker and Benjamin J. Taylor, "Secondary Boycott Analysis by Industry," *LLJ*, Oct. 1973; ———, "The Secondary Boycott Maze," *LLJ*, July 1974; B. Cushman, "Secondary Boycotts Under Taft-Hartley," *Syracuse LR*, Fall 1954; Ralph M. Dereshinsky, Alan D. Berkowitz, and Philip A. Miscimarra, *The NLRB and Secondary Boycotts* (rev. ed., Philadelphia: Univ. of Pennsylvania, Wharton School, Industrial Research Unit, LRPP Series no. 4, 1981); Laurence Gold, "The 'Logic' of the Connell Opinion," *NYU 29th Annual Conference on Labor*, ed. by Richard Adelman (New York: Bender, 1976); John S. Irving, Jr., "The Reach of the Secondary Boycott Prohibitions Under the LMRA and 'Labor Organization' Issues in Secondary Boycott Cases," *NYU 25th Annual Conference on Labor* (New York: Bender, 1973); Leonard S. Janofsky and Howard C. Hay, "Connell—Consistent with Past, Indicative of the Future," *NYU 29th Annual Conference on Labor*, ed. by Richard Adelman (New York: Bender, 1976); Irving Kovarsky, "The Supreme Court and the Secondary Boycott," *LLJ*, April 1965; Gregory Kramer, "The Section 8(b)(4) Publicity Proviso and *NLRB v. Servette*: A Supreme Court Mandate Ignored," *LLJ*, Oct. 1982; Douglas Leslie, "Right to Control: A Study in Secondary Boycotts and Labor Antitrust," *IR Law Digest*, Fall 1976; J. James Miller, "Legal and Economic History of the Secondary Boycott," *LLJ*, Aug. 1961; David Previant, "New Develoments in Secondary Boycotts," *NYU 23d Annual Conference on Labor*, ed. by Thomas Christensen and Andrea Christensen (New York: Bender, 1971); Philip Ross, "An Assessment of the Landrum-Griffin Act's Secondary Boycott Amendments to the Taft-Hartley Act," *LLJ*, Nov. 1971; Melvin J. Segal, "Secondary Boycott Loopholes," *LLJ*, March 1959; Arthur B. Smith, Jr., "Work Preservation Boycotts: 'The Drawing of Lines More Nice than Obvious,'" *Industrial Relations LJ*, Fall 1976; Irving Weschler, "Certain Aspects of Administration of Secondary Boycotts Under the Provisions of the Labor-Management Relations Act of 1947 and the Evolution of Doctrines of the United States Supreme Court" (M.B.A. thesis, NYU, 1956); Don A. Zimmerman, "The Changing Arsenal of Economic Weapons: Consequences for Section 8(b)(4), the Board and the Courts," *NYU 34th Annual National Conference on Labor*, ed. by Richard Adelman (New York: Bender, 1982).

See also BOYCOTT, BUCKS' STOVE AND RANGE CASE, HOT CARGO PROVISIONS, LAWLOR V. LOEWE.

secondary employment A term which has a variety of meanings. It is sometimes used as the equivalent of moonlighting, that is, working at a second job when the employee already holds a full-time job. It is also used to indicate employment which results as a byproduct of a major operation such as a construction operation or a refinery. The expenditure of funds in the primary industry leads to employment of a secondary nature elsewhere. The phrase occasionally is applied to industries which process materials on a secondary level and thereby provide employment. Thus, the production of cloth would be a primary operation, whereas the cutting, dyeing, or sewing operations might be considered secondary.

See also DOUBLE EMPLOYMENT.

secondary picketing The bringing of pressure by picketing an establishment which is not directly involved in a dispute but which has some business connection with a company with whom the union does have a dispute. It may be done either for organizational purposes or as incidental to a strike.

secondary strike A strike against an employer who deals with a company whose workers are out on strike. Although there is here an aspect of the sympathetic strike, it is frequently distinguished from it in that in a secondary strike there is a close business relationship between the employers involved. Usually one is a supplier to the other, or possibly a subsidiary, or otherwise intimately connected in the overall operations of the industry.

second injury provisions Language in state statutes which is designed to assist partially disabled employees to be rehired. Since such employees might be more prone to additional injury and possible total disability, employers occasionally are reluctant to hire them. Because of second injury provisions in some state laws, employees who receive another injury cannot hold the employer liable except for the additional partial disability. Other state laws may provide that the total available compensation because of the additional injury be smaller since the individual's total earning power should be reflected in the fact that there was an earlier disability.

Second International A group of labor and socialist parties from various countries organized in Paris in 1889 as an organization directed primarily against militarism. The Second International lost out to the incipient nationalism throughout the world. The organization was rebuilt in Hamburg in 1923 and its position has been that of the moderate or gradualist socialist parties. It excluded the Communists, who had formed the Third International.

Source references: Julius Braunthal, *History of the International, Vol. I: 1864–1914* (New York: Praeger, 1967); Russell E. Westmeyer, *Modern Economic and Social Systems* (New York: Farrar, Rinehart, 1940).

secretaries of labor *See* LABOR SECRETARIES.

Section 7(a) of the National Industrial Recovery Act *See* NATIONAL INDUSTRIAL RECOVERY ACT, SECTION 7(A).

Section 10(j) A provision in the Taft-Hartley Act which permits the NLRB to obtian injunctive relief when "there is reasonable cause to believe that the charges filed were true" and that injunctive relief is necessary to effectuate the policies of the Act.

Section 10(j) reads as follows:

> The Board shall have power upon issuance of a complaint as provided in subsection (b) charging that any person has engaged in or is engaging in an unfair labor practice to petition any district court of the United States (including the District Court of the United States for the District of Columbia) within any district wherein the unfair labor practice in question is alleged to have occurred or wherein such person resides or transacts business, for appropriate temporary relief or restraining order. Upon the filing of any such petition the court shall cause notice thereof to be served upon such person and thereupon shall have jurisdiction to grant to the Board such temporary relief or restraining order as it deems just and proper.

Section 14(b) Section 14(b) of the Taft-Hartley Act provides the channel through which individual states may enact "right-to-work" legislation. It reads as follows:

> Nothing in this act shall be construed as authorizing the execution or application of agreements requiring membership in a labor organization as a condition of employment in any State or Territory in which such execution or application is prohibited by State or Territorial law.

See also PREEMPTION, DOCTRINE OF; RIGHT TO WORK LAW.

Section 301 A provision in Title 3 of the Taft-Hartley Act which permits suits by and against labor organizations for violation of contract without imposition of the generally accepted federal court limitations on amount in controversy and citizenship of the parties.

The first paragraph of Section 301 reads:

> Suits for violation of contracts between an employer and a labor organization representing employees in an industry affecting commerce as defined in this Act, or between any such labor organizations, may be brought in any district court of the United States having jurisdiction of the parties, without respect to the amount in controversy or without regard to the citizenship of the parties.

Source references: O. S. Hoebreck, "Federal Courts Under Section 301," *Marquette LR*, Spring 1960; "Section 301(a) and the Federal Common Law of Labor Agreements," *Yale LJ*, April 1966; Michael I. Sovern, "Section 301 and the Primary Jurisdiction of the NLRB," *LLJ*, Jan. 1963.

Section 1981 The modern form of the Civil Rights Act of 1866, codified as 42 U.S.C. 1981.

See also CIVIL RIGHTS ACT OF 1866.

Section 1983 The modern form of the Civil Rights Act of 1871, codified as 42 U.S.C. 1983.

See also CIVIL RIGHTS ACT OF 1871.

secular unemployment Unemployment due to forces in the economic system which have long-run impact leading to a decline in employment. Four of these forces are listed by Professor Carroll R. Daugherty as (1) the rise of new industries and the decline of others, (2) the migration of industries to locations in new regions, (3) the concentration of businesses in large units through mergers and consolidations, and (4) the use of new machinery and new processes of production.

Source references: Carroll R. Daugherty, *Labor Problems in American Industry, 1948–1949 Impression* (Boston: Houghton Mifflin, 1948); Paul H. Douglas and Aaron Director, *The Problem of Unemployment*

(New York: Macmillan, 1931); Alvin H. Hansen, *Economic Stabilization in an Unbalanced World* (New York: Harcourt, Brace, 1932).

See also CYCLICAL UNEMPLOYMENT, FRICTIONAL UNEMPLOYMENT, FULL EMPLOYMENT, SEASONAL UNEMPLOYMENT, TECHNOLOGICAL UNEMPLOYMENT.

security A broad term which encompasses the types of union security in collective bargaining agreements, as well as individual economic and social security.

Source references: Daniel Bell, "The Workers' Search for Security," *MLR*, June 1963; William Hedley, "Security of Employment: The Workers' Charter," *Journal of Business Law*, Jan. 1963; Glenn W. Miller, "Appraisal of Collectively Bargained and Governmental Programs for Employee Security," *New Dimensions in Collective Bargaining*, ed. by Harold W. Davey, Howard S. Kaltenborn, and Stanley H. Ruttenberg (New York: Harper, IRRA Pub. no. 21, 1959); J. W. Myers, "Government and Voluntary Programs for Security," *Harvard BR*, March 1950.

See also SOCIAL SECURITY ACT, UNION SECURITY CLAUSES.

Security Officers; International Union of (Ind) Formerly known as the International Union of Guards and Watchmen (Ind), the present name was adopted in the late 1970s. It publishes the bimonthly *Newsletter*.

Address: 2404 Merced St., San Leandro, Calif. 94577. Tel. (415) 895–9905

sedentary occupation A job which does not require much physical activity and where the employee typically sits at a desk. Such jobs include bookkeeping, typing, etc. The automation revolution may result in many more occupations of this charater.

seizure *See* GOVERNMENT SEIZURE, PRESIDENTIAL SEIZURE.

selection interview One of the methods widely used in selecting persons for employment. It frequently will be used in addition to other selection techniques, including an evaluation of the person's previous record, various recommendations, or tests given by the employer or other groups which relate to the specific aspects of the job.

Source reference: Benjamin Balinsky, *The Selection Interview: Essentials for Management* (New Rochelle: Bruce, 1962).

See also EMPLOYMENT INTERVIEW.

selection of employees One of the major tasks of the personnel office and the supervisors directly concerned with new staff. It is the process of choosing the individual most likely to perform the job effectively and be able to fit into the operation of the company and cooperate with other employees. In addition, in some jobs a potential for promotion and advancement must be shown.

If the recruiting process has been effective and qualified individuals have been brought into the reviewing operation, the function of the selection process is to review these individuals—their records, their past achievements and potentials—and to give such other tests as are necessary to make sure that the person chosen is the person best suited for the position.

Source references: Philip Ash, "Selection Techniques and the Law: I. Discrimination in Hiring and Placement," *Personnel*, Nov./Dec. 1967; Charles Bahn, "The Economy of Scientific Selection," *PJ*, Aug. 1970; Lance A. Berger, "Beneath the Tip of the Iceberg: How to Handle the Employee Selection Decision," *Personnel*, Sept./Oct. 1977; Robert B. Best, "Don't Forget Those Reference Checks!" *Public Personnel Management*, Nov./Dec. 1977; Stephen J. Carroll, Jr. and Allan N. Nash, "Effectiveness of a Forced-Choice Reference Check," *Personnel Administration*, March/April 1972; George W. England and Donald G. Paterson, "Selection and Placement—The Past Ten Years," *Employment Relations Research*, ed. by Herbert G. Heneman, Jr., et al. (New York: Harper, IRRA Pub. no. 23, 1960); Leonard W. Ferguson, S. Rains Wallace, Jr., and Robert K. Zelle, "Selection and Turnover," *PJ*, March 1959; Lawrence R. Jauch, "Systematizing the Selection Decision," *PJ*, Nov. 1976; John H. Kirkwood, "Selection Techniques and the Law: II. To Test or Not to Test?" *Personnel*, Nov./Dec. 1967; Desmond D. Martin, William J. Kearney, and George D. Holdefer, *The Decision to Hire: A Comparison of Selec-*

tion Tools (Cincinnati: Univ. of Cincinnati, College of Business Administration, Reprint Series no. 45, 1971); Robert N. McMurray, *Tested Techniques of Personnel Selection* (Chicago: Dartnell, 1955); Mary Green Miner and John B. Miner, *Employee Selection Within the Law* (Washington: BNA, 1978); Thomas A. Petit and Terry W. Mullins, "Decisions, Decisions: How to Make Good Ones on Employee Selection," *Personnel*, March/April 1981; Scott T. Rickard, "Effective Staff Selection," *PJ*, June 1981; Lance W. Seberhagen, Michael D. McCollum, and Connie D. Churchill, *Legal Aspects of Personnel Selection in the Public Service* (Chicago: IPMA, Special Report, 1973); Robert D. Smith, "Models for Personnel Selection Decisions,"*PJ*, Aug. 1973; Erwin S. Stanton, *Successful Personnel Recruiting and Selection* (New York: AMACOM, 1977); Arthur A. Witkin, "Commonly Overlooked Dimensions of Employee Selection," *PJ*, July 1980.

See also "BOTTOM LINE," EMPLOYMENT INTERVIEW, EXIT INTERVIEW, PROMOTION, RECRUITING.

selective certification Used as an affirmative action measure in some jurisdictions, it allows employers to expand the eligible list for job vacancies through consideration of factors other than highest test scores. Such a device is thought to afford women and minorities greater opportunity to fill certain civil service positions.

Source references: Alice H. Cook and Joyce M. Najita, *Equal Employment Opportunity, Collective Bargaining and the Merit Principle in Hawaii* (Honolulu: Hawaii, Dept. of Personnel Services, 1979); Robert Freiberg (ed.), *The Manager's Guide to Equal Employment Opportunity* (New York: Executive Enterprises, 1977).

selective service The administrative machinery which gives effect to selective service laws or the manpower controls during a war or emergency periods.

Source references: David F. Bradford, *Deferment Policy in Selective Service* (Princeton: Princeton Univ., IR Section, Research Report Series no. 113, 1969); Michael Pancer, "What You Should Know About the Selective Service Law," *PJ*, Oct. 1969; Betty M. Vetter, "What Every Young Man Should Know About the Draft," *Occupational Outlook Quarterly*, Fall 1969.

self-administered (trusteed) plan Any pension or retirement plan funded through a trustee. The trustee may be an individual, a group, or bank. The funds are paid to the trustee yearly, and as pensions become due they are paid from the fund.

Source reference: BNA, *Pensions and Profit Sharing* (3d ed., Washington: 1964).

self-determination election Provisions in the National Labor Relations Act which permit craft or skilled or professional employees to determine through an election whether they wish to be included in a larger unit, generally the production unit, for bargaining purposes.

self-employed The gainfully occupied segment of the work force whose members work for themselves.

Source references: T. Scott Fain, "Self-Employed Americans: Their Number Has Increased," *MLR*, Nov. 1980; Irving Leveson, "The Supply of Self-Employed: A Study of Retail Managers," *Proceedings of the 20th A/M, IRRA*, ed. by Gerald Somers (Madison: 1968).

self-employment The act of being self-employed or working for oneself. Among those who are generally regarded as self-employed or engaged in self-employment are doctors, lawyers, farmers.

Source references: John E. Bregger, "Self-Employment in the United States, 1948–62," *MLR*, Jan. 1963; Victor R. Fuchs, "Self-Employment and Labor Force Participation of Older Males," *Journal of Human Resources*, Summer 1982; Marcia Levy, *Self-Employment in the Covered Work Force* (Washington: U.S. Dept. of HEW, SSA, Staff Paper 19, 1975); Gloria Stevenson, "Working For Yourself: What's It Like?" *Occupational Outlook Quarterly*, Spring 1973; U.S. Dept. of HEW, SSA, *Self-Employment and Retirement Age* (Washington: Research and Statistics Note no. 15, 1976); ———, *Self-Employment of Black Men, 1960 and 1970* (Washington: Research and Statistics Note no. 4, 1976).

self-insurance Assumption by a company or organization of its own risk instead of insuring through a general carrier or insurance company.

self-organization One of the essential features of collective bargaining. A protected right of employees to combine for the purpose of obtaining better wages, hours, and working conditions. The right of self-organization had been recognized long before the New Deal period in the 1930s. However, the full liberty of self-organization was not adequately protected by law so as to enforce it as a right. One of the earlier statements which attempted in part to enforce that right through limitation on the use of the injunction is set out in the Norris-LaGuardia Act of March 23, 1932. Section 2 provides as follows:

> Whereas under prevailing economic conditions, developed with the aid of governmental authority for owners of property to organize in the corporate and other forms of ownership association, the individual unorganized worker is commonly helpless to exercise actual liberty of contract and to protect his freedom of labor, and thereby to obtain acceptable terms and conditions of employment, wherefore, though he should be free to decline to associate with his fellows, it is necessary that he have full freedom of association, self-organization, and designation of representatives of his own choosing, to negotiate the terms and conditions of his employment, and that he shall be free from the interference, restraint, or coercion of employers of labor or their agents, in the designation of such representatives or in self-organization or in other concerted activities for the purpose of collective bargaining or other mutual aid or protection; therefore, the following definitions of, and limitations upon, the jurisdiction and authority of the courts of the United States are hereby enacted.

The foregoing language seemingly inspired the language subsequently incorporated in Section 7 of the National Labor Relations Act.

See also NATIONAL LABOR RELATIONS ACT.

selling out The phrase used to describe the action of a union leader or group which has settled a strike or negotiation on terms which are not popular with a majority of the workers. The term basically implies that the leaders accepted monetary inducements or obtained personal benefits from the settlement.

semi-industrial union A union which is neither completely a craft union nor an industrial union. One which combines the features of both.

semiskilled labor Labor which is between the highly skilled and unskilled. Employees in the semiskilled category, generally have some training but it is likely to have been short and sketchy. They frequently have manipulative skill, but their work is generally routine and well defined. They may require some training and exercise limited independent judgment, but do not generally approach the traditional skilled crafts.

senior executive service (SES) Term used to cover programs established in public employment to recruit and retain competent, qualified top-level managers. In California, it is called "Career Executive Assignment"; in Iowa, "Public Service Executive" program; in Oregon, "Executive Service"; in Wisconsin, "Career Executive Program"; and in the federal service, "Senior Executive Service." Finkle et al. note that the programs are "specific only in concept and very general in terms of operations."

The federal program was established by Title IV of the Civil Service Reform Act of 1978 and covers positions in the GS–16, 17, and 18 ranks and in level IV and V of the Executive Schedule. An objective of the federal SES is to insure that compensation, retention, and tenure are contingent upon executive success. Executives are appraised on the basis of individual and organizational performance. Executives electing to join the SES agree to accept reassignment to areas where they are needed and to give up the job security available to other federal employees. However, in return, SES members become eligible for performance awards which could amount to 20 percent of their basic salary. In addition, some SES members are eligible for presidential rank awards which carry one-time lump sum payments of up to $20,000.

Source references: Civil Service Reform Act of 1978; 5 U.S.C. 3131 et seq. (1982); John Birkenstock, Ronald Kurtz, and Steven Phillips, "Career Executive Assignments—Report of a California Innovation," *Public Personnel Management*, May/June 1975; Arthur L. Finkle, Herbert Hall, and Sophia S. Min,

"Senior Executive Service: The State of the Art," *Public Personnel Management*, Fall 1981; U.S. GAO, *Actions Needed to Enhance the Credibility of Senior Executive Service Performance Award Programs* (Washington: 1981).

seniority The length of service an individual employee has in a unit. Length of service frequently determines position when layoffs and rehires take place, and frequently is an important factor in promotions and transfers.

The seniority principle rests on the assumption that the individuals with the greatest length of service within the company should be given preference in employment.

"Straight seniority" applies to situations in which length of service is the only criterion and "qualified seniority" where factors other than length of service are considered. The phrase "top seniority" applies to special union representatives in order to assure that adequate union representation will be available in the plant while the individuals are serving as union representatives. Such top or "superseniority" applies only while the individual is in office and generally is exercised only in case of reductions in staff.

Seniority may be established for various units such as an individual craft or operation, department, entire plant, or in some cases all of the plants of a company in a particular geographic area.

Source references: James J. Bambrick, Jr., "Ford's Area-Wide Seniority Plan," *Management Record*, March 1954; Richard P. Brown, "A New Technique in Seniority Administration,"*ILRR*, Oct. 1955; Bonnie G. Cebulski, *Affirmative Action Versus Seniority—Is Conflict Inevitable?* (Berkeley: UC, Institute of IR, 1977); James A. Craft, "Equal Opportunity and Seniority: Trends and Manpower Implications," *LLJ*, Dec. 1975; Ben Fischer, "Affirmative Action v. Seniority, Seniority is Healthy," *LLJ*, Aug. 1976; J. Gordon Forester, Jr., "Protracted Litigation in Airline Seniority Disputes," *LLJ*, March 1979; Carl Gersuny, "Employment Security: Cases from Iago to Weber," *Journal of Labor Research*, Winter 1982; ———, "Origins of Seniority Provisions in Collective Bargaining," *LLJ*, Aug. 1982; James E. Jones, Jr., *Title VII, Seniority, and the Supreme Court: Clarification or Retreat?* (Madison: Univ. of Wisconsin, IRRI, Reprint 217, 1977); John A. Lapp, *How to Handle Problems of Seniority* (Deep River: NFI, 1946); John T. Lavey, "Seniority Today—Selected Litigation Risks for Employers and Unions," *Labor Law Developments 1982*, Proceedings of 28th Annual Institute on Labor Law, SLF (New York: Bender, 1982); Arthur A. Malinowski, "The *Teamsters* 703(h) Exemption: Does It Apply to Nonunion Employers?" *Employee Relations LJ*, Autumn 1981; Philomena M. Mullady, "Seniority—A Changing Concept?" *Personnel*, July 1956; Leonard R. Sayles, "Seniority: An Internal Union Problem," *Harvard BR*, Jan./Feb. 1952; "Seniority and Business Mergers: The Union's Duty of Fair Representation," *IR Law Digest*, Oct. 1968; "Seniority—Fair Play on the Job," *American Federationist*, Sept. 1961; Jonathan L. F. Silver, "Operation of the 'Escalator Clause' in Fringe Benefit Cases," *IR Law Digest*, April 1976; U.S. CSC, *Last Hired, First Fired: Layoffs and Civil Rights* (Washington: 1977); U.S. Dept. of Labor, BLS, *Major Collective Bargaining Agreements: Administration of Seniority* (Washington: Bull. 1425–14, 1973).

See also ALBEMARLE PAPER CO. V. MOODY, BONA FIDE SENIORITY SYSTEM, BUMPING, DEPARTMENTAL SENIORITY, "FREEDOM NOW" THEORY, FROZEN SENIORITY, INVERSE SENIORITY, LAYOFF, MEMPHIS FIRE DEPARTMENT V. STOTTS, OCCUPATIONAL SENIORITY, REEMPLOYMENT, RETROACTIVE SENIORITY, "RIGHTFUL PLACE," "STATUS QUO" THEORY, SUPERSENIORITY, TEAMSTERS V. U.S., TOP SENIORITY.

seniority clauses Provisions in collective bargaining agreements which apply the principle of seniority to the employment relationship. Typically such clauses relate an individual's length of service to job retention and recall in case of layoff. They also may make seniority a factor in promotion or transfer, in choice of vacation, and in other aspects of an individual's employment.

Source references: Sara Behman, "Affirmative Action v. Seniority, The Affirmative Action Position," *LLJ*, Aug. 1976; Richard N. Block, "The Impact of Seniority Provisions on the Manufacturing Quit Rate," *ILRR*, July 1978; Jack Hoover and William Leahy,

"Union Seniority Provisions and Discrimination," *Proceedings of the 31st A/M, IRRA*, ed. by Barbara Dennis (Madison: 1979); Irving Kovarsky, "Current Remedies for the Discriminatory Effects of Seniority Agreements," *IR Law Digest*, Jan. 1972; Marvin J. Levine, "The Conflict Between Negotiated Seniority Provisions and Title VII of the Civil Rights Act of 1964: Recent Developments," *LLJ*, June 1978; John W. McCaffrey, "Development and Administration of Seniority Provisions," *NYU 2d Annual Conference on Labor*, ed. by Emanuel Stein (Albany: Bender, 1949); A. P. Mitchem, "Seniority Clauses in Collective Bargaining Agreements," *Rocky Mountain LR*, Feb. 1949; U.S. Dept. of Labor, BLS, *Major Collective Bargaining Agreements: Seniority in Promotion and Transfer Provisions* (Washington: Bull. no. 1425–11, 1970).

seniority increases *See* AUTOMATIC WAGE ADJUSTMENT.

seniority list The schedules in a particular company listing the names of the individuals in the bargaining unit and the length of continuous service of each employee. The list indicates the priority of the individual based on continuous service within the plant or other unit depending on the particular contract provision.

The seniority lists may be set up on the basis of their actual operation in the plant, such as a departmental seniority list or a plantwide seniority list. The purpose is to let the individual employees know where they stand on the seniority roster so that they may protect their rights as set forth in the collective bargaining contract.

The seniority lists are generally available to the union shop steward or other union representative.

Source references: Thomas Kennedy, "Merging Seniority Lists," *Labor Arbitration and Industrial Change*, Proceedings of the 16th A/M, NAA, ed. by Mark Kahn (Washington: BNA, 1963); Dan H. Mater and Garth L. Mangum, "The Integration of Seniority Lists in Transportation Mergers," *ILRR*, April 1963.

seniority policy The statement by a company describing its seniority policy. Where the plant is organized and a collective bargaining agreement exists, the contract language spells out the nature of seniority and its application to various situations such as layoff, rehire, promotions, transfers, etc.

Source references: James J. Bambrick, "Experience Writes a Seniority Policy," *Management Record*, Sept. 1951; Frederick H. Harbison, *Seniority Policies and Procedures as Developed Through Collective Bargaining* (Princeton: Princeton UP, 1941).

seniority rights Privileges, rights, and other benefits which accrue to an individual because of length of service or in the performance of certain work. These rights may be construed and protected by arbitrators or the courts in interpreting the collective bargaining contract.

Source references: Benjamin Aaron, "Reflections on the Legal Nature and Enforceability of Seniority Rights," 75 *Harvard LR* 1532 (1962); Vincent J. Apruzzese, "A Management View of Employment Concepts in Conflict—Seniority v. Equal Opportunity," *Labor Law Developments 1976*, Proceedings of 22d Annual Institute on Labor Law, SLF (New York: Bender, 1976); Alfred W. Blumrosen, "Seniority Rights and Industrial Change," *Minnesota LR*, March 1963; Alan V. Friedman and Allen M. Katz, "Retroactive Seniority for the Identifiable Victim Under Title VII—Must Last Hired, First Fired Give Way," *NYU 28th Annual Conference on Labor*, ed. by Richard Adelman (New York: Bender, 1976); Eugene A. Hoffman, *Do the Seniority Rights of Employees Survive an Expired Contract?* (New York: NAM, 1961); Wayne E. Howard, "Seniority Rights and Trial Periods," *AJ*, Vol. 15, no. 2, 1960; Caroline Poplin, "Fair Employment in a Depressed Economy: The Layoff Problem," *IR Law Digest*, April 1976; Susan C. Ross, "Reconciling Plant Seniority with Affirmative Action and Anti-Discrimination," *NYU 28th Annual Conference on Labor*, ed. by Richard Adelman (New York: Bender, 1976); James E. Youngdahl, "How Can Seniority, Anti-Discrimination and Affirmative Action be Reconciled in a Layoff Economy: The Union Viewpoint," *NYU 28th Annual Conference on Labor*, ed. by Richard Adelman (New York: Bender, 1976).

seniority systems The procedures established in plants which attempt to protect the rights of individuals who have been with the company for long periods of time. Seniority systems exist not only in organized plants, but also in nonunion and unorganized plants.

Source references: Thomas R. Bagby, "The Supreme Court Reaffirms Broad Immunity for Seniority Systems," *LLJ*, July 1982; Robert Coulson, "The Emerging Role of Title VII Arbitration," *LLJ*, May 1975; Helen Elkiss, "Modifying Seniority Systems Which Perpetuate Past Discrimination," *LLJ*, Jan. 1980; Marvin Gittler, "What is a Bona Fide Seniority System Under the Civil Rights Statutes?" *Labor Law Developments 1981*, Proceedings of 27th Annual Institute on Labor Law, SLF (New York: Bender, 1981); Maryellen R. Kelley, "Discrimination in Seniority Systems: A Case Study," *ILRR*, Oct. 1982; NICB, *Seniority Systems in Nonunionized Companies* (New York: Studies in Personnel Policy no. 110, 1950); Paul J. Spiegelman, "Bona Fide Seniority Systems and Relief from 'Last Hired, First Fired' Layoffs Under Title VII," *Employee Relations LJ*, Autumn 1976; Stephen C. Swanson, "The Affect of the Supreme Court's Seniority Decisions,"*PJ*, Dec. 1977; Paul I. Weiner, "Seniority Systems Under *Teamsters* and *Bryant*," *Employee Relations LJ*, Winter 1980/81; David Ziskind, "Affirmative Action v. Seniority, Retroactive Seniority: A Remedy for Hiring Discrimination," *LLJ*, Aug. 1976.

seniority wage system Known as the nenkó wage system (length-of-service reward wage system) in Japan. According to Shimada, it is a "method of determining wages, salaries, and other rewards from employment based primarily on a worker's length of service, but partly on his age and education. With this system, a worker is assured of sufficient earnings to cover his needs over his life cycle. Thus, he is willing to commit himself to the employing firm over a long period of time and also has an incentive to learn on the job."

Source references: Tadashi Hanami, *Labor Relations in Japan Today* (Tokyo: Kodansha Int., 1979); OECD, *Manpower Policy in Japan* (Paris: 1973); Beatrice G. Reubens, "Manpower Training in Japan," *MLR*, Sept. 1973; Haruo Shimada, "Japanese Industrial Relations—A New General Model? A Survey of the English-Language Literature," *Contemporary Industrial Relations in Japan*, ed. by Taishiro Shirai (Madison: Univ. of Wisconsin Press, 1983).

See also ENTERPRISE UNIONISM, LIFETIME EMPLOYMENT SYSTEM.

Senn v. Tile Layers' Protective Union A decision handed down by the Supreme Court in 1937 by a 5-4 vote holding that a Wisconsin anti-injunction law was constitutional. The law previously had been held to violate the 14th Amendment by the Wisconsin Supreme Court.

Justice Brandeis stated the case as presenting "the question whether the provision of the Wisconsin Labor Code which authorized giving publicity to labor disputes, declaring peaceful picketing and patrolling lawful, and prohibit granting of an injunction against such conduct, violate as here construed and applied, the due process clause or equal protection clause of the 14th Amendment."

The Tile Layers' Union was attempting to organize the shop of Paul Senn, a contractor. They placed two to four pickets in front of his home where he had his office. Senn did most of the tile laying himself and the major question was whether he could be made to stop working at the trade and provide jobs to journeymen tile layers. Although the union had no recognition, the Court held that there was a labor dispute within the meaning of the Wisconsin statute and refused to find the Wisconsin statute unconstitutional.

Source references: Labor Code of Wisconsin Statutes 1935 (Wisconsin Laws 1931, Ch. 376; Laws 1935, Ch. 551); *Senn v. Tile Layers' Protective Union*, 301 US 468 (1937); Milton Handler, *Cases and Materials on Labor Law* (St. Paul: West Publishing, 1944).

sensitivity training A form of leadership training in which personal experience in a group is used to help individuals become more aware of themselves and of the manner in which they relate to others on the theory that effective leaders in an organization are more sensitive and more accurate perceivers of how others really think and feel than less effective leaders. Training sessions are guided by one or two "trainers" who attempt to initiate discussion and call attention to conflicts among the participants which block open communication. During the sessions, the group generally moves toward the expression of individuals' perceptions of each other, the revealing of and sharing of personal concerns and emotional conflicts, the recognition of common experience, and the discovery of numerous common difficulties in relating to persons in the members' daily routine.

Sensitivity training developed in the latter 1940s from the laboratory training programs of the summer leadership workshops conducted by the National Training Laboratory in Group Development.

Source references: Kurt W. Back, *Beyond Words; The Story of Sensitivity Training and the Encounter Movement* (New York: Russell Sage Foundation, 1972); Mary Ann Coghill, *Sensitivity Training, A Review of the Controversy* (Ithaca: NYSSILR, Cornell Univ., Key Issues Series no. 1, 1967); John E. Drotning, "Sensitivity Training: Some Critical Questions," *PJ*, Nov. 1966; Jack L. Rettig and Matt M. Amano, "A Survey of ASPA Experience With Management by Objectives, Sensitivity Training and Transactional Analysis," *PJ*, Jan. 1976; Burt K. Scanlan, "Sensitivity Training—Clarifications, Issues, Insights," *PJ*, July 1971; Louis J. Schuster, "Needed: More Sensitivity, Less Training," *PJ*, Aug. 1969; Irving R. Weschler and Jerome Reisel, *Inside a Sensitivity Training Group* (Los Angeles: UC, Institute of IR, Monograph Series no. 4, n.d.); Mary C. Westphal, "Reaction: Minority Sensitivity Training," *Public Personnel Review*, April 1970.

See also LABORATORY TRAINING, T-GROUP.

separability clause A clause in a labor contract which protects the validity of the rest of the contract should any part of it be held invalid.

See also SAVINGS CLAUSE.

separation The termination of employment on a permanent basis, which may be initiated by the employer or by the employee. It does not consider the cause or the party taking the initiative and therefore includes quits, layoffs, discharges, and resignations.

separation allowance *See* DISMISSAL COMPENSATION.

separation interview *See* EXIT INTERVIEW.

separation pay *See* DISMISSAL COMPENSATION.

separation rate *See* LABOR TURNOVER.

serfdom A form of bondage a step up from slavery, where the individual could be sold by his master.

The institution of serfdom was part of the manorial system. It involved a form of compulsory labor and service to the person who owned the land, the lord of the manor. However, the individual could not be sold as in slavery and had certain freedoms under the feudal system.

service credit *See* SENIORITY.

service division That part of the personnel department which concerns itself with providing a variety of personal services to the individual. These may include first aid, counseling, recreational programs, food services, the employee magazine, etc.

Service Employees' International Union (AFL-CIO) Organized in 1917 as the Building Service Employees' International Union and affiliated with the AFL in 1921. It adopted its present name in 1968. On August 19, 1974, the Illinois State Employees Association, a former affiliate of the Assembly of Governmental Employees, merged with the union, but withdrew on May 20, 1975.

The following unions merged with the Service Employees' Union: the International Jewelry Workers' Union (AFL-CIO) and the Oregon Public Employees Association (Ind) in 1980; the National Association of Government Employees (Ind) in 1982; and the California State Employees Association (Ind) in 1984. In 1981, 9 to 5, National Association of Working Women, affiliated with the union as District 925.

The union publishes the monthly *Service Employee* and *SEIU Leadership News Update*.

Address: 2020 K St., N.W., Washington, D.C. 20006. Tel. (202) 452–8750

See also DISTRICT 925, SERVICE EMPLOYEES' INTERNATIONAL UNION; 9 TO 5, NATIONAL ASSOCIATION OF WORKING WOMEN.

service fee Under the agency shop arrangement, a fixed amount, usually the equivalent of union dues which is agreed upon in negotiation between union and employer, paid by nonmembers of a union as a charge to defray the union's expenses in rendering services to nonmembers in the collective bargaining relationship. The service fee is a means of eliminating the "free rider" who does not belong to the union or pay union dues and fees but who benefits from union representation and union services by virtue of the legal obligation upon the union to represent all employees in the bargaining unit. The service fee arrangement has been extended to other union activities such as hiring hall fees and pensioner service fees.

Source references: George W. Cassidy, "Equity Considerations in Public Sector Union Security Arrangements: Should 'Free-Riders' Pay?" *Journal of Collective Negotiations in the Public Sector*, Vol. 5, no. 1, 1976; Charles Sovel, "Service Fees for Union Benefits," *NYU 21st Annual Conference on Labor*, ed. by Thomas Christensen (New York: Bender, 1969).

See also AGENCY SHOP, FAIR SHARE AGREEMENT.

service interruption insurance *See* MUTUAL STRIKE AID.

Servicemen's Readjustment Act of 1944 Popularly known as the G. I. Bill of Rights. It provides for various allowances including educational opportunities for veterans and special financial benefits.

service rating *See* EFFICIENCY RATING, MERIT RATING.

settlement A term generally applied to the agreement, mutually agreed upon between labor and management, resolving a particular dispute or, if a contract negotiation is involved, the mutual agreement on the basis of which a dispute is avoided, or if one has been in progress, is settled.

Settlement agreements may refer to adjustments which are reduced to writing and approved by a regional director of the NLRB in cases which involve a charge of an unfair labor practice. When the party who has engaged in the unfair labor practice agrees to make the necessary adjustment and the other party is willing to withdraw the charge, a settlement agreement may be reached closing the case.

set-up time An allowance frequently provided in contracts for the period during which an operator sets up the machine prior to running a job. Such allowances are made where the set-up time is not actually included in the time allowance for the job.

See also ALLOWED TIME.

seven-hour day The practice of some companies which work on a 39-hour week (seven-hour day, five days a week and half day or four hours on Saturday). It may also apply to companies which have a six-day week of seven hours or a 42-hour week schedule.

See also HOURS OF WORK.

706 agency The state or local fair employment authority recognized as a compliance agency under Section 706(c) of the Civil Rights Act of 1964. According to the EEOC Procedural Regulations, "The qualifications for designation under section 706(c) are as follows:

(1) That the State or political subdivision has a fair employment practice law which makes unlawful employment practices based upon race, color, religion, sex or national origin; and
(2) That the State or political subdivision has either established a State or local authority or authorized an existing State or local authority that is empowered with respect to employment practices found to be unlawful, to do one of three things: To grant relief from the practice; to seek relief from the practice; or to institute criminal proceedings with respect to the practice."

Discrimination charges must first be filed with, or deferred to, a 706 agency before the EEOC has jurisdiction.

Source references: Civil Rights Act of 1964, as amended, 42 U.S.C. 2000e–5 (1982); U.S. EEOC, "Procedural Regulations," 29 C.F.R. 1601.

See also DEFERRAL.

severability clause *See* SEPARABILITY CLAUSE.

severance interview *See* EXIT INTERVIEW.

severance pay *See* DISMISSAL COMPENSATION, LAYOFF PAY.

sex-based wage discrimination *See* PAY EQUITY.

sex differential A variation or difference in rates paid to men and women, made unlawful by the Equal Pay Act.

Source references: Andrea H. Beller, "EEO Laws and the Earnings of Women," *Proceedings of the 29th A/M, IRRA*, ed. by James Stern and Barbara Dennis (Madison: 1977); Walter Block and Walter Williams, "Male-Female Earnings Differentials: A Critical Reappraisal," *Journal of Labor Research*, Fall 1981; Ruth G. Blumrosen, "Wage Discrimination, Job Segregation, and Women Workers," *Employee Relations LJ*, Summer 1980; Gary D. Brown, "Discrimination and Pay Disparities Between White Men and Women," *MLR*, March 1978; ———, "How Type of Employment Affects Earnings Differences by Sex," *MLR*, July 1976; Martin Dooley and Peter Gottschalk, "Does a Younger Male Labor Force Mean Greater Earnings Inequality?" *MLR*, Nov. 1982; Marianne A. Ferber and Helen M. Lowry, "The Sex Differential in Earnings: A Reappraisal," *ILRR*, April 1976; Morley Gunderson, "The Influence of the Status and Sex Composition of Occupations on the Male-Female Earnings Gap," *ILRR*, Jan. 1978; Peter Henle and Paul Ryscavage, "The Distribution of Earned Income Among Men and Women, 1958–77," *MLR*, April 1980; Donald J. McNulty, "Differences in Pay Between Men and Women Workers," *MLR*, Dec. 1967; Nancy F. Rytina, "Earnings of Men and Women: A Look at Specific Occupations," *MLR*, April 1982; Henry Sanborn, "Pay Differences Between Men and Women," *ILRR*, July 1964; Sharon P. Smith, "Government Wage Differentials by Sex," *Journal of Human Resources*, Spring 1976; U.S. Dept. of Labor, BLS, *The Female-Male Earnings Gap: A Review of Employment and Earnings Issues* (Washington: Report 673, 1982); U.S. Dept. of Labor, Women's Bureau, *The Earnings Gap Between Women and Men* (Washington: 1979); Ruth Weyand, "Sex-Biased Wage Rates and Job Assignments," *Labor Law Developments 1975*, Proceedings of the 21st Annual Institute on Labor Law, SLF (New York: Bender, 1975).

See also COMPARABLE WORTH, EQUAL PAY ACT OF 1963, EQUAL PAY FOR EQUAL WORK, PAY EQUITY.

sex discrimination Practices, policies, or procedures that deny equal employment opportunity on the basis of sex. Under Title VII of the Civil Rights Act of 1964, discrimination on the basis of pregnancy, childbirth, or related medical conditions is included in the meaning of sex discrimination.

The EEOC Guidelines on Discrimination Because of Sex cites examples of such discrimination: labeling jobs as either "men's" or "women's" for hiring or promotion purposes, maintaining separate seniority lists based on sex, or discriminating between men and women on fringe benefits. Employment practices involving sexual harassment are also considered unlawful. Discrimination against homosexuals, however, is not prohibited by Title VII.

In addition to the Title VII ban on sex discrimination, Executive Order 11246 requires federal contractors to take affirmative action to ensure that employment practices are implemented without regard to sex and Executive Order 11478 prohibits discimination on the basis of sex in federal employment.

Source references: Executive Order 11246, 3 C.F.R. (1964–65 comp.) 339; U.S. EEOC, "Guidelines on Discrimination Because of Sex," 29 C.F.R. 1604; U.S. OFCCP, "Revised Order No. 4," 41 C.F.R. 60–2; ———, "Sex Discrimination Guidelines," 41 C.F.R. 60–20; Joan Abramson, *Old Boys—New Women, The Politics of Sex Discrimination* (New York: Praeger, 1979); Marianne A. Ferber and Carole A. Green, "Traditional or Reverse Sex Discrimination? A Case Study of a Large Public University," *ILRR*, July 1982; Vern E. Hauck, "*Burdine*: Sex Discrimination, Promotion, and Arbitration," *LLJ*, July 1982; Jennifer S. Macleod, "Sex Discrimination: What It is, How to Combat It," *Employee Relations LJ*, Spring 1976; Task Force on Working Women, *Exploitation from 9 to 5, Report of the Twentieth Century Fund Task Force on Women and Employment* (New York: Twentieth Century Fund, 1975); U.S. Commission on Civil Rights, *A Guide to*

Federal Laws Prohibiting Sex Discrimination (Washington: 1974); Benjamin W. Wolkinson and Dennis H. Liberson, "The Arbitration of Sex Discrimination Grievances," *AJ*, June 1982; Women's Labor Project, *Bargaining for Equality, A Guide to Legal and Collective Bargaining Solutions for Workplace Problems that Particularly Affect Women* (2d ed., San Francisco: 1981).

See also AFFIRMATIVE ACTION, AFSCME V. STATE OF WASHINGTON, BENNETT AMENDMENT, BONA FIDE OCCUPATIONAL QUALIFICATION (BFOQ), CIVIL RIGHTS ACT OF 1964, EXECUTIVE ORDER 11246, EXECUTIVE ORDER 11478, FEENEY CASE, GENERAL ELECTRIC V. GILBERT, GUNTHER CASE, IUE V. WESTINGHOUSE ELECTRIC CORP., MANHART CASE, NORRIS CASE, PREGNANCY DISCRIMINATION ACT, TITLE IX OF THE EDUCATION AMENDMENTS OF 1972.

"sex plus" discrimination Refers to the disparate treatment of employees because of sex by the imposition of employment criteria for one gender, but not for the other. Examples of "sex plus" discrimination include a policy of not accepting applications from women with pre–school age children, prohibiting employment of married female flight attendants, or requiring married female employees to take the husband's surname.

Source references: Allen v. Lovejoy, 553 F2d 522, 14 FEP Cases 1194 (1977); *Phillips v. Martin Marietta Corp.*, 400 US 542, 3 FEP Cases 40 (1971); *Sprogis v. United Airlines*, 444 F2d 1194, 3 FEP Cases 621 (1971).

sexual harassment According to the EEOC Guidelines on Discrimination Because of Sex, it is "Unwelcome sexual advances, requests for sexual favors, and other verbal or physical conduct of a sexual nature . . . when (1) submission to such conduct is made either explicitly or implicitly a term or condition of an individual's employment, (2) submission to or rejection of such conduct by an individual is used as the basis for employment decisions affecting such individual, or (3) such conduct has the purpose or effect of unreasonably interfering with an individual's work performance or creating an intimidating, hostile, or offensive working environment."

The guidelines hold the employer, its agents or supervisors responsible for the sexual harassment of employees "regardless of whether the specific acts complained of were authorized or even forbidden by the employer and regardless of whether the employer knew of or should have known of their occurrence." An employer, its agents or supervisory employees who knows or should have known of harassing conduct is also responsible for the conduct between fellow employees and possibly for the acts of nonemployees "unless it can show that . . . immediate and appropriate corrective action" was taken.

Sexual harassment in the workplace is considered a violation of Title VII of the Civil Rights Act of 1964. The courts have generally upheld sexual harassment claims and have found employers liable for the actions of supervisory employees.

Source references: Bundy v. Jackson, 641 F2d 934, 24 FEP Cases 1155 (1981); U.S. EEOC, "Guidelines on Discrimination Because of Sex," 29 C.F.R. 1604; Constance Backhouse and Leah Cohen, *Sexual Harassment on the Job; How to Avoid the Working Women's Nightmare* (Englewood Cliffs; PH, 1981); Ralph H. Baxter, Jr., "Judicial and Administrative Protections Against Sexual Harassment in the Work Place," *Employee Relations LJ*, Spring 1982; BNA, *Sexual Harassment and Labor Relations* (Washington: 1981); Marcia L. Greenbaum and Bruce Fraser, "Sexual Harassment in the Workplace," *AJ*, Dec. 1981; Michele Hoyman and Ronda Robinson, "Interpreting the New Sexual Harassment Guidelines," *PJ*, Dec. 1980; George K. Kronenberger and David L. Bourke, "Effective Training and the Elimination of Sexual Harassment," *PJ*, Nov. 1981; Donna E. Ledgerwood and Sue Johnson-Dietz, "The EEOC's Bold Foray into Sexual Harassment on the Job: New Implications," *Proceedings of the 33d A/M, IRRA*, ed. by Barbara Dennis (Madison: 1981); Jane M. Picker, "Sexual Harassment," *NYU 34th Annual National Conference on Labor*, ed. by Richard Adelman (New York: Bender, 1982); Robert W. Schupp, Joyce Windham, and Scott Draughn, "Sexual Harassment Under Title VII: The Legal Status," *LLJ*, April 1981; Gary R. Siniscalo, "Sexual Harassment and Employer Liability: The Flirtation that Could Cost a Fortune," *Employee Relations LJ*, Autumn 1980; Jay W. Waks and Michael G.

Starr, "Sexual Harassment in the Work Place: The Scope of Employer Liability," *Employee Relations LJ*, Winter 1981/82; ______, "The 'Sexual Shakedown' in Perspective: Sexual Harassment in its Social and Legal Contexts," *Employee Relations LJ*, Spring 1982.

See also SEX DISCRIMINATION.

shakedown time The period of time allowed after the installation or adjustment of a wage incentive plan to permit normal operation to iron out difficulties.

shape-up A method of hiring prevalent for many years in the longshore industry and common to the hiring of migratory farm workers. The procedure involved the lineup at least once a day of prospective employees in the form roughly of a half circle on the pier. The representatives of the employing steamship-stevedoring companies would pass among them and choose the ones they wanted to hire.

The shape-up has given way in most areas to the hiring hall and other procedures which provide a better organized and less inherently discriminatory form of hiring and rotation.

Source references: American Association of Port Authorities, Committee on Standardization and Special Research, *A Port Dictionary of Technical Terms* (New Orleans: 1940); Malcolm Johnson, *Crime on the Labor Front* (New York: McGraw-Hill, 1950); Charles P. Larrowe, *Shape-Up and Hiring Hall* (Berkeley: UC Press, 1955); Edward E. Swanstron, *The Waterfront Labor Problem* (New York: Fordham UP, 1938).

See also DISPATCHERS, HIRING HALL.

share-the-work *See* WORK SHARING.

Sheet Metal Workers' International Association (AFL-CIO) The organization was founded in January 1888 in Toledo, Ohio, as the Tin, Sheet, Iron and Cornice Workers International Association. The name was changed in 1896 to the Amalgamated Sheet Metal Workers International Association. It was changed again in 1903 to the Amalgamated Sheet Metal Workers' International Alliance. When the Coppersmiths International Union amalgamated with the Sheet Metal organization and the Brass and Metal Workers joined later, the name of the organization was changed to the Sheet Metal Workers' International Association by its convention in 1924. Its official publication is the *Sheet Metal Workers' Journal*, published monthly.

Address: 1750 New York Ave., N.W., Washington, D.C. 20006. Tel. (202) 783–5880

sheltered shops Workshops and employment areas, usually operated by charitable and nonprofit organizations which employ severely handicapped individuals in an atmosphere which approximates that of private industry. They seek to develop skills and adjustments which in some cases permit the individuals to obtain outside employment.

Source references: Harriet Cooperman and Mark Brossman, "The Utility of the Sheltered Workshop: The Need for Reform," *Industrial and Labor Relations Forum*, Winter 1975; John R. Kimberly, *Environmental Constraints and Organizational Structure: A Comparative Analysis of Rehabilitation Organizations* (Urbana: Univ. of Illinois, Institute of Labor and IR, Reprint Series 242, 1975); National Assn. of Sheltered Workshops and Homebound Programs, Inc., *Sheltered Workshops—A Handbook* (rev. ed., Washington: 1966); Gopal C. Pati and Glenn Morrison, "Enabling the Disabled," *Harvard BR*, July/Aug. 1982; U.S. Dept. of Labor, Manpower Administration, *Sheltered Workshops: A Pathway to Regular Employment* (Washington: Manpower Research Bull. no. 15, 1967); U.S. Dept. of Labor, Wage and Hour and Public Contracts Divisions, *Sheltered Employment in the United States Under Federal Minimum Wage Laws* (Washington: 1965); Xavier M. Vela, "Fair Labor Standards for the Handicapped," *LLJ*, July 1978.

Sherman Act of 1890 The Sherman Anti-Trust Act was passed in 1890 (26 Stat. 209), and its main function is set out in the first section of the statute which provides in part:

> Section 1. Every contract, combination in the form of trust or otherwise, or conspiracy, in restraint of trade or commerce among the several States, or with foreign nations, is hereby declared to be illegal; . . . . Every person who shall make any such contract or engage in any such combination or conspiracy hereby declared to be illegal shall be deemed guilty of a misdemeanor, and, on conviction thereof, shall be punished by fine not exceeding fifty thousand dollars, or by imprisonment not exceeding one

year, or by both said punishments, in the discretion of the court.

Section 2. Every person who shall monopolize, or attempt to monopolize, or combine or conspire with any other person or persons, to monopolize any part of the trade or commerce among the several States, or with foreign nations, shall be deemed guilty of a misdemeanor, and, on conviction thereof, shall be punished by fine not exceeding fifty thousand dollars, or by imprisonment not exceeding one year, or by both said punishments, in the discretion of the court.

Although it appeared that the statute was directed toward industry monopolistic and antitrust practices, the law was applied to labor unions and it was subsequently necessary to have special legislation passed (the Clayton Act) in order to offset court decisions under the Sherman Act. However, even the Clayton Act did not quite solve the problem under the antitrust laws.

Source references: Apex Hosiery Co. v. Leader, 310 US 469, 6 LRRM 647 (1940); *Bedford Cut Stone Co. v. Journeymen Stone Cutters' Assn. of North America*, 274 US 37 (1927); Edward Berman, *Labor and the Sherman Act* (New York: Harper, 1930); Louis B. Boudin, "The Sherman Act and Labor Disputes," 39 *Colorado LR* 1283 (1939) and 40 *Colorado LR* 14 (1940); Elliot Bredhoff, "Labor Unions Under the Sherman Act: The Supreme Court Will Take Another Look," *NYU 17th Annual Conference on Labor*, ed. by Thomas Christensen (Washington: BNA, 1964); David F. Cavers, "Labor v. the Sherman Act," 8 *Univ. of Chicago LR* 246 (1941); Malcolm Cohen, "Unions and the Antitrust Strawman," *LLJ*, Feb. 1963; Morris D. Forkosch, "The Revival of the Sherman Act and Its Application to Labor Organizations," *LLJ*, Oct. 1953; Samuel Gompers, "The Hatter's Case. The Sherman Law—Amend It or End It," *American Federationist*, March 1910; Charles O. Gregory, "The Sherman Act v. Labor," 8 *Univ. of Chicago LR* 222 (1941); Milton Handler, *Antitrust in Perspective, The Complementary Roles of Rule and Discretion* (New York: Columbia UP, 1957); William Letwin, *Law and Economic Policy in America; The Evolution of the Sherman Antitrust Act* (New York: Random House, 1965); Edward W. Merkel, "The Other Anti of Antitrust," *Harvard BR*, March/April 1968; B. C. Schmidt, "The Application of the Antitrust Laws to Labor: A New Era," 19 *Texas LR* 256 (1941); Harry Shulman, "Labor and the Anti-Trust Laws," 34 *Illinois LR* 769 (1940).

See also ALLEN-BRADLEY CASE; APEX HOSIERY CO. V. LEADER; CLAYTON ACT OF 1914; CORONADO COAL V. UNITED MINE WORKERS; HUTCHESON CASE; LAWLOR V. LOEWE; PENNINGTON CASE.

shift A regularly scheduled period of work during the 24-hour day for a plant. The shift has a fixed beginning and ending each day. The term may apply both to the work period and to the workers who are employed during that period.

In some industries, the shift may be referred to as a "trick" or a "tour."

The following shifts have generally been used and are recognized:

(1) day shift—one where the regularly scheduled hours are during daylight;
(2) evening shift—where the schedule ends at or near midnight;
(3) graveyard shift—sometimes called the night shift, where the work schedule starts at or near midnight.

A shift is referred to as a *fixed shift* when the employees remain on the same schedule for long periods of time. It is referred to as a *rotating shift* when crews change their hours at periodic intervals. It is referred to as a *split shift* when the daily work schedule is divided into two or more parts, and as a *swing shift* when it is the rotating shift or a fourth shift in a plant which operates on an around-the-clock basis in a seven-day period. The name is derived from the nature of the operation, since all four shifts or the special shift rotate or swing to different days and hours at specified intervals.

Source references: Roger Betancourt and Christopher Clague, "Multiple Shifts and the Employment Problem in Developing Countries," *ILR*, Sept./Oct. 1976; J. Carpentier and P. Cazamian, *Night Work, Its Effects on the Health and Welfare of the Worker* (Geneva: ILO, 1977); Thomas H. Ferry, "Management Teamwork in Shift Relationships," *PJ*, April 1966; Peter Finn, "The Effects of Shift Work on the Lives of Employees," *MLR*, Oct. 1981; Floyd C. Mann, "Shift Work and the Shorter Workweek," *Hours of Work*, ed. by

Clyde E. Dankert et al. (New York: Harper, IRRA Pub. no. 32, 1965); Janice Neipert Hedges and Edward S. Sekscenski, "Workers on Late Shifts in a Changing Economy," *MLR*, Sept. 1979; Marc Maurice, *Shift Work, Economic Advantages and Social Costs* (Geneva: ILO, 1975); Carol Medley, *Shift Workers: A Descriptive Analysis of Worker Characteristics* (Columbus: Ohio State Univ., Center for Human Resource Research, 1979); Herbert R. Northrup, James T. Wilson, and Karen M. Rose, "The Twelve-Hour Shift in the Petroleum and Chemical Industries," *ILRR*, April 1979; P. J. Sloane, "Economic Aspects of Shift and Night Work in Industrialised Market Economies," *ILR*, March/April 1978; Donald L. Tasto and Michael J. Colligan, *Shift Work Practices in the United States* (Washington: U.S. Dept. of HEW, Public Health Service, 1977); U.S. Dept. of HHS, Public Health Service, *The Twenty-Four Hour Workday: Proceedings of a Symposium on Variations in Work-Sleep Schedules* (Washington: 1981); William B. Werther, Jr., "Mini-Shifts: An Alternative to Overtime," *Management Review*, July 1976; Jadwiga Wojtczak-Jaroszowa, *Physiological and Psychological Aspects of Night and Shift Work* (Washington: U.S. Dept. of HEW, Public Health Service, 1977); W. McEwan Young, "Shift Work and Flexible Schedules: Are They Compatible?" *ILR*, Jan./Feb. 1980; John Zalusky, "Shiftwork—A Complex of Problems," *American Federationist*, May 1978.

See also OFF-SHIFT, SINGLE-SHIFT SYSTEM, SLIDE DAY, TWO-PLATOON SYSTEM.

shift, afternoon *See* AFTERNOON SHIFT.

shift, day *See* DAY SHIFT.

shift, fixed *See* FIXED SHIFT.

shift, graveyard *See* GRAVEYARD SHIFT.

shift, lobster *See* LOBSTER SHIFT.

shift, multiple *See* MULTIPLE SHIFT.

shift, night *See* NIGHT SHIFT.

shift, relief *See* RELIEF SHIFT.

shift, rotating *See* ROTATING SHIFT.

shift, split *See* SPLIT SHIFT.

shift, stub *See* STUB SHIFT.

shift, swing *See* SWING SHIFT.

shift-boss The foreman or supervisor on one of the shifts where a company operates on a multiple-shift basis.

shift differential A premium rate or compensation given to individuals who perform work on a schedule other than the regular day schedule. The payment may be a fixed cents-per-hour above the regular day shift or a percentage over the earnings of the regular day shift. Sometimes the premium is in the form of a shorter number of hours which are worked at the full rate of pay for the longer, standard shift. The premium is based on the inconvenience (and possibly irregular span) of the time at which the employee works.

Source references: Otto Hollberg, "Workweeks, Overtime and Shift Pay in 17 Labor Markets, 1957–58," *MLR*, Dec. 1958; "Shift Work and Shift Differentials in Canadian Manufacturing," *ILR*, April 1962.

See also NIGHT PREMIUM.

shift premium *See* SHIFT DIFFERENTIAL.

shift provisions Clauses in collective bargaining contracts dealing with the problems of multiple shifts.

Source references: John N. Gentry, "Shift Provisions in Major Union Contracts, 1958," *MLR*, March 1959; Arnold Strasser, "Provisions for Late Shifts in Manufacturing Industries," *MLR*, May 1965.

shine time The time which an individual employee waits to be sure that a replacement has arrived. This happens occasionally in multiple-shift operations where it is necessary to assure continuous operation and to protect the machine to be used by the replacement.

Shoe and Allied Craftsmen; Brotherhood of (Ind) 838 Main Street, Brockton, Mass. 02401. Tel. (617) 587–2606

Shoe Workers of America; United (AFL-CIO) Union formed in 1937 with the merger of the United Shoe and Leather Workers Union (organized in 1933) and the Shoe Workers Protective Union (formed in 1899). On March

5, 1979, the union merged with the Amalgamated Clothing and Textile Workers Union (AFL-CIO).

Source references: Horace B. Davis, *Shoes: The Workers and the Industry* (New York: International Publishers, 1940); Augusta E. Galster, *The Labor Movement in the Shoe Industry, Especially in Philadelphia* (New York: Ronald Press, 1924); E. Robert Livernash, "Collective Bargaining and Competitive Cost in the Shoe Industry," *MLR*, March 1957; Thomas L. Norton, *Trade Union Policies in the Massachusetts Shoe Industry, 1919–1929* (New York: Columbia UP, 1932).

See also CLOTHING AND TEXTILE WORKERS UNION; AMALGAMATED (AFL-CIO).

Shoe Workers' Union; Boot and (AFL-CIO) Efforts at organization of boot and shoe workers began late in the 18th century. The Federal Society of Journeymen Cordwainers organized in Philadelphia in 1794. It was involved in the conspiracy trials of 1806. Consolidation efforts on a national level were accomplished in 1835 with the formation of the National Cooperative Association of Journeymen Cordwainers. The introduction of machinery for shoemaking brought shoe workers into the Knights of St. Crispin, which was active in the movement to control the use of mechanization as it affected labor. Workers in the boot and shoe industry gravitated toward the Knights of Labor during its heyday and formed a National Trade Assembly in 1884. The group later withdrew from the Knights of Labor and formed the Boot and Shoe Workers in April 1895.

In September 1977, the union merged with the Retail Clerks International Union (AFL-CIO).

See also RETAIL CLERKS INTERNATIONAL UNION (AFL-CIO).

shop A place where work is done. The term sometimes is applied to the kind of union security which exists in a particular operation or shop, such as open shop, closed shop, preferential shop, union shop.

See also CLOSED SHOP, OPEN SHOP, PREFERENTIAL SHOP, UNION SHOP.

shop, agency *See* AGENCY SHOP.

shop, all-union *See* ALL-UNION SHOP.

shop, closed *See* CLOSED SHOP.

shop, closed anti-union *See* CLOSED ANTI-UNION SHOP.

shop, modified closed *See* MODIFIED CLOSED SHOP.

shop, modified union *See* MODIFIED UNION SHOP.

shop, open *See* OPEN SHOP.

shop, percentage *See* PERCENTAGE SHOP.

shop, preferential *See* PREFERENTIAL SHOP.

shop card A poster or card which is displayed by an employer to indicate that the work is being done under union conditions, sometimes referred to as union-shop card.

See also UNION LABEL (BUG).

shop chairperson The chief steward in the plant or chairperson of the department stewards. Frequently serves as chairperson of the stewards in dealing with higher management representatives in the settlement of grievances. The individual stewards are usually elected by the employees within the department or plant. The shop chairperson or chief steward is frequently elected by the department stewards to act as their chairperson and chief spokesperson.

See SHOP STEWARD.

shop club *See* CHAPEL.

shop committee In current usage it consists of a relatively small group of workers, elected on a shiftwide basis, to represent the employees in the handling of grievances and similar problems with plant management above the level of foreman. Frequently the shop chairperson may work with a shop committee in order to obtain a broader representation of the viewpoint of the rank and file.

In former usage, particularly during the period of employee representation plans and company unions, the shop committee was frequently a group (also elected by the employees) whose function was to handle grievances and related matters but served primarily as a substitute for collective bargaining.

Source references: Edward Berman, *Labor and the Sherman Act* (New York: Harper, 1930); Dorothea DeSchweinitz, *Labor and*

Management in a Common Enterprise (Cambridge: Harvard UP, 1949); Alexander Feller and Jacob E. Hurwitz, *How to Deal With Organized Labor* (New York: Alexander Pub., 1937); Orwell de R. Foenander, *Shop Stewards and Shop Committees: A Study in Trade Unionism and Industrial Relations in Australia* (Carlton: Melbourne UP, 1965); Elias Lieberman, *The Collective Labor Agreement* (New York: Harper, 1939); Harry Sangerman, "Employee Committees: Can They Survive Under the Taft-Hartley Act?" *LLJ*, Oct. 1973.

See also COMPANY UNION, EMPLOYEE REPRESENTATION PLANS, GRIEVANCE COMMITTEE, WORKERS' COUNCILS.

shop control *See* DISCIPLINE.

shop council *See* COMPANY UNION.

shop morale The general group attitude which is reflected in a cooperative working relationship where there is enthusiasm for achievement of the goals of the organization and loyalty to the organization and among individuals.

See also MORALE SURVEY.

shop rules *See* WORK RULES.

shop steward A representative of the union who carries out the responsibilities of the union in the plant at the department level. The steward generally handles grievances in their first stage, may collect dues, and performs other duties as required by the union. A steward is usually elected by the other members in the plant (or may be appointed by the union officers). The steward is protected while holding that position under the superseniority provisions with regard to layoff and frequently is paid for the time spent in handling grievances. The shop steward is also sometimes known as the union steward.

Source references: AFL-CIO, *AFL-CIO Manual for Federal Employees* (Washington: Pub. no. 138, 1982); Steven Briggs, "The Steward, the Supervisor, and the Grievance Process," *Proceedings of the 34th A/M, IRRA*, ed. by Barbara Dennis (Madison: 1982); Mary Elkuss, *You Are Now a Shop Steward* (New York: Amalgamated Clothing and Textile Workers Union, 1977); Herman Erickson, *The Steward's Role in the Union and a History of American Unions* (New York: Exposition Press, 1971); William H. Leahy, "Arbitration and Insubordination of Union Stewards," *AJ*, March 1972; ———, "Arbitration of Disputes Over Grievance Processing by Union Representatives," *AJ*, Vol. 26, no. 2, 1971; ———, "Landmark Cases Involving Union Representatives," *PJ*, April 1972; James E. Martin, "Effectiveness of Union Steward Training in the Public Sector: Results From a Multiple Case Study," *Journal of Collective Negotiations in the Public Sector*, Vol. 4, no. 2, 1975; R. J. Moore, "The Motivation to Become a Shop Steward," *BJIR*, March 1980; Al Nash, *The Union Steward: Duties, Rights, and Status* (Ithaca: NYSSILR, Cornell Univ., Key Issues Series no. 22, 1977); Arthur A. Sloane and Laurence B. Valant, "Changing Status of the Union Shop Steward," *PJ*, June 1965.

See also GRIEVANCE, PAY FOR SHOP STEWARDS, SHOP CHAIRPERSON, SUPERSENIORITY.

shop strike A strike which is limited to the employees of a single company.

See also STRIKE.

shorter hours *See* HOURS OF WORK, UNEMPLOYMENT.

shorter workweek The reduction of hours of work has been a major goal of workers everywhere for centuries and a specific goal of American labor for the last century and a half. The pressure during the 1960s for the reduction in hours of work and consequently a shorter workweek has been accelerated by increasing technological change and automation. Trade unions have sought to obtain a reduction of the present 40-hour week to 35 hours in order to provide more employment.

Source references: John M. Barry, "The Pressure Builds for Shorter Workweeks," *American Federationist*, Nov. 1961; Thomas R. Brooks, "The Shorter Workweek: Its Purpose Is Not More Leisure But More Jobs," *Commonweal*, Feb. 16, 1962; "Creating Jobs Through a Shorter Workweek," *American Federationist*, July 1965; Clyde E. Dankert, "Shorter Hours—In Theory and Practice," *ILRR*, April 1962; Marcia L. Greenbaum, *The Shorter Workweek* (Ithaca: NYSSILR, Cornell Univ., Bull. no. 50, 1963); Richard I.

Hartman and K. Mark Weaver, "Four Factors Influencing Conversion to a Four-Day Work Week," *Human Resource Management*, Spring 1977; Sar A. Levitan and Richard S. Belous, *Shorter Hours, Shorter Weeks: Spreading the Work to Reduce Unemployment* (Baltimore: Johns Hopkins UP, 1977); ———, "Thank God It's Thursday!" *Across the Board*, March 1977; David M. Maklan, *The Four-Day Workweek; Blue Collar Adjustment to a Nonconventional Arrangement of Work and Leisure Time* (New York: Praeger, 1977); ———, "How Blue-Collar Workers on 4-Day Workweeks Use Their Time," *MLR*, Aug. 1977; NAM, *The Issue of the Shorter Workweek* (New York: 1961); Stanley D. Nollen and Virginia H. Martin, *Alternative Work Schedules: Part 2: Permanent Part-Time Employment, Part 3: The Compressed Workweek;* An AMA Survey Report (New York: AMA, 1978); Riva Poor (ed.), *4 Days, 40 Hours and Other Forms of the Rearranged Workweek* (New York: New American Library, 1973); Carmen D. Saso, *4/40: The Four-Day Workweek* (Chicago: PPA, 1972); Gilbert V. Steward and John M. Larsen, "A Four-Day/Three-Day Per Work Application to a Continuous Production Operation," *Management of Personnel Quarterly*, Winter 1971; U.S. Dept. of Labor, BLS, *The Revised Workweek: Results of a Pilot Study of 16 Firms* (Washington: Bull. no. 1846, 1975); Kenneth E. Wheeler, Richard Gurman, and Dale Tarnowieski, *The Four-Day Week* (New York: AMA, Research Report, 1972); John Zalusky, "Shorter Hours—The Steady Gain," *American Federationist*, Jan. 1978; Joseph S. Zeisel, "The Workweek in American Industry, 1850–1956," *MLR*, Jan. 1958.

See also FOUR-DAY WORKWEEK, HOURS OF WORK, THIRTY-HOUR WEEK.

short-shift *See* PART-TIME EMPLOYMENT.

short-time employment *See* PART-TIME EMPLOYMENT.

short workweek benefit The supplemental unemployment benefits (SUB) plan, first negotiated by the United Auto Workers and the Ford Motor Company in 1955, grew out of organized labor's long-term goal to obtain a guaranteed annual wage for workers. SUB, privately financed by the employer, was conceived by the union as a means of supplementing the low level state unemployment insurance benefits and of eliminating the income difference between the salaried worker and the hourly wage production worker, who is more frequently subjected to layoffs and to seasonal variations in employment.

In 1961 a short workweek benefit was first negotiated as part of a United Auto Workers SUB plan. Under a short workweek benefit a worker is eligible for supplemental payments if he works less than a full 40-hour week. Under the auto plan, if the short workweek is scheduled by the employer to adjust employment to declining customer demand, the worker may receive a short workweek benefit of 75 percent of the hourly wage for each hour less than 40 not made available for work. If the short workweek is unscheduled, the worker is entitled to a supplemental benefit of 50 percent of the hourly wage for each hour less than 40 not worked.

Source references: Joseph M. Becker, *Guaranteed Income for the Unemployed, The Story of SUB* (Baltimore: Johns Hopkins Press, 1968); Rudolph Oswald, "SUB: Closing the Wage Loss Gap," *American Federationist*, Dec. 1966; Beverly K. Shaffer, "Experience with Supplementary Unemployment Benefits: A Case Study of the Atlantic Steel Company," *ILRR*, Oct. 1968; U.S. Dept. of Labor, BLS, *Major Collective Bargaining Agreements, Supplemental Unemployment Benefit Plans and Wage-Employment Guarantees* (Washington: Bull. no. 1425–3, 1965).

See also SUPPLEMENTAL UNEMPLOYMENT BENEFITS.

showing of interest Evidence of employee support that a union must present before a representation election will be held. The NLRB requires designation by at least 30 percent of the bargaining unit employees, usually in the form of signed and dated authorization cards. The NLRB also accepts designations in the form of signed petitions and union application cards.

Source reference: U.S. NLRB, *Rules and Regulations and Statements of Procedure* (Washington: 1982).

See also AUTHORIZATION CARD.

show pay *See* CALL-IN PAY.

shutdown The closing of a plant for any reason such as a strike, lockout, for the installation of new equipment or materials, as a result of economic and financial difficulty, or for inventory purposes, etc.

Occasionally the term "shutdown" has been limited to stoppages of production resulting primarily from the installation of new equipment, for the repair of machinery, and for the lack of either sufficient material or lack of sufficient orders; the closing of operations for other reasons has been listed as a stoppage, strike, or lockout. Shutdowns for reasons other than labor disputes occasionally are referred to as down periods.

See also DOWN PERIODS.

sick benefits *See* HEALTH BENEFIT PROGRAMS.

sick leave Time allowed off from work to an employee because of illness, accident, or some other incapacity. The time off is usually without compensation, after a stated period as established by company policy or under a collective bargaining agreement. The individual retains his job rights including seniority and other privileges.

Source references: Barron H. Harvey, "Two Alternatives to Traditional Sick Leave Programs," *PJ*, May 1983; Edgar H. Johnson, Jr., "Control of Sick Leave," *Personnel Administration*, Jan./Feb. 1969; Ronald A. Korner, "Buyback of Unused Sick Leave: A Cost Evaluation Technique," *PJ*, Nov. 1967; Raymond Krah, *Administrative Control of Sick Leave* (Chicago: Civil Service Assembly, Personnel Report no. 544, 1954); U.S. CSC, *Maternity/Sick Leave Provisions in Federal Agreements* (Washington: 1975); Donald R. Winkler, "The Effects of Sick-Leave Policy on Teacher Absenteeism," *ILRR*, Jan. 1980; William J. Woska, "Sick Leave Incentive Plans—A Benefit to Consider," *Public Personnel Review*, Jan. 1972.

See also ABSENTEEISM, LEAVE OF ABSENCE, PAID SICK LEAVE.

sickness insurance *See* MEDICAL CARE PLANS.

sickout Refers to large numbers of employees calling in sick or taking sick leave at the same time. This tactic was frequently used in early public sector bargaining relationships as a form of job action.

Source reference: The Twentieth Century Fund, *Pickets at City Hall* (New York: 1970).

See also BLUE FLU, JOB ACTION.

Siderographers; International Association of (AFL-CIO) Formed in 1899 in Washington D.C.

Address: 1134 Boulevard, New Milford, N.J. 07646. Tel. (212) 542–9200

signing the document Reference to a system employed in England whereby individuals were required to sign what was known in the United States as the yellow-dog contract—a contract which required the individual to refrain from joining a labor organization while in the employ of the company, and if a member, to sever relationships with the union.

Source references: Edward Wiech, *The American Miners' Association* (New York: Russell Sage Foundation, 1940); Samuel Yellen, *American Labor Struggles* (New York: Arno, c.1936, 1969).

See also YELLOW DOG CONTRACT.

silicosis A disease of the lungs resulting from breathing air which contains uncombined silicon dioxide dust. Silicosis at one time caused more fatalities than the combined effects of all other types of mining hazards. At present the danger has been reduced because of better ventilation and understanding of the ways in which silicosis is caused, and more scientific methods of handling the minute particles of dust.

Source references: Committee on Tuberculosis in Industry, *Industry, Tuberculosis, Silicosis and Compensation: A Symposium* (New York: National TB Association, 1945); William Gafafer (ed.), *Manual of Industrial Hygiene and Medical Services in War Industries* (Philadelphia: Saunders, 1943); Bethel McGrath, *Nursing in Commerce and Industry* (New York: Commonwealth Fund, 1946); Norman Taylor (ed.), *Stedman's Medical Dictionary* (17th rev. ed., Baltimore: William, Wilkins, 1949).

See also INDUSTRIAL DISEASE, INDUSTRIAL POISON.

simulation A procedure designed to approximate situations which might arise and provide methods of learning various processes as well as learning to be of help in such areas as selection and training. Games and other procedures are used as substitutes for the real thing.

Source references: AMA: *Simulation and Gaming: A Symposium* (New York: 1961); Richard F. Barton, *A Primer on Simulation and Gaming* (Englewood Cliffs, N.J.: PH, 1970); Mary Ann Coghill, *Games and Simulations in Industrial and Labor Relations Training* (Ithaca: NYSSILR, Cornell Univ., Key Issues Series no. 7, 1971); Paul S. Greenlaw, Lowell W. Herron, and Richard H. Rawdon, *Business Simulation in Industrial and University Education* (Englewood Cliffs, N.J.: PH, 1962); James L. McKenney, *Simulation Gaming for Management Development* (Boston: Harvard Univ., Graduate School of Business Administration, 1967); John H. Norton, "Simulation for Planning and Control," *Management Review*, Feb. 1972; John W. Plattner and Lowell W. Herron, *Simulation: Its Use in Employee Selection and Training* (New York: AMA, Management Bull. no. 20, 1962); Hindy Lauer Schachter, "Simulations for Training and Assessment: The Problem of Relevance to the Real World," *Public Personnel Management*, Vol. 9, no. 3, 1980; Gilbert G. Siegel, "Gaming Simulation in the Teaching of Public Personnel Administration," *Public Personnel Management*, July/Aug. 1977; Roger N. Wolff and George H. Haines, Jr., *The Executive Education Experience Using the Toronto Management Game* (Toronto: Univ. of Toronto, Faculty Management Studies, Reprint no. 39, 1974).

Sinclair Refining Co. v. Atkinson A Supreme Court decision holding that the Norris-LaGuardia Act prohibits federal courts from granting an injunction to enjoin a grievance dispute subject to a no-strike agreement.

The *Boys Markets* decision in 1970 overruled the *Sinclair* ruling.

Source reference: Sinclair Refining Co. v. Atkinson, 370 US 195, 50 LRRM 2420 (1962).

See also BOYS MARKETS CASE, SUITS FOR CONTRACT VIOLATION.

Sindermann case A Supreme Court decision holding that, Sindermann, a college professor who worked under a series of one-year contracts in the Texas state university system, the last four at Odessa Junior College, was entitled to a hearing for nonrenewal of appointment.

The Court ruled that Sindermann had a "genuine dispute," that there was reason to believe that the nonrenewal violated his constitutionally protected right of freedom of speech under the First and Fourteenth Amendments. The nonrenewal of appointment followed Sindermann's public disagreements with the policies of the college's Board of Regents.

The Court also held that unlike *Roth* (which was decided concurrently with *Sindermann*), the respondent raised "a genuine issue as to his interest in continued employment at Odessa Junior College. . . . In particular, the respondent alleged that the college had a *de facto* tenure program, and that he had tenure under that program. . . . [T]he respondent claimed legitimate reliance upon guidelines. . . . that provided that a person, like himself, who had been employed as a teacher in the state college and university system for seven years or more has some form of job tenure."

While proof of property interest did not entitle Sindermann to reinstatement, the Court said that "such proof would obligate college officials to grant a hearing at his request, where he could be informed of the grounds for his nonretention and challenge their sufficiency."

Source references: Perry v. Sindermann, 408 US 593 (1972); Commission on Academic Tenure in Higher Education, *Faculty Tenure; A Report and Recommendations* (San Francisco: Jossey-Bass, 1973); Walter S. Griggs and Harvey W. Rubin, "Legal Ramifications of the Tenure Crisis," *Journal of Collective Negotiations in the Public Sector*, Vol. 6, no. 2, 1977; Carol Herrnstadt Shulman, *Employment of Nontenured Faculty: Some Implications of Roth and Sinderman* (Washington: American Association for Higher Education, ERIC/Higher Education Research Report no. 8, 1973).

See also ACADEMIC TENURE, ROTH CASE.

single-company union Generally a labor union whose membership is limited to employees in one plant.

See also COMPANY UNION.

single-employer bargaining Collective bargaining arrangements limited to a single employer and a group of employees.

single-plant bargaining Bargaining which takes place between a union and management for one plant of a particular company.

See also COLLECTIVE BARGAINING, COMPANYWIDE.

single rate A wage rate which is the same for all workers employed on the same job or in the same job classification. The rate remains the same for the entire period that the individual is on that job and in that specific job classification.

The single rate is generally applied to qualified and experienced individuals. There is a lower rate for learners or apprentices.

See also RATE RANGE.

single-shift system A working arrangement limited to a regular five- or six-day week, with employees working for a specific daily period such as eight hours.

See also MULTIPLE SHIFT, SHIFT.

single-union bargaining Bargaining relationships in which only a single union takes part.

See also BARGAINING UNIT, MULTIPLANT BARGAINING.

single worker An individual worker who is without dependents. In dealing with statistics on average family income and standards of living for the average family, it is necessary to keep in mind that in the economy there are single workers whose needs are generally less than those of a worker with a family.

sister A union member of the female sex.

See also BROTHER.

sister lodge (local) A term used to refer to lodges (locals) of the same national or international union other than the speaker's own lodge or local union.

sit-down strike A work stoppage during which employees remain at their place of work and refuse to leave the company premises. Sit-down strikes during their heyday in the 1930s were not protected strikes under the National Labor Relations Act and the Supreme Court in the *Fansteel* case held that the right to strike did not extend to the use of the sit-down strike.

Source references: Louis Adamic, "Sit-Down," *The Nation,* Dec. 5 and 12, 1936; Sidney Fine, *Sit-Down: The General Motors Strike of 1936–1937* (Ann Arbor: Univ. of Michigan Press, 1969); Leon Green, "The Case for the Sit-Down Strike," *New Republic,* March 24, 1937; J. Woodford Howard, Jr., "Frank Murphy, and the Sit-Down Strikes of 1937," *Labor History,* Spring 1960; Daniel Nelson, "Origins of the Sit-Down Era: Worker Militancy and Innovation in the Rubber Industry, 1934–38," *Labor History,* Spring 1982; ———, "The Beginning of the Sit-Down Era: The Reminiscences of Rex Murray," *Labor History,* Winter 1974; Louis Stark, "Sit-Down," *Survey Graphic,* June 1937.

See also FANSTEEL CASE, STAY-IN STRIKE, STRIKE, WALKOUT.

sitting on the lid Act of containing, sometimes precariously, internal forces; maintaining an equilibrium, or the status quo.

situs picketing *See* PICKETING AT COMMON SITE (SITUS).

six-hour day AFL conventions supported the six-hour day as far back as 1913, although the major efforts for the six-hour day did not come until 1932 following the AFL proposals for the five-day week in 1926. The National Recovery Administration and the long period of depression after 1929 created further pressure to reduce the hours of work and to spread employment opportunities to those without jobs.

See also FAIR LABOR STANDARDS ACT OF 1938, HOURS OF WORK.

six-six plan Training programs which combine schooling and practical work on the job. Students attend classes for six months a year and spend the remaining six months on the job. Other plans provide a different distribution of education and practical work application.

Source reference: William Patterson and Marion H. Hedges, *Educating for Industry* (New York: PH, 1946).

See also TRAINING.

sixty-day notice Provision in Section 8(d)(1) of the amended National Labor Relations Act (Taft-Hartley Act) which requires giving 60 days' notice of intention to modify or cancel a contract.

The purpose of the 60-day notice is to reduce the number of strikes by providing an opportunity for the parties to inform each other of changes which either desires to make in the agreement which is about to terminate. It also puts on notice the federal and state mediation agencies that bargaining is to take place during this period. The 60-day notice is designed to continue the status quo during a period in which a real effort can be made to reach agreement.

sixty-percent rule Under Executive Order 10988 the percentage of eligible voters required by a federal agency to vote in an election to determine exclusive representation rights before the election is considered as valid.

Employee organizations objected to the 60 percent rule, since this varied from the procedures used by the NLRB in the private sector. The government agencies insisted that 60 percent of the eligible voters in the appropriate unit must vote before the election would be considered valid.

Some modification was made in the 60 percent rule as it applied to run-off elections. The election policy approved by the Civil Service Commission and the U.S. Department of Labor in run-off elections did not require the 60 percent rule, since presumably that rule had already been met in the original (first) election.

This rule was abolished by Section 10(a) of Executive Order 11491.

Source reference: Harold S. Roberts, *Labor-Management Relations in the Public Service* (Honolulu: Univ. of Hawaii Press, 1970).

size of loads *See* SLING LOAD, WORK LOAD.

skill A personal quality which reflects expertness in a particular field of knowledge, or in doing a particular job. It implies coordination of mind and body in the performance of complicated operations as well as the effective use of knowledge and technical ability. It may involve a high degree of dexterity on job operations as well as a high degree of precision and coordination.

One authority defines the term as follows: "The word skill is used with a variety of meanings. It may refer to practical ability in art or science . . . power to visualize and to perform as in the case of a toolmaker, sometimes [it may refer] to manual dexterity coupled with little or no technical knowledge, as with machine operators. Whatever the nature of skill, the word usually refers to the quality of performance. It is characterized by precision in coordination of the senses, knowledge and muscles involved. . . . There are three distinct kinds of skill: muscular, sensory, and thinking."

In the area of job evaluation the characteristics of skill include training, education, experience, initiative, dexterity, ingenuity, etc.

Source references: Eugene Benge, *Breaking the Skilled Labor Bottleneck* (New York: NFI, 1942); Russell W. Rumberger, "The Changing Skill Requirements on Jobs in the U.S. Economy," *ILRR*, July 1981.

See also ABILITY.

skill differential Differences in wage rates paid to workers in occupations which require varying levels of skill. The term may also apply to the differentials in wage rates of individuals in the same occupation, where higher rates are paid to those who perform the more complex activities.

See also WAGE DIFFERENTIALS.

skilled labor Workers who have mastered one of the traditional crafts, such as machinists, cabinet makers, etc., usually through apprenticeship training. These individuals also possess comprehensive knowledge of the job, are able to exercise judgment, have a high degree of manual dexterity, and frequently are capable of assuming substantial responsibility.

Source references: Max Carey, "The Crafts—Five Million Opportunities," *Occupational Outlook Quarterly*, Spring 1971; Andrew Dawson, "The Paradox of Dynamic Technological Change and the Labor Aristocracy in the United States, 1880–1914," *Labor History*, Summer 1979; Alan L. Gustman and Martin Segal, "The Skilled-Unskilled Wage Differential in Construction," *ILRR*, Jan. 1974; Allan F. Salt, "Estimated Need for Skilled Workers,

1965–1975," *MLR,* April 1966; Peter T. Schoemann, "The Crucial Need for Skilled Workers," *American Federationist,* Nov. 1962; Edgar Weinberg, "Reducing Skill Shortages in Construction," *MLR,* Feb. 1969; "What Some Companies Are Doing About the Skilled Labor Shortage," *Management Review,* Aug. 1967; William W. Winpisinger, "Correcting the Shortage of Skilled Workers," *American Federationist,* June 1980.

See also APPRENTICESHIP, JOURNEYMAN.

skills inventory, employee *See* INVENTORY OF EMPLOYEE SKILLS.

slave driver An individual who was responsible under the slave system for getting work performance from the slave. In its present application the term is applied to supervisors who demand of employees performance in excess of what the employees regard as a reasonable rate of operation.

slave labor A form of bondage that has existed in many stages of recorded history. Slaves may have been captives of war, individuals who were kidnapped, or those who were in bondage because of unpaid debts. In Europe as well as in the United States, slaves were used primarily in agriculture and they were dependent for their lives and subsistence on their masters.

Source references: Ronald L. Lewis, "The Use and Extent of Slave Labor in the Chesapeake Iron Industry: The Colonial Era," *Labor History,* Summer 1976; Patrick Montgomery, "Slavery—Still Very Much a Reality," *Free Labour World,* Oct. 1974; Bonnelu Philips, *Slave Labor* (New York: Appleton, 1918).

slave labor law A phrase used by labor leaders to indicate dislike of the Taft-Hartley Act.

slide day The day on which an individual employee changes from one to another shift.

sling load A longshore phrase describing the actual load placed on the sling which swings cargo from, or into, the hold of a ship. Longshore contracts contain lists of maximum sling loads for various products.

The size of the sling load was established for the purpose of safety in some situations and in others the size was designed to limit the actual amount of a product to be moved at any one time. With containerization and mechanization agreements, strict limitations on sling loads have been modified.

slowdown A concerted and deliberate effort by employees to reduce output and efficiency in order to obtain concessions from the employer. The slowdown is a modified form of strike, since it is designed to achieve the same general purpose through different techniques.

Source reference: Richard S. Hammett, Joel Seidman, and Jack London, "The Slowdown as a Union Tactic," *Journal of Political Economy,* April 1957.

See also CA' CANNY, GOLDBRICKING, RESTRICTION OF OUTPUT, "RULEBOOK" SLOWDOWN, SOLDIERING, STRIKE, WORK TO RULE.

slugger A type of fink used to assault and beat up strikers or union leaders.

See also FINK.

Smith-Connally Act *See* WAR LABOR DISPUTES ACT.

Smith-Hughes Act A statute passed in 1917 to promote the development of vocational education within the states. The government provided funds for matching state appropriations for vocational education programs.

See also VOCATIONAL EDUCATION.

snapper A term occasionally applied by workers to supervisors or foremen. The phrase is not widely used.

snap strike A brief and spontaneous stoppage of work by a group of employees, acting without authorization of the union.

See also QUICKIE STOPPAGE OR STRIKE, WILDCAT STRIKE.

snowballing A term for labor pirating, or employer efforts to entice workers from other employers in the same industry by paying above-standard wages and offering other inducements to switch jobs.

See also LABOR PIRACY.

Soccer League Players Association; Major Indoor Affiliated with the Federation of Professional Athletes (AFL-CIO).

Address: 1300 Connecticut Ave., N.W., Washington, D.C. 20036. Tel. (202) 463–2200

Soccer League Players Association; North American Affiliated with the Federation of Professional Athletes (AFL-CIO).

Address: 1300 Connecticut Ave., N.W., Washington, D.C. 20036. Tel. (202) 463–2200

Social and Rehabilitation Service Created in 1967 by a departmental reorganization order of the secretary of health, education, and welfare, the Service administered federal programs of technical and financial support to states, communities, organizations, and individuals by providing social, rehabilitation, income maintenance, medical, maternal and child care, family and child welfare, and other welfare services to the aged, children and youth, the disabled, and poor families.

The Service was abolished by the secretary's reorganization order of March 8, 1977.

social insurance Most authorities refer to social insurance as insurance devised by the state to give the wage earner and his dependents a minimum of income during periods when, through conditions largely beyond his control, the worker's earnings are impaired or cut off. Various forms of social insurance devised by the state are (1) workers compensation, (2) safety and health legislation, (3) unemployment insurance, (4) social security legislation.

Source references: Philip Booth, "Public Systems of Distributing Risks to Security," *MLR,* June 1963; William G. Bowen et al., *The Princeton Symposium on the American System of Social Insurance: Its Philosophy, Impact, and Future Development* (New York: McGraw-Hill, 1968); J. Douglas Brown, "The Role of Social Insurance in the United States," *ILRR,* Oct. 1960; Wilbur J. Cohen, "Economic Security for the Aged, Sick and Disabled: Some Issues and Implications," *Towards Freedom From Want,* ed. by Sar A. Levitan, Wilbur J. Cohen, and Robert J. Lampman (Madison: IRRA, 1968); Gerhard Colm, "The Economic Base and Units of Social Welfare," *MLR,* June 1963; Juan de Torres, "To Promote the General Welfare," *Conference Board Record,* July 1972; E. J. Faulkner, "Social Security and Insurance: Some Relationships in Perspective," *Journal of Insurance,* June 1963; J. Eldred Hill, Jr., "The Role and Impact of Federal Standards: Workmen's Compensation and Unemployment Compensation," *Proceedings of the 26th A/M, IRRA,* ed. by Gerald Somers (Madison: 1974); Merrill Murray, "Social Insurance Perspectives: Background Philosophy and Early Program Developments," *Journal of Insurance,* June 1963; Merrill G. Murray, *Income for the Unemployed, the Variety and Fragmentation of Programs* (Kalamazoo: Upjohn Institute for Employment Research, 1971); Robert Myers, *Social Insurance and Allied Government Programs* (Homewood: Irwin, 1965); Arthur Williams, Jr., "Social Insurance: Proper Terminology?" *Journal of Insurance,* March 1963; Chester A. Williams, Jr., John G. Turnbull, and Earl F. Cheit, *Economic and Social Security; Social Insurance and Other Approaches* (5th ed., New York: Wiley, 1982).

socialism A philosophy and a political movement which aim at collective organization of the community by providing that the means of production, distribution, and exchange of goods and services be owned, controlled, and operated in common ownership for the advantage of the group as a whole, rather than for the profit of individuals under competitive society.

The socialist movements have dissociated themselves from Marxism and have opposed the class struggle and the seizure of political power through force and violence. They also have rejected the idea of the dictatorship of the proletariat, and have aimed at gradual socialization of enterprise through existing capitalist institutions.

Source references: Robert J. Alexander, "Schisms and Unifications in the American Old Left, 1953–1970," *Labor History,* Fall 1973; David Brody (comp.), *The American Labor Movement* (New York: Harper & Row, 1971); Harry Fleischman, *Norman Thomas, A Biography* (New York: Norton, 1964); Chad Gaffield, "Big Business, the Working-Class, and Socialism in Schenectady, 1911–1916," *Labor History,* Summer 1978; Walter Galenson, "Why the American Labor Movement Is Not Socialist," *American Review,* Winter 1961; Morris Hillquit, Samuel Gompers, and Max J. Hayes, *The Double Edge of Labor's Sword* (New York: Arno, 1971); Harvey Klehr, "Leninism, Lewis Corey, and the Failure of American Socialism," *Labor His-*

tory, Spring 1977; John H. M. Laslett, "Reflections on the Failure of Socialism in the American Federation of Labor," *Mississippi Valley Historical Review,* March 1964; ———, "Socialism and the American Labor Movement: Some New Reflections," *Labor History,* Spring 1967; Charles Leinenweber, "The Class and Ethnic Bases of New York City Socialism, 1904–1915," *Labor History,* Winter 1981; Sally M. Miller, *Victor Berger and the Promise of Constructive Socialism, 1910–1920* (Westport, Conn.: Greenwood Press, 1973); Richard Oestreicher, "Socialism and the Knights of Labor in Detroit, 1877–1886," *Labor History,* Winter 1981; Roy Rosenzweig, "'Socialism in Our Time': The Socialist Party and the Unemployed, 1929–1936," *Labor History,* Fall 1979; Bertrand Russell, *Roads to Freedom: Socialism, Anarchism and Syndicalism* (3d ed., London: Allen, Unwin, 1966); James D. Young, "Daniel De Leon and Anglo-American Socialism," *Labor History,* Summer 1976.

Socialist Labor Party The Socialist Labor Party of North America, organized in 1877, had developed from the Social Democratic Working-Men's Party of North America, which had been in existence since 1874. The Party sought through a two-way attack to transform society and persuade American workmen to accept socialism. The first method was through trade union action and the second through direct political activity.

Source references: Selig Perlman and Philip Taft, *History of Labor in the United States, 1896–1932* (New York: Macmillan, 1935); Hubert Perrier, "The Socialists and the Working Class in New York: 1890–1896," *Labor History,* Fall 1981; Earl R. Sikes, *Contemporary Economic Systems* (New York: Holt, 1940); Russel E. Westmeyer, *Modern Economics and Social Systems* (New York: Farrar, Rinehart, 1940).

Socialist Trade and Labor Alliance A dual union established in 1895 by Daniel DeLeon, a lecturer on international relations at Columbia University. DeLeon in 1895 called on American unions to oppose the AFL and join his Socialist Trade and Labor Alliance.

According to Professors Millis and Montgomery, "DeLeon was denied control of the *Journal of the Knights of Labor,* allegedly promised him in return for socialist support . . . for head of the Order in 1894, and then in 1895, he was even refused a seat in the General Assembly." The Socialist Labor Party had a membership estimated variously between 15,000 to 30,000 members and was confined largely to a few socialist unions in and around New York City. The Socialist Trade and Labor Alliance disappeared from the scene at about the time that the Socialist Party was established in 1901.

Source reference: Harry A. Millis and Royal E. Montgomery, *Organized Labor* (New York: McGraw-Hill, 1945).

Social Security Act A federal statute enacted in 1935 establishing a national social insurance program and an agency to administer it. The program was devised to "provide some safeguard against the insecurity of modern life through cooperative action by federal and state governments, thus making possible the fullest consideration of the local economic and social problems . . . while maintaining a national unity of program and purposes."

A series of liberalizing amendments broadened the Act's coverage and expanded its benefits. Major programs currently provided under the Act include:

(1) Retirement insurance,
(2) Survivors insurance,
(3) Disability insurance,
(4) Hospital and medical insurance for the aged and disabled,
(5) Black lung benefits,
(6) Supplemental security income,
(7) Unemployment insurance,
(8) Public assistance,
(9) Food stamps,
(10) Child support enforcement,
(11) Maternal/child health and welfare,
(12) Workers compensation,
(13) Railroad retirement, sickness, and unemployment insurance,
(14) Veterans benefits, and
(15) Federal, state, and local government employees retirement.

Major amendments to the Act were enacted in 1983 to meet the financial problems of the social security program, the deficit of which was estimated to be $168 billion. The National Commission on Social Security Reform, established by the President, presented its recommendations to the President and the Congress on January 20, 1983. Based on these recommendations, Congress enacted the 1983 amendments which included, among others, provisions for a higher tax rate and taxable wage base, a decrease in benefits, taxation of some benefits, extension of coverage to federal employees hired after 1983 and employees of nonprofit organizations, raising the retirement age, revision of the cost-of-living adjustments of benefits, and non-withdrawal of state and local governments from the social security system.

Source references: Arthur J. Altmeyer, *The Formative Years of Social Security* (Madison: Univ. of Wisconsin Press, 1966); Robert M. Ball, "Social Security Cuts: Violating a Trust," *American Federationist*, June 1981; Philip Booth, *Social Security in America* (Ann Arbor: Univ. of Michigan–Wayne State Univ., Institute of Labor and IR, Policy Papers in Human Resources and IR 19, 1973); J. Douglas Brown, *Essays on Social Security* (Princeton: Princeton Univ., IR Section, Research Report series 123, 1977); ———, *The Genesis of Social Security in America* (Princeton: Princeton Univ., IR Section, 1969); Eveline M. Burns, "New Directions in Social Security," *NYU 14th Annual Conference on Labor*, ed. by Emanuel Stein (Albany: Bender, 1961); Colin D. Campbell (ed.), *Financing Social Security* (Washington: AEI, 1979); Wilbur Cohen, "Some Issues and Goals in Social Security," *ILRR*, July 1959; Wilbur J. Cohen, "Social Security 40 Years Later," *American Federationist*, Dec. 1975; Martha Derthick, *Policymaking for Social Security* (Washington: Brookings Institution, 1979); Robert J. Lampman, "The Future of Social Security, 1977–2050," *Proceedings of the 29th A/M, IRRA*, ed. by James Stern and Barbara Dennis (Madison: 1977); Mickey D. Levy, *Achieving Financial Solvency in Social Security* (Washington: AEI, Special Analysis 81–6, 1981); Allen D. Marshall, "Social Security at the Crossroads," *ILRR*, Oct. 1960; Ida C. Merriam, "Social Security and Social Welfare Indicators," *Annals*, Jan. 1978; Robert J. Myers, "Expansion or Contraction of Social Security: Serious Side Effects," *Annals*, May 1979; PH, *What the New 1983 Social Security Law Means to You and Your Employees* (Englewood Cliffs: 1983); Robert J. Pruim, *Social Security and the Public Employee; A Look at the Issues: Past, Present and Future* (Washington: Assembly of Governmental Employees, 1978); Shirley H. Rhine, *Social Security: Problems and Solutions* (New York: The Conference Board, Research Bull. 122, 1982); Burton W. Teague, "Social Insecurity," *Across the Board*, Sept. 1977; U.S. Congress, House, Committee on Ways and Means, *Staff Data and Materials Related to Social Security Financing* (Washington: 1983); U.S. Congress, Senate, Committee on Finance, *The Social Security Act and Related Laws, April 1982 Edition* (Washington: 1982); U.S. Congressional Budget Office, *Paying for Social Security: Funding Options for the Near Term* (Washington: 1981); U.S. Dept. of HHS, SSA, *Social Security Handbook* (7th ed., Washington: 1982); ———, *Social Security Programs Throughout the World, 1981* (Washington: Research Report 58, 1982); U.S. Dept. of HEW, SSA, *Social Security Financing and Benefits; Reports of the 1979 Advisory Council on Social Security* [with executive summary] (Washington: 1979); U.S. National Commission on Social Security, *Social Security in America's Future, Final Report of the National Commission* (Washington: 1981); U.S. National Commission on Social Security Reform, *Report of the National Commission on Social Security Reform* (Washington: 1983); Edwin E. Witte, *The Development of the Social Security Act* (Madison: Univ. of Wisconsin Press, 1962).

See also HELVERING V. DAVIS, STEWART MACHINE CO. V. DAVIS.

Social Security Administration Originally established as the Social Security Board by the Social Security Act of 1935 to administer the provisions of that Act, it became part of the Federal Security Agency in 1939. The Social Security Board was abolished in 1946; its title was changed to Social Security Administration (SSA) and its functions were placed under the Federal Security Administrator. In 1953 the Social Security Administration became a part of the newly created Department of Health, Education, and Welfare. The SSA was reorganized in 1963 and made responsible for retirement, survivors, and disability insurance and federal credit union programs. It was again reorganized on July 26, 1965, to accommodate the new federal health insurance programs. The SSA also administers the supplemental security income program for the aged, blind, and disabled.

The SSA administers its programs through 10 regional offices, six program service centers, and over 1,300 local offices.

With the reorganization of the Department of Health, Education, and Welfare in 1979, the SSA is currently part of the Department of Health and Human Services.

Address: 6041 Security Blvd., Baltimore, Md. 21235. Tel. (301) 876–6450

Source references: U.S. GAO, *Social Security Administration Should Improve Its Recovery of Overpayments Made to Retirement, Survivors, and Disability Insurance Beneficiaries* (Washington: 1979); ———, *The Social Security Administration Should Provide More Management and Leadership in Determining Who is Eligible for Disability Benefits, Department of Health, Education, and Welfare* (Washington: 1976).

social security tax Social security benefits are financed by a payroll tax levied equally on the employer and employee. The 1965 amendments to the Social Security Act called for a separate tax on both parties for the then newly created medicare program. Together with the Old Age, Survivors, and Disability Insurance (OASDI) taxes, these taxes are assessed on a percentage of employee earnings up to a given wage base. For example, the tax rate in 1983 was 6.70 percent on earnings up to $35,700. The 1983 amendments incorporated new tax schedules for 1984 to 1990 and later. Thus, the schedules increase employer-employee contributions from 7.00 percent in 1984 to 7.65 percent in 1990 and later; for the self employed from 14 percent in 1984 to 15.30 percent in 1990 and later. The taxable wage base which was $35,700 in 1983 will be recalculated annually to reflect increases in the consumer price index.

Source reference: PH, *What the New 1983 Social Security Law Means to You and Your Employees* (Englewood Cliffs: 1983).

social wage A phrase that has been used in two ways in America. One definition suggests that, in order for workers to have a fair share of the long-term increase in national income, workers' wages must rise proportionately with the increase in productivity or output per man-hour, rather than merely being adjusted to changes in the price level. A second definition implies that wages should achieve something beyond the bare necessities of life and obtain comforts and luxuries.

It is possible to combine these two usages if one assumes that obtaining comforts and luxuries is made possible through the increase in productivity.

Society of Professionals in Dispute Resolution (SPIDR) A private organization formed in 1972, SPIDR seeks to increase public understanding and acceptability of negotiation, collective bargaining, and the role of neutrals in dispute resolution procedures and promote development of "innovative" impasse resolution techniques.

SPIDR serves as a clearinghouse for information and publishes the quarterly *News* and special topic papers. Meetings are held annually and proceedings of the meetings are published.

Address: 1730 Rhode Island Ave., N.W., Suite 909, Washington, D.C. 20036. Tel. (202) 833–2188

Source reference: SPIDR, *The Public Interest and the Role of the Neutral in Dispute Settlement, Proceedings of the Inaugural Convention . . . , Reston, Virginia, October 17–19, 1973* (Washington: 1974).

soft job The description of a position which requires little application or ability and pays well.

soldiering Loafing or a deliberate reduction of output and waste of time by an employee. It generally is distinguished from the slowdown since it rarely is organized group action and does not involve bringing pressure upon the employer for the achievement of any particular purpose.

See also RUSHERS, SLOWDOWN.

sole bargaining rights The right of a union, either upon certification by the NLRB or a state agency, to represent employees in an appropriate bargaining unit. The union as sole or exclusive bargaining agent represents all of the employees in the bargaining unit, both union and nonunion, for purposes of negotiating an agreement and enforcing it.

See also CERTIFICATION, EXCLUSIVE BARGAINING AGENT, RECOGNITION.

solicitation of union members Efforts by a union to bring into membership workers who are not members of the union.

solidarity contract Called "the contract of solidarity" by Albert Tevoedjre, director of the International Institute for Labour Studies, it is a proposal for an agreement to promote cooperation among nations. Tevoedjre states that the "contract of solidarity is motivated principally by the search for a higher interest common to the parties concerned. . . . On the one hand, this global solidarity can be built up only on the bases of concrete commitment; on the other, it poses the principle of respect for the freedom of the parties, which implies autonomy on the basis of their respective identities and designs."

Source reference: "Towards Solidarity Contracts," *Labour and Society*, July/Oct. 1978.

solidarity of labor A term applied to efforts of unions to stand united for or against some particular program.

sound and tested rates A wage concept adopted toward the end of World War II by the National War Labor Board to provide wage flexibility and stabilization simultaneously. The "sound and tested rates" actually were so-called going rates for particular occupations in a given labor market area. The minimum of the range or the minimum of the bracket was established at the first major cluster of rates in a wage distribution. This cluster was considered to be the appropriate rate for the adjustment of interplant inequities. The regional boards were permitted to establish these sound and tested going rates and wage adjustments by agreement and disputed cases were measured against these rates.

See also HOLD-THE-LINE ORDER, LITTLE STEEL FORMULA.

South Dakota State Employees Organization (Ind) An organization affiliated with the Assembly of Governmental Employees. Its official publication is the *SDSEO Newsletter* (seven issues annually).

Address: P.O. Box 1021, Pierre, S.D. 57501. Tel. (605) 224–8241

Southern Labor Union (Ind) Its official monthly publication is *The Coal Miner*.

Address: P.O. Box 479, Oneida, Tenn. 37841. Tel. (615) 569–8335

southern wage differentials *See* NORTH-SOUTH WAGE DIFFERENTIALS.

Spanish-surnamed American *See* HISPANIC.

sparetime work *See* DOUBLE EMPLOYMENT, PART-TIME EMPLOYMENT, SECONDARY EMPLOYMENT.

specialization of labor A procedure for securing most efficient productive results through subdivision of personnel into logical and necessary units. It involves improved use of skills, simplification of job operations, and more extensive use of capital.

special permit rate An agreement under which a union worker from another jurisdiction is employed in a particular area, usually because of a labor shortage. The out-of-area worker receives the same rate as that paid to regular union workers in the area under a special permit granted by the union.

speeders *See* PACERS.

speed-up A term used by workers to describe efforts of employers to increase productivity without a corresponding increase in compensation. Speed-up is achieved either by increasing the workload of the individual, speeding up the assembly line, or, in piece-rate systems, cutting the rate.

Source reference: James Barnett, *Speeding Up the Workers* (New York: International Pamphlets, 1932).

See also STRETCH OUT.

speed-up boy *See* EFFICIENCY EXPERT.

spell-out time *See* REST PERIOD.

spendable earnings Total money earnings less amounts deducted, such as taxes. Frequently referred to as take-home earnings—the amount actually available for spending.

The BLS statistical series known as "spendable average weekly earnings," was discontinued in 1982. This earnings series represented take-home pay of workers having a specified number of dependents. To reach the figure, federal social security and income taxes were deducted from the individual's gross average weekly earnings.

Source references: "The Calculation and Uses of Spendable Earnings Series," *MLR*, April 1966; "Reagan Budget Slashes Could Mean Elimination of Several BLS Series," *Daily Labor Report*, No. 216, Nov. 9, 1981; U.S. Dept. of Labor, BLS, *Employment and Earnings, United States, 1909–78* (Washington: Bull. 1312–11, 1979); James R. Wetzel, "The Spendable Earnings of Factory Workers," *Employment and Earnings*, Feb. 1966.

See also EARNINGS, TAKE-HOME PAY.

Spielberg doctrine The policy of the NLRB to defer to an arbitrator's decision if it is found that (1) the arbitration proceedings are fair, (2) all parties agree to be bound by the arbitrator's decision, and (3) the arbitrator's decision is not repugnant to the purpose and policies of the National Labor Relations Act. A fourth criterion, that the arbitrator must rule on an unfair labor practice issue, if present, was added in 1963 with the *Raytheon* decision (140 NLRB 883, 52 LRRM 1129). Since *Raytheon*, the NLRB has changed its position several times in interpreting the arbitrator's responsibilities under the fourth criterion.

Source references: Electronic Reproduction Service, 213 NLRB 758, 87 LRRM 1211 (1974); *Olin Corp.*, 268 NLRB No. 86, 115 LRRM 1056 (1984); *Spielberg Manufacturing Co.*, 112 NLRB 1080, 36 LRRM 1152 (1955); *Suburban Motor Freight*, 247 NLRB 146, 103 LRRM 1113 (1980); M. J. Fox, Jr., Glenna M. Witt, and Thomas R. Fox, "The Deferral Policy Revisited . . . From Spielberg to Suburban Motor Freight," *Journal of Collective Negotiations in the Public Sector*, Vol. 11, no. 3, 1982; John C. Truesdale, "Is *Spielberg* Dead?" *NYU 31st Annual National Conference on Labor*, ed. by Richard Adelman (New York: Bender, 1978).

See also DEFERRAL.

spies *See* ESPIONAGE, STOOL PIGEON.

Spinners Union; International (Ind) It was organized in 1858 and remained in the AFL until 1919 when it was ousted for refusing to merge with the United Textile Workers. It reaffiliated with the AFL in 1937 but was suspended in the early 1950s. The union was disbanded in 1954.

split shift A daily work schedule which is not continuous but split into two or more working periods with a substantial time interval between the two. Split shifts are found in industries such as local transportation, where employees have to work a peak rush period in the morning and possibly one in the late afternoon. It applies also to some restaurant employees who may work several hours at noon and again several hours in the evening. Some agreements provide special compensation for employees working on split shifts.

split workweek A workweek which begins before and extends beyond the date of a semimonthly pay period.

sponsor An individual designated by an employer to assume major responsibility for the familiarization of a new employee with company policy, personnel procedures, and operation of the job.

Source reference: George D. Halsey, *Training Employees* (New York: Harper, 1949).

See also INDUCTION.

spotter In labor parlance a person hired by an employer to engage in labor espionage.

In other usage, a detective who is hired to detect dishonesty and irregularities at retail stores, etc.

Source references: U.S. Dept. of Labor, ETA, *Dictionary of Occupational Titles* (4th ed., Washington: 1977); Maurice H. Wessin, *Dictionary of American Slang* (New York: Crowell, 1934).

spreading work *See* SHORTER WORKWEEK, WORK SHARING.

stabilization of employment *See* EMPLOYMENT STABILIZATION.

staffing pattern *See* MANNING TABLE.

staggering of employment A procedure for reducing unemployment by dividing available work among all employees. It has been suggested that staggering is not a device which reduces unemployment but "only smears it more evenly."

staggering of hours A procedure for adjusting hours of employment in order to schedule work more evenly.

standard agreement *See* AGREEMENT, MASTER.

standard hour Term used in incentive wage plans. Points, manits, B's, and standard minutes are essentially the same; namely, each represents a man-minute's worth of work. A standard hour is 60 times as much work.

Source reference: Herbert J. Myers, *Simplified Time Study* (New York: Ronald Press, 1944).

See also INCENTIVE RATE.

standard of living Various classifications have been set up to describe the level or standard of living of various groups in any community. One grouping includes (1) poverty or pauper level, (2) minimum subsistence level, (3) minimum health-and-decency level, and (4) minimum comfort level.

Source references: Sheldon H. Danziger and Robert J. Lampman, "Getting and Spending," *Annals*, Jan. 1978; Marvin Friedman, *The Use of Economic Data in Collective Bargaining* (Washington: U.S. Dept. of Labor, LMSA, 1978); George H. Hildebrand, "The New Economic Environment of the United States and Its Meaning," *ILRR*, July 1963; Helen H. Lamale, "Workers' Wealth and Family Living Standards," *MLR*, June 1963; Herman P. Miller, *Rich Man, Poor Man* (New York: Crowell, 1971); Rufus E. Runzheimer, Jr., "Factoring Living-Cost Differentials into Salary Levels," *Personnel*, Jan./Feb. 1979; James H. Schultz and Guy Carrin, "The Role of Savings and Pension Systems in Maintaining Living Standards in Retirement," *Journal of Human Resources*, Summer 1972.

See also BARE (MINIMUM) SUBSISTENCE LEVEL, CONSUMER PRICE INDEX, FAMILY BUDGET, HEALTH AND DECENCY STANDARD OF LIVING, HELLER COMMITTEE FOR RESEARCH IN SOCIAL ECONOMICS.

standard rate The hourly rate of pay established for an occupation generally in a plant or industry through the process of collective bargaining, by regulation, by company rules, or by state or federal law. The standard rate sometimes is referred to as the union rate or the minimum rate for a qualified worker.

standard time The time, usually established by time and motion study, required for the average worker to perform a specific operation without undue fatigue. It applies to time under a wage incentive system where units of time rather than the number of items or pieces produced are utilized to establish premium or incentive earnings. Incentive earnings are obtained when the worker produces in less than the standard time; for example, a person would receive six hours' pay for performing a task in five hours where the standard set for the task is six hours. The incentive is based on the time saved over and above the standard time set for the job.

standard workweek *See* BASIC WORKWEEK, FAIR LABOR STANDARDS ACT OF 1938.

stand-by *See* ON-CALL TIME PAY.

stare decisis Literally means to abide by decided matters, the doctrine of following the judicial precedent for a point or principle of law. Normally, a court will follow the precedent established by a higher court. Stare decisis, Justice Frankfurter wrote in *Helvering v. Hallock*, "is a principle of policy and not a mechanical formula of adherence to the latest decision, however recent and questionable, when such adherence involves collision with a prior doctrine more embracing in its scope, intrinsically sounder, and verified by experience."

According to Elkouri and Elkouri, although arbitrators are not bound by prior awards, an arbitrator may choose to follow "authoritative" precedents: "In actual practice it is not at all uncommon for an arbitrator to preface the assertion of an established rule or principle with some statement such as 'it has become a well-accepted principle,' or 'it is a general rule that,' or 'the consensus is,' or 'the weight of authority is.' In doing this arbitrators frequently cite precedents, but just as frequently they cite few or no specific cases to support their assertion that the principle does in fact exist. Possibly the true significance of such statements lies in the fact that the arbitrator was willing to accept arbitration awards as a source of fundamental substantive principles."

Source references: Helvering v. Hallock, 309 US 106 (1940); Frank Elkouri and Edna Asper Elkouri, *How Arbitration Works* (4th ed., Washington: BNA, 1985); Katharine Seide, *A Dictionary of Arbitration and Its Terms* (Dobbs Ferry, N.Y.: Oceana Publications, 1970).

starting rate The rate of pay for an individual when first hired by a company.

State, County and Municipal Employees; American Federation of (AFL-CIO) Formed by a group of Wisconsin state employees in 1932. Under the leadership of Arnold Zander, the group subsequently affiliated with the AFL's American Federation of Government Employees. In 1936, the state and local government workers left AFGE and were granted a separate charter as a national union by the AFL and adopted the present name.

Initial concerns of AFSCME focused on white-collar employees, the merit system, and civil service legislation. Following the election of Jerry Wurf as president in 1964, AFSCME increased its nationwide organizing and collective bargaining efforts and supported the right of public employees to strike.

During the 1970s, AFSCME became known as the fastest growing union and the largest public sector union in the U.S., representing both white- and blue-collar employees. The Civil Service Employees Association of New York State, one of the larger independent public sector unions, affiliated with AFSCME in 1978. By 1982, AFSCME had 2,950 local unions with 80 district councils and a membership of nearly 1,100,000. The official monthly publication is *The Public Employee.*

Address: 1625 L St., N.W., Washington, D.C. 20036. Tel. (202) 429–1000

Source references: AFSCME, *A Chronology of Unionism in U.S. Public Employment* (Washington: 1974); Richard N. Billings and John Greenya, *Power to the Public Worker* (Washington: R. B. Luce, 1974); Harry A. Donoian, "The AFGE and the AFSCME: Labor's Hope for the Future?" *LLJ,* Dec. 1967; Joseph C. Goulden, *Jerry Wurf: Labor's Last Angry Man* (New York: Atheneum, 1982); Charles J. Janus, "AFSCME Attacks Proposition 13, Endorses New Dues Structure," *MLR,* Sept. 1978; Leo Kramer, *Labor's Paradox—The American Federation of State, County and Municipal Employees, AFL-CIO* (New York: Wiley, 1962); Sterling Spero and John M. Capozzola, *The Urban Community and its Unionized Bureaucracies* (New York: Dunellen, 1973); Arnold Zander, "Public Employees are Turning to Unionism," *American Federationist,* Aug. 1958.

state federations of labor State organizations established by the AFL and currently by the AFL-CIO, whose function is to represent the interests of unions within a particular state. They act as lobbying agents for promotion of legislation desired by unions within the state and also to oppose legislation which unions consider unfavorable. The state organizations attempt to coordinate the policies of unions within the state, and receive assistance from the national and international unions which have members within the state. Attempts have been made to coordinate the programs and policies of the state federations with that of the parent AFL-CIO body. The list of state federations with addresses follows.

Alabama Labor Council, 231 West Valley Ave., Birmingham, Ala. 35209.

Alaska State AFL-CIO, 900 W. Northern Lights, Anchorage, Alaska 99503.

Arizona State AFL-CIO, 520 W. Adams St., Phoenix, Ariz. 85003.

Arkansas State AFL-CIO, 1115 Bishop St., Little Rock, Ark. 72202.

California Labor Federation, 995 Market St., San Francisco, Calif. 94103.

Colorado AFL-CIO, 360 Acoma St., Denver, Colo. 80223.

Connecticut State AFL-CIO, P.O. Box 5278, Hamden, Conn. 06518.

Delaware State AFL-CIO, P.O. Box 581, 1 Bassett Ave., New Castle, Del. 19720.

Florida AFL-CIO, 135 S. Monroe St., Tallahassee, Fla. 32301.

Georgia State AFL-CIO, 501 Pulliam St., S.W., Atlanta, Ga. 30312.

Hawaii State AFL-CIO, 320 Ward Ave., Suite 205, Honolulu, Hawaii 96814.

Idaho State AFL-CIO, 225 North 16th St., Boise, Idaho 83702.

Illinois State Federation of Labor and Congress of Industrial Organizations, 300 North State St., Chicago, Ill. 60610.

Indiana State AFL-CIO, 1701 W. 18th St., Indianapolis, Ind. 46202.

Iowa Federation of Labor, 2000 Walker St., Suite A, Des Moines, Iowa 50317.

Kansas State Federation of Labor, 3830 South Meridian, Wichita, Kan. 67217.

Kentucky State AFL-CIO, 1317 Berry Blvd., Louisville, Ky. 40215.

Louisiana AFL-CIO, P.O. Box 3477, Baton Rouge, La. 70821.

Maine AFL-CIO, 72 Center St., P.O. Box 70, Brewer, Maine 04412.

Maryland State and D.C. AFL-CIO, 93 Main St., Annapolis, Md. 21401.

Massachusetts AFL-CIO, 8 Beacon St., Boston, Mass. 02108.

Michigan State AFL-CIO, 419 S. Washington Ave., Lansing, Mich. 48933.

Minnesota AFL-CIO, 175 Aurora Ave., St. Paul, Minn. 55103.

Mississippi AFL-CIO, P.O. Box 2010, Jackson, Miss. 39205.

Missouri State Labor Council, 208 Madison St., Jefferson City, Mo. 65101.

Montana State AFL-CIO, P.O. Box 1176, Helena, Mont. 59624.

Nebraska State AFL-CIO, 4660 S. 60th Ave., Omaha, Neb. 68117.

Nevada State AFL-CIO, P.O. Box 7467, Las Vegas, Nev. 89101.

New Hampshire State Labor Council, 366 Huse Rd., Manchester, N.H. 03103.

New Jersey State AFL-CIO, 106 W. State St., Trenton, N.J. 08608.

New Mexico State AFL-CIO, 5905 Marble Ave., N.E., Albuquerque, N.M. 87110.

New York State AFL-CIO, 451 Park Ave., South, New York, N.Y. 10016.

North Carolina State AFL-CIO, P.O. Box 10805, Raleigh, N.C. 27605.

North Dakota AFL-CIO, 1533 N. 12th St., Bismarck, N.D. 58501.

Ohio AFL-CIO, 271 East State Street, Columbus, Ohio 43215.

Oklahoma State AFL-CIO, 501 N.E. 27th St., Oklahoma City, Okla. 73105.

Oregon AFL-CIO, 1900 Hines St., S.E., Salem, Ore. 97302.

Pennsylvania AFL-CIO, 101 Pine St., Harrisburg, Pa. 17101.

Puerto Rico Federation of Labor, P.O. Box 1648, San Juan, Puerto Rico 00903.

Rhode Island AFL-CIO, 111 Park St., Providence, R.I. 02908.

South Carolina AFL-CIO, P.O. Box 6128, W. Columbia, S.C. 29171.

South Dakota State Federation of Labor, P.O. Box 58, 18th and Dakota South, Huron, S.D. 57350.

Tennessee State Labor Council, 535 Church St., Suite 800, Nashville, Tenn. 37219.

Texas State AFL-CIO, P.O. Box 12727, Austin, Tex. 78711.

Utah State AFL-CIO, 2261 S. Redwood Rd., Salt Lake City, Utah 84119.

Vermont State Labor Council, 149 State St., P.O. Box 858, Montpelier, Vt. 05602.

Virginia State AFL-CIO, 3315 W. Broad St., Richmond, Va. 23230.

Washington State Labor Council, 2815 2nd Ave., Seattle, Wash. 98121.

West Virginia Labor Federation, 501 Broad St., Charleston, W. Va. 25301.

Wisconsin State AFL-CIO, 6333 West Bluemound Road, Milwaukee, Wis. 53213.

Wyoming State AFL-CIO, 1904 Thomes Ave., Cheyenne, Wyo. 82001.

state industrial council The counterpart of the state federations of labor when the CIO was a separate parent organization. With the merger of the AFL-CIO the state federations of labor and the state industrial councils have been amalgamated.

state jurisdiction Authority of the state legislatures and state courts in the field of industrial relations.

See also FEDERAL-STATE JURISDICTION; PREEMPTION, DOCTRINE OF; RIGHT TO WORK LAW.

state labor relations act State laws dealing with labor relations similar to the National Labor Relations Act and sometimes known as "Little Wagner Acts."

Source references: Richard R. Nelson, "State Labor Legislation Enacted in 1982," *MLR*, Jan. 1983; Russell A. Smith and R. Theodore Clark, Jr., "Reappraisal of the Role of the States in Shaping Labor Relations Law," *Wisconsin LR*, Summer 1965.

See also BABY WAGNER ACTS.

statism A political theory which holds that the state should control the economic and social life of the nation in order to achieve maximum efficiency and social welfare. The term is used to describe trend or movement toward government control of economic life through greater planning or nationalization of major industries.

"status quo" theory One of three interpretations of Title VII of the Civil Rights Act of 1964 and its application to discriminatory seniority systems, it would leave the seniority rights of white workers intact, i.e., positions in the plant hierarchy already achieved would be preserved. Thus, relative to their white contemporaries who had been preferred, black incumbents could not improve their status. This view is often associated with the decision of the U.S. Court of Appeals for the Fifth Circuit in *Whitfield v. United Steelworkers Local 2708*.

According to this theory, an employer satisfies the requirements of Title VII by ending all "explicit" discrimination. In *Local 189, Papermakers v. U.S.*, the court noted that under a "status quo" theory, "whatever unfortunate effects there might be in future bidding by Negroes luckless enough to have been hired before desegregation would be considered merely as an incident of new extinguished discrimination." Thus, blacks whose jobs were in "black" lines of progression would not be able to count that time bidding for jobs in what had been "white" lines of progression.

Source references: Local 189, United Papermakers and Paperworkers v. U.S., 416 F2d 980, 1 FEP Cases 875 (1969); *Whitfield v. United Steelworkers Local 2708*, 263 F2d 546, 9 FEP Cases 1043 (CA 5, 1959); "Title VII, Seniority Discrimination, and the Incumbent Negro," 80 *Harvard LR* 1260 (1967).

See also "FREEDOM NOW" THEORY, "RIGHTFUL PLACE."

statute of laborers English laws designed to control wages and prices as a result of the Black Plague in the middle of the 14th century. The pestilence killed large numbers of workers and resulted in pressure to increase wages. The legislation in 1351 was designed to hold wages of workers at levels existing immediately prior to the Black Plague.

statute of limitations In law, a designated period of time within which an action can be brought before a court or other tribunal. The term has been much adapted. For instance, the requirement that charges of Taft-Hartley Act violations must be filed within six months of the alleged unlawful conduct commonly is called a "statute of limitations."

statutory arbitration *See* ARBITRATION, COMPULSORY.

statutory law Legislative enactments in the federal, state, and municipal jurisdictions.

See also COMMON LAW.

stay-in strike A strike during which employees remain in the plant. A sit-down strike that lasts for a substantial period of time is referred to as a "stay-in strike."

See also SIT-DOWN STRIKE.

Steel and Tin Workers; Amalgamated Association of Iron *See* STEELWORKERS OF AMERICA; UNITED (AFL-CIO).

Steel Labor Relations Board *See* NATIONAL STEEL LABOR RELATIONS BOARD.

steel strike Refers especially to the two unusually long steel strikes in American labor history, the (1919) strike at the end of World War I and the 1959–1960 strike.

Source references: David Brody, *Labor in Crisis: The Steel Strike of 1919* (Philadephia: Lippincott, 1965); Milton Derber, "Steel Strike Complicates 20 Years of Progress in Labor Relations," *Industrial Bulletin*, Nov. 1959; William Z. Foster, *The Great Steel Strike* (New York: Arno Press & The New York Times, 1969); Interchurch World Movement, *Public Opinion and the Steel Strike* (New York: Harcourt, Brace, 1921); "Labor Dispute and Settlement in the United States Steel Industry," *ILR*, July 1960; James P. Mitchell, "Background Statistics Bearing on the Steel Dispute," *MLR*, Oct. 1959; National Council of the Churches of Christ in the USA, Dept. of Church and Economic Life, *In Search of Maturity in Industrial Relations: Some Long-Range Ethical Implications of the 1959–1960 Dispute in the Steel Industry, The Report of a Special Committee* (New York: 1960); Albert T. Sommers, "Parallels to the Steel Strike," *Business Record*, Aug. 1959; "The Steel Board's Final Report on the 1959

Dispute," *MLR*, March 1960; United Steelworkers of America, *The 1959 Steel Strike* (Pittsburgh: Pamphlet no. PR–112, 1961).

Steelworkers of America; United (AFL-CIO) The steelworkers' organization in the United States goes back to the Amalgamated Association of Iron, Steel and Tin Workers of North America which was organized in Pittsburgh, Pennsylvania, in August 1876. It was an amalgamation of independent unions in the industry, which at that time included the United Sons of Vulcan, the Associated Brotherhood of Iron and Steel Heaters, Rollers and Roughers, the Iron and Steel Roll Hands Union, and the Nailers' Union.

The major efforts to organize the steel industry at the end of World War I were not successful. Organization of the industry finally followed the establishment by the CIO of the Steel Workers Organizing Committee (SWOC). The United Steelworkers of America in 1942 succeeded the organizing committee. In 1967, the unaffiliated International Union of Mine, Mill and Smelter Workers merged with the Steelworkers, adding some 30,000 members to the United Steelworkers of America.

On January 1, 1971, the United Stone and Allied Products Workers of America (AFL-CIO) merged with the union. District 50, an independent union formerly affiliated with the United Mine Workers of America, merged with the Steelworkers on August 9, 1972. The union's official publication is *Steelabor.*

Address: Five Gateway Center, Pittsburgh, Pa. 15222. Tel. (412) 562–2400

Source references: Larry T. Adams, "Abel-Dominated Convention Endorses No-Strike Policy, Seeks Job Guarantee," *MLR*, Nov. 1976; Eugene H. Becker, "Steelworkers Laud Import Restrictions, Ban Outsiders' Election Contributions," *MLR*, Dec. 1978; David Brody, *Steelworkers in America: The Nonunion Era* (Cambridge: Harvard UP, 1960); Robert R. R. Brooks, *As Steel Goes: Unionism in a Basic Industry* (New Haven: Yale UP, 1940); George H. Cohen, "The Secretary of Labor's Court Challenge to the Steelworkers' Meeting Attendance Rule: A Case Study of the Conflict Between Internal Union Self-Government and the Administration of the Landrum-Griffin Act," *NYU 26th Annual Conference on Labor,* ed. by Emanuel Stein and S. Theodore Reiner (New York: Bender, 1974); Glenn W. Gilman and James W. Sweeney, *Atlantic Steel Co. and United Steelworkers of America* (New York: NPA, Case Studies on the Causes of Industrial Peace no. 12, 1953); William Grogan, *John Riffe of the Steelworkers: American Labor Statesman* (New York: Coward-McCann, 1959); John Herling, *Right to Challenge; People and Power in the Steelworkers Union* (New York: Harper & Row, 1972); Robert S. Keitel, "The Merger of the International Union of Mine, Mill and Smelter Workers into the United Steelworkers of America," *Labor History,* Winter 1974; E. Robert Livernash, *Collective Bargaining in the Basic Steel Industry* (Washington: U.S. Dept. of Labor, 1961); George P. Shultz and Robert P. Crisara, *The LaPointe Machine Tool Co. and the United Steelworkers of America* (New York: NPA, Case Studies on the Causes of Industrial Peace no. 10, 1952); Jack Stieber, "Company Cooperation in Collective Bargaining in the Basic Steel Industry," *Proceedings of the 1960 Annual Spring Meeting, IRRA*, ed. by David Johnson (Madison: 1960); Vincent D. Sweeney, *The United Steelworkers of America: The First 10 Years* (Pittsburgh: The Union, 1946); ———, *The United Steelworkers of America: Twenty Years Later, 1936–1956* (Pittsburgh: The Union, 1956); Lloyd Ulman, *The Government of the Steel Workers' Union* (New York: Wiley, 1962); P. Alston Waring and Clinton S. Golden, *Soil and Steel* (New York: Harper, 1947).

Steelworkers trilogy A series of three Supreme Court decisions issued in 1960 establishing significant principles covering grievance arbitration which served to protect and strengthen grievance arbitration by limiting judicial participation in the process. These cases involved the United Steelworkers of America and the American Manufacturing Co., Warrior Gulf and Navigation Co., and Enterprise Wheel and Car Corp. The *American Manufacturing* and *Warrior Gulf and Navigation* cases involved actions to enforce agreements to arbitrate; the *Enterprise Wheel and Car* case involved an action to enforce an arbitration award. In *American Manufactur-*

ing, the Court stated that (1) courts should rule only on arbitrability questions, and (2) courts should not be involved in judging the merits of a grievance. The Court, in *Warrior Gulf and Navigation*, ruled that (1) if doubts exist on arbitrability, they should be resolved in favor of arbitration, and (2) grievances are arbitrable unless specifically excluded by the contract. *Enterprise Wheel and Car* provided that courts should not review the merits of an arbitration award "so long as it draws its essence from the collective bargaining agreement. When the arbitrator's words manifest an infidelity to this obligation, courts have no choice but to refuse enforcement of the award."

Source references: Steelworkers v. American Manufacturing Co., 363 US 564, 46 LRRM 2414 (1960); *Steelworkers v. Enterprise Wheel and Car Corp.*, 363 US 593, 46 LRRM 2423 (1960); *Steelworkers v. Warrior Navigation Co.*, 363 US 574, 46 LRRM 2416 (1960); Benjamin Aaron, "Arbitration in the Federal Courts: Aftermath of the Trilogy," 9 *UCLA LR* 360 (1962); Clarke W. Brinckerhoff, "Judicial Review of Labor Arbitration Awards After the Trilogy," *IR Law Digest*, April 1968; Charles O. Gregory, "Enforcement of Collective Agreements by Arbitration," 48 *Virginia LR* 883 (1962); Sam Kagel, "Recent Supreme Court Decisions and the Arbitration Process," *Arbitration and Public Policy*, Proceedings of the 14th A/M, NAA, ed. by Spencer Pollard (Washington: BNA, 1961); Robert A. Levitt, "The Supreme Court and Arbitration," *NYU 14th Annual Conference on Labor*, ed. by Emanuel Stein (Albany: Bender, 1961); Henry Mayer, "Labor Relations, 1961: The Steelworkers Case Re-Examined," *LLJ*, March 1962; Bernard D. Meltzer, "The Supreme Court, Arbitrability, and Collective Bargaining," 28 *Univ. of Chicago LR* 464 (1961); Charles J. Morris, "Twenty Years of Trilogy: A Celebration," *Decisional Thinking of Arbitrators and Judges*, Proceedings of the 33d A/M, NAA, ed. by James Stern and Barbara Dennis (Washington: BNA, 1981); Theodore J. St. Antoine, "Judicial Review of Labor Arbitration Awards: A Second Look at *Enterprise Wheel* and Its Progeny," *Arbitratrion—1977*, Proceedings of the 30th A/M, NAA, ed. by Barbara Dennis and Gerald Somers (Washington: BNA, 1978); Russell A. Smith and Dallas L. Jones, "The Impact of the Emerging Federal Law of Grievance Arbitration on Judges, Arbitrators, and Parties," 52 *Virginia LR* 831 (1966); ———, "The Supreme Court and Labor Dispute Arbitration: The Emerging Federal Law," 63 *Michigan LR* 751 (1965); Franklin B. Snyder, "What Has the Supreme Court Done to Arbitration?" *LLJ*, Feb. 1961.

See also ARBITRATION, GRIEVANCE.

Steelworkers v. Weber *See* WEBER CASE.

Stereotypers' and Electrotypers' Union of North America; International (AFL-CIO) The union was organized in 1902. It affiliated with the AFL with jurisdiction over all branches of stereotyping, electrotyping, and other methods of duplicate printing. On October 2, 1973, it merged with the International Printing Pressmen and Assistants Union of North America to form the International Printing and Graphic Communications Union (AFL-CIO).

See also PRINTING AND GRAPHIC COMMUNICATIONS UNION; INTERNATIONAL (AFL-CIO).

steward *See* SHOP STEWARD.

steward's privileges The special rights of the business agent or shop steward as established in the collective bargaining agreement.

See also SUPERSENIORITY.

Stewart Machine Company v. Davis A decision of the Supreme Court in 1937 which upheld the unemployment provisions of the Social Security Act providing for a payroll tax on employers.

Source reference: Stewart Machine Co. v. Davis, 301 Sup.Ct. 548 (1937).

stint wage system A form of wage payment on the basis of a particular task assigned to an individual to be performed during a single day. When the employee has completed the task, he is free to go home.

stock purchase plan *See* EMPLOYEE STOCK OWNERSHIP PLAN.

Stockyard Workers Association of America (Ind) This union merged with the Amalgamated Meat Cutters and Butcher Workmen of North America (AFL-CIO) in July 1954.

See also MEAT CUTTERS AND BUTCHER WORKMEN OF NORTH AMERICA; AMALGAMATED (AFL-CIO).

Stone and Allied Products Workers of America; United (AFL-CIO) The union merged with the United Steelworkers of America (AFL-CIO) on January 1, 1971.

See also STEELWORKERS OF AMERICA; UNITED (AFL-CIO).

Stone Cutters Association of North America; Journeymen (AFL-CIO) A small group of skilled journeymen organized in 1853. On February 1, 1968, the union affiliated with the Laborers' International Union of North America (AFL-CIO).

Source reference: George E. Barnett, *Chapters on Machinery and Labor* (Cambridge: Harvard UP, 1926).

See also LABORERS' INTERNATIONAL UNION OF NORTH AMERICA (AFL-CIO).

stool pigeon Generally a labor spy, someone either hired by a detective agency or by an employer to keep him informed on the activities of a union.

See also ANTI-UNION PRACTICES, BACK ROOM BOYS, ESPIONAGE, LAFOLLETTE COMMITTEE.

stoop labor Farm labor requiring kneeling or bending as in cotton picking or truck farming.

stopwatch method Refers to the procedure using stop watches in motion and time study in the establishment of wage incentives.

Source reference: "Exit Stopwatch, Enter 'Standard Data'," *American Federationist,* June 1962.

See also MOTION STUDY.

store order A form of scrip certificate which permits the employee to exchange the store order for goods at the company store.

See also COMPANY STORE, SCRIP.

Stove, Furnace and Allied Appliance Workers' International Union of North America (AFL-CIO) Formerly known as the Stove Mounters' International Union of North America (AFL-CIO). The official quarterly publication is the *Stove, Furnace & Allied Appliance Workers' International Union Journal.*

Address: 2929 South Jefferson Ave., St. Louis, Mo. 63118. Tel. (314) 664–3736

Source reference: James M. Roberts, "Meet the Stove Mounters," *American Federationist,* Jan. 1959.

Stove Mounters' International Union of North America (AFL-CIO) *See* STOVE, FURNACE AND ALLIED APPLIANCE WORKERS' INTERNATIONAL UNION OF NORTH AMERICA (AFL-CIO).

straight A term applied to nonunion members who share the benefits of collective bargaining but do not share the costs.

See also FREE RIDERS, RAND FORMULA.

straight day-work A method of wage payment in which the employer pays the employee a fixed amount for a day's work.

straight point method A method of job rating in which all of the job characteristics are considered to have the same importance and weight.

straight-time pay Regular time or wage payments, excluding overtime or other premiums. Sometimes referred to as the regular wage rate.

stranger picketing Picketing by individuals who are not employees of the company being picketed. Usually they belong to the union which is seeking to organize employees in the plant.

See also AMERICAN FEDERATION OF LABOR V. SWING.

straw boss A gang or group leader, a worker who takes the lead in a group which consists of himself and a small number of other employees. He performs all of the duties of the other workers and his supervisory activities are incidental to his production performance.

Source reference: U.S. Dept. of Labor, ETA, *Dictionary of Occupational Titles* (4th ed., Washington: 1977).

street badge An identification required under some state laws, in the form of a badge, which is worn by child workers who are permitted to engage in "street trades."

Street, Electric Railway and Motor Coach Employes of America; Amalgamated Association of (AFL-CIO) The union was organized in September 1892 in Indianapolis, Indiana, as the Amalgamated Association of Street Railway Employees. Following the development of electric power for street railways, the union changed its name to the Amalgamated Association of Street and Electric Railway Employes of America. The change took place in 1903. "Motor Coach" was added to its name in 1934.

On July 1, 1964, the name of the union was changed to the Amalgamated Transit Union (AFL-CIO).

Source reference: Amalgamated Association of Street, Electric Railway and Motor Coach Employes of America, *Golden Jubilee* (Detroit: 1942).

See also TRANSIT UNION; AMALGAMATED (AFL-CIO).

street trades A term applied to occupations, usually conducted by children, most of which are performed in the streets, such as newsboy, messenger, bootblack, refuse collector.

stress A term used to denote force, pressure, strain, or strong effort that contributes to long-term ill health.

In physics and engineering, stress means the force or pressure applied to an object. Robert L. Kahn uses the "engineering analogy" to describe job stress: "Increases in work load, for example, can be thought of as increments of stress, in much the same way that we might think of increasing weight on a bridge or building."

Noise, physical demand, responsibility, and time limitations are some of the factors that are considered to create job stress.

The term "burnout" is used to describe the state of emotional exhaustion resulting from job-related stress, a condition which may provoke health problems and reduce performance, or lead the employee to quit the job.

Source references: Herbert Benson and Robert L. Allen, "How Much Stress is Too Much?" *Harvard BR*, Sept./Oct. 1980; BenAmi Blau, "Understanding Midcareer Stress," *Management Review*, Aug. 1978; Cary Cherniss, *Staff Burnout, Job Stress in the Human Services* (Beverly Hills: Sage Pub., 1980); Cary L. Cooper, *The Stress Check; Coping with the Stresses of Life and Work* (Englewood Cliffs: PH, 1981); E. N. Corlett and J. Richardson (ed.), *Stress, Work Design, and Productivity* (New York: Wiley, 1981); Joseph Grimaldi and Bette P. Schnapper, "Managing Employee Stress: Reducing the Costs, Increasing the Benefits," *Management Review*, Aug. 1981; Robert L. Kahn, *Work and Health* (New York: Wiley, 1981); Harry Levinson, "When Executives Burn Out," *Harvard BR*, May/June 1981; Michael T. Matteson and John M. Ivancevich, "The How, What and Why of Stress Management Training," *PJ*, Oct. 1982; Beverly A. Potter, *Beating Job Burnout* (San Francisco: Harbor Pub., 1980); Heather R. Sailer, John Schlacter, and Mark R. Edwards, "Stress: Causes, Consequences, and Coping Strategies," *Personnel*, July/Aug. 1982; Rosalind M. Schwartz (ed.), *New Developments in Occupational Stress, Proceedings of the Conference . . .* (Los Angeles: UC, Institute of IR, 1979); Arthur B. Shostak, *Blue Collar Stress* (Reading, Mass.: Addison-Wesley, 1980); Jere E. Yates, *Managing Stress, A Businessperson's Guide* (New York: AMACOM, 1979).

See also OVERWORK, WORKAHOLIC.

stretch out A term synonymous with speedup. It is widely used in the textile industry and in industries using automatic machinery. Under the stretch-out system workers are required to take on additional responsibilities and to increase output without a corresponding increase in wage payments.

strike A temporary stoppage of work or a concerted withdrawal from work by a group of employees of an establishment or several establishments to express a grievance or to enforce demands affecting wages, hours, and/or working conditions. It is a concerted withdrawal of work, since it is the action of a group, and it is a temporary withdrawal, since the employees expect to return to work after the dispute has been resolved. Strikers consider themselves employees of the company with a right to return to the job once the dispute has been resolved.

Most of the state and local laws deal with the problem of public employee strikes. Many statutes attempt to spell out what constitutes a strike within the meaning of the statute, and some indicate the penalties which flow from strike action.

There are substantial differences of opinion by authorities as to the dates of early strikes in American labor history as well as to the unions involved. Those generally noted in the latter part of the 18th century are the New York Journeymen Tailors Strike of 1768, the New York Printers Strike of 1778, the Philadelphia Seamen's Strike of 1779, the New York Shoemakers Strike of 1785, and the Philadelphia Printers Strike of 1786. Selig Perlman in his *History of Trade Unionism in the United States* refers to the Philadelphia Printers Strike of 1786 as the first genuine labor strike.

Source references: Benjamin Aaron, *Collective Bargaining Where Strikes Are Not Tolerated* (Los Angeles: UC, Institute of IR, Reprint no. 225, 1972); ———, *The Strike: A Current Assessment* (Los Angeles: UC, Institute of IR, 1967); ———, "Strikes in Breach of Collective Agreements: Some Unanswered Questions," *Columbia LR*, June 1963; Walter E. Baer, *Strikes: A Study of Conflict and How to Resolve It* (New York: AMACOM, 1975); Eugene H. Becker, "Analysis of Work Stoppages in the Federal Sector, 1962–1981," *MLR*, Aug. 1982; John M. Capozzola, "Public Employee Strikes: Myths and Realities," *National Civic Review*, April 1979; Neil W. Chamberlain, *Social Responsibility and Strikes* (New York: Harper, 1953); Neil W. Chamberlain and Jane M. Schilling, *The Impact of Strikes* (New York: Harper, 1954); R. Theodore Clark, Jr., "Injunctive Relief: Some Practical Considerations," *Public Management*, Feb. 1976; ———, "Public Employee Strikes: Some Proposed Solutions," *LLJ*, Feb. 1972; Walter L. Daykin, "The Legal Aspects of Strikes," *LLJ*, Aug. 1960; P. K. Edwards, "The 'Social' Determination of Strike Activity: An Explication and Critique," *Journal of IR*, June 1979; Malcolm Fisher, *Measurement of Labour Disputes and Their Economic Effects* (Paris: OECD, 1973); Robert Booth Fowler, "Normative Aspects of Public Employee Strikes," *Public Personnel Management*, March/April 1974; Thomas P. Gies, "Employer Remedies for Work Stoppages that Violate No-Strike Provisions," *Employee Relations LJ*, Autumn 1982; Alvin H. Hansen, "Cycles of Strikes," *AER*, Dec. 1921; George W. Hartmann and Theodore Newcomb (ed.), *Industrial Conflict—A Psychological Interpretation* (New York: Cordon, 1939); Woodruff Imberman, "Strikes Cost More than You Think," *Harvard BR*, May/June 1979; Bruce E. Kaufman, "The Determinants of Strikes in the United States, 1900–1977," *ILRR*, July 1982; David B. McCalmont, "The Semi-Strike," *ILRR*, Jan. 1962; William B. Nelson, Gerald W. Stone, Jr., and J. Michael Swint, "An Economic Analysis of Public Sector Collective Bargaining and Strike Activity," *Journal of Labor Research*, Spring 1981; OECD, *Labour Disputes, A Perspective* (Paris: 1979); Public Service Research Council, *Public Sector Bargaining and Strikes* (6th ed., Vienna, Va.: 1982); Myron Roomkin, "Union Structure, Internal Control, and Strike Activity," *ILRR*, Jan. 1976; Robert N. Stern, "Toward an Empirical Merger: Sociological and Economic Conceptions of Strike Activity," *Proceedings of the 28th A/M, IRRA*, ed. by James Stern and Barbara Dennis (Madison: 1976); "Strikes: Myth vs. Reality," *American Federationist*, March 1963; Helene S. Tanimoto and Joyce M. Najita, *Guide to Statutory Provisions in Public Sector Collective Bargaining—Strike Rights and Prohibitions* (3d issue, Honolulu: Univ. of Hawaii, IRC, 1981); U.S. Dept. of Labor, BLS, *Analysis of Work Stoppages, 1979* (Washington: Bull. 2092, 1981); ———, *Exploring Alternatives to the Strike* (Washington: Reprint, 1973); ———, *Work Stoppages in Government, 1980* (Washington: Bull. 2110, 1981).

See also BLUE FLU, BOYCOTT, CONCILIATION, GRADUATED STRIKE, INDUSTRIAL CONFLICT, JOB ACTION, MEDIATION, MUTUAL STRIKE AID, NATIONAL EMERGENCY BOARDS, NATIONAL EMERGENCY DISPUTES, NO-STRIKE CLAUSE, PICKETING, PROFESSIONAL SANCTION, RIGHT TO STRIKE, "RULEBOOK" SLOWDOWN, SABOTAGE, SANCTION, SICKOUT, SLOWDOWN, STRIKE PENALTY, TURNOUT, VIOLENCE IN LABOR DISPUTES, WALKOUT.

strike, anti-certification *See* ANTI-CERTIFICATION STRIKE.

strike, economic *See* ECONOMIC STRIKE.

strike, enforcement *See* ENFORCEMENT STRIKE.

strike, general *See* GENERAL STRIKE.

strike, graduated *See* GRADUATED STRIKE.

strike, illegal *See* ILLEGAL STRIKE.

strike, industrywide *See* INDUSTRYWIDE STRIKE.

strike, jurisdictional *See* JURISDICTIONAL DISPUTE, JURISDICTIONAL STRIKE.

strike, multiplied *See* MULTIPLIED STRIKE.

strike, national emergency *See* NATIONAL EMERGENCY STRIKES.

strike, negative *See* NEGATIVE STRIKE.

strike, outlaw *See* OUTLAW STRIKE.

strike, partial *See* PARTIAL STRIKE.

strike, positive *See* POSITIVE STRIKE.

strike, quickie *See* QUICKIE STOPPAGE OR STRIKE.

strike, secondary *See* SECONDARY STRIKE.

strike, shop *See* SHOP STRIKE.

strike, sit-down *See* SIT-DOWN STRIKE.

strike, slow-down *See* SLOWDOWN.

strike, snap *See* SNAP STRIKE.

strike, stay-in *See* STAY-IN STRIKE.

strike, sympathy *See* SYMPATHETIC (SYMPATHY) STRIKE.

strike, unauthorized *See* UNAUTHORIZED STRIKE.

strike, unfair labor practice *See* UNFAIR LABOR PRACTICE STRIKE.

strike, wildcat *See* WILDCAT STRIKE.

strike aid *See* MUTUAL STRIKE AID.

strike benefits Union payments to regular members and sometimes to nonmember workers in the plant, who are out on strike, in order to help finance them during the work stoppage. Strike benefits also may refer to unemployment compensation and public assistance such as Aid to Families with Dependent Children (AFDC), food stamps, and medicaid benefits received by strikers. Eligibility and amount of such assistance vary according to each state.

The question has been raised whether strike benefits are taxable as income or should be considered as gifts and therefore not taxable as part of the workers' gross income. A decision of the Supreme Court in 1960 and a subsequent ruling by the Internal Revenue Service bear on this question. The Internal Revenue Service has modified a number of previous rulings dealing with strikes or lockout benefits. These revisions are the result of a decision by the Supreme Court in *U.S. v. Allen Kaiser* (363 US 299 (1960)). In that case a labor organization furnished strike benefits to an individual in the form of room rent and food vouchers. These benefits were given to a participating striker although he was not a member of the union. The Supreme Court held that the strike benefits given by the union were *gifts* within the meaning of Section 102(a) of the Internal Revenue Code of 1954 and therefore were not includable in the worker's gross income. The Internal Revenue Service in its revised Section 61, defining gross income, holds that in cases where the facts are substantially like those presented in the *Kaiser* case, "Strike benefit payments and lockout benefit payments made by the unions will be regarded as gifts and, therefore, [as] excludable from the gross income of the recipients. Other cases will be scrutinized to determine whether the payments constitute gross income for federal income tax purposes. However, the fact that benefits are paid only to union members will not, in and of itself, be considered a determinative factor."

The Tax Court, in a number of cases (among others, *J. N. Hager*, 43 TC 468, Dec. 27,215; *J. W. Godwin*, (DC) 65–1 USTC P9121; *M. J. Colwell*, 64 TC 534, Dec. 33,331), has held that strike benefits were not gifts and therefore were subject to gross income taxation.

Source references: James T. Carney, "The Forgotten Man on the Welfare Roll: A Study of Public Subsidies for Strikers," *IR Law Digest*, Summer 1974; Robert W. Clark III, "Welfare for Strikers: ITT v. Minter (Chicago)," *IR Law Digest*, July 1972; Edward R. Curtin, "National Union Strike Benefits, 1967," *Conference Board Record*, Sept. 1967; ———, *Union Initiation Fees, Dues and Per Capita Tax, National Union Strike Benefits* (New York: NICB, 1968); "IRS Adopts *Kaiser* Case Rule for Strike-Lockout Benefits," *Daily Labor Report*, No. 141, July 24, 1961; Steven C. Kahn, "The Case Against Welfare Assistance to Strikers," *Employee Relations*

LJ, Autumn 1975; Sheldon Kline, "Strike Benefits of National Unions," *MLR*, March 1975; Harry H. Rains, "Should Strikers Receive Unemployment Insurance Benefits?" *LLJ*, Nov. 1979; Armand J. Thieblot, Jr. and Ronald M. Cowin, *Welfare and Strikes, The Use of Public Funds to Support Strikers* (Philadelphia: Univ. of Pennsylvania, Wharton School of Finance and Commerce, Industrial Research Unit, LRPP series no. 6, 1972); Marc E. Thomas, "Strikers' Eligibility for Public Assistance: The Standard Based on Need," 52 *Journal of Urban Law* 115 (1974).

strike bill A proposed law presented to a legislative body attempting to regulate strikes or strike activity.

strike-bound A plant which is on strike or attempting to operate under strike conditions.

strikebreaker A person, not a regular employee, who accepts employment in a struck plant. A strikebreaker is distinguishable from a scab, who is an employee who continues to work during a strike. A strikebreaker may pretend to work, or may be a guard, or fink.

The purpose of strikebreaking is described by Professor Joseph Shister as follows:

> The purpose of strikebreaking is to destroy a union once formed. It should occasion no surprise to learn that employers bent on the destruction of a labor union utilize every possible tactic to break a strike. Crushing of the strike deals an irreparable blow to the labor union. This is particularly true where the issue in the strike is union recognition. Labor unions must first be recognized by employers as collective bargaining agencies before they can bargain collectively over economic issues. Since this is true, employers frequently have employed tactics calculated to break union recognition strikes.
>
> There are three major lines of approach to break strikes:
>
> (1) the fortification of a plant with munitions and private plant police, the latter hired not to protect property against theft, fire, and the like, but employed for the purpose of intimidating workers who would strike;
> (2) the hiring of professional strikebreakers; and
> (3) the breaking down of the morale of strikers by instituting back to work movements.

Source references: Jerry M. Cooper, "The Army as Strikebreaker—The Railroad Strikes of 1877 and 1894," *Labor History*, Spring 1977; Richard L. Ehrlich, "Immigrant Strikebreaking Activity: A Sampling of Opinion Expressed in the National Labor Tribune, 1878–1885," *Labor History*, Fall 1974; Ross E. Getman, "'The Mohawk Valley Formula': A Case Study of the Manipulation of Rumor," *Industrial and Labor Relations Forum*, June 1981; Benjamin Rubenstein, "Section 10(i)—A Modern Strikebreaking Weapon?" *LLJ*, Dec. 1960; Joseph Shister, *Government and Collective Bargaining* (New York: Lippincott, 1951); William M. Tuttle, Jr., "Some Strikebreakers' Observations of Industrial Warfare," *Labor History*, Spring 1966.

See also ANTI-STRIKEBREAKING ACT (BYRNES ACT), BACK-TO-WORK MOVEMENT, BERGOFF TECHNIQUE, FINK, JOHNSTOWN CITIZENS COMMITTEE, MOHAWK VALLEY FORMULA, SCAB, STRIKE GUARD.

strike committee A special group set up by a union to administer a current strike in all its aspects.

strike contingency plan Management policies and procedures to guide operations of a firm or plant in strike situations.

According to Perry et al., companies in the 1960s began to abandon the policy of non-operation during strikes. However, the lack of success in operating plants during this period "was sufficiently painful to force the firms to develop comprehensive operating plans. In all of the firms studied, planning for possible plant operation is now a routine element in the overall process of preparing for contract negotiation."

Although situations and needs vary among organizations, seven key areas according to Perry et al. appear to be covered by strike plans: production, shipping and receiving, maintenance, industrial relations, plant security, communications, and legal representation.

Source references: Joseph D. Levesque, "Municipal Strike Planning: The Logistics of Allocating Resources," *Public Personnel Management*, March/April 1980; Walter G. Mullins, *Strike Defense Manual* (Houston: Gulf Pub., 1980); Lee T. Paterson and John Liebert, *Management Strike Handbook* (Chicago: IPMA, PERL no. 47, 1974); Charles R. Perry, Andrew M. Kramer, and Thomas J. Schneider, *Operating During Strikes: Company Experience, NLRB Policies, and Governmental Regulations* (Philadelphia: Univ. of Pennsylvania, Wharton School, Industrial Research Unit, LRPP series no. 23, 1982); "Preparing a Strike Manual," *Public Management*, Feb. 1976; Louis E. Tagliaferri, "Plant Operation During a Strike," *Personnel Administration*, March/April 1972; H. W. Vanderbach, "Where to Next? Strike Planning," *PJ*, Nov. 1977.

strike duty Assignments made to members of the union during a strike. May include simple picketing, providing food, preventing violence, etc.

strike fund A reserve put aside, generally by the international union and occasionally by local unions, to defray the expenses of a strike when and if it occurs. Strike expenses cover strike benefits to individual members on strike, publicity costs, legal fees, and other miscellaneous expenses. The strike fund or reserve commonly is referred to as the union's "war chest."

Source references: AFL-CIO, *Beyond the Picket Line: How to Organize a Strike Assistance Program* (New York: 1958); ———, *Strike Publicity Guide for Local Unions* (Washington: 1959); Kirk R. Petshek and William Paschell, "Financing of Union Activities," *MLR*, Oct. 1952.

strike guard A term generally applied to professional strikebreakers, who are hired technically to protect nonstriking employees or plant property.

strike insurance *See* MUTUAL STRIKE AID.

strike notice A statement or declaration required by law, and occasionally under collective bargaining agreements, advising the employer that the union plans to go on strike within a specified period of time.

See also FEDERAL MEDIATION AND CONCILIATION SERVICE (FMCS), SIXTY-DAY NOTICE, WAR LABOR DISPUTES ACT.

strike pay Benefits paid to employees while on strike.

strike penalty Measures and actions usually taken against employees and unions for disobeying laws prohibiting strike activity or violation of no-strike provisions of collective bargaining agreements. In the public sector, the most common kinds of penalties assessed against employees are termination of pay while employees are on strike and imposition of disciplinary measures, including discharge, suspension, or demotion; for employee organizations, common penalties include loss of exclusive representative status, fines, and cancellation of check-off privileges for a specified period of time.

There are public sector laws which penalize unlawful strikes by denying employees reinstatement or placing conditions upon their reinstatement. Other statutory penalties include provisions for loss of tenure or of pay increases. Imprisonment and fines for violation of an injunction or court order issued to enjoin strike action are also forms of penalty under some public sector laws.

In some jurisdictions, the degree to which the public employer provokes a strike is taken into account by the administering agency or the courts, resulting in mitigation of the penalty.

Source references: Jerome T. Barrett and Ira B. Lobel, "Public Sector Strikes—Legislative and Court Treatment," *MLR*, Sept. 1974; David C. Ford (ed.), *Should We Jail Public Employees?* (New York: Workers Defense League, 1973); Wayne F. Foster, "Damage Liability of State or Local Public Employees' Union or Union Officials for Unlawful Work Stoppage," 84 *ALR*3d 336 (1978); Eva Robins, "Penalties in Strikes Against a Public Employer," *NYU 22d Annual Conference on Labor*, ed. by Thomas Christensen and Andrea Christensen (New York: Bender, 1970); Helene S. Tanimoto and Joyce M. Najita, *Guide to Statutory Provisions in Public Sector Collective Bargaining—Strike Rights and Prohibitions* (3d issue, Honolulu: Univ. of Hawaii, IRC, 1981); Andrew W. J. Thomson, *Strike and Strike Penalties in Public Employment* (Ithaca: Cornell Univ., NYSSILR, Public Employee Relations Report no. 2, 1967).

strike propensity The tendency of strikes to be more prevalent in some industries and some types of work than others. Efforts have been made to examine the characteristics of such industries and to compare relative strike prevalence among different countries at different stages of economic development.

Source references: R. O. Clarke, "Labour-Management Disputes: A Perspective," *BJIR,* March 1980; S. W. Creigh and Peter Makeham, "Foreign Ownership and Strike-Proneness: A Research Note," *BJIR,* Nov. 1978; C. Frederick Eisele, "Organization Size, Technology, and Frequency of Strikes," *ILRR,* July 1974; Robert A. McLean, "Interindustry Differences in Strike Activity," *IR,* Winter 1979; James L. Perry, "Public Policy and Public Employee Strikes," *IR,* Oct. 1977; Gaston V. Rimlinger, "International Differences in the Strike Propensity," *ILRR,* April 1959; Russell K. Schutt, "Models of Militancy: Support for Strikes and Work Actions Among Employees," *ILRR,* April 1982; James L. Stern and Craig Olson, "The Propensity to Strike of Local Government Employees," *Journal of Collective Negotiations in the Public Sector,* Vol. 11, no. 3, 1982; Robert N. Stern, "Intermetropolitan Patterns of Strike Frequency," *ILRR,* Jan. 1976.

See also STRIKE, WORK STOPPAGE STATISTICS.

striker An individual who is on strike.

strike replacements Individuals who are hired by the employer to replace workers on strike.

strike statistics *See* WORK STOPPAGE STATISTICS.

strike vote A poll of employees in the bargaining unit to determine whether they wish to go on strike. Votes usually are by secret ballot. Approval by more than a bare majority may be required. Many union constitutions provide special procedures for calling a strike.

Source references: Frank A. Anton, *Government Supervised Strike Votes,* A Study Prepared for the Dept. of Labour, Ottawa, Under the University Research Program (Toronto: CCH, 1961); Samuel H. Cohen, "The Strike Ballot and Other Compulsory Union Balloting," *LLJ,* March 1956; Herbert S. Parnes, *Union Strike Votes: Current Practice and Proposed Controls* (Princeton: Princeton Univ., IR Section, 1956); William Paschell, "Union Strike Vote Practices and Proposed Controls," *MLR,* June 1956.

See also WAR LABOR DISPUTES ACT.

striking on the job *See* CA' CANNY, SOLDIERING.

struck goods Goods produced or handled by a company whose workers are on strike.

See also HOT CARGO PROVISIONS.

struck shop A company or plant whose employees are out on strike.

struck work Similar to struck goods, where the products turned out or the work done is for an employer or company whose employees are on strike.

struck work clause A provision in the collective bargaining contract which permits employees to refuse to perform work farmed out by a struck company.

structural unemployment Structural unemployment is related to changes in the structure of the economy and tends to be difficult to control, long-term, and persistent. It is caused by the emergence of new industries and the decline of older ones, impact and growth of automation, relocation of industry, effects of foreign competition, and the entry of youth into the labor force. Structural unemployment is revealed in high unemployment rates among certain sectors of the population, for example, the uneducated, the unskilled, the poor, as opposed to other sectors, such as skilled workers. Structural unemployment involves some frictional problems, and for this reason structural unemployment is sometimes included in definitions of frictional unemployment although the latter tends to be short-run unemployment. The solution to structural unemployment requires, among other things, creating new job opportunities, training workers with marketable skills, and providing relocation allowances for displaced workers.

Source references: Arthur D. Butler, "Identifying Structural Unemployment: Comment," *ILRR,* April 1967; Eleanor Gilpatrick, "On the Classification of Unemployment: A View of the Structural-Inadequate Demand Debate," *ILRR,* Jan. 1966; ———, *Structural Unemployment and Aggregate Demand* (Baltimore: Johns Hopkins Press,

1966); R. A. Gordon, "Has Structural Unemployment Worsened?" *IR*, May 1964; Linda Hochman, "An Evaluation of Federal Programs Designed to Reduce Regional Unemployment of a Structural Nature," *Industrial and Labor Relations Forum*, Dec. 1972; Charles C. Killingsworth, "The Fall and Rise of the Idea of Structural Unemployment," *Proceedings of the 31st A/M, IRRA*, ed. by Barbara Dennis (Madison: 1979); ———, *Structural Unemployment in the United States* (Washington: U.S. Dept. of Labor, Manpower Administration, Seminar on Manpower Policy and Program, 1965); Alan Kistler, "Job Training in the '80s," *American Federationist*, Feb. 1980; Sar A. Levitan, "Structural Unemployment and Public Policy," *LLJ*, July 1961; Ray Marshall, "Employment Policies that Deal with Structural Unemployment," *MLR*, May 1978; Robert Plant, *Industries in Trouble* (Geneva: ILO, 1981); Vladimir Stoikov, "Increasing Structural Unemployment Re-Examined," *ILRR*, April 1966; Ernst W. Stromsdorfer, "Labor Force Adjustment to Structural Displacement in a Local Labor Market," *ILRR*, Jan. 1965; Ralph Turvey, "Structural Change and Structural Unemployment," *ILR*, Sept./Oct. 1977; U.S. National Commission for Employment Policy, *Sixth Annual Report to the President and the Congress Including Findings and Recommendations on Economic Development and Jobs for the Structurally Unemployed* (Washington: Report 10, 1980).

See also DISGUISED UNEMPLOYMENT, FRICTIONAL UNEMPLOYMENT, TECHNOLOGICAL UNEMPLOYMENT.

stub shift A work shift which has fewer hours than the regular shift.

See also SHIFT.

studebakerism A term which describes the industrial relations philosophy followed by Harold Vance, president, and Paul Hoffman, chairman of the executive committee, of the Studebaker-Packard Corporation. The policy held that it is more effective to resolve problems on the basis of cooperation for mutual benefit than on the basis of balance of power. The policy provided the union with a more active voice in management and a greater sense of responsibility and authority for union stewards and employees in the plant than in the general run of plants.

Source reference: Robert N. McMurry, "War and Peace in Labor Relations," *Harvard BR*, Nov./Dec. 1955.

student worker An employee of a company who is engaged in a training program or works while still engaged in a course of study.

Source references: Gary B. Brumback, "A Critical Look at a Federal Agency's Student Training and Employment Program," *Public Personnel Review*, Oct. 1969; Sanford Cohen and William C. Pyle, "An Indiana Program of Job Training and Work Experience for Students," *MLR*, Feb. 1963; Sigmund G. Ginsberg, "New York City's 1968 Summer Intern Program," *Public Personnel Review*, July 1969; Allan B. Mandelstramm and Rudolph C. Blitz, "Summer Employment of Students: A Local Study," *IR*, May 1967; Kopp Michelotti, "Young Workers: In School and Out," *MLR*, Sept. 1973; Anne McDougall Young, "School and Work Among Youth During the 1970's," *MLR*, Sept. 1980.

style development rate A trial or experimental rate which applies to work on new styles for which piece rates have not been established. The rate approximates average hourly earnings earned under previous piece rate operations.

subcontracting A procedure followed by many companies to sublet certain parts of the operation to subcontractors, rather than have the company's employees perform the work, frequently on the ground that the work can be performed more efficiently and with less expense to the main company. Many agreements negotiated between unions and companies specify the conditions under which work may be contracted out. One such agreement reads: "Work usually performed by employees in this bargaining unit will not be contracted out if it will result in layoff of the employees covered by this agreement."

The term privatization is used to refer to the subcontracting of public services to private industry. Services commonly "privatized" include, among others, building construction, janitorial services, and refuse collection.

Source references: Gerald Aksen, "Arbitration of Government Subcontracting Disputes," *AJ*, Vol. 20, no. 1, 1965; Walter F. Baer, "Subcontracting—Twilight Zone in the Management Function," *LLJ*, Oct. 1965; Stephen J. Barres, "Subcontracting: A Persistent Labor Problem," *LLJ*, Oct. 1967; James T. Bennett and Thomas J. DiLorenzo, "Public Employee Unions and the Privatization of 'Public' Services," *Journal of Labor Research*, Winter 1983; Herbert N. Bernhardt, "Subcontracting During the Term of a Contract: A Clash Between the NLRB and Arbitral Principle," *AJ*, March 1982; Herbert Burstein, "Subcontracting and Plant Removals," *LLJ*, June 1962; California Tax Foundation, *Contracting Out Local Government Services in California* (Sacramento: 1981); G. Allan Dash, Jr., "The Arbitration of Subcontracting Disputes," *ILRR*, Jan. 1963; ———, "Decisive Elements in Subcontracting Cases," *LLJ*, April 1963; Walter L. Daykin, "Subcontracting in Industry," *LLJ*, March 1963; Ronald Donovan and Marsha J. Orr, *Subcontracting in the Public Sector: The New York State Experience* (Ithaca: Cornell Univ., NYSSILR, Institute of Public Employment, Monograph no. 10, 1982); Guy Farmer, "Good Faith Bargaining Over Subcontracting," *Georgetown LJ*, Spring 1963; John H. Galligan and Irving H. Sabghir, "Subcontracting and the Obligation to Bargain Under New York's Taylor Law," *LLJ*, Dec. 1978; Robert F. Koretz, "How Issues of Subcontracting and Plant Removal Are Handled: By Courts," *ILRR*, Jan. 1966; Rosaline Levenson, "Do Private Contractual Services Substitute for Public Employees?" *Public Personnel Management*, May/June 1977; Barry A. Leibling, "Deciding Whether to Use Staff or Outside Vendor Services," *Management Review*, March 1982; Leon E. Lunden, "Subcontracting Clauses in Major Contracts, Parts I and II," *MLR*, June and July 1961; Lee C. Shaw and Irving M. Friedman, "Plant Removals and Subcontracting of Work," *LLJ*, April 1963; Anthony V. Sinicropi, "Revisiting an Old Battle Ground: The Subcontracting Dispute," *Arbitration of Subcontracting and Wage Incentive Disputes*, Proceedings of the 32d A/M, NAA, ed. by James Stern and Barbara Dennis (Washington: BNA, 1980); Paul D. Staudohar, "Subcontracting in State and Local Government Employment," *Journal of Collective Negotiations in the Public Sector*, Vol. 9, no. 3, 1980; U.S. Dept. of Labor, BLS, *Major Collective Bargaining Agreements: Subcontracting* (Washington: Bull. no. 1425–8, 1969); Saul Wallen, "How Issues of Subcontracting and Plant Removal Are Handled: By Arbitrators," *ILRR*, Jan. 1966.

See also FIBREBOARD CASE, PLANT MIGRATION, RUNAWAY SHOP.

subemployment A concept designed to estimate adequacy of employment, it was developed in 1966 in response to Secretary of Labor Willard Wirtz's directive that a study be made and a subemployment concept be developed to measure the severity of employment problems in city slums. The concept combines earnings and employment data into a single index so as to provide a "summary measure of the total problem of unemployment and low earnings," on the premise that "workers with low earnings may have problems of as much concern from the viewpoint of manpower policy as those of many workers with substantial unemployment."

The subemployed were to include the unemployed, those working full time but earning wages below the official poverty line, those working only part-time but seeking full-time work, and those of working age who stopped looking for work because they believed no work was available. According to Miller, "Subemployed persons are workers. They are not as well off, on average, as other workers, but their incomes are considerably higher than those of persons not in the labor force, who, except for discouraged workers, are not counted as subemployed. In this respect, the subemployment concept describes the employment and income-adequacy problems of the more affluent segment of the poverty area population."

Vietorisz et al. identify three major types of subemployment—(1) lack of individual opportunities for finding useful paid employment at a decent living wage, (2) inability of family heads to support their families adequately, and (3) underutilization of skill.

Source references: Sar A. Levitan and Robert Taggart, "The Hardship Index," *Across the Board*, Nov. 1976; Herman P. Miller, "Subemployment in Poverty Areas of Large U.S. Cities," *MLR*, Oct. 1973; Thomas Vietorisz et al., "Subemployment: Concepts,

Measurements, and Trends," *Proceedings of the 27th A/M, IRRA*, ed. by James Stern and Barbara Dennis (Madison: 1975).

See also WORKING POOR.

subminimum rate A wage rate below the minimum established for a particular occupation and industry or geographic area by law, collective bargaining agreement, or by policy or practice. Rates in this category might apply to substandard workers, learners, superannuated employees, or handicapped persons.

submission agreement *See* AGREEMENT, SUBMISSION.

subsistence allowance Payments to workers for expenses covering lodging, meals, and transportation. Allowances of this type may be based on a fixed per diem or may be reimbursed, within limits, on actual expenses incurred on all subsistence items. Such subsistence allowances may be available to institutional employees as well as to those on travel status. They may also apply to certain occupations which on occasion require payments in lieu of subsistence.

subsistence plane of living *See* BARE (MINIMUM) SUBSISTENCE LEVEL.

subsistence wage An amount of money, usually computed on a weekly basis, which is sufficient to keep an average working family in health and economic efficiency.

Source reference: John A. Hobson, *Work and Wealth: A Human Evaluation* (New York: Macmillan, 1926).

See also FAMILY BUDGET.

substandard employees Handicapped workers who do not meet the average or normal standards of production because of physical or mental handicaps. They usually are paid a rate lower than the regular rate for the job.

See also HANDICAPPED WORKER.

substandard rate A wage rate lower than the standard or prevailing rate. For example, under the Fair Labor Standards Act, handicapped workers may be paid less than the prevailing rate with the approval of the wage-hour administrator.

See also HANDICAPPED WORKER.

substantial evidence A phrase used in Section 10(e) of the Taft-Hartley Act, which states that the NLRB's findings of fact shall be conclusive if they are supported by "substantial evidence" considered on the record as a whole. Whether they are so supported is a question of law for the courts to decide.

Construing Section 10(e) in a 1951 case, the Supreme Court said that a reviewing court may set aside a Board order when "it cannot conscientiously find that the evidence supporting that decision is substantial, when viewed in the light that the record in its entirety furnishes, including the body of evidence opposed to the Board's view." The Court added, however, that a reviewing court may not "displace the Board's choice between two fairly conflicting views, even though the court would justifiably have made a different choice had the matter been before it *de novo*."

Source reference: Universal Camera Corp. v. NLRB, 340 US 474, 27 LRRM 2373 (1951).

successor employer An individual or corporation purchasing a company or its stock, leasing a business, forming a new company, or companies that merge or take over the operations of other companies determined to have inherited the predecessor's obligations under the National Labor Relations Act.

Despite changes in ownership or management, if control is retained by the same parties, the same products or services are produced/rendered, the same machinery and equipment are used, or the same supervisors and employees are employed, the successor is subject to the predecessor's obligations under the law.

The NLRB may impose the duty to bargain on the successor employer if the change in ownership leaves the identity of the business enterprise largely intact or the company's location does not change.

Although the courts have held that the substantive terms of a collective bargaining agreement may not be imposed on the new owner, the successor employer may be liable for a predecessor's unfair labor practices or may be compelled to arbitrate employee rights under the old contract.

Source references: John Wiley & Sons v. Livingston, 376 US 543, 55 LRRM 2769 (1964); *NLRB v. Burns International Security*

Services, 406 US 272, 80 LRRM 2225 (19'.2); *Howard Johnson Co. v. Hotel Employees*, 417 US 249, 86 LRRM 2449 (1974); Jules I. Crystal, "Successor and Assigns Clauses: Do They Actually Require that a Purchaser Adopt the Seller's Contract?" *LLJ*, Sept. 1982; Isaac N. Groner, "The Vanguard of the Labor Law of Corporate Successorships: The Burns Detective Agency Case," *NYU 24th Annual Conference on Labor* (New York: Bender, 1972); Saul G. Kramer and Aaron J. Schindel, "Bargaining Obligations and Corporate Transformations," *NYU 33d Annual National Conference on Labor*, ed. by Richard Adelman (New York: Bender, 1981); William A. Krupman and Roger S. Kaplan, "The Stock Purchaser After *Burns*: Must He Buy the Union Contract?" *LLJ*, June 1980; Jerome J. La Penna, "Bankruptcy and the Collective Bargaining Agreement," *NYU 29th Annual Conference on Labor*, ed. by Richard Adelman (New York: Bender, 1976); George Murphy, "Successorship and the Forgotten Employee: A Suggested Approach," *NYU 31st Annual National Conference on Labor*, ed. by Richard Adelman (New York: Bender, 1978); James Severson and Michael Willcoxon, "Successorship Under *Howard Johnson*: Short Order Justice for Employees," *Industrial Relations LJ*, Spring 1976; I. Herbert Stern, "Binding the Successor Employer to its Predecessor's Collective Agreement Under the NLRA," *IR Law Digest*, July 1972; Christina B. Whitman, "Contract Rights and the Successor Employer: The Impact of *Burns* Security," *IR Law Digest*, July 1973; J. Albert Woll, "From *Wiley v. Livingston* to *NLRB v. Burns*: The Evolving Labor Law of Successorship," *Labor Law Developments 1972*, Proceedings of 18th Annual Institute on Labor Law, SLF (New York: Bender, 1972).

successor union A union succeeding another (usually company-dominated) union. The term may also apply to a union which has won collective bargaining rights from an existing union and claims the rights under the existing contract.

See also COMPANY-DOMINATED UNION.

suggestion bonus Usually a cash bonus (although occasionally it may be in the form of company stock, government bonds, or in merchandise), for suggestions considered meritorious and which will promote more efficient operation or result in cost savings to the organization.

See also BONUS.

suggestion system An organized company program which is developed for many reasons, including the opportunity to provide employees the chance to present ideas, methods, or plans for the improvement of the company's product or services. The system provides machinery for the examination of such proposals and the determination of the amount of the award, and outlines procedures for putting the plans into effect. It has been found that suggestion systems, in some cases, have developed creative talents, have resulted in additional interest in the work of the company, and have produced greater cooperation.

It is believed that the suggestion system may provide an opportunity for indicating dissatisfaction with existing practices and procedures.

Source references: John C. Bobbitt, "Ways to Stimulate Suggestions," *PJ*, Jan. 1960; Harry O. Carr, "It Pays to Promote the Suggestion System," *Personnel Administration*, July 1959; Edward H. Downey and Walter L. Balk, *Employee Innovation and Government Productivity: A Study of Suggestion Systems in the Public Sector* (Chicago: IPMA, Personnel Report 763, 1976); Lee A. Graf, "Suggestion Program Failure: Causes and Remedies," *PJ*, June 1982; W. O'Connell, "Does Your Suggestion System Pay Its Way?" *Personnel*, Jan. 1962; Stanley J. Seimer, *Suggestion Plans in American Industry: The Role of the Foreman* (Syracuse: Syracuse UP, 1959); William Short, "How to Operate a Suggestion Plan Effectively," *PJ*, Oct. 1962; "Suggestion Systems, An Answer to Perennial Problems," *PJ*, July 1980; Milton A. Tatter, "Turning Ideas Into Gold," *Management Review*, March 1975; U.S. GAO, *The Federal Employee Suggestion System—Possibilities for Improvement* (Washington: 1978); William S. Wilcox, "Reducing Costs by Increasing Employee Suggestions," *PJ*, March 1958; Cecil T. Young, "Suggestion Systems: Boon or Bane?" *PJ*, March 1963.

suits for contract violation For many years suits to enforce collective bargaining contracts were kept to a minimum by the old common law rule that unions, like other unincorporated associations, could neither sue nor be sued as entities. Section 301 of the Taft-Hartley Act, however, gave the federal district courts jurisdiction of suits to enforce collective bargaining contracts. To make this right broadly available, Section 301 removed two prior jurisdictional impediments to such actions: (1) No longer need the amount in controversy be at least $3,000 and (2) the prior requirement that the opposing parties must be citizens of different states also was waived.

In the landmark *Lincoln Mills* case, the Supreme Court held that Section 301 gave the federal district courts jurisdiction to issue injunctions to enforce contract provisions for the arbitration of unsettled grievances. It also said that the federal courts should fashion a body of substantive law to apply in such contract enforcement suits. (*Textile Workers v. Lincoln Mills*, 353 US 448, 40 LRRM 2113 (1957)).

The Supreme Court later held, however, that an injunction to enforce a no-strike clause in a collective bargaining contract may not be issued in a suit brought under Section 301. This section, the Court said, did not repeal or narrow the provisions of the Norris-LaGuardia Act that deprive federal district courts of jurisdiction to issue injunctions against peaceful strikes. (*Sinclair Refining Co. v. Atkinson*, 370 US 195, 50 LRRM 2420 (1962)).

An employer, however, may sue for damages in a Section 301 action where a union strikes in violation of a no-strike clause. (*UAW v. Benton Harbor*, 242 F2d 536, 39 LRRM 2689 (CA 6, 1957), *cert. denied*, 355 US 814, 40 LRRM 2680 (1958)).

See also ENFORCEMENT OF AGREEMENT, LINCOLN MILLS CASE, NO-SUIT CLAUSE, SINCLAIR REFINING CO. V. ATKINSON, UNITED MINE WORKERS V. CORONADO COAL AND COKE CO.

sunshine bargaining Refers to public sector collective bargaining sessions being open to public view. The basic rationale for sunshine or open meeting legislation is to assure the democratic process by barring secrecy so that the public's faith in government is not undermined. Some argue, however, that sunshine bargaining may have a negative effect on the negotiation process.

Although all 50 states have enacted sunshine statutes protecting the right of the public to be present at meetings of public bodies, only a few include the collective bargaining process. Florida, in 1974, was the first state to extend sunshine provisions to both state and local government negotiations.

Source references: George W. Cassidy, "An Analysis of Pressure Group Activities in the Context of Open Meeting and Public Employee Relations Law," *Journal of Collective Negotiations in the Public Sector*, Vol. 8, no. 1, 1979; Julius N. Draznin, "Letting the Sunshine Into Collective Bargaining," *PJ*, Oct. 1976; Edward L. Suntrup, "New Dimensions in Sunshine Bargaining," *PJ*, March 1979.

See also GOLDFISH BOWL BARGAINING.

superannuated fund A pension fund set aside to provide income for workers who are retired because of age.

superannuated rate Rate paid to superannuated employees. It is a rate below that prevailing for regular employees. Superannuated rates are applied to individuals with long service who are in need or to those who are needed because of labor shortages. A rate of pay below the prevailing wage rate is justified because the older employees are unable to perform the regular duties of the job.

superannuated workers *See* OLDER WORKER.

superannuation *See* PENSION PLAN.

superseniority Special seniority which supersedes ordinary seniority and is not dependent on the length of service of the individual. It is sometimes referred to as synthetic seniority because it is not earned by the employee through length of service.

It is most frequently used for protection against layoffs of shop stewards and grievance committeemen, so that the union may have available individuals who are familiar with the problems of the company. Holders of the superseniority are protected in their employment during their term of union office.

Source references: George K. Leonard, "Practical Applications of Superseniority,"

LLJ, Jan. 1975; Max S. Wortman, "Superseniority—Myth or Reality?" *LLJ*, April 1967.

See also SENIORITY, TOP SENIORITY.

supervision The responsibility for directing the work of others in order to attain work objectives. The term is applied in a general way to those who direct the work of others.

Source references: Ted F. Anthony and Archie B. Carroll, "Preventing Supervision from Becoming an End-of-the-Line Job," *PJ*, June 1977; Lewis R. Benton, *Supervision and Management* (New York: McGraw-Hill, 1972); James M. Black and Guy B. Ford, *Front-Line Management: A Guide to Effective Supervisory Action* (New York: McGraw-Hill, 1963); Robert W. Eckles, Ronald L. Carmichael, and Bernard R. Sarchet, *Essentials of Management for First-Line Supervision* (New York: Wiley, 1974); Saul W. Gellerman, "Supervision: Substance and Style," *Harvard BR*, March/April 1976; Carl Heyel, *Management for Modern Supervisors* (New York: AMA, 1962); Louis V. Imundo, *The Effective Supervisor's Handbook* (New York: AMACOM, 1980); Brian R. Kay and Roy L. Clough, Jr., *Cases in Supervision* (New York: McGraw-Hill, 1962); Brian R. Kay and Stuart Palmer, *The Challenge of Supervision* (New York: McGraw-Hill, 1961); Douglas McGregor, *The Human Side of Enterprise* (New York: McGraw-Hill, 1960); Erin-Aine Miller and Rosalind Schwartz, *Effective Supervision; Principles and Skills, Impact of Collective Bargaining* (Los Angeles: UC, Institute of IR, 1977); Merle C. Nutt, *Meeting the Challenge of Supervision* (New York: Exposition Press, 1972); John M. Pfiffner and Marshall Fels, *The Supervision of Personnel: Human Relations in the Management of Men* (3d ed., Englewood Cliffs: PH, 1964); W. Richard Plunkett, *Supervision: The Direction of People At Work* (Dubuque: Brown, 1975); William M. Read, *Now You Are a Supervisor: A Dynamic Approach to Self-Improvement Dealing With the Human Side of Supervision* (Coatesville, Pa.: Pyramid Pub., 1962); Lawrence L. Steinmetz and H. Ralph Todd, Jr., *First-Line Management: Approaching Supervision Effectively* (Dallas: Business Publications, 1975).

See also ONE-TO-ONE ORGANIZATION.

supervisor A person having management responsibilities, usually including the right to hire and fire or to recommend such action. The Taft-Hartley Act in Section 2 (11) defines the term supervisor to mean ". . . any individual having authority, in the interest of the employer, to hire, transfer, suspend, layoff, recall, promote, discharge, assign, reward, or discipline other employees, or responsibility to direct them, or to adjust their grievances, or effectively to recommend such action, if in connection with the foregoing the exercise of such authority is not of a merely routine or clerical nature, but requires the use of independent judgment."

Source references: AMA, *Special Problems the Supervisor Must Handle*, Selected Reprints from AMA Periodicals (New York: 1966–1968); ———, *The Supervisor's Responsibilities in Labor Relations* (New York: 1963); Lester R. Bittel, *What Every Supervisor Should Know* (3d ed., New York: McGraw-Hill, 1974); Lester R. Bittel and Jackson E. Ramsey, "The Limited, Traditional World of Supervisors," *Harvard BR*, July/Aug. 1982; Martin M. Broadwell, *The New Supervisor* (2d ed., Reading, Mass.: Addison-Wesley, 1979); BNA, *Status of First-Level Supervisors* (Washington: PPF Survey no. 95, 1971); Archie B. Carroll and Ted F. Anthony, "An Overview of the Supervisor's Job," *PJ*, May 1976; Eunice C. Coleman and Maureen E. Campbell, *Supervisors: A Corporate Resource*, An AMA Management Briefing (New York: AMA, 1975); Charles E. Davis and Jonathan P. West, "Attitudinal Differences Among Supervisors in the Public Sector," *ILRR*, July 1979; Walter L. Daykin, "Legal Meaning of 'Supervisor' Under Taft-Hartley," *LLJ*, Feb. 1962; Ernest A. Doud and Edward J. Miller, "First-Line Supervisors: The Key to Improved Performance," *Management Review*, Dec. 1980; James W. Driscoll, Daniel J. Carroll, Jr. and Timothy A. Sprecher, "The First-Level Supervisor: Still 'the Man in the Middle'," *Sloan Management Review*, Winter 1978; Samuel Fried, "Limitations on the Right of Unions to Discipline Supervisors," 53 *Boston Univ. LR* 1019 (1973); George D. Halsey, *Selecting and Developing First-Line Supervisors* (New York: Harper, 1955); Charles W. Johnson, *The Supervisor: Key Management*

(Englewood Cliffs: PH, 1960); Philip C. Lederer, "Management's Right to Loyalty of Supervisors," *LLJ*, Feb. 1981; W. Earl Sasser, Jr. and Frank S. Leonard, "Let First-Level Supervisors Do Their Job," *Harvard BR*, March/April 1980; Laurence M. Smiley and Paul R. Westbrook, "The First-Line Supervisory Problem Redefined," *PJ*, Dec. 1975; Ernest N. Uhles, *How to Become an Effective Supervisor; A Survival Manual for the Man in the Middle* (New York: Exposition Press, 1971); William R. Van Dersal, *The Successful Supervisor in Government and Business* (3d ed., New York: Harper & Row, 1974); Robert L. Walker and James W. Robinson, "The First-Line Supervisor's Role in the Grievance Procedure," *AJ*, Dec. 1977.

See also FOREMAN.

supervisor rating *See* MERIT RATING.

supervisory training *See* FOREMAN TRAINING.

supper money An allowance provided to workers who work overtime and therefore are required to eat away from home.

supplemental benefits *See* FRINGE BENEFITS, PENSION, VACATIONS.

supplemental unemployment benefits Programs established by many companies which attempt to provide additional benefits for employees to supplement those received under state unemployment compensation laws. These plans are of two general types, the individual account and the pooled fund.

The individual account plan provides that contributions are credited to each employee's account and benefits paid to each worker are charged against that account. Any balance remaining in the account when the employee is terminated is paid to the individual.

Under pooled fund plans, benefits are paid from the fund to which the employer contributes. Individual employees are credited with the time they have worked and charged with the time for which they draw benefits. The credits and charges are determined independently of the company contribution and the terminated employee has no vested right to such contributions.

SUB plans are employer financed.

Source references: Emerson H. Beier, "Financial Aspects of SUB Plans," *MLR*, April 1966; Richard N. Block, "Job Changing and Negotiated Nonwage Provisions," *IR*, Oct. 1978; Audrey Freedman, "Reexamining Income Security: SUB vs. Guaranteed Work," *Conference Board Record*, May 1976; ———, *Security Bargains Reconsidered; SUB, Severance Pay, Guaranteed Work* (New York: The Conference Board, Report no. 736, 1978); Harry Malisoff, *The Financing of Extended Unemployment Insurance Benefits in the United States* (Kalamazoo: Upjohn Institute, 1963); John W. McConnell, "Initial Experience in Operation of Supplemental Unemployment Benefit Plans," *New Dimensions in Collective Bargaining*, ed. by Harold W. Davey, Howard S. Kaltenborn, and Stanley H. Ruttenberg (New York: Harper, IRRA Pub. no. 21, 1959); Beverly K. Schaffer, "Experience with Supplementary Unemployment Benefits: A Case Study of the Atlantic Steel Company," *ILRR*, Oct. 1968; U.S. Dept. of Labor, BLS, *Major Collective Bargaining Agreements: Supplemental Unemployment Benefit Plans and Wage-Employment Guarantees* (Washington: Bull. no. 1425–3, 1965).

See also GUARANTEED ANNUAL WAGE, SHORT WORKWEEK BENEFIT, TEMPORARY EXTENDED UNEMPLOYMENT COMPENSATION, UNEMPLOYMENT COMPENSATION.

supplementary training Training given to an employee beyond the basic training provided for in regular programs.

supplements to wages and salaries All additions or supplements to the basic wage or salary rate. For national income purposes, the U.S. Dept. of Commerce defines supplements as "employer contributions for social insurance and . . . other labor income." Such employer payments include old age, survivors, disability and hospital insurance; unemployment insurance; government retirement; and workers compensation. Labor income includes private pension and welfare funds contributions and directors' fees.

Source references: Robert G. Rice, "Skill, Earnings, and the Growth of Wage Supplements," *AER*, May 1966; U.S. Dept. of Commerce, Bureau of Economic Analysis,

Business Statistics 1979 (22d ed., Washington: 1980).

See also BENEFIT PLANS, FRINGE BENEFITS.

Supreme Court The court of last resort in the U.S. federal judicial system.

Source references: Benjamin Aaron, "Labor Law Decisions of the Supreme Court," *Labor Law Developments 1975*, Proceedings of the 21st Annual Institute on Labor Law, SLF (New York: Bender, 1975); Thomas G. S. Christensen, "The Supreme Court's Labor Law Decisions, 1979–1980 Term: 'A Rose is a Rose is a Rose,' But the Petals Sure are Different," *Labor Law Developments 1981*, Proceedings of the 27th Annual Institute on Labor Law, SLF (New York: Bender, 1981); Lawrence F. Doppelt, "Employee Interests in Labor Law: The Supreme Court Swings Back the Pendulum," *Industrial Relations LJ*, Summer 1976; William Feldesman, "The Supreme Court and Collective Bargaining Under the National Labor Relations Act," *LLJ*, May 1962; Alvin L. Goldman, *The Supreme Court and Labor-Management Relations Law* (Lexington, Mass.: Lexington Books, 1976); Carl F. Goodman, "Public Employment and the Supreme Court's 1976–77 Term," *Public Personnel Management*, Sept./Oct. 1977; Lee Modjeska, "Decisions of the Supreme Court, 1979–1980—Labor Relations and Employment Discrimination Law," *Industrial Relations LJ*, Vol. 4, no. 1, 1980; Joseph E. Moore, "The NLRB and the Supreme Court," *LLJ*, April 1969; Gregory J. Mounts, "Labor and the Supreme Court: Significant Decisions of 1979–80," *MLR*, April 1981; Albion G. Taylor, *Labor and the Supreme Court* (2d ed., Ann Arbor: Braun-Brumfield, 1961); Ralph K. Winter, Jr., "Judicial Review of Agency Decisions: The Labor Board and the Court," *IR Law Digest*, April 1969; Benjamin M. Ziegler (ed.), *The Supreme Court and American Economic Life* (Evanston: Row, Peterson, 1962).

surgical benefits Payments usually made by the employer providing for surgical care or cash allowances for such care. Surgical benefits are frequently included in overall health and insurance programs.

Source references: BNA, *Collective Bargaining Negotiations and Contracts*, Vol. 2, 44:5; U.S. Dept. of Labor, BLS, *Health and Insurance Plans Under Collective Bargaining: Surgical and Medical Benefits, Late Summer 1959* (Washington: Bull. no. 1280, 1960).

See also HEALTH BENEFIT PROGRAMS.

surplus value *See* LABOR THEORY OF VALUE.

surveillance *See* ESPIONAGE.

survivors' benefits Benefits available to widows and other survivors in case of death resulting from work injuries. Survivors' benefits also are paid under the Social Security Act.

Source references: Earl F. Cheit, "Work Injuries and Recovery: I. Survivors' Benefits—A Plan to Make Them Equitable," *MLR*, Oct. 1961; Harry L. Levin and Stanley S. Sacks, "Survivors' Benefits in Collectively Bargained Pension Plans," *MLR*, July 1962.

See also HEALTH BENEFIT PROGRAMS; OLD AGE, SURVIVORS, AND DISABILITY INSURANCE.

suspension A form of disciplinary action by an employer less drastic than discharge. It is frequently used as a warning to the individual that a continuation of certain conduct will result in ultimate discharge.

Source reference: AMA, *Constructive Discipline in Industry* (New York: Special Research Report no. 3, 1943).

See also DISCHARGE, DISCIPLINARY LAYOFF, FURLOUGH, LEAVE OF ABSENCE, TEMPORARY LAYOFF.

sweatshop A plant or place of work where the conditions are substantially below accepted standards. The conditions may be unhealthy or substandard in respect to both wages and working conditions. The general description of the sweatshop and its causes was set out by Professors Adams and Sumner as follows:

> The sweating system grew out of three essential conditions: (a) a crowded population in large cities; (b) contract work; and (c) inexpensive machinery. Newly arrived immigrants crowded in large cities and were the most helpless victims of the system, and, by their willingness to submit to almost any terms of employment in order to live, were the source of fierce competition which intensified the very evils under which they suffered. . . .
>
> There are three characteristic evils of the sweating system: (a) low wages, (b) long hours, (c) unsanitary workshops. In the last named evil

is implied a fourth, the danger to the health of the consumer from the use of sweatshop goods. . . .

A leading cause of the sweating system was undoubtedly the lack of competitive ability on the part of large numbers of wage-workers, a lack which was principally due to ignorance, absence of industrial training, and a low standard of life. A second cause was that in certain industries, the general rule that the big shop can produce more cheaply than the small ones did not hold good. Hence, the big shop eliminated extra costs by driving down wages to the subsistence point and below, by indefinitely prolonging hours, and by wholly neglecting sanitary conditions.

Source reference: Thomas S. Adams and Helen L. Sumner, *Labor Problems* (New York: Macmillan, 1912).

sweetheart contract *See* AGREEMENT, SWEETHEART.

swifts *See* PACERS.

Swing case *See* AMERICAN FEDERATION OF LABOR V. SWING.

swing shift A crew of workers (sometimes known as the fourth shift or crew) on continuous operation schedule. The name derives from the need to have at least one shift (or occasionally all four shifts, depending upon the nature of the swing) rotating to different days and hours at specified intervals.

Source reference: Paul and Faith Pigors, *Human Aspects of Multiple Shift Operations* (Cambridge: MIT, Dept. of Economics and Social Sciences, Publications in Social Sciences, Series 2, no. 13, 1944).

See also ROTATING SHIFT, SHIFT.

Switchmen's Union of North America (AFL-CIO) Founded as the Switchmen's Association in Chicago in 1877, its name was changed to the Switchmen's Mutual Aid Association of the United States of America in 1886. Following a lockout on the Chicago Northwestern Railroad and a strike on the Chicago, Burlington and Quincy Railroad in 1888, the Switchmen's Mutual Aid Association died in July 1894.

The present Switchmen's Union was established at a Kansas City meeting of various switchmen locals on October 23, 1894.

The union affiliated with the AFL on July 12, 1906. It also affiliated with the Canadian Labour Congress in 1935.

On January 1, 1969, the union and three other railroad unions—the Brotherhood of Locomotive Firemen and Enginemen, the Brotherhood of Railroad Trainmen, and the Order of Railway Conductors and Brakemen—merged to form the United Transportation Union.

See also TRANSPORTATION UNION; UNITED (AFL-CIO).

sympathetic (sympathy) strike Strike action by a union in support of the objectives of another organization, but in which dispute it has no direct or immediate interest and the possible benefits to itself from such strike are indirect and remote.

Source references: Michael H. Boldt, "*Design and Manufacturing Corporation:* The Multiplant Employer and Sympathy Strikes," *LLJ*, March 1982; Walter B. Connolly, Jr., "Section 7 and Sympathy Strikes: The Respective Rights of Employers and Employees," *LLJ*, Dec. 1974; Stig Gustafsson, "Sympathy Strikes—Are They Legal?" *Free Labour World*, March 1962; Elvis C. Stephens and Donna Ledgerwood, "Do No-Strike Clauses Prohibit Sympathy Strikes?" *LLJ*, May 1982; "Sympathy Strikes Under the Minnesota Public Employment Relations Act," 63 *Minnesota LR* 1023 (1979).

syndicalism A term for trade unionism in France. It is based largely on a revolutionary philosophy. The best known syndicalist union in the United States was the Industrial Workers of the World (IWW). The theory was to have syndicates or unions use their economic power for the purpose of obtaining control of industry.

Source references: Melvyn Dubofsky, "The Origins of Western Working Class Radicalism, 1890–1905," *Labor History*, Spring 1966; Patrick Renshaw, *The Wobblies* (Garden City: Doubleday, 1967); Bertrand Russell, *Roads to Freedom: Socialism, Anarchism and Syndicalism* (3d ed., London: Allen, Unwin, 1966); Henry C. Simons, "Some Reflections on Syndicalisms," *Journal of Political Economy*, March 1944; Fred Witney, "Labor and the Spanish Syndical System," *MLR*, Aug. 1966.

See also REVOLUTIONARY UNIONISM.

systemic discrimination Discrimination resulting from the system of employment policies and practices, though often neutral on their face, that serve to differentiate or to perpetuate a differentiation in terms of conditions of employment for applicants or employees because of race, color, religion, sex, national origin, disability, veteran status, or age. Examples of such practices include use of tests, educational requirements, height and weight restrictions.

The EEOC has adopted the following standards to determine possible systemic discrimination by employers and other persons subject to Title VII of the Civil Rights Act of 1964:

(1) Continuation of "policies and practices which result in low utilization of available minorities and/or women,"

(2) Employment of "a substantially smaller proportion of minorities and/or women [in comparison with] . . . other employers in the same labor market who employ persons with the same general level of skills,"

(3) Employment of "a substantially smaller proportion of minorities and/or women in . . . higher paid job categories than in . . . lower paid job categories,"

(4) "Maintenance of specific . . . policies and practices relating to the terms and conditions of employment that have an adverse impact on minorities and/or women, and are not justified by business necessity,"

(5) Employment practices which "have had the effect of restricting or excluding available minorities and/or women from significant employment opportunities, and who are likely to be used as models for other employers because of such factors as the number of their employees, their impact on local economy, or their competitive position in the industry," and

(6) Employers with "substantial numbers of employment opportunities," but "whose practices do not provide available minorities and women with fair access to these opportunities."

Source references: EEOC Compliance Manual (Chicago: CCH, 1982); U.S. OFCCP, *Federal Contract Compliance Manual* (Washington: 1979).

system unit A collective bargaining unit, usually in the utilities, such as transportation or communications industries.

systemwide unit A bargaining unit covering an entire system in the utilities area, transportation or communications.

T

TCE *See* TRANSPORTATION-COMMUNICATION EMPLOYEES UNION (AFL-CIO).

TDA *See* TRAIN DISPATCHERS ASSOCIATION; AMERICAN (AFL-CIO).

TDMM *See* TOOL, DIE AND MOLD MAKERS; INTERNATIONAL UNION OF (IND).

TIU *See* TELECOMMUNICATIONS INTERNATIONAL UNION (IND).

TMTF *See* TILE, MARBLE, TERRAZZO FINISHERS AND SHOPWORKERS AND GRANITE CUTTERS INTERNATIONAL UNION (AFL-CIO).

TNG *See* NEWSPAPER GUILD; THE (AFL-CIO).

TPS *See* TEXTILE PROCESSORS, SERVICE TRADES, HEALTH CARE, PROFESSIONAL AND TECHNICAL EMPLOYEES INTERNATIONAL UNION.

TRASOP *See* TAX REDUCTION ACT STOCK OWNERSHIP PLAN (TRASOP).

TRSOC *See* TRADEMARK SOCIETY, INC. (IND).

TUC *See* BRITISH TRADES UNION CONGRESS.

TVA *See* TENNESSEE VALLEY AUTHORITY.

TWI *See* TRAINING WITHIN INDUSTRY.

TWU *See* TRANSPORT WORKERS UNION OF AMERICA (AFL-CIO).

Taft-Hartley Act *See* LABOR MANAGEMENT RELATIONS ACT OF 1947.

tailor-made test Tests specially designed (tailor-made) to meet a particular situation when recruiting for a person of highly specialized skills or requirements.

See also TEST.

take-home pay The net amount of money which a worker receives in his pay check after all of the required deductions are made. Required deductions may include taxes, social security payments, union dues, insurance premiums, and other expenses which are deducted from his gross earnings.

See also ACTUAL WAGES, REAL WAGES, SPENDABLE EARNINGS.

tandem increases Adjustments or increases to certain employees or groups which correspond to increases granted to related employees.

tapered wage increases A wage stabilization technique devised by the World War II War Labor Board to maintain wage structure differentials when eliminating substandard conditions. In general, the principle was that the lower-paid workers received a higher wage adjustment than the better-paid workers. The "tapering" formula applied to all substandard cases in the New England shoe industry provided a one-cent hourly increase for employees earning 76 to 80 cents an hour, a 10-cent increase to those earning 40 cents an hour; rates for pieceworkers were to be adjusted from 1.3 percent for employees earning between 76 and 80 cents to 21.1 percent for those earning between 40 and 45 cents an hour.

Source reference: International Shoe Co., 14 WLR 309 (1944).

tardiness A form of absenteeism; lack of punctuality in arriving at the place of work. Some regard tardiness as any absence of less than one-half day.

Source reference: "Who Cares If You're Late to Work?" *Management Review*, April 1969.

See also ABSENTEEISM.

target The expected earnings to which piece rates are geared. The piece rate system may set a certain percentage of earnings above the base rate as a goal to be achieved by the average employee. This is referred to as the "target," or the expected earnings from use of a certain rate.

task A term used to describe a unit of work or effort exerted to achieve a specific purpose, such as setting up a machine to perform a certain job.

In wage incentive systems it is considered to be the amount of production per unit of time which is necessary to earn the base rate of pay.

See also STANDARD TIME.

task performed *See* FUNCTUS OFFICIO.

task time The determination of the time required for the average worker to perform a job according to the prescribed standard.

task work A plan in use in some operations where the employees are permitted to go home after they have completed their assignment task for the day. The plan is referred to as "uku pau" in Hawaii and is common in refuse collection work. Employees complete their day's work in substantially fewer than eight hours.

Tax Reduction Act stock ownership plan (TRASOP) A plan to provide employees with shares of company stock by allowing corporate tax credit based on a percentage of capital investment. TRASOPs were authorized by the Tax Reduction Act of 1975, which entitled employers to receive credit equal to 1 percent of their investment tax credit if such funds were invested in company stock on behalf of their employees.

The Tax Reform Act of 1976 provided added incentive by allowing an additional one-half percent tax credit if employee contributions to the TRASOPs were matched by employer contributions.

The Economic Recovery Tax Act of 1981 replaces TRASOPs with the payroll-based employee stock ownership plans (PAYSOPs).

Source references: Paul E. Burke, "TRASOPs: The Beautiful Benefit," *PJ*, March 1978; Theresa Thompson, "Time to Reassess Tax Credit for Employee Stock Ownership Plans," *Management Review*, Feb. 1982.

See also PAYROLL-BASED EMPLOYEE STOCK OWNERSHIP PLAN (PAYSOP).

Taylor differential piece-rate plan *See* DIFFERENTIAL PIECE-RATE PLAN.

Tayloresque A term describing either scientific management or the differential piece-rate system sponsored by Frederick W. Taylor.

Taylor Law Formally titled the Public Employees' Fair Employment Act, this New York state law covering public employment relations was approved on April 21, 1967, effective September 1, 1967. It repealed Section 108 of the New York Civil Service Law, commonly referred to as the Condon-Wadlin Law. Under the law, public employees are prohibited from striking, and penalties for violation are levied against the union and employees involved. The popular title of the law owes its origin to the commission appointed by Governor Nelson Rockefeller and chaired by Professor George W. Taylor of the Wharton School of Finance and Commerce, University of Pennsylvania.

Source references: Grace Sterrett Aboud and Robert E. Doherty, *Practices and Procedures Under the Taylor Law: A Practical Guide in Narrative Form* (Ithaca: Cornell Univ., NYSSILR, Institute of Public Employment, 1974); Richard M. Gaba, "Scope of Bargaining Under New York's Taylor Law," *Journal of Collective Negotiations in the Public Sector*, Summer 1974; Robert Helsby, "Impact of the Taylor Law on Public Schools (1968–1970)," *Journal of Collective Negotiations in the Public Sector*, Feb. 1972; New York State, Public Employment Relations Board, *Symposium on Police and Firefighter Arbitration in New York State, December 1–3, 1976* (Albany: 1977); ———, *What is the Taylor Law? . . . And How Does it Work?* (Albany: 1974); Harold S. Roberts, *Labor-Management Relations in the Public Service* (Honolulu: Univ. of Hawaii Press, 1970).

teacher negotiation *See* COLLECTIVE NEGOTIATION, PROFESSIONAL NEGOTIATION.

Teachers; American Federation of (AFL-CIO) In 1916, a group of eight teacher unions from the midwest and east coast formed the American Federation of Teachers and affiliated as a national union with the AFL.

The AFT first saw itself as a catalyst for the National Education Association (NEA) to advance the cause of the classroom teacher. Early AFT members were encouraged to attend NEA conventions and work within the Association. However, after indications that the NEA was not interested in following a union model, the AFT formed a close identification with organized labor and established a reputation as a strong advocate of collective bargaining for public school teachers.

In 1982, the AFT had 2,200 local unions and a membership of 551,359. It issues the *American Teacher* (monthly) and the *American Educator* (quarterly).

Address: 11 Dupont Circle, N.W., Washington, D.C. 20036. Tel. (202) 797-4400

Source references: American Federation of Teachers, *Teacher Strikes and Elections* (Washington: 1969); Carl A. Batlin, "American Federation of Teachers Endorses Merger Talks with NEA," *MLR*, Oct. 1973; Robert J. Braun, *Teachers and Power; The Story of the American Federation of Teachers* (New York: Simon and Schuster, 1972); Burton Butcher and Alan E. Schenker, "Faculty Bargaining at Four-Year Institutions: Differences Among Three National Bargaining Associations," *Journal of Collective Negotiations in the Public Sector*, Vol. 5, no. 2, 1976; William Edward Eaton, *The American Federation of Teachers, 1916–1961; a History of the Movement* (Carbondale: Southern Illinois UP, 1976); John Ligtenberg and Charles W. Miller, *Landmark Cases in the History of the American Federation of Teachers* (Washington: American Federation of Teachers, 1969); Michael H. Moskow, *Teachers and Unions* (Philadelphia: Univ. of Pennsylvania, Wharton School of Finance and Commerce, Industrial Research Unit, 1966); Philip Taft, *United They Teach; The Story of the United Federation of Teachers* (Los Angeles: Nash Pub., 1974).

team bonus system *See* GROUP BONUS.

Teamsters, Chauffeurs, Warehousemen and Helpers of America; International Brotherhood of (Ind) Organized in 1899 as the Team Drivers' International Union. A group seceded in 1901 and established the Teamsters National Union. The two organizations reunited in 1903 and formed the International Brotherhood of Teamsters. With the advent of automobiles, the union extended its jurisdiction to chauffeurs and truck drivers and in 1909 changed its name to the International Brotherhood of Teamsters, Chauffeurs, Stablemen and Helpers. It adopted its present name in 1940. The union was expelled from the AFL-CIO in December 1957.

Unions which have merged with the Teamsters include: the Allied Independent Union in January 1957, the American Communications Association in December 1966, and the Brewery Workers (AFL-CIO) on November 6, 1973.

The Laundry, Dry Cleaning and Dye House Workers International Union is affiliated with the Teamsters.

The official quarterly publication is the *International Teamster Magazine*.

Address: 25 Louisiana Ave., N.W., Washington, D.C. 20001. Tel. (202) 624–6800

Source references: Steven Brill, *The Teamsters* (New York: Simon and Schuster, 1978); Farrell Dobbs, *Teamster Power* (New York: Monad Press, 1973); Donald Garnel, *The Rise of Teamster Power in the West* (Berkeley: UC Press, 1972); Miles E. Hoffman, *A Contemporary Analysis of a Labor Union: International Brotherhood of Teamsters, Chauffeurs, Warehousemen and Helpers of America* (Philadelphia: Temple Univ., Labor Monograph no. 6, 1964); Ralph C. and Estelle D. James, *Hoffa and the Teamsters* (Princeton: Van Nostrand, 1965); ________, "Hoffa's Impact on Teamster Wages," *IR*, Oct. 1964; Robert D. Leiter, *The Teamsters Union* (New York: Bookman Associates, 1957); John D. McCallum, *Dave Beck* (Mercer Island, Washington: The Writing Works, Inc., 1978); Clark R. Mollenhoff, *Tentacles of Power, The Story of Jimmy Hoffa* (Cleveland: World Publishing, 1965); Sam Romer, *The International Brotherhood of Teamsters: Its Government and Structure* (New York: Wiley, 1962); Walter Sheridan, *The Fall and Rise of Jimmy Hoffa* (New York: Saturday Review Press, 1972); Philip Taft, *The Structure and Government of Labor Unions* (Cambridge: Harvard UP, 1954).

See also ALLIANCE FOR LABOR ACTION (ALA).

Teamsters v. U.S. A landmark Supreme Court decision in which the Court, for the first time, approved the use of statistical evidence in establishing a prima facie case of employment discrimination.

The Court also held the employer's seniority system to be bona fide because it applied "equally to all races and ethnic groups. . . . [T]he seniority system did not have its genesis in racial discrimination. . . . In these circumstances, the single fact that the system extends no retroactive seniority to pre-Act discriminatees does not make it unlawful."

The Court additionally ruled that retroactive seniority may be an appropriate remedy for individuals who had been discouraged from applying for more desirable jobs because of the employer's well-known discriminatory policies. It declared that "an incumbent employee's failure to apply for a job is not an inexorable bar to an award of retroactive seniority. Individual nonapplicants must be given an opportunity to undertake their difficult task of proving that they should be treated as applicants and therefore are presumptively entitled to relief accordingly."

Source references: Teamsters v. U.S., 431 US 324, 14 FEP Cases 1514 (1977); Michael J. Zimmer, "Teamsters: Redefinition and Retrenchment of Concepts of Discrimination," *NYU 30th Annual National Conference on Labor*, ed. by Richard Adelman (New York: Bender, 1978).

See also BONA FIDE SENIORITY SYSTEM, MEMPHIS FIRE DEPARTMENT V. STOTTS, SENIORITY.

Technical Engineers; American Federation of (AFL-CIO) Founded in 1918 as the International Federation of Technical Engineers, Architects' and Draftsmen's Unions (AFL), it adopted the name American Federation of Technical Engineers in the early 1950s. The union changed its name to the American Federation of Professional and Technical Engineers (AFL-CIO) in the early 1970s.

See also PROFESSIONAL AND TECHNICAL ENGINEERS; INTERNATIONAL FEDERATION OF (AFL-CIO).

technocracy A theory of economic and social organization in which industrial management would be scientifically controlled by engineers. The proponents of technocracy, called technocrats, argued that the economy was outmoded and that machines could be controlled to provide greater human benefits if the control were put in the hands of the technologists. Technocracy had a mild vogue in the early days of the New Deal.

technological change Changes in production methods which involve the use of new machinery and equipment for the purpose of increasing productivity. Professor Yoder holds that technological change involves "two types of development: increased power and enhanced efficiency in the use of power, result in changes in labor productivity and their variable is directly related to the displacement of workers and resulting unemployment."

Source references: Jules Backman, "Cushioning the Impact of Technological Change," *LLJ*, Sept. 1962; Derek Bok and Max D. Kossoris, *Methods of Adjusting to Automation and Technological Change, A Review of Selected Methods Prepared for the President's Committee on Labor-Management Policy* (Washington: U.S. Dept. of Labor, 1964); James R. Bright, "Evaluating Signs of Technological Change," *Harvard BR*, Jan./Feb. 1970; Robert E. Callahan, "A Management Dilemma Revisited: Must Business Choose Between Stability and Adaptability?" *Sloan Management Review*, Fall 1979; Ewan Clague and Leon Greenberg, "Technological Change and Employment," *MLR*, July 1962; Peter Drucker, *Technology, Management and Society; Essays* (New York: Harper & Row, 1970); Fe Josefina Dy, "Technology to Make Work More Human," *ILR*, Sept./Oct. 1978; Solomon Fabricant, *Measurement of Technological Change* (Washington: U.S. Dept. of Labor, Manpower Administration, Seminar on Manpower Policy and Program, 1965); Robert L. Heilbroner, *Automation in the Perspective of Long-Term Technological Change* (Washington: U.S. Dept. of Labor, Manpower Administration, Seminar on Manpower Policy and Program, 1966); Christopher T. Hill and James M. Utterback, "The Dynamics of Product and Process Innovation," *Management Review*, Jan. 1980; J. Herbert Hollomon, *Technical Change and American Enter-*

prise (Washington: NPA, Report no. 139, 1974); Louis B. Knecht, "The Worker in the Age of Communications, Part I: The Impact of Technology," *American Federationist*, July 1972; Dale D. McConkey, "The NLRB and Technological Change," *LLJ*, Jan. 1962; Markley Roberts, "Adjusting to Technological Change," *American Federationist*, Feb. 1973; ———, "Harnessing Technology: The Workers' Stake," *American Federationist*, April 1979; George P. Shultz and Arnold R. Weber, "Technological Change and Industrial Relations," *Employment Relations Research*, ed. by Herbert G. Heneman, Jr. et al. (New York: Harper, IRRA Pub. no. 23, 1960); Gerald G. Somers, Edward L. Cushman, and Nat Weinberg (ed.), *Adjusting to Technological Change* (New York: Harper, IRRA Pub. no. 29, 1963); George W. Taylor, "Collective Bargaining and Technological Change," *MLR*, Aug. 1962; U.S. Dept. of Labor, BLS, *Technology and Labor in Four Industries* (Washington: Bull. 2104, 1982); U.S. National Commission on Technology, Automation, and Economic Progress, *Technology and the American Economy, The Report of the Commission* (7 vol., Washington: 1966); Dale Yoder, *Labor Economics and Labor Problems* (2d ed., New York: McGraw-Hill, 1939).

technological unemployment Unemployment which results from changes in techniques of production that reduce the amount of labor required to produce an article.

The discussion centers around "automation," the term used to describe the trend away from hand to machine labor and new methods of developing labor-saving devices.

Source references: George B. Baldwin and George P. Shultz, "Automation—A New Dimension to Old Problems," *MLR*, Feb. 1955; George Bennett, "Unemployment, Automation and Labor-Management Relations," *Personnel Administration*, Sept./Oct. 1964; John I. Snyder, Jr., "Automation and Unemployment: Management's Quiet Crisis," *Management Review*, Nov. 1963; Richard C. Wilcock, "Fast Changing Technology—Its Impact on Labor Problems," *Pennsylvania Business Survey*, Dec. 1959.

See also AUTOMATION, CYCLICAL UNEMPLOYMENT, FRICTIONAL UNEMPLOYMENT, FULL EMPLOYMENT, MECHANIZATION, SEASONAL UNEMPLOYMENT, STRUCTURAL UNEMPLOYMENT, UNEMPLOYMENT.

Telecommunications International Union (Ind) Formerly known as the Alliance of Independent Telephone Unions (Ind). It issues the *TIU Health and Safety Hotline*, *TIU Legislative Report*, *TIU News*, and *TIU Newsletter*.

Address: 2341 Whitney Ave., Hamden, Conn. 06518. Tel. (203) 281–7945

Telegraphers' Union; The Commercial (AFL-CIO) Organized in Washington as the Commercial Telegraphers' Union of America in March 1903 as an amalgamation of two competing organizations, the International Union of Commercial Telegraphers and the Order of Commercial Telegraphers. The International Union of Commercial Telegraphers had organized in Chicago in June 1902 and the Order of Commercial Telegraphers was the outgrowth of the Brotherhood of Commercial Telegraphers which was sponsored by the Order of Railroad Telegraphers from 1897 to 1902. Since both organizations applied for a charter to the AFL in 1902, the AFL ordered a joint conference, which took place in March 1903 and resulted in amalgamation of the two unions.

The union changed its name to the Commercial Telegraphers' Union of North America in 1928, then to the Commercial Telegraphers' Union in the late 1940s, and then to The Commercial Telegraphers' Union (AFL-CIO) in the mid-1950s. Finally, in 1968 the union changed its name to the United Telegraph Workers (AFL-CIO).

See also TELEGRAPH WORKERS; UNITED (AFL-CIO).

Telegraph Workers; United (AFL-CIO) Formerly known as The Commercial Telegraphers' Union, the present name was adopted in 1968.

Its monthly publication is the *Telegraph Workers Journal*.

Address: 701 East Gude Dr., Rockville, Md. 20850. Tel. (301) 762–4444

Telephone Unions; Alliance of Independent (Ind) Founded in 1949, the name was changed to Telecommunications International Union.

See also TELECOMMUNICATIONS INTERNATIONAL UNION (IND).

Telephone Workers; National Federation of (Ind) *See* COMMUNICATIONS WORKERS OF AMERICA (AFL-CIO).

Television and Radio Artists; American Federation of A branch of the Associated Actors and Artistes of America (AFL-CIO). The union issues the quarterly *AFTRA Magazine*.

Address: 1350 Avenue of the Americas, New York, N.Y. 10019. Tel. (212) 265–7700

Teller Act *See* WELFARE AND PENSION PLANS DISCLOSURE ACT OF 1958 (TELLER ACT).

temporary arbitrator An individual who handles a single case for the parties in dispute. The assignment is completed upon presentation of the award. Sometimes referred to as an "ad hoc" arbitrator.

See also ARBITRATION, AD HOC; ARBITRATOR.

temporary disability An injury resulting in the temporary incapacity to perform work. Professor Reede divides temporary disabilities or losses into three broad categories in the following terms: "An injury of very short duration occasions a loss so slight that it can be borne by the worker. Injuries of medium duration (one week to a month) burden the worker unduly if he must shoulder them alone, but a substantial part of the loss can be borne by him. Injuries of long duration occasion losses so severe that few if any workers can bear them, and the larger proportion of the losses should be compensated."

Source references: Earl F. Cheit, *Medical Care Under Workmen's Compensation* (Washington: U.S. Dept. of Labor, Bureau of Labor Standards, Bull. no. 244, 1962); Arthur H. Reede, *Adequacy of Workmen's Compensation* (Cambridge: Harvard UP, 1947).

See also DISABILITY, PERMANENT DISABILITY.

temporary disability insurance An income maintenance program, usually providing for benefits measured by prior earnings payable in periods of sickness and injury incurred while engaged in non-work-connected activities. It is distinguished from health insurance which aims to minimize the cost of medical and hospital care and provides benefits measured primarily by the cost of the services needed. It is also distinct from disability benefits (cash payments for long-term cases) and workers compensation (both cash and service benefits for work-connected cases). Sometimes referred to as cash sickness benefits.

Under laws enacted by California, Hawaii, New Jersey, New York, Puerto Rico, and Rhode Island and by the federal government for railroad employees under the 1946 amendments to the Railroad Unemployment Insurance Act of 1938, benefits are provided over a limited period of time. New York, for example, provides benefits amounting to one-half the worker's average weekly wages, with a minimum of $20 and a maximum of $95 per week, for a maximum of 26 weeks; employees contribute one-half of one percent of the first $60 of weekly wages and the employer pays the balance of the cost. Other states permit private plans which may be financed by a commercial firm, a self-insured policy, or by a union or a union-management plan.

Source references: Robert J. Myers, *Social Insurance and Allied Government Programs* (Homewood: Irwin, 1965); PH, *Pension and Profit Sharing*, Vol. 1-A; Stefan A. Riesenfeld, *Temporary Disability Insurance* (Honolulu: Univ. of Hawaii, Legislative Reference Bureau, Report no. 1, 1969); Alfred M. Skolnik, "Income-Loss Protection Against Illness, 1948–66," *Social Security Bulletin*, Jan. 1968.

temporary employee A worker hired for a limited time only, frequently to meet a peak demand or special rush job. Such an employee is hired with the understanding that employment will end with completion of the particular task. A temporary employee does not accumulate seniority.

See also SEASONAL EMPLOYMENT, SENIORITY, WORK PERMITS.

temporary extended unemployment compensation Unemployment insurance provided by federal law to provide additional unemployment compensation to those who exhaust their rights under existing state law.

Under the Federal Supplemental Compensation (FSC) program authorized by the Tax

Equity and Fiscal Responsibility Act of 1982 (P.L. 97–248), effective September 12, 1982 to March 31, 1983, unemployment benefits were extended from 6 to 10 weeks. Benefit extensions differed among states and were determined by "high unemployment tests." Under the FSC program, benefits were extended to cover a maximum of 49 weeks—26 weeks of regular unemployment compensation, 13 weeks of extended benefits, and 10 weeks of FSC.

On March 29, 1983, President Reagan signed P.L. 98–13 to continue the FSC programs. The new law, which expired on September 30, 1983, extended the maximum duration of FSC to 14 weeks. The FSC program was extended to March 1985 by H.R. 3929.

Source references: Philip Booth, "Temporary Extended Unemployment Compensation Act of 1961—A Legislative History," *LLJ*, Oct. 1961; BNA, "Extra Jobless Aid to Go to 3 Million," *Employment and Training Reporter*, April 27, 1983; ———, "Extra 'UI' Payments for Jobless Begin," *Employment and Training Reporter*, Sept. 15, 1982.

See also UNEMPLOYMENT BENEFITS, UNEMPLOYMENT COMPENSATION.

temporary layoff A separation from employment at the instigation of the employer but without fault on the employee's part, usually of a short-term nature. It is assumed that the employee will be returned to the payroll when additional work becomes available.

See also DISCHARGE, DISCIPLINE, FURLOUGH, LAYOFF, SUSPENSION.

temporary restraining order *See* INJUNCTION.

Tennessee Valley Authority Established by the Tennessee Valley Authority Act of 1933, the first major program for a comprehensive river valley development in the United States. TVA first recognized and bargained with a group of unions in its early years, approximately a quarter century before the federal government set up collective bargaining procedures for other federal employees.

Source references: Roger L. Bowlby and William R. Schriver, "Bluffing and the 'Split-the-Difference' Theory of Wage Bargaining," *ILRR*, Jan. 1978; Michael L. Brookshire, "Bargaining Structure in the Public Sector: The TVA 'Model'," *Journal of Collective Negotiations in the Public Sector*, Vol. 5, no. 3, 1976; "TVA—The Controversial Success," *American Federationist*, April 1963; U.S. GAO, *Tennessee Valley Authority: Information on Certain Contracting and Personnel Management Activities* (Washington: 1976); Aubrey J. Wagner, "TVA Looks at Three Decades of Collective Bargaining," *ILRR*, Oct. 1968.

tenure An arrangement under which employment is continued until retirement, barring special circumstances such as dismissal for cause or financial exigency. Tenure is generally acquired through seniority and satisfactory job performance over a period of time.

In the public service, according to Stahl, security of tenure is required "to deal with the peculiar threats to security in governmental organizations—principally the danger of making employment contingent upon factors other than the performance of the worker. Meeting this danger was precisely the aim of the 'security of tenure' espoused by the early civil service reformers and implied in the tradition of 'merit system' laws."

Source reference: O. Glenn Stahl, *Public Personnel Administration* (4th ed., New York: Harper, 1956).

See also ACADEMIC TENURE, JOB TENURE.

terminal arbitration *See* ARBITRATION, TERMINAL.

terminal job *See* BLIND ALLEY JOBS, DEAD-END JOB.

termination The severing of an employee's relationship with an employer. It may be at the employee's initiative or that of the employer.

See also DISCHARGE, QUIT, RESIGNATION, RETIREMENT.

termination at will *See* EMPLOYMENT AT WILL.

termination clause *See* AGREEMENT DURATION.

termination interview *See* EXIT INTERVIEW.

termination pay *See* DISMISSAL COMPENSATION.

term of agreement *See* AGREEMENT DURATION.

test Any device or questionnaire, written or oral, for the purpose of measuring a person's abilities, interests, aptitudes, and other qualities for the purpose of hiring, placement, or for special training.

Source references: Betty R. Anderson and Martha P. Rogers (ed.), *Personnel Testing and Equal Employment Opportunity* (Washington: U.S. EEOC, 1971); Douglas D. Baker and David E. Terpstra, "Employee Selection: Must Every Job Be Validated?" *PJ*, Aug. 1982; W. Terence G. Bates, "A Systematic Approach to Personnel Selection," *ILR*, July/Aug. 1971; William C. Byham and Morton E. Spitzer, *The Law and Personnel Testing* (New York: AMA, 1971); W. Considine et al., "Developing a Physical Performance Test Battery for Screening Chicago Fire Fighter Applicants," *Public Personnel Management*, Jan./Feb. 1976; Zachary D. Fasman, "Public Employment Testing: Harmonizing the Discord Between Civil Service and Equal Employment," *Employee Relations LJ*, Spring 1976; Saul W. Gellerman, "Personnel Testing: What the Critics Overlook," *Personnel*, May/June 1963; Craig Haney, "Employment Tests and Employment Discrimination: A Dissenting Psychological Opinion," *Industrial Relations LJ*, Vol. 5, no. 1, 1982; Thelma Hunt and Clyde J. Lindley, "Documentation of Selection and Promotion Test Questions: Are Your Records Sagging?" *Public Personnel Management*, Nov./Dec. 1977; Peter Koenig, "Testing: The Industrial Psychologist's Headache," *Management Review*, Oct. 1974; Laurence Lipsett, "Guideposts for Personnel Testing," *PJ*, Nov. 1961; Maria Marcus, "The Myths Persist: The Relevancy of Testing; Lack of Sensitivity," *NYU 26th Annual Conference on Labor*, ed. by Emanuel Stein and S. Theodore Reiner (New York: Bender, 1974); James C. McBrearty, "Legality of Employment Tests: The Impact of *Duke Power Co.*," *LLJ*, July 1971; William R. Nelson, "Employment Testing and the Demise of the PACE Examination," *LLJ*, Nov. 1982; Robert W. Pranis, *Interpreting Test Results* (Chicago: Univ. of Chicago, IRC, Occasional Papers, no. 21, 1961); Harold H. Punke, "The Relevance and Broadening Use of Personnel Testing," *LLJ*, March 1974; David E. Robertson, "Employment Testing and Discrimination," *PJ*, Jan. 1975; Laura Rosenberg, "A Successful Experiment in Cooperative Testing, Research and Validation," *PJ*, Jan. 1975; Bonnie Sandman and Faith Urban, "Employment Testing and the Law," *LLJ*, Jan. 1976; James C. Sharf, "Do's and Don'ts in the Employment Process: The Current Status of Testing," *Employee Relations LJ*, Spring 1976; Jerome Siegel, *Personnel Testing Under EEO*, An AMA Research Study (New York: AMA, 1980); Andrew H. Souerwine, "More Value From Personnel Testing," *Harvard BR*, March/April 1961; Ray F. Travaglio, "Response Differences Among Employment Applicants," *PJ*, July 1970; U.S. GAO, *Federal Employment Examinations: Do They Achieve Equal Opportunity and Merit Principle Goals?* (Washington: 1979); William H. Warren, "*Albemarle v. Moody*: Where it All Began," *LLJ*, Oct. 1976; James Weitzul, "Employment Tests: Fair or Unfair Discrimination?" *Management Review*, Aug. 1980.

See also ABILITY TESTS, ACHIEVEMENT TEST, ALBEMARLE PAPER CO. V. MOODY, APTITUDE TESTS, BATTERY TESTS, GRIGGS V. DUKE POWER CO., INTELLIGENCE TESTS, KUDER PREFERENCE RECORD AND INTEREST SURVEYS, MANUAL AND MOTOR SKILL TESTS, MECHANICAL APTITUDE TESTS, PERFORMANCE TESTS, PERSONALITY INVENTORY, PSYCHOLOGICAL TESTING, TAILOR-MADE TEST, UNIFORM GUIDELINES ON EMPLOYEE SELECTION PROCEDURES.

test hands Employees used in motion study in order to determine the proper sequence of job operations to eliminate waste effort. They may be selected for time and motion studies in establishment of piece rates and job standards. A garment industry contract in New York provided for the use of test hands in the following clause:

> Should the employers and the price committee fail to agree on the price, the garment in dispute shall be submitted to a test: the "test hand" shall be chosen by agreement between the employer and price committee. The price of the garment to be determined by such "test hand" shall be equal to the established hourly

rate of the "test hand" multiplied by the number of hours it takes such "test hand" to make a garment. The price to be in no event less than such as would yield to the minimum operator $1.10 per hour for a continuous hour of work.

Texas and New Orleans Railway v. Brotherhood of Railway and Steamship Clerks A case which resulted from an action by the Railway Clerks in 1927 under Section 2 of the Railway Labor Act seeking an injunction against the Texas and New Orleans Railway Company. The union charged the company with having violated the Railway Labor Act by seeking to replace it with a company union for collective bargaining purposes. An injunction was granted, with which the company refused to comply. After contempt proceedings, the trial court issued a mandatory order for disestablishment of the company union as the collective bargaining agent. The case was carried up to the Supreme Court, which in 1930 ordered the company to bargain with the Railway Clerks rather than with the company union.

Source reference: Texas and NORR v. Brotherhood, 281 US 548 (1930).

Textile Processors, Service Trades, Health Care, Professional and Technical Employees International Union The union, known as the Laundry Workers' International Union, began as a directly affiliated AFL local in 1898 and was composed of shirt and collar workers in factories in Troy, New York. It expanded in 1900 into the Shirt, Waist and Laundry Workers' International Union. Up until 1909 it maintained jurisdiction over the making and laundering of shirts and collars. In 1909, jurisdiction of shirt manufacturing was taken over by the United Garment Workers of America and the original charter was surrendered and a new one granted which gave it jurisdiction over laundries only. The name of the union was changed to the Laundry Workers' International Union (AFL).

In May 1956, the International Association of Cleaning and Dye House Workers merged with the Laundry Workers, the combined union later changing its name to the Laundry, Cleaning and Dye House Workers International Union (AFL-CIO). The union was expelled from the AFL-CIO in December 1957. The name of the union was later changed to the Laundry, Dry Cleaning and Dye House Workers International Union (Ind) and in March 1962, it affiliated with the International Brotherhood of Teamsters. The present name was adopted in 1983.

Address: 360 North Michigan Ave., Chicago, Ill. 60601. Tel. (312) 726–9416

See also TEAMSTERS, CHAUFFEURS, WAREHOUSEMEN AND HELPERS OF AMERICA; INTERNATIONAL BROTHERHOOD OF (IND).

Textile Workers of America; United (AFL-CIO) Organized in Washington, D.C., in November 1901. The first national organization in the textile industry was the National Union of Textile Workers, formed in June 1896 from a group of directly affiliated AFL locals. This group did not stay in existence very long. Another organization was established at about the same time known as the American Federation of Textile Operatives and that union combined with AFL locals to form the United Textile Workers of America.

Its official publication is the *Textile Challenger*, issued semiannually.

Address: 420 Common St., Lawrence, Mass. 01840. Tel. (617) 686–2901

Textile Workers Union of America (AFL-CIO) A union which developed out of the activities in the late 1930s of the Textile Workers Organizing Committee, one of the numerous organizing committees established by the CIO after breaking from the AFL. Its nucleus was derived from dissident or former members of the United Textile Workers of America. The feud between these two unions is one of the classics of trade unionism in the United States. Both were AFL-CIO affiliates.

The American Federation of Hosiery Workers (AFL-CIO) merged with the union in April 1965. On June 3, 1976, the union merged with the Amalgamated Clothing Workers Union (AFL-CIO) to form the Amalgamated Clothing and Textile Workers Union (AFL-CIO).

Source references: John R. Commons Labor Reference Center, *The Textile Workers Union of America Papers: A Descriptive Guide* (Madison: State Historical Society of Wisconsin and Univ. of Wisconsin, Library Bull. No. 1, 1966); Richard Kelley, *Nine Lives for Labor* (New York: Praeger, 1956); George S. Paul, *American Velvet Company and Tex-*

tile Workers Union of America (New York: NPA, Causes of Industrial Peace Study No. 11, 1953); Textile Workers Union of America, *"Almost Unbelievable" . . . The Story of an Industry, a Union and a Law* (New York: 1961); ________, *The TWUA Story: They Said It Couldn't Be Done* (New York: 1964).

See also CLOTHING AND TEXTILE WORKERS UNION; AMALGAMATED (AFL-CIO).

T-group The T-Group (training group) is the core of many laboratory training programs. The T-Group is that portion of the program in which participants become involved in the dynamics of a small group with a minimum amount of structure and attempt to learn directly from the group experience.

Sensitivity training is that part of T-Group training which concentrates on the participants' becoming more aware of themselves and of the way they relate to others through the occasionally intense interaction with members of the training group.

Source references: Chris Argyris, "T-Groups for Organizational Effectiveness," *Harvard BR*, March/April 1964; L. P. Bradford, Jack R. Gibb, and Kenneth D. Benne (ed.), *T-Group Theory and Laboratory Method* (New York: Wiley, 1964); William F. Glueck, "Reflections on a T-Group Experience," *PJ*, July 1968; Stanley M. Herman, "What is This Thing Called Organization Development?" *PJ*, Aug. 1971; Spencer Klaw, "Two Weeks in a T Group," *Fortune*, Aug. 1961; Kenneth W. Thomas, *A Satire: The Phenomenology of the Confirmed Thinker, or "Catch-22 in a T-Group"* (Los Angeles: UC, Institute of IR, Reprint 264, 1977); K. G. Van Auken, Jr., "A Further View on Laboratory Education," *MLR*, March 1971.

See also LABORATORY TRAINING, SENSITIVITY TRAINING.

Theatrical Stage Employees and Moving Picture Machine Operators of the United States and Canada; International Alliance of (AFL-CIO) Eleven stage-hand locals organized the National Alliance of Theatrical Stage Employes in New York City in 1893. With the granting of a charter to a local in Canada, the Alliance in 1898 became the International Alliance of Theatrical Stage Employes.

When motion picture machine operators were organized, the International Brotherhood of Electrical Workers and the Stage Hands both claimed jurisdiction and after much difficulty, the American Federation of Labor at its 1914 convention granted jurisdiction over motion picture operators to the Stage Employes. The union then changed its title to the International Alliance of Theatrical Stage Employees and Moving Picture Machine Operators of the United States and Canada.

Its quarterly publication is the *Official Bulletin*.

Address: 1515 Broadway, Suite 601, New York, N.Y. 10036. Tel. (212) 730–1770

Source references: Robert O. Baker, "The International Alliance of Theatrical Stage Employes and Moving Picture Machine Operators of the United States and Canada" (Unpublished Ph.D. thesis, Univ. of Kansas, 1933); The International Alliance of Theatrical Stage Employes of the U.S., *50th Anniversary, 1893–1943* (New York: 1943).

Theory X and Theory Y Two sets of assumptions about human nature and human behavior developed by Douglas McGregor. According to McGregor, these assumptions influence the way management treats its employees and how effectively organizational objectives are achieved.

Under Theory X, the average person is assumed to dislike work, and because of this dislike, must be coerced, controlled, and directed to achieve the employer's objectives. The average person "prefers to be directed, wishes to avoid responsibility, has relatively little ambition, wants security above all." Management principles based on these assumptions focus on direction and control of employees through the exercise of authority. According to McGregor, management's reliance on authority can lead to resistance, restriction of output, and an indifference to organizational objectives on the part of employees.

Under Theory Y, work is assumed to be as natural as play or rest, and it is assumed that the average person will exercise creativity, self-direction, and responsibility in the service of objectives to which he or she is committed. Based on these assumptions, an effective manager tries to meet the needs of the organization by realizing the employee's human potential; management tries to create conditions increasing the personal commitment of employees to the success of the enterprise.

Source reference: Douglas McGregor, *The Human Side of Enterprise* (New York: McGraw-Hill, 1960).

Theory Z Title of book by William Ouchi in which he describes management that utilizes a consensual, participative decision-making process. According to Ouchi, the Theory Z approach to management "suggests that involved workers are the key to increased productivity."

Source references: Richard Tanner Johnson and William G. Ouchi, "Made in America (Under Japanese Management)," *Harvard BR*, Sept./Oct. 1974; Charles W. Joiner, Jr., "The Manager's Story of How He Made the Z Concept Work," *Management Review*, May 1983; William G. Ouchi, *Theory Z: How American Business Can Meet the Japanese Challenge* (Reading, Mass.: Addison-Wesley, 1981).

therblig An element of motion first classified by Frank G. Gilbreth. He classified the 17 basic types by setting out a symbol for each movement. He thought that these would be found in all kinds of work. A therblig is merely Gilbreth spelled backwards. The 17 elements of movements were: search, find, select, grasp, position, transport loaded, disassemble—take apart, use, assemble, inspect, preposition—prepare for next operation, release load, transport empty, wait—unavoidable delay, wait—avoidable delay, rest for overcoming fatigue, plan.

Third International A labor and socialist organization consisting of radical labor groups and leaders convened by Nicolai Lenin in Moscow in 1919. The Third International was oriented toward the world revolution which was expected by the Bolsheviks. It urged the establishment of communist parties in all countries and the infiltration of communists into trade unions in order to convert them to the cause. The Third International is sometimes known as the Communist International or the Comintern.

See also COMINTERN.

third round increases General demands for wage adjustments following the end of World War II. The third round of adjustments were those demanded by the unions in the major industries in 1948. (The "first round" was in 1946, the second, 1947).

See also FIRST ROUND INCREASES, FOURTH ROUND INCREASE.

thirty-hour week A move in the early 1930s to reduce the daily hours of work to six in order to stimulate recovery from economic depression. The bill introduced by Senator Hugo Black for the thirty-hour week passed the Senate in April 1933, but did not receive House support. The National Industrial Recovery Act sought to incorporate many of the proposals pending in Congress to stimulate the economy, including the sharing of work through reduction in hours.

Source references: William Green, *The Thirty Hour Week* (Washington: AFL, 1935); Labor Research Association, *The Case for the 30-Hour Week—With No Cut in Take-Home Pay* (New York: International Pub., 1960); Harold G. Moulton and Maurice Leven, *The Thirty Hour Week* (Washington: Brookings Institution, 1935).

See also SHORTER WORKWEEK.

thousand-hour clause *See* ONE-THOUSAND-HOUR CLAUSE.

threats and coercion *See* COERCION.

three position plan A procedure combining both training and promotion. It provides that every individual in the plant shall have three functions or three positions within the overall group. An individual belongs to the group next higher up as a learner, and spends part of the time in training for promotion to that job. The individual also belongs to the group below as a teacher, and part of that time is devoted to instructing others in that group who will move up to take that individual's place. Third, the individual works at the presently held position. The time in any one position depends upon the speed with which training takes place and the ability of the person to move ahead to the higher position.

three-shift system *See* SHIFT.

thrift plans Programs promoted or sponsored by employers to educate employees in financial matters and to promote saving.

See also SAVINGS PLAN.

tie up *See* SHUTDOWN, STRIKE.

Tile, Marble, Terrazzo Finishers and Shopworkers and Granite Cutters International Union (AFL-CIO) Formerly known as the International Association of Marble, Slate and Stone Polishers, Rubbers and Sawyers, Tile and Marble Setters' Helpers and Marble Mosaic and Terrazzo Workers' Helpers (AFL-CIO).

On January 7, 1980, The Granite Cutters International Association of America (AFL-CIO) merged with the union. Its bimonthly publication is the *Finishers' News*.

Address: 801 North Pitt St., Suite 116, Alexandria, Va. 22314. Tel. (703) 549–3050

time and a half pay Overtime or premium compensation of one and one-half times the regular rate for time worked as overtime under the Fair Labor Standards Act.

Source reference: U.S. Dept. of Labor, BLS, *Collective Bargaining Provisions: Hours of Work, Overtime Pay, Shift Operations* (Washington: Bull. no. 980–18, 1950).

See also FAIR LABOR STANDARDS ACT OF 1938, OVERTIME PAY.

time and motion study The analysis of motions and measurement of time required to perform a specific job with specified materials and equipment. The motions are watched and the time recorded to indicate the length of time required to perform the particular job or part of a job. Motion study is concerned primarily with an attempt to economize motions and thereby save time and increase output. Time study is concerned primarily with the measurement of the time required to perform specific operations.

Professor Barnes summarizes motion and time study primarily as "the analysis of the methods, of the materials, and of the tools and equipment used, or to be used, in the performance of a piece of work—an analysis carried on with the purpose of (1) finding the most economical way of doing this work; (2)standardizing the methods, materials, tools, and equipment; (3) accurately determining the time required by a qualified person working at a normal pace to do the task; and (4) assisting in training the worker in the new method."

Source references: Ralph M. Barnes, *Motion and Time Study* (6th ed., New York: Wiley, 1968); George W. Chane, *Motion and Time Study* (New York: Harper, 1942); Frank B. and Lillian M. Gilbreth, *Applied Time and Motion Study* (New York: Sturgis, Walton, 1917); Walter G. Holmes, *Applied Time and Motion Study* (New York: Ronald Press, 1938); U.S. Dept. of Labor, BLS, *Major Collective Bargaining Agreements: Wage-Incentive, Production-Standard, and Time-Study Provisions* (Washington: Bull. 1425–18, 1979); Kjell B. Zandin, "Better Work Management with MOST," *Management Review*, July 1975.

See also LEVELING, METHODS STUDY, MICROMOTION STUDY, MOTION ECONOMY, MOTION STUDY, STOPWATCH METHOD, TEST HANDS, TIME STUDY.

time basis Applies to wages received by employees on an hourly, weekly, or other time basis.

time clock An established work schedule which usually means a 5-day, 40-hour week, and 8-hour day. Compliance with the work schedule is monitored by a time clock that records the arrival and departure times of each employee. Beginning in the 1970s, employers started to experiment with or adopt new types of work schedules.

Source references: Jerome Rosow and Robert Zager, "Punch Out the Time Clocks," *Harvard BR*, March/April 1983; Gloria Stevenson, "Who's Changing the Face on the Timeclock?" *Occupational Outlook Quarterly*, Spring 1974.

See also FLEXTIME/FLEXITIME.

time limits May apply to many areas of collective bargaining but most frequently to the time limits set forth in the grievance procedure. Individuals or unions are required to submit grievances in successive steps within certain specified periods of time for grievances to be considered timely by the company or the arbitrator.

time lost on grievances Provisions in many contracts require pay to shop stewards or grievance committee members for the time necessarily spent in handling grievances during working hours. Limitations may be placed on the number of hours for which a company will compensate for time lost in handling grievances.

See also GRIEVANCE, OFFICIAL TIME, PAY FOR GRIEVANCE TIME, PAY FOR SHOP STEWARDS, RELEASED TIME.

time-off plan A plan or system for paying a fixed or constant wage to workers who work fluctuating workweeks by giving them time off to offset the overtime work. The phrase may also apply to time away from the job, by leave of absence, with permission of the company and without loss of seniority.

See also COMPENSATORY TIME OFF, LEAVE OF ABSENCE.

time standard *See* STANDARD TIME.

time study The attempt to make an accurate stop-watch study of each individual job to determine the best way of performing it. Time study procedure has been described in the following passage by Professor Reynolds:

> The first step is to standardize conditions on the job and to determine the best way of doing it through a methods analysis, including, but not limited to a study of workers' motions on the job. Operators on the job are then trained to use the proper methods until they do so naturally and automatically. This first step is essential to accurate time study, and can often by itself yield large increases in productivity. The next step is to select an operator who appears to be of average speed and ability, and to time his production over a long enough period so that variations in his speed of work can be averaged out. The worker will hardly ever take exactly the same time for two successive units of output. The only way to eliminate these irregular fluctuations in work speed is to time a considerable number of units and take an average. The actual work of timing jobs is a good deal more complex than this brief statement suggests. The timer does not simply measure the time required for the whole process of turning out a unit of output. He breaks the production process down into each separate movement of the worker's hands and body. The time required for each of these movements is recorded separately. This enables the observer to determine whether the worker is using the proper methods, whether he is using them consistently, whether certain motions are taking more time than they should normally take, and even whether the worker is deliberately "holding back" during the time study.

Source references: United Electrical, Radio and Machine Workers of America, *U.E. Guide to Wage Payment Plans, Time Study, and Job Evaluation* (New York: 1943); William Gomberg, *A Trade Union Analysis of Time Study* (Chicago: Science Research Associates, 1948); Bertram Gottlieb, *The Art of Time Study: An Exercise of Personal Judgment* (Iowa City: Univ. of Iowa, Center for Labor and Management, Monograph no. 2, 1966); Marvin E. Mundel, *Motion and Time Study: Principles and Practice* (New York: PH, 1950); James A. Parton, *Motion and Time Study Manual* (New York: Conover-Mast, 1952); Lloyd G. Reynolds, *Labor Economics and Labor Relations* (8th ed., Englewood Cliffs: PH, 1982).

See also JOINT TIME STUDY, MOTION STUDY.

time study analyst An individual who makes a detailed analysis of the time required for an average operator to perform a particular job with certain equipment and materials. The analyst may determine how many units of product each worker on a job should turn out during a specified period of time.

time study engineer A person who specializes and has been trained in motion and time study and has a proper background in engineering.

time wages A fixed wage based on an hour, day, week, or month paid for a specific job or occupation.

See also WAGE PAYMENT PLANS.

time-work contracts Agreements whereby payment is made by the hour without regard to amount of production.

tip A gratuity given to an employee by a customer in recognition of the satisfactory performance of personal service. It can also be given for the behavior customarily expected of a person in a particular situation. For example, a guest in a hotel, restaurant, or steamship may give a tip because it is expected and not necessarily because of the character of the service received from the employee.

tipple The place where loaded cars from the coal pits are tipped or dumped.

Title VII, Civil Rights Act of 1964 *See* CIVIL RIGHTS ACT OF 1964.

Title VII, Civil Service Reform Act of 1978 One of nine titles of the Civil Service Reform Act, Title VII represents the first legislated labor relations program for nonpostal federal employees. Title VII protects the right of federal employees to organize, bargain collectively, and participate in decision making. It also establishes the Federal Labor Relations Authority, expands the scope of negotiated grievance procedures, provides for union representation at certain investigatory interviews, and increases official time for employees representing unions in negotiations. Labor unions have the right to negotiate over personnel policies, practices, and conditions of employment. Subjects excluded from bargaining are governmentwide regulations and matters limited by law, or agency regulations for which a compelling need exists. Management, however, must negotiate the procedures that are to be followed in the exercise of its rights and the appropriate arrangements for employees adversely affected by management decisions.

Source references: Civil Service Reform Act of 1978, 5 U.S.C. 7101 et seq. (1982); Arthur L. Burnett, James A. Brodsky, and Brian Boru McGovern (ed.), *Labor-Management Relations, Civil Service Reforms, and EEO in the Federal Sector* (Washington: Federal Bar Assn., Committee on Public Sector Labor Relations, 1980); Charles J. Coleman, "The Civil Service Reform Act of 1978: Its Meaning and Its Roots," *LLJ*, April 1980; Henry B. Frazier III, "Labor-Management Relations in the Federal Government," *LLJ*, March 1979; Anthony F. Ingrassia, "Reflections on the New Labor Law," *LLJ*, Sept. 1979; Douglas M. McCabe, "Labor Relations, Collective Bargaining, and Performance Appraisal in the Federal Government Under the Civil Service Reform Act of 1978," *Public Personnel Management*, Summer 1984; U.S. Congress, House, Committee on Post Office and Civil Service, *Legislative History of the Federal Service Labor-Management Relations Statute, Title VII of the Civil Service Reform Act of 1978* (Washington: 1979).

See also CIVIL SERVICE REFORM ACT OF 1978, COMPELLING NEED, FEDERAL LABOR RELATIONS AUTHORITY (FLRA), MERIT SYSTEMS PROTECTION BOARD (MSPB), OFFICE OF PERSONNEL MANAGEMENT (OPM), OFFICIAL TIME, REORGANIZATION PLAN NO. 1 OF 1978, REORGANIZATION PLAN NO. 2 OF 1978.

Title IX of the Education Amendments of 1972 Prohibits discrimination on the basis of sex in any education program or activity that receives federal financial assistance. Educational institutions covered by the Act include "any public or private preschool, elementary, or secondary school, or any institution of vocational, professional, or higher education. . . ." Exceptions to Title IX coverage include religious and military schools, social fraternities or sororities, voluntary youth service organizations, father-son or mother-daughter activities.

In 1984, the Supreme Court ruled in *Grove City College v. Bell,* that federal tuition grants to college students did not trigger institution-wide coverage of programs under Title IX. Thus, only the financial aid office of the school was subject to Title IX compliance. This narrow interpretation limited the enforcement of Title IX only to those educational programs and activities directly receiving federal funds.

Source references: Education Amendments of 1972, as amended, 20 U.S.C. 1681–1686 (1982); *Grove City College v. Bell,* U.S. Sup.Ct. No. 92–792 (1984); *North Haven Board of Education v. Bell,* 456 US 512, 28 FEP Cases 1393 (1982); U.S. Dept. of Education, "Nondiscrimination on the Basis of Sex in Education Programs and Activities Receiving or Benefiting from Federal Financial Assistance," 34 C.F.R. 106; Martha Matthews and Shirley McCune, *Complying With Title IX: Implementing Institutional Self-Evaluation* (Washington: U.S. Dept. of HEW, Office of Education, 1977).

Tobacco Inspectors Mutual Association; Federal (Ind) The union merged with the National Federation of Federal Employees (Ind) on March 18, 1968.

See also FEDERAL EMPLOYEES; NATIONAL FEDERATION OF (IND).

Tobacco Workers International Union (AFL-CIO) Organized in Missouri in 1895 and affiliated with the AFL. On August 16, 1978, the union merged with the Bakery and Confectionery Workers' International Union of America (AFL-CIO) to form the Bakery, Confectionery and Tobacco Workers International Union (AFL-CIO).

See also BAKERY, CONFECTIONERY AND TOBACCO WORKERS INTERNATIONAL UNION (AFL-CIO).

Toledo Industrial Peace Board (Toledo Plan) Best known of the municipal conciliation plans, the Toledo Plan was established in April 1936 when the city of Toledo took over the Toledo Industrial Peace Board, an organization which had been active since July 1935. The board consisted of five employees, five employers, and eight members representing the public, all under a full-time director. Public members were appointed by the mayor on recommendations of the board. The prime objective was to promote industrial harmony and to act in an advisory capacity to the city on industrial relations matters. The board acted largely in a mediatory capacity, and meetings were not open to the public. The Toledo Plan was abandoned in 1943 following the advent of the National War Labor Board, the U.S. Conciliation Service, and the NLRB.

Source references: Ordinance No. 76–36, March 30, 1936 of Toledo, Ohio; Ed J. Bodette, "The Toledo Plan," *Employment Security Review*, Sept. 1940; Kurt Braun, *Labor Disputes and Their Settlement* (Baltimore: Johns Hopkins Press, 1955); Morton Goldberg, "The Preservation of Public Interest in Labor-Management Disputes," *Proceedings of the Annual Ohio Personnel Institute* (Columbus: Ohio State Univ., Bureau of Business Research, 1957); Edward McGrady, "How Peace Came to Toledo," *Atlantic*, July 1938; William L. Nunn, *Local Progress and Labor Peace* (New York: National Municipal League, 1941); ———, "Municipal Labor Boards of Toledo and Newark," *MLR*, Nov. 1939; Victor H. Rosenbloom, "How Cities Keep Industrial Peace," *LLJ*, Oct. 1952; Edmund Ruffin, "Toledo Industrial Peace Board," *Toledo City Journal*, Jan. 22, 1938.

Toledo Labor-Management-Citizens Committee This group was a resurrection of the old Toledo Industrial Peace Board established in response to the desire to prevent economic losses following the postwar strikes. A tripartite group of 18 representatives—six each from labor, management, and the public—was appointed in June 1945 to study community labor-management relations, and in February 1946 the group submitted a report which included a charter, a code of conduct for labor and management, and the suggestion that an ordinance be enacted which would recognize the proposed charter as the overall guide to industrial relations in the community. Under the procedures, union and management groups which endorsed the principles of the charter applied for a certificate and remained parties as long as they adhered to the provisions of the charter. The study committee became the permanent committee, but by 1954 following a major reorganization the Committee had expanded to 30 full members and 18 associate members. In addition to its mediation function, the Committee conducted representation elections and card checks and sponsored and conducted educational programs in industrial relations. Formal meetings of the Committee ended in October 1965, following which the Committee underwent reorganization.

Source references: Kurt Braun, *Labor Disputes and Their Settlement* (Baltimore: Johns Hopkins Press, 1955); Jerome Gross, "Charter of the Toledo Labor-Management-Citizens Committee," *ILRR*, April 1948; John F. Mead and Joseph Krislov, "The Toledo Labor Management Citizens Committee," *LLJ*, Nov. 1969; Victor H. Rosenbloom, "How Cities Keep Industrial Peace," *LLJ*, Oct. 1952; Toledo Labor-Management-Citizens Committee, *Annual Reports* (Toledo: 1946+); ———, *The Toledo Plan for Industrial Harmony* (Toledo: n.d.); Univ. of Toledo and Toledo Labor-Management-Citizens Committee, *Labor-Management Institutes*; an exposition of grievance procedure, mediation and arbitration, labor law (Toledo: 1955).

See also JAMESTOWN AREA LABOR-MANAGEMENT COMMITTEE.

tolling A form of job selling or kickback (somewhat similar to fee-splitting) engaged in by supervisors and superintendents in days past. Anti-kickback legislation has outlawed the practice.

See also ANTI-KICKBACK LAW (COPELAND ACT), KICKBACK.

Tool Craftsmen; International Association of (Ind) Founded in 1953, the union is affiliated with the National Federation of Independent Unions. Its quarterly publication is *The Tool and Die Journal.*

Address: 1915 Arrowline Ct., Bettendorf, Iowa 52722. Tel. (319) 332–6147.

Tool, Die and Mold Makers; International Union of (Ind) Founded in 1972, it publishes *The Indicator* monthly.

Address: 71 East Cherry St., Rahway, N.J. 07065. Tel. (201) 388–3323

tooling-up period Procedures in highly mechanized mass production such as automobile production in which the equipment and production machinery are tooled for the production of a new model.

tool maintenance time A time allowance permitted individual workers for the repair, overhauling, and maintenance of their tools.

top-down contract An agreement between an employer or employer group with the officer or head of the union without the participation of the rank and file.

See also AGREEMENT, SWEETHEART.

top seniority A form of preferential or superseniority extended to union officials by contract.

Such a clause might read thus:

> The union executive officers, chief shop stewards, grievance committee chairman, and bargaining committee members, the total of whom is not to exceed 30 in number, shall be given preferential seniority as follows:
>
> The above designated union officials shall be moved upon their respective seniority lists to the point equivalent to ten additional years of service. Since preferential seniority for such officials is granted in order to secure adequate union representation, such preferential seniority status shall operate only at the time of layoff, and for all other purposes of seniority consideration their regular seniority position shall be applied.

Source reference: Max S. Wortman, "Super Seniority—Myth or Reality?" *LLJ*, April 1967.

See also SUPERSENIORITY.

totality of conduct A policy or doctrine determined by the NLRB prior to the Taft-Hartley amendments that statements which may be noncoercive when standing alone may be found coercive when considered along with an employer's background of anti-union history. The Board attempts to consider the total record of action rather than the particular isolated statements made by an employer.

total man hours The cumulative or aggregate number of hours worked by a group of employees in a particular period.

See also MAN-HOUR.

tour A term not frequently used although "tour of duty" is familiar. The term "shift" is used as its equivalent. It is the work period of schedule of working hours for a particular employee or group of employees.

See also TRICK.

Toys, Playthings, Novelties and Allied Products of the United States and Canada; International Union of Dolls, (AFL-CIO) Formerly known as the International Union of Doll and Toy Workers of the United States and Canada (AFL-CIO). It changed its name to the International Union of Allied Novelty and Production Workers (AFL-CIO) in the 1970s.

See also NOVELTY AND PRODUCTION WORKERS; INTERNATIONAL UNION OF ALLIED (AFL-CIO).

trade *See* CRAFT, OCCUPATION.

Trade Act of 1974 The legislation replacing the Trade Expansion Act of 1962. According to Mitchell, the Act was enacted to counter the lowering of U.S. tariff rates which "left exposed a layer of nontariff barriers, such as quotas and similar government policies. . . . In addition, the entry of Britain and two other countries into the EEC [European Economic Community] . . . raised the potential for trade diversion and separate world trading blocs." Nontariff barriers had not been "explicitly considered" in previous trade legislation. The 1974 Act "provided new negotiating authority for the president, both on tariff and nontariff barriers. It provided for generalized tariff preferences, such as duty-free treatment of the products of less-developed countries over a ten-year period and most-favored nation treatment for imports from those communist countries not currently enjoying that status."

The Trade Act liberalized the administrative procedures and eligibility requirements for trade adjustment assistance and extended coverage of the program to communities. The administration of the Act is placed under the Department of Labor (for workers) and under the Department of Commerce (for trade-impacted communities).

Source references: Larry T. Adams, "Auto Workers Seek Government Aid for Laid-Off Workers, Ailing Industry," *MLR*, Sept. 1980; Marvin M. Fooks, "Trade Adjustment Assistance," *Proceedings of the 28th A/M, IRRA*, ed. by James Stern and Barbara Dennis (Madison: 1976); Peter Henle, "Trade Adjustment Assistance: Should It Be Modified?" *MLR*, March 1977; Elizabeth R. Jager, "Adjustment Assistance for Import-Impacted Workers," *Proceedings of the 28th A/M, IRRA*, ed. by James Stern and Barbara Dennis (Madison: 1976); Daniel J. B. Mitchell,' *Labor Issues of American International Trade and Investment* (Baltimore: Johns Hopkins UP, 1976); U.S. GAO, *Adjustment Assistance to Firms Under the Trade Act of 1974—Income Maintenance or Successful Adjustment?* (Washington: 1978); ———, *Restricting Trade Act Benefits to Import-Affected Workers Who Cannot Find a Job Can Save Millions* (Washington: 1980); ———, *Worker Adjustment Assistance Under the Trade Act of 1974—Problems in Assisting Auto Workers, Department of Labor* (Washington: 1978); ———, *Worker Adjustment Assistance Under the Trade Act of 1974 to New England Workers Has Been Primarily Income Maintenance* (Washington: 1978); U.S. National Commission for Manpower Policy, *Trade and Employment, A Conference Report* (Washington: Special Report no. 30, 1978).

See also TRADE EXPANSION ACT OF 1962.

trade adjustment assistance *See* TRADE EXPANSION ACT OF 1962.

trade agreement *See* AGREEMENT, COLLECTIVE.

Trade Expansion Act of 1962 In January 1962, President Kennedy sent a message to Congress recommending a revision of U.S. trade agreement legislation in light of new developments taking place since the reciprocal trade agreements program was initiated in 1934.

Among other provisions, the resulting legislation, enacted October 11, 1962, provided for an adjustment assistance program to help those firms and workers adversely affected by imports. The import-injured firms were offered technical and financial assistance, including direct loans and tax relief through the carryback of operating losses. In the case of workers, the Act provided compensation for partial or complete loss of employment, retraining to qualify the worker for other types of employment, and relocation allowances to aid a worker seeking employment in an area where the worker's skill may be in demand. The law was replaced by the Trade Act of 1974.

Source references: Christian A. Herter, "Kennedy Round: A Progress Report; Address, May 20, 1965," *U.S. Department of State Bulletin*, July 5, 1965; Kenneth C. Mackenzie, *Tariff-Making and Trade Policy in the United States and Canada: A Comparative Study* (New York: Praeger, 1968); Stanley D. Metzger, *Trade Agreements and the Kennedy Round* (Fairfax, Va.: Coiner Publications, 1964); "The New Trade Act: Tool to Expand Markets," *American Federationist*, Jan. 1963; William M. Roth, "Completing the Work of the Kennedy Round; Address, October 5, 1967," *U.S. Department of State Bulletin*, Oct. 30, 1967; Leonard Weiss, "Trade Expansion Act of 1962," *U.S. Department of State Bulletin*, Dec. 3, 1962.

See also TRADE ACT OF 1974.

Trademark Society, Inc. (Ind) P.O. Box 2631, EADS Station, Arlington, Va. 22202. Tel. (703) 557–9560

trades council A group of trade unions in a locality or geographic region which organizes usually for the purpose of dealing with an employers' association and to promote activities of mutual benefit to the members.

trade union An association of workers in a particular trade or craft organized to promote a common interest and to further that interest through negotiation of wages, hours, and other conditions of employment.

Source references: Irving Bernstein, "Trade Union Characteristics, Membership, and Influence," *MLR*, May 1959; Walter Galenson and Seymour Martin Lipset (ed.), *Labor and Trade Unionism: An Interdisciplinary Reader* (New York: Wiley, 1960); Robert F. Hoxie, *Trade Unionism in the United States* (2d ed., New York: Appleton, 1923); William H. Miernyk, *Trade Unions in the Age of Affluence* (New York: Random House, 1962); Selig Perlman, *History of Trade Unionism in the United States* (New York: Macmillan, 1922); Albert Rees, *The Economics of Trade Unions* (2d ed., Chicago: Univ. of Chicago Press, 1977); B. J. Widick, *Labor Today: The Triumphs and Failures of Unionism in the United States* (Boston: Houghton Mifflin, 1964); Leo Wolman, *Ebb and Flow in Trade Unionism* (New York: NBER, 1936).

See also INDUSTRIAL UNION, LABOR UNION.

Trade Union Educational League With the demise of the IWW at the end of World War I, there remained no union with a revolutionary philosophy in the country. In 1920 William Z. Foster, a communist leader, established an organization, the Trade Union Educational League, for the purpose of training leaders and propagandizing for the promotion of revolutionary unionism in the United States. The organization remained in operation until it modified its general policy in 1929 (on instructions presumably from the Red International) for the purpose of "uniting all revolutionary unions, minority groups, and individual militants." The organization established in August 1929 was the Trade Union Unity League.

trade union publications *Trade Union Publications*, a three-volume index of the journals and convention proceedings of 50 selected unions from the time of their origin until 1941, is an outstanding guide compiled by Lloyd G. Reynolds and Charles C. Killingsworth. The period indexed begins with 1850.

Large collections of trade union publications are to be found in the U.S. Department of Labor, The Library of Congress, the New York Public Library, the Wisconsin Historical Society Library, and the John Crerar Library in Chicago. Most university industrial relations centers or programs also maintain collections of current trade union publications.

Source references: George E. Barnett, *A Trial Bibliography of American Trade Union Publications* (Baltimore: Johns Hopkins Press, 1904, 1907); Univ. of Michigan, *Index to Labor Union Periodicals* (Ann Arbor: Bureau of IR, 1962–Feb. 1969 [monthly]); Lloyd G. Reynolds and Charles C. Killingsworth, *Trade Union Publications* (3 vol., Baltimore: Johns Hopkins Press, 1944); Eleanor H. Scanlan, "A Key to the Labor Press: Michigan Index to Labor Union Periodicals," *Management of Personnel Quarterly*, Fall 1968; "The 75th Anniversary of Labor's Magazine," *American Federationist*, Feb. 1969; U.S. Dept. of Labor, *American Trade Union Journals and Labor Papers* (Washington: 1964).

See also LABOR JOURNALISM.

Trade Union Unity League The Trade Union Unity League (TUUL) attempted to establish new industrial unions of groups which had previously been under the jurisdiction of the AFL. It not only supported dual unionism, but also promoted the dual-union strategy of boring from within. The TUUL was active from 1920 until 1935.

See also TRADE UNION EDUCATIONAL LEAGUE.

Train Dispatchers Association; American (AFL-CIO) Organized in 1917 as the Western Dispatchers' Association, the union adopted the present name in 1918. It publishes *The Train Dispatcher* (8 issues annually).

Address: 1401 S. Harlem Ave., Berwyn, Ill. 60402. Tel. (312) 795–5656

trainee An employee who is assigned to a prescribed training program to fit the individual to perform adequately the normal operations of a specified job. During the training period, as a "learner," the employee is paid less than the rate of the job for which the individual is being trained. This practice is sanctioned under the Fair Labor Standards Act.

In respect to factory work, for instance, a trainee is not to be confused with an apprentice, because ordinarily the trainee is not being prepared to handle a skilled, or craft, job.

Personnel practice has broadened the use of the term, and it is not uncommon to speak of "trainees" for advanced managerial positions.

training Systematic instruction and programs of activities and learning for the purpose of acquiring skills for particular jobs.

National efforts to provide training for the disadvantaged, displaced workers, youth, hard-core unemployed, minority groups, and women, among others, have been carried out by legislation such as the Manpower Development and Training Act of 1962, Comprehensive Employment and Training Act of 1973, and Job Training Partnership Act of 1982.

Source references: Curtis C. Aller et al., *Layoff Time Training: A Key to Upgrading Workforce Utilization and EEOC Affirmative Action* (Washington: U.S. Dept. of Labor, ETA, R & D Monograph 61, 1978); Charles Bahn, "The Counter Training Problem," *PJ*, Dec. 1973; Bernard M. Bass and James A. Vaughan, *Training in Industry: The Management of Learning* (Belmont: Wadsworth Publishing, 1968); Elizabeth B. Bolton and Luther Wade Humphreys, "A Training Model for Women—An Androgynous Approach," *PJ*, May 1977; BNA, *Training Programs and Tuition Aid Plans* (Washington: PPF Survey no. 123, 1978); William C. Byham and James Robinson, "Building Supervisory Confidence—A Key to Transfer of Training," *PJ*, May 1977; Kathleen Cooke, "A Model for the Identification of Training Needs," *Public Personnel Management*, July/Aug. 1979; Thomas J. DiLauro, "Training Needs Assessment: Current Practice and New Directions," *Public Personnel Management*, Nov./Dec. 1979; John E. Drotning and David B. Lipsky, "How Union Leaders View Job Training Programs," *MLR*, April 1971; Daniel M. Duncan, "Training Strategy and the 'System'," *PJ*, June 1972; Karl H. Ebel, "The Microelectronics Training Gap in the Metal Trades," *ILR*, Nov./Dec. 1981; Herbert M. Engel and Ronald W. James, "Negotiating for Employee Training and Development Programs: The New York State Experience," *Public Personnel Management*, March/April 1973; Daniel C. Feldman, "A Socialization Process that Helps New Recruits Succeed," *Personnel*, March/April 1980; Richard F. Fraser, John W. Gore, and Chester C. Cotton, "A System for Determining Training Needs," *PJ*, Dec. 1978; Kevin Fry, "Job Training—Stepping Up," *American Federationist*, May 1979; Albert C. Hyde and Jay M. Shafritz, "Training and Development and Personnel Management," *Public Personnel Management*, Nov./Dec. 1979; John L. Iacobelli, "Training Avoidance: Manpower Waste and Skill Shortage," *Proceedings of the 24th A/M, IRRA*, ed. by Gerald Somers (Madison: 1972); Frederic Jacobs and Donald Phillips, "Beyond the Little Red Schoolhouse," *Change*, July/Aug. 1979; J. M. Juran, "Product Quality—A Prescription for the West, Part I: Training and Improvement Programs," *Management Review*, June 1981; Sar A. Levitan and Garth L. Mangum (ed.), *The T in CETA, Local and National Perspectives* (Kalamazoo: Upjohn Institute for Employment Research, 1981); David B. Lipsky, "Employer Role in Hard-Core Trainee Success," *IR*, May 1973; Fred Luthans and Tim R. V. Davis, "Beyond Modeling: Managing Social Learning Processes in Human Resource Training and Development," *Human Resource Management*, Summer 1981; Laird W. Mealiea and John F. Duffy, "An Integrated Model for Training and Development: How to Build on What You Already Have," *Public Personnel Management*, Vol. 9, no. 4, 1980; Elizabeth J. Mitchell and Albert C. Hyde, "Training Demand Assessment: Three Case Studies in Planning Training Programs," *Public Personnel Management*, Nov./Dec. 1979; Charles A. Myers, *The Role of the Private Sector in Manpower Development* (Baltimore: Johns Hopkins Press, 1971); Gale E. Newell, "How to Plan a Training Program," *PJ*, May 1976; Felix A. Nigro and Lloyd G. Nigro, "The Trainer as a Strategist," *Public Personnel Management*, May/June 1974; Sylvia S. Small, "Statistical Effect of Work-Training Programs on the Unemployment Rate," *MLR*, Sept. 1972; Robert Taggart, *A Fisherman's Guide, An Assessment of Training and Remediation Strategies* (Kalamazoo: Upjohn Institute for Employment Research, 1981); U.S. Dept. of Labor, ETA, *Training Information for Policy Guidance* (Washington: R & D Monograph 76, 1980); U.S. National Center for Productivity and Quality of Working Life,

Productivity and Job Security: Case Studies of Continuing Education for Engineers, Technicians, and Managers (Washington: 1978); U.S. President, *Employment and Training Report of the President* (Washington: 1976); Arthur E. Wallach, "System Changes Begin in the Training Department," *PJ*, Dec. 1979.

See also COLD STORAGE TRAINING, COMPREHENSIVE EMPLOYMENT AND TRAINING ACT (CETA) OF 1973, FOREMAN TRAINING, INDUSTRIAL EDUCATION, INTRAPLANT TRAINING, JOB INSTRUCTION TRAINING, JOB METHODS TRAINING, JOB RELATIONS TRAINING, JOB SAFETY TRAINING, JOB TRAINING, JOB TRAINING PARTNERSHIP ACT (JTPA) OF 1982, LEADERSHIP TRAINING, MANAGEMENT DEVELOPMENT, MANPOWER DEVELOPMENT AND TRAINING ACT OF 1962, NATIONAL ALLIANCE OF BUSINESS (NAB), ON-THE-JOB TRAINING (OJT), PRE-EMPLOYMENT TRAINING, PROGRAMMED INSTRUCTION OR LEARNING, PROJECT METHOD, RETRAINING, SIX-SIX PLAN, TRADE ACT OF 1974, UNDERSTUDY, VERSATILITY TRAINING, VESTIBULE TRAINING, VOCATIONAL TRAINING.

training within industry A program which started as an emergency service during World War II. Its prime purpose was to assist defense industries to meet their manpower needs by training workers within each industry to make the fullest use of their skills.

Source references: Donald F. Lane, "TWI Programs vs. Contemporary Training Programs,"*PJ*, April 1961; U.S. War Manpower Commission, *The Training Within Industry Report 1940–45* (Washington: 1945); U.S. War Manpower Commission, Bureau of Training, Training Within Industry Service, *Bulletins and Outlines of the Service for War Plants and Essential Services* (Washington: 1945).

See also ON-THE-JOB TRAINING (OJT).

tramping committee Similar to walking delegates or union functionaries who check on activities of individuals, particularly during strikes, to make sure that no scabbing takes place. The phrase was used commonly in the early part of the 19th century.

transfer The shifting or movement of an employee from one job to another. Generallly the new assignment carries the same pay and privileges as the old. Transfers may be on a temporary basis, as when work is in short supply, or on a permanent basis when an individual seeks a job in another department or operation of the plant.

Source references: Michael A. Baer, "Employee Desires in Residential Relocation Situations," *Human Resource Management*, Fall 1974; Edward J. Bardi and Jack L. Simonetti, "The Game of Management Chess—Policies and Perils of Management Transfers," *PJ*, April 1977; BNA, *Employee Promotion and Transfer Policies* (Washington: PPF Survey no. 120, 1978); Lawrence W. Foster and Marilyn L. Liebrenz, "Corporate Moves—Who Pays the Psychic Costs?" *Personnel*, Nov./Dec. 1977; David B. Lipsky, "Interplant Transfer and Terminated Workers: A Case Study," *ILRR*, Jan. 1970; Harold Mack, "Transition Management in a Changing Environment," *PJ*, Sept. 1978; John M. Moore, "Transferring Minority Employees: Are They Being Treated Fairly?" *PJ*, Feb. 1975; Peter L. Mullins, "The Price Tag on Employee Transfers," *Personnel*, March/April 1969; Rudolph Oswald, "The Transfer Rights of Displaced Workers," *American Federationist*, July 1966; Robert A. Pitts, "Unshakle Your 'Comers'," *Harvard BR*, May/June 1977; Philip Taft, "Interplant Transfers in the Automobile Industry," *MLR*, March 1963; U.S. Dept. of Labor, BLS, *Major Collective Bargaining Agreements: Plant Movement, Transfer, and Relocation Allowances* (Washington: Bull. no. 1425–10, 1969).

See also PRODUCTION TRANSFER.

transfer card Card issued by a local union to a member in good standing, certifying eligibility to join another local of the same union in a different location.

Transit Union; Amalgamated (AFL-CIO) Formerly known as the Amalgamated Association of Street, Electric Railway and Motor Coach Employes of America (AFL-CIO), its present name was adopted on July 1, 1964.

Its monthly publication is *In Transit*.

Address: 5025 Wisconsin Ave., N.W., Washington, D.C. 20016. Tel. (202) 537–1645

Transportation Act of 1920 *See* ESCH-CUMMINS ACT.

Transportation-Communication Employees Union (AFL-CIO) Formerly known as The Order of Railroad Telegraphers, which changed its name in 1964 to the Transportation-Communication Employees Union. In 1969, the Transportation-Communication Employees Union merged with the Brotherhood of Railway, Airline and Steamship Clerks, Freight Handlers, Express and Station Employes (AFL-CIO).

See also RAILROAD TELEGRAPHERS; THE ORDER OF (AFL-CIO); RAILWAY, AIRLINE AND STEAMSHIP CLERKS, FREIGHT HANDLERS, EXPRESS AND STATION EMPLOYES; BROTHERHOOD OF (AFL-CIO).

Transportation Services and Allied Workers A former division of the Seafarers' International Union of North America (AFL-CIO), the union was dissolved in July 1967.

Transportation Union; United (AFL-CIO) Labor union formed on January 1, 1969, with the merger of four railway unions—the Brotherhood of Locomotive Firemen and Enginemen, the Brotherhood of Railroad Trainmen, the Order of Railway Conductors and Brakemen, and the Switchmen's Union of North America. The merger brought together an estimated 280,400 rail workers into the new union.

"By this move of unification, we expect to strengthen each craft within the union, and to give each man in the industry additional strength. . . . We will . . . be able to apply our united strength to solve our problems, not only the problems of our members but those also of our industry," stated Charles Luna, the first president of the new union.

On September 1, 1970, the Federated Council of the International Association of Railway Employees and Association of Railway Trainmen and Locomotive Firemen (Ind) merged with the union. Its official publication is the weekly *UTU News.*

Address: 14600 Detroit Ave., Cleveland, Ohio 44107. Tel. (216) 228–9400

Source reference: UTU Transportation News, January 4, 1969.

Transport Service Employees; United (AFL-CIO) Formerly known as the United Transport Service Employees of America (CIO). It merged with the Brotherhood of Railway, Airline and Steamship Clerks, Freight Handlers, Express and Station Employes (AFL-CIO) on September 26, 1972.

Transport Workers Union of America (AFL-CIO) Organized in 1934, it merged with the International Association of Machinists in 1936 but withdrew from the Machinists union a year later and affiliated with the CIO.

The United Railroad Workers of America (CIO) in October 1954, the International Air Line Stewards and Stewardesses Association (AFL-CIO) in 1961, and the Air Line Dispatchers Association (AFL-CIO) on March 15, 1977, have merged with the union.

The monthly publication is the *TWU Express.*

Address: 1980 Broadway, New York, N.Y. 10023. Tel. (212) 873–6000

Source references: Theodore W. Kheel and C. J. K. Turcoff, *Arbitration and Transit Peace* (Englewood Cliffs: PH, 1962); James J. McGinley, *Labor Relations in the New York Rapid Transit Systems, 1904–1944* (New York: King's Crown Press, 1949); Transport Workers Union of America, *TWU and Civil Rights* (New York: 1965).

travel allowance An allowance, usually for transportation expenses, to a worker who is required to travel on company business. Where an employer requests an individual to move to another locality or to work at another plant on a regular basis, the transportation expenses will include moving expenses.

Source references: BNA, *Employee Expense Allowances and Perquisites* (Washington: PPF Survey no. 124, 1979); Joseph A. Capolarello, "Employee Mileage Allowances: Too High or Too Low?" *PJ*, Feb. 1975; The Conference Board, *Transporting Employees: The Corporate Programs* (New York: Research Bulletin no. 131, 1983); Milton Reitzfeld, *Controlling Travel Costs*, An AMA Management Briefing (New York: AMA, 1982); Harold L. Seligman, "How to Control Runaway Travel Costs," *Management Review*, Jan. 1981.

See also EXPENSE ALLOWANCES.

travel time The time spent by an individual going to and from a designated point to his place of work. Travel time includes portal-to-portal time in mining and deadheading time on the railroads.

Source reference: U.S. Congress, House, Committee on Post Office and Civil Service, Subcommittee on Compensation, *Travel Time Compensation: Hearings*, Jan. 25, 26, 1966 (Washington: 1966).

See also MOVING ALLOWANCES, PORTAL-TO-PORTAL PAY.

Treasury Employees Union; National (Ind) Formerly known as the National Association of Internal Revenue Employees (Ind), the present name was adopted in the early 1970s. On June 9, 1975, the National Customs Service Association (Ind) merged with the organization. Its publications are the *Steward Update* (monthly), *Capitol Report* (monthly), and *NTEU Bulletin* (issued every three weeks).

Address: 1730 K St., N.W., Suite 1101, Washington, D.C. 20006. Tel. (202) 785–4411

trial examiner The official charged by the NLRB to conduct hearings following issuance of a complaint by the general counsel alleging that an employer or union has violated the Taft-Hartley Act by the commission of unfair labor practices. The trial examiner is, in effect, a "judge" in a court of first impression, although the hearing procedures in NLRB complaint ("C") cases are less formal than those in a court of law.

Powers given trial examiners by the Board include these: to administer oaths and affirmations; to grant applications for subpoenas, and to rule upon petitions to revoke subpoenas; to rule upon offers of proof and receive relevant evidence; to take or cause depositions to be taken; to regulate the course of the hearing "and, if appropriate or necessary, to exclude persons or counsel from the hearing for contemptuous conduct and to strike all related testimony of witnesses refusing to answer any proper question"; to dispose of procedural requests and similar matters, including motions of various kinds, and to dismiss complaints or portions thereof; to make and file decisions in conformity with Section 8 of the Administrative Procedure Act; to call, examine, and cross-examine witnesses, and to introduce into the hearing record documentary or other evidence; to request parties at any time during the hearing to state their positions on any issue in the case or theory in support thereof; and to take any other action necessary under the Board's Rules and Regulations.

Trial examiners have been known as administrative law judges since 1972.

See also ADMINISTRATIVE LAW JUDGE (ALJ).

trial examiner's decision Since September 3, 1963, NLRB trial examiners have issued decisions which are not reviewed by the Board unless exceptions to the decision are filed by a party or the parties to a case involving charges of unfair labor practices. Prior to that time the intermediate report (or recommended order) of a trial examiner did not have this status, although it was in almost identical form, stating the alleged violation of the statute, usually the background of the charges, findings of fact, and conclusions of law. If the parties to a complaint ("C") case accept the trial examiner's decision, that ends the matter. If, however, exception is taken to the decision, the Board must review the trial examiner's decision and issue a cease and desist (or dismissal) order of its own. A cease-and-desist order of the Board is subject to review by a circuit court of appeals, which may enforce, modify, or reject the order. The appellate decision then is subject to final review (on petition for certiorari) by the Supreme Court.

Trial examiners have been known as administrative law judges since 1972.

See also ADMINISTRATIVE LAW JUDGE (ALJ), INTERMEDIATE REPORT.

trial period The initial or probationary period for a new employee on the job. Provision is generally made that the first 30 days of employment will be on a probationary or trial basis and that (during the trial period) management has the discretion to discharge such employee without cause. During their probationary or trial periods employees generally have no recourse to the grievance machinery. The phrase "trial period" may also apply to a period of time during which a new piece rate is being worked on by incentive employees, and before the rate is made permanent.

See also PROBATIONARY EMPLOYEE.

trick Generally considered as synonymous with shift or tour.

tri-offer arbitration *See* ARBITRATION, TRI-OFFER.

tripartite boards A board composed of representatives of labor, management, and the public. The best known tripartite boards were the National War Labor Boards during World Wars I and II.

Source references: Robert G. Dixon, "Tripartitism in the National War Labor Board," *ILRR*, April 1949; George H. Hildebrand, "The Use of Tripartite Bodies to Aid Collective Bargaining," *MLR*, June 1961; ———, "The Use of Tripartite Bodies to Supplement Collective Bargaining," *LLJ*, July 1961; Joseph Lazar, Vincent Lombardi, and George Seltzer, "The Tripartite Commission in Public Interest Labor Disputes in Minnesota, 1940–1960," *LLJ*, May 1963; Edward Sussna, "Is Tripartite Bargaining Inevitable?" *LLJ*, May 1959; "The Use of Tripartite Boards in Labor, Commercial and International Arbitration," 68 *Harvard LR* 293 (1954).

troubled employee An individual with personal or work-related problems. The troubled employee's problems are generally more frequent and serious than those of the "normal" employee—higher rates of absence and tardiness, more accidents, inferior quality of work, low productivity, and interpersonal conflict. Alcoholism, drug abuse, emotional or mental illness, and marital and financial problems are some of the factors contributing to poor job performance of troubled employees.

Source references: Frank E. Kuzmits and Henry E. Hammons II, "Rehabilitating the Troubled Employee," *PJ*, April 1979; John H. Meyer and Teresa C. Meyer, "The Supervisor as Counselor—How to Help the Distressed Employee," *Management Review*, April 1982; James E. Petersen, "Insight: A Management Program of Help for Troubled People," *LLJ*, Aug. 1972; Robert W. Reardon, "Help for the Troubled Worker in a Small Company," *Personnel*, Jan./Feb. 1976.

trouble makers *See* AGITATOR.

trouble men Individuals who repair and service equipment. Sometimes called maintenance men and trouble shooters.

Truax v. Corrigan A decision of the Supreme Court in which the Court set aside an Arizona Supreme Court decision upholding the anti-injunction law passed by that state. The Arizona statute was modeled on Section 20 of the Clayton Act. Mass picketing by strikers occurred during a dispute at a restaurant in Bisbee and when the company sought an injunction to restrain picketing, it was denied by the Arizona courts on the ground that the Arizona statute forbade issuance of such an order. The Supreme Court on review of the case in a 5–4 decision, set aside the Arizona law because the prohibition of injunctions in the case of mass picketing was, the Court said, "a wrongful and highly injurious invasion of property rights." The Supreme Court held the State Supreme Court decision unconstitutional insofar as it interpreted the Arizona statute to prohibit injunctions against tortious and unlawful picketing.

Source reference: Truax v. Corrigan, 257 US 312 (1921).

See also PICKETING.

truck system A form of barter system whereby employees were paid their wages in goods or in scrip to be used at a store owned by the employer.

See also COMPANY STORE.

true accident A phrase used in handling employee liability or accident cases to describe an accident for which no one is to blame; that is, neither the employer nor the employee is responsible for its occurrence.

trusteeing The practice of attaching, through a court order, the wages of a debtor and collecting it directly from his employer.

See also GARNISHMENT.

trusteeship, union A trusteeship is a method of supervision or control whereby a labor organization suspends the autonomy of a subordinate group or body, under the constitution or bylaws of the organization.

As a result of abuses made public during the McClellan Committee hearings, the Congress enacted Title III of the Labor-Management Reporting and Disclosure Act of 1959, which sets forth the conditions under which the trusteeships may be established and continued. The law requires reporting and public disclosure by labor organizations of the stewardships involved in a trusteeship.

The law also holds it to be a crime either to count the votes of the delegates of a trusteed union unless they are democratically elected, or to transfer funds to the supervisory organization. The law also provides redress for the union member or subordinate body, either directly in the courts or through the secretary of labor.

Section 3 of the law defines "trusteeship" to mean "any receivership, trusteeship, or other methods of supervision or control whereby a labor organization suspends the autonomy otherwise available to a subordinate body under its constitution or bylaws."

Source references: Labor-Management Reporting and Disclosure Act, as amended, 29 U.S.C. 301–306 (1982); Harry P. Cohany and Irving P. Phillips, "Trusteeship Provisions in Union Constitutions," *MLR*, Nov. 1959; William J. Isaacson, "Union Trusteeships Under the Landrum-Griffin Act," *NYU 14th Annual Conference on Labor*, ed. by Emanuel Stein (Albany: Bender, 1961); Sar A. Levitan, "Union Trusteeships: The Federal Law and an Inventory," *LLJ*, Dec. 1960; Matthew A. Rooney, "A Fair Hearing Requirement for Union Trusteeships Under the LMRDA," *IR Law Digest*, Jan. 1974; Daniel L. Shneidman, "Union Trusteeships and Section 304(a) of the Landrum-Griffin Act," *LLJ*, June 1963; U.S. Dept. of Labor, Bureau of Labor-Management Reports, *Union Trusteeships: Report of the Secretary of Labor to the Congress* (Washington: 1962); U.S. Dept. of Labor, LMSA, *Union Officer Elections and Trusteeships Case Digest* (Washington: 1980); Arnold R. Weber, "Local Union Trusteeship and Public Policy," *ILRR*, Jan. 1961.

See also LABOR-MANAGEMENT REPORTING AND DISCLOSURE ACT OF 1959, MONITORSHIP.

tube bending formula A policy (formulated by the NLRB) which held that certain expressions of employers in opposition to unionism are not coercive or threatening and do not constitute improper interference within the meaning of the National Labor Relations Act. The term is derived from the name of the case in which the NLRB established the policy.

Source references: American Tube Bending Co. and IAM, 44 NLRB 121, 11 LRRM 61 (1942); *NLRB v. American Tube Bending Co.*, 134 F2d 993, 12 LRRM 615 (CA 2, 1943).

tuition aid Employer reimbursement of employee education expenses. Such aid is intended to encourage workers to improve job performance and to provide opportunities for upgrading and promotion. It is usually available to all full-time workers regardless of occupation or length of service and requires that courses be job-related. Employees may be reimbursed for the entire cost, or aid may depend of length of service, or on the grade received for the course, or as specified in the tuition aid plan. It is generally required that courses be taken at colleges and universities, trade schools, and correspondence schools. Courses offered by professional groups are also covered under some plans.

Source references: BNA, *Training Programs and Tuition Aid Plans* (Washington: PPF Survey no. 123, 1978); Richard A. Kaimann and Daniel Robey, "Tuition Refund—Asset or Liability?" *PJ*, Aug. 1976; "Tuition Reimbursement in Employee Productivity and OD: A Survey," *Public Personnel Management*, May/June 1977.

See also EDUCATIONAL LEAVE.

turnout A term equivalent to the term "strike." A familiar phrase in the early part of the 19th century.

turnover *See* LABOR TURNOVER.

twilight arbitration *See* ARBITRATION, TWILIGHT.

twilight zone *See* FEDERAL-STATE JURISDICTION; PREEMPTION, DOCTRINE OF.

two-platoon system Similar to a two-shift operation.

two-thousand-hour clause Same as the thousand-hour clause under the Fair Labor Standards Act, except that under the two-thousand-hour clause, overtime provisions did not apply up to 12 hours per day and 56 hours per week, if the union and the employer have entered into an agreement that no employee in the plant will be employed for more than a total of 2,000 hours in any period of 52 consecutive weeks. The Act presently permits employment up to 2,080 hours without overtime penalty. Employment up to 2,240 hours without overtime penalty is permitted if the collective bargaining agreement provides a specified minimum guarantee of hours of employment.

See also ONE-THOUSAND-HOUR CLAUSE.

two-tier wage structure A plan allowing reduced pay and benefits for new hires while maintaining or improving the wages, benefits, or job security of current employees. Unions have been reluctant to agree to two-tier wage structures, under which pay for newly-hired employees may be as much as 50 percent lower than the regular pay rate. Such plans, however, are sought by employers, who cite financial problems or the need to improve competition with nonunion companies. According to a 1983 Bureau of National Affairs Survey, about 5 percent of the surveyed contracts contained some form of two-tier wage structure.

Source references: "Analysis of 1983's Most Significant Events," *Retail/Services Labor Report*, January 9, 1984; "Analysis of What's Ahead in 1984," *Retail/Services Labor Report*, January 16, 1984.

two-year rule A rule established by the NLRB holding that the first two years of a collective bargaining agreement shall be considered a reasonable period during which claims by rival unions will not generally be considered.

See also CONTRACT-BAR RULE.

Typographical Union; International (AFL-CIO) A union organized in 1852 which claimed jurisdiction over most of the crafts in the printing trade. Bookbinders, stereotypers, photo-engravers, and pressmen formed their own internationals and separated from the ITU.

On January 1, 1979, the International Mailers Union (Ind) merged with the union. The official monthly publication is the *Typographical Journal.*

Address: 301 Union Blvd., Colorado Springs, Colo. 80910. Tel. (303) 636–2341

Source references: International Typographical Union, Executive Council, *Facts About International Typographical Union and a Chronological Digest of Its History* (Indianapolis: The Union, 1952); Harry Kelber and Carl Schlesinger, *Union Printers and Controlled Automation* (New York: Free Press, 1967); Seymour M. Lipset, Martin A. Trow, and James S. Coleman, *Union Democracy: The Internal Politics of the International Typographical Union* (Glencoe: Free Press, 1956); Jacob Loft, *The Printing Trades* (New York: Farrar, Rinehart, 1944); James M. Lynch, *Epochal History of the International Typographical Union* (Indianapolis: The Union, 1925); John McVicar, *Origin and Progress of the Typographical Union, 1850–1891* (Lansing: Thorp, 1891); George A. Tracy, *History of the Typographical Union* (Indianapolis: The Union, 1931).

U

UAPD *See* PHYSICIANS AND DENTISTS; UNION OF AMERICAN (IND).

UAW *See* AUTOMOBILE, AEROSPACE AND AGRICULTURAL IMPLEMENT WORKERS OF AMERICA; INTERNATIONAL UNION, UNITED (AFL-CIO).

UE *See* ELECTRICAL, RADIO AND MACHINE WORKERS OF AMERICA; UNITED (IND).

UFCW *See* FOOD AND COMMERCIAL WORKERS INTERNATIONAL UNION; UNITED (AFL-CIO).

UFW *See* FARM WORKERS OF AMERICA; UNITED (AFL-CIO).

UFWA *See* FURNITURE WORKERS OF AMERICA; UNITED (AFL-CIO).

UGCW *See* GLASS AND CERAMIC WORKERS OF NORTH AMERICA; UNITED (AFL-CIO).

UGW *See* GARMENT WORKERS OF AMERICA; UNITED (AFL-CIO).

UIS *See* UNEMPLOYMENT INSURANCE SERVICE (UIS).

UIU *See* UPHOLSTERERS' INTERNATIONAL UNION OF NORTH AMERICA (AFL-CIO).

UJH *See* HORSESHOERS; INTERNATIONAL UNION OF JOURNEYMEN (AFL-CIO).

ULP *See* UNFAIR LABOR PRACTICES.

UMW *See* MINE WORKERS OF AMERICA; UNITED (IND).

UPIU *See* PAPERWORKERS INTERNATIONAL UNION; UNITED (AFL-CIO).

URW *See* RUBBER, CORK, LINOLEUM AND PLASTIC WORKERS OF AMERICA; UNITED (AFL-CIO).

USA *See* STEELWORKERS OF AMERICA; UNITED (AFL-CIO).

UTU *See* TRANSPORTATION UNION; UNITED (AFL-CIO).

UTW *See* TELEGRAPH WORKERS; UNITED (AFL-CIO).

UTWA *See* TEXTILE WORKERS OF AMERICA; UNITED (AFL-CIO).

UWNE *See* UTILITY WORKERS OF NEW ENGLAND, INC.; BROTHERHOOD OF (IND).

UWU *See* UTILITY WORKERS UNION OF AMERICA (AFL-CIO).

"U" cases A designation used by the NLRB for petitions pending before the Board. "UD" cases involve petitions to rescind a union-shop authorization filed by an individual, a group, or a labor organization. "UC" cases involve petitions filed by a certified or currently recognized representative of a bargaining unit or by an employer of such bargaining unit employees to clarify an existing bargaining unit.

Source reference: U.S. NLRB, *A Guide to Basic Law and Procedures Under the National Labor Relations Act* (Washington: 1978).

See also "AC" CASES, "R" CASES.

umpire The term is synonymous with arbitrator. The terms arbitrator, impartial chairperson, and umpire frequently are used interchangeably. A distinction is made by some writers to the effect that the term "arbitrator" applies to individuals who are appointed to settle a particular dispute. Actually the term "ad hoc" arbitrator is used for that purpose whereas the terms "impartial chairperson" and "umpire" imply that the individual is on a permanent basis; that is, for the duration of the collective bargaining agreement.

A distinction frequently is made in the literature to the effect that the impartial chairperson who has served in some industries over long periods of time, has not only the function of arbitrating disputes arising under the contract, but may on occasion be brought into the negotiations to mediate or to make a final determination of substantive issues. The umpire may exercise similar functions but generally handles only grievance disputes.

See also ARBITRATION; ARBITRATION, AD HOC; IMPARTIAL CHAIRPERSON; PERMANENT ARBITRATOR; REFEREE.

Umpires Association; Major League (Ind) Organization formed in 1969 by the merger of the Association of National Baseball League Umpires (founded in 1963) and the Association of American League Umpires.

Address: 3 Girard Plaza, Suite 2106, Philadelphia, Pa. 19102. Tel. (215) 568–7368

unaffiliated union A local or national union which is not affiliated with AFL-CIO. Unaffiliated unions are called independent unions, but are to be distinguished from so-called independent unions which are company-dominated.

Source reference: U.S. Dept. of Labor, BLS, *Unaffiliated Intrastate and Single-Employer Unions, 1967* (Washington: Bull. no. 1640, 1970).

See also COMPANY-DOMINATED UNION, INDEPENDENT UNIONS.

unapproved wage increase Under wartime stabilization laws, a wage increase which, although not illegal, could not be used by the employer as a basis for requesting adjustments in prices.

unauthorized strike A strike which does not have the approval of the union and is in violation of the no-strike provision of the collective bargaining agreement. It is frequently referred to as a wildcat, illegal, quickie, or an outlaw strike.

Professor Shulman, umpire under the Ford Motor Company contract, in *Ford Motor Co.*, Opinion A–241, 6 LA 799 (1947), had the following comments to make on an illegitimate strike: "An illegitimate strike . . . is a serious blow against the union itself. It manifests lack of confidence in the union. It mars the union's efforts to achieve compliance by the company. It weakens the union's bargaining power in future negotiations. Illegitimate strikers must be told without equivocation that they are fighting the union as well as the company."

Source references: "Strike Control Provisions in Union Constitutions," *MLR*, May 1954; Samuel Yellen, *American Labor Struggle* (New York: Russell, 1956).

See also ILLEGAL STRIKE, OUTLAW STRIKE, QUICKIE STOPPAGE OR STRIKE.

unclassified service Positions not subject to civil service regulations and procedure, such as elected officials, heads of departments, appointees to special boards and commissions, including, according to Stahl, "experts who may be permanent or temporary employees working under special contract." Sometimes referred to as excepted or noncareer service.

Source references: O. Glenn Stahl, *Public Personnel Administration* (7th ed., New York: Harper & Row, 1976); U.S. Library of Congress, Congressional Research Service, *History of Civil Service Merit Systems of the United States and Selected Foreign Countries* (Washington: 1976).

See also CLASSIFIED SERVICE, EXEMPT CLASS.

undercover agents *See* ESPIONAGE, LABOR SPY.

underemployed An individual who is earning an income at subsistence level and is seeking employment at a higher level of earnings, or a part-time worker seeking full-time employment. Also refers to a worker whose ability and skill are not being fully utilized.

See also SUBEMPLOYMENT.

underemployment A condition sometimes existing in the economy in which there is inadequate utilization of available existing manpower. Such a situation either does not provide sufficient earnings to maintain the individual at a reasonable standard of living or does not adequately utilize the capacities and abilities of the persons in the labor market.

Source references: Curtis L. Gilroy, "Supplemental Measures of Labor Force Underutilization," *MLR*, May 1975; Claire C. Hodge and James R. Wetzel, "Short Workweeks and Underemployment," *MLR*, Sept. 1967; Ethel B. Jones, "The Elusive Concept of Underemployment," *Journal of Human*

Resources, Fall 1971; Ernesto Kritz and Joseph Ramos, "The Measurement of Urban Underemployment: A Report on Three Experimental Surveys," *ILR*, Jan./Feb. 1976; Harvey Leibenstein, "The Theory of Underemployment in Backward Economies," *Journal of Political Economy*, April 1957; U.S. Dept. of Agriculture, *Underemployment Estimates by County, United States, 1960* (Washington: Agriculture Economic Report no. 166, 1969); T. Vietorisz, R. Mier, and J. Giblin, "Subemployment: Exclusion and Inadequacy Indexes," *MLR*, May 1975.

See also MANPOWER, RETRAINING, SUBEMPLOYMENT.

underrepresentation According to the OFCCP, it refers to the employment of "substantially fewer minorities or women in a job area than might reasonably be expected by their representation in the contractor's work force, or relevant section of that work force; or by their availability for the jobs involved." The identification of job areas exhibiting underrepresentation is a part of the required work force analysis in an affirmative action program. "'Underrepresentation' is not the same as 'underutilization,' which is any numeric difference between availability and utilization. A substantial disparity is required for underrepresentation."

Source reference: U.S. OFCCP, *Federal Contract Compliance Manual* (Washington: 1979).

See also CONCENTRATION, GOALS AND TIMETABLES, UTILIZATION ANALYSIS.

understudy A form of on-the-job training where an individual acts as an assistant to the full-fledged journeyman who is engaged in the trade which the understudy is learning. When the journeyman is transferred or promoted, the understudy may take over the job. Sometimes the term applies to an individual brought into an organization to be trained to take over the job of a particular person who plans to retire.

under the hat agreement *See* AGREEMENT, SWEETHEART.

underutilization Defined by OFCCP as "[e]mployment of members of a race, ethnic or sex group in a job or job group at a rate below their availability. The concept of underutilization includes any numerical disparity, and is not limited by the 80% rule applicable to concepts such as adverse impact. Underutilization for contractors subject to 41 CFR 60–2 [Revised Order No. 4] is determined by conducting a job group analysis according to 41 CFR 60–2.11(b)."

Under the EEOC Uniform Guidelines on Employee Selection Procedures, federal enforcement agencies may infer that an employee selection process has adverse impact "if the user has an underutilization of a group in the job category, as compared to the group's representation in the relevant labor market or, in the case of jobs filled from within, the applicable work force." An affirmative action program may be one means of remedying underutilization.

Source references: U.S. EEOC, "Uniform Guidelines on Employee Selection Procedures," 29 C.F.R. 1607; U.S. OFCCP, "Revised Order No. 4," 41 C.F.R. 60–2; Oscar Ornati and Edward Giblin, "'Underutilization'—As Compared to What?" *Employee Relations LJ*, Summer 1977; U.S. OFCCP, *Federal Contract Compliance Manual* (Washington: 1979).

See also ADVERSE IMPACT, AVAILABILITY, REVISED ORDER NO. 4, UNDERREPRESENTATION, UTILIZATION ANALYSIS.

undocumented workers Aliens who do not have the required working papers. There is debate whether undocumented workers take "desirable" jobs, thus displacing domestic workers and contributing to unemployment, or whether they take jobs no one else would take. The NLRB and the courts have found that undocumented workers are "employees" under the National Labor Relations Act, and are entitled to form and join unions and elect bargaining representatives.

Source references: Amay's Bakery & Noodle Co., Inc., 227 NLRB 214, 94 LRRM 1165 (1976); *NLRB v. Sure-Tan, Inc.*, 583 F2d 355, 99 LRRM 2388 (1978); Charles B. Knapp, "Developing a National Policy to Deal With Undocumented Aliens," *Proceedings of the 30th A/M, IRRA*, ed. by Barbara Dennis (Madison: 1978); Albert Kutchins and Kate Tweedy, "No Two Ways About It: Employer Sanctions Versus Labor Law Protections for Undocumented Workers," *Industrial Rela-*

tions LJ, Vol. 5, no. 3, 1983; Ellen Sehgal and Joyce Vialet, "Documenting the Undocumented: Data, Like Aliens Are Elusive," *MLR*, Oct. 1980.

See also ALIEN LABOR, GUESTWORKER PROGRAM.

undue hardship Refers to a claim by employers that accommodating employees because of religion or handicap is detrimental to the conduct of business, i.e., will create an "undue hardship." Title VII of the Civil Rights Act of 1964 confers a duty upon employers "to reasonably accommodate" religious observances or practices unless there is "undue hardship" on business operations. Federal contractors may claim undue hardship in accommodating handicapped individuals or disabled veterans; according to the OFCCP, business necessity and financial expense may be considerations in determining undue hardship.

Source references: Civil Rights Act of 1964, as amended, 42 U.S.C. 2000e et seq. (1982); U.S. EEOC, "Guidelines on Discrimination Because of Religion," 29 C.F.R. 1605; U.S. OFCCP, "Affirmative Action Obligations of Contractors and Subcontractors for Handicapped Workers," 41 C.F.R. 60–741; ———, "Affirmative Action Program for Disabled Veterans and Veterans of the Vietnam Era," 41 C.F.R. 60–250.

See also ACCOMMODATION, BONA FIDE OCCUPATIONAL QUALIFICATION (BFOQ), REHABILITATION ACT OF 1973.

unemployable A term which seeks to identify individuals who cannot fit into the labor market and are unable to find employment. The term is often used interchangeably with the term hard-core unemployed and in juxtaposition with the term hard-core unemployed in the phrase "hard-core unemployables." The unemployables are those who experience difficulty in getting and retaining even an unskilled, low-wage, low-status job. They may have extreme educational deficiencies, be severely handicapped (physically or mentally), have a criminal record, have a high rate of absenteeism, have a problem with alcoholism or drugs, or be unable to adapt to the routine and responsibility needed to hold a job.

Source references: AMA, *How to Employ the "Unemployable" Successfully*, Selected Reprints from AMA Periodicals (New York: 1967–1968); Richard Beatty and Craig E. Schneier, "Training the Hard Core Unemployed Through Positive Reinforcement," *Human Resource Management*, Winter 1972; John L. Burns, "Benefits of Training the Hard-to-Employ," *Harvard BR*, May/June 1980; Nicholas DiMarco and David P. Gustafson, "Attitudes of Co-Workers and Management Toward Hard-Core Employees," *Personnel Psychology*, Spring 1975; Lucy N. Friedman and Carl B. Weisbrod, "A Way to Move Welfare Recipients into the Work Force," *Harvard BR*, Jan./Feb. 1978; Manpower Demonstration Research Corp., *Summary and Findings of the National Supported Work Demonstration* (Cambridge: Ballinger, 1980); John D. McGarr, Jr., "'Hire the Unemployables'—Corporate Slogan or Planned Program," *LLJ*, Oct. 1969; Fred H. Schmidt, "A Repair Shop for Unemployables," *IR*, May 1969; Robert C. Sedwick and Donald J. Bodwell, "The Hard-Core Employee—Key to High Retention," *PJ*, Dec. 1971; Bert C. Shlensky, "Employing the Ex-Offender," *Conference Board Record*, July 1974; Robert Taggart, *The Prison of Unemployment; Manpower Programs for Offenders* (Baltimore: Johns Hopkins UP, 1972); Keith C. Weir, "Hard Core Training and Employment," *PJ*, May 1971.

See also ALCOHOLISM, DISADVANTAGED WORKERS, DRUG ABUSE, EMPLOYABLE, HARD CORE OF UNEMPLOYMENT.

unemployed The Current Population Survey defines the unemployed as civilians 16 years and older "who had no employment during the survey week, were available for work, except for temporary illness, and (a) had made specific efforts to find employment sometime during the prior 4 weeks, or (b) were waiting to be called to a job from which they had been laid off, or (c) were waiting to report to a new job within 30 days."

The technical definitions of the unemployed are set by state unemployment offices to facilitate identification of individuals for the purpose of determining whether they qualify for unemployment benefits under state laws, the general criterion being whether a person is able and willing to work at a job which is reasonably related to the qualifications and under reasonable local standards. For the definition used to tabulate statistical data on unemployment, see *Concepts and Methods Used in Labor Force Statistics Derived from the Current Population Survey* (BLS Report 463, 1976) and *Manual for Developing Local Area Unemployment Statistics* (BLS, 1979).

The term "unemployed" has been variously defined by writers in the field of labor and is being refined constantly so that it may better reflect the labor market situation to assist in manpower utilization and to understand the nature and characteristics of those without employment.

A description of those regarded as unemployed by Professors Adams and Sumner in 1905 states that:

> The unemployed may conveniently be divided into four classes: (a) Skilled and efficient workmen who are temporarily out of employment owing to bad weather, "shut-downs," and other seasonal "vicissitudes of work in a normal state of trade;" (b) another group of industrious and efficient workmen, deprived of employment by prolonged industrial depression, revolution of fashion, introduction of new machinery, foreign competition, etc., who—although trustworthy and efficient—have no certain prospect of obtaining employment within a definite period; (c) a great mass of casual, unskilled laborers, morally, and too often physically, incapable of sustained work; and (d) the semi-criminal loafers, dependents and delinquents, in short the "unemployable."

Source references: Thomas S. Adams and Helen L. Sumner, *Labor Problems: A Text Book* (New York: Macmillan, 1905); E. Wight Bakke, *The Unemployed Worker* (New Haven: Yale UP, 1940); Barbara Becnel, "The Crime-Unemployment Cycle," *American Federationist*, Nov. 1978; "Better Yardsticks to Count the Unemployed," *American Federationist*, Nov. 1961; Kim B. Clark and Lawrence H. Summers, "Unemployment Reconsidered," *Harvard BR*, Nov./Dec. 1980; Gertrude Deutsch, "How the Unemployed Are Counted," *Business Record*, Dec. 1960; Herbert S. Parnes, *Unemployment Experience of Individuals Over a Decade: Variations by Sex, Race and Age* (Kalamazoo: Upjohn Institute for Employment Research, 1982); "The Scars of Unemployment," *American Federationist*, Oct. 1979; U.S. Congress, Joint Economic Committee, *Achieving the Goals of the Employment Act of 1946—Thirtieth Anniversary Review, Vol. 1—Employment. Paper no. 5—Estimating the Social Costs of National Economic Policy; Implications for Mental and Physical Health, and Criminal Aggression* (Washington: 1976); U.S. Dept. of Labor, BLS, *Job Loss and Other Factors Behind the Recent Increase in Unemployment* (Washington: Report 446, 1975).

See also LABOR FORCE, RETRAINING.

unemployment Attempts to define "employment" and "unemployment" have proven difficult, with the definitions to a large extent determined by sources of data used in developing the measures. The two basic sources used for statistics on current unemployment in the United States are (1) the Current Population Survey (CPS) conducted by the U.S. Bureau of the Census for the Bureau of Labor Statistics and (2) unemployment insurance (UI) data compiled from administration records of state employment security agencies.

Observations in the report, *Mobility and Worker Adaptation to Economic Change in the United States*, issued in July 1963, read in part as follows:

> The statistics from the Current Population Survey provide a basis for identifying in the Nation, as a whole, the personal characteristics (age, sex, marital status, color, etc.), and the occupational and other economic characteristics of both employed and unemployed persons in the population. . . . These are figures most widely quoted in discussions of American unemployment. Recognition needs to be given to their inclusiveness, and to the fact that some persons not generally counted in the unemployment statistics of other countries, such as new entrants in the labor force, youngsters in school, and housewives seeking temporary work, are included in this measure of unemployment.

Beginning with the data for January 1967, changes in the definitions of employment and unemployment were instituted in the CPS statistics in line with the basic recommendations of the President's Committee to Appraise Employment and Unemployment Statistics (The Gordon Committee) as set forth in its 1962 report, *Measuring Employ-*

ment and Unemployment. The previous sample of approximately 35,000 households was increased to 52,500 spread over 449 sample areas. In the previous CPS, the employment status of persons 14 years of age and over was measured; the lower age limit was raised to 16, although the CPS continues to collect and publish separately data for the 14- and 15-year-olds. Under the previous definition, persons were counted as unemployed if they had no job and were looking for work during the specific week of each month which is surveyed. Under the new definition, persons are counted as unemployed if (a) they were "engaged in some specific jobseeking activity (going to the Employment Service, applying to an employer, answering a want-ad, being on a union or professional register, etc.) within the past 4 weeks," (b) they were "waiting to start a new job within 30 days," or (c) they were "waiting to be recalled from layoff. In all cases, the individual must be currently available for work." The definition does not include inactive work seekers who would have been looking for work except for the belief that no work was available and such persons are not in the current labor force if they took no steps to find work in the past four weeks. Persons holding a job but not at work during the survey week are now classified as employed, even through they were seeking other jobs. For most analytical purposes, the new series is regarded as reasonably comparable to those of previous years.

Currently, the overall unemployment rate represents the number of unemployed as a percent of the labor force which includes members of the Armed Forces stationed in the United States. The CPS sample covers approximately 60,000 households.

The July 1963 report continues:

> Data from the unemployment insurance system provide a measure of unemployed workers who are receiving compensation during their period of joblessness. Data on unemployment from this source are published on a weekly basis for each of the States and on a monthly basis for each of the 150 major labor market areas. In addition, the Department of Labor publishes a monthly report presenting detailed information on personal and economic characteristics of the insured unemployed—sex, age, occupation, industry attachment, and duration of current spell of insured unemployment—by States. The information is obtained through the cooperation of the State and local offices of the State employment security agencies.
>
> Figures on unemployment insurance do not include persons who have exhausted their benefit rights, new workers who have not had sufficient work experience to establish eligibility for unemployment insurance, and persons who worked in establishments not covered by unemployment insurance systems. About 80 percent of all nonfarm employees are covered by unemployment insurance systems. Excluded are mainly those workers in agriculture, State and local governments, domestic service, self-employment, and unpaid family work. Also excluded are some who work in nonprofit organizations and in certain small firms. On the other hand some workers who receive benefits are partially employed and would not be counted as unemployed in the household survey.
>
> This presents a statistical problem in that total unemployment figures for the labor force are collected for the Nation as a whole, but not for individual areas. In order to provide information on total unemployment in greater geographic detail, a method has been developed for estimating total unemployment for states and local labor market areas using insured unemployment and payroll employment figures as a base. The national system of area classifications according to adequacy of labor supply is based primarily on these estimates. A total of 150 major labor market areas are classified on this basis for each month. . . .

The monthly report issued by the Department of Labor, presenting detailed information on personal and economic characteristics of the insured unemployed, has been expanded to include information on color and ethnicity of claimants. In 1980, over 97 percent of all wage and salary employment, including state and local government, was covered by unemployment insurance systems.

Prior to 1973, unemployment estimates were developed from UI data through a series of computational steps, termed the Handbook method, which was the only means used in developing state and local area labor force and unemployment estimates. The method involved a series of estimations based on data for three categories of unemployed workers: "(1) Those who were last employed in industries covered by State UI laws; (2) those who were last employed in noncovered industries; and (3) those who either entered the labor force for the first time, or reentered after a period of separation. . . . The covered category consists of those unemployed workers who are currently collecting UI benefits, have exhausted their benefits, have been disqualified from receiving benefits, and have delayed filing for benefits."

Beginning in 1973, a new system for developing labor force estimates was introduced which combined the Handbook method with the concepts, definitions, and estimation controls from the CPS. State samples were expanded, and "beginning in January 1978, monthly CPS data were introduced as the official labor force estimates at the statewide level for the 10 largest States—California, Florida, Illinois, Massachusetts, Michigan, New Jersey, New York, Ohio, Pennsylvania, and Texas; and for two areas—Los Angeles-Long Beach Standard Metropolitan Statistical Area (SMSA) and New York City." Under the federal-state cooperative program, the UI data base for all states and areas has been standardized "so that the Handbook method data is consistent with the concept and definition of unemployment used in the CPS. . . . Currently, monthly estimates of employment and unemployment are prepared in the State agencies for some 5,000 geographic areas which include all States, LMA's [labor market areas], and counties and cities with 50,000 or more population."

Monthly unemployment data are available in *Employment and Earnings* and the *Monthly Labor Review,* publications of the Bureau of Labor Statistics.

Source references: Solomon Barkin, *Emerging Unemployment Problems in the Western World* (Amherst: Univ. of Massachusetts, Labor Relations & Research Center, Reprint 65, 1981); Irving Bernstein (ed.), *Unemployment: Problems and Policies; Selected Papers* (Los Angeles: UC, Institute of IR, 1976); Clair Brown, "Unemployment Theory and Policy, 1946–1980," *IR,* Spring 1983; Kim B. Clark and Lawrence H. Summers, *The Dynamics of Unemployment,* A Report Prepared for the Office of the Assistant Secretary for Policy, Evaluation and Research (Washington: U.S. Dept. of Labor, 1981); Martin Feldstein, "The Economics of the New Unemployment," *The Public Interest,* Fall 1973; Robert H. Ferguson, *Unemployment: Its Scope, Measurement, and Effect on Poverty* (2d ed., Ithaca: NYSSILR, Cornell Univ., Bull. no. 53–2, 1971); Irving Leveson, *The Unemployment Problem: Its Nature, Extent and Responsiveness to Public and Private Initiatives* (Croton-on-Hudson: Hudson Institute, Special Issues in the Public Interest no. 1, 1977); Arthur M. Okun (ed.), *The Battle Against Unemployment* (rev. ed., New York: Norton, 1972); Frank C. Pierson, *The Minimum Level of Unemployment and Public Policy* (Kalamazoo: Upjohn Institute for Employment Research, 1980); Richard Rosen, "Identifying States and Areas Prone to High and Low Unemployment," *MLR,* March 1980; Paul M. Ryscavage, "Employment Problems and Poverty: Examining the Linkages," *MLR,* June 1982; Bernhard Schwab, "Dealing with Unemployment—What are the Alternatives?" *Sloan Management Review,* Summer 1979; Guy Standing, "The Notion of Voluntary Unemployment," *ILR,* Sept./Oct. 1981; U.S. Advisory Commission on Intergovernmental Relations, *The Federal Role in the Federal System: The Dynamics of Growth. Reducing Unemployment: Intergovernmental Dimensions of a National Problem* (Washington: 1982); U.S. Dept. of Labor, BLS, *BLS Handbook of Methods, Volume 1* (Washington: Bull. 2134–1, 1982); ______, *Employment and Unemployment: A Report on 1980* (Washington: Special Labor Force Report 244, 1981); ______, *Geographic Profile of Employment and Unemployment, 1981* (Washington: Bull. 2156, 1982); ______, *How the Government Measures Unemployment* (Washington: Report 505, 1977); ______, *Questions and Answers on Popular Labor Force Topics* (Washington: Report 522, 1978); ______, *Unemployment and Its Effect on Family Income in 1980* (Washington: Bull. 2148, 1982); U.S. Dept. of Labor, Manpower Adm., *Mobility and Worker Adaptation to Economic Change in the United States* (Washington: Research Bull. 1, 1963); U.S. National Commission on Employment and Unemployment Statistics, *Counting the Labor Force* (Washington: 1979); ______, *Counting the Labor Force: Readings in Labor Force Statistics, Appendix, Vol. III* (Washington: 1979); ______, *An Evaluation of Unemployment Data Needs in Macro Models,* by Jeffery M. Perloff and Michael L. Wachter (Washington:

Background Paper 17, 1978); U.S. President's Committee to Appraise Employment and Unemployment Statistics, *Measuring Employment and Unemployment* (Washington: 1962).

See also CURRENT POPULATION SURVEY (CPS), CYCLICAL UNEMPLOYMENT, DISCOURAGED WORKERS, EMPLOYMENT, FRICTIONAL UNEMPLOYMENT, HARD CORE OF UNEMPLOYMENT, LABOR FORCE, SEASONAL UNEMPLOYMENT, SECULAR UNEMPLOYMENT, STRUCTURAL UNEMPLOYMENT, SUBEMPLOYMENT, TECHNOLOGICAL UNEMPLOYMENT, UNEMPLOYED.

unemployment, cyclical *See* CYCLICAL UNEMPLOYMENT.

unemployment, disguised *See* DISGUISED UNEMPLOYMENT.

unemployment, frictional *See* FRICTIONAL UNEMPLOYMENT.

unemployment, normal *See* NORMAL UNEMPLOYMENT.

unemployment, persistent *See* PERSISTENT UNEMPLOYMENT.

unemployment, priority *See* PRIORITY UNEMPLOYMENT.

unemployment, seasonal *See* SEASONAL UNEMPLOYMENT.

unemployment, secular *See* SECULAR UNEMPLOYMENT.

unemployment, structural *See* STRUCTURAL UNEMPLOYMENT.

unemployment, technological *See* TECHNOLOGICAL UNEMPLOYMENT.

unemployment benefits Weekly dollar amounts available to unemployed workers under state unemployment compensation laws. The benefits provide a minimum and maximum weekly amount under the law. Some states also provide dependency allowances. Almost all of the states provide a maximum number of weeks of benefits available under their law.

Source references: AFL-CIO, Maritime Trades Dept., *Unemployment and the Worker* (Washington: 1975); Robert Black and Cyrus Karr, *Estimating Outlays for Unemployment Compensation Programs* (Washington: U.S. Congressional Budget Office, Technical Analysis Paper no. 1, 1976); Paul L. Burgess and Jerry L. Kingston, "The Impact of Unemployment Insurance Benefits on Reemployment Success," *ILRR*, Oct. 1976; Richard J. Butler and Thomas R. Sisti, "Impact of Experience Rating and UI Benefits on Unemployment: The Neglected Firm Side," *Proceedings of the 33d A/M, IRRA*, ed. by Barbara Dennis (Madison: 1981); Walter Corson and Walter Nicholson, *The Federal Supplemental Benefits Program; An Appraisal of Emergency Extended Unemployment Insurance Benefits* (Kalamazoo: Upjohn Institute for Employment Research, 1982); William Stanley Devino, *Exhaustion of Unemployment Benefits During a Recession* (East Lansing: Michigan State Univ., Labor and IRC, 1960); Ronald G. Ehrenberg and Ronald L. Oaxaca, "Impacts of Unemployment Insurance on the Duration of Unemployment and the Post-Unemployed Wage," *Proceedings of the 28th A/M, IRRA*, ed. by James Stern and Barbara Dennis (Madison: 1976); Gary S. Fields, "Direct Labor Market Effects of Unemployment Insurance," *IR*, Feb. 1977; Phyllis H. Fineshriber, "Impact on Unemployment Compensation of the Increased Labor Force Participation of Women," *Proceedings of the 31st A/M, IRRA*, ed. by Barbara Dennis (Madison: 1979); Arleen Gilliam, "The Need for an Adequate Unemployment Compensation System," *Proceedings of the 34th A/M, IRRA*, ed. by Barbara Dennis (Madison: 1982); Joseph E. Hight, "Insured Unemployment Rates, Extended Benefits, and Unemployment Insurance Exhaustions," *Proceedings of the 28th A/M, IRRA*, ed. by James Stern and Barbara Dennis (Madison: 1976); Jerry L. Kingston and Paul L. Burgess, "How Do UI Benefits Affect the Benefit Utilization Rate," *IR*, Feb. 1977; Richard A. Lester, *Implications of Labor Force Developments for Unemployment Benefits* (Princeton: Princeton Univ., IR Section, 1961); Paul A. Mackin, *Extended Unemployment Benefits* (Kalamazoo: Upjohn Institute for Employment Research, 1965); Stephen T. Marston, "Effects of Unemployment Benefits Paid to Voluntary Job Leavers," *IR*, Fall 1982; Wilbur D. Mills, "Aiding the Unemployed, the First Line of Defense," *American Federationist*, Aug. 1971; Merrill G. Murray, *The Duration of Unemployment Benefits* (Kalamazoo: Upjohn Institute for Employment Research, 1974); William Papier, "Standards for Improving Maximum Unemployment Insurance Benefits," *ILRR*, April 1974; George S. Roche, *Entitlement to Unemployment Insurance Benefits* (Kalamazoo: Upjohn Institute for Employment Research, 1973); U.S. Congress, House, Committee on Ways and Means, *Information on Unemployment and Unemployment Compensation Programs* (Washington: 1975); Edward D. Wickersham, "Legislative Implications of Recent Unemployment Benefits Agreements," *LLJ*, June 1956.

See also BENEFIT YEAR, GUARANTEED ANNUAL WAGE, OUT-OF-WORK BENEFITS, SUPPLEMENTAL UNEMPLOYMENT BENEFITS, TEMPORARY EXTENDED UNEMPLOYMENT COMPENSATION.

unemployment compensation Programs providing benefits to individuals who are unemployed through no fault of their own. The state systems provide payments to eligible employees from funds obtained by payroll taxes on employers.

Source references: A. J. Hayes, "Labor Looks at Unemployment Compensation," *American Federationist*, Nov. 1959; Richard A. Lester, "The Economic Significance of Unemployment Compensation, 1948–1959," *Review of Economics and Statistics*, Nov. 1960; ———, *The Economics of Unemployment Compensation* (Princeton: Princeton Univ., IR Section, 1962); ———, "Financing of Unemployment Compensation," *ILRR*, Oct. 1960.

See also SOCIAL SECURITY ACT, UNEMPLOYMENT INSURANCE.

unemployment data Information dealing with the problem of unemployment.

Source references: Robert W. Bednarzik and Richard B. Tiller, "Area Labor Market Response to National Unemployment Patterns," *MLR*, Jan. 1982; Norman Bowers, "Probing the Issues of Unemployment Duration," *MLR*, July 1980; John E. Bregger, "Unemployment Statistics and What They Mean," *MLR*, Nov. 1971; Glen G. Cain, "The Unemployment Rate as an Economic Indicator," *MLR*, March 1979; Ewan Clague, "Adequacy of Unemployment Data for Government Uses," *MLR*, Feb. 1962; Paul O. Flaim, "The Effect of Demographic Changes on the Nation's Unemployment Rate," *MLR*, March 1979; Paul O. Flaim and Christopher G. Gellner, "An Analysis of Unemployment by Household Relationship," *MLR*, Aug. 1972; Christopher G. Gellner, "Regional Differences in Employment and Unemployment, 1957–72," *MLR*, March 1974; Howard Hayghe, "New Data Series on Families Show Most Jobless Have Working Relatives," *MLR*, Dec. 1976; Francis W. Horvath, "Forgotten Unemployment: Recall Bias in Retrospective Data," *MLR*, March 1982; Stanley Lebergott, "Unemployment Data Needs for Planning and Evaluating Policy," *MLR*, Feb. 1962; Leonard A. Lecht et al., *Labor Force Yardsticks, A Guide to Policies for Reducing Unemployment* (New York: The Conference Board, Information Bull. 45, 1978); Geoffrey H. Moore, "A New Leading Index of Employment and Unemployment," *MLR*, June 1981; Noreen L. Preston, *The Help-Wanted Index: Technical Description and Behavioral Trends* (New York: The Conference Board, Report 716, 1977); Robert N. Ray, "Dispersion Tendencies in Occupational Unemployment Rates," *MLR*, April 1976; Julius Shiskin, "Employment and Unemployment: The Doughnut or the Hole?" *MLR*, Feb. 1976; Andrew M. Sum and Thomas P. Rush, "The Geographic Structure of Unemployment Rates," *MLR*, March 1975; U.S. Dept. of Commerce, *Unemployment Rates for States and Identifiable Local Governments Under Title I of the Public Works Employment Act of 1976 (PL 94–369)* (Washington: 1976); U.S. National Commission on Employment and Unemployment Statistics, *An Appraisal of New Sources of Employment and Unemployment Statistics*, by Morris M. Kleiner (Washington: Background Paper 32, 1979); ———, *Concepts and Data Needs; Counting the Labor Force, Appendix Volume 1* (Washington: 1980); ———, *Data Collection, Processing and Presentation: National and Local; Counting the Labor Force, Appendix Volume II* (Washington: 1980); ———, *Employment and Unemployment Statistics as Indexes of Economic Activity and Capacity Utilization*, by Richard Ruggles (Washington:

Background Paper 28, 1979); ———, *Employment and Unemployment Statistics for Nonmetropolitan Areas*, by Sigurd R. Nilsen (Washington: Background Paper 33, 1979); ———, *Employment and Unemployment Statistics in Collective Bargaining*, by Daniel Quinn Mills (Washington: Background Paper 10, 1978); ———, *Improving the Presentation of Employment and Unemployment Statistics*, by Geoffrey H. Moore (Washington: Background Paper 22, 1978); ———, *Measuring Types of Unemployment: Implications for Unemployment Statistics*, by Robert S. Goldfarb (Washington: Background Paper 8, 1978); ———, *Microeconomic Aspects of Employment and Unemployment Statistics*, by Frank P. Stafford (Washington: Background Paper 9, 1978); ———, *On the Seasonal Adjustment of Economic Time Series Aggregates: A Case Study of the Unemployment Rate*, by Estela B. Dagum (Washington: Background Paper 31, 1979); Ronald S. Warren, Jr., "A Method to Measure Flow and Duration as Unemployment Rate Components," *MLR*, March 1977; Martin Ziegler, "Efforts to Improve Estimates of State and Local Unemployment," *MLR*, Nov. 1977.

See also UNEMPLOYMENT.

unemployment insurance The program set up under the Social Security Act of 1935 providing a federal-state program. All of the states have established unemployment insurance funds which are supported through payroll taxes. Payments are available after a brief waiting period to individuals who are unemployed and they receive insurance or unemployment benefits for a number of weeks. Individuals who obtain unemployment insurance are required to report to the local Employment Service offices to indicate their availability to accept employment if employment opportunities are available. The detailed administration of unemployment insurance is handled under state laws.

Source references: Joseph M. Becker, *The Adequacy of the Benefit Amount in Unemployment Insurance* (Kalamazoo: Upjohn Institute, 1961); Saul J. Blaustein, *Job and Income Security for Unemployed Workers, Some New Directions* (Kalamazoo: Upjohn Institute for Employment Research, 1981); Philip Booth, "Unemployment Insurance and the Challenge of the 1960's," *Proceedings of the 14th A/M, IRRA*, ed. by Gerald Somers (Madison: 1962); Sol C. Chaikin, "Redesigning Unemployment Compensation," *American Federationist*, Nov. 1979; Jack Chernick and Charles R. Naef, "Legal and Political Aspects of the Integration of Unemployment Insurance and SUB Plans," *ILRR*, Oct. 1958; John D. Crosier, "Current Controversial Issues in Unemployment Insurance; Fund Solvency—Is Anyone Serious?" *Proceedings of the 34th A/M, IRRA*, ed. by Barbara Dennis (Madison: 1982); David L. Edgell and Stephen A. Wandner, "Unemployment Insurance: Its Economic Performance," *MLR*, April 1974; G. Joachim Elterich, "Estimating the Cost of Extending Jobless Insurance to Farmworkers," *MLR*, May 1978; Martin S. Feldstein, "Unemployment Insurance: Time for Reform," *Harvard BR*, March/April 1975; William Haber and Merrill G. Murray, *Unemployment Insurance in the American Economy: An Historical Review and Analysis* (Homewood: Irwin, 1966); Terrence C. Halpin, "The Effect of Unemployment Insurance on Seasonal Fluctuations in Employment," *ILRR*, April 1979; Daniel S. Hamermesh, *Jobless Pay and the Economy* (Baltimore: Johns Hopkins UP, 1977); ———, *Unemployment Insurance and the Older American* (Kalamazoo: Upjohn Institute for Employment Research, 1980); Joseph A. Hickey, "Unemployment Insurance Covers Additional 9 Million Workers," *MLR*, May 1978; Arnold Katz and Joseph E. Hight, "The Economics of Unemployment Insurance: A Symposium, Overview," *ILRR*, July 1977; Richard A. Lester and Philip Booth, "Is Unemployment Insurance Geared to Today's Unemployment Risks?" *Labor Market and Social Security* (Kalamazoo: Upjohn Institute, 1962); Paul J. Mackin, *Benefit Financing in Unemployment Insurance: A Problem of Balancing Responsibilities* (Kalamazoo: Upjohn Institute for Employment Research, 1978); Harry Malisoff, "The Challenge of Unemployment Insurance," *ILRR*, Oct. 1960; Charles E. McLure, Jr., "The Incidence of the Financing of Unemployment Insurance," *ILRR*, July 1977; Raymond Munts, "A New Role for Unemployment Insurance," *American Federa-*

tionist, June 1965; Raymond Munts and Irwin Garfinkel, *The Work Disincentive Effects of Unemployment Insurance* (Kalamazoo: Upjohn Institute for Employment Research, 1974); Daniel Nelson, *Unemployment Insurance: The American Experience, 1915–1935* (Madison: Univ. of Wisconsin Press, 1969); Arthur Padilla, "The Unemployment Insurance System: Its Financial Structure," *MLR*, Dec. 1981; Diana Runner, "Unemployment Insurance Laws: Legislative Revisions in 1982," *MLR*, Jan. 1983; Herman M. Somers, "Some Issues in the Improvement of the Federal-State Unemployment Insurance Program," *Proceedings of the 12th A/M, IRRA*, ed. by David Johnson (Madison: 1960); Tax Foundation, Inc., *Unemployment Insurance: Trends and Issues* (Washington: Research Pub. no. 35, 1982); U.S. Congress, Senate, Committee on Finance, *Staff Data and Materials Related to the Unemployment Compensation Program* (Washington: 1979); U.S. Congressional Budget Office, *Unemployment Compensation: A Background Report* (Washington: Background Paper 15, 1976); U.S. Dept. of Labor, ETA, *Financing America's Unemployment Compensation Program* (Washington: Unemployment Insurance Technical Staff Paper 4, 1979); ———, *Significant Provisions of State Unemployment Insurance Laws, July 4, 1982* (Washington: 1982); U.S. GAO, *Unemployment Insurance—Inequities and Work Disincentives in the Current System* (Washington: 1979); ———, *Unemployment Insurance—Need to Reduce Unequal Treatment of Claimants and Improve Benefit Payment Controls and Tax Collections* (Washington: 1978); U.S. National Commission on Unemployment Compensation, *Unemployment Compensation: Final Report* (Washington: 1980); ———, *Unemployment Compensation: Studies and Research, Vols. 1–3* (Washington: 1980); Upjohn Institute for Employment Research, *Strengthening Unemployment Insurance, Program Improvements;* Report on Recommendations of the Institute's Unemployment Insurance Research Advisory Committee (Kalamazoo: 1975); Clair Vickery, "Unemployment Insurance: A Positive Reappraisal," *IR*, Winter 1979; George M. Von Furstenberg, "Stabilization Characteristics of Unemployment Insurance," *ILRR*, April 1976; Wayne Vroman, "Unemployment Insurance: New Goals for the 1980s?" *Proceedings of the 31st A/M, IRRA*, ed. by Barbara Dennis (Madison: 1979); C. Arthur Williams, Jr., "Meeting the Risk of Unemployment: Changing Societal Responses," *Annals*, May 1979.

See also NEEDS TEST, SOCIAL SECURITY ACT, UNEMPLOYMENT BENEFITS.

Unemployment Insurance Service (UIS) A division of the Bureau of Employment Security, it was transferred from the Federal Security Agency to the Department of Labor in 1949. When the Bureau was abolished in 1969, the functions of the Bureau and the UIS were transferred to the Manpower Administration. It is currently a division of the Employment and Training Administration.

UIS administers, among other programs, the federal-state unemployment insurance system, trade adjustment assistance, and supplemental or extended benefit programs.

Source reference: U.S. Dept. of Labor, *The Anvil and the Plow, A History of the United States Department of Labor* (Washington: 1963).

See also EMPLOYMENT AND TRAINING ADMINISTRATION (ETA).

unemployment relief *See* RELIEF.

unfair employer An employer who is guilty of an unfair labor practice under federal, state, or local law or an employer who refuses to recognize a union, or employ its members.

See also UNFAIR LABOR PRACTICES, UNFAIR LISTS.

unfair goods Products or goods not produced under union conditions.

unfair labor practice proceeding A proceeding under federal, state, or local labor law to determine whether an employer or union is guilty of an unfair labor practice.

unfair labor practices Actions of employers or unions that are prohibited as unfair labor practices under federal, state, or local labor relations statutes. Section 8 of the Taft-Hartley Act enumerates the employer and union unfair labor practices under the federal law. There are six unfair labor practices of employers. In capsule form, they are:

(1) Interference with employee rights under the Act;
(2) Domination of unions;
(3) Discrimination against employees for union or concerted activities;
(4) Retaliation against employees for invoking their rights under the Act;
(5) Refusal to bargain with a majority representative of the employees; and
(6) Execution of hot-cargo agreements with unions.

The union unfair labor practices are more complicated, several being divided into parts on the basis of the objective of the action. In brief, they are:

(1) Restraining or coercing employees or employers in the exercise of their statutory rights;
(2) Causing an employer to unlawfully discriminate against an employee;
(3) Refusing to bargain with an employer;
(4) Striking, inducing others to strike, and threatening, coercing, or restraining any person for the objects of forcing an employer or self-employed person to join a union or enter into a hot-cargo contract, forcing any person to stop doing business with another person (secondary boycott), forcing another employer to bargain with a union not certified as bargaining agent, or forcing an employer to assign work to a particular union, trade, or craft (jurisdictional strike);
(5) Requiring employees covered by union-security agreements to pay excessive or discriminatory initiation fees;
(6) Causing an employer to pay for services not to be performed (featherbedding);
(7) Engaging in recognitional or organizational picketing where another union is lawfully recognized as bargaining agent, a valid election having been conducted within the preceding 12 months, or the picketing is conducted without an election petition being filed within a reasonable period of time.

The charges of unfair labor practices are adjudicated by the NLRB. If violations are found, cease and desist orders are issued, which are enforceable in the federal courts of appeals.

Source references: John L. Blackman, Jr., "Relative Severity of Employer Unfair Labor Practices," *LLJ*, Feb. 1971; BNA, *The Labor Reform Law* (Washington: 1959); J. Gary DiNunno, "J. P. Stevens: Anatomy of an Outlaw," *American Federationist*, April 1976; Charles A. Edwards, "Protection of the Complaining Employee: How Much is Too Much?" *Employee Relations LJ*, Autumn 1980; Carrol Hament, "Are Instructions to Supervisors to Commit Unfair Labor Practices Unlawful *Per Se*?" *LLJ*, May 1975; Dell Bush Johannesen, "Continuing Controversy: New Remedies for Old Unfair Labor Practices," *LLJ*, Feb. 1972; ———, "Disciplinary Fines as Interference with Protected Rights: Section 8(b)(1)(A)," *LLJ*, May 1973; Randall G. Kesselring and Paul Brinker, "Discriminatory Treatment of Employees Under Section 8(a)(2)," *LLJ*, Oct. 1979; ———, "Employer Domination Under Section 8(a)(2)," *LLJ*, June 1979; ———, "Financial and Material Support Under Section 8(a)(2)," *LLJ*, Jan. 1980; Bernard T. King, "Pre-Election Conduct—Expanding Employer Rights and Some New and Renewed Perspectives," *Industrial Relations LJ*, Summer 1977; Philip C. Lederer, "'*W'right* Line or Spur Track?" *LLJ*, Feb. 1982; "Liability Through Agency—The Needless Lawsuit?" *LLJ*, March 1981; Abbe David Lowell, "Dow Chemical: Restricting the Availability of Self-Help Measures in Labor Disputes," *IR Law Digest*, Summer 1977; H. L. Luxemberg and B. C. Roberts, "Unfair Labor Practices Under the Taft-Hartley Act—A Comparative Study," *Brooklyn LR*, Dec. 1947; Barry A. Macey, "Does Employer Implementation of Employee Production Teams Violate Section 8(a)(2) of the National Labor Relations Act?" *IR Law Digest*, Jan. 1975; Douglas S. McDowell and Kenneth C. Huhn, *NLRB Remedies for Unfair Labor Practices* (Philadelphia: Univ. of Pennsylvania, Wharton School, Industrial Research Unit, LRRP Series Report no. 12, 1976); Midwest Center for Public Sector Labor Relations, Indiana Univ., *Questions and Answers on Unfair Labor Practices, A Practitioner's Guide* (Bloomington: 1977); "New Standards for Domination and Support Under Section

8(a)(2)," *IR Law Digest*, July 1973; William S. Ostan, "Bargaining Orders: *Gissel* and *United Dairy Farmers* Revisited," *Employee Relations LJ*, Autumn 1982; William J. Payne and Donald F. Sileo, "Self-Enforcement Under the National Labor Relations Act: Disavowals of Unfair Labor Practice Conduct," *LLJ*, Dec. 1982; Sylvester Petro, "Employer Unfair Practices Under the Taft-Hartley Act," *LLJ*, April 1952, May 1952, and June 1952; Joseph A. Pichler and H. Gordon Fitch, "And Women Must Weep: The NLRB as Film Critic," *ILRR*, April 1975; George Schatzki, "Breach of Contract and Section 8(a)(5) of the National Labor Relations Act," *Labor Law Developments 1972*, Proceedings of the 18th Annual Institute on Labor Law, SLF (New York: Bender, 1972); ———, "NLRB Resolution of Contract Disputes Under Section 8(a)(5)," *IR Law Digest*, July 1972; Rex Weil, "Pretrial Discovery in NLRB Unfair Labor Practice Cases," *IR Law Digest*, Spring 1978.

See also LABOR MANAGEMENT RELATIONS ACT OF 1947.

unfair labor practice strike A work stoppage caused or prolonged, in whole or in part, by actions of the employer which are held to be unfair labor practices under federal, state, or local labor laws.

See also ECONOMIC STRIKE.

unfair lists Lists of either firms or products considered by a labor organization to be unfair to the union.

See also BUCKS' STOVE AND RANGE CASE.

unfunded A pension fund for which there has been no advance funding and from which payments are made when actual needs arise to pay the pensioners. A pay-as-you-go plan.

Source reference: BNA, *Pensions and Profit Sharing* (3d ed., Washington: 1964).

uniformed services Usually refers to police officers and fire fighters. The term "uniformed protective services" is sometimes used instead.

Source reference: Jack Stieber, *Public Employee Unionism: Structure, Growth, Policy* (Washington: Brookings Institution, 1973).

Uniform Guidelines on Employee Selection Procedures Jointly adopted in 1978 by the EEOC, the Civil Service Commission, the Department of Labor, and the Department of Justice, the Uniform Guidelines apply to persons subject to Title VII of the Civil Rights Act of 1964, Executive Order 11246, and other equal employment opportunity requirements of federal law. They do not apply to the Age Discrimination in Employment Act and the Rehabilitation Act of 1973. The guidelines are "designed to assist employers, labor organizations, employment agencies, and licensing and certification boards to comply with requirements of Federal law prohibiting employment practices which discriminate on grounds of race, color, religion, sex, and national origin [by providing] . . . a framework for determining the proper use of tests and other selection procedures." The guidelines apply only to employment selection procedures and not to questions of the lawfulness of a seniority system or to recruitment practices. Selection procedures covered include paper and pencil tests; assessment techniques such as performance tests, training programs, physical, educational, and work experience requirements; informal interviews; and unscored application forms.

The Uniform Guidelines take a "bottom line" approach in evaluating adverse impact based on the 80 percent rule, i.e., if the total selection process for a job does not adversely affect a protected group, the individual components "in usual circumstances" need not be evaluated or validated.

Source references: U.S. EEOC, "Uniform Guidelines on Employee Selection Procedures," 29 C.F.R. 1607; Thomas G. Abram, "Overview of Uniform Selection Guidelines: Pitfalls for the Unwary Employer," *LLJ*, Aug. 1979; R. Lawrence Ashe, Jr., "Job-Related Selection Procedures Under the Uniform Guidelines in the 1980s," *Labor Law Developments 1981*, Proceedings of the 27th Annual Institute on Labor Law, SLF (New York: Bender, 1981); Thomas P. Dhanens, "Implications of the New EEOC Guidelines," *Personnel*, Sept./Oct. 1979; Gary W. Florkowski, "Alternative Selection Procedures and the Uniform Guidelines: Improving the Quality of Employer Investigations," *Employee Relations LJ*, Spring 1983; Alan M. Koral, "Practical Application of the Uniform Guidelines: What to Do 'Til the Agency

Comes," *Employee Relations LJ*, Spring 1980; David E. Robertson, "New Directions in EEO Guidelines," *PJ*, July 1978; Stephen Rubenfeld, "The Uniform Guidelines: A Personnel Decision-Making Perspective," *Employee Relations LJ*, Summer 1981; Allan Sloan, "An Analysis of Uniform Guidelines on Employee Selection Procedures," *Employee Relations LJ*, Winter 1978/79; U.S. GAO, *Problems with Federal Equal Employment Opportunity Guidelines on Employee Selection Procedures Need to be Resolved* (Washington: 1978).

See also ALBEMARLE PAPER CO. V. MOODY, "BOTTOM LINE," CONSTRUCT VALIDITY, CONTENT VALIDITY, CRITERION VALIDITY, EIGHTY PERCENT (80%) RULE.

unilateral action Action taken by one of the parties to a collective bargaining relationship independently of the desires or wishes of the other, without notice or consultation.

Source reference: Malcolm H. Gotterer, "Union Reactions to Unilateral Changes in Work Measurement Procedures," *Personnel Psychology*, Winter 1961.

union *See* LABOR ORGANIZATION, LABOR UNION, NATIONAL AND INTERNATIONAL UNIONS.

union, certified *See* CERTIFICATION.

union, closed *See* CLOSED UNION.

union, company *See* COMPANY UNION.

union, company-dominated *See* COMPANY-DOMINATED UNION.

union, craft *See* CRAFT UNION.

union, dual *See* DUAL UNIONISM.

union, independent *See* INDEPENDENT UNIONS.

union, independent local *See* LOCAL INDEPENDENT UNION.

union, industrial *See* INDUSTRIAL UNION.

union, inside *See* INSIDE UNION.

union, internal affairs of *See* INTERNAL AFFAIRS OF UNIONS.

union, international *See* INTERNATIONAL UNION.

union, lobbying *See* LABOR LOBBY.

union, local *See* LOCAL UNION.

union, local industrial *See* LOCAL INDUSTRIAL UNION.

union, minority *See* MINORITY UNION.

union, national *See* NATIONAL UNION.

union, noncomplying *See* NONCOMPLYING UNION.

union, nonoperating *See* NONOPERATING UNION.

union, open *See* OPEN UNION.

union, paper *See* PAPER LOCALS.

union, parent *See* PARENT UNION.

union, plant *See* PLANT UNION.

union, semi-industrial *See* SEMI-INDUSTRIAL UNION.

union, single-company *See* SINGLE-COMPANY UNION.

union, successor *See* SUCCESSOR UNION.

union, unaffiliated *See* UNAFFILIATED UNION.

union agreement *See* AGREEMENT, COLLECTIVE.

union assessments *See* ASSESSMENTS.

union-association bargaining *See* ASSOCIATION AGREEMENT.

union baiting *See* ANTI-UNION PRACTICES.

union business agent *See* BUSINESS AGENT, SHOP CHAIRPERSON, SHOP STEWARD, TRAMPING COMMITTEE.

union button *See* BUTTON.

union certification *See* CERTIFICATION.

union committeeman *See* COMMITTEEMAN, SHOP STEWARD.

union constitution *See* CONSTITUTION AND BYLAWS.

union contract *See* AGREEMENT, COLLECTIVE.

union convention *See* CONVENTION, LABOR CONVENTION.

union decertification *See* DECERTIFICATION.

union democracy *See* DEMOCRACY.

union discipline The procedures and powers unions exercise over their constituent bodies and members. Most constitutions and bylaws establish procedures for review of cases where the union has applied sanctions and disciplined individual members.

Source references: Charles B. Craver, "The Boeing Decision: A Blow to Federalism, Individual Rights and Stare Decisis," *IR Law Digest,* Fall 1974; Francis T. Coleman, "Union Discipline Under Section 8(b)(1)(A) of the National Labor Relations Act: The Emergence of a New Trilogy," *IR Law Digest,* July 1971; Samuel Fried, "Limitations on the Right of Unions to Discipline Supervisors," *Boston Univ. LR,* Nov. 1973; Jeffrey L. Harrison, "Union Discipline and the Employer-Employee Relationship," *LLJ,* April 1971; Paul R. Hays, "The Union and Its Members," *NYU 11th Annual Conference on Labor,* ed. by Emanuel Stein (Albany: Bender, 1958); John Hutchinson, *George Meany and the Wayward* (Los Angeles: UC, Institute of IR, Reprint no. 224, 1972); Dell Bush Johanneson, "Disciplinary Fines as Interference with Protected Rights: Section 8(b)(1)(A)," *LLJ,* May 1973; Thomas J. Keeline, *NLRB and Judicial Control of Union Discipline* (Philadelphia: Univ. of Pennsylvania, Wharton School, Industrial Research Unit, LRPP Series Report no. 13, 1976); Leon E. Lunden, "Union Disciplinary Powers and Procedures: II. Trial Powers and Procedures at the Local Union Level," *MLR,* March 1963; Michael E. Norton, Jr., "Union Discipline of Supervisor Members," *IR Law Digest,* Jan. 1975; Stephen I. Schlossberg and Stanley Lubin, "Union Fines and Union Discipline Under the National Labor Relations Act," *NYU 23d Annual Conference on Labor,* ed. by Thomas Christensen and Andrea Christensen (New York: Bender, 1971); Martin C. Seham, "Limitations Upon and Directions of a Union's Right to Discipline its Members," *NYU 25th Annual Conference on Labor* (New York: Bender, 1973); Clyde Summers, "Disciplinary Powers of Unions," *ILRR,* July 1950; ———, "Disciplinary Procedures of Unions," *ILRR,* Oct. 1950; David A. Swankin, "Union Disciplinary Powers and Procedures: I. Ground for Trial of Members and Local Officers," *MLR,* Feb. 1963; Philip Taft, "Union Discipline," *NYU 26th Annual Conference on Labor,* ed. by Emanuel Stein and S. Theodore Reiner (New York: Bender, 1974); "Union Power to Discipline Members Who Resign," *IR Law Digest,* Jan. 1974; Harry H. Wellington, "Union Fines and Workers' Rights," *IR Law Digest,* Spring 1977.

See also DISCIPLINE, EXPULSION FROM UNION, LABOR-MANAGEMENT REPORTING AND DISCLOSURE ACT OF 1959.

union dues *See* DUES.

union education activity *See* LABOR EDUCATION.

union elections Procedures established by union constitutions and bylaws to govern the election of union officials. Typically the rules state eligibility requirements, tenure, how elections are to be conducted (secret ballot, referendum, etc.), procedures for determining and certifying results to the membership, and means of contesting a certified result.

A number of provisions of the Labor-Management Reporting and Disclosure Act of 1959 regulate the election of union officers with the prime objective to safeguard democratic processes within the union.

Regulations issued under Title IV set out procedures to cover the following problems in elections:

(1) Who must be elected and how often;
(2) Basic provisions for nominating procedures, including reasonable notice;
(3) Campaign rules;
(4) Election procedures, including the meaning of "membership in good standing" and what constitutes a "secret ballot";
(5) Procedure for protesting elections and how a challenge may be handled.

The Office of Labor-Management Standards Enforcement of the U.S. Department of Labor has a checklist on election procedures with a series of questions directed to labor organizations to ascertain whether they conform to the provisions of the law. The checklist reads as follows:

Are elections held within the 3-, 4-, or 5-year limit prescribed by the Act?

Do members receive reasonable opportunity for nomination, including notice of the:

A. Offices to be filed;

B. Time for submitting nominations;

C. Place for submitting nominations; and

D. Proper form for submitting nominations?

Do members have reasonable time to nominate candidates?

Do all members in good standing have an opportunity to be nominated, subject only to reasonable qualifications uniformly imposed?

Are rules governing eligibility for nomination fair, reasonable, and uniformly imposed?

Do all candidates have equal opportunity to use membership lists, distribute literature, and campaign for office?

If there is a union-shop, maintenance-of-membership, or similar agreement, do all bona fide candidates have the opportunity to inspect membership lists of all members covered by the union-security clause, once within 30 days before the election?

Are no funds received from dues, assessments, or similar levies used to promote the candidacy of any person? Are no employer funds so used?

Are all officers and all delegates to conventions at which they vote for officers elected by secret ballot?

Do all members in good standing have an opportunity to vote, limited only by reasonable rules uniformly imposed?

Are election notices mailed to members at least 15 days before elections?

Are candidates given the opportunity to have observers at each polling place and at each place where the ballots are counted?

Can members support candidates of their choice without being subject to penalty, discipline, improper interference, or reprisal of any kind?

Do election procedures conform to the constitution and bylaws and are they consistent with the provisions of the act?

If there are persons barred under sec. 504(a) of the LMRDA or 29 CFR 208.36, have they been disqualified from seeking and holding office?

Are the ballots of each local counted and a report showing the vote by locals published separately in elections required to be held by title IV of the act?

Are ballots and other election records preserved for at least 1 year?

Source references: Mary Dickenson, "The Effects of Parties and Factions on Trade Union Elections," *BJIR*, July 1981; Sara Gamm, "The Election Base of National Union Executive Boards," *ILRR*, April 1979; Leonard J. Lurie, "Union Elections—Some Unresolved Problems," *NYU 15th Annual Conference on Labor*, ed. by Emanuel Stein (Albany: Bender, 1962); Martha F. Riche, "Union Election Challenges Under the LMRDA," *MLR*, Jan. 1965; U.S. Dept. of Labor, LMSA, *Electing Union Officers* (Washington: Technical Assistance Aid no. 5, 1980); ———, *Union Election Cases Under the Labor-Management Reporting and Disclosure Act, 1966–1970* (Washington: 1972); ———, *Union Officer Elections and Trusteeships Case Digest* (Washington: 1980).

See also REPRESENTATION ELECTIONS.

union fees *See* FEES, INITIATION FEE.

union growth *See* UNION MEMBERSHIP.

union health and medical programs *See* HEALTH BENEFIT PROGRAMS, HEALTH INSURANCE.

union hiring hall *See* HIRING HALL.

union housing Provision of housing accommodations by unions for their members. Efforts have been made by both local and national unions to provide consumer goods and services at low cost. Some of these efforts have been particularly fruitful in the area of union housing. One of the best known enterprises of this kind is that of the Amalgamated Clothing and Textile Workers, which has built its own apartments in New York City for rental to its members.

union incorporation *See* INCORPORATION OF UNIONS.

union insignia *See* BUTTON, UNION LABEL (BUG).

union insurance plans *See* INSURANCE PLAN.

unionism *See* LABOR ORGANIZATION.

union jurisdiction *See* JURISDICTION, UNION.

union label agreement A procedure used to obtain standardized agreements with a degree of uniformity in wage and other working conditions through union label agreements which permit employers to use the label if they agree to the working conditions prescribed in the agreement.

Union Label and Service Trades Department One of the AFL-CIO trade and industrial departments. Its bimonthly publication is the *Label Letter.*

Address: AFL-CIO Building, 815 16th St., N.W., Washington, D.C. 20006. Tel. (202) 628–2131

See also AFL-CIO DEPARTMENTS.

union label (bug) The emblem attached to or printed on an article to indicate that it has been made by union labor or under union conditions. Unions in the garment and printing industries have been among the major supporters of the union label. The program to spread the use of the union label is supported by many unions. The union label department of the AFL was an indication of this interest as is the combined Union Label and Service Trades Department of the AFL-CIO.

Source references: Monroe M. Bird and James W. Robinson, "The Effectiveness of the Union Label and 'Buy Union' Campaigns," *ILRR,* July 1972; "Labor's Centennial 1881–1981: 100 Years with the Union Label," *American Federationist,* April 1981; Alexander Uhl, "The Union Label—Emblem of Dignity and Progress," *American Federationist,* May 1963.

See also BLACKLIST, FAIR LIST, JOINT LABEL, UNION LABEL AND SERVICE TRADES DEPARTMENT.

union label goods Goods produced under union conditions.

See also UNION LABEL (BUG).

union label shop An employer or company which agrees to use a union label on its product. An example of this is the National Coat and Suit Industry Recovery Board which uses such a union label.

union label trades International unions which encourage the use of the union label in their trades. The printing trades unions set up Allied Printing Trades Councils in various cities to promote and police use of the joint label.

union labor Workers organized in trade unions.

See also NONUNION EMPLOYEE.

Union Labor Party A political organization established in 1888 consisting of various remnants of the Greenback Party, some farm groups, and labor unions to take an active part in the presidential election of 1888. The group received some 150,000 votes out of a total of 11,000,000 cast in that election.

union leadership The individuals in the labor movement who have responsibility for guiding and directing the programs of their organizations, and give direction and inspiration to trade union enterprises and new developments generally. Professor C. R. Daugherty describes the characteristics of union leaders in the following statement:

> In an industrial world of rapid changes, great complexity, and frequent hostility, self-preservation depends on flexibility of methods for meeting new situations. There must be some union men continually on the watch during the period between conventions, men able to analyze and plan and make the right decisions quickly, who have brains, brawn, moral courage, and respect-inspiring personalities, who can command obedience and confidence—men in short who are good generals and good mixers. Unionists have realized that to get what they want they must have leaders of this kind. They have therefore elected and re-elected from among their members those who seemed most nearly to possess the desirable traits.

Source references: E. Wight Bakke, "Union Leadership and the Public Interest," *Proceedings of the 21st A/M, IRRA,* ed. by Gerald Somers (Madison: 1969); Jack Barbash (ed.), *Unions and Union Leadership: Their Human Meaning* (New York: Harper, 1959); Carroll R. Daugherty, *Labor Problems in American Industry* (Boston: Houghton Mifflin, 1948); George W. England, Naresh C. Agarwal, and Robert E. Trerise, "Union Leaders and Managers: A Comparison of Value Systems," *IR,* May 1971; Karen S. Koziara, Mary I. Bradley, and David A. Pierson, "Becoming a Union Leader: The Path to Local Office," *MLR,* Feb. 1982; Walter Licht and Hal Seth Barron, "Labor's Men: A Collective Biography of Union Officialdom During the New Deal Years," *Labor History,* Fall 1978; Joel Seidman and Daisy L. Tagliacozzo,

"Union Government and Union Leadership," *A Decade of Industrial Relations Research 1946–1956*, ed. by Neil W. Chamberlain, Frank C. Pierson and Theresa Wolfson (New York: Harper, IRRA Pub. no. 19, 1958); Warren R. Van Tine, *The Making of the Labor Bureaucrat: Union Leadership in the United States, 1870–1920* (Amherst: Univ. of Massachusetts Press, 1973).

See also BUSINESS AGENT, LABOR LEADER, UNION OFFICERS.

union leave Paid or unpaid excused leave for union representatives, shop stewards, and other recognized labor union officials to attend to union business, e.g., participating in union conventions.

union-made goods Products produced by unionized or organized employees.

See also UNION LABEL (BUG).

union maintenance clause *See* MAINTENANCE OF MEMBERSHIP, UNION SECURITY CLAUSES.

union-management cooperation *See* INDUSTRIAL PEACE, LABOR-MANAGEMENT COMMITTEE, LABOR-MANAGEMENT COOPERATION.

union-management relations *See* EMPLOYER-EMPLOYEE RELATIONS, INDUSTRIAL RELATIONS.

union membership All of those individuals who are members of a union. What constitutes membership depends on the provisions of the union constitution and bylaws and the practice of the individual national or local union. In some cases, membership requirements are somewhat rigid; in others they are quite flexible. Membership usually depends upon the payment of initiation fees, regular dues and special assessments, and maintaining the qualities expected of a union member. For some purposes, unions retain in membership individuals who are unemployed. They also have included veterans and others, even though their periodic dues payments or other qualifications for union membership have not been met.

Some unions allow retired members to retain full membership rights, including the right to vote at union conventions. While local union programs for retired members may consist only of social gatherings, most unions encourage projects which involve the retired worker in community services and educational and recreational activities.

Source references: AFL-CIO, *Union Membership and Employment, 1959–1979* (Washington: 1980); Joseph R. Antos, Mark Chandler, and Wesley Mellow, "Sex Differences in Union Membership," *ILRR*, Jan. 1980; Jack Barbash, "The Emergence of Urban Low-Wage Unionism," *Proceedings of the 26th A/M, IRRA*, ed. by Gerald Somers (Madison: 1974); Irving Bernstein, "The Growth of American Unions, 1945–1960," *Labor History*, Spring 1961; Harry P. Cohany, "Trends and Changes in Union Membership," *MLR*, May 1966; Walter G. Davis, "A New Look at Reaching the Union Member," *American Federationist*, May 1971; Eric Fine and Frederic Leffler, "The Accommodation of Skilled and White Collar Workers in Industrial Unions," *Industrial and Labor Relations Forum*, March 1973; J. H. Foegen, "Union Membership: Gain or Loss?" *Personnel Administration*, Jan./Feb. 1963; Richard B. Freeman and James L. Medoff, "New Estimates of Private Sector Unionism in the United States," *ILRR*, Jan. 1979; Richard A. Givens, "The Enfranchisement of Employees Arbitrarily Rejected for Union Membership," *LLJ*, Sept. 1960; William Glick, Philip Mirvis, and Diane Harder, "Union Satisfaction and Participation," *IR*, May 1977; Richard W. Hurd, "Strategies for Union Growth in Food Manufacturing and Agriculture," *Proceedings of the 26th A/M, IRRA*, ed. by Gerald Somers (Madison: 1974); Alan Kistler, "Trends in Union Growth," *LLJ*, Aug. 1977; Sheldon M. Kline, "Membership in Labor Unions and Employee Associations, 1972," *MLR*, Aug. 1974; Richard Korn, *A Union and Its Retired Workers: A Case Study of the UAW* (Ithaca: Cornell Univ., NYSSILR, Key Issues Series no. 21, 1976); Ruth Kornhauser, "Some Social Determinants and Consequences of Union Membership," *Labor History*, Winter 1961; Linda H. LeGrande, "Women in Labor Organizations: Their Ranks are Increasing," *MLR*, Aug. 1978; Anne H. Nelson, *Working Women in Organized Labor* (Ithaca: Cornell Univ., NYSSILR, Reprint Series no. 385, 1975); Marcus H. Sandver and Herbert G.

Heneman III, "Union Growth Through the Election Process," *IR*, Winter 1981; Paul E. Sultan, *The Disenchanted Unionist* (New York: Harper & Row, 1963); U.S. Dept. of Labor, BLS, *Earnings and Other Characteristics of Organized Workers, May 1980* (Washington: Bull. 2105, 1981); U.S. Dept. of Labor, LMSA, *Union Status and Benefits of Retirees* (Washington: 1973); U.S. EEOC, *Minority and Female Membership in Referral Unions, 1974* (Washington: Research Report no. 55, 1977); Barbara M. Wertheimer, *Search for a Partnership Role, Women in Labor Unions Today* (Ithaca: Cornell Univ., NYSSILR, Reprint Series no. 387, 1976).

See also ELIGIBILITY FOR UNION MEMBERSHIP, LIMITATION OF MEMBERSHIP, MEMBERSHIP IN GOOD STANDING, RESTRICTION OF MEMBERSHIP.

union membership, compulsory *See* COMPULSORY UNION MEMBERSHIP.

union membership drive Activities designed to obtain additional union members. Membership drives take place continually but occasionally special campaigns are staged to organize a particular industry, or a whole region.

See also ORGANIZING.

union membership dues and fees *See* DUES, FEES, INITIATION FEE.

union membership eligibility The rules defining eligibility to membership in a particular union generally are spelled out in the union constitution and bylaws. As a rule, persons actually working at the trade are accepted to membership.

Federal, state, and local legislation and administrative and judicial rulings have almost made obsolete most of the old-fashioned bases for denying union membership, such as sex, race, citizenship, or political affiliation. Some unions may require previous apprenticeship.

Source references: Julius Rezler, "Admission Policy of American Trade Unions Concerning Immigrant Workers," *LLJ*, May 1960; Clyde W. Summers, "Admissions Policies of Labor Unions," *Quarterly Journal of Economics*, Nov. 1946.

See also ELIGIBILITY FOR UNION MEMBERSHIP, RESTRICTION OF MEMBERSHIP.

union monopoly *See* LABOR MONOPOLY.

union officers The officers of trade unions.

The Landrum-Griffin Act in Section 3(n) defines officer to mean "any constitutional officer, any person authorized to perform the functions of president, vice president, secretary, treasurer, or other executive functions of a labor organization, and any member of its executive board or similar governing body."

Source references: NLRB v. Coca-Cola Bottling Co. of Louisville, 118 NLRB 1422, 37 LRRM 2585 (1956); Leon Applebaum and Harry R. Blaine, "Compensation and Turnover of Union Officers," *IR*, May 1975; Ronald Ehrenberg and Steven Goldberg, "Officer Performance and Compensation in Local Building Trades Unions," *ILRR*, Jan. 1977; Bernard Gernigon, *Tenure of Trade Union Office* (Geneva: ILO, 1977); Walter J. Gershenfeld and Stuart M. Schmidt, *Officer, Member and Steward Priorities for Local Unions: Congruities, Differences* (Philadelphia: Temple Univ., IR and Organizational Behavior Dept., 1981); Lois S. Gray, "Training of Labor Union Officials," *LLJ*, Aug. 1975; Clark Kerr, *Unions and Union Leaders of Their Own Choosing* (New York: Fund for the Republic, 1957); John M. McEnany, "The Fiduciary Duty Under Section 501 of the LMRDA," *IR Law Digest*, April 1976; Glen W. Miller and Edward J. Stockton, "Local Union Officer—His Background, Activities and Attitudes," *LLJ*, Jan. 1957; Marcus Hart Sandver, "Determinants of Pay for Large Local Union Officers," *IR*, Feb. 1978; Joel Seidman, "Discipline of Union Officers by Public Management," *AJ*, Dec. 1977; U.S. Dept. of Labor, LMSA, *Electing Union Officers* (rev. ed., Washington: Technical Assistance Aid no. 5, 1980).

See also BUSINESS AGENT, LABOR LEADER, SHOP CHAIRPERSON, SHOP STEWARD, UNION LEADERSHIP, U.S. V. ARCHIE BROWN.

union organizers *See* ORGANIZERS.

union participation in management Procedures to fulfill the concept of "partners in production." Some contracts have provided for participation by unions in matters usually thought of as being solely in the area of management prerogatives.

Source references: Neil W. Chamberlain, "The Union Challenge to Management Control," *ILRR,* Jan. 1963; Milton Derber, "Labor Participation in Management; Some Impressions of Experience in the Metal Working Industries of Britain, Israel and the United States," *Proceedings of the 17th A/M, IRRA,* ed. by Gerald Somers (Madison: 1965); Milton Derber, W. E. Chalmers and Milton T. Edelman, "Union Participation in Plant Decision-Making," *ILRR,* Oct. 1961; John R. P. French et al., "An Experiment on Participation in a Norwegian Factory," *Human Relations,* Feb. 1960; Henry L. Nunn, *Partners in Production: A New Role for Management and Labor* (Englewood Cliffs: PH, 1961).

See also CODETERMINATION, LABOR-MANAGEMENT COOPERATION, MANAGEMENT RIGHTS, PARTICIPATIVE MANAGEMENT.

union pension plans *See* PENSION PLAN.

union periodicals *See* LABOR JOURNALISM, TRADE UNION PUBLICATIONS.

union policies Those basic and underlying guides which are the cornerstone of the philosophy adopted by trade unions to assist in their growth and development. Union policies have direct impact on labor-management relations and it is necessary for management to understand these basic policies in order to resolve problems of mutual concern.

union political action *See* AFL-CIO COPE; POLITICAL ACTION, UNION.

union political education *See* POLITICAL EDUCATION, UNION.

union power A phrase frequently used during major strikes or to describe actions of strong unions to indicate the extent to which unions are able to bring economic pressure on management or on the community in achieving their purposes.

Source references: Philip D. Bradley (ed.), *The Public Stake in Union Power* (Charlottesville: Univ. of Virginia Press, 1959); John M. Court, *The Problems of Union Power* (Washington: Labor Policy Association, 1961); Scott Greer, *Last Man In: Racial Access to Union Power* (Glencoe: Free Press, 1959); David B. Lipsky (ed.), *Union Power and Public Policy* (Ithaca: NYSSILR, Cornell Univ., 1975); Melvin Lurie, "Government Regulation and Union Power: A Case Study of the Boston Transit Industry," *Journal of Law and Economics,* Oct. 1960; William H. Miernyk, "The Need for a New Look at Union Power," *LLJ,* Nov. 1959; Daniel L. Shneidman, "Application and Limitation of Union Power," *LLJ,* July 1971.

union racketeering *See* LABOR RACKETEER, RACKETEERING.

union rate The hourly single rate for an occupation, trade, or craft which has been agreed to in collective bargaining.

See also MINIMUM RATES, RATE FOR THE JOB.

union recognition *See* EXCLUSIVE BARGAINING AGENT, RECOGNITION.

union referral *See* HIRING HALL, REFERRAL.

union registration *See* REGISTRATION REQUIREMENTS.

union regulation *See* REGULATION OF LABOR UNIONS.

union representative *See* BUSINESS AGENT.

union responsibility Those acts and protections required of unions by public law or democratic practice to safeguard individual members of the union or the general public.

Source references: Jack Barbash, *The Public Responsibility of Unions in Respect to Their Internal Affairs* (Madison: Univ. of Wisconsin, IR Research Center, Reprint Series no. 16, 1960); Marvin Hill, Jr., "The Union's Duty to Process Discrimination Claims," *AJ,* Sept. 1977; Charles A. Kothe, *Labor-Management Responsibilities in a Competitive World* (New York: NAM, 1962); Boyd Leedom, "Aspects of Government Regulation and Union Responsibility," *LLJ,* April 1959; Emanuel Stein, "Ethical Aspects of Union Policy and Conduct," *Annals,* Jan. 1966; U.S. Commission on Civil Rights, *Nonreferral Unions and Equal Employment Opportunity* (Washington: 1982); U.S. Dept. of Labor, LMSA, *Rights and Responsibilities Under LMRDA* (Washington: 1967); Edwin A. Witte, "The Responsibilities of Labor and Management," *Proceedings of the 9th Annual Labor-Management Conference and 10th*

Anniversary of the Institute of Management and Labor Relations (New Brunswick: Rutgers Univ., Institute of Management and Labor Relations, 1957).

See also DUTY OF FAIR REPRESENTATION, RIGHTS OF UNION MEMBERS.

union rights Those freedoms of action or freedoms from restraint which individual union members or organizations claim are theirs by constitutional right, statute, or practices recognized over a period of time. Among these might be the rights of assembly, freedom to speak, to form a union, and to strike.

union rules and regulations Internal law developed by individual unions consistent with the union's constitution. These rules cover a wide range, from qualifications for membership to discipline for infraction of the rules. They may specify what work is to be done by whom, and otherwise regulate conduct on the job. Federal legislation, notably the Landrum-Griffin Act, undertakes to prevent denial or abuse of the rights of individual members by union officials.

union scale *See* UNION RATE.

union security clauses Provisions in collective bargaining agreements which aim to protect the union against employers, nonunion employees, and/or raids by competing unions.

Typical union security clause is the union shop.

In the absence of such provisions, employees in the bargaining unit are free to join or support the union at will, and in union reasoning, receive union negotiated benefits at no personal expense, thus getting a "free ride."

Source references: Patricia N. Blair, "Union Security Agreements in Public Employment," *IR Law Digest*, Summer 1975; Mary Ann Coghill, *Efforts to Repeal 14(b): A Review of Legislative Action by the 89th Congress on the Controversial Taft-Hartley Section* (Ithaca: NYSSILR, Cornell Univ., 1966); I. J. Gromfine, "Union Security Clauses in Public Employment," *Proceedings of NYU 22d Annual Conference on Labor*, ed. by Thomas Christensen and Andrea Christensen (New York: Bender, 1970); Thomas R. Haggard, *Compulsory Unionism, The NLRB, and the Courts; A Legal Analysis of Union Security Agreements* (Philadelphia: Univ. of Pennsylvania, Wharton School, Industrial Research Unit, LRPP Series Report no. 15, 1977): Kurt L. Hanslowe, David Dunn, and Jay Erstling, *Union Security in Public Employment: Of Free Riding and Free Association* (Ithaca: Cornell Univ., NYSSILR, Institute of Public Employment, IPE Monograph no. 8, 1978); Margie Ransom McCloskey and Richard S. Rubin, "Union Security in the Public Sector: Types, Problems, Trends," *Journal of Collective Negotiations in the Public Sector*, Vol. 6, no. 4, 1977; Mark A. Moore, "The Conflict Between Union Discipline and Union Security," *LLJ*, Feb. 1967; Joyce M. Najita and Dennis T. Ogawa, *Guide to Statutory Provisions in Public Sector Collective Bargaining—Union Security* (Honolulu: Univ. of Hawaii, IRC, 1973); Nels E. Nelson, "Union Security in the Public Sector," *LLJ*, June 1976; Daniel H. Pollitt, "Union Security in America," *American Federationist*, Oct. 1973; Philip L. Ross, "Caesar and God: A Statutory Balance—Union Security and Religious Discrimination Under the Title VII Requirement of Reasonable Accommodation," *Industrial Relations LJ*, Summer 1979; Bonnie L. Siber, "The Security of Unions and Equal Employment Opportunity: Can the Two Exist," *Industrial and Labor Relations Forum*, Oct. 1974; Paul E. Sultan, "The Union Security Issue," *Public Policy and Collective Bargaining*, ed. by Joseph Shister, Benjamin Aaron and Clyde W. Summers (New York: Harper, IRRA Pub. no. 27, 1962); William D. Torrence, "More Comments on Union Security and Management Authority," *LLJ*, April 1961; U.S. Dept. of Labor, BLS, *Major Collective Bargaining Agreements: Union Security and Dues Checkoff Provisions* (Washington: Bull. 1425–21, 1982); Glenn A. Zipp, "Rights and Responsibilities of Parties to a Union-Security Agreement," *LLJ*, April 1982.

See also ABOOD V. DETROIT BOARD OF EDUCATION, AGENCY SHOP, CLOSED SHOP, FAIR SHARE AGREEMENT, FREE RIDERS, HIRING HALL, MAINTENANCE OF MEMBERSHIP, MODIFIED CLOSED SHOP, OPEN SHOP, PREFERENTIAL HIRING, PREFERENTIAL SHOP, RIGHT TO WORK LAW, SERVICE FEE, UNION SHOP.

union shop A form of union security which permits employers to hire workers of their choice but requires all new employees to become members of the union within a specified period of time, usually 30 days. It also requires the individual to remain a member or pay union dues for the duration of the collective bargaining agreement.

Source references: Sanford Cohen, "Union Shop Polls: A Solution to the Right-to-Work Issue," *ILRR,* Jan. 1959; Robert J. Connerton, "Union Shop Agreements in Right-to-Work States," *NYU 23d Annual Conference on Labor,* ed. by Thomas Christensen and Andrea Christensen (New York: Bender, 1971); James B. Dworkin and Marian N. Extejt, "The Union-Shop Deauthorization Poll: A New Look After 20 Years," *MLR,* Nov. 1979; Ronald L. Miller, "Right-To-Work Laws and Compulsory Union Membership in the United States," *BJIR,* July 1976; Chester A. Morgan, "The Union Shop Deauthorization Poll," *ILRR,* Oct. 1958; Allan G. Pulsipher, "The Union Shop: A Legitimate Form of Coercion in a Free-Market Economy," *ILRR,* July 1966.

See also AGENCY SHOP, ALL-UNION SHOP, MODIFIED UNION SHOP.

union shop, modified *See* MODIFIED UNION SHOP.

union-shop card A card issued by a union to an employer to be displayed to indicate that the employer is operating under union conditions. It is used most often in service industries, restaurants, etc. It is analogous to use of a union label on production items.

union-shop elections Employee elections required under the original Taft-Hartley Act before a union could negotiate a union shop agreement. This procedure was eliminated by Congress in 1951.

Source reference: John A. Hogan, "The Meaning of the Union Shop Elections," *ILRR,* April 1949.

union steward *See* SHOP STEWARD.

union trusteeship *See* TRUSTEESHIP, UNION.

union wage *See* UNION RATE.

union work card A card given an employee to indicate that the individual is employable as a member in good standing of the union.

unit appropriate for bargaining *See* APPROPRIATE UNIT, BARGAINING UNIT.

United Labor Party A political party sponsored largely by Henry George which supported him when he ran for election as mayor of New York in 1886. Its prime philosophy was the single tax and the basic argument that those values which arise from society's growth, including property values, should belong to the community and should be retrieved by taxation.

United Mine Workers v. Coronado Coal and Coke Co. In the *Coronado* case the Supreme Court established the principle that an unincorporated association, a trade union, could be sued for damages. The *Coronado* suit under the Sherman Act which might have involved some $2 million in damages, actually was settled for only $27,500, after 13 years of litigation.

Source references: United Mine Workers v. Coronado Coal and Coke Co., 259 US 344 (1922); Edward Berman, *Labor and the Sherman Act* (New York: Harper, 1930).

See also SUITS FOR CONTRACT VIOLATION.

United States Air Traffic Controllers Organization *See* PROFESSIONAL AIR TRAFFIC CONTROLLERS ORGANIZATION.

University Professors; American Association of (Ind) *See* AMERICAN ASSOCIATION OF UNIVERSITY PROFESSORS (AAUP) (IND).

unlicensed personnel Merchant seamen who are below "officer" rank and are not required to have a government license to work.

unskilled labor Persons performing simple manual operations which may be learned readily and who have no identifiable craft or skill. Sometimes referred to as common labor.

See also SKILLED LABOR.

upgrading A procedure used to advance employees more rapidly than usual in order to utilize their greater skills and abilities in higher rated positions. It is an organized and systematic procedure for promotion of qualified employees, particularly when it is difficult to obtain experienced help as during periods of tight labor supply. Upgrading is a form of promotion or advancement of employees to secure the maximum utilization of their ability.

Source references: Randyl D. Elkin, *Negative Effects and Occupational Upgrading in a Collective Bargaining Environment* (Ames: Iowa State Univ., IRC, WP 1973–03, 1973); Samuel B. Marks, "Employer Techniques for Upgrading Low-Skill Workers," *Proceedings of the 21st A/M, IRRA*, ed. by Gerald Somers (Madison: 1969); Joseph A. Schiffhauer, "Developing Human Resources Through an Employee Upgrading Program," *PJ*, March 1972; U.S. Dept. of Labor, Manpower Administration, *A Handbook for Upgrading Low-Skilled Workers* (Washington: Research and Demonstration Findings no. 13, 1971); ———, *Upgrading—Problems and Potentialities: The R & D Experience* (Washington: Monograph 40, 1970).

Upholsterers' International Union of North America (AFL-CIO) Founded in 1892, it affiliated with the AFL in 1900. The official quarterly publication is the *UIU Journal.*

Address: 25 North Fourth St., Philadelphia, Pa. 19106. Tel. (215) 923–5700

uplift unionism Unionism concerned with positive steps to improve the conditions of workers. Improvement may be implemented in many areas, including old-age benefits, insurance, recreational activities, health improvements. Its prime purpose, according to Professor Furniss, is to "elevate the moral, intellectual, and social life of the worker, to improve the conditions under which he works, to raise his material standards of living, give him a sense of personal worth and dignity, secure for him the leisure for culture, and insure him and his family against loss of decent livelihood by reason of unemployment, accident, disease, or old age."

Professor Daugherty sums up his view of the general aims of uplift or welfare unionism in the following paragraph:

> Welfare [or uplift] unionism is found to have the following general aims: general improvement of workers' terms of employment, general elevation of material conditions of living, provision of security in the face of risks of industry, better health, more leisure, greater opportunities for intellectual development and education, more chances for stimulating social contacts with fellow workers. The attainment of these ultimates is to be brought about by working for such immediate objectives as laws making safe and sanitary shop conditions compulsory, laws establishing minimum wages for all occupations and classes of workers; laws establishing the eight-hour day or forty-hour week; abolition of sweatshops, the peaceful settlement of industrial dispute; social insurance; the democratization of government through direct election of high officers and through wider use of the initiative, referendum, and recall; stricter control of banks and stock exchanges; free textbooks and free education; more complete protection of women and children in industry; limitations on the court's power to declare labor legislation unconstitutional; and less expensive methods of securing justice from the courts.

Source references: Carroll R. Daugherty, *Labor Problems in American Industry* (New York: Houghton Mifflin, 1933); Edgar S. Furniss, *Labor Problems* (New York: Houghton Mifflin, 1925); Raymond and Mary Louise Munts, "Welfare History of the I.L.G.W.U.," *Labor History*, Spring 1968 (Special Supplement); Jerome Wolf, *Ferment in Labor* (New York: Glencoe Press, 1968).

U.S. Anthracite Coal Commission *See* ANTHRACITE COAL COMMISSION.

U.S. Arbitration Act A statute passed on February 12, 1935, "to make valid and enforceable written provisions or agreements for arbitration of disputes arising out of contracts, maritime transactions, or commerce among the states or territories or with foreign nations."

Source references: United States Arbitration Act, as amended, 9 U.S.C. 1–14, 201–208 (1982); Ernest G. Allen and Seymour Philip Kaye, "The U.S. Arbitration Act and Collective Bargaining Agreements," *AJ*, Vol. 4, no. 1, 1949; George C. Barbesi, "Arbitration and Ocean Marine Cargo Subrogation," *AJ*, Vol. 16, no. 2, 1961; Herbert Burstein, "The United States Arbitration Act: A Re-Evaluation," *LLJ*, July 1958; Robert Coulson, *Labor Arbitration; What You Need to Know* (New York: AAA, 1973); ———, "Prima Paint: An Arbitration Milestone," *AJ*, Vol. 22, no. 4, 1967; Joseph E. De Sio, "Specific Enforcement of Arbitration Under the U.S. Arbitration Act," *NYU 8th Annual Conference on Labor*, ed. by Emanuel Stein (Albany: Bender, 1955); "Proposed United States Labor Arbitration Act," *Challenges to*

Arbitration, Proceedings of the 13th A/M, NAA, ed. by Jean McKelvey (Washington: BNA, 1960).

U.S. Atomic Energy Labor-Management Relations Panel *See* ATOMIC ENERGY LABOR-MANAGEMENT RELATIONS PANEL.

U.S. Board of Mediation The name of the three-member board as set up under the Railway Labor Act of 1926.

See also NATIONAL MEDIATION BOARD, RAILWAY LABOR ACT.

U.S. Bureau of Apprenticeship and Training *See* BUREAU OF APPRENTICESHIP AND TRAINING (BAT).

U.S. Bureau of Employees' Compensation *See* BUREAU OF EMPLOYEES' COMPENSATION.

U.S. Bureau of Employment Security *See* BUREAU OF EMPLOYMENT SECURITY.

U.S. Bureau of International Labor Affairs *See* BUREAU OF INTERNATIONAL LABOR AFFAIRS.

U.S. Bureau of Labor Standards *See* BUREAU OF LABOR STANDARDS.

U.S. Bureau of Labor Statistics *See* BUREAU OF LABOR STATISTICS.

U.S. Bureau of Old Age and Survivors Insurance *See* BUREAU OF OLD AGE AND SURVIVORS INSURANCE.

U.S. Bureau of Retirement and Survivors Insurance *See* BUREAU OF OLD AGE AND SURVIVORS INSURANCE.

U.S. Children's Bureau *See* CHILDREN'S BUREAU.

U.S. Civil Service Commission (CSC) An agency created by the Civil Service Act of 1883, which authorized the President to appoint three commissioners, by and with the advice and consent of the Senate, to aid him in the preparation of rules governing the filling of positions which shall be filled "from among those graded highest" in examinations.

An act of March 3, 1871 (16 Stat. 514; 5 U.S.C. 631), had previously authorized the President to prescribe regulations for the admission of persons into the civil service. The first examination was held in April 1872.

The commission's authority was later broadened by legislation and executive orders. Reorganization Plan 5 of 1949 provided for the designation of a chairman and prescribed the functions of the chairman and the commissioners. Over the years the commission's role was broadened to include such federal personnel management activities as job classification, status and tenure, pay comparability, awards, training, labor-management relations, equal employment opportunity, health and life insurance programs, and retirement.

Reorganization Plan No. 2 of 1978 abolished the CSC and transferred its functions to the Merit Systems Protection Board and the Office of Personnel Management.

Source references: Donald R. Harvey, *The Civil Service Commission* (New York: Praeger, 1970); Paul P. Van Riper, *History of the United States Civil Service* (Evanston: Row, Peterson, 1958).

See also MERIT SYSTEMS PROTECTION BOARD (MSPB), OFFICE OF PERSONNEL MANAGEMENT (OPM).

U.S. Commission on Civil Rights Established under the Civil Rights Act of 1957 as an independent, bipartisan, factfinding agency of the executive branch. In 1983, it was reconstituted as an eight-member body, four members appointed by the President and four by Congress.

The commission has investigatory and information gathering functions pertaining to discriminatory actions based on color, race, religion, sex, age, handicap, and national origin, and it has authority to hold hearings and to issue subpoenas "for the production of documents and the attendance of witnesses."

Source references: "Organization and Functions of the Commission," 45 C.F.R. 701; "Program Recommendations of Linda Chavez, Staff Director of Reconstituted U.S. Commission on Civil Rights," *Daily Labor Report*, No. 5, Jan. 10, 1984; U.S. Commission on Civil Rights, *Promises and Perceptions, Federal Efforts to Eliminate Discrimination Through Affirmative Action* (Washington: 1981).

U.S. Conciliation Service *See* FEDERAL MEDIATION AND CONCILIATION SERVICE (FMCS).

U.S. Council of Economic Advisers *See* COUNCIL OF ECONOMIC ADVISERS.

U.S. Department of Education *See* EDUCATION, DEPARTMENT OF.

U.S. Department of Health and Human Services *See* HEALTH AND HUMAN SERVICES, DEPARTMENT OF.

U.S. Department of Health, Education and Welfare *See* HEALTH, EDUCATION AND WELFARE; DEPARTMENT OF.

U.S. Department of Labor *See* LABOR DEPARTMENT, U.S.; LABOR SECRETARIES.

U.S. Division of Labor Standards *See* BUREAU OF LABOR STANDARDS.

U.S. Economic Development Administration *See* PUBLIC WORKS AND ECONOMIC DEVELOPMENT ACT OF 1965.

U.S. Employment and Training Administration *See* EMPLOYMENT AND TRAINING ADMINISTRATION (ETA).

U.S. Employment Service The U.S. Employment Service within the Department of Labor was created by an act of Congress in 1933. The prime function of the service is the establishment of a national employment system and cooperation with states in setting up public employment agencies.

Although the Employment Service is considered the product of the act of June 6, 1933, in actuality it has a history going back to 1907 when it was used by the Bureau of Immigration as a means of placing immigrants on farms. In January 1915, jurisdiction of the service was extended to cover all occupations and all classes of workers.

It was not until June 1933, however, that a national employment system was established by act of Congress. This statute created the U.S. Employment Service in the Department of Labor and displaced the Federal Employment Service, which had offices in the states that were conducted independently.

A major reorganization of the Manpower Administration, effective March 17, 1969, established a new service known as the U.S. Training and Employment Service (USTES), which combined the major programs and functions of the U.S. Employment Service and the Bureau of Work-Training Programs. The USTES was abolished by the secretary of labor in 1971.

The Employment Service, through its nearly 2,500 local public employment offices, provides training, placement, recruitment, and counseling services. The Service operates job training and vocational education programs; administers the Work Incentive (WIN) program jointly with the Department of Health and Human Services; provides employment services to workers adversely affected by imports, under authority of the Trade Act of 1974; and provides counseling, referral, and placement through its Apprenticeship Information Centers.

Source references: Wagner-Peyser Act, as amended, 29 U.S.C. 49 et seq. (1982); Leonard P. Adams, *The Public Employment Service in Transition, 1933–1968; Evolution of a Placement Service Into a Manpower Agency* (Ithaca: NYSSILR, Cornell Univ., 1969); Neale Baxter, "Job-Flo: How to Learn If There's a Job in Dallas When You're Jobless in Des Moines," *Occupational Outlook Quarterly*, Summer 1976; Frank H. Cassell, *The Public Employment Service: Organization in Change* (Ann Arbor: Academic Publications, 1968); William Haber and Daniel H. Kruger, *The Role of the U.S. Employment Service in a Changing Economy* (Kalamazoo: Upjohn Institute, 1964); Peter G. Petro (ed.), *The Changing Mission of the United States Employment Service: Increasing Productivity and Improving the Operation of the Labor Market, Report of Symposium Presentations, Discussions and Recommendations on Occasion of the 40th Anniversary Observance of the United States Employment Service* (Washington: U.S. Dept. of Labor, ETA, 1977); U.S. Dept. of Labor, Manpower Administration, *The Employment Service, Forty Years of Progress* (Washington: 1973).

See also U.S. TRAINING AND EMPLOYMENT SERVICE, WAGNER-PEYSER ACT.

U.S. Employment Standards Administration *See* EMPLOYMENT STANDARDS ADMINISTRATION (ESA).

U.S. Equal Employment Opportunity Commission *See* EQUAL EMPLOYMENT OPPORTUNITY COMMISSION.

U.S. Equal Employment Opportunity Coordinating Council *See* EQUAL EMPLOYMENT OPPORTUNITY COORDINATING COUNCIL.

U.S. Fair Employment Practice Committee *See* FAIR EMPLOYMENT PRACTICE COMMITTEE.

U.S. Federal Committee on Apprenticeship Training *See* FEDERAL COMMITTEE ON APPRENTICESHIP TRAINING.

U.S. Federal Emergency Administration of Public Works *See* FEDERAL EMERGENCY ADMINISTRATION OF PUBLIC WORKS.

U.S. Federal Emergency Relief Administration *See* FEDERAL EMERGENCY RELIEF ADMINISTRATION (FERA).

U.S. Federal Employment Stabilization Board *See* FEDERAL EMPLOYMENT STABILIZATION BOARD.

U.S. Federal Labor Relations Authority *See* FEDERAL LABOR RELATIONS AUTHORITY (FLRA).

U.S. Federal Labor Relations Council *See* FEDERAL LABOR RELATIONS COUNCIL (FLRC).

U.S. Federal Mediation and Conciliation Service *See* FEDERAL MEDIATION AND CONCILATION SERVICE (FMCS).

U.S. Federal Security Agency *See* FEDERAL SECURITY AGENCY.

U.S. Federal Service Impasses Panel *See* FEDERAL SERVICE IMPASSES PANEL (FSIP).

U.S. Federal Works Agency *See* FEDERAL WORKS AGENCY.

U.S. Joint Congressional Committee on the Economic Report *See* JOINT CONGRESSIONAL COMMITTEE ON THE ECONOMIC REPORT.

U.S. Labor-Management Services Administration *See* LABOR-MANAGEMENT SERVICES ADMINISTRATION (LMSA).

U.S. Manpower Administration *See* MANPOWER ADMINISTRATION, DEPARTMENT OF LABOR.

U.S. Maritime Labor Board *See* MARITIME LABOR BOARD.

U.S. Merit Systems Protection Board *See* MERIT SYSTEMS PROTECTION BOARD (MSPB).

U.S. Missile Sites Labor Commission *See* MISSILE SITES LABOR COMMISSION.

U.S. National Air Transport Adjustment Board *See* NATIONAL AIR TRANSPORT ADJUSTMENT BOARD.

U.S. National Commission for Employment Policy *See* NATIONAL COMMISSION FOR EMPLOYMENT POLICY.

U.S. National Commission on Social Security Reform *See* NATIONAL COMMISSION ON SOCIAL SECURITY REFORM.

U.S. National Commission on Technology, Automation, and Economic Progress *See* NATIONAL COMMISSION ON TECHNOLOGY, AUTOMATION, AND ECONOMIC PROGRESS.

U.S. National Defense Mediation Board *See* NATIONAL DEFENSE MEDIATION BOARD.

U.S. National Labor Board *See* NATIONAL LABOR BOARD.

U.S. National Labor-Management Panel *See* NATIONAL LABOR-MANAGEMENT PANEL.

U.S. National Labor Relations Board *See* NATIONAL LABOR RELATIONS BOARD.

U.S. National Mediation Board *See* NATIONAL MEDIATION BOARD.

U.S. National Railroad Adjustment Board *See* NATIONAL RAILROAD ADJUSTMENT BOARD.

U.S. National Recovery Administration *See* NATIONAL RECOVERY ADMINISTRATION.

U.S. National Steel Labor Relations Board *See* NATIONAL STEEL LABOR RELATIONS BOARD.

U.S. National Wage Stabilization Board *See* NATIONAL WAGE STABILIZATION BOARD.

U.S. National War Labor Board *See* NATIONAL WAR LABOR BOARD.

U.S. National Youth Administration *See* NATIONAL YOUTH ADMINISTRATION.

U.S. Occupational Safety and Health Administration *See* OCCUPATIONAL SAFETY AND HEALTH ACT (OSHA) OF 1970.

U.S. Office of Education *See* OFFICE OF EDUCATION.

U.S. Office of Federal Contract Compliance Programs *See* OFFICE OF FEDERAL CONTRACT COMPLIANCE PROGRAMS (OFCCP).

U.S. Office of Labor-Management and Welfare-Pension Reports *See* OFFICE OF LABOR-MANAGEMENT AND WELFARE-PENSION REPORTS.

U.S. Office of Labor-Management Standards Enforcement *See* OFFICE OF LABOR-MANAGEMENT STANDARDS ENFORCEMENT.

U.S. Office of Personnel Management *See* OFFICE OF PERSONNEL MANAGEMENT (OPM).

U.S. Office of Price Administration *See* OFFICE OF PRICE ADMINISTRATION.

U.S. Office of Vocational Rehabilitation *See* OFFICE OF VOCATIONAL REHABILITATION.

U.S. Pension and Welfare Benefits Programs *See* PENSION AND WELFARE BENEFIT PROGRAMS, U.S. DEPARTMENT OF LABOR.

U.S. Pension Benefit Guaranty Corp. *See* PENSION BENEFIT GUARANTY CORP. (PBGC).

U.S. Petroleum Labor Policy Board *See* PETROLEUM LABOR POLICY BOARD.

U.S. Presidential Railroad Commission *See* PRESIDENTIAL RAILROAD COMMISSION.

U.S. President's Advisory Committee on Labor-Management Policy *See* PRESIDENT'S ADVISORY COMMITTEE ON LABOR-MANAGEMENT POLICY.

U.S. President's Committee on Employment of Physically Handicapped *See* PRESIDENT'S COMMITTEE ON EMPLOYMENT OF THE HANDICAPPED.

U.S. President's Committee on Employment of the Handicapped *See* PRESIDENT'S COMMITTEE ON EMPLOYMENT OF THE HANDICAPPED.

U.S. President's Committee on Equal Employment Opportunity *See* PRESIDENT'S COMMITTEE ON EQUAL EMPLOYMENT OPPORTUNITY.

U.S. President's Committee on Youth Employment *See* PRESIDENT'S COMMITTEE ON YOUTH EMPLOYMENT.

U.S. President's Committee to Appraise Employment and Unemployment Statistics *See* UNEMPLOYMENT.

U.S. President's Task Force on Employee-Management Relations in the Federal Service *See* EXECUTIVE ORDER 10988.

U.S. Public Works Administration *See* PUBLIC WORKS ADMINISTRATION (AUTHORITY).

U.S. Railroad Labor Board *See* RAILROAD LABOR BOARD.

U.S. Rehabilitation Services Administration *See* REHABILITATION SERVICES ADMINISTRATION.

U.S. Social and Rehabilitation Service *See* SOCIAL AND REHABILITATION SERVICE.

U.S. Social Security Administration *See* SOCIAL SECURITY ADMINISTRATION.

U.S. Supreme Court *See* SUPREME COURT.

U.S. Training and Employment Service The USTES was established by the secretary of labor's Order No. 14–69, effective March 17, 1969, to "handle all employment, work-experience and training programs that are the responsibility of the Labor Department" within the Manpower Administration. Major functions of the U.S. Employment Service and the Bureau of Work-Training Programs were combined into this service.

The USTES administered "such programs as on-the-job training under the Manpower Development and Training Act, New

Careers, Operation Mainstream, Neighborhood Youth Corps, Work Incentive Programs, Apprenticeship Outreach, Concentrated Employment Programs, and Job Opportunities in the Business Sector (JOBS) with the National Alliance of Businessmen."

The USTES was abolished by the secretary of labor in 1971. The job training programs are currently administered by the Employment and Training Administration.

Source references: Harvey Kahalas and David L. Groves, "A Historical and Factor Analytic View of the Employment Service," *LLJ*, Sept. 1974; "Nixon and Shultz Announce Reorganization of Labor Department's Manpower Functions," *Daily Labor Report*, No. 49, March 13, 1969; D. Alton Smith, *Measuring the Benefits of Job Banks* (Princeton: Princeton Univ., IR Section, WP no. 50, 1974).

U.S. Unemployment Insurance Service *See* UNEMPLOYMENT INSURANCE SERVICE (UIS).

U.S. v. Archie Brown A decision by the Supreme Court in June 1965 which held unconstitutional Section 504 of the Landrum-Griffin Act. Under that section persons who are or had been members of the Communist Party were barred from union office. The Court ruled that Section 504 was void as a bill of attainder.

Source reference: U.S. v. Archie Brown, 381 US 437, 85 SCt. 1707 (1965).

U.S. v. Darby Lumber Co. A decision of the Supreme Court in February 1941 which held that the minimum wage provisions of Section 6 of the Fair Labor Standards Act and the hours provisions of Section 7 did not violate the due process clause of the Fifth Amendment.

Source reference: U.S. v. Darby Lumber Co., 312 US 451 (1941).

U.S. v. Debs *See* PULLMAN STRIKE.

U.S. Wage Adjustment Board *See* WAGE ADJUSTMENT BOARD.

U.S. Wage and Hour Division *See* WAGE AND HOUR DIVISION.

U.S. War Manpower Commission *See* WAR MANPOWER COMMISSION.

U.S. Women's Bureau *See* WOMEN'S BUREAU.

U.S. Works Progress Administration *See* WORKS PROGRESS ADMINISTRATION.

U.S. Works Projects Administration *See* WORKS PROGRESS ADMINISTRATION.

Utah Public Employees Association (Ind) An organization affiliated with the Assembly of Governmental Employees. Its monthly publications are *The Utah Public Employee* and *Courier*.

Address: 1000 Bellwood Lane, Murray, Utah 84107. Tel. (801) 264–8732

Utah School Employees Association (Ind) An organization affiliated with the American Association of Classified School Employees (Ind). Its bimonthly publication is the *USEA Review*.

Address: 15 East 10200 South, Sandy, Utah 84070. Tel. (801) 566–8822

Utility Workers of New England, Inc.; Brotherhood of (Ind) Founded in 1934, the union publishes the quarterly *Labor*.

Address: 212 Union St., Providence, R.I. 02903. Tel. (401) 751–6829

Utility Workers Union of America (AFL-CIO) Established in 1945, its official monthly publication is *Light*.

Address: 815 16th St., N.W., Suite 605, Washington, D.C. 20006. Tel. (202) 347–8105

utilization analysis A work-force review to determine whether minorities and women are underutilized in certain jobs or classifications. This analysis measures a company's work force against the available qualified workers in the relevant work force. It is a required element of any affirmative action plan developed under Revised Order No. 4.

Source references: U.S. OFCCP, "Revised Order No. 4," 41 C.F.R. 60–2; ———, *Federal Contract Compliance Manual* (Washington: 1979).

See also AVAILABILITY, UNDERUTILIZATION.

V

vacating an award Procedure for setting aside an arbitration award. State law may specify grounds on which awards may be set aside. These include procurement of an award by corruption, fraud, or undue means; an award based on partiality; failure to provide either party with a fair hearing; or arbitrators exceeding their powers.

See also ARBITRATION AWARD, ENFORCEMENT OF ARBITRATION AGREEMENT.

vacation pay Pay for specified periods of time off from work, under either contract provisions or company policy. The practice of "granting" vacations to employees is believed to have originated with bookkeepers, whose work activities the employer wanted to check. Vacation, and particularly paid vacation, for many years was almost exclusively a privilege of white-collar employees. During World War II the National War Labor Board extended the practice of paid vacations to production workers. Currently it is a major "fringe" benefit throughout industry. Wartime wage controls necessitated the development of such fringe benefits. The board reasoned that vacations with pay were not inflationary, and that after a period of rest an employee would return to work capable of increased productive effort. The usual vacation award was one week with pay after one year's service, two weeks after five years.

Source reference: "Annual Vacations With Pay," *ILR*, Aug. 1962; NICB, *Time Off With Pay* (New York: Studies in Personnel Policy no. 196, 1965); U.S. Dept. of Labor, BLS, *Collective Bargaining Agreements: Paid Vacation and Holiday Provisions* (Washington: Bull. no. 1425–9, 1969).

See also PAID VACATION PLAN.

vacations Specific periods during which employees are relieved of job obligations without loss of any benefit or privilege of employment, and usually with pay. An old theory has it that vacations provide periods of rest, following which employees can apply themselves to their jobs with renewed vigor. A more recent theory has it that extra-long vacations for senior employees afford means of providing employment to individuals who otherwise would be jobless. Vacations are not to be confused with leaves of absence, which generally are without pay unless geared to activities calculated to improve job performance.

Vacation practices vary widely. These variations can be examined in publications of the U.S. Department of Labor and of such private establishments as The Bureau of National Affairs, Inc., Commerce Clearing House, Inc., and others.

Source references: Seymour Brandwein, "Longer Vacations Are Coming," *American Federationist*, Aug. 1956; BNA, *Paid Holiday and Vacation Policies* (Washington: PFF Survey no. 130, 1980); Mary Ann Coghill, *The Shorter Work Year: A Review of Current Trends Toward Extended Vacations* (Ithaca: Cornell Univ., NYSSILR, Technical Reports Series, 1965); William L. Daykin, "Vacation Rights Under Collective Bargaining Agreements," *AJ*, Vol. 17, no. 1, 1962; Donald F. Farwell and Daniel L. Harbour, *Extended Vacations: An Innovation in Collective Bargaining* (Washington: BNA, 1964); Rick Galleher, "Time Off: More Vacations and Holidays," *American Federationist*, Jan. 1974; Arthur Haulot, "The Staggering of Annual Holidays with Pay," *ILR*, March/April 1979; Philip Kienast, "Extended Leisure for Blue Collar Workers: A Look at the Steelworker's Extended Vacation Program," *LLJ*, Oct. 1969; "Longer Vacations Through Bargaining," *American Federationist*, Dec. 1962; NICB, *Paid Vacation Practices* (New York: Studies in Personnel Policy No. 116, 1961); Rudolph Oswald, "The Growth of Longer Vacations," *American Federationist*, Nov.

1967; John E. Shea, "The Rise and Fall of Extended Vacation Plans," *Personnel*, Jan./Feb. 1967; Arthur A. Sloane, "Trends Toward More Liberalized Vacations," *Personnel*, Jan./Feb. 1966; John Zalusky, "Vacations-Holidays: Tools in Cutting Work Time," *American Federationist*, Feb. 1977.

See also PAID VACATION PLAN, SABBATICALS, UNEMPLOYMENT.

Vaca v. Sipes The 1967 Supreme Court decision that laid down rules concerning (1) individual employee rights in suits alleging a breach of union contract by an employer, (2) the elements which constitute a breach of the union's duty of fair representation, and (3) the liability to be borne by the union and employer in such cases.

The Court stated that an employee may sue an employer for breach of the union contract under Section 301 of the Labor Management Relations Act if the employee had attempted to exhaust the grievance procedure but was prevented by the union's "wrongful" refusal to process the grievance. It was ruled, however, that refusal to take a grievance to arbitration did not in itself constitute wrongful union conduct. The Court held that the individual employee "has no absolute right to have his grievance arbitrated under the collective bargaining agreement," and it must be shown that the union's conduct was "arbitrary, discriminatory, or in bad faith" in order to establish the union's breach of duty of fair representation.

It was also held by the Court that the "governing principle" in awarding damages in breach of duty suits

> is to apportion liability between the employer and the union according to the damage caused by the fault of each. Thus, damages attributable solely to the employer's breach of contract should not be charged to the union, but increases if any in those damages caused by the union's refusal to process the grievance should not be charged to the employer.

Source references: Vaca v. Sipes, 386 US 171, 64 LRRM 2369 (1967); "Individual Control Over Personal Grievances Under *Vaca v. Sipes*," *IR Law Digest*, Oct. 1968; Jack L. Kroner, "The Individual Employee: His 'Rights' in Arbitration After *Vaca v. Sipes*," *NYU 20th Annual Conference on Labor*, ed. by Thomas Christensen (Albany: Bender, 1968).

Variety Artists; American Guild of A branch of the Associated Actors and Artistes of America (AFL-CIO). Its quarterly publication is the *AGVA Newsletter*.

Address: 184 5th Ave., New York, N.Y. 10010. Tel. (212) 675–1003

See also BURLESQUE ARTISTS ASSOCIATION.

Vermont State Employees Association (Ind) An organization affiliated with the Assembly of Governmental Employees. It publishes the *V.S.E.A. Voice* (quarterly) and *V.S.E.A. Update* (monthly).

Address: 513 State St., Montpelier, Vt. 05602. Tel. (802) 223–5247

versatility training A form of training in which workers are given a wide variety of tasks and trained in a number of related jobs. The purpose is to make these individuals more flexibly useful throughout the plant in time of difficulty or when bottlenecks develop, and to enable them to fit into any part of the organization with a minimum degree of difficulty.

See also FLYING SQUADRON.

vertical movement (promotion) The advancement or promotion of individuals from a lower to a higher grade.

vertical rating *See* MUTUAL RATING.

vertical union *See* INDUSTRIAL UNION.

vested rights Rights of a financial character, such as an individual's stake in a pension plan, which are accured to him after a stated period (5, 10, or 15 years, for example). This "vested" sum is irrevocably the individual's, regardless of his quitting employment before becoming eligible—in the example of a pension plan—for retirement.

Source references: Donald M. Landay and Harry E. Davis, "Growth and Vesting Changes in Private Pension Plans," *MLR*, May 1968; U.S. Dept. of Labor, BLS, *Coverage and Vesting of Full-Time Employees Under Private Retirement Plans: Findings from the April 1972 Survey* (Washington: Report 423, 1973); ———, *Labor Mobility and Private Pension Plans: A Study of Vesting, Early Retirement, and Portability Provisions*

(Washington: Bull. 1407, 1964); "Vesting of Private Pensions: Implications for Public Policy," *MLR,* March 1965.

vestibule school A training quarters or school where employees, primarily unskilled and semiskilled, are taught to operate certain types of equipment and machinery under conditions which approximate those in the actual plant, but where the machines are located away from the plant site. This permits a learning process free from actual working pressures and away from the noise and clamor of a large work room. It is used where on-the-job training does not lend itself to training effectively.

See also TRAINING.

vestibule training Training done in a vestibule school.

veteran of the Vietnam era Defined by the Vietnam Era Veterans Readjustment Assistance Act as "an eligible veteran any part of whose active military, naval, or air service was during the Vietnam era." An "eligible veteran" is "a person who (A) served on active duty for a period of more than 180 days and was discharged or released therefrom with other than a dishonorable discharge, or (B) was discharged or released from active duty because of a service-connected disability."

Also defined by the OFCCP as "a person who served on active duty for a period of more than 180 days, any part of which occurred between August 5, 1964 and May 7, 1975, and was discharged or released therefrom with other than a dishonorable discharge; or who was discharged or released from active duty for a service-connected disability if any part of such active duty was performed between August 5, 1964 and May 7, 1975; and who was so discharged or released within 48 months preceding an alleged violation of the Vietnam Era Veterans' Readjustment Assistance Act of 1974, the affirmative action clause, or the regulations issued pursuant to the Act."

Source references: Vietnam Era Veterans Readjustment Assistance Act of 1974, 38 U.S.C. 2011–2014 (1982); U.S. OFCCP, *Federal Contract Compliance Manual* (Washington: 1979).

veteran's preference Advantages in employment and promotion both in the civil service and private employment to veterans of the armed forces who are honorably discharged. Preferential treatment has also been given to veterans by some unions who accept them into membership without initiation fees and in some cases have waived formal apprenticeship where the veteran had acquired reasonable skill in the trade while serving in the armed forces.

See also FEENEY CASE.

Vietnam Era Veterans Readjustment Assistance Act of 1974 Originally enacted in 1972, the law prohibits employment discrimination against qualified disabled veterans and veterans of the Vietnam era by certain government contractors and federal agencies. Employers with federal contracts in the amount of $10,000 or more are required to "take affirmative action to employ and advance in employment qualified special disabled veterans and veterans of the Vietnam era." Federal agencies are required to draw up and implement an affirmative action program for the hiring, placement, and advancement of veterans covered by the law.

Source references: Vietnam Era Veterans Readjustment Assistance Act of 1974, as amended, 38 U.S.C. 2011–2014 (1982); U.S. OFCCP, "Affirmative Action Program for Disabled Veterans and Veterans of the Vietnam Era," 41 C.F.R. 60–250.

See also ACCOMMODATION, DISABLED VETERAN, OFFICE OF FEDERAL CONTRACT COMPLIANCE PROGRAMS (OFCCP), VETERAN OF THE VIETNAM ERA.

vigilante groups *See* BACK-TO-WORK MOVEMENT, MOHAWK VALLEY FORMULA, STRIKEBREAKER.

villeinage *See* SERFDOM.

violation of agreement *See* ABROGATION OF AGREEMENT, ARBITRATION AWARD, ENFORCEMENT OF AGREEMENT, SUITS FOR CONTRACT VIOLATION.

violence in labor disputes Physical force applied to persons and property; bloodshed, and even murder. While not unknown, these incidents are not typical of strikes today; but the history of American unionism is well-studded with them, notably in cases where armed force has been brought to bear on strikers.

Professor Albion Taylor states that "an analysis of the causes of violence in connection with strikes shows that it usually arises from acts of an irritating character, acts that are an affront to the personal dignity of workers, such as interference with the freedom of assemblage, the employment of professional strikebreakers, and the use of state militia to quell strikes. Violence is seldom premeditated, except on the part of revolutionary or predatory unionism."

Source references: Louis Adamic, *Dynamite: The Story of Class Violence* (New York: Viking Press, 1931); Robert V. Bruce, *1877: Year of Violence* (New York: Bobbs-Merrill, 1959); Morris D. Forkosch, "Violence in Labor-Management Relations," *LLJ*, Feb. 1962; George W. Hartmann and Theodore Newcomb (ed.), *Industrial Conflict—A Psychological Interpretation* (New York: Cordon, 1939); Robert Hunter, *Violence and the Labor Movement* (New York: Arno Press & The New York Times, 1969); Philip Taft, "Violence in American Labor Disputes," *Annals*, March 1966; Albion G. Taylor, *Labor Problems and Labor Law* (2d ed., New York: PH, 1950); Armand J. Thieblot, Jr. and Thomas R. Haggard, *Union Violence: The Record and the Response by Courts, Legislatures, and the NLRB* (Philadelphia: Univ. of Pennsylvania, Wharton School, Industrial Research Unit, LRPP Series no. 25, 1983); Edwin Witte, *The Government in Labor Disputes* (New York: McGraw-Hill, 1932).

See also BOYCOTT, HERRIN MASSACRE, INDUSTRIAL CONFLICT, LAFOLLETTE COMMITTEE, PICKETING, REVOLUTIONARY UNIONISM, STRIKE.

Virginian Railway Co. v. System Federation No. 40 A decision of the Supreme Court which upheld the provisions of the Railway Labor Act as applied to a ruling of the National Mediation Board certifying an outside union for collective bargaining and requiring the company not to bargain with its company union.

Source reference: Virginian Railway v. System Federation No. 40, 300 US 515, 1 LRRM 743 (1937).

visits by union representatives *See* ACCESS TO PLANT BY UNION REPRESENTATIVES, SHOP STEWARD.

visual aids Devices to accelerate the learning process utilizing the sense of sight. These may include films, charts, and slides.

Source references: "Audio Visual Media for Labour Education" *Free Labour World*, July/Aug. 1971; John W. Brophy, "Television Video Tape Recorder—New Tool for Training in Business and Industry," *PJ*, Sept. 1971; Walton N. Hershfield, "Video-Sonic Instructional Techniques for Training Personnel," *PJ*, Feb. 1967; Robert H. Hess, "A Supervisory Development Program—On Video Tape," *PJ*, Jan. 1977; James J. Jehring, "Audio-Visual Materials in Industrial and Labor Relations," *ILRR*, Oct. 1952; Richard Kritzer, "The Use of Videotape in Behavioral Change," *Public Personnel Management*, July/Aug. 1974; Thomas F. Stroh, *The Use of Video Tape in Training and Development* (New York: AMA, Research Study no. 93, 1969).

vocation A person's business, profession, or occupation.

See also OCCUPATION.

vocational counselor An individual who helps a worker, student, or applicant for a position to choose, prepare for, and enter an occupation.

The *Dictionary of Occupational Titles* defines a vocational counselor, in part, as a person who "counsels individuals and provides group educational and vocational guidance services, . . . refers students to placement service [and] assists individuals to understand and overcome social and emotional problems." A vocational-rehabilitation counselor "counsels handicapped individuals to provide vocational rehabilitation services . . . and evaluates handicapped applicants to determine degree of handicap, eligibility for service, and feasibility of vocational rehabilitation." The *Standard Occupational Classification Manual* describes vocational and educational counselors as those individuals "assisting students or workers in self-understanding, self-development, and career planning by presenting educational and occupational information."

The U.S. Employment Service attempts through counseling to assist workers in making satisfactory occupational choices and in finding employment in their chosen fields.

Source references: Lloyd H. Lofquist and George W. England, *Problems in Vocational Counseling: The Application of Research Findings* (Dubuque: William C. Brown, 1961); Gloria Stevenson, "Counseling Black Teenage Girls," *Occupational Outlook Quarterly,* Summer 1975; U.S. Dept. of Commerce, Office of Federal Statistical Policy and Standards, *Standard Occupational Classification Manual* (Washington: 1980); U.S. Dept. of Education, *Vocational Counseling for Displaced Homemakers, A Manual* (Washington: 1980); U.S. Dept. of Labor, ETA, *Dictionary of Occupational Titles* (4th ed., Washington: 1977); Mary Ellen Verheyden-Hilliard, *Professional Development Programs for Sex Equity in Vocational Education* (Washington: U.S. Dept. of HEW, Office of Education, Information series no. 148, 1979); Harold L. Wilensky, "Careers, Counseling and the Curriculum," *Journal of Human Resources,* Winter 1967.

See also U.S. EMPLOYMENT SERVICE.

vocational diagnosis The analysis by a vocational technician or counselor of an individual's aptitudes, experience, interests, and education in order to assist the individual in making a vocational choice.

vocational education Programs to teach people the fundamentals of particular skills, to train them in new skills, and to develop effective teachers in vocational education.

Source references: J. Stanley Ahmann, *Needs Assessment for Program Planning in Vocational Education* (Washington: U.S. Dept. of HEW, Office of Education, Information Series no. 154, 1979); Roger L. Bowlby and William R. Schriver, "Academic Ability and Rates of Return to Vocational Training," *ILRR,* April 1973; Paul V. Braden and Krishan K. Paul, *The Role of Vocational Education in the Nation's Economic Development* (Washington: U.S. Dept. of HEW, Office of Education, Information Series no. 150, 1979); Samuel M. Burt, *Industry and Community Leaders in Education, The State Advisory Councils on Vocational Education* (Kalamazoo: Upjohn Institute for Employment Research, 1969); Mary A. Golladay and Rolf M. Wulfsberg, *The Condition of Vocational Education* (Washington: U.S. Dept. of HEW, National Center for Education Statistics, 1981); John T. Grasso, *The Contributions of Vocational Education, Training and Work Experience to the Early Career Achievements of Young Men* (Columbus: Ohio State Univ., Center for Human Resource Research, 1975); Leonard A. Lecht, *Occupational Choices and Training Needs; Prospects for the 1980s* (New York: Praeger, 1977); Sar A. Levitan, *Vocational Education and Federal Policy* (Kalamazoo: Upjohn Institute, 1963); Rudy Oswald, "Labor's Stake in Vocational Education," *American Federationist,* Aug. 1975; Griff D. Pitts, "How to Select a Private Vocational School," *Occupational Outlook Quarterly,* Summer 1976; William R. Schriver and Roger L. Bowlby, "Vocational Training and the Income-Education Linkage," *IR,* May 1972; Carl J. Shaefer and Jacob J. Kaufman (ed.), *Vocational Education: Social and Behavioral Perspectives; a Report Prepared for the Massachusets Advisory Council on Education* (Lexington: Mass.: Heath, Lexington Books, 1971); Gerald G. Somers and J. Kenneth Little (ed.), *Vocational Education: Today and Tomorrow* (Madison: Center for Studies in Vocational and Technical Education, Univ. of Wisconsin, 1971); JoAnn M. Steiger and Sara Cooper, *The Vocational Preparation of Women, Report and Recommendations of the Secretary's Advisory Committee on the Rights and Responsibilities of Women* (Washington: U.S. Dept. of HEW, 1975); David W. Stevens, *The Coordination of Vocational Education Programs with CETA* (Washington: U.S. Dept. of HEW, Office of Education, Information Series no. 151, 1979); U.S. Dept. of Education, *Resource Guide for Vocational Educators and Planners* (Washington: 1980); U.S. Dept. of HEW, *Education for a Changing World of Work: Report of the Panel of Consultants on Vocational Education* (Washington: 1963); U.S. Dept. of HEW, National Institute of Education, *The Planning Papers for the Vocational Education Study* (Washington: Vocational Education Study Pub. no. 1, 1979); U.S. Dept. of HEW, Office of Education, *New Thrusts in Vocational Education* (Washington: 1971); U.S. GAO, *What is the Role of Federal Assistance for Vocational Education? Office of Education, Department of Health, Education, and Welfare* (Washington: 1974); U.S. National Advisory Council on Vocational

Education, *Increasing Sex Equity, the Impact of the 1976 Vocational Education Amendments on Sex Equity in Vocational Education* (Washington: 1981); U.S. National Commission for Employment Policy, *The Federal Role in Vocational Education* (Washington: Report no. 12, 1981).

See also CAREER EDUCATION, INDUSTRIAL EDUCATION, SMITH-HUGHES ACT.

vocational guidance Programs and activities which assist and direct individuals toward a vocational choice.

Source references: Stephen D. Anderson, "Planning for Career Growth," *PJ*, May 1973; Ruth Barry and Beverly Wolf, *An Epitaph for Vocational Guidance: Myths, Actualities, and Implications* (New York: Columbia Univ., Teachers College, 1962); Philip G. Benson and George C. Thornton III, "A Model Career Planning Program," *Personnel*, March/April 1978; Robert L. Darcy, "A Classroom Introduction to the World of Work," *Occupational Outlook Quarterly*, Winter 1972; Donald Dillon, "Toward Matching Personal and Job Characteristics," *Occupational Outlook Quarterly*, Winter 1972; Eli Ginzberg, *Career Guidance: Who Needs It, Who Provides It, Who Can Improve It* (New York: McGraw-Hill, 1971); Thelma C. Lennon, *Guidance Needs of Special Populations* (Washington: U.S. Dept. of HEW, Office of Education, Information Series no. 145, 1979); Norman R. Miller, "Career Guidance—A Means of Tapping Hidden Potential," *Personnel*, July/Aug. 1964; Margaret Nolte, "Work Study Programs in Colleges and Universities," *PJ*, Dec. 1967; Henry G. Pearson, " 'Person Skills' vs. Job Techniques—An Answer to Student Orientation," *PJ*, May 1978; Donald E. Super, *The Psychology of Careers* (New York: Harper, 1957); Robert L. Thorndike and Elizabeth Hagen, *Ten Thousand Careers* (New York: Wiley, 1959).

vocational rehabilitation Programs designed for and directed to the thousands of individuals who become physically disabled each year and who need to be retrained and prepared for new jobs. Prior to passage of the Federal Vocational Rehabilitation Act of 1920, some efforts had been made by the states in this area. With passage of the Social Security Act of 1935 and subsequent amendments, substantial sums were made available to meet the administrative costs of approved state vocational rehabilitation programs and to share the expenses of actual rehabilitation programs.

The Vocational Rehabilitation (Smith-Fess) Act of 1920 was to aid the industrially disabled and provide funds to augment rehabilitation programs being started by several states. In 1943, with the passage of the LaFollette-Barden Act the present Vocational Rehabilitation Program was established. Services were extended to include the blind and the mentally handicapped, and the definition of rehabilitation services was expanded to include medical restoration and all services necessary to return the disabled person to satisfying, gainful employment.

Source references: Ronald W. Conley, "A Benefit-Cost Analysis of the Vocational Rehabilitation Program," *Journal of Human Resources*, Spring 1969; Vernon Hauck and Irving Kovarsky, *Epilepsy and Employment* (Iowa City: Univ. of Iowa, Center for Labor and Management, Research Series V, 1975); A. J. Jaffe (ed.), *Workmen's Compensation and Vocational Rehabilitation* (New York: Columbia Univ., Bureau of Applied Research, 1961); Sar A. Levitan and Robert Taggart, "Employment Problems of Disabled Persons," *MLR*, March 1977; Garth L. Mangum and Lowell M. Glenn, *Vocational Rehabilitation and Federal Manpower Policy* (Ann Arbor: Univ. of Michigan–Wayne State Univ., Institute of Labor and IR, Policy Papers in Human Resources and IR no. 4, 1967); National Institutes on Rehabilitation and Health Services, *Report of the National Workshop on Rehabilitation and Workmen's Compensation* (Washington: 1971); Louise M. Neuschutz, *Vocational Rehabilitation for the Physically Handicapped* (Springfield, Ill.: Charles C. Thomas, 1959); U.S. Congress, Senate, Committee on Labor and Public Welfare, *Administration of the Vocational Rehabilitation Act for Fiscal Year 1972* (Washington: 1973); George N. Wright, Kenneth W. Reagles, and Kenneth R. Thomas, "The Wood County Project: An Expanded Rehabilitation Programme for the Vocationally Handicapped," *ILR*, July/Aug. 1971.

See also REHABILITATION ACT OF 1973, REHABILITATION SERVICES ADMINISTRATION,

VIETNAM ERA VETERANS READJUSTMENT ASSISTANCE ACT OF 1974, WORKERS COMPENSATION.

Vocational Rehabilitation Administration *See* OFFICE OF VOCATIONAL REHABILITATION.

vocational training Activities and programs, including curriculum and actual training and operations, to give a person the skill needed to perform a particular job.

See also TRAINING.

volitional test A criterion used by California courts to determine the question of unemployment insurance eligibility where strikes or lockouts result in unemployment. The rule requires the California Unemployment Insurance Appeals Board to determine whether the employer or the union first applies the economic weapon.

Source reference: John Morrell & Co. v. California Unemployment Insurance Appeals Board, Civ. 24023, Cal. Ct. Appeal (1967).

See also UNEMPLOYMENT COMPENSATION.

voluntarism Herbert Harris suggests that "voluntarism" is to labor what "laissez-faire" is to business. Voluntarism was the policy of Samuel Gompers and the AFL. It reflected the idea that workers were to rely basically on their trade union strength and their ability to use the strike, boycott, and other activity to achieve their demands through collective bargaining. Government intervention was regarded as undesirable.

This philosophy was due largely to the historical background which indicated that by and large government intervention was usually on the side opposed to unions and the objectives they sought to achieve. It was assumed that since government intervention was objectionable, unions therefore should build their organizations so they could rely on their own economic strength.

The basic philosophy of voluntarism has given ground so that unions not only have accepted government intervention and government support, but seek favorable legislation in addition to gains made through collective bargaining.

Even during the period of voluntarism, unions sought government protection of their right to organize for the purpose of collective bargaining. Note the statement of the 1914 AFL convention's committee on resolutions, which said in part: "We have tried in this country, as working men have endeavored to do in others, to secure through legislation a guarantee that our rights to organize and to trade union effort should not be interfered with. That has been one form of legislation which the trade union movement has most heartily and effectively applied."

Source references: AFL, *Report of the Proceedings of the 34th Annual Convention of the American Federation of Labor, 1914* (Washington: 1915); Samuel Gompers, *Seventy Years of Life and Labor: An Autobiography* (New York: Dutton, 1943); Herbert Harris, *Labor's Civil War* (New York: Knopf, 1940); Bernard Mandel, *Samuel Gompers, A Biography* (Yellow Springs, Ohio: Antioch Press, 1963); Michael Rogin, "Voluntarism: The Political Functions of an Antipolitical Doctrine," *ILRR*, July 1962; David J. Saposs, "Voluntarism in the American Labor Movement," *MLR*, Sept. 1954.

voluntary arbitration *See* ARBITRATION, VOLUNTARY.

voluntary association A group of individuals who join together to develop and extend their common interests.

voluntary check-off A form of check-off which requires individual employees to authorize their employers to make such deductions from their pay. This is required under Section 302 of the Taft-Hartley Act.

See also AUTOMATIC CHECK-OFF, CHECK-OFF, INVOLUNTARY CHECK-OFF, RAND FORMULA.

voluntary retirement *See* RETIREMENT, VOLUNTARY.

voluntary union membership Membership which individuals are free to undertake or free to give up. The opposite is true of compulsory union membership.

Source references: Chamber of Commerce of the U.S., *The Case for Voluntary Unionism* (Washington: 1955); John E. Coogan, *Voluntary Unionism for Free Americans* (Washington: National Right to Work Committee, 1960); George Rose, "The Legal Protection of

Voluntary Union Membership," *LLJ*, May 1960.

See also COMPULSORY UNION MEMBERSHIP, MEMBERSHIP IN GOOD STANDING, UNION MEMBERSHIP.

voting laws With reference to employees, state laws which require employers to allow workers time off during the day in order to cast their ballots.

voting procedure, NLRB Procedures followed by the NLRB in conducting employee elections. A brochure issued by the Board in 1984 to instruct prospective voters explains the procedures thus:

General Information

Prior to any election conducted by the NLRB there will be posted at the place of your work a Notice of Election issued by the NLRB to inform you of:

The *date, hours, and place* of the election,
The *payroll period* for *voter eligibility*,
A description of the *voting unit* of employees,
General rules as to *conduct of elections*.

There is a sample ballot on the Notice of Election which, except for color, is a reproduction of the ballot you will receive when you vote.

You should read the Notice of Election so that you will be familiar with the ballot.

The Voting Place

In the voting place will be a table, a voting booth, and a ballot box. At the table there will be observers for the union and the employer and a representative of the NLRB, each of whom will be wearing an official badge. The observers' badges will have "Observer" on them. The NLRB representative will wear an "Agent" badge.

The Agent is in charge of the election. If you have questions, talk only with the Agent.

The Voting Procedure

1. Go to the voting table, standing in line if necessary.
2. Give your name, and clock number if you have one, to the observers. The observers will find your name on the voting list and tell the Agent your name has been found. If any questions are asked, talk only with the Agent. Do not argue with the observers.
3. After your name has been checked off, go to the Agent to obtain your ballot.
4. Go into the vacant voting booth. Mark the ballot with *one X only*. Do *not* sign the ballot. Fold the ballot to hide the mark and leave the voting booth taking your ballot with you.
5. Put your ballot in the ballot box yourself. Do not let anyone else touch it.
6. Leave the polling place.

You will notice that only the Agent handled the blank ballots and only *you* handled your marked ballot. Once your marked ballot is in the ballot box it becomes mixed with all other ballots in the box and cannot be identified. *No one can determine how you have voted.*

Challenged Ballots

Questions sometimes arise about eligibility of certain persons. Any observer or the NLRB representative can challenge an individual's right to vote. This challenge, however, must be for good cause and not for personal reasons; for example, a name may not appear on the eligibility list because of a clerical error.

If your vote is challenged, take your ballot into the booth, mark it, fold it to keep the mark secret, and return to the voting table. The Agent will give you a challenged ballot envelope on the stub of which are written your name and clock number and the reason for the challenge. *You* put the ballot in the envelope. *You* seal the envelope, and *you* deposit it in the ballot box.

You will note that while your name is on the stub of the envelope it is *not* on the ballot.

Secrecy of your vote is maintained because if challenged ballots must be counted and if later investigation reveals challenged voters are eligible to vote, the stub containing the name and clock number of the individual voter is first torn off and discarded. All challenged ballot envelopes are then mixed together. The ballots are then removed and counted by the Board Agent. By this method secrecy is maintained.

Rights of Employees

You are entitled to vote your free choice in a fair, honest, secret-ballot election.

The National Labor Relations Board is the agency of the United States Government which protects that right as well as other important rights guaranteed by the National Labor Relations Act.

Under Section 7 of the National Labor Relations Act, employees have the right:

To self-organization,
To form, join, or assist labor organizations,
To bargain collectively through representatives of their own choosing.
To act together for the purposes of collective bargaining or other mutual aid or protection.
To refuse to do any or all of these things. However, the union and employer, in a State where such agreements are permit-

ted, may enter into a lawful union-security clause requiring employees to join the union.

The National Labor Relations Board wants all eligible voters to be familiar with their rights under the law and wants both employers and unions to know what is expected of them when it holds an election.

When an election is held, the Board protects your right to a free choice under the law. Improper conduct, such as described [below], will not be permitted. We expect all parties to Board elections to cooperate fully with this Agency in maintaining basic principles of a fair election as expressed by law. The National Labor Relations Board as an agent of the United States Government does not endorse any choice in the election.

Protection of Your Rights

The Board applies rules to keep its elections fair and honest. If agents of either unions or employers interfere with your right to a free, fair, and honest election, the election can be set aside by the Board. Where appropriate the Board provides other remedies, such as reinstatement for employees fired for exercising their rights, including backpay from the party responsible for their discharge.

The following are examples of conduct which interfere with the rights of employees and may result in the setting aside of the election:

Threatening loss of jobs or benefits by an employer or a union,

Promising or granting promotions, pay raises, or other benefits, to influence an employee's vote by a party capable of carrying out such promises,

An employer firing employees to discourage or encourage union activity or a union causing them to be fired to encourage union activity,

Making campaign speeches to assembled groups of employees on company time within the 24-hour period before the election,

Incitement by either an employer or a union of racial or religious prejudice by inflammatory appeals,

Threatening physical force or violence to employees by a union or an employer to influence their votes.

Source references: Gloria Busman, *Union Representatives' Guide to NLRB RC and CA Cases* (Los Angeles: UC, Institute of IR, Policy and Practice Publication, 1977); John E. Drotning, "NLRB Policy Toward Employer Objections to Election Misconduct," *LLJ*, June 1965; Julius Getman, Stephen B. Goldberg, and Jeanne B. Herman, *Union Representation Elections: Law and Reality* (New York: Russell Sage Foundation, 1976); Malcolm Lassman, "Employer Petitions for NLRB Elections and the Board's Disclaimer Doctrine," *LLJ*, June 1966; Jay S. Siegel, "Problems and Procedures in the NLRB Election Process," *Labor Law Developments 1968*, Proceedings of the 14th Annual Institute on Labor Law, SLF (New York: Bender, 1968); James P. Swann, Jr., *NLRB Elections: A Guidebook for Employers* (Washington: BNA, 1980); U.S. NLRB, *Information to Voters in Elections Conducted by the National Labor Relations Board* (Washington: 1962); ———, *Rules and Regulations and Statements of Procedures, Series 8, as amended* (Washington: 1982); ———, *Your Government Conducts an Election* (Washington: 1984).

See also REPRESENTATION ELECTIONS.

W

WA *See* WATCHMEN'S ASSOCIATION; INDEPENDENT (IND).

WCL *See* WORLD CONFEDERATION OF LABOUR (WCL).

WFTU *See* WORLD FEDERATION OF TRADE UNIONS (WFTU).

WGA *See* WRITERS GUILD OF AMERICA (IND).

WISU *See* WESTINGHOUSE INDEPENDENT SALARIED UNIONS; FEDERATION OF (IND).

WLB *See* NATIONAL WAR LABOR BOARD.

WPA *See* WORKS PROGRESS ADMINISTRATION.

WPPW *See* PULP AND PAPER WORKERS; ASSOCIATION OF WESTERN (IND).

WSE *See* WEATHER SERVICE EMPLOYEES ORGANIZATION; NATIONAL.

WWML *See* LATHERS INTERNATIONAL UNION; THE WOOD, WIRE AND METAL (AFL-CIO).

wage The price paid for a particular type of work or service rendered by an employee. In technical usage the price paid to executive and professional employees is included in wages, although some suggest that this type of compensation be listed as salary. In common usage, the term "wage" applies to compensation to unskilled, semiskilled, and skilled workers, who are paid on an hourly or incentive basis. Payments to white-collar employees and professionals are generally referred to as salary.

Source references: John T. Dunlop, *American Wage Determination: The Trend and Its Significance* (Washington: Chamber of Commerce of the U.S., 1947); Michael P. Fogarty, *The Just Wage* (London: Chapman, 1961); Walter Galenson, *A Primer on Employment and Wages* (New York: Vintage Books, 1966).

See also SALARIED EMPLOYEE, SALARY RATE.

wage, natural Economists of the classical school generally distinguished between the market price of labor and its natural price. The natural price, according to David Ricardo, "is that price which is necessary to enable laborers, one with another to subsist and perpetuate their race, without either increase or diminution."

According to Malthus, the natural or necessary price of labor is "the price which is necessary, in order that at the condition of society, there should be on the average a sufficient number of laborers to meet the existing demand."

Source references: Paul H. Douglas, Curtice N. Hitchcock, and Willard E. Atkins, *The Worker in Modern Economic Society* (Chicago: Univ. of Chicago Press, 1923); Paul K. Grosser, *Ideologies and American Labor* (London: Oxford UP, 1941); Michael Wermel, *The Evolution of the Classical Wage Theory* (New York: Columbia UP, 1939).

See also IRON LAW OF WAGES, SUBSISTENCE WAGE.

Wage Adjustment Board A specialized agency within the National War Labor Board during World War II to handle the problems of wage stabilization and regulation in the building and construction industry.

Source reference: U.S. Dept. of Labor, *The Termination Report of the National War Labor Board* (3 vol., Washington: 1947).

wage adjustment plans Provisions in collective bargaining agreements for the modification or change of wages in accordance with certain specified criteria. Among the most frequently used is the cost of living adjustment measured by changes in the Consumer Price

Index. Other criteria used include changes in the cost of materials or the price of the commodity.

Source reference: William A. Howard, "Wage Adjustment and Profit Rates: An Error-Learning Approach to Collective Bargaining," *ILRR*, April 1969.

See also ANNUAL IMPROVEMENT FACTOR, AUTOMATIC WAGE ADJUSTMENT, COST-OF-LIVING ADJUSTMENT, ESCALATOR CLAUSE, GRADUATED WAGE, LONGEVITY PAY, PERMISSIVE WAGE ADJUSTMENT.

wage advance plans A wage payment plan in which an employee may draw pay prior to the performance of actual work. This may be an advance payment on a new employee's first week's salary. Advances may be provided to individuals during the slack season for work to be performed during the regular season. In some cases services may already have been rendered, but are paid for in advance of the regular payday which may still be a few days or a week ahead.

wage analysis A periodic study and examination of wages which may include wage rates of specific occupations, wage differentials and relationships, long-range trends and variations among skills, and a variety of other wage data. The general purpose is to determine the basis for company policy or to establish or modify a compensation or wage schedule. It may be done in preparation for collective bargaining.

wage analyst A person technically qualified to examine and evaluate wage data.

Wage and Hour Act *See* FAIR LABOR STANDARDS ACT OF 1938.

Wage and Hour and Public Contracts Divisions *See* WAGE AND HOUR DIVISION.

Wage and Hour Division A division of the Employment Standards Administration, U.S. Department of Labor, it is responsible for the administration and enforcement of the Fair Labor Standards Act and the Walsh-Healey Act. The division is also responsible for predetermination of prevailing wage rates for federal construction contracts subject to the Davis-Bacon Act.

After the Public Contracts Division was consolidated with the Wage and Hour Division on August 21, 1942, it was known as the Wage and Hour and Public Contracts Divisions until May 1971, when the Public Contracts Division was absorbed by the Wage and Hour Division. It maintains 10 regional offices.

Address: Room S–3502, 200 Constitution Ave., N.W., Washington, D.C. 20210. Tel. (202) 523–8305

Source reference: U.S. Dept. of Labor, *The Anvil and the Plow, A History of the United States Department of Labor* (Washington: 1963).

See also EMPLOYMENT STANDARDS ADMINISTRATION (ESA).

wage and salary administration The broad range of wage and salary determination and supervision within a particular plant. The responsibility also includes the implementation of wage and salary adjustments. In order to assure full information about trends in wages and salaries, data are collected on prices and the cost of living. There is also frequent review and analysis of the job structure and job rates in the plant. The wage and salary administration division, usually within the personnel department, is responsible for the continuing analysis of major factors involved in work and payment within the company.

Source references: David W. Belcher, *Compensation Administration* (Englewood Cliffs: PH, 1974); ______, *Wage and Salary Administration* (2d ed., Englewood Cliffs: PH, 1962); Charles W. Brennan, *Wage Administration: Plans, Practices and Principles* (Homewood: Irwin, 1963); BNA, *Wage and Salary Administration* (Washington: BNA, PPF Survey no. 131, 1981); Bruce R. Ellig, "Compensation Management: Its Past and Its Future," *Personnel*, May/June 1977; Richard I. Henderson, "The Changing Role of the Wage and Salary Administrator," *Personnel*, Nov./Dec. 1976; ______, *Compensation Management: Rewarding Performance in the Modern Organization* (Reston, Va.: Reston, 1976); Elizabeth Lanham, *Administration of Wages and Salaries* (New York: Harper, 1963); Edward E. Lawler, III, "New Approaches to Pay: Innovations that Work," *Personnel*, Sept./Oct. 1976; ______, *Pay and Organization Development* (Reading, Mass.:

Addison-Wesley, 1981); U.S. Dept. of Labor, BLS, *Major Collective Bargaining Agreements: Wage Administration Provisions* (Washington: Bull. 1425–17, 1978); Kenneth O. Warner and J. J. Donovan (ed.), *Practical Guidelines to Public Pay Administration* (2 vol., Chicago: PPA, 1963); David Weeks, *Compensating Employees: Lessons of the 1970's* (New York: The Conference Board, Report 707, 1976).

See also SALARY ADMINISTRATION.

wage and salary stabilization The programs developed by government during periods of crisis, such as during World War II, for the purpose of keeping wages and prices in some stable relationship and to avoid inflationary pressures which arise because of the transformation of the productive capacity of the economy toward war materials and the necessary curtailment of consumer goods.

See also WAGE STABILIZATION.

wage arbitration *See* ARBITRATION, WAGE.

wage assignment *See* ASSIGNMENT OF WAGES, GARNISHMENT.

wage attachment *See* GARNISHMENT.

wage award *See* ARBITRATION; ARBITRATION, WAGE.

wage bargaining The factors which influence the actual determination of wages in collective bargaining. They include the relative economic power of labor and management in negotiations, competitive conditions of the industry, knowledge of the labor market, bargaining skill of the parties, etc. How the wage bargain is arrived at is a matter of central concern in the field of industrial relations and may influence general wage policy.

Source references: Mario F. Bognanno and James B. Dworkin, *Comments on "Who Wins in Wage Bargaining"* (Minneapolis: Univ. of Minnesota, IRC, WP no. 74–06, 1974); James A. Craft, *Information Disclosure and the Role of the Accountant in Collective Bargaining* (Pittsburgh: Univ. of Pittsburgh, Graduate School of Business, Reprint no. 374, 1981); Lily Mary David and Victor J. Sheifer, "Estimating the Cost of Collective Bargaining Settlements," *MLR*, May 1969; Peter Feuille, Wallace E. Hendricks, and Lawrence M. Kahn, "Wage and Nonwage Outcomes in Collective Bargaining: Determinants and Tradeoffs," *Journal of Labor Research*, Spring 1981; Marvin Friedman, *The Use of Economic Data in Collective Bargaining* (Washington: U.S. Dept. of Labor, LMSA, 1978); Daniel S. Hamermesh, "Who 'Wins' in Wage Bargaining?" *ILRR*, July 1973; Harold M. Levinson, *Determining Forces in Collective Bargaining* (New York: Wiley, 1966); Lloyd G. Reynolds, "Wage Bargaining, Price Changes, and Employment," *Proceedings of the 1st A/M, IRRA*, ed. by Milton Derber (Champaign: 1949); George W. Taylor, "Criteria in the Wage Bargain," *NYU 1st Annual Conference on Labor*, ed. by Emanuel Stein (Albany: Bender, 1948); "Wage Bargaining—Review and Preview," *American Federationist*, Feb. 1962.

wage board employees Federal government employees in trades, crafts, or labor occupations whose rates of pay are fixed and adjusted administratively in accordance with prevailing area rates. Sometimes referred to as government blue-collar employees. The term "wage board" grew out of the government agency practice of utilizing survey boards to determine prevailing area wage rates in setting wage rates for these employees.

Under the Federal Wage System established by P.L. 92–392 (1972), pay rates for wage board or blue-collar employees are based on prevailing private sector rates within local areas. Surveys to gather data on local rates are conducted by joint labor-management groups. The Federal Prevailing Rate Advisory Committee, composed of equal numbers of management and labor representatives and headed by a chairperson appointed by the director of the Office of Personnel Management (OPM), advises the OPM "on a wide variety of policy matters related to the Federal Wage System."

Source references: Harry A. Donoian, "A New Approach to Setting the Pay of Federal Blue-Collar Workers," *MLR*, April 1969; Harold Suskin (ed.), *Job Evaluation and Pay Administration in the Public Sector* (Chicago: IPMA, 1977).

See also CLASSIFICATION ACT EMPLOYEES, FEDERAL WAGE SYSTEM.

wage boards Neutral boards established primarily as arbitral boards, but sometimes as boards of conciliation, for the purpose of establishing minimum wages in order to raise the wages of unorganized employees who are dragging rates down and to encourage organization. They have been widely used in Australia and Great Britain through the trade boards.

Wage boards are not prevalent in the United States, although wage-board procedure is utilized under the Fair Labor Standards Act, and also occasionally in the states to deal with minimum wages in certain industries.

Source references: George W. Hartmann and Theodore Newcomb (ed.), *Industrial Conflict—A Psychological Interpretation* (New York: Cordon, 1939); Dorothy Sells, *British Wage Boards* (Washington: Brookings Institution, 1939).

wage brackets *See* SOUND AND TESTED RATES.

wage chronologies A series of studies instituted by BLS in 1948 to show for limited periods the rates of wages, the pattern of wage changes and related benefit and plant practices.

The *Directory of Wage Chronologies From 1948 to June 1969* published in 1969, indicates the wage chronology reports by specific employers or groups of employees, the period covered in the survey, the report number, as well as its first publication as a *Monthly Labor Review* article.

Source references: U.S. Dept. of Labor, BLS, *A Directory of Wage Chronologies, 1948–June 1969* (Washington: 1969); ———, *Major BLS Programs—A Summary of Their Characteristics, 1969 Edition* (Washington: 1969).

wage collection Procedures established by state departments of labor and frequently by law to assure that individuals working for wages receive the full amount of money due them. The regulations may apply to the frequency of the wage payment intervals and require explicit indication to the employee of the amount earned and of any deductions from the wages due. Wage collection problems arise frequently in the case of fly-by-night enterprises, which seek to defraud individual wage earners. In some cities, legal aid societies have assisted employees to collect the wages due them.

wage control The phrase usually applies to efforts by government to stabilize wages at existing levels or at levels which would create a minimum of inflationary pressure. The phrase is also applied occasionally to efforts made by unions to stabilize wages by obtaining uniform wage rates by geographic regions or by industry.

See also WAGE-PRICE POLICY, WAGE STABILIZATION.

wage criteria The factors which are taken into consideration by labor and management in wage negotiations. Among factors usually raised at the bargaining table are the employer's ability to pay, productivity of employees, substandard wages, price changes, company profits, competition, and the like.

Source references: Jules Backman, *Wage Determination: An Analysis of Wage Criteria* (Princeton: Van Nostrand, 1959); John T. Dunlop, "The Economies of Wage Dispute Settlement," *Law and Contemporary Problems*, Spring 1947; A. L. Gitlow, "Wage Criteria: Their Validity in Wage Determination," *PJ*, Nov. 1956; Morton Singer, "Labor Arbitration: The Need for Universal Wage Criteria," *LLJ*, June 1951; Sylvia Wiseman, "Wage Criteria for Collective Bargaining," *ILRR*, Jan. 1956.

See also WAGE BARGAINING.

wage cut A reduction in wages. Unions generally oppose wage cuts made in order to keep a company in business, particularly since this might result in subsidizing incompetent or inefficient management. However, under some circumstances unions agree to the reduction of wage rates in order to maintain employment for their members.

Professor S. H. Slichter in *Union Policies and Industrial Management* indicated three situations in which unions have agreed to accept wage cuts:

1. In some cases firms were urgently in need of immediate relief from competitive pressure. Reductions of costs through improvements in efficiency take time. In a small number of such cases the union consented to temporary

general reductions in wages. It was understood that the old rates would be restored as soon as the finances of the firm permitted it.
2. In every piecework shop there are bound to be some rates which are out of line and which yield earnings disproportionate to the skill of the job—sometimes too high and sometimes too low. It has been the policy of the union to resist cuts in rates that were too high and to trade reductions in these rates for increases in rates that had proved to be too low. Now, in order to help union employers find ways of cutting their costs, it modified its attitude toward the high rates. It came to regard them as special privileges accruing to a very few members of the union by which these members profited at the expense of the other members and hence was willing to accept cuts in such rates.
3. Recognition by the union that it must help its employers compete with non-union employers led to a marked change in the policy of the union in setting new piece rates.

Source reference: Sumner H. Slichter, *Union Policies and Industrial Management* (Washington: Brookings Institution, 1941).

wage decisions The decisions on wage policy reached either by international unions or major companies. These decisions can have major impact on a wide variety of economic conditions in the community.

Source reference: George P. Shultz and Charles A. Myers, "Union Wage Decisions and Employment," *AER*, June 1950.

See also WAGE BARGAINING.

wage deductions Sums withheld by an employer from the gross earnings of employees to pay certain charges levied against them or which they have authorized. The deductions include such items as taxes and union dues.

See also CHECK-OFF.

wage deferral *See* DEFERRED WAGE INCREASE.

wage determination The practices and procedures used to fix wage rates in collective bargaining. In nonunion situations, determination is simply by unilateral employer action or, in some cases, through third-party determination, such as arbitration. The techniques and procedures for wage determination depend upon the particular needs of a company and may involve not only a major review of the job structure of an entire plant, but also levels of wages, and comparisons with other companies in the same industry or geographic area. During periods of national emergency or war, wage determinations usually are made by public tribunals which establish general policy.

Source references: John T. Dunlop, *Wage Determination Under Trade Unions* (New York: Augustus M. Kelley, 1966); Otto Eckstein and Thomas A. Wilson, "The Determination of Money Wages in American Industry," *Quarterly Journal of Economics*, Aug. 1962; Henry S. Farber, *Individual Preferences and Union Wage Determination: The Case of the United Mine Workers* (Princeton: Princeton Univ., IR Section, WP 99, 1977); Wallace Hendricks, *Labor Market Structure and Union Wage Levels* (Champaign: Univ. of Illinois, Institute of Labor and IR, 1975); ———, *Unionism, Oligopoly and Rigid Wages* (Urbana: Univ. of Illinois, Institute of Labor and IR, Reprint Series no. 290, 1981); William A. Howard and N. Arnold Tolles, "Wage Determination in Key Manufacturing Industries, 1950–70," *ILRR*, July 1974; George E. Johnson, "The Determination of Wages in the Union and Non-Union Sectors," *BJIR*, July 1977; Harry C. Katz, "Municipal Pay Determination: The Case of San Francisco," *IR*, Winter 1979; D. Quinn Mills, "The Problems of Setting General Pay Standards: An Historical Review," *Proceedings of the 26th A/M, IRRA*, ed. by Gerald Somers (Madison: 1974); Daniel J. B. Mitchell, "Some Empirical Observations of Relevance to the Analysis of Union Wage Determination," *Journal of Labor Research*, Fall 1980; Melvin W. Reder, "Wage Determination in Theory and Practice," *A Decade of Industrial Relations Research, 1946–1956*, ed. by Neil W. Chamberlain, Frank C. Pierson and Theresa Wolfson (New York: Harper, IRRA Pub. no. 19, 1958); W. Earl Sasser and Samuel H. Pettway, "Case of Big Mac's Pay Plans," *Harvard BR*, July/Aug. 1974; Albert Schwenk, *The Influence of Selected Industry Characteristics on Negotiated Settlements* (Washington: U.S. Dept. of Labor, BLS, Staff Paper no. 5, 1971); Stuart O. Schwietzer, "Factors Determining the Interindustry Structure of Wages," *ILRR*, Jan. 1969; Robert E. Sibson, *Wages and Salaries: A Handbook for Line Managers* (rev. ed., New York: AMA, 1967); George W. Taylor and Frank C. Pierson (ed.), *New Concepts in Wage Determination* (New York: McGraw-Hill, 1957).

See also RATE SETTING.

wage developments The U.S. Department of Labor, Bureau of Labor Statistics, issues a series of monthly reports on wage adjustments made throughout the country. One of these is the monthly periodical entitled *Current Wage Developments.*

It reports the current wage changes in various industries and includes details by industry, union, and company or association, showing the effective dates of changes, the approximate number of workers involved, and the wage adjustments made.

wage differentials Variations among wage rates due to a variety of factors—job content, geographic location, skill, industry, company, sex. Union efforts often are directed to the elimination of wage differentials traceable to factors other than those resulting from differences in the amount of effort or skill required to perform the work.

Source references: John Abowd and Orley Ashenfelter, *Unemployment and Compensating Wage Differentials* (Princeton: Princeton Univ., IR Section, WP 120, 1979); Orley Ashenfelter and Richard Layard, *Incomes Policy and Wage Differentials* (Princeton: Princeton Univ., IR Section, WP 138, 1980); Farrell E. Bloch and Mark S. Kuskin, "Wage Determination in the Union and Nonunion Sectors," *ILRR*, Jan. 1978; Daniel S. Hamermesh, *White Collar Unions and Occupational Wage Differentials* (Princeton: Princeton Univ., IR Section, WP no. 16, 1969); C. Russell Hill, "Migrant-Nonmigrant Earnings Differentials in a Local Labor Market," *ILRR*, April 1975; Toivo P. Kanninen, "Wage Differentials Among Labor Markets," *MLR*, June 1962; John E. Maher, "Union, Nonunion Wage Differentials," *AER*, June 1956; Joanne Martin, "The Fairness of Earnings Differentials: An Experimental Study of the Perceptions of Blue-Collar Workers," *Journal of Human Resources*, Winter 1982; Harry Ober, "Occupational Wage Differentials, 1907–1947," *MLR*, July 1948; Craig A. Olson, "An Analysis of Wage Differentials Received by Workers on Dangerous Jobs," *Journal of Human Resources*, Spring 1981; Robert Ozanne, "A Century of Occupational Differentials in Manufacturing," *Review of Economics and Statistics*, Aug. 1962; Joseph F. Quinn, *Pay Differentials Among Mature Workers in the Public and Private Sectors* (Madison: Univ. of Madison, Institute for Research on Poverty, Discussion Paper 445–77, 1977); Albert Rees, *Compensating Wage Differentials* (Princeton: Princeton Univ., IR Section, WP 41, 1973); Lloyd G. Reynolds, "Wage Differences in Local Labor Markets," *AER*, June 1946; Paul M. Ryscavage, "Measuring Union-Nonunion Earnings Differences," *MLR*, Dec. 1974; David E. Shulenberger, Robert A. McLean, and Sara B. Rasch, "Union-Nonunion Wage Differentials: A Replication and Extension," *IR*, Spring 1982; Mark S. Sieling, "Clerical Pay Differentials in Metropolitan Areas, 1961–80," *MLR*, July 1982; Sharon P. Smith, *Government Wage Differentials* (Princeton: Princeton Univ., IR Section, WP 65, 1975); ———, "Pay Differentials Between Federal Government and Private Sector Workers," *ILRR*, Jan. 1976; Robert W. Van Giezen, "A New Look at Occupational Wages Within Individual Establishments," *MLR*, Nov. 1982; Stephen W. Welch, "Union-Nonunion Construction Wage Differentials," *IR*, Spring 1980.

See also CIVIL RIGHTS ACT OF 1964, EQUAL PAY ACT OF 1963, GEOGRAPHIC WAGE DIFFERENTIALS, HISTORICAL WAGE DIFFERENTIALS, INTERCITY DIFFERENTIAL, NORTH-SOUTH WAGE DIFFERENTIALS, OFF-SHIFT DIFFERENTIAL, RACE DIFFERENTIAL, REGIONAL (WAGE) DIFFERENTIAL, SEX DIFFERENTIAL, SHIFT DIFFERENTIAL, SKILL DIFFERENTIAL.

wage disputes Disagreements between labor and management over wages or wage rates.

wage dispute settlement Procedures and techniques to resolve wage disputes.

Source references: John T. Dunlop, "The Economics of Wage-Dispute Settlement," *Law and Contemporary Problems*, Spring 1947; A. H. Raskin, "An Effective Way to Settle Wage Disputes?" *Challenge*, Feb. 1961.

See also DISPUTE ADJUSTMENT.

wage drift Term generally used to describe the differential change in average earnings levels over time as measured against negotiated changes. The difference between the level of actual earnings and the level at which earnings would be if formal general wage changes alone are taken into account is likened to an upward drift.

wage escalation Upward movement of wages through use of an adjustment clause such as a cost of living escalator provision, a deferred wage increase, or an "annual productivity factor."

Source references: Jules Backman, "Wage Escalation and Inflation," *ILRR*, April 1960; H. M. Douty, "The Growth, Status, and Implications of Wage Escalation," *MLR*, Feb. 1953; Joseph W. Garbarino, "Wage Escalation and Wage Inflation," *Proceedings of the Business and Economic Statistical Section of the American Statistical Association*, Dec. 1959.

See also ESCALATOR CLAUSE.

wage floor A minimum wage established either through collective bargaining, below which an individual cannot be hired, or the legal minimum established under such laws as the Fair Labor Standards Act or state minimum wage laws.

Source references: J. F. Kennedy, "Floor Beneath Wages Is Gone: Fair Labor Standards and Walsh-Healey Acts," *New Republic*, July 20, 1953; Jacob Mincer, *The Economics of Wage Floors* (Cambridge: NBER, WP 804, 1981).

See also FAIR LABOR STANDARDS ACT OF 1938.

wage garnishment *See* GARNISHMENT.

Wage-Hour Law *See* FAIR LABOR STANDARDS ACT OF 1938.

wage incentive plans *See* INCENTIVE CONTRACTS, INCENTIVE RATE, INCENTIVE WAGE, MANIT.

wage increase *See* ACROSS-THE-BOARD INCREASE, TAPERED WAGE INCREASES.

wage indexation *See* COST-OF-LIVING ADJUSTMENT.

wage inequality A disparity between the rates paid to workers whose responsibilities and duties are identical or nearly so. Under wage stabilization during World War II "inequality" was a basis for granting wage adjustments. Inequality of wage rates existed on an intraplant or interplant basis. One method of resolving inequalities was to establish wage brackets of sound and tested rates.

Collective bargaining agreements may provide procedures to review and eliminate wage inequalities.

See also SOUND AND TESTED RATES.

wage laws Statutes concerned with determination of minimum wages. The Fair Labor Standards Act is one such law. Many states have minimum wage laws.

See also FAIR LABOR STANDARDS ACT OF 1938.

wage leadership A single dominant company or a group of companies may negotiate settlements which establish the pattern or leadership, not only for that industry, but possibly also for related industries. Follow-the-leader wage adjustments are usual in some industries.

The phrase sometimes is applied to a company which maintains a policy of wage leadership in the industry or geographic area.

wage level The general plane or going rate of wages received by individuals in a geographic area, in an industry, a single establishment, or an occupation. The determination of the relative uniformity or level is based on the average rates paid within that occupation, geographic area, or industry. Some industries and occupations have high wage levels whereas others have low wage levels.

wage mediation Efforts by a third party to resolve differences on wages. Mediators, unlike arbitrators, merely assist the parties in reaching agreement. They have no authority to make determinations.

wage movements Upward or downward changes in wages over periods of time. Efforts have been made to measure these changes, not only in particular industries or occupational groups, but also between organized and unorganized sectors in the community.

Source references: Joseph Altonji and Orley Ashenfelter, *Wage Movements and the Labor Market Equilibrium Hypothesis*

(Princeton: Princeton Univ., IR Section, WP no. 130, 1979); Martin Segal, "Unionism and Wage Movements," *Southern Economic Journal*, Oct. 1961.

See also WAGE DEVELOPMENTS.

wage negotiations Collective bargaining negotiations concerned primarily with determination of wages.

Source references: James J. Bambrick, Jr. and D. K. Lippman, *What Happened in 1949 Wage Negotiations* (New York: NICB, Studies in Personnel Policy no. 105, 1950); Pao Lun Cheng, "Wage Negotiation and Bargaining Power," *ILRR*, Jan. 1968; Richard A. Lester, "Negotiated Wage Increases, 1951–1967," *The Review of Economics and Statistics*, May 1968; Sumner H. Slichter, *Basic Criteria in Wage Negotiations* (Chicago: Chicago Assn. of Commerce and Industry, 1947).

See also WAGE BARGAINING.

wage patterns The wage structures or relationships among the various jobs in a given industry or geographic area. Also applies to situations in which a major company negotiates a wage increase that becomes the wage pattern for an entire industry or geographic area.

Source references: Kenneth Alexander and John E. Maher, "The Wage Pattern in the United States, 1946–1957," *ILRR*, July 1962; Maurice C. Benewitz and Alan Spiro, "The Wage Pattern in the United States, 1946–1957," *ILRR*, Oct. 1962; John E. Maher, "The Wage Pattern in the United States, 1946–1957," *ILRR*, Oct. 1961.

See also PATTERN BARGAINING, WAGE DEVELOPMENTS.

wage payment plans Systems of wage payment either on the basis of time worked or the amount of work done on an individual or group incentive basis.

Source references: Chris J. Berger and Donald P. Schwab, "Pay Incentives and Pay Satisfaction," *IR*, Spring 1980; Robert J. Greene, "Which Pay Delivery System is Best for Your Organization?" *Personnel*, May/June 1981; Robert B. McKersie, "Wage Payment Methods of the Future," *BJIR*, June 1963; George T. Milkovich and Michael J. Delaney, *A Note on Determining Employee Preferences for Alternative Compensation Forms* (Minneapolis: Univ. of Minnesota, IRC, WP 73–03, 1973); John H. Pencavel, *Work Effort and Alternative Methods of Remuneration* (Princeton: Princeton Univ., IR Section, WP no. 63, 1975); United Electrical, Radio and Machine Workers, *UE Guide to Wage Payment Plans, Time Study and Job Evaluation* (New York: 1943).

See also BONUS, INCENTIVE WAGE, INDIVIDUAL AGREEMENT, STINT WAGE SYSTEM, STRAIGHT DAY-WORK.

wage policy The formalized practice and statements of general principles laid down by a company, industry, or unit of government concerning all matters involving wages. It also may mean the programs, practices, and theories of trade unions as they affect wages and wage movements. In periods of rapid price movements and during war periods, the government's concern relates to stabilization of wages and prices as a support to reasonable acceleration of the economy.

Source references: Barton J. Bernstein, "The Truman Administration and Its Reconversion Wage Policy," *Labor History*, Fall 1965; H. M. Douty, "Some Problems of Wage Policy," *MLR*, July 1962; W. Frank, "A National Wages Policy: Some Legal Implications," *Journal of Business Law*, April 1962; Joseph W. Garbarino, *Wage Policy and Long-Term Contracts* (Washington: Brookings Institution, 1962); Gottfried Haberler, "Incomes Policy and Inflation, Some Further Reflections," *Proceedings of the 24th A/M, IRRA*, ed. by Gerald Somers (Madison: 1972); J. R. Hicks, "Economic Foundations of Wage Policy," *Economic Journal*, Sept. 1955; George H. Hildebrand, "Wage Policy and Economic Activity," *MLR*, Feb. 1959; Richard A. Lester, *Company Wage Policies* (Princeton: Princeton Univ., IR Section, 1948); Benjamin C. Roberts, *National Wages Policy in War and Peace* (London: Allen, Unwin, 1958); Arthur M. Ross, *Trade-Union Wage Policy* (Berkeley: UC Press, 1948); Laurence S. Seidman, "The Case for a Tax-Based Incomes Policy," *Sloan Management Review*, Winter 1979.

wage preference Priorities under the common law and most state statutes which give a worker a prior claim on a bankrupt estate for wages due because of work performed within a reasonable period prior to the bankruptcy. Except for claims by the government for taxes, costs of administration, and preservation of the estate, wage claims have preference over other obligations of the estate.

wage-price policy The general principles set out by government enunciating standards of noninflationary price and wage behavior to attain full employment, with appeals to labor and business for compliance. The main element of wage-price controls is to keep hourly wage increases in line with the average long-term gains in output per man-hour.

In the United States the use of mandatory wage and price controls has been mainly restricted to wartime. In 1971, however, President Nixon implemented the first peacetime system of mandatory wage and price controls in U.S. history. This program, put in effect on August 6, 1971, imposed a 90-day freeze on wages, salaries, fringe benefits, prices, and rents. The Cost of Living Council, a cabinet-level group, was established to oversee the program. Other bodies, such as the Price Commission, composed of all public members, and the Pay Board, a tripartite body, were created to administer Phases I through IV of the Nixon program, which was extended to April 30, 1974.

A voluntary wage price standards program administered by the Council on Wage and Price Stability was instituted by President Carter on October 24, 1978. President Reagan terminated this program on January 29, 1981.

Source references: AFL-CIO, *Meany on Controls* (Washington: 1972); John T. Dunlop, "Wage and Price Controls as Seen by a Controller," *LLJ*, Aug. 1975; Craufurd D. Goodwin (ed.), *Exhortation and Controls; The Search for a Wage-Price Policy, 1945–1971* (Washington: Brookings Institution, 1975); C. Jackson Grayson, Jr., *Confessions of a Price Controller* (Homewood: Dow Jones-Irwin, 1974); Robert W. Kopp, "The Impact of the Phase II Mandatory Pay Controls on Collective Bargaining," *NYU 26th Annual Conference on Labor*, ed. by Emanuel Stein and S. Theodore Reiner (New York: Bender, 1974); John Kraft and Blaine Roberts (ed.), *Wage and Price Controls, The U.S. Experiment* (New York: Praeger, 1975); Robert F. Lanzillotti, Mary T. Hamilton, and R. Blaine Roberts, *Phase II in Review, The Price Commission Experience* (Washington: Brookings Institution, 1975); Edward S. Mason, "Some Reflections on the Wage-Price Problem," *Proceedings of the 1st A/M, IRRA*, ed. by Milton Derber (Champaign: 1949); D. Quinn Mills, "Comprehensive Wage-Price Policy," *Sloan Management Review*, Winter 1979; Daniel J. B. Mitchell, "Phase II Wage Controls," *ILRR*, April 1974; Paul Prasow, *The Impact of Wage Guidelines—Controls on Collective Bargaining* (Los Angeles: UC, Institute of IR, Reprint no. 292, 1980); George P. Shultz and Kenneth W. Dam, "Reflections on Wage and Price Controls," *ILRR*, Jan. 1977; James W. Smith, "The Nixon Administration's Wage Controls: A Labor Viewpoint," *LLJ*, Aug. 1973; Herbert Stein, "Price-Fixing as Seen by a Price-Fixer," *Across the Board*, Dec. 1978; Lucretia Dewey Tanner and Mary Converse, "The 1978–80 Pay Guidelines: Meeting the Need for Flexibility," *MLR*, July 1981; U.S. Council on Wage and Price Stability, *Evaluation of the Pay and Price Standards Program* (Washington: 1981); ———, *Second-Year Price Standards: A Compendium* (Washington: 1980); U.S. GAO, *The Voluntary Pay and Price Standards Have Had No Discernable Effect on Inflation* (Washington: 1980); Jay W. Waks, "Guide to the Pay Standard: The Seven Percent Solution," *Employee Relations LJ*, Summer 1979; Arnold R. Weber, *In Pursuit of Price Stability; The Wage-Price Freeze of 1971* (Washington: Brookings Institution, 1973); Arnold R. Weber and Daniel J. B. Mitchell, *The Pay Board's Progress, Wage Controls in Phase II* (Washington: Brookings Institution, 1978); Kenneth Young and Rudy Oswald, "Controls: An Unfair Program Gets Worse," *American Federationist*, Feb. 1979.

wage progression A system that provides wage increases automatically after a certain length of service. The increases sometimes are referred to as longevity or seniority increases.

See also AUTOMATIC PROGRESSION, MERIT INCREASE.

wage-push inflation The characterization by some economists of certain types of inflationary movement. It suggests that the prime mover is the pressure of wages. Others suggest that the cause is "price-pull" inflation by use of the other blade of the wage-price shears.

Source references: Ralph C. James, "Market Structures and Wage-Push Inflation," *ILRR*, July 1960; Alfred Kuhn, "Market Structures and Wage-Push Inflation," *ILRR*, Jan. 1959; Howard D. Marshall, "Checking Wage-Push Inflation," *LLJ*, Jan. 1960; Walter A. Morton, "Wage-Push Inflation," *Proceedings of the 11th A/M, IRRA*, ed. by Gerald Somers (Madison: 1959).

wage range *See* RATE RANGE.

wage rate The established or regular rate of pay for a given unit of time or effort on the job, exclusive of premium payments. Payments may be made on a time basis or by incentive rates.

Source reference: J. Pen, *The Wage Rate Under Collective Bargaining* (Cambridge: Harvard UP, 1959).

See also OCCUPATIONAL RATE, PREVAILING RATE, PROBATIONARY RATE, SINGLE RATE.

wage rate bracket *See* SOUND AND TESTED RATES.

wage rate determination The process of establishing wage rates, usually through collective bargaining.

Source reference: Edwin E. Witte, "Criteria in Wage Rate Determination," *Washington Univ. LQ*, Fall 1949.

See also WAGE BARGAINING.

wage rate structure *See* WAGE STRUCTURE.

wage relationships Efforts are made to explain wage relationships by assessment of market influences, including the impact of the economic power respectively of labor and management in wage determination. The term also describes internal wage-job relationships of a plant.

Source references: Donald J. Blackmore, "Occupational Wage Relationships in Metropolitan Areas," *MLR*, Dec. 1968; Clark Kerr, "Wage Relationships—The Comparative Impact of Market and Power Forces," *The Theory of Wage Determination*, ed. by John T. Dunlop (New York: Macmillan, 1957); Philip Ross, "Labor Market Behavior and the Relationship Between Unemployment and Wages," *Proceedings of the 14th A/M, IRRA*, ed. by Gerald Somers (Madison: 1962).

wage reopening clause A provision in collective bargaining agreements which permits either party, but usually the union, to reopen the contract during its term to renegotiate wages. This is particularly true when unions and employers have negotiated contracts for long terms. Unless the contract makes provision for automatic adjustments, it is usual to make some provision to reopen it in order to avoid freezing wages for a long period, and to take care of unusual circumstances which might result from rapid price movements or a period of wage instability.

See also ANNUAL IMPROVEMENT FACTOR, ESCALATOR CLAUSE, LONG-TERM CONTRACT, REOPENING CLAUSE.

wage restitution *See* BACK PAY.

wage review A periodic review of the performance of individuals to determine those eligible for increases because of merit or for promotion to higher-rated jobs.

See also JOINT WAGE REVIEW COMMITTEE, MERIT INCREASE.

wages, aggregate All wage payments earned by wage earners during a specified period.

wages, real *See* REAL WAGES.

wage settlement *See* WAGE BARGAINING.

wages-fund theory A theory of wages popular during Malthus' time stating that there was a fixed lump of wages for employees in any country in any year. Any effort by one group of workers to increase its share (through organization or economic pressure) therefore would merely result in reducing the share available to other workers.

Source references: Charles Gide and Charles Rist, *A History of Economic Doctrines* (London: Harrap, 1915); Lewis H. Haney, *History of Economic Thought* (New York: Macmillan, 1949); William A. Scott, *The Development of Economics* (New York: Appleton-Century, 1933).

wage spillover Refers to the influence of wage rates in "key" industries or bargaining units on the wages in other industries or units. Wage spillover occurs where union wage settlements set a pattern for nonunion wages, or if wages in the private sector set a pattern for public sector pay.

The degree of spillover may depend on such factors as labor and product market conditions and union power.

Source references: Clifford H. Anderson, "Wage Spillover Mechanisms: A U.S.-Canadian Analysis," *IR*, May 1972; John Lawler, "Wage Spillover: The Impact of Landrum-Griffin," *IR*, Winter 1981; Daniel J. B. Mitchell, *Unions, Wages, and Inflation* (Washington: Brookings Institution, 1980).

See also RIPPLE EFFECT.

wage stabilization The systematic and organized effort of government to maintain stable economic conditions by assurance of reasonable relationships between wages and prices. During World War II Congress passed the Stabilization Act in October 1942 which permitted the President to issue general orders to stabilize prices, wages, and salaries. Executive Order 9250 was issued on October 3, 1942 as an attempt to keep wages at the level that existed on September 15, 1942.

Voluntary wage adjustments were precluded. But the National War Labor Board was limited in adjusting wages to those necessary to "correct maladjustments or inequalities, to eliminate substandards of living, to correct gross inequities, or to aid in the effective prosecution of the war." The board's wage stabilization program had to be developed within that general framework.

During the Korean War in 1950, the President by Executive Order established the Economic Stabilization Agency on September 9, 1950, which included a Wage Stabilization Board. This was enlarged to an 18-member board on April 21, 1951, which was tripartite in character. It had jurisdiction not only over wage disputes, but over nonwage issues which threatened or affected defense efforts.

Source references: Isaac N. Groner, "The Legal Basis for Wage Stabilization Board Operations," *NYU 5th Annual Conference on Labor*, ed. by Emanuel Stein (Albany: Bender, 1952); Clark Kerr, "Governmental Wage Restraints: Their Limits and Uses in a Mobilized Economy," *AER*, May 1952; Richard A. Lester, "Collective Bargaining Under Stabilization," *NYU 4th Annual Conference on Labor*, ed. by Emanuel Stein (Albany: Bender, 1951); Moses Lukaczer, "Planning for Wage Stabilization," *LLJ*, Feb. 1957; Henry Mayer, "Impact of the Control Program on Collective Bargaining," *NYU 5th Annual Conference on Labor*, ed. by Emanual Stein (Albany: Bender, 1952); C. Wilson Randle, "The Impact of Wage Stabilization Upon Bargaining Practices," *LLJ*, Sept. 1951; Bruno Stein, "Wage Stabilization in the Korean War Period: The Role of Subsidiary Wage Boards," *Labor History*, Spring 1963; U.S. Wage Stabilization Board, *Wages in a National Emergency—The Why and How of Wage Stabilization* (Washington: 1952); Harry Weiss, "The Wage Stabilization Program," *NYU 4th Annual Conference on Labor*, ed. by Emanuel Stein (Albany: Bender, 1951).

See also NATIONAL WAGE STABILIZATION BOARD, WAGE-PRICE POLICY.

Wage Stabilization Board *See* NATIONAL WAGE STABILIZATION BOARD.

wage structure Douty states that "Among its several meanings, the term 'structure' implies a series of relationships. The wage structure of a plant or an office or, more broadly, of a national economy can be viewed as a series of wage rates designed to compensate workers for the varying skills and abilities required in the production process. . . . The concept of structure also has dimensional aspects. In the case of wages, the significant dimension is the number of workers at each rate in the scale. A wage structure is defined, therefore, not only by a series of hierarchy of rates, but also by the relative importance of each rate."

Source references: H. M. Douty, *The Wage Bargain and the Labor Market* (Baltimore: Johns Hopkins UP, 1980); John T. Dunlop, "The Task of Contemporary Wage Theory," *The Theory of Wage Determination* (New York: Macmillan, 1964); Joseph Garbarino, "A Theory of Inter-Industry Wage Structure Variation," *Quarterly Journal of Economics*, May 1950; Robert J. Gordon, *Why U.S. Wage and Employment Behavior Differs From That in Britain and Japan* (Cambridge: NBER, WP 809, 1981); George H. Hildebrand, *External Influence and the Determination of the Internal Wage Struc-*

ture (Ithaca: NYSSILR, Cornell Univ., Reprint 142, 1964); Ephraim Kleiman, "Wages and Plant Size: A Spillover Effect?" *ILRR*, Jan. 1971; Marvin Kosters, Kenneth Fedor, and Albert Eckstein, "Collective Bargaining Settlements and the Wage Structure," *LLJ*, Aug. 1973; Robert Livernash, "Stabilization of Internal Wage Rate Structure," *ILRR*, Jan. 1954; Patrick R. Pinto and Benjamin H. Lowenberg, "Pay: A Unitary View," *PJ*, June 1973; Felice Porter and Richard L. Keller, "Public and Private Pay Levels: A Comparison in Large Labor Markets," *MLR*, July 1981; Lloyd G. Reynolds and Cynthia H. Taft, *The Evolution of the Wage Structure* (New Haven: Yale UP, Studies in Economics, Vol. 6, 1955); Myra H. Strober, "Economic Development and the Hierarchy of Earnings," *IR*, Feb. 1973; Harold Suskin (ed.), *Job Evaluation and Pay Administration in the Public Sector* (Chicago: IPMA, 1977).

wage survey Wage studies which are based on the collection, tabulation, and analysis of original wage data on a company, geographic, industry, or national basis. The type of survey will depend on the purpose for which the material is to be utilized. It is of crucial importance that the materials provide reliable data, which will prove useful to labor and management in their negotiations as well as to economists interested in understanding the changing pattern of wages throughout the country.

Source references: American Compensation Association, *"Compensation" Pay Survey* (Scottsdale: 1981); Jack Blackman and Martin R. Gainsbrugh, *Behavior of Wages* (New York: NICB, 1948); Michael E. Borus, "Response Error in Survey Reports of Earnings Information," *Journal of the American Statistical Association*, Sept. 1966; Kenneth E. Foster, "The Plus Side of Salary Surveys," *Personnel*, Jan./Feb. 1963; William A. Groenekamp, "How Reliable Are Wage Surveys," *Personnel*, Jan./Feb. 1967; Harold A. Hovey and Elizabeth Dickson, *Comparing Compensation in Major American Cities: Study Methodology* (Washington: Urban Institute, WP 09–5115–01, 1978); Toivo P. Kanninen, "New Dimensions in BLS Wage Survey Work," *MLR*, Oct. 1959; Deborah B. Talbot, "Improved Area Wage Survey Indexes," *MLR*, May 1975; Joseph C. Ullman, "Using Turnover Data to Improve Wage Surveys," *PJ*, Oct. 1966; U.S. Dept. of Labor, BLS, *Major BLS Programs—A Summary of Their Characteristics, 1969 Edition* (Washington: 1969); ———, *Profiles of Occupational Pay: A Chartbook* (Washington: Bull. 2037, 1979); Virginia L. Ward, "Area Sample Changes in the Area Wage Survey Program," *MLR*, May 1975.

See also COMMUNITY WAGE SURVEY.

wage theories Hypotheses developed by economists and political scientists to explain wage rates and movements and the basis for wage payments. Numerous theories have been propounded. Among the best known are the Bargaining Theory of Wages, the Iron Law of Wages, the Marginal Productivity Theory of Wages, and the Residual Claimant Theory of Wages.

See also BARGAINING THEORY OF WAGES, IRON LAW OF WAGES, MARGINAL PRODUCTIVITY THEORY OF WAGES, RESIDUAL CLAIMANT THEORY (WAGES), WAGES-FUND THEORY.

wage trends *See* WAGE MOVEMENTS.

Wagner Act *See* NATIONAL LABOR RELATIONS ACT.

Wagner-Connery Act *See* NATIONAL LABOR RELATIONS ACT.

Wagner-Lewis bill An unemployment compensation bill proposed in February 1934. President Roosevelt felt that additional study was necessary before any major legislation should be enacted, and in June 1934 a Committee on Economic Security was established. The recommendations of this committee were incorporated in the bill which later became known as the Social Security Act of 1935.

Source references: Abraham Epstein, *Insecurity—A Challenge to America* (New York: Random House, 1938); Maxwell S. Stewart, *Social Security* (New York: Norton, 1939).

See also SOCIAL SECURITY ACT.

Wagner-Peyser Act The Act establishing the U.S. Employment Service in 1933 to assist in the development of a nationwide system of public employment offices to bring workers and employers together.

The U.S. Employment Service establishes policies and develops methods and procedures for the coordination and guidance of a nationwide system of public employment offices operated by state agencies which are affiliated with the U.S. Employment Service within the Employment and Training Administration of the U.S. Department of Labor.

The six major functions of the U.S. Employment Service include:

(1) Placement service,
(2) Employment counseling and selective placement service,
(3) Provision of special services to veterans,
(4) Industrial services,
(5) Supplying labor-market information, and
(6) Community participation.

Source reference: Wagner-Peyser Act, as amended, 29 U.S.C. 49 et seq. (1982).

See also JOB TRAINING PARTNERSHIP ACT (JTPA) OF 1982, U.S. EMPLOYMENT SERVICE.

waiting period (time) This phrase has a variety of meanings. Among them are: (1) a cooling-off period prior to calling a strike, which may be required by law or by collective bargaining agreement; (2) the period under sickness and accident insurance prior to an employee becoming eligible to receive payments; (3) the period of time before an employee receives unemployment insurance payments; (4) idle time because of a breakdown in machinery or because of a delay in receiving materials.

See also COOLING-OFF PERIOD, UNEMPLOYMENT COMPENSATION.

walking delegate *See* BUSINESS AGENT, TRAMPING COMMITTEE.

walkout The term is used as synonymous with strike. It is more akin to a quickie or a wildcat strike, since there is usually no formal procedure involved in calling the walkout. It is more a spontaneous reaction to a specific problem in the plant rather than the calculated or planned action of a strike.

Wall Paper Craftsmen and Workers of North America; United (AFL-CIO) The Wall Paper Craftsmen merged with the International Brotherhood of Pulp, Sulphite and Paper Mill Workers (AFL-CIO) on April 29, 1958.

See also PULP, SULPHITE AND PAPER MILL WORKERS; INTERNATIONAL BROTHERHOOD OF (AFL-CIO).

Walsh-Healey Act of 1936 Statute enacted by Congress to establish labor standards for work performed on government manufacturing and supply contracts. It applies to employees working on government contracts in excess of $10,000 for materials, articles, supplies, equipment, or naval vessels. Office and custodial employees are not covered, and the exemptions under the Fair Labor Standards Act for executive, administrative, and professional employees also are applied under this Act. A number of types of contracts, including those for "perishable" commodities, those with common carriers and communications companies, and those for purchase of commodities in the "open market," are specifically exempt from the Act's requirements.

Under the minimum-wage standard, covered employees must be paid at least the prevailing minimum wage rates as determined by the secretary of labor. They also must be paid time and one-half their "basic" rate for work in excess of eight hours a day or 40 hours a week, whichever is greater. Learners, handicapped workers, and apprentices may be employed at rates below the applicable minimum rate in accordance with special regulations issued under the Act.

The child-labor provisions forbid the employment of both female and male minors under the age of 16 on government work. The Act also forbids their employment on government contracts where the working conditions are unsanitary, hazardous, or dangerous to the health and safety of the employees.

The under secretary of labor is authorized to investigate and decide cases involving alleged violations of the Act. The government may sue to recover liquidated damages found due in such proceedings in the federal courts, or it may deduct the damages from the amount due the contractor under his contract. For minimum-wage and overtime-pay violations, the liquidated damages equal the underpayments to employees. A penalty of $10 a day is assessed for each day a minor or convict is knowingly employed on government work. Serious and willful violators are subject to the blacklist penalty barring them from participation in government contracts for a period of three years. The Act is administered by the Wage and Hour Division in the Department of Labor.

Like the Fair Labor Standards and Davis-Bacon Acts, the Walsh-Healey Act was amended by the Portal-to-Portal Act to specify standards for determining compensable working time and to provide additional defenses to liability under the Act, including a two-year statute of limitations on liquidated damage claims.

Source references: Walsh-Healey Public Contracts Act, as amended, 41 U.S.C. 1952, Secs. 35–45 (1982); Carroll L. Christenson and Richard A. Myren, *Wage Policy Under the Walsh-Healey Public Contracts Act: A Critical Review* (Bloomington: Indiana UP, 1966); Rudolf Modley and James R. Patton, Jr., "Problem Child Among Labor Laws: The Walsh-Healey Act," *Duke LJ*, Spring 1963; Herbert C. Morton, *Public Contracts and Private Wages: Experience Under the Walsh-Healey Act* (Washington: Brookings Institution, 1965); U.S. Congress, Senate, Committee on Labor and Human Services, *Walsh-Healey Act/Contract Work Hours Standards Act Amendments, 1981, Hearings* (Washington: 1981).

See also PORTAL-TO-PORTAL PAY ACT, PREVAILING RATE.

War Labor Board *See* NATIONAL WAR LABOR BOARD.

War Labor Disputes Act Also known as the Smith-Connally Act, which gave statutory recognition to the National War Labor Board and provided for special elections before a strike could be called (even though labor and management had agreed to a no-strike, no-lockout understanding as a basis for establishing the National War Labor Board). The Act also limited political contributions by unions and, more importantly, provided for seizure of plant facilities under certain conditions.

See also GOVERNMENT SEIZURE.

War Manpower Commission The agency during World War II which had responsibility for integrating the manpower resources of the country for the most effective utilization of workers. The Commission directed the Selective Service System and tried to channel workers into industries engaged in the production of war materials.

Source reference: Avery Craven and Walter Johnson, *The United States, Experiment in Democracy* (Boston: Ginn, 1950).

See also EMPLOYMENT CONTROLS, MANPOWER.

Washington Job Protection Agreement A plan negotiated in 1936 by railroad carriers and 21 unions to provide displacement and severance allowances to employees required to accept new positions or separation from employment because of "coordination." "Coordination" is defined under the agreement as "joint action by two or more carriers whereby they unify, consolidate, merge or pool in whole or in part their separate railroad facilities or any of the operations or services previously performed by them through such separate facilities." A 90-day written notice of any coordination is required of the carrier to its employees and to the representatives of the employees. The 1936 agreement, in part or in its entirety, is still utilized to deal with technological, organizational, or operational changes.

Source reference: BNA, *Collective Bargaining Negotiations and Contracts,* Vol. 2, 53:511.

Washington Public Employees Association (Ind) Formerly known as the Washington State Employees Association, it is affiliated with the Assembly of Governmental Employees. Its monthly publication is *The Sentinel.*

Address: 114 West 10th St., Olympia, Wash. 98501. Tel. (206) 943–1121

wash-up time *See* CLEAN-UP PERIOD.

watch The period during which a seaman is on duty. It is comparable in normal operations to the work period or the shift.

Watchmen's Association; Independent (Ind) 9519 4th Ave., Brooklyn, N.Y. 11209. Tel. (718) 836–3508

Watch Workers Union; American (Ind) An organization affiliated with the National Federation of Independent Unions.

Address: 617 West Orange St., Lancaster, Pa. 17603. Tel. (717) 392–7255

Watson-Parker Act *See* RAILWAY LABOR ACT.

Weather Service Employees Organization; National A branch of the National Marine Engineers' Beneficial Association (AFL-CIO). Its official publication is *The Four Winds*.

Address: 444 North Capitol St., Washington, D.C. 20001. Tel. (202) 783–3131

Weber case The case in which the Supreme Court endorsed a contractual affirmative action plan negotiated between Kaiser Aluminum and Chemical Corp. and the United Steelworkers Union that reserved 50 percent of the openings in a job training program for black employees. The Court held that the affirmative action plan and Title VII of the Civil Rights Act of 1964 worked "to break down old patterns of racial segregation and hierarchy. Both were structured to 'open employment opportunities for Negroes in occupations which have been traditionally closed to them.'" The Court found the affirmative action plan to be a "permissible" plan because it "does not unnecessarily trammel the interests of the white employees. The plan does not require the discharge of white workers and their replacement with new black hires. Nor does the plan create an absolute bar to the advancement of white employees; half of those trained in the program will be white. Moreover, the plan is a temporary measure; it is not intended to maintain racial balance, but simply to eliminate a manifest racial imbalance. Preferential selection of craft employees . . . will end as soon as the percentage of black skilled craft workers . . . approximates the percentage of blacks in the local labor force."

Source references: United Steelworkers of America v. Weber, 443 US 317, 20 FEP Cases 1 (1979); Michael R. Fonthan, "After Weber: An Analysis of the Supreme Court's Endorsement of Racial Preference for Minorities," *Labor Law Developments 1980*, Proceedings of 26th Annual Institute on Labor Law, SLF (New York: Bender, 1980); Thomas R. Knight, "Title VII and Private Voluntary Remedial Preferences: The Impact of *Weber* and *Bakke*," *Industrial and Labor Relations Forum*, June 1980; Terry Leap and Irving Kovarsky, "What is the Impact of *Weber* on Collective Bargaining?" *LLJ*, June 1980; Neil D. McFeeley, "Weber Versus Affirmative Action?" *Personnel*, Jan./Feb. 1980; Thompson Powers, "Implications of *Weber*—'A Net Beneath,'" *Employee Relations LJ*, Winter 1979/80.

See also BAKKE CASE.

"we do not patronize" lists *See* BLACKLIST, BOYCOTT, BUCKS' STOVE AND RANGE CASE, WHITELIST.

weighted point method A job rating and evaluation procedure which examines the various component parts of the job, including such items as skill, responsibility, and effort, and weighs them according to their importance in a particular operation.

See also JOB EVALUATION, POINT PLAN.

Weingarten case A 1975 Supreme Court ruling upholding an NLRB decision that under Section 7 of the National Labor Relations Act, employees have the right to union representation at an investigatory interview if they reasonably believe the investigation will result in disciplinary action.

The Civil Service Reform Act of 1978 extends *Weingarten* rights to federal employees. In addition, each federal agency is annually required to inform its employees of their right to such representation.

Source references: NLRB v. Weingarten, Inc., 420 US 251, 88 LRRM 2689 (1975); David M. Cohen, "The Right to Representation: *Weingarten* and the Federal Employee," *LLJ*, Jan. 1979; Wallace B. Nelson, "Union Representation During Investigatory Interviews," *AJ*, Sept. 1976; Lewis H. Silverman and Michael J. Soltis, "Weingarten: An Old Trumpet Plays the Labor Circuit," *LLJ*, Nov. 1981; K. Bruce Stickler, "Investigating Employee Misconduct—Must the Union Be There?" *Employee Relations LJ*, Autumn 1977.

Welders of America; National Union, United (Ind) *See* WELDORS; INTERNATIONAL UNION, UNITED (IND).

Weldors; International Union, United (Ind) The union was formerly known as the National Union, United Welders of America (Ind). It merged with the International Union of Operating Engineers (AFL-CIO) on March 1, 1968.

See also OPERATING ENGINEERS; INTERNATIONAL UNION OF (AFL-CIO).

welfare activities *See* HEALTH BENEFIT PROGRAMS.

welfare and pension plans *See* PENSION PLAN, WELFARE PLANS.

Welfare and Pension Plans Disclosure Act of 1958 (Teller Act) A federal statute passed in 1958, effective January 1, 1959, which covered all nongovernmental welfare and pension plans affecting more than 25 employees. The Act provided for the registration, reporting, and disclosure of employee welfare and pension benefit plans and pertinent data.

The law was repealed with the enactment of the Employee Retirement Income Security Act of 1974.

Source references: Welfare and Pension Plans Disclosure Act, as amended, 29 U.S.C. 301–309 (1982) (repealed, 88 Stat. 851 (1974); matters formerly covered by the Welfare and Pension Plans Disclosure Act are now covered by the Employee Retirement Income Security Act of 1974, Pub. L. 93–406, Sept. 2, 1974, 88 Stat. 829 (codified as amended in scattered sections of 5, 18, 26, 29, 31, and 42 U.S.C.); U.S. Dept. of Labor, *Legislative History of the Welfare and Pension Plans Disclosure Act of 1958, as Amended by Public Law 87–420 of 1962* (Washington: 1962).

See also EMPLOYEE RETIREMENT INCOME SECURITY ACT (ERISA) OF 1974.

welfare funds Funds generally established through collective bargaining which provide various health and welfare benefits, including death benefits and pension funds.

Source references: David Dubinsky, "Safeguarding Union Welfare Funds," *American Federationist*, July 1954; Gordon M. Kaufman and Roy Penchansky, "Simulation Study of Union Health and Welfare Funds," *Industrial Management Review*, Fall 1968; William Pearl, "Welfare and Pension Funds Come of Age," *LLJ*, March 1961.

See also PENSION FUND, PENSION PLAN.

welfare management A phrase used to describe activities and programs of employers to improve the comfort, convenience, and welfare of their workers. It is sometimes referred to as paternalism, particularly where the welfare programs are developed as a substitute for collective bargaining or as a means to discourage employee organization.

See also PATERNALISM, EMPLOYER.

welfare plans Health and benefit plans which may include life insurance, hospital, medical, and surgical protection, paid sick leave, pensions, and other welfare benefits for employees. Programs may be financed through joint contributions or solely by employers.

The Employee Retirement Income Security Act (ERISA) of 1974 defines a welfare plan as "any plan, fund, or program . . . established or maintained by an employer or by an employee organization, or by both . . . for the purpose of providing for its participants or their beneficiaries, through the purchase of insurance or otherwise, (A) medical, surgical, or hospital care or benefits, or benefits in the event of sickness, accident, disability, death or unemployment, or vacation benefits, apprenticeship or other training programs, or day care centers, scholarship funds, or prepaid legal services, or (B) any benefit described in section 302(c) of the Labor Management Relations Act, 1947 (other than pensions on retirement or death, and insurance to provide such pensions)." In 1981, some 4.5 million welfare plans covering 152 million participants came under the purview of ERISA.

Source references: Arthur J. Deric (ed.), *The Total Approach to Employee Benefits* (New York: AMA, 1967); T. J. Gordon and R. E. LeBleu, "Employee Benefits, 1970–1985," *Harvard BR*, Jan./Feb. 1970; Elsie Hoexter, *Administrative Expenses of Welfare and Pension Plans, A LMSA Study Report* (Washington: U.S. Dept. of Labor, LMSA, 1974); Jacob Sheinkman, "Fringe Benefits and Welfare Plans," *NYU 22d Annual Conference on Labor*, ed. by Thomas Christensen and Andrea Christensen (New York: Bender, 1970); U.S. Dept. of Labor, LMSA, *Employee Retirement Income Security Act, 1981 Report to Congress* (Washington: 1982).

See also EMPLOYEE BENEFITS, EMPLOYEE RETIREMENT INCOME SECURITY ACT (ERISA)

OF 1974, HEALTH AND WELFARE FUNDS, HEALTH BENEFIT PROGRAMS.

welfare policies *See* PUBLIC ASSISTANCE.

welfare (uplift) unionism *See* UPLIFT UNIONISM.

West Coast Hotel Company v. Parrish *See* ADKINS V. CHILDREN'S HOSPITAL.

West Coast Longshore Mechanization Agreement An agreement negotiated between the Pacific Maritime Association and the International Longshoremen's and Warehousemen's Union which attempts to cope with some of the problems presented by mechanization and automation in longshore operations.

Source references: Lincoln Fairley, *Facing Mechanization: The West Coast Longshore Plan* (Los Angeles: UC, Institute of IR, Monograph Series 23, 1979); ———, "The ILWU-PMA Mechanization and Modernization Agreement," *LLJ*, July 1961; ———, *"Problems of the West Coast Longshore Mechanization Agreement," MLR*, June 1961; William Glazier, "Automation and the Longshoremen: A West Coast Solution," *Atlantic Monthly*, Dec. 1960; Paul Hartman, *Collective Bargaining and Productivity: The Longshore Mechanization Agreement* (Berkeley: UC Press, 1969); ILWU, *Information and Union Comment on the 1960 Mechanization and Modernization Fund Agreement Between the Longshoremen of the Pacific Coast and the Steamship and Stevedoring Employers* (San Francisco: 1960); "Mechanisation Clause in New United States Dockworkers' Agreement," *ILR*, July 1962.

See also MECHANIZATION.

Westinghouse Electric Corp.; IUE v. *See* IUE V. WESTINGHOUSE ELECTRIC CORP.

Westinghouse Independent Salaried Unions; Federation of (Ind) Its official annual publication is *The Regulator*.

Address: 505 Manor Building, Pittsburgh, Pa. 15219. Tel. (412) 471–3815

whipsawing A union stratagem to obtain benefits from a number or group of employers by applying pressure to one. The objective is to win favorable terms from the one employer and then use it as a pattern or base to obtain the same or greater benefits from the other employers, under the same threat of pressure (including a strike) used against the first employer.

Whirlpool Corp. v. Marshall A 1980 Supreme Court case upholding Occupational Safety and Health Act regulation 29 C.F.R. Sec. 1977.12, giving employees the right to refuse to work if (1) there is reasonable apprehension that the conditions of work constitute a real danger of death or serious injury, (2) there is insufficient time to utilize normal enforcement procedures under the Occupational Safety and Health Act of 1970, and (3) prior attempts to get the employer to remedy the dangerous conditions fail. The Court found the regulation to be consistent with the purposes of the Act and enforceable under Sec. 11(c)(1), which prohibits the discharge of or discrimination against any employee who exercises "any right afforded by" the Act.

The case involved the discipline of two employees who had refused a directive to work on a wire screen that they claimed was unsafe. The Court ruled that the two employees "were clearly subjected to 'discrimination' " when written reprimands were placed in their employment files.

Source references: Whirlpool Corp. v. Marshall, 445 US 1, 8 OSHC 1001 (1980); Larry Drapkin, "The Right to Refuse Hazardous Work After *Whirlpool*," *Industrial Relations LJ*, Vol. 4, no. 1, 1980; Kenneth Kirschner, "Workers in a *Whirlpool*: Employees' Statutory Rights to Refuse Hazardous Work," *LLJ*, May 1980.

See also OCCUPATIONAL SAFETY AND HEALTH ACT (OSHA) OF 1970.

whistleblower An employee who discloses improper employer practices or policies. Defective products, corruption, and cost overruns are among practices that have been exposed by whistleblowers.

The Civil Service Reform Act of 1978 includes provisions to protect federal employees against reprisal for such disclosure. Some state laws also provide similar protections for whistleblowers.

Source references: Mitchell J. Lindauer, "Government Employee Disclosures of Agency Wrongdoings: Protecting the Right to Blow the Whistle," *IR Law Digest*, April

1976; Melissa Patack, "Employees and Freedom of Speech," *Industrial and Labor Relations Forum,* Vol. 13, no. 1, 1978; Kenneth D. Walters, "Your Employees' Right to Blow the Whistle," *Harvard BR,* July/Aug. 1975.

white-collar employee A broad category of employees other than production and blue-collar workers, usually office, clerical, sales, semitechnical and professional, and minor supervisory employees.

The *Standard Occupational Classification Manual* developed by the U.S. Department of Commerce eliminated the use of the broad categorization of occupations such as white collar and blue collar for the 1980 Census and the Current Population Survey beginning in January 1983. As Breggar explains, "the framers of the [*Standard Occupational Classification Manual*] had explicitly intended to finally purge these titles because of the favorable impression given by 'white-collar' versus the more pejorative notion of 'blue-collar'. . . . Another misleading aspect . . . is the unevenness and largely misunderstood aspects of each; among other things, they are incorrectly assumed by many to exhaust occupational coverage (there are also the service and farm groupings)."

Source references: John E. Bregger, "Labor Force Data From the CPS to Undergo Revision in January 1983," *MLR,* Nov. 1982; Thomas R. Brooks, "New Fit to the White Collar," *Management Review,* Nov. 1963; BNA, *Practices for White-Collar Employees* (Washington: PPF Survey no. 69, 1963); Arthur J. Corazzini, "Equality of Employment Opportunity in the Federal White-Collar Civil Service," *Journal of Human Resources,* Fall 1972; Arthur J. Gartaganis, "Federal White-Collar Occupations," *MLR,* Aug. 1968; Christopher G. Gellner, "Occupational Characteristics of Urban Workers," *MLR,* Oct. 1971; David B. Johnson and James L. Stern, "Why and How Workers Shift from Blue-Collar to White-Collar Jobs," *MLR,* Oct. 1969; Karen Kelly, "A White-Collar Recession?" *Conference Board Record,* Sept. 1971; Jurgen Kocka, *White Collar Workers in America, 1890–1940, A Social-Political History in International Perspective* (Beverly Hills: Sage Publications, 1980); Edward Mandt, "Managing the Knowledge Worker of the Future," *PJ,* March 1978; C. Wright Mills, *White Collar: The American Middle Class* (New York: Oxford UP, 1951); Martin E. Personick and Carl B. Barsky, "White-Collar Pay Levels Linked to Corporate Work Force Size," *MLR,* May 1982.

See also WHITE-COLLAR UNIONISM.

white-collar exemptions Provisions of the Fair Labor Standards Act which permit overtime exemptions for professional, administrative, and executive employees.

Source reference: U.S. Dept. of Labor, Wage and Hour and Public Contracts Divisions, *White Collar Exemptions Under the Fair Labor Standards Act, as amended, 1961* (Washington: 1961).

white-collar unionism An inexact term that may be used to describe the process of organizing white-collar workers, the collective bargaining procedures and objectives of white-collar unions, or even some philosophy thought to be peculiar to white-collar, as contrasted to production-worker, unions. Usually the term is associated with organizing efforts.

Source references: Marina Angel, "White-Collar and Professional Unionization," *LLJ,* Feb. 1982; Albert A. Blum, *Management and the White-Collar Union* (New York: AMA, Research Study no. 63, 1964); Albert A. Blum et al., *White-Collar Workers* (New York: Random House, 1971); Clark C. Caskey, "White-Collar Employees—A Union Dilemma and a Management Challenge," *Management of Personnel Quarterly,* Spring 1962; H. M. Douty, "Prospects for White-Collar Unionism," *MLR,* Jan. 1969; Eric Fine and Frederic Leffler, "The Accommodation of Skilled and White Collar Workers in Industrial Unions," *Industrial and Labor Relations Forum,* March 1973; Harold J. Gibbons, Everett M. Kassalow, and Joel Seidman, *Developments in White Collar Unionism* (Chicago: Univ. of Chicago, IRC, Occasional Papers no. 24, 1962); Daniel S. Hamermesh, "White-Collar Unions, Blue-Collar Unions, and Wages in Manufacturing," *ILRR,* Jan. 1971; Eileen B. Hoffman, *Unionization of Professional Societies* (New York: The Conference Board, Report no. 690, 1976); Everett M. Kassalow, "New Union Frontier: White-Collar Workers," *Harvard BR,* Jan./Feb. 1962; ———, "White-Collar Unions and the Work Humanization Movement," *MLR*, May 1977; Donald J. Petersen, "Labor Trends: White Collar Unionization and the Pay Board," *Personnel*, July/Aug. 1972; Carl Dean Snyder, *White-Collar Workers and the UAW* (Urbana: Univ. of Illinois Press, 1973); Erwin S. Stanton, "White Collar Unionization: New Challenges to Management," *PJ*, Feb. 1972; George Strauss, "White Collar Unions Are Different," *Harvard BR*, Sept./Oct. 1954; Adolf Sturmthal (ed.), *White-Collar Trade Unions* (Urbana: Univ. of Illinois Press, 1966).

See also WHITE-COLLAR EMPLOYEE.

whitelist May refer to a list, maintained by employers, of workers who are eligible for employment primarily because they are not union members. It may also be a list of employers who are fair to the union or who are organized and use the union label. Whitelists are the reverse of blacklists and unfair or "do not patronize" lists.

See also BLACKLIST, FAIR LIST, UNION LABEL (BUG).

Whitley councils *See* JOINT INDUSTRIAL COUNCIL.

wholesale price index A BLS statistical series showing changes in wholesale prices over periods of time.

Source references: Allan D. Searle, "Weight Revisions in the Wholesale Price Index, 1890–1960," *MLR*, Feb. 1962; U.S. Council on Wage and Price Stability, *The Wholesale Price Index: Review and Evaluation* (Washington: 1977).

See also CONSUMER PRICE INDEX.

wildcat strike A work stoppage, generally spontaneous in character, by a group of employees without union authorization or approval. Frequently it is called by a group of employees because of some problem such as the disciplining of a union member. A wildcat strike may exist where a local union has supported a strike but has not received the approval of the national or international union. A wildcat strike generally is in violation of the collective bargaining agreement. The nature of these strikes is described briefly by Professor Reynolds in the following language:

> Unauthorized or "outlaw" strikes sometimes occur because of lack of discipline on the part of new union members. This happened in many of the new industrial unions during the late thirties. Workers who had long stood in fear of their employers found it exhilarating to sit down on the shop floor over every dispute rather than wait for the slower grievance procedure to operate. It takes some time to educate new unionists to the fact that collective bargaining involves responsibilities as well as rights.

Peterson observes:

> In addition to their fear of the consequences of public disapproval, the "wildcat" nature of this form of strike action imperiled the union's influence upon the workers themselves. By their very nature such strikes are not compatible with stable collective bargaining relationships for they enable a few workers, without notice to the union or to the employer, to tie up operations in entire plants. When they occur in organized plants, they represent a rebellion against the union as much as against the employer because they antithesize the orderly grievance adjustment procedures established by the union's contract with the employer.

Source references: James B. Atleson, "Work Group Behavior and Wildcat Strikes: The Causes and Functions of Industrial Civil Disobedience," *IR Law Digest*, Summer 1974; Jack Barbash, *Labor Unions in Action* (New York: Harper, 1948); Richard A. Givens, "Liability of Individual Employees for Wildcat Strikes?" *Employee Relations LJ*, Spring 1979; William B. Gould, "The Status of Unauthorized and Wildcat Strikes Under the NLRA," *Cornell LQ*, Spring 1967; Alvin W. Gouldner, *Wildcat Strike: A Study in Worker-Management Relationships* (New York: Harper, 1954); John S. Greenebaum, "New Influences at the Bargaining Table: The Rebellious Rank and File," *Personnel*, March/April 1972; Morrison Handsaker, "Arbitration and Discipline for Wildcat Strikes: A Reply Article," *LLJ*, May 1963; Garth L. Mangum, "Taming Wildcat Strikes," *Harvard BR*, March/April 1960; Florence Peterson, *Survey of Labor Economics* (rev. ed., New York: Harper, 1951); Lloyd G. Reynolds, *Labor Economics and Labor Relations* (4th ed., Englewood Cliffs: PH, 1964); Steven Rummage, "Union Officers and Wildcat Strikes: Freedom from Discriminatory Discipline," *Industrial Relations LJ*, Vol. 4, no. 2, 1981; Evan J. Spelfogel, "Wildcat Strikes and Minority Concerted Activity—Discipline, Damage Suits, and Injunctions," *Labor Law*

Developments 1973, Proceedings of the 19th Annual Institute on Labor Law, SLF (New York: Bender, 1973).

See also SNAP STRIKE, STRIKE, UNAUTHORIZED STRIKE.

"willing and able" clause A provision in the United Mine Workers contract of 1947 designed to offset provisions of the Taft-Hartley Act which permit suits for violation of contract. The union hoped through this clause to eliminate possible damage suits resulting from work stoppages arising under the contract. Some unions attempted in their agreement negotiations following Taft-Hartley to limit the actual amount of damages which could be assessed in case of contract violation.

UMW's able-and-willing clause provided in part:

> It is the intent and purpose of the parties hereto that this agreement will promote and improve industrial and economic relationships in the bituminous coal industry and to set forth herein the basic agreements covering rates of pay, hours of work, and conditions of employment to be observed between the parties, and shall cover the employment of persons employed in the bituminous coal mines covered by this agreement during such time as such persons are able and willing to work.

Source reference: "Industry-Wide Bargaining Revived in Coal As Operators Give UMW Its 'Best Contract,'" *Daily Labor Report,* No. 132, July 8, 1947.

See also SUITS FOR CONTRACT VIOLATION.

Wilson v. New The case in which the Supreme Court upheld the constitutionality of the Adamson Act.

Source reference: Wilson v. New, 243 US 332 (1917).

See also ADAMSON ACT.

Wire Weavers Protective Association; American (AFL-CIO) This union merged with the United Papermakers and Paperworkers (AFL-CIO) in February 1959.

See also PAPERMAKERS AND PAPERWORKERS; UNITED (AFL-CIO).

Wisconsin Employment Peace Act A comprehensive labor relations statute adopted by the state of Wisconsin in 1939. It is the predecessor of the Taft-Hartley Act. The Wisconsin Employment Relations Commission administers the act and also serves as the administrative agency for the Municipal Employment Relations Act (since 1962) and the State Employment Labor Relations Act (since 1967).

Source references: Wisconsin Employment Peace Act, effective May 5, 1939, as amended; Justin C. Smith, "The Background and Events Leading Up to the Passage of the Wisconsin Employment Peace Act," *LLJ,* Jan. 1961; ———, "Putting the Wisconsin Employment Peace Act into Effect: The First Ten Years," *Marquette LR,* Winter 1962/63.

Wisconsin School for Workers Education program started in 1924 when the Madison YWCA and faculty members of the University of Wisconsin economics department conducted a summer school for eight working women in Madison. The program was continued with a six-week summer program in 1925, involving 42 working women and was known as the Wisconsin School for Women Workers in Industry. In 1927, the Workers College in Milwaukee, established by the Milwaukee Federated Trades Council in 1922, and the School for Women Workers in Industry were combined as the School for Workers. Professor John R. Commons, chairman of the faculty committee of the School for Women Workers in Industry, and Henry Ohl, president of the Wisconsin State Federation of Labor, were instrumental in establishing the School for Workers.

From a largely summer school program, the School for Workers became part of the University of Wisconsin extension division in 1944. Extension courses are conducted on the campus and throughout the state by full-time staff members of the school.

Current course offerings of the school include comparable worth, computers for local unions, ergonomics, occupational health and safety, job stress, time study, job evaluation, union administration, collective bargaining, and contract negotiation.

Address: 422 Lowell Hall, 610 Langgon St., Madison, Wisconsin 53703. Tel. (608) 262–2111

Source references: Robert Ozanne, *The Wisconsin Idea in Workers' Education* (Madison: Univ. of Wisconsin, IR Research Center, 1961); Lawrence Rogin and Marjorie

Rachlin, *Labor Education in the United States* (Washington: National Institute of Labor Education, 1968).

withholding Any deduction from an employee's gross wage which is withheld by his consent or by provision of law.

Wobblies *See* INDUSTRIAL WORKERS OF THE WORLD.

Wolff Packing Company v. Court of Industrial Relations Decisions handed down by the Supreme Court in 1923 and 1925 involving the Kansas law providing for compulsory arbitration of labor disputes in certain industries said to be "affected with a public interest." In the 1923 decision, the Court held the law unconstitutional, as violative of the 14th Amendment to the federal Constitution, insofar as it permitted the fixing of wages for a packing house through compulsory arbitration. In the 1925 decision, the Court also held unconstitutional the provision of the law authorizing an administrative board to fix hours of labor in industries relating to food, clothing, and fuel whenever a controversy arises between employer and employees.

Source references: Wolff Packing Co. v. Court of Industrial Relations, 262 US 522 (1923) and 267 US 552 (1925); Harold S. Roberts, *Compulsory Arbitration of Labor Disputes in Public Utilities* (Honolulu: Univ. of Hawaii, IRC, 1949).

See also KANSAS COURT OF INDUSTRIAL RELATIONS.

women in industry In 1983, some 48.5 million women workers, 16 years of age and older, comprised more than 43 percent of the civilian labor force and 52.9 percent of the total female population in the United States, compared to 63 million men workers representing 56 percent of the total labor force and 76.4 percent of the male population. The unemployment rate for women was 9.2 percent and for men, 9.9 percent.

Labor force participation was highest among women in the 25–34 (13.7 million) and 35–44 years (10.2 million) age brackets.

Approximately 41.5 million (or 52.7 percent) of white women were in the labor force in 1983, with a 7.9 percent unemployment rate; there were 5.6 million (or 54.2 percent) black women with 18.6 percent unemployment; and 3.2 million (or 48.5 percent) Hispanic women with 14.2 percent unemployment.

By occupation, the largest number of women (20.1 million) were employed in technical, sales, and administrative support jobs—5.6 million of whom were in sales and 13.1 million in clerical and administrative support. Some 7.1 million women were employed in service occupations (not including private household and protective services); 3.2 million as machine operators, assemblers, and inspectors; and 6.1 million as elementary and secondary school teachers.

By family characteristics, approximately 24.2 million wives were employed in 1983, 54 percent of whom had children under 18 years of age. Some 5 million working women maintained families, 65 percent of whom had children under 18 years of age.

In the nonagricultural industries, labor force participation of married women was 22.3 million; widowed, divorced, or separated women, 7.8 million; and single women, 10.4 million.

Median weekly earnings of full-time women wage and salary workers in the latter part of 1983 were:

- Managerial and professional—$363 ($550 for men)
- Technical, sales, and administrative support—$247 ($402 for men)
- Service—$176 ($258 for men)
- Precision production, craft, and repair—$243 ($404 for men)
- Operators, fabricators, and laborers—$207 ($316 for men)
- Farming, forestry, and fishing—$175 ($198 for men)

Since the 1960s, women have claimed the largest share of labor force growth and it is projected that women will account for 7 of 10 additions to the labor force in the 1980s.

From 1950 to 1977, the number of years an average 20-year-old woman could be expected to spend in the labor force nearly doubled from 14½ to 26 years. The worklife of a 20-year old man, on the other hand, fell from 41½ to 37 years. A woman, thus, could expect to spend 45 percent of her life working in 1977 compared to 27 percent in 1950.

State legislation was once intended to protect the woman worker, restrict the number of hours a woman could work, or restrict the kind of job a woman could hold, but current federal legislation prohibits such discrimination based on sex. The Equal Pay Act of 1963 calls for equal pay for equal work regardless of sex and Title VII of the Civil Rights Act of 1964 prohibits discrimination in employment on the basis of race, color, religion, national origin, or sex. Executive Order 11246 also forbids employment discrimination on the basis of sex by federal contractors.

Source references: "Annual Averages—Household Data," *Employment and Earnings*, Jan. 1984; Howard Davis, "Employment Gains of Women by Industry, 1968–78," *MLR*, June 1980; Paul O. Flaim and Howard N. Fullerton, Jr., "Labor Force Projections to 1990: Three Possible Paths," *MLR*, Dec. 1978; C. F. Fretz and Joanne Hayman, "Progress for Women—Men Are Still More Equal," *Harvard BR*, Sept./Oct. 1973; Juanita Morris Kreps and Robert Clark, *Sex, Age, and Work: The Changing Composition of the Labor Force* (Baltimore: Johns Hopkins UP, Policy Studies in Employment and Welfare no. 23, 1975); Jerolyn R. Lyle and Jane L. Ross, *Women in Industry; Employment Patterns of Women in Corporate America* (Lexington, Mass.: Lexington Books, 1973); Ann R. Miller, "Changing Work Life Patterns: A Twenty-Five Year Review," *Annals*, Jan. 1978; Ruth Gilbert Shaeffer and Edith F. Lynton, *Corporate Experiences in Improving Women's Job Opportunities* (New York: The Conference Board, Report no. 755, 1979); Adele Simmons et al., *Exploitation From 9 to 5, Report of the Twentieth Century Fund Task Force on Women and Employment* (New York: Twentieth Century Fund, 1975); Ralph E. Smith (ed.), *The Subtle Revolution, Women at Work* (Washington: Urban Institute, 1979); C. Paul Sparks, "Employment and Utilization of Women," *Employee Relations LJ*, Spring 1976; U.S. Congress, Joint Economic Committee, *American Women Workers in a Full Employment Economy, A Compendium of Papers* (Washington: 1977); U.S. Dept. of Labor, BLS, *U.S. Working Women: A Databook* (Washington: Bull. 1977, 1977); ———, *Women at Work: A Chartbook* (Washington: Bull. 2168, 1983); U.S. Dept. of Labor, ETA, *The Socioeconomic Status of Households Headed by Women, Results from the National Longitudinal Surveys* (Washington: R&D Monograph 72, 1979); ———, *Women at Work* (Washington: R&D Monograph 46, 1977); U.S. Dept. of Labor, Manpower Adm., *Dual Careers, A Longitudinal Study of Labor Market Experience of Women, Volumes 1–5* (Washington: Research Monograph 21, 1970–1981); ———, *Years for Decision: A Longitudinal Study of the Educational and Labor Market Experience of Young Women, Volumes 1–3* (Washington: Research Monograph 24, 1971, 1974, 1976); U.S. Dept. of Labor, Women's Bureau, *Employment and Economic Issues of Low Income Women: Report of a Project* (Washington: 1978); ———, *Employment Goals of the World Plan of Action: Developments and Issues in the United States; Report for the World Conference on the United Nations Decade for Women 1976–1985* (Washington: 1980); ———, *The Employment of Women: General Diagnosis of Developments and Issues* (Washington: 1980); ———, *Twenty Facts on Women Workers* (Washington: 1980); Elizabeth Waldman and Beverly J. McEaddy, "Where Women Work—An Analysis by Industry and Occupation," *MLR*, May 1974; Phyllis A. Wallace (ed.), *Women in the Workplace* (Boston: Auburn House, 1982); Barbara Mayer Wertheimer (ed.), *Labor Education for Women Workers* (Philadelphia: Temple UP, 1981).

See also COALITION OF LABOR UNION WOMEN (CLUW); COMPARABLE WORTH; FEDERALLY EMPLOYED WOMEN (FEW); NATIONAL COMMISSION ON WORKING WOMEN; NATIONAL COMMITTEE ON PAY EQUITY; NATIONAL ORGANIZATION FOR WOMEN (NOW); 9 TO 5, NATIONAL ASSOCIATION OF WORKING WOMEN; OCCUPATIONAL SEGREGATION; PAY EQUITY; SEX DISCRIMINATION.

Women's Bureau First established in 1918 as the Woman in Industry Service; made a permanent part of the U.S. Department of Labor by Congress in June 1920. The statute authorizes the bureau "to formulate standards and policies which shall promote the welfare of wage-earning women, improve their working conditions, increase their efficiency, and advance their opportunities for profitable employment . . . the Bureau shall have authority to investigate and report to the said [Labor] Department upon all matters pertaining to the welfare of women in industry."

Women's Trade Union League *See* NATIONAL WOMEN'S TRADE UNION LEAGUE.

Woodworkers of America; International (AFL-CIO) A group which withdrew from the United Brotherhood of Carpenters and Joiners in 1937 and affiliated with the CIO. It drew most of its membership from the Pacific Northwest.

The union's monthly publications are the *International Woodworker* and *B.C. Lumberworker*.

Address: 1622 North Lombard St., Portland, Ore. 97217. Tel. (503) 285–5281

wop American slang for a common laborer or immigrants from southern Europe, especially Italy.

work Considered one of the basic institutions of life, work was defined by a special task force to the secretary of health, education, and welfare as "an activity that produces something of value for other people." Although sometimes used interchangeably with "labor," work may refer to a broader idea than the effort for which one is paid. Work can also function to create or contribute to self-esteem and shape a sense of identity. The special task force found that the lack of work or meaningless work may create a host of social and economic problems, including worker alienation, alcoholism, drug abuse, and low productivity.

Source reference: Work in America, Report of a Special Task Force to the Secretary of Health, Education, and Welfare (Cambridge: The MIT Press, 1973).

See also LABOR.

workaholic A word coined in 1971 by Wayne Oates in *Confessions of a Workaholic* to describe someone whose work occupies an inordinate amount of time and interest. Cherrington notes that the identifying feature of a workaholic is an "irrational commitment to excessive work." A workaholic is someone with an uncontrollable compulsion to work.

Source references: David J. Cherrington, *The Work Ethic; Work Values and Values that Work* (New York: AMACOM, 1980); Wayne Oates, *Confessions of a Workaholic* (New York: World Pub., 1971).

See also STRESS.

work assignment The assignment by the employer, in the absence of a limiting collective bargaining agreement or practice, of work to be performed by a particular group or classification of employees. With the objective of protecting employers from being caught in the middle of union disputes over job assignments, Section 8(b)(4)(D) of the Taft-Hartley Act made it an unfair labor practice for a union to attempt by picketing or striking to force an employer to assign work to one group of employees rather than to another.

Congress, however, declined to rely solely on the machinery provided to remedy other unfair labor practices and added a unique preliminary step for handling Section 8(b)(4)(D) charges. Section 10(k) provides that before passing upon the unfair practice charge, the NLRB first must "determine the dispute" unless the parties "have adjusted or agreed upon methods for voluntary adjustment of the dispute."

In making a "determination of the dispute" in the 10(k) phase of such proceedings, the NLRB for several years confined itself merely to determining whether the striking union was lawfully entitled to compel assignment of the work to its members by virtue of a contract or NLRB certification. It refrained from making affirmative awards of the disputed work.

In 1961, however, the Supreme Court told the Board that its policy was not correct. The Court held that where two or more unions are claiming the right to perform work and the case is brought before the Board, it is the Board's duty to decide which group is right "and then specifically to award such tasks in accordance with its decision." (*NLRB v. Radio Engineers Union* [Columbia Broadcasting System], 364 US 573, 47 LRRM 2332 (1961)).

The NLRB made its initial determinations under the new policy the following year. At that time, the Board said that it would not "formulate rules" for making job assignments. Each case, it added, "will have to be decided on its own facts." But the Board did say that it would "consider all relevant factors in determining who is entitled to the work in dispute, e.g., the skills and work involved, certifications by the Board, company and industry practice, agreements between unions and between employers and unions, awards of arbitrators, joint boards, and the AFL-CIO in the same or related cases, the assignment made by the employer, and the efficient operation of the employer's business." (*IAM, Lodge No. 1743 and J. A. Jones Construction Co.*, 135 NLRB 1402, 49 LRRM 1684 (1962)).

In a decision handed down in 1964, the Supreme Court made clear, however, that the jurisdiction of the NLRB in the work-assignment disputes was not exclusive. It held that a union that represents production and maintenance employees may compel arbitration, by a suit brought in a state court, of a grievance asserting that technical employees represented by another union are performing production and maintenance work, even though the dispute may involve matters within the jurisdiction of the NLRB. Arbitration is available as an alternative remedy to an NLRB proceeding, whether the dispute be regarded as one involving work assignments or as one involving representation, the Court said. (*Carey v. Westinghouse Electric Corp.*, 375 US 261, 55 LRRM 2042 (1964)).

The Building Trades Department of the AFL-CIO established a National Joint Board for Settlement of Jurisdictional Disputes to deal with the special problems of that industry. In 1965, the operating plan for the Joint Board was revised, and a committee of the American Bar Association's Section of Labor Relations Law suggested that, henceforth, the NLRB should give greater weight to decisions of the Joint Board.

Source references: Plumbing Contractors Assn. of Baltimore, 93 NLRB 1081, 27 LRRM 1514 (1951); Charles Albano, "Try It You'll Like It," *Public Personnel Management*, Sept./Oct. 1973; American Bar Association, "Report of the Special Committee on the Building and Construction Industry," *Section of Labor Relations Law, 1965 Proceedings* (Chicago: 1965); Lloyd H. Bailer, "The Right to Assign Employees in One Job Classification to Jobs in Another Classification," *ILRR*, Jan. 1963; Solomon Barkin, "Handling Work Assignment Changes," *Harvard BR*, Summer 1947; Milton Rubin, "The Right of Management to Split Jobs and Assign Work to Other Jobs," *ILRR*, Jan. 1963; Charles T. Schmidt, Jr., "What Is the Current Status of Work Assignment Disputes?" *LLJ*, May 1965; Saul Wallen, "The Arbitration of Work Assignment Disputes," *ILRR*, Jan. 1963.

See also JURISDICTIONAL DISPUTE, "R" CASES.

work clothing Provisions in some contracts, often for safety reasons, requiring the employer to provide the clothing to be worn on the job by the employee and in some cases requiring the employer to pay for laundering or cleaning.

work councils *See* JOINT INDUSTRIAL COUNCIL.

workday Refers to the time spent by employees at their place of employment. The Fair Labor Standards Act refers to a "workday" as any consecutive 24 hours. The Walsh-Healey Rulings and Interpretations state that "the term 'day' means a workday of 24 consecutive hours beginning at the same time each calendar day." The Wage and Hour Interpretative Bulletin on the Portal-to-Portal Act defines workday as "the period between the commencement and completion on the same workday of an employee's principal activity or activities. It includes all time within that period whether or not the employee engages in work throughout all of that period. For example, a rest period or a lunch period is part of the 'workday.'"

Source references: "Wage and Hour Interpretative Bulletin," 29 C.F.R. Section 790.6(b); "Wage and Hour Regulations," 29 C.F.R. Sec. 516.2(a)(7); Walsh-Healey Act Rulings and Interpretations, No. 3, Sec. 42(b)(2).

See also BASIC WORKDAY.

worker A broad term designating an individual who works for wages or salary and performs services or work for an employer. A broader definition would encompass all activities of individuals which bring some monetary compensation or work satisfaction.

Source references: Reinhard Bendix, "Managers, Workers and Ideas in the United States," *Research in Industrial Human Relations*, ed. by Conrad M. Arensberg et al.

(New York: Harper, IRRA Pub. no. 17, 1957); Neil W. Chamberlain, *Labor* (New York: McGraw-Hill, 1962); Paul Fraisse, "Of Time and the Workers," *Harvard BR*, May/June 1959; Eli Ginzberg and Hyman Berman, *The American Worker in the Twentieth Century: A History Through Autobiographies* (New York: Free Press of Glencoe, 1963); Melvin Kranzberg and Joseph Gies, *By the Sweat of Thy Brow: Work in the Western World* (New York: Putnam, 1975); Richard B. Morris (ed.), *The U.S. Department of Labor Bicentennial History of the American Worker* (Washington: U.S. Dept. of Labor, 1976); Ross Stagner et al., *The Worker in the New Industrial Environment* (Ann Arbor: Foundation for Research on Human Behavior, 1962); Louis Terkel, *Working: People Talk About What They Do All Day and How They Feel About What They Do* (New York: Pantheon Books, 1974).

See also EMPLOYEE, LABOR.

worker analysis *See* JOB ANALYSIS.

worker education *See* INDUSTRIAL EDUCATION, LABOR EDUCATION.

worker participation Efforts to permit employee participation in the management of business. It may apply to safety plans, handling production problems, or actual managerial decisions.

Source references: Milton Derber, "Labor Participation in Management," *Proceedings of the 17th A/M, IRRA*, ed. by Gerald Somers (Madison: 1965); George P. Shultz, "Worker Participation on Production Problems: A Discussion of Experience With the 'Scanlon Plan,'" *Personnel*, Nov. 1951; Ludwig Teller, *Worker Participation in Business Management* (Washington: U.S. Congress, House, Committee on Education and Labor, 1961).

See also CODETERMINATION, EMPLOYEE REPRESENTATION PLANS, MANAGEMENT RIGHTS, PARTICIPATIVE MANAGEMENT, SCANLON PLAN.

workers compensation The basic principles of workers compensation were developed in Germany around 1883 and spread to various parts of Europe. Workers compensation came into being when the common law provisions of employer liability became inadequate and when it was found that an injured worker could recover damages only if it could be proven that the accident or injury was caused by the negligence of the employer. The first United States compensation law was enacted by Congress in 1908, but it applied only to a limited group of federal employees. Major developments in workers compensation legislation took place in the states and the state of New Jersey was one of the first to establish a law in 1911.

The prime purpose of workers compensation is to provide financial aid through a system of insurance to compensate employees for damages or injuries incurred in the course of employment.

Most employers insure workers compensation risks through private insurance companies and set aside funds to make such insurance a part of the general cost of operating their businesses. Present laws of the states make workers compensation available without regard to negligence or carelessness of the individual or liability on the part of the employer. They cover both injuries and occupational diseases.

Source references: Monroe Berkowitz, *Workmen's Compensation: The New Jersey Experience* (New Brunswick: Rutgers UP, 1960); Merton C. Bernstein, "Report of the National Commission on State Workmen's Compensation Laws, Introduction," *Proceedings of the 25th A/M, IRRA*, ed. by Gerald Somers (Madison: 1973); John F. Burton, Jr., "Federal or State Responsibility for Workers' Compensation?" *Proceedings of the 29th A/M, IRRA*, ed. by James Stern and Barbara Dennis (Madison: 1977); Chamber of Commerce of the U.S., *Analysis of Workers' Compensation Laws, 1983 Edition* (Washington: 1983); James R. Chelius, "The Influence of Workers' Compensation on Safety Incentives," *ILRR*, Jan. 1982; ______, *Workplace Safety and Health, The Role of Workers' Compensation* (Washington: AEI, Studies 174, 1977); Martin W. Elson and John F. Burton, Jr., "Workers' Compensation Insurance: Recent Trends in Employer Costs," *MLR*, March 1981; Albert Kutchins, "The Most Exclusive Remedy is No Remedy at All: Workers' Compensation Coverage for Occupational Diseases," *LLJ*, April 1981; National Institutes on Rehabilitation and Health Services, *Report of the National*

Workshop on Rehabilitation and Workmen's Compensation, 1971 (Washington: 1971); James R. O'Brien, "The Case for Federal Job Injury Standards," *American Federationist,* Dec. 1972; Richard Robblee, "The Dark Side of Workers' Compensation: Burdens and Benefits in Occupational Disease Coverage," *Industrial Relations LJ*, Winter 1978; Barrett Seeley, "The Drift in Workers' Compensation," *American Federationist,* Sept. 1979; Herman M. Somers and Anne R. Somers, *Workmen's Compensation* (New York: Wiley, 1954); U.S. Dept. of Labor, *White Paper on Workers' Compensation, A Report on the Need for Reform of State Workers' Compensation* (Washington: 1974); U.S. National Commission on State Workmen's Compensation Laws, *Compendium on Workmen's Compensation* (Washington: 1973); ———, *The Report of the National Commission on State Workmen's Compensation Laws* (Washington: 1972); ———, *Supplemental Studies for the National Commission on State Workmen's Compensation Laws, Volumes I–III,* by Peter S. Barth et al. (Washington: 1973); C. Arthur Williams, Jr., *Insurance Arrangements Under Workmen's Compensation* (Washington: U.S. Dept. of Labor, Bureau of Labor Standards, Bull. no. 317, 1970); Norman J. Wood, "Workmen's Compensation and Mental Injury," *LLJ*, Oct. 1977.

See also ACCIDENT FREQUENCY RATE, ACCIDENT PREVENTION, COMPENSABLE INJURY, CONTRIBUTORY NEGLIGENCE, EMPLOYERS' LIABILITY, FARWELL V. BOSTON & WORCESTER RAILROAD CO., INDUSTRIAL ACCIDENT, INDUSTRIAL DISEASE, TEMPORARY DISABILITY INSURANCE.

workers' councils A form of co-determination and employee-management cooperation. It has received a good deal of attention in Germany and has been tried in some of the communist countries, such as Poland and Yugoslavia.

Source references: "Competence of Workers' Councils in Regard to the Removal of Managers of Undertakings from Their Posts in Yugoslavia," *ILR,* Feb. 1962; A. Delperee, "Joint Committees in Belgium," *ILR,* March 1960; Milton Derber, "Worker Participation in Israeli Management," *IR,* Oct. 1963; Paula Hann, "How a Works Council Works," *Management Review*, April 1975; ILO, *Consultation and Co-operation Between Employers and Workers at the Level of the Enterprise* (Geneva: Labour-Management Series no. 13, 1962); Karl Kummer, "Works Councils in Austria," *ILR*, Feb. 1960; N. S. Ross, "Joint Consultation and Workers' Control," *The Political Quarterly,* Jan./March 1956; Frank H. Stephen (ed.), *The Performance of Labor-Managed Firms* (New York: St. Martin's Press, 1982); Adolf Sturmthal, *Workers' Councils* (Cambridge: Harvard UP, 1964); ———, "The Workers' Councils in Poland," *ILRR*, April 1961.

work ethic A belief that honest labor and effort to do good work is important and fulfilling. Barbash writes that there is no fixed definition of the work ethic but the term is used in the following context: "1. Work as an end in itself which, it is expected, will be rewarded eventually with material success; key meanings under this head include the centrality of work, the dignity of work however menial, work as a calling. 2. Pride in good quality workmanship, hard work, 'an instinct of workmanship,' satisfaction in work. 3. Adherence to the discipline of work: punctuality, obedience, diligence, industriousness."

Source references: Jack Barbash, "Which Work Ethic?" *The Work Ethic—A Critical Analysis* (Madison: IRRA, 1983); Milton R. Blood, *Work Values and Job Satisfaction* (Berkeley: UC, Institute of IR, Reprint no. 344, 1970); Rogene A. Buchholz, "The Work Ethic Reconsidered," *ILRR*, July 1978; David J. Cherrington, *The Work Ethic; Work Values and Values That Work* (New York: AMACOM, 1980); John A. Fossum, "Urban-Rural Differences in Job Satisfaction," *ILRR*, April 1974; Stuart B. Kaufman, "Samuel Gompers vs. Horatio Alger: Defining the Work Ethic," *American Federationist*, Feb. 1981; Thomas A. Kochan, David B. Lipsky, and Lee Dyer, "Collective Bargaining and the Quality of Work: The Views of Local Union Activists," *Proceedings of the 27th A/M, IRRA*, ed. by James Stern and Barbara Dennis (Madison: 1975); Sar A. Levitan, "The Work Ethic Lives!" *Across the Board,* Aug. 1979; Mark G. Mindell and William I. Gorden, *Employee Values in a Changing Society,* An AMA Management Briefing (New

York: AMA, 1981); Walter S. Neff, "Work and the Human Condition: Understanding Difficulties in Work Adaptation," *Management of Personnel Quarterly*, Spring 1971; Barry Z. Posner, W. Alan Randolph, and Max S. Wortman, Jr., "A New Ethic for Work? The Worth Ethic," *Human Resource Management*, Fall 1975; Daniel T. Rodgers, *The Work Ethic in Industrial America, 1850–1920* (Chicago: Univ. of Chicago Press, 1974); Marsha Sinetar, "Management in the New Age: An Exploration of Changing Work Values," *PJ*, Sept. 1980; George Strauss, *Workers: Attitudes and Adjustments* (Berkeley: UC, Institute of IR, Reprint no. 384, 1974); Dale Tarnowieski, *The Changing Success Ethic* (New York: AMA, Survey Report, 1973).

work experience The sum total of the type of work performed by individuals and groups. Manpower potentials are derived from total work experience, work training, education, and ability of employees to perform effectively.

Source references: T. Aldrich Finegan, "The Work Experience of Men in the Labor Force: An Occupational Study," *ILRR*, Jan. 1964; U.S. Dept. of Labor, BLS, *Work Experience and Earnings in 1975 by State and Area* (Washington: 1978); Anne McDougall Young, "Work Experience of the Population in 1978," *MLR*, March 1980.

work force *See* LABOR FORCE.

Work Incentive Program (WIN) A program authorized by the Social Security Amendments of 1967 to remove recipients of Aid to Families With Dependent Children (AFDC) from the welfare rolls into productive employment. Under the original program, public welfare agencies referred registrants for the WIN program "and emphasis tended to be upon the provision of classroom training and other aids to employability development, rather than upon immediate job placement." The 1971 amendments to the Social Security Act redirected the WIN program and required all persons 16 years of age and older receiving or applying for AFDC relief to register in the WIN program. In addition, the "emphasis was shifted from employability development to job placement at the earliest point feasible."

The program is jointly administered by the U.S. Departments of Labor and Health and Human Services.

Source references: Gary L. Appel and Robert E. Schlenker, "An Analysis of Michigan's Experience with Work Incentives," *MLR*, Sept. 1971; Sar A. Levitan and David Marwick, "Work and Training for Relief Recipients," *Journal of Human Resources*, Volume VIII, Supplement, 1973; Sar A. Levitan, Martin Rein, and David Marwick, *Work and Welfare Go Together* (Baltimore: Johns Hopkins UP, 1972); Bradley R. Schiller, "Lessons from WIN: A Manpower Evaluation," *Journal of Human Resources*, Fall 1978; Georgina M. Smith, *The WIN Program, Job Training for Welfare Mothers* (New Brunswick: Rutgers Univ., Institute of Management and Labor Relations, 1972); U.S. Dept. of Labor, ETA, *Implementing Welfare Employment Programs: An Institutional Analysis of the Work Incentive (WIN) Program* (Washington: R&D Monograph 78, 1980); ———, *The Work Incentive (WIN) Program and Related Experiences, A Review of Research with Policy Implications* (Washington: R&D Monograph 49, 1977); U.S. Dept. of Labor and U.S. Dept. of HEW, *WIN: 1968–1978, A Report at 10 Years, Ninth Annual Report to the Congress on Employment and Training Under Title IV of the Social Security Act October 1, 1977–September 30, 1978* (Washington: 1979).

working class A broad term describing groups of individuals in a society who must labor for a living. The term is often used to refer to a distinct social class formed by similar earnings, work environment, education, and level of job skills. Stricker includes the following categories of workers in the working class: clerical, sales, craftsmen and foremen, operatives, private household workers, other service workers, farm laborers and foremen, and laborers. Dawson defines the working class to include manufacturing, mechanical, trade, transportation, agricultural, domestic, and personal service occupations.

In Marxist literature, the term refers to the group of "property-less" workers forming the basic organizing unit for revolutionary movements.

Source references: Stanley Aronowitz, *False Promises, The Shaping of American Working Class Consciousness* (New York: McGraw-Hill, 1973); Andrew Dawson, "The Paradox of Dynamic Technological Change and the Labor Aristocracy in the United States, 1880–1914," *Labor History*, Summer 1979; William Form, *Sociological Research and the American Working Class* (Urbana-Champaign: Univ. of Illinois, Institute of Labor and IR, Reprint no. 307, 1983); David Montgomery, "To Study the People: The American Working Class," *Labor History*, Fall 1980; Frank Stricker, "Affluence for Whom—Another Look at Prosperity and the Working Class in the 1920s," *Labor History*, Winter 1983.

See also PROLETARIAT.

working employer An individual who, although he employs others in connection with work which he directs, also takes an active part in the performance of that work. Some contractors perform that role, especially if they have come up from the ranks and are skilled craftsmen.

working force The term refers to the total number of workers on a particular project or operation and sometimes to the average number of employees, either on a monthly or annual basis. Where averages are determined, one procedure is to add the number of employees on the payroll at the beginning of the period covered to the number at the end of the period and divide by two. If the beginning and ending periods are not affected by unusual circumstances, such as a period of depression or a cutback in production, this normally will provide a satisfactory measure of the work force of particular plants.

See also LABOR FORCE.

working foreman A supervisory employee who performs the role of foreman and also engages in a limited amount of actual production work. Collective bargaining contracts frequently limit such work. Particularly in times of high unemployment, unions attempt to restrict the amount of production work performed by supervisory employees.

See also FOREMAN.

working hours *See* WORKING TIME.

Workingmen's Protective Union An organization established in 1847 by John Kualback for the purpose of encouraging cooperatives. The name of the organization was changed in 1849 to the New England Protective Union. In addition to its cooperative aspects, the organization was concerned with land reform and establishment of the 10-hour day.

Source references: Robert F. Hoxie, *Trade Unionism in the United States* (New York: Appleton, 1931); Harry A. Millis and Royal E. Montgomery, *Organized Labor* (New York: McGraw-Hill, 1945); Albert Sonnichsen, *Consumers' Cooperation* (New York: Macmillan, 1919).

See also CONSUMERS' COOPERATIVE.

working poor People who are employed but earn income below the poverty level. The working poor does not include low-paid workers who have families with adequate income, such as teenagers supported by parents or people who work to supplement an adequate family income or retirement income. According to Bluestone et al., a high wage earner may belong to the working poor because of the large number of dependents that income supports.

Source references: Barry Bluestone, William M. Murphy, and Mary Stevenson, *Low Wages and the Working Poor* (Ann Arbor: Univ. of Michigan–Wayne State Univ., Institute of Labor and IR, Policy Papers in Human Resources and IR no. 22, 1973); Sar A. Levitan and Richard S. Belous, *More than Subsistence: Minimum Wages for the Working Poor* (Baltimore: Johns Hopkins UP, 1979); Steven Sternlieb and Alvin Bauman, "Employment Characteristics of Low-Wage Workers," *MLR*, July 1972.

See also POOR, SUBEMPLOYMENT.

working schedule, flexible Arrangements between employer and union to permit modification of the schedule by lengthening or shortening or shifting the schedule in order to provide greater flexibility to meet changes in production conditions.

The personnel aspects of work schedules which require policy decisions by management according to Pigors and Myers are:

(1) length of the work day and work week per employee;

(2) payment for overtime and for Saturday and Sunday work as such;
(3) number of shifts and the hours when they start;
(4) making night shifts as attractive as possible;
(5) fixed vs. rotating shifts;
(6) basis for shift assignments and shift transfers;
(7) desirability of scheduled rest periods; and
(8) paid vacations and paid holidays.

Source references: Fred Best, "Preferences on Worklife Scheduling and Work-Leisure Tradeoffs," *MLR,* June 1978; Janice Neipert Hedges, "New Patterns for Working Time," *MLR,* Feb. 1973; Paul Pigors and Charles A. Myers, *Personnel Administration* (3d ed., New York: McGraw-Hill, 1956); U.S. National Center for Productivity and Quality of Working Life, *Alternatives in the World of Work* (Washington: 1976).

See also FLEXTIME/FLEXITIME, HOURS OF WORK, PAID VACATION PLAN, SHIFT.

working stiff A colloquial expression designating an ordinary worker or wage earner.

working time The time spent by a worker who is entitled to pay under the Fair Labor Standards Act, the Walsh-Healey Act, or under the collective bargaining agreement. Under the Portal-to-Portal Act, the time which is compensable is determined by contract, law, practice, or custom.

In a case involving union solicitation rules, the NLRB held that working time "connotes periods when employees are performing actual job duties, periods which do not include the employees' own time such as lunch and break periods." In the same case, the Board also stated that working hours "connotes periods from the beginning to the end of the workshifts, periods that include employees' own time."

Source reference: Our Way, Inc., 268 NLRB No. 61, 115 LRRM 1009 (1983).

See also FAIR LABOR STANDARDS ACT OF 1938, HOURS OF WORK, PORTAL-TO-PORTAL PAY ACT.

Working Women *See* 9 TO 5, NATIONAL ASSOCIATION OF WORKING WOMEN.

work injuries *See* INDUSTRIAL ACCIDENT.

work load The quantitative measure of the amount of work performed, measured by the hour or day. It may be the measure to determine wages or productivity of employees in the plant. The term frequently refers to a normal or standard output, representing reasonably efficient productivity and work output without undue risk to the health or safety of the individual.

Source references: John R. P. French, Jr., John Tupper, and Ernst F. Mueller, *Work Load of University Professors* (Ann Arbor: Institute of Social Research, Univ. of Michigan, 1965); U.S. Dept. of Labor, BLS, *Major Collective Bargaining Agreements: Wage-Incentive, Production-Standard, and Time-Study Provisions* (Washington: Bull. 1425–18, 1979).

work measurement Procedures, generally statistical and technical in nature, to measure the actual output of individuals as well as the design and measurement of work methods appropriate for optimum performance. It may apply to the amount of work to be performed by a worker in a given period of time.

Source references: Adam Abruzzi, *Work, Workers and Work Measurement* (New York: Columbia UP, 1956); Richard M. Crossan and Harold W. Nance, *Master Standard Data: The Economic Approach to Work Assignment* (New York: McGraw-Hill, 1962); Ken Davies, "An Approach to Clerical and Nonmanual Work Measurement," *Management Review,* July 1975; R. Randall Hoffman, "MJS: Management by Job Standards," *PJ,* Aug. 1979; Buddy L. Jackson, "Determining Efficiency Through Work Sampling," *Management Review,* Jan. 1972; Vincent G. Reuter, "Staffing and Training for Work Study," *PJ,* Feb. 1971; David Sirota and Alan D. Wolfson, "Adequate Grievance Channels: Overcoming the Negative Effects of Work Measurement on Employee Morale," *Human Resource Management,* Summer 1972; Henry S. Woodbridge, Jr., "Whittling Clerical Costs," *Personnel,* Jan./Feb. 1972; Samuel L. Young, "A Program for Making Clerical Time Count," *Management Review,* Oct. 1971; Kjell B. Zandin, "Better Work Management with MOST," *Management Review,* July 1975.

See also TIME AND MOTION STUDY.

workmen's compensation *See* INSURANCE, WORKERS COMPENSATION; WORKERS COMPENSATION.

work periods *See* HOURS OF WORK.

work permits Certificates issued to a child by school officials or state departments of labor permitting employment for specified periods of time and under specific controls as to hours and working conditions.

See also CHILD LABOR, PERMIT CARD.

work practices *See* BOGUS (TYPE) WORK, LIMITATION OF OUTPUT, MAKE-WORK PRACTICES, RESTRICTION OF OUTPUT.

work relief An assistance program for unemployed individuals or families which provides them with an opportunity for work. The assistance given is through actual employment on some public works project established by the federal, state, or local government. It has been contended by some that this is a better expedient than direct relief given merely in the form of money or goods without any requirement that the individual perform some work which is useful and valuable to the community and satisfying to the worker.

Source references: B. S. Howard, *The WPA and the Federal Relief Policy* (New York: Russell Sage Foundation, 1943); James M. Williams, *Human Aspects of Unemployment and Relief* (Chapel Hill: Univ. of North Carolina Press, 1933).

See also RELIEF, UNEMPLOYMENT, WORKS PROGRESS ADMINISTRATION.

work restriction Planned or tacit action by employees to limit output in order to "stretch the work" or to extend employment opportunities, or to bring pressure on the employer to grant economic concessions.

Professor Groat provided a simplified explanation of work restriction in the following statement: "If there are 20 houses to paint, the jobs will last longer if five men are put on than if double the number are set to work. If there is an order for 500 pairs of shoes, the job will last longer if the men take their time than if they rush the work. In this very concrete way it is easy for a workman whose outlook is no wider than the narrow bit of work that he does to insist on putting a limit to his efforts in order to make the job last longer. Wider considerations do not influence him. For him, it is quite simply personal. He has a family to provide for. When work is scarce the employer lays off men. He may be laid off at the end of the very job on which he is working."

Professor Peterson distinguishes two types of work restrictions; one which is essentially a slowdown strike and the other relating to job scarcity and the prolongation of job opportunities. She states in part that work restriction is "a tacit understanding or planned movement among a group of employees to limit output below the standard of efficiency which could be maintained without risk to health and safety. Restriction of output may be (1) a temporary act to gain an immediate definite concession from the employer in which case it takes on the nature of a slowdown strike; (2) an effort to prolong a job and prevent unemployment. Where workers are imbued with the idea of permanent scarcity of jobs, rules which directly or indirectly curtail production may be introduced in the union's constitution or agreements with employers."

Source references: George G. Groat, *Organized Labor in America* (New York: Macmillan, 1916); Florence Peterson, *American Labor Unions* (2d rev. ed., New York: Harper, 1963); John R. Van de Water, "Legal and Managerial Control of Work Restrictions in Industry," *LLJ*, Sept. 1963.

See also LIMITATION OF OUTPUT, MAKE-WORK PRACTICES, RESTRICTION OF OUTPUT.

work rules The regulations in accordance with which work is done. The phrase applies generally to conditions of work which are incorporated in collective bargaining agreements at union insistence for the primary purpose of maximizing employment opportunities and to protect the employee's own job.

Source references: Solomon Barkin, "Work Rules: A Phase of Collective Bargaining," *LLJ*, May 1961; The Conference Board, *Personnel Practices III: Employee Services, Work Rules* (New York: Information Bull. no. 95, 1981); Pearce Davis, "Arbitration of Work Rules Disputes," *AJ*, Vol. 16, no. 2, 1961; Lincoln Fairley, "West Coast Longshore Work Rules," *ILRR*, Oct. 1962; Ben Fischer, "Work Rules: The On-the-Job Realities," *American Federationist*, June 1961; William Gomberg, "The Work Rule Problem and Property Rights in the Job," *MLR*, June 1961; ———, "The Work Rules and Work

Practices Problem," *LLJ*, July 1961; Paul T. Hartman, "Union Work Rules: A Brief Theoretical Analysis and Some Empirical Results," *Proceedings of the 19th A/M, IRRA*, ed. by Gerald Somers (Madison: 1967); Morris A. Horowitz, *Manpower Utilization in the Railroad Industry: An Analysis of Working Rules and Practices* (Boston: Northeastern Univ., Bureau of Business and Economic Research, 1960); Charles C. Killingsworth, "The Modernization of West Coast Longshore Work Rules," *ILRR*, April 1962; Max D. Kossoris, "Working Rules in West Coast Longshoring," *MLR*, Jan. 1961; E. Robert Livernash, "The General Problem of Work Rules," *Proceedings of the 14th A/M, IRRA*, ed. by Gerald Somers (Madison: 1962).

See also FEATHERBEDDING, MAKE-WORK PRACTICES, MANAGEMENT RIGHTS.

work satisfaction The enjoyment and satisfaction individuals experience as a result of their work. Efforts have been made through psychological and other studies to determine the extent to which certain types of rewards may act as the equivalent of work satisfaction or ways in which employees may feel that their particular contribution to total output is something about which they can feel a sense of accomplishment and pride.

Source references: Robert Blaunder, "Work Satisfaction and Industrial Trends in Modern Society," *Labor and Trade Unionism: An Interdisciplinary Reader*, ed. by Walter Galenson and Seymour M. Lipset (New York: Wiley, 1960); Robert E. Carlson et al., *The Measurement of Employment Satisfaction* (Minneapolis: Univ. of Minnesota, IRC, Minnesota Studies in Vocational Rehabilitation, Bull. no. 35, 1962); Abraham Zaleznik, *Worker Satisfaction and Development* (Boston: Harvard Univ., 1965).

See also JOB SATISFACTION.

works councils *See* WORKERS' COUNCILS.

work sharing A plan whereby available work is spread among all of the workers in the group in order to prevent or reduce the extent of a layoff when production requirements result in a substantial decline in available work. The arrangement essentially involve an even or equitable distribution of work in lieu of layoffs.

Source references: Robert Bednarzik, "Worksharing in the U.S.: Its Prevalence and Duration," *MLR*, July 1980; Fred Best, *Work Sharing; Issues, Policy Options and Prospects* (Kalamazoo: Upjohn Institute for Employment Research, 1981); Fred Best and James Mattesich, "Short-Time Compensation Systems in California and Europe," *MLR*, July 1980; Alfred W. Blumrosen and Ruth G. Blumrosen, "Layoff or Work Sharing: The Civil Rights Act of 1964 in the Recession of 1975," *Employee Relations LJ*, Summer 1975; Sar A. Levitan and Richard S. Belous, "Work-Sharing Initiatives at Home and Abroad," *MLR*, Sept. 1977; Alan H. Lochner, "Short-Time Compensation: A Viable Alternative to Layoffs," *PJ*, March 1981; Maureen E. McCarthy and Gail S. Rosenberg, *Work Sharing Case Studies* (Kalamazoo: Upjohn Institute for Employment Research, 1981); Nancy J. McNeff et al., "Alternatives to Employee Layoffs: Work Sharing and Prelayoff Consultation," *Personnel*, Jan./Feb. 1978; Clyde W. Summers and Margaret C. Love, "Work Sharing as an Alternative to Layoffs by Seniority: Title VII Remedies in Recession," *IR Law Digest*, Winter 1977; U.S. Dept. of Labor, BLS, *Major Collective Bargaining Agreements: Layoff, Recall, and Worksharing Procedures* (Washington: Bull. 1425–13, 1972).

See also EMPLOYMENT STABILIZATION, JOB SHARING, LAYOFF, LUMP OF LABOR THEORY, REDUCTION IN HOURS, SHORTER WORKWEEK.

work simplification The systematic organization of work methods, tools, materials, equipment, and working conditions to achieve the most efficient operation consistent with high quality and minimal fatigue. It requires the maximum utilization of motion and time study as well as painstaking industrial organization, both on the technical and human aspects.

Source references: Cecil E. Goode, "Greater Productivity Through the Organization of Work," *Personnel Administration*, Jan./Feb. 1964; Joseph M. Madden, "What Makes Work Difficult?" *PJ*, July/Aug. 1962; Charles O. Reynolds, *Work Simplification for Everyone* (Coatesville, Pa.: Pyramid Pub., 1962); W. Clements Zinck, *Dynamic Work*

Simplification (New York: Reinhold Pub., 1962).

See also TIME AND MOTION STUDY.

work spreading *See* WORK SHARING.

Works Progress Administration A federal agency established under the Emergency Relief Act of 1935 to provide employment for individuals who were either on relief or in need of assistance. The purpose of the Works Progress Administration (WPA) was to provide direct employment on public projects to the unemployed who under normal circumstances would be eligible for relief. In 1939 the program was renamed the Works Projects Administration under the Federal Works Agency. It was liquidated in December 1942.

Source reference: Donald S. However, *The WPA and Federal Relief Policy* (New York: Russell Sage Foundation, 1943).

See also FEDERAL WORKS AGENCY, PUBLIC WORKS ADMINISTRATION (AUTHORITY), PUBLIC WORKS AND ECONOMIC DEVELOPMENT ACT OF 1965, UNEMPLOYMENT.

Works Projects Administration *See* WORKS PROGRESS ADMINISTRATION.

work stoppage *See* STRIKE.

work stoppage statistics BLS published until 1981 monthly and annual data on all work stoppages occurring in the United States, involving as many as six workers and lasting a full day or shift or longer. Figures were presented by month and by year on (1) the number of stoppages beginning in the month or year, and the number of stoppages in effect during the month or year; (2) numbers of workers involved in stoppages beginning in the month or year, and the numbers of workers involved in stoppages in effect during the period; and (3) the number of man-days of idleness during the month or year, and man days of idleness as a percent of estimated total working time.

Since 1982, BLS data are limited to work stoppages involving 1,000 or more workers, which are reported on a monthly basis in the *Monthly Labor Review* and *Current Wage Developments*. The annual publications, *Analysis of Work Stoppages, 1979* and *Work Stoppages in Government, 1980,* were the last issues in the series published.

Beginning with 1967, estimates of employment have been used based on (1) wage and salary workers in the civilian work force and on (2) the private nonfarm sector. The new private nonfarm sector series approximates the former BLS series, which excluded government and agricultural workers from employment totals, but accounted for time lost by such workers while on strike. The "total economy" measure of strike idleness includes government and agricultural workers in both the employment count and the idleness ratios. Data on the private nonfarm sector excludes agricultural and government workers from the employment count and also from calculation of percentage of working time lost.

The data presented by BLS do not measure the indirect or secondary effect on other establishments or industries whose employees are made idle as a result of material or service shortages.

BLS does not distinguish between stoppages of work by "strikes" or "lockouts." The Bureau's figures include both types of stoppages. The total number of workers involved in strikes in a given year could include workers counted more than once, if they were involved in more than one stoppage during the year. In 1949, for example, 365,000 to 400,000 coal miners struck on three different occasions, and they accounted for almost 1.2 million of the year's total of 3.0 million workers involved in work stoppages.

Idleness as a percent of working time: In computing man-hours of idleness as a percent of working time—the "idleness rate"—the Bureau computes working time by multiplying the average number of workers employed during the year in nonfarm establishments, exclusive of government, by the number of days typically worked by most employees. In the computations, Saturdays (when customarily not worked), Sundays, and established holidays as provided in most union contracts are excluded.

Duration: Although only workdays are used in computing man-days of total idleness, duration is expressed in terms of calendar days, including non-workdays.

Geographical data: Stoppages occurring in more than one state are listed separately by BLS in each state affected. The workers and man-days of idleness are allocated among each of the affected states. The same procedure is followed in allocating data on stoppages occurring in more than one industry, industry group, or metropolitan area.

Source references: Joseph W. Bloch and Julian Malnak, "The Dimensions of Major Work Stoppages," *MLR*, April 1961; Paul H. Douglas, "An Analysis of Strike Statistics, 1881–1921," *Journal of the American Statistical Association*, Sept. 1923; P. K. Edwards, "The End of American Strike Statistics," *BJIR*, Nov. 1983; Howard N. Fullerton, "'Total Economy' Measure of Strike Idleness," *MLR*, Oct. 1968; Desmond W. Oxnam, "International Comparisons of Industrial Conflict: An Appraisal," *Journal of IR*, July 1965; U.S. Dept. of Labor, BLS, *BLS Handbook of Methods* (Washington: Bull. 1910, 1976); ———, *Work Stoppages: Fifty States and the District of Columbia, 1927–62* (Washington: Report 256, 1963).

work to rule A British form of slowdown in which all rules are scrupulously observed and work on days off, Sundays, and outside regular shifts is refused.

See also "RULEBOOK" SLOWDOWN.

workweek The scheduled number of working hours, or the normally expected hours of employment for the week or in any seven-day period, during which an employee is expected to work and beyond which overtime or premium pay is paid.

A representative contract clause follows:

(1) The work day shall be 24 consecutive hours and eight (8) hours shall constitute the regular day's work.

(2) Forty (40) hours shall constitute a regular week's work and a regular week's work shall be performed on five (5) consecutive days, which shall be normally Monday to Friday, inclusive, and such other regularly scheduled work days to such extent and at such hours as may be required by the Company.

(3) Eight (8) hours shall constitute the regular day's work, which hours shall be consecutive except for time out for meals. Meal periods shall not be considered as breaking the continuity in determining whether or not an employee has worked in excess of eight (8) consecutive hours, but such employees, shall not be paid for the meal period except during extended overtime periods.

(4) All work in excess of eight (8) hours in any work day, or in excess of eight (8) consecutive hours, or any work performed after an employee's normal quitting time shall be considered as overtime and shall be paid for at the rate of one and one-half (1½) times the regular straight time hourly rate for the first four (4) hours of such overtime, and at two (2) times the regular straight time hourly rate for all work in excess of such four (4) hours of overtime in any work day.

(5) The first eight (8) hours of all scheduled work performed on the designated sixth (6th) day of the work week shall be paid for at one and one-half (1½) times the regular straight time hourly rate and all work in excess of eight (8) hours on the designated sixth (6th) day shall be paid for at two (2) times the regular straight time hourly rate.

All hours of scheduled work performed on the seventh (7th) day of the work week shall be paid for at two (2) times the regular straight time hourly rate.

Source references: Gerhard Bry, *The Average Workweek as an Economic Indicator* (New York: NBER, Occasional Papers no. 69, 1959); Ben A. Buisman, "4-Day, 40-Hour Workweek: Its Effect on Management and Labor," *PJ*, Nov. 1975; Richard M. Devens, Jr., "The Average Workweek: Two Surveys Compared," *MLR*, July 1978; Janice Neipert Hedges, "Changes in the Number of Days in the Workweek, 1973–76," *MLR*, April 1977; ———, "How Many Days Make a Workweek?" *MLR*, April 1975; ———, "The Workweek in 1979: Fewer But Longer Workdays," *MLR*, Aug. 1980; Thomas J. Kniesner, "The Full-Time Workweek in the United States, 1900–1977," *ILRR*, Oct. 1976; Daniel E. Taylor and Edward S. Sekscenski, "Workers on Long Schedules, Single and Multiple Job Holders," *MLR*, May 1982.

See also BASIC WORKWEEK, ENGLISH WORKWEEK, FAIR LABOR STANDARDS ACT OF 1938, FIVE-DAY WORKWEEK, FORTY-HOUR WEEK, FOUR-DAY WORKWEEK, HOURS OF

WORK, NOMINAL WORKWEEK, NORMAL WORKWEEK, SHORTER WORKWEEK, SPLIT WORKWEEK, THIRTY-HOUR WEEK.

World Confederation of Labour (WCL) An international organization of trade unions founded at The Hague in 1921 and dedicated "to achieve a social order in conformity with Christian principles." Formerly known as the International Federation of Christian Trade Unions (CISC were its French initials), its membership was open to all workers believing in God, and the federation combined both genuine trade unions as well as associations of Catholic workers and exile groups which did not carry out trade union functions. During the 1960s, "the CISC adopted a secular programme, and in 1968 it chose the new name of World Confederation of Labour." According to Windmuller, "it adopted a militant secular programme based on humanist, socialist, and syndicalist ideas. It also sought to alter the balance of its programme and the composition of its membership by enlarging its activities in the less developed countries." In 1969, it was estimated that the WCL represented about 14 million workers in 76 countries.

Regional WCL organizations currently exist in Latin America (CLAT) and Asia (BATU). In 1974, the WCL lost its European regional body (EO) when its affiliates joined the European Trade Union Confederation and its African organization, PAWC, which was forced to dissolve under pressure from African governments.

Source references: Efren Cordova, "The Changing Character of the Christian International," *Relations Industrielles*, Jan. 1968; Emil Joseph Kirchner, *The Trade Union as a Pressure Group in the European Community* (Westmead, Eng.: Saxon House, 1977); George C. Lodge, *Spearheads of Democracy, Labor in the Developing Countries* (New York: Harper, 1962); Eli Marx and Walter Kendall, *Unions in Europe* (Sussex, Eng.: Univ. of Sussex, Centre for Contemporary European Studies, 1971); U.S. Dept. of Labor, BILA, *Directory of Christian Trade Unions (CISC)* (rev. ed., Washington: 1963); John P. Windmuller, "International Trade Union Movement," *Comparative Labour Law and Industrial Relations*, ed. by R. Blanpain (Washington: BNA, 1982); ———, "International Trade Union Organizations: Structure, Functions, Limitations," *International Labour*, ed. by Solomon Barkin et al. (New York: Harper, IRRA Pub., 1967).

See also EUROPEAN TRADE UNION CONFEDERATION (ETUC), INTERNATIONAL CONFEDERATION OF FREE TRADE UNIONS (ICFTU), WORLD FEDERATION OF TRADE UNIONS (WFTU).

World Federation of Trade Unions (WFTU) Founded in 1945 with the British Trades Union Congress (TUC), the Soviet federation of labor unions (AUCCTU), and the CIO as its principal members. Opposed to the WFTU communist-oriented policy, both the British TUC and the CIO withdrew from the organization in 1949 and joined with other groups to form the International Confederation of Free Trade Unions (ICFTU). According to Windmuller, the WFTU's primary affiliates since 1949 "have been the labour organisations in countries governed by Communist parties and allied to the Soviet Union." It is estimated to have a membership of over 200 million.

Source references: Adolf Sturmthal, "The Crisis of the WFTU," *ILRR*, July 1948; John P. Windmuller, *American Labor and the International Labor Movement, 1940 to 1953* (Ithaca: Cornell Univ., NYSSILR, Cornell International Industrial & Labor Relations Report no. 2, 1954); ———, "Foreign Affairs and the AFL-CIO," *ILRR*, April 1956; ———, "International Trade Union Movement," *Comparative Labour Law and Industrial Relations*, ed. by R. Blanpain (Washington: BNA, 1982).

See also EUROPEAN TRADE UNION CONFEDERATION (ETUC), INTERNATIONAL CONFEDERATION OF FREE TRADE UNIONS (ICFTU), INTERNATIONAL FEDERATION OF TRADE UNIONS (IFTU), WORLD CONFEDERATION OF LABOUR (WCL).

wrap-up clause *See* ZIPPER CLAUSE.

Wright Line *See* MIXED MOTIVE CASES.

Writers Guild of America (Ind) Comprised of two units—Writers Guild of America, East, Inc. and Writers Guild of America, West, Inc. The respective divisions issue the *Writers Guild of America, East Newsletter* (11 times a year) and the monthly *Writers Guild of America, West, Inc.*

Addresses: Writers Guild of America, East, Inc., 555 West 57th St., New York, N.Y. 10019. Tel. (212) 245–6180; Writers Guild of America West, Inc., 8955 Beverly Blvd., Los Angeles, Calif. 90048. Tel. (213) 550–1000

written grievances Grievances which are reduced to writing. This may be required by collective bargaining contracts. Grievances may be initially handled orally and then put in writing if not settled. Some hold that it might be possible to reduce the number of grievances if they were handled on a less formal basis and were not reduced to writing.

Source reference: Robert B. McKersie and William W. Shropshire, Jr., "Avoiding Written Grievances: A Successful Program," *Journal of Business,* April 1962.

wrongful discharge An "unjust" termination of an employee. Wrongful discharge may include (1) violation of public policy—for example, termination for whistleblowing, union activity, or refusal to participate in illegal acts; (2) violation of provisions contained in a labor agreement, personnel manual, or company handbook; or (3) breach of a promise of employment.

Source references: BNA, *The Employment-At-Will Issue* (Washington: 1982); Susan L. Catler, "The Case Against Proposals to Eliminate the Employment at Will Rule," *Industrial Relations LJ*, Vol. 5, no. 4, 1983; Marco L. Colosi, "Who's Pulling the Strings on Employment at Will?" *PJ*, May 1984.

See also EMPLOYMENT AT WILL, JUST CAUSE.

Wyoming Public Employees Association (Ind) Formerly known as the Wyoming State Employees Association (Ind), it is affiliated with the Assembly of Governmental Employees. Its official publication is the *WPEA Reporter.*

Address: 408 West 23rd St., Cheyenne, Wyo. 82001. Tel. (307) 635–7901

Y

yellow dog contract An agreement (either written or oral) between an employer and a worker which provides that as a condition of employment the worker will refrain from joining a union or, if the worker is a member, will leave the organization. The purpose of the yellow dog contract is essentially to prevent employees from organizing. Under the Norris-LaGuardia Act (Section 3), the yellow dog contract is not enforceable. Section 3 of that law states:

> Any undertaking or promise, such as is described in this section, or any other undertaking or promise in conflict with the public policy declared in section 2 of this Act, is hereby declared to be contrary to the public policy of the United States, shall not be enforceable in any court of the United States and shall not afford any basis for the granting of legal or equitable relief by any such court, including specifically the following:
>
> Every undertaking or promise hereafter made, whether written or oral, express or implied, constituting or contained in any contract or agreement of hiring or employment, between any individual, firm, company, association, or corporation, and any employee or prospective employee of the same, whereby
>
> (a) Either party to such contract or agreement undertakes or promises not to join, become, or remain a member of any labor organization or of any employer organization, or
>
> (b) Either party to such contract or agreement undertakes or promises that he will withdraw from an employment relation in the event that he joins, becomes, or remains a member of any labor organization or of any employer organization.

Source references: Norris-LaGuardia Act, Act of March 23, 1932, Ch. 90, 72d Cong., 1st Sess., as amended; Joel I. Seidman, *The Yellow Dog Contract* (Baltimore: Johns Hopkins Press, 1932).

See also ADAIR V. UNITED STATES, BALLEISEN CONTRACTS, COPPAGE V. KANSAS, ERDMAN ACT, EXCHANGE BAKERY V. RIFKIN, IRONCLAD AGREEMENT (CONTRACT), NORRIS-LAGUARDIA ACT.

Yeshiva University case A 1980 Supreme Court ruling which held that full-time faculty at Yeshiva University are managerial employees without collective bargaining rights under the National Labor Relations Act.

The Court noted that the Yeshiva University faculty exercised authority "which in any other context unquestionably would be managerial." According to the Court, the faculty decided what courses would be offered, when they would be scheduled, and to whom they would be taught; determined teaching methods, grading policies, and matriculation standards; and on occasion, faculty views determined the size of student body, the tuition to be charged, and the location of a school. "To the extent the industrial analogy applies, the faculty determines within each school the product to be produced, the terms upon which it will be offered, and the customers who will be served," the Court added.

Source references: NLRB v. Yeshiva University, 444 US 672, 103 LRRM 2526 (1980); Carlene A. Clarke, "The *Yeshiva* Case: An Analysis and an Assessment of Its Potential Impact on Public Universities," *Journal of Higher Education*, Sept./Oct. 1981; Joel M. Douglas, "Distinguishing *Yeshiva*: A Troubling Task for the NLRB," *LLJ*, Feb. 1983; ———, "Faculty Collective Bargaining in the Aftermath of Yeshiva," *Change*, March 1981; John A. Gray, "Managerial Employees and the Industrial Analogy: *NLRB v. Yeshiva University*," *LLJ*, July 1982; David Roots and Ira Michael Shepard, "Yeshiva: A Legal Analysis," *Journal of the College and University Personnel Association*, Summer 1980; Edward L. Suntrup, "*NLRB v. Yeshiva University* and Unionization in Higher Education," *Industrial Relations LJ*, Vol. 4, no. 2, 1981.

Youngstown Sheet and Tube Co. v. Sawyer Decision of the Supreme Court holding that the President has no power to order seizure of the basic steel industry's plants during peacetime and in the absence of congressional authorization.

Source reference: Youngstown Sheet & Tube v. Sawyer, 343 US 579, 30 LRRM 2172 (1952).

See also GOVERNMENT SEIZURE.

young workers Individuals who have entered the labor market and are either seeking employment or are starting on their first jobs. While there is no technical definition of young workers based on age, the lowest age brackets of data from the Current Population Survey are generally given as those 16 to 19 years and 20 to 24 years. According to Ruebens et al., "the size of youth population, divided into the age groups 15 to 19 and 20 to 24, provide the basis for assessing the changing numbers and proportions of young people who are enrolled in educational institutions or are participating in the labor force."

Source references: Arvil V. Adams and Garth L. Mangum, *The Lingering Crisis of Youth Unemployment* (Kalamazoo: Upjohn Institute for Employment Research, 1978); Norman Bowers, "Young and Marginal: An Overview of Youth Employment," *MLR*, Oct. 1979; Richard B. Freeman and David A. Wise, *Youth Unemployment, NBER Summary Report* (Cambridge: NBER, 1980); Carol Leon, "Young Adults: A Transitional Group with Changing Labor Force Patterns," *MLR*, May 1978; Sar A. Levitan, *Youth Employment Act* (Kalamazoo: Upjohn Institute, 1963); Garth Mangum and John Walsh, *Employment and Training Programs for Youth: What Works Best for Whom?* (Washington: U.S. Dept. of Labor, ETA, 1978); Joseph A. Raelin, *Building a Career, the Effect of Initial Job Experiences and Related Work Attitudes on Later Employment* (Kalamazoo: Upjohn Institute for Employment Research, 1980); Beatrice G. Reubens, John A. C. Harrison, and Kalman Rupp, *The Youth Labor Force, 1945–1995, A Cross-National Analysis* (Totowa, N.J.: Allanheld, Osmun, 1981); Kezia Sproat, "Using National Longitudinal Surveys to Track Young Workers," *MLR*, Oct. 1979; Clarence Thomas, "Minorities, Youth, and Education," *Journal of Labor Research*, Fall 1982; U.S. Congressional Budget Office, *Improving Youth Employment Prospects: Issues and Options* (Washington: 1982); U.S. Dept. of HEW, Education Division, *Indicators of Youth Unemployment and Education in Industrialized Nations* (Washington: 1978); U.S. Dept. of Labor, BES, *Counseling and Employment Service for Youth* (Washington: 1963); U.S. Dept. of Labor, ETA, *Conference Report on Youth Unemployment: Its Measurement and Meaning* (Washington: 1978); ———, *Youth Serving the Community: Realistic Public Service Roles for Young Workers* (Washington: R&D Monograph 68, 1979); U.S. Dept. of Labor, Manpower Administration, *Career Thresholds, A Longitudinal Study of the Educational and Labor Market Experience of Male Youth, Volumes 1–6* (Washington: Research Monograph 16, 1970–1977); U.S. National Commission for Manpower Policy, *From School to Work: Improving the Transition* (Washington: 1976); U.S. Vice President's Task Force on Youth Employment, *A Review of Youth Employment, Programs and Policies: Volume I* (Washington: 1980); Diane N. Westcott, "The Youngest Workers; 14- and 15-Year-Olds," *MLR*, Feb. 1981; Work in America Institute, *Job Strategies for Urban Youth, Sixteen Pilot Programs for Action* (Scarsdale: 1979); Anne McDougall Young, "Labor Force Patterns of Students, Graduates, and Dropouts, 1981," *MLR*, Sept. 1982.

Youth Administration, National *See* NATIONAL YOUTH ADMINISTRATION.

Z

zero defects program Program to motivate employees to complete a job without error through (1) employee identification of the causes of job errors, (2) suggestions for correction, and (3) rewards for high quality of work.

Source references: AMA, *Zero Defects, Doing It Right the First Time* (New York: Management Bull. 71, 1965); Gerald V. Barrett and Patrick A. Cabe, "Zero Defects Programs: Their Effects at Different Job Levels," *Personnel*, Nov./Dec. 1967; Stanley J. Birkin, "Let's Admit It: Zero Defects is no Panacea!" *Public Personnel Management*, March/April 1974; P. J. Cathey, "Quality Control: A Zero-Defects Program," *Management Review*, Nov. 1963; Hubert M. Childress, "Zero Defects: Guide or Gimmick?" *Management Review*, July 1966; Edgar F. Huse, "Do Zero Defects Programs Really Motivate Workers?" *Personnel*, March/April 1966; Joseph L. Mazel, "Setting Up a Zero Defects Program," *Management Review*, Sept. 1965; Lloyd A. Swanson and Darrel Corbin, "Employee Motivation Programs: A Change in Philosophy?" *PJ*, Nov. 1969.

zinger An extraneous issue introduced near the close of collective bargaining negotiations or included in the final-offer arbitration package. According to Najita, it may be "an item which could never be negotiated or expect to be won in conventional arbitration."

According to Stern, it is "a demand which standing alone would be rejected but which within the package as a whole is not sufficiently important to cause the arbitrator to select the position of the other party."

Source references: Peter Feuille, *Final Offer Arbitration* (Chicago: IPMA, PERL 50, 1975); Joyce M. Najita, *Compulsory Arbitration and the Resolution of Impasse Disputes Involving Firefighters and Police in Hawaii* (Honolulu: Univ. of Hawaii, 1976); James Stern, "3-State Study by Profs Boosts Compulsory Arb," *LMRS Newsletter*, Sept. 1975.

zipper clause An abbreviated form of the waiver provision in a collective bargaining agreement, sometimes referred to as a "wrap-up" clause, considered to denote waiver of the right of either party to require the other to bargain on any matter not covered in an agreement during the life of the contract, thus limiting the terms and conditions of employment to those set forth in the contract. A clause of this type would read:

> This contract is complete in itself and sets forth all the terms and conditions of the agreement between the parties hereto.

Source references: The Beacon Journal Publishing Co. and Newspaper Delivery Drivers, Chauffeurs and Handlers Local Union No. 163 TCWH (Ind), 164 NLRB 734, 65 LRRM 1126 (1967); *The Borden Co. and Local Union No. 274, International Brotherhood of Teamsters, Chauffeurs, Warehousemen and Helpers (AFL)*, 110 NLRB 802, 35 LRRM 1133 (1954); *New York Mirror and N.Y. Newspaper Printing Pressmen's Union No. 2, IPPA (AFL-CIO) and Publishers' Assn. of New York City*, 151 NLRB 834, 58 LRRM 1465 (1965); Walter P. Loomis and Joseph German, "Management's Reserved Rights and the NLRB—An Employer's View," *LLJ*, Nov. 1968.

See also REOPENING CLAUSE.

General Source References

Aaron, Benjamin, Joseph R. Grodin, and James L. Stern (ed.). *Public-Sector Bargaining.* (Washington: Bureau of National Affairs, IRRA series, 1979).

American Arbitration Assn. *The Future of Labor Arbitration in America.* (New York: 1976).

American Bar Assn. Section of Labor Relations Law. *The Developing Labor Law: The Board, The Courts, and the National Labor Relations Act,* edited by Charles J. Morris et al. (2d ed., Washington: Bureau of National Affairs, 1983).

Anderson, Arvid and Hugh D. Jascourt. *Trends in Public Sector Labor Relations, Vol. 1, 1972–73.* (Chicago: International Public Management Assn. and the Public Employment Relations Research Institute, 1975).

Atherton, Wallace N. *Theory of Union Bargaining Goals.* (Princeton: Princeton University Press, 1973).

Bacharach, Samuel B. and Edward J. Lawler. *Bargaining; Power, Tactics and Outcomes.* (San Francisco: Jossey-Bass, 1981).

Bakke, E. Wight. *Mutual Survival; The Goal of Unions and Management.* (2d ed., Hamden, Conn.: Archon Books, 1966).

Bakke, E. Wight, Clark Kerr, and Charles W. Anrod. *Unions, Management, and the Public.* (3d ed., New York: Harcourt, Brace, 1967).

Barbash, Jack. *Labor's Grass Roots, A Study of the Local Union.* (New York: Harper, 1961).

Barkin, Solomon (ed.). *Worker Militancy and Its Consequences, 1965–75.* (New York: Praeger, 1975).

Beal, Edwin F. and James P. Begin. *The Practice of Collective Bargaining.* (6th ed., Homewood: Irwin, 1982).

Becker, Esther R. *Dictionary of Personnel and Industrial Relations.* (New York: Philosophical Library, 1958).

Benn, A. E. *The Management Dictionary.* (New York: Exposition Press, 1952).

Bernstein, Irving. *The Lean Years; A History of the American Worker, 1920–1933.* (Boston: Houghton Mifflin, 1960).

______. *The Turbulent Years; A History of the American Worker, 1933–1941.* (Boston: Houghton Mifflin, 1970).

Blanpain, R. (ed.). *Comparative Labour Law and Industrial Relations.* (Washington: Bureau of National Affairs, 1982).

Blaxall, Martha and Barbara Reagan (ed.). *Women and the Workplace: The Implications of Occupational Segregation.* (Chicago: University of Chicago Press, 1976).

Bloom, Gordon F. and Herbert R. Northrup. *Economics of Labor Relations.* (9th ed., Homewood: Irwin, 1981).

Blum, Albert A. (ed.). *International Handbook of Industrial Relations: Contemporary Developments and Research.* (Westport, Conn.: Greenwood Press, 1981).

Bok, Derek C. and John T. Dunlop. *Labor and the American Community.* (New York: Simon and Schuster, 1970).

Brown, J. Douglas. *Essays on Social Security.* (Princeton: Princeton University, Industrial Relations Section, 1977).

Bulmer, Charles and John L. Carmichael, Jr. (ed.). *Employment and Labor-Relations Policy* (Lexington, Mass.: Lexington Books, 1980).

Casselman, P. H. *Labor Dictionary.* (New York: Philosophical Library, 1949).

Chamberlain, Neil W. *Sourcebook on Labor.* (New York: McGraw-Hill, 1958).

Cohen, Sanford. *Labor in the United States.* (3d ed., Columbus: Merrill, 1970).

Cole, David L. *The Quest for Industrial Peace.* (New York: McGraw-Hill, 1963).

Commons, John R. *The Economics of Collective Action.* (Madison: University of Wisconsin Press, 1970).

Commons, John R. et al. *Documentary History of American Industrial Society.* (Cleveland: Arthur H. Clark Co., 1910).

Commons, John R. and Associates. *History of Labour in the United States.* (4 vol., New York: Macmillan, 1935–1946).

Cox, Archibald, Derek C. Bok, and Robert A. Gorman. *Cases and Materials on Labor Law.* (9th ed., Mineola, N.Y.: Foundation Press, 1981).

Davey, Harold W. et al. *Contemporary Collective Bargaining.* (4th ed., Englewood Cliffs: Prentice-Hall, 1982).

De Menil, George. *Bargaining: Monopoly Power Versus Union Power.* (Cambridge: MIT Press, 1971).

Derthick, Martha. *Policymaking for Social Security.* (Washington: Brookings Institution, 1979).

Drucker, Peter F. *The Age of Discontinuity.* (New York: Harper, 1969).

———. *The Practice of Management.* (New York: Harper, 1954).

Dulles, Foster R. *Labor in America.* (3d ed., New York: Crowell, 1966).

Dunlop, John T. *Dispute Resolution, Negotiation and Consensus Building.* (Dover, Mass.: Auburn House, 1984).

———. *Industrial Relations Systems.* (New York: Holt, 1958).

Elkouri, Frank and Edna Asper Elkouri. *How Arbitration Works.* (4th ed., Washington: Bureau of National Affairs, 1985).

Fairweather, Owen. *Practice and Procedure in Labor Arbitration.* (2d ed., Washington: Bureau of National Affairs, 1983).

Flippo, Edwin B. *Personnel Management.* (5th ed., New York: McGraw-Hill, 1984).

Freeman, Richard B. *Labor Economics.* (2d ed., Englewood Cliffs: Prentice-Hall, 1979).

French, Wendell. *The Personnel Management Process: Cases on Human Resources Administration.* (2d ed., Boston: Houghton Mifflin, 1982).

Garbarino, Joseph W. *Faculty Bargaining; Change and Conflict.* (New York: McGraw-Hill, 1975).

Garraty, John A. *Unemployment in History: Economic Thought and Public Policy.* (New York: Harper & Row, 1978).
Getman, Julius G. *Labor Relations; Law, Practice and Policy.* (Mineola, N.Y.: Foundation Press, 1978).
Getman, Julius G., Stephen B. Goldberg, and Jeanne B. Herman. *Union Representation Elections: Law and Reality.* (New York: Russell Sage Foundation, 1976).
Gibbons, Muriel K. et al. (ed.). *Portrait of a Process—Collective Negotiations in Public Employment.* (Fort Washington, Pa.: Public Employment Relations Service, Labor Relations Press, 1979).
Ginzberg, Eli (ed.). *Employing the Unemployed.* (New York: Basic Books, 1980).
Ginzberg, Eli and Hyman Berman. *The American Workers in the Twentieth Century, A History Through Autobiographies.* (New York: Free Press of Glencoe, 1963).
Gitlow, Abraham L. *Labor and Manpower Economics.* (3d ed., Homewood: Irwin, 1971).
Goldberg, Arthur J. *AFL-CIO: Labor United.* (New York: McGraw-Hill, 1956).
Hausman, Leonard J. et al. (ed.). *Equal Rights and Industrial Relations.* (Madison: IRRA, 1977).
Hill, Herbert. *Black Labor and the American Legal System.* (Washington: Bureau of National Affairs, 1977).
Horton, B. J., Julian Ripley, Jr., and N. B. Schnapper. *Dictionary of Modern Economics.* (Washington: Public Affairs Press, 1948).
Jacks, Stanley M. (ed.). *Issues in Labor Policy;* Papers in Honor of Douglass Vincent Brown. (Cambridge: MIT Press, 1971).
Jacobs, Paul. *The State of the Unions.* (New York: Atheneum, 1963).
Jascourt, Hugh D. (ed.). *Government Labor Relations: Trends and Information for the Future. Volume 1, 1975 to 1978.* (Oak Park, Ill.: Moore Pub. and Public Employment Relations Research Institute, 1979).
Kaye, Seymour P. and Arthur Marsh (ed.). *International Manual on Collective Bargaining for Public Employees.* (New York: Praeger, 1973).
Kerr, Clark, John T. Dunlop, Frederick H. Harbison, and Charles A. Myers. *Industrialism and Industrial Man.* (Cambridge: Harvard University Press, 1960).
Kerr, Clark and Jerome M. Rosow (ed.). *Work in America: The Decade Ahead.* (New York: Van Nostrand Reinhold, 1979).
Kochan, Thomas A. *Collective Bargaining and Industrial Relations.* (Homewood: Irwin, 1980).
Kochan, Thomas A., Daniel J. B. Mitchell, and Lee Dyer (ed.). *Industrial Relations Research in the 1970s: Review and Appraisal.* (Madison: IRRA, 1982).
Kornhauser, Arthur, Robert Dubin, and Arthur M. Ross (ed.). *Industrial Conflict.* (New York: McGraw-Hill, 1954).
Kreps, Juanita M., Gerald G. Somers, and Richard Perlman. *Contemporary Labor Economics: Issues, Analysis, and Policies.* (Belmont, Calif.: Wadsworth, 1974).

Lester, Richard A. *As Unions Mature.* (Princeton: Princeton University Press, 1958).

———. *Economics of Labor.* (2d ed., New York: Macmillan, 1964).

Levitan, Sar A. *The Great Society's Poor Law; A New Approach to Poverty.* (Baltimore: Johns Hopkins Press, 1969).

Lewin, David, Peter Feuille, and Thomas Kochan. *Public Sector Labor Relations: Analysis and Readings.* (2d ed., Sun Lakes, Ariz.: Thomas Horton & Daughters, 1981).

Lieberman, Myron. *Public-Sector Bargaining, A Policy Reappraisal.* (Lexington, Mass.: Lexington Books, 1980).

Likert, Rensis. *New Patterns of Management.* (New York: McGraw-Hill, 1961).

Livernash, E. Robert (ed.). *Comparable Worth: Issues and Alternatives.* (Washington: Equal Employment Advisory Council, 1980).

Lloyd, Cynthia B. (comp.). *Sex, Discrimination, and the Division of Labor.* (New York: Columbia University Press, 1975).

Lloyd, Cynthia B. and Beth T. Niemi. *The Economics of Sex Differentials.* (Irvington, N. Y.: Columbia University Press, 1979).

Loewenberg, J. Joseph and Michael H. Moskow. *Collective Bargaining in Government: Readings and Cases.* (Englewood Cliffs: Prentice-Hall, 1972).

Mangum, Garth L. *The Emergence of Manpower Policy.* (New York: Holt, Rinehart and Winston, 1969).

Marshall, F. Ray, Allan M. Carter, and Allan G. King. *Labor Economics, Wages, Employment, and Trade Unionism.* (4th ed., Homewood: Irwin, 1980).

Martin, Benjamin and Everett M. Kassalow (ed.). *Labor Relations in Advanced Industrial Societies: Issues and Problems.* (Washington: Carnegie Endowment for International Peace, 1980).

McGregor, Douglas. *The Human Side of Enterprise.* (New York: McGraw-Hill, 1960).

Mills, Daniel Quinn. *Government, Labor and Inflation: Wage Stabilization in the United States.* (Chicago: University of Chicago Press, 1975).

———. *Labor-Management Relations.* (2d ed., New York: McGraw-Hill, 1982).

Mitchell, Daniel J. B. *Unions, Wages, and Inflation.* (Washington: Brookings Institution, 1980).

Moynihan, Daniel P. (ed.). *On Understanding Poverty: Perspective From the Social Sciences.* (New York: Basic Books, 1969).

Munnell, Alicia H. *The Future of Social Security.* (Washington: Brookings Institution, 1977).

National Planning Assn. *Causes of Industrial Peace Under Collective Bargaining; Case Studies.* (Washington: 1948–1953).

Nesbitt, Murray B. *Labor Relations in the Federal Government Service.* (Washington: Bureau of National Affairs, 1976).

Palgrave, Robert H. I. *Palgrave's Dictionary of Political Economy,* edited by Henry Higgs. (new ed., 3 vol., London: Macmillan, 1926).

Perlman, Richard. *Labor Theory.* (New York: Wiley, 1969).

Perlman, Selig. *A History of Trade Unionism in the United States.* (New York: Macmillan, 1937).

———. *A Theory of the Labor Movement.* (New York: Kelley, 1949).

Pierson, Frank C. *Unions in Postwar America, An Economic Assessment.* (New York: Random House, 1967).

Prasow, Paul and Edward Peters. *Arbitration and Collective Bargaining: Conflict Resolution in Labor Relations.* (2d ed., New York: McGraw-Hill, 1983).

Reynolds, Lloyd G. *Labor Economics and Labor Relations.* (8th ed., Englewood Cliffs: Prentice-Hall, 1982).

Reynolds, Lloyd G. and Charles C. Killingsworth. *Trade Union Publications.* (3 vol., Baltimore: Johns Hopkins Press, 1944–45).

Rezler, Julius. *Automation and Industrial Labor.* (New York: Random House, 1969).

Roberts, Harold S. *Labor-Management Relations in the Public Service.* (Honolulu: University of Hawaii Press, 1970).

Ross, Arthur M. (ed.). *Employment Policy and the Labor Market.* (Berkeley: University of California Press, 1965).

Rowan, Richard L. (ed.). *Readings in Labor Economics and Labor Relations.* (4th ed., Homewood: Irwin, 1980).

Ruttenberg, Stanley H. *Manpower Challenge in the 1970s: Institutions and Social Change.* (Baltimore: Johns Hopkins Press, 1970).

Schick, Richard P. and Jean J. Couturier. *The Public Interest in Government Labor Relations.* (Cambridge: Ballinger, 1977).

Schlei, Barbara Lindemann and Paul Grossman. *Employment Discrimination Law.* (2d ed., Washington: Bureau of National Affairs, 1983).

Schrank, Robert. *Ten Thousand Working Days.* (Cambridge: MIT Press, 1978).

Schwartz, Robert J. *The Dictionary of Business and Industry.* (New York: Forbes, 1954).

Seide, Katharine (ed.). *A Dictionary of Arbitration and Its Terms, Labor-Commercial-International.* (Dobbs Ferry, N.Y.: Oceana Publications, 1970).

Seidman, Joel I. (ed.). *Trade Union Government and Collective Bargaining.* (New York: Praeger, 1970).

———. *Union Rights and Union Duties.* (New York: Harcourt, Brace, 1943).

Selekman, Benjamin M., Sylvia K. Selekman, and Stephen H. Fuller. *Problems in Labor Relations.* (2d ed., New York: McGraw-Hill, 1958).

Seligman, Edwin R. A. (ed.). *Encyclopedia of the Social Sciences.* (15 vol., New York: Macmillan, 1930–1935).

Shafritz, Jay M. *Dictionary of Personnel Management and Labor Relations.* (Oak Park, Ill.: Moore Pub., 1980).

Sills, David A. (ed.). *International Encyclopedia of the Social Sciences.* (17 vol., New York: Macmillan and the Free Press, 1968).

Sloane, Arthur A. and Fred Witney. *Labor Relations.* (3d ed., Englewood Cliffs: Prentice-Hall, 1977).

Smith, Arthur B. Jr. *Employment Discrimination Law, Cases and Materials.* (Indianapolis: Bobbs-Merrill, 1978).

Smith, Ralph E. (ed.). *The Subtle Revolution: Women at Work.* (Washington: Urban Institute, 1979).
Somers, Gerald G. (ed.). *Collective Bargaining: Contemporary American Experience.* (Madison: IRRA, 1980).
———. (ed.). *Essays in Industrial Relations Theory.* (Ames: Iowa State University Press, 1969).
Spero, Sterling D. *Government as Employer.* (Carbondale: Southern Illinois University Press, 1972).
Spero, Sterling D. and John M. Capozzola. *The Urban Community and Its Unionized Bureaucracies.* (New York: Dunellen, 1973).
Stahl, O. Glenn. *Public Personnel Administration.* (7th ed., New York: Harper & Row, 1976).
Stein, Bruno. *Social Security and Pensions in Transition: Understanding the American Retirement System.* (New York: Free Press, Macmillan, 1980).
Stern, James L. et al. *Final Offer Arbitration: The Effects on Public Safety Employee Bargaining.* (Lexington, Mass.: Lexington Books, 1975).
Stieber, Jack. *Public Employee Unionism.* (Washington: Brookings Institution, 1973).
Stieber, Jack, Robert B. McKersie, and D. Quinn Mills (ed.). *U.S. Industrial Relations 1950–1980: A Critical Assessment.* (Madison: IRRA, 1981).
Strauss, George et al. (ed.). *Organizational Behavior: Research and Issues.* (Madison: IRRA, 1974).
Suskin, Harold (ed.). *Job Evaluation and Pay Administration in the Public Sector.* (Chicago: International Personnel Management Assn., 1977).
Taft, Philip. *Organized Labor in American History.* (New York: Harper, 1964).
———. *The Structure and Government of Labor Unions.* (Cambridge: Harvard University Press, 1954).
Terkel, Louis. *Working: People Talk About What They Do All Day and How They Feel About What They Do.* (New York: Pantheon Books, 1974).
Treiman, Donald J. *Job Evaluation: An Analytic Review.* (Washington: National Academy of Sciences, 1979).
Trieman, Donald J. and Heidi I. Hartmann (ed.). *Women, Work, and Wages: Equal Pay for Jobs of Equal Value.* (Washington: National Academy Press, 1981).
Twentieth Century Fund. *How Collective Bargaining Works.* (New York: 1942).
U. S. Dept. of Labor. Bureau of Labor Statistics. *Brief History of the American Labor Movement.* (Washington: Bull. 1000, 1970).
———. *Glossary of Current Industrial Relations and Wage Terms.* (Washington: Bull. 1438, 1965).
Vladeck, Judith P. and Stephen C. Vladeck (ed.). *Collective Bargaining in Higher Education—The Developing Law.* (New York: Practising Law Institute, 1975).
Walton, Richard E. and Robert B. McKersie. *A Behavioral Theory of Labor Negotiations.* (New York: McGraw-Hill, 1965).
Webb, Sidney and Beatrice Webb. *The History of Trade Unionism.* (rev. ed., London: Longmans, Green, 1920).

Wellington, Harry H. and Ralph K. Winter, Jr. *The Unions and the Cities.* (Washington: Brookings Institution, 1972).

Whyte, William H., Jr. *The Organization Man.* (New York: Simon and Schuster, 1956).

Wilson, Wesley M. *The Labor Relations Primer.* (Homewood: Dow Jones-Irwin, 1973).

Witte, Edwin E. *Social Security Perspectives, Essays,* edited by Robert J. Lampman. (Madison: University of Wisconsin Press, 1962).

Wolfbein, Seymour L. (ed.). *Emerging Sectors of Collective Bargaining.* (Braintree, Mass.: Mark Pub., 1970).

Woytinsky, W. S. *Employment and Wages in the United States.* (New York: Twentieth Century Fund, 1953).

Yoder, Dale and Paul D. Staudohar. *Personnel Management and Industrial Relations.* (7th ed., Englewood Cliffs: Prentice-Hall, 1982).

BNA's Labor Services

Users of the *Dictionary* who desire more information on specific topics or who wish to keep abreast of current developments in areas of interest should consult BNA's loose-leaf subscription services. Each service has its own index and guide to the user.

Following is a list of BNA's Labor Services.

Affirmative Action Compliance Manual for Federal Contractors. This monthly service provides updates on affirmative action developments plus a comprehensive reference manual containing the official regulations and directives issued by the Labor Department's Office of Federal Contract Compliance Programs.

Benefits Today. This biweekly resource provides a comprehensive overview and analysis of significant trends and developments relating to the management of employee benefit plans. It provides news on the latest legislative, regulatory, and judicial developments and examples of successful plans and policies being used in benefit management by companies nationwide.

BNA Pension Reporter. This weekly publication reports on the latest pension developments in Washington and the states. It covers court activity, regulatory developments, legislative and administrative moves, standards, agency opinions, as well as reports on meetings of professional organizations.

BNA Policy and Practice Series. This is an 11-binder reference and notification service for the employee relations executive covering both legislative, administrative, and judicial regulation, as well as practical policies being used by companies across the nation. It consists of separate sections dealing with personnel management, compensation, wages and hours, fair employment practices, and labor relations. Two newsletters—the weekly *Bulletin to Management* and the biweekly *Fair Employment Practices Summary of Latest Developments* —cover current developments, case studies, statistics, and analysis of trends.

BNA's Employee Relations Weekly. This is a weekly report on conditions and developments affecting the workplace with the emphasis on analysis of trends and how-to techniques.

Collective Bargaining Negotiations and Contracts. This is a two-binder reference service with a biweekly newsletter designed to provide ongoing information to help unions and management prepare, negotiate, and administer collective bargaining agreements. It is tied to an extensive database that includes information from BNA's library of more than 3,000 current collective bargaining contracts and from current wage and benefit settlements.

Construction Labor Report. This weekly notification service monitors bargaining and labor relations developments affecting the construction industry.

Daily Labor Report. Each business day, this 30–40 page report provides information on the latest developments in labor relations from Washington and across the country. It is the nation's only daily reporting service on labor developments.

EEOC Compliance Manual. This monthly service provides updates on affirmative action developments plus a comprehensive reference manual containing the text of the internal policy manual used by the Equal Employment Opportunity Commission.

Employee Benefits Cases. This weekly service provides the text of federal and state court decisions dealing with employee benefits as well as rulings from arbitrators and the NLRB. The rulings are digested and indexed using the same system developed by BNA's *Labor Relations Reporter.*

Employment and Training Reporter. This weekly reporting and reference service provides news, analysis, and technical assistance relating to federal, state, and local job training programs and related activities by private industry.

Fair Employment Practice Service. This is a two-binder reference service supplemented with a biweekly newsletter that covers EEO developments, including court decisions (full text), EEOC rulings (digests), federal and state laws and regulations (full text), and guidelines on how the laws are being enforced and on policies and practices being used by companies and unions.

Government Employee Relations Report. This is one-binder reference service and a weekly notification report covering the law and practice of labor relations in the public sectors—federal, state, and local.

The Government Manager. This is a biweekly bulletin that provides employee relations guidance for government managers.

Job Safety and Health. This is a one-binder reference manual supplemented with a biweekly bulletin covering job safety and health laws and policies and practices being used by companies and unions.

Labor Arbitration Reports. This weekly information service has been published since 1946 to provide the text of significant awards by labor arbitrators. Research in the 85-volume library of past awards is facilitated by BNA's cumulative digest and index system. Current biographical data on labor arbitrators is included.

Labor Relations Reporter. This notification and reference service has been published since 1937 to cover decisions and nondecisional information dealing with labor relations, fair employment practices, labor arbitration, and wages and hours. The complete service includes weekly reports, 14 binders for decisional advance sheets and reference manuals, bound casebooks, and cumulative digests and indexes.

Retail/Service Labor Report. This weekly notification service reports on union and management activities affecting employee relations in the retail and service industries.

Union Labor Report. This service for union officials provides a two-binder reference manual and a weekly bulletin reporting on labor laws and regulations, grievances, bargaining, organizing, and economic data. Also included is a quarterly newsletter for union stewards.

White Collar Report. This weekly notification service reports on labor relations developments affecting clerical, technical, health care, and professional employees.

The Bureau of National Affairs, Inc., also publishes numerous book titles in the field of labor-management relations. Where appropriate, these titles are cited under the source references of individual entries within the *Dictionary*.